BIG BOOK OF Windows Hacks

First Edition

Preston Gralla

BEIJING • CAMBRIDGE • FARNHAM • KÖLN • PARIS • SEBASTOPOL • TAIPEI • TOKYO

BIG BOOK OF WINDOWS HACKS

by Preston Gralla

Published by Make:Books, an imprint of Maker Media, a division of O'Reilly Media, Inc.
1005 Gravenstein Highway North, Sebastopol, CA 95472.

O'Reilly books may be purchased for educational, business, or sales promotional use.
For more information, contact our corporate/institutional sales department:
800-998-9938 or *corporate@oreilly.com*.

Print History
October 2007
First Edition

Publisher: Dale Dougherty
Associate Publisher and Executive Editor: Dan Woods
Editor: Brian Jepson
Copy Editors: Mary Anne Weeks Mayo & Nancy Kotary
Creative Director: Daniel Carter
Designer: Alison Kendall
Production Manager: Terry Bronson
Indexer: Patti Schiendelman

ISBN-10: 0-596-52835-3
ISBN-13: 978-0-596-52835-5

CONTENTS

PREFACE xiii

How to Use This Book xiii

How This Book is Organized xiv

Conventions Used in This Book xvi

Using Code Examples xvi

We'd Like to Hear from You xvii

CHAPTER 01: STARTUP AND SHUTDOWN 18

HACK 01: Change Your Windows Vista Boot Screen 18

HACK 02: Change your Windows XP Boot Screen 21

HACK 03: Speed Up Boot and Shutdown Times 22

HACK 04: Run Windows Vista Without Activation for 120 Days 25

HACK 05: Bypass the Windows Vista and XP Logon Screen on Multi-Account PCs 27

HACK 06: Speed Up Startup by Halting Startup Programs and Services 29

HACK 07: BIOS Hacks for Faster Bootup 34

HACK 08: Hack an Unhackable BIOS 36

HACK 09: Upgrade Your Flash BIOS 38

HACK 10: The Secrets of Windows Vista's BCDEDIT 42

HACK 11: Customize Windows XP Multiboot Startup Options 45

HACK 12: Hack Windows Vista Multiboot Systems with VistaBootPRO 50

HACK 13: Move Partitions Around on Vista Without Destroying It 53

HACK 14: Transforming Your Windows XP Laptop into a Dual-Boot XP/Ubuntu Linux System 54

CHAPTER 02: HACKING THE INTERFACE 62

HACK 15: Hack Your Way Through Windows Vista's Aero Interface 62

HACK 16: A Grab Bag of Great Vista Interface Hacks 66

HACK 17: Turn Windows Into a 3D Virtual Desktop 70

HACK 18: Hack Your Way Through the Interface with the Registry Editor 72

HACK 19: Customize the Windows XP GUI with Tweak UI 75

HACK 20: Control the Control Panel 78

HACK 21: Hack the Start Menu and Taskbar 82

HACK 22: Hacking Gadgets 84

HACK 23: Force the Slide Show Gadget to Play Videos as Well as Images 88

HACK 24: Play YouTube Videos in the Feed Headlines Gadget 92

HACK 25: Carry Your Gadgets with You on a USB Flash Drive 94

HACK 26: Automatically Build Any Vista Gadget from the Web 96
HACK 27: Yes, You *Can* Hack Windows Vista's Screensavers 99
HACK 28: Extend Your Screen Real Estate with Virtual Desktops 100
HACK 29: Force Older Programs to Use XP Common Controls 103
HACK 30: Run Linux Inside Windows Without Dual Booting 105
HACK 31: Run Mac OS X on Windows Vista 111
HACK 32: Go Retro: Run Windows 3.11 in Windows Vista 116
HACK 33: Instant Linux 124

CHAPTER 03: WINDOWS EXPLORER, MANAGING FILES, AND SEARCH 134

HACK 34: A Power User's Hidden Weapon: Improve the Context Menu 134
HACK 35: More Hacks for Improving Windows Vista's Context Menu 137
HACK 36: Open an Administrator Command Prompt Anywhere in Windows Explorer 138
HACK 37: Generate Folder and File Listings for Printing or Editing 140
HACK 38: Only the Shadow Knows: Using Windows Shadow Copy 143
HACK 39: Control Windows Explorer with Command-Line Shortcuts 146
HACK 40: Move User Directories to a Separate Partition or Drive 150
HACK 41: Hack Your Partitions in Windows Vista 152
HACK 42: Get More Hard-Disk Space by Using NTFS Compression 155
HACK 43: Power Up Search in Windows Vista 158
HACK 44: Quick Way To Speed Up Windows Vista Search 164
HACK 45: Use Start ++ To Juice Up Windows Vista Search 165
HACK 46: Find Files Faster in Windows XP by Mastering the Indexing Service's Query Language 167
HACK 47: Secrets of Windows Vista's Sync Center and Offline Files 172

CHAPTER 04: INTERNET EXPLORER, THE WEB AND THE INTERNET 180

HACK 48: Clear Up Router Congestion and Increase Your Bandwidth 180
HACK 49: Surf Anonymously, Without a Trace — For Free 182
HACK 50: Use OpenDNS for Faster, Safer Web Browsing 187
HACK 51: Tweak DNS Settings for Faster Internet Access 190
HACK 52: Kill Viruses, Spyware, and Web Bugs — For Free 193
HACK 53: Keep Your Google Search History Private 198
HACK 54: Fix Internet Explorer 7 Add-In Woes 201
HACK 55: Kill Badly Behaving Items on the Internet Explorer Tools Menu 203
HACK 56: Hack Printouts in Internet Explorer 7 204
HACK 57: Hack Internet Explorer with the Group Policy Editor 207
HACK 58: Hack Firefox 210
HACK 59: Stop Firefox Memory Leaks 216
HACK 60: Build Your Own Firefox Search Engine 220
HACK 61: Build Your Own Internet Explorer Search Engine 224
HACK 62: Make Java-based Apps Play Nice with Vista 228
HACK 63: Where Did HyperTerminal Go? 229
HACK 64: Mash Up Google Calendar and Other Online Calendars with Windows Vista's Calendar 231

HACK 65: Import Internet Calendars into Outlook 235
HACK 66: Create Custom RSS Feeds from Newsgroups and Online Forums 238

CHAPTER 05: NETWORKING 246

HACK 67: Quick Fix for a Sluggish Router 246
HACK 68: Give the World Access to a Server or PC Behind Your Home Router 249
HACK 69: Give Your Home Server a Hostname 252
HACK 70: Get Quick Access to Network Connections in Windows Vista 254
HACK 71: Teach XP to Play Nice on Networks with Vista 256
HACK 72: Teach All Your Networks to Get Along 261
HACK 73: Control Another Windows XP PC with Remote Access 264
HACK 74: Control Another Windows Vista PC with Remote Access 268
HACK 75: Reboot Your Network Settings 271
HACK 76: Troubleshoot Network Connections with ping, tracert, and pathping 271
HACK 77: Troubleshoot Network Connections with netsh, netstat, and ipconfig 275
HACK 78: Prioritize Packets to Improve Voice Quality 279
HACK 79: Sound Like Darth Vader While You VoIP 281
HACK 80: Record VoIP Calls 282
HACK 81: Make Skype Work with Personal Firewalls 283
HACK 82: Improve Skype Service Quality 285
HACK 83: Automatically Forward Skype Voicemail 288

CHAPTER 06: EMAIL 290

HACK 84: Instantly Compress Files You Send via Email 290
HACK 85: Put Your Bloated Outlook Mailbox On a Diet 291
HACK 86: Stay Off Spam Lists 294
HACK 87: Prevent Your Newsletter from Being Blocked as Spam 296
HACK 88: Block International Spam 297
HACK 89: Open Blocked File Attachments in Outlook and Outlook Express 300
HACK 90: Remove Exchange messaging From Outlook 2007 304
HACK 91: Publish Your Outlook Calendar to the Web 304
HACK 92: Turn Gmail into a Universal Inbox 308
HACK 93: Use Gmail as a POP3 Server 310
HACK 94: Use Gmail as a Virtual Hard Drive 312
HACK 95: Import Your Contacts into Gmail 313
HACK 96: Import Mail into Gmail 319

CHAPTER 07: WEB AND THE INTERNET 324

HACK 97: Turn Your Home Router into an Enterprise-Level Powerhouse 324
HACK 98: Troubleshoot Wireless Interference Woes, and Extend Your Range 333
HACK 99: Impersonate Another Computer on the Network 336
HACK 100: Protect Yourself Against "Free Wi-Fi" Scammers 339
HACK 101: Protect Your Home Wi-Fi Network 343
HACK 102: Turn On Wi-Fi Encryption 349

HACK 103: Go Wardriving for Wi-Fi Access....351
HACK 104: Solve Hotspot Email Woes....354
HACK 105: Protect Yourself at Hotspots....357
HACK 106: Hacking Wi-Fi Antennas....361
HACK 107: Using a Bluetooth Headset in Vista....368

CHAPTER 08: SECURITY....374

HACK 108: Hack Windows Vista's User Account Control....374
HACK 109: Unlock the Super-Secret Administrator Account....377
HACK 110: Root Out Rootkits....378
HACK 111: Kill Spyware and Pests With Your Bare Hands....381
HACK 112: Hacking Windows Vista's Outbound Firewall....386
HACK 113: Punch an Escape Hole Through Your Firewall....389
HACK 114: Track Firewall Activity with a Windows Firewall Log....394
HACK 115: Protect Your Privacy by Removing Windows Vista Metadata....398
HACK 116: Kill Annoying Software Registration Reminders....400
HACK 117: Use Vista's BitLocker with a USB Key....401
HACK 118: Hide Folders and Files with the Encrypting File System....404
HACK 119: Set Up a Virtual Private Network....409

CHAPTER 09: APPLICATIONS, HOME SERVER, AND BACKUP....416

HACK 120: Fast Hacks for Word 2007....416
HACK 121: Blog Using Word 2007....418
HACK 122: Create Reusable "Building Blocks" in Word 2007....421
HACK 123: Say Hello to Your New Word 2007 Commands....423
HACK 124: Shrink Supersized Pictures in Office Docs....429
HACK 125: Grab Real-Time Stock Quotes in Excel....431
HACK 126: Open and Create Office Docs Without Word or Excel....433
HACK 127: Roll Your Own PDFs....435
HACK 128: Customize Windows Home Server Backups....438
HACK 129: Make a Remote Connection to Windows Home Server Over the Internet....441
HACK 130: Take Remote Command of a PC Using Window Home Server....445
HACK 131: Hacking Windows Vista Backups....448
HACK 132: Use Windows XP's Ntbackup in Windows Vista....450
HACK 133: Best Backup Plans for Your PC....453
HACK 134: Control How Much Disk Space Windows Vista Uses for System Restore....458
HACK 135: Run 16-Bit DOS and Windows Applications....460
HACK 136: Emulate the Nintendo Entertainment System on a PC....463
HACK 137: Emulate the Game Boy on Your PC....468

CHAPTER 10: GRAPHICS AND MULTIMEDIA 472

HACK 138: Set Up Your PC To Record TV Shows 472
HACK 139: Remove Commercials from Recorded TV Shows 479
HACK 140: Make Your Own TV Show Mashup 483
HACK 141: Burn Recorded TV Shows Directly from Windows Media Center to DVD 490
HACK 142: Rip DVDs into Media Center 492
HACK 143: Quick Fix for Video and Animation Woes 498
HACK 144: Choose the Right Settings for Publishing Your Movie in Windows Movie Maker 498
HACK 145: Upload Your Video to YouTube 501
HACK 146: Turn VHS Tapes into DVD Movies 505
HACK 147: Store Any Type of File on Your Zune 509
HACK 148: Watch Any DVD on Your Zune 510
HACK 149: Delete Music from Your PC without Deleting It from Your Zune 511
HACK 150: Play YouTube Videos on your Zune 512
HACK 151: Copy Recorded TV Shows To Your Zune 513
HACK 152: Organize Your Photos with Metadata 514
HACK 153: Use RAW Photos in Windows Photo Gallery 519
HACK 154: Play It Loud 520
HACK 155: Convert Vinyl and Tapes to MP3s 522

CHAPTER 11: SYSTEM PERFORMANCE 524

HACK 156: Strip the Crud Out of Your Windows Install 524
HACK 157: Hack Multicore Performance 527
HACK 158: Speed Up Your PC with ReadyBoost 529
HACK 159: Force Windows Vista to Use Any Flash Drive for ReadyBoost 532
HACK 160: Get the Most Out of Your RAM 535
HACK 161: Improve Defragging in Windows XP 539
HACK 162: Look, Ma, No Hands! How To Automate Defrag in Windows XP 541
HACK 163: Schedule Defragging in Windows Vista 544
HACK 164: Defragment a Single File 545
HACK 165: Track Down Vista System Woes 547
HACK 166: Track System Performance with the XP Performance Console 550
HACK 167: Track Performance and Reliability with the Vista Reliability Monitor 553
HACK 168: Speed Up System Performance with the Task Manager 556
HACK 169: Manage the Paging File 562
HACK 170: Speed It Up with RAID 565

CHAPTER 12: HARDWARE 568

HACK 171: Mod Your PC's Case 568
HACK 172: Use Your Zune as a USB Hard Drive 573
HACK 173: Install a Larger Disk in Your Zune 573
HACK 174: Troubleshoot Hardware with Device Manager 578
HACK 175: Uncover Hidden Hardware with the Device Manager 583
HACK 176: Get a Comprehensive List of all Your Drivers 586

HACK 177: Turn off Hybrid Sleep Mode in Windows Vista 588
HACK 178: A Quick Way to Overclock your PC 590
HACK 179: Keep It Cool 591
HACK 180: Overclock Any Video Card 599
HACK 181: Install a Video Card 599
HACK 182: Top Hardware Troubleshooting Hacks 603

CHAPTER 13: THE REGISTRY AND GROUP POLICY EDITOR . . 610

HACK 183: Don't Fear the Registry 611
HACK 184: Hack Away at the Registry 617
HACK 185: Safely Edit the Registry Using .reg Files 619
HACK 186: Better Registry Backups 622
HACK 187: Track and Restore Registry Changes 623
HACK 188: Hack Away at Windows with the Group Policy Editor 624

CREDITS 627
INDEX 633

PREFACE

What good is software and hardware if you can't hack it? In my book (literally), it's no good at all.

Windows-related software and hardware is eminently hackable. As you'll see, you can hack just about anything. Want to completely redo Windows Vista's (or Windows XP's) interface? I'll show you how. How about hacking the dreaded Vista User Account Control prompt, ReadyBoost, or Windows Aero? It's in here as well. Want to mod your PC's case, do some serious Zune hacking, replace your home router's firmware to give it enterprise-level features, hack your BIOS, speed up Internet access for free, take control of your wireless network, and more? That's all in here as well, and plenty more, to boot. (And yes, there are plenty of hacks for booting your PC as well, including setting up multiboot systems and mastering Windows Vista's bizarre new BCD store for bootup.)

You'll find hundreds of hacks in this book. Some are simple enough so that you can do them in a few minutes. Some take some serious time and thought, such as how to build your own Windows Vista gadgets. But all of them are useful or entertaining. You'll learn how to get far more out of Windows-related software and hardware, and have fun in the process.

The hundreds of hacks you'll find inside are useful, frequently entertaining, and will save you countless hours at the keyboard. Whether you want to speed up your PC, customize the Windows interface, hack your wired and wireless network, get more out of the Web, make better use of email, use the Registry to bend the operating system to your will, record TV shows and burn DVDS, or use Windows for countless other useful tasks, you'll find what you're looking for here. And each hack doesn't just show you *how* to do something; it also teaches *why* it works. Each hack is a starting point, rather than an ending point, so that you can apply the knowledge you've gained to create new hacks of your own. Try it out: who knows, in the next edition of this book, you might get a hack of your own published.

The book covers Windows Vista and Windows XP, as well as hardware that works with both, including laptops, desktops, the Zune, and more. It also covers other Microsoft software, including Microsoft Office and Windows Home Server.

How to Use This Book

You can read this book from cover to cover if you like, but each hack stands on its own, so feel free to browse and jump to the different sections that interest you most. If there's a prerequisite you need to know about, a cross-reference will guide you to the right hack. If you're not familiar with the Registry yet, or you want a refresher, you might want to spend some time in Chapter 13 to get a good grounding.

How This Book Is Organized

This book is not a mere tips-and-tricks compendium that tells you where to click, where to drag, and what commands to type. It takes advantage of Windows' flexibility and new features, recognizes that there are specific tasks you want to accomplish with the operating system and related hardware and software, and offers bite-size pieces of functionality you can put to use in a few minutes. It also shows how you can expand on their usefulness yourself. To give you this kind of help, the book is organized into 13 chapters:

Chapter 1, Startup and Shutdown

Want to change the picture that appears on your bootscreen, create a multiboot system for multiple Windows versions as well as Linux, speed up startup and shutdowns, or hack your BIOS? You'll find all that in this chapter, as well as the Registry, to enable you to control many different aspects of startup and shutdown, customize multiboot options, and learn the deep, dark secrets of Vista's BCD store—and how to get around it.

Chapter 2, Hacking the Interface

Want to bend Windows Vista's Aero interface to your will? You'll find that in this chapter, along with ways to hack XP's interface as well. You'll also learn how to create 3D virtual desktops and control the Control Panel, Start menu and Taskbar. And for gadget freaks—that's Vista gadgets—you'll find plenty of hacks, including how to have a gadget play YouTube videos. You'll also discover how to easily build a gadget from any gadget or widget on the Web. Mac lovers will find out how to run Mac OS X on Windows, and those who want to go retro can find out how to run Windows 3.11.

Chapter 3, Windows Explorer, Managing Files, and Search

If you haven't given much thought to Windows Explorer or searching in Windows, so much the worse for you. As you'll see in this chapter, there are plenty of ways you can hack both. You'll be able to power up the context menu, hack your partitions and redirect your user folders in Visa, use Windows Shadow Copy to restore files, and more. As for search, you'll find out how to speed it up, and add amazing new features via a simple add-in. The chapter also demystifies the confusing and rarely used Sync Center, and shows how to get more disk space using NTFS compression.

Chapter 4, Internet Explorer, the Web, and the Internet

Face it: you live on the Web and Internet, so why not make the most of it? In this chapter, you'll find plenty of ways to improve your life online, including how to increase your bandwidth for free by clearing up router congestion, hacking DNS for lightning-fast Web access; how to build your own Internet; and Firefox Explorer search applets, protect yourself by surfing anonymously without a trace; and plenty more. You'll also find out how to keep your Google searches private, fix a variety of Internet Explorer woes, stop Firefox memory leaks, and even build a Google screensaver.

Chapter 5, Networking

If you've got a small network, you need this chapter. The first hack alone will make it worth your while; you'll be able to fix a sluggish router in a few simple steps. The chapter also tells you how to make XP and Vista get along on a network, give the world access to a server behind your router, use remote access to control distant computers, and use command-line tools for trouble-free network operations. You'll also find plenty of hacks for using Voice over Internet Protocol (VoIP) to make inexpensive phone calls, including plenty of Skype hacks.

Chapter 6, Email

Email—can't live with it, can't live without it . . . and in this chapter, you'll learn many ways to get more out of it. Here's where you'll find out how hack Gmail, including using it as a universal inbox; put your bloated Outlook folders on a diet; slam spam; instantly compress files for faster sending; open blocked file attachments in Outlook, Outlook Express, and Windows Mail; and much more.

Chapter 7, Wireless

It's an unwired world, and Windows is at the center of it. This chapter offers plenty of great wireless hacks, including one that shows you how to turn your $50 router into an enterprise-level powerhouse by replacing its firmware. You'll also find out how to build your own antenna, extend the range of your wireless network, spoof your MAC address, and protect yourself against "free WiFi" scammers as well as protect your home wireless network. And if you have trouble sending email from hot spots, there's a hack for you. There's plenty more here as well, including setting up a Bluetooth headset in Windows Vista.

Chapter 8, Security

It's a nasty world out here. There are snoopers, intruders, and malware writers looking to turn your PC into a spam-spewing zombie. But this chapter helps you fight them off and also shows how to customize how you use security. Don't like the way that User Account Control (UAC) works in Vista? No problem—I'll show you how to hack it. Want to go mano a mano against spyware and kill it with your bare hands? I'll show you how to do that as well. You'll also find out how to unlock Windows Vista's super-secret Administrator account, root out rootkits, hack the Windows Vista (and XP) firewall, and use Vista's BitLocker encryption technology with a USB key. There are also hacks on encrypting your PC, setting up your own virtual private network (VPN), and more.

Chapter 9, Applications, Home Server, and Backup

An operating system by itself is a poor thing. What makes it go are applications, and you'll find out how to hack them in this chapter. Want to hack Microsoft's Home Server? You'll find ways to do that. Want to blog with Word 2007 and use Excel to grab live data from the internet? You'll learn to do that as well, along with finding out how to create reusable building blocks in Word 2007. You'll also see how to shrink supersized pictures in Office, hack Windows backups, use Windows XP's Ntbackup in Windows Vista, and more

Chapter 10, Graphics and Multimedia

While you weren't watching, Windows and related technologies became a multimedia powerhouse, ripe for the hacking. This chapter probably has the highest coolness factor of the entire book. You'll find out how to record TV shows, edit out commercials, and even "mash up" several TV shows—what happens when you combine *Lost* with *House*? You'll be able to do it. You'll also discover plenty of Zune hacks, including how to record TV shows to watch on the Zune, how to exchange any file using Zune's built-in Wi-Fi, and how to watch any DVD on your Zune. You'll also discover how to copy DVDs to your hard disk, save YouTube videos to your PC (and your iPod and Zune), and transfer movies from old tapes to DVDs. There are plenty more hacks as well.

Chapter 11, System Performance

When it comes to PCs, there are only three important speeds—fast, faster, and fastest. This chapter shows you how to make sure that your PC always runs in the fastest lane. Want to strip the crud out of your Windows install? It's here. You'll also learn how to hack dual core performance and speed up your PC with ReadyBoost. The chapter also shows you how to get the most out of your RAM, speed up your hard disk, and use a variety of tools for tracking down system woes and fixing them.

Chapter 12, Hardware

Hardware hacks: just the sound of it can make grown men and women shiver—visions of sizzling soldering irons, of system boards, cards, and cables scattered in an unholy mess, of a PC turned into toast. But as you'll see in this chapter, it's easier to do than you might think. You'll find out how to mod your PC's case like a hot rodder, replace your Zune's hard drive with a bigger one, troubleshoot hardware problems, overclock your PC and video card, cool down overclocked PCs, and plenty more.

Chapter 13, The Registry and Group Policy Editor

If you're going to hack Windows, you'll need to use the Registry. It's that simple. This chapter goes beyond merely teaching you how to use the Registry and how it's organized (although it covers that in detail). It also shows you how to hack the Registry itself—for example, by offering hacks on how to use *.reg* files to edit the Registry safely, and how to track and restore Registry changes. Additionally, you'll find out how to use the Group Policy Editor for hacking.

Conventions Used in This Book

This book uses the following typographical conventions:

Italic

Used to indicate new terms, URLs, filenames, file extensions, directories, and folders.

`Constant width`

Used to show code examples, verbatim searches and commands, the contents of files, and the output from commands.

Gray

Used in examples and tables to show commands or other text that should be typed literally.

`Constant width gray`

Used in examples, tables, and commands to show text that should be replaced with user-supplied values.

Pay special attention to notes set apart from the text with the following icons:

 This icon indicates a tip, suggestion, or general note. It contains useful supplementary information or an observation about the topic at hand.

 This icon indicates a warning or note of caution.

The slider icons, found next to each hack, indicate the relative complexity of the hack:

Easy:

Intermediate:

Expert:

Using Code Examples

This book is here to help you get your job done. In general, you may use the code in this book in your programs and documentation. You do not need to contact us for permission unless you're reproducing a significant portion of the code. For example, writing a program that uses several chunks of code from this book does not require permission. Selling or distributing a CDROM of examples from O'Reilly books does require permission. Answering a question by citing this book and quoting example code does not require permission. Incorporating a significant amount of example code from this book into your product's documentation does require permission.

We appreciate, but do not require, attribution. An attribution usually includes the title, author, publisher, and ISBN. For example: "Big Book of Windows Hacks, by Preston Gralla. Copyright 2007 O'Reilly Media, Inc., 978-0-596-52835-5."

If you feel your use of code examples falls outside fair use or the permission given above, feel free to contact us at permissions@oreilly.com.

Acknowledgments

A writer without an editor is a lonely thing, and for this book I've been lucky enough to enjoy the companionship and editorial insight and guidance of Brian Jepson. Brian has been far more than an editor on the book: He has written hacks, made my hacks better, been an invaluable technical resource, served as a technical reviewer, and even worked on the cover design. For all I know, he ran the presses as well.

Thanks also go to Brian Sawyer, who was the book's first editor before he moved to another position. And I'd like to thank Nancy Kotary and Mary Anne Mayo, who copyedited the manuscript, Terry Bronson, who shepherded this book through production, and Alison Kendall for the design and layout of the book.

Finally, as always, thanks go to my wife Lydia, my daughter Mia, and my son Gabe. Without them, is anything worth hacking?

We'd Like to Hear from You

Please address comments and questions concerning this book to the publisher:

O'Reilly Media, Inc.

1005 Gravenstein Highway North

Sebastopol, CA 95472

(800) 998-9938 (in the United States or Canada)

(707) 829-0515 (international or local)

(707) 829-0104 (fax)

We have a web page for this book that lists errata, examples, and any additional information. You can access this page at: http://www.makezine.com/go/bbowinhacks

To comment or ask technical questions about this book, send email to *bookquestions@oreilly.com*

Maker Media is a division of O'Reilly Media devoted entirely to the growing community of resourceful people who believe that if you can imagine it, you can make it. Consisting of Make Magazine, Craft Magazine, Maker Faire, and the Hacks series of books, Maker Media encourages the Do-It-Yourself mentality by providing creative inspiration and instruction.

For more information about Maker Media, visit us online:

MAKE: www.makezine.com

CRAFT: www.craftzine.com

Maker Faire: www.makerfaire.com

Hacks: www.hackszine.com

01 STARTUP AND SHUTDOWN

How much do you think about the way you start up and shut down Windows? After all, what's to think about—push a few buttons and you're done, right?

Wrong. As you'll see in this chapter, starting up and shutting down Windows is absolutely hackable. Whether you want to be more productive or just have fun, there's plenty to hack. Want to change the Windows Vista and Windows XP boot screen? You can do it. Tired of waiting for your PC to start up and shut down? You can speed it up. Want to boot into multiple operating systems, create a dual-boot Linux-Windows laptop, and customize your multiboot options? You can do that as well. In this chapter, you'll even learn about hardware startup hacks that show you how to tweak your BIOS.

HACK 01: Change Your Windows Vista Boot Screen

V Tired of seeing the same old Windows Vista logo every time you start Windows Vista? Here's how you can replace it with any one you want—for free.

Start Windows Vista. Stare at the same boring boot screen you've seen approximately 2,984 times. Ho-hum. Another day of computing.

It doesn't need to be that way. You can create your own boot screen for Windows Vista, or use a graphic you find online. And it's easy to do.

First you'll need to create or find a graphic for your new boot screen. You'll need two versions of the graphic, one 1024 x 768 pixels, and one 800 x 600 pixels. They must be in 24-bit *.bmp* format.

If you can't create them yourself, use Google's image search (go to Google, then click the Images link and do your search). In your search results, under each image, you'll see the dimensions of the graphic, so you'll be able to know ahead of time whether it's the right size (Figure 1-1). Note that if you come across a graphic in *.jpg* format, you can still use it, because you can have Internet Explorer save it as a *.bmp*.

You can save time by finding just one file, a 1024 x 768 pixel image. You can then use your graphics software to make a copy of the file as an 800 x 600 pixel file, so that you'll have two files, one 1024 x 768, and the other 800 x 600 . A great tool for doing this is the free IrfanView (www.irfanview.com). When you open a file in IrfanView, select Image→Resize/Resample, click 800 x 600 pixels on the right side of the screen, and click OK. Then save the file with a new name, making sure not to overwrite your original file.

In Internet Explorer, right-click the image you want to use, select Save Picture As, and in the Save As Type drop-down, select *.bmp*. Then save the file.

After you have both files, download, install, and run the free Vista Boot Logo Generator (www.computa.co.uk/staff/dan/?p=18). Click each of the "Browse for image" buttons and select your two graphics. You'll see a screen like the one shown in Figure 1-2. Select File→Save Boot Screen As and

Figure 1-1.
Searching Google for an image to use for your boot screen

Figure 1-2.
Selecting a new boot screen for Windows Vista

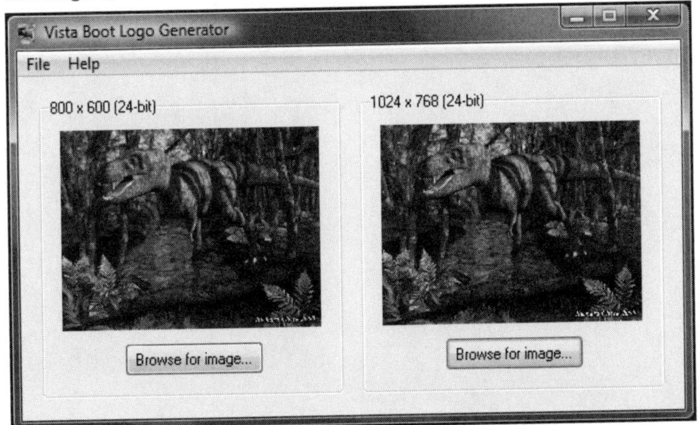

QUICK HACK

TURN ON WINDOWS VISTA'S HIDDEN BOOT SCREEN

If you don't want to go to the trouble of building your own boot screen, but aren't happy with the default one for Windows Vista, there's another solution: turn on Windows Vista's hidden boot screen. It's called Aurora, because it looks like Aurora Borealis, also known as the Northern Lights. To turn it on, run the MSCONFIG utility, and on the Boot tab, select "No GUI boot" and click OK. From now on, you'll use the hidden Windows Vista boot screen (if you've previously replaced the *winload.exe.mui* file with your own boot screen, you'll need to restore the original to see the Aurora screen).

save the file to any location on your hard disk. over. The program does not save the files as graphics, and instead will save them both as a single file, *winload.exe.mui*.

Now that the file is saved, copy it to *C:\Windows\System32\en-US*. There will already be a file in that folder named *winload.exe.mui*, so make sure that you back up the original and replace it with this new one.

Windows Vista may not allow you to overwrite the *winload.exe.mui*, file. If that's the case, follow the directions in "Troubleshooting," later in this hack.

Now run the MSCONFIG utility: type MSCONFIG in the Search box or at the command prompt and press Enter. Click the Boot tab, select "No GUI boot," and click OK, as shown in Figure 1-3. You'll be asked to restart Windows. Click Restart, and you'll see your new boot screen in living, full-color glory.

Whenever you run MSCONFIG to make a system change, it configures itself to run automatically on the next reboot. Because MSCONFIG requires administrative privileges, it can't start automatically, and you'll get a notification that "Windows has blocked some startup programs." Click the blocked startup program icon in the notification area, choose the System Configuration Utility, and let it run. You'll get a dialog window explaining that you've made changes to your startup configuration (and you can also tell MSCONFIG to stop showing this message at startup).

Troubleshooting

When you try to copy *winload.exe.mui* to *C:\Windows\System32\en-US*, you might get a permissions error of some sort, preventing you from copying the file. And even if you don't get an error, when you restart Windows, you might not see your boot screen. If either of those things happens to you, follow this advice. It will solve the permissions problem.

First, run the command prompt as an administrator, by typing `cmd` at the Search box, and pressing Ctrl-Shift-Enter. Then type the following at the command prompt, and press Enter:

```
takeown /f C:\Windows\System32\en-US\winload.exe.mui
```

You'll get a message that you now have ownership of *C:\Windows\System32\en-US\winload.exe.mui*. Next, type the following at the command prompt (where `yourname` is your username), and press Enter:

```
cacls C:\Windows\System32\en-US\winload.exe.mui /G yourname:F
```

Figure 1-3.
The last step in changing your Windows Vista boot screen

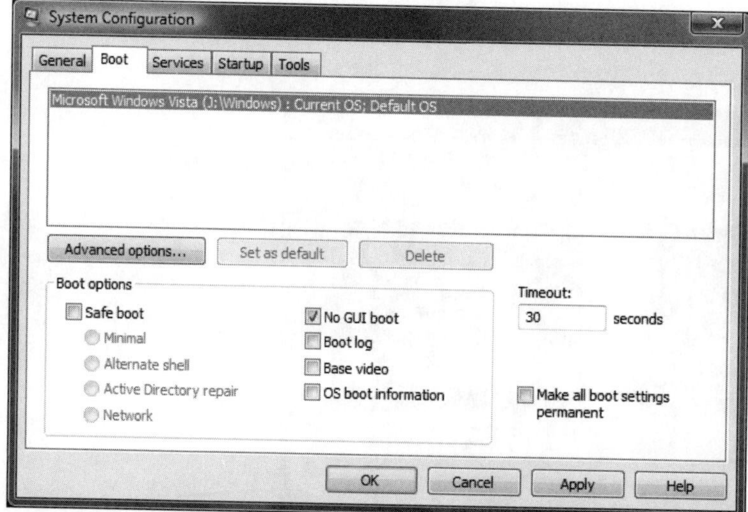

You'll be asked whether you want to proceed. Press the Y key and then press Enter. You'll get this:

```
processed file: C:\Windows\System32\en-US\winload.exe.mui
```

You can now go ahead and copy *winload.exe.mui* to *C:\Windows\System32\en-US*, and then proceed with the rest of the hack.

See Also

- "Change Your Windows XP Boot Screen" **[Hack #2]**

HACK 02: Change Your Windows XP Boot Screen

XP Windows XP users can change their boot screens with this free software. Say good-bye to the boring Windows XP logo.

Windows XP users get as tired of their boot screens as Windows Vista users do—so if you're a Windows XP user, this hack is for you. It'll show you how to easily change your boot screen.

Download, install, and run the free program BootSkin (www.stardock.com/products/bootskin).

A screen like the one shown in Figure 1-4 appears. Scroll to any boot screen and click Preview to see a larger view of it. Once you've found one you want to use as your boot screen, click Apply.

The next time you boot, you'll see your new boot screen. But you're not limited to the boot screens in the program. Click Browse boot screen library, and you'll be brought to a page from the WinCustomize BootSkins Gallery that has thousands of boot skins. It's shown in Figure 1-5.

Figure 1-4.
Choose your new Windows XP logo here

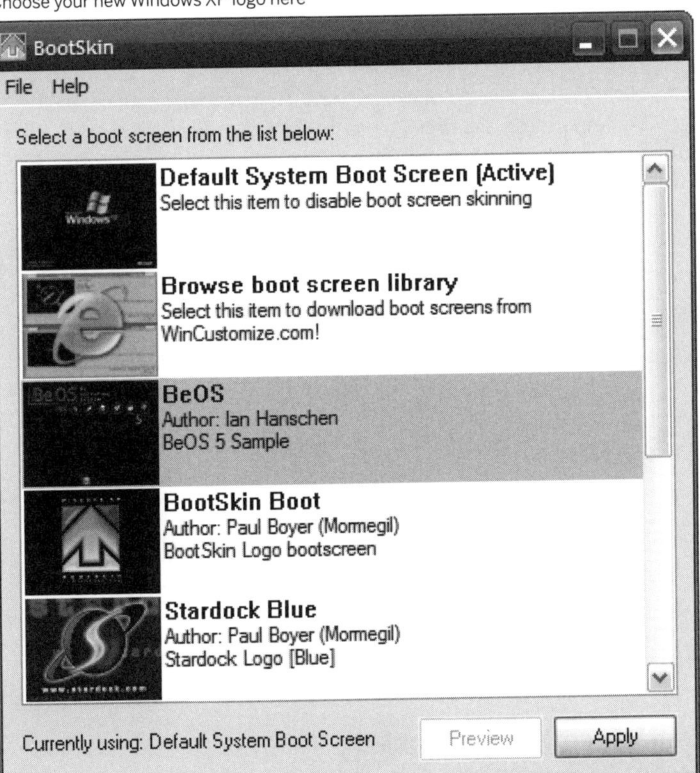

> **QUICK HACK**
>
> **FIND ALL YOUR SOFTWARE PRODUCT KEYS**
>
> When you install Windows and many pieces of software, such as Microsoft Office, you'll need to type in long, impossible-to-remember product keys that you get on a label on the DVD case, or sent to you via email. At times, you'll need these product keys, when you want to upgrade, or get technical support, for example. But keeping track of them can be impossible. Run the free software program Keyfinder (www.magicaljellybean.com); it will peer into your system and tell you your Windows keys, Office keys, and keys for other software as well. It works with Windows XP, Microsoft Office and 32-bit versions of Windows Vista, as well as other programs. However, it won't work with 64-bit Windows Vista (as of this writing). For that, you'll need to use the free Windows Product Key Viewer (www.rjlsoftware.com/software/utility/winproductkey/download.shtml).

Figure 1-5.
Browsing for a new Windows XP boot screen

Click one you want to download and you'll see a larger preview of it. Click the Download button, and from the screen that appears, click the "Click link to download" link. Then save the boot screen on your PC. In BootSkin, select File→Import from file, and browse to and select your downloaded boot screen. You'll get a notice that the screen was imported. The new boot screen will now show up in the program, and you can use it in the same way as you can any other boot screen.

You can have BootSkin choose a random boot screen every time you start Windows XP. Choose File→Random boot screen at startup.

See Also

- "Change Your Windows Vista Boot Screen" **[Hack #1]**

HACK 03: Speed Up Boot and Shutdown Times

V XP Shorten the time it takes for your desktop to appear when you turn on your PC—and make Windows shut down faster.

No matter how fast your PC boots, it's not fast enough. Here are several hacks to get you right to your desktop as quickly as possible after startup, whether you use Windows XP or Windows Vista.

Confirm That Boot Defragmentation Is Enabled

There's a simple way to speed up Windows startup: make your system do a boot defragment, which puts all the boot files next to one another on your hard disk. When boot files are in close proximity to one another, your system will start faster.

On most systems, boot defragment should be enabled by default, but it might not be on yours, or it might have been changed inadvertently. To make sure that boot defragment is enabled on your system, launch the Registry Editor by typing regedit at the Start Search box or a command prompt (see Chapter 13 for details) and go to:

```
HKEY_LOCAL_MACHINE\SOFTWARE\Microsoft\Dfrg\BootOptimizeFunction
```

Edit the `Enable` string value to Y if it is not already set to Y. Exit the Registry and reboot. The next time you reboot, your computer will perform a boot defragment.

 I've found many web sites recommending a way of speeding up boot times for Windows XP that might in fact slow down the amount of time it takes to boot up and probably slow down launching applications as well. The tip recommends going to your *C:\WINDOWS\Prefetch* directory and emptying it every week. Windows uses this directory to speed up launching applications. It analyzes the files you use during startup and the applications you launch, and it creates an index to where those files and applications are located on your hard disk. By using this index, Windows can launch files and applications faster. So, by emptying the directory, you are most likely slowing down launching applications. In my tests, I've also found that after emptying the directory, it takes my PC a few seconds *longer* to get to my desktop after bootup. You'll also slow down launching files and opening applications, and interfere with Windows Vista ReadyBoost. (See "Speed Up Your PC with ReadyBoost" **[Hack #158]** and "Force Windows Vista to Use Any USB Flash Drive for ReadyBoost" **[Hack #159]**.)

Hack Your BIOS for Faster Startups

When you turn on your PC, it goes through a set of startup procedures in its BIOS before it gets to starting Windows. So, if you speed up those initial startup procedures, you'll make your system start faster.

You can speed up your startup procedures by changing the BIOS with the built-in setup utility. How you run this utility varies from PC to PC, but you typically get to it by pressing either the Delete, F1, or F10 key during startup. You'll come to a menu with a variety of choices. Here are the choices to make for faster system startups:

Quick Power On Self Test (POST)
When you choose this option, your system runs an abbreviated `POST` rather than the normal, lengthy one.

Change Your Boot Order
If you change the boot order so that your BIOS checks the hard disk first for booting, it won't check any other devices, and will speed up your startup time.

Boot Up Floppy Seek
Disable this option. When it's enabled, your system spends a few extra seconds looking for your floppy drive—a relatively pointless procedure, especially considering how infrequently you use your floppy drive.

Boot Delay
Some systems let you delay booting after you turn on your PC so that your hard drive gets a chance to start spinning before bootup. Most likely, you don't need to have this boot delay, so turn it off. If you run into problems, however, you can turn it back on.

Fine-Tune Your Registry for Faster Startups

Over time, your Registry can become bloated with unused entries, slowing down your system startup because your system loads them every time you start up your PC. Get a Registry cleanup tool to delete unneeded Registry entries and speed up startup times. Eusing Free Registry Cleaner (www.eusing.com/free_registry_cleaner/registry_cleaner.htm), shown in Figure 1-6, is an excellent

Figure 1-6.
Cleaning the Registry with Eusing Free Registry Cleaner

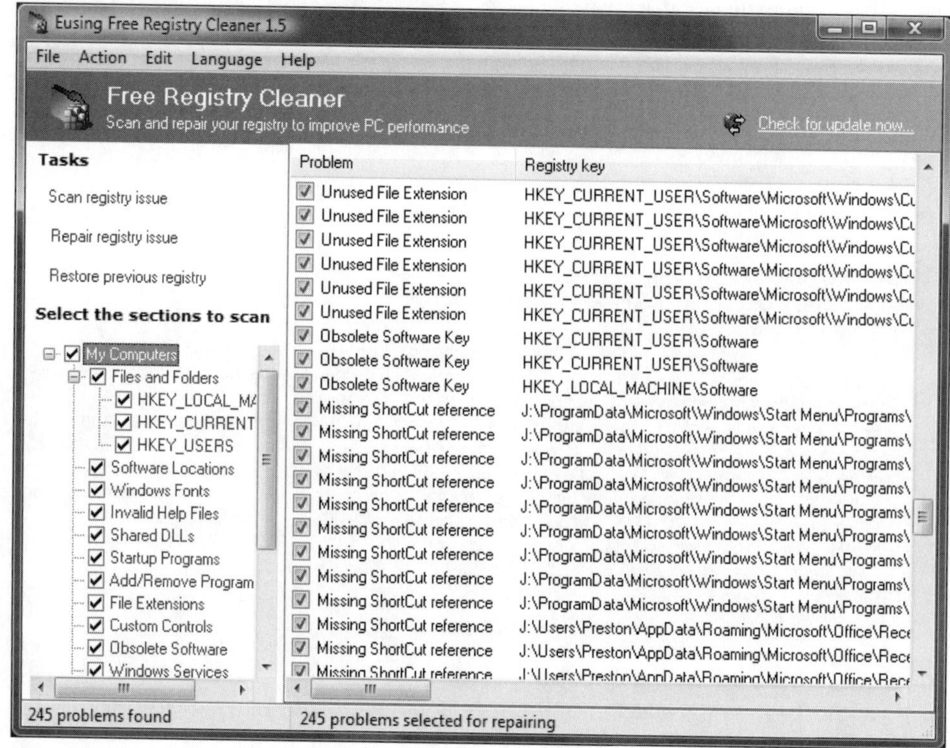

Registry cleanup tool. It combs your Registry for outdated and useless entries and then lets you choose which entries to delete and which to keep. It also lets you restore your Registry if you run into a problem.

Speed Up Shutdown Times

It's not only startup times that you'd like to speed up; you can also adjust things so that your system shuts down faster. If shutting down XP takes what seems to be an inordinate amount of time, here are a couple of steps you can take to speed up the shutdown process:

Don't have Windows clear your paging file at shutdown

For security reasons, you can have Windows clear your paging file (*pagefile.sys*) of its contents whenever you shut down. Your paging file is used to store temporary files and data, but when your system shuts down, information stays in the file. Some people prefer to have the paging file cleared at shutdown, because sensitive information (such as unencrypted passwords) sometimes ends up in the file. However, clearing the paging file can slow shutdown times significantly, so if extreme security isn't a high priority, you might not want to clear it.

To shut down Windows without clearing your paging file, run the Registry Editor and go to:

```
HKEY_LOCAL_MACHINE\SYSTEM\CurrentControlSet\Control\Session Manager\Memory Management
```

Change the value of `ClearPageFileAtShutdown` to `0`. (It may already be set to this.) Close the Registry and restart your computer. Whenever you turn off Windows from now on, the paging file won't be cleared, and you should be able to shut down more quickly.

 One simple way to speed up shutdown (and startup) times is to not ever actually shut down your PC. Instead, use sleep or hibernate modes. They use very little power, and shut down and start up your PC far more quickly than when you shut off the power completely.

Sometimes it takes Windows a long time to shut down because it's waiting to see whether a service will stop on its own before prompting you to manually shut it down. Windows, by default, waits 20 seconds before prompting you, which can sometimes seem interminable. You can hack the Registry to have Windows ask you sooner than 20 seconds. Run the Registry Editor and go to:

```
HKEY_LOCAL_MACHINE\SYSTEM\CurrentControlSet\Control
```

Look for the `WaitToKillServiceTimeout` value. By default, it's set to `20000` (20,000 milliseconds). Change it to another number, in milliseconds—such as `15000`, which would have Windows wait 15 seconds instead of 20 before prompting you. It's a good idea to start off lowering the number in increments of not more than five seconds, to see how your computer responds. And don't set it to lower than `5000`, or you might lose data or your PC might not shut down properly.

Turn off unnecessary services

Services take time to shut down, so the fewer you run, the faster you can shut down. For information on how to shut them down, see "Speed Up Startup by Halting Startup Programs and Services" [Hack #6].

See Also

- "BIOS Hacks for Faster Bootup" [Hack #7]
- "Speed Up Startup by Halting Startup Programs and Services" [Hack #6]

HACK 04: Run Windows Vista Without Activation for 120 Days

V Don't like to be forced to activate Windows Vista after 30 days? With this simple hack, you can extend that period to a full 120.

When you install Windows Vista, you're asked whether you want to "activate" the operating system right away. When Windows Vista activates, it contacts Microsoft servers over the Internet, and registers itself with Microsoft. At that point, Windows is tied to your specific hardware configuration, such as your motherboard, hard drive, and other pieces of hardware. If you make major changes to your hardware, such as installing a new motherboard, you'll have to reactivate Windows.

 If you don't like the idea of having your PC contact Microsoft servers over the Internet, you can instead call Microsoft to have Windows activated.

You don't have to activate Windows Vista when you install it. You can do it any time in the next 30 days. But if you don't do it after 30 days, you'll get a warning, and after that, Windows won't function fully. Many people don't like the activation process because it ties Windows to their hardware configuration, and they like putting off activation. Also, if someone knows they're going to do a major overhaul of their hardware in a few months, they'd also like to put off activation, because they'll then only have to activate Windows again.

There's a simple command-line tool that will allow you to extend your activation so that you can use Windows for a full 120 days with activating it. The Windows Software Licensing Management Tool is the Visual Basic script *slmgr.vbs*, found in *C:\Windows\system32*.

To run it, start a command prompt as an administrator by typing cmd in the Search box and right-clicking the icon that appears at the top of the Start menu and selecting "Run as administrator."

At the command prompt, type this command and press Enter:

```
slmgr -rearm
```

You'll see the message, "Command completed successfully. Please restart the system for the changes to take effect." Reboot, and your activation period will be extended for 30 additional days. You'll be able to do this three times, which means you'll be able to run Vista without activation for 120 days.

After you type in your commands, nothing will seem to happen for a while, perhaps a minute or more. Don't worry; nothing's wrong. *slmgr.vbs* take a while to go about doing its business.

After you reboot, you can check whether your time was extended using *slmgr.vbs* to report on the state of your system's activation. Type this command and press Enter:

```
slmgr -xpr
```

A screen appears telling you how long you have to wait until you have to activate Windows.

Several people have reported that you can put off activation for a year or more, using a Registry hack. On a PC that has yet to have Windows activated, open the Registry Editor, and go to `HKEY_LOCAL_MACHINE\SOFTWARE\Microsoft\Windows NT\CurrentVersion\SL`. Look for the key named `SkipRearm` and change the value from 00000000 to 00000001. Exit the Registry, then use the slmgr command as described earlier to push out the activation deadline 30 days. You may now be able to keep doing this indefinitely. There's a chance that Microsoft will close this hack off, by the way, and it may be short-lived.

Hacking the Hack

You can use the *slmgr.vbs* command to perform other tasks related to your Windows license and activation. For example, type this command:

```
slmgr -dli
```

and you'll be shown information about your Windows Vista license, as in Figure 1-7. Table 1-1 lists other switches you can use in concert with slmgr and what each does.

Table 1-1 Switches for *slmgr*

SWITCH	WHAT IT DOES
-ipk <product key>	Installs a product key, or replaces an existing product key with a new one
-upk	Uninstalls the current product key
-ato	Activates Windows

Figure 1-7.
A short version of the license information for a PC

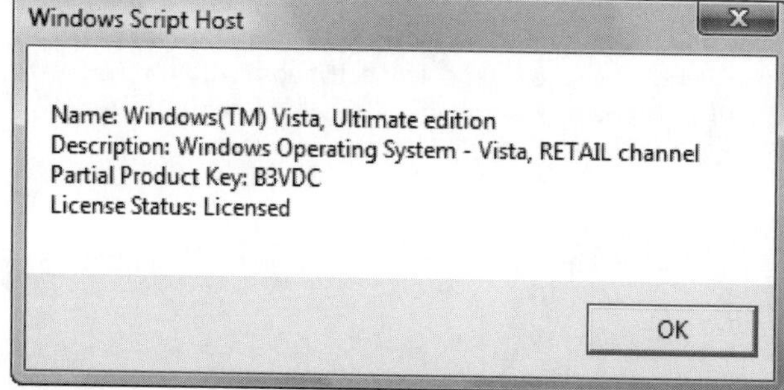

Table 1-1 Switches for *slmgr* *(continued)*

SWITCH	WHAT IT DOES
-dli	Displays basic license information
-dlv	Displays detailed license information
-xpr	Displays the expiration date for the current license

HACK 05: Bypass the Windows Vista Logon Screen on Multiaccount PCs

V Having to type in your logon information on a system with two or more user accounts can be a pain. This hack shows you how to tell Windows Vista to log on to your primary account immediately.

When you have more than one user account on a Windows Vista PC, every time you restart your PC, you'll be presented with a welcome screen listing all the accounts on the machine, forcing you to click one and type in your logon information.

But what if, like many people, you use one primary account nearly all the time, and use others only on occasion—and you'd like to bypass the screen listing all the user accounts and be logged in automatically? You're apparently out of luck; Windows Vista can't seem to do it.

Figure 1-8.
The User Accounts screen lists all your user accounts, and lets you customize them

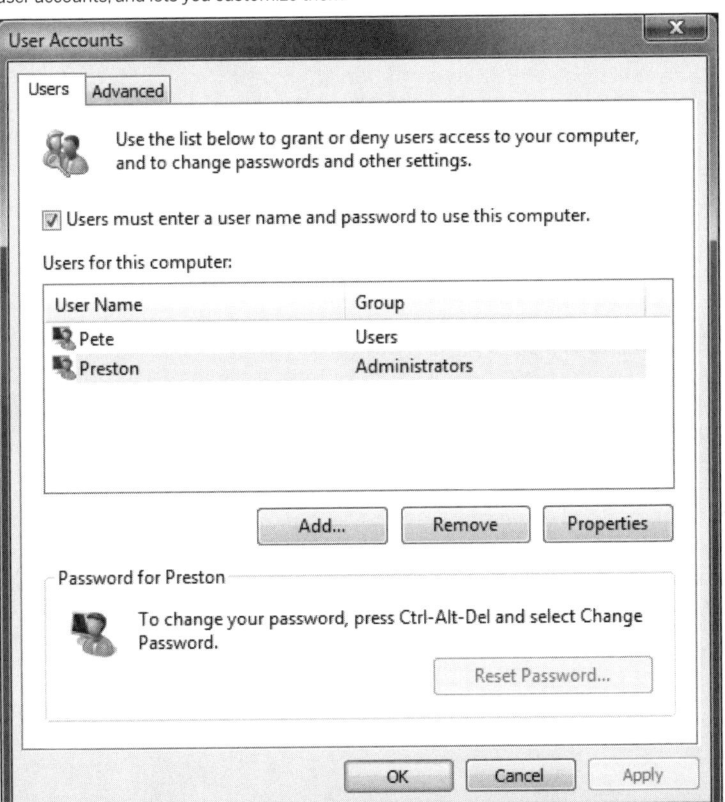

Remember, if you use auto logon, anyone can user your PC without your password, so only use this hack if you're sure that no one will log on and do harm to your system. This is particularly relevant if you use an administrator account to auto logon, because that account can do many things to a Windows Vista system that a normal account can't do.

Actually, though, it can, as you'll see in this simple hack. Follow it, and you'll automatically log in to your primary account, and then be able to switch to any other account when you wish:

1. At the Search box or a command prompt, type control userpasswords2. The User Accounts screen, shown in Figure 1-8, appears.

2. On the User Accounts tab, highlight the account that you want to automatically log on with, then uncheck the box next to "Users must enter a user name and password to use this computer."

3. The Automatically Log On dialog box appears, as seen in Figure 1-9. Type in the password for the account that you want to log on automatically. If the account shown isn't the one that you want to log on automatically, type in the username and password for the account that you want to use. Click OK.

4. From now on, you'll automatically log in using that account. When you're logged in, if you want to switch to another account, use Fast User Switching by clicking the Start button, then clicking the arrow in the lower righthand corner of the Start menu, and selecting "Switch User." You'll come to a screen listing all users on your PC, where you can log in as any other user.

Auto Logons for Domain-Connected PCs

If you're on a company network and part of a domain, the "Users must enter a user name and password to use this computer" choice won't appear on the User Accounts screen, because domain users always have to enter a username and password to log on to their computer. So this hack won't work for them.

However, there is a way for even domain users to automatically log on, by using any of several command-line utilities. Good ones include Autologon for Windows (www.microsoft.com/technet/sysinternals/utilities/Autologon.mspx), and autologon.exe (shellrevealed.com/files/folders/code/entry4411.aspx).

See Also

- "Unlock the Super-Secret Administrator Account" **[Hack #109]**

Figure 1-9.
Telling Windows Vista which account should automatically log on

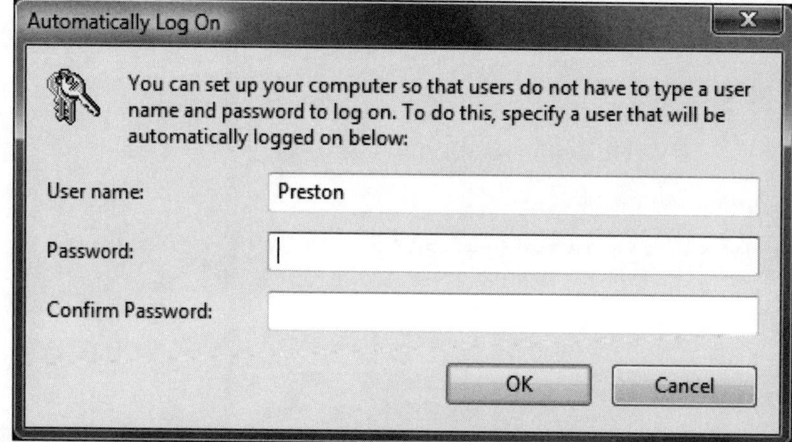

HACK 06: Speed Up Startup by Halting Startup Programs and Services

V XP Increase your PC's performance and speed up startup times by shutting off applications and services that you don't need.

One of the best ways to speed up your PC without having to spend money on extra RAM is to stop unnecessary programs and services from running whenever you start your PC. When too many programs and services run automatically every time you start up your system, startup itself takes a long time—and too many programs and services running simultaneously can bog down your CPU and hog your memory.

Some programs, such as antivirus software, should run automatically at startup and always run on your computer. But many other programs, such as instant messenger software, serve no purpose by being run at startup. And while you need a variety of background services running on your PC for Windows to function, there are many unnecessary services that run on startup. For example, on many Windows XP systems, the Wireless Zero Configuration Service runs to automatically configure a wifi (802.11) network card, even though no such card is present in the system. (Windows Vista does away with the Wireless Zero Configuration Service entirely.)

Eliminating Programs that Run at Startup

The task of stopping programs from running at startup is particularly daunting because there is no single place you can go to stop them all. Some run because they're put in the *Startup* folder, others because they're part of logon scripts, still others because of Registry settings, and so on. But with a little bit of perseverance, you should be able to stop them from running.

Cleaning Out the Startup Folder

Start by cleaning out your *Startup* folder. In Windows XP, it is in *C:\Documents and Settings*`<User Name>`*\Start Menu\Programs\Startup*, where `<User Name>` is your Windows logon name. In Windows Vista, find it in *C:\Users*`<User Name>`*\\AppData\Roaming\Microsoft\Windows\Start Menu\Programs\Startup* where `<User Name>` is, again, your Windows logon name. Delete the shortcuts of any programs you don't want to run on startup. As with any shortcuts, when you delete them, you're deleting only the shortcut, not the program itself. (You can also clear out the startup items in Windows XP by going to Start→Programs→Startup and deleting items you want to remove. In Windows Vista, go to Start→All Programs→Startup.)

To stop Windows from loading any programs in the *Startup* folder, hold down the Shift key during bootup. No programs in the *Startup* folder will run, but the items will still remain there so that they will start up as they would normally the next time you boot.

Next, clean out any tasks that have been automatically scheduled to run. In Windows XP, you'll find them in your *Scheduled Tasks* folder. Go to *C:\WINDOWS\Tasks*, and delete the shortcuts of any programs that you don't want to run.

In Windows Vista, you'll have to run the Task Scheduler, and delete tasks from there. Go to the Control Panel→System and Maintenance→Schedule Tasks. The Task Scheduler appears. Click "Task Scheduler Library" to display the tasks that have been scheduled, as shown in Figure 1-10. Look for any tasks that you don't want to run. In particular, look at the Triggers column and see whether any tasks are listed "At system startup." Such tasks start every time you run your PC. To see details about the task, including what it does, the executable file, how often it is scheduled, and so on, double-click it and look through the various tabs.

Figure 1-10.
Look for any tasks that are scheduled to run at startup in Windows Vista's Task Scheduler, and delete them if they're unnecessary

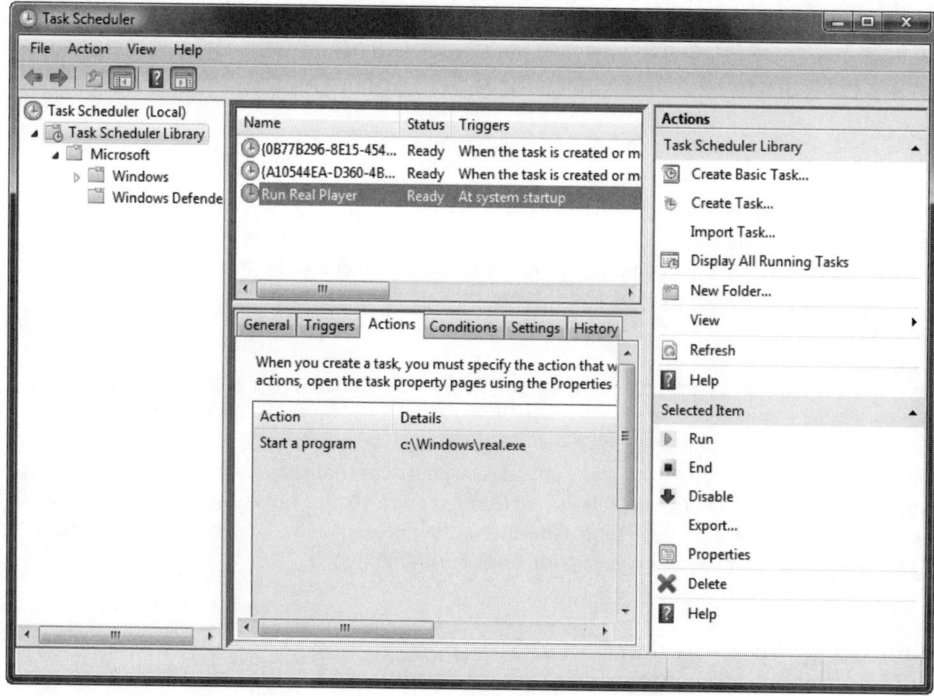

When you've identified a task you don't want to run on startup, highlight it, click Delete, and click OK when you're prompted.

Using the System Configuration Utility

Taking the previous steps will stop the obvious programs from running at startup, but it won't kill them all. The best tool for disabling hidden programs that run on startup is the Startup tab in the System Configuration Utility, shown in Figure 1-11. To run it in either Windows XP or Windows Vista, type msconfig at the Search box in the Start menu, in a command prompt or in the Run box and press Enter. (If that doesn't work, first do a search for *msconfig.exe*, and then when you find the file, double-click it.)

To stop a program from running at startup, go to the Startup tab in this utility and uncheck the box next to the program. It can sometimes be difficult to understand what programs are listed on the Startup tab. Some, such as America Online, are clearly labeled. But often, you'll see a phrase or collection of letters, such as *fs20*. That's the name of the running file—in this case, *fs20.exe*, which is Free Surfer Companion, a pop-up killer, cache manager, and surfing utility.

To get more information about a listing, expand the width of the Command column near the top of the Startup tab. Expand it enough and you'll see the startup command that the program issues, including its location, such as *C:\Program Files\Free Surfer\fs20.exe*. The directory location should be another hint to help you know the name of the program.

When stopping programs from running at startup, it's best to stop them one at a time rather than in groups. You want to make sure that you're not causing any system problems by stopping them. So, stop one and restart your PC. If it runs fine, stop another and restart. Continue doing this until you've cleared all the programs you don't want to run automatically.

Figure 1-11.
The Startup tab of the System Configuration Utility

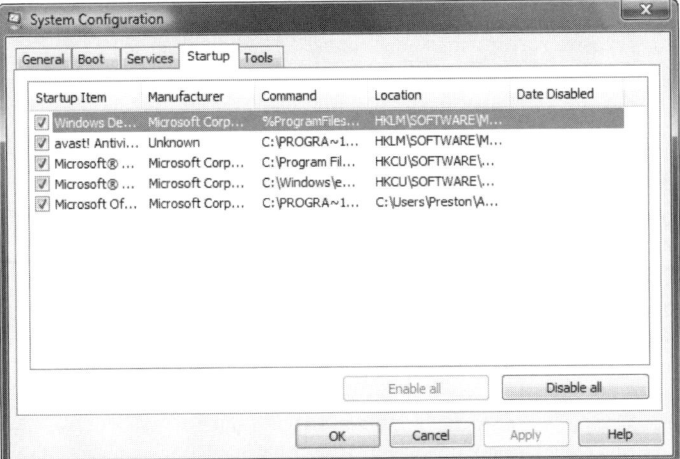

Each time you uncheck a box and restart your PC, you'll get a warning stating that you've used the System Configuration Utility to disable a program from starting automatically. If you don't want to see that warning, disable it by checking the box in the dialog box itself.

After you've used the System Configuration Utility to identify programs that run upon startup, you might want to try disabling them from within the programs themselves. Run each program that starts automatically, and see if you can find a setting that allows you to prevent it from running on startup. For example, to get rid of Apple QuickTime's startup item, right-click the QuickTime icon in the notification area, select QuickTime Preferences, go to the Advanced tab, and uncheck the box labeled "Install QuickTime icon in system tray."

Using the Registry to Halt Programs Running on Startup

Even the System Configuration Utility won't necessarily let you identify and kill all programs that run on startup. You might also need to hack the Registry to disable them. To do so, Launch the Registry Editor by typing regedit at the Start Search box or a command prompt (see Chapter 13 for details) and go to `HKEY_CURRENT_USER\Software\Microsoft\Windows\CurrentVersion\Run`. The right pane will contain a list of some of the programs that run automatically at startup. The Data field tells you the path and name of the executable so that you can determine what each program is. Right-click any program you don't want to run, and choose Delete. That will kill any programs that run and are specific to your account. To kill programs that run for every user of the system, go to `HKEY_LOCAL_MACHINE\SOFTWARE\Microsoft\Windows\CurrentVersion\Run` and follow the same instructions for deleting other programs that you don't want to run at startup.

Shutting Off Services that Run at Startup

Constantly running in the background of Windows are *services*—processes that help the operating system run, or that provide support to applications. Many of these services launch automatically at startup. Although you need many of them, many aren't required and can slow down your system when they run in the background.

You can prevent services from running at startup by using the System Configuration Utility, similar to how you halt programs from running at startup, but using the Services tab instead of the Startup tab. When you go to that tab, you'll see a very long list of services, most of which Windows requires to run. A good way to weed out unnecessary services is to see which services weren't created by Microsoft, which aren't required by Windows, and which have been installed by a third party. You can then decide which to stop and which to run. To see non-Microsoft services, click "Hide all Microsoft services." You'll see a list like the one shown Figure 1-12.

The System Configuration Utility is useful, but it doesn't necessarily list every service that launches on startup. A bigger problem is that turning off services is more of a shot in the dark than disabling programs. When you disable a program, you can get a sense of what the program does. But when you turn off a service through the System Configuration Utility, there's often no way to know what it does (or did).

A better way of turning off services at startup is via the Services Computer Management Console, shown in Figure 1-13. Run it by typing services.msc at the command prompt or Search box. The Services Computer Management Console includes a description of all services so that you can know ahead of time whether a particular service is one you want to turn off. It also lets you pause the service so that you can test out your machine with the service off to see whether it's needed.

After you run the console, click the Extended tab. This view shows you a description of each service in the left pane when you highlight the service. The Startup Type column shows you which services launch upon startup—any services with "Automatic" in that column. Click the top of that column to sort together all the services that automatically launch on startup. Then highlight each service and read the descriptions.

When you find a service that you want to turn off, right-click it and choose Properties. In the Properties dialog box that appears, choose Manual from the "Startup type" drop-down list. The service won't start automatically from now on (unless another service requires it in order to start), but you can start it manually via the console. If you want the service disabled so that it can't be run, choose Disabled. (If you disable a service that a critical Windows service depends on, that service won't be able to start either, which could cause problems.)

To test the effects of turning off the service, turn off any services you don't want to run by clicking "Stop the service" in the left pane, or by right-clicking the service and choosing Stop. Note that some services can't be stopped while the system is running. You'll have to set them to "manual" and reboot to see the effect of turning them off.

Table 1-1 lists some common services you might want to halt from running at startup. Note that some run on Windows XP, some on Windows Vista, and some on both.

Figure 1-12.
A list of all non-Microsoft services running on a Windows Vista PC

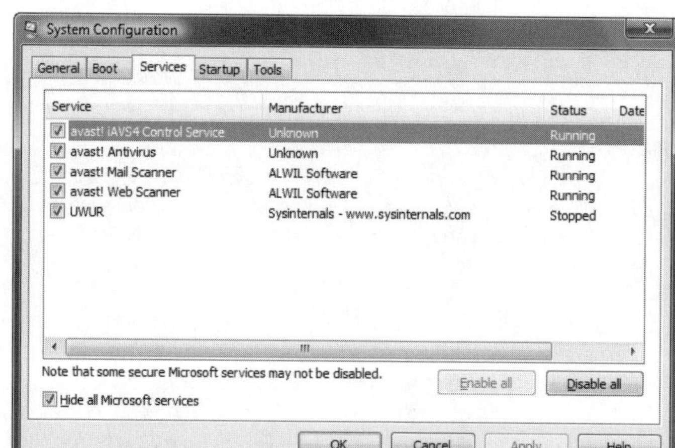

Figure 1-13.
The Services Computer Management Console

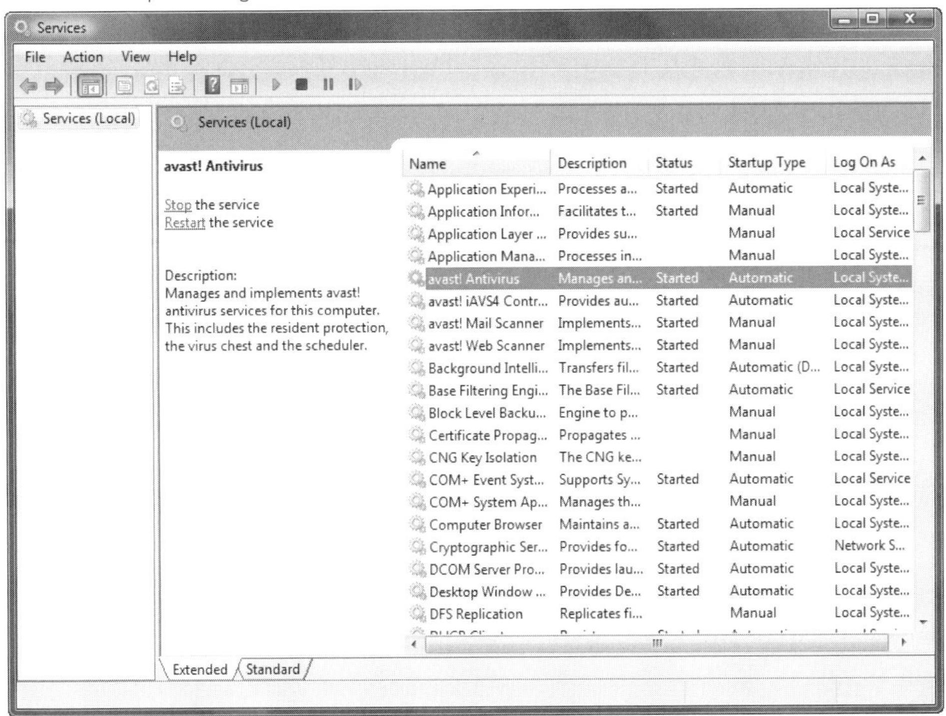

Table 1-1 Services you might want to turn off

SERVICE	WHAT IT DOES
Portable Media Serial Number	Retrieves the serial number of a portable music player attached to your PC.
Remote Registry	Allows remote users to modify Registry settings on the computer.
Uninterruptible Power Supply	Manages an Uninterruptible Power Supply (UPS) connected to your PC.
Windows Error Reporting Service	Turns on error reporting and delivery of solutions if your system crashes or hangs.
Telnet	Allows a remote user to log in to your computer and run programs. (This service is not on all versions of Windows.)
Wireless Zero Configuration Service	Automatically configures a wi-fi (802.11) network card. You'll still be able to use your wi-fi card if you use this, but you won't automatically connect to Wi-Fi networks. (Windows XP only)
Messenger	Turns on the Messenger service, which can be used to deliver spam via pop-ups. (This is not the instant messaging program Windows Messenger.)
Pen Service	The Tablet PC Pen Input Service.
Infrared monitor service	Supports the use of infrared devices with your PC.

HACKING YOUR BIOS

Your system's BIOS (Basic Input/Output System) is firmware stored in a chip on your PC that handles basic system start-up—in essence, it gets your computer's hardware ready so that the operating system can load on it. What's important to understand about the BIOS is that it runs before Windows runs, and handles the basic tasks of recognizing and configuring your hardware.

There are ways to hack your BIOS **[Hack #3]** so that your PC starts up more quickly. In the next three hacks, you'll dig deeper into BIOS hacking, including upgrading a flash BIOS, and hacking a BIOS that appears to be unhackable.

HACK 07: BIOS Hacks for Faster Bootup

V XP Some of the stuff your computer does at boot time is of no use. Disable those features to boot faster.

The system BIOS does a lot of work in the P.O.S.T. (Power On Self Test) phase before it gets your system to the point where it reads boot-up information from a disk drive to load an operating system. Some of the things that happen in P.O.S.T. have nothing to do with system performance, other than impeding the process of getting to the operating system to run your applications. Intel, AMD, AMI, Award/Phoenix, and the PC manufacturers were aware of this waste of time, evaluated the events involved, and in many cases took steps to reduce the number of items and the amount of time the startup process takes. To that end, there are a handful of changes you can make in order to boot up faster.

Disable Extended Tests

Many systems offer the option of allowing an in-depth test of system memory and components (an extended test) or zipping through the system and getting to bootup as quickly as possible. With RAM as reliable and economical as it is (and having so much of it) and having plug-and-play operating systems like Windows—and, to some extent, current versions of Linux—the Quick Test mode is more than adequate, and preferred for faster boot times. This parameter is shown in Figure 1-14, and specifies the depth, and thus the time involved, for testing system RAM and finding and checking the basic components of the system—COM and LPT ports and such.

Configure Drive Detection

Most BIOSes provide the capability to automatically search for, identify, and configure different types of drives across multiple IDE and Serial ATA connections. This parameter setting usually shows up as AUTO in the IDE configuration choices. If you leave the parameter for all four possible IDE or Serial ATA devices set to AUTO, your BIOS will waste a lot of time searching for nonexistent devices. For faster boot times set the parameter to NONE, as shown in Figure 1-15, for any unused interfaces and connections that have nothing attached to them.

Figure 1-14.
Settings for the fastest P.O.S.T.

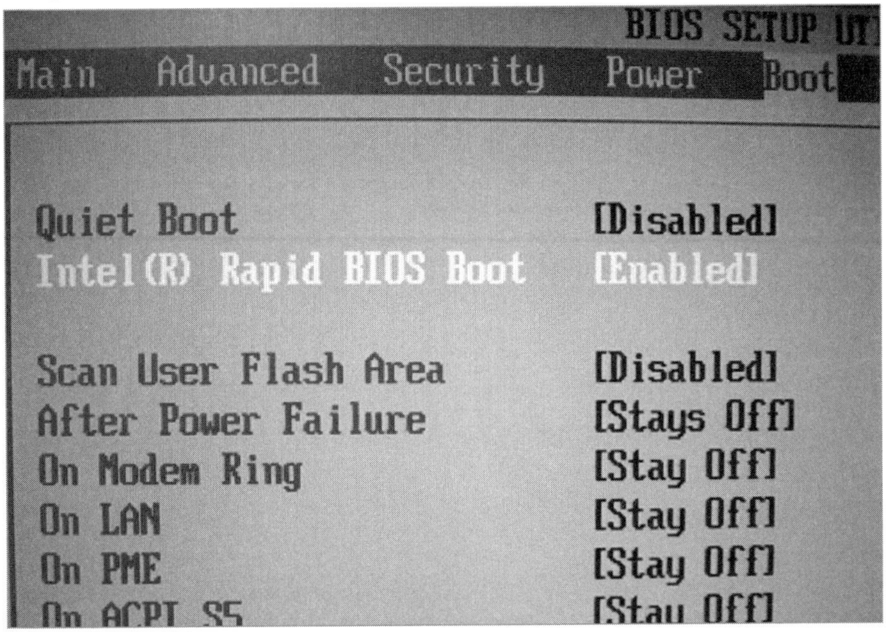

Figure 1-15.
Set any unused IDE devices to NONE to speed boot time

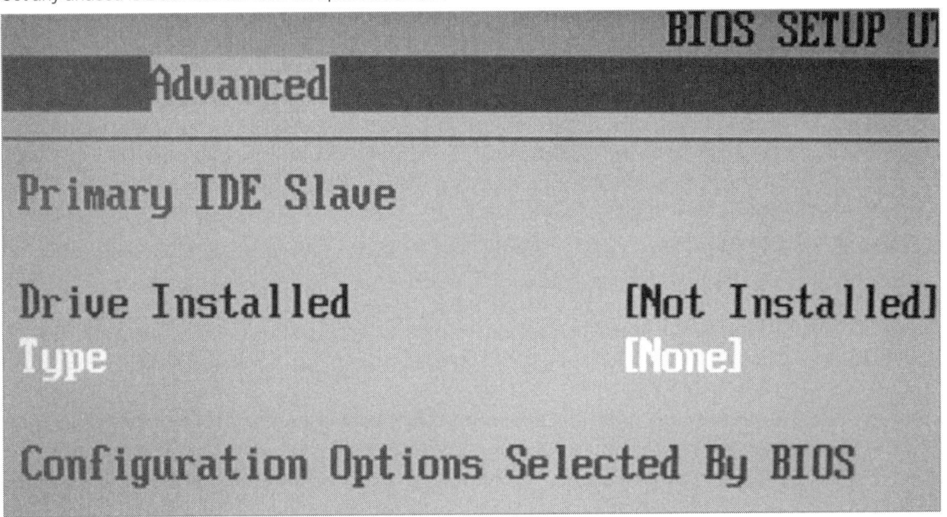

User BIOS Regions

This parameter, if it exists in your setup program, instructs the BIOS to search upper DOS memory (between 640 KB and 1 MB) for the existence of additional BIOS extension code. Such code exists on SCSI host adapters and on network cards that provide the ability to boot from a network server. Most PC users never encounter a SCSI interface, and neither do systems configured to boot over a LAN through a network card, so there don't set this parameter to anything but No, Off, or Disabled —and save yourself a couple more seconds at boot time.

See Also

- "Speed Up Boot and Shutdown Times" **[Hack #3]**

— Jim Aspinwall, from PC Hacks (O'Reilly)

HACK 08: Hack an Unhackable BIOS

 You may be able to find a BIOS upgrade to work around that unhackable, squeaky clean OEM BIOS.

If you want to do hardware and BIOS hacking, you may run into problems because your BIOS may not support a variety of hacks. A "dumbed-down" BIOS setup gives you few options to choose from, while a truly hackable BIOS gives you parameters aplenty.

> If you're willing to spend a lot of time hacking you may want to replace your existing BIOS with a Linux-based one, LinuxBIOS. For details, see linuxbios.org/Documentation.

Most no-name, "white-box," do-it-yourself PC system boards come littered with hackable bits through switches, jumpers, or the BIOS. These boards are the subject of the majority of hacks, overclocking, modifications, BIOS upgrades and just plain "geeking out" on what a PC can be made to do. You'll get hours of enjoyment fiddling with every bit and parameter you can find, and perhaps encounter hours or days of frustration if one of your hacks causes you to lose data or massive quantities of that soft furry stuff atop your head.

If you've got an OEM system—one with a recognizable and sustained brand name such as Compaq, Dell, Gateway, HP, IBM, NEC, Sony, or Toshiba, chances are good that you will not find any parameters worth hacking on—you've got a dumbed-down BIOS.

The unhackable BIOS exists for one very simple reason: the manufacturer wants this PC to work for the broadest, simplest set of PC users. In other words, it does not want to have to bear the cost of support calls related to hacked BIOS settings: completely understandable for a family PC, but very frustrating if you're a real techie and wish to experiment.

All hope may not be lost. Many vendors use the same or a similar version of system boards that you can get off the shelf or by mail order. For instance, I have an HP Pavilion system that uses an Asus A7V-M and, by coincidence, an individually boxed Asus A7V that I bought to build into my own case. The HP Pavilion A7V-M board uses a dumbed-down Award BIOS, and the boxed board uses a fully hackable Award BIOS. The dumbed-down BIOS in the HP does not allow me to change CPU or memory timing, which are critical to the overclocking hacks in Chapter 12.

BIOS upgrades can afford you the benefit of new hacking capabilities, provide fixes to known bugs, or provide support for newer features and hardware such as larger hard drives. Furthermore, these upgrades may come with bootable CD-ROM support that may not be included in the original BIOS.

If the P.O.S.T. display for your system board does not show either the AMI, Award, MR BIOS, or Phoenix brand name (see Figure 1-16) when it boots up, you're probably stuck—no hacking allowed. If you do see the brand name of the BIOS, you may be in luck, as you may be able to take advantage of this hack by getting an upgraded BIOS from ESupport.com at www.esupport.com.

ESupport.com provides a small program they call the BIOS Agent that can sniff out details of your present BIOS. They also have a list of tips to help you identify your BIOS if their program cannot do it. The best way to identify your Award BIOS is from the absolute version number that appears at the bottom of your screen at boot time, as shown in Figure 1-17. You can press the Pause/Break key on most PCs to stop the system from booting up so you can copy down this information. From that information, their sales department can tell you if they can provide an upgraded BIOS, and perhaps what additional features you might get with it.

The unfortunate part of getting a new BIOS from ESupport.com is that you cannot merely download the BIOS code and upload it into your PC as you can with BIOS updates from the motherboard maker. An ESupport.com BIOS upgrade will come to you in the mail already installed on a memory chip, which reduces the chances of someone making an unauthorized copy of their work. If your system board's BIOS memory chip is soldered onto the board, as shown in Figure 1-18, or is not

QUICK HACK 

BOOT INTO A DIFFERENT VERSION OF WINDOWS QUICKLY

If you run multiple versions of Windows on your PC—for example, Windows XP and Windows 98—you know how annoying it is to go through the reboot routine when you want to boot into a different operating system than the one you're currently using. Restart (www.gabrieleponti.com/software/index.html#restart) comes to the rescue. It appears as a green icon in your system tray. Click it to see all your available operating systems, choose the one you want to boot into, and the program reboots your PC into the operating system that you chose. It works with Windows 95, 98, Me, NT, 2000, XP and 2003 Server, but not yet with Windows Vista.

Figure 1-16.
A typical Award BIOS boot screen. The true version number of the BIOS is shown in the lower-left corner.

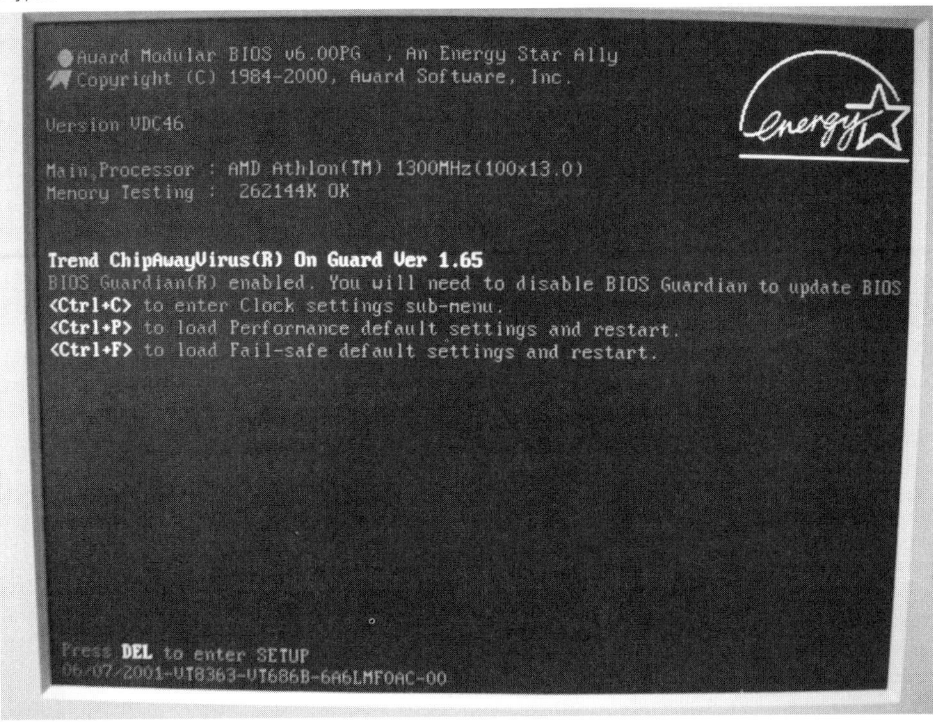

Figure 1-17.
The true version number of the BIOS

Figure 1-18.
This Phoenix BIOS chip is a Flash ROM that cannot be removed from the board. It can only be updated electronically.

Figure 1-19.
A replaceable/upgradeable socket-mounted Award BIOS chip.
Note the CMOS memory battery and CMOS reset jumper above chip.

mounted in a chip socket, as shown in Figure 1-19, you will likely not be able to purchase a BIOS upgrade from ESupport.com.

You may notice two sets of numbers referring to the version of Award or Phoenix BIOS running your system. The number at the top of the screen, like 4.51, 6.0PG, or similar, is a gross representation of the base BIOS code set used to create the specific BIOS version you have. You need to locate and note the longer multicharacter number that indicates the specific version for your system board. For the Award BIOS, this number is almost always displayed in the lower-left corner of the screen. For the Phoenix BIOS, this number typically appears near the top of the screen with other system board manufacturer's information.

See Also

- "Upgrade Your Flash BIOS" **[Hack #9]**

— Jim Aspinwall, from PC Hacks (O'Reilly)

HACK 09: Upgrade Your Flash BIOS

V XP Resolve system-level bugs and overcome feature limitations by upgrading your BIOS.

Sometimes a vendor learns of problems or limitations only after a product gets to market and is used in a lot of different situations. Nearly every system board and PC system on the market undergoes at least one significant revision of the BIOS after the product has been released for sale.

Most of us think nothing of seeking out the latest patches and updates for our application software and hardware drivers in hopes of solving a problem, gaining a feature, or boosting performance, but rarely do we think of updating the software and internal drivers that make our system board tick—the system BIOS.

I highly recommend visiting the web site of the manufacturer of your PC system or system board, or even ESupport.com's web site, to learn what the latest revision of BIOS is for your PC and the issues the revision addresses. You may find one or more clues that can help you solve problems or gain new or proper functionality of your system for a few minutes of browsing and downloading time.

Do not bother visiting the BIOS makers' web sites looking for BIOS updates. AMI and Award/Phoenix supply only the tools and services for system board and PC makers to create their own BIOS code specific to each individual system board. You wouldn't think of calling Microsoft, makers of the Visual Studio program development tools, about support or upgrades for software made by Adobe, Intuit, Symantec, or other software makers who use the Visual Studio tools. Nor would you call Sears about problems with your house built with a Craftsman hammer. And so it is with the BIOS companies. A good resource for identifying your system board is the www.motherboards.org web site.

In most cases, except getting a BIOS upgrade from ESupport.com, getting a BIOS update and the software program to load the update into your PC are free from every system board and PC maker's web site. Because many of the devices you add to a system after the initial purchase are too new to be known to or supported by system board vendors, BIOS upgrades are issued to fix anything from an all-out serious bug that prevents some aspect of the system board from working to enhancing the detection or size of certain types of disk drives, or adding extra support for plug-and-play or power management functions. These items should be spelled out in a readme or BIOS revision description file associated with the particular BIOS version that you download.

Updating the system BIOS involves overwriting the BIOS code currently stored on the system board and replacing it with new code. This process has the potential to render your system board useless if there is an error or interruption while the update is occurring. If the BIOS file you download is incomplete or corrupt in any way, you will not be able to properly load the BIOS into the system board.

Part of the overall BIOS upgrade process may include backing up the current BIOS onto disk. If your system does not behave correctly after the upgrade, you can flash it with a new, good BIOS file or use the original backed-up BIOS file to go back to a known good state. Depending on your motherboard's capabilities, you may or may not be able to recover from a flashing accident. Intel provides a downloadable recovery BIOS, which can recover certain Intel motherboards after a failed BIOS upgrade. You can locate your recovery BIOS by visiting downloadfinder.intel.com, navigating to your motherboard, and selecting the recovery BIOS, if one is available.

A typical BIOS file can be as large as 4 MB, depending on features. They can be downloaded or used via a bootable CD containing the BIOS file and update program.

Some BIOS upgrade programs are available for use under Windows; this approach, although convenient and more user-friendly, has the risk of failing due to a crash, conflict, or other instability within Windows. I recommend using a DOS-based BIOS upgrade program if it is available. A good bet is to use a USB flash DOS-bootable pen drive. For details, see www.bootdisk.com/pendrive.htm.

Some BIOS update programs create their own bootable diskettes and execute the upgrade process automatically so you need supply only the diskette. Once you have downloaded the BIOS file (usually a .BIN file extension type) and BIOS update program to your hard drive, follow the instructions provided with the upgrade (most users will start at the following Step 8 after launching a Windows-based BIOS updater) or all of the following steps to update your system's BIOS.

Be sure that your computer is plugged into a UPS (Uninterruptible Power Supply) or (if it's a notebook) has a full battery charge. All it takes is a power outage during a BIOS upgrade to render your motherboard useless.

1. If you need to install your BIOS upgrade from a DOS environment, prepare a formatted DOS boot diskette (otherwise, run the Windows-based upgrade program and skip to Step 8). Any version of DOS should do, but making a DOS 6.22, Windows 95, 98, or Me startup diskette would be most common. You can also make an MS-DOS startup disk using the format program in Windows XP (run `format` from the Command Prompt) or Windows Vista (run `format` from an Administrator Command Prompt **[Hack #36]**), or downloading boot diskette images from www.bootdisk.com.

2. If in Windows, go to the A: drive.

3. In DOS or Windows, delete the following files from the diskette to make room for the BIOS files:
   - *All ASPIxxxx.SYS files*
   - *All BTxxxxxx.SYS files*

» *OAKCDROM.SYS*
» *RAMDRIVE.SYS*
» *EBD.CAB*
» *SMARTDRV.EXE*
» *CONFIG.SYS*
» *AUTOEXEC.BAT*

4. Copy the specific BIOS (.BIN) file to the diskette.

5. Copy the BIOS upgrade program to the diskette.

6. Restart the PC with the diskette in the drive so that the system boots from the floppy. You may need to change the boot device order first.

7. At the DOS prompt type in the name of the BIOS upgrade program and press the Enter key to run it. You should be presented with a text menu of options.

8. One of the options should be to copy the existing FLASH ROM BIOS to disk as a backup—do this. (Often the upgrade process will automatically prompt to copy a backup of the BIOS to disk.)

9. Select the option to program the new BIOS file into the FLASH ROM. If you are presented with the option, and you did not already make a backup of the existing BIOS, do so now.

10. Follow the prompts to upgrade your BIOS. In some cases, you need to provide the name of the new BIOS file and let the program copy the file into the FLASH ROM.

11. When the programming process completes, remove the diskette from the drive and restart the PC. If your computer displays the BIOS version at boot time, you should notice the new BIOS version appear on screen.

12. Go into the BIOS setup program. Verify or set the date, time, and other parameters that you're familiar with and restart the PC. You're done with the BIOS upgrade.

Don't forget to check the web site of your video card, disk drive, printer, and USB-connected product vendors for any BIOS or firmware updates for these devices.

— Jim Aspinwall, from PC Hacks (O'Reilly)

HACKING MULTIBOOT SYSTEMS

One of Windows' more useful features is its ability to boot multiple operating systems. You may want to use multiple operating systems on your PC for a variety of reasons—your virtual private network (VPN) from work may work only with Windows XP, for example, but you run Windows Vista. Maybe you need to test software on different systems. Perhaps you're a cross-platform developer, working in Linux as well as Windows.

Or, on the other hand, you might like to boot into multiple operating systems simply because you can. After all, there's often great pleasure to be had in simply doing something for its own sake.

The keys to multibooting are Windows' boot loaders and boot managers. After you create a multiboot system, when you start up your PC, one of these programs takes over, and displays a menu of choices of installed operating systems. Scroll to the one you want, select it, and you're ready to go.

In this section of the book, you'll learn how to hack multiboot systems. You'll see how you can set up and run a dual-boot Windows XP–Linux PC, and a dual-boot Windows XP–Windows Vista PC, as well as how to hack startup options for multiboot systems.

There are similarities in how you customize Windows XP and Windows Vista multiboot systems—you can use the *Msconfig.exe* utility and the Startup and Recovery tab of the System Properties dialog box (Windows Vista's version is shown in Figure 1-20) to edit multiboot as well as basic startup options for both, for example.

To get to the Startup and Recovery tab in Windows XP, right-click My Computer, select Properties, select the Advanced tab, and click the Settings button in the Startup and Recovery section. In Windows Vista, right-click Computer, select Properties, click Advanced System Settings, and on the Advanced tab, click the Settings button in the Startup and Recovery section.

But the similarities are skin-deep. As you'll see in [Hack #10] Windows Vista has introduced an entirely new startup and boot system, the Boot Configuration Data (BCD) store. The BCD store controls how Windows Vista starts, including multiboot configurations. In Windows XP, all this information was contained in a text file called *boot.ini*, which was far easier to edit than BCD. *Msconfig.exe* and the Startup and Recovery tab let you edit the basics of BCD. But to do more than that, you'll have to

Figure 1-20.
Editing boot options in Windows Vista

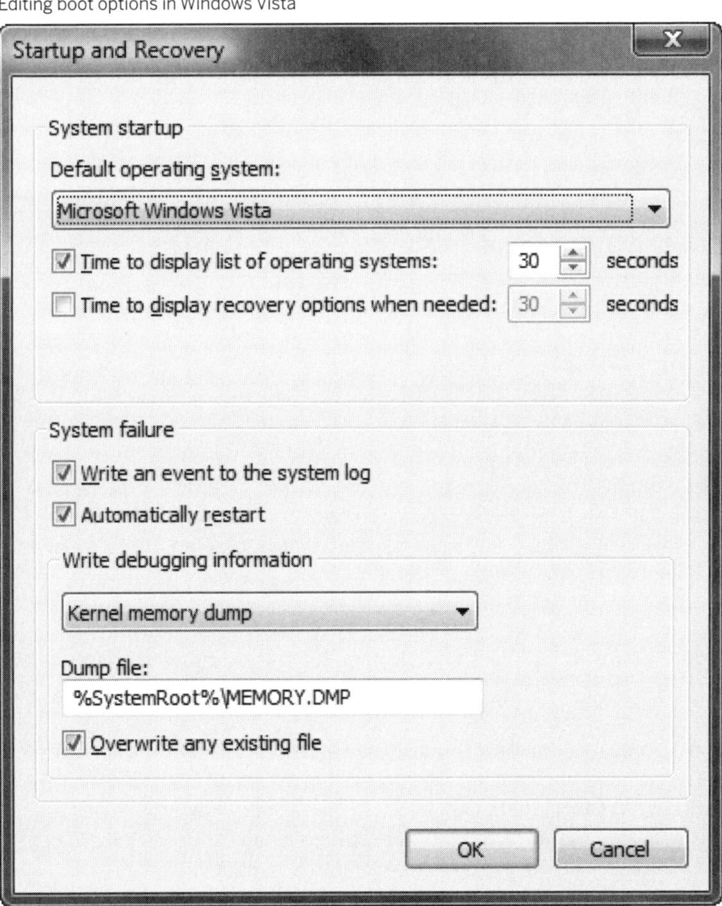

wrestle with BCDEDIT, a command-line tool that is one of the most complex and confounding you'll ever come across. Suffice it to say that even grown men and women have been known to weep just thinking of touching it. Fortunately, there are some alternatives.

Why did Microsoft make such a major change to the way Windows handles bootup? It wanted to develop a common way to handle devices not just with the traditional BIOS, but that use a new firmware model called the Extensible Firmware Interface (EFI). The *boot.ini* method couldn't work on EFI. A BCD store, however, can be used on both systems. BCDEDIT can handle EFI as well as BIOS-based PCs.

On a computer with a traditional BIOS, the BCD store is found in the *\Boot\Bcd* directory of the active partition. On an EFI-based system, it is found in the EFI system partition.

For customizing complex boot tasks in Windows Vista, your best bet is to use the free VistaBootPRO **[Hack #12]** But for simpler matters, it's worth learning the basics of BCDEDIT **[Hack #10]**. Another good choice is EasyBCD (neosmart.net).

OK, enough background. Time to get hacking.

HACK 10: The Secrets of Windows Vista's BCDEDIT

V Baffled by Windows Vista's BCDEDIT command-line tool for customizing multiboot startups? Who isn't? Here's an easy guide to its basics.

If you're only looking to customize the basics of your Windows Vista multiboot system, there's no need to download and install VistaBootPRO **[Hack #12]**. You can, instead, directly hack the BCD store using BCDEDIT.

Before you get started, you need a little introduction to the BCD store, and how BCDEDIT lets you edit it. The BCD is made up of a series of objects, each of which is a boot environment application, such as a boot manager. Each object, in turn, is made up of a series of elements. And each element has an attribute that tells how it will be used.

For example, the Windows Boot Manager in the BCD handles the initial startup of the PC, and displays a multiboot menu. One of the elements in the Windows Boot Manager is *timeout*, which determines how long to display the multiboot menu before loading the default operating system. The timeout element's option is a number, such as 30, which determines how long (in seconds) to display the screen.

There's one more thing you need to know about the BCD. When you use BCDEDIT to edit the BCD, you often need to use a GUID (Globally Unique Identifier) of an object of some kind. For example, a partition on a PC has its own GUID, which looks something like this: *{b37c75ca-dd09-11d8-9a7e-1030581395c7}*.

BCDEDIT wasn't designed for users, and instead was designed for system administrators who need to set up multiple Windows Vista systems. BCDEDIT and the BCD store are used not only for handling multiboot systems, but also for managing all aspect of Windows startup. System administrators can write scripts using BCDEDIT to automate complex tasks for multiple machines.

That GUID for the partition is unique. But there are also GUIDs that are predefined, and are exactly the same from PC to PC. For example, the Windows Legacy OS Loader, used to load Windows XP and Windows 2000, always has the GUID *{466f5a88-0af2-4f76-9038-095b170dc21c}*. To make it somewhat easier to use BCD, aliases represent these universal, predefined GUIDs. So instead of using *{466f5a88-0af2-4f76-9038-095b170dc21c}*, you can use the alias *{ntldr}*.

With that background behind us, it's time to actually use BCDEDIT. It's a command-line tool, and you need to run it as an administrator. Type cmd at the Search box on the Start menu, right-click the cmd icon that appears at the top of the Start menu, and select Run as administrator.

Before doing any editing, it's a good idea to back up the BCD store, so that you can late restore it, if you do any kind of damage. Create a folder for the BCD store on another drive or a removable disk. In our example, we'll say that you're going to back it up to your *D:* drive. So create a folder called *\BCD Backup* on your *D:* drive. Once you've done that, type this command and press Enter to back up the BCD store to it:

```
bcdedit /export "D:\BCD Backup\Bcd Backup"
```

If you later need to restore the BCD store, type this command:

```
bcdedit /import "D:\BCD Backup\Bcd Backup"
```

Next, take a look at how your multiboot system is set up. At the command line, type bcdedit and press Enter. You'll see a listing like this:

```
Windows Boot Manager
--------------------
identifier              {bootmgr}
device                  partition=C:
description             Windows Boot Manager
locale                  en-US
inherit                 {globalsettings}
default                 {current}
resumeobject            {657290bb-767a-11db-b48e-f34163468438}
displayorder            {ntldr}
                        {current}
toolsdisplayorder       {memdiag}
timeout                 30

Windows Legacy OS Loader
------------------------
identifier              {ntldr}
device                  partition=C:
path                    \ntldr
description             Earlier Version of Windows

Windows Boot Loader
-------------------
identifier              {current}
device                  partition=J:
path                    \Windows\system32\winload.exe
description             Microsoft Windows Vista
locale                  en-US
inherit                 {bootloadersettings}
osdevice                partition=J:
systemroot              \Windows
resumeobject            {657290bb-767a-11db-b48e-f34163468438}
nx                      OptIn
```

We're not going to edit most of this. We're going to change only the basics, because a full explanation of how to use BCDEDIT is well beyond the scope of this book. And besides, there are much easier ways to work with the BCD store **[Hack #12]**.

Note all the listings with curly braces { } around them. These are GUIDs. Most are aliases, such as *{ntldr}*.

The first main listing is *Windows Boot Manager*, which handles the initial startup. The elements underneath it detail its path, the language it's in, and so on. It's mainly self-explanatory. The next listing, *Windows Legacy OS Loader*, is the loader used to load Windows XP or Windows 2000. The final listing, *Windows Boot Loader*, is used to load Windows Vista.

So what does this entire listing tell us? The multiboot window will be displayed for 30 seconds, as you can see in the *timeout* listing of 30 under *Windows Boot Manager*. Windows Vista is the default operating system that loads after 30 seconds if no action is taken. You can tell that because the *default* listing in *Windows Boot Manager* is *{current}*—and as you can see, the identifier directly under *Windows Boot Loader* is *{current}* and its description is *Microsoft Windows Vista*.

On the multiboot menu that appears when the PC starts, the first listing will be for the previous version of Windows, and the text will read Earlier Version of Windows. The second listing will be for Windows Vista, and the text will read Microsoft Windows Vista.

You can tell that because the *displayorder* under *Windows Boot Manager* is *{ntldr}* first, and *{current}* second. And if you look in the description of *Windows Legacy OS Loader*, you'll see Earlier Version of Windows, and in the *description* of *Windows Boot Loader*, you'll see Microsoft Windows Vista.

To make changes with BCDEDIT, you use a variety of switches. For details, type bcdedit /?, and you'll get a list of switches, and how to use them. You need to use the switches in concert with GUIDs and attributes. For example, if you wanted to change the boot menu so that instead of displaying Earlier Version of Windows, it displayed Windows XP, you'd issue this command and press Enter.

```
bcdedit /set {ntldr} description "Windows XP"
```

Similarly, if you wanted to change the menu so that it displayed Windows Vista Ultimate instead of Microsoft Windows Vista, you'd issue this command and press Enter:

```
bcdedit /set {current} description "Windows Vista Ultimate"
```

To change the amount of time the menu appears before booting into the default operating system to 20 seconds, type this command and press Enter:

```
bcdedit /timeout 15
```

To have your PC boot into Windows XP instead of Windows Vista as the default operating system, type this command and press Enter:

```
bcdedit /default {ntldr}
```

To change the display order of the multiboot menu, so that the Windows Vista entry appears first, and the Windows XP entry appears second, type this command and press Enter:

```
bcdedit /displayorder {current} {ntldr}
```

After you make your changes, they'll take effect the next time you reboot.

See Also

- "Hack Windows Vista Multiboot Systems with VistaBootPRO" **[Hack #12]**
- "Customize Windows XP Multiboot Startup Options" **[Hack #11]**

HACK 11: Customize Windows XP Multiboot Startup Options

XP Edit or create a startup menu that lets you choose which operating system to boot into in multiboot systems, or create a menu that lets you choose different startup options for your single operating system if you have only XP installed.

If you've installed another operating system (in addition to XP) on your system, your PC starts up with a multiboot menu, which allows you to choose the operating system you want to run. The menu stays live for 30 seconds, and a screen countdown tells you how long you have to make a choice from the menu. After the 30 seconds elapse, it boots into your default operating system, which is generally the last operating system you installed.

You can customize that multiboot menu and how your PC starts by editing the *boot.ini* file, a hidden system file, to control a variety of startup options, including how long to display the menu, which operating system should be the default, whether to use the XP splash screen when XP starts, and similar features. And as you'll see later in this hack, you can also use the file to create a startup menu that will allow you to choose from different versions of your operating system—for example, one that you'll use for tracking down startup problems, and another for starting in Safe Mode.

The *boot.ini* file is a plain-text file found in your root *C:* folder. You might not be able to see it because it's a system file, and if you can see it, you might not be able to edit it because it's a read-only file. To make it visible, launch Windows Explorer, choose View→Tools→Folder Options→View, and select the Show Hidden Files and Folders radio button. To make it a file you can edit, right-click it in Windows Explorer, choose Properties, uncheck the Read-Only box, and click OK. For a quicker way, right-click My Computer, choose Advanced-→Startup and Recovery Settings, and then click Edit to edit the boot.ini file. That way, you don't need to remember to set the permissions back the way you found them.

Editing Files

To edit the file, open it with a text editor such as Notepad. Following is a typical *boot.ini* file for a PC that has two operating systems installed on it—Windows XP Home Edition and Windows 2000 Professional:

```
[boot loader]
timeout=30
default=multi(0)disk(0)rdisk(0)partition(1)\WINDOWS
[operating systems]
multi(0)disk(0)rdisk(0)partition(1)\WINDOWS="Microsoft Windows XP Home Edition" /fastdetect
multi(0)disk(0)rdisk(0)partition(2)\WINNT="Windows 2000 Professional" /fastdetect
```

As you can see, there are two sections in the file: `[bootloader]` and `[operating systems]`. To customize your menu and startup options, edit the entries in each section. Before editing *boot.ini*, make a copy of it and save it under a different name (such as *boot.ini.old*) so that you can revert to that if you cause problems when you edit the file.

Following are details about how to edit the entries in each section:

`[boot loader]`

This section controls how the boot process works; it specifies the default operating system and how long a user has to make a selection from a boot menu, if a boot menu has been enabled. The `timeout` value specifies, in seconds, how long to display the menu and wait for a selection before loading the default operating system. If you want a delay of 15 seconds, for example, enter `15` for the value. Use a value of `0` if you want the default operating system to boot immediately. If you want the menu to be displayed indefinitely and stay onscreen until a selection is made, use a value of `-1`. The `default` value specifies which entry in the `[operating systems]` section is the default operating system. (The `default` value is used even if there is only one operating system in the `[operating systems]` section.) To change the default operating system, edit the setting: in the preceding example, to `default=multi(0)disk(0)rdisk(0)partition(2)\WINNT`.

So, in this example, if you change the menu settings so that the screen appears for ten seconds before loading the default operating system, and the default operating system is Windows 2000 Professional, the section reads:

```
[boot loader]
timeout=10
default=multi(0)disk(0)rdisk(0)partition(2)\WINNT
```

`[operating systems]`

This section specifies which operating systems are present on the computer, and detailed options for each one. XP uses the Advanced RISC Computing (ARC) path to specify the location of the boot partition. In the preceding example, the ARC path is:

```
multi(0)disk(0)rdisk(0)partition(1)\WINDOWS
```

The first parameter, which identifies the disk controller, should be `0`. The second parameter, the `disk` parameter, should also be `0`. The `rdisk` parameter specifies the disk number on the controller that has the boot partition. The numbers start at `0`. So, if you have two or more hard disks installed and the second hard disk has the boot partition, the setting is `rdisk(1)`. The `partition` parameter identifies the partition number of the boot partition. Partitions start with the number 1. The final section, which in the example is `\WINDOWS`, specifies the path to the folder where the operating system is installed.

To the right of the ARC path in the example is `="Microsoft Windows XP Home Edition"` `/fastdetect`. The words within quotes are what will appear on the boot menu next to the entry. To customize the text on the menu, you can change these words to whatever you wish—for example, "My Favorite Operating System." The `/fastdetect` switch disables the detection of serial and parallel devices, which allows for faster booting. The detection of these devices isn't normally required in XP, because the functions are performed by plug-and-play drivers, so it's generally a good idea to use the `/fastdetect` switch. The `/fastdetect` switch is only one of many switches that you can use in the *boot.ini* file to customize how the operating system loads. Table 1-2 lists others you can use (see www.microsoft.com/technet/sysinternals/information/bootini.mspx for more details).

Table 1-2 Switches for *boot.ini*

SWITCH	WHAT IT DOES
/3GB	On 32-bit systems, increases the size of the user process address space to 3GB and reduces the size of the system address space to 1GB.
/BASEVIDEO	Starts Windows using the standard VGA driver. It's most useful if you can't boot normally because of a video driver problem.
/BAUDRATE=RATE	Specifies the baud rate for remote kernel debugging and enables kernel-mode debugging.
/BOOTLOG	Logs information about the boot process to the *ntbtlog.txt* file in the *C:\Windows* folder.
/BOOTLOGO	Enables an installable splash screen (*C:\Windows\Boot.bmp*).
/BREAK	Used with kernel debugging. Sets a breakpoint at HAL initialization.
/BURNMEMORY=N	Specifies the amount of memory (in megabytes) by which to reduce the amount of memory.
/CHANNEL=N	Used with /DEBUGPORT=1394. Specifies which IEEE1394 (also known as FireWire or i.Link) channel to use for kernel debugging communications.
/CLKLVL	Configures HAL to use a level-sensitive rather than edge-sensitive clock for hardware interrupts.
/CMDCONS	Boots the recovery console.
/CRASHDEBUG	Loads the debugger at boot, but the debugger remains inactive unless a crash occurs.
/DEBUG	Loads the debugger at boot and runs it.
/DEBUGPORT=[PORT]	Specifies the port for kernel-mode debugging, and enables it. You can specify a COM port or 1394 for IEEE1394.
/EXECUTE	Disables no-execute protection. (See /NOEXECUTE.)
/FASTDETECT	Disables the detection of serial and parallel devices.
/INTAFFINITY	Configures HAL to set its interrupt affinity to send interrupts only to the highest-numbered processor.
/KERNEL=FILENAME /HAL=FILENAME	Allows you to override the filename for the HAL or kernel image.
/LASTKNOWNGOOD	Equivalent to selecting the LastKnownGood boot option.
MAXMEM=N	Specifies the maximum amount of RAM that Windows can use.
/MAXPROCSPERCLUSTER=N	Forces cluster-mode APIC addressing, except on systems with an external 82489DX APIC.
/MININT	Instructs the Windows Preinstallation Environment to load the SYSTEM registry hive as volatile (changes to hive are not made permanent).
/NODEBUG	Stops the debugger from loading.

Table 1-2 Switches for *boot.ini* *(continued)*

<table>
<tr><th>SWITCH</th><th>WHAT IT DOES</th></tr>
<tr><td><code>/NOEXECUTE</code>
<code>/NOEXECUTE=[OPTIN|OPTOUT|ALWAYSON|ALWAYSOFF]</code></td><td>Configures no-execute protection on 32-bit processors that support it. You can specify this option alone (which turns it on) or with an option:
OPTIN: Enables protection on core system images and images that have been enabled in the Data Execution Prevention dialog.
OPTOUT: Enables protection on all images except those that have been enabled in the Data Execution Prevention dialog.
ALWAYSON: Enables protection on all images.
ALWAYSOFF: Disables protection.</td></tr>
<tr><td><code>/NOGUIBOOT</code></td><td>Does not allow the splash screen to load during boot.</td></tr>
<tr><td><code>/NOLOWMEM</code></td><td>Prevents Windows from initializing the VGA driver during the boot process.</td></tr>
<tr><td><code>/NOPAE</code></td><td>Prevents Windows from using the Physical Address Extension (PAE) version of the kernel.</td></tr>
<tr><td><code>/NOSERIALMICE=[COMx|COMx,COMy,...]</code>
<code>/NOSERIALMICE</code></td><td>Disables the serial mouse on the specified (or all) ports.</td></tr>
<tr><td><code>/NUMPROC</code></td><td>Specifies the maximum number of processors to enable.</td></tr>
<tr><td><code>/ONECPU</code></td><td>Forces Windows to use only one CPU.</td></tr>
<tr><td><code>/PAE</code></td><td>Forces Windows to use the Physical Address Extension (PAE) version of the kernel.</td></tr>
<tr><td><code>/PCILOCK</code></td><td>Prevents Windows from dynamically assigning IO and IRQ resources, leaving such choices up to the BIOS.</td></tr>
<tr><td><code>/RDPATH=PATH</code></td><td>Specifies the path to a system disk image (may be on a network drive), which the system will boot from. You can use <code>/RDIMAGEOFFSET=N</code> to specify the offset of the system image.</td></tr>
<tr><td><code>/REDIRECT</code></td><td>Tells Windows to send boot information to the serial port and accept system management commands through that port.</td></tr>
<tr><td><code>/SAFEBOOT:switch</code></td><td>Forces Windows to boot into the safe mode specified by the <code>switch</code> parameter, which can be <code>minimal</code>, <code>network</code>, <code>dsrepair</code>, or <code>minimal(alternateshell)</code>. In <code>minimal</code> safe mode, only the minimum set of drivers necessary to start XP are loaded. In <code>network</code> safe mode, networking drivers are loaded in addition to the minimum set of drivers. In <code>dsrepair</code> safe mode, Windows restores Active Directory from a backup. In <code>minimal(alternateshell)</code> the minimum set of drivers are loaded and XP boots into the command prompt.</td></tr>
<tr><td><code>SCSIORDINAL:n</code></td><td>Specifies the SCSI ID of the controller.</td></tr>
<tr><td><code>/SDIBOOT=PATH</code></td><td>Specifies the RAM disk image in a System Disk Image file.</td></tr>
</table>

Table 1-2 Switches for *boot.ini* (*continued*)

SWITCH	WHAT IT DOES
/SOS	Displays the name of each driver as it loads and gives descriptions of what is occurring during the boot process. It also offers other information, including the XP build number, the service pack number, the number of processors on the system, and the amount of installed memory.
/TIMERES=N	Sets the resolution of the system timer in hundreds of nanoseconds.
/USERVA=N	Specifies the amount (in MB) of the address space available to applications.
/WIN95	Boots the Consumer Windows boot sector in *Bootsect.dos*.
/WIN95DOS	Boots the MS-DOS boot sector in *Bootsect.dos*.
/YEAR=N	Specifies the year. Handy for Y2K testing, and maybe even Y2K38 testing!

When you've finished editing the *boot.ini* file, save it. The next time you start your computer, its settings will go into effect.

In this example, if we want the menu to appear for 45 seconds, the default operating system to be Windows 2000, and the XP splash screen to be turned off when we choose to load XP, the *boot.ini* file should look like this:

```
[boot loader]
timeout=45
default=multi(0)disk(0)rdisk(0)partition(2)\WINNT
[operating systems]
multi(0)disk(0)rdisk(0)partition(1)\WINDOWS="Microsoft Windows XP Home" /fastdetect /noguiboot
multi(0)disk(0)rdisk(0)partition(2)\WINNT="Windows 2000 Professional" /fastdetect
```

Create a Startup Menu Even If You Have Only One Operating System

Even if you have only one operating system, you can create a boot menu that will let you choose to load your operating system with different parameters. For example, for menu choices, you might have your normal operating system, a mode that lets you trace any startup problems, and Safe Mode. To give yourself the option of operating systems with different parameters, create separate entries for each new operating system choice. For example, for the version of the operating system that traces potential startup problems, you could create this entry:

```
multi(0)disk(0)rdisk(0)partition(1)\WINDOWS="Trace Problems XP Home" /fastdetect /bootlog /sos
```

This entry creates a startup log and displays information about the drivers and other operating system information as it loads.

For the version of the operating system that loads in Safe Mode but still allows networking, you could create this entry:

```
multi(0)disk(0)rdisk(0)partition(1)\WINDOWS="Safe Start XP Home" /fastdetect /safeboot:network
```

Figure 1-21.
The System Configuration Utility

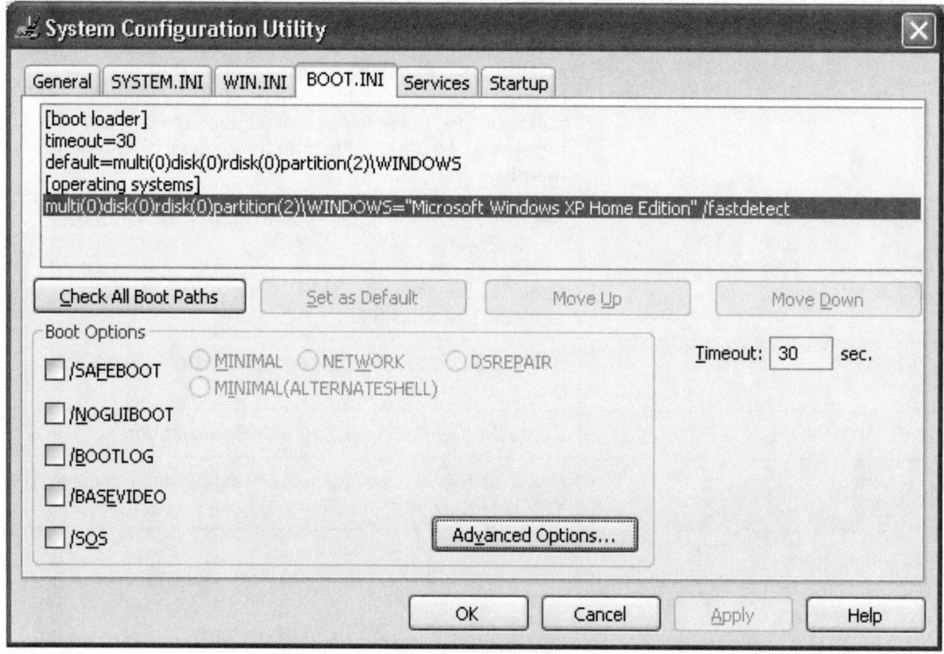

The *boot.ini* file would look like this, assuming that you want the menu to display for 30 seconds and you want normal XP startup to be the default:

```
[boot loader]
timeout=30
default=multi(0)disk(0)rdisk(0)partition(1)\WINDOWS
[operating systems]
multi(0)disk(0)rdisk(0)partition(1)\WINDOWS="Microsoft Windows XP Home Edition" /fastdetect
multi(0)disk(0)rdisk(0)partition(1)\WINDOWS="Trace Problems XP Home" /fastdetect /bootlog /sos
multi(0)disk(0)rdisk(0)partition(1)\WINDOWS="Safe Start XP Home" /fastdetect /safeboot:network
```

If you're leery of using a text editor to edit *boot.ini* directly, you can use the System Configuration Utility **[Hack #6]** instead. Type **msconfig** at a command prompt or in the Run box and click the BOOT.INI tab, shown in Figure 1-21. You'll be able to add several switches (but not as many as you can if you edit the *boot.ini* file yourself using a text editor).

See Also

- "Hack Windows Vista Multiboot Systems with VistaBootPRO" **[Hack #12]**
- "The Secrets of Windows Vista's BCDEDIT" **[Hack #10]**

HACK 12: Hack Windows Vista Multiboot Systems with VistaBootPRO

V You don't need to wrestle with BCDEDIT if you want to change how Windows Vista boots, especially on a multiboot system. Use the free VistaBootPRO instead.

As you've seen **[Hack #10]** hacking the way that Windows Vista boots is pretty tough if your only tool is the command-line interface.

There's a much better solution than going *mano a mano* with BCDEDIT. Use the free VistaBootPro (www.vistabootpro.org), which offers a simple, graphical way to hack multiboot systems. Think of VistaBootPRO as a front-end to BCDEDIT. When you make changes using VistaBootPRO, you're actually editing your BCD store, as if you were using BCDEDIT.

Before using VistaBootPro, it's a good idea to get a basic understanding of what the BCD store **[Hack #10]** is and does.

The first thing you should do after installing VistaBootPRO is to back up your existing BCD store. That way, if anything goes amiss when you use the program, you can easily revert to your previous store. To back up your BCD store, click the Backup/Restore Center in VistaBootPRO. A screen like the one shown in Figure 1-22 appears. Click the Save button to save a copy of your store with the file name *VPB_Backup.bcd* to the root folder. You can also browse to a different folder and save it there. To restore to the BCD store you've saved, click the Restore button, click Search, and browse to *VPB_Backup.bcd*, and then follow the directions for restoring to it.

You can also use the command line to save your BCD store to a removable drive or disk, for more safety. Create a folder for the BCD store: for example, *D:\BCD Backup*. Next, launch an administrator's command prompt, and type `bcdedit /export "D:\BCD Backup\Bcd Backup"`. That will back up the store. To restore it, type this command: `bcdedit /import "D:\BCD Backup\Bcd Backup"`. For more details, see "The Secrets of Windows Vista's BCDEDIT" **[Hack #10]**.

Using VistaBootPRO is quite straightforward. To see your BCD store information, click View Settings. For a basic overview of your BCD store, and how your system is set to boot, select Overview, as shown in Figure 1-23. It describes, in plain English, how your system is set to boot, and shows you the basic settings in the BCD store **[Hack #10]**. Select Detailed to see more BCD settings, and select All for a comprehensive list.

Figure 1-22.
Before using VistaBootPRO to change your boot settings, back up your BCD store

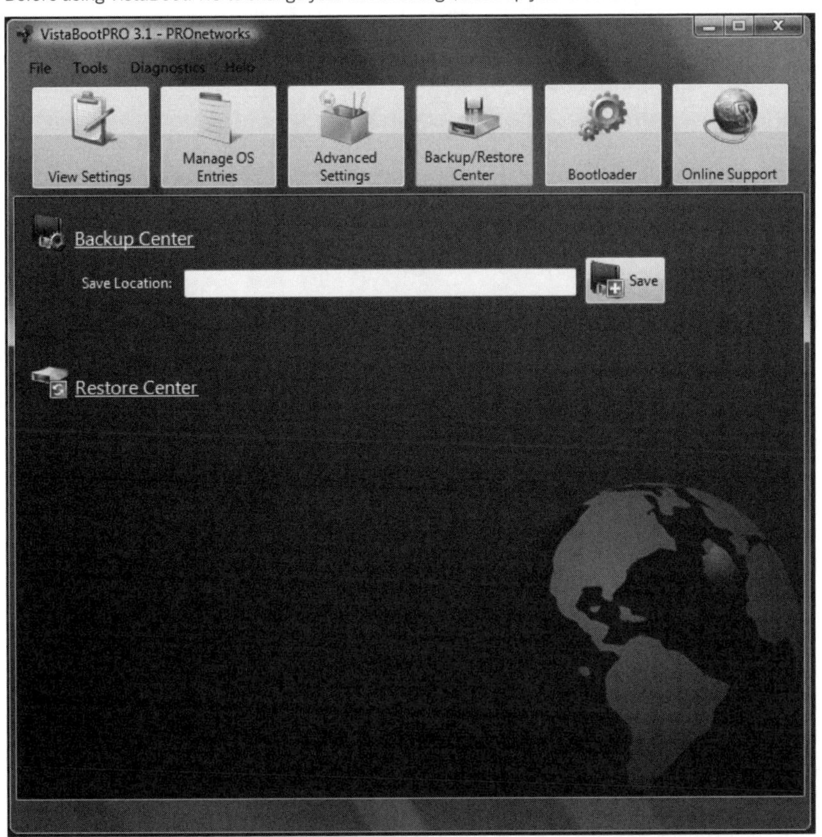

Figure 1-23.
An overview of the BCD store, and how Windows Vista boots

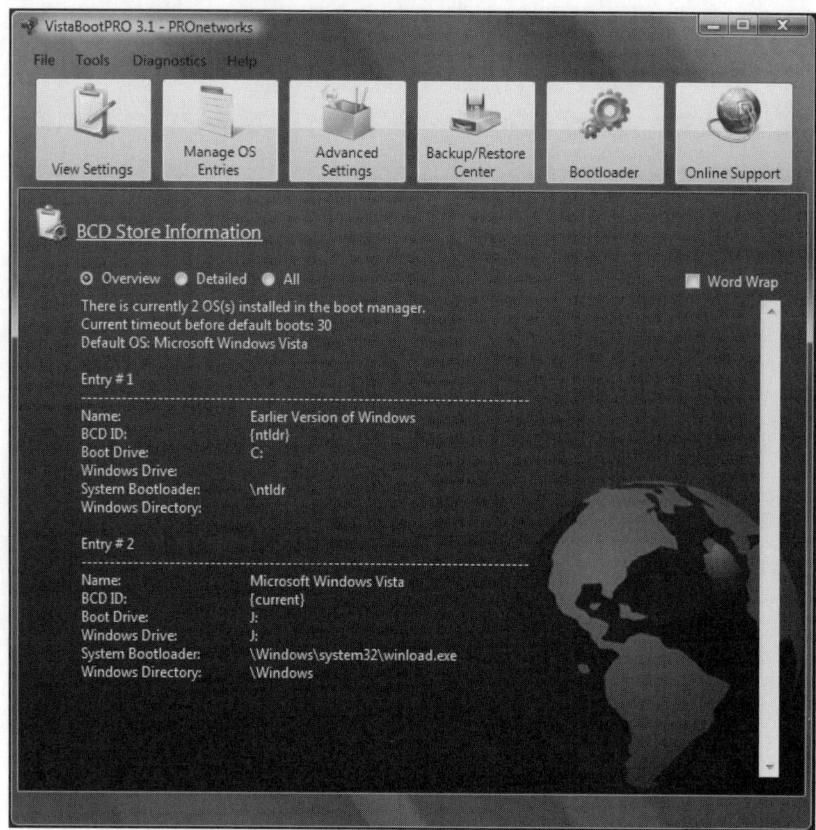

Click "Manage OS Entries" to get to the most important part of VistaBootPRO. Here's where you can change the order of the boot menu that appears when your PC starts, set one of the operating systems to be the default, rename any of your operating system list entries, and change the amount of time the menu displays before you boot into your default operating system. As you can see in Figure 1-24, the use of this screen is quite straightforward. Make your changes and click Apply, and the next time you restart your PC, your new boot settings take effect.

The Advanced Settings button contains mainly esoteric options, but it's the place to go if you want to debug the boot process, enable or disable the boot GUI mode, allow or disallow the use of unsigned drivers in the 64-bit version of Windows Vista, along with similar options.

The final button, Bootloader, will let you uninstall the Windows Vista bootloader, in case you have a dual-boot system, and want to revert to the boot loader of the previous version of Windows.

See Also

- "The Secrets of Windows Vista's BCDEDIT" **[Hack #10]**
- For another good tool for multiboot and editing BCD, get the free EasyBCD (neosmart.net/dl.php?id=1)

Figure 1-24.
Configuring the most important multiboot options

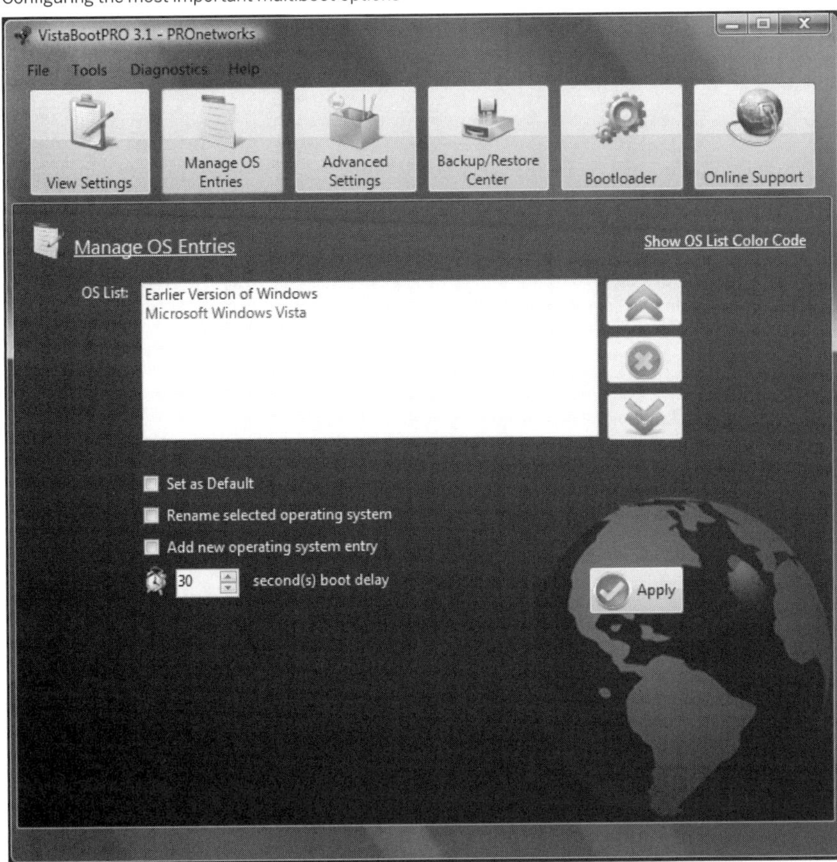

HACK 13: Move Partitions Around on Vista Without Destroying It

V Resizing partitions in Vista can lead to a meltdown—you may not be able to boot. Here's how to resize and still boot up, problem-free.

One of the cool things about Vista is its ability to resize partitions using *diskmgmt.msc*. This trick works great for those times when you need to shrink or grow a partition. Unfortunately, if you need to move things around as I did this weekend, you won't be able to use the built-in tool.

I needed to delete a partition I wasn't using and also give more space to my Vista partition. So I turned to the trusty Gparted (gparted.sourceforge.net), a free alternative to tools like Partition Magic. (Partition Magic doesn't work in Vista, by the way.) It performed the partitioning flawlessly, but Vista refused to boot after that. I was prepared for that, thanks to the Gparted Vista HOWTO (gparted.free.fr/screenshots/VISTA/Howto_move_VISTA.html), and had my Vista boot DVD ready to perform the post-Gparted operation:

- Boot up the installation DVD
- Choose the repair option
- Let the installation DVD repair the disk automatically when prompted to do so.

This process let Vista boot, but there was still a problem . . . one that I remember from messing up drive letter assignments in previous versions of Windows: Vista booted up and took me to the login screen, but wouldn't show my desktop. (In theory, the HOWTO should have worked perfectly, but I have a dual-boot Vista/XP system, and things got confused.)

So I had to do one more set of tasks:

- Log in
- Hit Ctrl-Alt-Del to get Task Manager to appear (the desktop will not appear normally when the drive letter is messed up)
- Use Task Manager to run Regedit and make my way to `HKEY_LOCAL_MACHINE\SYSTEM\MountedDevices` and fix the drive letter assignments.

The drive letter assignments can be tricky, because you probably need to do something like rename *\DosDevices\C:* to *\DosDevices\D:* and vice versa, but you can't have duplicate names, so you'll need to change one of them to something temporary, like:

- *\DosDevices\C:* to *\DosDevices\X:*
- *\DosDevices\D:* to *\DosDevices\C:*
- *\DosDevices\X:* to *\DosDevices\D:*

Once I did that, I rebooted, and all was right with the world!

— Brian Jepson

HACK 14: Transforming Your Windows XP Laptop into a Dual-Boot XP/Ubuntu Linux System

XP Here's how to turn your Windows XP into a Linux dual-boot wonder.

For those of us who do considerable work in the Linux environment, a Windows-only notebook is far from ideal. I worked with Unix on Windows packages such as Uwin and Cygwin for several years, but I finally decided I wanted a full Linux installation on my notebook.

I started with my aging Toshiba laptop (which had about 90 percent of its 30GB disk filled) and, without losing any data, turned it into a dual-boot XP/Ubuntu Linux system with a shared partition where many of my user files were accessible whether I was using XP or Ubuntu. This made the laptop much more versatile, which is ideal for a developer who works in Linux but must also work in Windows for certain applications or for Windows-based development. A few months later, the monitor on that machine gave out. I bought a new HP notebook and transformed it into a dual-boot XP/Ubuntu Linux system right away.

This hack describes the steps I took to complete the dual-boot conversions.

Prerequisites: Disk Space and CDs

As you might expect, a dual-boot computer requires more disk space than a computer running just one operating system. I don't recommend performing an XP/Linux dual-boot conversion with a drive smaller than the 30 GB that my older notebook had. A system with more than 60 GB disk space is a more ideal starting point.

When reconfiguring operating systems on a hard drive, you must be able to boot the system using a CD that has appropriate tools for disk partitioning, file editing, and so on. I used the System Rescue CD (www.sysresccd.org/Main_Page), a Gentoo Linux 2.4 Live CD (www.gentoo.org) with system utilities including QtParted, GRUB, LILO, archiving tools, editors, CD tools, Perl 5.8, CaptiveNtfs, and others. I downloaded the ISO image file using Windows and made my CD using Alex Feinman's excellent ISO Recorder (isorecorder.alexfeinman.com/isorecorder.htm). I downloaded the installation ISO file for Ubuntu 5.10, "The Breezy Badger," at Ubuntu's download page (www.ubuntu.com/getubuntu/download). Again, I made the CD using ISO Recorder.

Windows Disk Preparations

If you're converting a Windows system that you've used for some time, the disk may be nearly full, and the files will likely be scattered across it. To install Linux, you need to divide the disk into multiple partitions. One way to do this is to destructively repartition the entire disk, but then you have to reinstall Windows and all of your Windows software—not a pleasing prospect. A better solution is to resize the Windows NTFS partition, then add new partitions for Linux, Linux swap space, and a FAT32 shared partition.

Because my Toshiba notebook's disk was 90 percent full, the first thing I had to do was remove files. If you're in this situation, see how much space you can free up by:

- Backing up all critical files (or performing a full system backup if you have capability to do that).
- Removing Windows software that you never use and never plan to use, using "Add or Remove Programs" ("Uninstall a program" in Vista) in the Windows Control Panel or the uninstallation programs that came with the software.
- Removing unneeded data files.
- Moving documents, data files, and project workspaces (for example, software development directories) that you can later store temporarily in the new shared partition to another computer.
- Emptying the Windows Recycle Bin.
- Doing all of these things decreased my Windows disk usage to 10 GB, leaving 18 GB free. However, the files were still scattered across the disk.

Before you can resize the NTFS partition, you must move all files to the "front" of the disk. You can see the locations of files on your disk by running the Windows Defragmenter utility. Go to Start→All Programs→Accessories→System Tools→Disk Defragmenter to launch the defragmenter. Figure 1-25 illustrates my disk usage after the defragmentation cycle completed.

The files were not as completely packed into the "front" of the disk (the left side of the Defragmenter diagram) as I would have expected. A little research revealed that the Windows Defragmenter applies a less-comprehensive defragmenting approach than is available in some commercial programs. I decided to rerun the Windows Defragmenter. After three more runs, my disk usage looked more like Figure 1-26.

This result looked adequate. More than half of the disk was available for my Linux installation, Linux swap, and the shared FAT32 partition.

One problem that you may encounter in defragmenting a Windows disk using the Windows Defragmenter is unmovable files (the green bars, if you're looking at your results) located in inconvenient locations (on the right side of the display, near the end of your disk). The two most common unmovable laptop files are the Windows operating system paging file (*pagefile.sys*) and the hibernation file (*hiberfil.sys*), which stores the system state when the XP operating system goes into "hibernate" mode. An easy solution is to temporarily remove these files, then reinstall them after you've resized the NTFS partition. If you need help with this, see my blog entry "Moving the Unmovable: Windows Disk Defragmentation Strategies" (lyratechnicalsystems.com/?p=9).

Figure 1-25.
Notebook disk usage after running the Windows disk defragmenter

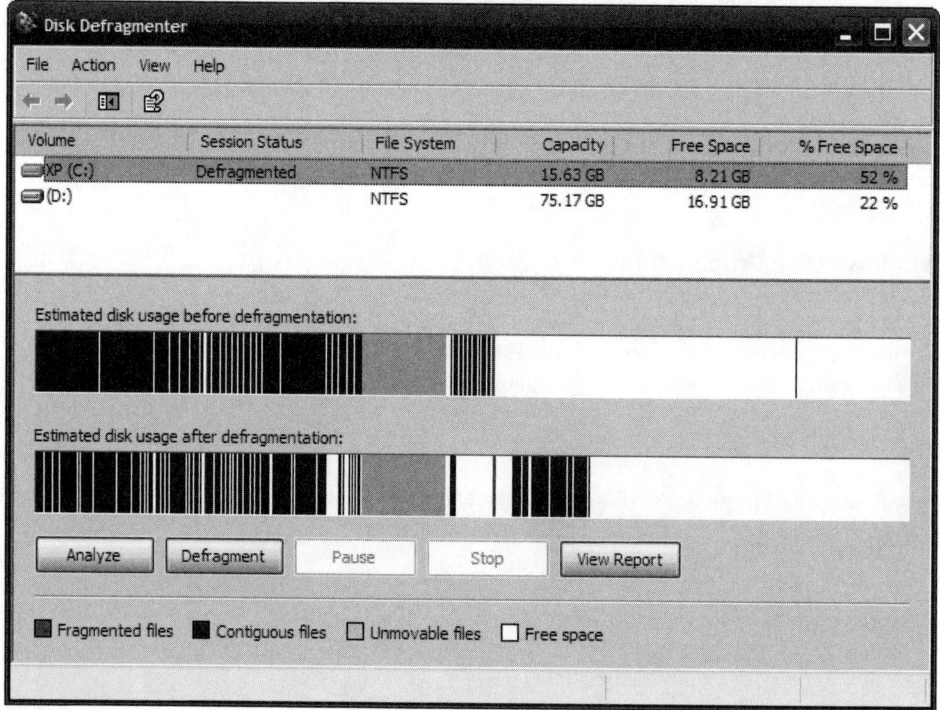

Figure 1-26.
Notebook disk usage after four Windows disk defragmenter runs

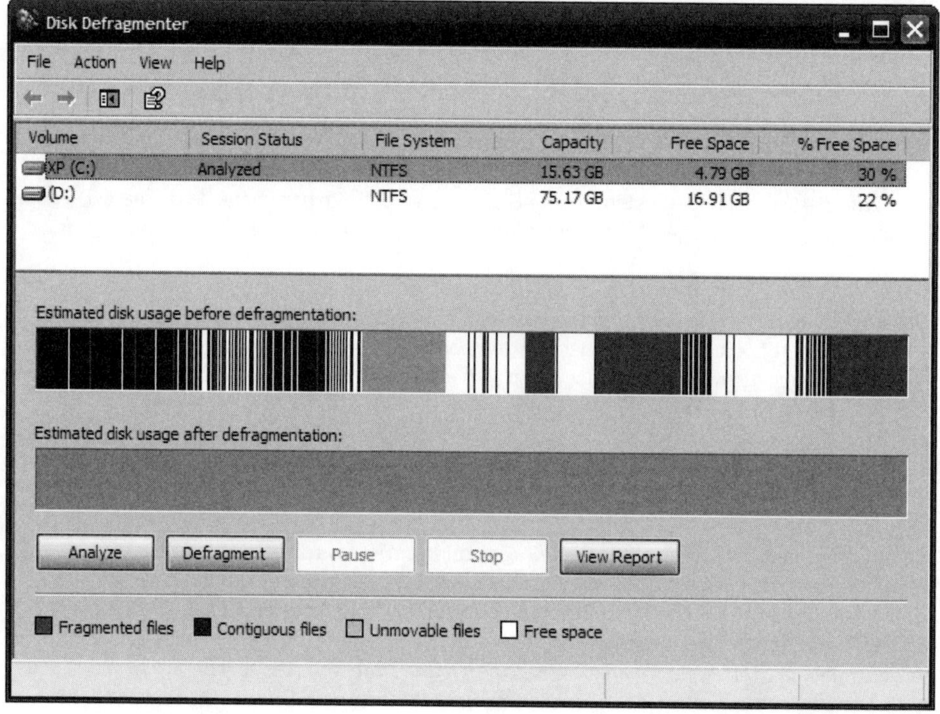

Dual-Boot Computer Disk Partitioning

When sizing your partitions, consider the following:

- **Windows NTFS partition:** Provide adequate space for the full operating system (including anticipated future patches), installation of all applications you want, and plenty of extra space (just to be safe).
- **Linux ext3 partition:** Provide adequate space for the full operating system; for convenience, allow enough space for software installation in the default install locations (*/usr/bin*, and so on).
- **Linux Swap:** Follow the standard rule of allocating swap—twice your RAM.
- **Shared FAT32 partition:** Don't make this too small. For example, if your email will reside on the shared partition, that alone can quickly occupy gigabytes of disk space.

Although people often recommend creating a separate partition for the */home* directory, I chose to let */home* reside on the root partition, in this case. Most of the data that I would normally store in a Linux */home* directory is actually in the shared FAT32 partition on my dual-boot systems, leaving */home* relatively empty.

Here are the partition sizes I used for my two notebooks:

PARTITION	TOSHIBA (30 GB DRIVE)	HP (80 GB DRIVE)
Windows NTFS	18 GB	19 GB
Linux ext3	5 GB	30 GB
Linux swap	1 GB	2 GB
FAT32 (shared)	5 GB	25 GB

Once you've decided on partition sizes, boot the system using the System Rescue CD. When the rescue CD presents the boot: prompt, I recommend entering fb800 nodetect:

```
boot: fb800 nodetect
```

This setting bypasses a full search for the devices on your computer. When I tried the default boot with my new HP, the system displayed the message "USB and PCI hotplugging" and froze, forcing me into a hard power-down. My Knoppix 3.7 LiveCD also failed to complete its boot on the HP, using the default options. Because I don't plan to work with USB or hotplug devices, there is no need to detect them.

After the rescue CD boots, you'll see a Linux command prompt. Enter run_qtparted to launch the QtParted disk partitioning application. (Documentation and screen shots are available from the project's site at qtparted.sourceforge.net.)

Select the Windows partition (this was */dev/hda* on both my systems), and resize it: select Operations→Resize, enter the new partition size (observe your units, MB or GB), and click OK.

Next, create a second primary partition, of type ext3, for the new Ubuntu system: highlight the "02" partition, and select *Operations→Create*. Set "Create as" to "Primary Partition" (so that the Linux system can boot), select "ext3" as the partition type, give the drive a sensible partition label, enter the partition size, and click OK. Create the Linux swap partition by highlighting number 03 and selecting Operations→Create. Select "linux-swap" as the partition type, select the swap size, and click OK.

Finally, create the FAT32 partition that both operating systems will share. Highlight number "04" and select Operations→Create. Set the partition type to FAT32, provide a label, and allow the partition to use the remainder of the disk.

Now, study the color-coded diagram at the top of the QtParted window. The sizes of the colored partition regions should match what you expect to see based on your disk space allocation design. If there is any doubt, you can select Device→Undo to undo your changes, or exit QtParted and start over.

When you're absolutely certain that everything looks correct, select Device→Commit. The QtParted program will warn you that all partitions must be unmounted. The hard drive partitions won't be mounted if you went directly from the CD boot to *run_qtparted*. Click Yes to commit your changes.

A progress window appears, and QtParted displays various messages as it performs the repartioning operations. It took about ten minutes to repartition my 30 GB Toshiba drive into the four new partitions, but on my HP all operations completed in about a minute. If everything works, QtParted displays "Operations completed successfully." Click OK, then select File→Quit to exit QtParted.

Enter shutdown -r now to shut down the system. At this point, you might want to reboot to verify that your Windows system is still bootable. Windows should boot fine if you selected an adequate resize partition size based on the final Windows defragmentation map. At boot time, Windows may detect the change in disk partition size and begin to run the *chkdsk* utility. Let this continue so that Windows can reset its internal information about available disk drives.

After Windows has completed its analysis of the new disk partitions and booted into its normal operating mode, open Explorer and look at the identified drives. You should see the resized boot drive, plus a new drive letter that designates the FAT32 partition you created using QtParted.

Installing Ubuntu Linux

To install Ubuntu Linux, reboot the system with the Ubuntu boot CD in the drive. At the Partition disks screen, select "Manually edit partition table." On my systems, Ubuntu found these partitions:

- ntfs */media/hda1*
- ext3 */media/hda2*
- swap *swap*
- fat32 */media/hd4*

The ntfs partition is the resized Windows partition. The ext3 partition is where you want to install Ubuntu. Make sure you set the mount point to */* for this partition, set the bootable flag to on, and let Ubuntu format the partition. For the FAT32 partition, specify a mount point such as */share*. When the configuration settings are correct, select Finish partitioning and write changes to disk. The installer will format the ext3 and swap partitions.

Installing GRUB and Making Ubuntu Bootable Using the Windows Bootloader

The remainder of the Ubuntu install is straightforward, until you must choose whether to install the GRUB bootloader to the Master Boot Record (MBR). To be extra protective of my working Windows installation, I chose not to install GRUB to my MBR, which led me to a screen titled Install the GRUB boot loader on a hard disk. Here, I identified my Ubuntu partition:

```
(hd0,1)
```

In GRUB's zero-based drive identification convention, this indicates the first disk drive (drive hd0), second partition (partition 1).

After installing GRUB, Ubuntu will request a reboot to complete its installation running from the hard drive. On both of my systems, the reboot produced the ominous message "Missing operating system." This message is the result of Ubuntu having set its own partition as the active partition. The Windows bootloader, which is still installed in the master boot record, cannot boot Windows, because the Windows partition is not flagged as active; the Windows bootloader also has no knowledge of the Ubuntu operating system, so that cannot boot, either.

To make the system bootable into both Windows and Ubuntu, reboot into the System Rescue CD. Run QtParted, select the Windows partition (for example, */dev/hda1*), and select Operations→Set Active. Select Device→Commit to commit your changes. The QtParted progress window will display the operations, ending with Operations completed successfully. Exit QtParted, but don't shut down.

Now you must copy data from the Ubuntu partition to a file that the Windows bootloader can use for booting Ubuntu. The FAT32 partition, which is accessible to both Linux and Windows, is useful. At the System Rescue CD command prompt, mount the FAT32 partition:

```
# mkdir /mnt/share
# mount -t msdos /dev/hda4 /mnt/share
```

 On your system, the */dev* identification of the FAT32 drive may differ. Mount using the correct partition designation for your system.

Make a file containing data copied from the boot sector of your Linux drive (substitute your Linux drive designation if it is not */dev/hda2*):

```
# dd if=/dev/hda2 of=/mnt/share/ubuntu.bin bs=512 count=1
```

If you enter:

```
# ls -l /mnt/share
```

you should see the file *ubuntu.bin* with size 512 bytes.

Now configure the Windows bootloader. Shut down the system and let Windows boot. Copy the *ubuntu.bin* file from the FAT32 Windows drive to drive *C:*. Next, edit the system startup settings. Open the Control Panel, select System, and go to the Advanced tab. Click the Startup and Recovery settings button. Click the Edit button to edit the startup options file manually (Figure 1-27).

Clicking Edit loads the *boot.ini* file into Notepad. Add a new line at the end of the file:

```
C:\UBUNTU.BIN="Ubuntu Linux"
```

Save the file and close Notepad. Make sure the "Time to display list of operating systems" has a value of at least 5 or 10, to give yourself plenty of time to select the operating system at boot time. Click OK to save the Startup settings.

You now have a dual-boot XP/Ubuntu notebook computer. Reboot the computer and select Ubuntu Linux to complete the installation and configuration of Ubuntu. Linux configuration issues vary for different computers.

Figure 1-27.
Navigating to edit the Windows bootloader startup settings

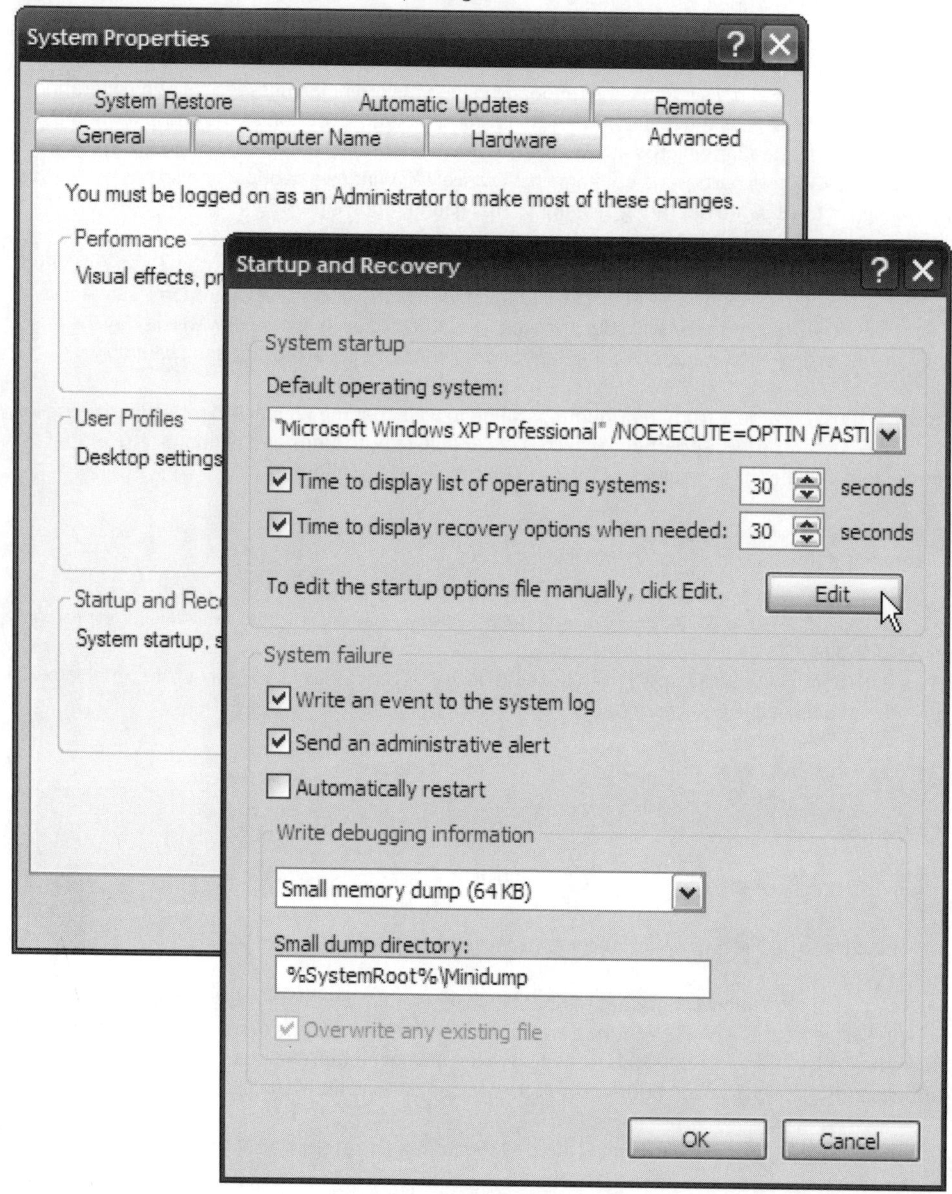

Accessing the Shared Partition from Ubuntu

Ubuntu mounts the shared FAT32 partition at boot time:

```
kevin@lyrahpnx:~$ df
Filesystem           1K-blocks      Used Available Use% Mounted on
/dev/hda2             30233928   1766828  26931288   7% /
tmpfs                   517816        16    517800   1% /dev/shm
tmpfs                   517816     12588    505228   3% /lib/modules/2.6.12-9-386/volatile
/dev/hda1             19451896   3548380  15903516  19% /media/hda1
/dev/hda4             25916224       160  25916064   1% /share
```

By default, the root user owns the partition:

```
kevin@lyrahpnx:~$ ls -l /share
total 48
drwxr-xr-x  2 root root 16384 2006-02-09 11:03 Recycled
drwxr-xr-x  3 root root 16384 2006-02-09 11:03 System Volume Information
-rwxr-xr-x  1 root root   512 2006-02-09 10:56 ubuntu.bin
```

You won't be able to access the shared partition from Ubuntu Linux using your normal login name unless you change this.

The simplest solution is to have the */share* partition mounted at boot time specifying your login ID as the owner. First, display your user ID record from */etc/passwd* (substitute your user name for kevin):

```
kevin@lyrahpnx:~$ grep kevin /etc/passwd
kevin:x:1000:1000:Kevin Farnham,,,:/home/kevin:/bin/bash
```

The third and fourth items are the user ID and group ID; these are necessary when you modify the mount command in */etc/fstab*.

Because *fstab* is a critical Linux system file, make a backup copy of your working version before you edit the file. Then, edit *fstab* (use *sudo*, because root owns the file), and change the options section for the */share* entry to defaults,uid=uuuu,gid=gggg, where uuuu is your user ID and gggg is your group ID. Here's my revised */etc/fstab* (note the */dev/hda4 /share* entry):

```
kevin@lyrahpnx:/etc$ cat fstab
# /etc/fstab: static file system information.
#
# <file system> <mount point>   <type>  <options>       <dump>  <pass>
proc            /proc           proc    defaults        0       0
/dev/hda2       /               ext3    defaults,errors=remount-ro 0       1
/dev/hda1       /media/hda1     ntfs    defaults        0       0
/dev/hda4       /share          vfat    defaults,uid=1000,gid=1000        0       0
/dev/hda3       none            swap    sw              0       0
/dev/hdb        /media/cdrom0   udf,iso9660 user,noauto     0       0
```

When you reboot into Ubuntu, the */share* partition will be mounted with your user name having full ownership and full access.

Conclusion

Converting a single disk-drive notebook computer into a dual-boot Windows XP/Ubuntu Linux system requires advance planning and careful execution of multiple sequences of steps. However, the benefit of being able to boot either Windows or Linux on a portable system, and to share data between the two, is well worth the effort for people who work in both realms.

See Also

- Installing and Configuring Ubuntu on a Laptop (www.linuxdevcenter.com/pub/a/linux/2005/11/17/ubuntu_laptop.html)
- "Run Linux Inside Windows without Dual Booting" **[Hack #30]**
- "Instant Linux" **[Hack #33]**

— Kevin Farnham

02 HACKING THE INTERFACE

To many people, Windows' user interface *is* the operating system. It's what you interact with all day, and more than anything else, it determines how pleased or displeased you are with your life at the keyboard. It also greatly affects your productivity.

It's also just plain fun to hack. There are nearly infinite possibilities for hacking. For example, in Windows Vista, do you like Sidebar gadgets? If so, you'll find a slew of ways here to hack them, including building gadgets yourself and hacking them so that they'll do thing such as display YouTube videos.

You'll also learn how to hack most other aspects of both the Windows XP and Windows Vista interface. In this chapter, you'll learn how to hack your way to a better GUI—one that reflects your own preferences, not the market-driven designs of Microsoft engineers. You'll even learn how to run Linux and the Mac operating system right inside Windows. And if you'd like to go retro, you'll see how to run Windows 3.11 inside it as well.

HACK 15: Hack Your Way Through Windows Vista's Aero Interface

V Don't like the way Vista's nifty new Aero interface works? Not to worry—here's how to bend it to your will.

Windows Vista's new Aero interface, which features animated windows with transparent borders and cool features such as Windows Flip 3-D, which shows all open windows in full three-dimensional glory on your desktop, may be the best part of the new operating system.

Better yet, what you see is *not* what you get, because there are plenty of secret ways you can hack it. Whether you want to change the size of transparent window borders or slow down window animations, you can now bend it to your will.

Hack Aero's Glass Borders

The borders around system windows, such as dialog boxes and the Control Panel, are transparent in Windows Vista's Aero interface. You're not stuck with those border sizes, though; you can shrink them or make them larger:

1. Right-click the Desktop and select Personalize.
2. Click Windows Color and Appearance.
3. Click "Open classic appearance properties" for more color options.

4. From the dialog box that appears, make sure that Windows Aero is selected as the color scheme. Click the Advanced button on the right side of the dialog box.

5. Select "Border Padding" in the Item drop-down box, as shown in Figure 2-1. To change the size of the border, type a new size for the border. (The default is 4.) Click OK, then OK again. The sizes of the borders will now change.

You can change more about the borders than just their size, including their transparency and color. Right-click the desktop and select Personalize→Window Color and Appearance (see Figure 2-2). To change the transparency of window borders, move the color intensity slider to the left to make them more transparent, and to the right to make them more translucent. Choose a color for your windows on the top of the screen, or custom-build a color by clicking Show color mixer, and then moving the sliders to mix your own color. To turn off transparency, uncheck, the box next to "Enable transparency."

Figure 2-1.
Adjusting Aero's glass borders

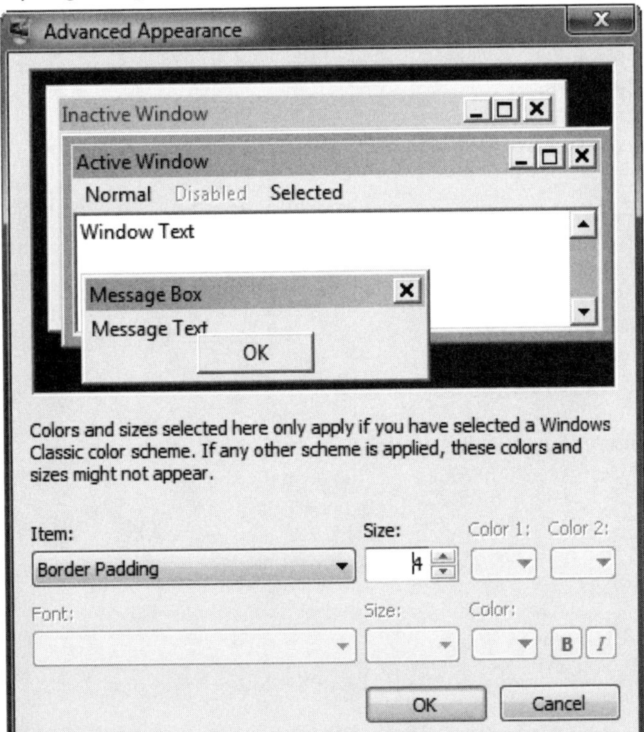

Figure 2-2.
Moving the slider to change the amount of transparency in window borders

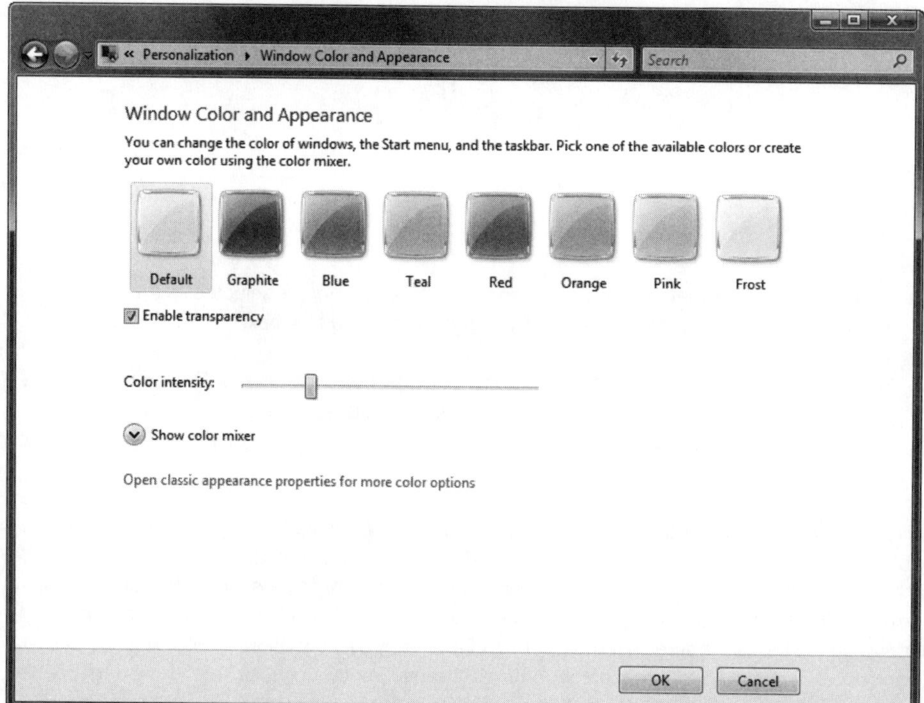

Make Windows Animation Go Slo-Mo

Here's a nifty little hack that has absolutely no purpose except for pure entertainment and eye candy value. It will slow down the animations that occur when windows minimize and maximize to and from the Taskbar, and you hold down the Shift key.

Launch the Registry Editor Registry Editor by typing regedit at the Start Search box or a command prompt (see Chapter 13 for details) and then:

1. Go to `HKEY_CURRENT_USER\Software\Microsoft\Windows\DWM`.
2. Select Edit→New DWORD (32-bit) Value, and create a new DWORD called AnimationsShiftKey.
3. Give it a value of 1.
4. Close the Registry Editor.
5. Log off of Windows and then log back in again, or else reboot.
6. Hold the Shift key and minimize or maximize a window. The animation will be slowed down considerably. To make the animation go at normal speed, let go of the shift key.

> **QUICK HACK**
>
> **HACK VISTA'S BLINKING CURSOR**
>
> Windows Vista's blinking cursor can be razor thin, and sometimes it can be very hard to find it, especially if you're using a laptop. But it's easy to make the cursor thicker—pretty much as thick as you want. Select Control Panel→Ease of Access→Optimize visual display. Scroll toward the bottom of the screen, until you come to "Make things on the screen easier to see."
>
> In the box next to "Set the thickness of the blinking cursor," select a number. The larger the number, the fatter the cursor. You'll see a preview of the cursor in the box next to the box. Click Save. The cursor throughout Windows Vista will now be fatter and easier to see.

Speed Up Windows Aero

One problem with Windows Aero is that it may slow down your system. If you want, you can turn it off:

1. Right-click the Windows desktop and select Personalize→Window Color and Appearance.
2. Click "Open classic appearance properties" for more color options.
3. In the Color scheme drop-down box, choose Windows Vista Basic or Windows Standard, and click OK. Aero will now be turned off.

But what if there are some things you like about Aero, such as windows animations, but others you don't like, such as transparent windows? You can turn off some Aero features to speed up your PC, but leave others on that you like using. To do it, select Start→Computer→System Properties. Click Advanced system settings, then in the Performance section, click the Settings button. A screen like the one shown in Figure 2-3 appears. Uncheck those features that you want to turn off, then click OK.

Figure 2-3.
Choosing which Windows Aero features you want to use

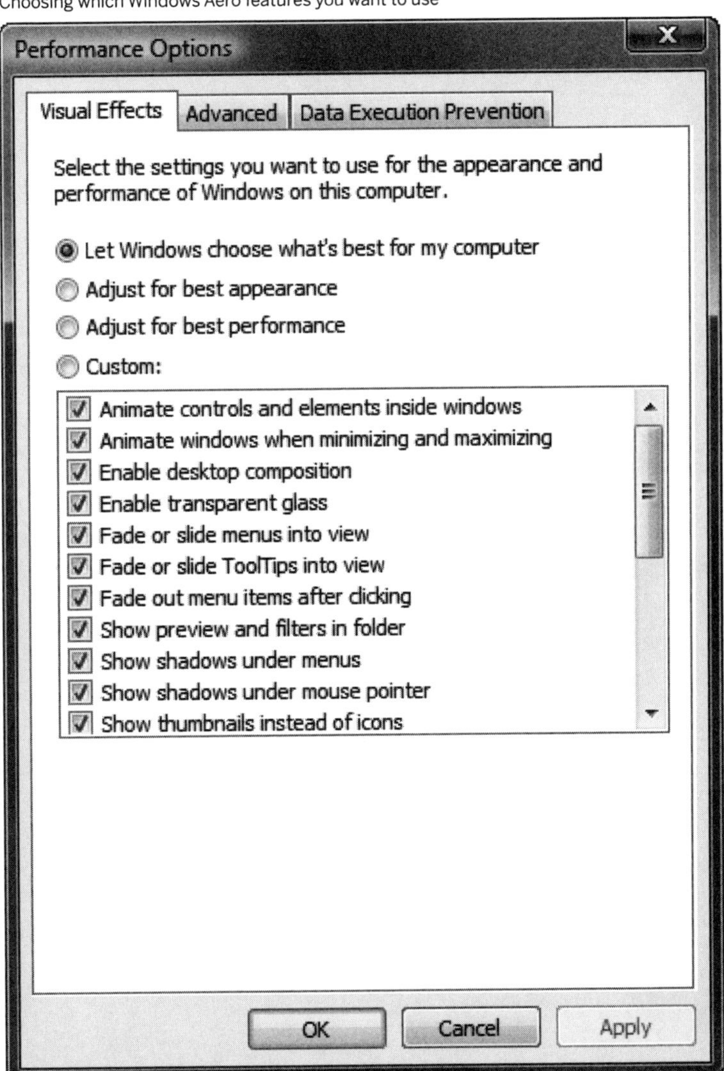

HACK 16: A Grab Bag of Great Vista Interface Hacks

V Want more ways to mold Windows Vista's interface to your wishes? There's plenty for you here.

Windows Vista's interface is just begging you to hack it. Whether you want to change ClearType settings, remove desktop icons or more, there's something here you'll like.

Hack ClearType

There's one universal truth you can say about ClearType—most people either hate it or love it. With Windows Vista, this font-smoothing technology, designed primarily for laptops and LCDs, is turned on by default. Some people complain that ClearType makes text hard to read and fuzzy; others say it makes text far easier on the eyes.

You can, however, turn off ClearType. To do it through the GUI, right-click the desktop and select Personalize→Windows Color and Appearance→Open classic appearance properties for more color

Figure 2-4.
Turning off ClearType

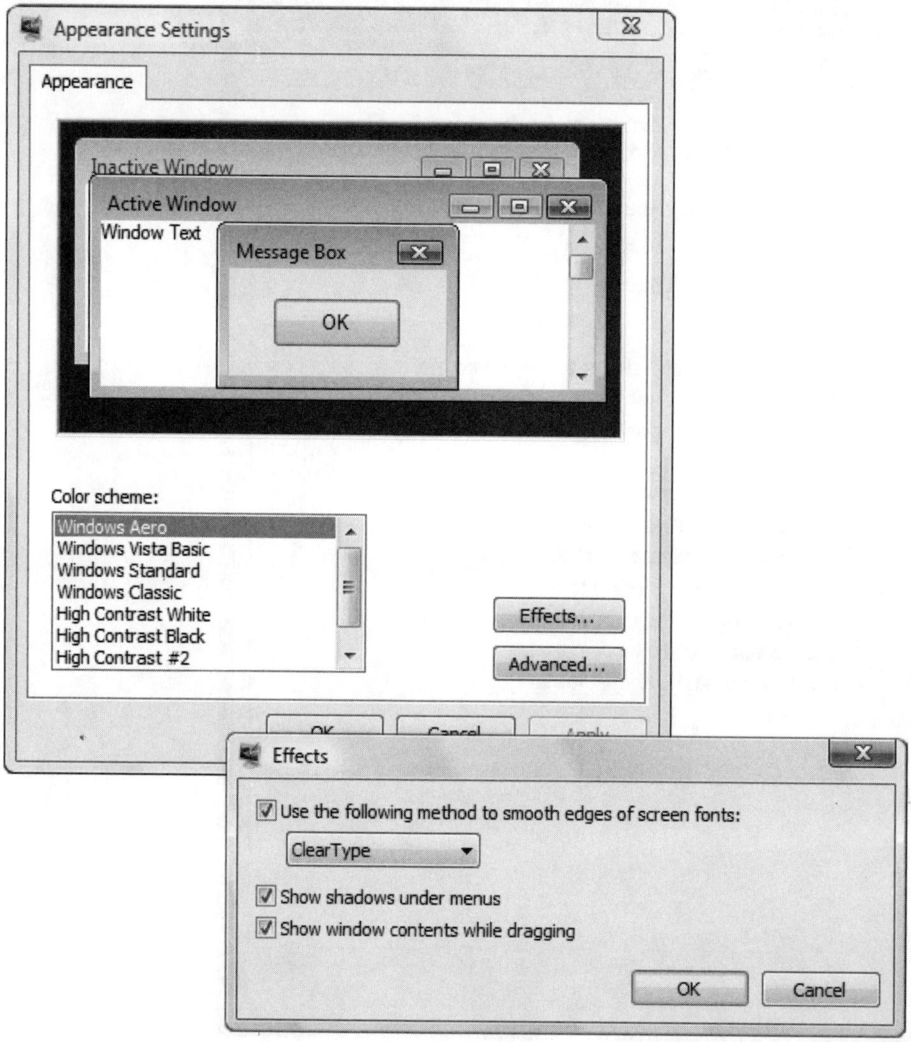

Figure 2-5.
Tuning ClearType on Windows Vista

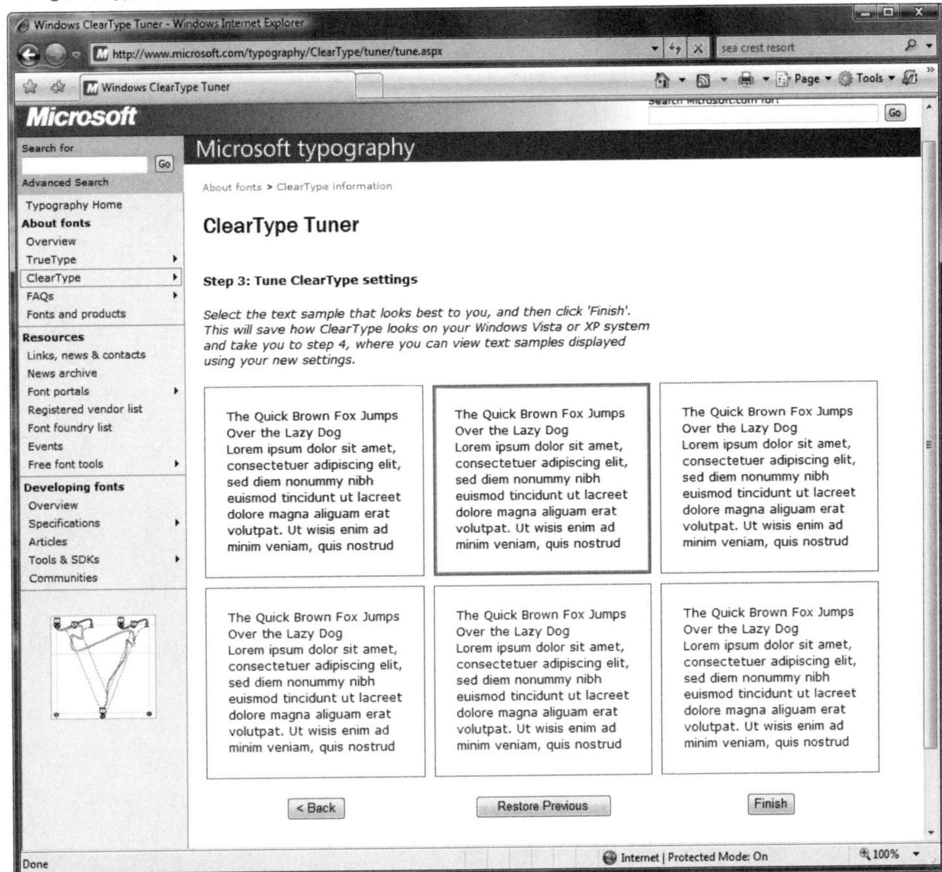

options→Effects. The screen shown in Figure 2-4 appears. In the drop-down box, select Standard, and click OK and OK again. ClearType is now turned off.

You can also turn off ClearType using the Registry. Launch the Registry Editor by typing regedit at the Start Search box or a command prompt (see Chapter 13 for details). Go to `HKEY_CURRENT_USER\Control Panel\Desktop`. Set the `FontSmoothing` value to `1`, and set the `FontSmoothingType` to `1`. Exit the Registry and reboot.

If you want to use ClearType, but would like to fine-tune the way it displays type, go to the ClearType Tuner at www.microsoft.com/typography/ClearType/tuner/tune.aspx. You'll be walked through a series of screens like the one shown in Figure 2-5. In each screen, you'll have a choice of which type looks best. Choose it and click Next until the last screen, where you'll click Finish.

When you visit the ClearType Tuner web site, you'll be prompted to install an ActiveX control for tuning ClearType. Even if you don't install the ActiveX control, you'll be able to tune ClearType straight from the web site, without the control.

If you prefer the Registry approach, you can hack the Registry to tune ClearType as well. To do it this way, launch the Registry Editor by typing regedit at the Start Search box or a command prompt (see Chapter 13 for details). Go to `HKEY_CURRENT_USER\Control Panel\Desktop`. Set the `FontSmoothingOrientation` value to `0` if you have a CRT monitor, `1` if you have an LCD monitor, or `2` if you have a BGR monitor (which is extremely rare). Unless you know you have a BGR monitor, don't use `2`. The `FontSmoothingGamma` value sets the brightness. You can set it to anything between `1000` and `2000`. (Higher is brighter.) Exit the Registry. You might need to reboot for the

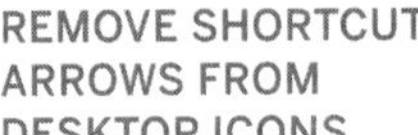

REMOVE SHORTCUT ARROWS FROM DESKTOP ICONS

If you don't like the annoying arrows that appear on icons on your Windows Vista desktop, it's easy to get rid of them. Download the free Vista Shortcut Overlay Remover (www.frameworkx.com/Frameworkx/solution.aspx?id=632). It will let you reduce or remove the arrows that appear on shortcuts on your Windows Vista Desktop. Run the program, then select whether you want a small, light arrow or no arrow at all for shortcuts, and click Apply. Then log off and log back on again, and your changes will take effect. Run the program again and select the normal-sized arrow if you want the default shortcut arrows back.

changes to take effect. For the `FontSmoothingGamma` value, you may need to experiment until you have the right brightness for your system.

 This Registry-editing technique works on Windows XP as well as Windows Vista.

Remove the Text from Desktop Icons

Don't like the presence of text beneath the icons on your desktop? It's easy to remove them. Right-click an icon and select Rename. Then, while holding down the Alt key, type 255 on the keypad, then click the icon. The text will disappear from your desktop. If you're using a laptop, you'll need to turn on numlock, and use the K key for the letter 2, and the I key for the letter 5, to enter 255. Figures 2-6 and 2-7 show the original and result.

Figure 2-6.
Now you see the text . . .

Figure 2-7.
. . . and now you don't.

 This hack works on Windows XP as well as Windows Vista.

Use Checkboxes to Select Items in Windows Explorer

If you often use Windows Explorer to perform actions on multiple files at once, such as copying or deleting, you'll appreciate a different way to select multiple files—via check box rather than having to hold down Ctrl while you select each.

To turn on the feature, in Windows Explorer select Organize→Folder and Search Options→View. Scroll to the bottom of the screen, and check the box next to "Use check boxes to select items." Click OK. From now on, as you move your cursor in Windows Explorer, a check box shows up next to each file. To select the file, check the box. Select as many files as you'd like, and then perform an operation on multiple files as you would normally. Figure 2-8 shows the hack in action.

Kill the File Deletion Confirmation Box

When you're using User Account Control (UAC) and you want to delete a file, you have to run the metaphorical gauntlet before you can actually delete the file. First the delete confirmation box

Figure 2-8.
Selecting multiple files using check boxes

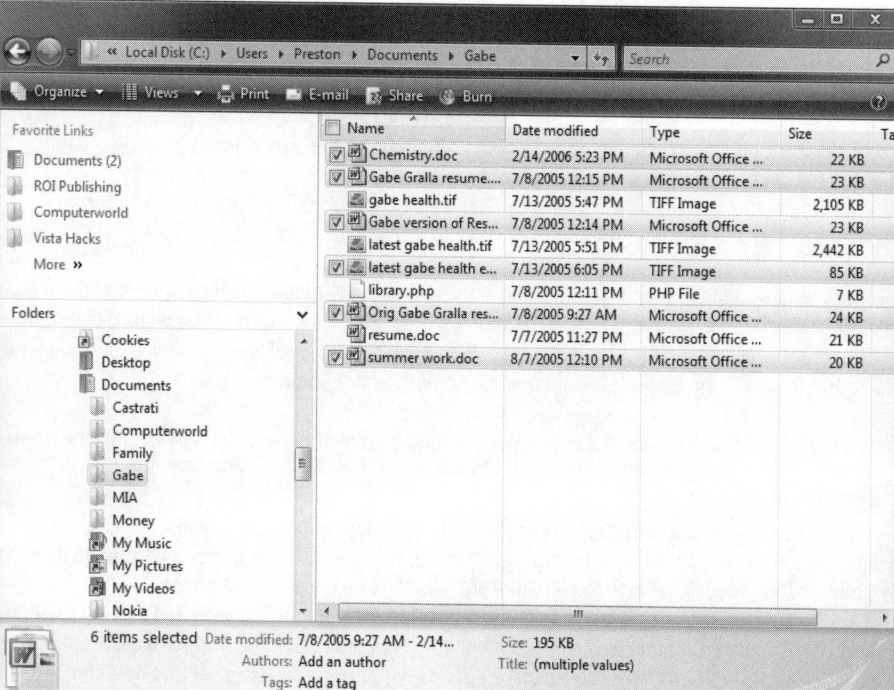

> **QUICK HACK**
>
> **ANIMATE WINDOWS VISTA'S NETWORK ICON**
>
> Here's a quick way to see whenever you're sending or receiving data over your network—animate the network icon that sits in the system tray. Right-click the icon and select Turn on activity animation. Whenever data is being sent or received, the icon will subtly light up. To turn off the animation, right-click the icon and select Turn off activity animation.

appears, and then after that the UAC authorization box appears. If you'd like, you can eliminate the delete confirmation box.

Right-click the Recycle Bin, select Properties, and uncheck the box next to "Display delete confirmation dialog" (see Figure 2-9). Then click OK. From now on, no boxes will appear when you delete a file—any file, not just system files. So be careful before making this change. You could, of course, use the Recycle Bin to restore any files you accidentally deleted.

If you turn off the delete confirmation dialog box, make sure that you don't also select "Do not move files to the Recycle Bin." If you do that, when you delete a file accidentally, you won't be able to restore it from the Recycle Bin.

Get Back Your Favorite Desktop Icons

Windows Vista does away with a number of familiar desktop icons from previous versions of Windows, such as My Documents, My Computer, and My Network. (In Windows Vista, there is no "My" in from of them—they're Documents, Computer, and Network.) If you feel nostalgic for them, it's easy to get them back. Right-click the desktop and select Personalize. On the lefthand side of the screen, select Change Desktop Icons. The screen shown in Figure 2-10 appears. Check the boxes next to the icons you want to appear, and click OK.

Figure 2-9.
Killing the delete confirmation dialog box

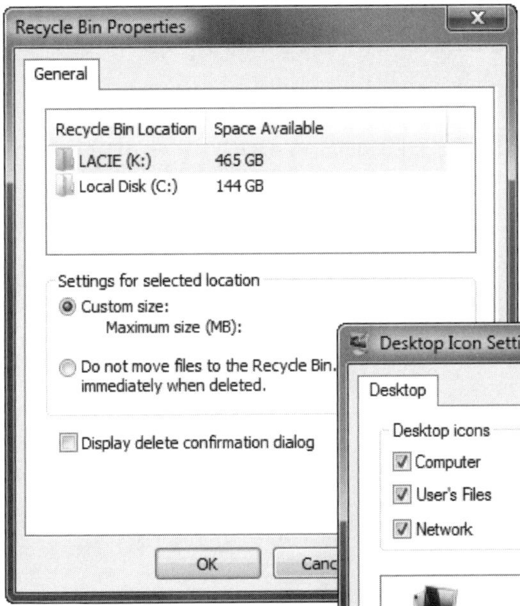

Figure 2-10.
Adding some of your old favorite desktop icons to Windows Vista

QUICK HACK

CHANGE THE REGISTRATION NAME AND COMPANY NAME IN WINDOWS

Your copy of Windows includes a registration name (your name), and your company name, if Windows was installed by your company. You'll see them if you right-click My Computer (in Windows XP), or Computer (in Windows Vista) and select Properties. You can change them both with a Registry hack. Launch the Registry Editor by typing regedit at the Start Search box or a command prompt (see Chapter 13 for details). Go to `HKEY_LOCAL_MACHINE\Software\Microsoft\Windows NT\CurrentVersion`. Edit the `RegisteredOwner` string and type the name you want to be for the registered owner. Then do the same for the `RegisteredOrganization` string. Exit the Registry, and the changes will take effect.

Speed Up Windows Flip 3D

Windows Flip 3D is one of Windows Vista's coolest new features, but if your hardware isn't up to snuff, its operation can be jagged and sluggish. You can speed it up and smooth its animations by limiting the number of windows it displays in 3D.

Launch the Registry Editor by typing regedit at the Start Search box or a command prompt (see Chapter 13 for details). Go to `HKEY_CURRENT_USER\Software\Microsoft\Windows\DWM`. Create a new DWORD and name it `Max3Dwindows`. Set the value to the maximum number of windows you want displayed. If you have severe performance problems, set it at 4; you can always increase the number later. Exit the Registry Editor. You'll need to restart Vista's Desktop Windows Manager (DWM) for the change to take effect. Launch an elevated command prompt by typing cmd in the search box and pressing Ctrl-Shift-Enter. Type net stop uxsms and press Enter. Then type net start uxsms and press Enter. You can also instead restart your PC.

With the new settings in effect, Windows Flip 3D will displays only the number of windows you've told it to. If you have more windows open than the maximum, as you scroll through your windows, new will replace the old. For example, if you have six windows open, only four will be displayed. As you scroll through them, new ones replace the ones that scroll off.

See Also

- "Hack Your Way Through Windows Vista's Aero Interface" **[Hack #15]**

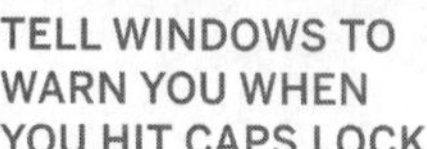

TELL WINDOWS TO WARN YOU WHEN YOU HIT CAPS LOCK

One of the more annoying experiences in Windows is accidentally hitting the Caps Lock key, and accidentally typing all capital letters. There's a simple way that you can have Windows beep at you when you've accidentally hit it. In Windows XP, select Control Panel→Accessibility Options→Accessibility Options, and at the bottom of the screen, check the box next to Use Toggle Keys and click OK. In Windows Vista, select Control Panel→Ease of Access→Change how your keyboard works. Then check the box next to Use Toggle Keys and click Save.

HACK 17: Turn Windows into a 3D Virtual Desktop

V XP Think Windows Flip 3D is cool? You ain't seen nothing yet. This freebie lets you turn Windows Vista and Windows XP into virtual 3D desktops.

Virtual desktops **[Hack #28]** are a great way to make your life at the keyboard far more productive. But being productive isn't always what life is all about—sometimes it's about fun as well.

The program DeskSpace (previously named, oddly, Yod'm 3D) gives you the best of both worlds. It lets you create four virtual desktops, and places each desktop on a virtual 3D cube that you can rotate through space to switch among them, as you can see in Figure 2-11. You can zoom in and out of the cube, and even move windows between desktops. And you can even move windows between your virtual desktops. Download a beta of this program from www.otakusoftware.com/deskspace/index.html. It's a *.zip* file, and the program requires installation. Unzip it to a folder, and then double-click the executable file, and the program runs. The first screen you'll see is a configuration screen, shown in Figure 2-12.

You'll be sent to the Activation key tab, which lets you specify the hot key you'll use to activate the program, and set other options, such as whether to start the program with Windows. The options here are self-explanatory, and the default hotkey combination is Shift-Ctrl. The other tabs are self-explanatory as well. DeskSpace lets you zoom in and out on the virtual cube; the Zoom tab lets you set options such as the increments for zooming in and out, and similar options. The Display tab lets you set a variety of options related to the display, including whether to use a widescreen or standard background, and settings related to anti-aliasing, whether to use hardware acceleration, and similar options.

To use the program, press and hold the hotkey (by default it's Ctrl-Shift). Your screen will shrink very slightly. To shrink the screen even further, press the up arrow; to make it larger after you've shrunk it, press the down arrow. To switch directly to another virtual desktop, press the right arrow key to move to the virtual desktop to the right of you, and the left arrow key to move to the virtual desktop to the left of you, while you're still holding down the hotkey.

Figure 2-11.
DeskSpace lets you create virtual desktops on a 3D cube, and quickly switch among them

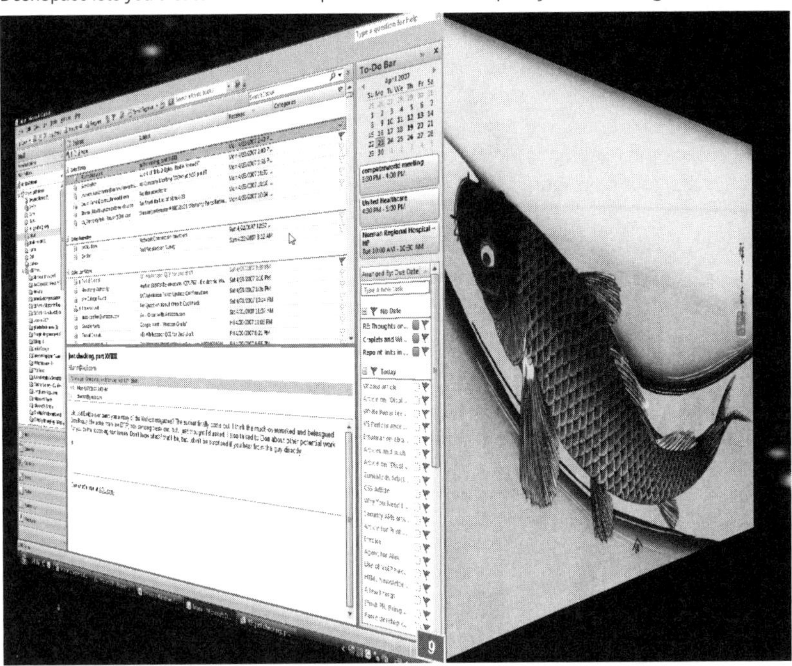

Figure 2-12.
DeskSpace configuration

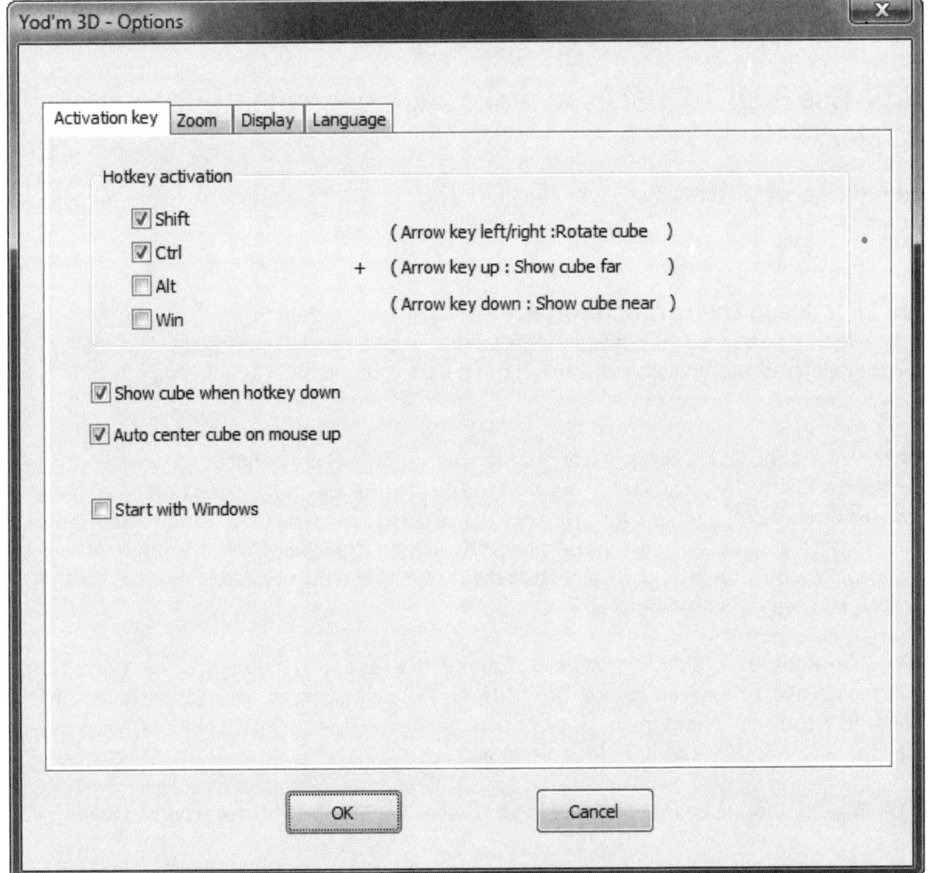

QUICK HACK

QUICKLY RESIZE WINDOWS VISTA ICONS

Not happy with the size of the icons on the Windows Vista desktop, or in Windows Explorer? It's a snap to change their size. Press the Ctrl key and scroll your mouse wheel (or trackpad equivalent) forward to enlarge the icons, or toward you to shrink them. You'll have sizes to choose from.

If you'd prefer to rotate the virtual 3D cube through space, when you're holding down the Shift key, press the left mouse button and use the mouse to rotate the cube.

Once you're in a new virtual desktop, change your settings however you'd like, run applications, and so on. You can then switch from desktop to desktop.

To change your settings, click the program's icon in the system tray and select options. To exit the program, click the icon and select Exit. Your current desktop will stay intact, but your other three virtual desktops will close down. You won't lose data; any open applications and file on those virtual desktops will automatically be sent to your current desktop.

You can also perform these nifty tricks with DeskSpace:

Switch an application or window between virtual desktops
First, make sure that the application or window isn't maximized. Then click the title bar, and while still holding it down, press the DeskSpace hotkey. Now, using your mouse, drag the application or window to the virtual desktop where you want it to reside. Then release the Ctrl-Shift key.

Shift to any active application on any virtual desktop
To do this, click the DeskSpace icon. A list of the windows and applications open in other virtual desktops will appear. Select the one you want to switch to, and you'll be immediately sent there.

See Also

- "Extend Your Screen Real Estate with Virtual Desktops" **[Hack #28]**

HACK 18: Hack Your Way Through the Interface with the Registry Editor

V XP Use Registry hacks to make a ton of great interface changes.

Hidden in the mazes of the Registry are countless ways to hack XP's interface. Following are some of my favorites.

Hide All Icons in the Notification Area

The system tray, also called the notification area, is the small area on the far-right side of the taskbar, in which utilities and programs that run in the background, such as antivirus software, display their icons.

I don't find it a particularly intelligent use of screen real estate, so I prefer not to see the icons there. To hide them, run the Registry Editor **[Hack #184]** and go to `HKEY_CURRENT_USER\Software\Microsoft\Windows\CurrentVersion\Policies\Explorer` (you may need to create the Explorer key if it does not already exist). Among other things, this key controls the display of objects throughout Windows. Create a new `DWORD` called `NoTrayItemsDisplay`. Assign it a value of `1`. (A value of `0` will keep the icons displayed.)

While you're at the `HKEY_CURRENT_USER\Software\Microsoft\Windows\CurrentVersion\Policies\Explorer` key, you can also delete the My Recent Documents icon (called Recent Items in Windows Vista) on the Start menu. Create a new `DWORD` called `NoRecentDocsMenu`. Assign it a value of `1`. (A value of `0` will keep the icon displayed.)

Exit the Registry, log out, and log back in again, to have either (or both) of these changes take effect.

Figure 2-13.
Hiding inactive icons

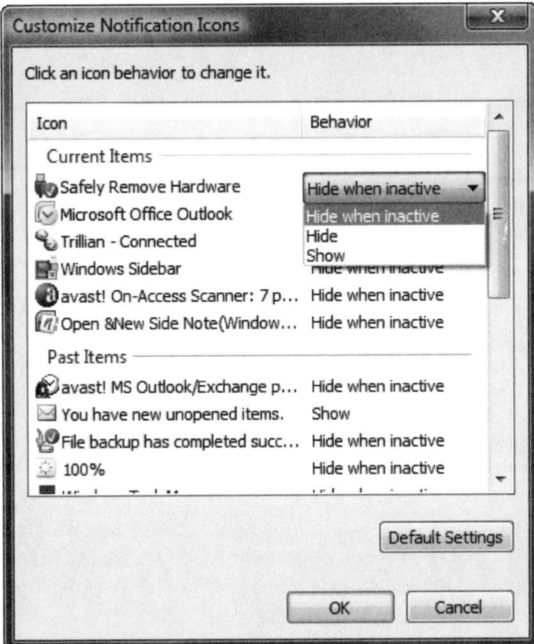

Hide Only Certain Icons in the Notification Area

You might want to display some icons in the notification area but hide others. If so, you can hide icons on a case-by-case basis. You'll do it by delving through menus, though, not by hacking the Registry. Right-click the taskbar and choose Properties→Taskbar. The Taskbar and Start Menu Properties dialog box appears. This dialog box, as the name implies, lets you control how the taskbar and Start menu look and function.

In the Notification Area tab of the dialog box, check the box next to "Hide inactive icons," then click Customize. The Customize Notifications dialog box appears as shown in Figure 2-13.

Click the program's listing in the Behavior column, and choose from the drop-down menu to hide the icon when the program is inactive, to always hide it, or to never hide it. Click OK twice. Your changes will take effect immediately.

Add Specific Folders to the Open Dialog Box

When you use certain Windows applications (such as Notepad) to open a file, on the left side of the Open dialog box are a group of icons and folders (such as My Documents, My Recent Documents, Desktop, My Computer, and My Network) to which you can navigate to open files.

 If you're not a fan of the Registry, there's an easier way to add folders to the open dialog boxes, or to remove folders from dialog boxes in XP—use the Tweak UI power toy [Hack #19]. Even if you are a Registry fan, it's easier to use Tweak UI to do this than it is using the Registry.

Good idea, bad implementation. Do you really keep documents in My Computer? Unlikely, at best. It would be much more helpful if you could list only those folders that you use, and if you could choose to put *any* folder there, not just ones Windows decides you need.

In fact, you can do it with a Registry hack. It'll let you put just the folders of your choosing on the left side of the Open dialog box. Note that when you do this, it will affect Windows applications such as Notepad and Paint that use the Open and Save common dialog boxes. However, it won't affect Microsoft Office applications and other applications that don't use the common dialog boxes.

QUICK HACK

ADD FOLDERS TO OFFICE'S DIALOG BOXES

It's easy to add your favorite folders to Microsoft Office Open and Save dialog boxes. If you have Microsoft Office 2007, open an Open or Save dialog box, and then drag a folder from the bottom Folders section to the Favorite Links section at the top. In earlier versions of Microsoft Office, open an Open or Save dialog box, highlight the folder that you want to add, and select Tools→Add to My Places.

Run the Registry Editor and go to HKEY_CURRENT_USER\Software\Microsoft\Windows\CurrentVersion\Policies\comdlg32. This is the key that determines how common dialog boxes are handled. You're going to create a subkey that will create a customized location for the folders, and then give that subkey a series of values, each of which will define a folder location.

This works with XP only, not with any version of Windows Vista. Fortunately, you can drag folders to the Vista Favorite Links in any Save or Open dialog box, as well as in Explorer.

To start, create a new subkey underneath HKEY_CURRENT_USER\Software\Microsoft\Windows\CurrentVersion\Policies\comdlg32 called Placesbar, and create a String value for it named Place0. Give Place0 a value of the topmost folder that you want to appear on the Open dialog box; for example, C:\Projects.

Next, create another String value for Placesbar called Place1. Give it a value of the second folder that you want to appear on the Open dialog box. You can put up to five icons on the Open dialog box, so create new String values up to Place4 and give them values as outlined in the previous steps. When you're done, exit the Registry. You won't have to reboot for the changes to take effect.

If you do not want any folders to appear in common Open dialog boxes, you can specify that as well. In HKEY_CURRENT_USER\Software\Microsoft\Windows\CurrentVersion\Policies\comdlg32, create a new DWORD value called NoPlacesBar and give it a value of 1. Exit the Registry. If you want the folders back, either delete NoPlacesBar or give it a value of 0.

Turn Off System Beeps

To me, the system beeps that my PC makes when it encounters certain system errors are like balloon tips—gnatlike annoyances that I can do without. So I turn them off using a Registry hack. Run the Registry Editor, go to HKEY_CURRENT_USER\Control Panel\Sound, and find the Beep and ExtendedSounds String values. Set each value to No. Exit the Registry and reboot. The beeps will no longer sound.

Use Your Own Graphic for Your User Account

This one isn't a Registry hack, but I couldn't resist putting it in here, as it's one of the more useful ways to customize the interface. The Windows graphic for your user account on the Start menu might not be to your taste, and your choice of other graphics to display there isn't particularly inspiring, either. After all, not everyone wants to be pictured as a rubber duckie, a snowflake, or a pair of horses.

But you're not limited to Windows-supplied pictures for your user account; you can use any *.gif*, *.jpg*, *.png*, or *.bmp* image. In this hack, I'll show you how to use your own picture.

To change your User Account picture to any one that you want in Windows XP, from the Control Panel, choose User Accounts, pick the account you want to change, choose "Change my picture," then choose "Browse for more pictures." Navigate to the picture you want to use and click OK.

In Windows Vista, choose Control Panel→User Accounts and Family Safety→Change your account picture. Then select "Browse for more pictures," navigate to the picture you want to use, and click OK. Figure 2-14 shows the screen you'll use to change your picture; it also shows the customized User Account picture I use during the winter holiday season.

For those interested in saving keystrokes, there's a quicker way to get to the screen letting you customize your picture. Click your account picture in either Windows XP or Window Vista, and a screen appears that lets you change your user account.

Figure 2-14.
Changing your User Account picture

HACK 19: Customize the Windows XP GUI with Tweak UI

XP Want to bend XP's interface to your will without getting your hands into the Registry or having to excavate menus three levels deep? Then get this supremely useful freebie from Microsoft and create your own customized version of XP.

There are countless ways to customize XP's interface, including Registry hacks and menus and options hidden many layers deep. But if you're the kind of person who lives in the express lane, juices up on double espressos, and wants to hack away at the interface fast, you need Tweak UI.

 Download Tweak UI for free from Microsoft at www.microsoft.com/windowsxp/downloads/powertoys/xppowertoys.mspx. It's part of a suite of free, unsupported utilities from Microsoft called XP PowerToys, but it's far and away the best one.

Tweak UI lets you tweak not only the interface, as the title suggests, but also many other system settings, such as how Internet Explorer's search works, whether to automate your logon upon system startup, and whether to enable CD autoplay so that the CD immediately starts up whenever you pop it into your drive. In this hack, you'll learn how to use it and apply that knowledge to create a speedy, stripped-down version of XP. Figure 2-15 shows Tweak UI in action, customizing the display of thumbnail pictures in Windows Explorer.

I don't have room to show you all the powers of Tweak UI, but here are some of the highlights:

- The General section lets you control XP's animated effects, fades, and shadowing. Also worthwhile in that section is "Show Windows version on desktop." Check the option and it displays, in the lower-right portion of your screen, your exact version of XP—for example, "Windows XP Home Edition Build 2600.xpsp1.020828-1920 (Service Pack 1)," as shown in Figure 2-16. I find it useful for knowing whether I need to add XP Service Packs, or for providing the information to tech support. You'll have to log off or restart your PC before it will display your version.

Figure 2-15.
Customizing the size and quality of thumbnails in Windows Explorer

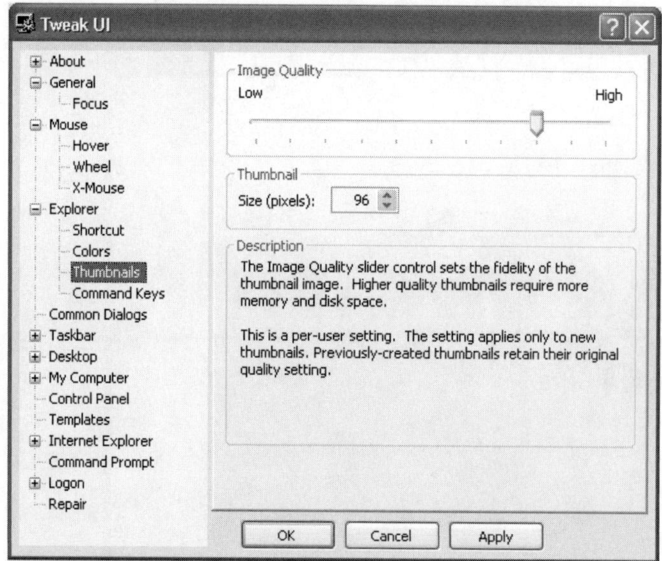

Figure 2-16.
Displaying the exact version
and build of XP on your desktop

Windows XP Home Edition
Build 2600.xpsp1.020828-1920 (Service Pack 1)

You can also force the operating system to display your exact version and build of XP on your desktop by using a Registry hack. Run the Registry Editor **[Hack #184]**. Go to `HKEY_CURRENT_USER\Control Panel\Desktop`, and find the `DWORD` value `PaintDesktopVersion`. Change the value to `1`. Exit the Registry and then log out and back in again. To remove the version and build number, change the value back to `0`. In beta versions of XP, the value was turned on by default, but when the product shipped, it was turned off.

- In Tweak UI, you also can hide desktop icons that seemingly can't be deleted from the desktop, such as the Internet Explorer, Microsoft Outlook, My Computer, My Documents, My Network Places, and Recycle Bin icons. To do this, go to the Desktop section and uncheck the boxes next to the icons you want to vanish. You won't have to log off for the changes to take effect.

QUICK HACK 

CHECK IF YOU'RE LOGGED IN AS AN ADMINISTRATOR

Not sure whether you're logged in as an administrator in Windows? Right-click the Start button, and if on the menu that appears you see Open All Users, you're an administrator; if it merely says Open, you're not.

As of this writing, Microsoft hadn't yet created a version of Tweak UI for Windows Vista, but is expected to do so at some point.

- In the Explorer section, customize the taskbar and desktop by enabling or disabling balloon tips and specifying which programs will be allowed to show up on the Frequently Used Programs List, among other customizations.
- Customize how Windows Explorer looks and functions by controlling the quality of image thumbnails; changing the way shortcuts look; determining whether to include Help, Recent Documents, and Logoff on the Start menu; and many similar options.

There's a lot more as well; to find it all, download it and try it all out.

Create a Speedy, Stripped-Down Interface with Tweak UI

Although it's fun to use Tweak UI to fiddle with the UI, its real power becomes apparent when you use it to create your own customized XP interfaces. For example, you might be the type who is concerned about only one thing when you use your PC: pure functionality. You want to get your work done fast, and you don't want to be bothered by the extra frou-frous that XP throws in your way and that slow down your system. Here's how to create a speedy, stripped-down interface using Tweak UI:

Turn off animations, fades, and similar features

Animations and fades are pretty, but they require system resources and slow down your system. You can turn off a wide variety of these animations and fades from the General section of Tweak UI. Uncheck the boxes next to all of them—"Enable menu animation," "Enable menu selection fading," "Enable tooltip animation," and the many others listed there.

Speed up right-click menu displays, hovers, and other mouse actions

If you want menus to appear with absolutely no delay when you right-click an object or icon, go to the Mouse section and move the Menu speed slider all the way to the left. Test how fast the menus will display by right-clicking the test icon. From this section, you can also increase your mouse sensitivity so that it responds more quickly to your clicks and drags. In the Mouse Sensitivity section, decrease the numbers next to Double-Click and Drag, and see the results by double-clicking the test icon.

The Mouse section also lets you change the mouse's sensitivity to "hovering"—for example, displaying a tool tip when you hover your mouse over an icon. To speed up the hover display, highlight Hover underneath the Mouse section, then decrease the numbers next to "Hover sensitivity" and "Hover time." Test out your settings using the test icon.

Decrease the image quality of thumbnails in Windows Explorer

Windows Explorer uses up RAM when it displays thumbnails, which can slow down your system, because the RAM could instead be used for your applications or the operating system itself. Use Tweak UI to give thumbnails the minimum amount of RAM only. Go to the Explorer→Thumbnails section and in the Image Quality area, move the slider all the way to the left, to the lowest setting for image quality. Decrease the thumbnail size, in pixels.

You can also completely turn off thumbnails so that they aren't displayed in Windows Explorer. From Windows Explorer, choose View→Details, or choose View→List.

Delete unnecessary desktop icons

Desktop icons take up RAM and clutter your interface, so you want as few of them as possible on your desktop for a stripped-down implementation of XP. You can delete most desktop icons, but some of them such as Outlook and Internet Explorer apparently can't be deleted. However, Tweak UI lets you delete them. Go to the Desktop section and uncheck the boxes next to the icons that you want off the desktop.

Hide Control Panel applets

The Control Panel is filled with applets that you will rarely, if ever, use, and that clutter up the interface, making it more difficult to find the applets you do want to use. To hide applets, go to the Control Panel section and uncheck the boxes next to the applets that you want to hide. (You can force the Registry to do the same thing—see "Control the Control Panel" **[Hack #20]**. That hack also shows you how you can run the applets, even after you've removed their icons.)

Clean up the right-click New menu

When you right-click the desktop and choose New, you can automatically create a new document by choosing from a submenu. That submenu can offer many choices of which document types to create, depending on the applications you have installed on your PC and how those applications handle their installation process. In many instances, those choices can be little more than clutter, because you might rarely need to create new documents of certain types in this way. Strip down that submenu to the essentials so that it has only those document types that you frequently create. Choose Templates, and uncheck the boxes next to the document types you rarely create. For example, most people rarely use the Briefcase, but that is one of your choices, so remove that unless you regularly move files using it. (To add power to the right-click context menu in Explorer, see "A Power User's Hidden Weapon: Improve the Context Menu" **[Hack #34]**.)

Enable autologon

If you're the primary person who uses your PC, you can enable autologon so that you're logged on automatically when the system starts. Choose Autologon from the Logon section, check the box next to "Log on automatically at system startup," and make sure your username, domain, and password are correct.

HACK 20: Control the Control Panel

V XP Whether you're a fan of Vista's new Control Panel or XP's old Control Panel (or even if you're a fan of neither), there's a lot you can do to make it more palatable—like hiding applets you never use, recategorizing the ones you do use, and displaying all applets in a simple-to-use cascading menu.

The Control Panel: love it or hate it. It's a very simple way to organize all the applets and features of Windows. But the Control Panel's several-layer organization forces you to click far too many times to get to the applet you want. And its clutter of applets that you may use rarely, if ever, makes it even more difficult and confusing.

You can always click the Switch to Classic View button to do away with the new design, but the Classic View has its problems as well: its long, alphabetized list of thumbnails is just as difficult to navigate as the new Control Panel.

The solution? Start by cleaning up the Control Panel, hiding applets that you use rarely. Note that when you hide the applets, you can still use them; you just won't see their icons in the Control Panel.

In this hack, you'll not only find out ways you can control the Control Panel, but you'll also see how you can apply that knowledge to create different customized Control Panels.

Hide Unused Applets with the Registry in Windows XP

To hide unused applets using the Registry in Windows XP, launch the Registry Editor by typing regedit at the Start Search box or a command prompt (see Chapter 13 for details). Go to `HKEY_LOCAL_MACHINE\SOFTWARE\Microsoft\Windows\CurrentVersion\Control Panel\don't load`.

The key, as its name implies, determines which Control Panel applet icons are *not* loaded into the Control Panel. You'll still be able to run those applets from the command line, and they may also appear in other places, such as XP's Common Tasks shown on the left side of the Control Panel window, after you hide them (as explained later in this hack)—you just won't be able to see their icons in the Control Panel.

To hide an applet, create a new `String` value whose name is the filename of the applet you want to hide. For example, to hide the Mouse Control dialog box, the `String` value would be *main.cpl*. See Table 2-1 for a list of Control Panel applets and their filenames. Note that some of these may be available on Windows XP, and some on Windows Vista, and more are available on both.

Table 2-1 Control Panel applets and their filenames

APPLET	FILENAME
Accessibility Options	*access.cpl*
Add Hardware Wizard	*hdwwiz.cpl*
Add or Remove Programs	*appwiz.cpl*
Display Properties	*desk.cpl*
Game Controllers	*joy.cpl*
Internet Properties	*inetcpl.cpl*

Table 2-1 Control Panel applets and their filenames *(continued)*

APPLET	FILENAME
Mouse Properties	*main.cpl*
Network Connections	*ncpa.cpl*
ODBC Data Source Administrator	*odbccp32.cpl*
Phone and Modem Options	*telephon.cpl*
Power Options Properties	*powercfg.cpl*
Region and Language Options	*intl.cpl*
Sound and Audio Devices	*mmsys.cpl*
Speech Properties	*sapi.cpl*
System Properties	*sysdm.cpl*
Time and Date Properties	*timedate.cpl*
User Accounts	*nusrmgr.cpl*

Create separate String values for each applet you want to hide, then exit the Registry. The applets will vanish from the Control Panel. To make a hidden applet appear again, delete its string value from this same registry key.

Hide Unused Applets with the Group Policy Editor

If you have XP Professional or Windows Vista Enterprise, Business or Ultimate editions, you don't need to get your hands dirty with the Registry to hide unused applets; instead, you can use the Group Policy Editor to accomplish the same task. (See Chapter 13 for more details about how to use the Group Policy Editor.) The Group Policy Editor is primarily used for setting network and multiuser policies and rights, but it can also be used to customize the way Windows looks and works. Run the Group Policy Editor by typing `gpedit.msc` at the Run prompt or the command line.

Once you've run it, go to `User Configuration\Administrative Templates\Control Panel`, double-click "Hide specified Control Panel applets" and choose Enabled. After you click Enabled, choose Show→Add and type in the Control Panel filename (which you can find in Table 2-1) for each applet you want to hide. (In Windows Vista, type in the full name of the applet, not the *.cpl* filename). Click OK in each dialog box that appears. When you exit the Group Policy Editor, the specified applets will no longer appear in the Control Panel.

This technique is best for when you want to hide only a few applets. If you want to hide most of the applets and want to display a few, there's another method you might want to try. Run the Group Policy Editor and go to `User Configuration\Administrative Templates\Control Panel`, the section that handles the Control Panel. As you can see when you get there, you can do a lot more than hide the Control Panel's unused applets in this section of the Group Policy Editor; you can also control many other aspects of how the Control Panel looks and functions.

Now right-click "Show only specified Control Panel applets," and choose Properties. You'll see the screen pictured in Figure 2-17.

Get ready for a bit of counterintuitive selecting. To disable Control Panel applets, you must choose the Enabled radio button because you're enabling the feature to show only certain Control Panel applets. Strange, but true.

QUICK HACK 

HOW TO RUN HIDDEN APPLETS

Hiding applets cleans up the Control Panel, but leaves you with another problem—what if you need to run an applet whose icon you've hidden? It's simple: at the Run box or command line, type in the name of the applet you want to run—such as `Inetcpl.cpl` for the Internet Properties applets—and press Enter. See Table 2-1 for a list of filenames.

Figure 2-17.
Disabling Control Panel applets in the Group Policy Editor

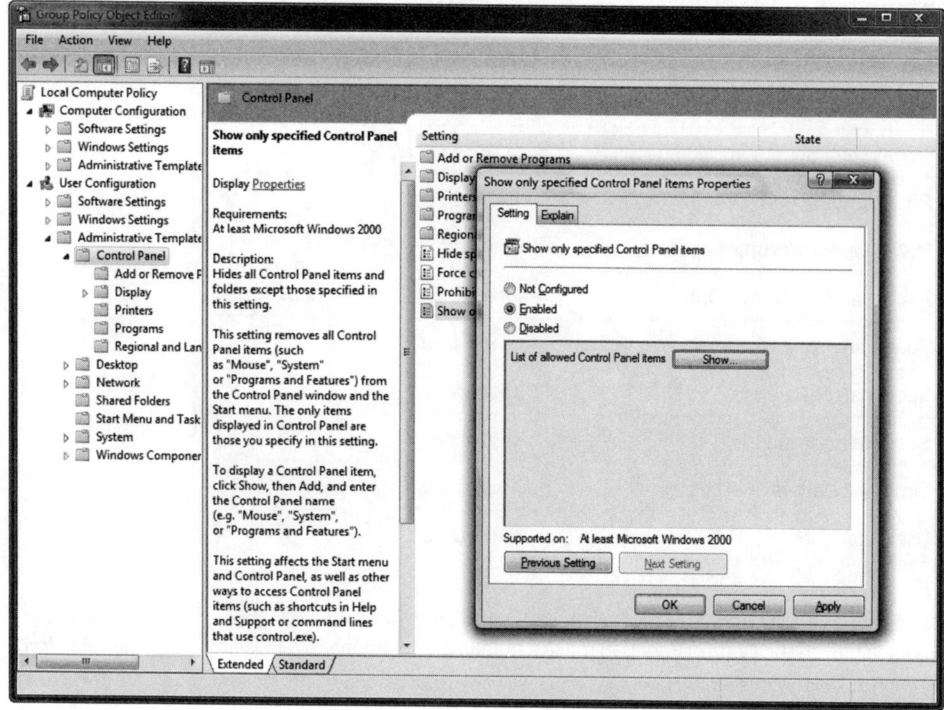

To decide which applets to show, click the Show button. The Show Contents screen appears. Click Add, and you're ready to list all the Control Panel applets that you want to appear. For each item that you want to appear, type in its Control Panel filename, which you can find in Table 2-1. For example, if you want the Time and Date dialog box to appear, type in `timedate.cpl`. In Windows Vista, you'll need to type in the name of the Control Panel applet, Date and Time.

 On Windows XP, you can also use Tweak UI to hide Control Panel applets.

When you've listed all the Control Panel applets that you want to appear, click OK and exit the Group Policy Editor. Only the applets you've chosen to display now appear in the Control Panel.

To customize other aspects of how the Control Panel works, follow the same instructions as outlined previously—right-click the item you want to change, choose Properties, and pick your options.

Recategorize Control Panel Applets

Hiding applets goes only partway toward cleaning up the Control Panel. You can also recategorize applets and put them in any category you want. For example, by default, the Mouse Properties applet can be found in the Printers and Other Hardware category, but if you prefer that it instead be found in Accessibility Options, you can move it there.

To put an applet into any category you want, you need two pieces of information: the filename of the applet (for example, *main.cpl* for the Mouse Properties dialog box), and the Registry value for each Control Panel category (for example, `0x00000007 (7)` for Accessibility Options). For the filename of each applet, see Table 2-1. For the Registry value for each Control Panel category, see Table 2-2. With these two pieces of information in hand, you can recategorize any or all Control Panel applets.

Table 2-2 Control Panel categories and their Registry value data

CONTROL PANEL CATEGORY	VALUE DATA
Accessibility Options	0x00000007 (7)
Add or Remove Programs	0x00000008 (8)
Appearance and Themes	0x00000001 (1)
Date, Time, Language, and Regional Options	0x00000006 (6)
Network and Internet Connections	0x00000003 (3)
Other Control Panel Options	0x00000000 (0)
Performance and Maintenance	0x00000005 (5)
Printers and Other Hardware	0x00000002 (2)
Sounds, Speech, and Audio Devices	0x00000004 (4)
User Accounts	0x00000009 (9)
No category	0xffffffff

To recategorize a Control Panel applet, launch the Registry Editor by typing regedit at the Start Search box or a command prompt (see Chapter 13 for details). Go to `HKEY_LOCAL_MACHINE\SOFTWARE\Microsoft\Windows\CurrentVersion\Control Panel\Extended Properties` and locate the key `{305CA226-D286-468e-B848-2B2E8E697B74}2` (`System.ControlPanel.Category` in Vista), which is the container that holds all Control Panel categories.

Now find the Registry key of the applet you want to recategorize. The filename of the applet will appear on the end of the key; for example, `%SystemRoot%\system32\main.cpl` is the Mouse Properties dialog box. Turn to trusty Table 2-1 for a list of other filenames for Control Panel applets.

Change the key's `DWORD` value to the value of the Control Panel category into which you want the applet to appear, as shown in Table 2-2. For example, if you want the applet to appear in the Performance and Maintenance category, give it a value of `5`. The value will then be displayed in the Registry as `0x00000005(5)`. When you're done, exit the Registry. The applet will now appear in the new category.

Display Control Panel Applets in a Cascading Menu

If you're a "just the facts, ma'am" type, you'll want to bypass the Control Panel altogether. Rather than clicking effete icons, you can instead force Windows to display Control Panel applets in a cascading menu when you choose Control Panel from the Start button, as shown in Figure 2-18.

To force the Control Panel to display as a cascading menu, right-click the taskbar and choose Properties→Start Menu. Click the Customize button (in Windows XP, you'll need to choose the Advanced tab). In the Control Panel heading, choose "Display as a menu." Click OK twice.

Build Customized Control Panels

Armed with all this Control Panel hackery, you can build customized Control Panels. For example, you can build a Control Panel for computer newbies, which hides the more technical applets and categories. Hide the applets in the Network and Internet Connections category, the Performance and Maintenance category, and the Sounds, Speech, and Audio Devices category—that way, newbies can't get into trouble by making changes that will affect the system in unexpected ways.

QUICK HACK 

TWEAK VISTA TO YOUR HEART'S CONTENT

If you want to hack and tweak Windows Vista without having to dig into the Registry, Group Policy Editor, or even too deeply into the user interface, there's a simple solution: Get the free TweakVI (www.totalidea.com/content/tweakvi/tweakvi-index.html). It offers countless tweaks, including the Start menu, Internet Explorer, your CPU's cache, and plenty more.

Figure 2-18.
Turning the Control Panel into a cascading menu for quick access to applets

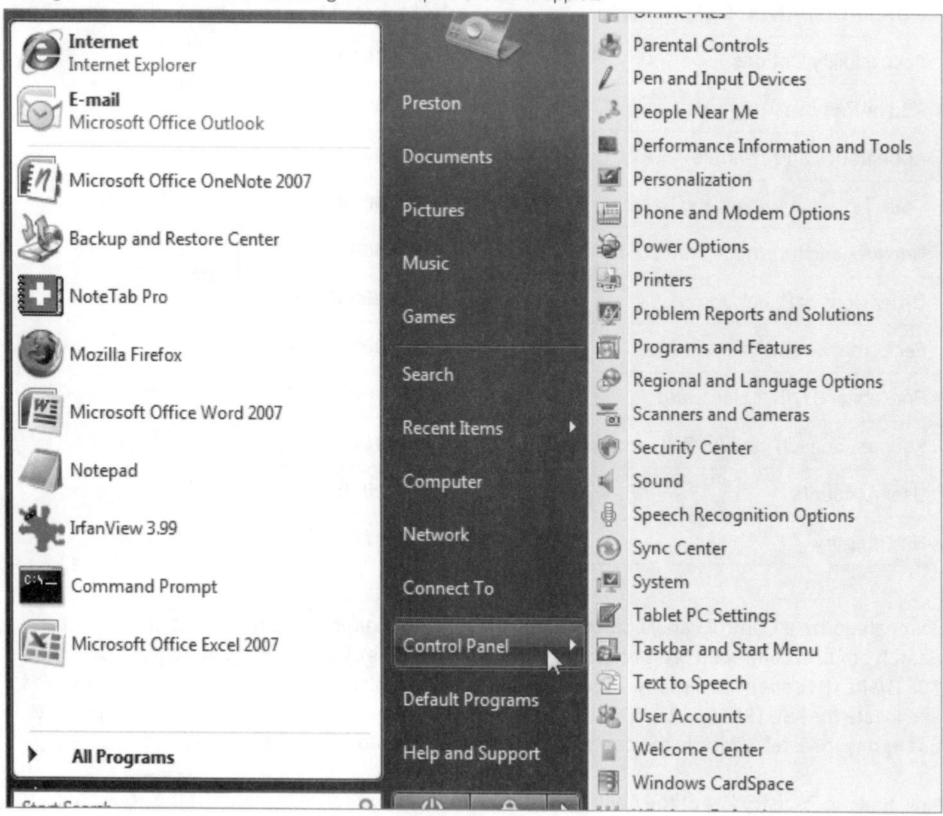

For system administrators, group all system-type applets into a single category, such as Network and Internet Connections. You'll probably want to keep all the existing applets there but also add the Administrative Tools, Scheduled Tasks, and System applets to it, as well as the Printers and Faxes applet. (If the administrator has to handle other hardware, such as scanners, add the Scanners and Cameras applet as well.)

For those who like to hack their systems and want instant, stripped-down access to customization tools, take all the applets that are now in Network and Internet Connections, and all those in Performance and Maintenance, and group them into the Appearance and Themes category. Then force the Control Panel to display as a cascading menu, and all of the hackery-type applets will be available instantly, because the Appearance and Themes category is at the top of the cascading menu and all the relevant applets are available directly from it.

HACK 21: Hack the Start Menu and Taskbar

V XP The Group Policy Editor gives you instant access to changing dozens of interface settings. Here's how to use it to create your own personalized Start menu and taskbar.

The Group Policy Editor does more than just customize the Control Panel **[Hack #20]**; it gives you control over many aspects of Windows' interface as well—in particular, the Start menu and taskbar. In fact, it gives you quick access to more than three dozen separate settings for them in Windows XP, and 64 settings in Windows Vista.

Run the Group Policy Editor by typing `gpedit.msc` at the Run prompt or command line. Go to `User Configuration\Administrative Templates\Start Menu and Taskbar`. As you can see in Figure 2-19, the right pane displays all the settings you can change. If you click the Extended tab at the bottom of the screen, you'll be shown a description of the setting that you've highlighted, along with an explanation of each option. Settings you can customize include showing the Pictures (in XP, My Pictures) icon, the Run menu, and the Music icon on the Start menu; locking the taskbar so that it can't be customized; and many others. To change a setting, double-click it and choose your options from the menu that is displayed.

There's not room in this hack to go into detail about each setting you can change, so I'll tell you about some of my favorites. I've never been a big fan of My Documents (Documents in Vista), My Pictures (Pictures in Vista), and My Music (Music in Vista) in on the Start menu in Windows. In fact, I never use those folders, so there's no point having them on the Start menu. The settings in the Group Policy Editor let you get rid of them.

If you share your PC with other people, the Group Policy Editor is a great way to make sure no one can change the Start menu and taskbar except you. So, when you have the Start menu and taskbar working the way you want, they'll stay that way until you want to change them. Enable "Prevent changes to Taskbar and Start Menu settings," and no one will be able to change their settings except you (or another user who has administrator privileges). Select "Remove drag-and-drop context menus on the Start Menu," and no one except you will be able to remove or reorder items on the Start menu. You can even stop anyone else from shutting down Windows by selecting "Remove and prevent access to the Shut Down command." (Of course, they can still shut down your PC the old-fashioned way: by using the power switch.)

Among the many entries here are a lot of pointless ones, by the way. You can remove the Logoff entry on the Start menu, for example, which certainly isn't high on my list of must-haves. But who knows—you might want to do that, or make any of the many other changes the Group Policy Editor allows. Go in there yourself and muck around; you'll find plenty to change.

Figure 2-19.
Customizing the Start menu and taskbar in the Group Policy Editor

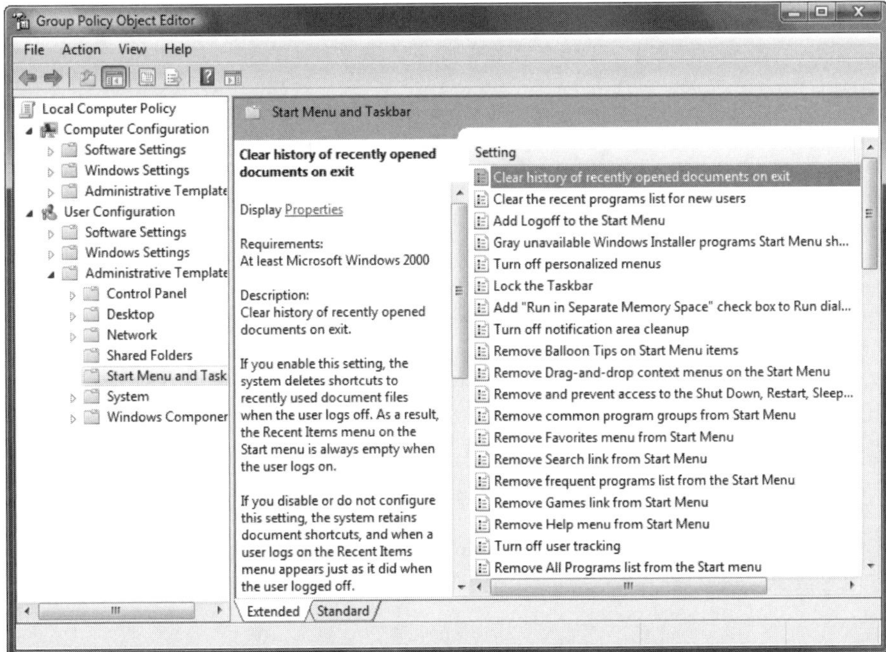

Hack the Windows XP Taskbar with Tweak UI

You can use Tweak UI to hack the Windows XP taskbar, to a limited degree. Go to its Taskbar section, and you can disable or enable balloon tips, and enable or disable warnings when you're low on disk space. Underneath the Taskbar section, you'll find a Grouping subsection that controls how taskbar "grouping" works. When you run too many programs with too many files open, all of them can't fit individually on the taskbar. So XP groups files from the same application with each other. For example, if you have four Word files open, it shows only a single icon for Word on the taskbar, with the number 4 inside it. Click the icon, and a list of all four files pops up. You can then choose which to open. Tweak UI lets you control how that grouping works; you can decide whether to first group applications with the most windows, or instead first group applications that you use the least. You can also choose to group all applications with two or more windows open, three or more windows open, and so on.

HACK 22: Hacking Gadgets

V One of the most useful new features of the Windows Vista interface is the Sidebar and its gadgets, which live on the right side of the Desktop.

Figure 2-20.
A group of Gadgets on the Sidebar

Gadgets are convenient little applets that usually deliver live information to you without you having to lift a finger—for example, current stock information or the weather, RSS feeds, and so on. Figure 2-20 shows a typical example of gadgets on the Sidebar.

You may think that you need programming expertise to hack gadgets, but you don't. With an understanding of how gadgets work and the advice in these hacks, you'll be able to do it easily.

You won't need any special expertise to complete these hacks, or any special software either. You'll use Notepad, which comes with Windows. The hacks won't take long, and will introduce you to the openness of the Sidebar gadget platform. By "openness," I mean that you can take any gadget, copy its code, and then modify it to become your own.

Gadgets are really just miniature browser windows, but a bit more powerful. Hats off to Microsoft for the decision to make gadgets using this simple browser framework. Microsoft could have easily written this platform to use any number of other technologies, making the gadget code unavailable to the naked eye. Keeping the gadget code in this framework means the code can be shared, modified, and improved upon.

We'll be hacking several system gadgets that ship with Windows Vista. As you'll see, though, you won't actually touch the gadgets themselves. Instead, you'll copy them and then make changes to the copies of the gadgets. That means you can always get your gadgets back to their original state. (For details, seethe upcoming section "Uninstalling and Restoring Gadgets.")

In the following hacks, you are going to modify the Slide Show gadget to let it display video files and launch those videos in the default video folder. After this, you'll move on to make the built-in Feed Headlines gadget allow you to see YouTube video feeds. It requires a little bit of copying and pasting, but that's going to be the extent of the coding required. This exercise is intended to give you enough confidence to move on and start hacking gadgets on your own for your specific needs.

When you make that gadget that you can't live without, remember to share it with the rest of world on the Windows Live Gallery (gallery.live.com) web site. The only requirement for submitting gadgets is that you sign up for a Windows Live (formerly Passport) account.

Lastly, you'll learn how to take your gadgets with you on a flash memory device such as a USB key. You'll really want this if you make a great gadget and you want to use it at home and work, but want to keep their settings with you wherever you go.

Concepts You Need to Know Before Hacking Gadgets

Windows Vista has three main gadgets folders. Each gadget lives in its own subfolder beneath one of those main folders. Each gadgets subfolder contains the information and files needed to run that gadget.

Here are Windows Vista's three main gadget folders:

- A built-in gadgets folder (*C:\Program Files\Windows Sidebar\Gadgets*) that contains subfolders with all the built-in gadgets that ship with the operating system. These built-in gadgets cannot be modified, but new gadgets can be added to the built-in gadget folder.
- A shared gadgets folder (*C:\Program Files\Windows Sidebar\Shared Gadgets*). This folder is shared with all users of the PC. Gadgets in the subfolders underneath it are shared with all users. Once you have developed a new gadget and want everyone using that machine to have access to it, place it in this folder.
- The user gadgets folder (*C:\Users*`username`*\AppData\Local\Microsoft\Windows Sidebar\Gadgets*), which contains all the gadgets installed by that user. By default, this is a hidden folder. It is only accessible to the logged-in user. Every user has his own gadgets folder. Gadgets that are placed here can be accessed only by the logged-in users. In the following hacks, this is where you'll create new gadgets.

The subfolder for each gadget is named after the gadget itself, followed by the *.Gadget* extension. For example, Windows Vista's built in Calendar gadget's folder is *Calendar.Gadget*. It lives underneath the built-in *C:\Program Files\Windows Sidebar\Gadgets*, along with all of the other built-in gadgets, as shown in Figure 2-21.

The built-in gadgets folder has 11 subfolders, each of which contains one of Windows Vista's built-in gadgets:

- *Calendar.Gadget*
- *Clock.Gadget*
- *Contacts.Gadget*
- *CPU. Gadget*
- *Currency.Gadget*
- *Notes.Gadget*
- *PicturePuzzle.Gadget*
- *RSSFeeds.Gadget*
- *SlideShow.Gadet*
- *Stocks.Gadget*
- *Weather.Gadget*

Built-in Versus User-Installed Gadgets

There is really no standard terminology for dealing with gadgets, but to make things easier to understand, I'm going to refer to two types of gadgets: built-in gadgets, and user-installed gadgets.

Adding gadgets to the sidebar can be addicting, but be careful not to add too many of them. Gadgets are mini applications that run all the time, and each one uses up memory and CPU time. Consider several default gadgets. The clock polls the system time every minute or every second depending on whether the seconds hand is displayed. The Feed Headlines gadget changes its view every 30 seconds, and the Slideshow switches out images every 30 seconds. And that's just a start. So before adding a new gadget to the sidebar, consider whether it's something you really need to run.

Built-in gadgets are those that ship with Vista, and as previously explained, are found in subfolders underneath *C:\Program Files\Windows Sidebar\Gadgets*. These gadgets cannot be deleted from the operating system, and they cannot be modified, except through controls on the gadget itself when it lives on the Sidebar.

Figure 2-21.
Windows Vista's built-in Gadgets folder

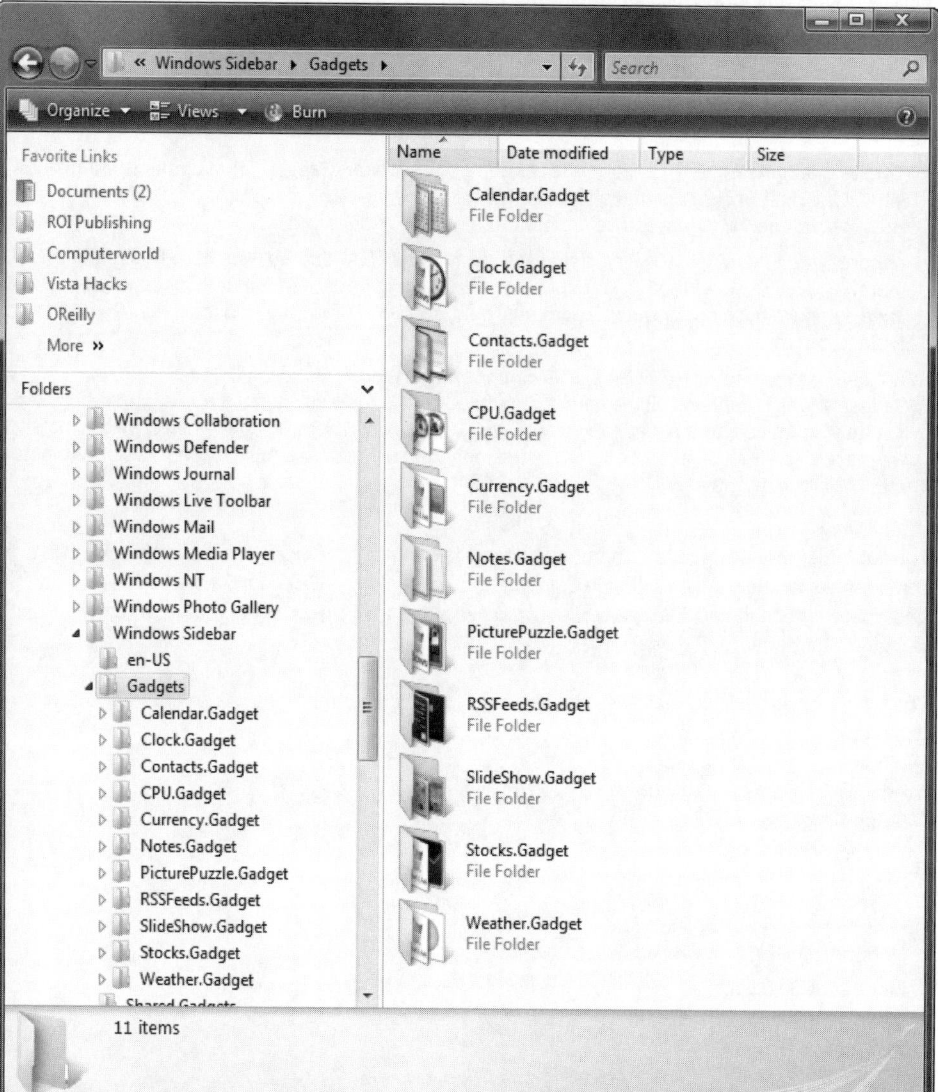

QUICK HACK

GET A BETTER CPU GADGET

The CPU Gadget that ships with Windows Vista does a nice job of showing you how what percent of your CPU's capabilities you're currently using, and how much RAM you're using. But what if you have a dual-core CPU? The gadget shows overall use, but not per CPU. That's where the Multi Meter (Dual Core) Gadget comes in. It show you what percent of each of your CPU's capabilities are being used at any one time, along with overall RAM use. At the top of the Windows Vista Sidebar, click the + sign, and from the Gadget Gallery, click "Get more gadgets online." Then browse for the Multi Meter (Dual Core) Gadget. It's very popular, so it's most likely right on the front page. If not, you'll find it in the Tools and Utilities category.

User-installed gadgets are those a user has created or downloaded and installed. Depending on whether they can be used by everyone on the computer or only by the person who created or installed them, they are found in either the shared gadgets folder (*C:\Program Files\Windows Sidebar\ Shared Gadgets*) or the user gadgets folder (*C:\Users*`username`*\AppData\Local\ Microsoft\WindowsSidebar\Gadgets*). These gadgets can be deleted or modified.

Understanding gadget.xml

All gadgets have a configuration file called *gadget.xml* that lives in a subfolder underneath the gadgets subfolder. The name, icon and almost any other information about the gadget's appearance is contained in this file. You can't change the name of *gadget.xml*; if you do, the gadget will not appear in the Gadget Gallery or on the Sidebar. There should be only one *gadget.xml* file per gadget.

Gadget Settings

Basic settings about how gadgets work on the Sidebar are stored in a text file called *settings.ini*. The Sidebar keeps information about the state of each gadget in this file, such as whether a gadget is docked or undocked, the order of the gadgets in the sidebar, and specific customization for each gadget. For example, if you have a weather gadget installed, the file stores the geographic location for which you want to track the weather. When you make changes to any Sidebar or gadget configuration, that new information is stored in a *settings.ini* file.

Each main gadgets folder (*C:\Program Files\Windows Sidebar\Gadgets*, *C:\Program Files\Windows Sidebar\Shared Gadgets*, and (*C:\Users*`username`*\AppData\Local\Microsoft\Windows Sidebar\Gadgets*) has its own *settings.ini* file. The *settings.ini* files in *C:\Program Files\Windows Sidebar\Shared Gadgets* and (*C:\Users*`username`*\AppData\Local\Microsoft\Windows Sidebar\Gadgets* contain settings to tell how gadgets should be displayed for either all users, or an individual user. The purpose of the *settings.ini* file in *C:\Program Files\Windows Sidebar\Gadgets* is somewhat different than the *settings.ini* files in *C:\Program Files\Windows Sidebar\Shared Gadgets* and *C:\Users*`username`*\AppData\Local\Microsoft\Windows Sidebar\Gadgets*. It stores the default settings for the Sidebar, not the current settings, and it can't be edited. It's used to restore the Sidebar to its initial, default state, if something should go amiss.

Uninstalling and Restoring Gadgets

Removing a gadget from the Sidebar is simple; hover your mouse over it and click the X, or right-click the gadget and select Close Gadget. Doing either of these things, though, won't remove the gadget from your PC—only from the Sidebar.

To uninstall a gadget, first get to the Gadget Gallery by clicking the + sign at the top of the Sidebar. Then right-click the gadget you want to uninstall, and select Uninstall as shown in Figure 2-22.

What actually happens to that gadget varies according to whether it's a user-installed gadget or a built-in one. A user-installed gadget will be taken out of the Gadget Gallery window and the entire gadget directory will be moved to the Recycle Bin. A built-in gadget will be taken out of the gadget Gallery window but the gadget will not be moved from its original location. This means that all of the original gadgets can always be restored.

To restore any built-in gadgets that you've uninstalled, with the Sidebar displayed, right-click an empty area of the Sidebar, choose Properties, and click "Restore gadgets installed with Windows." You can use this to your advantage by uninstalling a default gadget after you have created a new

Figure 2-22.
Uninstalling a Gadget

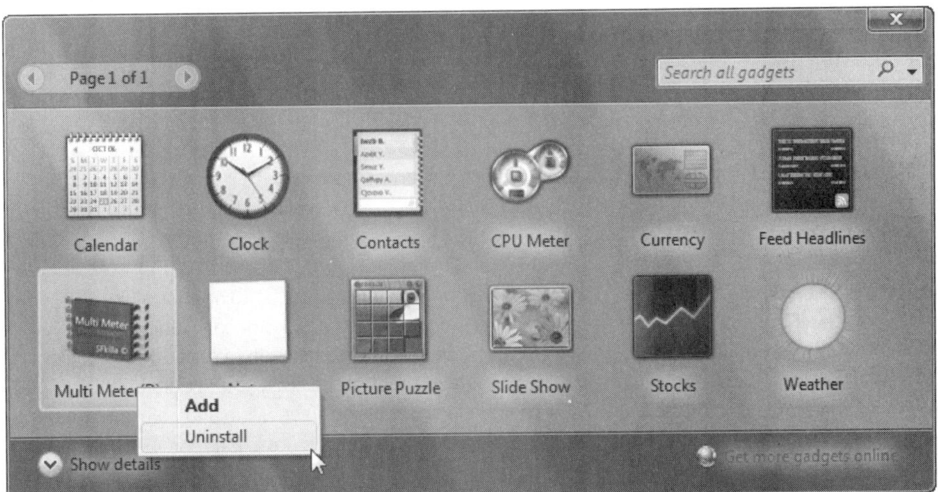

copy and have hacked it by adding new functionality. This approach assures you that you will never lose your original version and can always return to it. This way you can hack without fear of ruining something beyond repair.

— John Moscarillo

HACK 23: Force the Slide Show Gadget to Play Videos as Well as Images

V Windows Vista's built-in Slide Show gadget automatically displays a changing array of photos on your PC. Here's how to make it cycle through videos as well.

Windows Vista's built-in Slide Show gadget displays pictures as a constantly changing slideshow from any folder on your PC, one after another, as a thumbnail right inside the gadget, as you can see in Figure 2-23.

We're going to hack it so that it displays thumbnails of videos as well as pictures in the slide show. It won't actually play the video inside the gadget. Instead, when you click the video, it will launch Windows Media Player (or whatever you use as your default media player), with the video inside it. To do this, start with the code for the built-in Slide Show gadget.

First, copy the entire *SlideShow.Gadget* folder from *C:\Program Files\Windows Sidebar\Gadgets* to *C:\Users*`username`*\AppData\Local\Microsoft\Windows Sidebar\Gadgets*. Then rename it to *SlideShowPlayer.Gadget*.

The name you give to the new folder doesn't really matter; it won't affect the functioning of the gadget. You only have to make sure that it ends in a *.Gadget* extension.

You now have two identical Slide Show gadgets on your PC. If you were to open the Gadget Gallery by clicking the + sign at the top of the Sidebar, you'd see two identical gadgets. This can get confusing, so you're going to rename one of them—the gadget you're going to modify to display videos.

To change the name of the gadget in the Gadget Gallery, you edit its *gadget.xml* file. Go to *C:\Users*`username`*\AppData\Local\Microsoft\Windows Sidebar\Gadgets\SlideShowPlayer.Gadget* and navigate to the *en-US* subfolder beneath it. (That's assuming you're using a U.S. version of Vista. If you're using a different version, go to the folder that matches your Vista version and language.) Open *gadget.xml* In Notepad. On the third line from the top, you will see the following line:

```
<name>Slide Show</name>
```

Change this to:

```
<name>Slide Show Player</name>
```

Save and close this file. Open the Gadget Gallery. (If it's already open, close it, and then open it again.) You'll now see two Slide Show gadgets, but one will be called Slide Show Player. That's the gadget you're going to modify.

Now it's time to modify the gadget so that it displays videos. Use Notepad to open the file *slideShow.js* in *C:\Users*`username`*\AppData\Local\Microsoft\Windows Sidebar\Gadgets\SlideShowPlayer.Gadget\en-US\js*. You're going to edit some code here, so to make things easier, turn on Notepad's Status Bar, which displays the line number of the code you're editing. In Notepad, select View→Status Bar. At the lower-right part of the screen, you'll see a line and column number, telling you at exactly what line you are in the file, as you can see in Figure 2-24.

Figure 2-23.
Vista's Slide Show gadget

Figure 2-24.
Editing the *slideShow.js* file, with the Status Bar turned on, as you can see in the lower-right part of the screen

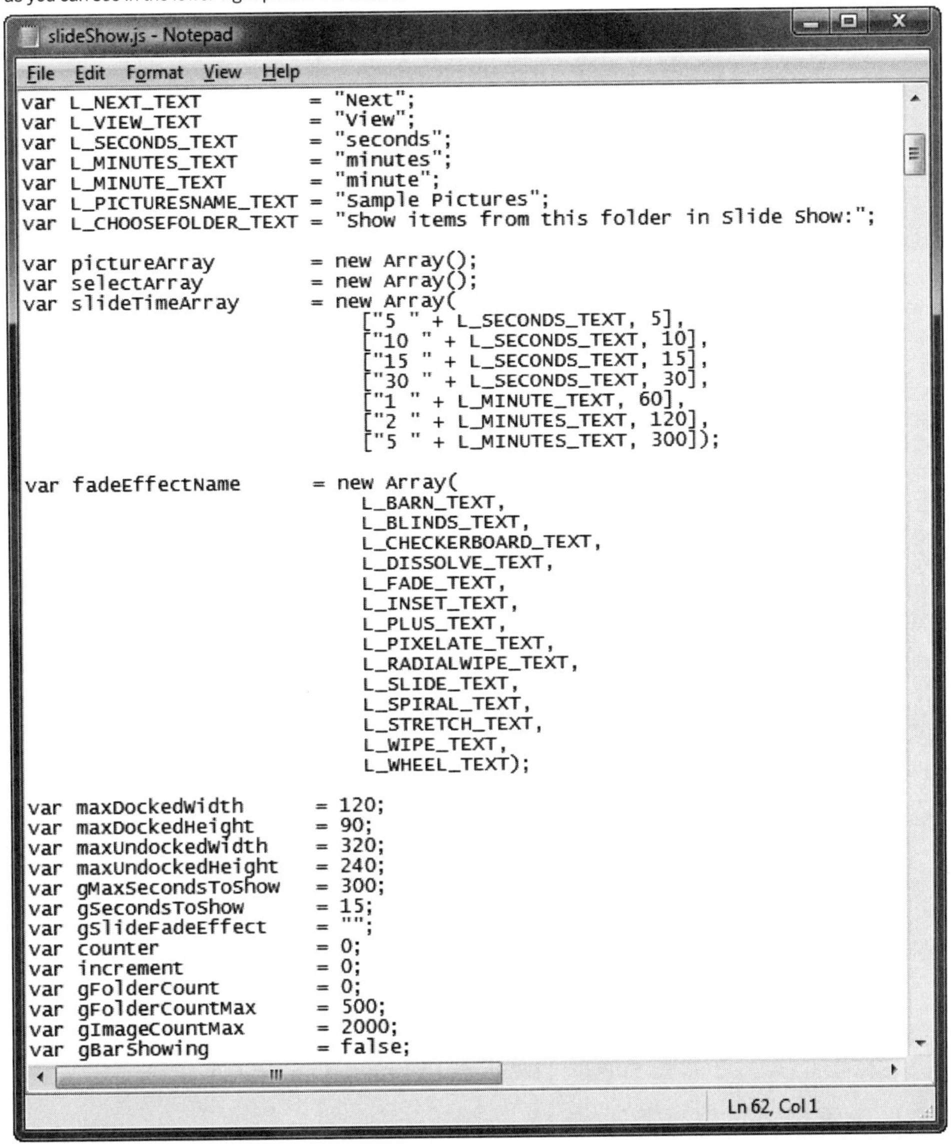

slideShow.js - Notepad

File Edit Format View Help

```
var L_NEXT_TEXT         = "Next";
var L_VIEW_TEXT         = "View";
var L_SECONDS_TEXT      = "seconds";
var L_MINUTES_TEXT      = "minutes";
var L_MINUTE_TEXT       = "minute";
var L_PICTURESNAME_TEXT = "Sample Pictures";
var L_CHOOSEFOLDER_TEXT = "Show items from this folder in Slide Show:";

var pictureArray        = new Array();
var selectArray         = new Array();
var slideTimeArray      = new Array(
        ["5 " + L_SECONDS_TEXT, 5],
        ["10 " + L_SECONDS_TEXT, 10],
        ["15 " + L_SECONDS_TEXT, 15],
        ["30 " + L_SECONDS_TEXT, 30],
        ["1 " + L_MINUTE_TEXT, 60],
        ["2 " + L_MINUTES_TEXT, 120],
        ["5 " + L_MINUTES_TEXT, 300]);

var fadeEffectName      = new Array(
        L_BARN_TEXT,
        L_BLINDS_TEXT,
        L_CHECKERBOARD_TEXT,
        L_DISSOLVE_TEXT,
        L_FADE_TEXT,
        L_INSET_TEXT,
        L_PLUS_TEXT,
        L_PIXELATE_TEXT,
        L_RADIALWIPE_TEXT,
        L_SLIDE_TEXT,
        L_SPIRAL_TEXT,
        L_STRETCH_TEXT,
        L_WIPE_TEXT,
        L_WHEEL_TEXT);

var maxDockedWidth      = 120;
var maxDockedHeight     = 90;
var maxUndockedWidth    = 320;
var maxUndockedHeight   = 240;
var gMaxSecondsToShow   = 300;
var gSecondsToShow      = 15;
var gSlideFadeEffect    = "";
var counter             = 0;
var increment           = 0;
var gFolderCount        = 0;
var gFolderCountMax     = 500;
var gImageCountMax      = 2000;
var gBarShowing         = false;
```

Ln 62, Col 1

There's a lot of code in this file—980 lines worth. But don't worry, you'll be changing only four lines and adding only four lines. Go to lines 62 and 63. Change this:

```
var maxUndockedWidth    = 320;
var maxUndockedHeight   = 240;
```

to:

```
var maxUndockedWidth    = 220;
var maxUndockedHeight   = 195;
```

Notepad makes it easy to jump to any line in a file. Select Edit→Go To, type in the line number to which you want to jump, and click OK.

Now go to line 697 and change this:

```
var imageNameArray =  new Array(".jpg", ".jpeg", ".jpe", ".gif", ".png",  ".bmp");
```

to:

```
var imageNameArray = new Array(".avi", ".wmv", ".jpg", ".jpeg", ".jpe", ".gif", ".png",  ".bmp");
```

By making this change, you're telling the gadget to play videos in the *.avi* and *.wmv* formats, as well as displaying graphics files it already displays.

Now go to line 278, and add the following two lines:

```
with(picture.style)
        width=320,height=240;
```

Next, go to line 309 (give or take a line or two depending on how many lines you used to add the new line). Add the following text:

```
with(picture.style)
        width=120,height=90;
```

That's it—you've just created a gadget that displays videos as well as graphics in a slideshow. Open the Gadget Gallery and add the new Slide Show Player to the Sidebar by double-clicking it or dragging it to the Sidebar. If you've pointed your Slide Show Player gadget to a folder that has only graphics in it and no videos, it won't appear to do anything different than it has previously. But if you point it to a folder that has either *.avi* or *.wmv* files in it, the gadget will play those video. To change the folder that it points to, hover your mouse over the gadget and click the small wrench icon. From the screen that appears, click the button labeled "..." and browse to a folder with video in it, then click OK.

If there is a video format supported by your built-in media player that you'd like your new Slide Show Player gadget to play, add that extension to the one line that contains the file types, where you added *.avi* and *.wmv* file types. The gadget will now display these new files.

Now that it's working, test it out. Figure 2-25 shows the player displaying a thumbnail of a video as it cycles through photos and videos in a folder.

Click the magnifying glass icon that appears when hovering over the gadget, and the video launches in Windows Media Player, as you can see in Figure 2-26.

Figure 2-25.
The new gadget displaying a thumbnail of a video

Hacking the Hack

As I explained earlier, it's easy to change the folder that the gadget uses to display pictures and videos. But if you remove the gadget from the sidebar, and then add it again, the gadget will default back to Pictures, rather than Videos.

If you'd like the default folder to always be My Videos (or another folder of your choosing), you can edit *slideShow.js* again. Open it in Notepad and go to line 30 and change this line:

```
var L_PICTURESNAME_TEXT = "Sample Pictures";
```

to:

```
var L_PICTURESNAME_TEXT = "Sample Videos";
```

Then go to line 164 and change this:

```
var myPicturesObj = System.Shell.knownFolder("pictures").Self;
```

Figure 2-26.
Double-click the video thumbnail, and Windows Media Player opens and plays the video

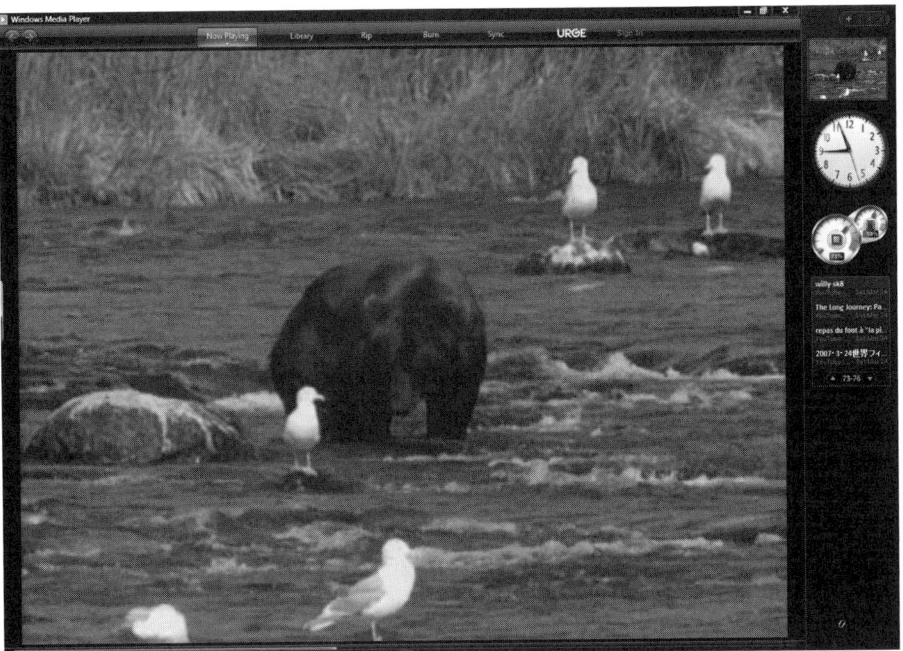

to:

```
var myPicturesObj = System.Shell.knownFolder("videos").Self;
```

Next, go to line 371 and change:

```
this.myPicturesFolder = samplePictPath + "\\Pictures\\Sample Pictures";
```

to:

```
this.myPicturesFolder = samplePictPath + "\\Videos\\Sample Videos";
```

Finally, go to line 474 and change:

```
imagePathAndName = slideSettings.myPicturesFolder + "\\Garden.jpg";
```

to:

```
imagePathAndName = slideSettings.myPicturesFolder + "\\Butterfly.wmv";
```

See Also

- "Play YouTube Videos in the Feed Headlines Gadget" **[Hack #24]**
- "Carry Your Gadgets with you on a USB Flash Drive" **[Hack #25]**
- "Automatically Build any Vista Gadget from the Web" **[Hack #26]**

— John Moscarillo

Play YouTube Videos in the Feed Headlines Gadget

V Are you a big fan of YouTube? This hack provides a way to see its videos right in a gadget.

The Feed Headlines gadget is one of the most useful gadgets of all. It grabs all of your RSS feeds, and displays their headlines, one after another, as well as the name of the RSS feed, right in the Sidebar. Click any feed and it "flies out" to reveal a synopsis of the post, as you can see in Figure 2-27. Click the headline or the synopsis, and you'll go straight to the post online.

Increasingly, RSS feeds are used not just to let people read blogs, but to distribute media as well, such as podcasts or YouTube videos. An enclosure tag in the RSS feed links to the media, so that the media can be downloaded directly from the RSS feed. In the case of YouTube, Macromedia's Flash player is used to play the videos. In this hack, you'll tell the gadget to use Flash to play the video.

Windows Vista's Feed Headlines RSS gadget can't handle enclosures. But with the knowledge you gained from **[Hack #23]**, you'll be able to use the Feed Headlines gadget to play media. In this hack, I'll show you how to play YouTube videos from an RSS feed using the Feed Headlines gadget.

As with the last hack, you'll copy code from a built-in gadget, and then edit it; in this instance, the Feed Headlines gadget. First copy the entire *RSSFeeds.Gadget* folder from *C:\Program Files\Windows Sidebar\Gadgets* to *C:\Users*`username`*\AppData\Local\Microsoft\Windows Sidebar\Gadgets* Then rename it to *RSSVideo.Gadget*.

The name you give to the new folder doesn't really matter; it won't affect the functioning of the gadget. You only have to make sure that it ends in a *.Gadget* extension.

You now have two identical Feed Headlines gadgets on your PC. If you were to open the Gadget Gallery by clicking the + sign at the top of the Sidebar, you'd see two identical gadgets. This can get confusing, so you're going to rename one of them—the gadget you're going to modify to play YouTube videos.

To change the name of the gadget in the Gadget Gallery, edit its *gadget.xml* file. Go to *C:\Users*`username`*\AppData\Local\Microsoft\Windows Sidebar\Gadgets\ RSSVideo.Gadget* and navigate to the *en-US* subfolder. (Assuming you're using a U.S. version of Vista. If you're using a different version, go to the folder that matches your Vista version and language.) Open *gadget.xml* In Notepad. On the third line from the top you will see the following line:

```
<name>Feed Headlines</name>
```

Change this to:

```
<name>Feed Videos</name>
```

Save and close this file. Open the Gadget Gallery. (If it's already open, first close it, then open it again.) You'll now see two Feed Headlines gadgets, but one will be called Feed Videos. That's the gadget you're going to modify.

Follow the directions from the previous hack for opening and editing a *.js* file with Notepad. In this instance, you're going to open *RSSFeeds.js* in *C:\Users*`username`*\AppData\Local\Microsoft\Windows Sidebar\Gadgets\ RSSVideo.Gadget\en-US\js*.

Go to line 1108 and look for this text:

```
flyoutDiv.getElementById("flyoutMain").innerHTML = currentFeed.Description;
```

Leave that text as is. Add this code directly beneath it:

Figure 2-27.
The Feed Headlines gadget displays your RSS feeds. Click it and it "flies out" to reveal a synopsis of a post.

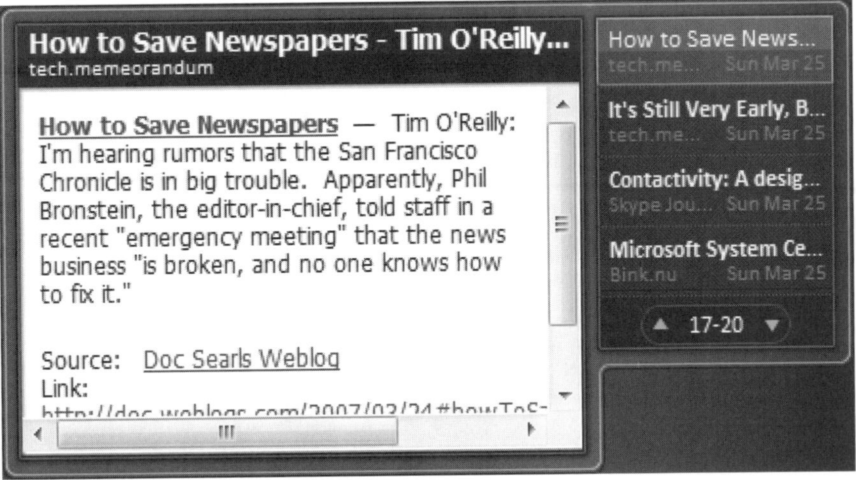

Figure 2-28.
At first, the new RSS gadget looks just like the old gadget

```
var swfObject = '';
var tempSWF = currentFeed.Enclosure.URL;
if(tempSWF != null)
{
  swfObject =
    '<object classid="clsid:d27cdb6e-ae6d-11cf-96b8-444553540000"' +
    'codebase="http://fpdownload.macromedia.com/pub/shockwave/cabs/' +
    'flash/swflash.cab#version=9,0,0,0" '+
    'width="255" height="196" id="swfObject" align="middle">'+
    '<param name="allowScriptAccess" value="sameDomain" />'+
    '<param name="movie" value="'+tempSWF+'" />'+
    '<param name="quality" value="high" />'+
    '<param name="bgcolor" value="#ffffff" />'+
    '</object>';
}
flyoutDiv.getElementById("flyoutMain").innerHTML = swfObject +
  currentFeed.Description;
```

That's all the coding you need to do. Open the Gadget Gallery and add the new Feed Videos gadget to the Sidebar. It will not appear any different—you will see RSS headlines as usual, as you can see in Figure 2-28.

Click the RSS headline from YouTube to make it "fly out" (if you don't see any YouTube headlines, subscribe to a YouTube RSS Feed using Internet Explorer), and you'll see that it looks just like a video on YouTube, as shown in Figure 2-29. Click the Start button, and the video plays, as you can see in Figure 2-30.

You don't need to change how you subscribe to RSS feeds to use this hack; subscribe to the feeds as you would normally, using Internet Explorer. But now you can subscribe to YouTube video feeds and view them in the gadget. You can get a list of them at www.youtube.com/rssls.

See Also

- "Force the SlideShow Gadget to Play Videos as Well as Images" [Hack #23]
- "Carry Your Gadgets with you on a USB Flash Drive" [Hack #25]
- "Automatically Build any Vista Gadget from the Web" [Hack #26]

— John Moscarillo

Figure 2-29.
The YouTube video, waiting to be played in the gadget's "fly out"

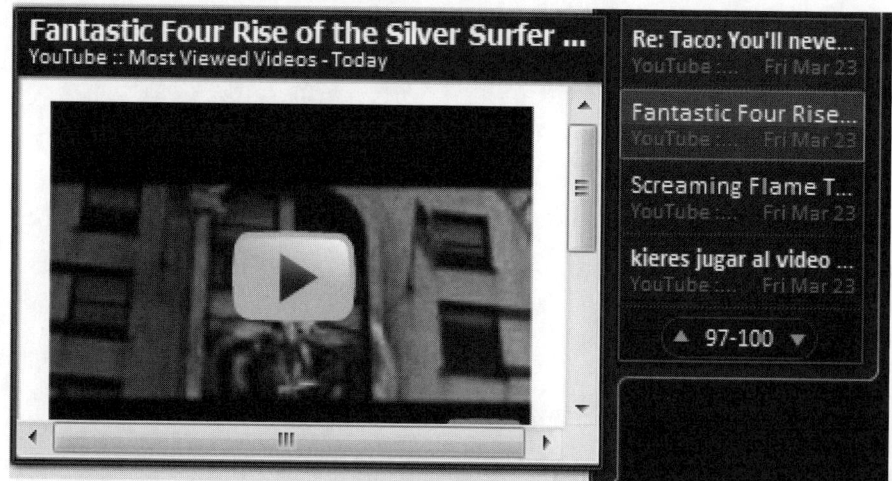

Figure 2-30.
The YouTube video

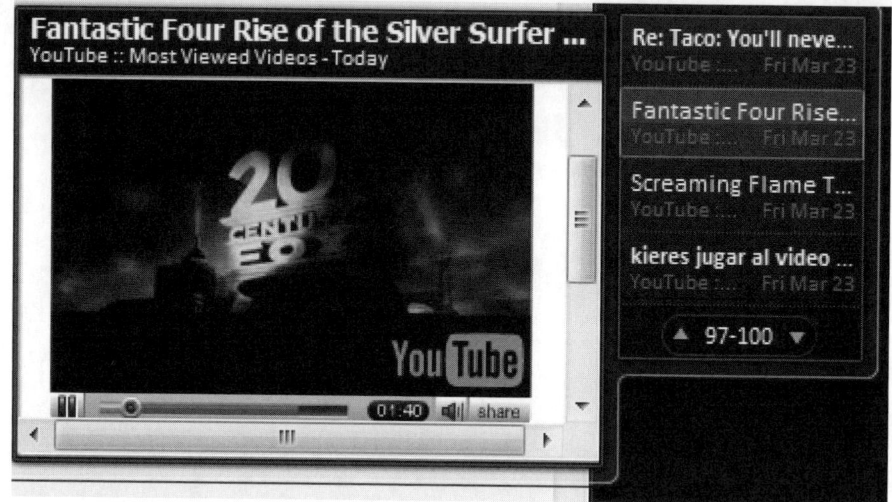

HACK 25: Carry Your Gadgets with You on a USB Flash Drive

V Wherever you go, you can carry your favorite gadgets with you on a flash drive. Just pop the drive into another PC, and voilà! the Sidebar and all your favorite gadgets are ready to go.

If you're such a big fan of your gadgets that you want to take them with you wherever you go, you can put your Sidebar and gadget settings on a USB drive, then pop that drive into any other Windows Vista PC—and all your Sidebar settings will be intact, along with all of your gadgets. This hack shows you how to do that with a USB drive, but you could also use it for any flash device, such as an SD card.

One nice use of this is to play family video and photos on any Vista PC, using the gadgets you created in "Force the Slideshow Gadget To Play Videos as Well as Images" **[Hack #23]**. You could put all your family videos and photos on the flash drive, and have the Slide Show gadget cycle through them.

Plug the USB drive into your PC and create a folder called *sblocal* on it—if you have a USB drive that uses your *E:* drive, the new directory would *E:\sblocal*.

Copy the contents of *C:\Users*username*\AppData\Local\Microsoft\Windows Sidebar* and all its subfolders contents to *E:\sblocal*. Make sure that you copy all the files and subfolders.

Open the *settings.ini* file in *E:\sblocal* using Notepad. You're going to make a few changes to the file, so that when you plug your USB drive into another PC, Windows Vista will know to look on the USB drive itself for your gadget information, not to its own local folders.

 If you only use Windows Vista's built-in default gadgets, you won't need to edit the *settings.ini* file.

In *settings.ini*, there are several lines that tell Windows Vista where to find gadget information. They all begin with this text:

```
PrivateSetting_GadgetName=
```

and following that, will be a folder location. So the entire line may look like this:

```
PrivateSetting_GadgetName=%PROGRAMFILES%\windows
```

Any time you see that line, leave it alone. It's pointing to the default location for Windows, and you don't want to change that.

In other instances, you'll see a line that looks like this:

```
PrivateSetting_GadgetName=%PROGRAMFILES%\windows sidebar\gadgets\Clock.gadget
```

You're going to leave lines that include that folder location alone also. It's pointing to the folder for built-in gadgets. Because that folder is the same on every copy of Vista, you shouldn't change it.

Instead, you should look for lines that have a different folder location—your own user gadget folder. So the line would look like this:

```
PrivateSetting_GadgetName="C:%5CUsers%5username%5CAppData%5CLocal%5CMicrosoft%5CWindows%20Sidebar%
5CGadgets%5CRSSVideo.Gadget"
```

In this instance, username would actually be your username. Every time you come across that folder location for the `PrivateSetting_GadgetName=` line, you should change this:

```
C:%5CUsers%5username%5CAppData%5CLocal%5CMicrosoft%5CWindows%20Sidebar%5CGadgets%5C
```

to:

```
%GADGETS_USER%%5C
```

In other words, you would change this entire line:

```
PrivateSetting_GadgetName="C:%5CUsers%5username%5CAppData%5CLocal%5CMicrosoft%5CWindows%20Sidebar%5
CGadgets%5CRSSVideo.Gadget"
```

to this entire line:

```
PrivateSetting_GadgetName="%GADGETS_USER%%5CRSSVideo.Gadget"
```

After you go through the file and make all the changes, close it.

Now you need to create a way for the Sidebar on each machine you visit to find the gadgets, by creating a *.cmd* file. This step opens a command window and tells the system where to find the gadgets.

Create a new file in Notepad called *sb.cmd*. Type in this text, exactly as you see it:

```
pushd %~dp0
set GADGETS_SETTINGS=%~dp0
set GADGETS_USER=%~dp0\gadgets
start sidebar
popd
```

Store it in the same folder as *settings.ini*, which in this example is in *E:\sblocal*.

To see this hack in action on the PC that it's currently plugged into, exit the Sidebar by right-clicking it and choosing Exit, then double-clicking the *sb.cmd* file in *E:\sblocal*. To use your gadgets on any other Windows Vista PC, plug the USB drive into a USB port, exit the Sidebar, then double-click the *sb.cmd* file.

 Exiting the Sidebar is different than "closing" it. When you "close" the Sidebar, it is still running, but isn't displayed. For example, when you return to the Desktop, sometimes the Sidebar won't appear, but its icon will still be in the Taskbar. (If the icon is in the Taskbar, the Sidebar is still running in the background.) So make sure to exit the Sidebar by right-clicking its icon and choosing Exit before you double-click the *sb.cmd* file.

GIVE WINDOWS XP TASKBAR THUMBNAILS LIKE WINDOWS VISTA

If you're a Windows XP user, and crave the live thumbnail feature of Windows Vista, worry not—there's a simple way to do it. The free Visual Tooltip (http://chsalmon.club.fr/index.php?en/Visual-tooltip-about) does it for you. Visual Tooltip even gives you features that Windows Vista's live thumbnails don't have, such as moving the thumbnails anywhere on the Desktop, adding them to a floating "dock bar," and rotating them. The program also works with Windows Vista, so Windows Vista users can teach their live thumbnails new tricks.

See Also

- "Force the SlideShow Gadget to Play Videos as Well as Images" **[Hack #23]**
- "Play YouTube Videos in the Feed Headlines Gadget" **[Hack #24]**
- "Automatically Build any Vista Gadget from the Web" **[Hack #26]**
- "Speed Up Your PC with ReadyBoost" **[Hack #159]**

— John Moscarillo

HACK 26: Automatically Build Any Vista Gadget from the Web

V There are thousands of gadgets and widgets that run on web sites such as Google, Yahoo, and others. Here's how you can magically transform them into Windows Vista gadgets that live in your Sidebar.

The Web is alive with gadgets and widgets—there are hundreds or thousands of them on web sites including Google, Yahoo, and many others. There is no common standard for building gadgets and widgets, though. That means that if you come across a widget or gadget that you'd like to run on your Windows Vista sidebar, you're out of luck. It just won't run there . . . or wouldn't until now.

A free program called the Amnesty Generator (amnesty.mesadynamics.com/GeneratorWin.html) takes gadgets and widgets you find on the Web and transforms them so that you can run them as Windows Vista gadgets, right on your Sidebar.

In this hack, you'll see how to take a Google gadget, and transform it into a Windows Vista gadget for your sidebar.

Download Amnesty Generator, install it, and run it. From the screen that appears, choose a web site whose gadgets or widgets you want to browse, and find one that you want to run as a Windows Vista gadget. The site will open in your browser. For this example, look on the Google Gadget site (www.google.com/ig/directory?synd=open) for a gadget.

Find a gadget you want to transform, then click Add to Your Web Page. A page will appear with a preview of the gadget, as well as information about it, including its name and size, and possibly some customization options. I'm a fan of retro games, and I found a Space Invaders–type game. I'll use that as an example of how to turn a Google gadget into a Windows Vista gadget.

Click Get the Code at the bottom of the page. The code will appear on the page, as you can see at the bottom of Figure 2-31.

Copy the code that appears, and paste it into Amnesty Generator in the appropriate box in Step 2 of the application, as you can see in Figure 2-32. Press the Tab key, and Step 3 will be automatically populated, including the gadget name, width, and height. Change the name of the gadget if you like, but it's not a good idea to change the dimensions, because if you do, it might not work properly. Click the Browse button to find a graphic that will display as the gadget's picture in the sidebar. If you don't have a suitable one, go into in Internet Explorer, right-click the gadget's image on the Google gadget page, select Save Picture As..., and save the picture to your hard disk. Then when you click on Browse in Amnesty Generator, select that picture.

When you're done, click Generate. The gadget won't show up yet in the Sidebar; it's been placed in the Gadget Gallery. Click the + sign at the top of the Sidebar to open the Gadget Gallery, and you'll see your new gadget, as shown in Figure 2-33.

Figure 2-31.
The bottom of the page displays the code you'll need to transform this Google Gadget into a Windows Vista gadget

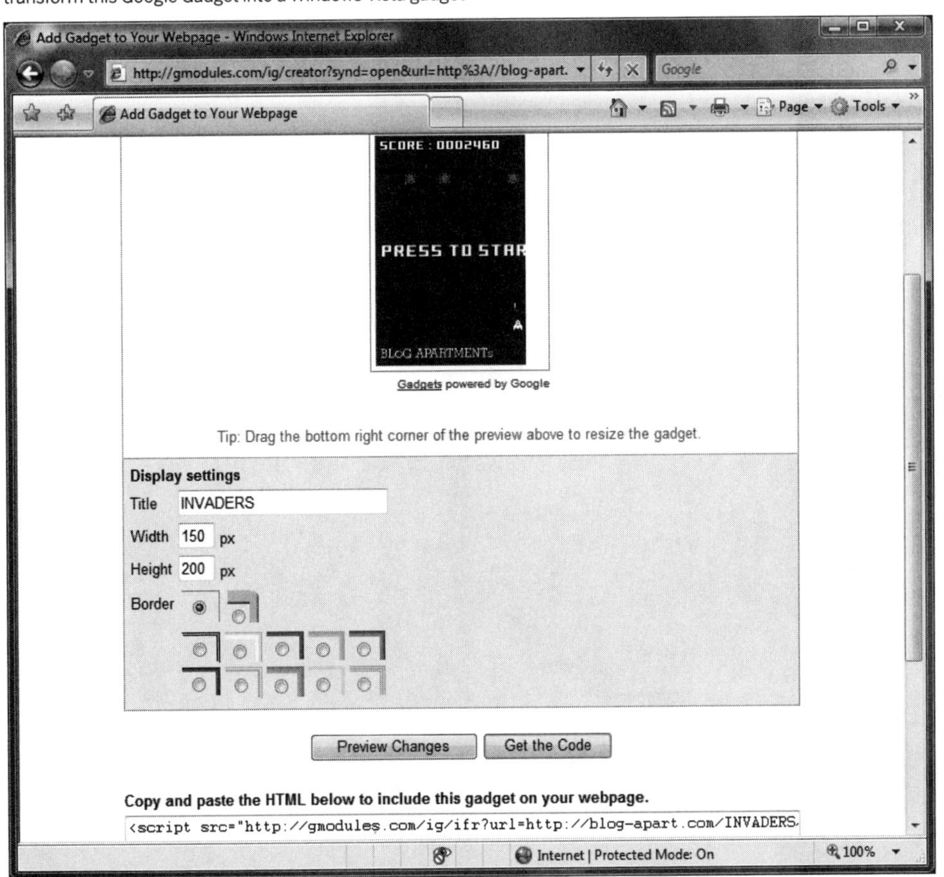

Figure 2-32.
Using Amnesty Generator to build your Windows Vista gadget

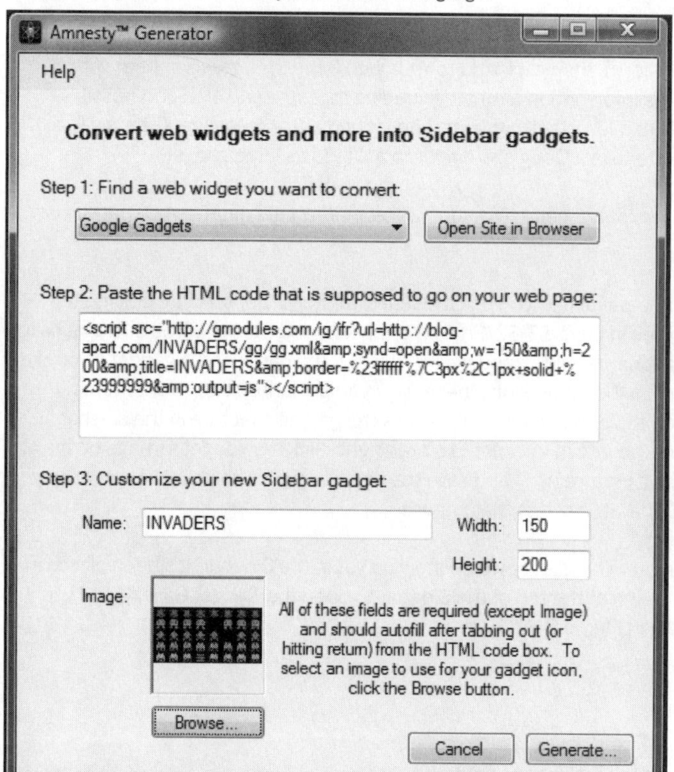

Figure 2-33.
The new gadget in the Gadget Gallery

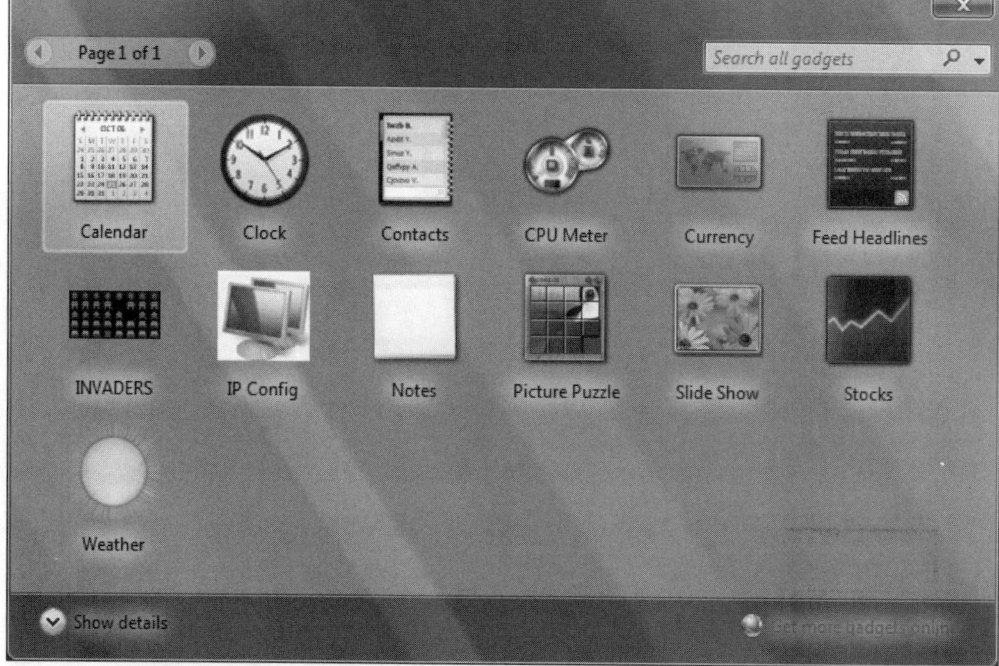

QUICK HACK

REMOVE SHORTCUT ARROWS FROM YOUR ICONS

If the large shortcut arrows on your desktop icons offend your aesthetic sensibility, get rid of them in Windows Vista, using the free FxVisor (www.frameworkx.com/Frameworkx/solution.aspx?id=632). Run it, and you can choose to either make the shortcut arrow smaller and lighter, or remove it altogether. The program doesn't work with Windows XP, but XP users can use Microsoft's free Tweak UI (www.microsoft.com/windowsxp/downloads/powertoys/xppowertoys.mspx, as mentioned earlier) to accomplish the same thing. Run it and choose Explorer→Shortcut. Choose the light arrow if you want the arrows to be smaller and lighter, or None to remove it completely.

Add the gadget to your sidebar by double-clicking it or dragging it to the Sidebar. It's now ready to be used as a Windows Vista gadget, as you can see in Figure 2-34.

You can use the gadget in the same way as you can any other. If you find that it's causing problems, uninstall it. Go to the Gadget Gallery, right-click it, and select Uninstall. By the way, not every gadget you find on the Web will be able to be converted and run properly. There's no way to know ahead of time which will work and which won't, so you'll have to find out by trial and error.

HACK 27: Yes, You *Can* Hack Windows Vista's Screensavers

Think you can't customize Windows Vista's screensavers? Think again—this hack shows you how.

Here's a dare for you: Try to customize Windows Vista's built-in screensavers, such as the Bubbles screensaver or the Ribbons screensaver. Right-click the desktop, choose Personalize→Screen saver, choose either Bubbles or Ribbons from the drop-down list, and click Settings. You'll be greeted with the message: "This screen saver has no options you can set."

For some inexplicable reason, Microsoft gives you no apparent way to customize either of these screensavers, such as by changing how the bubbles look, or the number or thickness of the ribbons.

With a little bit of Registry magic, you can in fact customize both. For the Bubbles screensaver, for example, you can make the bubbles metallic or keep them transparent; specify whether the bubbles should have shadows; and display the bubbles against the desktop or against a solid black background. For the Ribbon screensaver, you can change the number and thickness of the ribbons

To customize the Bubbles screensaver, launch the Registry Editor by typing regedit at the Start Search box or a command prompt (see Chapter13 for details) and then follow these steps:

1. Go to `HKEY_CURRENT_USER\Software\Microsoft\Windows\CurrentVersion\Screensavers\Bubbles`.

2. Select Edit→New DWORD (32-bit) Value, and create a new DWORD called MaterialGlass. Give it a value of 1 for glassy, transparent bubbles, or a value of 0 for metallic bubbles.

3. Create a DWORD called ShowShadows, and give it a value of 1 to display shadows below the bubbles, or a value of 0 to have no shadow displayed.

4. Create a DWORD called ShowBubbles and give it a value of 1 to show the bubbles on the desktop, or a value of 0 to show them against a solid black background.

Your new settings will take effect immediately.

To hack the Ribbons screensaver, open the Registry Editor and follow these steps:

1. Go to `HKEY_CURRENT_USER\Software`

2. `\Microsoft\Windows\CurrentVersion\Screensavers\Ribbons`. Select Edit→New DWORD (32-bit) Value, and create a new DWORD called NumRibbons. Click Decimal, and then type in the number of ribbons you want to be displayed. The minimum number of ribbons is 1; the maximum is 256.

3. Create a DWORD called RibbonWidth, click Decimal, and then type in a number to determine the width of each ribbon. The smaller the number, the narrower the ribbon.

Figure 2-34.
The new gadget played in the Sidebar

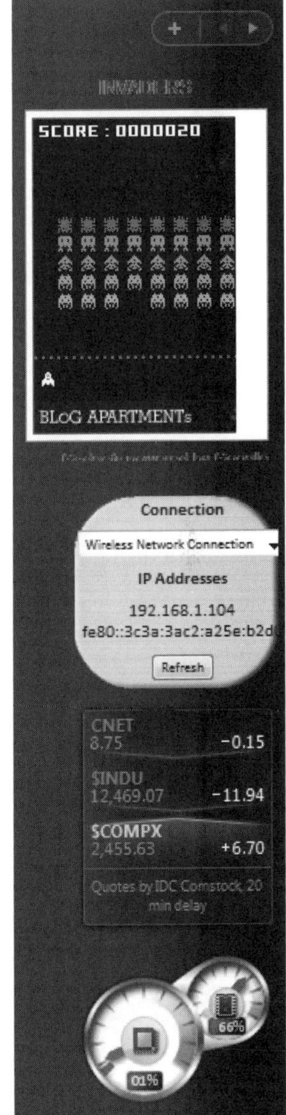

Your new settings will take effect immediately.

To hack the Mystify screensaver, open the Registry Editor and go to `HKEY_CURRENT_USER\Software\Microsoft\Windows\CurrentVersion\Screensavers\Mystify`. Select Edit→New DWORD (32-bit) Value, and create a new DWORD called NumLines. Click Decimal, and then type in the number of lines you want to be displayed. The greater the number of lines, the more "psychedelic"-looking the screensaver will be. Your new settings will take effect immediately.

To hack the Aurora screensaver, open the Registry Editor and go to `HKEY_CURRENT_USER\Software\Microsoft\Windows\CurrentVersion\Screensavers\Aurora`. Select Edit→New DWORD (32-bit) Value, and create a new DWORD called NumLayers. Click Decimal, and then type in a number. The higher the number, the greater the brightness of the Aurora.

Your new settings will take effect immediately.

For all screensavers, to revert to your original settings, delete the Registry keys that you created.

See Also

- "Hack Your Way Through Windows Vista's Aero Interface" **[Hack #15]**

QUICK HACK

TURN THE SLEEP BUTTON INTO A POWER OFF BUTTON

In Windows Vista, when you click the Start button, a series of buttons appear on the right-hand side of the screen to let you log off, put your PC to sleep, turn off your PC, and so on. The leftmost of those buttons looks a lot like an Off button, but depending on your configuration, it may not in fact turn off your computer—it may only put your PC to "sleep," a low-power type of hibernation mode. If you'd prefer that the button instead turn off your PC, open a command prompt, then type powercfg.cpl,1, and press Enter. You can also select Control Panel→System Maintenance→Change what the power buttons do, select Shut Down from the Power button drop-down list, and click Save Changes.

HACK 28: Extend Your Screen Real Estate with Virtual Desktops

XP Virtual desktops allow you to stretch your screen real estate well beyond its normal size, as well as to organize different views of your workspace.

At any point during the day, I might be writing software, listening to music, purchasing computer equipment, messing with my GPS and software, playing computer games with my son, or working with my editor. Sometimes, I'm doing all those things at once. It's a wonder I can keep all the windows organized. Fortunately, I don't have to do all the organizing myself.

The Virtual Desktop Manager (VDM) gives me a way to organize the work I'm doing, using up to four switchable desktops. VDM is part of the unsupported PowerToys collection from Microsoft that includes Tweak UI.

Download VDM from www.microsoft.com/windowsxp/downloads/powertoys/xppowertoys.mspx and install it on your machine. You will not notice anything new. You have to activate its toolbar before you can begin using it. To activate VDM, right-click the taskbar at the bottom of the screen and select Toolbars→Desktop Manager, as shown in Figure 2-35.

Figure 2-35.
Activating the Virtual Desktop Manager

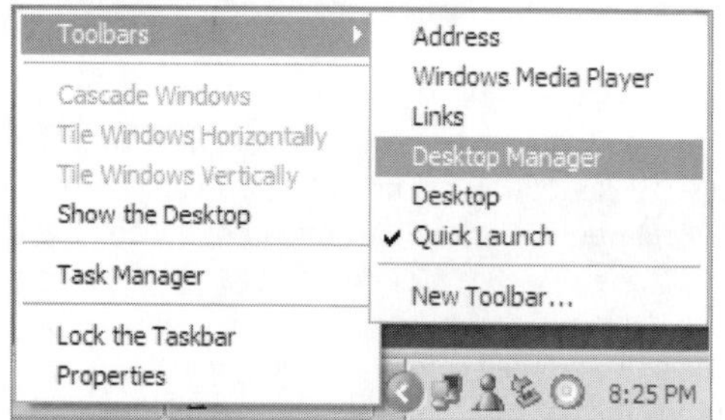

After you activate VDM, you will notice a new toolbar on the taskbar at the bottom of the screen, as shown in Figure 2-36. To switch between desktops, click one of the numbered blue buttons. At first, the desktops will all appear, the same because you haven't done anything in them to make them unique.

Click button 1 and then launch your web browser. Next, click button 2 and then open your email program. Next, click button 3 and then double-click the My Computer icon. Now, click the green button with an icon of a grid on it. Your screen should look something like Figure 2-37. Click one of the four images of the desktop to switch to that virtual desktop.

Without changing a single option, VDM is a very useful addition to Windows XP. But if you don't twiddle with it, you can't really call yourself a hacker, now, can you? If you right-click any of the buttons on the VDM toolbar, as shown in Figure 2-38, you can configure VDM to suit your needs.

Figure 2-36.
The Virtual Desktop Manager toolbar

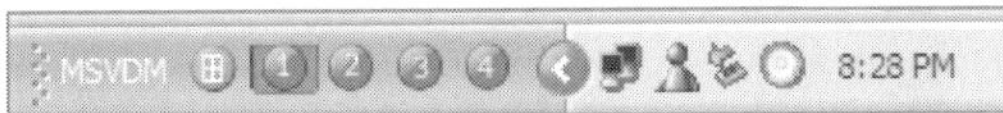

Figure 2-37.
The Virtual Desktop Manager preview screen

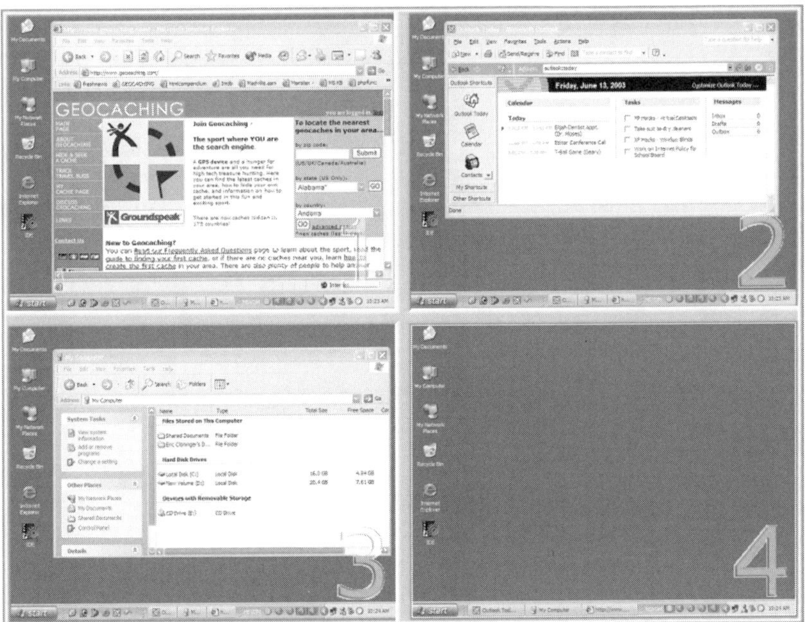

Figure 2-38.
The Virtual Desktop Manager toolbar configuration menu

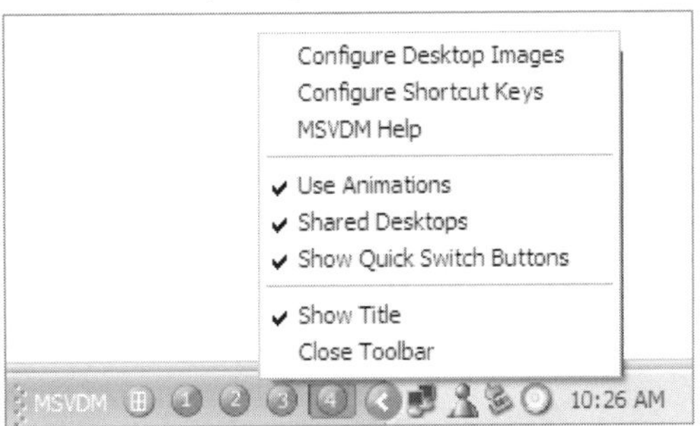

QUICK HACK

CREATE VIRTUAL DESKTOPS IN WINDOWS VISTA

If you want to create virtual desktops in Windows Vista, there's a way to do it. Download the Vista Virtual Desktop Manager from http://www.codeplex.com/vdm.

Your desktop has a background image that you can set as you wish. When you purchased your computer or installed Windows XP, the background image was a grassy hill with a blue sky or an image supplied by the computer manufacturer. Because VDM provides you with four separate desktops, you can customize each with a different background image. If you choose the Configure Desktop Images item from the toolbar's menu, you will see the dialog box shown in Figure 2-39.

To change the background for one of the virtual desktops, specify which desktop area you want to change on the left side of the window. Then locate a file from the list on the left. The list of images comes from both *C:\WINDOWS\Web\Wallpaper* and *C:\Documents and Settings*`username`*\My Documents\My Pictures*. If you want to use a picture that's not in the list, click the Browse button and locate the file. However, you might find that VDM changes your original background picture to a solid color when you first run it. Just change it back to your preferred background.

Look at Figure 2-39; notice that desktop 3 is shown in gray. This color is how VDM informs you that you have no background image set for the desktop. When you switch to that desktop, the background will be whatever color you have selected in your display properties.

In addition to pressing the numbered buttons, you can use keyboard shortcuts to switch between the desktops. Hold down the Windows key (if your keyboard has one; if it doesn't, you can change the key assignments, as explained next) and one of the number keys 1 through 4 to switch to the appropriate desktop. To switch to the VDM preview screen, hold down the Windows key and press V. To change the key assignments that switch between the desktops, choose Configure Shortcut Keys from the toolbar menu and use the dialog box shown in Figure 2-40.

I'm not a big fan of animation on my computer when I'm trying to work. I don't like wasting CPU cycles, and I don't like waiting for them to finish. (Also, it reminds me of the talking paperclip in older versions of Microsoft Word.) So I generally turn off all animation in the Windows desktop and in Explorer. If you want to speed up the switch between virtual desktops, uncheck the menu item named Use Animations.

Look at Figure 2-37 again. Notice that each separate desktop has taskbar buttons for every program that is running. VDM does this so that you can move running programs between the desktops. I prefer each desktop to have taskbar buttons for programs that run on that desktop. To enable this, right-click VDM on the taskbar and uncheck the menu item named Shared Desktops.

If you would rather rely on keyboard shortcuts and reclaim space on the taskbar, right-click VDM and uncheck the Show Quick Switch Buttons menu item.

Figure 2-39.
Virtual Desktop Manager background image settings

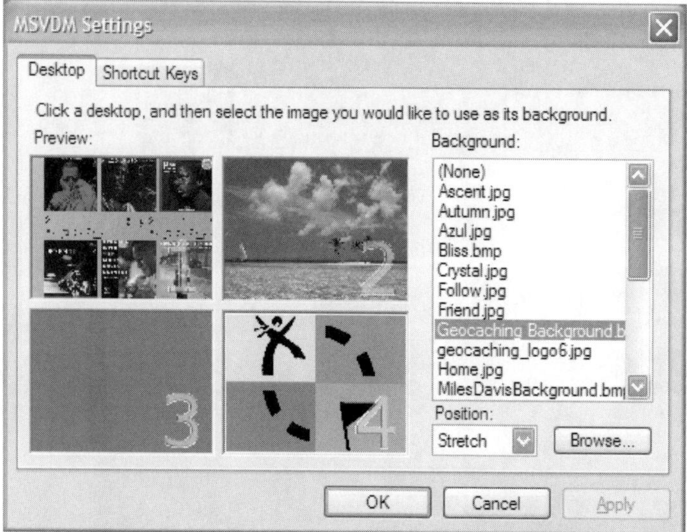

Figure 2-40.
Virtual Desktop Manager shortcut key settings

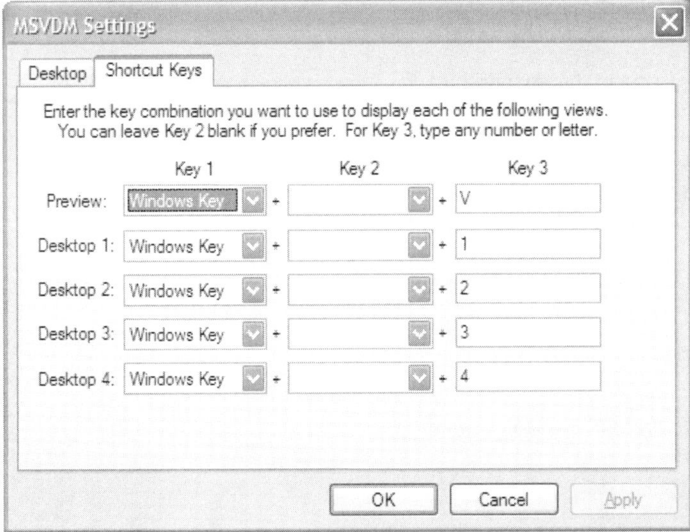

You should keep the following things in mind when using VDM:

- If you choose a background image using the Settings dialog, the VDM settings override the background image settings in the Display Properties dialog (your previous image won't be selected anymore; you'll have to reselect it).
- If you use background images, the act of switching between desktops will be noticeably slower.
- Shortcuts and icons on the desktop will show up on all virtual desktops.
- If you have programs that float above all other windows on the screen (such as a program with an Always On Top option), they will show up on all desktops.
- Windows Media Player using the MiniPlayer skin is one of those programs that float above everything else. If you turn on the Windows Media Player toolbar and then minimize the player, a smaller version of the player appears on the taskbar and becomes available to all desktops.

See Also

- An excellent virtual desktop is DeskSpace (www.otakusoftware.com/deskspace/). It works with Vista as well as XP, and lets you place your virtual desktop on a 3D cube.
- Another popular product is the shareware application Cool Desk. It costs $24.95 and supports up to nine separate desktops. You can download Cool Desk at www.shelltoys.com/virtual_desktop/index.html.
- One of the more interesting desktop managers is Vern. Vern is free to download, but the author asks users who enjoy it to contribute. You can download Vern from www.oneguycoding.com/vern.
- "Turn Windows into a 3D Virtual Desktop" **[Hack #17]**

— Eric Cloninger

HACK 29: Force Older Programs to Use XP Common Controls

XP Older Windows programs look ancient and outdated in XP, because they don't use the XP-style buttons and checkboxes. Here's how to make them use XP common controls.

When you run an older program in XP, the operating system applies an XP-type frame around it, with rounded title bars. But the older program itself still uses its older-style interface. You can, however, force older programs to use XP-type common controls for things such as checkboxes and buttons. You'll have to create a manifest file (a specifically formatted XML file) and place it in the same directory as the older file.

Example 2-1 shows the code to put in your manifest file. For `Program Name`, enter the name of the program, and for `Description of Program`, enter a description for the program.

Example 2-1 Creating a manifest file

```
<?xml version="1.0" encoding="UTF-8" standalone="yes"?>
<assembly xmlns="urn:schemas-microsoft-com:asm.v1" manifestVersion="1.0">
<assemblyIdentity
    version="1.0.0.0"
    processorArchitecture="X86"
    name="Program Name"
    type="win32"
/>
<description>Description of Program</description>
<dependency>
    <dependentAssembly>
        <assemblyIdentity
            type="win32"
            name="Microsoft.Windows.Common-Controls"
            version="6.0.0.0"
            processorArchitecture="X86"
            publicKeyToken="6595b64144ccf1df"
            language="*"
        />
    </dependentAssembly>
</dependency>
</assembly>
```

To create the file, open Notepad, copy the text into it, and save it to the same folder as the executable file of the program you want to force to use XP common controls. Give it the same name as the program's executable file, but with an extension of *.manifest*. For example, if the program's executable file is named *oldprogram.exe*, give the manifest file the name *oldprogram.exe.manifest*.

QUICK HACK

BEST WAY TO CAPTURE WINDOWS VISTA SCREENS

Commercial and free tools for capturing Windows Vista screens don't do the operating system justice. For one thing, as a rule, they don't capture the shadows around windows. For another, they won't capture both the currently selected window, and the parent windows. There's a free and simple solution: Window Clippings (www.windowclippings.com). Not only will it capture shadows and parent windows, but does a great job with transparent windows as well.

RUNNING OTHER OPERATING SYSTEMS INSIDE WINDOWS

Dedicated Windows hackers often aren't happy running just one operating system—they want to run at least one other, such as Linux or Mac OS X. But setting up dual-boot systems can be more headache than it's worth, if you want to run those operating systems only occasionally.

In the next hacks, you'll learn how to run Linux, Mac OS X, and even Windows 3.11 inside your current version of Windows, without having to dual boot.

HACK 30: Run Linux Inside Windows Without Dual Booting

V XP Want to run Linux without the hassle of setting up and maintaining a dual-boot system? With Microsoft Virtual PC, it's easy to do.

Setting up a dual Linux-Windows Vista system isn't for the faint of heart—or even for the strong of heart, for that matter. In fact, it can take a good deal of work to set up a dual-boot Linux-Windows XP system [Hack #14] as well.

But if you want to run Linux on your PC, there's no need to go to the hassle of installing a dual-boot system. You can run Linux right inside of Windows Vista, using Microsoft Virtual PC. To do it, you install the free Microsoft Virtual PC, then install Ubuntu Linux as a virtual operating system inside it. As you'll see, it's not that tough to do.

Another good bet for running Linux on top of Windows is to install the free VMware Server (www.vmware.com), and then run Linux inside it. VMware Server offers more support for a wider variety of Linux distributions than does Microsoft Virtual PC.

As with the related hack in Chapter 1, you're going to install Ubuntu, a free, popular version of Linux that has a Mac-like feel to it. As of this writing, both Ubuntu 6.06 LTS and 7.04 are available. If you run into any trouble with 7.04, install version 6.06, which is likely to be more stable under Virtual PC (and just as well supported; the LTS stands for Long-Term Support).

Download Ubuntu Version 6.06 from www.ubuntu.com/getubuntu/download. It downloads as an *.iso* file. There are two ways to use that *.iso* file to install Ubuntu. One is to burn it to disc, and then use the disc to install Ubuntu, after you've installed Microsoft Virtual PC. The other way is to use the *.iso* file directly from your PC without burning to disc.

If you choose the disc-burning method, there are a number of programs that you can use to burn the *.iso* file to disc, but my favorite is ImgBurn (www.imgburn.com). After you install it and have downloaded the Ubuntu *.iso* file, run the program and put a blank CD or DVD in your drive. Click the + button in ImgBurn near the top of the screen, and navigate to and select the *.iso* file. Then click the Write button near the bottom of the screen. ImgBurn will burn the file to disc (see Figure 2-41).

To use the *.iso* file method, follow the instructions in this hack until your machine starts booting. Then, as it's booting, click CD→Capture ISO Image, and select the Ubuntu ISO image. Then select Action→Reset to reboot the virtual machine from the ISO image. You can then follow along with this hack as though you'd booted from a real CD.

Figure 2-41.
Burning the Ubuntu *.iso* file to disc

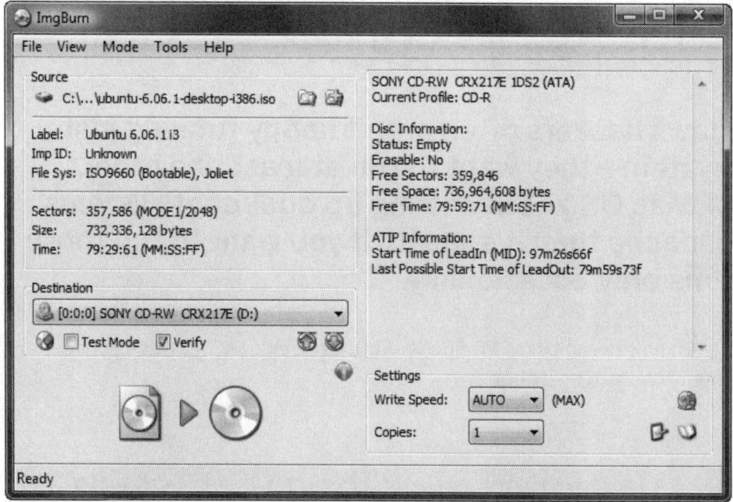

Figure 2-42.
Creating a virtual machine

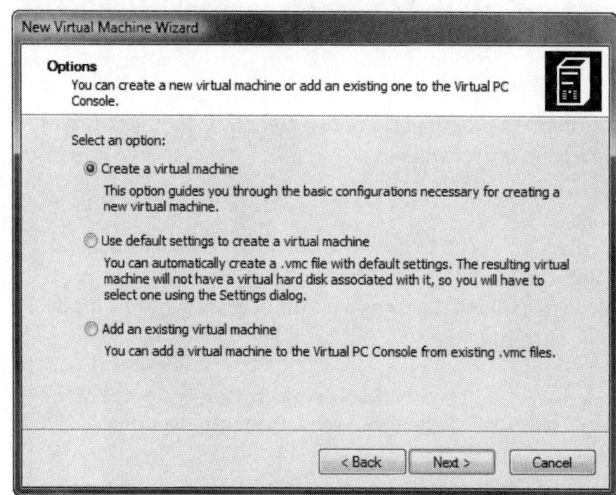

Now download and install Microsoft Virtual PC (www.microsoft.com/windows/products/winfamily/virtualpc/default.mspx).

Microsoft Virtual PC doesn't run on every version of Windows XP or Windows Vista. It works with Windows XP Professional, Windows XP Tablet PC, Windows Server 2003, Windows Vista Business, Windows Vista Enterprise, and Windows Vista Ultimate.

When you first run Virtual PC, a wizard appears that will help you install and configure a new virtual machine—in this instance, Ubuntu. Click Next when the wizard appears. A screen appears (Figure 2-42), asking whether you want to create a virtual machine, add a virtual machine, or use the default settings for creating a virtual machine. Select "Create a virtual machine."

In the next screen, you'll be asked to name your new virtual machine. Name it Ubuntu 6.06, and click Next. In the following screen (Figure 2-43), choose the operating system you'll install. Ubuntu or Linux won't be listed, so from the drop-down list, select Other, then click Next.

In the screen that follows, you're told that the default RAM that will be devoted to your new virtual machine is 128 MB. That's too little. You need at least 256 MB. If you are planning to work with

Figure 2-43.
Make sure to choose Other from this screen when selecting the operating system that you're going to install

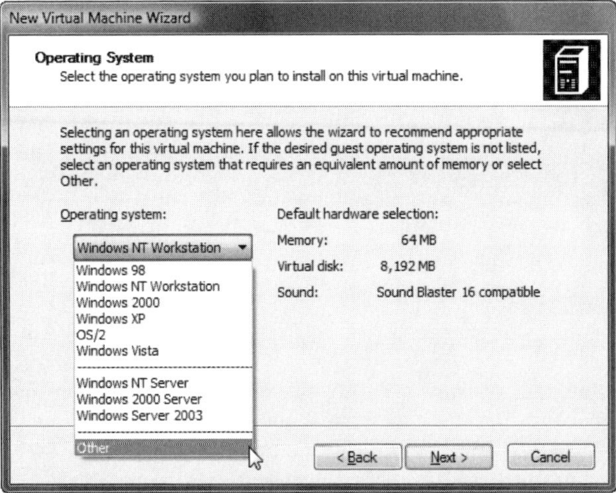

Figure 2-44.
Adjusting the amount of RAM to give your new virtual machine

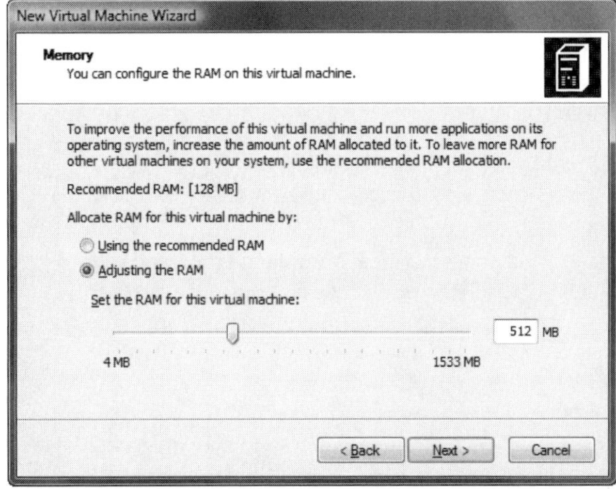

graphics, a better bet is 512 MB. Keep in mind, though, that the RAM you devote to your virtual machine is taken away from the rest of Windows. So you'll need to balance your need for RAM in Windows with Ubuntu's need for RAM.

To adjust the amount of RAM, click "Adjusting the RAM," then move the slider to the amount of RAM you want to give to the Ubuntu virtual machine, or type in the amount you want to use (Figure 2-44). Then click Next.

A screen appears asking if you want to use an existing virtual disk, or if you would rather create a new one. A virtual hard disk is a file with the *.vsd* extension that is stored on your physical hard disk, and that contains the Ubuntu operating system files, any applications you install, and any data files. Select "A new virtual hard disk," and click Next.

A screen will appear asking you to name your new *.vsd* file, and asking where you would like to store it. Accept the default. You'll also be told the default size of your new *.vsd* file. Unless you need a great deal more space for files than Microsoft Virtual PC gives you, accept the default, and click Next. From the next screen that appears, click Finish.

Figure 2-45.
The Virtual PC Console

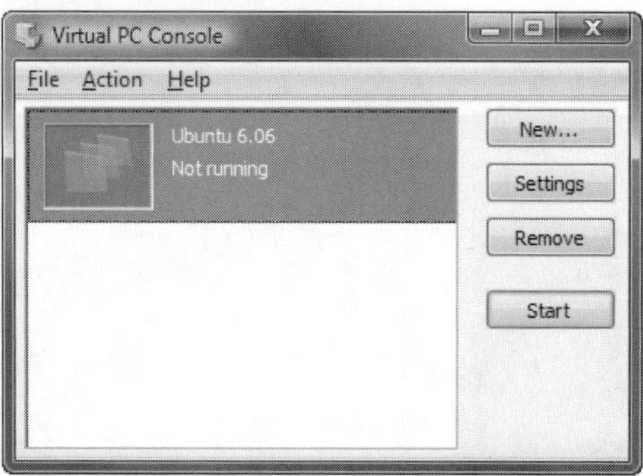

You'll see a small screen called the Virtual PC Console, with a listing for your new virtual machine in it (see Figure 2-45). Now you'll have to install the operating system into it. Place the Ubuntu installation disk you burned into your CD or DVD drive. If you have auto-play enabled, you may get an autorun popup in Windows; don't run the disc's setup program. Highlight your Ubuntu 6.06 listing in the Virtual PC Console, and click Start. Wait several minutes until you get a prompt to reboot, then press the space bar. A screen like the one shown in Figure 2-46 will appear.

Select Start Ubuntu in safe graphics mode. Be careful not to choose "Start or install Ubuntu." If you do, your graphics will be garbled. Wait several minutes while the installation starts. A screen like that shown in Figure 2-47 will appear. Click the Install button. From the screen that appears, select your language, then click the Forward button.

To move the focus of your mouse cursor into the Ubuntu window in Microsoft Virtual PC, click anywhere inside the window. To move the focus of the mouse cursor back to Windows, press the right Alt key on your keyboard.

In the next series of screens, you'll be asked to choose your location and time zone, and your keyboard. Make your selection, clicking Forward each time you make a choice. You'll come to a screen like the one shown in Figure 2-48. Type in your name, username, password, and so on, then click Forward.

Next you'll be asked how you want to partition your hard disk (see Figure 2-49). Don't be scared by this screen. You're partitioning your virtual hard disk, not your real one, so select "Erase entire disk" and click Forward.

Finally, you'll come to a screen showing you the options you've chosen for installing Ubuntu. To change any of these, click the Back button repeatedly until you come to the option you want to change, then click Forward to get back to this screen. When you've chosen all your options, click Install.

Installation will take some time. At the end, you'll be told to restart your computer. Remember, though, that you're restarting only the virtual machine, not your real computer. Take your installation disc out of the drive and click the "Restart now" button. You'll now be able to use Ubuntu. It comes with a number of applications preinstalled, including Firefox, the OpenOffice.org application suite, games, graphics editors, and more. Figure 2-50 shows Ubuntu up and running.

See Also

- "Transform Your Windows XP Laptop into a Dual-Boot XP/Ubuntu Linux System" **[Hack #14]**
- "Run Mac OS X on Windows Vista" **[Hack #31]**
- "Instant Linux" **[Hack #33]**

Figure 2-46.
Installing Ubuntu

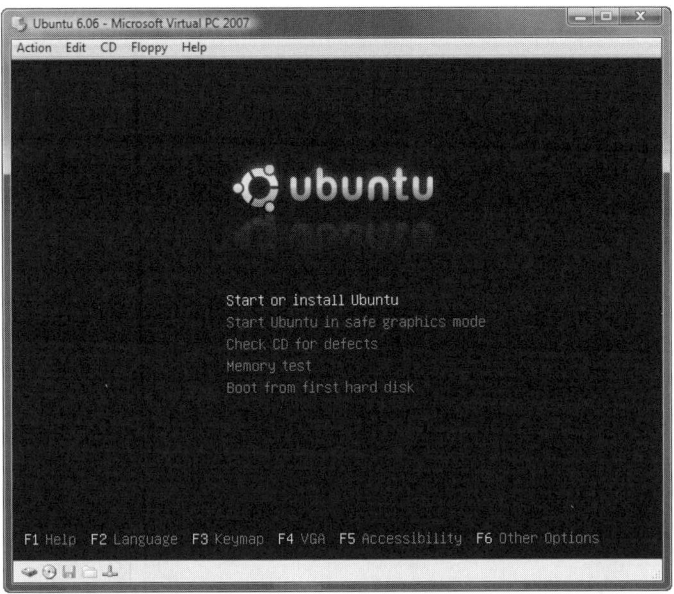

Figure 2-47.
Click the Install button to begin the Ubuntu installation

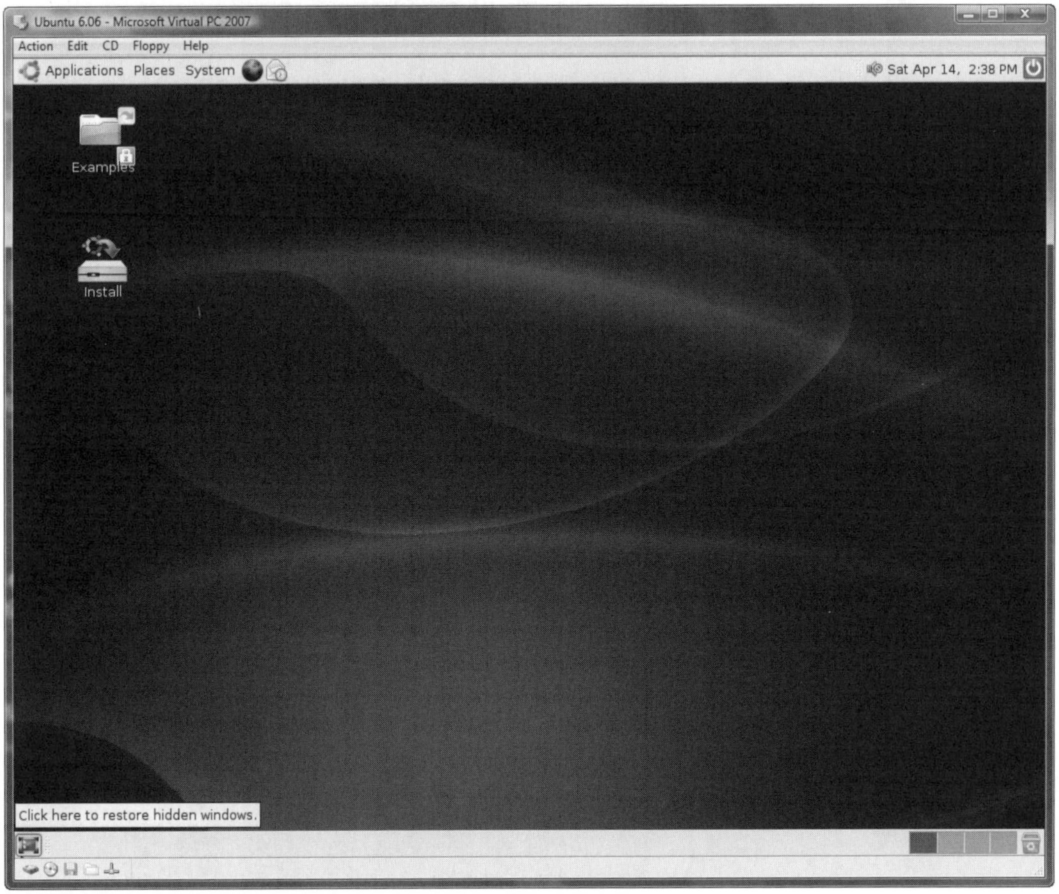

Figure 2-48.
Choose a name, password, and machine name

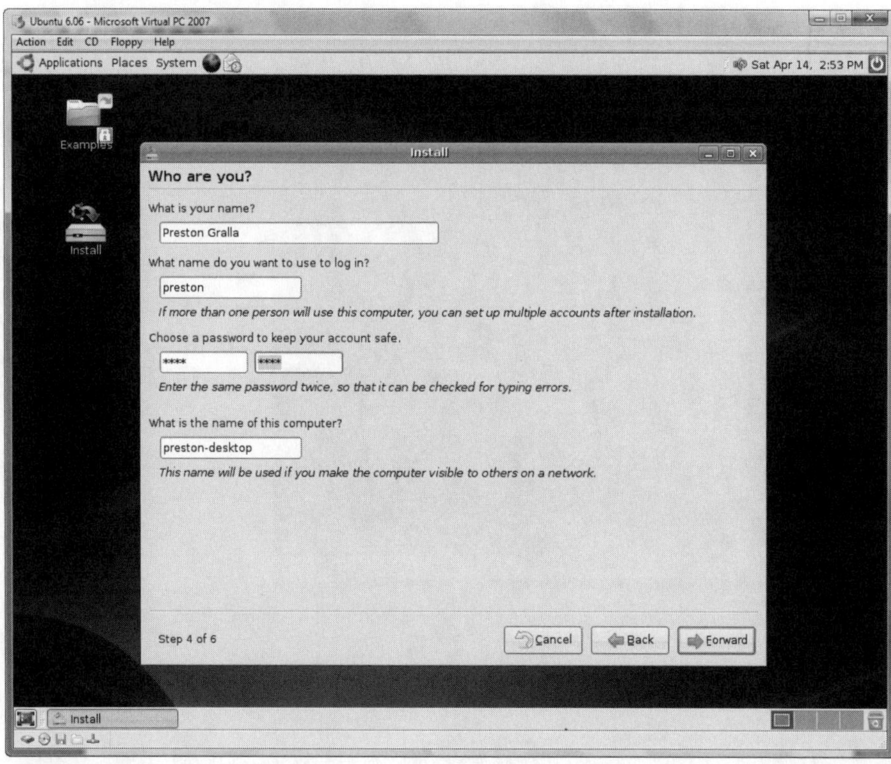

Figure 2-49.
Never fear—you're erasing or partitioning your virtual hard disk, not the real thing

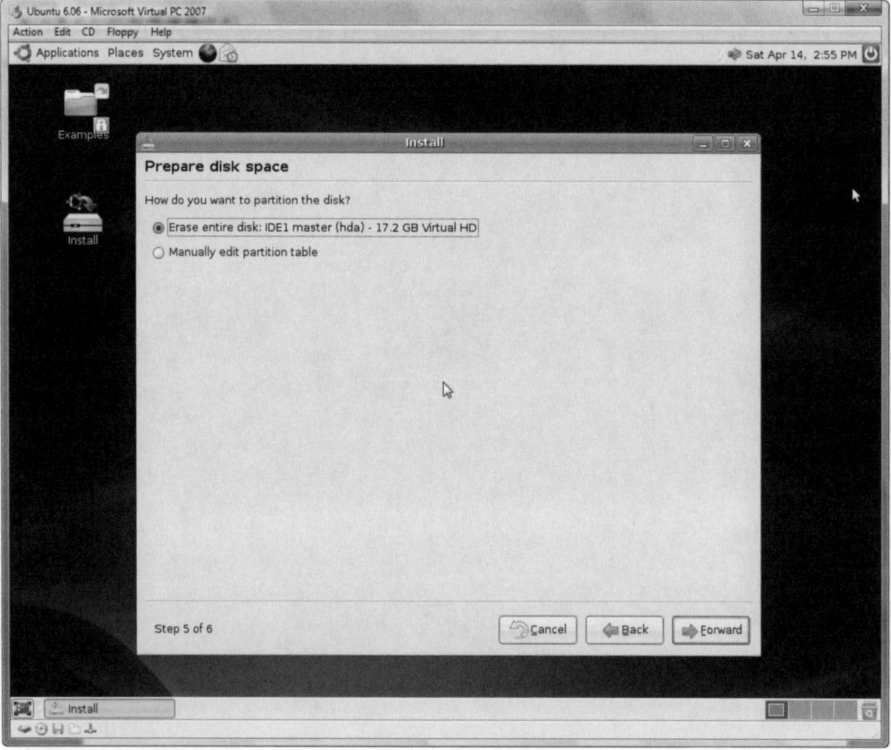

Figure 2-50.
Ubuntu is ready to go!

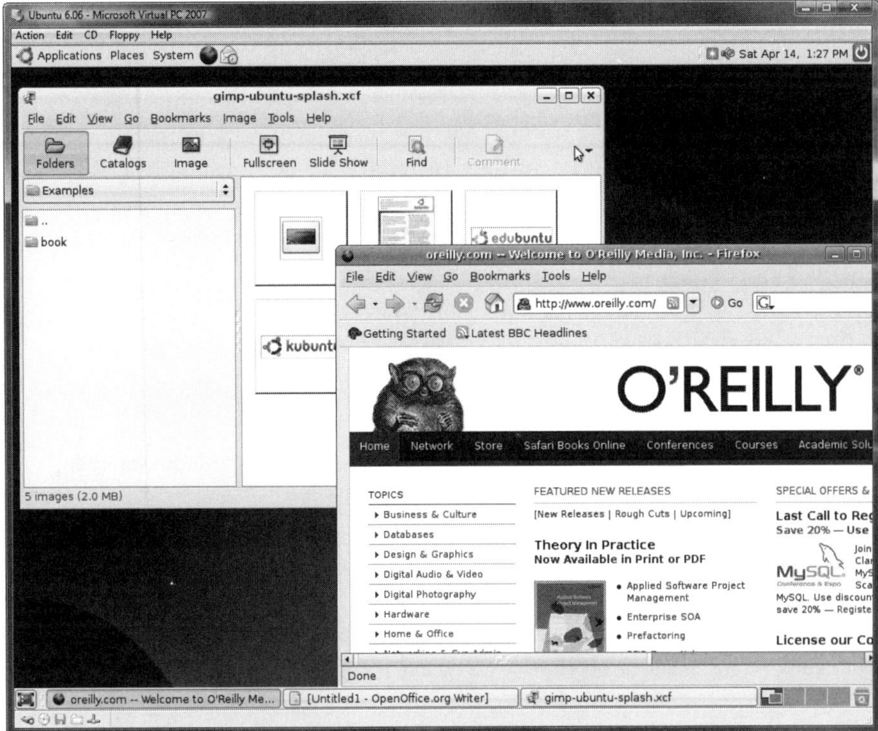

HACK 31: Run Mac OS X on Windows Vista

V In this hack, you will learn how to install the PowerPC version of Mac OS X on your Windows Vista PC, using PearPC.

For quite a long time, many Windows users have been clamoring for the opportunity to run the Mac OS X operating system on their Windows PCs. Because Mac OS X was designed to run on a different CPU architecture (PowerPC), running Mac OS X directly on Intel's CPU did not work. It wasn't until recently that PC users saw a ray of hope, when Apple announced that it was moving to Intel's CPU architecture and would port Mac OS X to run natively on Intel's x86 CPU architecture. However, the joy was short-lived, as Mac OS X can still run properly only on Apple's customized hardware, not commodity PCs that run Windows.

A quick and easy way of running Mac OS X on your current PC hardware is to run it in an emulator capable of emulating the PowerPC CPU architecture. While popular virtualization software programs such as Virtual PC and VMware have been on the market for a long time, none support Mac OS X. Fortunately, an Open Source project, PearPC, makes it possible to run Mac OS X on Windows.

PearPC is an architecture-independent PowerPC platform emulator. It is released under the General Public License (GPL), a free-use free software license. PearPC emulates the PowerPC architecture by using a JIT (Just-in-Time) emulator to dynamically translate PowerPC code into x86 code.

Installing Mac OS X on Windows Vista

To run Mac OS X on your Windows Vista PC, you need a reasonably fast machine, because Mac OS X will be running under emulation, and there is a performance penalty compared to running it natively on a Mac.

 The steps for installing Mac OS X on Windows Vista are largely the same for installing it on Windows XP, so you can use this hack as the basis for installing it on Windows XP as well.

My test system used for this hack comprises the following:

- Intel Pentium D 830 Dual Core Processor 3GHz
- 250 GB SATA II HDD (7200 RPM)
- 2 GB Memory
- NVIDIA GeForce 6200 TurboCache

Downloading PearPC

The first step to getting Mac OS X running is to download the PowerPC Architecture Emulator (PearPC) from pearpc.sourceforge.net/downloads.html. The current version number at this time of writing is 0.4. Download the *pearpc-0.4-win32-jitc.zip* file and extract it to a folder—say, *C:\PPC*.

 Throughout this hack, I use the working directory of *C:\PPC* for all PearPC-related activities.

The important files to note in the *C:\PPC* folder are *ppc.exe* (which is the PearPC emulator) and *ppccfg.example* (which contains the sample configuration to start PearPC).

Preparing the Mac OS X Installation Disk

Once PearPC has been downloaded and extracted, get out your Mac OS X installation disk. In this hack, I use Mac OS X v10.4 Tiger. If you have an older version of Mac OS X, such as v10.3 Panther, the installation instructions should still work.

Create ISO Images for Mac OS X Installation DVD

You are now ready to extract the content of the installation DVD into an *.iso* image. For this, you can use your favorite disk-imaging application, such as Nero. I used UltraISO from www.ezbsystems.com/ultraiso (from where you can obtain a free trial of the software).

Once UltraISO is downloaded and installed, launch UltraISO from Start→Programs→UltraISO→UltraISO. Go to the Tools menu, select Make CD/DVD Image... (see Figure 2-51).

In the Make CD/DVD Image dialog, select the drive containing the Mac OS X installation DVD and check the Standard ISO (.ISO) option (see Figure 2-52). Specify the output filename of the *.iso* image and click Make to start the extraction process. In my case, I extracted the *.iso* image to *C:\PPC* and named it *Mac OS X Install DVD.iso*.

Once the extraction is complete, you should now see the *.iso* image in the *C:\PPC* folder.

Preparing the Hard Disk Image File

Now that the Mac OS X Installation DVD ISO image is created, you should prepare a hard disk image to use for your installation. This image represents the hard disk on which you will install Mac OS X. The challenge in this step is that although it is easy to create a new disk image to use for Mac OS X, you must format it before it can be used. Thus, unless you already have a Mac, you will not be able to create this image easily.

Fortunately, there are some ready-made disk images that you can use. If you are installing Mac OS X 10.3 Panther, you can download a 6 GB disk image from os-emulation.net/pearpc/web/downloads/6gb.exe—this is not an image containing the OS, but rather a direct link to an empty disk image that has been formatted for Mac OS X use. If you are installing Mac OS X 10.4 Tiger, you can download a 6 GB disk image from os-emulation.net/pearpc/web/downloads/tiger.exe. These ready-made disk images are self-extracting .exe files, and when executed, they extract into a 6 GB disk image. Hence, make sure you have the necessary disk space before extracting them.

Figure 2-51.
Using UltraISO to make disk images

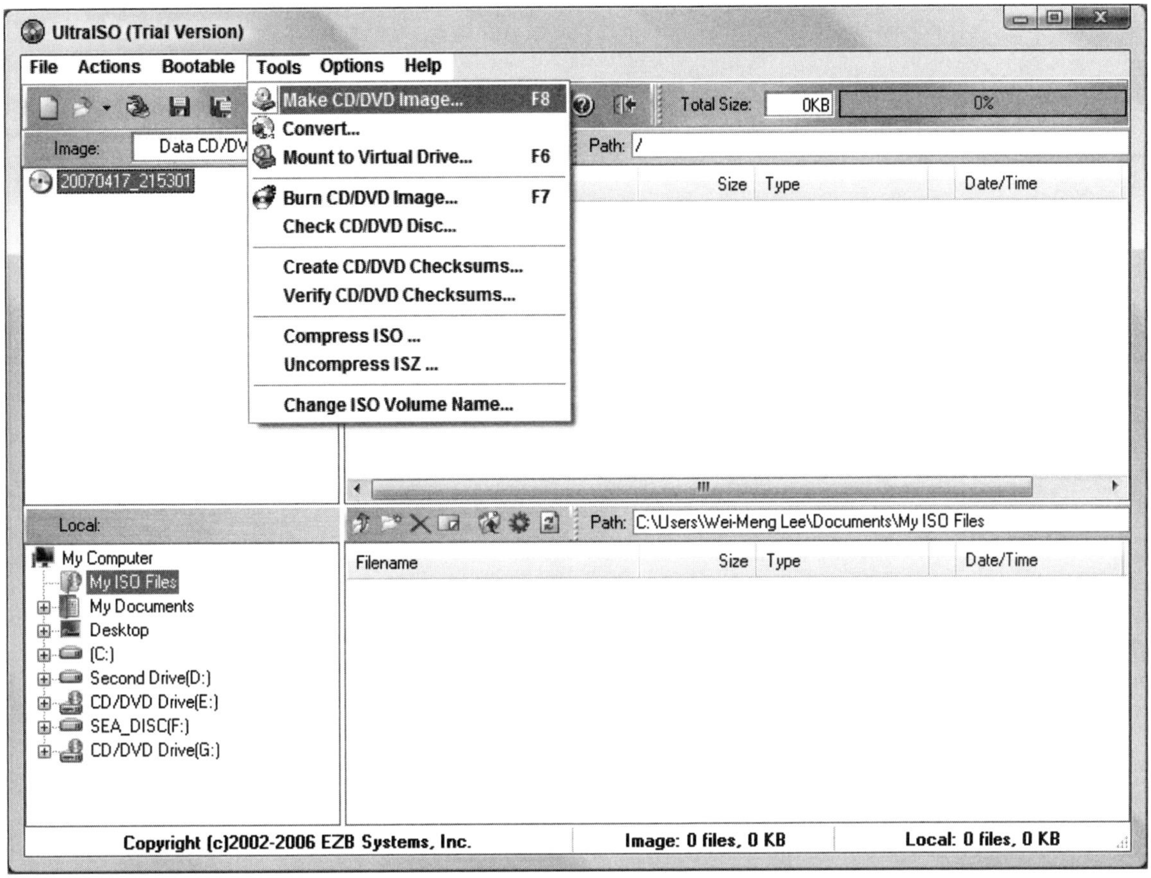

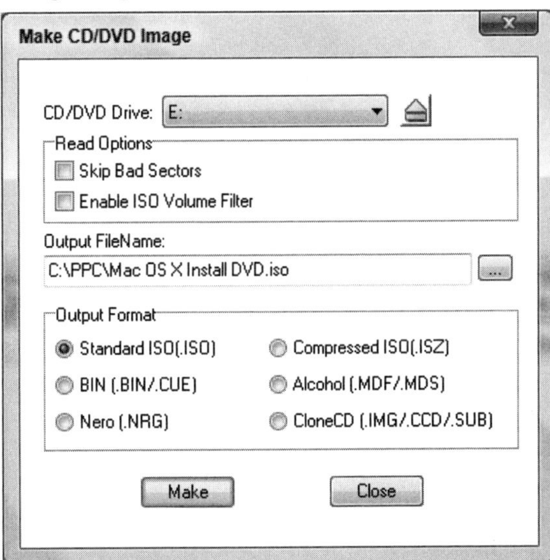

Figure 2-52.
Making an image of the installation disk

I am installing Mac OS X v10.4 Tiger, so I downloaded the *tiger.exe* file and saved it to *C:\PPC*. Once your download is complete, double-click on *tiger.exe* and start the image-expansion process. You will see a prompt showing you that that image will be extracted to *C:\pearpc*. However, you have a chance to change the output directory in the next screen. Click OK.

In the next screen, you can specify the folder where to store the expanded image. Change it to *C:\PPC* and click Extract. When the expansion is done, the *C:\PPC* directory will now contain the *tiger.img* image.

Modifying the Configuration File

You are now almost ready to start the installation process. But before you do that, you need to modify the configuration file.

Locate the *ppccfg.example* configuration file in the *C:\PPC folder*. This configuration file contains sample settings for PearPC to launch Mac OS X. Open it using WordPad (not Notepad).

Locate the settings below and change their values as shown in bold:

```
pci_ide0_master_installed = 1
pci_ide0_master_image = "C:\PPC\tiger.img"

pci_ide0_slave_installed = 1
pci_ide0_slave_image = "C:\PPC\Mac OS X Install DVD.iso"
pci_ide0_slave_type = "cdrom"
```

Basically, you are telling PearPC the location of your hard disk image and installation *.iso* image. Save the changes in WordPad.

Booting Up Mac OS X

You are now ready to set up Mac OS X. Go to the Command Prompt. Change to the *C:\PPC* directory and type the following command:

```
C:\PPC>ppc ppccfg.example
```

This command starts PearPC with the settings specified in the configuration file. You should see a PearPC 0.4 window appear, containing a series of text. After a while, you should see the boot-up screen of Mac OS X (see Figure 2-53).

Proceed as instructed on the screen. The installation can take quite a while (especially if you have a slow machine), so be patient. When the installation is done, PearPC automatically closes.

Installing Mac OS X

You are now ready to boot up Mac OS X for the first time. But before you do that, modify the configuration file (*ppccfg.example)* like so and disable the drive containing the *.iso* image:

```
pci_ide0_slave_installed = 0
```

Back on the command line, start PearPC again:

```
C:\PPC>ppc ppccfg.example
```

If the previous installation process goes without a hitch, you should see the welcome screen, as shown in Figure 2-54. Proceed with the configuration for first-time use.

Figure 2-53.
Mac OS X booting up

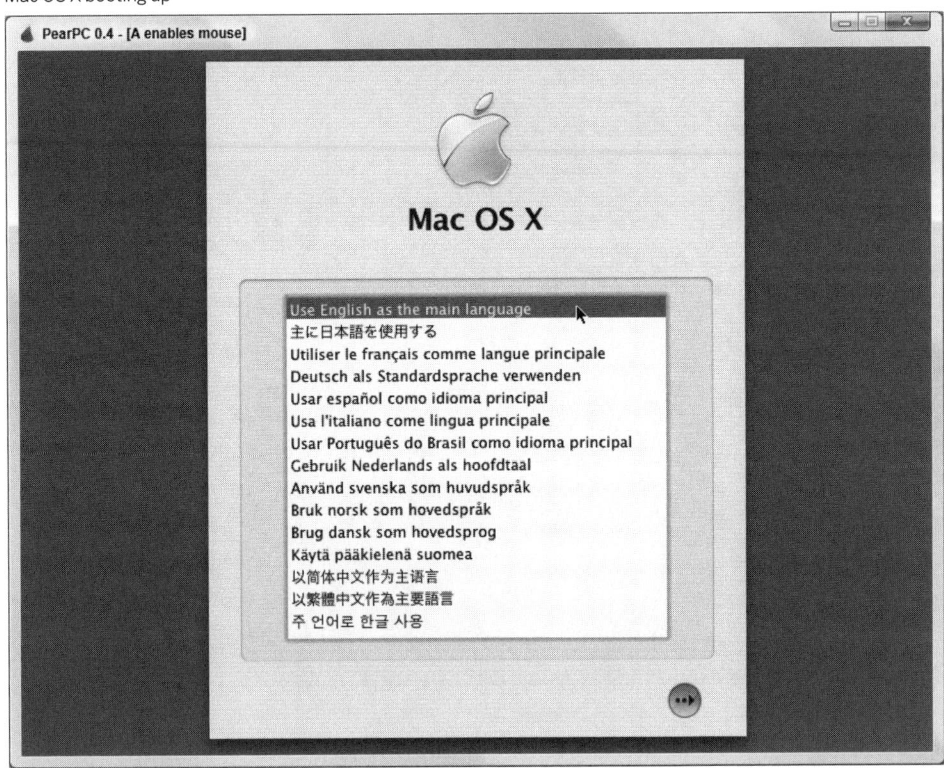

Figure 2-54.
Configuring Mac OS X

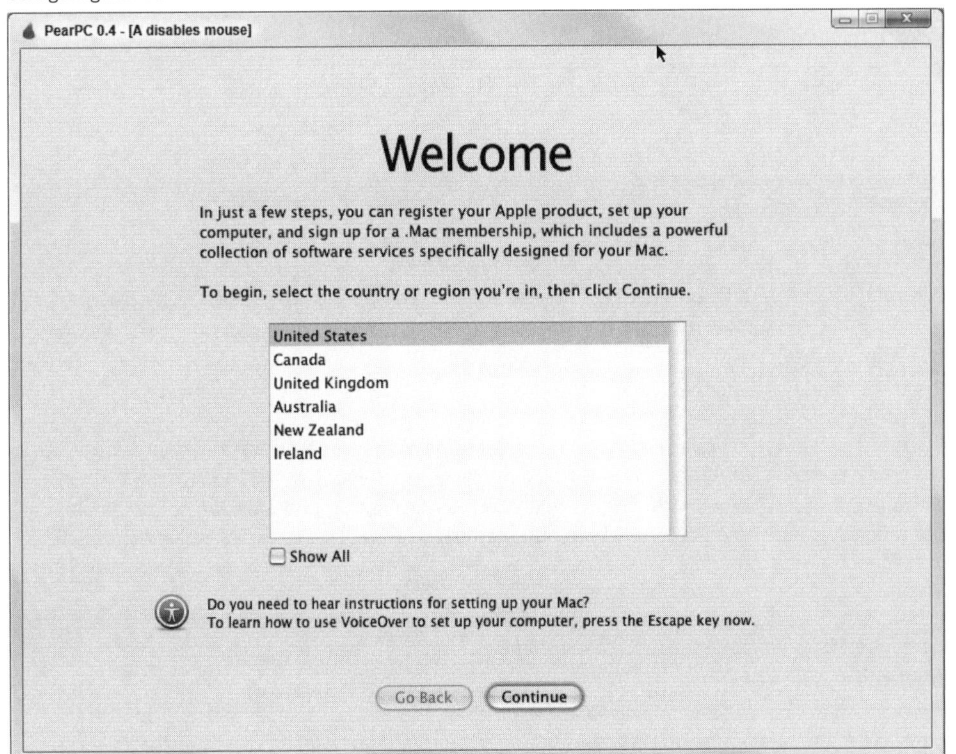

Figure 2-55.
Mac OS X running inside Windows Vista

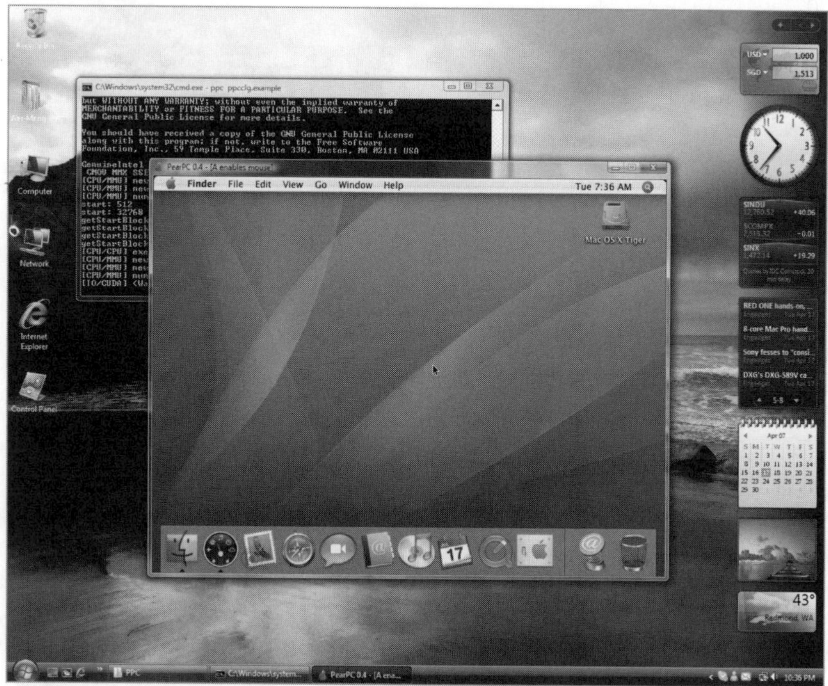

When the configuration is done, you should now have a functional Mac OS X! Figure 2-55 shows the glory and the proof that Mac OS X works with PearPC in Windows Vista. Have fun!

See Also

- *Running Mac OS X on Windows*, www.oreilly.com/catalog/runningmacpc/.

— Wei-Meng Lee

HACK 32: Go Retro: Run Windows 3.11 in Windows Vista

V Miss the good old DOS and Windows 3.11 days? If for some reason you want to relive the old memories of yesteryear, this hack shows you how you can get Windows 3.11 alive and kicking in Windows Vista.

Microsoft Windows has gone through a few generations of changes, starting from Windows 1.0 to the current Windows Vista. It is unlikely that you will reformat your hard disk to install the older OSes, but improvements in virtualization technologies have made it possible for you to run older operating systems in the comfort of your current system. You can now run OSes like Windows 95 and Windows 3.11 in Windows Vista. In this hack, I will show you how you can install Windows 3.11 on Vista.

Installing Virtual PC

To run Windows 3.11 in Vista, you can use a virtual machine such as Virtual PC or VMware. In this hack, I demonstrate how to do it using Microsoft Virtual PC. Microsoft has made Virtual PC 2007 free of charge to download. Download Virtual PC from www.microsoft.com/windows/products/

winfamily/virtualpc/default.mspx. If the location has changed, perform a search for "Download Virtual PC 2007" and you will be able to locate the URL to download it.

Once Virtual PC 2007 is downloaded and installed, launch it from the Start Menu. To get started, create a new virtual machine. You'll create one specifically for use with Windows 3.11. Click on the New... button and the New Virtual Machine Wizard will launch (see Figure 2-56). Click Next to proceed.

In the Options dialog, choose "Create a virtual machine" and click Next. Specify a name and location for the virtual machine. Type in "Windows 3.11" and click Next. Under the operating system drop-down list, use the default of "Other" and click Next. Use the recommended amount of RAM (128 MB) and click Next. Create a new virtual hard disk by selecting "A new virtual hard disk" and click Next. Use the default location and filename for the new virtual hard disk and click Next. That's it! Click Finish to complete the virtual machine creation step.

The steps for installing Windows 3.11 on Vista are largely the same for installing it on Windows XP, so you can follow these instructions to install it on Windows XP.

Obtaining DOS

Now that your virtual machine is created, you need to boot it up. Unlike Windows 95, Windows XP, and Vista, Windows 3.11 is not an operating system in itself. It runs on top of DOS, and thus you need to install DOS on the virtual machine before you can install Windows 3.11.

Instead of searching high and low for MS DOS (which may not be available for sale off the shelf), download a free, legal, DOS-compatible operating system called FreeDOS (www.freedos.org/freedos/files/). You can download an ISO image of FreeDOS from www.ibiblio.org/pub/micro/pc-stuff/freedos/files/distributions/1.0/ (select *fdbasecd.iso*).

Figure 2-56.
Creating a new virtual machine in Virtual PC 2007

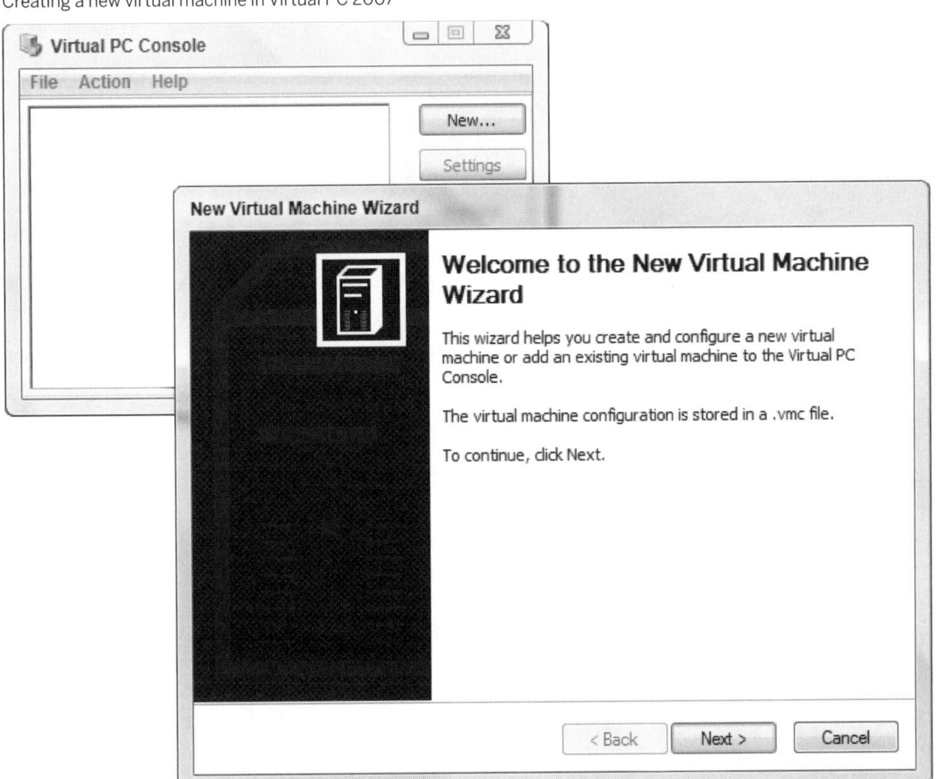

Obtaining Windows 3.11

Microsoft no longer sells Windows 3.11, so you'll probably need to get your copy of Windows 3.11 from eBay. A quick search showed several copies being sold, along with DOS, for under $30.

If you are one of the lucky ones with original installation disks (3.5-inch floppy disks) and the drive to use them in, your life is a little easier. MSDN subscribers are also in luck. You can download Windows 3.11 from the MSDN subscribers' download site.

In any case, you will need a disk tool to create the images for Windows 3.11 for use in Virtual PC 2007. I used UltraISO, as seen in a previous hack.

 If you're looking for a free tool for creating *.iso* images, try ImgBurn (www.imgburn.com).

Windows 3.11 on Floppy Disks

If you have Windows 3.11 on floppy disks, you would need to save all the files on the disks as disk images so that Virtual PC can read from them. With UltraISO downloaded and installed, launch UltraISO from Start→Programs→UltraISO→UltraISO.

Insert the first disk of the Windows 3.11 installation disks into your floppy disk drive, and in UltraISO, click on the Bootable menu item and select Make Floppy Image... (see Figure 2-57). You will be asked to specify a name for the image. Repeat this step for all the installation disks.

 Most newer PCs today do not come with floppy disk drives. If yours doesn't have one, you can buy a clever USB-based floppy disk drive. Plug it into your USB port, and you can use floppy disks. Plenty are available on eBay for under $15, and they're available on many other sites as well.

Windows 3.11 in a Directory

To test this hack out, I downloaded Windows 3.11 from MSDN. It's available as a single executable file that extracts all the necessary files into a folder. Assuming that all the files are now extracted to the *C:\Users\Wei-Meng Lee\Downloads\Win3.11* folder, launch UltraISO and drag all the files and drop it onto it (see Figure 2-58).

In UltraISO, click File→Save As... and enter a name for the ISO image. I named the file *Windows 3.11.iso* (for simplicity, I save it to the Desktop). This will create an ISO image containing all the Windows 3.11 installation files.

Installing DOS

Now that both the installation images for DOS and Windows 3.11 are ready, let's install FreeDOS onto the newly created virtual machine. Double-click on the Windows 3.11 virtual machine in Virtual PC to launch the virtual machine (see Figure 2-59).

To install FreeDOS, you need to capture the FreeDOS ISO image so that the virtual machine can boot from it. To do so, select CD→Capture ISO Image.... Select *fdbasecd.iso* and click Open.

If FreeDOS boots correctly, you should see the screen shown in Figure 2-60.

Next, type "1" and press Enter to boot FreeDOS from the ISO image. Select "1. Install to harddisk using FreeDOS SETUP (default)" and press Enter. You will be asked to select a language and keyboard layout. Select English (US) and press Enter. Select "Prepare the harddisk for FreeDOS 1.0 Final by running XFDisk" and press Enter. In the XFDisk options dialog, press Enter. Under the Options menu, select New Partition and then select Primary Partition. Enter the maximum size: 1637, for the partition and press Enter. Press Enter to initialize the new partition. When asked if you want to initialize the whole partition, select No and press Enter. Press F3 to exit. You will be asked if you want to write the partition table to the hard disk now. Select YES and press Enter. Select YES to restart the virtual machine.

Figure 2-57.
Creating a floppy disk image for Windows 3.11 disk 1

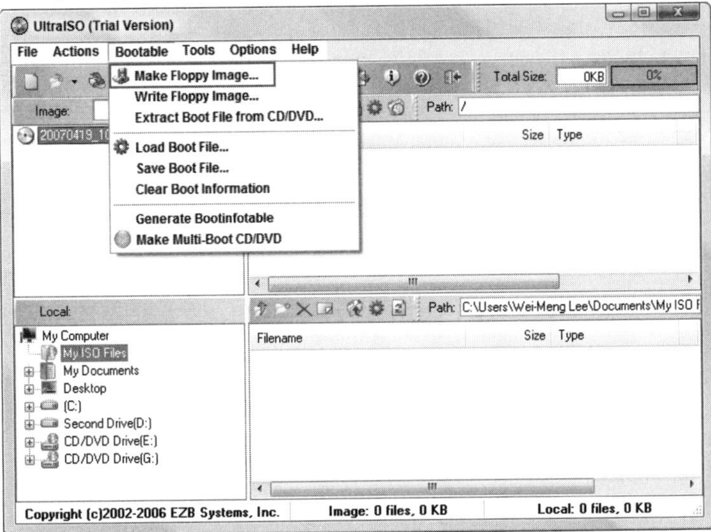

Figure 2-58.
Dragging and dropping the Windows 3.11 installation files onto UltraISO

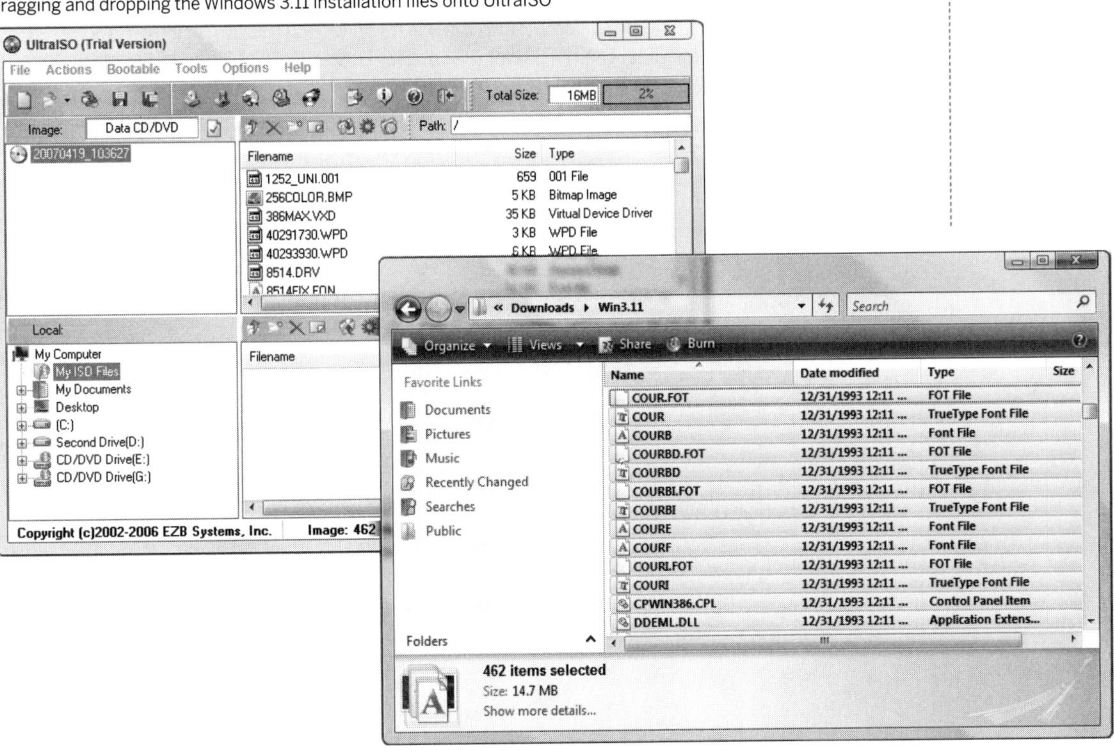

You have now partitioned your hard disk and your virtual machine will now be rebooted. In the boot up screen, type "1" to boot from the FreeDOS ISO image. Next, you'll format the newly created partition. Select "1. Install to hard disk using FreeDOS SETUP (default)" and press Enter. You will be asked to select a language and keyboard layout. Select English (US) and press Enter. In the next screen, when prompted to format your hard disk, select Yes. Select "Continue with FreeDOS installation" (see Figure 2-61) and press Enter.

Now select "Start installation of FreeDOS 1.0 Final." In the next couple of screens, select the default options by pressing the Enter key.

When done, you will be asked to reboot the virtual machine. In the boot-up screen, type "h" to boot from the hard disk. You will see three options to boot up (see Figure 2-62; the fourth option is not selectable). Select option 3 and press Enter.

If everything is installed property, you should now see the command prompt (see Figure 2-63). Congratulations—FreeDOS is now set up properly.

Installing Windows 3.11

With FreeDOS installed, you are now ready to install Windows 3.11. In Virtual PC, select CD→Capture ISO Image. You will now specify the Windows 3.11 ISO image that you have created earlier.

If you have created the disk images for the Windows 3.11 installation disk, select Floppy→Capture Floppy Disk Image.... In this hack, I am using the ISO image created for the Windows 3.11 files downloaded from MSDN.

In DOS mode, change the directory to D: and type "setup", like this:

```
C:\>d:
D:\>setup
```

You should now see the setup screen of Windows 3.11 (see Figure 2-64). Follow the steps outlined on the screen. When the installation completes, you will be asked to reboot. Click the Reboot button. After rebooting, be sure to select the third boot up option: "Load FreeDOS including HIMEM XMS-memory driver."

At the C:\ prompt, type `win /S` to start Windows 3.11 in standard mode.

```
C:\>win /S
```

Figure 2-65 shows Windows 3.11 in action!

For more information on running Windows 3.11 on FreeDOS, see wiki.fdos.org/Main/Windows.

See Also

- "Instant Linux" **[Hack #33]**

— Wei-Meng Lee

Figure 2-59.
Launching the newly created virtual machine

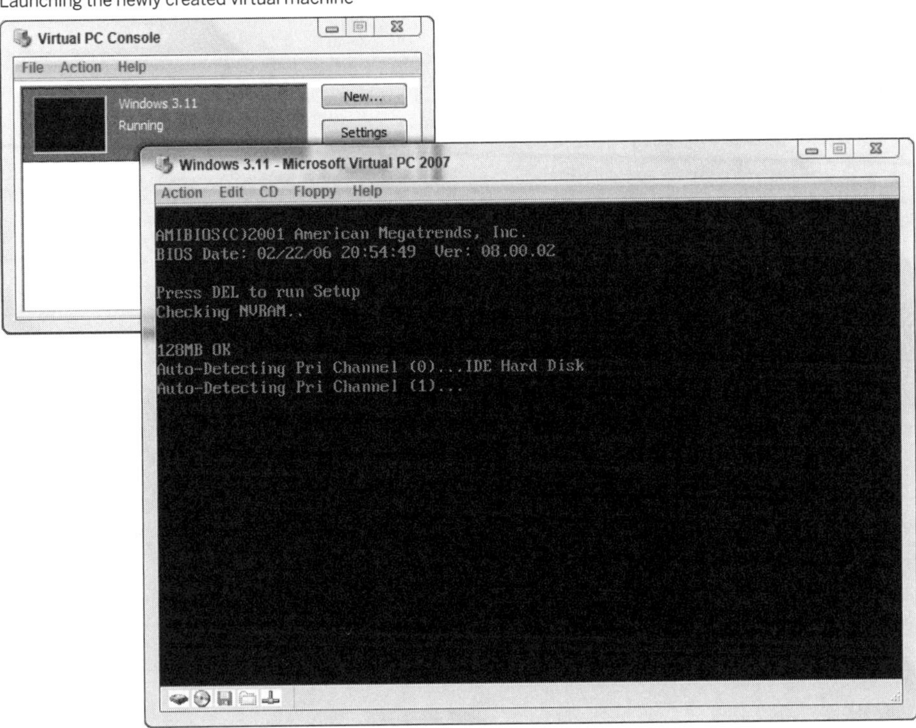

Figure 2-60.
Booting FreeDOS for the first time

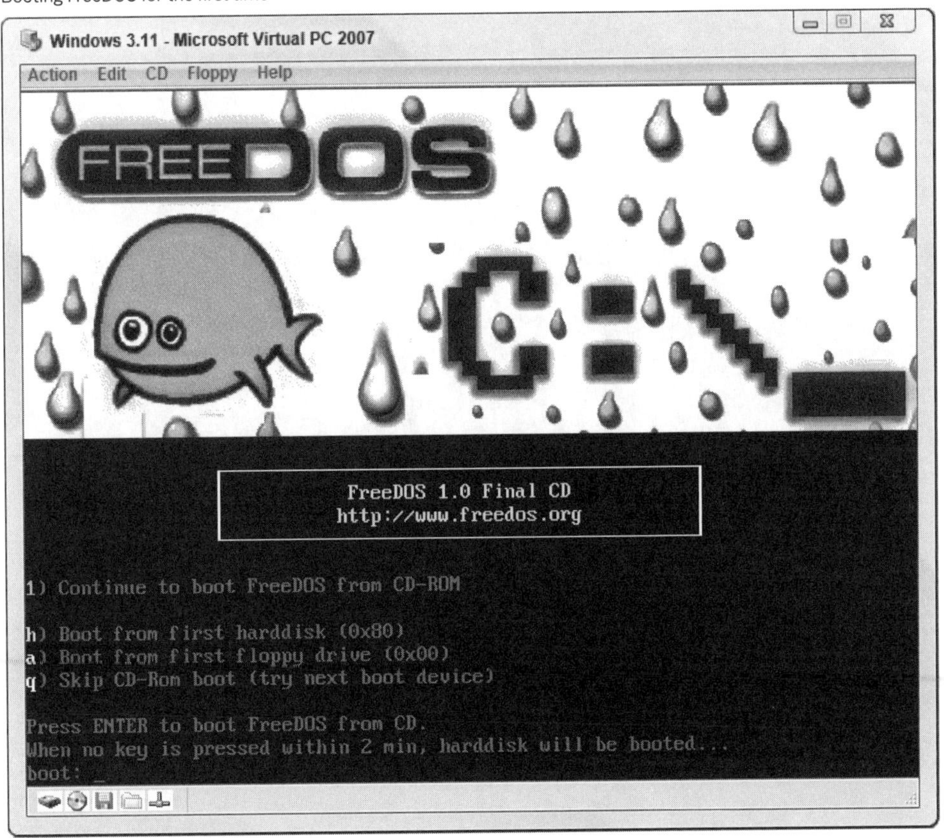

Figure 2-61.
Installing FreeDOS onto the hard disk

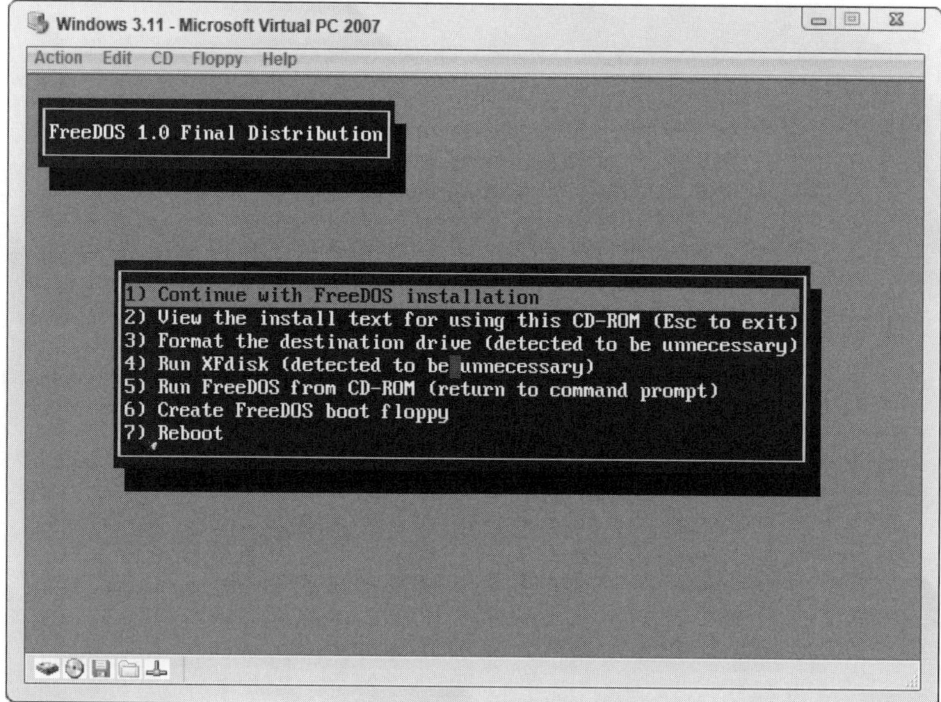

Figure 2-62.
FreeDOS boot-up options

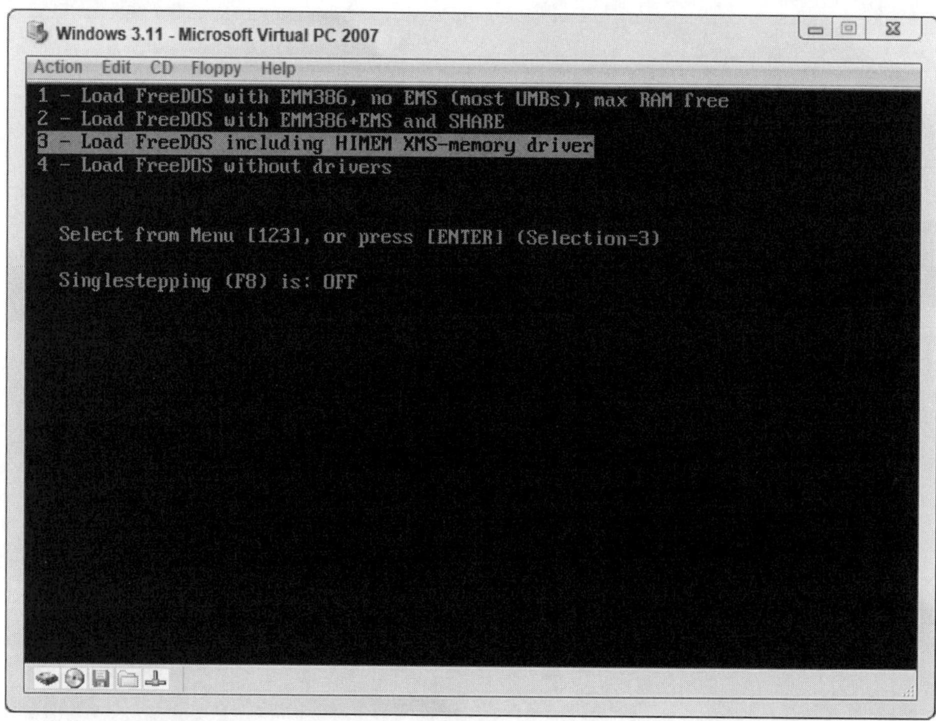

Figure 2-63.
Booting into FreeDOS

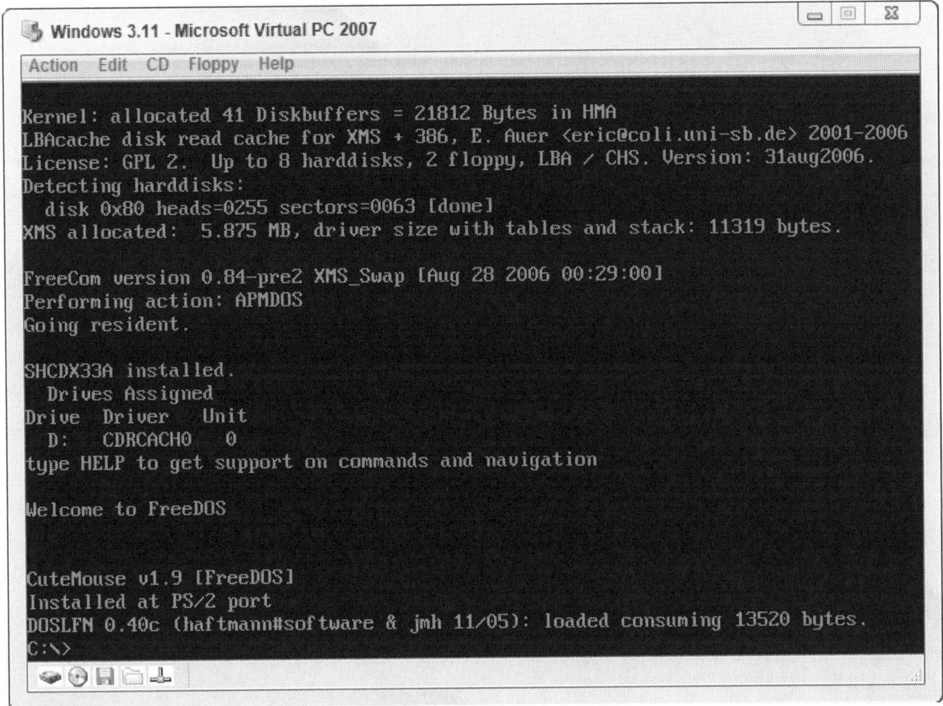

Figure 2-64.
Setting up Windows 3.11

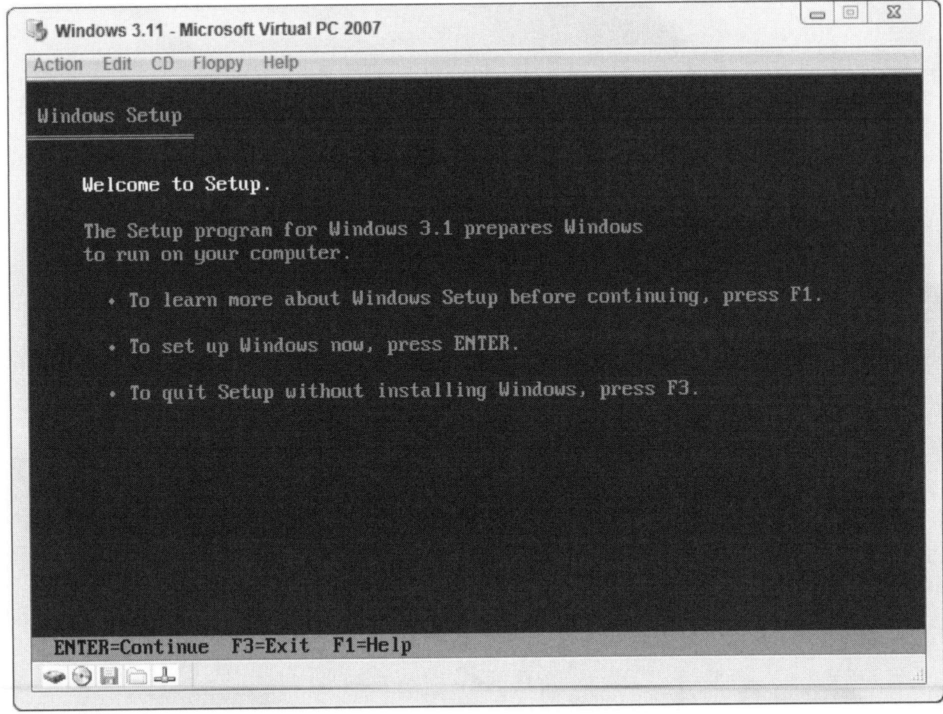

Figure 2-65.
Windows 3.11 in all its glory

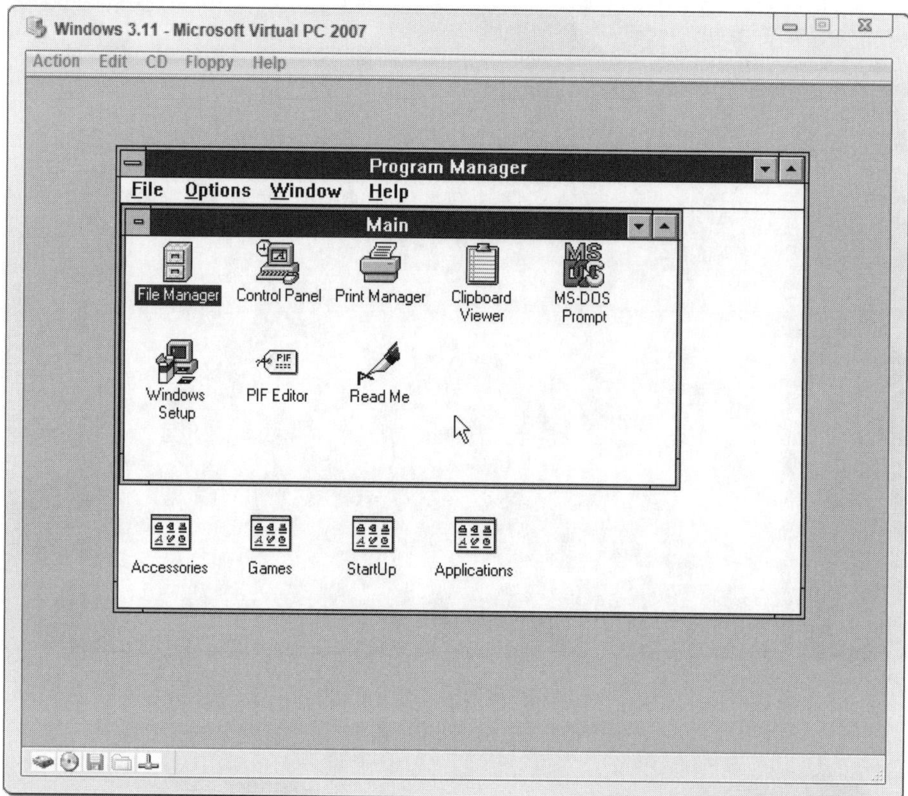

HACK 33: Instant Linux

V XP Want to know what all the fuss is about when it comes to Linux? Here's an easy way to try it out and use it, without installing software on your PC; it runs straight from a CD or DVD.

The Linux operating system inspires intense devotion among its adherents. There's good reason for that: it's fast, it's free, it hasn't been subject to the same kinds of security woes that bedevil Windows computers, and it can be just plain fun.

Of course, it can be just plain maddening as well. And the thought of installing an entirely new operating system alongside Windows or reformatting your hard disk . . . let's just say that unless you really know you want to use Linux, you probably don't want to go there.

But there's a way to get instant Linux: use the free software called Knoppix. It runs straight from a CD or DVD, so you don't need to do any installation at all. Just boot your computer from the disc, and voilà: instant Linux.

If you want to know more about Knoppix, such as how to use it to run Linux and make it easier to repair and recover your computer when it has problems, get a copy of Knoppix Hacks, 2nd Edition, by Kyle Rankin (O'Reilly), from which this hack is excerpted.

Download Knoppix

To obtain the latest version of Knoppix, download the CD or DVD image from one of Knoppix's mirrors or order a disk copy. If you have an unmetered broadband Internet connection and a CD-

R/RW or DVD-R/RW drive, download the CD or DVD image; it's the best way to get Knoppix. A collection of mirrors listed at www.knopper.net/knoppix-mirrors/index-en.html provides images in ISO format over http, ftp, or rsync. If you use BitTorrent (a peer-to-peer file-sharing application designed for large files), you can use the Knoppix torrent link on this page. When you click on a mirror you are taken to a licensing agreement page. Have your lawyer read through the software license (your lawyer reviews all of your software licenses before you accept them, right?), click Accept to proceed, and then choose a file from the list that is presented.

If you don't have an unmetered broadband Internet connection, or you don't have a CD or DVD writer, or you just don't want to bother with downloading and burning a disc, you can receive a Knoppix CD or DVD through the mail from a number of third-party vendors. There is a list of vendors to choose from at www.knopper.net/knoppix-vendors/index-en.html. These vendors are unaffiliated with the Knoppix project itself, and also offer other Linux distributions on CD and DVD. When ordering, make sure that the version the vendor is offering is the latest version by comparing its release date with the latest release on one of the Knoppix mirrors. You can purchase a Knoppix CD for $1.50 or a DVD for $5 plus shipping, which is a small price to pay if you want to avoid the hassle of downloading and burning a disc.

In addition to the latest version of Knoppix, most mirrors host a few past images along with their MD5sum, which you can use to verify that the file downloaded correctly and is an exact copy of the original file. An *MD5sum* is a checksum created from a large stream of data using the MD5 algorithm and is often used to verify that large files downloaded correctly. Practically speaking, an MD5sum-generating program takes your Knoppix ISO file and creates a fingerprint that only that specific file is capable of making. Changing even a single bit affects the MD5sum; therefore, if any error occurs during the download process, the generated sum is different from the one listed on the mirror. If both MD5sums match, the file you have is exactly like the file on the mirror.

There are a number of utilities to create an MD5sum under Windows. One such tool can be found at www.md5summer.org. Once you install this program, run it, navigate to the Knoppix ISO you wish to verify, and click OK. On your Linux machine, you will probably find that the `md5sum` utility is already installed. (Mac OS X has a similar utility, `md5`, that will print out the MD5sum so you can compare it to what's in the *.md5* file.) You'll need to install it, if it is not. Once `md5sum` is installed, make sure that the *.md5* file from the mirror is in the same directory as the image, and then type:

```
$ md5sum -cv KNOPPIX_V5.1.1CD-2007-01-04-EN.iso.md5

KNOPPIX_V5.1.1CD-2007-01-04-EN.iso OK
$
```

If the MD5sums match, you are dropped back to a prompt; otherwise, you receive the following error:

```
$ md5sum -cv KNOPPIX_ V5.1.1CD-2007-01-04-EN.iso.md5

KNOPPIX_V5.1.1CD-2007-01-04-EN.iso FAILED
md5sum: 1 of 1 file(s) failed MD5 check
$
```

You can also generate an MD5sum from the command line by typing:

```
$ md5sum KNOPPIX_V5.1.1CD-2007-01-04-EN.iso
379e2f9712834c8cef3efa6912f30755  KNOPPIX_V5.1.1CD-2007-01-04-EN.iso
```

Compare the MD5sum you generate to the corresponding *.md5* file from the mirror. If both match, you have a complete ISO and are ready to burn a disc.

When trying to decide which CD to choose, it helps to understand the scheme Knoppix uses for naming CD images. Here is an example ISO filename:

```
KNOPPIX_V5.1.1CD-2007-01-04-EN.iso
```

Deciphering the filename isn't tricky, and can be quite informative. In the aforementioned example, *KNOPPIX* is followed by the current version—in this case *5.1.1*. After that is *CD* or *DVD*, denoting whether this is the CD or DVD release. Following the version and type is a date stamp, which indicates the CD image's release date; in this example, the CD was released on January 04, 2007. These date stamps indicate the incremental version mentioned earlier. After the date stamp, there is a language code, in this case EN for English. Knoppix is a German project, and although the default language can be changed with cheat codes at boot time, the Knoppix project releases both German and English CDs to save English-speaking users from having to enter a language code at every boot. English-speaking users should download images with the EN language code, and German-speaking users should download images with the DE language code. Everyone else can choose either image and type a language code at boot time.

Select the latest version of Knoppix by clicking on the filename. The 700 MB file can take anywhere from a few hours to a day to download, depending on the speed of your Internet connection and the current load on the selected mirror. The 4 GB DVD image obviously takes substantially longer and is recommended only for high-speed Internet connections.

You can burn the Knoppix ISO to a CD or DVD using your favorite disc-burning software. It is important that you select the "burn image" or equivalent option in your disc-burning software. Do not select the option to burn a data CD or DVD; you will end up with a CD or DVD containing a single ISO file, which will not boot.

Boot Knoppix from a CD

For some computers, booting Knoppix is as simple as putting the CD in the CD-ROM drive or the DVD in the DVD-ROM drive and restarting the computer. For some computers, however, booting Knoppix might require changing the boot order in the BIOS. The BIOS is the screen that appears when you first boot a machine, and it usually lists the amount of RAM and the hard drives it detects. Older systems that don't support booting from a CD require that you boot from a floppy.

If your computer supports booting from a CD-ROM or DVD-ROM, but won't boot Knoppix by default, your problem is probably the system boot order setting in the BIOS. To change the boot order and save it, you must enter the BIOS setup, which you can do at boot time by pressing a special key. Some BIOSes tell you at boot time which key to press to change BIOS settings; the common ones are Esc, F2, and Del.

Once in the BIOS, find the section that changes boot device order. On some BIOSes, this setting is changed by selecting a tab along the top labeled Boot, and on others the option may be named "Boot device order" or something similar. Once you have found this setting, move the CD-ROM or DVD-ROM device so that it is listed before any hard drives. If you can't find or change this option, or you need other information specific to you system, refer to the BIOS manual that should have come with your computer or motherboard (you can often find out the BIOS key by searching Google for your computer model and the word "BIOS"). Once you have changed the boot device order, save your settings (doing this should also reboot the computer), and after your system boots and detects the Knoppix disc, you will be placed at the Knoppix boot prompt.

Boot Knoppix from a Floppy

Some older computers do not support booting directly from a CD-ROM. For these computers, you must first create a boot floppy that enables the system to boot off of the Knoppix disc. With older versions of Knoppix, there were tools available to allow you to create a boot floppy, but unfortunately the Linux kernel has gotten so large that it won't all fit on a single floppy. Although there are still ways to split the kernel across floppy disks, an easier approach is to use the Smart Boot Manager (SBM), a tool that creates a boot floppy that can boot just about any optical disc. To create an SBM boot floppy, go to their download page at btmgr.sf.net/download.html and download either the Binary Linux *sbminst* file to create the floppy from a Linux system, or the Binary DOS *sbminst.exe* file to create it from Windows.

To create an SBM floppy under Linux, insert a blank floppy into the drive and then run the following commands:

```
$ chmod a+x /path/to/sbminst
$ /path/to/sbminst -d /dev/fd0
```

Change */path/to/smbinst* and */dev/fd0* to reflect where you downloaded *sbminst* and your floppy device, respectively. Note that you may have to run *sbminst* as the root user if your regular account does not have permission to write to the floppy device.

To create an SBM floppy under Windows, insert a blank floppy into the drive, click Start→Run (under Vista, you can type this into the search field and press Return; you may need to use an Administrator Command Prompt: press Ctrl-Shift-Return instead of Return to get one) and run cmd.exe, and then, in the Command Prompt window that opens, type:

```
sbminst -d 0
```

With the floppy disk created and still inserted into the floppy drive, reboot the machine and boot off of the floppy. In the GUI that appears, you will see a number of options and devices listed. Use the arrow keys to move down to the CDROM device and hit Enter to boot the Knoppix CD.

The Knoppix Boot Prompt

Once you have booted from either a CD, DVD, or a floppy, you are presented with the Knoppix boot screen, as shown in Figure 2-66.

To boot directly into Knoppix, either hit Return or wait a few seconds, and Knoppix starts the boot process. At this boot prompt, you can enter special Knoppix cheat codes (see www.knoppix.net/wiki/Cheat_Codes) to control the boot process. Press F2 or F3 at this prompt to display some of the cheat codes.

As Knoppix boots, it displays colorful output while it detects your hardware. Once it has detected and set up your hardware, it automatically launches into the desktop environment and finishes by opening a web browser showing Knoppix documentation. At this point, you can launch programs, browse the Web, and play games. When you log out of the desktop environment, Knoppix shuts down and ejects the disc for you. If you use a floppy to boot Knoppix, remember to eject it—otherwise, the next time you start your computer, it will try to boot into Knoppix again, which you might not want automatically.

Explore the Desktop

Now you've booted from Knoppix. What's next? It's time to figure out what these windows, icons, and strange panels are for, and then to explore on your own. After you boot, you should be looking at the default Knoppix desktop, as shown in Figure 2-67.

The Desktop

Probably the first element that grabs your attention is the Konqueror web browser window that opens when K Desktop Environment (KDE) is started. KDE is one of the two most popular desktop environments for Linux (GNOME is the other). KDE's job is to manage your complete desktop environment. It draws your wallpaper, provides you with access to your programs through the menus and icons on the desktop, and manages the windows that appear once you launch an application. Once KDE starts, the first thing you see is the Knoppix help page. This web page contains information and help for Knoppix in many different languages, and includes links to sites to purchase Knoppix CD or DVDs, as well as get additional information. The help is available offline, which makes it very useful even when your network connection isn't working.

Figure 2-66.
The Knoppix boot screen

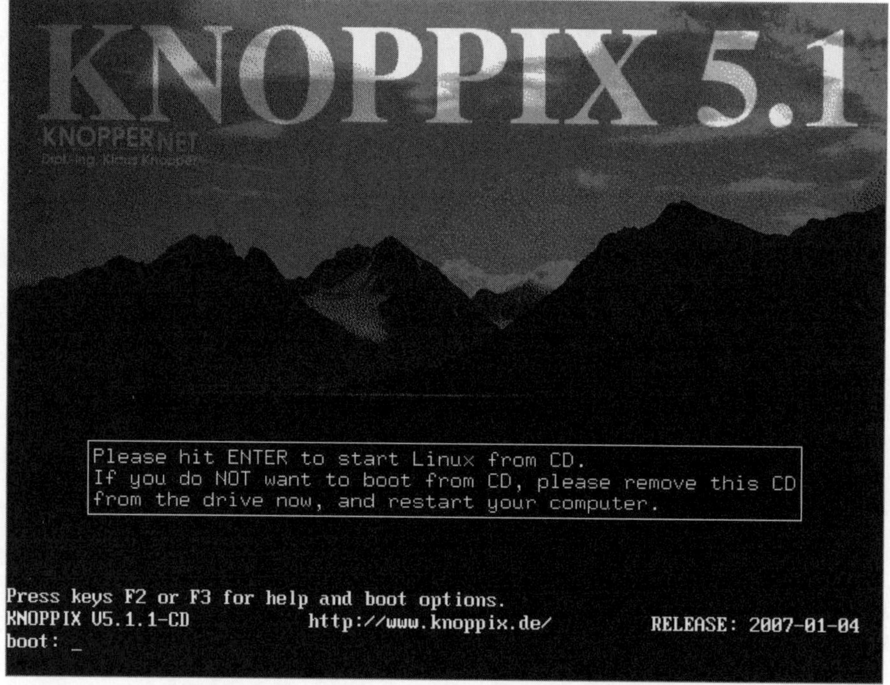

The desktop itself contains shortcuts to the hard drives, CD/DVD-ROMs, and floppy drives on your system (Figure 2-67). Click on any of the drive icons to automatically mount the drive as read-only and open up the mounted filesystem in Konqueror. Under KDE, the default is set to open a directory or launch a file with a single click, which might take some adjustment if you are used to double-clicking icons on the desktop. As Knoppix defaults to mounting these filesystems read-only, you can view and open the files you see, but you can't edit, delete, or move any of the files on these filesystems. You can, however, copy the files to your desktop and edit them from there. To make these filesystems writable, right-click on the drive icon and select "Change read/write mode." The right-click menu also gives you options to unmount and, if the device is a CD or DVD, to eject it.

The K Menu

The KDE panel spans the entire bottom portion of your screen. On the left of the panel is the K Menu, represented by the K Gear icon. Click on this icon to display the K Menu, which contains most of the graphical applications and some of the command-line applications within Knoppix organized into categories such as Editors, Games, Internet, and Settings (Figure 2-68). If you are new to KDE, Linux, or Knoppix, explore each of the categories in this menu and get acquainted with how all of the applications on the CD are organized.

At the top of the K Menu is a section reserved for recently used applications. As you run programs from within the K Menu, their icons show up in this section to provide quick access if you wish to run them again. Below this section is the applications section with submenus for each of the following items:

Development

Contains applications specifically useful for programming.

Editors

Lists a variety of text editors, including vim, Emacs, Joe, and many others to satisfy most—if not all—of the text-editor zealots out there (myself included).

Figure 2-67.
Desktop icons

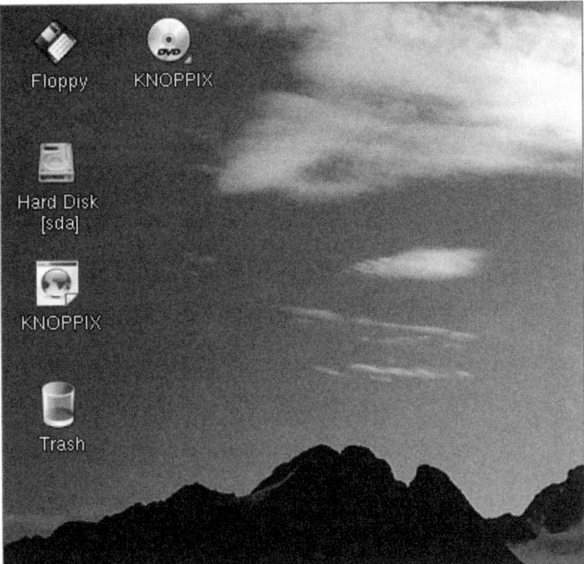

Emulators
Contains the different computer emulators included with Knoppix, such as Bochs. Though this would seem to be a fitting place for the program *Wine*, which allows you to run Windows programs on Linux, you won't find it here. That is because technically, Wine Is Not an Emulator.

Games
Who says Linux doesn't have games? Knoppix includes several, from arcade games to board games and card games. It is easy to get lost in this menu, only to emerge hours later—but don't spend *too* much time here, as there are more submenus to cover.

Graphics
Contains many different graphics applications, from painting programs to scanning programs and image manipulation applications (such as the GIMP).

Help
Provides some basic help applications that let you access info and manual pages for the different programs in Knoppix. For general desktop help, use the K Menu Help icon instead of the applications here.

Internet
Contains a slew of Internet applications, from web browsers to instant messengers and video conferencing applications.

KNOPPIX
Provides all of the Knoppix-specific applications that allow you to run particular configuration applications, start services, and special-purpose Knoppix utilities. This menu is also accessible from the penguin icon on the KDE panel.

Multimedia
Contains all of the multimedia applications—players for CDs, MP3s, and videos; mixers; and sound manipulation programs.

Office
Provides all of the applications useful in an office setting, including the complete OpenOffice.org suite.

Figure 2-68.
The K Menu

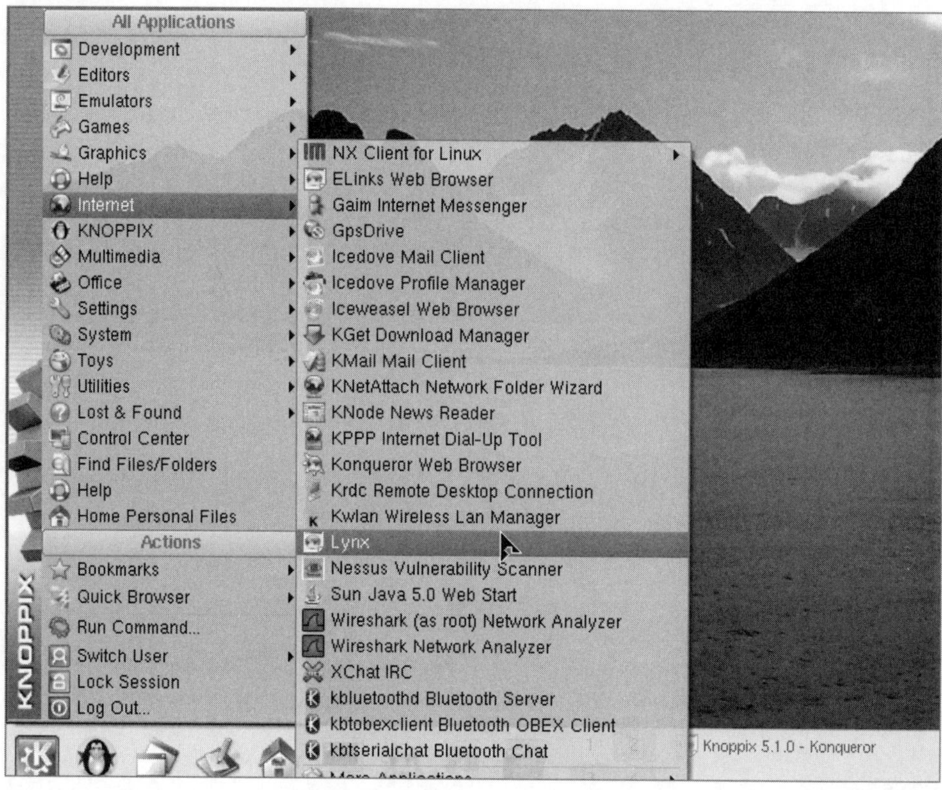

Settings

Not to be confused with the System or Utilities menus, this menu contains applications specifically for changing KDE settings.

System

Contains many useful applications for different aspects of system administration, including security scanners and backup utilities. Many of the programs in this menu require or give root privileges, so use these applications with caution.

Toys

Provides a few fun applications that don't really qualify as games, including the famous *xeyes* program, which creates two eyes on the desktop that follow the movement of your mouse.

Utilities

Displays utilities that aren't necessarily geared toward system administration, such as calculators and clocks.

After Utilities, instead of more application submenus, you find icons that run specific KDE applications:

Control Center

A quick shortcut to the KDE Control Center used to change KDE Settings.

Find Files

Runs the KDE *find* utility, a useful program for searching through your system for misplaced files.

Help
Launches the KDE Help Center, a useful program for getting KDE-specific help and asking questions such as "How do I resize my panel?"

Home Personal Files
Opens your home directory in the Konqueror file manager.

Below the application section of the K Menu is the actions section, which organizes a few special-purpose menus for KDE:

Bookmarks
Allows you to quickly access and edit bookmarks both in the Konqueror and Mozilla web browsers.

Quick Browser
Similar to the bookmark submenu, this provides quick access to your filesystem in a menu form. Click on one of the directory icons to launch Konqueror in that directory.

Run Command . . .
Opens a window that lets you type in a quick command you want to run without having to open a full shell. The keyboard shortcut Alt-F2 brings up the same dialog.

Switch User
KDE allows fast switching between different desktop users, but as there is only a single user on the default Knoppix desktop, there are no other users to switch to.

Lock Screen
Locks your screen, requiring a password to get back in. Because Knoppix doesn't use passwords by default, this feature has been disabled since Knoppix 3.2.

Log Out
Launches the log out dialog, which lets you log out of the desktop, reboot, or halt the machine.

The K Menu is worth investigating thoroughly. Browse through the different categories and try out the huge library of programs Knoppix includes. Everything runs from the CD or DVD, so you can't really harm anything with your experiments. Now that you are familiar with the K Menu, let's move on to the other parts of the Knoppix desktop.

The Panel

The panel is the gray bar along the bottom of the screen containing the K Menu and other items. The panel is like an extensible Windows taskbar. It allows for applets to be embedded in it; the default Knoppix panel (visible at the bottom of Figure 2-68) has several of these. To the immediate right of the K Menu are two other menus; the first has a penguin icon and is a shortcut to the KNOPPIX submenu. The next menu lists all of the applications open across all desktops. To lower all visible applications, click on the next icon, which looks a bit like a desk with a pencil on it. Click the icon again to raise all application windows. Next to those icons are many shortcut icons for applications in the K Menu. These are meant to provide quick access to commonly run applications. Right-click any of these icons to display a context menu that gives you the option to move or delete the icons. Drag and drop icons from the K Menu to add them to the panel.

To the right of the application icons is a box with the numbers 1, 2, 3, and 4 in it. This is known as a desktop pager, and it allows you to quickly switch desktops by clicking on the appropriate number. If you prefer, Ctrl-Tab cycles through your applications and Ctrl-Shift-Tab cycles through the desktops. By default, Knoppix has four virtual desktops that allow you to reduce clutter by grouping open programs onto different desktops. The pager highlights the active desktop so that you don't get lost.

Next to the pager is the task list, which shows all of your open applications. Click on the program name to raise and lower the program window. Right-click any of the windows in the task list to see a list of actions you can perform on that window, such as closing, maximizing, and moving the window to a different desktop.

After the task list are a few useful applets grouped in the system tray. Many applications that run in the background put an icon here to allow you quick access to the program's options. First, you see a flag to represent the KDE keyboard tool that lets you change which keyboard locale you are using on the desktop. Next, you see a screen display applet. Click this applet to change screen resolution and monitor frequency on the fly. If you have a detected sound card, you will see a speaker icon that represents the KDE mixer applet, which lets you change your volume settings. If Knoppix is unable to configure your sound card, the mixer applet has a red slash through it. Finally, at the far right of the panel is a clock. Before you can adjust the date and time, you must create a root password. To do so, click K→Knoppix→"Set password for root," or open a terminal window and type this:

```
knoppix@ttyp0[knoppix]$ sudo passwd
Enter new UNIX password:
Retype new UNIX password:
Passwd: password updated successfully
```

Experiment with the panel. Click and drag icons to move them around on the panel. Drag the applet handles to move them. Right-click icons and applets to see a list of options for the applet, including removing it from the panel completely. Drag icons from the desktop or the K Menu and drop them on the panel to add them. To resize the panel, right-click it and choose a size from the Size menu. Remember that all of the changes that you make are not persistent unless you save your Knoppix configuration.

See Also

- *Knoppix Hacks, 2nd Edition* by Kyle Rankin (O'Reilly)
- "Transform Your Windows XP Laptop into a Dual-Boot XP/Ubuntu Linux System" **[Hack #14]**
- "Run Linux Inside Windows Without Dual Booting" **[Hack #30]**

— Kyle Rankin

03 WINDOWS EXPLORER, MANAGING FILES, AND SEARCH

Do you ever give thought to Windows Explorer? Most likely not. You use it countless times a day but probably never really think about it. The same holds true for managing your files and searching for files.

But hacking Windows Explorer, the search feature, and the way you manage files is one of the simplest ways to get more out of Windows. You'll be able to find files faster, hack the Windows Explorer right-click menu, straighten out the mysterious *shadow copies* in Windows Vista, and do much more as well.

HACK 34: A Power User's Hidden Weapon: Improve the Context Menu

V XP The context menu in Windows XP and Windows Vista is underused by many. But with these four additions and edits to the menu, it'll turn into a powerhouse that you'll use every day.

Windows Explorer's right-click context menu is one of the most basic of all Windows XP and Windows Vista tools. It provides many shortcuts for whenever you want to take action on a file or a folder. But the right-click menu is missing several basic options, such as the ability to choose the folder where you want to move or copy the chosen file. And when you install new applications, they have a nasty habit of adding their own options that you'll rarely use in the right-click menu.

The end result: a right-click context menu cluttered with options and lacking several basic useful ones. But you can extend the power of the menu with these four hacks.

Add "Copy To Folder" and "Move To Folder" Context Menu Options

I spend a lot of time copying and moving files between folders. More often than not, when I click a file in Explorer, I want to copy or move it to another folder. That means I spend a good deal of time dragging files around or copying and pasting them.

But with a Registry hack, you can save yourself time: you can add Copy To Folder and Move To Folder options to the right-click context menu. When you choose one of the options from the menu, you browse to any place on your hard disk to copy or move the file to, and then send the file there. To add this option, run the Registry Editor [Hack #183]), and go to `HKEY_CLASSES_ROOT\AllFilesystemObjects\shellex\ContextMenuHandlers`. The `shellex` name tells you that it's a shell extension key that lets you customize the user shell or the interface. Create a new key called `Copy To`. Set the value to `{C2FBB630-2971-11d1-A18C-00C04FD75D13}`. Create another new key called `Move To`. Set the value to `{C2FBB631-2971-11d1-A18C-00C04FD75D13}`. Exit the Registry. The changes should take effect immediately. The Copy To Folder and Move To Folder options will appear. When you right-click a file and choose one of the options, you'll be able to move or copy the file, using a dialog box like the one shown in Figure 3-1.

Figure 3-1.
Specifying a destination using the Copy To Folder option

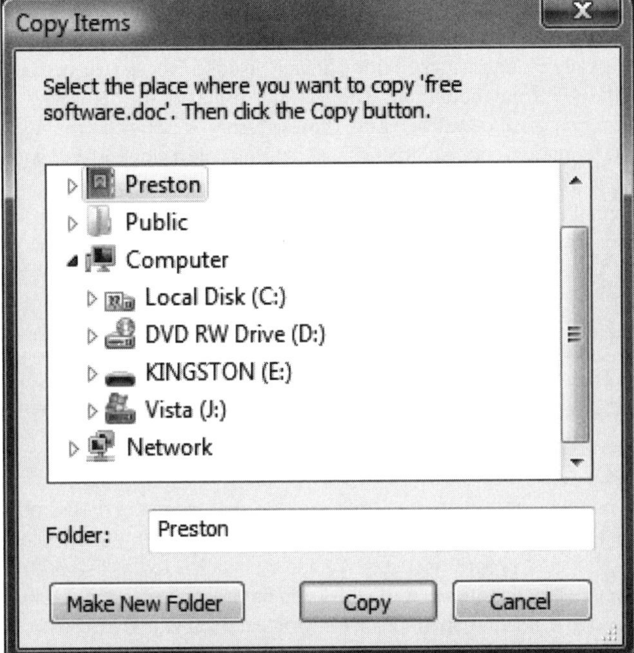

Add and Remove Destinations for the "Send To" Option

The right-click context menu does have one useful option, Send To, which allows you to send the file to any one of a list of programs or locations—for example, to a drive, program, or folder.

It would be nice to edit that list, adding new locations and programs and taking away existing ones that you never use. How locations and programs show up on the menu at first appears to be somewhat of a mystery, but in fact, it's easy to hack.

The approach is different in Windows XP versus Windows Vista. In Windows XP, go to *C:\Documents and Settings*`username`*\SendTo*, where `username` is your username. In Windows Vista, go to *C:\Users*`username`*\AppData\Roaming\Microsoft\Windows\SendTo*. In both cases, the folder will be filled with shortcuts to all the locations you find on your Send To context menu. To remove an item from the Send To menu, delete the shortcut from the folder. To add an item to the menu, add a shortcut to the folder by highlighting the folder, choosing File→New→Shortcut (on Vista, you'll need to press Alt to get the File menu to appear) and following the instructions for creating a shortcut. The new setting takes effect immediately; you don't have to exit Windows Explorer for it to go into effect.

Open the Command Prompt from the Right-Click Menu

I began computing in the days of DOS, and I still can't give up the command prompt. When it comes to doing down-and-dirty tasks such as mass deleting or renaming of files, nothing beats it. I find myself frequently switching back and forth between Windows Explorer and the command prompt.

Often, when using Windows Explorer, I want to open the command prompt at the folder that's my current location. That takes too many steps: opening a command prompt and then navigating to my current folder. However, there's a quicker way: you can add an option to the right-click context menu that opens a command prompt at your current folder. For example, if you were to right-click the *C:\My Stuff* folder, you could then choose to open a command prompt at *C:\My Stuff*.

On Vista, you can already do this. Hold down Shift when you right-click a folder window, and a new option appears on the context menu: Open Command Window Here.

To add the option, run the Registry Editor [Hack #183], then go to `HKEY_LOCAL_MACHINE\Software\Classes\Folder\Shell`. Create a new key called `Command Prompt`. For the default value, enter whatever text you want to appear when you right-click a folder—for example, `Open Command Prompt`. Create a new key beneath the `Command Prompt` key called `Command`. Set the default value to `Cmd.exe /k pushd %L`. That value launches *Cmd.exe*, the XP command prompt. The `/k` switch executes the command that follows but leaves the prompt running in interactive mode. That is, it lets you issue commands from the command prompt; the command prompt isn't being used to issue only a single command and then exit. The `pushd` command stores the name of the current directory, and `%L` uses that name to start the command prompt at it finally, exit the Registry. The new menu option shows up immediately. Note that it won't appear when you right-click a file; it shows up only when you right-click a folder.

Although many of us like fussing around with the Registry rather than doing things the easy way, there's also a way to add this option to your right-click context menu without editing the Registry. For Windows XP, download and install a free copy of Microsoft's Open Command Window Here PowerToy from www.microsoft.com/windowsxp/downloads/powertoys/xppowertoys.mspx. Many other PowerToys on that page are covered elsewhere in this book.

Clean Up the "Open With" Option

When you right-click a file, one of the menu options is Open With, which provides a list of programs for you to open the file with. This list changes according to the type of file you're clicking. Depending on the file type, the list can get long because programs frequently add themselves to this list when you install them. To make things worse, there are times when the listed programs aren't applicable. For example, do you really want to open a *.jpg* bitmap graphics file with Microsoft Word? I think not.

You can clean up the Open With list using a Registry hack. Run the Registry Editor, and go to `HKEY_CURRENT_USER\Software\Microsoft\Windows\CurrentVersion\Explorer\FileExts`. Look for the file extension whose Open With list you want to edit, and find its `OpenWithList` subkey—`HKEY_CURRENT_USER\Software\Microsoft\Windows\CurrentVersion\Explorer\FileExts\.doc\OpenWithList`, for example. The subkey has an alphabetical list of `String` values. Open each value, and examine the value data. It is the name of one of the programs on the Open With list (`Winword.exe`, for example). Delete any entry that you don't want to appear. Don't delete the value data; delete the `String` value listing. In other words, if the value data for the `String` value is `Winword.exe`, delete the entire string rather than just the value data. Exit the Registry.

In some cases, you may see an entry for OpenWithProgIds instead of OpenWithList. These ProgIds are more obscure shorthand for the programs they are associated with. For example, the entry for *.rtf* includes two ProgIds: rtffile (the default handler for RTF files: WordPad) and Word.RTF.8 (Microsoft Word).

See Also

- "More Hacks for Improving Windows Vista's Context Menu" [Hack #35]

HACK 35: More Hacks for Improving Windows Vista's Context Menu

V There's a simple, hidden way to improve your context menu in Windows Vista, and you won't have to touch the Registry.

Windows Vista users: Want more options for the context menu in Windows Vista? They're easy to get to. Hold down the Shift key as you right-click a file; you get several new menu options, as you can see circled in Figure 3-2.

Here are the new options you get and what each does:

Open as Read-Only
As the name says, this option opens the file as a read-only file.

Pin to Start Menu
This option pins a shortcut to the file in the top section of the Start menu. To remove the shortcut to the file from the Start menu, right-click the shortcut, and select "Remove from this list."

Add to Quick Launch
This option adds a shortcut to the file to the Quick Launch toolbar on the left side of the Taskbar. To remove the shortcut, right-click it, and choose Delete.

Copy as Path
This option copies the filename and path to the Windows clipboard; for example, *C:\Budget\2007 memo.xls*. You can then paste the text wherever you want.

Note that not every option will appear on every file you select. For example, Open as Read-Only will not appear when you select an executable file.

See Also

- "A Power User's Hidden Weapon: Improve the Context Menu" [Hack #34]

Figure 3-2.
These new options appear on the Context menu when right-clicking a file

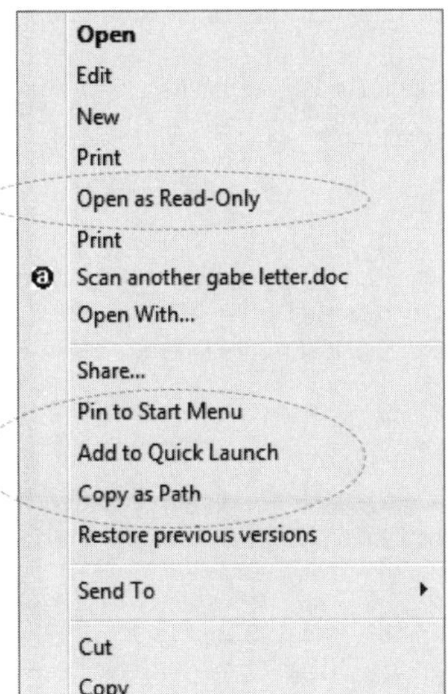

QUICK HACK

RESIZE DESKTOP ICONS WITH EASE

You may know that you can resize Vista's desktop icons by right-clicking the desktop and selecting Personalize→Adjust font size, then choosing either the default size (96 dpi) or a larger size (such as 120 dpi). But if you then click Custom DPI, you can choose from a much larger range by selecting a percentage from the drop-down list.

There's an even faster way to resize your desktop icons. Click the desktop, hold down the Control key, and use your mouse's scroll wheel to resize your icons by making them smaller (move the scroll wheel towards you) or larger (move the scroll wheel away from you).

HACK 36: Open an Administrator Command Prompt Anywhere in Windows Explorer

V Need to launch an administrator prompt on the fly in Windows Vista when you're deep inside a folder? Here's an easy way to do it.

Command-line junkies get frustrated easily by User Account Control because so many command-line tools require you to open an administrator command prompt. Particularly frustrating are instances when you're using Windows Explorer, and you realize that you need to launch an administrator command-line prompt at a particular folder, especially one that's nested several levels deep. You'll have to go through the annoying steps required to launch an administrator command prompt [Hack #108], then go through the equally annoying steps of using the CD command to get to the right folder. Then you can finally get to work.

There's a simpler way. A command-line hack will let you add a right-click option to Windows Explorer called Open Administrator Command Prompt Here. That way, you'll just need to right-click in the folder in which you want to open an administrator prompt, make your selection, and the prompt . . . well, the prompt opens promptly.

First, launch the Registry Editor by typing regedit at the Start Search box or a command prompt (see Chapter 13 for details). Go to `HKEY_CLASSES_ROOT\Directory\shell`, and create a new key called `runas`. After you create the key, double-click the Default string, and give it the value `Open Administrator Command Prompt Here`.

Next, in that new key, create a new string value called `NoWorkingDirectory`. Leave the value data field blank. Your Registry should look like Figure 3-3. Underneath the key you just created, `HKEY_CLASSES_ROOT\Directory\shell\runas`, create a new key called `command`. Double-click the key's default value, enter the following text, and click OK:

```
cmd.exe /k "pushd %L && title Command Prompt"
```

Figure 3-4 shows you what the Registry looks like.

Next, go to `HKEY_CLASSES_ROOT\Drive\shell` and create a new key called `runas`. After you create the key, double-click the Default string, and give it the value `Open Administrator Command Prompt Here`.

Next, in that new key, create a new string value called `NoWorkingDirectory`. Leave the value data field blank. The new string name should be `NoWorkingDirectory`, and the value data field should be blank.

Underneath the key you just created, `HKEY_CLASSES_ROOT\Drive\shell\runas`, create a new key called `command`. Double-click the key's default value, enter this, and click OK:

```
cmd.exe /k "pushd %L && title Command Prompt"
```

Exit the Registry. Open Windows Explorer, and right-click any folder or drive. There will now be a new menu choice, Open Administrator Command Prompt Here, as you can see in Figure 3-5. Click it; an administrator command prompt will open, and you'll be at the folder you just right-clicked.

Hacking the Hack

If you don't want to do all that editing to the Registry, you can create a *.reg* file that when double-clicked automatically creates all the proper Registry entries for you. Open Notepad, and type in this:

```
Windows Registry Editor Version 5.00
[HKEY_CLASSES_ROOT\Directory\shell\runas]
@="Open Administrator Command Prompt Here"
```

Figure 3-3.
Your Registry after your first round of editing

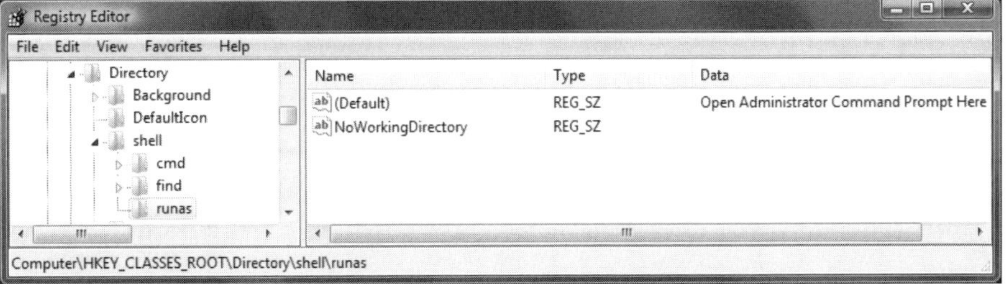

Figure 3-4.
Your Registry after the next round of editing

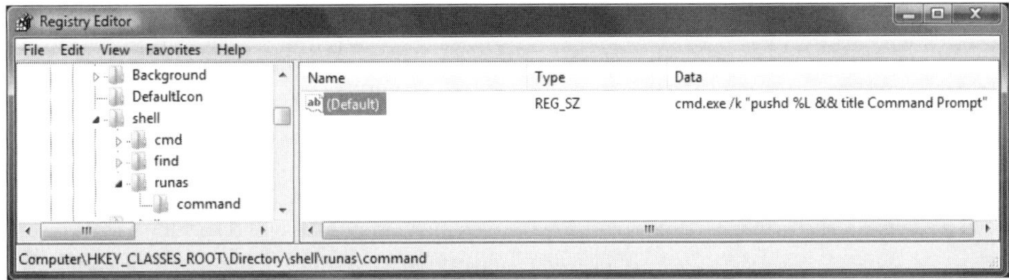

Figure 3-5.
The right-click menu, with a new choice for opening an administrator prompt at the current folder

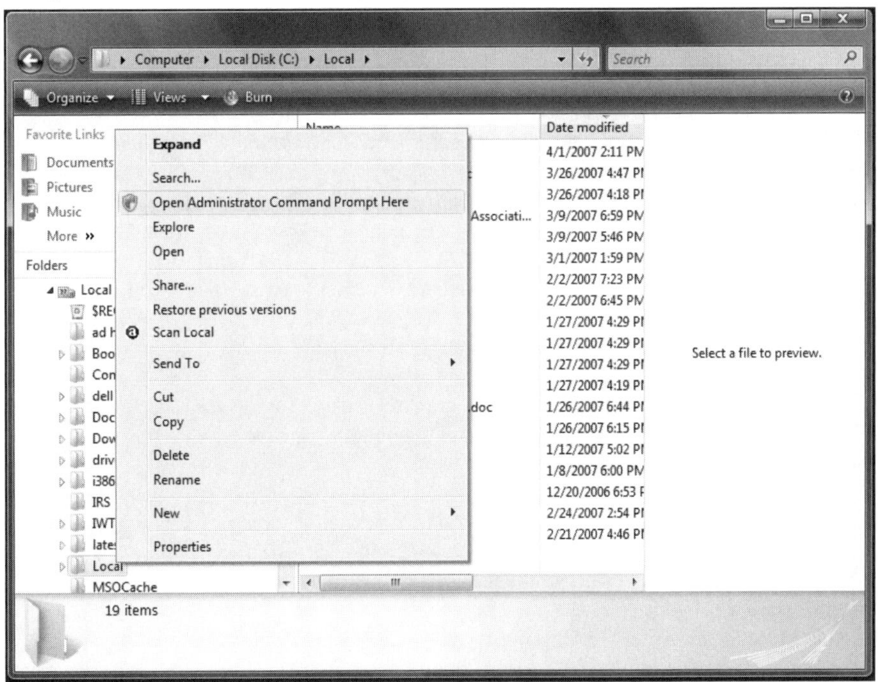


```
"NoWorkingDirectory"=""
[HKEY_CLASSES_ROOT\Directory\shell\runas\command]
@="cmd.exe /k \"pushd %L && title Command Prompt\""
[HKEY_CLASSES_ROOT\Drive\shell\runas]
@="Open Administrator Command Prompt Here"
"NoWorkingDirectory"=""
[HKEY_CLASSES_ROOT\Drive\shell\runas\command]
@="cmd.exe /k \"pushd %L && title Command Prompt\""
```

Give the file a name with the extension *.reg*, such as command *prompt.reg*. Double-click it, and the changes will be applied to the Registry.

See Also

- "A Power User's Hidden Weapon: Improve the Context Menu" **[Hack #34]**
- "More Hacks for Improving Windows Vista's Context Menu" **[Hack #35]**

HACK 37: Generate Folder and File Listings for Printing or Editing

XP V Longtime PC users and former Mac OS 9 users alike are often shocked when they realize there's no easy, built-in option to print a list of files in a folder in Windows. This hack creates a context-menu right-click option to create such a list, which you can then edit, copy, paste, and—most usefully—print.

How many times have you been browsing through directories in Windows Explorer and wished that you could generate a text file or printout listing the files and folders? It seems like such a simple request that it's amazing the option isn't available. You don't believe me? Right-click a folder, and see for yourself whether there is an option to list or print the structure. There isn't, but there is a workaround that doesn't require any third-party software. Here's how to create a context menu item that when clicked, generates a printable (and editable) text-file listing of the selected directory.

Windows XP

To create the entry in the context menu, you must first create a *batch file*. A batch file is a text file with the extension *.bat* that contains a sequence of commands for a computer operating system. The format for the batch file is:

```
dir /a /-p /o:gen >filelisting.txt
```

The name of the *.txt* file can be whatever you like. In this example, I've used *filelisting.txt*, but it could just as easily be *filelist*, *listoffiles*, *namedfiles*, or even *Wally* if you enjoy the bizarre in your filenaming schemes. Once you've decided on the filename, create the file in Notepad, as shown in Figure 3-6.

Save the file in your *WINDOWS* folder, as shown in Figure 3-7, making sure to use the *.bat* extension and not the default *.txt* extension. It's important to set the options "Save as type" to All Files and "Encoding" to ANSI.

Now that we have the *.bat* file created, the next step is to make it functional and easily accessible by integrating it into the context menu that opens when a right-click is executed. Open Windows Explorer, and choose Tools→Folder Options→File Types tab→Folder→Advanced→New to open the New Action box shown in Figure 3-8.

In the Action box, type the name that you want to appear in the context menu. Once again, you have wide latitude in choices; something like Create File Listing is probably most useful, but you can name yours something more confusing if you like. Browse to the location of the *.bat* file you created, and select it in the box labeled "Application used to perform action." Click OK, and you'll see that Create File Listing (or whatever you chose as an action name) has been added as one of the actions in the Edit File Type window, as shown in Figure 3-9. Do the standard Windows dance of clicking OK again to close all the open windows.

Figure 3-6.
Creating a batch file in Notepad

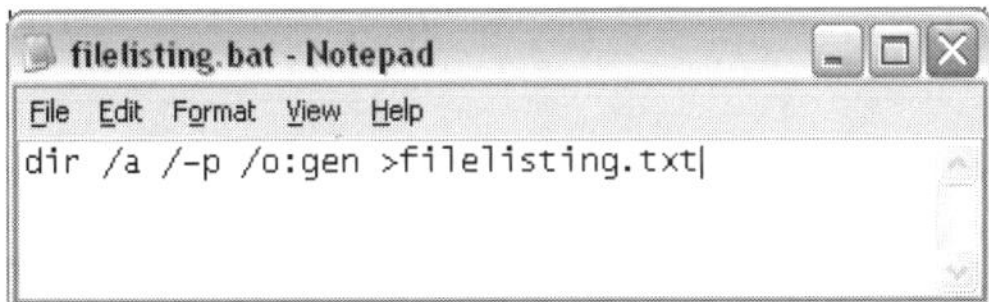

Figure 3-7.
Saving *filelisting.bat*

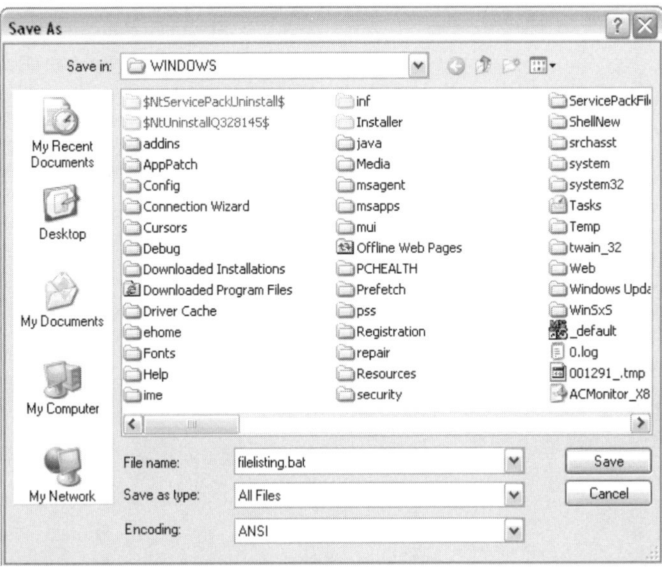

Figure 3-8.
Creating a new action for the context menu

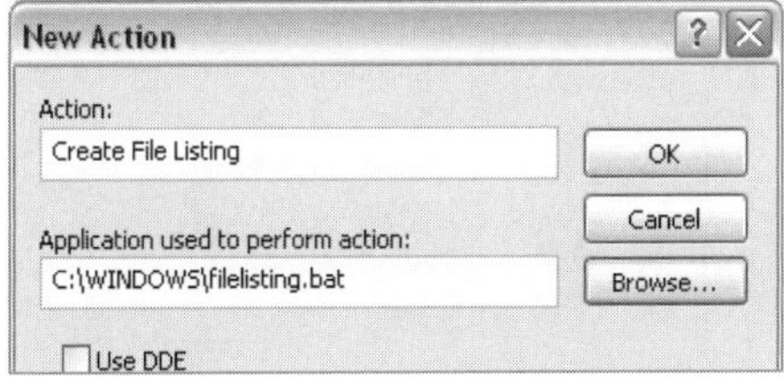

If for any reason you want to remove the Create File Listing entry from the context menu, edit the Registry **[Hack #183]**. Navigate to `HKEY_CLASSES_ROOT\Folder\shell\Create_File_Listing`, and delete the `Create_File_Listing` key in the left pane. Close RegEdit, and reboot to complete removal.

Vista

On Vista, you'll need to manipulate the Registry to get this to work. The steps are basically the same as shown in "Open an Administrator Command Prompt Anywhere in Windows Explorer" **[Hack #36]**, but you'll be adding an entry only to the Directory key, not to both the Directory and Drive keys.

Use Notepad to create a file called *dirlisting.reg* with the following contents:

```
REGEDIT4
[HKEY_CLASSES_ROOT\Directory\shell\filelisting]
@="Create File Listing"
[HKEY_CLASSES_ROOT\Directory\shell\filelisting\command]
@="cmd /c dir \"%L\" /a /-p /o:gen >  filelisting.txt"
```

Double-click the file to import it into the Registry, and you're ready to go.

To remove this entry, you need to delete the `HKEY_CLASSES_ROOT\Directory\shell\filelisting` key.

Running the Hack

That's it! Congratulations. You've created a new item on the context menu that's ready to go to work. So, now that it's there, what can you do with it?

Open up Windows Explorer. Navigate to whatever folder you want to use as the basis for the file list, and right-click to open the context menu. Click the Create File Listing item (see Figure 3-10), and the list will be generated and displayed at the bottom of the open Notepad window as *filelisting.txt*. Figure 3-11 shows the file listing generated from the Sample Music folder shown in Figure 3-10. Because it's a text file, it can be fully edited, copied, pasted, printed, and so on, for any purpose.

— Jim Foley

Figure 3-9.
The revised Edit File Type box with your new action

Figure 3-10.
Your new context menu action: Create File Listing

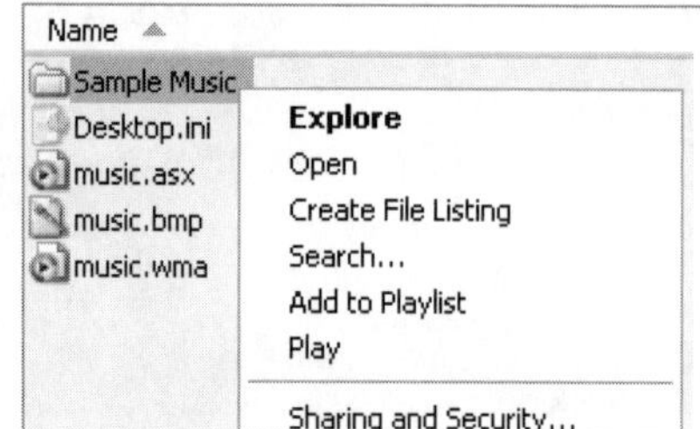

Figure 3-11.
The generated file listing, all ready for editing and printing

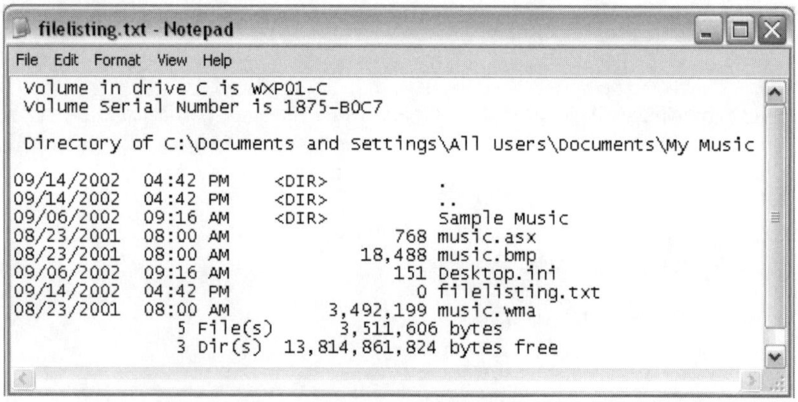

filelisting.txt - Notepad

File Edit Format View Help

```
 Volume in drive C is WXP01-C
 Volume Serial Number is 1875-B0C7

 Directory of C:\Documents and Settings\All Users\Documents\My Music

09/14/2002  04:42 PM    <DIR>          .
09/14/2002  04:42 PM    <DIR>          ..
09/06/2002  09:16 AM    <DIR>          Sample Music
08/23/2001  08:00 AM               768 music.asx
08/23/2001  08:00 AM            18,488 music.bmp
09/06/2002  09:16 AM               151 Desktop.ini
09/14/2002  04:42 PM                 0 filelisting.txt
08/23/2001  08:00 AM         3,492,199 music.wma
               5 File(s)      3,511,606 bytes
               3 Dir(s)  13,814,861,824 bytes free
```

HACK 38: Only the Shadow Knows: Using Windows Shadow Copy

V Built right into the Business, Enterprise, and Ultimate editions of Windows Vista is a way to retrieve earlier versions of documents.

The danger most of us think of when it comes to files is a system crash. But that's a relatively rare occurrence. More commonly, we make changes to a file that we shouldn't make, and then wish that we had some way to turn on the Wayback Machine and retrieve that earlier version.

If you've got the Business, Enterprise, or Ultimate edition of Windows Vista, you've got that Wayback Machine built right into your PC. It's called *shadow copies*. In Windows XP, only those who are connected to a corporate network can use shadow copies, and then only if it's been set up properly. And in Windows XP, you have to restore the copies from a server.

In Windows Vista, no server is needed: they're stored invisibly on your PC.

The good news about the shadow copy feature in Windows Vista is that it works. The bad news is that there is a pretty severe limitation to it: shadow copies are not made constantly—only when the system takes a Restore Point snapshot. Shadow copies are also made every time you do a backup using the Windows Backup program. So you won't necessarily have many previous versions of a file from which to choose if you want to use a shadow copy.

As an example, let's say Windows Vista is set up to create a Restore Point every night at midnight. You've been working on a budget spreadsheet for several days. Yesterday, you made four changes to it—one at 1 p.m., one at 2 p.m., one at 3 p.m., and the final one at 4 p.m. Today, you made one more change. You suddenly realize that you want a copy of the document that you made yesterday at 2 p.m.

You can't do it. You can get to the only last version of your file from yesterday, the one you made at 4 p.m. That was the last time you changed the file, and that's the version that was made when a snapshot was taken of your Restore Point.

Surprisingly, shadow copies don't take up as much disk space as you might imagine. Windows Vista stores only the incremental changes in the files, not entire files themselves—significantly reducing the hard-disk space devoted to them.

Using Shadow Copies to Restore Files

In order to use shadow copies, the feature must first be turned on, so check whether your system is set up to create restore points. Select Control Panel→System and Maintenance→System→System Protection; a screen like that shown in Figure 3-12 appears. Make sure that the box is checked next to the drive or drives that contain your files, and click OK.

If you haven't turned on system restore points, shadow copies are still made if you schedule backups. Choose Control Panel→"Backup your computer" to see whether you've scheduled backups. If not, click "Back up files," and follow the prompts for creating a regularly scheduled backup.

To view the shadow copies of a file, right-click it, and select Properties→Previous versions. A screen like that shown in Figure 3-13 will appear.

What you'll see depends on whether any shadow copies were made, when they were made, and whether any backup copies were made. Windows Vista assigns a certain amount of disk space to shadow copies and restore points, and puts files there on a first-in, first-out basis. So if a shadow

Figure 3-12.
Turn on System Protection to create shadow copies

QUICK HACK 

QUICK ZOOM IN WINDOWS EXPLORER AND INTERNET EXPLORER

Here's a quick way to zoom in on anything when you're using Windows Explorer or Internet Explorer. Hold down the Ctrl key and scroll your mouse wheel away from you, and you'll zoom in. To zoom out, hold down the mouse key and scroll your mouse wheel toward you, and you'll zoom out.

copy of the file was made months ago, but the file hasn't been touched since, you may not see any shadow copies because the shadow copy may have been automatically deleted to make way for newer files.

Assuming, though, that changes were made to the file relatively recently, and that you also back up your PC regularly, you'll see the screen like that shown in Figure 3-13. Listed will be the time and date each copy of the file was made, as well as whether the copy is a shadow copy or a backup copy. You'll be able to restore any version, whether it is a shadow copy or a backup copy. The only difference, as you'll see, is in how you restore the file.

If you use a dual-boot system, it will be very difficult for you to use shadow copies. Whenever you boot into a different system from Windows Vista, all of your shadow copies are wiped out and unavailable. The same holds true for your restore points; they're wiped out as well.

Because you can selectively disable System Protection on a drive-by-drive basis, you can work around this problem by telling each operating system to disable System Protection on the other operating system's drive. So, if Vista is installed on C:, and XP is installed on D:, you need to tell Vista to disable System Protection on drive D: and tell XP to disable System Protection on drive C:.

This is an accident-prone scheme, and a simple mistake can wipe out all of your shadow copies. So if you need to use more than one operating system on your PC, and don't need direct access to PCI, AGP, PCI Express, FireWire, or PC Card/Express Card devices in all your operating systems, consider installing Virtual PC **[Hack #30]** and running the other operating system as a virtual machine.

Before you restore a shadow copy, it's a good idea to first take a look inside. Just knowing the date and time a copy was made won't necessarily tell you much about the content of the file itself. Double-click the file, and it opens in the application that created it. Take a look at the file itself, then decide if you want to restore to this version of the file.

If you'd like, you can restore the file right from the application itself. Choose Save As, and then either overwrite the original file or save the shadow copy under a different name or to a new location.

Figure 3-13.
The list of shadow copies and backup copies

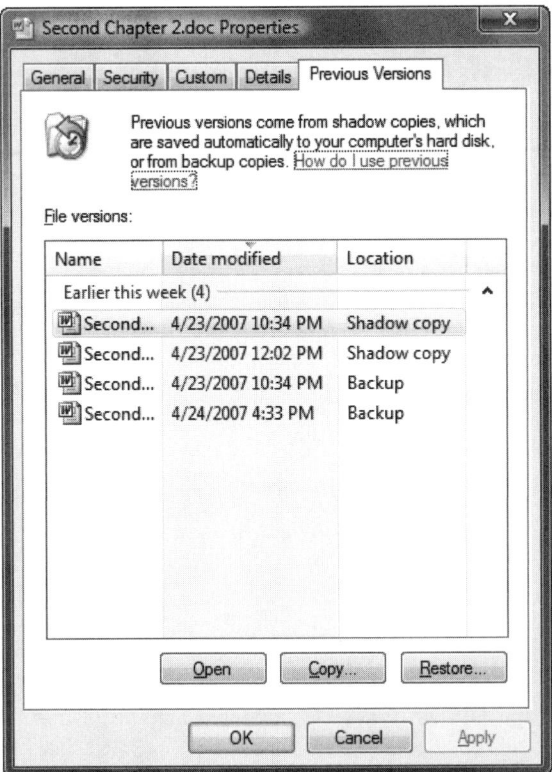

You can open only shadow copies this way. If you double-click a backup copy, nothing happens.

There's another way to restore a shadow copy of a file. Right-click the file on the screen shown in Figure 3-13, and choose Copy. A screen like that shown in Figure 3-14 appears. Select where you want to save the file, and save a copy of it.

You can also instead restore a shadow copy right over the existing file by clicking Restore. However, be very careful before you do this because you'll lose your existing version of the file, and you won't be able to get it back. Subsequently, I never restore files this way: you shouldn't either.

For backup files, your only choice is to restore them. Click the file on the screen shown in Figure 3-13 and click Restore. After a moment, a screen like that shown in Figure 3-15 appears. You can replace your existing file, or instead, save a copy of it and still retain the original file. If you choose to save a copy, it will have the same filename, but with (2) just before the extension, like this: *Budget 2007 (2).xls*.

Shadow copies aren't made for certain files and folders in Windows, in particular system files and folders. So, for example, no shadow copies are made of *C:\Windows* or the files within it.

You restore folders using shadow copies precisely the same way you do files. The only difference is that you'll restore an entire folder, rather than a single file.

Hacking the Hack

Here's a nifty trick: You can restore shadow copies of a file or folder even if you've deleted it, although you'll need to know the name of the parent folder if you want to do so. Open Windows Explorer, and navigate to the parent folder. Right-click somewhere in the folder, without selecting a file or folder, and click "Restore previous versions." Double-click the previous version of the folder which holds the folder or file you want to restore. Then drag the file or folder you want to restore to

Figure 3-14.
Choosing a location for restoring a shadow copy of a file

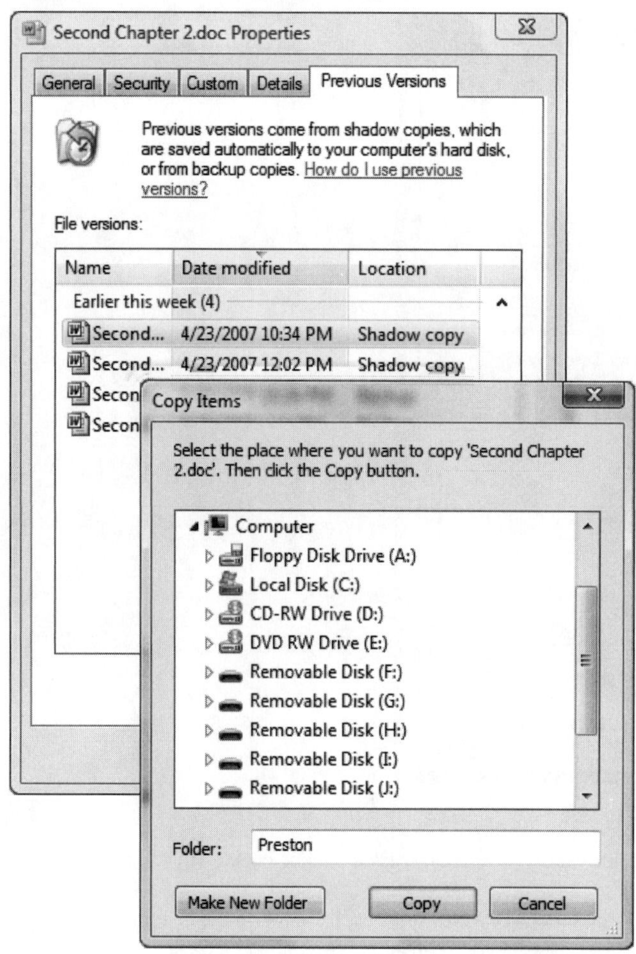

a different location—for example, to your desktop or to another folder. That's all it takes; the file or folder has now been restored to its new location.

HACK 39: Control Windows Explorer with Command-Line Shortcuts

V XP Create customized Explorer views from the command line, and save your favorite views in desktop shortcuts.

I rarely open Windows Explorer in its default view. Instead, I generally want to open it at a specific location, with a specific set of viewing features—for example, with the Folders bar in the left side on or off.

That's why I launch Windows Explorer from the command line, along with a set of switches for controlling how it opens. I also create desktop shortcuts out of these command-line launches so that my favorite views are always only a couple of clicks away.

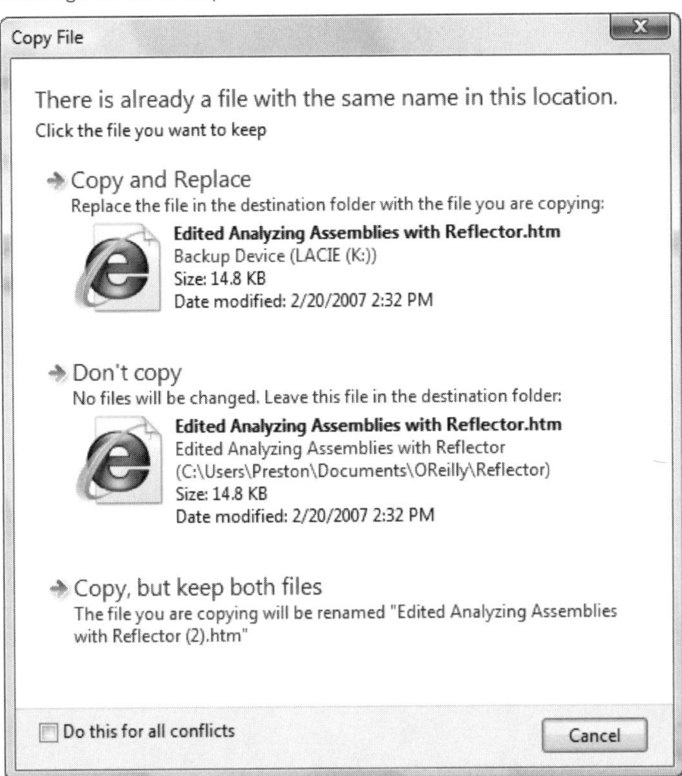

Figure 3-15.
Restoring a file from backup

For example, when I'm using Windows XP, and I want to open Windows Explorer to the *C:\Power Tools Book\Hacks* subfolder only, with no folders above it, and using the Folders bar, I open the command prompt and issue this command:

```
explorer /e,/root,c:\Power Tools Hacks
```

Because Windows Explorer differs between Windows XP and Windows Vista, switches don't necessarily work the same in each operating system. Throughout this hack, I've indicated any differences between the two.

To quickly open the current directory in Explorer from the command prompt, type:

```
start .
```

The `start` command opens a file (or directory) with the default handler. In this case, it opens the current directory (`.`) with Explorer. When I do that, the view pictured in Figure 3-16 appears.

Compare that view with the default view I get when I launch Windows Explorer in Windows XP the normal way (shown in Figure 3-17).

Not only does the Explorer view in Figure 3-16 open to a specific subfolder, but it also shows no folders above it. In contrast, Figure 3-17 shows the entire structure of my hard disk and opens to *C:*. I use the view in Figure 3-16 when I want to work exclusively on a specific subfolder and want to get to it quickly.

This is just one of the many uses for launching Windows Explorer from the command line with switches; no doubt you'll be able to find other uses for it. You'll be able to use it not only with the command line and with desktop shortcuts, but also if you run scripts and batch programs.

The syntax for running Explorer from the command line with switches is:

```
explorer  [/n]  [/e] [,root,object] [[,/select],subobject]
```

You don't have to use any switches; you can type `explorer` by itself, though doing that launches your default Explorer view.

Here is an explanation of how to use the switches and syntax:

`/n`
This switch opens Windows Explorer without displaying the Folders bar. Instead, it launches the view shown in Figure 3-18. (Windows XP only.)

`/e`
This switch opens Windows Explorer, displaying the Folders bar. (Windows XP only.)

`/root`,*object*
This switch opens Windows Explorer to a specific object, such as a folder, without displaying the folders above it, as shown in Figure 3-16. You can also use globally unique identifiers (GUIDs) with this switch, as explained later in this hack.

`[[/select]`,*subobject*`]`
This switch opens Windows Explorer to a specific file or folder that is then highlighted or expanded. You can use the `subobject` switch only without the `/select` parameter. When you use the `/select` parameter, the branches are not expanded, the folder is highlighted, and the subobject is highlighted in the right pane.

Create Desktop Shortcuts for Explorer

Typing command-line shortcuts can quickly give you a case of carpal tunnel syndrome, so a better idea is to run them as desktop shortcuts. Right-click the desktop, choose New→Shortcut, and in the location box, type the Explorer command-line syntax you want to use. Click Next, and give the shortcut a descriptive name—for example, "Hacks folder"—and click OK.

Figure 3-16.
Opening Windows Explorer to a specific folder with a specific view

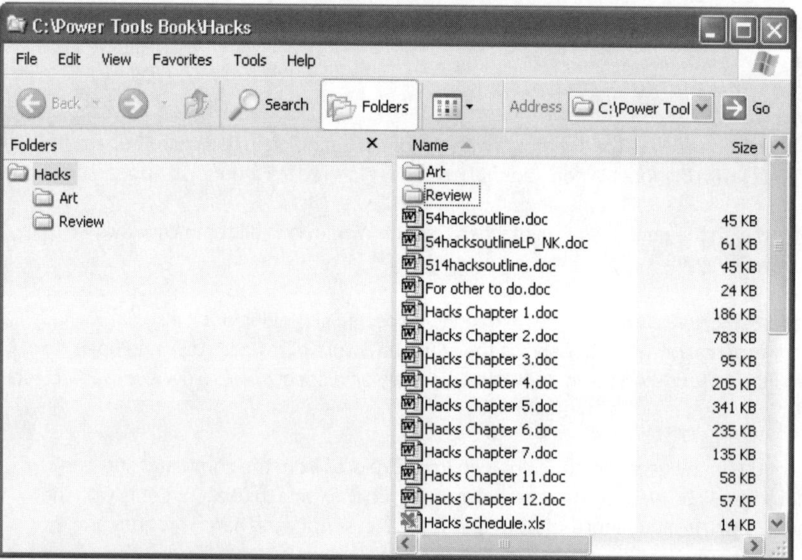

Figure 3-17.
My default for launching Windows Explorer

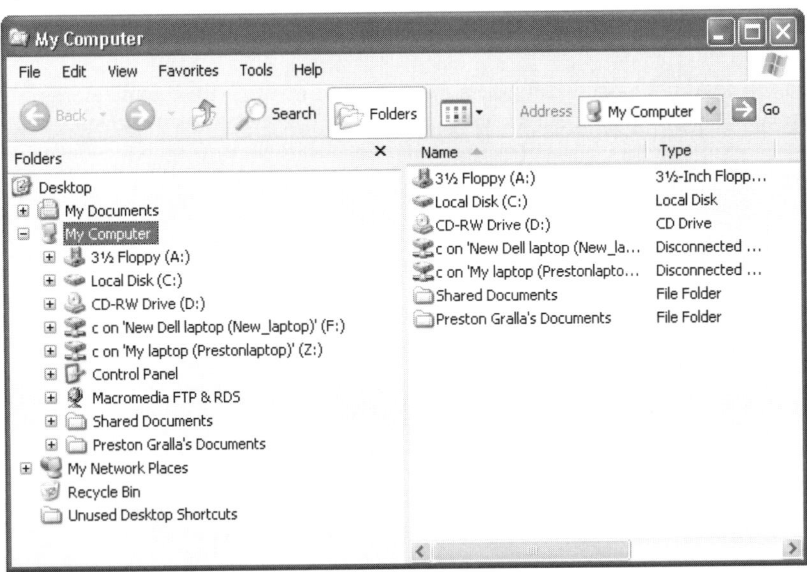

Figure 3-18.
The view of Explorer using the `/n` switch

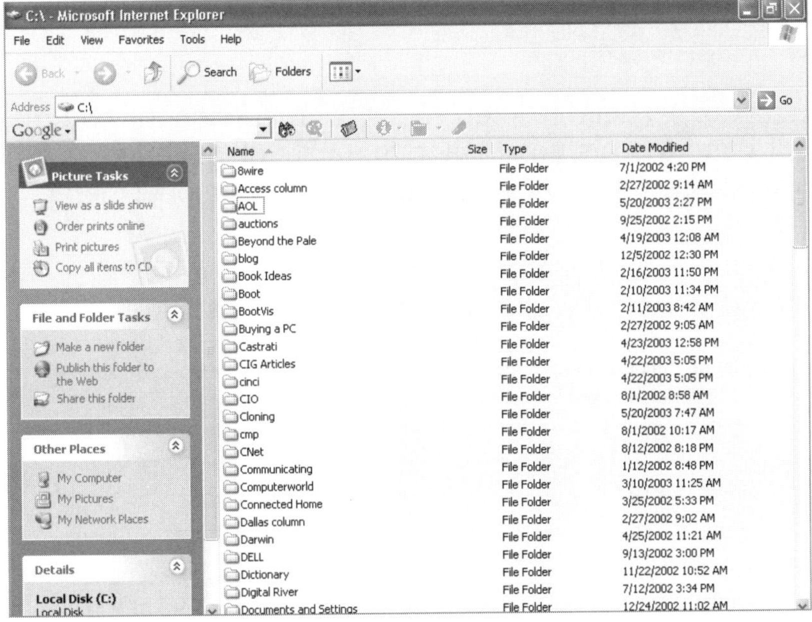

Using Globally Unique Identifiers with Command-Line Switches

You might want to open Explorer to certain system folders, such as My Network Places. To do so, run `explorer` from the command line and follow it with a space, two colons, and the GUIDs that identify specific system folders, like this:

```
explorer ::{208D2C60-3AEA-1069-A2D7-08002B30309D}
```

That command opens Windows Explorer to My Network Places in Windows XP, and Network in Windows Vista.

If you're using switches, similarly put a space and two colons in front of the GUID, like this:

```
explorer /e, ::{208D2C60-3AEA-1069-A2D7-08002B30309D}
```

You can use GUIDs in desktop shortcuts, batch files, and scripts, as well as at the command line. Table 3-1 lists the GUIDs for various system folders.

Table 3-1. GUIDs for system folders

Folder Name	GUID
My Computer (Computer in Windows Vista)	{20D04FE0-3AEA-1069-A2D8-08002B30309D}
My Network Places (Network in Windows Vista)	{208D2C60-3AEA-1069-A2D7-08002B30309D}
Network Connections	{7007ACC7-3202-11D1-AAD2-00805FC1270E}
Printers and Faxes (Printers in Windows Vista)	{2227A280-3AEA-1069-A2DE-08002B30309D}
Recycle Bin	{645FF040-5081-101B-9F08-00AA002F954E}
Scheduled Tasks	{D6277990-4C6A-11CF-8D87-00AA0060F5BF}

HACK 40: Move User Directories to a Separate Partition or Drive

V XP There's no real need to keep your documents on the same drive as your Windows system; in fact, there are plenty reasons to keep them separate. Here's how to relocate your personal folders to another drive.

If you follow the Windows default for storing your personal files, you keep them on the same drive as your Windows system. This can make life very difficult if your main hard disk crashes, and you need to recover. Recovering the data and system simultaneously can be problematic. In addition, if you upgrade or reinstall Windows, keeping your data on the same drive as your PC can cause headaches, particularly if you want to do a clean install of a new operating system. In short, it can cause problems for people who frequently muck around in their system doing hardware upgrades, setting up dual boot systems, upgrading their operating system, adding a second drive, and just generally hacking around.

You can, though, relocate your user folders so that they are on another drive on your system. Your applications will know they're stored there and go about their merry way as normal. The only difference is that your data will be safer than it was previously.

Relocating Folders in Windows Vista

In Windows Vista, by default your personal data is stored in various folders underneath *C:\Users*`username`. So, for example, your Favorites are stored in *C:\Users*`username`*\Favorites*, and your documents are stored in folders underneath *C:\Users*`username`*\Desktop\Documents.*

To redirect your folders to another drive:

1. Create the folder or folders on the drive to which you want the documents, Favorites, and so on, directed.

2. Right-click each folder on the other drive, and choose Properties→Security. Highlight your user account, click the Edit button, and make sure that it has full control over the folder, so that you can read and write to it, as shown in Figure 3-19.

3. On the drive in which you want to relocate folders, right-click a folder you want to redirect, such as *C:\Users*`username`*\Favorites*, and choose Properties→Location. You'll see the current location as shown in Figure 3-20.

4. Click the Move button, and select the drive and folder to which you want the folder relocated. A dialog box will ask whether you want to move all your files from your old location to your new location. Click Yes, then click OK. The folder will be relocated.

5. Do this for all the folders you want to relocate.

Using the Registry to Relocate Folders in Windows XP and Windows Vista

If you want to relocate folders in Windows XP, your best bet is to use a Registry hack. The same hack will work with Windows Vista, so you can use it instead of going through the steps outlined earlier in this hack.

Figure 3-19.
Giving full permission to modify a folder

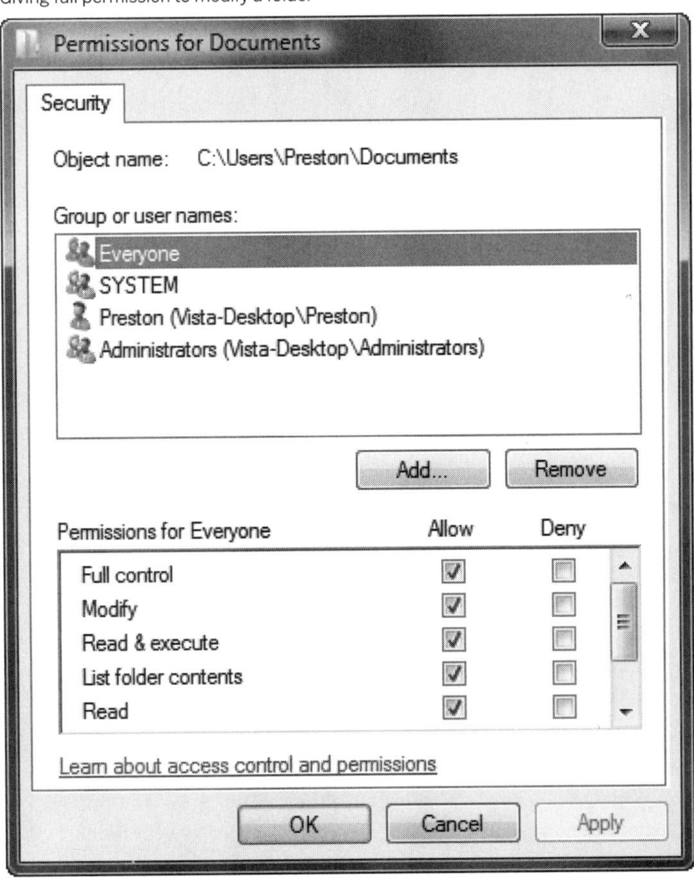

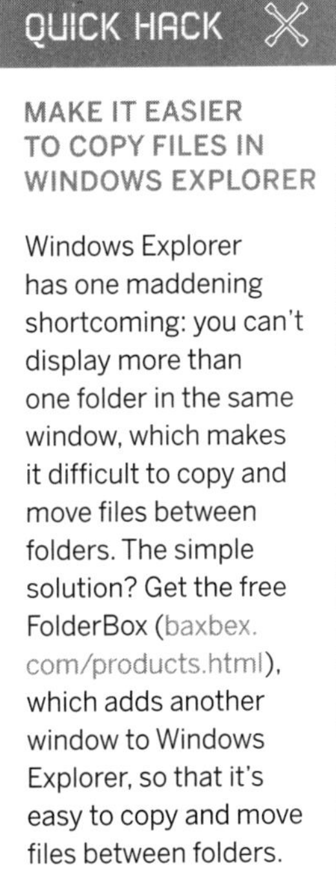

QUICK HACK

MAKE IT EASIER TO COPY FILES IN WINDOWS EXPLORER

Windows Explorer has one maddening shortcoming: you can't display more than one folder in the same window, which makes it difficult to copy and move files between folders. The simple solution? Get the free FolderBox (baxbex.com/products.html), which adds another window to Windows Explorer, so that it's easy to copy and move files between folders.

Figure 3-20.
Redirecting the Favorites folder

1. Create the folder or folders on the drive to which you want the documents, Favorites, and so on, redirected.

2. Launch the Registry Editor by typing regedit at the Start Search box or a command prompt (See Chapter 13 for details).

3. Go to `HKEY_CURRENT_USER\Software\Microsoft\Windows\CurrentVersion\Explorer\User Shell Folders`.

4. Locate the Registry key for the folder that you want to redirect. For example, the location for Favorites is in the Registry key `Favorites` and has the value `%USERPROFILE%\Favorites`, while the location for your Documents folder is in the Registry key `Personal` and has the value `%USERPROFILE%\My Documents`.

5. Change the values in the Registry keys to the locations of the folders you created, where you want the folders redirected. Exit the Registry. You may need to reboot or log off and back on for the change to take effect.

HACK 41: Hack Your Partitions in Windows Vista

V Windows Vista gives you tools to change, shrink, and manage your partitions. Here's how to use them.

Among Windows Vista's improvements over Windows XP is this big one: you can finally manage your disk partitions. Let's say, for example, you have one honking big hard disk set up as one partition, and you want to divide it into pieces. You may want to do this as a way to separate your data from your operating system, so that if you need to reinstall Windows Vista, upgrade it, and so on, you can do so without affecting your data.

Windows XP couldn't do this for you. You had to rely on a program such as Symantec's Partition Magic (www.partitionmagic.com) or the free GParted LiveCD (gparted.sourceforge.net). But Windows Vista includes a very nifty built-in tool for managing partitions—the Disk Management Console. There's plenty you can do with it. In this hack, I'll show you how to use it to shrink a partition and create a new one:

1. Open the Disk Management Console by typing diskmgmt.msc at a command prompt or in the Run box and pressing Enter. The Disk Management Console appears, and lists all the hard drives on your PC, including external hard drives and USB flash drives, as shown in Figure 3-21.

2. Right-click the partition you want to manage. You'll have a variety of options, depending on your system setup and the kind of partition you're going to manage. Some options will be grayed out, depending on the partition, as you can see in Figure 3-22. For example, if your right-click a boot partition, the Format option will not be available to you.

3. Choose Shrink Volume. After a few moments, Figure 3-23 appears. Make your choice as to how much you want to shrink the drive. You'll be shown the volume of the drive after you shrink it at the bottom of the screen. Click Shrink after you've made your choice.

4. The Disk Management Console will now show a new entry—an Unallocated Space block to the right of the volume you just shrank.

5. Right-click the Unallocated Space block, and choose New Simple Volume. A wizard will launch that prompts you through turning the unallocated space into a new partition, including assigning a drive letter, using all the available space on it, formatting the volume, and so on.

If you want to save time when creating your new partition, at the last step in the wizard, choose "Perform a quick format." This will save a considerable amount of time during the formatting.

Figure 3-21.

The Disk Management Console lists all hard disks on your PC, including external drives.

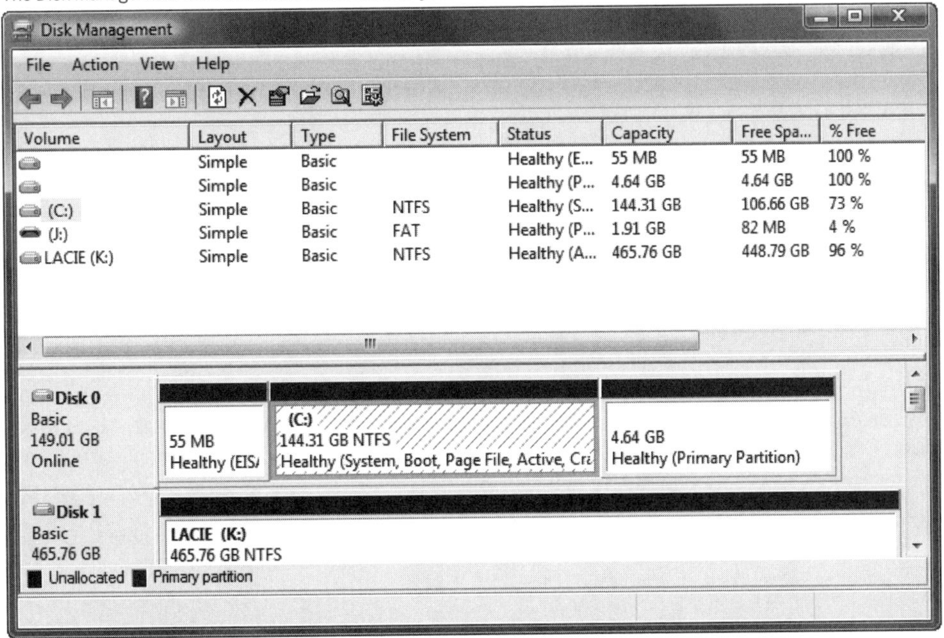

Figure 3-22.
Options for managing a partition.

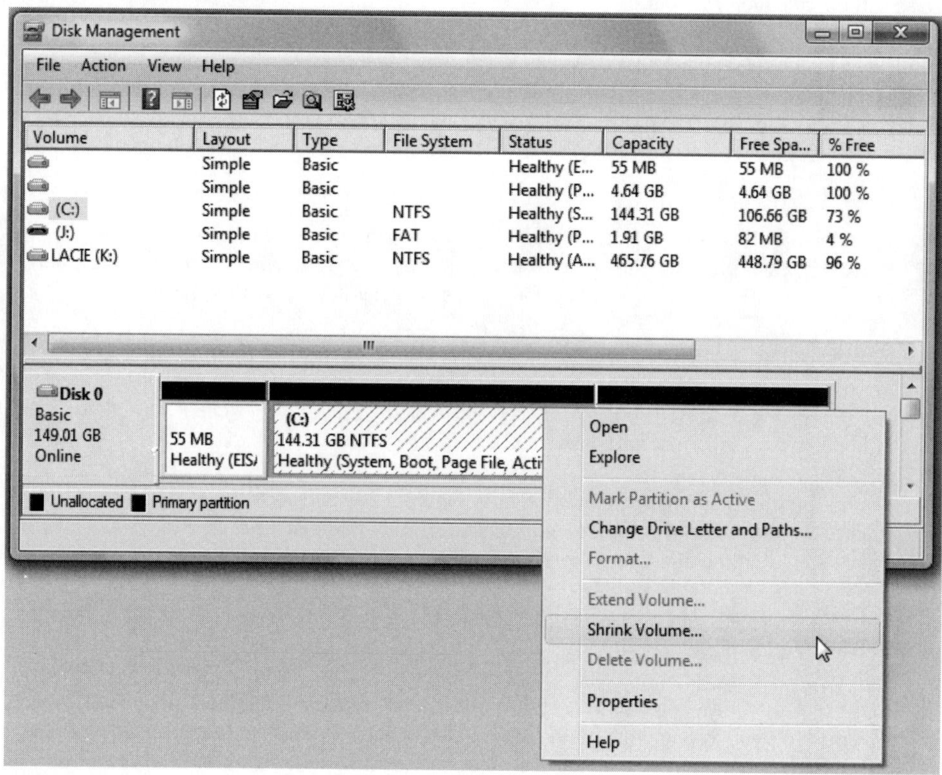

Figure 3-23.
Shrinking the C: drive

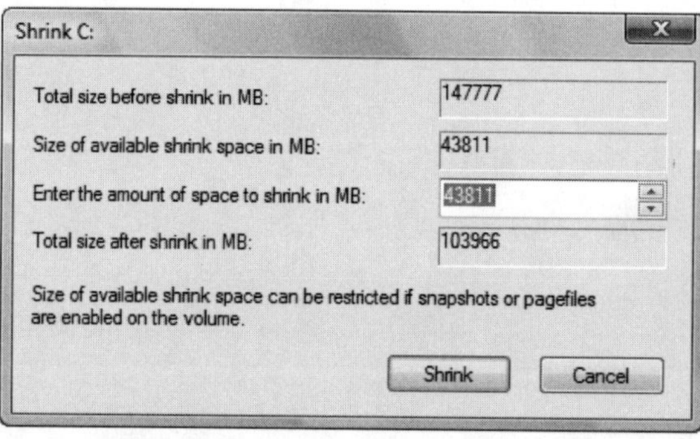

Unfortunately, there are some limits to Vista's built-in partition management tools (for example, you can't move partitions around). Fortunately, the free GParted LiveCD works with Vista, although you may need to take some additional steps as described in this hack:

www.hackszine.com/blog/archive/2007/04/move_partitions_around_on_vist.html

You can do anything you want with your new partition. You could use it to move data off the partition [Hack #40] with your operating system to the new partition. That way, if you need to reinstall or upgrade Windows Vista, your data won't be affected.

If you've been a fan of Partition Magic and want to use it on Windows Vista, don't bother. Partition Magic won't work with Windows Vista, and Symantec has said it will not develop the program to be compatible with the operating system.

HACK 42: Get More Hard-Disk Space by Using NTFS Compression

V XP The quickest and easiest way to give your system more room is to use Windows' built-in compression scheme for NTFS disks. Here's how to use it—and how to convert your existing disk to NTFS if it doesn't already use it.

If you need more hard-disk space, don't buy another hard disk right away. First, consider using NTFS (NT File System) compression, which can give significantly more hard-disk space by compressing all the files on your PC. NTFS's on-the-fly compression capabilities can shrink the size of individual files and folders, or entire drives. When you use it, the files or folders will be compressed when they're on your hard disk to save space, but they will be decompressed automatically when you use them and then compressed again when stored on your hard disk. This means that, unlike with a compression program such as WinZip (www.winzip.com), you don't have to deal with decompressing as well as compressing files. You can also easily turn compression on and off.

Note that NTFS compression isn't available with a FAT32 filesystem, so if you have a FAT32 system you first have to convert to NTFS, as explained later in this hack. If you're not sure which filesystem your volume uses, right-click your volume in Explorer, choose Properties→General, and look for the information next to File System.

How much disk space can you save by using NTFS compression? That depends largely on the kinds of files you have on your system. Bit-mapped graphics files are very compressible, so you'll save quite a bit of hard-disk space if you have many of them. Document files, such as Word files, are also reasonably compressible, while certain kinds of files, such as PDF (Adobe Acrobat) files and images compressed with a lossy compression scheme such as JPEG, are barely compressible at all.

 If you use NTFS compression on a file, the file can't be encrypted using Windows' encrypting capabilities, so be careful not to compress any files that you want to encrypt.

In tests on my own PC, I found that bit-mapped *.tif* graphics files were compressed by more than 80 percent: a folder full of them shrunk from 295 MB to 57 MB. Word files shrunk by 66 percent: a folder full of them shrunk from 131 KB to 44 KB. PDF files, by way of contrast, hardly compressed at all: a group of them shrunk by just more than 6 percent, from 5.59 MB to 5.27 MB.

When you use compression, you might notice a slight drop in system performance. There might be a slight lag when opening or closing files, depending on the speed of your system because the files have to be decompressed for you to open them and compressed when you save them. With newer systems, though, you probably won't notice a lag. On my now-aging Pentium 1.8GHz desktop, for example, I don't see a difference between working with files that have been compressed and working with files that haven't been compressed.

You can use NTFS compression on individual files, folders, and entire disks. To use NTFS compression on a file or folder, right-click the file or folder in Windows Explorer and choose Properties→General→Advanced. You'll see the screen shown in Figure 3-24.

Check the box next to "Compress contents to save disk space," click OK, and click OK again when the Properties dialog box appears.

If you want to compress an entire drive, right-click it in Windows Explorer and choose Properties→General→"Compress drive to save disk space." You'll be asked for confirmation, and then every folder and file on the drive will be compressed, one after another. Depending on the size of the drive, the procedure can take several hours. You can continue to use Windows while the compression takes place. During that time, however, you might be notified that a file is in use, so you'll need to

QUICK HACK 

MANAGE PARTITIONS DURING INSTALLATION

If you're doing a clean install, you can create partitions during the Windows Vista installation process, and create one also for your data so that you don't need to create one later on. During the installation process, when you get to the "Where do you want to install Windows" screen, click "Drive options (advanced)". You'll see a set of tools along the bottom of the screen for managing partitions. Click New to create a new partition, choose a size for the partition, and then click Apply. Your new partition will be created.

Figure 3-24.
Enabling compression on files and folders to save hard-disk space

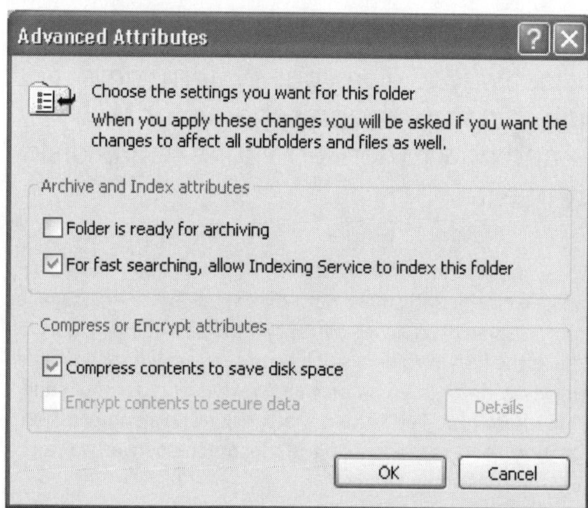

close it (if it's a file you're working on) so that Windows can compress it. There will be some files that Windows and other programs are using, and the only way to close them it to shut down items in the notification area and temporarily stop as many services as possible **[Hack #6]**. Even so, you'll find a few files that you can't loosen Windows' grip on.

By default, Windows visually differentiates between compressed files and decompressed files; compressed files are shown in blue. If for some reason your compressed files aren't blue, and you want them to be, from Windows Explorer choose Tools→Folder Options→View, scroll down, and select the checkbox next to "Show encrypted or compressed NTFS files in color."

How Compressing Folders Affects Underlying Files

When you compress files in a folder, they are all, obviously, compressed. But things can get confusing when you mix compressed folders and decompressed folders on a hard disk, or when you have compressed files in decompressed folders and vice versa. What happens, for example, when you move a decompressed file into a compressed folder, or move a compressed file from a compressed folder into a decompressed folder? The possibilities can set your head spinning. Here are the rules that apply when you're mixing compressed and decompressed files and folders:

- Files copied into a compressed folder are automatically compressed.
- New files created in a compressed folder are automatically compressed.
- Files moved into a compressed folder from a separate NTFS volume are automatically compressed.
- Files moved into a compressed folder from the same NTFS volume retain their compression settings. So, if the file was compressed, it will remain compressed. If the file was not compressed, it will not be compressed.
- If you move a file from a compressed folder to a decompressed folder in the same NTFS volume, the file will remain compressed.
- If you move a file from a compressed folder to a decompressed folder on a different NTFS volume, the file will no longer be compressed.
- Files copied or moved from a compressed folder on an NTFS volume to a FAT32 volume are decompressed.

Checking How Much Disk Space NTFS Compression Saves

When you compress a file or folder, it doesn't appear that you're actually saving any disk space; when you view a file listing in Windows Explorer, the size of the compressed files will remain the same as they were before compression. In fact, though, the files have been compressed, and space has been saved. Explorer reports on only the decompressed file size, not the compressed file size. To see the compressed size of a file or folder, right-click it in Windows Explorer, and choose Properties→General. You'll see two listings of the file size, one titled "Size" and the other titled "Size on disk." The "Size on disk" listing reports on the compressed size of the file, while the "Size" listing reports on the decompressed size, as shown in Figure 3-25.

When to Use ZIP Files and When to Use NTFS Compression

Another way to gain extra space on your hard disk is to use Windows' built-in ZIP capabilities. ZIP is an industry standard for file compression, and it compresses files much more effectively than NTFS does. In tests, I found that ZIP compression shrunk graphics files twice as effectively as NTFS compression; the resulting ZIP files were half the size of the NTFS-compressed files.

But that doesn't mean you should use ZIP compression all the time; there are times when using NTFS compression is a better bet. When files are zipped, for example, you can't open them in their application by double-clicking them. First you have to open the ZIP archive and then double-click the file. As a general rule, zipped files are not as convenient to use and handle as NTFS-compressed files. The exception is that ZIP lets you archive a group of files into a single folder, which you can then send to others via email or on disk.

What does this mean? On a day-to-day basis, NTFS compression is a better bet for files you frequently use. However, there are a number of reasons to use ZIP files instead:

- When you need to send a large file or files to someone via email. You can zip all the files into a single archive and send that along.

Figure 3-25.
Viewing the true size of a compressed file

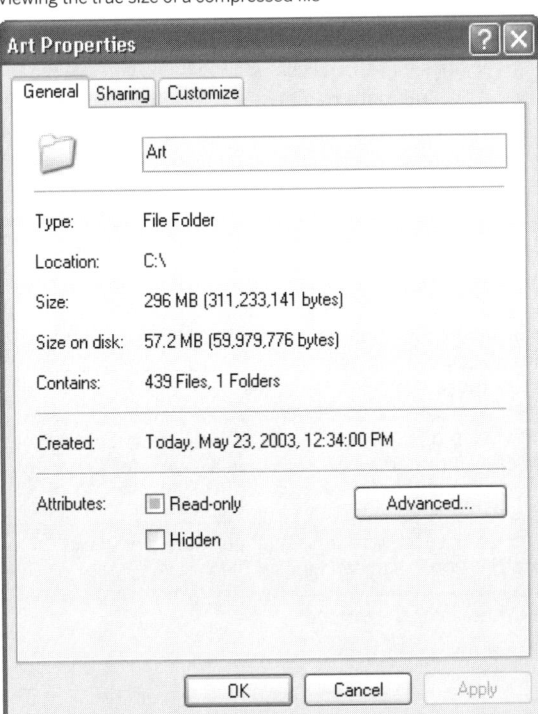

- For storing files that you rarely use. You can create ZIP archives to store the files and then delete the originals.
- For gaining the maximum amount of disk space. If hard-disk space is at a premium, you'll save much more with ZIP files.
- When you want to compress and also encrypt files. You can't encrypt files that have NTFS compression; you can encrypt files that have been zipped.

If you decide to use ZIP files, consider getting a copy of WinZip. It's easier to use than Windows' built-in ZIP compression and offers many more features, including several levels of compression, built-in links to email, and much more.

Hacking the Hack

If you convert to NTFS, here's a Registry hack for increasing its performance. Whenever you view a directory on an NTFS volume, the filesystem updates the date and timestamp to show the last time the directory was accessed. If you have a very large NTFS volume, this continual updating process can slow system performance. To disable automatic updating, run the Registry Editor, and go to `HKEY_LOCAL_MACHINE\SYSTEM\CurrentContolSet\Control\Filesystem`. Look for `NtfsDisableLastAccessUpdate`. If it's not present, create it as a `DWORD`. Set the value to 1.

> **QUICK HACK**
>
> **CONVERT YOUR HARD DISK TO NTFS**
>
> To use Windows compression or encryption, you have to use NTFS. But if you have a different filesystem, such as FAT32, you're not left out: you can convert it to NTFS with the `convert` utility. To convert a volume to NTFS, at a command prompt (on Vista, you need to start an Administrator Command Prompt [Hack #108]), type:
>
> ```
> convert d:
> /fs:ntfs
> ```
>
> where `d:` is the volume you want to convert.
>
> You can also use a number of parameters along with the utility:
>
> /v runs the utility in verbose mode, which provides information about the volume being converted.
>
> `/nosecurity` sets the security privileges on the converted disk so that its files and folders can be used by anyone.
>
> /x prevents another user from accessing the drive over the network while you're converting it, which would disrupt the conversion. (This parameter dismounts the drive from the network.)

HACK 43: Power Up Search in Windows Vista

V Search is embedded into every level of Windows Vista, but it can be confusing to use. Here's how to hack and master Vista's search to get lightning-fast and accurate results.

One of Windows Vista's greatest improvements over Windows XP is its new, far more powerful search. In many instances, all you need to do is type in a word or two, and voilá, your results appear.

Of course, this being Windows, things aren't really quite that simple. There are numerous ways to search in Windows, and at first it's not at all clear when you should use which. Should you use the Search box inside Windows Explorer? The one inside Internet Explorer? The Start Search box that appears when you click the Start button? How about choosing Start→Search, to go straight to the Search Folder and advanced Search screen?

Table 3-2 shows the major ways you can perform a search in Windows Vista, and recommendations on when to use which.

Table 3-2. Different ways to search

Search box in Windows Explorer	Best for searching inside individual folders and subfolders because it searches only the current folder and subfolders. Also best for searching on filenames.
Start→Search (leads to Search Folder and Advanced Search)	Best for performing complex searches across multiple folders, and for when you want to save a search for future use.
Start Search box on the Start menu	Best for quick searches across multiple folders or of the Internet. Not good for searching for filenames.
Search box in Internet Explorer	Best for searching the Internet.

Windows Vista performs a search while you type your search term into a search box. So as you type the letters "gran", for example, it will display all files that have "gran" in them and will narrow the search as you type more letters into the box.

Hacking the Index

When you do a search for a file on your computer, you aren't actually searching your entire hard disk. Instead, you're searching the Windows Vista index, which makes searching lightning-fast.

There are some instances in which you will search outside the index. For example, when you perform a search inside a folder, you also search the filenames inside the folder, not just the index. And as explained later, you can also expand your search to nonindexed locations if you wish.

But although the index makes searching lightning-fast, it can cause some confusion, as well. By default, your entire PC is not indexed, because doing that defeats the purpose of the index; the index would get so large that it would slow down your search.

By default, the following is indexed:

- Your user folder (*\Users*`username`): This contains your Documents, Music, Pictures, and Videos folders, as well as Contacts, Favorites, and the hidden AppData folder, that contains your Windows Mail messages, Firefox profiles, and other application-specific data.
- Offline files: These are files stored on a server or network drive that you have configured to be available offline.
- The contents of your Start menu.

That's well and good, but what happens if you don't store files and folders underneath your user folder: what if you store in other places on your hard disk? Then you won't find them when you perform a search, unless you specifically search for them outside the index, which of course defeats the purpose of the index.

There is a solution, however. You can add any folders you want to the index (and take them away, as well.) Here's how to do it:

1. Go to the Indexing Options screen by choosing Control Panel→System and Maintenance→ Indexing Options. You'll see a list of all the locations that are currently being indexed.
2. If you don't see the folder you want indexed, select Modify→Show all locations. A screen like Figure 3-26 appears. Expand your *C:* or other drive to show the folders on your hard disk.
3. Check boxes next to any folders you want added to the index, click OK, and then close. The folders will now be added to the search index. You can also exclude folders by unchecking them.

There's more you can do to the index as well, by going to the Advanced Options screen. (Get there by choosing Control Panel→System and Maintenance→Indexing Options→Advanced.) From the Index Settings tab, you can index encrypted files, rebuild the index, and change the location of the index. You can also tell the index how to handle two words that are otherwise identical except that one has an accent mark (known as a *diacritic*), and the other doesn't. You can tell the index to treat them as separate words or as the same word (the default).

The File Types tab lets you set which file types should be indexed, and for each file type, whether the contents and properties of the file should be indexed or just the properties.

If you find that when you search, you're not finding files that you know are in your index, the index may have been damaged. To solve the problem, you'll need to rebuild it: Select Advanced→Index Settings→Rebuild.

Figure 3-26.
Adding folders to the search index

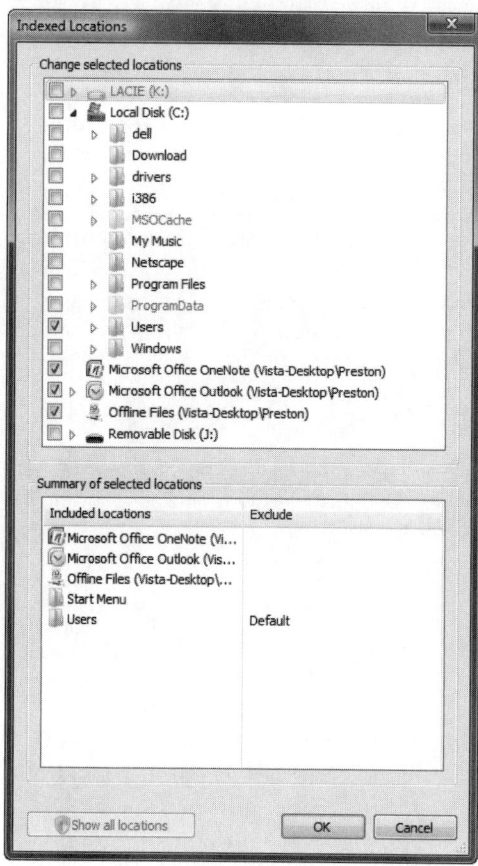

Creating Saved Searches

Do you regularly do the same searches over and over—for example, look for all emails from a certain person or all documents having to do with your 2007 budget? If so, you can save yourself plenty of time by doing the search just once and then going back to that search without having to type it in again. This is a particularly big time saver if you regularly do the same complex search.

To begin, choose Start→Search. You'll be sent to the Search Results folder, which starts as a blank Windows Explorer screen, with a Search Pane turned on. Type in your search terms, or else click Advanced Search to perform more advanced searches, such as searching by date, size, tags in a document, and so on. You can also use the buttons across the top of the screen to filter your searches. For example, to show only emails, click Email; to show only pictures, click Picture; and so on.

After you do your search, and it completes, you can save it. Click Save Search on the toolbar just above the search results, and you can save the search. (See Figure 3-27 for an advanced search being saved). You save it as a file with the *.search-ms* extension. By default, they are saved in the *\Users*`username`*\Searches* folder, but you can save them to any other folder as well.

There are several ways to return to a saved search. You can, of course, open Windows Explorer, navigate to where you've saved the *.search-ms.* file, and double-click it. There's a faster way, though. In Explorer's Navigation pane, click More under Favorite Links, and choose Searches. You'll be sent to the *\Users*`username`*\Searches* folder, and a list of all saved searches will appear—not only those that you've created, but those that Windows Vista has already pre-created for you as well, including searches for all recent documents, recent email, recent music, and so on.

Figure 3-27.
Saving a search so that you can later return to it

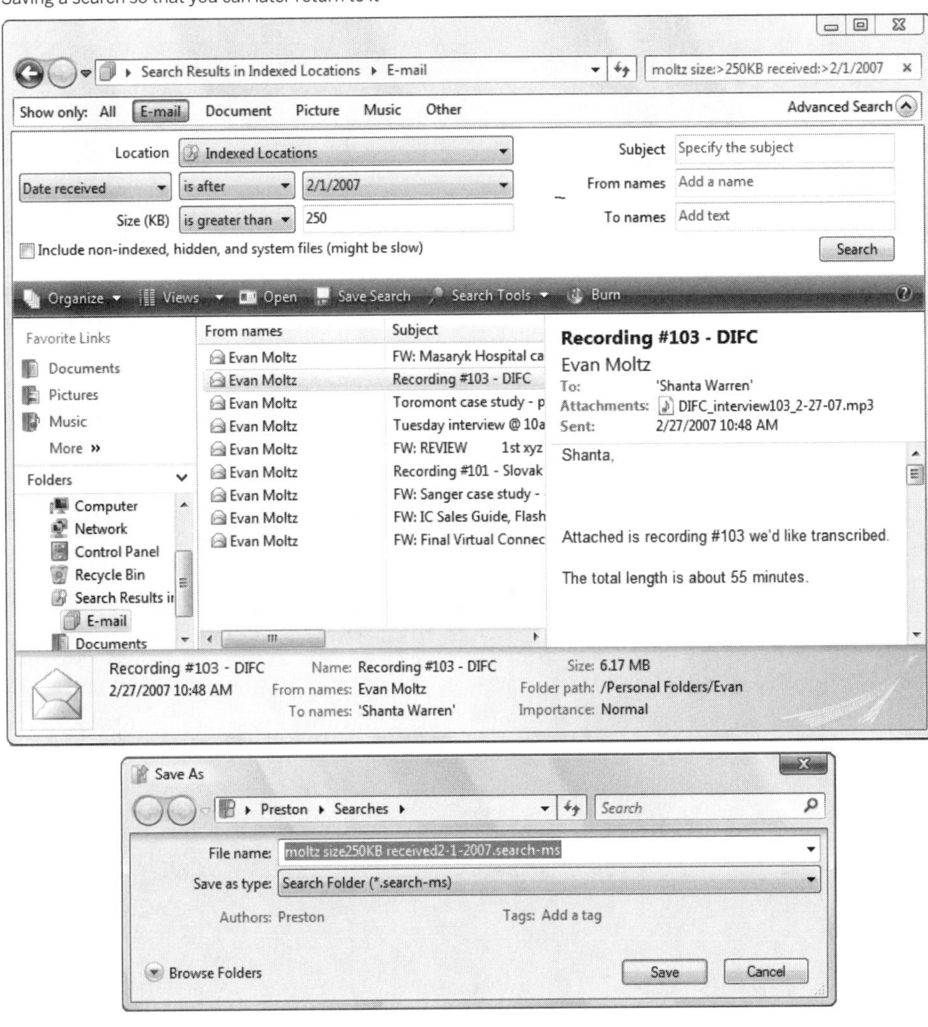

You don't have to choose Start→Search to do searches; you can simply type your search into the search box when you're in Windows Explorer. But when you do that, you'll only search the current folder, not your entire hard disk. In fact, this is a very good way to perform targeted searches: Open Windows Explorer, and go to the folder where you want to search, then search from there.

Note that you can save searches, not only when you use Start→Search, but when inside any folder in Windows Explorer as well. Your searches will be saved by default to your Search folder, no matter where you start your search.

Using Search Properties and Syntax

A very good way to find what you want quickly is to search through file properties (filename, file author, and so on) and to use a specialized syntax that makes finding files easier. You can search on any metadata associated with any files, as a quick way to find what you want. Table 3-3 shows many of the common properties you can search on and how to search using them.

Table 3-3. Search properties

Property	Property description	How to search for it
Filename	The name of the file.	Type part or all of the filename. To find a file named *budget.xls*, you could type `budg` or `.xls`.
Kind of file	The file type, such as Document, Picture, Video, or Music.	Type the kind of file; for example, Music for any music files.
File extension	The file extension, such as *.xls*, *.doc*, *.jpg*, and so on.	Type the filename extension. You can also use wildcards, for example, `*.mp3`.
Tags	Words or phrases you or others add to files to describe them.	Type a tag to see a list of files that have the matching tag.
Author	The person who created the file.	Type the name of the author.
Date Modified	The last date that the files were edited	Type Modified: 8/07/2008 to find files modified on that date. You can also only type in the month and day (Modified: 8/07), the year (Modified: 2008), today (Modified:today), or day of week (Modified:monday).
Contents	Any text that appears in a document..	Type in any word or phrase. You'll see a list of files that contain that text.

You can use these properties along with the proper syntax to narrow the searc. For example, to search for files that have the name "budget" in them, you would type this:

```
Name:budget
```

To search for files with the tag of "budget" you would type:

```
Tag:budget
```

To find files modified on November 7, 2006, you would type:

```
Modified:11/07/2006
```

You can also use Boolean filters—AND, NOT, OR; comparisons: >, <; and grouping: " ", ( )—and can combine them with searching for file properties. When using Boolean filters, you have to capitalize AND, NOT, and OR.

If you want to forgo complex searches and remembering search syntax, you can also use what is called natural language search, the ability to search for files using plain English, rather than complex syntax. For example, instead of typing

```
Kind:music artist:(Gluck or Salieri)
```

You could type:

```
Music by Gluck or Salieri
```

If you want to do that, you have to turn on natural language search using the Search tab of the Folder Options window. To do it, select Windows Explorer→Organize→Folder and Search Options→Search. Then check the box next to "Use natural language search," then click OK.

Hacking Search Options

You can also change the most basic things about how search works, for example, whether to display partial matches and how to handle searching nonindexed locations. Select Windows Explorer→Organize→Folder and Search Options→Search. You'll see three sections, as shown in Figure 3-28. Here's what each do, and what you need to know about them:

What to search

This section controls how Search handles filenames and file contents.In some circumstances it searches only through the actual names of files, and in other circumstances, it searches through the names of files, and well as through the contents of files. By default, it searches filenames and contents in indexed locations, and filenames only in nonindexed locations. This section, however, lets you change that behavior. Keep in mind that if you choose to always search through filenames and contents of non-indexed files, it may slow your search considerably because searching nonindexed files can be sluggish.

How to search

This controls a variety of search behaviors. You can include or not include subfolders when typing in the Search box; find or not find partial matches; and choose not to use the Index when searching (doing this will slow search down considerably, but casts a wider net).

In addition, it lets you use natural language search, as I previously explained.

Figure 3-28.
Configuring search options

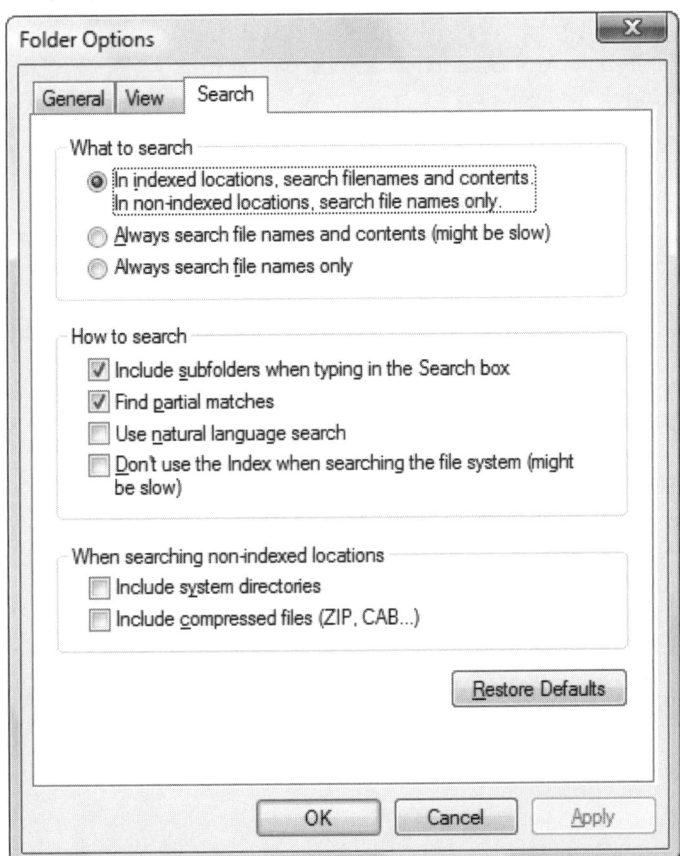

QUICK HACK

BETTER WINDOWS FLIP AND FLIP 3D

Here's a way to power up the Windows Flip (Alt-Tab) and Windows Flip 3D (Windows Key-Tab) keyboard shortcuts: add in the Ctrl key (Ctrl-Alt-Tab for Windows Flip, and Ctrl-Windows Key-Tab for Windows Flip 3D). Use the Ctrl key, and the task switchers will stay onscreen, so that you can scroll through your open windows and select using your mouse or arrow keys, without having to keep holding down the Alt or Windows key.

Figure 3-29.
Customizing Windows Vista search on the Start menu

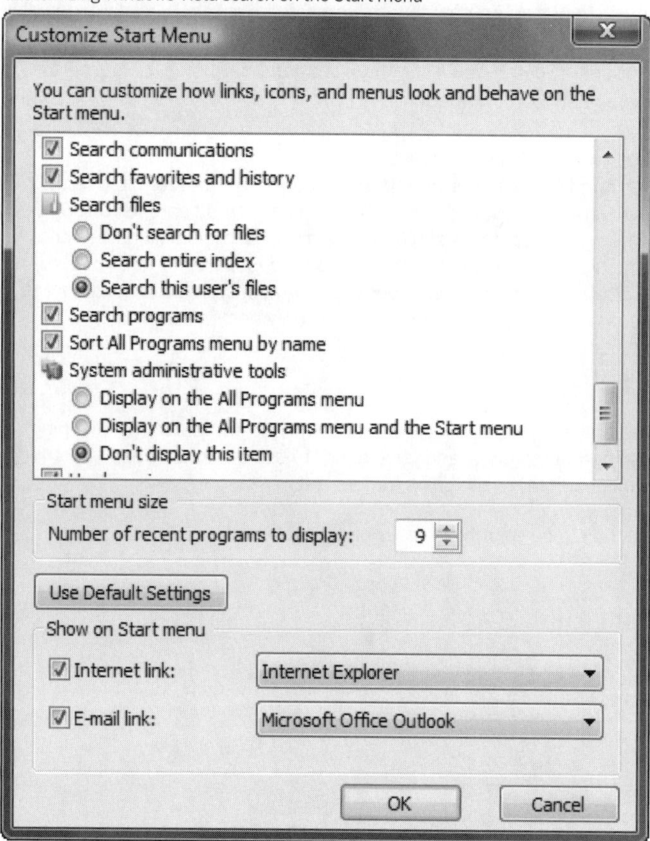

When searching non-indexed locations

You can choose to include or not include system directories and compressed files when searching through non-indexed areas. Including them will slow down search performance, but will be a broader search.

See Also

- "Find Files Faster in Windows XP by Mastering the Indexing Service's Query Language" **[Hack #46]**

HACK 44: Quick Way To Speed Up Windows Vista Search

V Windows Vista search can bog down if you've got plenty of files, emails, contacts, and more on your hard disk. Here's a simple way to make searching zippy again.

The first month or so after you've installed Windows Vista, its search feature seems lightning-fast. But then, over time, it gradually slows down. Is it simply getting tired?

No. The problem is that as you accumulate files, programs, emails, contacts, and more, Windows Vista has a lot more data to search through, and that slows it down. Its search feature even searches through your Favorites and your browsing history.

QUICK HACK

GET A BETTER WINDOWS EXPLORER

If you're not happy with Windows Explorer as a file manager, try out the free UltraExplorer (www.mustangpeak.net). It works with Windows XP as well as Windows Vista, sports a completely customizable interface, and includes lots of extras, such as a command-line window, a history window with a list of folders you've recently visited, a tabbed interface that lets you work with different folders in different tabs, and much more.

Most of the time when you do searches, you use the Search box on the Start menu, and those are most likely the times when you're looking for fast results. So I'll show you how to speed up searches launched from the Start menu.

First, decide what information you're looking for when you do a search from the Start menu's search box. Are you always looking to run a program? For a file? An email message? After you decide that, right-click the Start button, and choose Properties. Click Customize next to the Start menu entry, and the Customize Start Menu dialog box appears. Scroll toward the bottom, and you'll see the entries like those shown in Figure 3-29.

Uncheck boxes next to any type of content you don't want to search. For example, if you only want to search for programs, uncheck the boxes next to Search communications, and Search favorites and history, and select "Don't search for files." If you only want to search for files, uncheck the boxes next to Search programs, Search communications, and Search favorites and history. Click OK when you're done, and OK again. Searches will speed up considerably.

See Also

- "Power Up Search in Windows Vista" [Hack #43]
- "Find Files Faster in Windows XP by Mastering the Indexing Service's Query Language" [Hack #46]

HACK 45: Use Start ++ To Juice Up Windows Vista Search

V Turbocharge your searches with this freebie from one of Microsoft's Windows Vista architects.

Windows Vista's search box on the Start menu is one of the operating system's most useful new tools. It makes it easy to search your PC for files, programs, emails, and contact, and also to search the Web as well.

The free Start++ (brandontools.com) turbocharges that search box. It lets you create shortcut commands and aliases to perform all kinds of tasks, both on your PC and the Internet. It can do more than just search and can combine searches with automated tasks. For example, if you install the program and then type play Beethoven in the Start box, it searches for all files on your PC that have the keyword Beethoven, writes a playlist (*.MU3*) file that includes all the results, then opens the playlist in Windows Media Player and starts playing the music.

To start, download, install, and run the free Start++. You'll see it running in your system tray. Do a normal search, and you won't notice a difference at all; Search functions the way it normally does. But you can use its built-in "search startlets" and "command startlets" to automate tasks and searches. As the names imply, search startlets are shortcuts for for searches, and command startlets are shortcuts for commands.

To see what's available, right-click the Start++ icon, and select Configure. The screen shown in Figure 3-30 appears.

Here we're on the command startlets tab. A command startlet is essentially a shortcut that launches a more complicated command. A number have already been built, as you can see. To search Wikipedia for Cecilia Bartoli, type w Cecilia Bartoli, and press Enter. To run a command from the administrator command prompt, type sudo, followed by the command you want to run.

Build Your Own Command Startlet

You can also easily create your own command startlets. I'll show you how to build one to search the Netflix DVD rental site, but you can use the same technique to build one of your own.

QUICK HACK 

COPY AND PASTE YOUR PATH

In Windows Vista, Windows Explorer's new "breadcrumbs" in the Address Bar is great for navigation, but what if you want to copy and paste your current path into a document? There appears to be no way to do it? Not only that, but it uses a kind of alias feature to hide the first part of your path. It's easy to see your full path as text, though, and to copy and paste it. Click inside the Address Bar to the right of the rightmost breadcrumb entry. Your full path will now appear as text and be highlighted, so you can copy it. For example, in breadcrumbs the path may have been `username`*\Documents\Budget 2008*, but as text it shows up as *C:\Users*`username`*\Documents\Budget 2008*. Not only can you copy the text, but you can type any folder name into the Address Bar now, and navigate straight to it. Note that this hack won't work with some special locations such as Network and Computer.

Figure 3-30.
Search ++'s command startlets

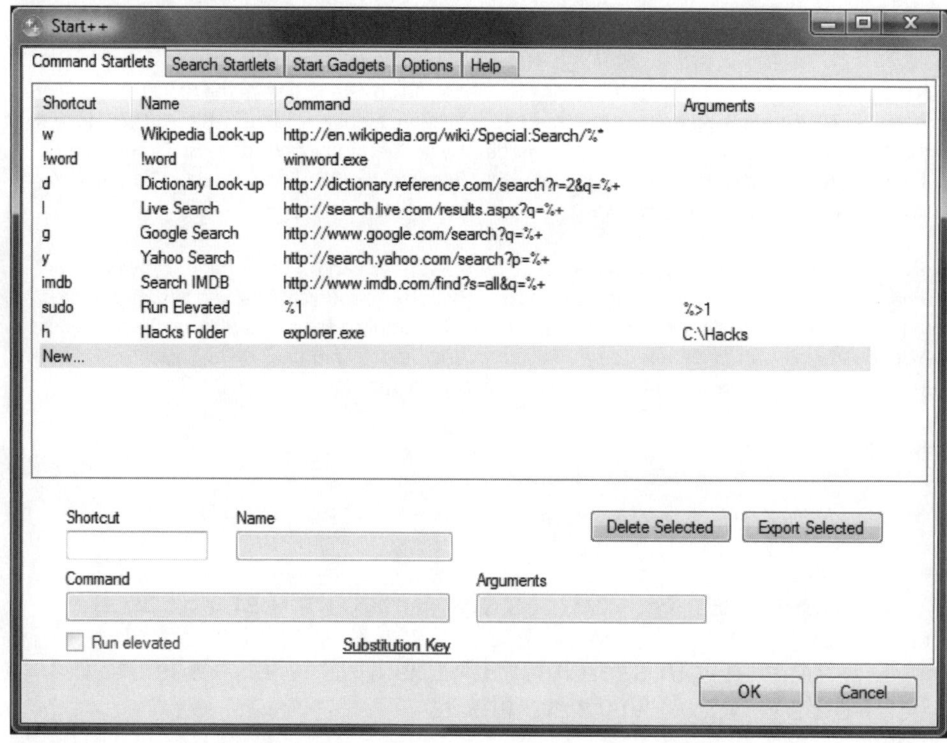

Figure 3-31.
The Start ++ Search Startlets tab.

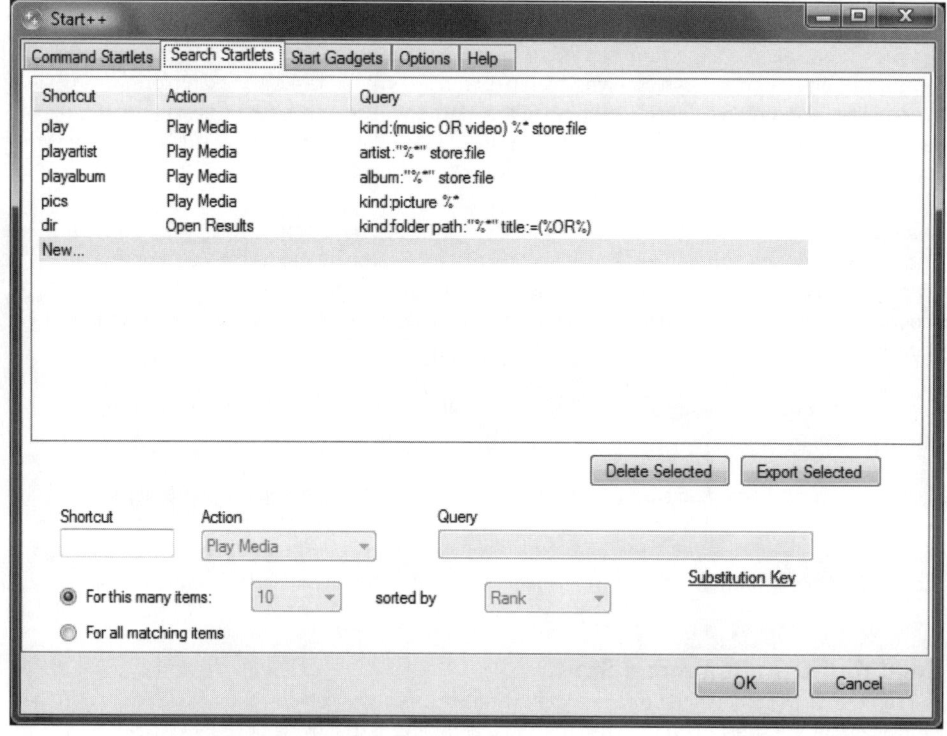

First we need to understand the search syntax used by Netflix. Go to the site, and type in a search term, for example `Bogart`. Look at the URL of the results. Here's what you'll see:

```
http://www.netflix.com/Search?v1=bogart
```

This tells us the search syntax that Netflix uses, which is `http://www.netflix.com/Search?v1=`, followed by the search term. Now that we know that, we can build our command startlet.

Click New. In the Shortcut box, type in the shortcut text you want to use to launch the command, in our example, we'll use nf. Then in the Name box, give the command startlet a name; we'll name it Netflix Search. Now in the Command box, type in the command you want the command startlet to run. Here's where to put the search syntax. In this case, you need to enter this:

```
http://www.netflix.com/Search?v1=%+
```

The `%+` tells the Netflix search engine to take whatever search term you type in, and append it to the end of `http://www.netflix.com/Search?v1=`.

We're not going to use any arguments, so leave that box blank. Click OK.

Now, when you type nf Bogart at the Search box on the Start menu and press Enter, you'll do a search of Netflix for the term Bogart.

Using Search Startlets

Search startlets are far more complicated than command startlets. To see what's available to you, click the Search startlets tab, as shown in Figure 3-31.

As you can see, you have a number of search startlets already written for you. Search startlets are used primarily for playing media, although they can be used for other purposes as well. The play command, for example, searches for media with the keyword or keywords you type in, then plays them in Windows Media Player. So type in play Beatles, and Windows Vista will search for all your media with the keyword Beatles, and then play them, one after another, in Windows Media Player. The search startlets available to you are all straightforward and self-explanatory.

You can also write search startlets of your own. As when creating a command startlet, click New, then fill in the form at the bottom of the screen. In the drop-down Action field on the form, you can tell Windows Vista to perform one of two actions: to either play the media in your default media player such as Windows Media Player or else to open the results in a folder. In the Query box, type in the query you want an action taken on. Then at the bottom of the screen, you have options for the number of items to open or play, and how to sort the results.

HACK 46: Find Files Faster in Windows XP by Mastering the Indexing Service's Query Language

XP Got a hard disk filled with many files and no easy way to find what you want quickly? Use XP's Indexing Service and its query language to get what you want—fast.

Packrats like me (and my editor) have a hard time finding exactly what they want on their hard disks. I have thousands of files there, some dating back close to 10 years, which I dutifully copy to a new system every time I upgrade my hardware. After all, who knows when I might need to find the list of books I planned to take out of the library in 1996?

XP's Search Companion is too slow, and the kinds of searches it can perform are fairly limited. It can't find files based on properties such as when the file was last printed or the word count of a file, or using a sophisticated search language.

The Indexing Service, first used with Microsoft Internet Information Services (IIS), is a far more powerful tool. It can perform searches hundreds of times faster and includes an exceedingly sophisticated query language you can use for performing searches. It works by indexing the files on your disk, and then, when you do a search, it queries that index rather than searching through your entire hard disk. The indexes the service creates are called *catalogs*.

By default, the Indexing Service is turned off. To activate it, first run the Search Companion by choosing Start→Search. From the screen that appears, choose Change Preferences→With Indexing Service. If the With Indexing Service option isn't available, and instead you see Without Indexing Service, it means the Indexing Service is already turned on.

When you activate the Indexing Service, it won't be available immediately. First it has to build an index, which can take a substantial amount of time, depending on the number of files on your hard disk and your processor speed. It's best to start the Indexing Service and leave your computer on overnight so that it can complete indexing.

To turn off the Indexing Service from the Search Companion, choose Change Preferences→Without Indexing Service. When you do that, you'll use the normal Search Companion. The index will remain intact; when you do a search, you just won't search through it. You can always turn the index back on when you want.

Using the Indexing Service's Query Language

The Indexing Service's query language is a sophisticated language, letting you search on file properties—such as the author of documents or the number of bytes in a document—using Boolean operators and other search criteria.

The language uses tags to define search criteria. For example, to search for the phrase "That dog won't hunt," the query would be:

```
{phrase} That dog won't hunt {/phrase}
```

You can search for text in the query language using either `phrase` or `freetext`. A `phrase` search searches for the exact words in the exact order, like this:

```
{phrase} old dog barks backwards {/phrase}
```

The search results will include only files whose text includes that exact phrase.

A `freetext` expression search looks for any words in the phrase and returns files that have any one of the words in the phrase. It works like the Boolean `OR` operator. So, the query:

```
{freetext} old dog barks backwards {/freetext}
```

returns many more searches than the `phrase` query, because it returns results that contain any of the words in the phrase.

Searching Using Properties

The Indexing Service's query language's power is contained in the way it can search not just for text, but also for document properties. The syntax for searching using properties in a query is:

```
{prop name=property name} query {/prop}
```

where `property name` is the name of the property, such as those listed in Table 3-4, and `query` is the text you're searching for. For example, to search for all documents last edited by Preston Gralla, you would enter:

```
{prop name=DocLastAuthor} Preston Gralla {/prop}
```

Queries can use *and ? wildcard characters, as well as Unix-style regular expression queries (for more on regular expressions, see *Mastering Regular Expressions* from O'Reilly). To use these wildcards, you must use the **{regex}** tag, like this:

```
{prop name=filename} {regex} *.xl? {/regex} {/prop}
```

The Indexing Service indexes not just the text of each document but also all the summary information associated with each document. (To see summary information for any document, right-click the document, and choose Properties→Summary.) In addition to searching for properties in the summary, you can also search for the properties found in Table 3-4, which lists the most important properties you can use to search.

Table 3-4. Important properties for searching via the Indexing Service

Property	Description
`Access`	The last time the document was accessed.
`All`	All available properties. Works with text queries but not numeric queries.
`AllocSize`	The total disk space allocated to the document.
`Contents`	The contents of the document.
`Created`	The time the document was created.
`Directory`	The full directory path in which the document is contained.
`DocAppName`	The name of the application in which the document was created.
`DocAuthor`	The author of the document.
`DocByteCount`	The number of bytes in the document.
`DocCategory`	The type of document.
`DocCharCount`	The number of characters in the document.
`DocComments`	Comments made about the document.
`DocCompany`	The name of the company for which the document was written.
`DocCreatedTime`	The time spent editing the document.
`DocHiddenCount`	The number of hidden slides in a PowerPoint document.
`DocKeyWords`	The keywords in the document.
`DocLastAuthor`	The name of the person who last edited the document.
`DocLastPrinted`	The time the document was most recently printed.
`DocLineCount`	The number of lines contained in the document.
`DocLastSavedTm`	The time the document was last saved.

Table 3-4. Important properties for searching via the Indexing Service *(continued)*

Property	Description
DocManager	The name of the manager of the document's author.
DocNoteCount	The number of pages with notes in a PowerPoint document.
DocPageCount	The number of pages in the document.
DocParaCount	The number of paragraphs in the document.
DocPartTitles	The names of document parts, such as spreadsheet names in an Excel document or slide titles in a PowerPoint slide show.
DocRevNumber	The current version number of the document.
DocSlideCount	The number of slides in a PowerPoint document.
DocTemplate	The name of the document's template.
DocTitle	The title of the document.
DocWordCount	The number of words in the document.
FileName	The filename of the document.
Path	The path to the document, including the document filename.
ShortFileName	The 8.3-format name of the document.
Size	The size of the document, in bytes.
Write	The date and time the document was last modified.

Searching Using Operators and Expressions

The query language also lets you use a variety of operators and expressions for both text and numbers:

`EQUALS` and `CONTAINS` operators

When you're creating a query using text, you can use the `EQUALS` and `CONTAINS` operators to narrow your search. Use the `EQUALS` operator when you want the exact words matched in the exact order, like this:

```
{prop name=DocTitle} EQUALS First Draft of Final Novel {/prop}
```

This query finds all documents with the title "First Draft of Final Novel." The query won't find a document with the title "Final Draft of First Novel" or "First Draft of Novel." The `EQUALS` operator works like the `phrase` expression.

Use the `CONTAINS` operator when you want to find any of the words in the document, in the same way you would use the `freetext` expression.

Relational operators

Use the following relational operators when you're searching using numbers:

=	Equal to
!=	Not equal to
<	Less than

<= Less than or equal to

> Greater than

>= Greater than or equal to

Date and time expressions

You can use the following formats when searching using dates and times:

```
yyyy/mm/dd hh:mm:ss
yyyy-mmmm-dd hh:mm:ss
```

You can also use date and time expressions in combination with relational operators—for example, to look for files that were created within the last two days:

```
{prop name=Created} >-2d {/prop}
```

Table 3-5 lists the date and time abbreviations you can use.

Table 3-5. Date and time expressions that work with relational operators

Abbreviation	Meaning	Abbreviation	Meaning
Y	Year	D	Day
Q	Quarter	H	Hour
M	Month	N	Minute
W	Week	S	Second

Boolean operators

The query language also uses the Boolean operators detailed in Table 3-6.

Table 3-6. Boolean operators used by the Indexing Service's query language

Boolean operator	Short form	Long form
AND	&	AND
OR	|	OR
Unary NOT	!	NOT
Binary NOT	&!	AND NOT

Use the unary NOT to negate a term. For example, to search for all documents that do not have seven PowerPoint slides, use the query:

```
{prop name=DocSlideCount} NOT = 7 {/prop}
```

Use the binary NOT to narrow a search, by combining two properties in a query. For example, to search for all documents with an author of "Preston Gralla" that are not titled Chapter 10, use this query (on one line):

```
{prop name=DocAuthor} Preston Gralla {/prop} NOT
{prop name=DocTitle} Chapter 10 {/prop}
```

Alternative verb forms

You can use the double-asterisk wildcard (**) to search for alternative forms of verbs in a document. For example, the query:

```
{prop name=Contents} run** {/prop}
```

returns all documents with the word "ran" or the word "run."

Ranking the Order of Search Results

If you're doing a search likely to return many results, you'll want the most-relevant searches to appear at the top of the results, and the least relevant to appear at the bottom. You can determine the relative importance of each term in your search and have the results weighted by that importance using the `weight` tag. Note that it does not get a closing `{/weight}` tag:

```
{weight value=n} query
```

The value parameter ranges between `0.000` and `1.000`.

If you are searching for the three terms "fire," "ice," and "slush," and you want to weight "fire" most heavily, "ice" second-most heavily, and "slush" least heavily, you can use this syntax (on a single line) in your query:

```
{weight value=1.000}fire AND {weight value=.500}ice AND {weight value=.250}slush
```

Editing the Indexing Service's Noise Filter

You can force the Indexing Service to ignore more words when you search, or you can have it ignore fewer words, simply by editing a text file. In a text file called *noise.eng*, usually found in *C:\Windows\System32*, you can find the list of words the Indexing Service ignores. (The extension *.eng* is for English. You can find noise filters from other languages as well—for example, *noise.deu* for German, *noise.fra* for French, and so on.)

The *noise.eng* file contains common articles, prepositions, pronouns, conjunctions, various forms of common verbs, and similar words. Open it in Notepad or another text editor, add words you want it to ignore, and delete words you don't want it to ignore. Then save the file, and the Indexing Service will follow your new rules.

See Also

- "Power Up Search in Windows Vista" **[Hack #43]**

HACK 47: Secrets of Windows Vista's Sync Center and Offline Files

V If you have multiple PCs and need to keep files synchronized among them, the Windows Vista Sync Center and Offline Files is the way to go.

If you work on multiple PCs, you know how difficult it can be to keep files in sync among them. For example, if you have a laptop and a desktop, you may want to work on the same set of files on them, without having to remember to copy them from one machine to another. It's too easy to make mistakes when trying to manually copy multiple files back and forth. More often than not, you end up overwriting a new file with an old one.

Figure 3-32.
Windows Vista's Sync Center

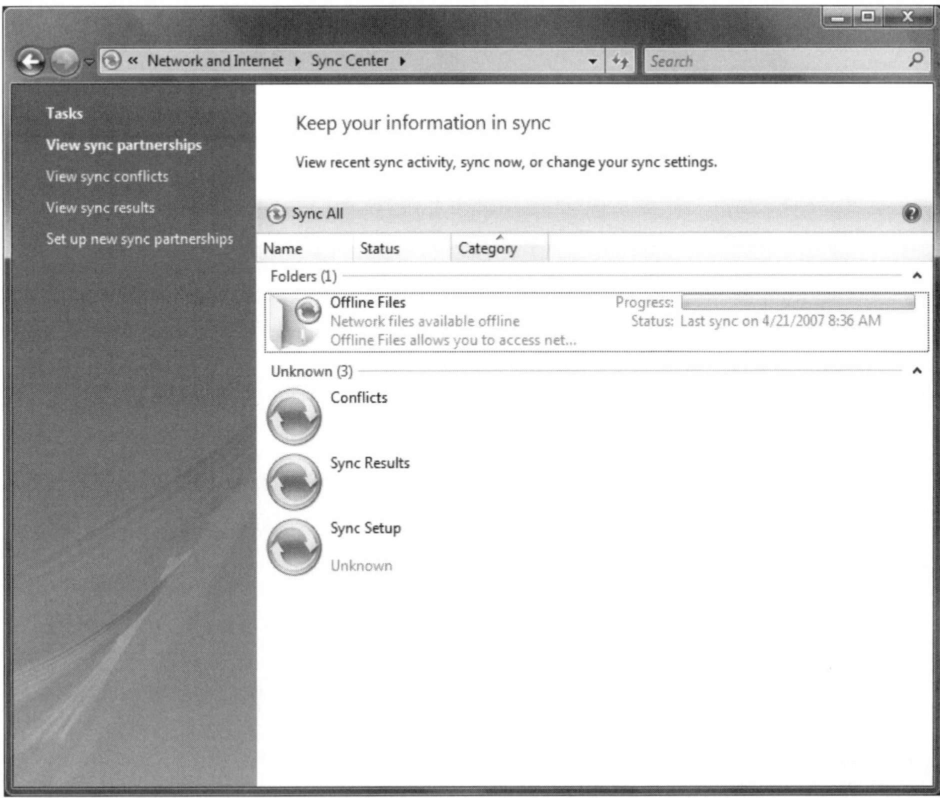

The offline files feature isn't available in Windows Vista Home Basic and Windows Vista Premium.

Windows Vista includes two related features that make it easy to keep files in sync: offline files and the Sync Center (Figure 3-32). In order to use them, your PCs have to be connected to the same network.

In this hack, you'll see how you can use offline files and the Sync Center on a small peer-to-peer network like one you have at home. Offline files work differently in a larger corporate network.

The Sync Center can also be used to synchronize files between your PC and multimedia devices and portable storage devices. In this hack, however, you'll learn how to use it to keep files in sync among PCs.

The Sync Center synchronizes files across a network, via offline files. With offline files, you can get access to files on a shared folder, even if PC or laptop is not currently connected to the network. Offline files allow you to open files, work on them when you're disconnected, and then update them at a later time when the connection has been reestablished.

The name offline files is somewhat misleading, because in fact, copies of the offline files are in fact stored on your local PC, and then synchronized to the other PC when you connect both to the network, and tell Windows Vista to synchronize them.

When you make a shared network folder available offline, you actually save those files to your own PC. When you make changes to them on your own PC or the shared network folders, they are kept in sync. Naturally, you could just save remote files on your own hard disk manually, edit them, and then transfer them manually to their original locations, replacing older versions where necessary. However, Windows Vista's support for offline files is much more convenient than doing all that manually.

QUICK HACK 

USE SYNCTOY FOR QUICK SYNCS

There's another way to synchronize folders—and you can do it in Windows XP as well as in Windows Vista. Get the free Microsoft SyncToy www.microsoft.com/windowsxp/using/digitalphotography/prophoto/synctoy.mspx. It's simpler than the Sync Center, and lets you synchronize files with a click or two.

Figure 3-33.
Enabling offline files

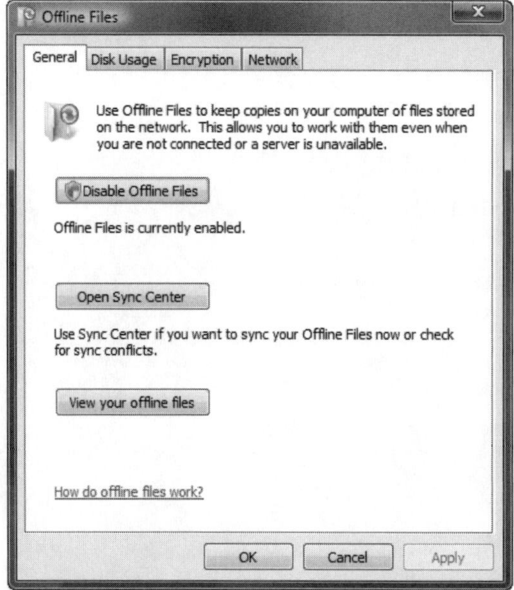

Figure 3-34.
Turning on file sharing

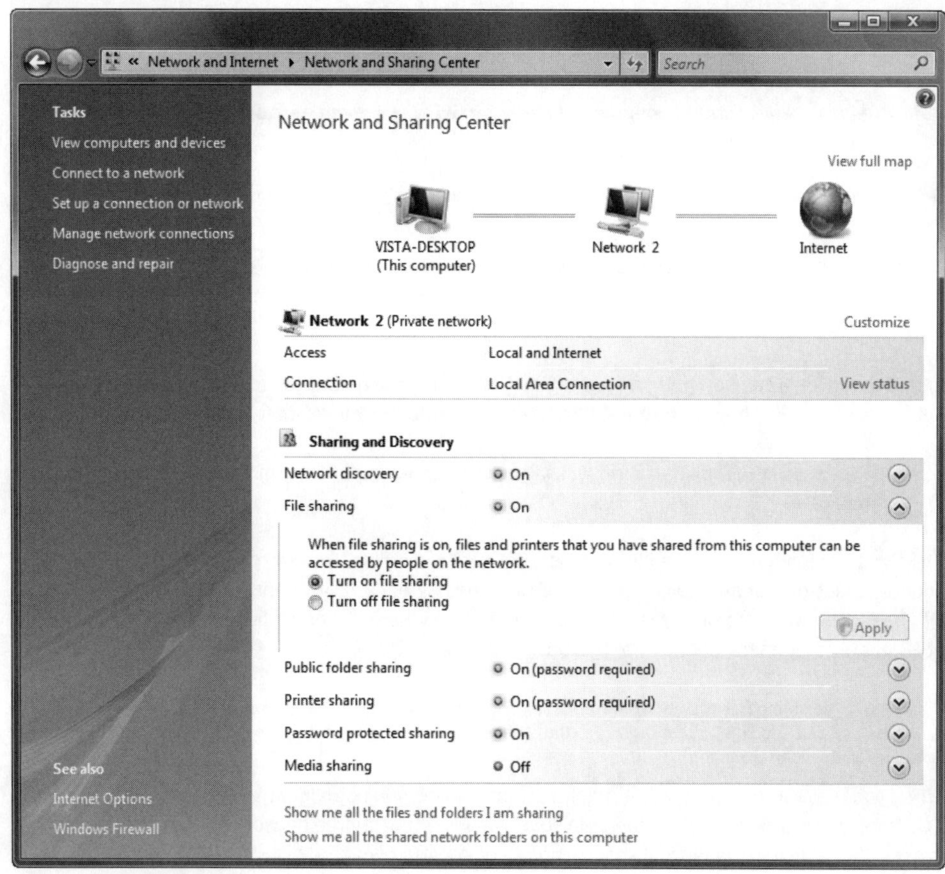

Figure 3-35.
Enabling sharing for a folder in Windows Vista

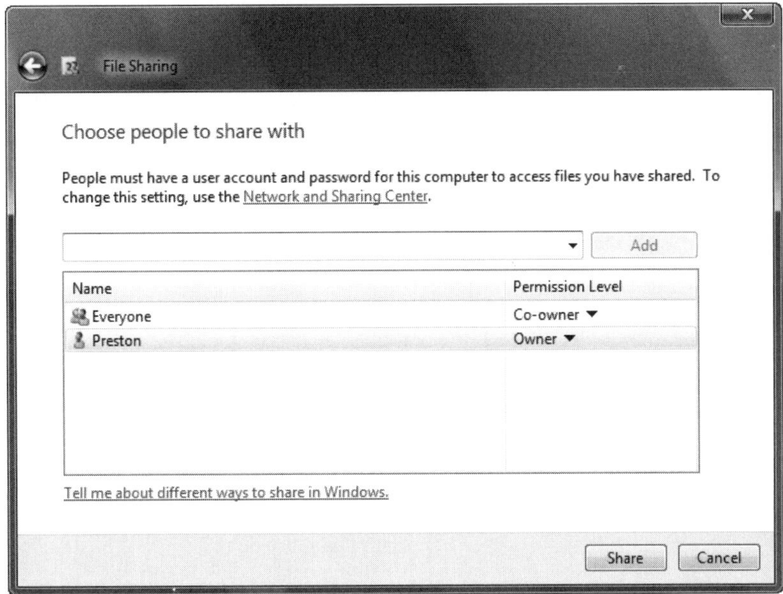

Setting Up Offline Files

In this hack, I assume you have two PCs, a desktop and a laptop. You mainly use the desktop, but there are times when you want to be able to work on your laptop away from your home or office. You'd like to be able to use offline files and the Sync Center to synchronize files between the two of them.

The first thing you should do is make sure that offline files are enabled on both your desktop and laptop PC. Select Control Panel→Network and Internet→Offline Files, and the screen shown in Figure 3-33 appears.

The top button should read Disable Offline Files, which means that they are enabled. If instead it reads Enable Offline Files, click the button to enable offline files.

Only those files and folders that you've decided to share can be accessed as offline files, so now you need to designate certain files and folders to be shared. In this example, you're going to share only files from the desktop PC, but you can do it for both computers if you want. Go to Control Panel→ Network and Internet→Network and Sharing Center. Click the down arrow across from File Sharing, and you'll see the screen shown in Figure 3-34.

Select "Turn on file sharing," and click Apply. You've now enabled file sharing. If you want to password-protect your files and folders so that only those people with an account and password can access them, click the down arrow next to "Password protected sharing" and select "Turn on password protected sharing."

Your folders and files aren't shared yet. You need to designate which folders and files you want to share. Right-click it, and select Share. A screen like that shown in Figure 3-35 appears.

This screen shows you who is allowed to access the folder. You can add accounts by typing their name into the box and clicking Add. When you're done, click Share.

The folder can now be shared with anyone on the network. But the folder still isn't available as offline files; you need to take one more step.

Figure 3-36.
Making files available offline

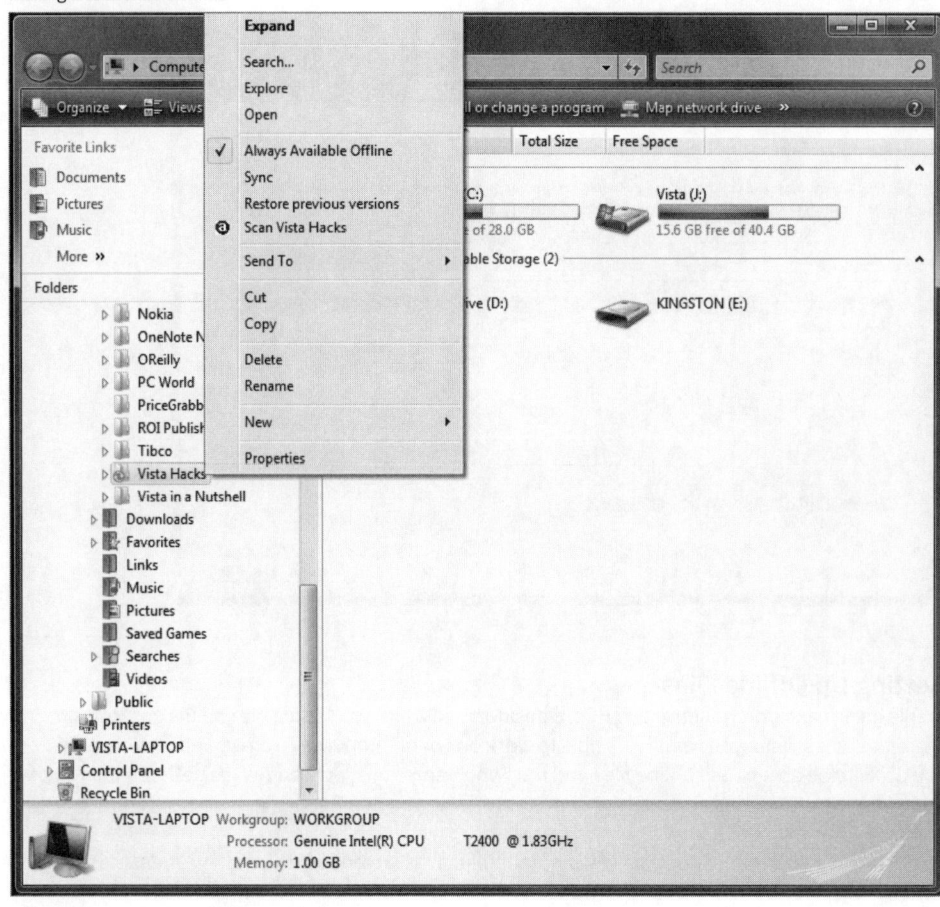

Figure 3-37.
Preparing to sync your offline files

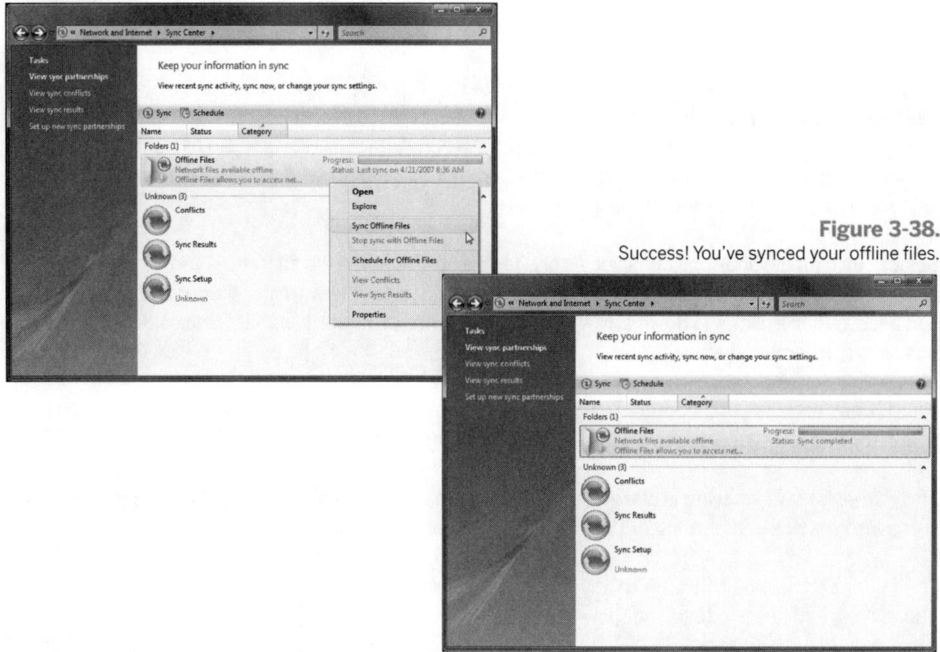

Figure 3-38.
Success! You've synced your offline files.

Go to your laptop PC, open Windows Explorer, and click Network. Connect to your desktop PC, and navigate to the shared folder that you want to be available as offline files. If you've enabled password-protected sharing, you'll have to type in an account name and password before you get there.

Right-click the shared folder that you want to be available as offline files, and select Always Available Offline so that a check box shows up next to it (Figure 3-36). Windows Vista will now make copies of those files and put them in the offline files area of your laptop. When it's done, you'll notice that the folder now has a small circular green icon on it; that indicates it's available offline.

Using the Sync Center

The simplest and safest way to work with offline files is via the Sync Center. When you use the Sync Center, you can be sure that you're always working on the latest version of offline files, and that they're kept in sync on both machines.

Open the Sync Center by selecting Control Panel→Network and Internet→Sync Center. Look for the Offline Files icon. To its right, you'll see the status of the last time the offline files were synced with your local PC. It's a good idea before working with offline files to first sync them.

 You can also sync Offline Files without having to go through the Sync Center. Select the Offline File or folder you want to sync, and select Sync.

To sync them, right-click anywhere in the Offline Files area, and select Sync Offline files, as shown in Figure 3-37. Depending on how many files need to be synced, and their sizes, they'll now be synced, and you'll be notified about the successful sync, as shown in Figure 3-38.

Windows Vista has to make decisions about how to sync files; here are the rules that it follows when files are synced between PCs:

- If the files are different, Sync Center decides which version of each file to keep and copies that version of the file to the other location (overwriting the version there). Unless you have set up the sync partnership differently, it keeps the most recent version and overwrites the older version.
- If a file has changed in both locations, Sync Center flags it as a sync conflict, then asks you which version to keep.
- If the files are identical in both locations, Sync Center takes no action.
- If you have added a new file to one location but not to the other, Sync Center copies the file to the other location.
- If you have deleted a file from one location but not from the other, Sync Center deletes the file from the other location.

Now that you've synced the files, you can disconnect from the network, take your laptop with you, and work on them. The offline files are now stored on your local PC. To get to them, open the Sync Center, double-click the Offline Files icon, then navigate to the folder with your offline files. It will appear with a small green icon next to it, as you can see in Figure 3-39.

Figure 3-39.
The folder with the small green circular icon has used offline files in it

OReilly	4/24/2007 7:00 AM	File F
PC World	2/18/2007 3:55 PM	File F
PriceGrabber	4/22/2007 11:52 PM	File F
ROI Publishing	3/18/2007 5:54 PM	File F
Tibco	4/11/2007 8:14 PM	File F
Vista Hacks	4/27/2007 9:32 AM	File F
Vista in a Nutshell	4/8/2007 8:46 PM	File F
desktop.ini	2/18/2007 12:46 PM	Confi

QUICK HACK 

HIDE YOUR DRIVE LETTERS

Don't like to see the drive letters next to your hard drives in Windows Explorer? It's easy to turn them off. In Windows Explorer, choose Organize→Folder and Search Options→View, uncheck the box next to Show drive letters, and click OK.

If you want the Sync Center to automatically sync files for you, right-click anywhere in the Offline Files area, and select Schedule for Offline Files. Follow the wizard to create a schedule. You'll be able to schedule syncs to occur at a particular time and day (every day at 2 p.m., for example), or else when a specific event occurs, such as every time you log onto the PC or when you connect to the network.

Work with the files as you would normally. When you connect back to the network, open the Sync Center, and sync the files, as previously outlined. They'll now be synced back to your desktop PC.

As you can see from Figure 3-39, the Sync Center does more than just show you your Offline Files. It also reports on the results of syncs, not just with offline files but with devices such as portable music players and USB drives as well. On the left side of the screen, you'll see a variety of options. Here's what they are, and what each does:

View sync partnerships

This is the main screen, which displays all the sync partnerships, including recent activity.

Figure 3-40.
Resolving a sync conflict

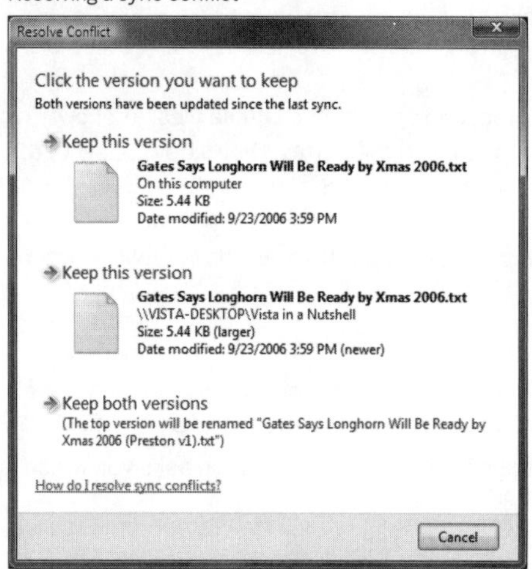

Figure 3-41.
Reviewing sync history

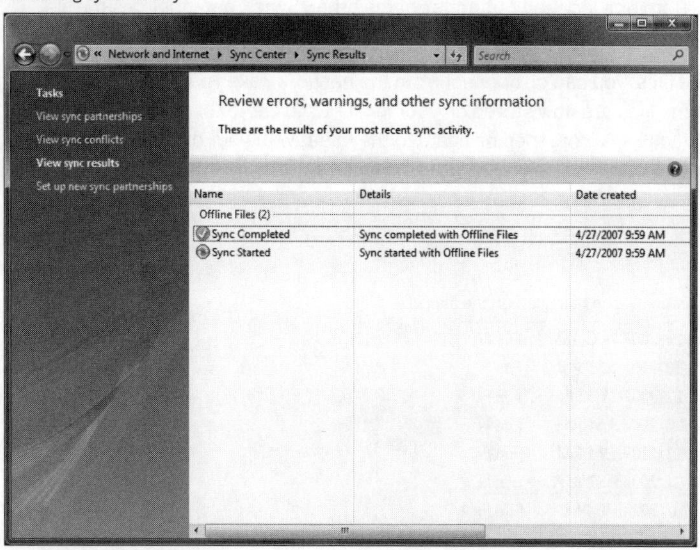

Figure 3-42.
Setting space limits on offline files

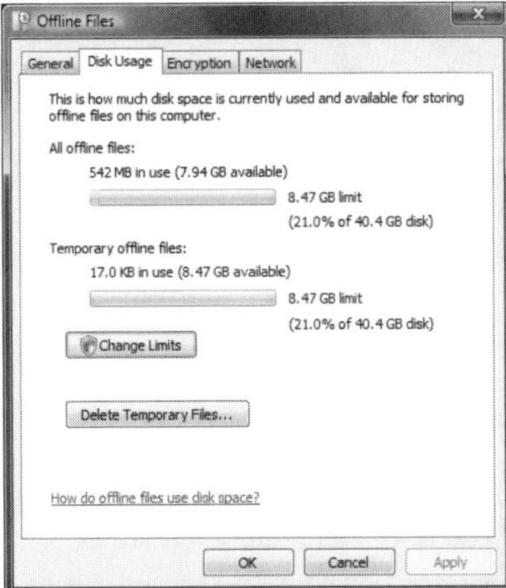

View Sync conflicts

If files cannot be synced because differences can't be reconciled between the different versions stored on different devices or shared folders, the conflicts will be listed here, along with any details about the conflicts. For example, if you've changed a document on your PC since the last sync, and a different change was made to the same document on an offline folder or mobile device, that will be listed as a conflict. Select the conflict, click Resolve, and the Conflict Resolution dialog box opens (Figure 3-40), which lets you determine which version of the file to keep or whether to keep both under different filenames.

View Sync results

This displays the history of your syncs. In addition to showing you successful syncs, as shown in Figure 3-41, errors and warnings are displayed here as well.

Set up new Sync partnerships

This screen shows any devices available for synchronizing. Before you can perform a sync, you first need to set up a partnership from this screen. Click the device or folders for which you want to set up a sync partnership, then click Set up and follow the directions.

Hacking the Hack

Windows Vista gives you control over the amount of space to devote to offline files and lets you set several other options related to them as well. To get to them, choose Control Panel→Network and Internet→Offline Files. Click the Disk Usage tab. You'll be shown how much disk space you currently have devoted to offline files, as well as the maximum amount of space for offline files (see Figure 3-42).

To change the amount of space you want to devote to offline files, click Change limits. From the screen that appears move the slider to set your disk usage limits. You can also encrypt your offline, files from the Encryption tab.

04 INTERNET EXPLORER, THE WEB, AND THE INTERNET

We all live on the Web. And so in this chapter, you'll find hacks that make using the Web even better. You'll find hacks for protecting your privacy when you surf, giving Internet Explorer a face-lift, hacking Firefox, building your own Internet Explorer and Firefox search tools, speeding up your surfing for free, and much more.

HACK 48: Clear Up Router Congestion and Increase Your Bandwidth

V A congested home router can reduce your Internet bandwidth and lead to packet loss. Here's how to turn on a hidden Windows Vista feature to clear it up.

Your broadband ISP may promise you 5-megabit Internet access and above, but if you've got a router prone to congestion, you may be getting nowhere near those speeds. Routers can get congested if their incoming packet buffers get full. When this happens, the router drops packets, and bandwidth suffers. In addition, streaming media such as videos may drop packets, and the video may appear jerky, or you may not be able to view it all.

Windows Vista includes a hidden feature, called Explicit Congestion Notification (ECN) that can help clear up the problem. Microsoft even claims that ECN can help speed up downloads and improve the reliability of data transfer when your router isn't congested. ECN is turned off by default because not all home routers support it, and if you turn it on with a nonsupported router, you can cause even worse connection problems.

There is a way, however, to find out if your router supports ECN and then to turn on ECN from the command line.

To find out if your router supports ECN, you need to run the Internet Connectivity Evaluation Tool. Make sure you're logged in to Windows Vista as an administrator. Then go to www.microsoft.com/windows/using/tools/igd/default.mspx and agree to the terms. When you agree, on the page that appears, Microsoft will attempt to install an ActiveX control. Your Internet Explorer security settings will most likely block the attempt. The Information Bar will light up yellow. Click it, and from the menu that appears (Figure 4-1), select Install ActiveX Control.

Follow the prompts for installing the software. A new web page will appear. Click Start Test. After several minutes of testing, you'll see a results screen like the one shown in Figure 4-2.

Scroll to the Traffic Congestion Test section. If your router passes the test, you can safely turn on ECN. If not, you can't.

Figure 4-1.
Telling Internet Explorer to install the Internet Connectivity Evaluation Tool

Internet Connectivity Evaluation Tool - Windows Internet Explorer
http://www.microsoft.com/windows/using/tools/igd/results.ms
catalyst case study
catalyst cas...
Advanced F...
Internet ...
Page
Tools
This website wants to install the following add-on: 'IGDTool 1.3.
add-on and want to install it, click here...
u trust the website and the
Install ActiveX Control...
What's the Risk?
More information
Quick Links

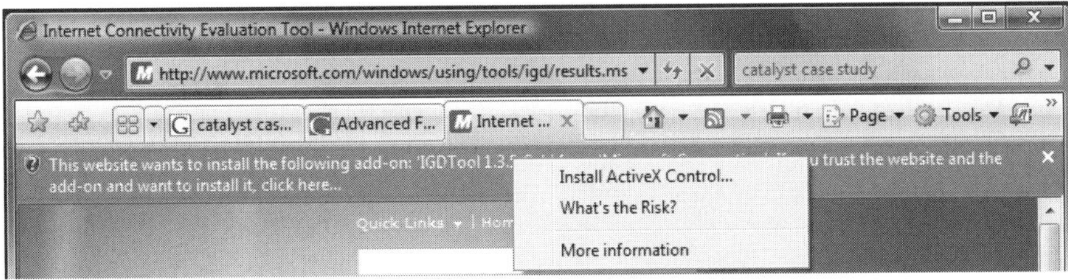

Figure 4-2.
You've passed the ECN test

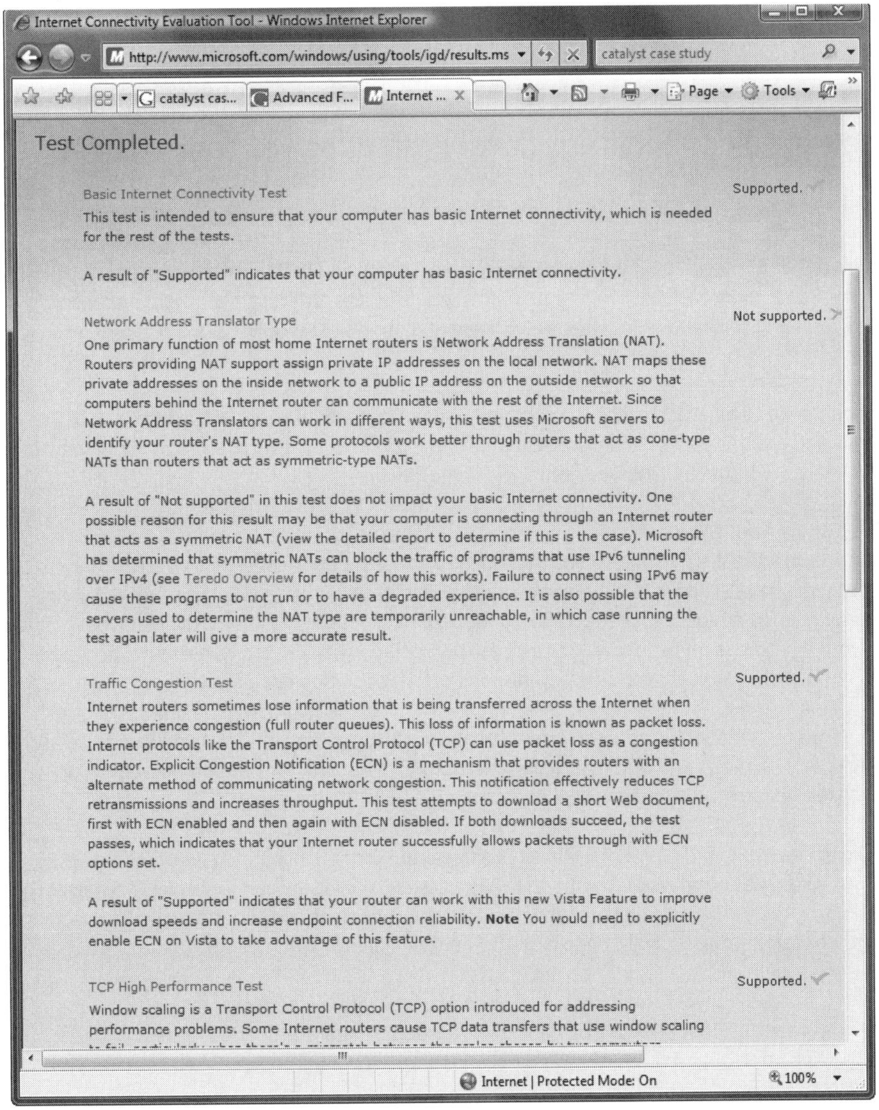

Internet Connectivity Evaluation Tool - Windows Internet Explorer
http://www.microsoft.com/windows/using/tools/igd/results.ms
catalyst case study
catalyst cas...
Advanced F...
Internet ...
Page
Tools
Test Completed.
Basic Internet Connectivity Test
Supported.
This test is intended to ensure that your computer has basic Internet connectivity, which is needed for the rest of the tests.
A result of "Supported" indicates that your computer has basic Internet connectivity.
Network Address Translator Type
Not supported.
One primary function of most home Internet routers is Network Address Translation (NAT). Routers providing NAT support assign private IP addresses on the local network. NAT maps these private addresses on the inside network to a public IP address on the outside network so that computers behind the Internet router can communicate with the rest of the Internet. Since Network Address Translators can work in different ways, this test uses Microsoft servers to identify your router's NAT type. Some protocols work better through routers that act as cone-type NATs than routers that act as symmetric-type NATs.
A result of "Not supported" in this test does not impact your basic Internet connectivity. One possible reason for this result may be that your computer is connecting through an Internet router that acts as a symmetric NAT (view the detailed report to determine if this is the case). Microsoft has determined that symmetric NATs can block the traffic of programs that use IPv6 tunneling over IPv4 (see Teredo Overview for details of how this works). Failure to connect using IPv6 may cause these programs to not run or to have a degraded experience. It is also possible that the servers used to determine the NAT type are temporarily unreachable, in which case running the test again later will give a more accurate result.
Traffic Congestion Test
Supported.
Internet routers sometimes lose information that is being transferred across the Internet when they experience congestion (full router queues). This loss of information is known as packet loss. Internet protocols like the Transport Control Protocol (TCP) can use packet loss as a congestion indicator. Explicit Congestion Notification (ECN) is a mechanism that provides routers with an alternate method of communicating network congestion. This notification effectively reduces TCP retransmissions and increases throughput. This test attempts to download a short Web document, first with ECN enabled and then again with ECN disabled. If both downloads succeed, the test passes, which indicates that your Internet router successfully allows packets through with ECN options set.
A result of "Supported" indicates that your router can work with this new Vista Feature to improve download speeds and increase endpoint connection reliability. Note You would need to explicitly enable ECN on Vista to take advantage of this feature.
TCP High Performance Test
Supported.
Window scaling is a Transport Control Protocol (TCP) option introduced for addressing performance problems. Some Internet routers cause TCP data transfers that use window scaling
Internet | Protected Mode: On
100%

To turn on ECN, first run an elevated command prompt by typing cmd at the Search box and pressing Ctrl-Shift-Enter. Then at the command line, type this command, and press Enter:

```
netsh interface tcp set global ecncapability=enabled
```

When you turn on ECN, you turn it on only for the computer on which you've issued the command, not on the entire network. If you want other Windows Vista PCs on the network to be able to take advantage of ECN, you'll need to turn it on at each of the PCs.

The command prompt will respond with an OK. ECN will now be enabled. If you notice a degradation in performance, you can turn off ECN by typing this command at an elevated command prompt and pressing Enter:

```
netsh interface tcp set global ecncapability=disabled
```

See Also

- For a good explanation of how ECN works, see this "Cable Guy" article: www.microsoft.com/technet/community/columns/cableguy/cg1006.mspx.
- For an explanation of the Internet Connectivity Evaluation Tool, see this Microsoft Knowledge Base article: support.microsoft.com/kb/932134/en-us.

HACK 49: Surf Anonymously, Without a Trace—For Free

V XP Feel like people are watching you? On the Web, they probably are. Follow this advice for protecting your online privacy.

The punchline to an old cartoon is "On the Internet nobody knows you're a dog," but these days, that's no longer true. It's easier than ever for the government, web sites, and private businesses to track exactly what you do online, know where you've visited, and build up comprehensive profiles about your likes, dislikes, and private habits. And with the federal government increasingly demanding online records from sites such as Google and others, your online privacy is even more endangered.

But you don't need to be a victim; there are things you can do to keep your surfing habits anonymous and protect your online privacy. In this hack, you'll find out how to keep your privacy to yourself when you use the Internet, without spending a penny.

What They Know About You

Whenever you surf the Web, you leave yourself open to being snooped upon by web sites. They can track your online travels, know what operating system and browser you're running, find out your machine name, uncover the last sites you've visited, examine your history list, delve into your cache, examine your IP address and use that to learn basic information about you such as your geographic location, and more. To a great extent, your Internet life is an open book when you visit.

Sites use a variety of techniques to gather and collate this information, but the two most basic are examining your IP address and placing cookies on your PC. Matching your IP address with your cookies makes it easier for them to create personal profiles.

If you'd like to see what kind of information sites can gather about you, head to two sites that peer into your browser and report what they find. The Privacy.net Analyzer (www.privacy.net/analyze), shown in Figure 4-3, gathers and displays basic information, such as your operating system, screen resolution, what site brought you to Privacy.net's Analyzer, general system setup, and so on.

BrowserSpy (gemal.dk/browserspy) delves even deeper into your system, and even reports on whether you have certain software on your system, such as RealPlayer and Adobe Acrobat, including version information.

QUICK HACK

CONVERT HTML FILES TO PLAIN TEXT

There are times when you'll want to convert an HTML file to a plain text file, for example, if you've got text on a page that you need for a purpose other than using it on a web site; for example, to use the same text in a newsletter. But stripping HTML out of a page is time-consuming and tedious. There's a simple answer: Get the free HTMLAsText (www.nirsoft.net/utils/htmlastext.html). Run the program, type in the HTML filename and location, and where you want the text file output, and it does the job for you. Command-line junkies can even run it from the command line.

Figure 4-3.
Here's just some of the information web sites know about you

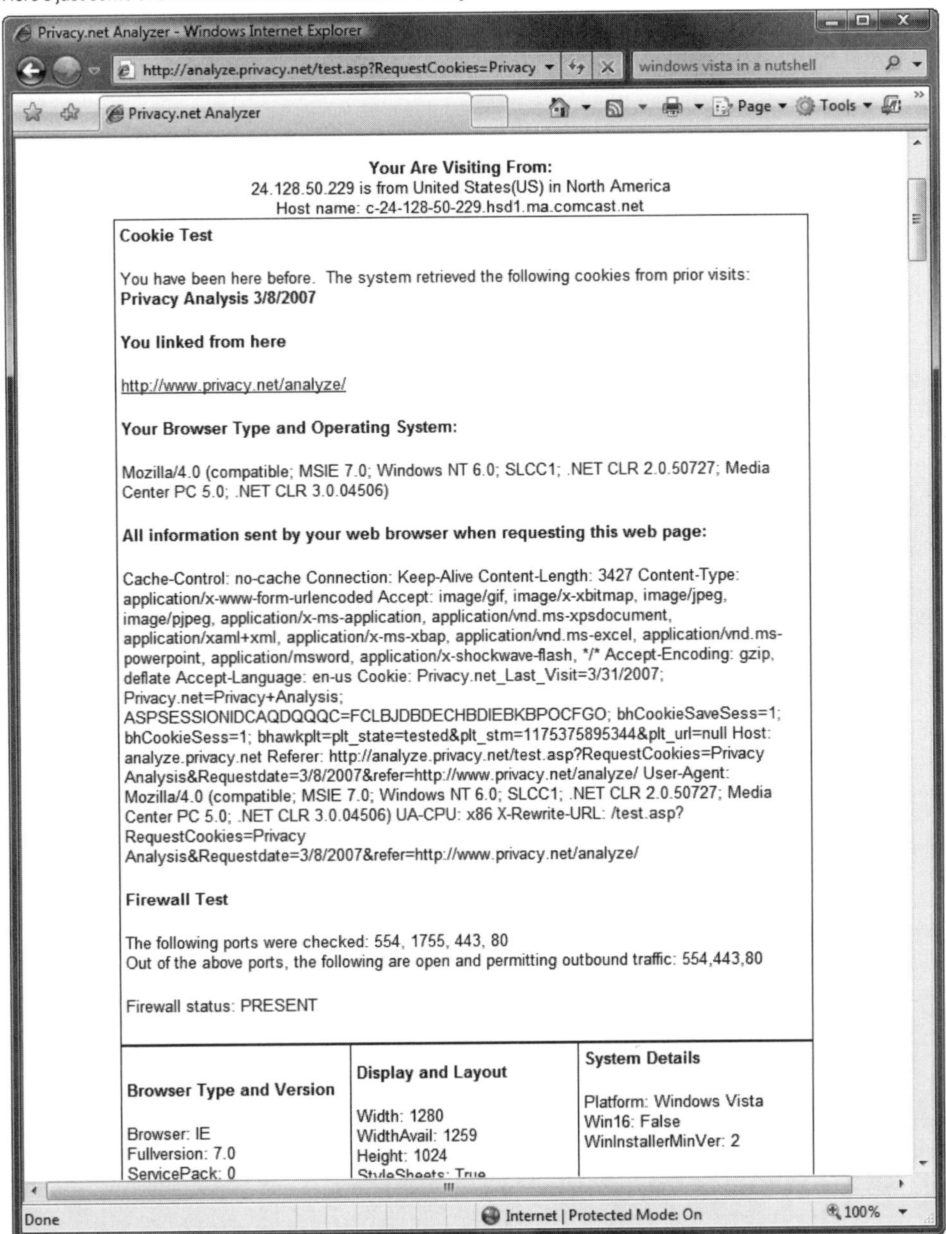

Protect Yourself: Surf Anonymously

The best way to make sure web sites can't gather personal information about you and your computer is to surf anonymously using an anonymous proxy server that sits between you and the web sites you visit. When you use an anonymous proxy server, your browser doesn't contact a web site directly. Instead, it tells a proxy server which web site you want to visit. The proxy server then contacts the web site, and when you get the web site's page, you don't get it directly from the site. Instead, it's delivered to you by the proxy server. In that way, your browser never directly contacts the web server whose site you want to view. The web site sees the IP address of the proxy server, not your PC's IP address. It can't read your cookies, see the referring page, or examine your clipboard because your PC is never in direct contact with it. You're able to surf anonymously, without a trace.

There are three primary ways to use anonymous proxy servers. You can configure your browser to use an anonymous proxy server (or else get software to configure it for you); you can visit a web site, which does the work of contacting the server; or you can download software which ensures your anonymity when you use the Internet. We'll look at how to do each.

Keep Yourself Anonymous with Tor

Tor (tor.eff.org) is the best free software you can find for being anonymous when you use the Web. When you use Tor, all your communications, (not just Web surfing, but also instant messaging and other applications) is in essence bounced around a giant network of Tor servers called "onion routers," until it's impossible for sites or people to be able to track your activities.

Setting up Tor is straightforward. Download a package that includes not just Tor, but other software you need to work in concert with it, such as Privoxy, a proxy program. All the software is self-configuring, so you won't need to muck around with port settings or the like. Tor runs as a small icon in your system tray. To start Tor, right-click it, and choose Start from the menu that appears; to stop it, right-click, it and choose Stop.

Once it starts, simply use the Internet as you normally would. If you're super-paranoid, you can regularly change your Tor "identity," to make it even harder for anyone to track your travels. Right-click the Tor icon, and select "New Identity"; that's all it takes.

Tor includes a nice bandwidth tool as well, that has nothing to do with anonymity but graphs your bandwidth use. Right-click the Tor icon, and choose Bandwidth Graph. You can see it in action, along with Tor's right-click context menu, in Figure 4-4.

Firefox users will want to download the Torbutton (https://addons.mozilla.org/firefox/2275/), which lets them turn Tor on and off from directly within Firefox.

I've found only one drawback to Tor; at times, I've noticed a slowdown in surfing when using it. But that comes and goes, and slowdowns aren't that extreme. So if you're worried about your privacy when you surf, it's a great bet.

Web Sites That Let You Surf Anonymously for Free

A number of free web sites offer free anonymous surfing via proxy servers. The benefits of these sites are obvious: when you surf, you're anonymous. But there are some drawbacks as well. Surfing

Figure 4-4.
Tor keeps you safe when surfing
and has extras such as a bandwidth graph

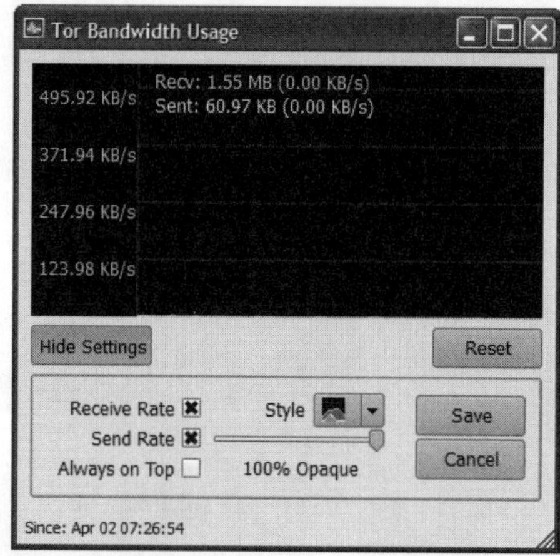

tends to be slower, and in some cases very slow. And when you use these web sites, some sites you visit from them don't display properly.

The sites all work pretty much the same. Head to them, and in a box, type the web site you want to visit. From that point on, you'll be surfing anonymously; the site does the work of using an anonymous proxy server for you.

The Cloak (www.the-cloak.com) is one such service. It lets you customize exactly how anonymous you want to be and what surfing technologies you want to leave on or off. It goes beyond providing anonymity and can also protect you in other ways, for example, by turning off Java and Javascript, or even blocking banner ads. As you can see in Figure 4-5, you can configure all that yourself, before you even start to surf.

Once you do that, you type in the address you want to visit, and you're off. As you browse in your

Figure 4-5.
Configuring anonymous surfing with The Cloak

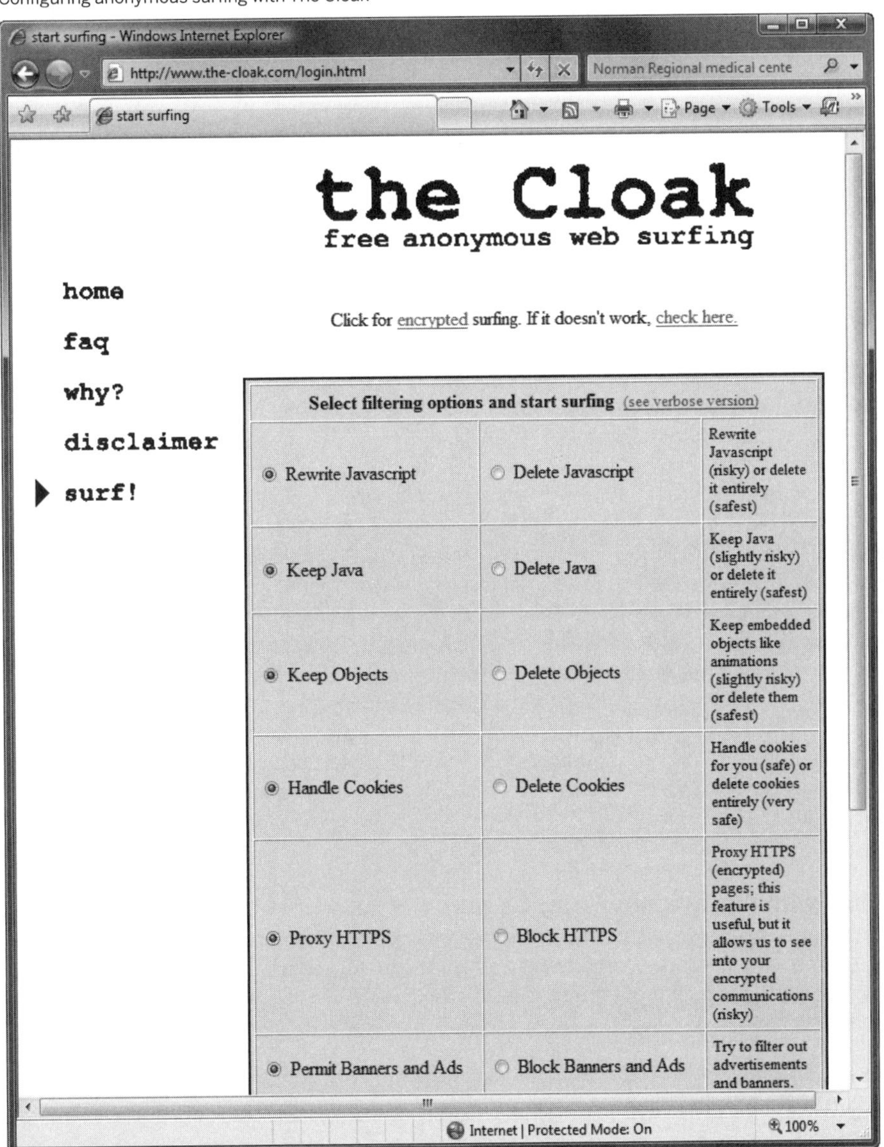

browser's address bar, you'll notice an odd URL that contains The Cloak's URL as well as the site you're visiting. For example, if you visit CNN, you'll see something like this:

```
http://www.the-cloak.com/Cloaked/+cfg=31/http%3A//www.cnn.com/
```

Note that if you want to remain anonymous during your surfing session after you visit the first web site from The Cloak, you'll have to only click links. If you type a URL directly into the address bar, The Cloak will no longer work.

The Cloak is free but has some limitations. You'll surf more slowly than normally, and the slowdown may become noticeable. One reason is that the site also offers a for-pay service, and so it throttles down free users, while letting those who pay surf without a throttle. And the site may also limit the amount of time you surf anonymously as well, depending on whether many users are logged in simultaneously.

Use Your Browser with an Anonymous Proxy

If you don't like the limitations imposed on you by sites like The Cloak, or would simply prefer to configure anonymous surfing yourself, you can easily set up your browser to use an anonymous proxy server that sits between you and the sites you visit.

To use an anonymous proxy server in concert with your browser, first find an anonymous proxy server. Hundreds of free, public proxy servers are available, but many frequently go offline or are very slow. Many sites compile lists of these proxy servers, including Public Proxy Servers (www.publicproxyservers.com/page1.html) and Atom InterSoft proxy server list (www.atomintersoft.com/products/alive-proxy/proxy-list). To find others, do a Google search.

I prefer the Atom InterSoft proxy server list because it provides more information about each server. It lists server uptime percentage and the last time the server was checked to see if it was online.

Find the server with the highest percentage of uptime. Write down the server's IP address and the port it uses. For example, if you see 24.236.148.15:80, the IP address is 24.236.148.15, and the port number is 80.

In Internet Explorer, select Tools→Internet Options, click the Connections tab, and click the LAN Settings button (see Figure 4-6). Check the box next to "Use a proxy server for your LAN". In the Address field, type in the IP address of the proxy server. In the Port field, type in its port number. Check the box next to "Bypass proxy server for local addresses"; you don't need to remain anonymous on your local network (and if your local network is a private network, the proxy server won't be able to connect to any of your internal web servers anyhow). Click OK and then OK again to close the dialog boxes. Now when you surf the Web, the proxy server will protect your privacy. Keep in mind that proxy servers can make surfing the Web slower, depending on the proxy you're using.

In Firefox, select Tools→Options→Advanced, click the Network tab, and click the Settings button. Choose "Manual proxy configuration", enter the proxy information (IP address and port number), and click OK and then OK again

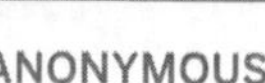

SEND ANONYMOUS EMAIL

Proxy servers and other anonymizing tools are useful for web surfing, but what if you want to send anonymous email—for example, if you're a "whistle blower" and don't want your identity known? Use an anonymous remailer such as the web-based Anonymouse's AnonEmail (anonymouse.org/anonemail.html), or the downloadable QuickSilver (quicksilvermail.net).

Problems with Anonymous Proxy Servers

If you set up your browser to use anonymous proxies, as I just outlined, you need to keep in mind that there's one potential danger: theoretically, a hacker could set up a proxy server and then use it to capture information about the Web sites you visit. And if you type in usernames and passwords, he could steal those as well.

I haven't heard of this actually happening in the real world, but you should be aware that it's a possibility. Using software such as Tor or a free proxy server such as The Cloak won't expose you to this danger; only the use of public proxy servers does.

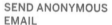

Figure 4-6.
Setting up Internet Explorer to surf the Web anonymously

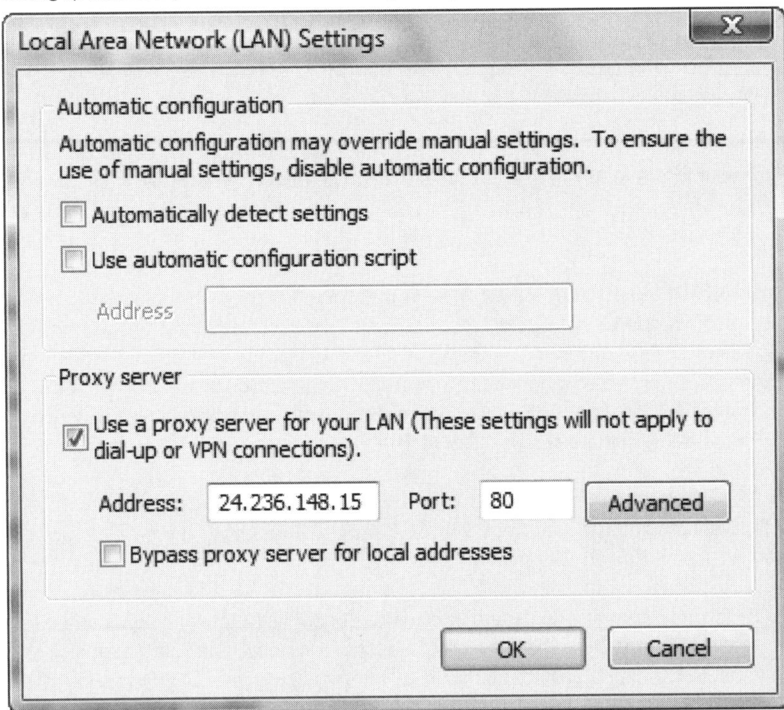

How can you protect yourself against this? Before using a proxy server, do a Google search on its name and address, to see if there are any reports about hackers using it. And it's also a good idea to only use a server that has been on the lists a long time because hackers are not likely to keep a server running a long time without being caught or shutting it down. The other option is to use the proxy only for casual surfing and not use a proxy when you connect to a service that requires a username and password.

See Also

- For a very good all-around resource about how to protect your privacy online, check out the Electronic Privacy Information Center's Online Guide to Practical Privacy Tools (www.epic.org/privacy/tools.html). It has plenty of links to software and sites to help protect your privacy.

HACK 50: Use OpenDNS for Faster, Safer Web Browsing

V XP Hard to believe but true: this free service speeds up your web surfing, helps protect you against phishing, and more.

Your DNS settings **[Hack #51]** can make a big difference how fast you can surf web sites. Here's another way to speed up web access by hacking DNS—and you'll get bonuses, such as antiphishing protection.

To do so, all you need to do is use the DNS servers run by the free OpenDNS service (www.opendns.com) for your ISP's DNS servers. OpenDNS has a monster DNS cache, and DNS servers located around the globe, so you may be able to retrieve IP addresses from it more quickly than from the default DNS servers your ISP points to. And, as you'll see later in this hack, you get all kinds of other benefits, such as automatically fixing URLs typos for you; for example, type www.yahoo.cmo into your address bar, and you'll be sent to www.yahoo.com, instead of getting a page error.

OpenDNS sounds too good to be true; why is the company offering this free service? In essence, it's betting that every once in a while, you'll type in a URL that doesn't exist and isn't a typo. When you type in a URL that isn't valid, and can't be fixed via OpenDNS's typo-fixing features, on the error page that appears, you'll see search results as well as clearly labeled advertisements delivered by OpenDNS. The service makes money on those ads. In addition, the company may at some point also offer additional, for-pay services in addition to its DNS service, although it claims it will never charge for its basic DNS service.

You don't need to visit the OpenDNS Web site to use its service. You only need to configure Windows Vista, Windows XP, or your home router to use its DNS servers. The following sections show how to do it.

Configure OpenDNS in Windows Vista and Windows XP

To use OpenDNS servers in Windows Vista, select Control Panel→Network and Internet→Network and Sharing Center. Click the View status link on the right side of the screen. The Local Connection Status screen appears. Click Properties, and the Local Area Connection Properties screen appears. Highlight Internet Protocol Version 4 (TCP/IP v4), click Properties, and at the bottom of the screen select "Use the following DNS server addresses" (Figure 4-7). For the Preferred DNS server, enter this address: `208.67.222.222`.

For the Alternative DNS server, enter this address: `208.67.220.220`. Click OK, and then click Close and Close again. Restart your PC for the settings to take effect.

In Windows XP, select Control Panel→Network and Internet Connections→Network Connections, right-click your network connection from the Network Connections window, and select Properties. From the network connection dialog box that appears, click Internet Protocol (TCP/IP) and click Properties. The screen you'll see will be the same as the one in Windows Vista, shown in Figure 4-7. Follow the same directions as for Windows Vista, and reboot.

Configure OpenDNS In Your Router

When you configure a PC to use OpenDNS, only that PC will be able to use the OpenDNS servers. If you want all of the PCs on your network to use the servers, you can tell your router to use the OpenDNS servers, and then all of your PCs on the network will follow suit. That way, you also won't have to configure each individual PC.

Figure 4-7.
Telling Windows Vista to use the OpenDNS servers

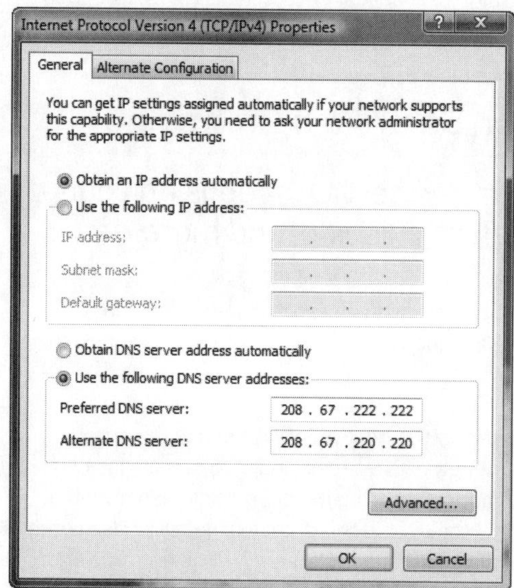

The way you do this will vary from router to router. Generally, though, you'll log into your router, look for the DNS settings, and then use the OpenDNS settings of 208.67.222.222 for the primary DNS server and 208.67.220.220 for the alternative DNS server.

On Linksys WRT54GX4, and many other Linksys routers, log into your router by going to 192.1681.1, and use admin as the password, leaving the user name blank. Scroll down the page until you come to the Static DNS 1 and Static DNS 2. (Figure 4-8). Click Save Settings. Restart your router and the PCs on your network, and they will begin using the OpenDNS DNS servers.

Hacking the Hack

After you've configured your DNS servers, you don't need to do anything special to use OpenDNS; your PC will do it automatically. In addition to faster surfing, you'll also get antiphishing protection; you'll be alerted when you visit a known phishing site. Note that your browser's antiphishing capabilities take precedence over OpenDNS's, so if your browser does a good job of blocking phishing sites, you may never see OpenDNS block a phishing site.

When you make a typo in the domain when entering a URL into your address bar, OpenDNS will try to fix it. So if you type in www.yahoo.cmo, you'll be sent to www.yahoo.com, and if you type in www.craigslist.og, you'll be sent to www.craigslist.org.

Figure 4-8.
Change the Static DNS settings in order to have your network use OpenDNS DNS servers

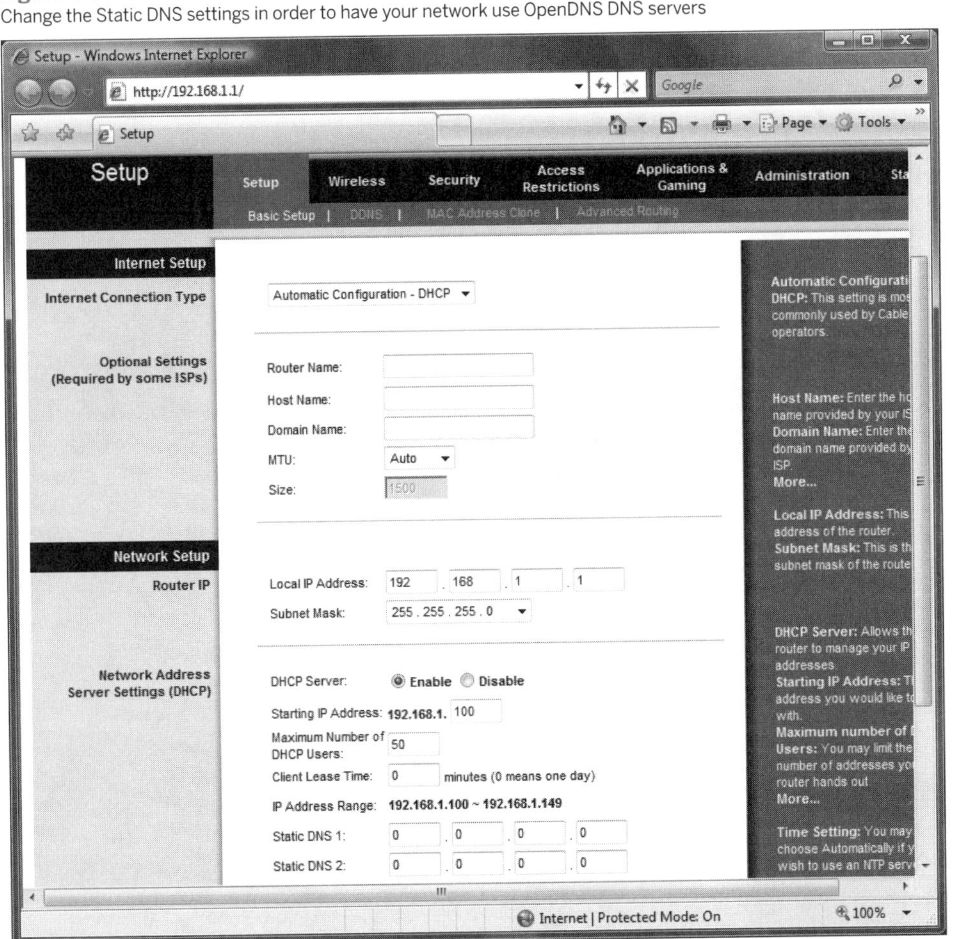

You can also create surfing shortcuts that let you visit web sites by typing in a few characters rather than a full URL. First register with the site. Then log in and click My Account, and then click the Shortcuts link. From the page that appears (Figure 4-9), type in the shortcut text in the top box and the URL in the bottom box, and click Create Shortcut. From now on, when you type the shortcut text into your browser window, you'll be sent to the full URL. You can also add the OpenDNS bookmarklet (found at the bottom of the page) to your browser, and in that way, create a shortcut for whichever page you happen to be viewing at the moment.

See Also

- "Tweak DNS Settings for Faster Internet Access" **[Hack #51]**

HACK 51: Tweak DNS Settings for Faster Internet Access

V XP Here's a handful of DNS hacks for speeding up access to web sites.

You use the Web by typing in hostnames such as www.oreilly.com, but web servers and Internet routers can't understand plain English words, so they need those letters translated into numeric IP addresses. Whenever you type in a hostname, such as www.oreilly.com, it needs to be resolved to its IP address, such as 208.201.239.37. DNS servers provide that name resolution automatically and behind the scenes as you surf the Web.

There are several ways you can hack your DNS settings so that you can get faster web access.

Figure 4-9.
Creating an OpenDNS shortcut

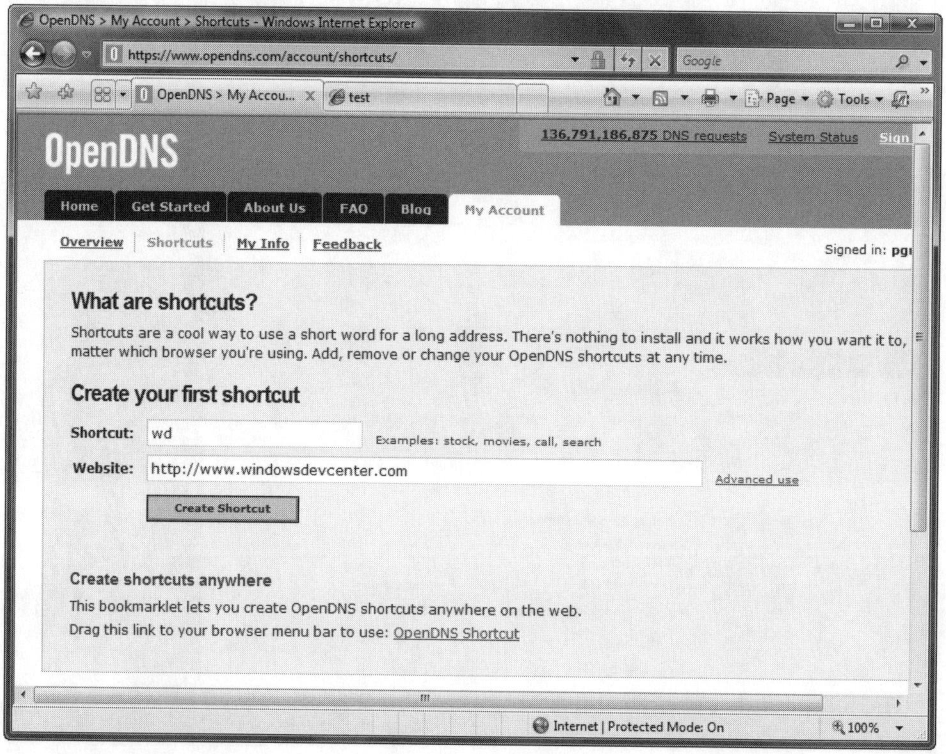

Speed Up Web Access with a HOSTS File

It takes time to send your request to a DNS server, have the server look up the proper IP address to resolve the name, and then send the IP address back to your PC. You can eliminate that delay by creating or editing a local *HOSTS* file on your own PC that contains hostnames and their corresponding IP addresses. When you create a *HOSTS* file, Windows will first look there to check if there's an entry for the hostname, and if it finds it, it will resolve the address itself. That way, Windows won't have to go out to a DNS server and wait for the response before visiting a web site. The *HOSTS* file is a plain-text file you can create or edit with a text editor such as Notepad.

You'll find an existing *HOSTS* file in *C:\Windows\System32\Drivers\Etc\HOSTS* in both Windows XP and Windows Vista. (If you upgraded to Windows XP from Windows 2000, it's located in *C:\Winnt\System32\Drivers\HOSTS*). The file has no extension; it is named only *HOSTS*. Open it in Notepad and enter the IP addresses and hostnames of your commonly visited web sites, like this:

```
208.201.239.37      oreilly.com
209.87.181.103      simtel.net
```

On Vista, you'll need to run Notepad as Administrator before you open the file. Locate Notepad's shortcut in the Start Menu, right-click on it, and choose Run as Administrator.

Each entry in the file should be on one line. The IP address should be in the first column, and the corresponding hostname in the next column. At least one space should separate the two columns. You can add comments to the file by preceding the line with a #, in which case the entire line will be ignored by the file, or by putting a # after the hostname, in which case only the comment after will be ignored. You might want to comment on individual entries—for example:

```
130.94.155.164            gralla.com    #still in beta
```

When you're finished editing the file, save it to its existing location.

Make sure to check your *HOSTS* file regularly and keep it up-to-date, or else you might deny yourself access to certain web sites. For example, if the www.gralla.com web site were to change its IP address but your *HOSTS* file kept the old, incorrect address, your browser would not be able to find the site because it would be given the wrong addressing information. You can confirm the IP address of each site periodically using the *nslookup* command-line utility (start a command prompt, type nslookup `hostname`, and you'll get one or more IP addresses for that site).

Adjust Windows' DNS Cache Settings

As a way of speeding up DNS, when you visit a site Windows puts the DNS information into a local DNS cache on your PC. So, when you want to go to a site, Windows first looks in its local DNS cache, called the *resolver cache*, to see whether the DNS information is contained there. That way, if it finds the information locally, it doesn't have to query a remote DNS server to find an IP address. The cache is made up of recently queried names and entries taken from your *HOSTS* file.

The cache contains both *negative* and *positive* entries. Positive entries are those in which the DNS lookup succeeded, and you were able to connect to the web site. If when Windows looks in the cache, it finds a positive entry, it immediately uses that DNS information and sends you to the requested web site.

You can view the contents of the resolver cache by opening up a command prompt and running the command ipconfig /displaydns.

Negative entries are those in which no match was found, and you end up getting a "Cannot find server or DNS" error in your browser. Similarly, when Windows looks in the cache and finds a negative entry, it gives you the error message without bothering to go out to the site.

Negative entries can lead to problems. When you try to make a connection to a site that has a negative entry in your cache, you'll get an error message, even if the site's problems have been resolved, and it's now reachable.

You can solve this problem, though, using a Registry hack. By default, Windows caches negative entries for five minutes. After five minutes, they're cleared from your cache. However, you can force Windows to not cache these negative entries so that you'll never run into this problem. Run the Registry Editor **[Hack #183]**, and go to `HKEY_LOCAL_MACHINE\SYSTEM\CurrentControlSet\Services\Dnscache\Parameters`. Create a new `DWORD` value with the name `NegativeCacheTime` and give it a value of `0`. (The value might already exist. If it does, edit its value to `0`.) The `DWORD` determines how much time, in seconds, to keep negative entries in the DNS cache. If you like, you can have the entries stay alive for one second by giving the `DWORD` a value of 1.

After you're done editing, exit the Registry. To make the change take effect, restart your computer, or flush your cache by issuing the command ipconfig /flushdns **[Hack #77]** at a command prompt (on Vista, you'll need to open an Administrator command prompt by right-clicking on its shortcut in the Start Menu and choosing Run as Administrator).

That command will flush your DNS cache; all the entries, both positive and negative, will be flushed, and it will be empty until you start visiting web sites. Negative entries, however, will not be added to the cache if you've given the `DWORD` a value of `0`.

You can also use the Registry to control the amount of time positive entries are kept in the DNS cache. By default, they are kept for 24 hours. To change the default, go to `HKEY_LOCAL_MACHINE\SYSTEM\CurrentControlSet\Services\Dnscache\Parameters` again and create a `DWORD` value called `MaxCacheEntryTtlLimit`. (If it's already present, just edit the value.) For the value, enter the amount of time you want the entry to remain, in seconds, making sure to use Decimal as the base.

Fix DNS Problems

Sometimes, when you can't connect to a web site, the cause is a DNS problem. There are things you can do to solve these problems, though. If you're having trouble connecting to a site, you can find out if DNS is a potential culprit by first pinging the site to which you can't connect: issue the `ping` command at the command prompt, like this:

```
ping www.zdnet.com
```

If the site is live, you'll get an answer like this:

```
Pinging www.zdnet.com [206.16.6.252] with 32 bytes of data:

Reply from 206.16.6.252: bytes=32 time=119ms TTL=242
Reply from 206.16.6.252: bytes=32 time=79ms TTL=242
Reply from 206.16.6.252: bytes=32 time=80ms TTL=242
Reply from 206.16.6.252: bytes=32 time=101ms TTL=242

Ping statistics for 206.16.6.252:
    Packets: Sent = 4, Received = 4, Lost = 0 (0% loss),
Approximate round trip times in milli-seconds:
    Minimum = 79ms, Maximum = 119ms, Average = 94ms
```

If it's not, you'll get a response like this:

```
Ping request could not find host. Please check the name and try again.
```

If you know the IP address of the site, you can try using its IP address instead of its name. If you ping a site's IP address and it's live, but you can't connect to it with your browser or ping it by name, a DNS problem might be the reason. If you suspect you're having a DNS problem, take the following actions:

Check your HOSTS file

If your *HOSTS* file contains an incorrect or outdated listing, you won't be able to connect. Even if you don't recall adding listings to a *HOSTS* file, it still might contain listings because some Internet accelerator utilities edit them without telling you. Open your *HOSTS* file with Notepad and see if the site you can't connect to is listed there. If it is, delete the entry, and you should be able to connect.

Check your DNS settings

Make sure your DNS settings are correct for your ISP or network. Find out from your ISP or network administrator what yours are supposed to be. Then, to find your current DNS settings, double-click the problem connection in the Network Connections folder, choose Support→Details (on Vista, click "View status" next to the connection in the Network and Sharing Center, then click Details), and look at the bottom of the tab to find your DNS servers. If they don't match what they're supposed to be, right-click the problem connection and choose Properties (on Vista, click Properties from the dialog that appears when you click "View status"). Then, highlight Internet Protocol Version 4 (TCP/IPv4), and choose Properties. Change the DNS servers to the proper ones, or choose "Obtain DNS server address automatically" if your ISP or network administrator tells you to.

Flush your DNS cache

The problem might be related to your DNS cache, so flush it out. To flush the cache, type `ipconfig /flushdns` at a command prompt.

Find out if your ISP is having DNS problems

The cause might be your ISP. One possibility is that one of its DNS servers is down, and you're trying to access the downed server. Ping each of your ISP's DNS servers and, if any of them don't respond, remove them from your DNS list, using the DNS server settings described earlier in this list (see "Check your DNS settings").

Reboot your router, access point, or cable modem

Many broadband routers and wireless access points have their own DNS server built-in. Even it gets confused sometimes. If all else fails, try powering down your router, access point, and/or cable or DSL modem. Wait about a minute and turn them back on to see if it clears up the problem.

HACK 52: Kill Viruses, Spyware, and Web Bugs—For Free

V XP You don't have to spend a penny to keep your PC safe from viruses, spyware and web bugs. Fight back with these tips and tools—for free.

How much money do you think you spend on security software for your PC? It's a lot more than you think. Start off with your antivirus software. Typically, it costs you $40 a year, and $60 or more a year if you use one that includes a firewall as well. Next add in your antspyware package, which not uncommonly puts you back another $40 or so.

That adds up to $100 a year. Think of it as a security tax on your PC.

The truth is, though, you don't need to spend a penny if you want to keep your PC safe against viruses, spyware, and the annoying pests known as web bugs. Home users can get software that does it for free, and does every good a job as expensive, for-pay software. And you can also use some hard-won advice to keep your PC safe as well. The rest of this hack shows you how to do it.

Kill Viruses Dead

Big-name antivirus software such as Norton AntiVirus or McAfee VirusScan forces you to pay for a subscription every year, but they have another drawback as well. They also tend to suck up a lot of system resources and use plenty of RAM, and your PC can take a big performance hit from them just to keep itself protected.

There's a better way. Use avast!, nifty antivirus software that's free for personal use and that takes up so few system resources and RAM you won't even notice it's there. Download it from www.avast.com, and follow the installation instructions. It includes seven different shields, and it's a good idea to install and use them all. Once avast! is running, you can customize each shield. Double-click the avast! icon running in the System Tray and from the screen that appears, select the shield you want to customize. To change the sensitivity of the scanner—how aggressively the shield should act—move the slider. Move it to the left to make it less sensitive, and to the right to make it more sensitive. To customize the shield even further, click the Customize button. The dialog box that appears will vary according to the shield you're customizing. For example, in Figure 4-10, you can see the dialog box for the Microsoft Outlook/Exchange shield, which lets you change many options, such as which messages to scan, how to scan attachments, and so on.

Note, by the way, that before you install avast!, you'll need to first uninstall whatever antivirus software you're already using; otherwise it might not work properly.

Protect Yourself Against Spyware

For most people, *spyware* has replaced viruses or worms as the most-feared and obnoxious danger on the Internet. A relatively few number of people become infected by viruses or worms, but it seems as if almost everyone you know has been hit by some kind of spyware.

Spyware is a catch-all phrase that encompasses many different types of obnoxious programs. The least intrusive of the bunch report on your surfing activity to a web site, which tracks what you do and then delivers ads to your PC based on your interests. But increasingly, they are becoming more intrusive. Some of them spawn pop-up swarms of ads that appear so quickly they overwhelm your PC, slowing it down and making it unusable. Others hijack your browser home page so that no matter what you do, you're sent to a home page of the hijacker's choosing, which might be a pornographic site, or perhaps a web site that spawns even more pop ups. And some kinds of spyware, called *keyloggers*, literally spy on you by watching every keystroke you make, and then send that information to someone on the Internet.

Even more fearsome is spyware that turns your PC into a "bot" or a "zombie" and forces it to spew out tens of thousands or more pieces of spam, all without your knowledge.

But you don't have to be a victim; there's a good deal you can do to protect yourself, and you won't have to spend a penny to do it:

Get a free spyware detector and eradicator

One of the best and most popular free program is Ad-Aware, available from www.lavasoft.com. It checks your system for spyware, finding not only program files, but also Registry entries and cookies. After it does a check, you can choose which spyware problems you want the program to fix, and it'll go about its work, deleting files, folders, and cookies, and fixing Registry entries. Because no one spyware-killer is perfect, I suggest getting another free one, Spybot Search & Destroy, from www.spybot.info. If you're a Vista user, you already have a free piece of antispyware, Windows Defender, pictured in Figure 4-11, on your system. If you use an earlier version of Windows, get a free copy of Windows Defender at www.windowsdefender.com.

Be vigilant about what you download

There are plenty of free programs available on the Internet, but not all have good intentions in mind. Some are spyware. So be careful before downloading any free software. Go to reputable download sites, such as the download library run by PC World (www.pcworld.com/downloads) or to www.download.com and read the descriptions and reviews, to make sure the software doesn't carry a spyware load. In addition, head to the Index of Known Spyware page run by Gibson Research at grc.com/oo/spyware.htm, the SpywareGuide at www.spywareguide.com/product_list_full.php, and the Spyware Warrior List of spyware at spywarewarrior.com/rogue_anti-spyware.htm for a list of spyware programs.

QUICK HACK 

YES, YOU CAN REMOVE NORTON ANTIVIRUS

Sometimes Norton AntiVirus acts like the undead, you simply can't remove it and using Windows built-in uninstallation program or Norton's uninstallation routine simply doesn't work. There's a simple solution: use the free Norton Removal Tool, designed to rid your PC of Norton 2003 software or later. Get it at tinyurl.com/6oq8f.

Figure 4-10.
Customizing how avast! scans email for viruses

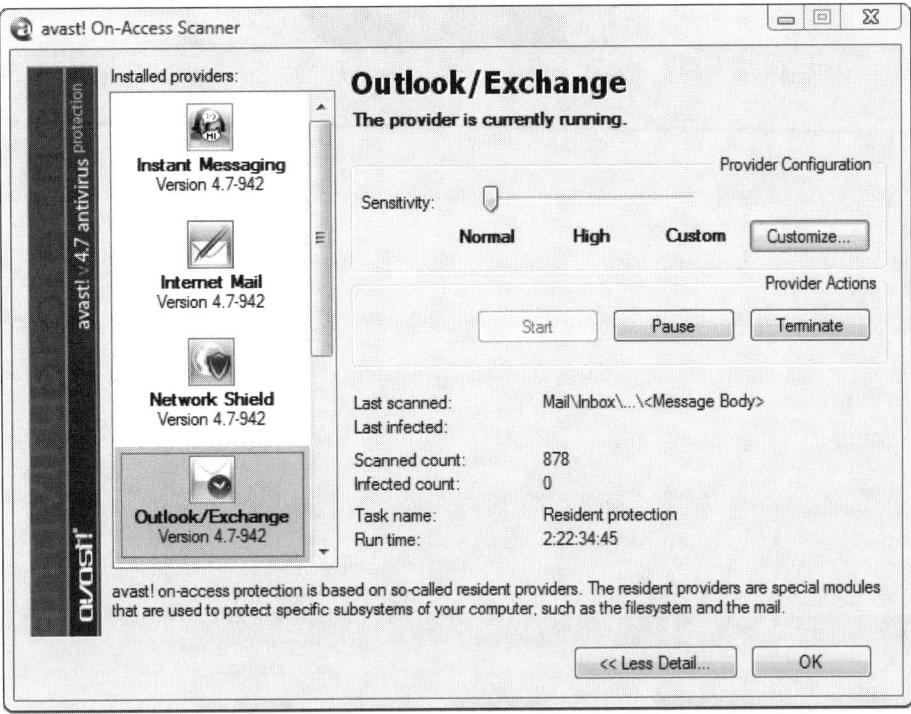

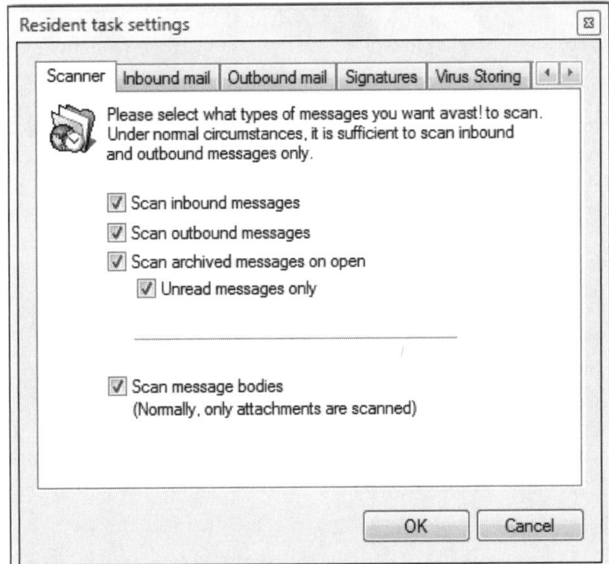

Use a personal firewall such as ZoneAlarm

A personal firewall will let you block any program on your system from contacting the Internet without your approval. With one installed, spyware can't "phone home" and alert others to your surfing habits. Windows XP's Windows Firewall doesn't have this capability, so you can't use it to block spyware. Windows Vista's Windows Firewall is better than XP's at blocking these kinds of outbound connections, but it may not block all of them. For maximum safety, get a free firewall such as ZoneAlarm's from www.zonealarm.com.

Figure 4-11.
Windows Defender protects against spyware and also lets you see what programs run when you start your PC

Kill pop ups

Pop-up ads are a common way of delivering spyware. Click a pop up, and you might get infected with spyware. So, kill pop ups. Internet Explorer 7 and Internet Explorer 6 with XP Service Pack 2 both include pop-up killers, as does Firefox. But keep in mind that sometimes pop-ups make it through their pop-up killers. If one does, close it down and don't click anything inside it (especially fake close buttons; be sure to use the real Windows controls in the upper corners of the window).

Be wary of files and links sent in instant messages

Increasingly, spyware is propagated via instant messaging programs. Spyware can in essence take over someone's instant messaging program and then send itself to everyone on the buddy list, either as an executable file or a link—and it appears that a person, rather than spyware is sending the file or link. So before clicking a link or using a file sent via instant messaging, double-check with your friend that he is actually sending you something, and that spyware hasn't done the job.

Stop drive-by downloads

A web site might attempt to download software to your PC without your knowledge, and it might carry a spyware payload. Internet Explorer 7 and Internet Explorer 6 with XP Service Pack 2 both include tools to stop drive-by downloads, as does Firefox. However, they're not necessarily 100 percent effective. So don't click links sent to you in spam, which can lead to sites with drive-by downloads.

Watch Out for Web Bugs

Web bugs are invisible bits of data, frequently a single pixel in size (sometimes called *clear GIFs*), that can track all your activities on a web site and report them back to a server. They are one of the more pernicious ways your online activities can be tracked, no matter which browser you're using. Sometimes, the web site the bugs send information to isn't the one that contains the web bug; for example, a web bug might send information back to an online advertising network.

Web bugs can send the following information back to a server:

- The IP address of your computer
- The URL of the page on which the web bug is located, so they know you visited the page

- The time the web bug was viewed, so they know exactly when you visited the page
- The URL of the web bug image
- The type of browser you have
- The values of certain cookies (generally only cookies set by the web site that the bug resides on)

A free piece of software called Bugnosis (www.bugnosis.org) will alert you whenever it comes across web bugs on pages you visit. It reports on the URL the bug reports to, and, for some bugs, it lets you click a link it creates so that you can send an email of complaint to the web site that runs the bug. It runs inside Internet Explorer as a toolbar and doesn't work with any other browsers.

The software can't actually protect you against web bugs, but it can alert you when you visit pages that use them, so you'll know to stay away from them in the future. When you visit a site, the Bugnosis toolbar reports on the number of suspicious items that might be web bugs. To see detailed information about each suspicious item and web bug, click the down arrow next to the Bugnosis logo, and choose Bugs Found in This Session. You'll see a list of every suspicious web bug, as you can see in Figure 4-12. Click the item, and you'll see a more detailed description, and an analysis on whether the item is truly a web bug or only suspicious.

Bugnosis can't actually block web bugs; it can only alert you to their presence. If you want your privacy protected when you surf the Web, your best bet is to surf anonymously **[Hack #49]**.

See Also

- If you want to keep up with the most recent spyware news and research, visit the Web site of perhaps the foremost spyware researcher in the world, Ben Edelman, at www.benedelman.org.

Figure 4-12.
Bugnosis in action

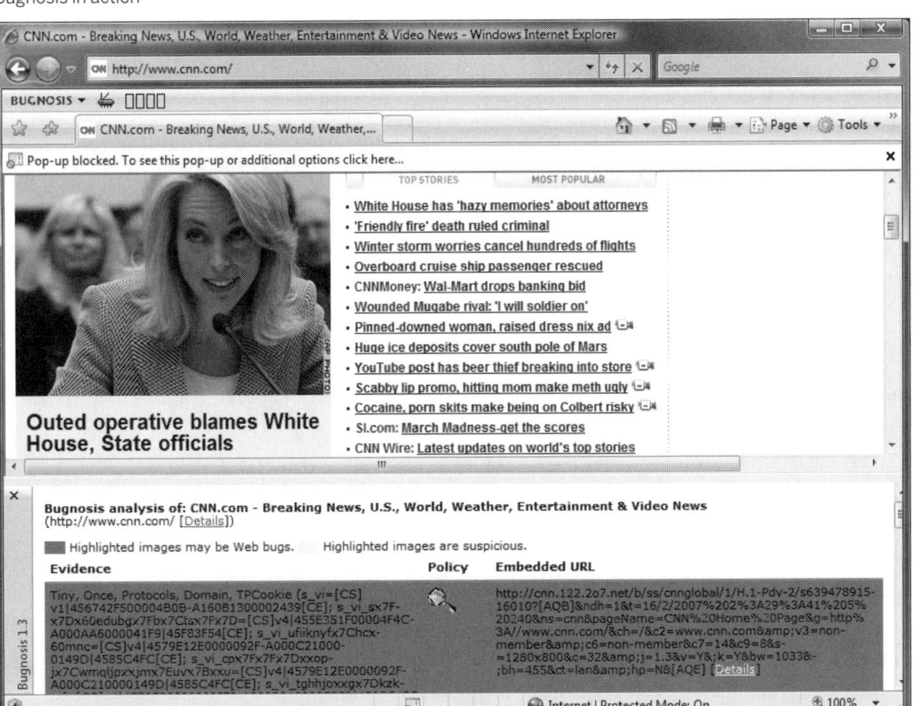

HACK 53: Keep Your Google Search History Private

V XP Worried that Google knows too much about you—and that the feds can subpoena that data? Fear not: here are seven steps you can take to keep your search history to yourself.

Most of us live in Google. We do all our searches in Google. We may use Google's Gmail email program. And we may use any of the many other myriad Google services.

This means that Google may know more about you than your mother does. Even if you trust Google and don't worry that it knows so much about your life, keep in mind that the U.S. government has been getting increasingly aggressive about issuing subpoenas that demand search histories.

So if you're worried about your Google search records falling into the wrong hands, here's what you can do to make sure they don't contain private information

Don't Log into Google When You Search

If you log into Google before you search, you make it easy for it to build a comprehensive profile about you because it knows your identity as you search. This includes not only Google but the entire ecosystem of its services, including Gmail, online office software, blogging services and more.

For privacy's sake, never do searches when you're logged into any Google services. So, for example, when you're logged into Gmail, don't search the Internet.

As a practical matter, this may be difficult to do, so another option is to use one browser such as Firefox for a service like Gmail, and another such as Internet Explorer for doing Google searches. That way, it will be much harder for the search engine to correlate your identity with your searches.

 For maximum safety, use an "anonymizing" service or software **[Hack #49]**.

If you don't like the idea of using two browsers, you can set up different profiles in your browser—one for using Gmail or another Google service, and the other for doing actual searches. Then use two instances of the browser, one with one profile, and the second with a different profile. That way, Google won't be able to correlate your searches with your identity.

Firefox lets you create separate profiles, but Internet Explorer doesn't, so you won't be able to use this technique in Internet Explorer. In Firefox, use the Profile Manager to create separate profiles. To do so, open a command prompt, and navigate to the directory in which Firefox is installed. (Depending on your version, it may be in *C:\Program Files\Mozilla Firefox*.) Type firefox.exe -ProfileManager, and press Enter. The Profile Manager, as shown in Figure 4-13, appears. Click Create Profile, and follow the wizard to create your profile. Create as many profiles as you like, and then use different profiles for searching and for using mail and other search engine services.

After you've created your profiles, you can run separate instances of Firefox using this command: firefox.exe -no-remote -P `profilename`. For example:

```
firefox.exe -no-remote -P default
firefox.exe -no-remote -P private
```

Block Google Cookies

Even if you don't log into Google, it can track your searches because it uses cookies to track your searches from session to session. Ultimately, that information can be used with information from your ISP about your IP address to build a profile about you.

Figure 4-13.
Creating a profile with Firefox's Profile Manager

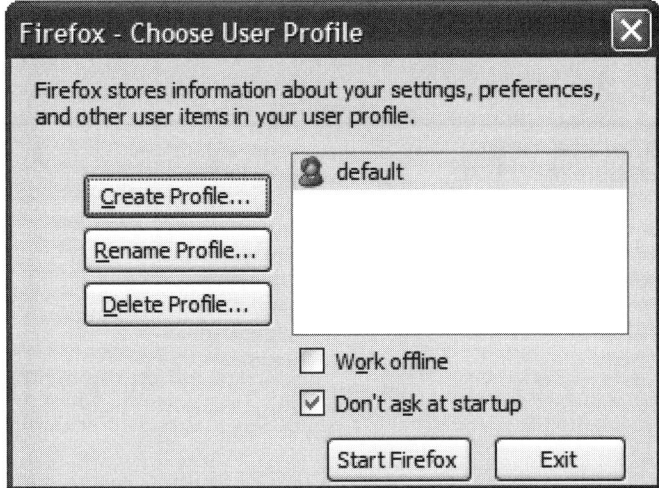

What to do? You could, of course, delete all your cookies before you visit Google. But that would kill all cookies, not just those related to Google. That can be problematic because cookies can be quite useful, for example, logging you into some sites automatically or saving your preferences on how you use sites.

Your ISP knows your IP address (even if you have a dynamically assigned address, it can correlate the time that you visit a given web site with whichever IP address you happen to have at that time), which means that it can track all the web sites you visit. That's bad enough for your privacy, but if you also use its search engine, it can correlate your IP address to your searches, and build an even more comprehensive profile about you. That profile may be available to anyone with a subpoena. So don't use an ISP's search engine (for example, search.comcast.net).

A simpler solution is to block only Google from placing cookies on your PC. How you do it varies from browser to browser. In Internet Explorer 7, for example, choose Tools→Internet Options, click the Privacy tab, then click the Sites button. In the "Address of website" box, type in www.google.com, and click Block (see Figure 4-14). Do the same for google.com. From now on, when you visit Google, it won't be allowed to place a cookie on your hard disk, and it won't be able to track your searches.

In Firefox 2, select Tools→Options, select the Privacy tab, and click Exceptions. Then type www.google.com into the "Address" of web site box, and click Block. Do the same for google.com.

(If you use another search engine, by the way, you can use this same technique to keep its cookies off your hard disk as well.)

Note that because Google won't be placing cookies on your hard disk, you may not be able to use various Google services, such as Gmail.

Here's the easiest way to make sure that information about your searches can't be used to build a personal profile about you: use a search engine that doesn't retain a history of your searches. That's what www.ixquick.com promises. It says it deletes all information about your searches within 48 hours, so the information simply isn't around for anyone to use. If the feds subpoena the data, there's nothing they get.

Figure 4-14.
Blocking Google from placing cookies on your hard disk

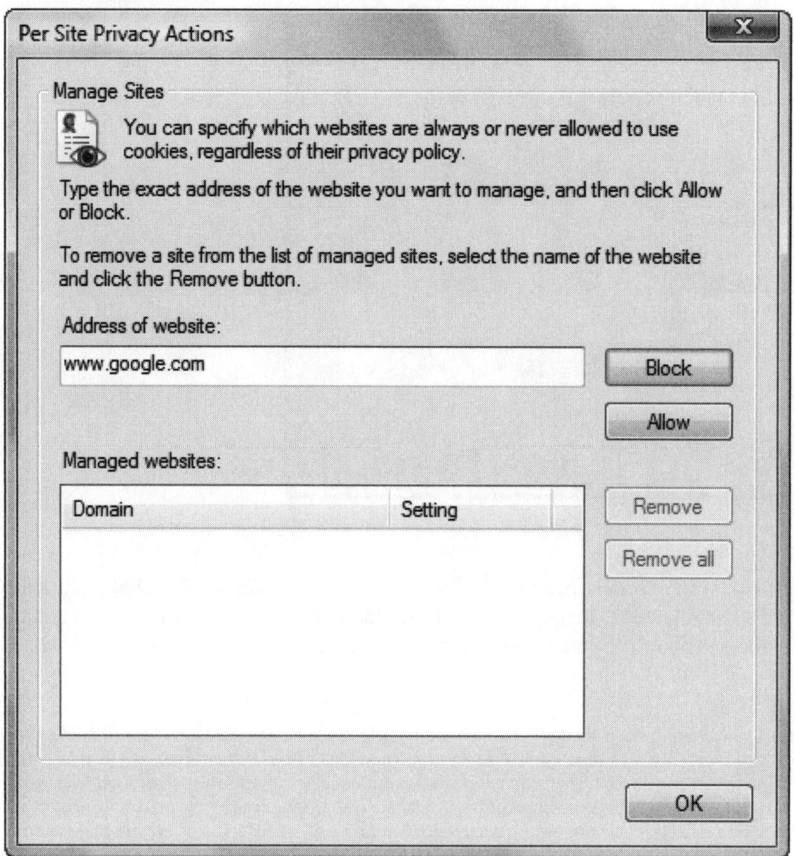

If you're a Firefox user, you can also use the CustomizeGoogle extension that among other things, anonymizes you when you use Google so that your searches can't be tracked. It's free; get it at www.customizegoogle.com.

Limit Your Google Services

Google has numerous services you can sign up for, including an RSS reader called Google Reader, and Google Groups, which lets you read newsgroups and other discussion groups. The more Google services like this you sign up for, the more information Google knows about you; in addition to your searches, it will know what blogs and newsgroups you read, for example. This makes it that much easier for the search giant to create a profile about you. So either don't sign up for those services, or else create separate Google accounts for each of them, so that the search engine can't correlate all your interests.

Also, think carefully before turning on Google's Search History feature. Search History lets you revisit all your searches, and shows what you've searched for every day. When you use Search History, anyone who guesses your password and logs in as you can see the all the searches that you've done on Google. If you're worried that that search history may fall into the wrong hands or be subpoenaed by the government, simply don't use the service.

Don't Include Personal Information in Your Searches

We've all "Googled" ourselves at times, just to see what's out there on the Web about us. But every time you use personal information in a search, such as your name, address, and so on, you make it easy for Google to know who you are and then correlate searches with your name. If Google only knows you by your cookie, it can be hard to personally identify you. But search for your name a lot, and it won't be too hard to correlate your identify with your searches.

 If you absolutely must do a search about personal information or do a search that is sensitive for some other reason, don't do it at home or at work. Instead, go to a public hot spot, and do the search from there. Make sure to use a hot spot that doesn't require you to log in or else your privacy can be compromised.

See Also

- "Surf Anonymously Without a Trace" [Hack #49]

HACK 54: Fix Internet Explorer 7 Add-In Woes

V XP If Internet Explorer 7 crashes or appears sluggish, the cause may be an errant toolbar or add-in. Follow these steps to weed out the problem and fix it.

There's a world of add-ins and toolbar extensions for Internet Explorer 7—and there's also a world of pain. If you notice Internet Explorer 7 slowing down, crashing, or exhibiting other odd behavior, the problem may be one of these add-ins or toolbars.

You can, though, figure out whether any of them are causing problems and then get rid of the ones that are problematic. The first step is to determine whether a toolbar or add-in is causing the problem. Do it by running Internet Explorer in no add-ons mode by choosing Start→All Programs→ Accessories→System Tools→Internet Explorer (No Add-ons). If you're able to run Internet Explorer without problems, an add-in or toolbar is causing the problem.

 If you still experience problems when using No Add-on mode, your best bet is to search the Microsoft Knowledge Base. Go to support.microsoft.com/search, and do a search for the kind of problem you're experiencing.

Next, use Internet Explorer 7's IE's Manage Add-ons feature to selectively disable add-ons until you find out which add-in or toolbar is the bad guy. Close Internet Explorer and restart it, but restart it normally this time, not in No Add-on mode. Select Tools→Manage Add-Ons→Enable or Disable Add-Ons. You'll see a list of all the add-ons that are currently loaded in Internet Explorer (Figure 4-15). Highlight one, click Disable, and click OK and OK again. You'll have to restart Internet Explorer for the change to take effect.

If Internet Explorer works without any problems, you've uncovered the cause of the problem. Instead of merely leaving the add-on disabled, though, you should remove it from your system. Use the Control Panel's normal Add/Remove program feature to remove it.

If disabling that add-on doesn't solve the problem, you should enable the add-on you've just disabled, then disable a different one. Select Tools→Manage Add-Ons→Enable or Disable Add-Ons. The screen shown in Figure 4-16 will list the add-on that you've disabled under the Disabled heading. Highlight it and click Enable. Then disable another add-on as previously outlined, and see if solves the problem. Keep disabling and enabling add-ons until you find the one that's causing the problem.

Hacking the Hack

If all else fails, you can reset Internet Explorer to its default settings, so that it reverts to the way it was when it was first installed on your PC. Select Tools→Internet Options→Advanced, and click the Reset button (Figure 4-17).

See Also

- "Kill Badly Behaving Items from the Internet Explorer Tools Menu" [Hack #55]

> **QUICK HACK**
>
> **SOLVE IE 7 WEBSITE WOES**
>
> Some web sites get confused when you visit them using Internet Explorer 7 because the sites still expect to see Internet Explorer 6 instead, and so you may not be able to use the site. A simple download will let you visit those sites in Internet Explorer 7, by fooling them into thinking you're actually using Internet Explorer 6. Go to tinyurl.com/qhawa, and download and install the User Agent String Utility. When you run it, it launches a new instance of Internet Explorer that tells a web site that it's Version 6, even though it's Version 7.

Figure 4-15.
Selectively disable add-ons and toolbars from this screen.

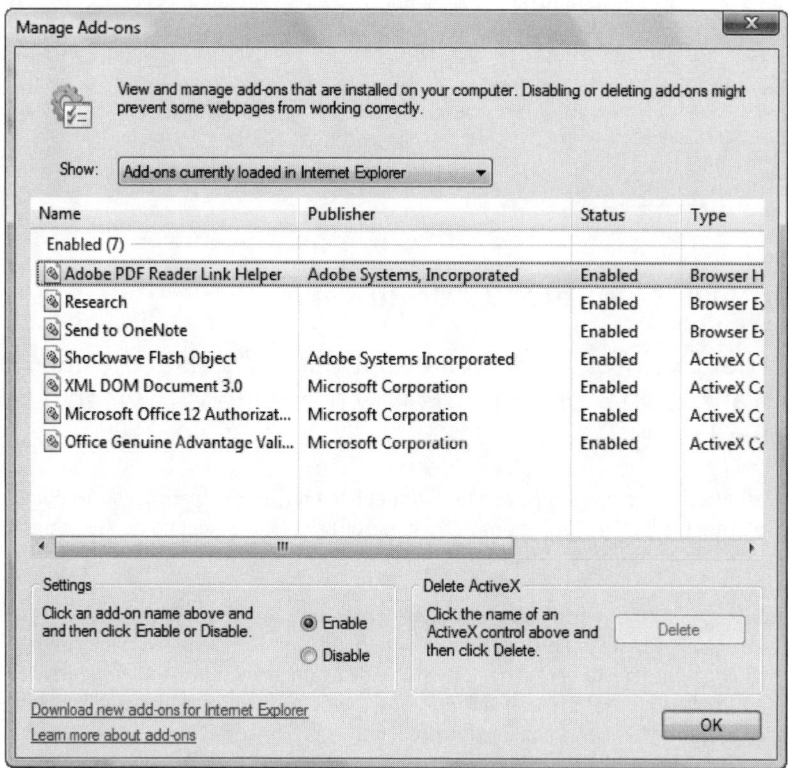

Figure 4-16.
The list of disabled and enabled add-ons

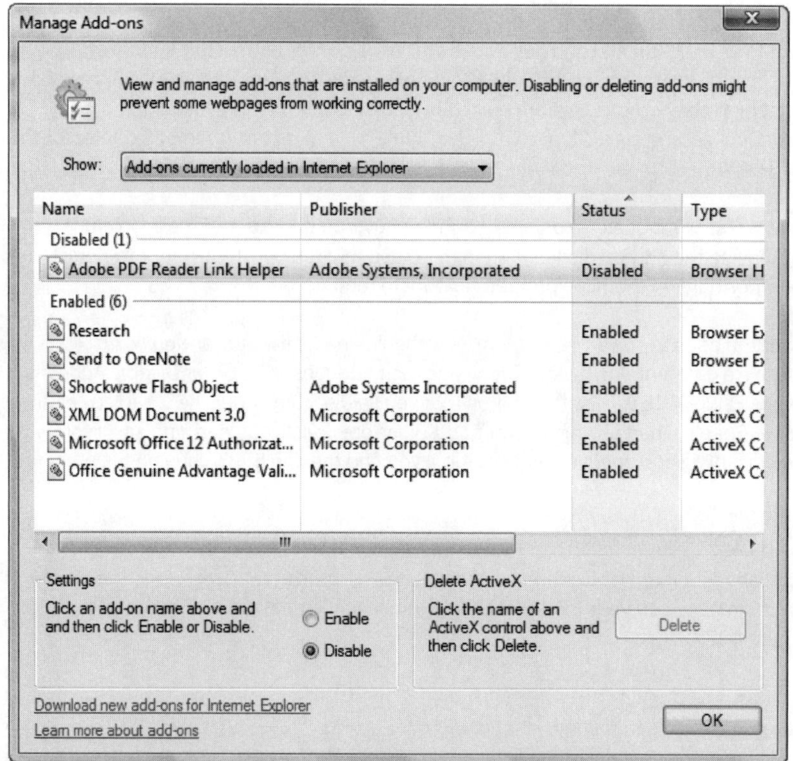

Figure 4-17.
Choosing the nuclear option: Resetting Internet Explorer to its default state

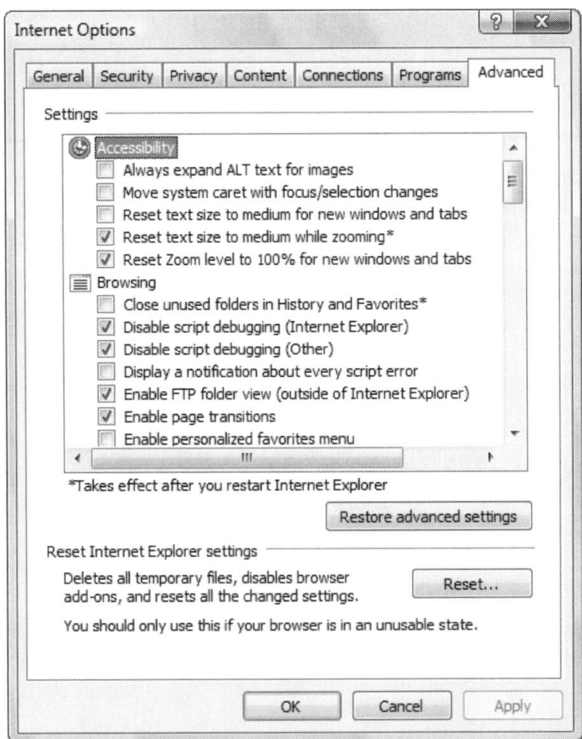

HACK 55: Kill Badly Behaving Items on the Internet Explorer Tools Menu

V XP Some toolbars leave behind their traces on the Internet Explorer Tools menu. Here's how to kill them.

Some toolbars and add-ins behave very badly: they install entries for themselves on your Tools menu that can't be removed, even if you uninstall the toolbar or add-in itself. Several people, for example, have complained that the PartyPoker.com listing remains on the Tools menu, even after the add-on itself has been removed.

You can remove them by editing the Registry, though. First uninstall the toolbar or add-in. If its listing remains on the Tools menu, launch the Registry Editor by typing `regedit` at the Start Search box or a command prompt (see Chapter 13 for details). Go to `HKEY_LOCAL_MACHINE\SOFTWARE\Microsoft\Internet Explorer\Extensions`. You'll see several keys named with what appear to be random letters and numbers, enclosed in brackets, as you can see in Figure 4-18.

Highlight each of the keys, and examine their keys and values. Somewhere you should see the name of the add-in, the file location, and so on. When you find the offending key, highlight it, and click Delete to remove it from the Registry. Make sure to delete the entire key—for example, `{2670000B-7450-4f3c-8181-5663EE9C6C49}`—and not individual strings and values. Then exit the Registry. You'll need to restart Windows Explorer, and possibly Windows itself, for the change to take effect.

See Also

- "Fix Internet Explorer 7 Add-In Woes" **[Hack #54]**

Figure 4-18
Listings of Internet Explorer extensions in the Registry

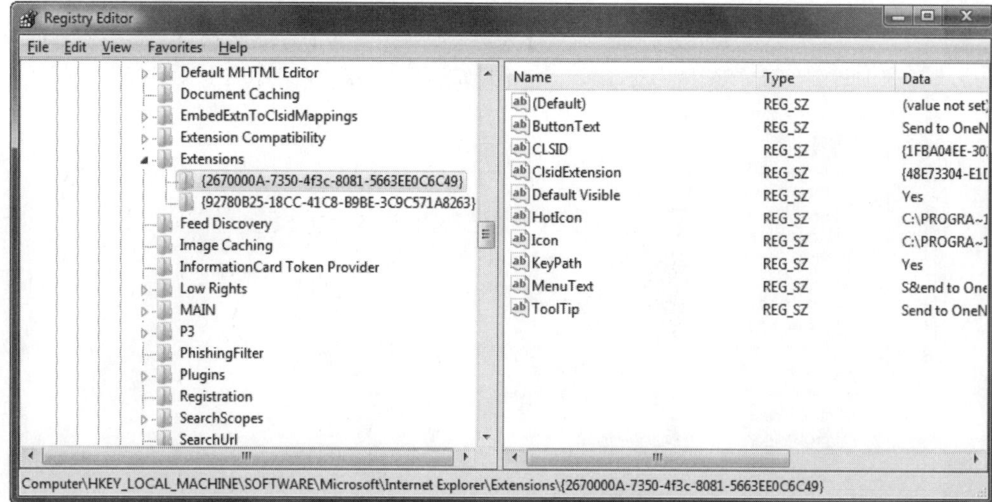

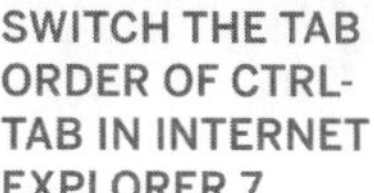

SWITCH THE TAB ORDER OF CTRL-TAB IN INTERNET EXPLORER 7

When you have multiple tabs open in Internet Explorer 7 and press Ctrl-Tab, you cycle through your tabs in order, starting with the one to the right of your current tab. This can be annoying, though, if you want to switch to the most recently used tab, instead of the one to the right. To tell Internet Explorer 7 to switch to the most recent tab when you press Ctrl-Tab, select Tools→Internet Options→Advanced. Then check the box next to "Use most recent order" when switching tabs with Ctrl-Tab. Close Internet Explorer, and restart it in order for the change to take effect.

HACK 56: Hack Printouts in Internet Explorer 7

V XP Take advantage of the new printing capabilities of Internet Explorer 7.

The most ballyhooed feature of Internet Explorer 7 was the addition of tabbed browsing, but little noticed was another great addition as well—better control over printing. Given how much printing most of us do, and what a poor job browsers generally do when printing web pages, this is a very big deal.

Internet Explorer 7 lets you change a variety of things about the way you print web pages, including whether to print a header or footer, what to put in the header and footer, whether to print thumbnails of web pages, and so on.

To change these options, click the printer icon at the top of Internet Explorer, and choose Print Preview. A screen like the one shown in Figure 4-19 appears.

The icons across the top give you basic control over printing and how pages will be displayed in print preview. Most are self-explanatory, such as printing in landscape or portrait mode, whether to preview one page at a time, two pages at a time, and so on.

To turn headers and footers on and off, click the fifth icon from the left, or press Alt-E. You'll see the display change to reflect whether the headers and footers will print.

If you'd like, you can customize those headers and footers, and not just print the default. To do it, click the Page Setup icon (the one that looks like a gear, the fourth from the left). The screen shown in Figure 4-20 appears.

Look at the Header and Footer input boxes: they tell Internet Explorer what to print in the header and footer. By default, here's what's in the header box:

```
&w&bPage &p of &P
```

Here's what's in the footer box:

```
&u&b&d
```

Figure 4-19
The Print Preview screen

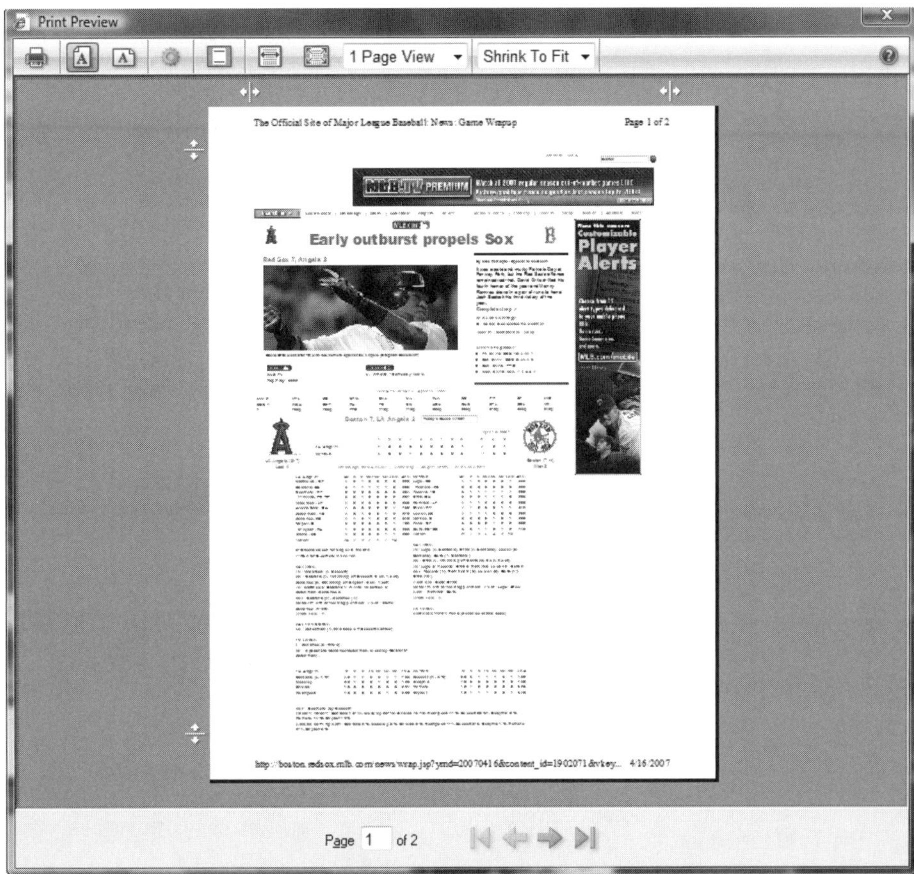

Figure 4-20
The Page Setup screen

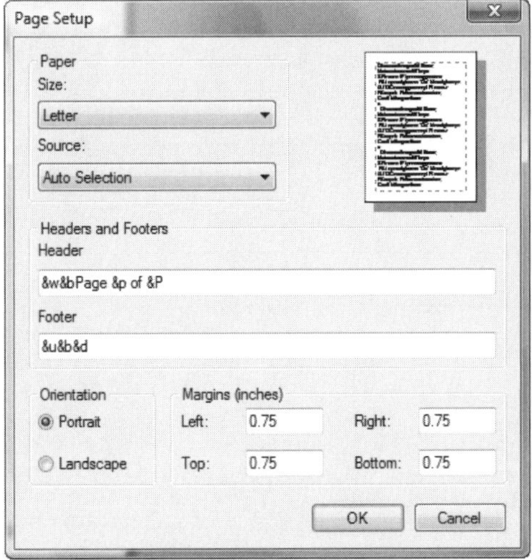

The code in the header box tells Internet Explorer to:

- Print the window title (&w)
- Print the word "Page" and align it and the rest of the text to the right (&bPage)
- After a space, print the page number (&p)
- After another space, print the total number of pages (&P)

The code in the footer box tells Internet Explorer to:

- Print the URL (&u)
- Print the date in short-date format (&b&d)

So, for example, if you visit the front page of the www.redsox.com web site on April 16, 2007, the window title was The Official Site of the Boston Red Sox: Homepage, and the front page, if printed, was four pages long, the header would print out this:

```
The Official Site of the Boston Red Sox:Homepage          Page 1 of 4
```

The footer would print out like this:

```
http://www.redsox.com                                        4/16/2007
```

By changing the text in the header and footer boxes, you can change what prints out. Here's the list of options available to you:

&w	Window Title
&u	URL of the current page
&d	The date in short format (4/16/2007)
&D	The date in long format, including the day of the week (Monday, April 16, 2007)
&t	Time in clock format (5:26:43 PM)
&T	Time in 24-hour format (17:26:43 PM)
&p	Current page number
&P	Total number of pages
&b	Right-align the following text
&b&b	Center the text inside the &bs
&&	An ampersand (&)

So in our example of the Red Sox page, this header:

```
I visited &w on &D.
```

would print this:

```
I visited The Official Site of the Boston Red Sox:Homepage on Monday, April 16, 2007
```

This footer:

```
I printed Page &p at &T
```

Would print this:

```
I printed Page 1 at 17:26:43 PM.
```

FIX PRINTING PROBLEMS IN INTERNET EXPLORER 6

When Internet Explorer 7 prints a web page, it automatically resizes it so that the entire page prints out, with no text missing. Not so Internet Explorer 6, though. That earlier version of the browser often cuts text off the right-hand side of the page. To fix the problem, choose File→Page Setup, and in the Margins (inches) section at the bottom of the box, reduce the right and/or left margins. The default is 0.75 inches, so try 0.5 inches for the right margin and see if it helps. Click OK once you've made your changes. You can check whether it will print properly by previewing the page (File→Print Preview). Keep changing the margins until the entire page prints out correctly.

HACK 57: Hack Internet Explorer with the Group Policy Editor

V XP Windows Vista's, and Windows XP Professional's Group Policy Editor lets you tweak Internet Explorer in countless ways—from changing its logo and background, to changing its titlebar text, and beyond.

The Group Policy Editor (See Chapter 13) is a powerful tool for making all kinds of tweaks to Windows. Although it was designed primarily for administrators on networks to make changes to groups of computers en masse, it's a great tool for tweaking and hacking individual machines as well. It can make all kinds of secret tweaks to Internet Explorer and makes it easy to customize many different aspects of Internet Explorer's behavior and appearance from one central place, without having to edit the Registry or delve deep into menus, dialog boxes, and options. You can customize how Internet Explorer looks and works for each individual account on the machine, or just for a single account if there is only one.

Group Policy Editor is available on Windows XP Professional, but not the Home edition. It's available on Windows Vista Enterprise, Business, and Ultimate, but not Home Basic or Home Premium.

That means you'll be able to create customized versions of IE for a variety of different purposes. For example, you can create customized browsers for your children, or for a business if you run or administer a small business.

Run the Group Policy Editor by typing gpedit.msc at a command line, the Run box, or the Search box, and pressing Enter. When it opens, go to `User Configuration\Windows Settings\Internet Explorer Maintenance`. There are five categories of Internet Explorer settings you can modify:

- Browser User Interface
- Connection
- URLs
- Security
- Programs

To change individual settings, browse to any of the categories, then from the right pane choose the setting you want to configure—for example, the browser title. Double-click the setting, and then fill out the dialog box, such as the one shown in Figure 4-21, which lets you change Internet Explorer's static and animated logos.

You can change quite a few settings with the Group Policy Editor. Next, we'll take a look at what the best of each category can do.

Browser User Interface

As the name implies, this section lets you customize Internet Explorer's interface. This section, as a whole, lets you create your own customized version of Internet Explorer. For example, you can create a version of IE specifically for one of your children—take a digital photo of her and use it as the background for the toolbar, crop a headshot photo of her and use it as the animated custom logo, and change the browser title to put her name on it. You can make three types of tweaks in this section:

Browser Title

This option lets you customize Internet Explorer's titlebar text, though only to a limited degree; you can add your name or your company's name to a text string of "Microsoft Internet Explorer provided by." For example, you can have the titlebar read "Microsoft Explorer provided by Preston Gralla."

Figure 4-21.
Using the Group Policy Editor to change Internet Explorer's settings

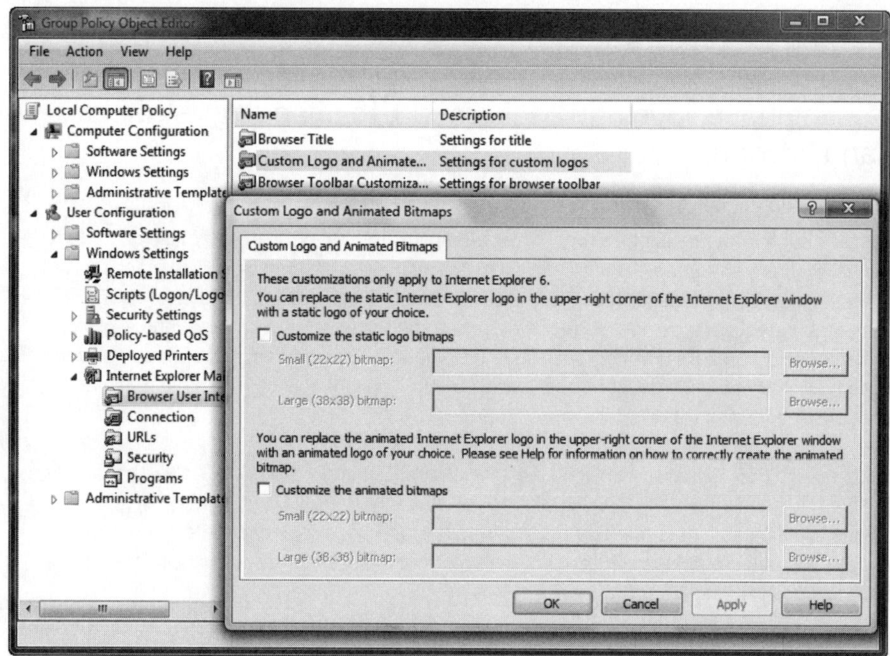

When you do this, Outlook Express will have the same title as well. Because you need to have that initial text string, this isn't a great hack unless you're a computer manufacturer and want to brand the browser.

Custom Logo

This setting lets you replace Internet Explorer's static and animated logo with logos of your own. Note that to do this, you'll first have to create the logos yourself. You'll have to create them in bitmap (*.bmp*) format in two sizes, 22 by 22 pixels and 38 by 38 pixels.

Browser Toolbar Customizations

You can use your own bitmap as the background to the Internet Explorer toolbar. Additionally, you can delete the existing toolbar buttons and add buttons of your own. You don't have to worry if the bitmap you want to use is not the same size as the toolbar. Internet Explorer will accommodate it—for example, by tiling a graphic that is smaller than the toolbar so that it appears multiple times.

You can only change the custom logo and browser toolbar in Internet Explorer 6; the customizations don't work on Internet Explorer 7. However, you can change the browser title in both Internet Explorer 6 and Internet Explorer 7.

Connection

This section lets you customize Internet Explorer's connection settings, which you would otherwise have to go to several places to set:

Connection Settings

This lets you customize your existing Internet connection settings and import them for another use on the PC. It's useful if you're the only user of the machine; it's intended to help you set up other accounts' connection settings. If you have a network at home, for example, you could copy the settings from one machine to every other machine on the network.

Automatic Browser Configuration

This is purely an administrator's tool. It lets you automatically change browser configurations on users' machines.

Proxy Settings

This lets you tell Internet Explorer to use proxy servers. You can also set up proxy servers [Hack #49] from within Internet Explorer. .

User Agent String

This lets you customize the user agent string that is sent to web sites whenever you visit them. The user agent string gives out basic information about your operating system and browser to the web site so that the site can better track usage statistics. Using this setting lets you append a specific text string to your PC's user agent string.

URLs

This section is mainly for administrators, so if you don't need administrative tools you can pretty much forgo it. If you are an administrator, it will let you specify IE settings for multiple machines, such as setting a home page for all, specifying a URL they will go to when Help is chosen, and populating their Favorites with those of your choice. If you run a small business, you can use these settings to build a business-specific browser for all your employees. For example, set the home page to be your company's home page or populate Favorites with intranet pages or other pages your employees need to access regularly, such as benefits information.

Favorites and Links

This lets you create a Favorites folder and links, or import them. It's primarily an administrator's tool, since it doesn't add much extra functionality to the normal way you can manage Favorites.

Important URLs

You can specify the starting page, create your own customized Search bar, and create a Help page that will display when someone clicks Help→Online Support. Again, this is primarily an administrator's tool.

Security

Here's where to set Internet Explorer security settings. You can change these settings from directly within Internet Explorer just as easily as changing them here—unless you need to change the settings for several accounts, in which case this is the place to go.

Security Zones and Content Rating

You can customize both security zones and content ratings, which limit sites with objectionable content from being visited. This is primarily an administrator's tool because these settings can be edited easily from inside Internet Explorer by choosing Tools→Internet Options→Security and Tools→Internet Options→Content. But it's ideal for parents who have networks at home and want to customize different security settings for their children's computers. You can set a higher level of security for children's computers and a lower level for parents' PCs.

Authenticode Settings

This lets you designate specific credential agencies and software publishers as trustworthy. This is primarily an administrator's tool because these settings can be edited easily from inside Internet Explorer by choosing Tools→Internet Options→Security and Tools→Internet Options→Content→ Certificates.

Programs

Once again, this section is mainly for administrators. It lets you change default programs for multiple machines. So, for users who require only a simple email program, you can set the default to be Outlook Express. For other users, you can set it as Outlook or a third-party email program.

Programs

This lets you change the default programs to be used for purposes such as email, HTML editing, and others. This is primarily an administrator's tool because these settings can be edited easily by choosing Tools→Internet Options→Programs.

HACK 58: Hack Firefox

V XP The free browser Firefox has gained millions of adherents since its release because of its security features, customizability, and features that Internet Explorer lacks. Here's a grab bag of hacks for powering it up.

The popular open source Firefox browser (available for download from www.mozilla.org/products/firefox and shown in Figure 4-22) has gained millions of followers. It's an immensely customizable piece of software, and is just *begging* to be hacked.

This hack, and the others in this book, primarily cover Firefox 2.0. However, much of the hacks can also be applied to earlier—and later—versions of Firefox as well.

In this hack, you'll learn how to add new features with Firefox extensions, and how to hack the interface with a hidden stylesheet.

Using Firefox Extensions

Perhaps the most remarkable feature of Firefox is its ability to use *extensions*. Extensions are free add-ins that give the browser all kinds of new features. Because Firefox is open source, anyone can write an extension, and developers all over the Internet have put their creativity to use. There are hundreds of them, and new ones are added every day (by the time you read this, more than 1,000 extensions could be available). They add a mind-boggling array of capabilities, such as telling you

Figure 4-22.
Firefox cries out: Hack me, please!

the real URL of a site you're visiting so that you won't be the victim of a phishing exploit, letting you navigate the Web using *mouse gestures* so that you can browse by moving your mouse rather than by clicking, blocking ads, and much more.

How to find extensions? In Firefox, choose Tools→Add-Ons→Get Extensions. You'll be sent to a web page that lists extensions by category, and also lists the most popular and most recent one. This is the official Firefox extensions site, but it's not the only place you can find extensions. You can find them on other places on the Web as well, notably at extensionroom.mozdev.org.

Browse to the extension you want to install and click Install. If you want more information about the extension before you install it, click the title of the extension, and you'll be sent to a page with more information about it; from there, you can also download the extension (see Figure 4-23).

After you click Install Now, the screen shown in Figure 4-24 appears.

Click Install Now, and after several moments, the extension will be installed and will appear in your Extensions window, as shown in Figure 4-25. The extension won't work yet; first you have to close Firefox and restart it.

When you restart Firefox, the extension will start working. Many extensions allow you to customize their options. So, immediately after installing an extension, you should do that. To customize the options for an extension, choose Tools→Add-ons, select the extension you want to customize, and choose Options. If you want to uninstall an extension, select it, click Uninstall, and then click OK. You'll have to close Firefox and restart for the extension to uninstall.

Figure 4-23.
Finding the Adblock Plus extension

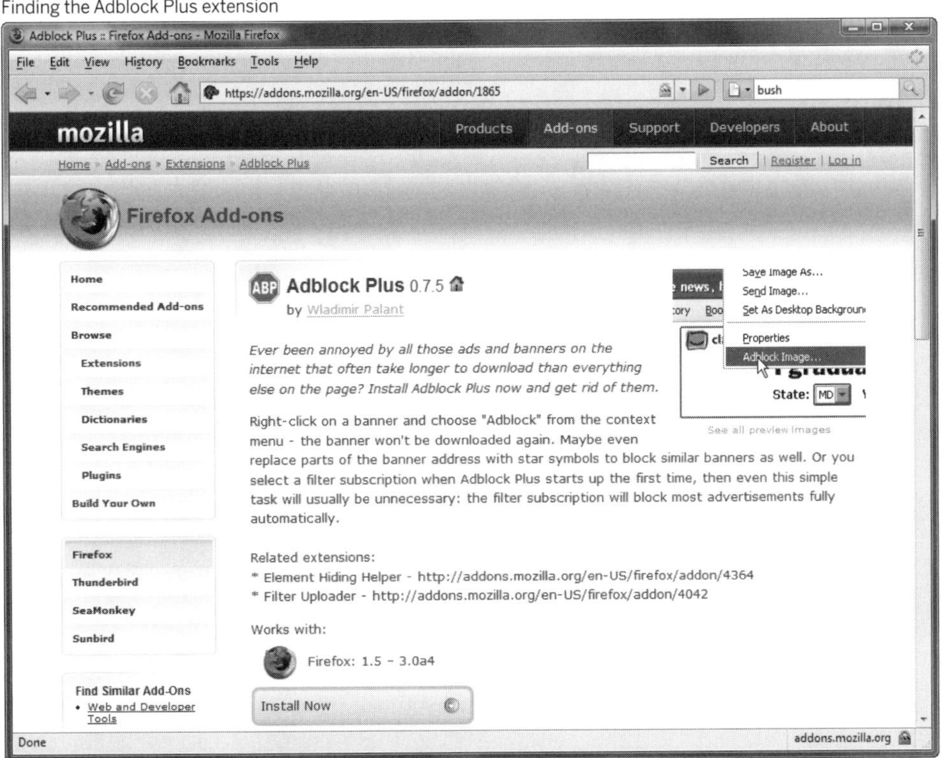

Figure 4-24.
Starting to install the extension

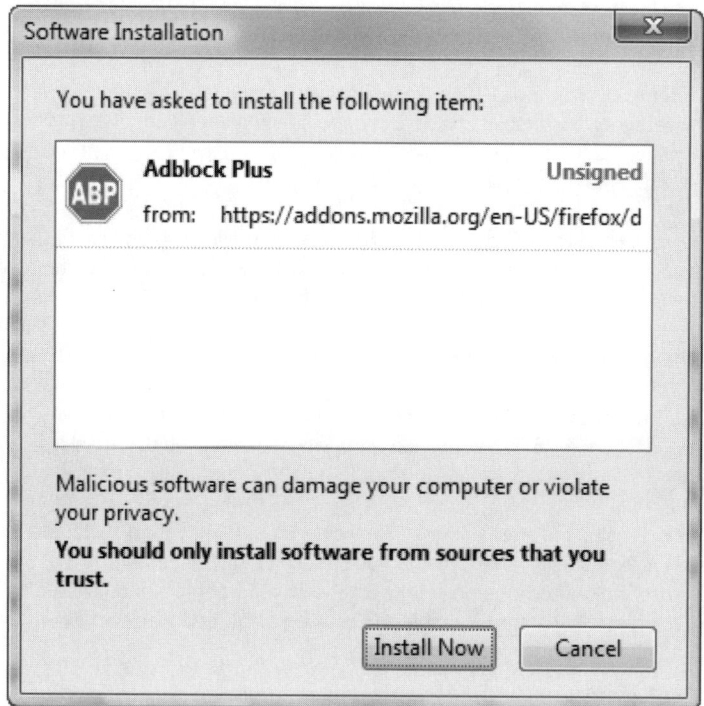

Figure 4-25.
The installed extension

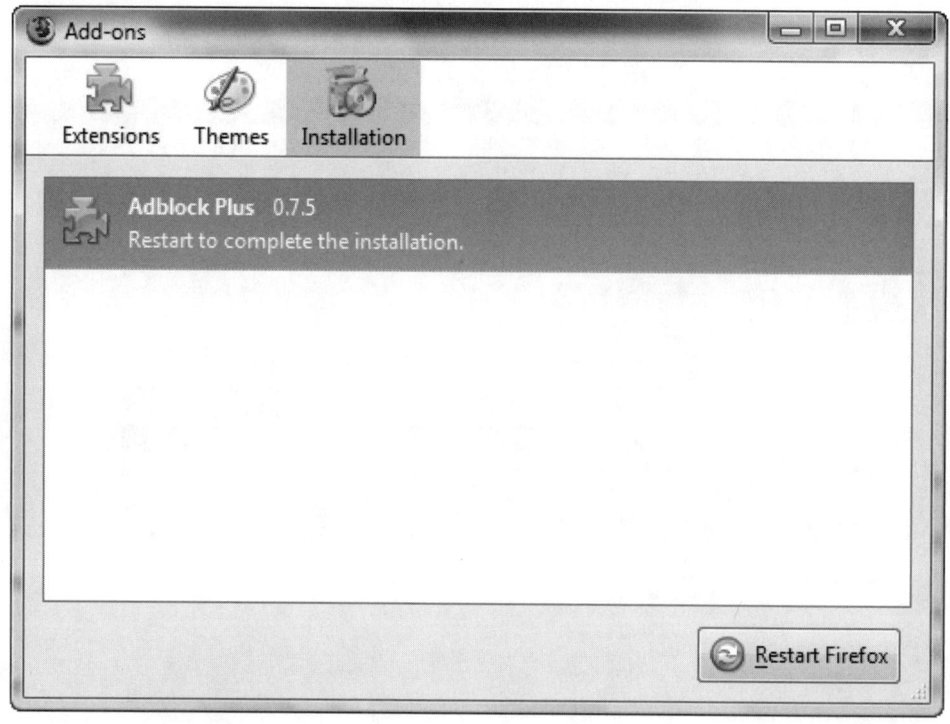

Hundreds of extensions are available, and everyone has their favorites. Here are a few of mine:

Firefox Showcase

This lets Firefox display thumbnails of all your open web sites and tabs, something that Internet Explorer can do, but Firefox, by itself, can't.

Session Manager

How many times have you closed down Firefox—or had Firefox crash—only to wish that you could recreate your last browsing session? That's what this nifty extension does. You can restore entire sessions, and you can even reopen a single tab that you accidentally closed.

IE Tab

Despite the popularity of Firefox, Internet Explorer remains the dominant browser. Because of this, some sites are designed to work with Internet Explorer and don't display well in Firefox. This extension will run Internet Explorer as a tab right inside Firefox, so you can continue to use Firefox for visiting other sites.

Cooliris Previews

Not sure if you want to visit a web site linked from the one you're currently on? Want to preview a YouTube video without having to leave your current page? Then this extension (Figure 4-26) is for you. Mouse over a link, and a small icon appears to the link's right. Highlight the icon, and you'll see a preview of the site.

Mouse Gestures

Instead of clicking your way around the Web, you can use mouse gestures. Hold down the mouse button and make a gesture with your mouse, and you can open and close windows, navigate from page to page, and more. So, for example, to close a tab, you would hold down the right-mouse button and move the mouse in a reverse "L" motion, and the tab would close.

Figure 4-26.
The Cooliris extension in action

Hacking the Firefox Interface

It's easy to apply *themes* to Firefox, which give it different colors and graphics. To apply a theme, choose Tools→Add-Ons→Themes→Get Themes, and you'll be sent to a web site with many different themes. When you find a theme you want, click its title, and you'll be sent to a page with more information, which sometimes includes a preview. You can install the theme from that by clicking Install Now. Click Restart Firefox after the theme downloads. This will make the theme available, but won't actually put it into use.

Select Tools→Add-Ons→Themes, and you'll see a list of all your themes (Figure 4-27). Highlight any to see a preview. Click Use Theme, restart Firefox, and the theme will be applied (Figure 4-28).

Firefox lets you do more than just change the theme. You can also hack the interface. Firefox's interface can be controlled by a cascading style sheet (CSS), a file that contains instructions on how Firefox should display. By editing that file, you can change Firefox's appearance.

The file is named *userChrome.css*, and for it to work, it needs to be located in a special folder underneath the folder that contains your Firefox profile. In Windows XP, the folder is *C:\Documents and Settings*`UserName`*\Application Data\Mozilla\Firefox\Profiles\xxxxx\chrome*, where `UserName` is your XP account name, and the *xxxxxx* will be random string of numbers and characters. In Windows Vista, the folder is *C:\Users*`UserName`*\AppData\Roaming\Mozilla\Firefox\Profiles\xxxxxx\chrome*. As with Windows XP, `UserName` is your Vista account name, and the *.xxxxxx* is a random string of numbers and characters.

When you install Firefox, there is no *userChrome.css* file in that folder. Instead, you'll find a file named *userChrome-example.css*. Save a copy of that file as *userChrome.css*, and edit it to change Firefox's interface. It's a plain-text file, so you can edit it with Notepad. Following are some of the hacks you can make by editing the file. If you don't already have a *userChrome.css*, you can start off with a blank text file, and name it *userChrome.css*.

Note that it's a good idea, when putting in this code, to put in a reminder for yourself so that later on you remember what it does. You have to tell *userChrome.css* to ignore your reminder so that it doesn't try to interpret it as code. So, surround your comments with `/*` to begin and `*/` to end, like this:

```
/* This is a comment */
```

Put Your Own Graphic on the Firefox Toolbar

If you don't like the plain background of Firefox's toolbar, you can put your own graphic there. Type the following into the *userChrome.css* file, and put the graphic you want to use—for instance, *background.gif*—in the same directory as *userChrome.css*:

```
/* Change the toolbar graphic */
menubar, toolbox, toolbar, .tabbrowser-tabs {
   background-image: url("background.gif") !important;
   background-color: none !important;
   }
```

Figure 4-27.
Turning on the Red Sox theme

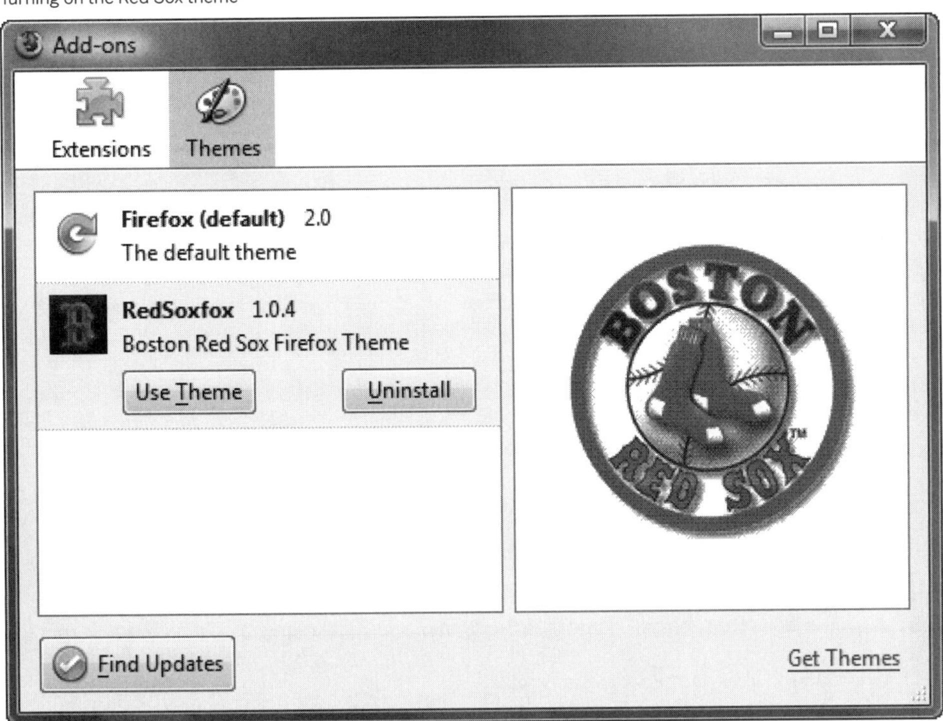

Figure 4-28.
Can't get a ticket to Fenway Park? Use the Red Sox Firefox theme instead.

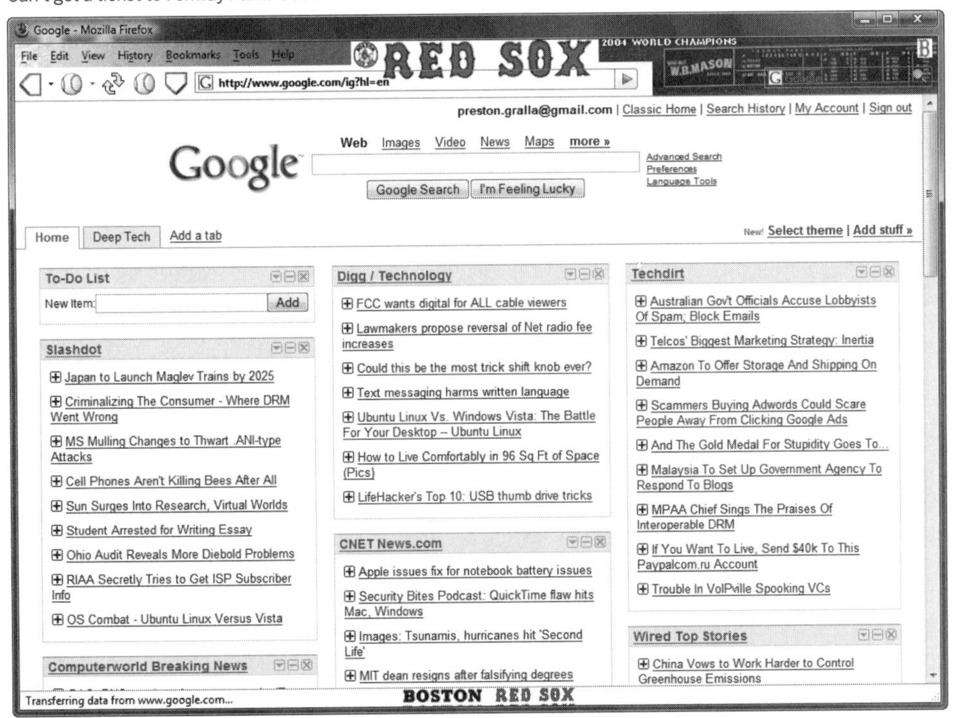

Make It Easier to Find the Active Tab

If you use many tabs when you browse, sometimes it can be difficult to distinguish the active one. So, you can make that tab stand out more by making its border red, and gray out the background tabs. Type the following into the *userChrome.css* file:

```
/* Change color of active tab */
tab{
   -moz-appearance: none !important;
}
tab[selected="true"] {
   background-color: rgb(222,100,100) !important;
   color: black !important;
}

/* Change color of normal tabs */
tab:not([selected="true"]) {
   background-color: rgb(200,196,188) !important;
   color: gray !important;
}
```

Kill Bookmark Icons

You can kill the icons that normally appear to the right of your bookmarks on the bookmarks menu:

```
/* Kill bookmark icons in the bookmarks menu */
menuitem.bookmark-item > .menu-iconic-left {
  display: none;
}
```

Naturally, you wouldn't necessarily use all these hacks in concert with one another. But you could, of course. Figure 4-29 shows what Firefox looks like after we've added the hacks to the *userChrome.css* file.

You can hack Firefox using the *userChrome.css* file in several additional ways. For more, go to www.mozilla.org/support/firefox/tips and www.mozilla.org/unix/customizing.html.

HACK 53: Stop Firefox Memory Leaks

V XP Firefox is notorious for leaking memory and causing system slowdowns. Here's how to fix the problem.

Through the years there has been a continuing Firefox problem that never seems to get fixed. It "leaks" memory; that is, it uses up RAM but then never releases it for other programs to use. A well-behaved program will release RAM when it no longer needs it, but Firefox sometime won't do it. In this hack, you'll teach Firefox how to behave.

First you'll want to know if Firefox is, in fact, leaking memory. If you notice general slowdowns on your PC after you've been running Firefox for a while, that may be the cause of the problem. You can also run Task Manager, to see how much RAM Firefox is using. Press Ctrl-Alt-Delete to run it. (In Windows Vista, you'll have to click Start Task Manager after you press Ctrl-Alt-Delete.)

Click the Processes tab, and see how much RAM Firefox is using (Figure 4-30). As a general rule, Firefox shouldn't be taking up much more than 80MB of RAM or so. If it does, you may have a Firefox leak problem.

Figure 4-29.
Firefox, after the userChrome.css file has been edited

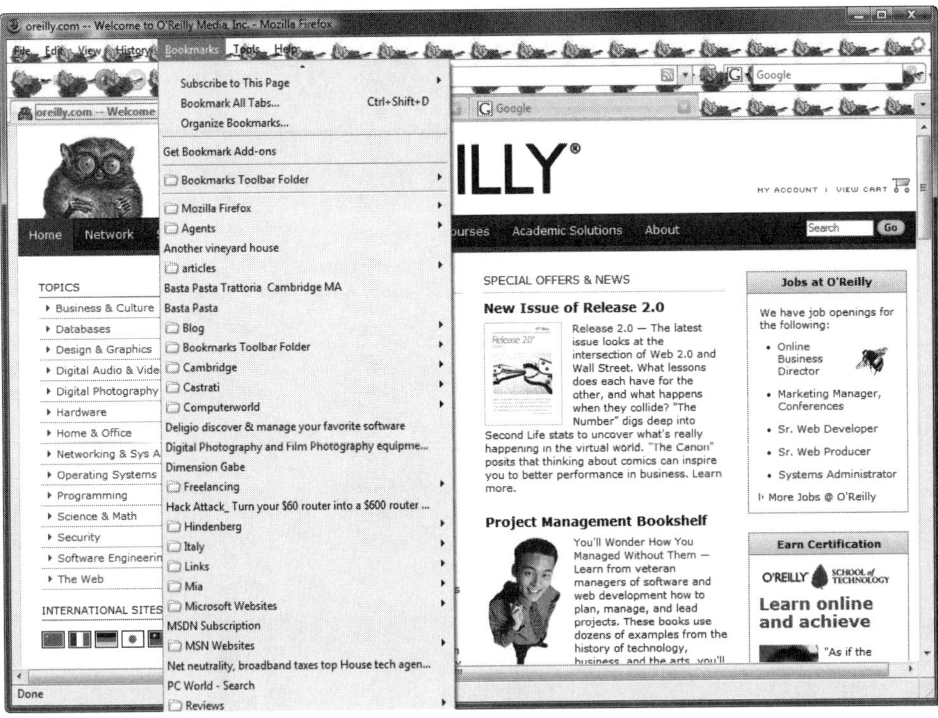

Fix Your Extensions

The most likely causes of RAM leaks are Firefox extensions. Also, if you've installed lots of extensions, you may be using unnecessary RAM. To see your list of installed extensions, select Tools→Add-Ons (Figure 4-31). If you see extensions that you never or rarely use, get rid of them by clicking Uninstall. You should also update your extensions, in case newer, sleeker versions are available. Click Find Updates, and update any that are outdated.

The problem may also be a badly behaving extension, one that sucks up too much memory or CPU time. Go to kb.mozillazine.org/Problematic_extensions, and you'll see a list of problematic extensions. If you're using any, remove them.

If you've done this, and you're still having problems, there's one more way to check whether extensions are the culprit. Exit Firefox, and then start it in Safe Mode by going to the command prompt, navigating to *C:\Program Files\Mozilla Firefox* (or wherever Firefox live, and typing this command and pressing Enter:

```
firefox -safe-mode
```

A screen like that shown in Figure 4-32 appears. Click Continue in Safe Mode. Firefox will now start with it add-ons disabled. Run the Task Manager again, and see how much RAM is being used. If a great deal less RAM is now being used than before, one of your extensions might be the culprit. Try disabling them individually, and restart after you disable each to see if you can find the cause of the problem. To disable any, select Tools→Add-Ons, clicked Disabled next to the extension you want to turn off, and start Firefox normally. See if that solves the problem.

Figure 4-30.
Good news: no Firefox leak here

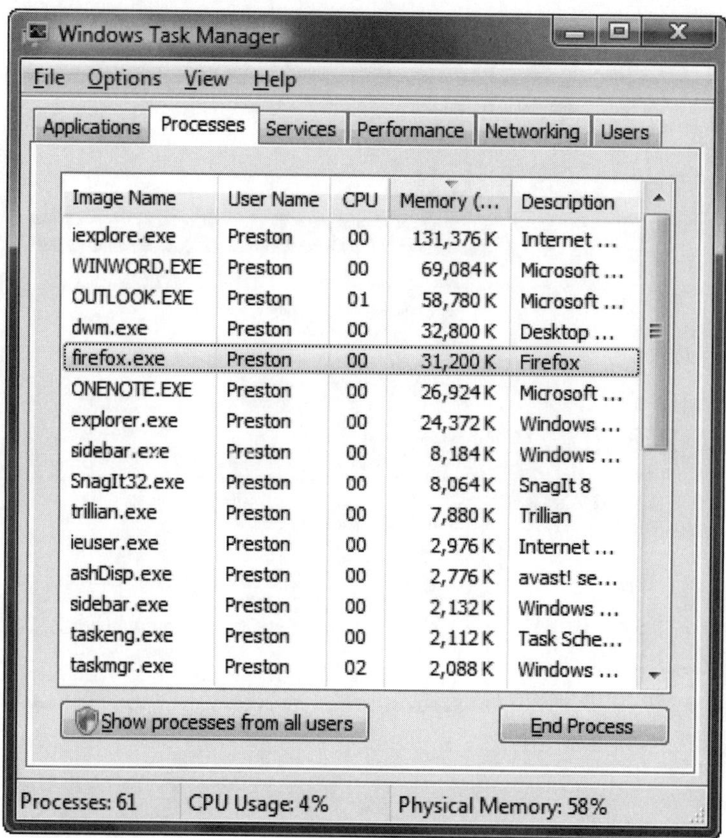

Figure 4-31.
This one's clean: Firefox running with few extensions

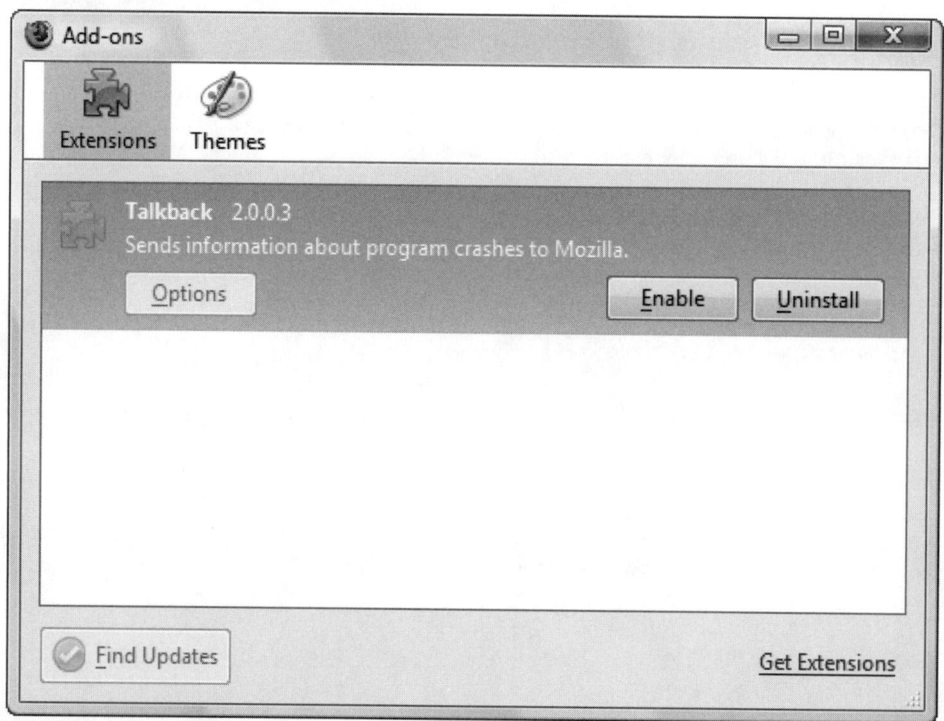

Figure 4-32.
Starting Firefox in Safe Mode

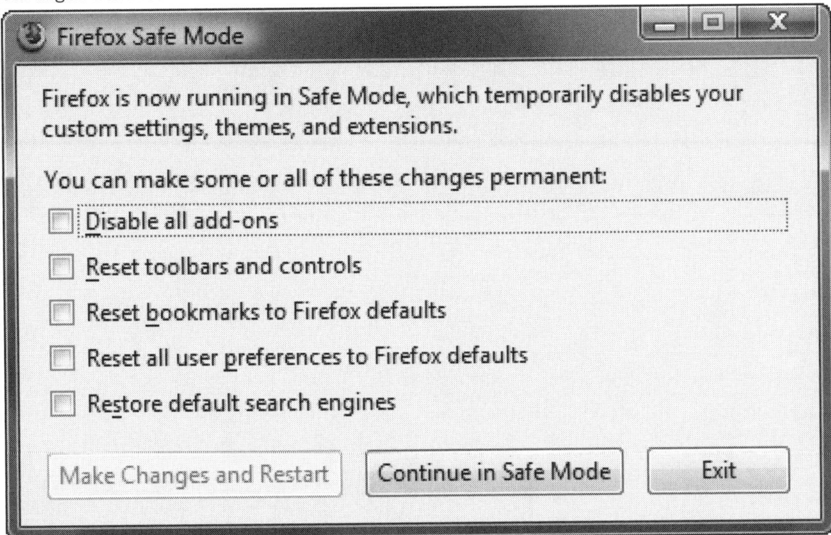

Limit Your Cache

One more cause of the problem could be the amount of cache you've devoted to Firefox. To fix it, first type about:config into the Firefox address bar. Firefox will open the about:config page, that lets you change many of Firefox's settings (Figure 4-33).

At the top of the page, in the Filter box, type browser.cache.memory.enable. You'll see the setting for your browser cache. Its value should be `true`, which means it's enabled. If it instead has a value of `false`, double-click it to turn the value to true.

Now that you've done that, you're going to create a new setting that will let you limit the amount of RAM that Firefox uses for its cache. Right-click an empty portion of the screen, and select New→Integer. In the New integer value dialog box that appears, type browser.cache.memory.capacity and click OK. Next, the Enter integer dialog box appears, asking that you type in a value. If you type in -1, Firefox will calculate the size of your cache based on the amount of RAM on your system. In Firefox 2.0, systems with 512 MB of RAM will get 14 MB of cache, 1 GB of RAM will get 18 MB of cache, 2 GB of RAM will get 24 MB of cache, and 4GB of RAM will get 30 MB of cache. There's no need to type in -1, though, because that's the default setting. Instead, enter a value that's smaller than the default, in kilobytes. So if you have a 2-GB system, for example, you might try typing in 18432, which will be 18 MB of RAM.

Next, right-click an empty portion of the screen, and choose New→Boolean. Give it a value name of `config.trim_on_minimize` and set the value to `true`. In Windows Vista, when you minimize a window, the memory use for that window is supposed to be reduced, but Firefox, by default, doesn't follow this behavior. By creating this value and setting it to `true`, you'll tell Firefox to release memory when it is minimized.

Now restart Firefox to put your settings into effect.

Finally, if all else fails, you should regularly close down Firefox and restart it. When you close Firefox, you'll release all the memory it used, and so you'll start from scratch with RAM when you restart. If you do this regularly, download and install the Tab Mix Plus extension (https://addons.mozilla.org/en-US/firefox/addon/1122), which restores browsing sessions after you shut down. That way, when you restart Firefox, you'll be able to open all the sites you were visiting when you last closed it down.

Figure 4-33.
The hidden Firefox configuration screen

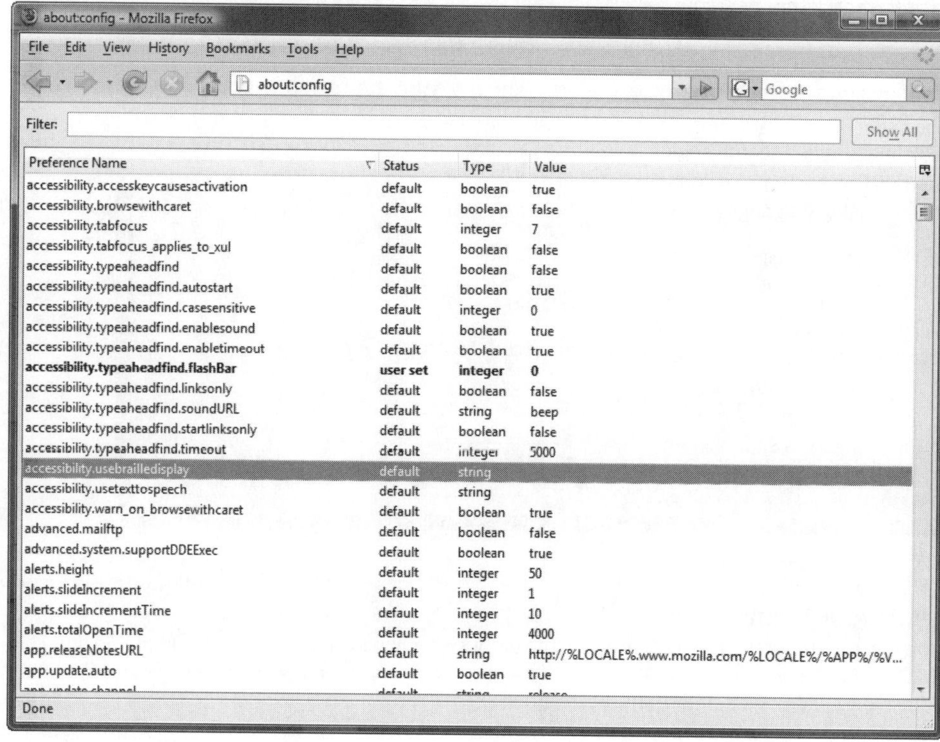

HACK 80: Build Your Own Firefox Search Engine

V XP Firefox's built-in search box lets you search Google from wherever you are. You don't have to settle for that built-in searching, though, because you can build your own Firefox search engine plug-in to search through any site from the Google search box.

Take a look at the upper-right corner of your Firefox browser. You'll see a nifty search box called the Search Bar that lets you search Google by typing in a search term. Better yet, you don't have to settle for searching just Google that way. You can search through other sites as well by installing a specific search engine add-in for that site to the Search Bar. So, instead of using Google to search the Internet, for example, you can use Wikipedia (http://www.wikipedia.com) or eBay (http://www.ebay.com).

Firefox 2.0 and higher use a new XML-based method for creating search engines with *OpenSearch Description* files, which are XML documents that describe search engines and the URL syntax of queries. However, the technique outlined in this hack will also work with Firefox 2.0, as well as with earlier versions of Firefox. In addition, it's easier to build a Firefox search engine using this method than the XML-based method.

And you're not limited to search sites. You can also search through an individual site. So, for example, you can search through Amazon.com (http://www.amazon.com), Live.com (http://www.live.com), or the sports site ESPN (http://www.espn.com) from that box as well. All you need to do is find and add the right search engine plug-in.

To do so, click the down arrow next to the G in the search box, choose Manage Search Engines, and then click the "Get more search engines" link. You'll be sent to https://addons.mozilla.org/en-US/firefox/browse/type:4/, which is a directory of search engines you can use in Firefox. Browse or search until you find one you want; then click its link. You'll get a dialog box like that shown in Figure 4-34, asking whether you want to add it to the Search Bar. Click Add, and it'll be added.

To choose which search engine to use in the Search Bar, click the down arrow next to the G in the Search Bar, and choose your search engine from the list. Then, type in a search term, and you'll search using that engine. The engine will stay there as your default until you choose another one.

 Go to mycroft.mozdev.org for even more search engines you can add to Firefox.

All that's well and good. But why settle for a search engine that's already been written? It's not that hard to write a plug-in of your own.

To get started, open a new file in a text editor such as Notepad. Give it the name of the site for which you're building a search engine, and give it the extension *.src*. In this instance, we're going to build a search engine for searching the federal government's White House site, so we'll call it *White House.src*. Save it in the folder *C:\Program Files\Microsoft Firefox\searchplugins*.

 If you're using Windows Vista, you'll have to run Notepad as an administrator if you want to save the file to *C:\Program Files\Microsoft Firefox\searchplugins*. To run Notepad as an administrator, find its shortcut in the Start Menu, right-click it, and choose Run as administrator.

The first line of the plug-in should be the search tag `<search`. So the first line of your file looks like this:

```
<search
```

Next, name your plug-in using this syntax:

```
name="My Plugin"
```

But replace `My Plugin` with the name of the plug-in you're writing. In this instance, we're calling it `White House`.

Now, describe your plug-in using this syntax:

```
description="My Plugin - My First Search Plugin"
```

The plug-in now looks like this:

```
<search
name="White House"
description="Search www.whitehouse.gov"
```

Figure 4-34.
Adding a new search engine to the Firefox Search Bar

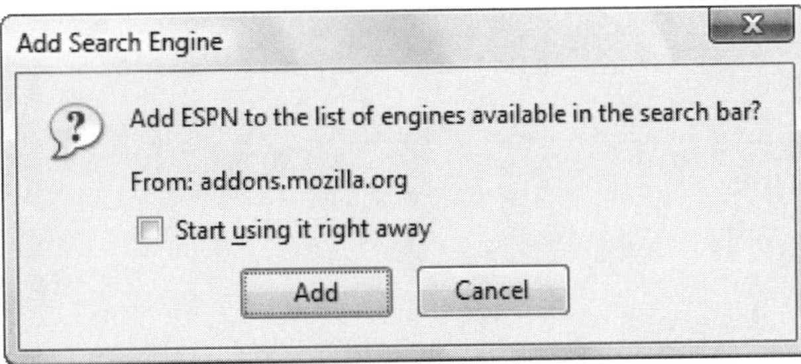

Now you have to tell the plug-in what action to take when you type in a search term and press Enter. What you're doing here is telling it how to search the site. To get this information, go to the site for which you want to build a search engine. Do a search, and look at the first part of the resulting URL, the portion before the first question mark (?). That's what will tell what action your search engine should take. For the http://www.whitehouse.gov site, that first part of the URL before the ? is http://www.whitehouse.gov/query.html.

Here's the syntax:

```
action="http://myplugin.faq/search"
```

So, in our instance, the line looks like this:

```
action="http://www.whitehouse.gov/query.html"
```

Now you need to put in the name of the search form. This will be the name of the site you're on, written with the following syntax:

```
searchForm="http://myplugin.faq"
```

Again, in this instance, this is:

```
searchForm="http://www.whitehouse.gov"
```

Underneath that, put the following code:

```
method="GET"
```

This tells the plug-in to use the GET method of searching, which is the only method supported, so there's no choice here. After that line, close off the search tag with a closing tag: >

So, here's what the plug-in looks like so far:

```
<search
name="White House"
description="Search www.whitehouse.gov"
action="http://www.whitehouse.gov/query.html"
searchForm="http://www.whitehouse.gov"
method="GET"
>
```

Now you need to add a line that tells the site's webmasters and administrators someone is searching the site using the plug-in. So, put in this line:

```
<input name="sourceid" value="Mozilla-search">
```

Next, you need to tell your plug-in what syntax to use when searching for the text you'll type into the Search Bar. This varies from site to site. Again, take a look at the URL that you get after you search the site. Look for whatever falls between the first ampersand (&) and your search term. For the www.whitehouse.gov site, it is qt.

Here's the syntax for this line:

```
<input name="query" user="">
```

So, in our instance, the line looks like this:

```
<input name="qt" user="">
```

Now you need to close off the entire search section with a closing </search> tag:

```
</search>
```

Here's what the final file looks like:

```
<search
name="White House"
description="Search www.whitehouse.gov"
action="http://www.whitehouse.gov/query.html"
searchForm="http://www.whitehouse.gov"
method="GET"
>

<input name="sourceid" value="Mozilla-search">
<input name="qt" user="">

</search>
```

That's it; you're done. Close Firefox, and restart it. Click the down arrow at the Search Bar, and your search engine plug-in will show up. Select it, type in your search term, press Enter, and you'll search the site.

Hacking the Hack

When you right-click the down arrow on the Search Bar, you'll see that many plug-ins have a small icon next to them. Yours doesn't, however. That's because you haven't created an icon for it. Create a 16x16 pixel icon, give it the same name as your plug-in, and save it as either a *.jpg* or *.png* graphics file. Then, put it in the *C:\Program Files\Microsoft Firefox\searchplugins* folder. So, in this instance, you'd create one called *White House.jpg*.

You can find ready-made icons in the right size, although not the right format, right on the Web. When you visit many web sites, you'll see in your web browser a small icon to the left of the http://; that same icon might show up next to the http:// on your Favorites list because the sites use something called a *favicon* that the browser displays.

You can find the favicon for the site, save it to your PC, convert it to *.jpg* or *.png* format, and use it for your search engine plug-in. To find the favicon for a site, go to *http://www.*`website`*.com/favicon.ico*, where `website` is the Favorite you want an icon for. For example, go to www.oreilly.com/favicon.ico for the O'Reilly icon. Keep in mind, though, that not all web sites have favicons, so you won't be able to do this for every site.

If you're using Firefox to get the icon, a dialog box will open, asking what to do with the file. Save it to your hard disk. If you're using Internet Explorer, you'll open the icon itself in your browser. Right-click it, choose Save Picture As, and save it on your hard disk.

It'll be in *.ico* format, so you need to convert it to *.jpg* or *.png*. An excellent program for doing this is IrfanView, available from www.irfanview.com. When you store the file, make sure it's in *C:\Program Files\Microsoft Firefox\searchplugins*.

See Also

- If you'd like, you can share your plug-in with others and have it available for download from the mycroft.mozdev.org/download.html site. To do so, you'll have to add some code to your plug-in. For details, go to mycroft.mozdev.org/deepdocs/quickstart.html#firstplugin. The page also has more detailed instructions for creating your search plug-in.
- "Build Your Own Internet Explorer Search Engine" **[Hack #61]**

QUICK HACK 

CREATE A FAVICON FOR YOUR WEB SITE

When you visit certain web sites, a small icon appears in the far left of the address bar, branding and identifying your site. It's easy to create one if you want one for your web site. If you're handy with graphics software, create a 16 x 16 pixel icon, and name it *favicon.ico*. If you're not handy, or just want the job done quickly, go to www.chami.com/html-kit/services/favicon, and click the Browse button to upload a source graphics file or photo you want turned into a *favicon.ico* file. Then click Generate FavIcon.ico. No matter which way you create the file, upload it to the folder that contains your web page. Then open the HTML of the page, and place this code between <head> and </head>:

```
<link rel="shortcut
icon" href="favicon.
ico" >
```

When visitors come to your site, they'll see the icon in the address bar of their browsers.

HACK 61: Build Your Own Internet Explorer Search Engine

V XP Not happy with the search providers built in to Internet Explorer 7? Then build one of your own, and see how you can share your newly created search provider with the world.

Internet Explorer 7 includes an Instant Search box that allows you to search from a list of search providers. Several are included by default right inside Internet Explorer. There are a number of others, written by Microsoft, that you can add as well.

But if your needs go beyond what can be provided by search providers such as Google, you can custom-build your own, so wherever you are on the Internet, you can search any site you want. In this hack, you'll learn to build your own, and then let anyone else use it as well.

To add additional search providers to the ones already in Internet Explorer, click on the drop down list located at the upper right of the screen, and select Find More Providers. (Figure 4-35).

On the web site that appears, you can select from a list of search providers available. As you'll see in this hack, you can also create your own custom search provider from here as well.

For example, in my blog at weimenglee.blogspot.com, I have a search text box at the top that allows readers to search within my blog (see Figure 4-36). This is a useful feature that allows me to find postings that I have made some time back.

Instead of going to my blog to search, I would like to be able to search directly from IE's search text box. In other words, I want to package this search service as a search provider so that I can add it to IE.

First, as I explained earlier in the hack, when you select Find More Providers, a web page appears. Next, open up another tab in Internet Explorer, and in that tab, visit the web site for which you want to build a search engine. Then, enter the search string TEST, making sure that you put the word in all capital letters.

In my case, I type TEST into the search textbox in my blog. My blog host is Blogger.com, and it returns a list of search results. The URL of the search result is:

http://search.blogger.com/?as_q=TEST&ie=UTF-8&ui=blg&bl_url=weimenglee.blogspot.com&x=17&y=11

Paste the search result URL into the Add Search Providers to Internet Explorer 7 page (accessible by selecting Find More Providers, as shown earlier in Figure 4-35). Give your custom search provider a name (see Figure 4-37).

Click Install to install the new search provider into your IE. You will be prompted to confirm this action (see Figure 4-38). Click Add Provider.

Internet Explorer will now contain the newly added search provider. I can now search my blog by typing the search term directly into the search box in IE (see Figure 4-39); I no longer need to visit my blog first and then search from there.

Distributing Your Search Provider

Now that you have created your own custom search provider, you might want to share it with your friends, family, and business associates. But first, let's take a look at how the search architecture in IE 7 works.

Figure 4-35.
Looking for more search providers

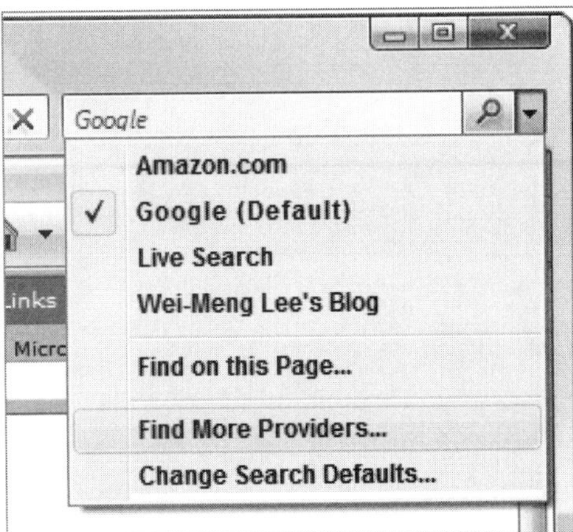

Figure 4-36.
Searching within a blog in Blogger.com

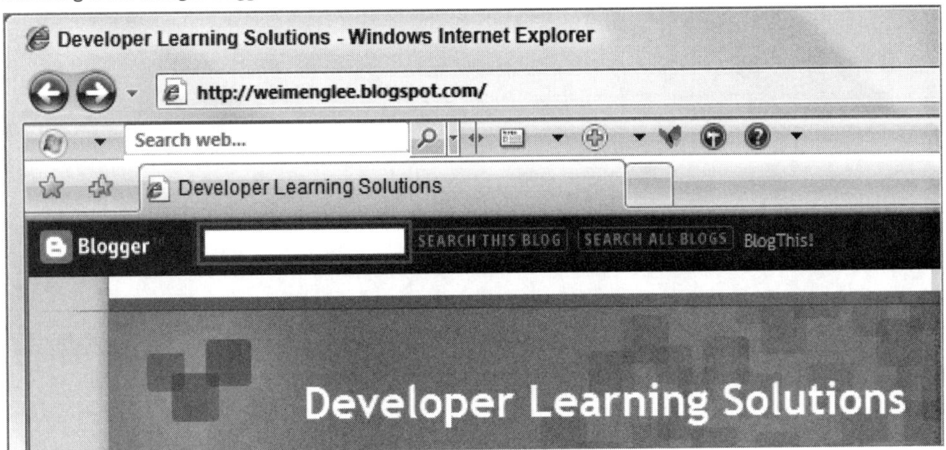

Figure 4-37.
Creating your own custom search provider

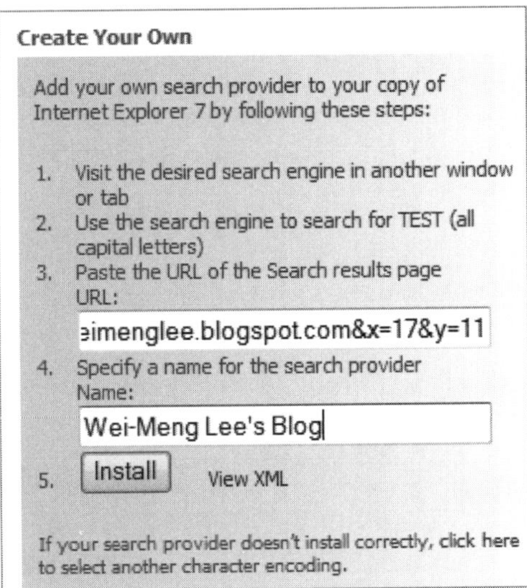

Figure 4-38.
Confirm adding the search provider

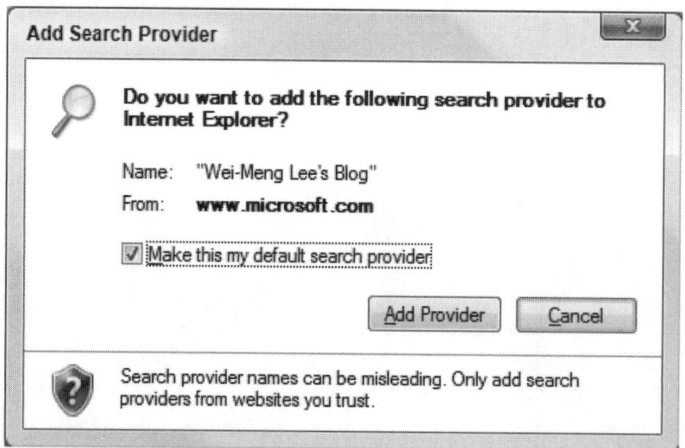

Figure 4-39.
Searching my blog within IE

The new search architecture in IE 7 uses *OpenSearch Description* files, which is a simple XML document describing search engines and the URL syntax of queries. In Figure 4-37 if you click on the View XML link, you will see the content of the OpenSearch Description file, as shown here:

```
<?xml version="1.0" encoding="UTF-8"?>
<OpenSearchDescription xmlns="http://a9.com/-/spec/opensearch/1.1/">
   <ShortName>Wei-Meng Lee's Blog</ShortName>
   <Description>Wei-Meng Lee's Blog provider</Description>
   <InputEncoding>UTF-8</InputEncoding><Url type="text/html" template="http://search.blogger.com/»
?as_q={searchTerms}&amp;ie=UTF-8&amp;ui=blg&amp;bl_url=weimenglee.blogspot.com&amp;x=17&amp;y=11"/>
</OpenSearchDescription>
```

This XML content describes the search provider that you have just created. IE 7 uses this XML content to add a new search provider to your browser.

To distribute this new search provider to the outside world, first save the above XML content to a file and name it as, say, *WMLBlogSearch.xml*.

Next, upload this file to a publicly available server, such as your own web site. For example, I have uploaded the file to my blog at: weimenglee.blogspot.com/WMLBlogSearch.xml.

In the final step you need to embed this XML file in a HTML file. Here, I have created a file named *Index.html* and embedded the URL to the XML file within a `<link>` element, like this:

```
<HTML>
   <HEAD>
      <link title="Wei-Meng Lee's Blog Search" rel="search"
         type="application/opensearchdescription+xml"
         href="http://weimenglee.blogspot.com/WMLBlogSearch.xml" >
   </HEAD>
   <BODY> <!-- Document body goes here --> </BODY>
</HTML>
```

Note that the `rel` attribute must be set to "search" and the `type` attribute set to "application/opens earchdescription+xml". The value of the `title` attribute will be used to describe your custom search provider.

You can now publish this *Index.html* file to your web site (or you can simply email it to whomever you want to install this new search provider).

When a user loads this *Index.html* file, he will see your custom search provider as well as an option to add it to his IE (see Figure 4-40).

Figure 4-40.
Viewing the new search provider

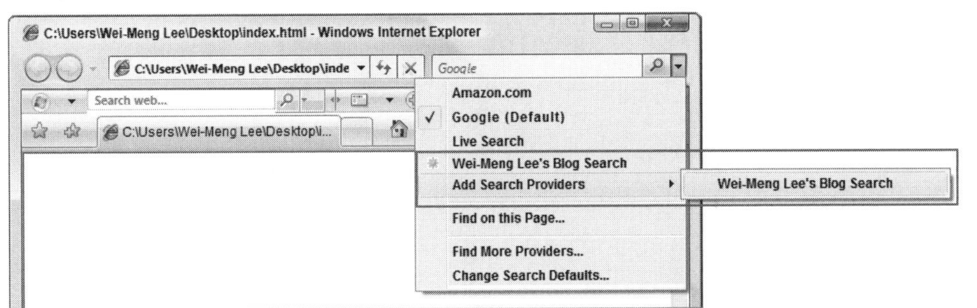

> **QUICK HACK**
>
> **TEST YOUR WEB SITE IN MULTIPLE BROWSERS**
>
> If you've got a web site, you'd like to know that it will work with many different browsers, including multiple versions of Internet Explorer, multiple versions of Firefox, and so on. Rather than having to install all those browsers on different PCs, you can instead go to the site Browsershots.org (www.browsershots.org). Type in the URL of your site, and choose the browsers with which you want to see the site. You'll then be able to see how the site looks in all the browsers; it can take a while, because your request is added to a queue, and you have to wait until your job is completed.

Clicking on Add Search Providers→Wei-Meng Lee's Blog Search will add the new search provider to IE.

See Also

- Search Provider Extensibility in Internet Explorer 7

msdn.microsoft.com/library/default.asp?url=/workshop/browser/external/overview/ie7_opensearch_ext.asp

- Add Search Providers to Internet Explorer 7

www.microsoft.com/windows/ie/searchguide/en-en/default.mspx

—Wei-Meng Lee

HACK 62: Make Java-based Apps Play Nice with Vista

V You no longer need to be bedeviled by Java-based apps shutting down Aero.

One of the surprises about Vista's Aero interface is that it will shut itself off when you run an older application that isn't compatible with Aero. When this happens, you'll see a notification appear telling you "The color scheme has been changed to Windows Vista Basic... click here for more information." When you click the notification, the dialog shown in Figure 4-41 appears.

In most cases, the only thing you can do is live with this problem until the application developer releases a new version. However, some Java-based applications have this problem, and the good news is that you can fix it yourself. First, you need to install the latest and greatest version of the Java Runtime Environment (JRE) from java.sun.com. Once you've done that, you have two choices:

Reconfigure the software to use the new JRE

If the software you're using has a "Java not included" option, install that instead. You might have to follow some extra instructions to set it up (such as setting a `JAVA_HOME` environment variable), but when you're done, everything should work fine.

Copy the new JRE into the software's install directory

Dig into the software you've installed, and look for a *java* or *jre* subfolder. You'll need to find your JRE installation (such as *C:\Program Files\Java\jre1.6.0_01*). Copy everything from there into the misbehaving software's *jre* or *java* folder (you should make a backup of this folder first). Here's how it's done at the Command Prompt, using Processing (www.processing.org) as an example:

```
C:\>cd \processing-0123

C:\processing-0123>ren java java.old

C:\processing-0123>xcopy /s "\Program Files\Java\jre1.6.0_01" java
Does java specify a file name or directory name on the target
(F = file, D = directory)? D
\Program Files\Java\jre1.6.0\COPYRIGHT
\Program Files\Java\jre1.6.0\LICENSE
...
```

However you decide to do it, the next time you run the troublesome app, it should now appear in all its Aero-enabled glory!

—Brian Jepson

Figure 4-41.
Why Aero got shut off

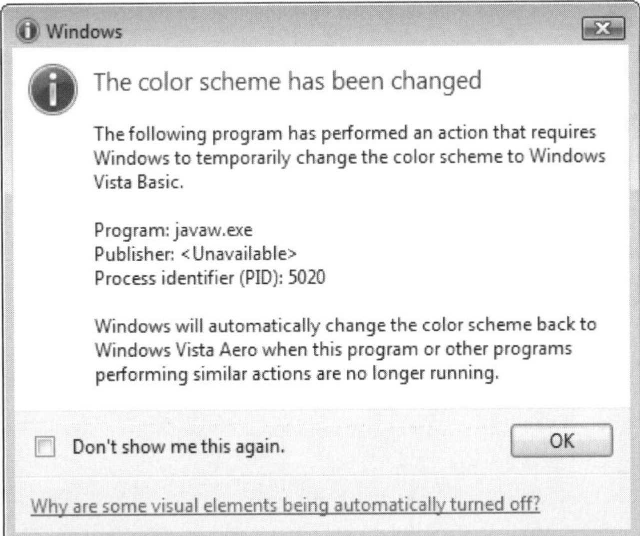

HACK 63: Where Did HyperTerminal Go?

V If you need to do any work over a serial or USB-to-serial port on Vista, you'll find that an old friend has gone missing.

Although the serial port is a vestigial component for many users, there are many people with devices that still communicate this way: analog modems, cellular modems, embedded computers, and more. On Windows XP and earlier versions, you could always turn to HyperTerminal to communicate with a serial port. In Vista, it's gone.

Fortunately, there are a couple of free replacements: PuTTY, the popular (and free) Telnet and SSH client, recently added support for serial ports. And you can still get HyperTerminal directly from its creator, Hilgraeve.

To use PuTTY to connect to a serial port, get the latest version from www.chiark.greenend.org.uk/~sgtatham/putty. When you run PuTTY, choose Serial as the Connection Type, and specify the COM port and speed, as shown in Figure 4-42.

Click Open, and you'll be connected to the port. Figure 4-43 shows a serial terminal session with a Lantronix CoBox Micro embedded Ethernet device.

If you find yourself longing for HyperTerminal, you can download a free (for personal use) version of HyperTerminal from www.hilgraeve.com/htpe. Figure 4-44 shows HyperTerminal Private Edition running on Windows Vista.

—Brian Jepson

QUICK HACK

SIMULTANEOUSLY DOWNLOAD MANY FILES IN INTERNET EXPLORER

Internet Explorer 7 on Windows XP, and earlier versions of Internet Explorer won't let you download more than two files at a time. (The Internet Explorer in Windows Vista doesn't have this limitation.) If you're a big downloader, this can be exceedingly annoying. However, a simple Registry hack will let you download as many files at a time as you'd like. Exit Internet Explorer, and launch the Registry Editor by typing regedit at the Start Search box or a command prompt (See Chapter 13 for details). Let's assume that you want to be able to download 10 files at a time. Go to `HKEY_CURRENT_USER\Software\Microsoft\Windows\CurrentVersion\Internet Settings`. Create a new DWord value called `MaxConnectionsPer1_0Server`. Give it a value of `10`. Then create another DWord value called `MaxConnectionsPerServer`. Also give it a value of `10`. Exit the Registry. You should now be able to download as many files up to 10 files at a time.

Figure 4-42.
Choosing the COM port in PuTTY

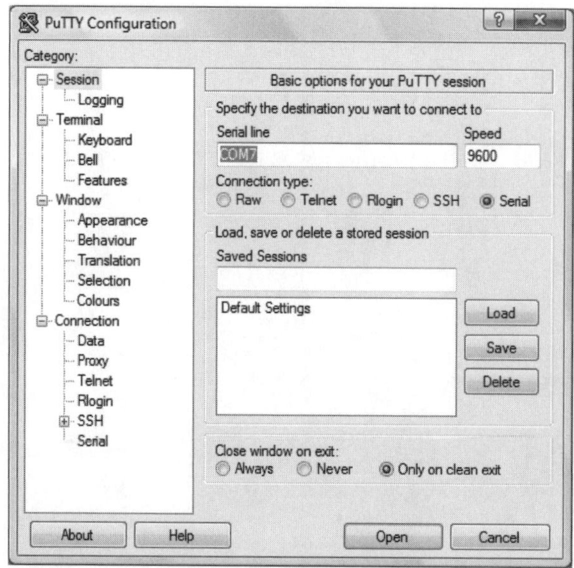

Figure 4-43.
Connecting to a Lantronix embedded Ethernet device

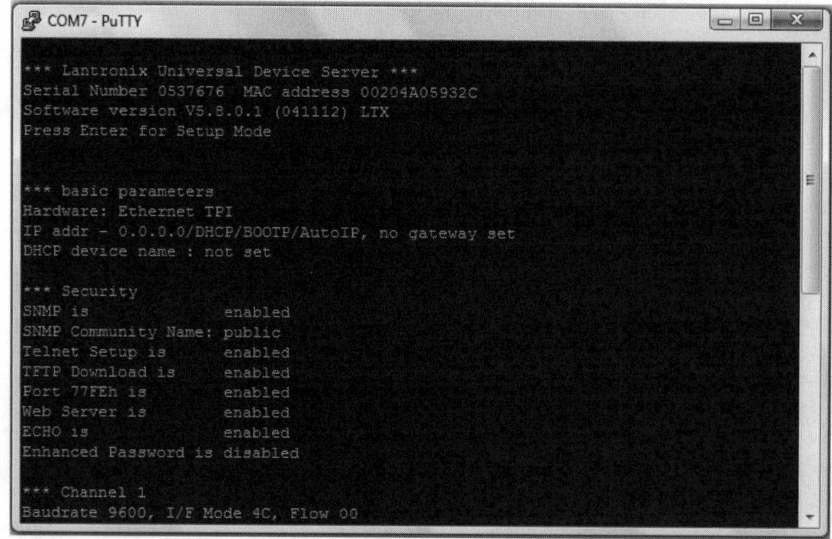

Figure 4-44.
Bringing back HyperTerminal

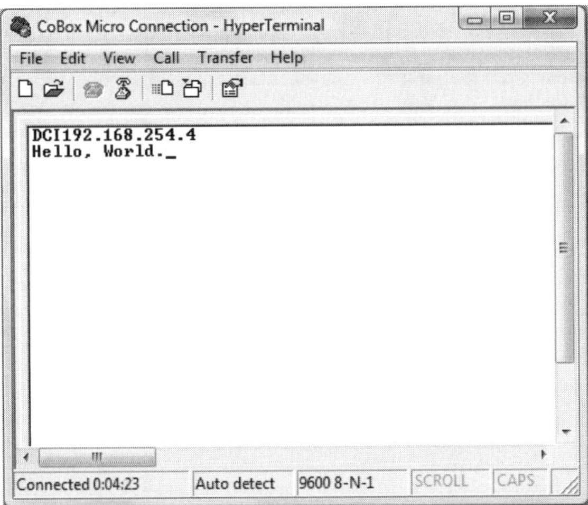

HACK 84: Mash Up Google Calendar and Other Online Calendars with Windows Vista's Calendar

V Online calendars such as Google's can pipe live information to you. Here's how to combine them with the Windows Vista calendar.

The Windows Calendar in Windows Vista is quite slick, but it has one shortcoming: you can't have it automatically update with information from the Web. Many online calendars, such as Google Calendar, have been designed for group scheduling and calendaring, and this inability of the Windows Calendar to do online updates puts a big crimp in it.

However, there's a fix. You can link your Windows Calendar to Google Calendar by subscribing to it. Then, whenever changes are made in your Google Calendar or other online calendar, they'll be automatically made in your Windows Calendar as well.

In addition, you can subscribe to any of the many public online calendars as well—for example, the playoff schedule of your favorite sports team.

The key to all this is the iCalendar (*.ics*) format (often referred to as iCal, which also happens to be the name of the Mac-based calendar). You'll tell Windows Calendar to subscribe to an *.ics* file, and Windows takes care of the rest.

In this hack, we'll start off with an empty Windows Calendar, with no information or appointments in it, as you can see in Figure 4-45.

We're going to subscribe to a Google Calendar, shown in Figure 4-46, that's chock full of appointments. It's a shared calendar, and so regularly gets updated by others.

First we need to find the address of the Google Calendar. In Google Calendar choose Settings→ Calendars. If you have more than one calendar, you'll see multiple ones here. Click the one you want to subscribe to, and you'll see a page like the one shown in Figure 4-47.

Click the Private Address ICAL button for your calendar. A screen like the one shown in Figure 4-48 appears. Copy the URL. Note that it ends in an *.ics* extension.

Figure 4-45.
An empty Windows Calendar

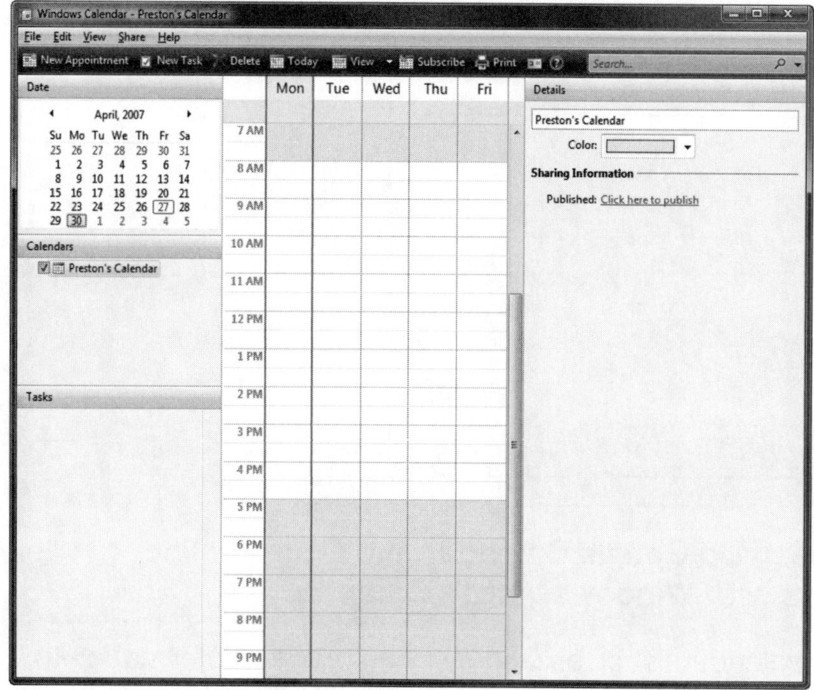

Figure 4-46.
The Google calendar, filled with appointments

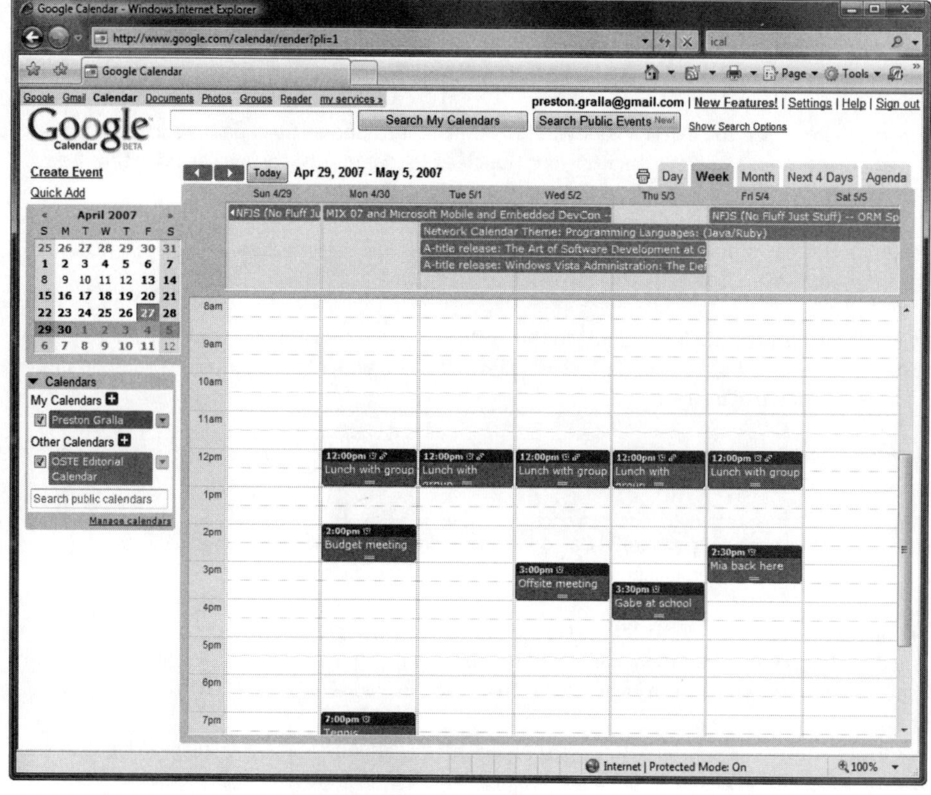

Figure 4-47.
From this page, you'll get the calendar's URL

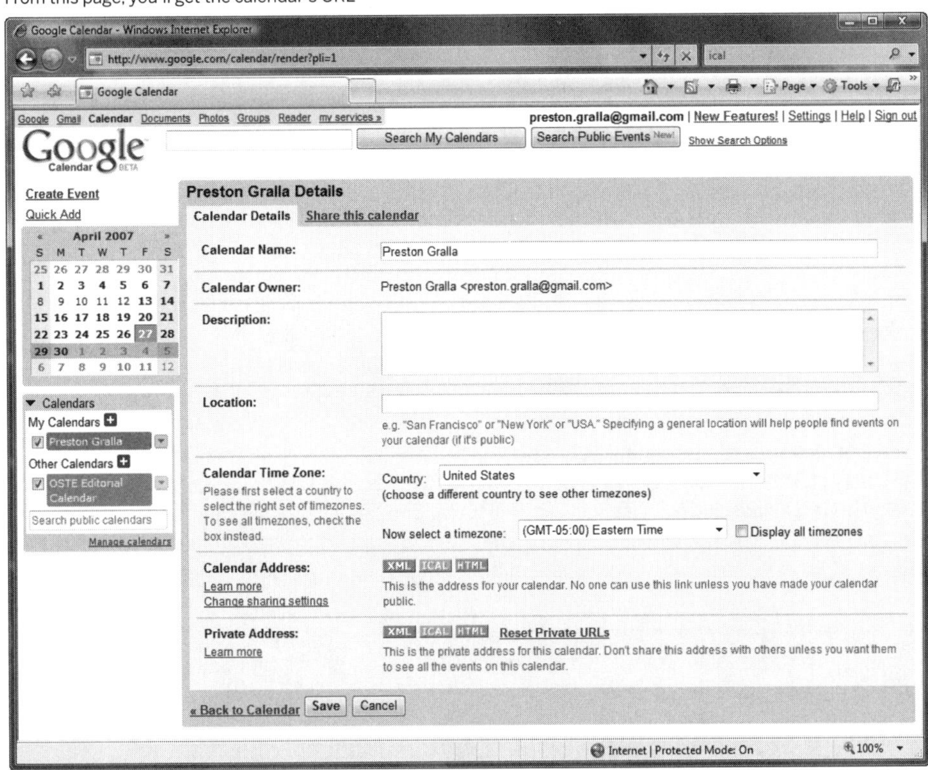

Figure 4-48.
Getting the URL for your calendar

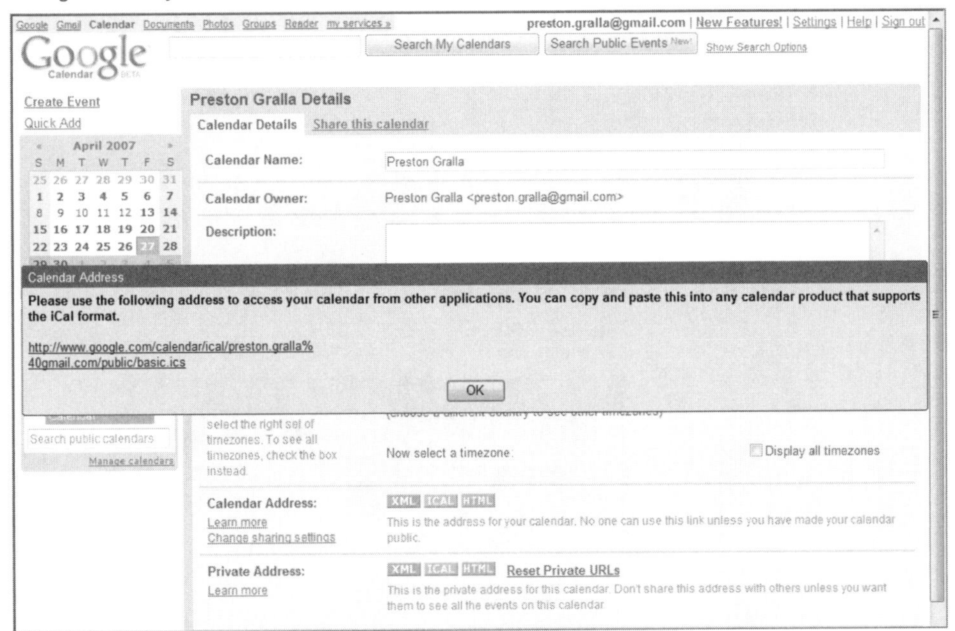

Now go to Windows Calendar, and click Subscribe. A screen like that shown in Figure 4-49 will appear.

Copy the URL into the box, and click Next. From this screen (Figure 4-50) you'll configure your settings, including how often the calendar should update (you can choose every 15 minutes, every hour, every day, every week, or No update), and whether to include Reminders and Tasks. Then click Finish.

The calendar will be imported into your Windows Calendar, as you can see in Figure 4-51. It will automatically update on the schedule that you set.

Hacking the Hack

There are plenty of public calendars that you can subscribe to—thousands of them, in fact, in just about every category you can imagine. They're as mainstream as schedules of your favorite sports teams (webcal://ical.mac.com/lembree/Boston%20Red%20Sox%202007.ics for the 2007 schedule of the Boston Red Sox fans) or as off-the-beaten-track as a calendar of important dates in Austrian politics (webcal://ical.mac.com/WebObjects/iCal.woa/Carlton32200532Fixture.ics). There are several places on the Web you can find them. One great site is icalshare.com. You can also go to a site run by Microsoft with a list of calendars, although it's somewhat limited. In Windows Calendar, click Subscribe, and from the screen that appears, click "Windows calendar website."

Figure 4-49.
Subscribing to your Google Calendar

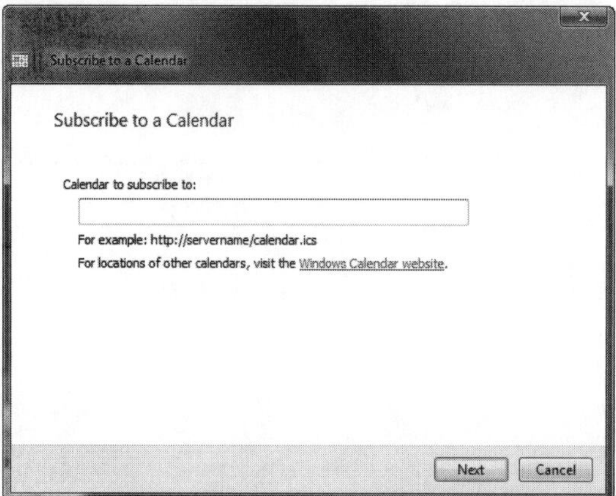

Figure 4-50.
Configuring your calendar

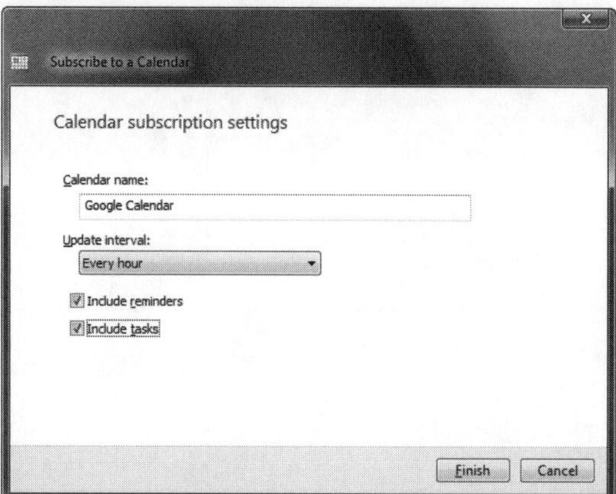

Figure 4-51.
Google Calendar, now live in your Windows Calendar

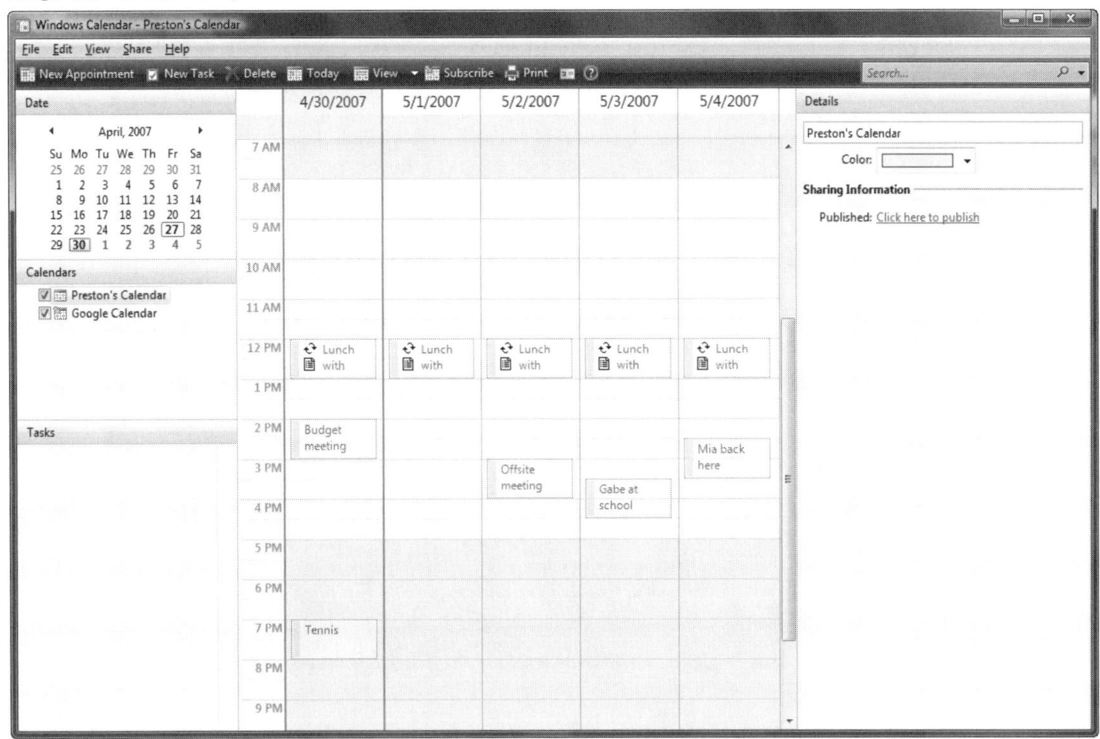

HACK 65: Import Internet Calendars into Outlook

V XP Outlook can perform the same trick with Internet calendars that Windows Calendar can.

If you use Outlook's calendar rather than Windows Calendar, you can still subscribe to Internet-based calendars. As with Windows Calendar, the magic happens because of the *.ics* format.

If you visit a site that lists public Internet calendars such as icalshare.com, subscribing to an Internet calendar is exceptionally easy. Click the Subscribe link next to the calendar, and it will be imported into Outlook. Depending on your security settings and which version of Windows and Internet Explorer you use, after you click the link, you must first allow the web site to communicate with your PC, as you can see in Figure 4-52.

Click Allow, and you'll be prompted to confirm the subscription. Select Yes, and the calendar will be imported into Outlook.

> If you click Advanced, you'll be able to configure a variety of settings, such as changing the folder name for the calendar, typing in a description, deciding whether to allow attachments to be downloaded, and so on.

Not all calendars have subscription links, though. Google Calendar, for example, doesn't. If there's a calendar you want to subscribe to, but it doesn't have a subscription link, first get the iCal URL **[Hack #64]**. Then in Outlook, select Tools→Account Settings→Internet Calendars. Click New and in the box that appears, copy the URL into the box (Figure 4-53).

Next, click Add, and the Subscription options page appears (Figure 4-54). Click OK, and the calendar will be imported.

Figure 4-52.
An Internet calendar, attempting to communicate with Outlook.

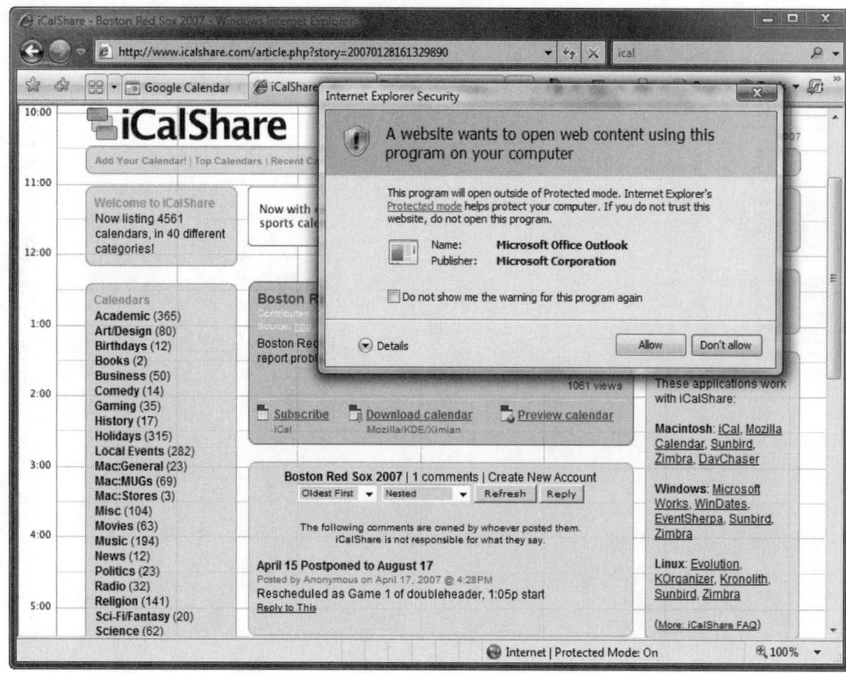

Figure 4-53.
Manually inputting the .ics file into Outlook

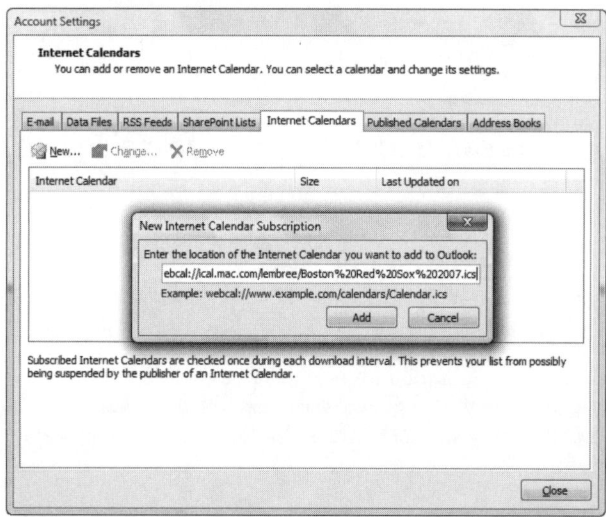

Viewing Multiple Calendars in Outlook

How you view calendars varies somewhat from version to version of Outlook, and a complete description of how to view them in every version of Outlook is beyond the scope of this book. So I'll describe how to view them in Outlook 2007.

Click Calendar in the left pane of Outlook 2007, and your new calendar will show up in the Other Calendars section in the left pane. Check the box next to it, and both calendars will show up side by side. (Figure 4-55).

Figure 4-54.
Finalizing your subscription options for an Internet calendar

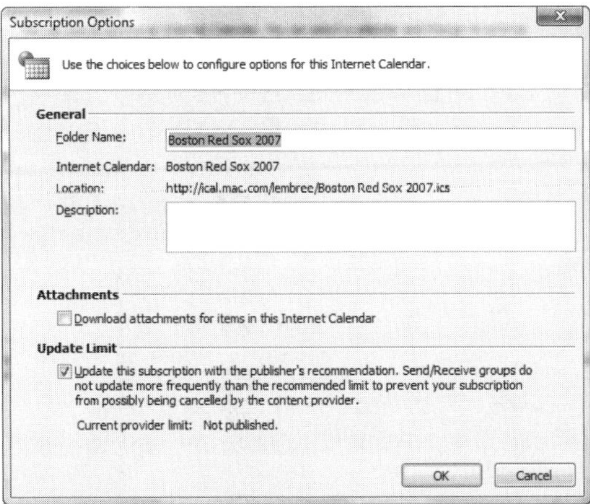

Figure 4-55.
Multiple calendars in Outlook

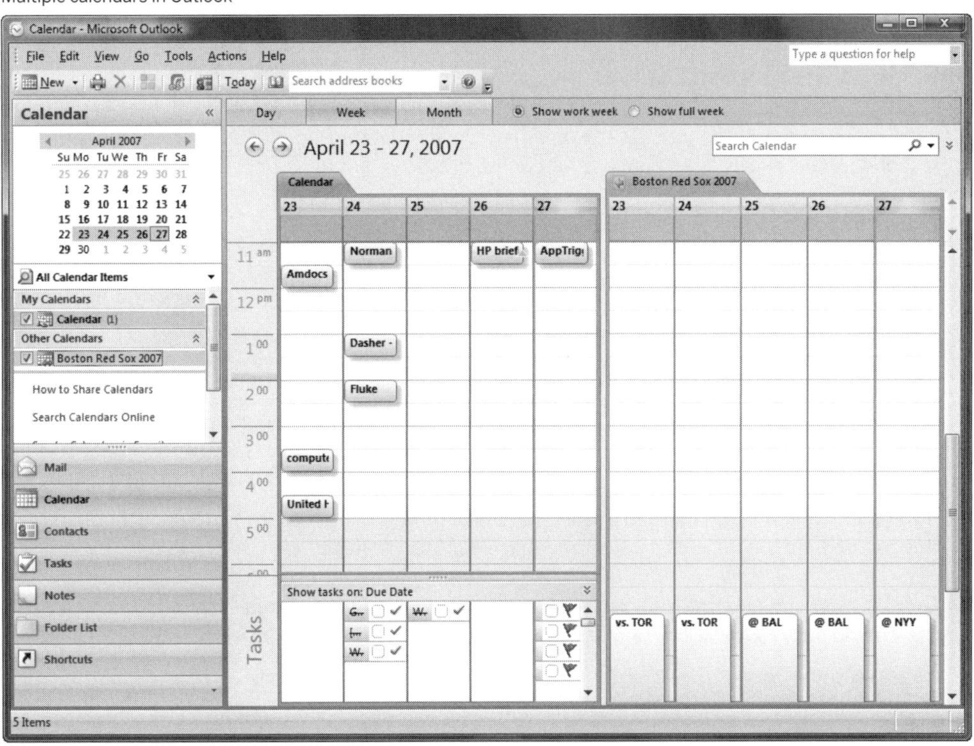

From here, you can drag and drop events between calendars. To display only one calendar, uncheck the box of the other one. And to remove a calendar, select Tools→Account Settings→Internet Calendars, highlight the calendar you want to delete, and click Remove.

HACK 86: Create Custom RSS Feeds from Newsgroups and Online Forums

V XP Here's how to get the best of both worlds: get newsgroup posts and online discussions delivered to you via RSS

I originally started using RSS to streamline how I read information on the Internet. I came across RSSBus (www.rssbus.com) when I was trying to determine whether I could create an RSS feed of other things I use regularly so I could have more power over how I managed them. I was surprised at how little time it took me to install the application, download and load an add-on, and get access to new ways of viewing and managing data.

In this hack, I'll show you how to use RSSBus to create an RSS feed from content on the Internet such as newsgroups. This will let you use an RSS reader, or even the RSS reader built into Internet Explorer 7, to get content delivered right to your desktop.

If all you're after is a quick and easy way to get an RSS feed for a newsgroup, visit news.google.com, where you can get RSS feeds for any group or Usenet newsgroup. But as you'll see in this hack, RSSBus can do much more.

RSSBus Desktop and Server

There is a desktop and server version of the product, but I am only going to discuss the desktop version. RSSBus Desktop consists of a small web server that runs on your desktop. It will only respond to local feed requests but has full connectivity to go out to any local or external source to get the feed input.

If you need a product with which multiple people can access an RSS feed you have created from other remote systems, you must use the server version.

Installation

The installation process is relatively quick and easy. The Microsoft .NET Framework 2.0 is a pre-requisite (but 3.0 would be fine also). Once the install is complete, you'll be presented with a screen to start the desktop version.

If you want to have RSSBus automatically start each time your system starts up, copy the Start Server icon from the RSSBus program menu to your Startup folder.

Once the application is installed and running, you have access to an administrative console via the Start menu or by right-clicking on the icon near the system clock as seen in Figure 4-56.

Whenever the application is started, the administration console will also open in your preferred web browser.

Understanding RSSBus Components

RSSBus had three main components: connectors, scripts and templates.

Connectors are libraries that implement one or more related operations. Operations can be thought of as procedures.

For example, one of the connectors, FileOps, which provides a library of operations for managing such things as files and directories. Here are the operations it provides:

- fileCopy: Copies the existing source file to a new destination
- fileCreate: Creates a text file, and optionally writes to it
- fileDelete: Deletes a file or directory

Figure 4-56.
Accessing the RSSBus Console

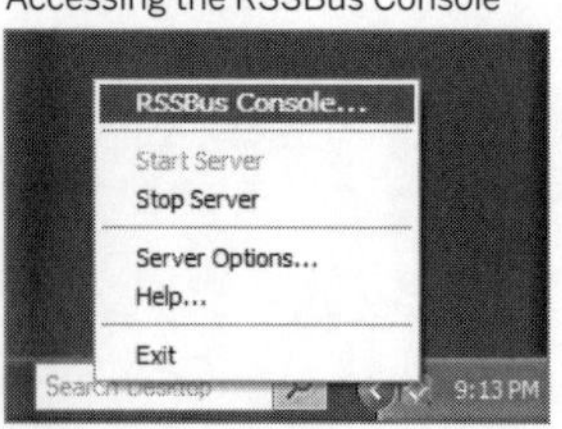

- fileListDir: Lists the files and directories in the specified path
- fileRead: Reads a text file, and pushes the data out

RSSBus comes with a large number of customizable set of connectors that provide operations for things like filesystem access, email, FTP, HTTP, and databases.

Here's a listing of all bundled connectors:

- CsvOps: Operations for managing delimited record files
- EncOps: Operations for encoding/decoding data using various formats
- ExcelOps: Operations that read and write data to Excel spreadsheets
- FileOps: Operations for managing files and directories
- FtpOps: Operations for transferring files to and from FTP servers
- GcalOps: Operations that provide access to Google calendar
- GsheetOps: Operations that provide access to Google spreadsheets
- GtalkOps: Operations that provide access to Google talk services
- ImapOps: Operations for receiving email messages from IMAP mail servers
- ImOps: Operations for instant messaging (Jabber, SMS, etc.)
- LdapOps: Operations for connecting to LDAP directories
- MediaOps: Operations that provide information about digital media files
- NntpOps: Operations for reading and posting newsgroup articles
- OfxOps: Operations for accessing bank accounts and financial services
- OracleOps: Operations for accessing Oracle databases
- PaypalOps: Operations that provide access to PayPal payment services
- PopOps: Operations for receiving email messages from POP servers
- SmtpOps: Operations for sending SMTP email
- SqlOps: Operations for connecting to SQL Server databases
- SysOps: Operations for system management (processes, memory, etc.)
- TsvOps: Operations for managing simple tab-separated file databases
- XmlOps: Operations that process XML files

Scripts

In their simplest form, the data from connectors is exposed via a well defined URL using RSBScript *scripts*. These scripts have an *.rsb* extension assigned to them, and can be created with any simple text editor, or by using the built-in editor in the administration console.

The script has constructs, called keywords, that allow data fetching (`rsb:call`), data modification (`rsb:set`) and data publishing (`rsb:push`). You will see an example a bit later in which all of these constructs are used in a Windows PowerShell script.

Templates

If displaying the feed output in an HTML format is not the preferred method, *templates* can be used to present the feed in alternate formats such as Word documents, Excel spreadsheets, or even a source code file.

The RSSBus Administration Console

Once open in a web browser, the administration console provides a tabbed view of the RSSBus configuration, as shown in Figure 4-57. There is a welcome, connectors, feeds and profile tab.

Figure 4-57.
The RSSBus console

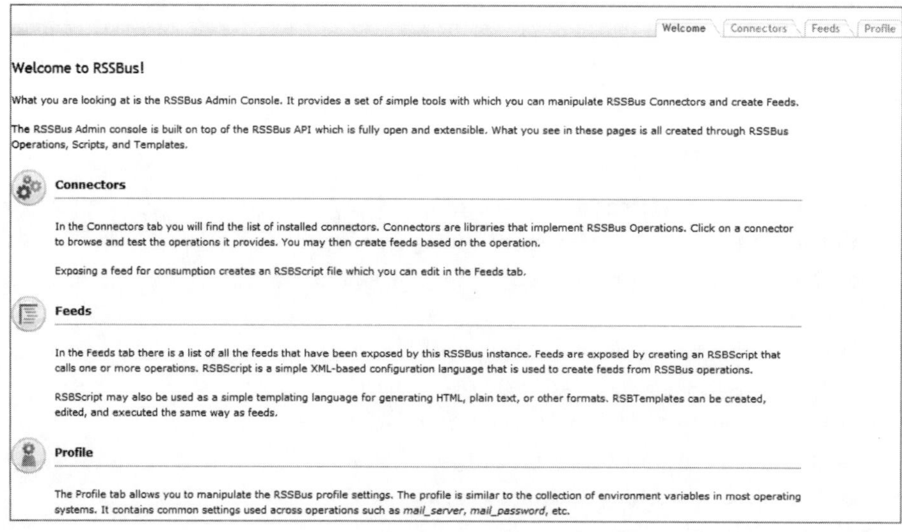

The connectors tab lists all available connectors along with all their supported operations.

The feeds tab lists all available feeds as well as the available templates. This is the tab where a built-in editor is available.

Configuring an RSS Feed of an NNTP Newsgroup

With that background, let's get to the hack. We'll start by creating a feed for an NNTP newsgroup.

For this hack, we'll create an RSS feed from `microsoft.public.windows.powershell` (available from the Microsoft news servers).

One simple way to get started is to take a script that someone else has written, and edit it for your own use. That's what's we're doing to do.

Go to www.rssbus.com, and scroll toward the bottom of the page. On the left side, you'll find a contributions section. Here you'll find various connectors, scripts/feeds, and templates that others have written. Click the Scripts/Feeds link, and from the page that appears, click Usenet Newsgroup Feed. You'll come to a page that has the script. The page shows the script itself and also has a download link. Don't copy and paste the script because it can cause hard-to-diagnose errors. Instead, click the download link, and save the script to your PC.

I won't list the entire script here; you can look at it when you download it. But you only need to change a single line to customize it to create an RSS feed of your favorite newsgroup.

Use the RSSBus built-in editor available in the feed tabs of the administration console to edit the newly downloaded script, which is named *Usenet_Newsgroup_Feed.rsb*. Change this one line of text:

```
<input name="currentgroup" default="microsoft.public.dotnet.languages.csharp"/>
```

to:

```
<input name="currentgroup" default="microsoft.public.windows.powershell"/>
```

Now just run the script, and it will download the latest 10 posts in the newsgroup into an RSS feed.

You can read the feed in your own RSS reader, or you can view it directly from the RSSBus administration console. Going to the feeds tab, then clicking on the *Usenet_Newsgroup_Feed.rsb* (the default name), will show some buttons such as "test" and "show feed" as shown in Figure 4-58.

From here, clicking on "show feed" provides several viewing alternatives. For our purposes, we will choose to see our feed as RSS. The resulting output is shown in Figure 4-59.

To subscribe to this feed, click the title shown in Figure 4-59, and Figure 4-60 appears, which provides the subscribe link that allows for any desktop RSS reader to subscribe to the original feed. (Because RSSBus desktop runs as a service on your local machine, web-based readers such as Bloglines and Google Reader won't be able to connect to it.)

If you click on any of the items in the RSS feed, the Usenet posting is opened up in your preferred newsgroup reader or browser as shown Figure 4-61.

Figure 4-58.
Viewing the script in RSSBus

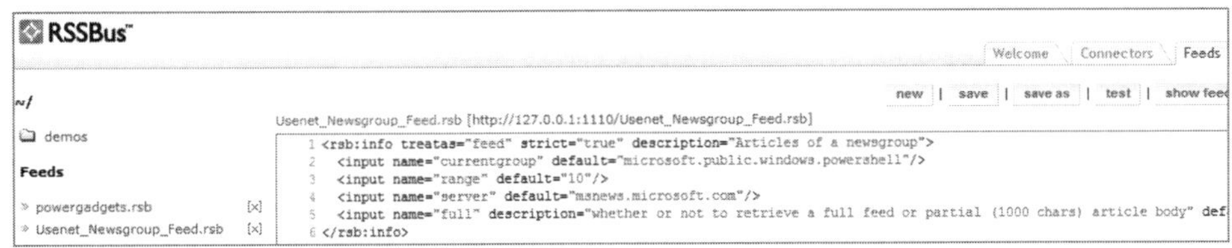

Figure 4-59.
Viewing the RSS feed inside RSSBus

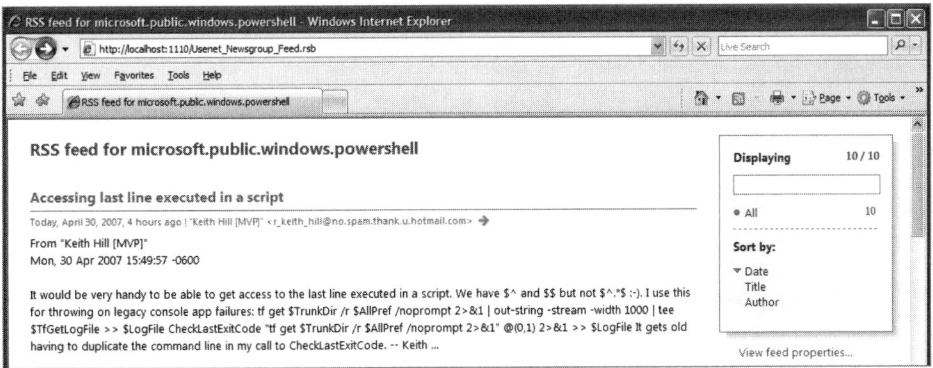

Figure 4-60.
Subscribing to the feed

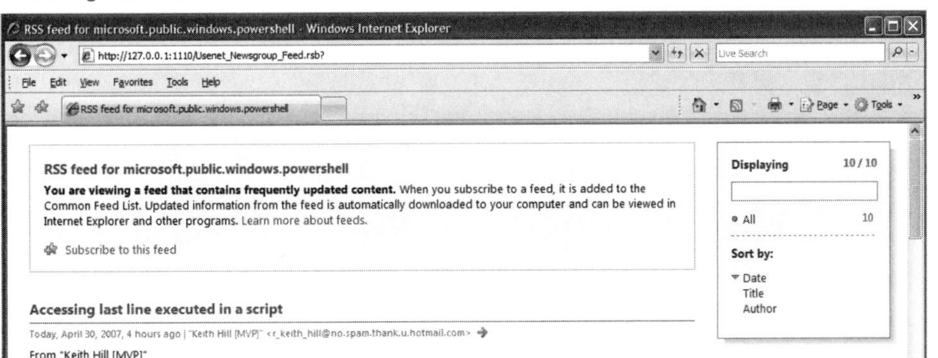

Figure 4-61.
Clicking a Usenet posting opens it up in your default newsgroup reader

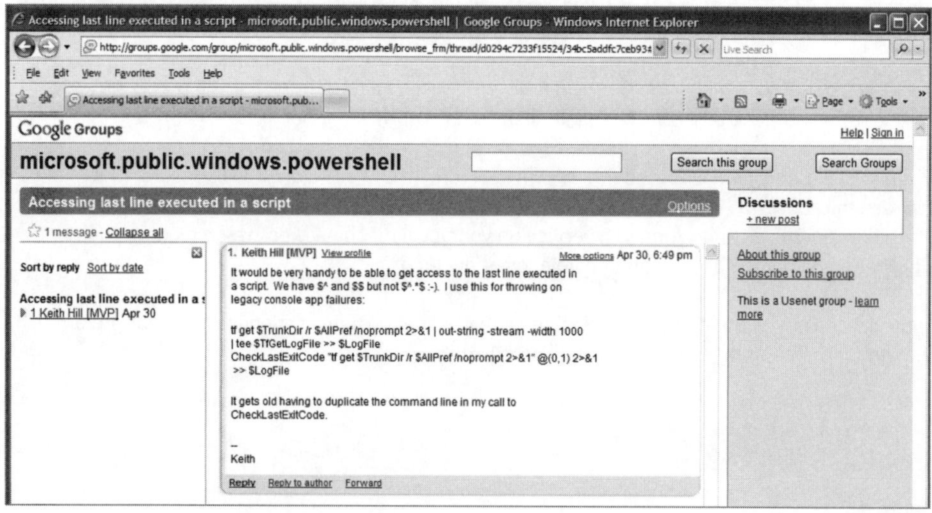

Create an RSS Feed to Community Server Forums

Community Server (www.communityserver.org) is a great product for creating online communities. It's used as a community support forum by PowerGadgets (www.powergadgets.com), one of my favorite Windows PowerShell add-ons.

A new production release of Community Server was released in mid-April 2007. I was not able to verify whether everything I indicate below still applies directly to the 2007 version also.

Community Server allows you to get RSS feeds from all the available forums via the RSS feed icon. After using RSS feeds to get updates, I realized that only new threads were showing in the RSS feed. I wanted to see new threads and new posts as well. But to see new posts, I had to sign up for an RSS feed to each and every thread. That's just too much work, and I wanted to automate this.

With the help of Windows PowerShell, I wrote a script to parse the RSS feed of each forum, and pull out the address of each thread, then using that information, I pieced together what the RSS feed to the thread itself would be. I then used all that information to create an RSBScript to give me all the forums' threads and posts in a single RSS feed.

Here's my Windows PowerShell script for doing it. I've commented it thoroughly:

```
$ErrorAction=$ErrorActionPreference

# I set this temporarily, otherwise, I have seen
# some errors I can't explain.
$ErrorActionPreference="silentlycontinue"

# Set the location for the RSBscript.
$feed_script="C:\rssbus\www\powergadgets.rsb"

# Make sure to delete the above file first.
if(Test-Path $feed_script){
 Remove-Item $feed_script
}

# Set a counter.
$j=1
```

```
# Start off the listing of RSS feeds with all the known forums.
$rss_feeds= `
@("http://powergadgets.com/csPg/forums/rss.aspx?ForumID=4&Mode=0",
"http://powergadgets.com/csPg/forums/rss.aspx?ForumID=5&Mode=0",
"http://powergadgets.com/csPg/forums/rss.aspx?ForumID=6&Mode=0",
"http://powergadgets.com/csPg/forums/rss.aspx?ForumID=14&Mode=0")
# This is the format used for the RSS feeds for individual threads.
$rss_url="http://powergadgets.com/csPg/forums/rss.aspx?ForumID="

# Create an array.
$threads=@()

# 1. We need to loop through each forum feed above.
# 2. We use a cmdlet named get-rss from www.nsoftware.com/powershell
# to retrieve the RSS feeds. You may still be able to apply for a not
# for resale non-commercial license through their site.
# 3. After having looked directly at the information provided in the
# feed, we piece back together some information to get the feed to
# the thread itself.
# 4. We add each of these new RSS feeds to an array.
for($i=0;$i -lt $rss_feeds.count;$i++)
{
  $threads+=(get-rss $rss_feeds[$i]|ForEach-Object `
  {
   $forum=$rss_feeds[$i].split('/.=&')[8]
   $thread=$_.link.split('/.')[7]
   ${rss_url}+${forum}+"&PostID="+${thread}
  })
}

# We add the new RSS feeds we've found to our original list
# of RSS feeds.
$rss_feeds+=$threads

# We also add the RSS feed to their blog.
$rss_feeds+="http://powergadgets.com/csPg/blogs/MainFeed.aspx"

# Now, we create the RSBscript that will be read by RSSBus
# using the proper syntax.
$rss_feeds|?{$_ -notmatch "^$"}|ForEach-Object `
 {
  Add-Content -path $feed_script -value `
  "<rsb:set item=`"input`" attr=`"feed#$j`" value=`"$_`" />"
  $j++
 }

# We add a few more lines to close up our RSBscript properly.
Add-Content -path $feed_script -value `
  "<rsb:call op=`"feedUnion`" in=`"input`">"
Add-Content -path $feed_script -value "<rsb:push />"
Add-Content -path $feed_script -value "</rsb:call>"

# Reset to previous value.
$ErrorActionPreference=$ErrorAction
```

Running the Windows PowerShell script creates an RSBScript that gives a combined view of all the RSS feeds for each forum and to each thread. That way, I get to see every post that shows up.

In the administration console, the new RSBScript (*powergadgets.rsb*) is automatically picked up as being in the proper directory for RSBScript and having the *.rsb* extension as shown in Figure 4-62.

—Marco Shaw

Figure 4-62.
The script, ready for running

05 NETWORKING

A PC by itself is a poor and lonely thing . . . which is why these days, most people have more than one PC at home, and many of them hooks their PCs and printers together via a home network, most commonly using a home router.

Today, for better or worse, you're more than an owner of a PC; you're a network administrator as well, even if you don't really know it. If you've ever wrestled with hooking up your network or trying to share files and folders, then you know the pain of a network administrator.

In this chapter, you'll find a wide variety of network hacks, including many hacks for optimizing your router and network, command-line and other tools for troubleshooting networks, tweaking settings for faster Internet access, and much more. There's also a sizable section on hacking phone calls made via Voice over Internet Protocol (VoIP) calls using the popular VoIP program Skype.

Note that you'll find many other networking-related hacks in other chapters, notably in Chapters 4, 7, 8, and 9.

HACK 67: Quick Fix for a Sluggish Router

V XP Does your router slow to a crawl, and speed up only when you restart it . . . only to have it slow down again? The reason for the slowdown may surprise you. Here's a hack that shows you how to fix it.

Several years ago, I had what seemed to be an unsolvable conundrum. For no apparent reason, and at odd times, my Internet access would slow to a crawl. I'd get fed up, restart the router, and it would speed up again. After a certain amount of time, it would slow down again.

Baffling, indeed.

Then I noticed that these slowdowns occurred only when my son was using his computer. The light bulb went off. He was using file-sharing software. The issue, though, wasn't what you might think, that he was using up too much available bandwidth, although that contributed to the problem.

The issue was that file-sharing software can quickly fill up and overwhelm routing tables in the router, and slow the entire network to a crawl. That's why restarting the router speeds up things: it cleans out the routing table. But if file-sharing and peer-to-peer (P2P) software is still being used, the problem can recur.

If your router similarly slows to a crawl, you should first try to see if file-sharing software is causing the problem. Depending on the router you use, you can probably see all the inbound and outbound traffic between your network and the Internet, on a PC-by-PC basis, by peeking into the router's logs. If you see a single PC with a constant stream of inbound and outbound URLs, it's a sign that file-sharing is going on.

In this hack, I'll show you how to check the logs on a Linksys router. If you have a different router, check its documentation for how to do it. First log into the Linksys administrator's setup screen by going to http://192.168.1.1 in your browser, and typing in your username and password. (The default is no username, and admin as the password.) If you've configured your network to use a different network range, replace 192.168.1.1 with the address of your router. Next, check the IP addresses of all the computers on your network, so that you can match the traffic log to each PC. Click the DHCP tab. Depending on your model of router, this might appear right at the top of your screen when you log into the router. Next, click the DHCP Client Table. A small browser window will pop up, showing you the IP address and hostname of each PC on your network, as you can see in Figure 5-1.

Now that you know the IP address of each computer on your network, it's time to check the router logs. Click the Log tab, choose the Enable radio button, and click the Apply button. (If the log is already enabled, you can skip this step.)

Check your incoming and outgoing logs. Click on Incoming Access Log to see the incoming traffic, by IP address, and the Outgoing Access Log to see outgoing traffic. Click the Refresh button every few seconds. If, each time you click the button, you notice more new outgoing URLs, someone may be using file-sharing. It's a better bet to check the Outgoing Access Log rather than the Incoming Access Log, because that's typically what causes the problem. In particular, look for many outgoing connections from a single PC, with new ones being added all the time.

Figure 5-1.
Here's how to find the IP address of every PC and device on your network. The 192.168.1.8 entry refers to a PS2 game system, which doesn't have a host name.

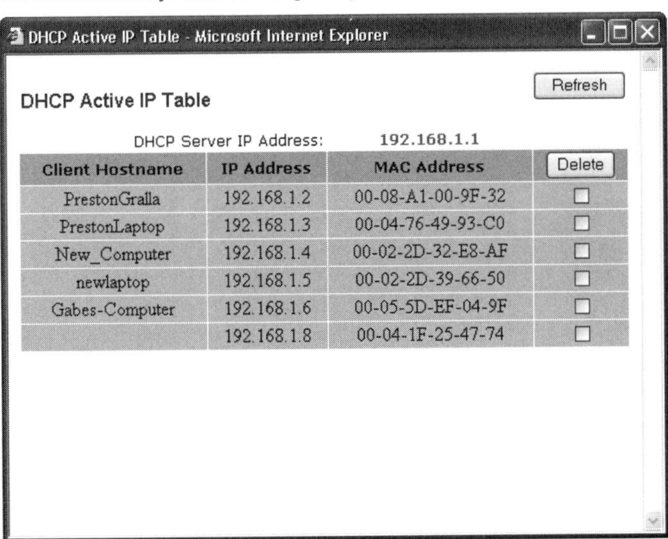
DHCP Active IP Table - Microsoft Internet Explorer

DHCP Active IP Table

Refresh

DHCP Server IP Address: 192.168.1.1

Client Hostname	IP Address	MAC Address	Delete
PrestonGralla	192.168.1.2	00-08-A1-00-9F-32	☐
PrestonLaptop	192.168.1.3	00-04-76-49-93-C0	☐
New_Computer	192.168.1.4	00-02-2D-32-E8-AF	☐
newlaptop	192.168.1.5	00-02-2D-39-66-50	☐
Gabes-Computer	192.168.1.6	00-05-5D-EF-04-9F	☐
	192.168.1.8	00-04-1F-25-47-74	☐

Even if someone isn't actively using a computer, file-sharing software can be the culprit causing slowdowns. Not uncommonly, teens leave file-sharing software going all the time, even when they're at school. In that case, the outgoing connections will again be the cause of the problem—another reason to check the Outgoing Access Log, rather than the incoming.

Figure 5-2 shows the outgoing log.

Once you've confirmed that's the problem, you can take action. You can, of course, simply ban file-sharing or peer-to-peer applications, but as any parent knows, that's a losing proposition.

One simple solution is to tell your child to only use file-sharing overnight, when people are not using your network. That way, when the network is in use during the day, it won't get bogged down.

You can also try to change some network settings on your router that may clear up the problem. Unfortunately, though, most routers don't let you manipulate these settings because their firmware won't allow it. However, if you've replaced your router's firmware with the Open Source DD-WRT [Hack #97] firmware (www.dd-wrt.com), you can do it.

If you've got DD-WRT installed, log in to your router, select Administration→Management, and scroll down to the IP Filter Settings area, as you can see in Figure 5-3.

Set Maximum Ports to 4096, and TCP Timeouts and UDP Timeouts both to 90. Click Save Settings, and then click Reboot Router. The new settings will take effect, and should solve the problem.

How does this help? The default for maximum ports on routers are often only 512, and TCP and UDP timeouts not uncommonly are set at the maximum, 3600. Making the change will increase the maximum number of available ports, but more important is that it will close any inactive connections after 90 seconds.

Figure 5-2.
Here's the outgoing traffic log. Plenty of connections from a single PC, so file-sharing is going on.

Outgoing Log Table - Microsoft Internet Explorer

Outgoing Log Table   Refresh

LAN IP	Destination URL/IP	Service/Port Number
192.168.1.6	80.161.55.188	1454
192.168.1.2	rms.adobe.com	HTTP
192.168.1.6	67.117.152.247	2252
192.168.1.6	80.51.236.181	3592
192.168.1.6	207.36.208.158	6969
192.168.1.3	63.211.66.69	HTTP
192.168.1.6	217.226.57.97	3254
192.168.1.6	sc.musicmatch.com	HTTP
192.168.1.2	rms.adobe.com	HTTP
192.168.1.6	212.127.132.184	4542
192.168.1.2	rms.adobe.com	HTTP
192.168.1.6	83.25.2.20	4851
192.168.1.2	rms.adobe.com	HTTP
192.168.1.6	220.235.11.22	4809
192.168.1.6	66.31.152.194	4834
192.168.1.6	sc.musicmatch.com	HTTP
192.168.1.2	rms.adobe.com	HTTP
192.168.1.6	62.104.83.91	59593
192.168.1.6	sc.musicmatch.com	HTTP
192.168.1.2	rms.adobe.com	HTTP
192.168.1.6	80.54.86.62	1077

Figure 5-3.
Change these settings if P2P applications are slowing down your router

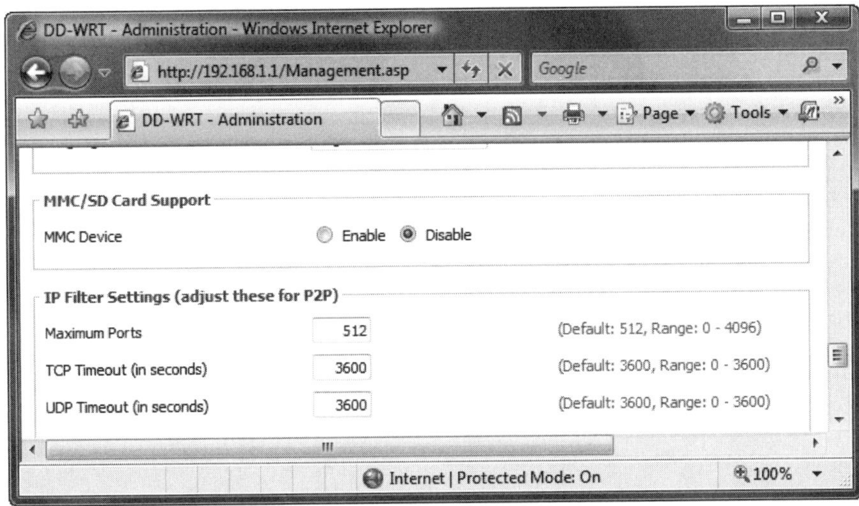

If you use some instant messaging clients such as AIM or ICQ, the timeout settings might cause connection problems. You may need to set the timeouts between 300 to 600. But you'll have to balance that with the need for faster timeouts for P2P applications, so be prepared to experiment.

HACK 68: Give the World Access to a Server or PC Behind Your Home Router

V XP If you've set up a server at home and want others to access it remotely, or if you want to remotely access or control a PC on your network, you're out of luck: your home router will block you. This hack shows you how to cut a hole through it.

One of your home router's best features can cause big problems if for some reason you need to get access to a PC remotely or if you want to make a server (such as a web server) you've set up available to the world.

That feature is *Network Address Translation* (NAT), in which the router's single, external IP address is shared among all the computers on the network, but each computer has its own internal IP address, invisible to the Internet. For example, to the Internet each computer looks as if it has the address of 66.32.43.98, but internally they have different addresses, such as 192.168.1.100, 192.168.1.101, and so on. The routers have built-in Dynamic Host Configuration Protocol (DHCP) servers that assign the internal IP address. Even though these internal IP addresses are cut off from the rest of the Internet, NAT allows the PCs to communicate with the Internet, and NAT also offers protection to PCs on the network. To the rest of the Internet, each PC has the IP address of the router, so each PC's resources can't be attacked or hijacked; they're essentially cloaked.

Unless a vulnerability is found in your particular router model, your network is safe from attack (this is why it's important to visit your router vendor's web site and apply the latest updates; if you are using custom firmware for your router, you can get updates from the project that supplied you with the custom firmware).

But if you have servers on your network that need to provide Internet-related services such as an FTP or web server, or if you need to allow certain PCs to be connected to the Internet for specific purposes (such as for playing multiplayer games), or need to get access to one of the PCs on your network from a remote location, you'll run into trouble because they don't have IP addresses that can be seen by the rest of the Internet.

However, with this hack, you can use your router to forward incoming requests to the right device (computer, video game system, server appliance, etc.) on your network. For example, if you have a web server or FTP server, and you want people to be able to connect to them, you'll be able to route incoming requests directly to those servers. PCs on the Internet will use your router's IP address, and your router will then route the requests to the proper device on your network. Normally, the devices would not be reachable because the IP addresses they are assigned by the router are internal LAN addresses, unreachable from the Internet.

Not all routers include this capability, so that might or might not work with yours. Check your router and its documentation. The feature is often called *port forwarding* or *mapping*.

For this hack, I'll use a Linksys router as an example. The instructions are for the WRT54GX4, but instructions will be similar for all other Linksys routers. To start, log into your administrator's screen by going to http://192.168.1.1 in your browser, and typing in your username and password. (The default is no username, and admin as the password.) If you've configured your network to use a different network range, replace 192.168.1.1 with the address of your router. Choose Applications & Gaming→Port Range Forwarding, and you'll see the screen shown in Figure 5-4.

When this feature is enabled, the router examines incoming requests, sees what port they're directed to (for example, port 80 for HTTP), and then routes the request to the proper device.

Fill in each device's IP address, the protocol used to connect to it (TCP, UDP, or both), and the port or port range you want forwarded to it. It's also a good idea to disable DHCP on each device to which

Figure 5-4.
Forwarding incoming requests to the proper server or device

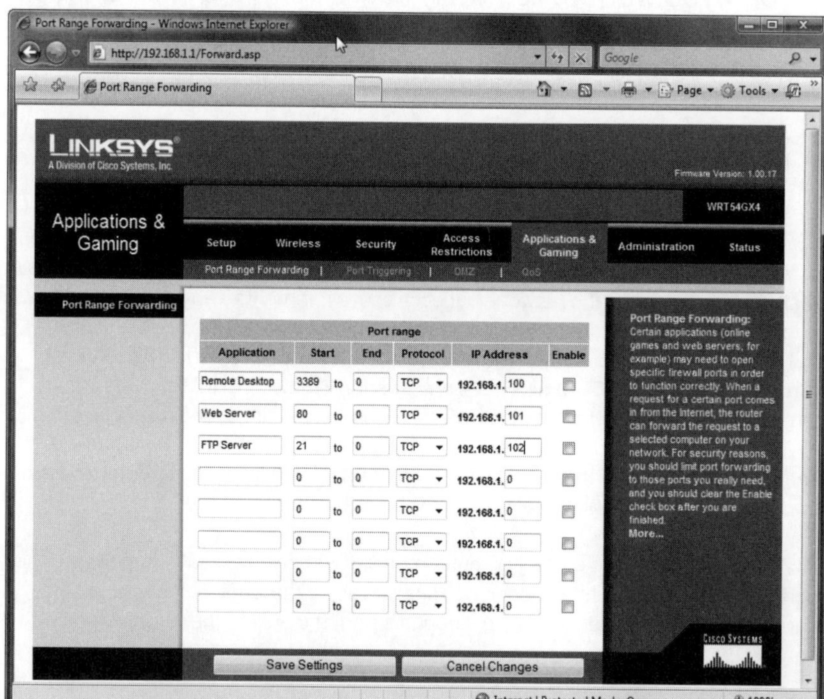

you want to forward requests and instead give them static internal IP addresses. If you continue to use DHCP instead of assigning them a static IP address, the IP addresses of the servers or devices might change and would therefore become unreachable. Check your router's documentation on how to force it to assign static IP addresses to specific devices.

If you're not sure of the IP address of your server or other device, open a command prompt on it, then type ipconfig and press Enter (on Linux or Mac OS X, open a terminal and type ifconfig). You'll then see its IP address; if the device has multiple network interfaces, look for the one that you intend to use, which should be the active interface.

Table 5-1 lists port addresses for common Internet services. For a complete list of ports, go to www.iana.org/assignments/port-numbers.

Table 5-1. Common Internet TCP ports

PORT NUMBER	SERVICE
7	Echo
21	FTP
22	SSH
23	Telnet
25	SMTP
42	Nameserv, WINS
43	Whois, nickname
53	DNS
79	Finger
80 or 8080	HTTP
81	Kerberos
101	HOSTNAME
110	POP3
119	NNTP
143	IMAP
161	SNMP
162	SNMP trap
1352	Lotus Notes
2500	Instiki Wiki
3389	Windows Remote Desktop (XP and Vista)
5631	PCAnywhere data
5632	PCAnywhere
5900 and higher	VNC remote control
6881 to 6990	BitTorrent

See Also

- "Give Your Home Server a Hostname" **[Hack #69]**

HACK 69: Give Your Home Server a Hostname

V XP Make sure the web site or other kind of Internet server you run at home is always available to the world.

If you run your own web server, mail server, or other kind of server at home and are connected to the Internet via a cable modem or DSL modem, people frequently might not be able to find your server. That's because, typically, broadband ISPs assign you a dynamic IP address that changes regularly, even if you don't reboot your router (see "Give the World Access to a Server or PC Behind your Home Router" **[Hack #68]** for details on setting up a server behind a home router). Because your IP address constantly changes, there is no way for people to connect to you. One day your public IP address might be 66.31.42.96, the next it might be 66.41.42.136, and if people don't know your server's current IP address they won't be able to find it. You won't be able to solve the problem by getting your own domain (such as www.gralla.com) and publishing that because DNS servers won't be able to keep track of your changing IP address either. If people type in your domain name, the servers won't be able to report on your IP address, and again, your server can't be reached.

There is a way to solve the problem, however: you can map your server's hostname to a dynamic IP address, using *Dynamic DNS* (DDNS). When you do this, it doesn't matter that your IP address changes; when people type in your web site's URL, they will be forwarded to your new IP address automatically.

You can do this for free by signing up with a DDNS service that provides automatic mapping. A number of services will do it for free, such as No-IP.com (www.no-ip.com). When you sign up for the service, you choose a hostname for your server and give that hostname out to people who want to connect to the server. Whatever name you choose will end in .no-ip.com—for example, gralla.no-ip.com. Figure 5-5 shows how simple it is to assign a hostname.

Figure 5-5.
Assigning a hostname

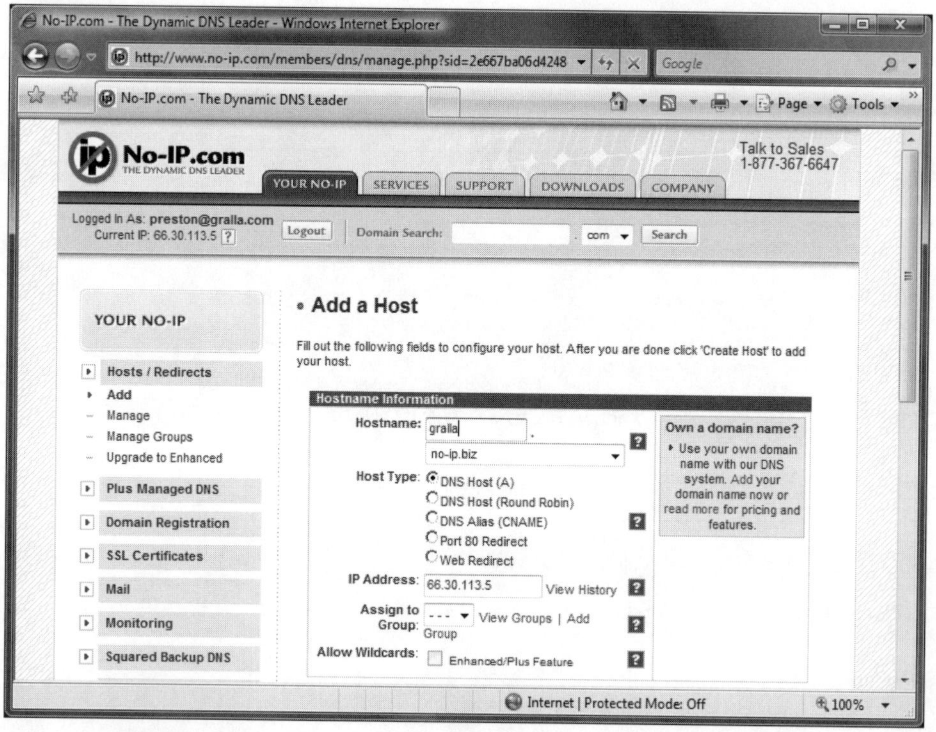

After you get your hostname, you download client software that periodically monitors your IP address (every three seconds). It reports on your server's current IP address to the No-IP.com site. Whenever the IP address changes, it reports that new IP address to the site. Figure 5-6 shows the client in action.

No-IP.com gives you a hostname in one of the domains that it manages (such as zapto.org and no-ip.com). The DNS records for your host have a very short time-to-live (TTL) so that No-IP can update them fairly quickly when your IP address changes. The person contacting your site will not have to do anything different from what she normally does; she just types in your URL and is connected to your site.

If you own a domain and want to map that hostname to a dynamic IP address instead of using a No-IP.com address, you'll have to sign up for No-IP.com's No-IP Plus service for $24.95 a month.

If you're using a router at home to share Internet access among several PCs, you might run into problems using the service. Many routers use NAT, in which all PCs on the network share a single external Internet address but are assigned internal network addresses. The No-IP.com client will track your external address, but because that single address is used by all PCs on the network, not just the server, incoming traffic won't be routed to your server. You can fix the problem by using the port forwarding feature [Hack #68] of your router to send the incoming traffic to the server.

You might run into another problem as well: when you try to test your server by connecting to it from a PC inside your network, you might not be able to connect to it. That's because you might not be able to connect to the external IP address from inside the network. If this happens, the only solution is to connect to the site from a PC outside your network or ask a friend to connect to it.

One more thing to watch out for: if you're behind a firewall, the No-IP.com client might have trouble connecting back to the No-IP.com site to report on your changing IP address. If you're using a

Figure 5-6.
The No-IP client monitoring an IP address.

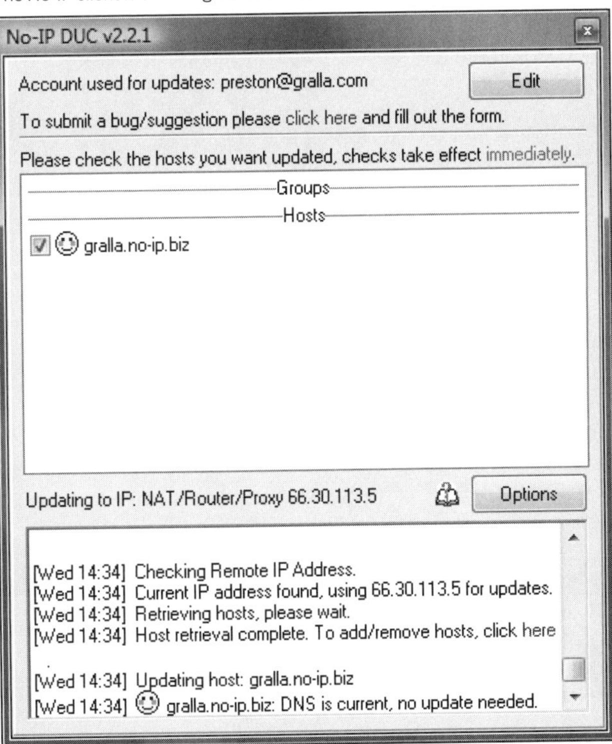

firewall such as ZoneAlarm, configure it to allow the client to make outbound connections. Also, depending on the firewall you use, you might need to configure it to open TCP port 8245 because that's the port the client uses to contact No-IP.com with your new IP address.

Hacking the Hack

If you use a Linksys router, consider using the DynDNS service (www.dyndns.com) instead of No-IP.com. Many Linksys routers include a built-in client for working with DynDNS, so you won't have to download separate software for it. (How you configure it depends on your router; check your user manual for instructions.)

There are a few anomalies you'll need to keep in mind. You may have to upgrade the router's firmware, because earlier versions of firmware from Linksys and other router manufacturers had significant problems that led DynDNS to block routers running those older versions. DynDNS has a list of certified routers at www.dyndns.com/support/clients/hardware/.

Other routers have support for DDNS services built in as well, so check your router manufacturer to see if it has any.

See Also

- "Give the World Access to a Server or PC Behind your Home Router" **[Hack #68]**

HACK 70: Get Quick Access to Network Connections in Windows Vista

V Tired of constant clicking when you want to get to a network connection, such as another PC on your network? Here are faster ways to get there.

If you've got a small home or small office network, you may often find yourself wanting to connect to another computer, device, or folder on a computer or device, to do something like open or copy a file. Too often, though, it takes a long time to get to that connection via a circuitous click path via Windows Explorer.

There are far quicker ways to get there. Perhaps the fastest is to put the connections right on your Start menu. Start off by opening the Network connections folder, shown in Figure 5-7, by choosing Start→Network.

To put a link to any of your network connections on the Start menu, drag the connection to the Start button. When the Start menu pops up, drag the connection to where you want it to be linked. As you drag it, the connection will appear transparent, and a shortcut icon will appear, as you can see in Figure 5-8.

Drop the connection to a spot near the top of the Start menu on the left side. Make sure that it appears above the thin, horizontal gray line. Anything placed above the line stays there permanently until you remove it; links below the line move on and off of the Start menu, depending on how frequently they are used. You can see the link toward the top of Figure 5-9.

If you'd prefer that the connection appear as a shortcut on the desktop, right-click the connection in the Network folder, and choose Create Shortcut.

You can also put a shortcut on your Desktop to a drive or folder on another computer. In the Network folder browse to the drive or folder, right-click it, and select Create Shortcut.

Figure 5-7.
The Network connections folder

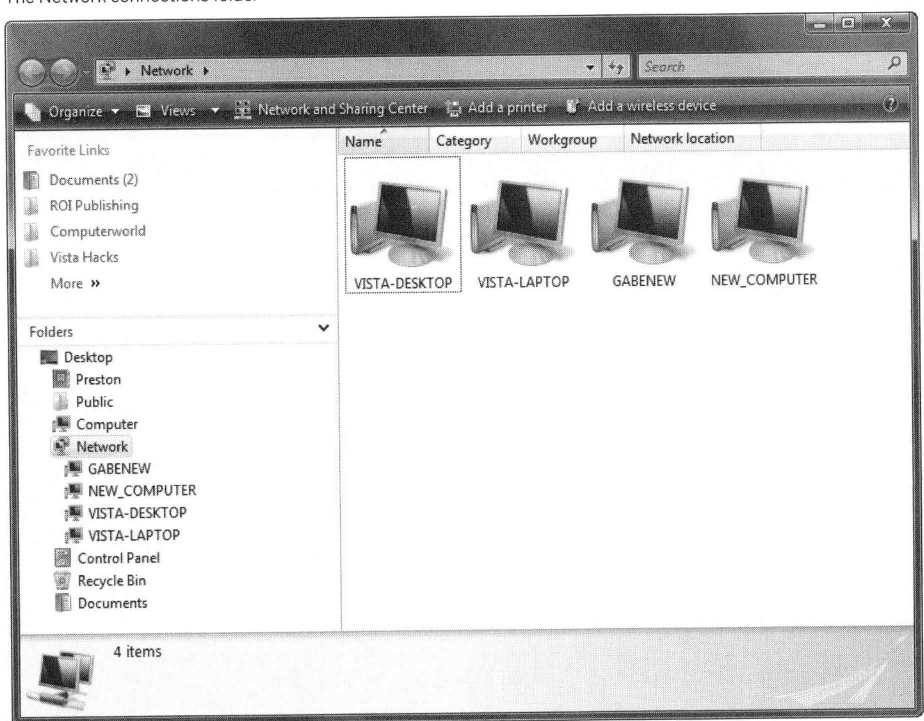

Figure 5-8.
Creating a link to a network connection on the Start menu

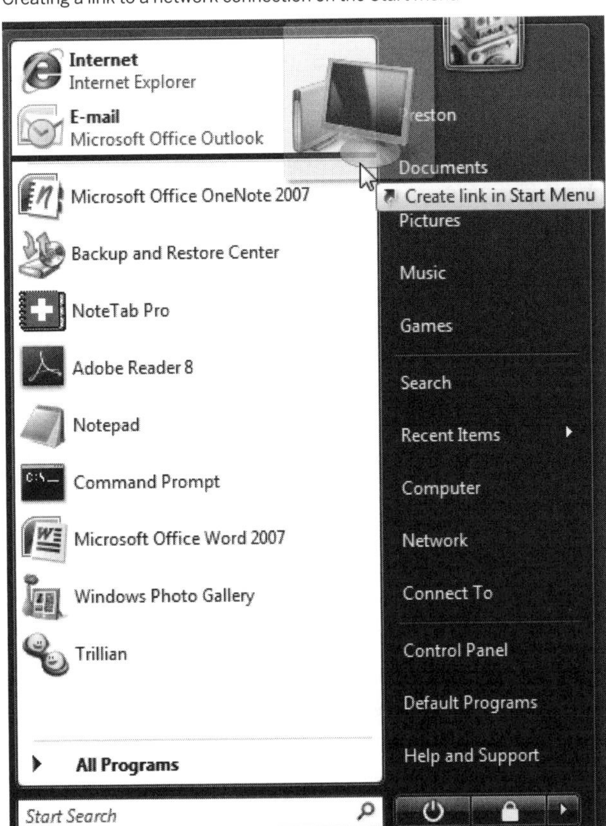

For another fast way to get to a drive or folder, you can map it as a network drive, such as G:, or H:. That way, it will show up throughout your computer in the same way local drives do in Windows Explorer as well as within applications.

To map a drive or folder as a network drive, open the drive or folder in Windows Explorer or via the Network connections folder. Right-click it, and select Map Network Drive. A dialog box, shown in Figure 5-10, appears. Select a drive letter from the drop-down list, and click Finish. The folder or drive will now show up as a drive letter on your local PC. If you want to reconnect automatically to the folder or drive every time you log on, make sure the box next to "Reconnect at logon" is checked.

Hacking the Hack

You can also add links to Internet locations, such as web sites, FTP servers, or other locations, right inside Windows Explorer. Open Windows Explorer to your computer (click Start→Computer), and right-click in the right pane. Select Add a Network Location. A wizard appears. Click Next, and on the next screen, select "Choose a custom network location," and click Next. On the next screen, type in the address of the Internet location, such as http://www.example.com/share. Make sure to include the http://, or ftp:// if it's an FTP server. Then click Next, and the shortcut will be added. You can also create shortcuts to locations on your network. Click the browse button, and select the network location. Or if you know the location, you can type it directly in, such as *\\PetePC\share* for the shared folder on the PetePC PC on your network.

HACK 71: Teach XP to Play Nice on Networks with Vista

V XP On networks, Windows XP and Windows Vista cooperate about as well as cats and dogs. But you can teach them to get along.

Can't we all just get along? That could well be the theme of problems you'll face when you mix Windows XP and Windows Vista on the same peer-to-peer home or small office network. It may be difficult for you to find your Windows XP PCs from Windows Vista when you're on the network and vice versa. And Windows XP PCs won't properly show up on Windows Vista's extremely useful network map—if they even show up at all.

This hack covers peer-to-peer networks such as the ones you'll set up at home with a home office router. It doesn't cover the large server-based networks you'll typically have at work.

The first problem is that the default name for your workgroup on the network has been changed from Windows XP Home to Windows Vista. In Windows XP Home, the default name for the network is `Mshome`; in Windows Vista, it is `Workgroup`. (It is `Workgroup` for Windows XP Professional.)

The naming conventions for peer-to-peer networks in Windows are extremely confusing. In Windows XP, if you go to My Network Places, you'll see one or more networks, including Microsoft Windows Network, and possibly Microsoft Terminal Services and Web Client Network. To see all the PCs on your network, click Microsoft Windows Network, and you'll then see workgroups. If it's a Windows XP Home-only network, you'll see `Mshome` as a workgroup; click it to see all the other PCs on your network. If you're on a network with Windows Vista or XP Professional PCs, you'll also see `Workgroup` listed as a workgroup.

In Windows Vista, by contrast, when you go to your Network folder, you won't see your workgroup name; you'll see only the PCs connected to your network. And you'll see all the PCs connected to all workgroups, including Windows XP Home PCs connected to the `Mshome` workgroup. You won't see the default workgroup name `Workgroup` listed.

The fix for this problem is easy; you can change the name of the workgroup on Windows XP Home to match the name of your Windows Vista network. On Windows XP, right-click My Computer, click the Computer Name tab, then click Change. The screen shown in Figure 5-11 appears. In the Workgroup box, type in the name of your Windows Vista network name. If you're leaving it as the default used

Figure 5-9.
The link, placed on the Start menu

Figure 5-10.
Mapping a network drive

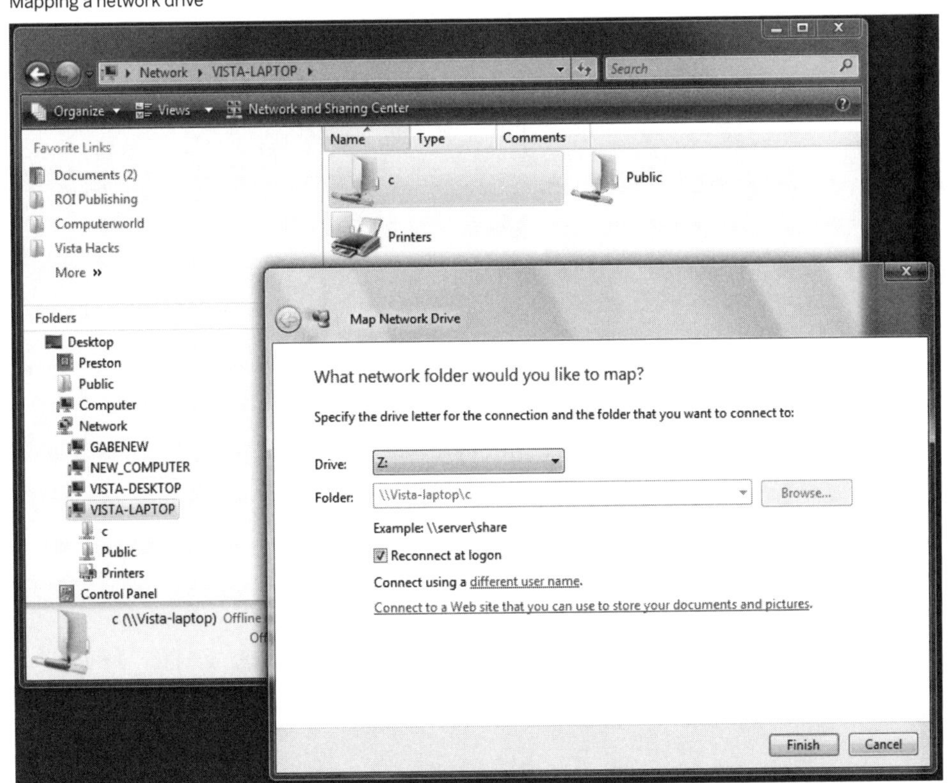

Figure 5-11.
Changing the name of your workgroup in Windows XP

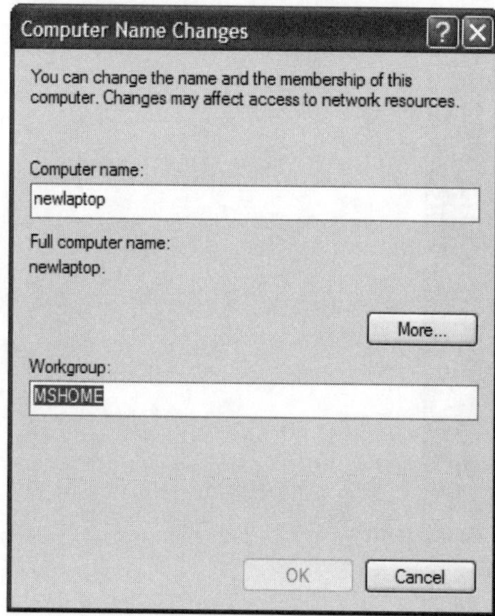

Figure 5-12.
Success: you've changed your workgroup name

in Windows Vista, type in `Workgroup`. If you're not using the Windows Vista default, change it to whatever name you've given your Windows Vista network, and click OK.

After you click OK, you'll see the confirmation dialog shown in Figure 5-12. Click OK again, then restart your PC.

If for some reason you want to change the name of your workgroup in Windows Vista, right-click Computer, and select Properties (or select Control Panel→System and Maintenance→"See the name of this computer"). You'll see the name of your PC as well as its workgroup name. Click Change settings, then from the screen that appears, click Change. In the dialog box shown in Figure 5-13, type in the new name for your workgroup, and click OK.

As with Windows XP, you'll get a confirmation that the name has been changed (Figure 5-14). You'll have to restart your PC for the changes to go into effect.

Making sure that both Windows XP and Windows Vista are on the same workgroup will go partway toward making the PCs get along on your network but won't go all the way. A bigger problem has to do with the new Windows Vista network map.

The network map is possibly the best addition that Windows Vista has made. To get there, select Control Panel→Network and Internet→Network and Sharing Center→"View full map". A screen like one shown in Figure 5-15 appears.

Figure 5-13.
Changing the name of your workgroup in Windows Vista

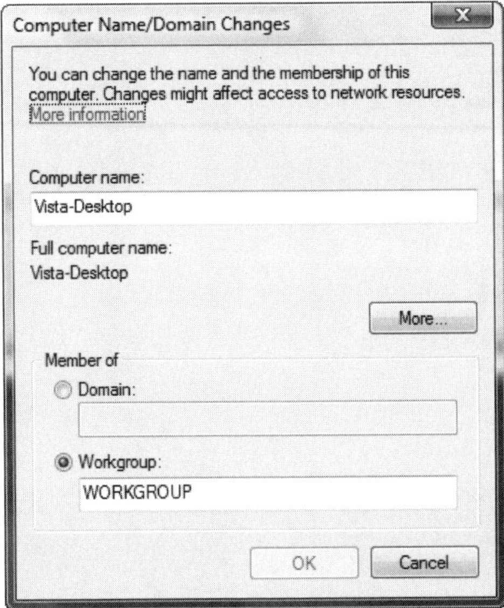

Figure 5-14.
You've just changed the name of your Windows Vista workgroup

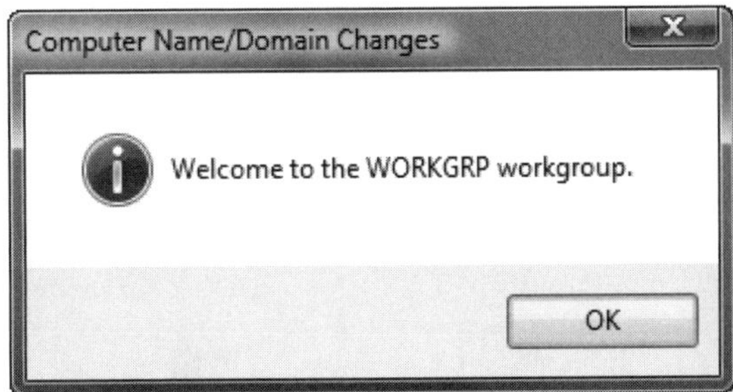

Figure 5-15.
Windows Vista's network map

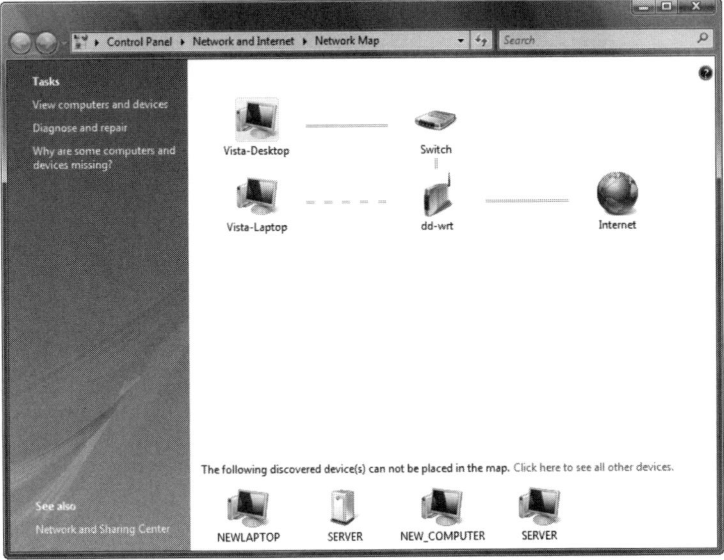

Figure 5-16.
Hovering your mouse over a PC in the network map

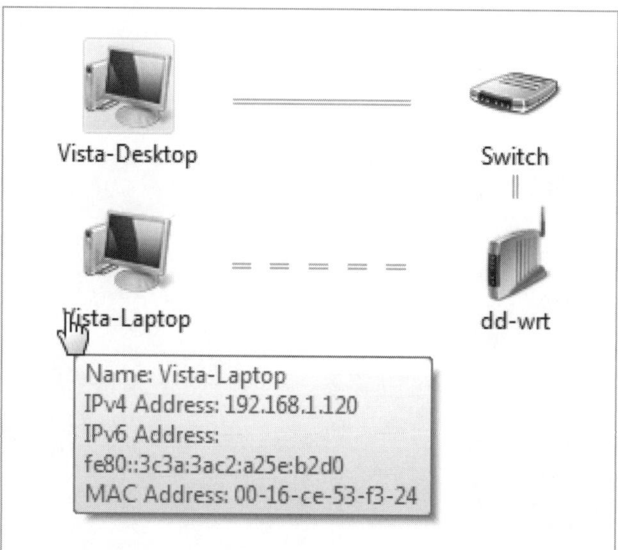

Figure 5-17.
An XP computer now can be placed directly on the network map

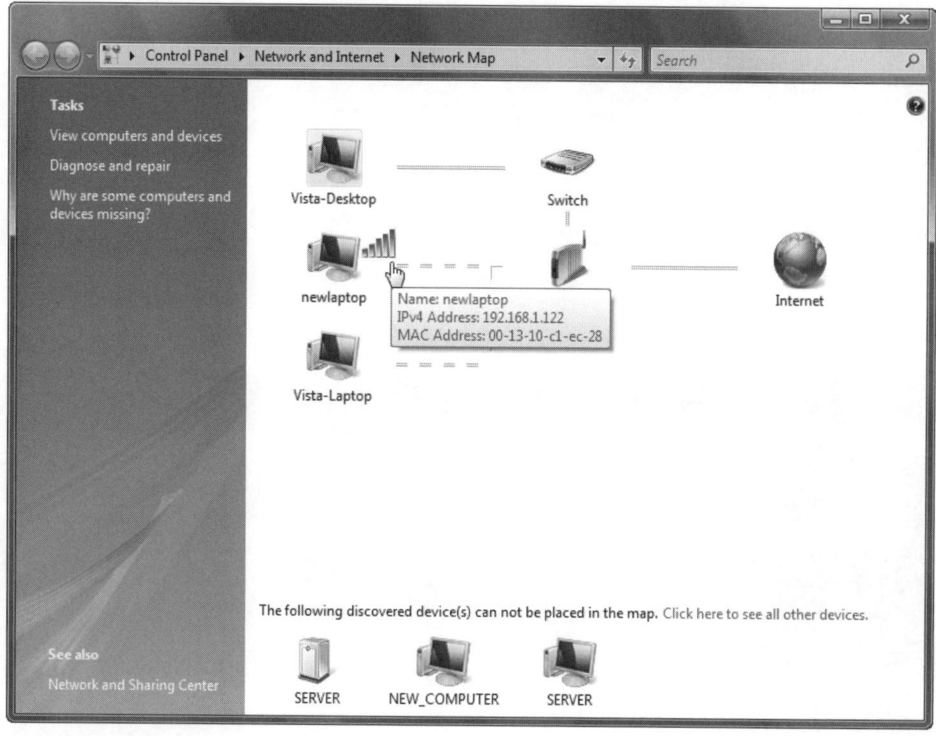

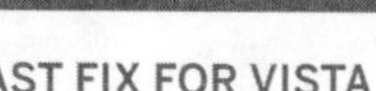

QUICK HACK

FAST FIX FOR VISTA NETWORK WOES

If you're using Windows Vista, and you've had problems copying large files over your network, getting disconnected from the network, or similar problems, the culprit may be a new Windows Vista feature called *auto-tuning*. Auto-tuning, in most cases, speeds up connections over your network. But it may also cause problems as well. To see if it's the cause of your woes, and to fix it, open an administrator's command prompt by typing `cmd` at the Search box and pressing Ctrl-Shift-Enter. Then at the command prompt, type this command: `netsh int tcp set global autotuninglevel=disabled`. Reboot your PC. If it doesn't solve the problem, you can turn auto-tuning back on by typing this at an administrator's command prompt and rebooting: `netsh int tcp set global autotuninglevel=normal`.

The map shows you all the PCs and devices attached to your network—those in your entire network, not just your workgroup. This map is more than nice to look at; it's extremely useful as well. Hover your mouse over any device, and you'll be shown information about it, such as its name, IP address, and MAC address, as shown in Figure 5-16. Click a PC, and you'll connect to it; then you'll see the shared folders to which you have access.

Ah, but there's a rub here. Look back at Figure 5-15. Notice, at the bottom of the screen, that there are a number of devices listed. Windows Vista has found them, but doesn't quite know what to make of them. It can't figure out where they fit in on the network. And it won't give you any information about them if you hover your mouse over them.

What gives?

The problem is that in order to discover information about devices, Windows Vista uses a new protocol, called Link Layer Topology Discovery (LLTD). LLTD is built in to any Windows Vista PC, which is why they show up properly on the network map. However, LLTD isn't built in to Windows XP, which is why they don't show up properly.

You can fix the problem by downloading and installing the Layer Topology Discovery (LLTD) Responder (tinyurl.com/2b3lkn). Install it, (restart your PC), and your Windows XP PC will show up on the network map, properly located, with the mouse hover in full working order (Figure 5-17).

HACK 72: Teach All Your Networks to Get Along

V XP If you've got multiple networks and want to tie them together into a seamless whole, here's what you can do.

If your house looks anything like mine, you've got PCs, printers, and routers sprawling everywhere. Maybe you've got an old router upstairs to which you've connected three PCs, a wireless network downstairs, PCs with wireless adapters scattered hither and yon, and wired PCs connected to the router. One of your upstairs PCs has a wireless adapter, and is connected to your downstairs wireless network and also to your upstairs router.

You desperately need to share folders and printers between your downstairs wireless PCs and your wired PCs upstairs, but they're on different networks. You could run out to Best Buy or Staples, but it's a holiday and you need to hook this up right away! You seem to be out of luck.

In fact, though, you're not out of luck. In Windows, you can easily create what's called a *network bridge* to connect your networks so that they work like one big network. You can do it in both Windows XP and Windows Vista. In this example, we'll connect two networks, a wired and a wireless one.

In order to bridge networks, you need a PC with connections to both networks. A laptop is ideal for this, because most include a built-in wireless adapter as well as a built-in Ethernet adapter. But even if you have a desktop it's easy to do; just plug a PCI network adapter into a free PCI slot, or even a USB network adapter into a free USB slot.

You can't add a VPN connection, a dial-in connection, or a direct cable connection to a network bridge.

First, go to your Network Connections folder (Figure 5-18). In Windows XP, get there by choosing Control Panel→Network and Internet Connections→Network Connections. In Windows Vista, get there by choosing Control Panel→Network and Internet→Network and Sharing Center→Manage network connections.

To bridge your connections, click on one connection, and while holding down the Ctrl key, click any other connections you want to add to the bridge. Then right-click, and select Bridge connections. After a short while, a new icon will show up in the folder, the network bridge, as you can see in Figure 5-19).

INSTALL INTERNET INFORMATION SERVICES (IIS) ON WINDOWS VISTA

Windows Vista ships with Internet Information Services, a web server as well as other types of servers, including an FTP server—but where is it? It doesn't seem to be installed anywhere in the operating system. It is, in fact, there, but it's waiting to be installed. Select Control Panel→Programs→Turn Windows features on or off. From the Windows Features screen that appears, check the box next to Internet Information Services. (If you only want to install certain components, such as just a web server, or just an FTP server, click the + sign and check boxes next to those components you want to install.) Then click OK, and IIS will be installed. Note that Home Premium edition of Windows Vista can accept only five simultaneous inbound connections, and the Home Basic edition doesn't come with IIS. All other versions of Vista come with IIS and can accept 10 simultaneous inbound connections.

Figure 5-18.
The Network Connections folder in Windows XP, with multiple network connections

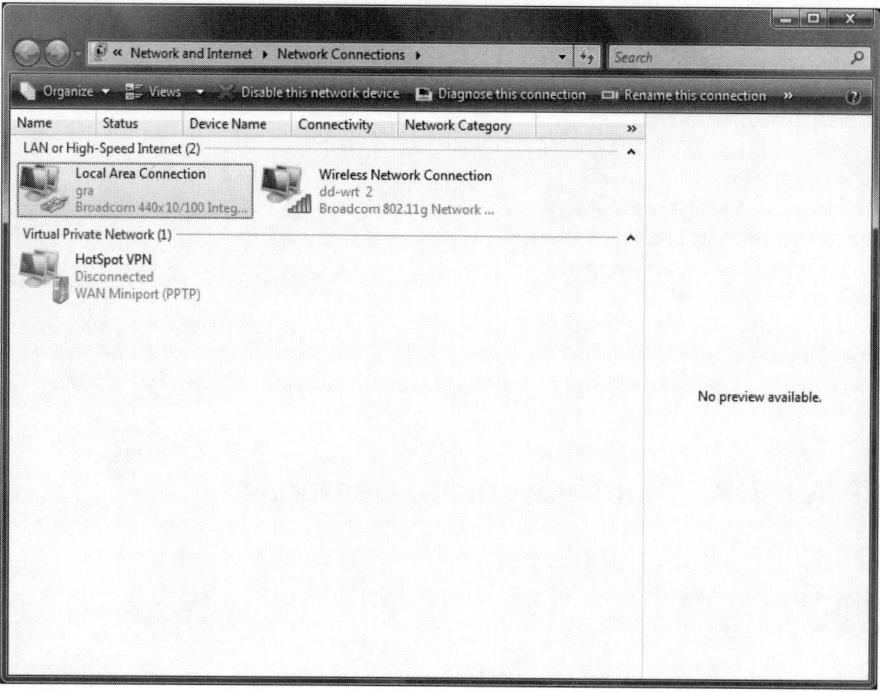

Figure 5-19.
The two networks have been bridged

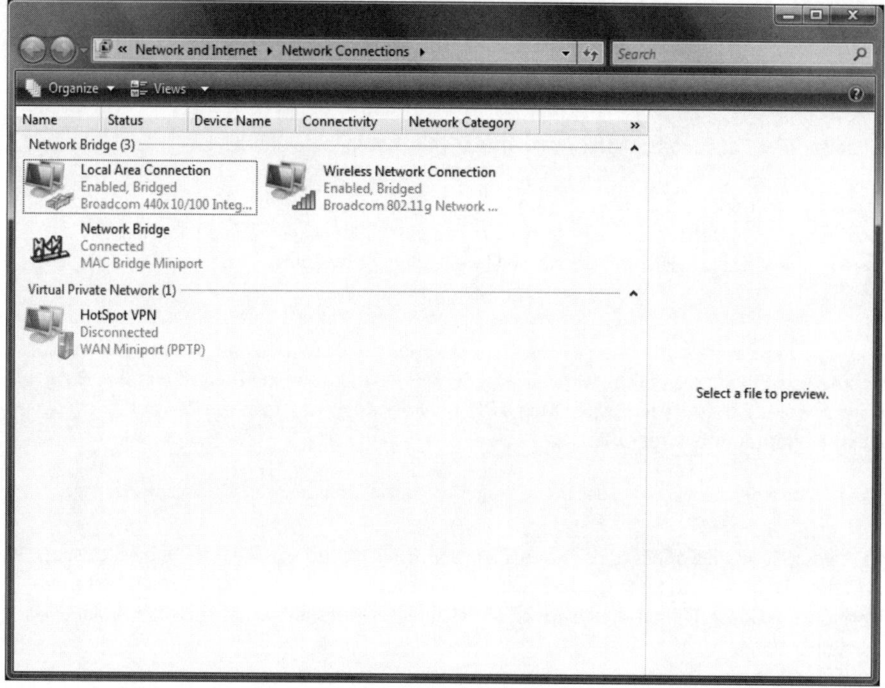

You'll now be able to treat the two networks as if they were one, and PCs from one network will be able to share folders and resources with PCs from the other.

From now on, you won't be able to change the properties or configuration for any individual network connection in the Network Connections folder; instead, you'll have to change them through the network bridge. If you right-click the Wireless Network Connection and choose Properties, you'll get the screen shown in Figure 5-20.

You'll have to do any configuration through the bridge itself, which now has several sets of configuration information, one for each connection. Right-click the network bridge icon, select Properties, and you'll see a screen like that shown in Figure 5-21. From here, you can configure each individual connection, by selecting it and clicking Configure.

To remove any connections from the bridge, right-click the connection, and select Remove from Bridge. To add a new connection, right-click the connection, and select Add to Bridge. If you want to kill the network bridge entirely, right-click it, and select Delete.

Figure 5-20.
When you set up a network bridge, you can no longer configure individual connections

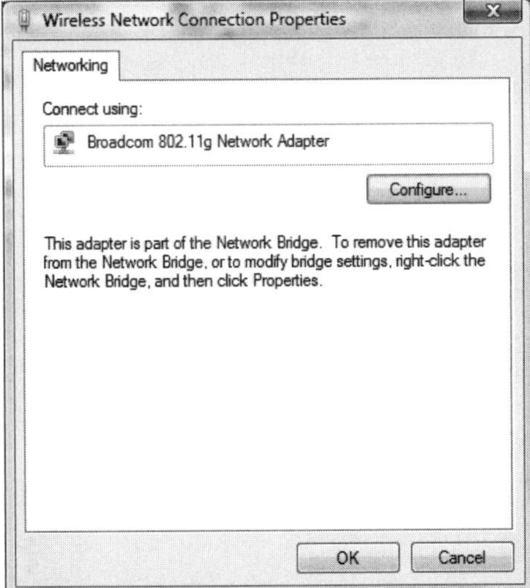

Figure 5-21.
The network bridge contains configuration information for each bridged connection

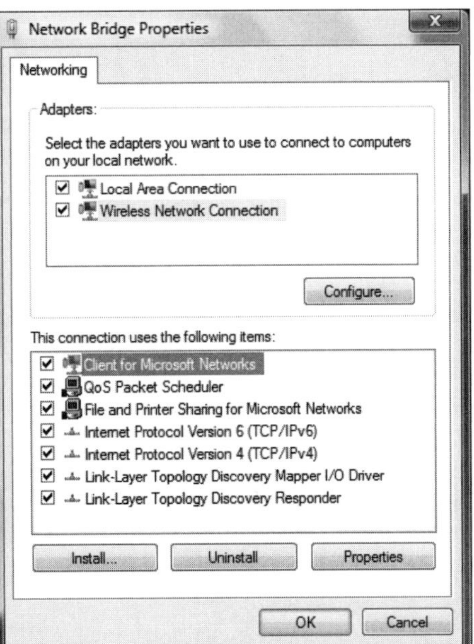

HACK 73: Control Another Windows XP PC with Remote Access

XP You can control a computer—virtually moving its mouse and typing on its keyboard—over the Internet, using Windows XP's built-in features.

When you are at work, wouldn't it be nice if you could log on to your home computer to check your email or find a file you took home? How about using your home or office desktop computer from your laptop on the road? You can use a remote control program to access another computer over the Internet, viewing its screen on your screen and giving commands via your mouse and keyboard. Windows XP comes with a feature called Remote Desktop, which you'll learn to use in this hack.

The computer you will control is called the *remote server*, and the computer you are actually sitting in front of is the *remote client*. Windows XP comes with a remote client program (Remote Desktop Connection), and Windows XP Professional comes with a remote server (Remote Desktop) that works with one client at a time—that is, one computer can "take over" your computer remotely (with luck, it'll be you doing the takeover!).

Remote Access Server (RAS) on Windows NT or 2000 servers and the Routing and Remote Access utility on Windows Server 2003 both act as remote servers that allow multiple remote clients to connect.

Windows XP Home Edition can't act as a remote server; if you need to be able to access a Home Edition system remotely, you need to upgrade to Windows XP Professional or use a third-party program. I recommend VNC, the small, open source program available at www.realvnc.com.

Configuring the Windows XP Remote Server

If you want to control your Windows XP Professional system remotely, set it up as a remote server. Using an administrator user account, choose Start→Control Panel→Performance and Maintenance→System (or press the Windows-Break key), click the Remote tab, select the "Allow users to connect remotely to this computer" checkbox in the Remote Desktop section of the tab to enable incoming connections, and click Select Remote Users if you want to control which user accounts can be used by remote clients. (Windows automatically allows connections from the current user, along with all user accounts in the local Administrators and Remote Desktop Users groups.)

Normally, remote clients connect to the server via a local area network or a permanent Internet connection. However, you can also configure the remote server to accept incoming phone calls if you have a dial-up modem. Create a dial-up connection that accepts incoming calls by running the New Connection Wizard (click "Create a new connection" from the task pane in the Network Connections window). Choose "Set up an advanced connection" as the Network Connection Type, choose "Accept incoming connections," choose your modem, choose whether to accept VPN connections [Hack #119], and choose which user accounts the incoming connection can connect to.

Firewalls usually refuse remote access connections so if you want your remote server to be accessible from the Internet, you need to open a port in your computer's firewall and quite often in your router [Hack #68]. Remote Desktop uses port 3389. If you use Windows XP's built-in Windows Firewall, select Control Panel→Security Center, scroll to the bottom of the screen, and click Windows Firewall. Then click the Advanced tab to get to the Advanced Settings dialog box. In the Network Connection Settings section, click Settings, and you'll see a screen like that shown in Figure 5-22. Click the Remote Desktop checkbox; if the Service Settings dialog box appears, just click OK.

Figure 5-22.
Telling Windows XP's Firewall to allow remote connections

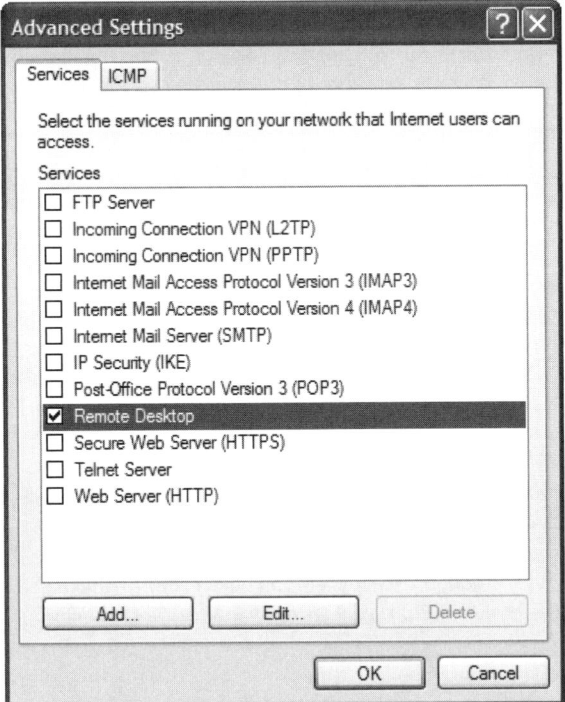

If you want to change the Remote Desktop server port to a number other than 3389 (perhaps to decrease the likelihood of malicious hackers breaking through it), see the Microsoft Knowledge Base Article Q187623 (at support.microsoft.com, type the article number in the "Search the Knowledge Base" box). You can also get to the article directly at support.microsoft.com/kb/187623/en-us.

When you connect from your remote client (described later in this hack), you need to provide a domain name or IP address. If it's a PC on your own network, type in the computer name or its local IP address when you use the client. But if you'll be connecting over the Internet, it's a little more complicated, because your PC's IP address changes each time you connect, and the computer doesn't have a domain name. One solution is to have someone at the remote server display the Network Connections window; right-click the Internet connection; choose Status from the shortcut menu; click the Support tab; and call, IM, or email you with the IP address that appears. However, this solution is no good if no one is available to do this. And as a practical matter, no one will be available to do it.

Instead, you can sign up for a dynamic DNS service **[Hack #69]**, such as at www.dyndns.com or www.tzo.com. The dynamic DNS service at DynDNS.com gives you a free domain name in the form `yourname.dyndns.org` (they offer several dozen domain names to which you can add your name). No-IP.com (www.no-ip.com) offers a similar service. TZO.com provides a subdomain at `yourname.tzo.com` for $25 per year. You install a small utility on your computer that automatically tells the dynamic DNS whenever your computer's IP address changes.

One final configuration note: when a client connects to your server via Remote Desktop, the user logs into one of the Windows XP user accounts. You can't log into accounts that have no password. Choose which account you want remote users to log into, and give it a password.

QUICK HACK

CONTROL MULTIPLE PCS WITH ONE KEYBOARD AND MOUSE

If you've got multiple PCs—or a mix of PCs and Macs—and you'd like to control them all with one mouse and keyboard, you can do it without having to set up remote connections. Download the open source program Synergy (synergy2.sourceforge.net) and install its server component on the PCs whose mouse and keyboard you want to control other PCs and Macs. Then install the client component on each PC and Mac you want to control. After that, you configure all the PCs and Macs to work with the server. Amazingly enough, you'll be able to move your mouse cursor to the edge of your monitor, then keep moving it, and the cursor will appear on the PC or Mac toward which you moved the cursor. You can then control that PC or Mac. You can even copy and paste between machines.

Configuring Your Router

If you're going to connect over the Internet to take control of your PC, you'll need to configure your home router so that you can get to the PC. You do this by configuring your home router to forward all traffic from specific ports to the internal IP address **[Hack #68]** of your home server (such as 192.168.1.1). When we refer to ports here, we're not talking about a physical plug on your PC. Instead, a port is a virtual connection used by the Internet. You'll need to tell the router to forward TCP ports 4125 and 443 to the internal IP address of the PC that you want to control. To find a computer's IP address, type ipconfig /all at a command prompt.

Setting Up the Remote Client

To set up the remote client software that comes with Windows XP, connect to the Internet and then choose Start→All Programs→Accessories→Communications→Remote Desktop Connection. (If it's not there, you need to install it from your Windows CD.) In the Remote Desktop Connection window, type the domain name or IP address of the server computer, and click Connect. Then type that computer's name (if you're controlling a PC over a local network) or that computer's IP address/hostname (if connected to the Internet).

Log on with the Windows XP user account and password for the remote server. You can also speed up logging in: when you run the Remote Desktop Connection, click Options, and you'll see a screen like Figure 5-23. Type in all the login information here, click Connect, and you'll be automatically logged in. You can also save the connection information so that you won't need to type in username password, and so on, in the future. Click the Save As button, save an *.rdp* file, and in the future, from

Figure 5-23.
Log in to your remote desktop connection from this screen

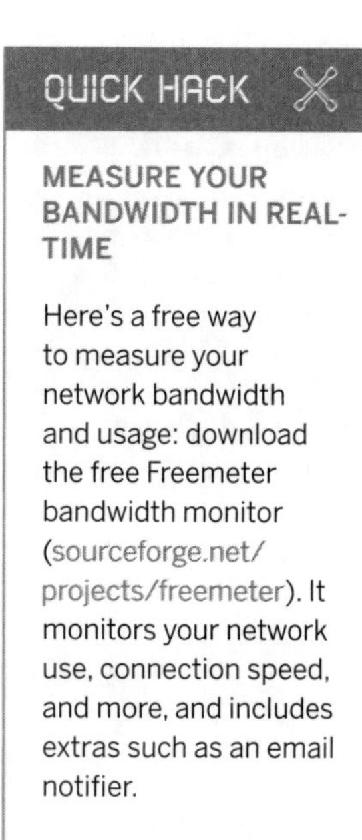

QUICK HACK

MEASURE YOUR BANDWIDTH IN REAL-TIME

Here's a free way to measure your network bandwidth and usage: download the free Freemeter bandwidth monitor (sourceforge.net/projects/freemeter). It monitors your network use, connection speed, and more, and includes extras such as an email notifier.

this screen, you can open the file, and you'll make the connection. This is especially useful if you make remote connections to more than one PC.

When you make a Remote Desktop Connection, you're logging onto a remote PC using your account on it. If someone on the PC logs on, your remote connection will be terminated.

Your computer screen now shows what's on the screen of the server computer. A connection bar appears as a button on the screen, showing the IP address of the remote server, along with Minimize, Restore, and Maximize buttons you can use to resize the remote client window. You can remotely connect not only to Windows XP PCs, but Windows Vista PCs as well. Figure 5-24 shows an XP PC taking control of a Windows Vista PC.

Once you're connected, you can cut and paste information from the remote client window to other windows. You can also use local files in your remote session; your local disk drives appear in My Computer (Windows Explorer). When you print from the remote client, the print job goes to your default local printer, not to the printer on the server. To end the connection, close the window in which the connection is being made.

— *Margaret Levine Young*

See Also

- "Control Another Windows Vista PC with Remote Access" **[Hack #74]**
- "Make a Remote Connection to Windows Home Server Over the Internet" **[Hack #129]**
- "Give Your Home Server a Hostname" **[Hack #69]**
- "Take Remote Command of a PC Using Window Home Server" **[Hack #130]**

Figure 5-24.
Taking remote control of a Windows Vista PC, using Windows XP

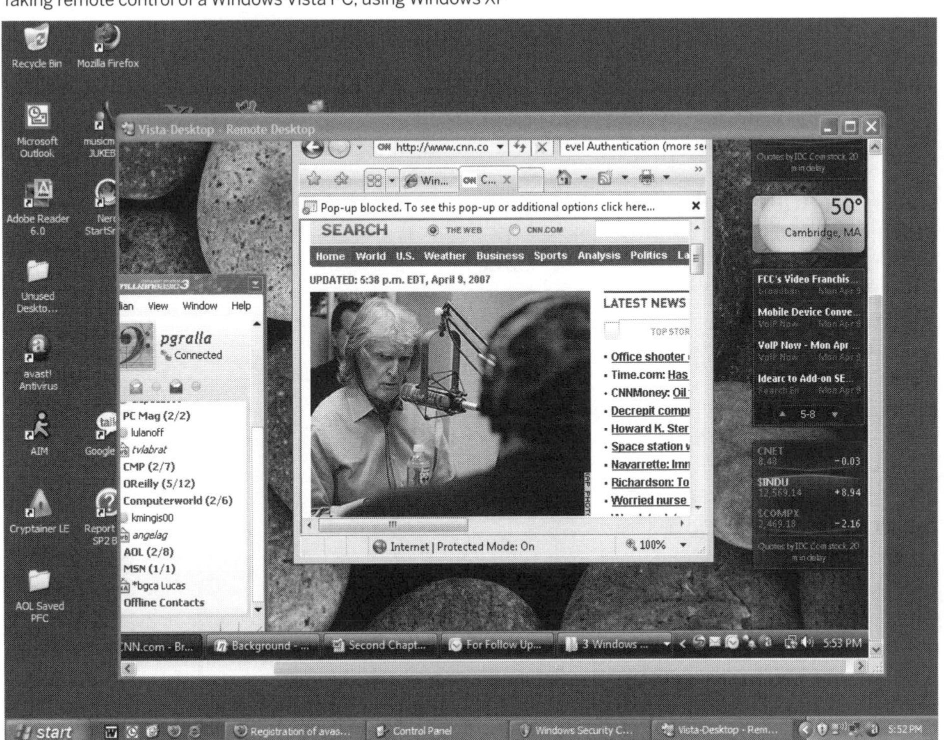

HACK 74: Control Another Windows Vista PC with Remote Access

V Windows Vista offers remote control as well. Here's how to do it.

In "Control Another Windows XP PC with Remote Access" [Hack #73], you found the benefits of remotely controlling a PC using another machine, and you've seen how to do it in Windows XP. It's just as easy, or maybe even easier, to do it with Vista, as you'll see in this hack.

Remote control in Windows Vista works much like it does in Windows XP. You run a server on a machine you want to control, then run a client a machine that you want to do the controlling.

> If you run Windows Home Basic or Windows Home Premium, you're out of luck; neither includes the remote server feature, and so a PC with either can't be controlled remotely with built-in remote features. You'll need Windows Business, Windows Enterprise, or Windows Ultimate if you want your machine to be controlled remotely; or you could use VNC, available from www.realvnc.com. However, Windows Home Basic and Windows Home Premium both include clients (as do Windows Business, Windows Enterprise, and Windows Ultimate), so you can use them to take remote control of another PC.

Configuring the Windows Vista Remote Server

To configure a computer to accept incoming connections via Remote Desktop Connection, go to Control Panel→System and Maintenance→Allow Remote Access, and in the Remote Desktop section, select "Allow connections from computers running any version of Remote Desktop (less secure)," or "Allow connections only from computers running Remote Desktop with Network Level Authentication (more secure)" (see Figure 5-25).

The Windows Vista Remote Desktop client supports Network Level Authentication, so if you're going to connect to the PC only with Windows Vista, you can use the secure connection. Windows XP clients, as a general rule, don't support Network Level Authentication. To find out if any Remote Desktop client support Network Level Authentication, run the client itself, click the small icon in the upper left-corner of its screen, and click About. If your client supports Network Level Authentication, it will say so, as you can see in Figure 5-26.

By default, all users with administrator privileges on your PC can make remote desktop connections to it. To enable access for other users, click Select Users from the screen shown in Figure 5-25, click Add from the screen that appears, and add them.

Configure Your Router

If you're going to connect over the Internet to take control of your PC, you'll need to configure your home router so that you can get to the PC. You do this by configuring your home router to forward all traffic from specific *ports* to the internal IP address of your home server (such as 192.168.1.1). When we refer to ports here, we're not talking about a physical connection on your PC. Instead, a port is a virtual connection used for network connections.

You'll need to tell the router to forward [Hack #68] TCP ports 4125 and 443 to the internal IP address of the PC that you want to control. To find its IP address, at a command prompt, type ipconfig /all.

Setting Up the Remote Client

Once a computer has been set up, you can connect to it by opening Remote Desktop Connection and typing that computer's name or IP address. Run the Remote Desktop Connection by selecting Start→All Programs→Accessories→Remote Desktop Connection. Type in the name or IP address of the computer to which you want to connect, then log in. Click Options to specify a username, password, domain (only for Windows Server domains), and even to save your connection settings to a file so you can connect more easily later. You can save the connection profile for a particular connection by clicking Save As. This creates a Remote Desktop Profile (*.rdp*) file, which you can

Figure 5-25.
Setting up a Windows Vista PC to accept remote connections

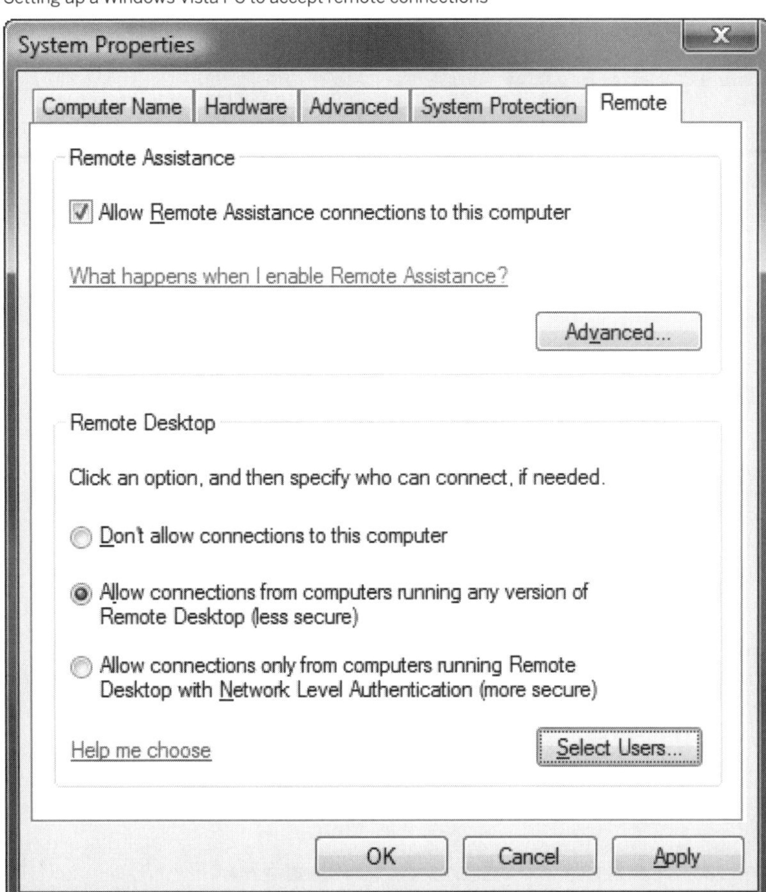

Figure 5-26.
This client supports Network Level Authentication

Figure 5-27.
The Windows Vista Remote Desktop client

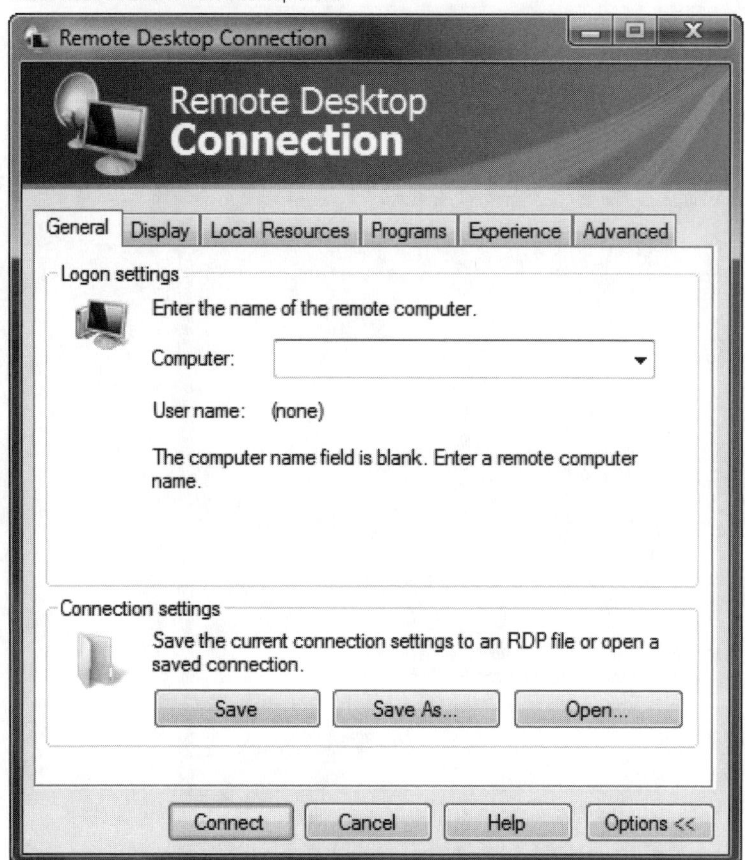

double-click to start the connection without having to retype the connection information. Right-click any *.rdp* file, and select Edit to return to the Properties dialog for the profile. (By default, the files are saved in your Documents folder).

Figure 5-27 shows the Windows Vista Remote Desktop client.

As with the Windows XP client, once you're connected, you can cut and paste information from the remote client window to other windows. You can also use local files in your remote session; your local disk drives will appear in Windows Explorer. Additionally, when you print from the remote client, the print job goes to your default local printer, not to the printer on the server.

 When you make a Remote Desktop Connection, you're logging onto a remote PC using your account on it. If someone on the PC logs on, your remote connection will be terminated.

To end the connection, close the window in which the connection is being made.

See Also

- "Control Another Windows XP PC with Remote Access" **[Hack #73]**
- "Make a Remote Connection to Windows Home Server Over the Internet" **[Hack #129]**
- "Give Your Home Server a Hostname" **[Hack #69]**
- "Take Remote Command of a PC Using Window Home Server" **[Hack #130]**

HACK 75: Reboot Your Network Settings

V XP Sometimes, when you've been assigned an IP address by a DHCP server, your PC doesn't appear to be on the network, and you can't get Internet or network access. Renewing your IP address often solves the problem.

If you're on a network, but you can't send or receive data, use any network resources, or visit the Internet, the culprit might be a problem with your DHCP-assigned IP address. The simplest way to fix it is to renew the IP address: get rid of the old one, and ask the DHCP server to send along a new one.

Before trying this, first make sure you're using a DHCP-assigned IP address rather than a static one. In Windows XP, right-click My Network Places, and choose Properties to get to the Network Connections folder. Right-click your current network connection, and choose Properties. On the General tab, select Internet Protocol (TCP/IP), and choose Properties. On the General tab, the radio button next to "Obtain an IP address automatically" will be selected if you're using DHCP.

In Windows Vista, right-click Network, select Properties, then from the Network and Sharing Center, click View status. On the Local Connection Properties dialog box, click Properties, and highlight Internet Protocol Version 4 (TCP/IPv4). Click Properties, and on the General tab, the radio button next to "Obtain an IP address automatically" will be selected if you're using DHCP.

After you've confirmed you're using DHCP, release your current IP address by typing `ipconfig /release` at a command prompt. The `ipconfig` command is an all-purpose command that lets you solve many network-related problems [Hack #77]. To renew the address and get a new IP address from the DHCP server, type `ipconfig /renew` at a command prompt. Your new IP address should fix the problem.

To find your new IP address, type `ipconfig` at a command prompt. In Windows XP, you can also select your connection in the Network Connections folder, click "View status of this connection," and click the Support tab. You'll see a screen that shows your new IP address and confirms it was assigned by a DHCP server. In Windows Vista, you can look for your IP address on the network map. To get there, choose Control Panel→Network and Internet→Network and Sharing Center→"View full map" as shown in Figure 5-28.

> **QUICK HACK**
>
> **INSTANTLY REBOOT YOUR NETWORK SETTINGS**
>
> Windows XP and Windows Vista both include a way to reboot your network settings without having to use the ipconfig command- line tool. In Windows XP, right-click My Network Places, choose Properties, and from the screen that appears right-click your network connection and select Repair. In Windows Vista, choose Control Panel→Network and Internet→ Network Sharing Center→"Diagnose and repair."

HACK 76: Troubleshoot Network Connections with ping, tracert, and pathping

V XP When you need help tracking down network connection problems, the command line is the place to go.

If you're having problems with your network and network connections, and you need troubleshooting help, forget the GUI tools; they don't offer enough help. To get to the root of the problems, you're going to have to get down and dirty with command-line tools. `ping` and `tracert` are familiar tools that you might have used on occasion, but you might not know the depth of their power or the switches available to use with them. And you probably haven't heard of `pathping`, a quasi-combination of the two commands.

Troubleshoot TCP/IP Problems with ping

The quickest, most commonly used, and, frequently, most helpful TCP/IP troubleshooting tool is the command-line tool `ping`. Use `ping` to find out whether the resource or server you're trying to

Figure 5-28.
Confirming your IP address in Windows Vista

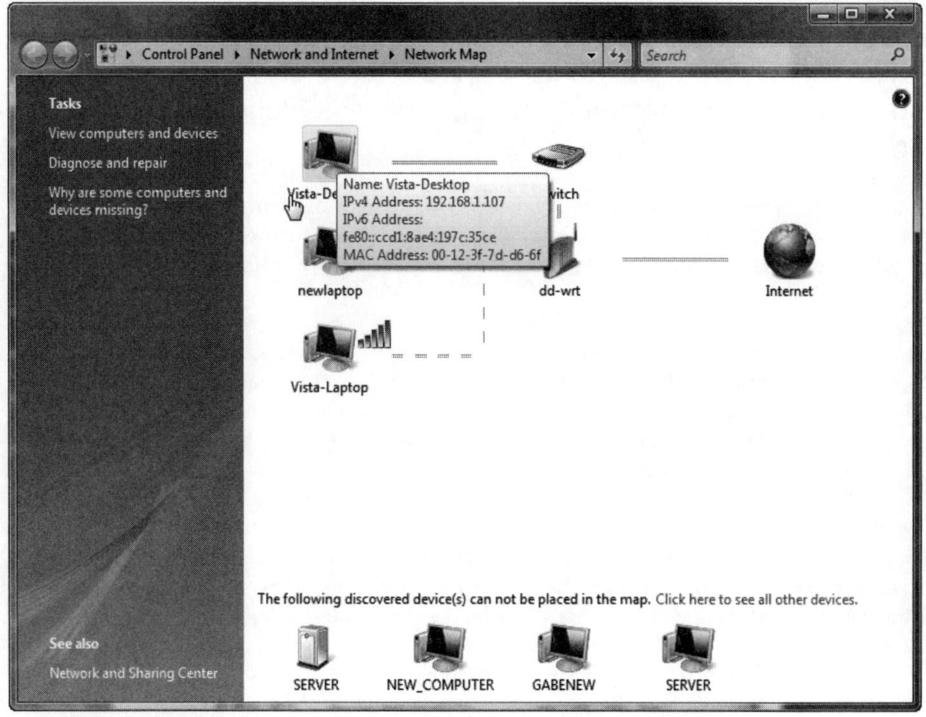

connect to on your network or the Internet is active, and to see if there are any problems with the hops along the way to that resource or server. `ping` sends Internet Control Message Protocol (ICMP) Echo Request messages to the destination you're checking on, receives responses in return, and reports to you information about the connection path between you and the destination and how quickly the packets made their trip. For example, if you are having trouble getting email from a server, your first step in troubleshooting should be to ping the server to see whether the server is live, and to see how responsive it is. To use `ping`, open the command prompt and type: `ping target`, where `target` is either a hostname or an IP address—for example, pop3.catalog.com, zdnet.com, or 209.217.46.121. In response, you'll get information in this format:

```
Pinging zdnet.com [206.16.6.208] with 32 bytes of data:

Reply from 206.16.6.208: bytes=32 time=83ms TTL=242
Reply from 206.16.6.208: bytes=32 time=73ms TTL=242
Reply from 206.16.6.208: bytes=32 time=91ms TTL=242

Ping statistics for 206.16.6.208:
    Packets: Sent = 3, Received = 3, Lost = 0 (0% loss),
Approximate round trip times in milli-seconds:
    Minimum = 73ms, Maximum = 91ms, Average = 82ms
```

If the host isn't active, instead of getting this report, you'll get the message "Request timed out."

If you enter a hostname, `ping` reports back with its IP address and then gives details about its four attempts to contact the host, a measurement of how long (in milliseconds) the packet took to make the round trip between your PC and the host, the TTL information about each packet, and a summary of its findings.

The TTL field can tell you how many hops the packets took to get from your PC to its destination. TTL initially specified the amount of time a packet could live, in seconds, before it expired, as a way to make sure packets didn't simply bounce around the Internet forever and create traffic jams. However, it can be reinterpreted to mean the maximum number of hops a packet will be allowed to take before it reaches its destination. The default number is 255. Each time a packet takes another hop, its TTL is reduced by one. The TTL number that `ping` reports is the packet's final TTL when it reaches its destination. To find out the number of hops a packet takes, subtract its initial TTL (by default, 255) from the TTL reported by `ping`. In our example, the packets took 13 hops to get to their destination.

You can use `ping` with switches, like so:

```
ping -a -l 45 208.201.239.237
```

This command changes the packet size sent from its default size of 32 bytes to 45 bytes, and resolves the IP address to a hostname; it lists the IP address's hostname in the output.

`ping` has a wide variety of useful switches that you can use for all kinds of troubleshooting. You use the basic `ping` command to check whether an Internet or network resource is live and to see if there are any delays in reaching it. But, as Table 5-2 shows, you can use `ping` and its switches for many other purposes as well—for example, to find out the IP address of a hostname, and vice versa.

Table 5-2. Useful ping switches

SWITCH	WHAT IT DOES
`-a`	Resolves an IP address to a hostname.
`-f`	Turns on the Don't Fragment flag for a packet. This lets you send packets that don't get broken up, and it can be useful when you want to test whether packets of a certain size are getting through.
`-i value`	Sets the value of the TTL field, using a number from `0` to `255`. When you use this option, note that the `ping` report will report back as if it were set to `255`. For example, if you set a TTL of `20`, and the packet takes 15 hops, the TTL value `ping` reports will be `240`.
`-l value`	Specifies the size of the ping message in bytes.
`-n count`	Specifies the number of ICMP Echo Request messages sent, instead of the default number of `4`.
`-r count`	Displays the IP addresses of the hops taken along the route to the destination. Specify a number between `1` and `9`. If the number of actual hops exceeds the number you specify, you will get a "Request timed out" message.
`-s count`	Displays a timestamp for the Echo Request and the Echo Reply Request for hops along the route. Specify a number between `1` and `4`. If the number of actual hops exceeds the number you specify, you will get a "Request timed out" message.
`-t`	Keeps sending the Echo Request message continually until stopped by pressing Ctrl-Break, Pause, or Ctrl-C.
`-w value`	The maximum amount of time (in milliseconds) to wait for an Echo Reply message for each Echo Request message before issuing a timeout message. The default is `4000` (4 seconds).

Trace Your Network and Internet Data Path with tracert

Frequently, you encounter a connection problem over your network or the Internet not because your final destination is down, but because there's a problem with a router somewhere between you and your final destination. For troubleshooting those kinds of problems, use `tracert`. It displays the path that data takes en route to the server or service you're trying to reach, either on your network or across the Internet. As with `ping`, it does this by sending ICMP Echo Request messages to the destination you're checking on. To use it, type `tracert destination` at a command prompt, where `destination` can be either an IP address or a hostname. Following is a typical response from a `tracert` command:

```
Tracing route to redir-zdnet.zdnet.com [206.16.6.208]
over a maximum of 30 hops:

  1     9 ms   11 ms    10 ms  10.208.128.1
  2     8 ms    8 ms     7 ms  bar02-p0-1.cmbrhe1.ma.attbb.net [24.128.8.53]
  3     9 ms    *       32 ms  bar03-p7-0.wobnhe1.ma.attbb.net [24.147.0.193]
  4     8 ms   14 ms     9 ms  12.125.39.213
  5    12 ms   10 ms     9 ms  gbr2-p70.cb1ma.ip.att.net [12.123.40.102]
  6    25 ms   26 ms    24 ms  gbr4-p80.cb1ma.ip.att.net [12.122.5.65]
  7    36 ms   39 ms    64 ms  gbr4-p40.cgcil.ip.att.net [12.122.2.49]
  8    33 ms   33 ms    48 ms  gbr3-p60.cgcil.ip.att.net [12.122.1.125]
  9    72 ms   80 ms    78 ms  gbr3-p30.sffca.ip.att.net [12.122.2.150]
 10    72 ms   77 ms    73 ms  idf26-gsr12-1-pos-6-0.rwc1.attens.net [12.122.255.222]
 11    76 ms   78 ms    79 ms  mdf3-bi4k-2-eth-1-1.rwc1.attens.net [216.148.209.66]
 12    73 ms   72 ms    74 ms  63.241.72.150
 13    72 ms   74 ms    71 ms  redir-zdnet.zdnet.com [206.16.6.208]
```

If the destination can't be reached, you will get the message "Destination unreachable."

As you can see, `tracert` shows the IP address and hostname address of each hop, along with timing data for each hop. If you're having problems on your network, this can help you locate the source of the problem; if a hop has a particularly long delay, you know that's the cause.

You can use several switches with `tracert`, like this:

```
tracert -d -h 45 zdnet.com
```

This command traces to zdnet.com, displaying only the IP addresses of each router and specifying a maximum number of 45 hops en route to the destination. Table 5-3 shows the most useful `tracert` switches.

Table 5-3. Useful tracert switches

SWITCH	WHAT IT DOES
-d	Does not display the hostname of each router
-h `value`	Sets a maximum number of hops for the trace to the destination
-w `value`	Sets the maximum amount of time in milliseconds to wait for a reply

Troubleshoot Network Problems with pathping

The `pathping` command works like a combination of `ping` and `tracert`. Type `pathping` from the command line, like this: `pathping target`, where `target` is either a hostname or an IP address—pop3.catalog.com or 209.217.46.121, for example. You then get a two-part report: first a list of every hop along the route to the destination, and then statistics about each hop, including the number of packets lost at each hop. It uses switches—for example:

```
pathping -n -w 1000 oreilly.com
```

This command tells pathping to not resolve the IP addresses of routers, and to wait one second (1,000 milliseconds) for an Echo Reply message. Table 5-4 lists the most important pathping switches.

Table 5-4. Useful pathping switches

SWITCH	WHAT IT DOES
-n	Does not display the hostname of each router.
-h value	Sets a maximum number of hops for the trace to the destination. The default is 30 hops.
-w value	Sets the maximum amount of time (in milliseconds) to wait for a reply.
-p	Sets the amount of time (in milliseconds) to wait before a new ping is issued. The default is 250.
-q value	Sets the number of ICMP Echo Request messages to transmit. The default is 100.

See Also

- "Troubleshoot Network Connections with netsh, netstat, and ipconfig" **[Hack #77]**

HACK 77: Troubleshoot Network Connections with netsh, netstat, and ipconfig

V XP Here are a few more command-line tools for tracking down problems with your network connection.

In addition to well-known command-line network utilities such as ping, tracert, and pathping **[Hack #76]**, three additional all-purpose utilities can help you troubleshoot network connections: netsh, netstat, and ipconfig.

Use netsh to Troubleshoot Network and Internet Connections in Windows XP

netsh is a wide-ranging command-line diagnostic tool that has an exceedingly large number of commands available. (For a complete list of available commands, use Windows XP Help and Support and search for netsh.) Here you'll learn the most interesting commands.

The most instructive of the netsh commands are the netsh diag commands. (Note that these are available in Windows XP, but not in Windows Vista.) Use them to find information about your PC's network setup, such as finding the IP address of its mail server, newsgroup server, DNS server, and similar resources.

There are two ways to use netsh: directly from the command line with all its switches, or first getting to the netsh console by typing netsh at the command line and then typing the command from the netsh> prompt that appears. For example, you could type netsh diag show adapter at the command line, which lists every network adapter on your PC, or you could get to the netsh> prompt and type diag show adapter.

Use the netsh command to connect to the resources and then get information about them. For example, to find the IP address of your DNS servers, type `netsh diag show dns`; to find the IP address of your mail server, type `netsh diag connect mail`.

Table 5-5 lists the most useful of the `netsh diag` commands. Precede each with `netsh diag`. Note that each one have many switches associated with them.

Table 5-5. Useful netsh diag commands

COMMAND	WHAT IT DOES
`connect ieproxy`	Establishes a connection to Internet Explorer's proxy server, if one exists
`connect mail`	Establishes a connection to the default Outlook Express mail server
`connect news`	Establishes a connection to the default Outlook Express newsgroup server
`ping adapter`	Establishes a connection with the named adapter
`ping dhcp`	Establishes a connection with a DHCP server
`show adapter`	Lists all the adapters on the PC
`show all`	Lists all the network objects defined for the local PC, such as adapters, network clients, servers, modems, and other objects
`show dhcp`	Lists all the DHCP servers for the specified adapter
`show dns`	Lists all the DNS servers for the specified adapter
`show gateway`	Lists all the gateways for the specified adapter

Use netstat to Get Information About Open Network Connections

If you want to get a snapshot of all incoming and outgoing network connections, use the `netstat` command. At a command prompt, type `netstat`. It lists all connections, including the protocol being used, the local and Internet addresses, and the current state of the connection, like this:

```
Active Connections
Proto  Local Address       Foreign Address        State
TCP    PrestonGralla:1031  localhost:2929         ESTABLISHED
TCP    PrestonGralla:2887  192.168.1.103:netbios-ssn  TIME_WAIT
TCP    PrestonGralla:2899  www.oreillynet.com:http  ESTABLISHED
TCP    PrestonGralla:2900  www.oreillynet.com:http  ESTABLISHED
TCP    PrestonGralla:2932  mail.attbi.com:pop3    ESTABLISHED
TCP    PrestonGralla:2936  vmms2.verisignmail.com:pop3  ESTABLISHED
```

It will help you know whether connections are live, the network or Internet device to which they're connected, and which local resource is making the connection. It's best suited for when you're troubleshooting network problems and want to find out whether certain ports are open, why certain computers on the network are having connection problems, and similar issues. You can use command-line switches with `netstat`. For example, you can display open ports and open connections with `netstat -a`. Table 5-6 lists `netstat` switches.

Table 5-6. Useful netstat switches

SWITCH	WHAT IT DOES
-a	Displays all open connections and ports.
-b	Displays the application (such as *firefox.exe*) responsible for the connection.
-e	Displays Ethernet statistics about packets transmitted and received. Can be combined with the -s switch.
-f	Vista only. Displays fully qualified domain names for remote addresses.
-n	Displays the addresses and ports in numeric, IP address form.
-o	Displays the process identifier (PID) that owns each connection.
-p proto	Displays the connections used by the protocol, which can be IP, IPv6, ICMP, ICMPv6, TCP, TCPv6, UDP, or UDPv6.
-r	Displays the network's routing table.
-s	Displays statistics for each protocol. It lists all statistics for all protocols, but you can list only those for a specified protocol if you combine it with the -p switch.
-t	Vista only. Displays current connection offload state.
-v	Used with -b. Displays DLLs along with application names.
interval value	Runs netstat repeatedly, pausing value seconds between each new display. To stop the display, press Ctrl-C.

Use ipconfig to Troubleshoot TCP/IP

One of the most powerful tools for analyzing and troubleshooting TCP/IP problems is the ipconfig command-line utility. It provides information about each of your adapters, including the assigned IP address, subnet mask, default gateway, MAC address, DNS servers, whether DHCP is enabled, and a variety of other data. To see basic information about your adapters, type ipconfig at a command prompt, and you'll see information like this:

```
Windows IP Configuration
Ethernet adapter Local Area Connection:
        Connection-specific DNS Suffix  . : ne1.client2.attbi.com
        Link-local IPv6 Address . . . . . : fe80::1569:46d4:f862:4837%8
        IPv4 Address. . . . . . . . . . . : 192.168.1.100
        Subnet Mask . . . . . . . . . . . : 255.255.255.0
        Default Gateway . . . . . . . . . : 192.168.1.1
```

As you can see, ipconfig provides basic information about your IP address, subnet mask, default gateway, and a connection-specific DNS suffix, if any. However, you can get much more detailed information using the /all switch, like this: ipconfig /all. For most troubleshooting purposes, use the /all switch. You get a much more comprehensive listing, as shown here:

```
Windows IP Configuration
        Host Name . . . . . . . . . . . . : PrestonGralla
        Primary Dns Suffix  . . . . . . . :
        Node Type . . . . . . . . . . . . : Mixed
        IP Routing Enabled. . . . . . . . : No
        WINS Proxy Enabled. . . . . . . . : No
Ethernet adapter Local Area Connection:
        Connection-specific DNS Suffix  . : ne1.client2.attbi.com
```

```
Description . . . . . . . . . . . : CNet PRO200WL PCI Fast Ethernet Adapter
Physical Address. . . . . . . . . : 00-08-A1-00-9F-32
Dhcp Enabled. . . . . . . . . . . : Yes
Autoconfiguration Enabled . . . . : Yes
IP Address. . . . . . . . . . . . : 192.168.1.100
Subnet Mask . . . . . . . . . . . : 255.255.255.0
Default Gateway . . . . . . . . . : 192.168.1.1
DHCP Server . . . . . . . . . . . : 192.168.1.1
DNS Servers . . . . . . . . . . . : 204.127.202.19
                                    216.148.227.79
Lease Obtained. . . . . . . . . . : Wednesday, June 27, 2007 9:11:29 AM
Lease Expires . . . . . . . . . . : Wednesday, July 04, 2007 9:11:29 AM
```

You can also use ipconfig to release and renew DHCP addresses, and to perform other troubleshooting functions as well. For example, to renew an adapter's IP address, use this command:

```
ipconfig /renew "adapter name"
```

where adapter name is the name of the adapter whose IP address you want to renew. Make sure to put quotes around the adapter name and use spaces if there is more than one word in the adapter name. Table 5-7 lists other switches you can use with ipconfig.

Table 5-7. Command-line switches for ipconfig

SWITCH	WHAT IT DOES
/all	Displays complete TCP/IP configuration information
/displaydns	Displays information from the DNS resolver cache **[Hack #51]**
/flushdns	Clears the DNS resolver cache
/registerdns	Refreshes all DHCP leases and reregisters DNS names
/release "adapter"	Releases the IPv4 address for the specified adapter
/renew "adapter"	Renews the IPv4 address for the specified adapter
/release6 "adapter"	Releases the IPv6 address for the specified adapter
/renew6 "adapter"	Renews the IPv6 address for the specified adapter
/setclassid "adapter" newclassid	Resets the DHCP Class ID for the specified adapter
/showclassid "adapter"	Displays the DHCP Class ID for the specified adapter

See Also

- "Troubleshoot Network Connections with ping, tracert, and pathping" **[Hack #76]**

VOIP HACKS

The Internet and home networks are increasingly used to place VoIP calls, for free or very low cost. There are many VoIP services available and many different kinds of VoIP software that let you call others. The most popular by far, though, is Skype (www.skype.com). This next section gives you a variety of VoIP hacks, mostly about how to hack Skype. If you haven't tried it yet, give it a try; it's free to download and install. You can make calls to other Skype users for free, and can make calls across the United States and the world for extremely low cost.

HACK 78: Prioritize Packets to Improve Voice Quality

V XP Voice traffic competes for available bandwidth on your broadband connection. If there is not enough bandwidth, packets get dropped.

Voice Over IP media streams require a constant, uninterrupted data flow. This data flow is composed of UDP packets that each carry between 10 and 30 milliseconds of sound information. Ideally, each packet in a media stream is evenly spaced and of the same size. In a perfect world, a packet never arrives out of sequence or gets dropped. VoIP media packets are framed in a highly precise, performance-sensitive way, described in more detail in *Switching to VoIP* (O'Reilly). Dropped packets and *packet jitter* (packets arriving out of order) cause problems—big problems—for an ongoing call. These problems can cause the voices on the call to sound robotic, to cut in and out, or to go silent altogether.

Most of the packet-drop problems you encounter while VoIPing are the fault of your bandwidth-limited ISP connection—the link from the ISP's network to your broadband router. If you're downloading songs to your iPod, surfing the O'Reilly Network, and patching your *World of Warcraft* client all at once, you won't have enough bandwidth left over to support a VoIP call, but there's a way to curb all those applications' thirst for bandwidth so that you can still VoIP successfully. Read on.

To maximize call quality, the network connection carrying VoIP media packets must be as reliable and consistent as possible. The data link to the ISP should treat all voice media traffic with *high priority*. That is, a VoIP packet gets handled first, as it is more important than another packet—say, for your BitTorrent upload. If the data link is swamped and is out of capacity to carry any more data, less important packets are discarded before more important ones. The net result—for high-priority services such as voice—is better Quality of Service, or QoS. Several standards exist to ensure that QoS can occur in a broadband VoIP setup, chief among them: Type of Service (ToS) and 802.1p.

If your broadband router is relatively new, it might support these standards, so that enabling packet prioritization is just a matter of flipping some configuration switches.

Prioritize Packets on a Linksys Broadband Router

ToS is a feature of Ethernet switches that permits packets tagged as high priority to be handled first, maximizing their QoS. 802.1p is a similar concept, but tends to hang around on routers, not switches. The Linksys BEFSR81 broadband router is a device that supports 802.1p. It sells for less than $100 USD online, and you can probably find one secondhand on eBay for even less.

In fact, setting up priorities on this router is a snap, thanks to Linksys' usual snazzy web-based interface. Once you get the router unboxed and hooked up, use the web interface to locate the QoS screen. (You'll see it after you click on the Advanced Configuration button and the QoS tab.)

The QoS screen contains two sections: one that allows you to establish queuing priorities for packets depending on their TCP/UDP port numbers, and one that allows you to alter the queuing priority depending upon which Ethernet switch port the traffic originated from. That is, since this router has a built-in switch, you can prioritize some of its eight Ethernet ports using the lower half of the QoS screen.

If your current router doesn't offer QoS features, you may be able to upgrade its firmware to DD-WRT open source software **[Hack #97]**. In addition to offering QoS capabilities, the software also allows you to set your VoIP application to receive the highest priority when routing packets.

Prioritize RTP Traffic

Most VoIP media streams are carried by Real-time Transport Protocol (RTP) packets. To raise the priority of RTP traffic, enter the port numbers 5004 and 5005, each on its own line, in the section labeled "Application-based QoS," and click on the High Priority radio button for each. After restarting the router, all RTP traffic sent from the router will be handled before any other traffic. This technique is especially good if your LAN has multiple VoIP devices that send media streams through the router.

Prioritize All the Traffic from Your VoIP ATA

If you have only a single VoIP device to support, it might be best if you tell the router to prioritize traffic by Ethernet port instead of by application, as in the preceding paragraph. Specifically, you want your router to prioritize traffic that comes from the Ethernet port to which your ATA is connected. To do so, use the High Priority and Low Priority radio buttons for the numbered Ethernet ports. Set them up however you want, and reboot the router.

Prioritize All the Traffic from an Attached Ethernet Switch

By setting the priority of a particular Ethernet port, you are telling the router to prioritize anything from the device connected on this port, even if this device is another switch. So, an easy way to give priority to all your dedicated VoIP devices, such as IP phones and ATAs, is to connect them all to the same switch and then connect that switch to a high-priority Ethernet port on the router.

Prioritize Traffic on a Standalone Switch

Many workgroup Ethernet switches offer QoS features that used to be found only on advanced "managed" switches. These days, inexpensive switches like the NETGEAR GS605 provide support for ToS and 802.1p. By placing such a switch between your broadband router and your VoIP device, with voice traffic prioritized, you can ensure that outbound voice streams get sent to your broadband router before anything else.

What Happens When VoIP Passes Your Router

Unfortunately, no matter how well prioritized and orderly your VoIP media traffic is when it's forwarded by your broadband router, it still might get slowed down, ripped up, and otherwise tattered as it makes its way across the Internet. The same is true of media packets that come from the Internet to your router—the packets carrying the voice of the person speaking to you. Because you're *receiving*—not transmitting—those packets, you can't really prioritize them. That's the responsibility of the routers that carried the packet to your router, and many routers on the Net these days are ignorant of QoS.

In short, you can control traffic sent from your network, but not traffic sent from other networks to yours. At first blush, this sounds like a threat to broadband VoIP, but over the last few years, many have discovered that the outbound traffic is all you really need to prioritize to ensure success with a broadband TSP. This is because most broadband ISPs limit the amount of outbound (upstream) bandwidth available to each customer to discourage customers from hosting high-traffic services on their residential broadband connections.

So, there's usually less available bandwidth for sending than for receiving. The VoIP media stream most likely to suffer as a result is the outbound stream, the one carrying your voice to the person on the other end of the call. As such, it's appropriate to prioritize outbound traffic to make up for the limits many ISPs force on outbound bandwidth.

See Also

- "Improve Skype Service Quality" **[Hack #82]**

— *Theodore Wallingford, from* VoIP Hacks

HACK 79: Sound Like Darth Vader While You VoIP

V XP Using Audio Voice Cloak, you can sound like Darth Vader—or like Alvin and the Chipmunks—while you talk online.

Star Wars Episode III: Revenge of the Sith hit the screens right around the time I first tried this hack. When I filed into the very first midnight screening of the movie at my local cineplex, I was particularly excited by the prospect of again hearing the voice of the galaxy's most dysfunctional father. There's just something about James Earl Jones and the flange effect.

After all, who hasn't looked into a mirror in a private moment and said, "*I* am your father!" a few times? OK, maybe you're not as big a Star Wars geek as I am, but if you are a closet Wookiee lover, I've got the perfect hack for you to use the next time you chat with fellow fans.

If you think spy movies are cooler than *Star Wars* movies, you can also use this hack to make yourself sound like one of those disguised-voice phone informants that sound a lot like, well, Darth Vader.

Gold Software's nifty voice-changing tool, Blaze Audio Voice Cloak, lets you tweak your speaking voice, adding pitch shifting, EQ, echo, and other sound effects in real time (Figure 5-29). If you have Windows, you're in luck. Download and install it from www.gold-software.com/download5903.html. Launch it and, after the shareware commercial, you'll be able to click the Voice Effects button to reveal all of the sound-altering controls available to you. The program uses the default microphone input, so if you're using a nonstandard microphone channel for your telephony or online chat, you'll need to click the Recording Source button and select the right input.

While you tinker with the software's settings, you can monitor yourself with the aptly titled Monitor Your Voice button. Beware: you'd better put on a pair of headphones, or you'll get feedback.

To get the most authentic Vader imitation (short of hiring Ben Burtt, the famed sound effects guru from Lucasfilm), you'll want a slightly southerly pitch shift (drag the pitch slider down a notch or two) and a flange effect (click the Flange Off button to toggle it on). Finally, click the Center button on the Equalization panel to flatten (or "reset") the equalizer. Then, monitor your speech to hear how you sound. You should have the familiar, convincing tone of a half-machine Sith Lord.

Figure 5-29.
Audio Voice Cloak's main interface

Now, fire up your Yahoo! chat client, or AIM and surf on over to the closest chat room. Since AVC passes the modified audio through in real time, you can chat live as Darth, or you can raise the pitch shift to sound like a chipmunk. And don't discount the immaturity factor: if you have kids who chat with their buddies online, this could be a lot of fun!

— *Theodore Wallingford, from* VoIP Hacks

HACK 80: Record VoIP Calls

V XP Want to record your VoIP calls? You'll need a little outside software assistance.

If you constantly forget things (which I do), or you're a private investigator (which I'm not), you might have wondered how to record calls so that you can listen to them later. Recording calls on traditional phones and IP phones is a simple matter of analog electronics, but recording softphone and instant-messenger voice calls is another matter entirely. Of course, you can set an old-fashioned tape recorder on your desk and press the Record button, but come on! In our digital world, there's got to be a better way, right?

Of course there is. You can find a handful of useful recorder apps at www.download.com and www.downloadsquad.com that can record WAV files and MP3s from any sound input or output on your Windows PC. One such application is Total Recorder (www.totalrecorder.com) (see Figure 5-30) developed by High Criteria. In its default configuration, Total Recorder will record only the output (the person on the other end of the call), not your voice.

To alleviate this, click Total Recorder's Recording Source and Parameters button, and then check the "Record also input stream" checkbox. This way, your recording will be sure to contain both sides of the call. The "Remove silence" checkbox will enable a feature that doesn't save moments of silence into the recording. This might be useful if you record a ton of calls and review them regularly, as waiting through unneeded silence would certainly slow this process and use up more hard-disk space.

A real time-saver is found by checking "Convert using Recording Parameters specified below" and then clicking the Change button. In the dialog window that appears, you can adjust the sound

Figure 5-30.
Total Recorder can save audio recordings from MSN Messenger, Yahoo! Messenger, AIM, Skype—you name it

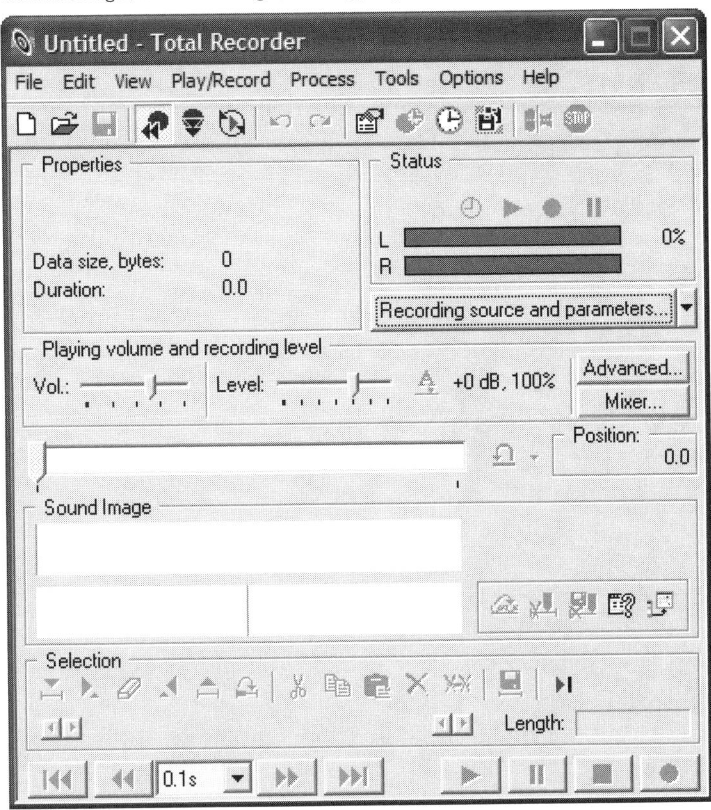

resolution and the output format. Just about every sound codec you'd want is supported, from Windows Media to MP3.

— *Theodore Wallingford, from* VoIP Hacks

HACK 81: Make Skype Work with Personal Firewalls

V XP Skype is rather good at working with firewalls without the need for any additional configuration, but sometimes it needs a little help.

Many VoIP applications simply don't work from behind a firewall or Network Address Translation device. And many, if not most, broadband Internet users operate from behind one or the other, or both!

Skype does a good job of transcending these barriers to communication, mostly without any additional configuration, but Skype is not foolproof in this respect. This hack will help you if you're having problems getting Skype to work from behind a firewall.

Firewall problems are most often signaled by Skype error #1102, "Skype cannot be started;" though #1101, 'No connection," and #1103, 'No connection," are also common. These errors mean that your Internet connection is down or misconfigured, you are behind a restrictive firewall or proxy that is

Figure 5-31.
Telnet prompt

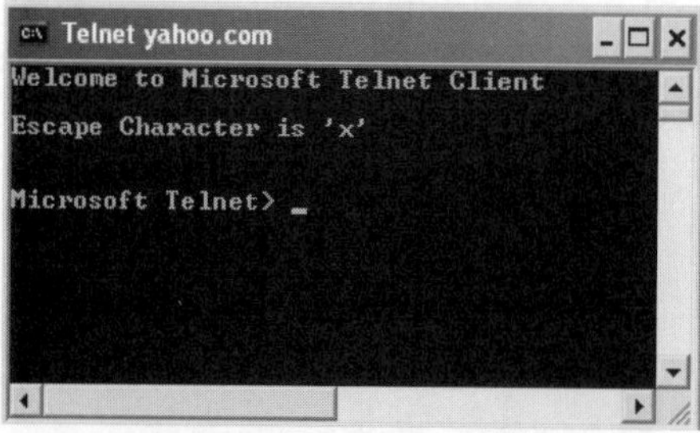

blocking Skype's access to the Internet, or your network or Internet service provider is somehow blocking Skype.

To learn more about the nature of your Internet connection, and how it might be blocking Skype, you can try these tests:

Other Peer-to-Peer (P2P) applications
Are other P2P-type applications also blocked? If the answer is yes, it's likely that your firewall is blocking all P2P-type traffic, including Skype. Otherwise, it is more likely that the problem is a network problem specific to Skype.

Telnet
From a command or shell prompt, enter telnet -ex yahoo.com 80. If the screen goes blank, enter 'x", and you should be greeted with a telnet prompt (see Figure 5-31). If you are, it means that you are able to make direct connections over the network without needing a proxy, so you likely have a Skype-specific Internet connection problem.

Broadly speaking, there are two types of firewall: those implemented in software that run on your desktop machine, and those implemented as part of some piece of network hardware (router, proxy, etc.). First, I'll discuss the general requirements for all types of firewall needed for Skype to work, and then I'll discuss software firewalls and hardware firewalls in turn.

At a minimum, Skype requires unrestricted access to outgoing *Transmission Control Protocol* (TCP) ports above 1024, or to ports 80 and 443. Skype prefers the former but can live with the latter. Skype's voice quality and functionality will be improved if, in addition, your firewall is open for two-way *User Datagram Protocol* (UDP) traffic on all ports above 1024. These are the first things you should check.

 Whether Skype should try to use TCP ports 80 and 443 is controlled through its options. Select Skype→Tools→Options...→Connection.

When Skype is installed, it randomly chooses a port above 1024 on which to listen for incoming traffic. You can inspect the port Skype has chosen on your machine by selecting Tools→Options...→Connection. If you don't want to open up all ports above 1024 for Skype, you can open only the specific port Skype has chosen for TCP and/or UDP traffic.

Software firewalls run on your machine and monitor incoming and outgoing Internet traffic for malicious activity. Moreover, applications that connect to the Internet from your machine are also monitored and, indeed, are usually blocked from connecting until you give them explicit permission. Windows XP (SP2) and Windows Vista come with their own firewalls that are turned on by default. Several firewall applications are available from independent vendors and from open source projects.

 When you upgrade Skype to a newer version, this may be detected by your firewall, and you may be prompted to give permission again for Skype to access the Internet.

Skype has a number of user guides for configuring the following popular software-only firewalls that run on Windows:

- Windows XP SP2 Firewall
- Norton Personal Firewall
- ZoneAlarm Pro
- McAfee Firewall Pro

You can find these guides at www.skype.com/help/guides/firewall.html.

Giving advice on configuring hardware-based firewalls is problematic because of the sheer variety of equipment in existence. Really, the advice comes down to opening the correct ports for Skype to use and making sure that port 80, if used, is not configured to pass only *HyperText Transport Protocol* (HTTP) traffic. Skype doesn't use HTTP. For the specifics of how to open ports and filter protocols, you will have to refer to the documentation for your firewall hardware.

Another known issue arises when your machine becomes a Skype super node, which is something over which you have no control. Super nodes are regular Skype clients that change their behavior, and in the process consume more network resources, to make Skype's global network work properly. Without super nodes, Skype would not work as well as it does, or perhaps not at all. But this may be of little comfort if *you* are one of the super nodes! The problem arises when a super node has so many incoming network requests—specifically, large numbers of TCP connections—that your router/firewall is overwhelmed. This is particularly true if your hardware has fairly minimal onboard processing power.

See Also

- Additional guidance on router/firewall configuration is available at www.skype.com/security/guide-for-network-admins.pdf.

— *Andrew Sheppard, from* Skype Hacks

HACK 82: Improve Skype Service Quality

V XP Supporting several Skype users on the same outgoing Internet connection may require implementation of bandwidth rationing (per user) using Quality of Service (QoS) to maintain good call quality.

The Internet is a shared resource, even for a single user. Web browsing, file downloads, streaming audio, and Skype calls are all vying for use of the data pipe. When several machines share the same Internet connection, this conflict over how bandwidth is shared among the competing users can be exacerbated. Certain activities, such as file downloads, are not bandwidth or latency critical in the sense that a slow file download is still a file download! In contrast, for VoIP applications such as Skype, being squeezed for bandwidth and latency by other applications might result in poor call quality.

Clearly, some way to prioritize Internet traffic is needed so that VoIP data packets get precedence over all other types of data packet. This is the goal of QoS, which seeks—in advance—to guarantee a certain level of service in terms of bandwidth and latency, plus other secondary characteristics, such as error rates. In this hack, I'll focus only on QoS for bandwidth and latency. Improving bandwidth and latency for Skype VoIP traffic will always improve voice-call quality.

What makes QoS difficult in the case of Skype is that it doesn't use any fixed port numbers for outgoing traffic. QoS normally works by binding the port numbers used by an application to a QoS feature built into the router **[Hack #78]**, which then takes care of prioritizing traffic for those fixed ports. However, for the outgoing part of a call, Skype uses available ports above and including 1024; that is, it randomly selects the UDP and/or TCP ports it needs between and including port numbers 1024 and 65535. QoS typically needs fixed ports to operate, so traditional QoS doesn't work for Skype.

However, it is possible to set up a "QoS-like" service for Skype by selectively rationing bandwidth.

For a single user, one way of setting up a QoS-like service is to use a bandwidth-shaping tool such as NetLimiter (www.NetLimiter.com/). Using such a tool, you can divvy up your available bandwidth among the applications running on your computer that require Internet bandwidth. Specifically, you can make sure there's always enough bandwidth left over for Skype to work, and work well in terms of call quality.

Let's look at a concrete example. Figure 5-32 shows the available Internet bandwidth for a machine. Let's play it safe, and say that there's 1,400 Kbps of available bandwidth, both uplink and downlink. If we reserve, say, 250 Kbps for Skype, that means we can allocate the remaining 1,150 Kbps of bandwidth among the remaining applications running on the machine that require Internet access. Using a tool such as NetLimiter, you can do this very easily. With the limits shown in Figure 5-33, no matter what else is being done on the machine, there should always be enough bandwidth left over for Skype to work well.

For multiple machines and users that share an Internet connection, you can put a similar method of budgeting and bandwidth rationing in place by using nothing more than simple arithmetic and by running NetLimiter on each machine. That way, no matter what any machine is doing in terms of accessing the Internet, no Skype call will be squeezed out, so to speak, and good call quality can be maintained for all users.

Hacking the Hack

Measuring, budgeting, and enforcing bandwidth limits with a tool such as NetLimiter can become tedious and a less-than-optimal way to manage your overall bandwidth when more than a handful of machines are involved. Fortunately, network devices are coming onto the market that effectively implement QoS in hardware by prioritizing Internet traffic based on monitoring data packet characteristics, rather than using fixed port numbers.

Such devices sit between your router and your broadband Internet connection and divide Internet traffic into streams of packets having different characteristics. Then, they give priority to those packets whose delivery is time-sensitive, such as the VoIP packets Skype uses. Best of all, these devices are Plug and Play (PnP), requiring little or no user configuration.

Hawking Technology claims its HBB1 Broadband Booster provides improvements of up to 400%, in terms of uplink throughput, for certain types of applications that use the Internet. The HBB1 improves upstream traffic only, and does not differentiate between different machines or applications, so you can't fine-tune Internet traffic prioritization as you can with tools such as NetLimiter. It is worth remembering that most asymmetric broadband Internet connections (especially cable and DSL, but also cellular connections such as EVDO) have substantially less uplink bandwidth than downlink bandwidth, so the HBB1's focus on upstream traffic improvement makes sense. These units do work and are an inexpensive method for implementing QoS for a group of Skype users that share a Digital Subscriber Line (DSL) or cable broadband connection.

— *Andrew Sheppard, from* Skype Hacks

Figure 5-32.
Available bandwidth as measured by www.speedtest.net

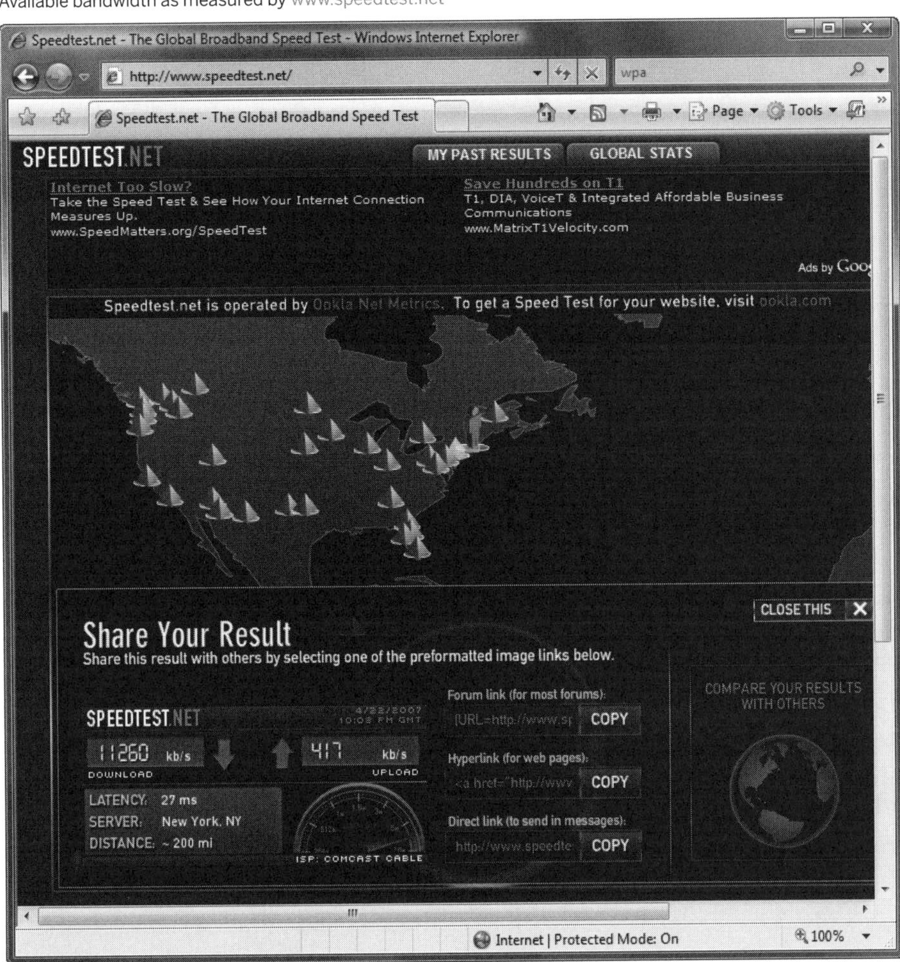

Figure 5-33.
Using NetLimiter to ration bandwidth

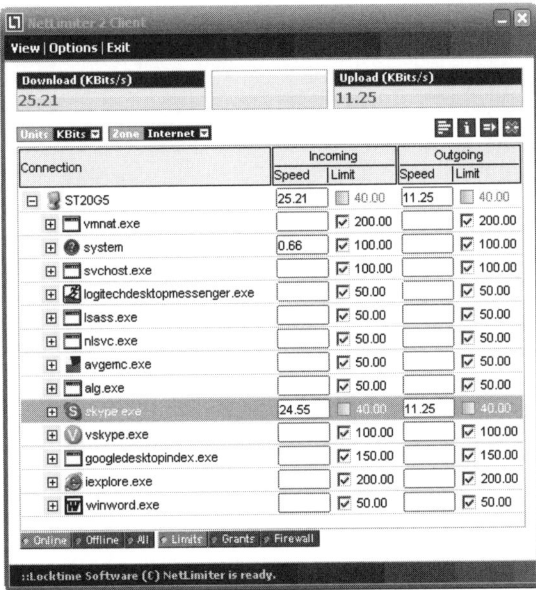

HACK 83: Automatically Forward Skype Voicemail

V XP Have all incoming voicemail forwarded to an email address of your choice as soon as it arrives.

This is one of those features you feel sure should be built into Skype, but isn't. Until it is, you'll need a Skype add-on to do the job, and for automatically forwarding all your voicemail to an email address, there is no better tool than Pamela Professional (€17.50, about $22, from www.pamela-systems.com).

Skype uses a proprietary and undocumented (outside of Skype, at least) format for its voicemail audio files, which have a *.dat* file extension and can normally be found in this folder: *C:\Documents and Settings*`Username`*\Application Data\Skype*`Skypename`*\voicemail*, where `Username` is the name used to log on to the machine, and `Skypename` is the name used to log on to Skype. This is unfortunate, as it means you cannot easily listen to, archive, or exchange Skype voicemail outside of Skype.

Setting up voicemail forwarding in Pamela is simplicity itself. Select Pamela→Tools→Options→Email forwarding, and set up how, and to what email address, you want your voicemail forwarded (see Figure 5-34).

Pamela forwards your voicemail as *.wav* files, which you can play easily by opening them (in your default player for *.wav* files, for example Windows Media Player) from directly within the received email (see Figure 5-35), or by saving them to disk for later. Just right-click on the *.wav* file attachment and choose Open or Save As.

Pamela uses a format for the name of the attached voicemail audio file that tells you a good deal about who left you voicemail, and when. Its format is *msg_*`skypename_dd_mmm_yyyy_hh_mm_ss.wav`, where `skypename` is the name of the Skype user who left the voicemail, `dd_mm_yyyy` is the date on which the voicemail was left, and `hh_mm_ss` is the time at which the voicemail was left.

— *Andrew Sheppard, from* Skype Hacks

Figure 5-34.
Setting up voicemail forwarding using Pamela

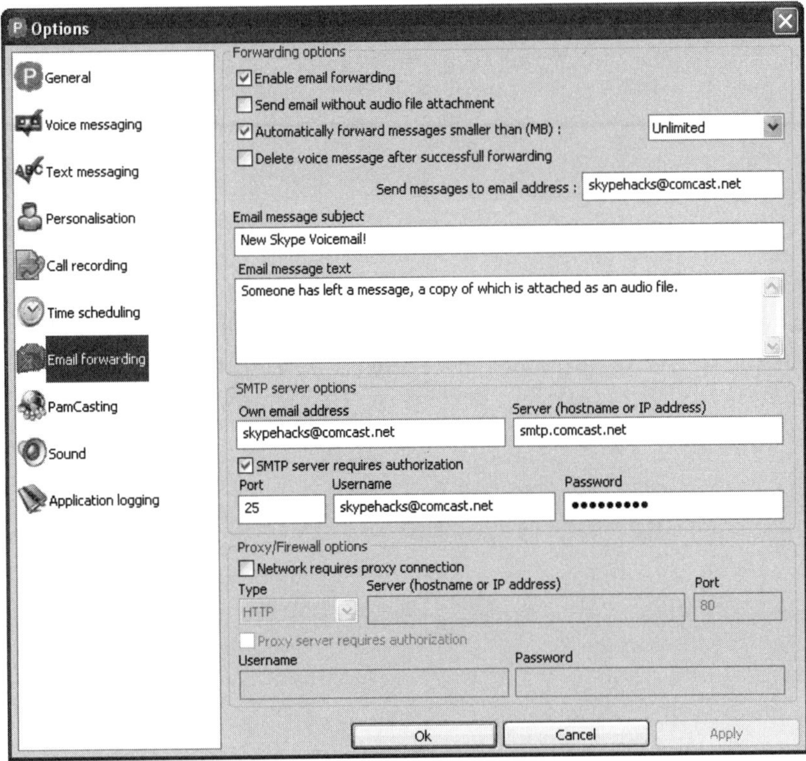

Figure 5-35.
Playing voicemail (in this case, using RealPlayer) forwarded by Pamela, directly from the email message

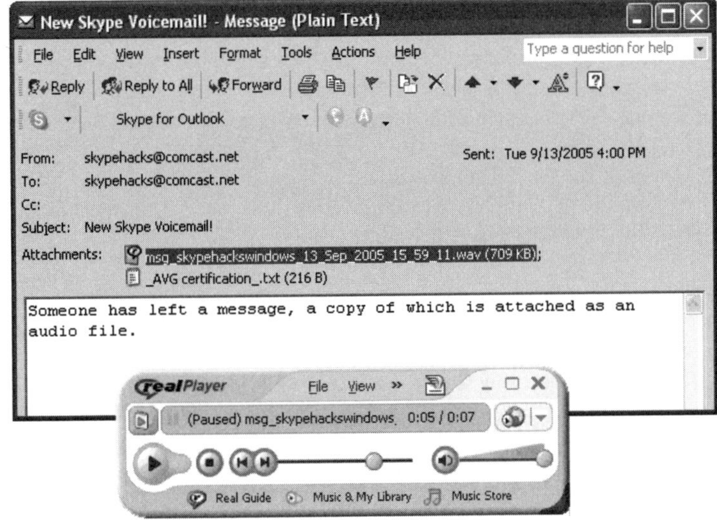

06 EMAIL

Email—can't live with it, can't live without it. Can you name another technology that has so dramatically changed the way we communicate? It makes it immeasurably easier to keep in touch with friends and family, and to do business. And it makes life extremely annoying . . . just think of spam.

The odds are that you're not getting the most out of your email. Spam may bedevil you, Outlook may block you from getting attachments, and if you're a Gmail user, you spend too much time doing unnecessary tasks.

This chapter shows you how to hack Gmail, Outlook, Outlook Express and more, and tells you how to fight spam. And there's plenty more as well.

HACK 84: Instantly Compress Files You Send via Email

V XP Got fat files you need to send via email? Here's a way to zip them in a snap.

When it comes to big files via email, your Internet service provider (ISP) is not your friend. Try to send a file or group of files as attachments over a certain file size, and your ISP or corporate email system will not let you send it—or else the recipient's email system will refuse to accept it.

What to do? Compress the files using built-in ZIP compression. But doing that can be a tiring process. First find the files, then zip them, then open Outlook, Outlook Express, or Windows Mail, then send the attachment. You've got better things to do with your life.

There's a way, however, to zip them in a single stop, from right within Outlook, Outlook Express, or Windows Mail, or your email program. It works in Windows XP as well as Windows Vista.

Create your email message as you would normally. Click the attachment icon, highlight all the files you want to send, and right-click the group (or the single file, if you're sending only one). Then select Send To→Compressed (zipped) Folder, as shown in Figure 6-1. The files will be zipped, and the ZIP file will be given the name of the first file in the group. Rename it if you want. Then select the ZIP file, click Insert, and send it on its merry way.

See Also

- "Shrink Supersized Pictures in Office Docs" [Hack #124]

Figure 6-1.
Compressing a group of files in Outlook before sending them

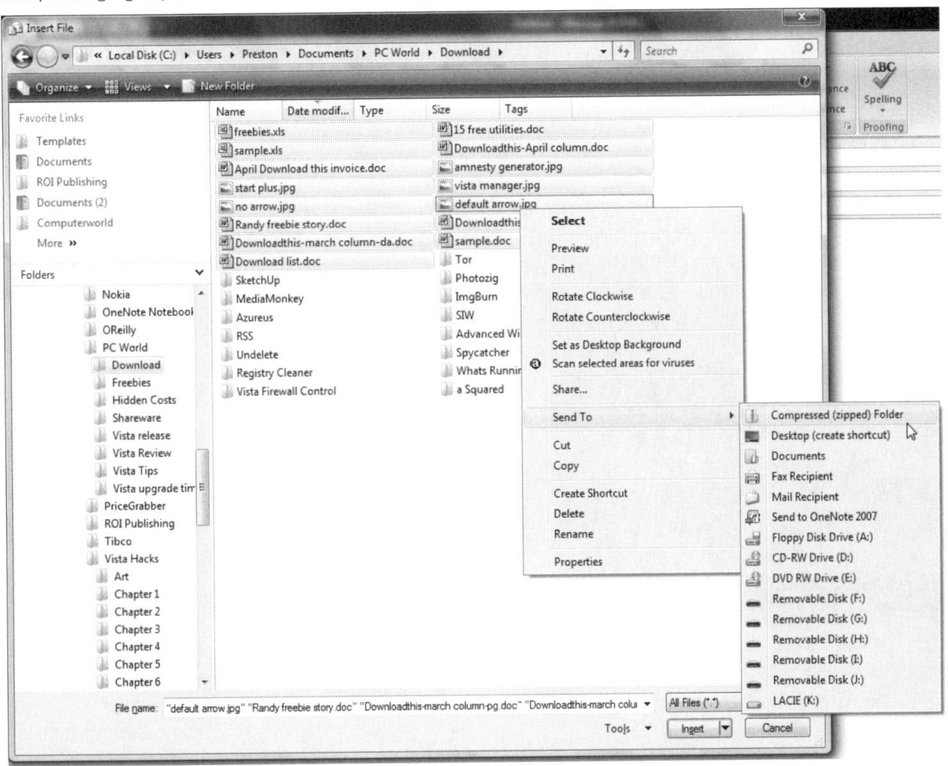

HACK 85: Put Your Bloated Outlook Mailbox On a Diet

V XP Email mailboxes very quickly grow to massive proportions. But with a few simple steps, you can reduce the size of a bloated Outlook mailbox.

With all the email you send and receive, and considering the size of your attachments, your Outlook mailbox can very quickly grow to an alarming size. As a general rule, Outlook mailboxes come in one of three sizes: Too Large, Way too Large, and Bloated Beyond Belief.

If you're like me, yours is Bloated Beyond Belief. Sizes of 400 MB or more aren't at all uncommon.

This hack applies to Outlook 2003 and Outlook 2007.

When this happens, you're not only taking up precious disk space. You're also hurting your PC's performance. Outlook can take a long time to load, and if you use Windows Vista, you could be slowing down overall search because you're clogging up the search index.

You can, however, put your bloated Outlook mailbox on a diet and slim it down. First, see how large it is. Outlook stores its data in *.pst* files, and by default the main Outlook data file is *Outlook.pst*. In Windows Vista you'll find the file in *C:\Users*`username`*\AppData\Local\Microsoft\Outlook*, where `username` is your account name. In Windows XP, it's in *C:\Documents and Settings*`username`*\Application Data\Microsoft\Outlook*. Look at the file size to see just how bloated it has become.

Now it's time to do the slimming. Select Tools→Mailbox Cleanup, and the screen shown in Figure 6-2 appears. Think of it as Outlook's diet center.

First, find out where the fat is. Click View Mailbox Size, and the screen shown in Figure 6-3 appears. That shows you the size of all your Outlook folders. This way, you can see which folder is most bloated. Using that information, you can go to your largest folders and delete as many files from there as possible.

A major cause of mailbox bloat is attachments. Graphics, PowerPoint slides, videos, audio files—all of these contribute to Outlook obesity. Select "Find items larger than..." and choose a file size, then click find. A screen appears that lists all emails that are that size or larger. Unfortunately, they're not grouped by size, but you can easily regroup them so that the largest files are on top. Grab the edge of the Size column and move it to the right, until you reveal the entire width of the column. Then click the Size heading. You'll reorder all the files in order of descending size, with the largest on top (Figure 6-4). You can now scroll through them, starting with the largest, deleting any that you no longer need. If you want to fine-tune your search for large files, you can use the search tools at the top of the screen, so that you can find large files by date, sender, day and time, and so on.

After you do that, get back to the screen shown in Figure 6-2. You can search for old files by selecting "Find items older than..." typing in the age of emails you want to find, and clicking Find. You can then delete older emails you no longer need.

The screen also lets you empty your deleted items folder and delete any duplicate emails.

Be wary of the AutoArchive button. When you click it, Outlook archives old email, without any kind of warning. Archiving files doesn't actually shrink your total Outlook file size; it only moves older files to an Archive folder. So although it shrinks the size of your *Outlook.pst* file, it creates an *Archive.pst* file, and you haven't really shrunk anything. To find your archived files, look in the folders underneath Outlook's *Archive Folders*.

Figure 6-2.
Here's Outlook's diet center

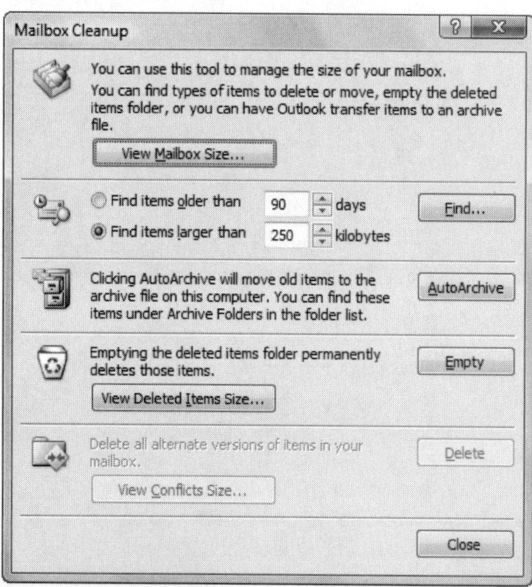

Emails in your archived folders will be deleted on a schedule set by Outlook. If you don't want older files automatically deleted, you should turn off that feature. To do it, choose Tools→Options→Other and click AutoArchive. From there, you can change the settings that automatically delete files.

Figure 6-3.
Finding the largest folders in Outlook

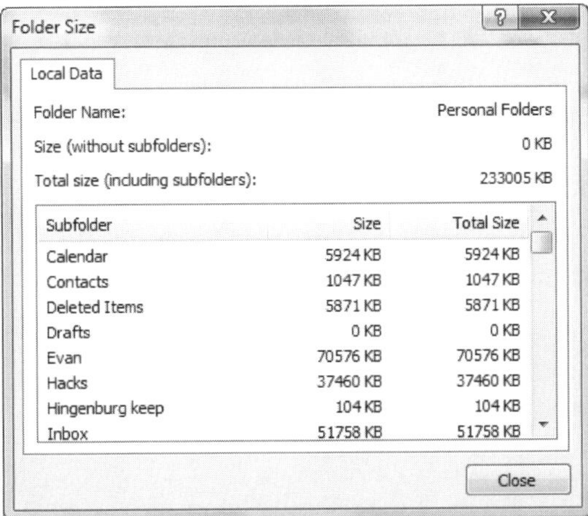

Figure 6-4.
Finding the largest attachments in Outlook

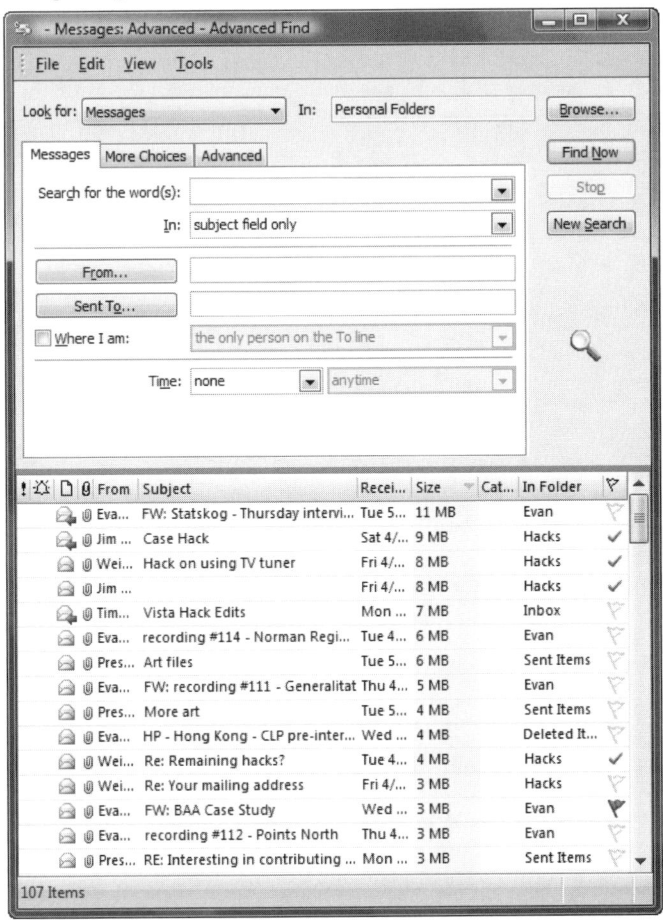

AutoArchive causes another problem as well: it makes it harder to search your mailbox. Let's say you want to find an email you've sent. Normally, you could just go to your Sent folder, and search for files there. But if those files have been archived, they won't be found. You'll also have to go to *Archive Folders\Sent*, and search from there as well. That doubles the amount of time you'll spend searching.

Outlook 2007 also includes a very quick and handy way to find files with large attachments so you can delete them. Go to Search Folders, and then click the "Larger than 100 KB" folder. You'll see all large emails, sorted by size, with the largest at the top. Simply delete any you don't want.

HACK 86: Stay Off Spam Lists

V XP When it comes to spam, prevention is the best cure. Simple steps can keep you off spam lists.

Unless you enjoy getting lots of mail from friendly Nigerian millionaires willing to share the wealth, or really *do* want to enlarge certain very private body parts, you'd like to stay away from spam. Sure, built-in spam filters in Outlook and other email software help, as does third-party anti-spam software. But no matter how good they are, spam will always get through.

There's no way to avoid spam, but there are ways to cut down on the amount you receive. And one of the best ways to do that is to stay off spam lists in the first place.

How do you end up on spam lists? The most common way, according to a comprehensive study done by the Center for Democracy & Technology, is that your email address is "harvested" by spammers who use programs to automatically scan web pages and gather email addresses from them. Those addresses are then sold to other spammers. The result: you're targeted by dozens of spam lists.

To stay off spam lists, try and keep your email address out of the public eye. If possible, don't put your email address on a public web site. If you post to Usenet newsgroups, don't use your real email address: you can instead get a free account at any of the free mail sites such as Yahoo, Hotmail or Gmail, and use those to post.

However, if there's a reason that you need to have your email address on a public web site, you can hide your address from spammers, even when it's in plain view.

At one time, you could get away with spelling out your email address—for example, you could write "preston at gralla dot com" instead of *preston@gralla.com*. Automated harvesting programs weren't smart enough to grab your address that way.

But times have changed, and some spammers have figured out ways to get around it. So another solution is to use inline JavaScript to generate your email address when the web page loads. Spam harvester bots see only a `<script>` tag, but users see *bob@bob.com*. Here's an example of the code you can pop in:

```
<script type="text/javascript" language="javascript">
<!--
  {
    document.write(String.fromCharCode(60,97,32,104,114,101,102,61,
    34,109,97,105,108,116,111,58,98,111,98,64,98,111,98,46,99,111,
    109,34,62,98,111,98,64,98,111,98,46,99,111,109,60,47,97,62))
  }
//-->
```

```
</script>
<noscript>
<a href = "mailto:%62%6F%62%40%62%6F%62%2E%63%6F%6D">email me</a>
</noscript>
```

To get your own bit of code so that your name is spelled out, go to the JavaScript generator from www.u.arizona.edu/~trw/spam/spam.htm. Feed it your email address, and it generates the JavaScript, ready for you to use.

Another solution is to use HTML characters for your address rather than plain-text characters. That way, a person who visits the page can see the email address, because HTML translates the underlying code into a readable address, but an automated harvester won't be able to read it (unless the author of that harvester is reading this book). To use HTML characters, you need to use the ANSI characters and precede each character by &#. Separate each HTML character by a (;) and leave no spaces between characters. So, for example, in HTML, the *preston@gralla.com* address would be:

```
&#112;&#114;&#101;&#115;&#116;&#111;&#110;&#64;&#103;&#114;&#97;&#108;&#108;&#97;&#46;&#099;&#111;
&#109
```

Keep in mind, though, that if you use HTML characters to spell out your email address, you won't be able to put HTML `mailto:` links; that requires the text to be actually spelled out rather than using HTML characters. One solution is to use an email form that doesn't expose your email address, although spambots have found workarounds for this as well. A better solution is to use what is called a CAPTCHA for the form, which requires that someone type in a response to a question in order to complete the task. Whenever you visit a site that asks you type in text displayed on a page, that's a CAPTCHA. A number of sites offer free CAPTCHA services, including captchas.net and recaptcha.net (and by using reCAPTCHA, you're helping to digitize scanned books).

Table 6-1 lists common ANSI codes that you'll need for most email addresses.

Table 6-1. Common ANSI codes

A	65	N	78	a	97	n	110	@	64
B	66	O	79	b	98	o	111	.	46
C	67	P	80	c	99	p	112	0	48
D	68	Q	81	d	100	q	113	1	49
E	69	R	82	e	101	r	114	3	51
F	70	S	83	f	102	s	115	4	52
G	71	T	84	g	103	t	116	5	53
H	72	U	85	h	104	u	117	6	54
I	73	V	86	i	105	v	118	7	55
J	74	W	87	j	106	w	119	8	56
K	75	X	88	k	107	x	120	9	57
L	76	Y	89	l	108	y	121		
M	77	Z	90	m	109	z	122		

For a more comprehensive list of ANSI codes and special HTML characters, go to www.alanwood.net/demos/ansi.html.

QUICK HACK

USE A DISPOSABLE EMAIL ADDRESS FOR SITE REGISTRATIONS

Many sites require that you register before you can view their content, and in order to complete the registration process, you'll have to click a link sent to you via email. The problem with this is that some sites then spam you with messages or sell your address to others who may bombard you with unwanted email. The solution: use a disposable email address from BugMeNot that you use only for that link, and that doesn't get sent to your real mail address. When you have to register for a site, use an email address that ends in @bugmenot.com, such as thisonen@bugmenot.com. Then go to email.bugmenot.com, type in the address, and you'll be able to read, and click on, the email sent to you. Note that the emails sent to you at the disposable address stay live for only 24 hours, so make sure to check it within a day of when you register for a site.

HACK 87: Prevent Your Newsletter from Being Blocked as Spam

V XP Your newsletter is important, so make sure that it isn't treated like spam.

Spam has become so much of a problem that ISPs and mail providers such as Google and Yahoo! use spam filters that kill much spam before it ever reaches your inbox. This is a good thing, unless you have a newsletter you send out to customers, friends, or family, and it gets blocked as spam. Making matters even more difficult for newsletter writers is that even if the newsletter makes it through ISP spam filters, spam filters in email programs and security software may kill it as well.

There are steps you can take to make it more likely that your newsletter won't get blocked as spam. Spam tends to have certain common characteristics. You can do your best to make sure that your newsletter doesn't have those characteristics and won't be blocked. These tips will help:

Watch your language
Don't use the kind of words that got your mouth washed out with soap as a kid.

Don't overuse capitalization
THIS MIGHT LOOK LIKE SPAM to a spam filter. So use the proper conventions for capitalization.

Don't overuse punctuation marks
Use too many exclamation points and question marks, especially in a row, like this !!?!, and the newsletter is more likely to be considered spam.

Avoid spam phrases
Some phrases are commonly used by spammers, such as "free investment," "cable converter," or even "stop snoring." Use them, and your newsletter is more likely to be considered spam. For a list of phrases to ignore, head to www.wilsonweb.com/wmt8/spamfilter_phrases.htm.

Link to domain names instead of IP address
If you have links in your newsletter, always use the domain name, such as www.oreilly.com, rather than the IP address, such as 208.201.239.37.

Use simple HTML
A lot of HTML code in a newsletter can set off spam filters, so keep it simple.

Check if you're on blacklists
Many spam filters use blacklists to help determine what's spam. If you end up on a blacklist, your newsletter won't get through to people using antispam software, and many mail providers and antispam tools use these to block spam as well. Here's a list of the most common ones: www.spews.org, www.spamhaus.org/sbl/index.lasso, www.abuse.net/lookup.phtml, www.njabl.org/lookup.html, and blackholes.bruli.net. If you find your IP address or domain on any of the lists, contact the site, and ask how to be taken off the list. Also, if you check the headers of any bounces you receive as a result of blacklisting, you may find a URL of the blacklist with a link to instructions for removal.

Encourage your subscribers to whitelist you
Many mail services and applications will allow their users to add senders to a whitelist; email from anyone on this list will almost always get through. In some cases, putting your email address in their mail program or service's address book is all it takes.

Use their full name
Put the recipient's first and last name at the top of each message ("Dear so-and-so") you send. If there's one thing that most spammers have in common, it's that they only know your email address (unless your email address is an obvious concatenation of your first and last name). Some spam filters will count on this fact and be more likely to flag as spam messages containing phrases such as "Dear PayPal user" rather than the recipient's full name.

You can also test your newsletter yourself. Subscribe to as many email addresses as you have (Google Mail, the email address you get from your ISP, your school or work address if it won't get you in trouble, etc.). Then, send yourself a copy of the newsletter. When you receive it, look for an option in your email program to view the original message, full headers, raw source, or something along those lines. Some email services will add spam scores/status to the email headers, such as "X-Spam-Status:". If it was categorized as spam, look in the mail headers for cryptic details such as "HOST_MISMATCH_COM." Google these terms, and you'll probably find some helpful details that explain what you did to anger the spam filter.

HACK 88: Block International Spam

V XP Annoyed by spam sent to you in foreign languages? No problem—block it forever.

Spam by itself is annoying enough. But getting spam sent to you in a language you can't understand could well send you through the roof. And because a good deal of spam comes from overseas, you could be getting a lot of this kind of spam. Figure 6-5 is an example of overseas spam that has become increasingly common.

Luckily, it's easy to block international spam in Outlook and Windows Vista's Windows Mail. The way you block it is similar in each.

Figure 6-5.
What does this email say? It may well be offering to increase the size of your private body parts. Overseas spam like this is becoming increasingly common.

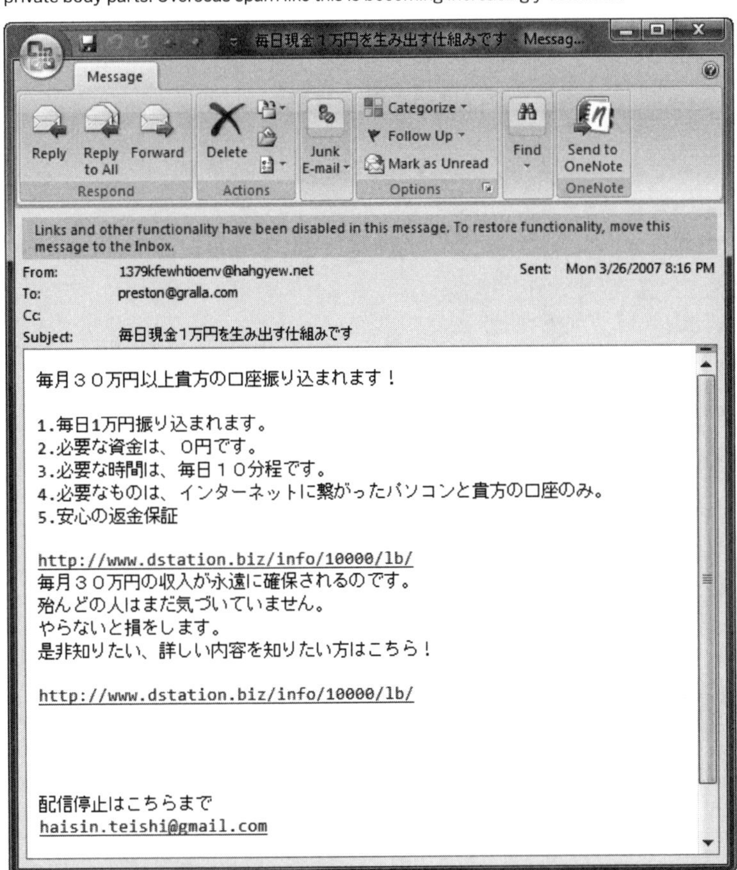

In Windows Outlook 2007, select Actions→Junk E-mail→Junk E-mail Options and click the International tab. You'll see a screen like the one shown in Figure 6-6.

Click Blocked Encodings List (see Figure 6-7). This lets you block mail that is encoded in various language sets. So, for example, if you don't read Japanese, Chinese, Vietnamese, and other languages, there's no point in accepting mail that uses those language sets. Check the boxes next to all languages you want to block, and click OK.

Next click Blocked Top-Level Domain List. The screen shown in Figure 6-8 appears.

This lets you block mail that has email addresses from specific countries. Be very careful here: this screen may or may not be of any use to you, and you don't want to block legitimate mail. A lot of spam that appears to originate overseas may not in fact have the domain of the true sender because spammers often use "bots" to send spam—PCs that they've essentially turned into spam-spewing zombies. So using this screen may not offer much help. In addition, it may also block legitimate mail sent to you from a foreign country. Still, if you absolutely know you get spam from certain foreign domains and that you'll never receive legitimate mail from them, check boxes next to each domain, and click OK.

You block international spam in Windows Mail and Outlook Express in a similar way. In Windows Mail, choose Tools→Junk Mail. Then choose the International tab, and you'll have options like those in Outlook 2007.

Figure 6-6.
The first step in stopping international spam

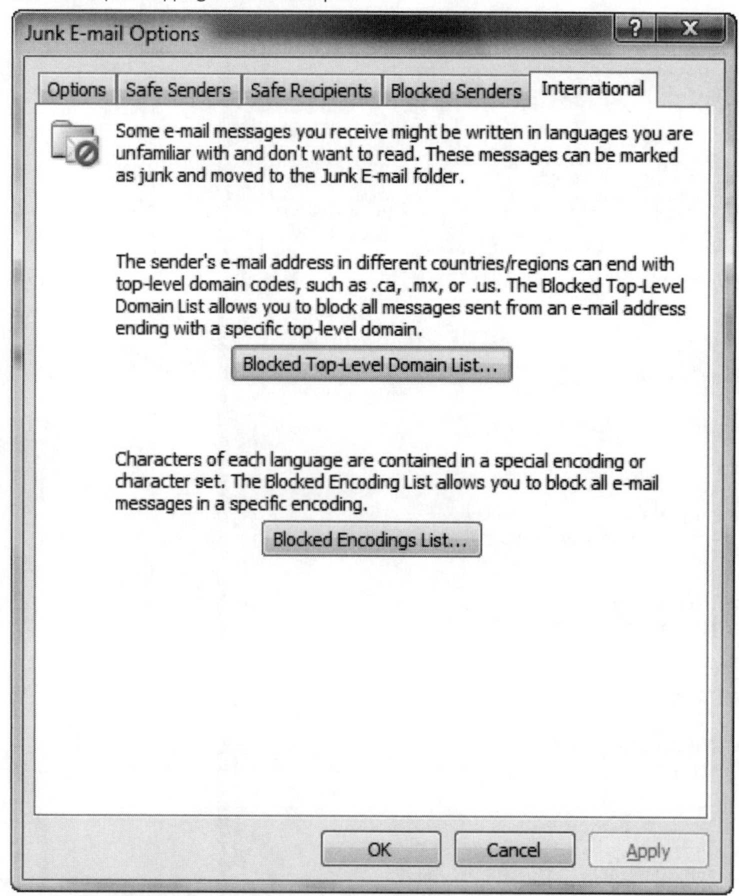

Figure 6-7.
This screen lets you block mail that uses a variety of different language sets

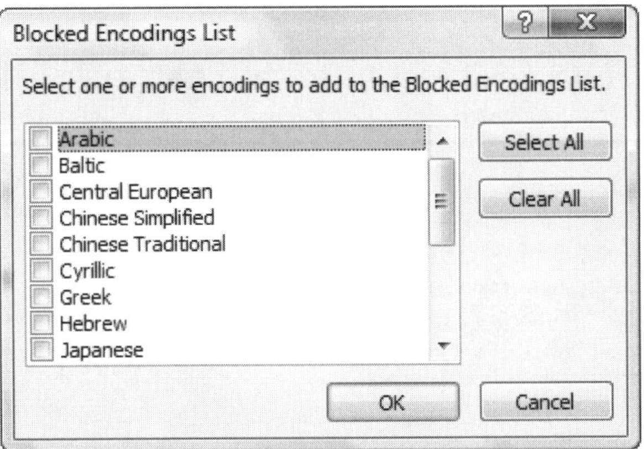

Figure 6-8.
This screen lets you block spam that originates from certain countries

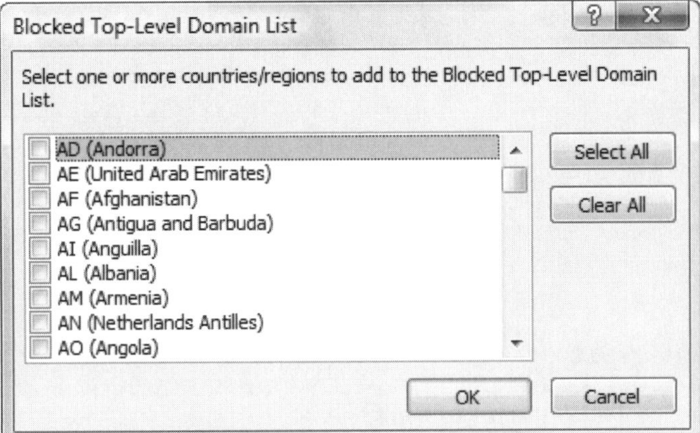

QUICK HACK

CAN A SERVICE CHECK WHETHER YOUR NEWSLETTER IS CONSIDERED SPAM?

A free service called SpamCheck (spamcheck.sitesell.com) claims that it can tell you whether a newsletter you send is likely to be considered spam [Hack #87]. Send the newsletter via email to spamcheck-thatswise@sitesell.net. Start the subject line with the word TEST, and make sure that it's capitalized. (After the word TEST, include the subject line you will normally include.) You'll get back an analysis of your newsletter, with an overall rating of how likely it is to be considered spam, as well as specific recommendations for how to fix your newsletter so it won't be considered spam.

How accurate is the service? Not very. I sent it multiple pieces of spam, and it didn't give any of them a bad enough rating to be considered spam. One of the pieces of spam even contained the subject line "Cure for Erectile Dysfunction," which is pretty much universally considered as spam.

However, it does offer an analysis of your newsletter, and the tips it gives are useful, so it's worth a shot for that.

HACK 89: Open Blocked File Attachments in Outlook and Outlook Express

V XP Force Outlook and Outlook Express to let you open a wide variety of file attachments that they normally block.

The world is full of nasty email-borne worms and viruses, and everyone certainly needs to be protected from them. But Microsoft, in the latest versions of Outlook and Outlook Express, takes a Big Nurse, draconian approach to the problem; it refuses to let you open a large number of file attachments sent to you via email, including those ending in *.exe*, *.bat*, and many other common file extensions. The theory is that it's possible a file with one of those extensions might be dangerous, so you shouldn't be allowed to open *any* file with that extension. That's like banning all cars because some people sometimes get into accidents.

When you try to open a file with one of those blocked extensions, you get the following error message: "Outlook blocked access to the following potentially unsafe attachments." Then you get a list of the attachments in your email that you can't open.

Depending on your version of Outlook, Outlook Express and Windows Mail, and whether you've applied a Service Pack update, your version might or might not exhibit this behavior. Some older versions don't act this way; all newer versions do, including Windows XP Service Pack 2 (SP2) and Windows Vista.

The simplest way to know whether your version acts this way is to see what happens when you get one of the blocked file attachments. If it's allowed to go through, there's no need to use this hack. If it's blocked, get thee to the keyboard. Outlook and Windows Mail/Outlook Express handle the problem differently, so we'll take a look at each.

Force Outlook to Let You Open Blocked File Attachments

Outlook assigns a level of risk to every file attachment sent to you. Level 1 is considered unsafe, so Outlook blocks your access to Level 1 attachments; you won't be able to open these files. Level 2 is considered a moderate risk, and you won't be able to open those files directly. Instead, you have to save the files to disk, and then you'll be able to open them. I'm not clear on how that increases security, but that's what Microsoft has done. Oh, and there's another oddball fact about Level 2: no file types are considered Level 2 risks. The only way for a file to be considered at that risk level is if you use Outlook in concert with a Microsoft Exchange Server, and the administrator uses his administration tools to put file extensions into that risk category. The administrator is also the only person who can take file extensions out of the category. So, you can pretty much ignore that category, unless you have some convincing official reason for changing your company's policy. Any file types not in Levels 1 and 2 are considered "other," and you can open them normally.

To force Outlook to let you open blocked file attachments, use this Registry hack. Before starting, you need to know the list of Level 1 file attachments that Outlook blocks. They're listed in Table 6-2. Just to make things more confusing, depending on your version of Office and what Service Pack you've installed, not all of these extensions can be blocked.

> **QUICK HACK**
>
> **PASTE BOILERPLATE TEXT INTO YOUR EMAILS**
>
> If you commonly use the same text frequently in your emails, for example, when answering the same question from people, you'll want this freebie. PhraseExpress stores text and phrases you commonly use, and pops them right into your email. Get it, and use it for free from www.phraseexpress.com.

Table 6-2. Blocked file extensions in Outlook

EXTENSION	FILE TYPE
.ade	Microsoft Access project extension
.adp	Microsoft Access project
.app	Visual FoxPro application
.asx	Windows Media audio/video
.bas	Microsoft Visual Basic class module
.bat	Batch file
.chm	Compiled HTML Help file
.cmd	Windows Command script
.com	MS-DOS program
.cpl	Control Panel extension
.crt	Security certificate
.csh	Unix shell extension
.exe	Executable program
.fxp	Visual FoxPro compiled program
.hlp	Help file
.hta	HTML program
.inf	Setup information
.ins	Internet Naming Service
.isp	Internet Communications settings
.js	Jscript file
.jse	Jscript Encoded Script file
.ksh	Unix shell extension
.lnk	Shortcut
.mda	Microsoft Access add-in program
.mdb	Microsoft Access program
.mde	Microsoft Access MDE database
.mdt	Microsoft Access workgroup information
.mdw	Microsoft Access workgroup information
.mdz	Microsoft Access wizard program
.msc	Microsoft Common Console document
.msi	Microsoft Windows Installer package
.msp	Microsoft Windows Installer patch
.mst	Microsoft Windows Installer transform; Microsoft Visual Test source file

Table 6-2. Blocked file extensions in Outlook *(continued)*

EXTENSION	FILE TYPE
.ops	Office XP settings
.pcd	Photo CD image; Microsoft Visual compiled script
.pif	Shortcut to MS-DOS program
.prf	Microsoft Outlook profile settings
.prg	Visual FoxPro program
.reg	Registry entries
.scf	Windows Explorer command
.scr	Screensaver
.shb	Shell Scrap object
.shs	Shell Scrap object
.url	Internet shortcut
.vb	VBScript file
.vbe	VBScript Encoded script file
.vbs	VBScript file
.wsc	Windows Script Component
.wsf	Windows Script file
.wsh	Windows Script Host Setting file

Decide which file extension you want to be able to open from within Outlook, and close Outlook if it's running. Then launch the Registry Editor by typing regedit at the Start Search box or a command prompt (see Chapter 13 for details). Go to `HKEY_CURRENT_USER\Software\Microsoft\Office\10.0\Outlook\Security`, if you're using Outlook 2003. If you're using Outlook 2007, go to `HKEY_CURRENT_USER\Software\Microsoft\Office\12.0\Outlook\Security`. Create a new `String` value called `Level1Remove`. In the `Value Data` field, type the name of the file extension you want to be able to open, for example, *.exe*. You can add multiple file extensions; if you do, separate them with semicolons, but no spaces, like this: `.exe;.bat;.pif`. Use Table 6-2 as a guide for which blocked file extensions you want to be able to open.

When you're done, exit the Registry, and reboot. Now you'll be able to open the file extensions you specified.

There's also an Outlook add-in that will let you open blocked email attachments without having to edit the Registry. The Attachment Options add-in, available from www.slovaktech.com/attachmentoptions.htm, lets you visually change which attachments you can open, and it also lets you set an additional option—having Outlook ask you whether you want to open certain file extensions on a case-by-case basis, instead of blocking them or automatically opening them. The author asks that you send a $10 donation if you use the add-in.

If you know the person sending you a certain attachment, you can also have him zip the file and resend it to you. That way, you're getting a file with a *.zip* file extension, which will get through.

Force Windows Mail and Outlook Express to Let You Open Blocked File Attachments

Like Outlook, Vista's Windows Mail in Vista, prevents you from opening certain email file attachments. Certain versions of Outlook Express might prevent this as well.

If you have installed Windows XP Service Pack 1 or Service Pack 2, Outlook Express Service Pack 1, or Internet Explorer 6 Service Pack 1, you'll be blocked from opening certain email file attachments in Outlook Express. Also, if you have a newer version of XP, you might be blocked.

With Windows Mail and Outlook Express, unlike with Outlook, you won't be able to determine on an extension-by-extension basis which attachments you can open. Instead, you can tell the program to let you open all blocked extensions, or you can tell it to stop you from opening any blocked extensions.

You follow the same steps for Windows Mail as for Outlook Express if you want to be able to open blocked attachments. Choose Tools→Options→Security to open the dialog box shown in Figure 6-9. Clear the box next to "Do not allow attachments to be saved or opened that could potentially be a virus." Click OK.

You might have to close Windows Mail or Outlook Express and restart it for the settings to take effect.

Figure 6-9.
Forcing Windows Mail to let you open all email attachments

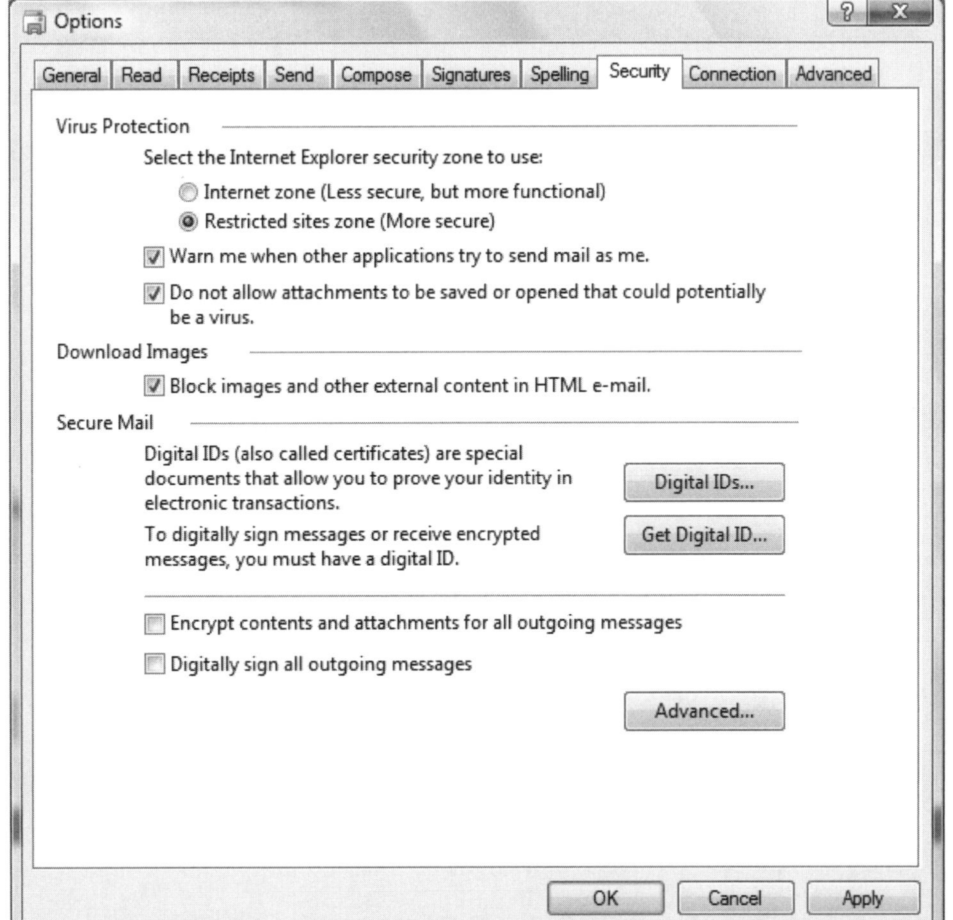

QUICK HACK

SEND ANY SIZE FILE VIA EMAIL

ISPs limit the size of files you can send or receive via email, sometimes at about 5 MB or so, and in some cases even smaller. What to do if you need to send larger files? Use the free SendThisFile service (www.sendthisfile.com). After you register, and you want to send a large file, log into the site, fill in a form that will send an email, and upload your large file. An email will be sent to the person who you want to receive the file. The email won't include the file itself; instead it will include a link. When they click the link, they'll download the large file from the www.sendthisfile.com site. There's no limit on file size or number of files you can send this way.

HACK 90: Remove Exchange Messaging From Outlook 2007

V XP If you don't use Outlook as part of a corporation, you don't need Microsoft Exchange Unified Messaging. Here's how to remove it.

If you are using Outlook at home or elsewhere with a POP or IMAP account, and don't use Microsoft Exchange, your version of Outlook 2007 may be using unnecessary system resources and RAM by running Microsoft Exchange Unified Messaging. Microsoft Exchange is a corporate email server, and if you don't use Exchange, there's no need to run that service inside Outlook 2007.

It's easy to remove it, though. Just follow these steps:

1. Select Tools→Trust Center→Add-Ins.
2. At the bottom of the page, select COM Add-ins from the drop-down list, and click Go. A screen like the one shown in Figure 6-10 appears.
3. Uncheck the box next to Microsoft Exchange Unified Messaging, and click OK. This will disable it. If you instead want to remove it from your system, highlight it, and click Remove. When you exit Outlook and restart, it should be disabled.

It's a good idea to first disable Microsoft Exchange Unified Messaging and run Outlook for several days with it disabled before you decide to remove it. If you have problems with Outlook, you can enable it by following the steps in this hack, and checking the box next to it. If you find, however, that Outlook runs fine without it after several days, you can remove it.

HACK 91: Publish Your Outlook Calendar to the Web

V XP Want to share your calendar with the world? Here's a quick way to do it in Outlook.

A calendar by itself is a lonely thing. The point of a calendar, after all, is not just to keep your own schedule, but also so that others can know your doings and schedule as well. If you keep your calendar in Outlook 2007, it's easy to publish it on the Web.

There are several ways you can publish your calendar, including publishing it on the Office Online service or to any web site of your choosing. This hack shows you how to do both.

Figure 6-10.
Removing the Exchange plug-in

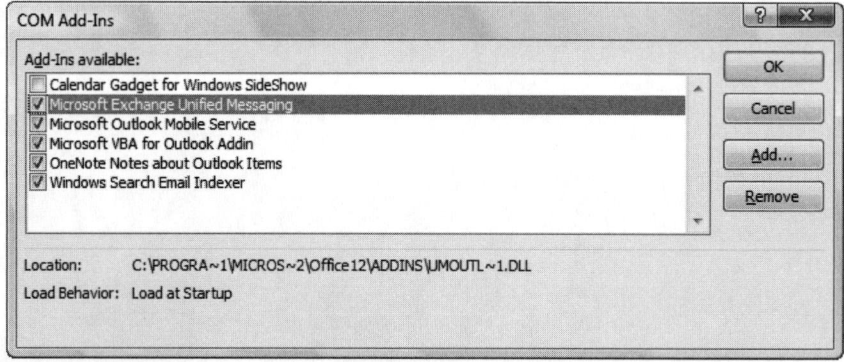

Publish Your Calendar to Office Online

Office Online is a Microsoft web site with a variety of tools, tips, and help for using Microsoft Office. One of its free services is the Microsoft Office Outlook Calendar Sharing Service, which lets you share your calendar with anyone and control who can see your calendar. Here's how to publish your calendar on Office Online and share it with others:

1. In Outlook go to your calendar, and click Publish My Calendar in the left-hand pane. A wizard appears that will walk you through the process of publishing your calendar.

2. Click Sign In. From the page that appears, if you already have a Windows Live ID, type in your email address and password. If you don't have a Windows Live ID, you'll be prompted to create one and sign in.

3. After you sign in, the form shown in Figure 6-11 appears. Choose the time span for the calendar, and the permissions for who can view it (whether anyone or just select people can view it). Click the arrow next to Detail to choose how much detail to show, in other words, whether to show actual appointments and descriptions, or instead terms like "free" and "busy," or a limited amount of details.

4. By default, your calendar automatically updates itself periodically on Office Online to reflect changes you make to it in Outlook. If you'd prefer that it not update at all, click Advanced, and select Single Upload, and click OK.

Figure 6-11.
Publishing your Outlook calendar to Office Online

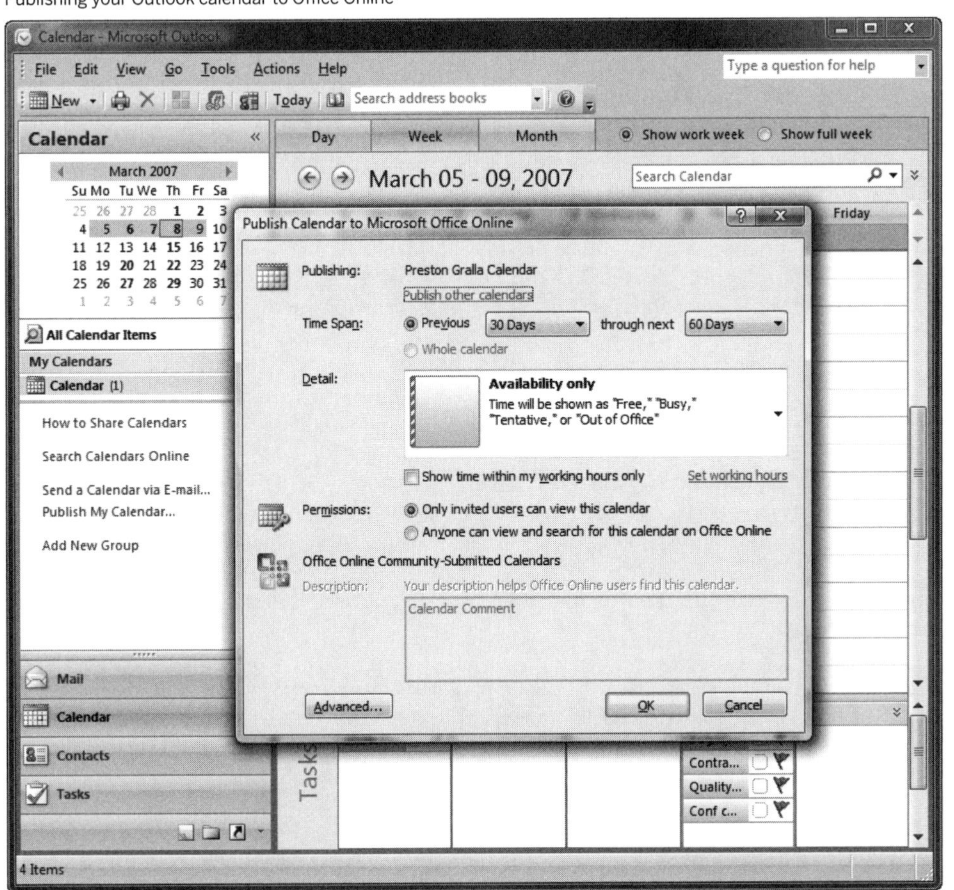

Figure 6-12.
The calendar available online

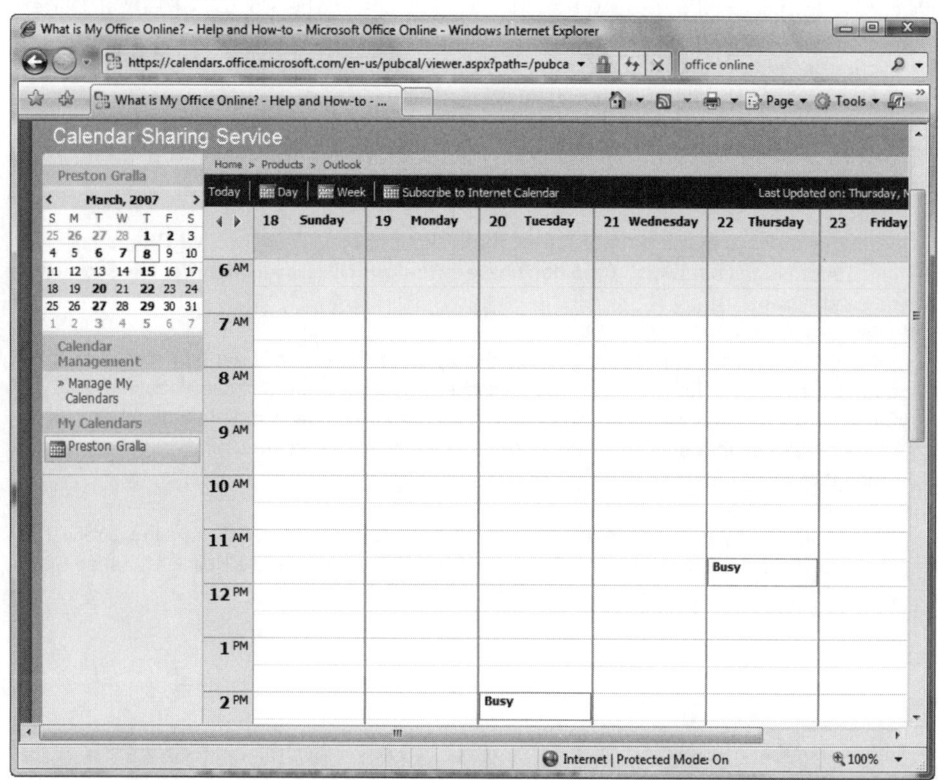

5. When you're ready to publish your calendar, click OK. The calendar will be uploaded to the Web. You'll next get a notice asking if you would like to send out an invitation to others to view your calendar online. Click Yes if you want to send an invitation.

6. To see your calendar, sign into Office Online at office.microsoft.com with the account you used to create the calendar. Click the Outlook Calendar Sharing Service on the left side of the page, then from the page that appears, click your calendar, and you'll see it, as shown in Figure 6-12.

7. To let others view the calendar, send them the URL.

Publish Your Calendar to Any Web Site

You can also publish your calendar to any web site as well. When you use this technique, you save your calendar as an HTML page, and then publish it as you would any other HTML page.

When you're in the calendar, choose File→Save as Web Page. The screen shown in Figure 6-13 appears.

Chose the duration of the calendar, any appointment details you wish to include, and give it a title. If you want the calendar to have a background graphic, check the box next to "Use background graphic," and browse to the graphic. Name the file, and change the location for the HTML file that will be created by clicking the Browse button and browsing to a new location.

> You must give the calendar an extension of *.htm* or *.html*. The filename cannot have any spaces in it (for example, this wouldn't work: *my calendar.html*). Instead, you can use an underscore character if you want a space, like this: *my_calendar.html*.

Figure 6-13.
Filling in the form to create the HTML code for your calendar

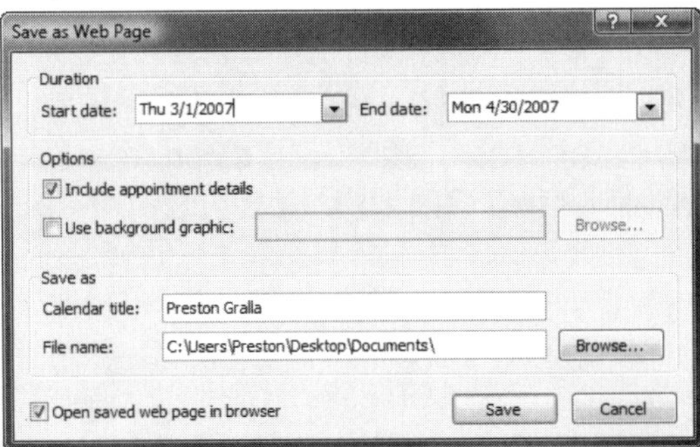

Figure 6-14.
A preview of what a calendar looks like created via HTML

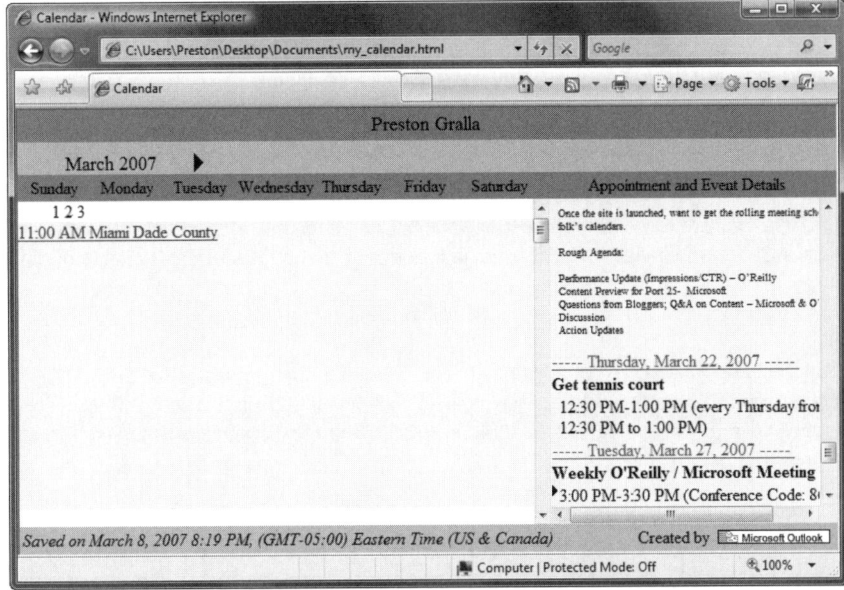

To see a preview of your calendar in your browser, make sure the box next to "Open saved web page" in browser is checked. After you've made your selections, click Save.

When you publish your calendar as an HTML page, it won't auto-update, as it does in Office Live. You'll have to save the calendar again as an HTML file and post it to a web server so that others can see the most recent version of the calendar.

If you've chosen to see a preview of your calendar, it will display in your web browser, as shown in Figure 6-14. You can now take the HTML file and post it to a web server, as you would any other HTML file.

GMAIL HACKS

The best free web-based email service in the world is Gmail, hands-down. It gives you as much storage as you'll ever need, lets you search through your mail using Gmail's powerful search tools, and much more.

Gmail may look simple and straightforward, but there's plenty you don't know about it. You can use it just like a POP3 account or as an extension of your hard drive. You can also import your mail and accounts into it, or use it as a universal inbox. You'll find that and more in the following hacks.

HACK 92: Turn Gmail into a Universal Inbox

V XP Have multiple email accounts and are tired of checking them all? Now you can use Gmail as a universal inbox and check all your mail from one interface.

Lots of people have multiple email accounts—one at work, one at home, and perhaps one or more provided by organizations such as an alumni association or civic group. Often, people check these accounts using a mail client. But what if you'd like to be able to see all your mail from all your accounts from a web site, in fact from the best web mail program there is—Gmail? It's easy to do.

Using Gmail as a universal inbox is a good idea for many reasons. Even if you use email software with each account, you can use Gmail to preview mail from all your accounts, without actually downloading the mail into your mail client. So you'll be able to go to Gmail and see all the mail you have from everywhere before downloading.

In addition, you can save copies of all your mail from all your accounts in your Gmail account for easy searching, so that you have access to that mail no matter where you are. You can do this even if you use a mail client for your mail. For example, you can have the mail copied into Gmail, and also downloaded into your mail client.

If you like web mail rather than a mail client, you could instead use Gmail to read all your mail.

It's pretty straightforward to do. Keep in mind, though, that you can only use Gmail to read mail from other accounts that offer POP3 access. If they don't offer POP3 access, as is the case with many web mail sites, you won't be able to use Gmail as a universal inbox.

To do so, log into Gmail, then click Settings and click Accounts. In the "Get mail from other accounts" section, click "Add another mail account." Enter the email address of the account you want to add, and click Next Step. A screen like Figure 6-15 will appear.

Fill in your username, password, and location of the account's POP server.

If you're going to also be accessing the mail from the account you just added through a mail client, or through the account's own web interface account, check the box next to "Leave a copy of retrieved message on the server". When you check this box, you'll be able to read the mail in Gmail, but the mail will stay on the server so that you can download it with your mail client or read it through the account's web interface.

Figure 6-15.
Adding an email account to Gmail

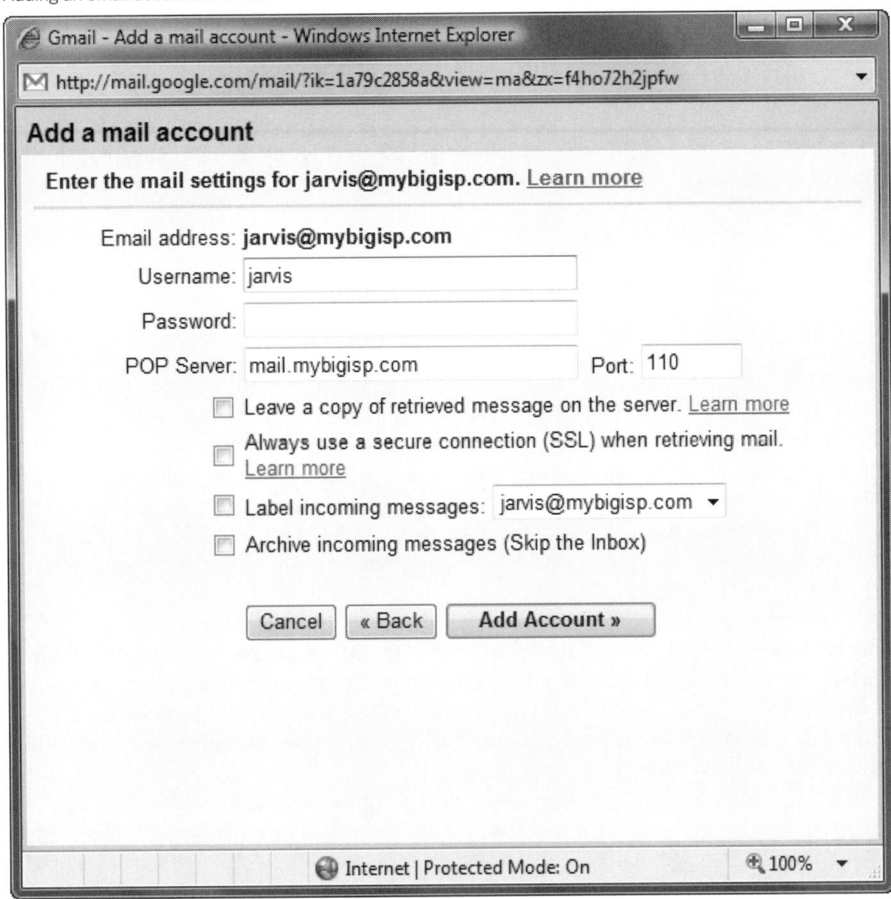

If you're going to be accessing the mail for the account only through your Gmail account, leave the box unchecked.

Check the box next to "Always use a secure connection (SSL) when retrieving mail". This ensures that your mail won't be snooped on.

 Your POP3 email server may not support SSL connections, so you may have to leave this box unchecked.

If you want all incoming messages from the account to carry a label—such as the name of the account—check the box next to "Label incoming messages". In Gmail, a label works much like a folder. All mail that carries the same label can be viewed by clicking on the label in Gmail. There will already be a predefined label of the email address of the new account. You can select a different label or create a new one by making a selection from the drop-down list. If you choose, you can have messages bypass your inbox and go straight to your Gmail archive. Do this if you want to use Gmail primarily for searching through mail. When you've made all your selections, click Add Account.

After your account has been added, you can set it up so that even if you compose mail in Gmail, it will appear to be from the account you just added. When a message appears asking if you want to create a custom "From address", click Yes, and follow the instructions.

Gmail will now check your account, and its mail will show up in Gmail. To stop Gmail from checking the mail, click Settings, click Accounts, then click delete next to the account.

Use Gmail as a POP3 Server

V XP Get the best of both worlds: combine Gmail with your normal email software such as Outlook.

Tempted by Gmail but aren't ready to give up your email software? No problem. You can use Gmail as a normal POP3 account, just like the one you have with your workplace or mail service provider.

You'll first have to configure Gmail to let you do it, and then you'll have to tell your email software to retrieve the mail.

In Gmail, click Settings and then click the Forwarding and POP link at the top of the page. The screen shown in Figure 6-16 appears.

If you want your email software to retrieve all the email you've ever received on Gmail, choose Enable POP for all mail. Be very careful before making this selection. Remember, Gmail gives you over 2 GB of storage, so if you've received a lot of mail, you could end up downloading gigabytes of mail when you make your first connection to Gmail using your email software. Also keep in mind that even if you have only a little mail in your Inbox, that's not all the email you have in your Gmail account. Most of your mail is in the Archive folder, and you might have hundreds or thousands of messages there, even if they're not currently showing in your Inbox.

If you choose "Enable POP only for mail that arrives from now on", only those messages you receive after this point will be downloaded to your email software. It's a much safer choice. If you want some old mail downloaded, you can always go into your Gmail account and forward the mail to yourself. That way, the forwarded mail will be treated as new mail and will be downloaded, while all the rest of your old mail won't be downloaded.

Figure 6-16.
Configuring Gmail for POP3 access

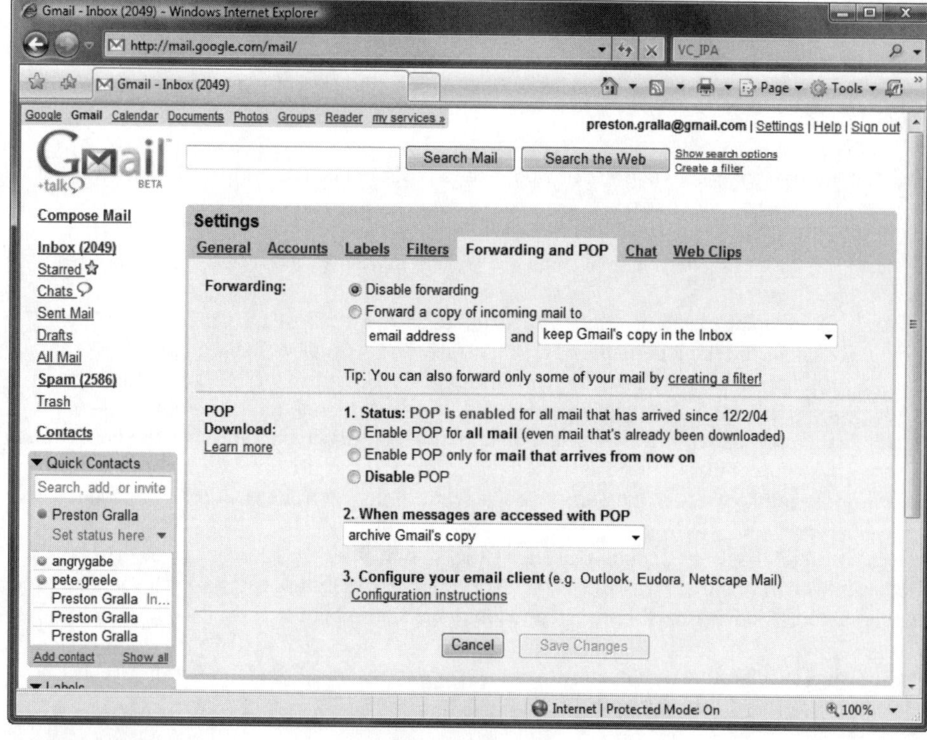

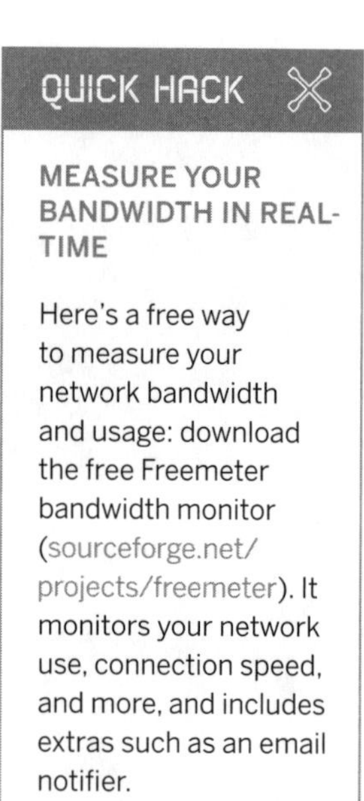

QUICK HACK

MEASURE YOUR BANDWIDTH IN REAL-TIME

Here's a free way to measure your network bandwidth and usage: download the free Freemeter bandwidth monitor (sourceforge.net/projects/freemeter). It monitors your network use, connection speed, and more, and includes extras such as an email notifier.

Next, make your choice about what should happen to your Gmail messages: should they be kept on the Gmail server, and if they are, should they be kept in the Inbox or in the Archived mail? Here are your choices:

Keep Gmail's copy in the Inbox
This leaves all new mail on the Gmail server in your Gmail Inbox. That way, even after you download it to your PC, it will stay in the Gmail Inbox on the Web as if you hadn't read it.

Archive Gmail's copy
This leaves all new email on the Gmail server, but instead of putting it into your Inbox, it moves it to your Archived mail. So, whenever you visit Gmail on the Web, if you want to see the mail, go to your Archive.

Delete Gmail's copy
This deletes the mail from Gmail.

Now it's time to configure your email program to get your Gmail mail. You set it up as you do any other new mail account. If your email software asks for for your POP3 server, use `pop.gmail.com`, and for your SMTP server, use `smtp.gmail.com`. When setting it up, tell your software to use a secure connection (SSL) for both SMTP and POP3.

So, for example, here's how you would set up Outlook 2007 for POP3 Gmail. (The instructions are nearly identical for earlier versions of Outlook.) After you've enabled POP3 access in Gmail, launch Outlook and choose Tools→Account Settings. Click New. From the Choose E-Mail Service screen that appears, enter your name, your Gmail address, and your password. Click Next, and you're done.

If that doesn't work for some reason, and you can't send and receive email, you'll need to manually enter your server information. Back on the screen where you entered your name, Gmail address and password, check the box next to "Manually configure server settings or additional server types". From the screen that appears, select Internet E-mail, and click Next. You'll see a screen like one shown in Figure 6-17.

In the User Information section, type in your name and Gmail address. In the Server information area, for the Account type, choose POP3. In the Incoming mail server box, type `pop.gmail.com` and in the Outgoing mail server box, type `smtp.gmail.com`. In the Logon Information area, enter

Figure 6-17.
Setting up POP3 access in Outlook 2003

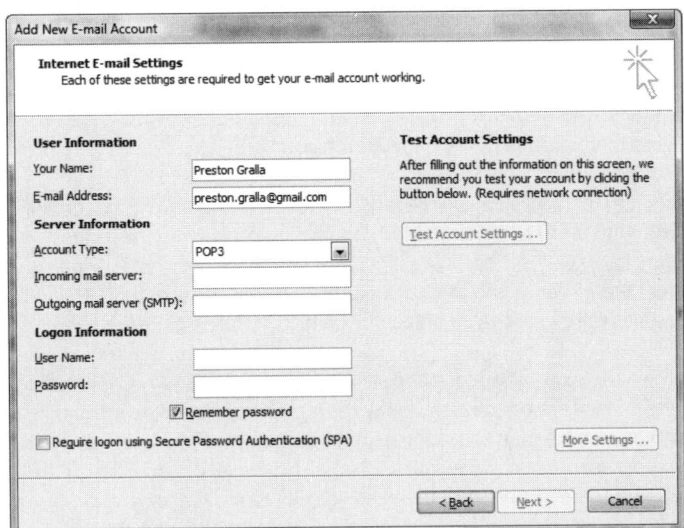

your Gmail username and password. Check the box next to Remember password. Check the box next to "Require logon using Secure Password Authentication (SPA)". Click More Settings, choose the Advanced tab, and check the box next to "This server requires an encrypted (SSL) connection". Then click OK, click Next and then Finish. Now you should be able to send and receive mail using Gmail.

HACK 94: Use Gmail as a Virtual Hard Drive

V XP Extend your hard drive into cyberspace with this free add-in.

With all of that extra space on Gmail, wouldn't it be nice to use some of it for storage rather than mail?

You can, with a free piece of software called GMail Drive shell extension. Download it from www.viksoe.dk/code/gmail.htm, and install it.

 Google doesn't look kindly on people who use software like this to turn Gmail into extra storage for your PC. In fact, it may lock your account if it finds you doing this. For details, see item #3 in mail.google.com/support/bin/answer.py?answer=43692.

After you install it, run Windows Explorer. A new drive will appear, called the Gmail Drive. Double-click it, and type in your Gmail password and username. If you don't want to have to log in every time you click the drive, check the box next to Auto Login.

You can use the Gmail drive as you can any other folder on your hard drive. (You'll of course have to be connected to the Internet for it to work.) This means you can copy files to it using Windows Explorer in the same way that you do any other files, and you can create subfolders as well.

 The Gmail drive looks like any hard drive on your system, but remember that it's a virtual drive and you're connected to it over the Internet. So, you can transfer files to it only at the speed of your Internet connection. On a dial-up connection, this will be exceedingly slow.

When you view the contents of your Gmail drive, the icons for the files won't necessarily look like the normal ones. Instead of showing the native icons for each file type (such as pieces of paper for Word files), in some instances, they'll show as gear-type icons.

When you copy a file to your Gmail drive, you're actually creating an email and posting it to your account. The email will appear in your Inbox, with the file as an attachment. If you want to open any of the files from inside Gmail, click the email to view it, and then click the Download button. The file will be downloaded to your PC. Using Gmail as a virtual drive can make your Inbox pretty messy. Luckily, you can create a filter that will automatically route the files to your archived mail folder. That way, you'll never see them in your Inbox, and they'll be in your archives.

The emails with the files attached to them all show up preceded by the letters GMAILFS. So, create a filter that will move all files with that prefix to your archived mail by first clicking Create a Filter from the top of the Gmail screen. In the Subject box, type `GMAILFS`, check the box next to "Has attachment," and then click Next Step. Then check the box next to "Skip the Inbox (Archive it)", and then click Create Filter. All your files will be sent straight to your Archive, bypassing the Inbox.

You can also have them labeled so that you know at a glance which files you copied from your hard disk. Before clicking Create Filter, check the box next to "Apply the label." From the drop-down box next to it, select New Label, and from the screen that appears, type in the label name (such as Hard Drive), and click OK. From the drop-down list, choose your new label. Now click Create Filter. The files will be archived but will also have the label next to them, so you can easily view only your files by clicking the Hard Drive label when you log into Gmail.

 It's not a good idea to use Gmail as your hard drive if you're going to use POP3 to retrieve your email from Gmail with your email software. If you do that, whenever you retrieve email from Google, you'll also retrieve all the files you've copied to Google when you used it as a virtual hard drive, which can be hundreds of megabytes.

See Also

- Many other free add-ins extend the functionality of Gmail—for example, to notify you when you have mail in Gmail, to keep a to-do list, and so on. Find them at www.marklyon.org/gmail/gmailapps.htm.

HACK 95: Import Your Contacts into Gmail

V XP Data entry's a drag. Export your contacts from an existing web mail service, desktop email application, or database, and import them into your Gmail address book.

Possibly the most annoying aspect of moving into any new web mail home is bringing all your family, friends, and business contacts along with you. The average end user has been trained not to expect any sort of import utility, so he instead sighs and settles in for an evening of data entry.

Gmail, as with most post-1990s web mail applications worth their salt, provides a facility that imports all those contacts in just a few clicks; just how many clicks depends on where you're exporting them from. Gmail accepts only one format: comma-separated values (CSV). Thankfully, CSV is about as low a common denominator you could wish for; Yahoo! Address Book, Outlook, Outlook Express, Mac OS X Address Book (with a little help from a free application), Excel, and many other applications, web or otherwise, speak CSV.

 Gmail's Help documentation on the subject of importing contacts is sure to keep up with the needs of its users, so keep an eye on "How do I import addresses into my Contacts list?" (gmail.google.com/support/bin/answer.py?answer=8301).

Anatomy of a Contacts CSV

First, a quick tour of a typical contacts CSV file as consumed by Gmail's import tool.

CSV files, as the name suggests, are little more than garden-variety text files in which data is listed one record per line, each field separated by (you guessed it!) a comma. The simplest of all *contacts.csv* files might look something like this:

```
name,email
Rael Dornfest,rael@oreilly.com
Tara Calishain,tara@researchbuzz.com
...
```

The first line lists field names—in this case, name and email address. Each line thereafter is a single person or entity (business, organization, etc.) in your contacts list with a corresponding name and email address.

Gmail accepts various formats of contact entry, recognizing some of the more common fields such as name, email address, phone, birthday, etc. Here's a slightly more detailed *contacts.csv*:

```
first name,last name,email address,phone
Rael,Dornfest,rael@oreilly.com,(212) 555-1212
Tara,Calishain,tara@researchbuzz.com, (212) 555-1213
...
```

Notice that name is split into first- and last-name fields, email is called *email address*, and there's a phone field too.

Unless you're going to be using Gmail as your main contacts database, you don't need to import more than name and email address (something akin to the first *contacts.csv* example) to find it useful.

When you export your contacts via CSV, Google adds identifying information for each field it exports. Here are the field names it exports: Name, E-mail, Notes, Description, Email, IM, Phone, Mobile, Pager, Fax, Company, Title, Other, Address.

Assuming you have a CSV file to work with (if you don't, skip to the next sections for some guidance), importing is a snap.

From the main Gmail screen in your web browser, click the Contacts link on the left side of the page. The Contacts page opens, listing all of (or none of, if you don't yet have any) your existing Gmail contacts. These may have been entered by hand, gleaned from incoming and outgoing mail, or imported at some earlier date. Figure 6-18 shows a Contacts page with no contacts in it yet.

Click the Import link at the top right of the page, and a new window pops up with the Import Contacts dialog.

From the new window, click the Browse... (or equivalent) button when prompted to do so, as shown in Figure 6-19 and find your CSV file on your computer's hard drive. (Just what this looks like depends on your operating system and browser, but essentially you're just choosing a file much like you would from any application.) Click the Import Contacts button and—Bob's your uncle (that's "Tada!" for my readers)—you should see a confirmation that all went according to plan, and your contacts have been imported into your Gmail address book.

Click the Close link, and you'll see your now fully stocked contacts list. If you're looking at your Frequently Mailed contacts, you might need to click the All Contacts link above your addresses to see the new entries; after all, they're not frequently mailed yet! Figure 6-20 shows mine after I imported the second sample CSV at the beginning of this hack.

Figure 6-18.
A blank Gmail Contacts page

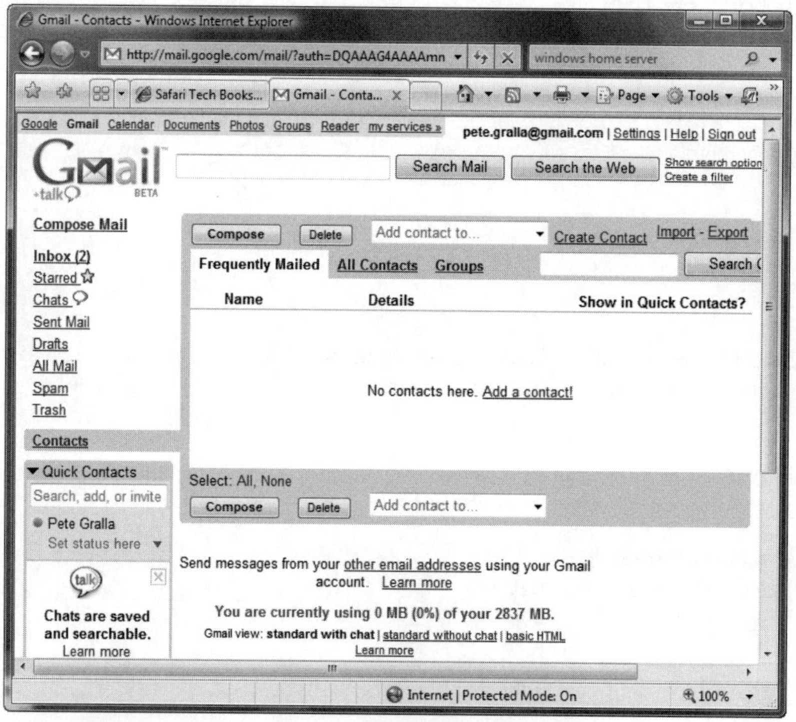

Figure 6-19.
Finding that CSV file

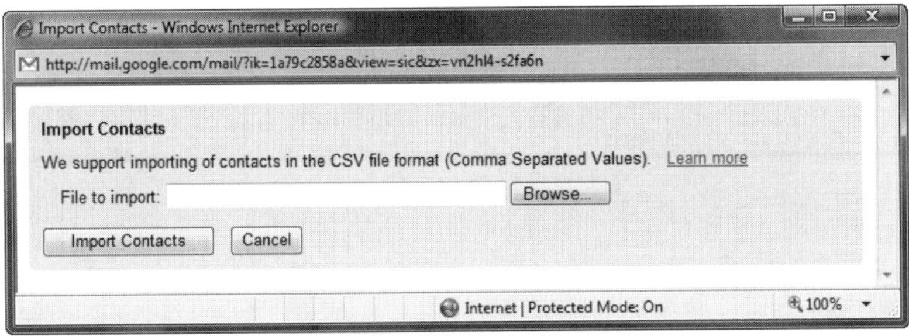

Figure 6-20.
The Contact page, with the contacts imported

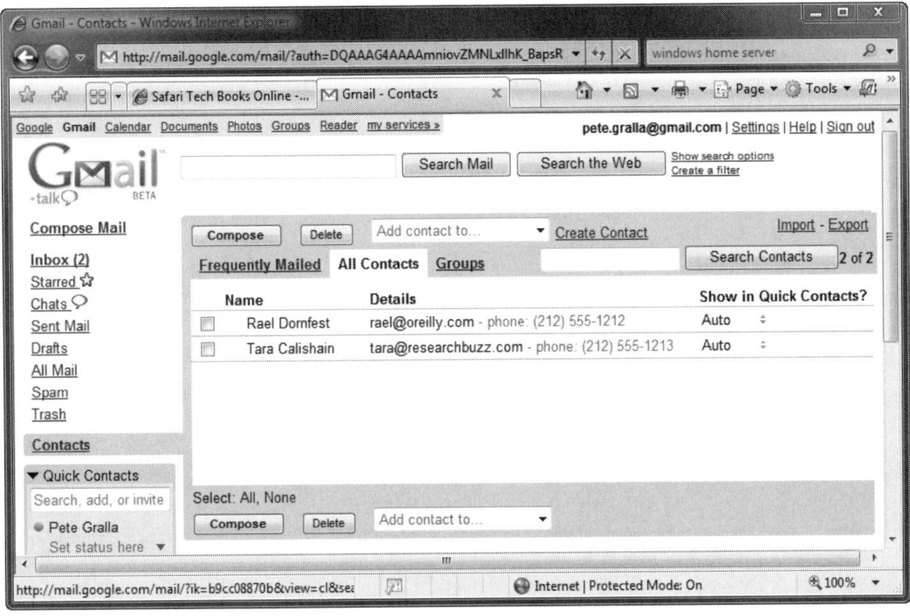

Delete any number of contacts by clicking their associated checkboxes and clicking the Delete button. Edit a contact by hovering over the name or clicking on the name, which brings up the hovering box shown in Figure 6-21.

Click Contact Details then the "edit contact information" link to change anything about the listing. From the Edit Contact page, you can click Add More Contact Info to fill in details about the contact, such as work and home phone, fax, address, or just about any other bit of information you'd like to add. Figure 6-22 shows the Edit Contact page with extended information.

And you can always type in a contact or three by hand using the Create Contact link on the front Contacts page.

Now whenever you start typing a known contact's name into the To, Cc, or Bcc field of a new message, Gmail autocompletes it for you. No need to remember that cousin Adam is adamg@ozziesurfers.co.au or that Auntie Joan is joan42@tepidmail.com.

Figure 6-21.
The hovering contact box

Figure 6-22.
Adding extended information to a contact

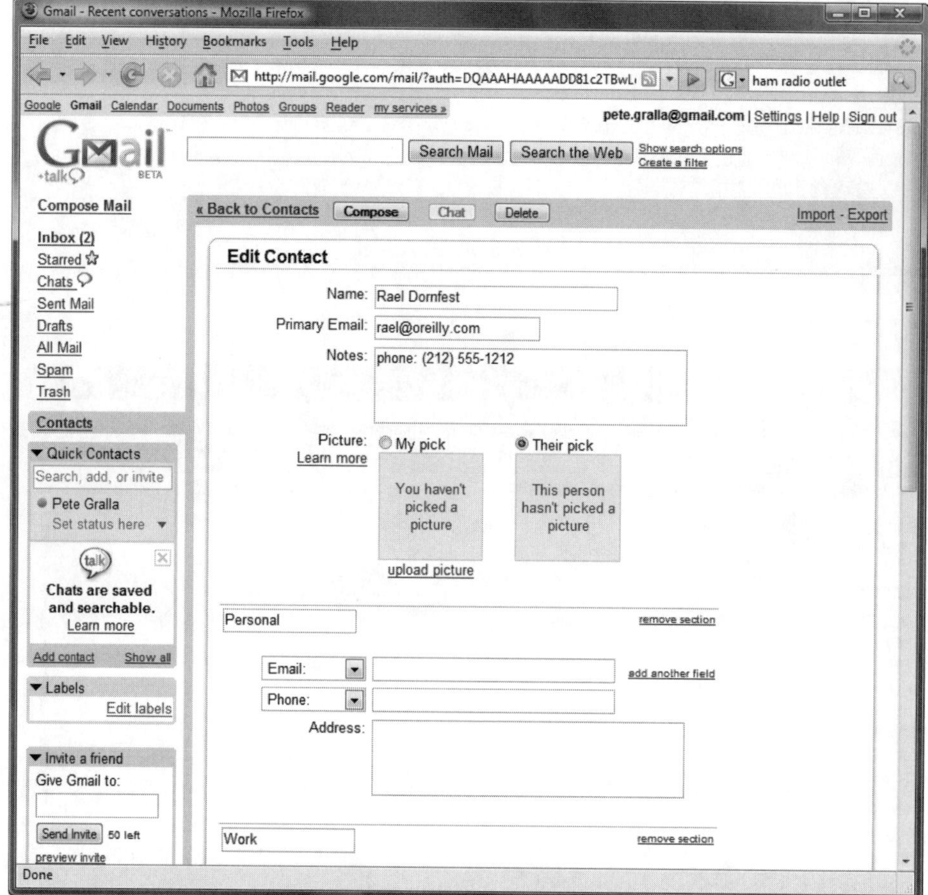

Out of Outlook, Outlook Express, and Windows Mail

Both Outlook Express and Outlook in Windows can export their address books as CSV.

In Outlook Express, select File→Export→Address Book, choose Text File (Comma Separated Values) as your output format and click the Export button.

In Outlook, select File→Import and Export, choose "Export to a file," click Next, select Comma Separated Values (Windows) as your output format, and click Next again. An Export Wizard then guides you the rest of the way to saving your contacts as a CSV file. Figure 6-23 shows Outlook exporting contacts as a CSV.

In Windows Mail, select File→Export→Windows Contacts, and from the screen that appears, choose CSV (Comma Separated Values), then click the Export button and follow the prompts. Feed the file to Gmail as described earlier.

Hopping Out of Windows Live Hotmail

Windows Live Hotmail can export a contact list as a CSV file, so that's all you'll need to do. Log into Windows Live Hotmail, then click Contacts. Then on the upper right side of your screen, click the down arrow next to Options, and select Export Contacts. From the screen that appears, then from the resulting dialog box, name and save your file. Then import the file into Gmail, as you would any other CSV file.

Figure 6-23.
Exporting contacts in Outlook

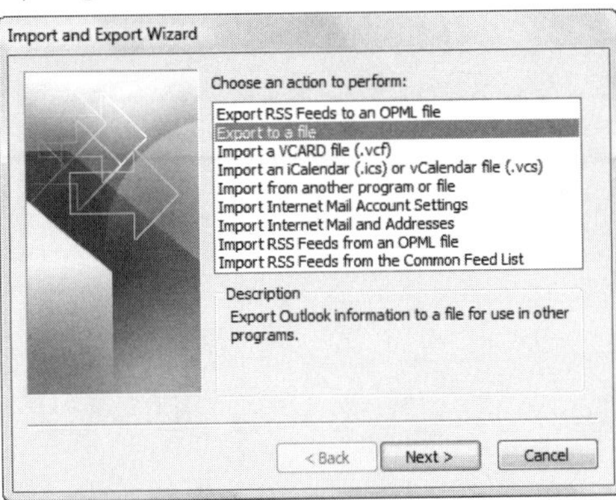

Yumping from Yahoo!

Yahoo! Address Book exports directly to CSV.Log into Yahoo! and in the upper right corner of the page select Options→Mail Options. From the page that appears, select Contact Options, then click Import/Export. Scroll to the Export section of the page, and next to Yahoo! CSV, click Export Now (Figure 6-24).

You'll be asked whether you want to open or save the file, as shown in Figure 6-25. Choose to save it, then navigate to the folder to which you want the file saved.

Now go ahead, and import that CSV using the Gmail import tool, described earlier.

 I do apologize for the bad "Yumping" pun, but "Yahoo!" doesn't leave you much room for alliterated action verbs: yodeling? yanking?

Hand-Crafting a CSV

If your contacts exist in some form with no obvious path to CSV, you can always export them in any way you can, arriving at some point at either a plain-text file that you can manipulate by hand—tedious, but possible—or something Excel can read. If you can get to Excel, you can get to CSV; to massage the data into a form similar to that discussed at the beginning of this hack, select File→Save As and save as "CSV (Comma delimited)."

Last-Ditch Effort

If, for whatever reason, you can't massage your contacts into CSV form or use Gmail's Import Contacts tool, there is a (admittedly grotty) way to get all your contacts to Gmail using email itself.

Send out a single email message, preferably one that announces your intention, to (on the To: line) your Gmail account (or one that forwards to your Gmail account), copying all your contacts on the Bcc: line. Bcc stands for Blind Carbon-Copy, which means that your recipients will not see each other's addresses. You may have to hunt around for the Bcc option. For example, in Outlook, you'll see it in the Select Names dialog that appears when you click the Cc button.

 You should probably batch these so you have some semblance of privacy; you don't want your family to see all of your business associates' addresses and vice versa. Send a separate message for contacts of a sensitive nature.

Figure 6-24.
Using the Yahoo! Address Book's Import/Export feature

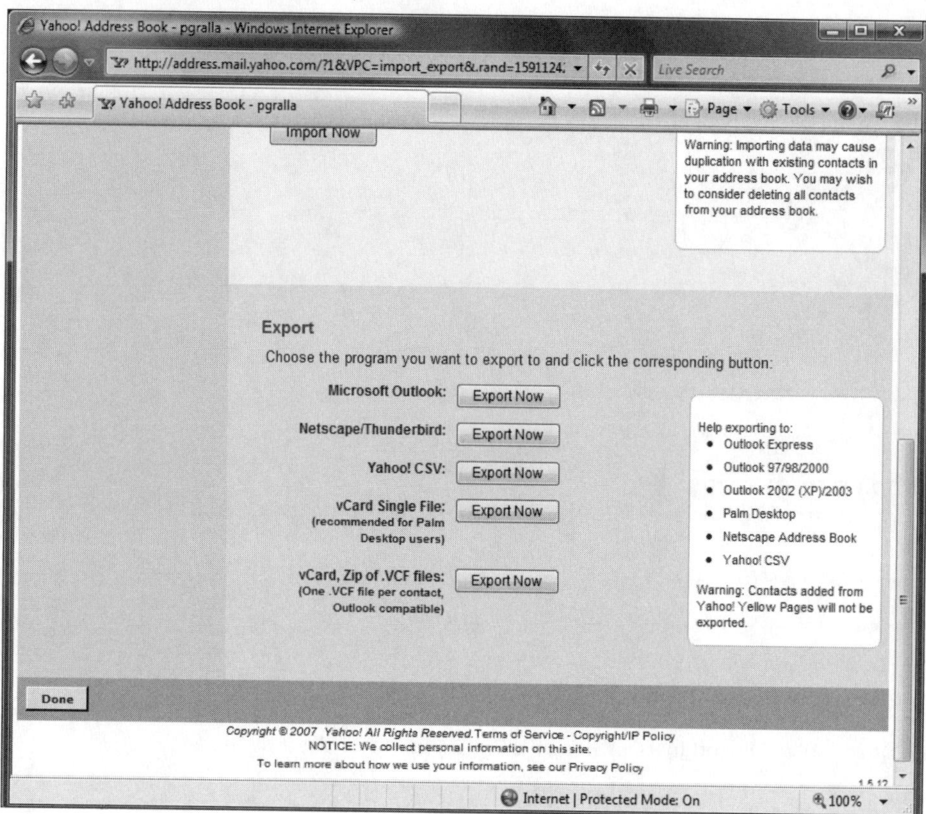

Figure 6-25.
Exporting as Yahoo! CSV

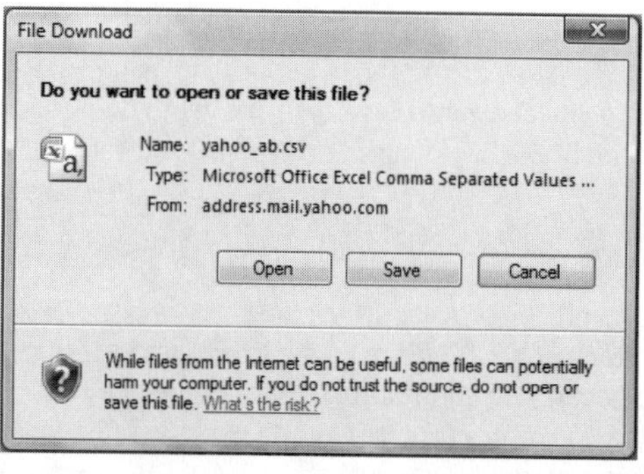

When you receive the message at Gmail, open it and choose "Reply to all." Write something explanatory again and send it off.

Gmail automatically adds to your contact list the names and email addresses of the people you send email to from Gmail, so you've just added all of those people to your Gmail address book.

Again, this is a rather annoying way (annoying to your friends, family, and business contacts) to get your contacts list to Gmail, so it should be regarded as a last-ditch effort. And since many people are cautious about who they give their email address out to, be sure to use the Bcc option instead of Cc.

—Rael Dornfest and Justin Blanton, from Google Hacks

> **QUICK HACK**
>
> **DISABLE WINDOWS MAIL'S SPLASH SCREEN**
>
> Is there any purpose to the splash screen that appears when you start Windows Mail in Windows Vista? If so, I haven't found it. If you'd like to disable it, Launch the Registry Editor by typing regedit at the Start Search box or a command prompt (See Chapter 13 for details). Go to `HKEY_CURRENT_USER\Software\Microsoft\Windows Mail`). Add the DWORD value `NoSplash` and give it a value of 1.

HACK 98: Import Mail into Gmail

V XP Moving to Gmail doesn't have to mean starting from scratch. Forward mail in bulk from your computer or other web mail service to your Gmail account.

The most enticing feature of Gmail is probably its ability to perform Google-style searches on your own Inbox. Over two gigabytes of free space is intriguing, but it's not much when you consider that you have far more than that available to you on even your most outdated PC. And I'd warrant that not even its snazzy Ajax interface is enough to tear you away from your existing web mail service, which would force you to uproot and start over.

Gmail doesn't currently provide a way to import your existing email archive (web mail service or desktop mailbox). While you might have already considered forwarding all that mail to your Gmail account, just how to do so—even forwarding just the few hundred "important" messages—presents quite a problem.

Not so, thanks to hacks such as the Google Mail Loader for forwarding desktop mail and web mail intermediaries, YPOPs! for Yahoo! Mail and MSN email, and GetMail for Hotmail.

Forward Desktop Mail

The Google Mail Loader (www.marklyon.org/gmail; GNU Public License) is a point-and-click application that reads your existing mail files on your computer and forwards the messages to Gmail—one every two seconds, so as not to overload or otherwise annoy the Gmail servers. It does so without deleting mail from your local computer; a copy of each and every message is sent to Gmail. You can even set it to drop uploaded messages into your Gmail Inbox or Sent Mail folder.

GML is cross-platform and understands multiple mailbox formats:

- Mbox (used by Netscape, Mozilla, Thunderbird, and many other email applications)
- MailDir (Qmail and others)
- MMDF (Mutt)
- MH (NMH)
- Babyl (Emacs RMAIL)
- Microsoft Outlook, via a utility such as PST Reader (www.mailnavigator.com/reading_ms_outlook_pst_files.html), which converts Outlook's PST files to Mbox format

Installing the Hack

Download the Windows version (www.marklyon.org/gmail/download.htm).

Running the Hack

Because Google Mail Loader works directly with your email application's mailboxes, you need to figure out where they live before you can go much further. Consult your email app's preferences or documentation or just dig around—both on your hard drive and by googling for `"outlook express" mailbox files location`, replacing `outlook express` with the name of your email program.

You also need to make sure your mailbox files are in a format that Google Mail Loader can read, as listed in the beginning of this hack. If there's any conversion to do, do it now. For instance, use PST Reader (www.mailnavigator.com/reading_ms_outlook_pst_files.html) to turn Outlook and Outlook Express PST files into mBox format.

With mailbox files in hand, launch Google Mail Loader by double-clicking *gmlw.exe* on Windows or typing `python gmlw.py` on the Unix or Mac OS X command line. Figure 6-26 shows Google Mail Loader running under Windows.

Work your way down the settings on the left half of the GML window:

1. The default SMTP server (that's the sendmail server, the one used to send your messages to Gmail) of smtp.google.com works for most users. If, for some reason, you are required by your local network administrator or ISP to use their outgoing mail server, replace the default with the appropriate address. If your outgoing mail server requires authentication, click the Requires Authentication checkbox, and fill in your username and password.

2. Click the Find button, and point GML at your mailbox file. If your email application uses MailDir format, select any file inside your MailDir directory.

3. From the File Type pull-down menu, choose your mailbox type (Figure 6-27). There are two versions of Mbox format: one is stricter about the file format and is therefore more accurate, while the other is more lenient and works better on some Mbox files.

For some of the history of mailbox file formats, read Jamie Zawinski's "mail summary files" at www.jwz.org/doc/mailsum.html.

4. If you don't know what format your mail application uses, try Googling for `mail format pine`, replacing `pine` with your mail app's name. (Pine uses Mbox, by the way.)

5. GML can upload both your incoming and outgoing mail. Choose "Mail I Received" from the Message Type pull-down menu, and messages are dropped into your Gmail Inbox and appear to be from the original sender, just as they did in your email application's mailbox. If you choose Mail I Sent, the messages are relabeled as coming from your Gmail address and appear in your Gmail Sent Mail folder.

Figure 6-26.
Google Mail Loader

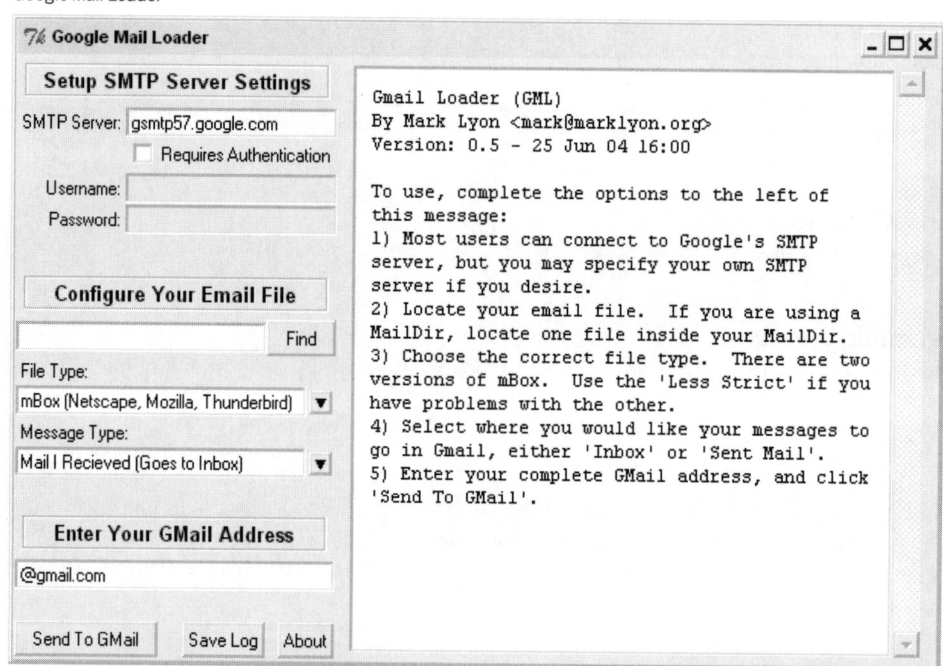

Figure 6-27.
Selecting your mailbox file type

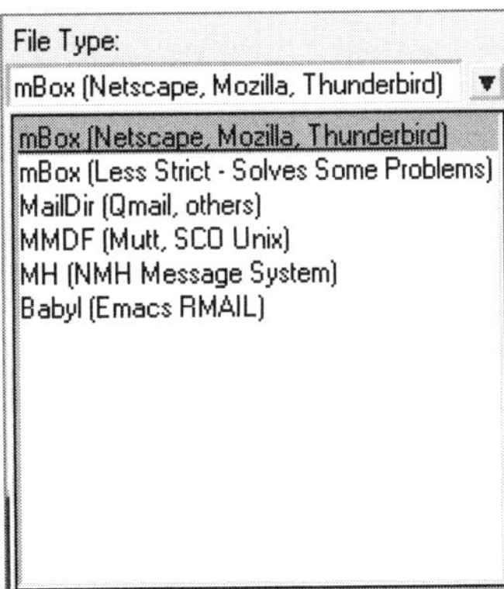

Gmail automatically labels incoming messages as Inbox. There's no way, unfortunately, for an external application to change this behavior, so messages imported as Mail | Sent are labeled as both Sent Mail and Inbox, and appear in both places. Keep in mind that there is only one copy of the message stored, and sent mail is relabeled so as to appear to be from your Gmail address, not your old email address.

If you Archive the copy you see in your Gmail Inbox, it will appear only in Sent Mail (and Archive, of course).

6. Type in your full Gmail address (e.g., *hank@gmail.com*).
7. Click the Send to Gmail button, and the application will start sending messages, one every two seconds. The delay is necessary to prevent flooding of Google's servers.

If you're interested in the details, click the Save Log button to save the contents of the output window to a file for later review.

There are, as with any hack of this sort, some issues worth noting:

- The timestamp of imported messages in your Gmail Inbox is the same as when the message was received by Google. Inside the message itself, however, the original date is still preserved. You can search for parts of dates to retrieve matching messages: `Aug 94`, for instance, finds all messages from August of 1994.
- The number of messages in your Inbox does not match the number GML reports as sent. This is because the number of GML reports is the number of new threads, not of individual messages. Gmail automatically groups related messages as they arrive.
- Some people, especially users of Mozilla or Firefox, report problems with their Mbox files being corrupt. I have tracked down a Python script (www.marklyon.org/gmail/cleanmbox.py) that cleans up most of these problems.
- Importing mail from Outlook is a bit spotty. I recommend one of two things: import your Outlook mail into Outlook Express and then into the open source Thunderbird mail application (www.mozilla.org/products/thunderbird), or use PST Reader or the like to convert your Outlook mail to Mbox.

Hacking the Hack

If you're a command-line jockey or don't particularly relish installing the various prerequisites (Python Mega Widgets) necessary to run the graphical version of Google Mail Loader, there's a text-only version available at www.marklyon.org/gmail/old/default.htm.

The only requirement for the command-line GML is Python (www.python.org).

Migrate from an Existing Web Mail Service

Despite attempts by your existing web mail service to entice you to stay, Gmail beckons with its gigabytes of storage, powerful search, rich web interface, and chance of grabbing a better email address than `raelity973@`. That said, you're loath to leave behind the last year or three's email. Well, in some cases, you can indeed take it with you, thanks to some nice donateware web-to-POP mail utilities. These intermediaries operate in one of two ways:

- The utility sits between your desktop email application and web mail service, allowing you to download all your mail to your computer, after which you can use the Google Mail Loader to feed it to Gmail.
- The utility combines these two steps into one, grabbing all your web mail and forwarding it in bulk to your Gmail account.

While there are no doubt any number of these utilities, two we stumbled across were GetMail and YPOPs!

If you use Yahoo! Mail, you can try out YPOPs! (yahoopops.sourceforge.net; donateware), a POP mail proxy that sits between your preferred email application and Yahoo! Mail. It's available for Windows, Mac OS X, Linux, and Solaris. The Windows version self-installs, while the others require that you compile from source code, so they are a little more difficult for the uninitiated to get up and running.

Move any messages you want to download and carry across to Gmail into your Yahoo! Mail Inbox and mark them as unread.

On Windows, run YPOPs! after installation. A little icon appears in your Windows taskbar; double-click it to get to the settings, shown in Figure 6-28.

While you can go ahead and make a few changes in the settings, YPOPs! runs right out of the box without any further configuration.

Now simply set up a POP mail account as you would any other, except that you point to YPOPs! running locally as your mail server—both incoming and outgoing. The YPOPs! site has details on configuring most email clients, and you can find them by clicking the Configure Mail Clients link on the left side of the YPOPs! home page (www.ypopsemail.com).

Once you have downloaded all your web mail to your computer, use the Google Email Loader to send all the contents of your local inbox to Gmail.

See Also

- GmailerXP (gmailerxp.sourceforge.net; donateware) is the be-all and end-all of Gmail/Windows integration, providing a full-featured frontend to your Gmail email, importing and uploading legacy messages to Gmail, new mail notification, and so on.
- gExodus (blog.codefront.net/archives/2004/06/23/gexodus-02-some-new-features-for-gmail-mbox-import-tool) is an Mbox-to-Gmail importer that's similar to Google Mail Loader, with the added feature of custom subject-line prefixes for imported mail, which allows you to tag the subject of all imported mail with `[home-import]`, for example, and set up filters and searches for that group of emails.

— *Mark Lyon, Justin Blanton, and Rael Dornfest, from* Google Hacks

Figure 6-28.
YPOPs! proxies POP mail requests

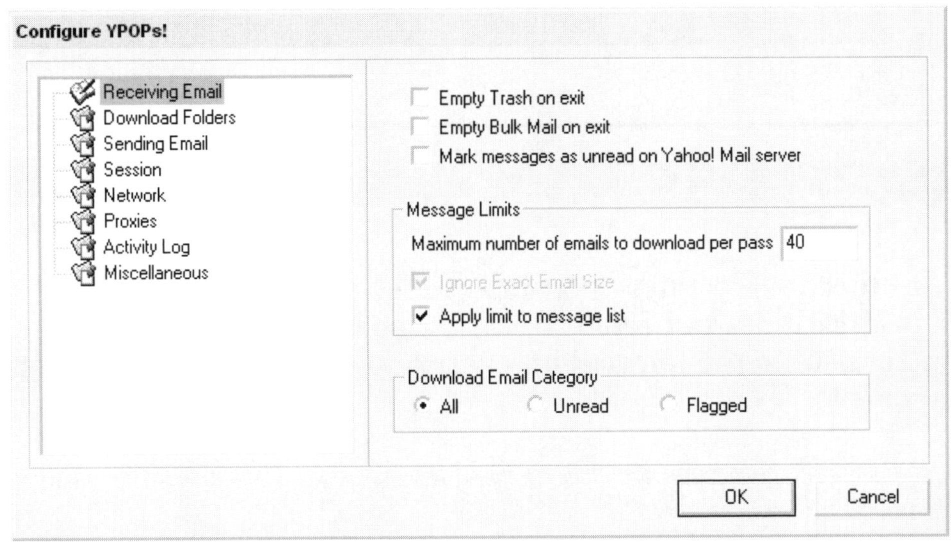

07 WIRELESS

Was there ever a time when you needed wires to connect to a network? It doesn't seem so, yet not so long ago the only way to connect to the Internet or a network was to plug in an Ethernet cable.

Thankfully, that's no longer the case. Wireless networking, via the 802.11 Wi-Fi standard has become ubiquitous. And that means it's ripe for hacking.

In this chapter, you'll find all kinds of wireless hacks. Want to give your homely home router the features of an enterprise powerhouse without spending a penny? You'll find out how to do it. Looking to build your own super-powerful Wi-Fi antenna? Yes, it's here. You'll also find out how to go wardriving for free Wi-Fi access, how to protect yourself at free hotspots, how to protect your home wireless network, and much more.

HACK 97: Turn Your Home Router into an Enterprise-Level Powerhouse

V XP Hidden in your inexpensive home router is a powerhouse waiting to break out. Here's how to give it extremely powerful features for free.

Home routers are as much a commodity computing item as you can find. Not uncommonly, they cost $50 or less, and they're usually simple, straightforward devices that are easy to use and set up, and don't offer a whole lot of extras.

Surprise—there's a lot more power lurking in that router than you realize. Many home routers have far more capabilities than you can imagine and can do many of the tricks that powerful, multihundred dollar enterprise routers can do. So why can't you get at them? Because of the *firmware* built into the router. Firmware is the software burned directly into the router itself. There's no big demand for fancy tricks for a simple home device, and if the capabilities were added, router makers would likely see a big upsurge in tech support calls. As a result, much of the hardware's capabilities go untapped, although Linksys has made a nod to the power user community by releasing some routers that work with open source firmware—as you'll see in this hack.

So how can you get at all that power? You can replace your router's firmware with the open source DD-WRT firmware. You'll get all kinds of new capabilities, including boosting your router's signal, improving network performance, giving yourself remote shell access to the router, and far more.

Keep in mind that there's a chance that you could do serious damage to your router if things go wrong during the firmware upgrade. You could even "brick" your router—break it so badly that it will no longer work.

Figure 7-1.
The Linksys WRT54GL router, just waiting to be hacked

Get the Right Router

The first step is to make sure your router can be upgraded, or else buy one that does. Not all routers can have their firmware upgraded to DD-WRT. Many, in fact, can't. Some routers from the same manufacturer can be upgraded, and some can't. To make things even more confusing, even the same *models* of routers from some manufacturers can be upgraded, while others can't, depending on the hardware version and the underlying operating system. For example, some versions of the Linksys WRT54G can use DD-WRT, while others can't because of changes to the underlying hardware.

So how to know which router can handle it? The best source of information about everything to do with DD-WRT is the exceedingly helpful and detailed DD-WRT Wiki (www.dd-wrt.com/wiki). Head to the Supported Devices page (www.dd-wrt.com/wiki/index.php/Supported_Devices) to see if it will work with your router. Make sure to click the link on your model number for more details. That will be the only way for you to make sure your model really is supported; the page explains how you can find out your model's hardware version, firmware, and capabilities, and will explain whether it will work with DD-WRT.

Install the Firmware

Once you've confirmed that your model can handle DD-WRT, it's time to install the firmware. The instructions for installing firmware vary from router to router, and even between firmware versions of the same router. So you should find the detailed instructions for your specific model on the DD-WRT Wiki site at the Installation page (www.dd-wrt.com/wiki/index.php?title=Installation).

The overall directions are largely the same for all routers, with variants. In this hack, I'll use the Linksys WRT54GL router, hardware version 1.1, shown in Figure 7-1. Even if you have a WRT54GL router, the instructions may vary somewhat from these instructions, depending on your hardware version. For details, and how to find out your hardware version, see the Linksys WRT54G/GL/GS/GX page on the DD-WRT Wiki (www.dd-wrt.com/wiki/index.php/Linksys_WRT54G/GL/GS/GX).

 The Linksys WRT54G was the first home router that released its firmware source code under the Open Source GNU GPL license, which lets programmers freely modify its firmware. Many versions of the WRT54G also use Linux as the underlying operating system.

Set up your router, connect it to the Internet, and connect your PC to the router. Make sure that you connect your PC to it via an Ethernet port, not wirelessly. If you try to upgrade the firmware wirelessly, you could be in for very serious trouble and could well brick your router. Also, never use an *https* (secure) connection for upgrading the firmware. Only use *http*.

 To make sure that you don't upgrade your firmware wirelessly, use a PC that doesn't even have a wireless adapter on it. If you don't have a PC without a wireless adapter, disable the wireless adapter (check the manufacturer's web site for details) or disconnect from the wireless network. If you don't disable the wireless adapter, you could accidentally end up upgrading the firmware with the wireless rather than wired connection.

Download the latest edition of the firmware from the DD-WRT site (www.dd-wrt.com/dd-wrtv2/downloads.php). As I explained previously, check the specific installation instructions for your router because depending on your specific router model and hardware version, you may need to download slightly different versions of DD-WRT. In some instances, you'll have to download two versions of DD-WRT—a "mini" firmware version to bootstrap the standard firmware version (which you'll also need to download).

For the WRT54GL hardware versions 1.1, download the latest generic firmware version. For other versions of the WRT54GL, such as hardware versions 1, you'll need to download both the mini and standard. Check the Linksys WRT54G/GL/GS/GX page on the DD-WRT Wiki (www.dd-wrt.com/wiki/index.php/Linksys_WRT54G/GL/GS/GX) for details.

After you download and install the firmware, reset your router to its factory defaults. First log into the administrator screen at http://192.168.1.1 (if you've configured your router to use a different network range, use the IP address of your router). Then go to Administration→Factory Defaults, select Yes, and Save Settings. See Figure 7-2.

Next, do a hard reset of your router by holding down its reset button, which you can find on the back of the router. Hold it down for 30 seconds.

Now you're ready to flash the firmware. Before you do it, though, turn off any antivirus or firewall software on the PC you're doing the flashing from. If antivirus or firewall software interrupts the firmware flash for any reason you could damage your router. And again, remember to do the firmware flash only over a wired connection, not a wireless one.

Log into the administrator screen, and select Administration→Firmware Upgrade. Click the Browse button, and select the firmware you downloaded, as shown in Figure 7-3. The firmware will end with a *.bin* extension. For my router, I selected the generic version of the firmware, *dd-wrt.v23_generic.bin*, because that's what is required by this router and hardware version.

Click Upgrade, and then don't do anything. If you do anything at all while the firmware is being upgraded, you could damage your router. The upgrade will take several minutes. Next, you should see a screen telling you that the firmware upgrade was successful. Click Continue.

You'll be asked to log in again. Your username and password will be reset from what it was previously. The username will be *root*, and the password *admin*. However, you may not be able to log in just yet: reset your router by holding down its reset button for 30 seconds. After it reboots, you should now be able to log in to your router, and when you do, the new firmware will be up and running.

Troubleshoot the Firmware Upgrade

In the ideal world, your firmware should now be upgraded. Not all of us, though, live in the ideal world. And so you may run into problems when you upgrade your firmware. For example, when

Figure 7-2.
Resetting the Linksys WRT54GL to its factory default settings

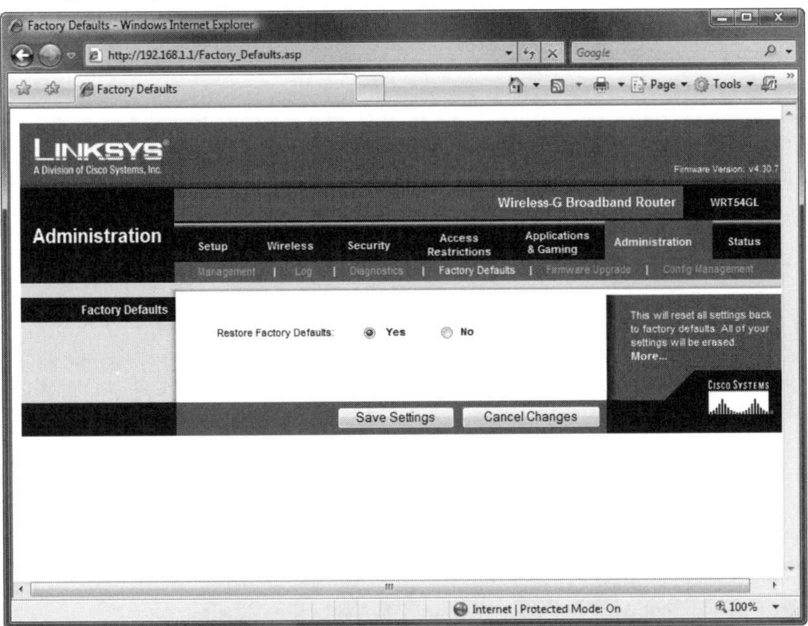

Figure 7-3.
Installing the DD-WRT firmware

I upgraded my WRT54GL, a screen appeared telling me that the upgrade was successful. But I couldn't log in to the router, even after resetting it. Following advice on the Recover from a Bad Flash page on the DD-WRT Wiki (www.dd-wrt.com/wiki/index.php/Recover_from_a_Bad_Flash#WRT54G), I unplugged the router's power cord, held down the reset button, then while holding it down plugged the power cord back in and held the reset button for five seconds. I then released the button, and waited a minute. Then I logged into the router, and the DD-WRT screen appeared. I was in!

Hack the Router

When you log into the router using *root* as the username, and *admin* as the password, you'll see a completely different screen than what you saw with the default firmware, so you know you're using the new firmware. Figure 7-4 shows the screen you'll see.

As you can see, you're not in the world of your old router firmware. For a start, there's a great deal more detail here about your router and network. For example, look down at the bottom of the screen. You'll see a list of all the wired and wireless PCs on your network, including their IP addresses. For wireless PCs, you'll also see the signal strength of their wireless connections. There's far more information here as well, such as the number of wireless packets sent and received, and the number of errors.

There are countless things you'll be able to do with DD-WRT firmware. Here I'll cover some of the high points, but there's plenty else you can do as well, so take the time to poke around the DD-WRT Wiki, as well as the DD-WRT documentation (www.informatione.gmxhome.de/DDWRT/Standard/V23final/help/index.html).

Figure 7-4.
You're not in Linksys land anymore: DD-WRT's Control Panel offers you far more tools and information than your former firmware

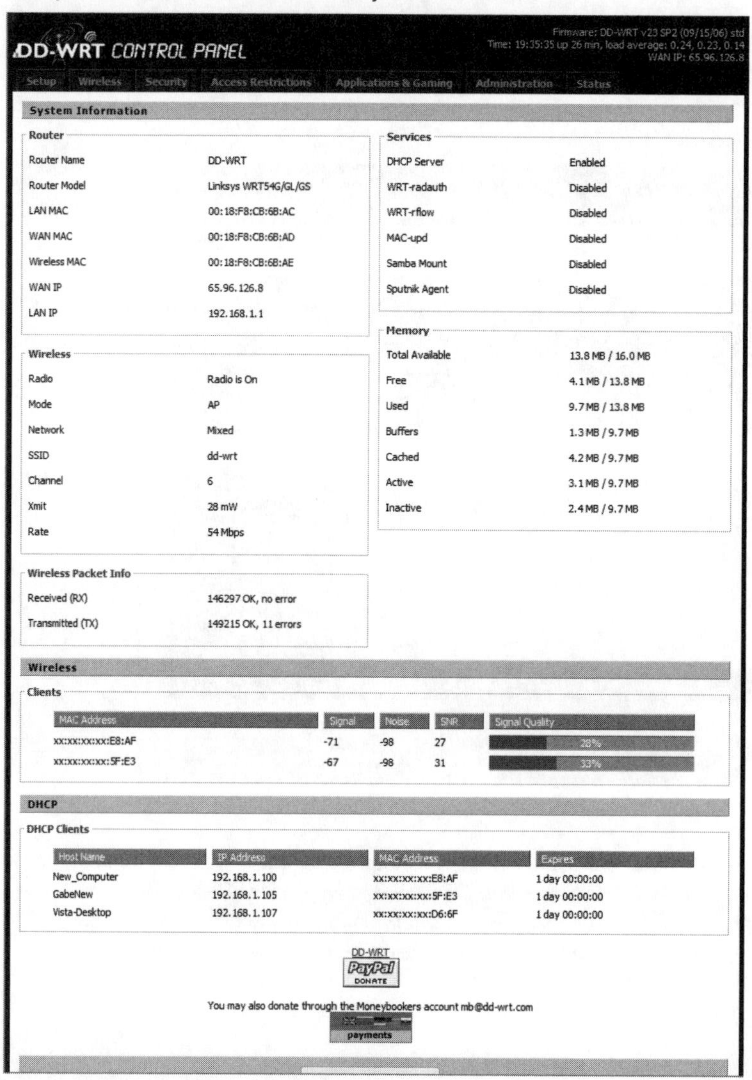

Juice Up Your Wireless Signal

The biggest problem most people have with their wireless router is that the signal is too weak in certain places. This is a particular problem if you live in a house. Your router might be downstairs, and upstairs rooms may have weak signals. Not uncommonly, you'll find near dead spots in your house as well. The DD-WRT solves the problem easily; it lets you bump up the power of your wireless signal.

To do it, log into the DD-WRT Control Panel, and select Wireless→Advanced Settings. Scroll down to Xmit Power, as shown in Figure 7-5.

In Linksys, the default is 28 mW (milliwatts). You can crank it up well beyond that; the range is between 0 and 251 mW. But don't crank it up all the way, or even close to all the way. If you do, you could quickly burn out your router because the higher the mW rating you use, the more heat your radio chipset will generate. The DD-WRT documentation says that using up to 70 mW should be safe in most cases. You may want to start lower than that, and keep increasing it until you find that the wireless signal is strong throughout your house. Click Save Settings every time you make a change.

Improve Network Performance

Several other settings on the Advanced Settings tab may help improve the performance of your wireless network. Changing the Beacon Interval setting can help if wireless clients are getting poor performance. The beacon is a wireless packet the router sends out as a way to synchronize the network. The default setting is 100 milliseconds. Change it to 50 milliseconds if you have wireless clients with poor reception.

It's essential to change your username and password from the default of *root* and *admin*. To do so, select Administration→Management, and type in the new username and password in the Router Password section.

If you have a network with from only one to three wireless PCs on it, you can also improve performance by allowing Frame Burst. This enables packet bursting, which can increase overall network speed. But if you have more than three clients, this will actually decrease throughput. By default it's turned off; select Enable if you want it on. When you're done, click Save Settings.

Figure 7-5.
The Advanced Settings screen lets you increase your wireless signal and set other advanced options for wireless

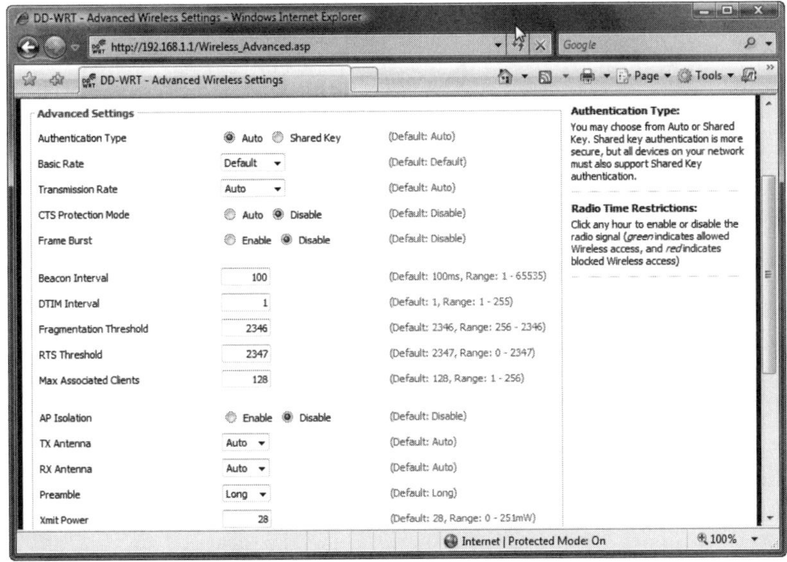

Improve Security by Auto-Turning Off Wireless Signals

When you're not at home or when you're sleeping, you most likely don't turn off your wireless network. If you're worried that bandwidth vampires or network crackers will steal your bandwidth or break into your network when you're not around, you can schedule your router to stop transmitting at certain times of the day and night. Wired connections will still work, but wireless connections won't.

On the Advanced Settings screen, scroll down to Radio Time Restrictions, and click Enable. A timeline of all the hours in the day will appear, as you can see in Figure 7-6. Click on all the hours that you want wireless access disabled. That hour will show up red. When you're done, click Save Settings.

Optimize Bandwidth for Certain Applications and PCs

DD-WRT includes very powerful Quality of Service features that let you ensure that certain applications and PCs get the most bandwidth when they need it. This is particularly helpful for Voice over Internet Protocol applications such as Skype that need all the bandwidth they can get in order to get as high a voice quality as possible. You have numerous options for QoS and can prioritize network bandwidth not only by application, but by PC as well.

For the basic setup, select Applications and Gaming→QoS, and select Enable next to Start QoS. Then select the WAN from the Port drop-down list, if it's not already selected. Figure 7-7 shows the QoS screen.

If you want to optimize your network for gaming, check the box next to Optimize for Gaming. This enables QoS for a group of TCP and UDP ports used in some games.

Next, fill in the uplink and downlink boxes. For each box, enter 85 percent of the bandwidth your ISP gives you. For example, if you have a 1.5-megabit download speed and 256-Kbps upload speed, enter 218 for uplink and 1306 for downlink. Make sure not to confuse the two, because if you do, you'll dramatically decrease your download speeds.

The rest of the screen lets you optimize your bandwidth for certain applications, certain PCs on your network, and by other criteria. To give a certain application, such as Skype, high priority, click Add, then select the application from the list that appears, as shown in Figure 7-8. Click Add, and it will be added to the Services Priority List. From the Priority drop-down box, select the priority you want to give it. The highest priority is Exempt, and the lowest is Bulk.

Figure 7-6.
Restricting wireless access to your network during certain parts of the day

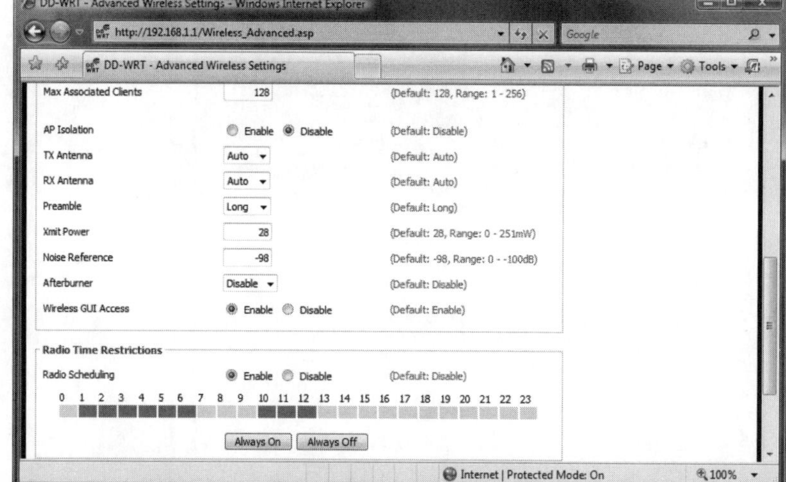

QUICK HACK 

FIND YOUR TRUE BANDWIDTH SPEEDS

Your ISP may promise you certain upload and download speeds, but how good is their real-world performance (there are many factors outside your ISP's control that affect performance)? There's a simple way to find out. Go to a free online speed test. There are quite a few available, so it's a good idea to go to several. Good ones are DSL Reports (www.dslreports.com/stest), the CNet Bandwidth Meter Test (reviews.cnet.com/7004-7254_7-0.html), and the Speakeasy Speed Test (www.speakeasy.net/speedtest) They're also useful for determining your bandwidth when configuring QoS.

Figure 7-7.
Using QoS Settings to optimize bandwidth

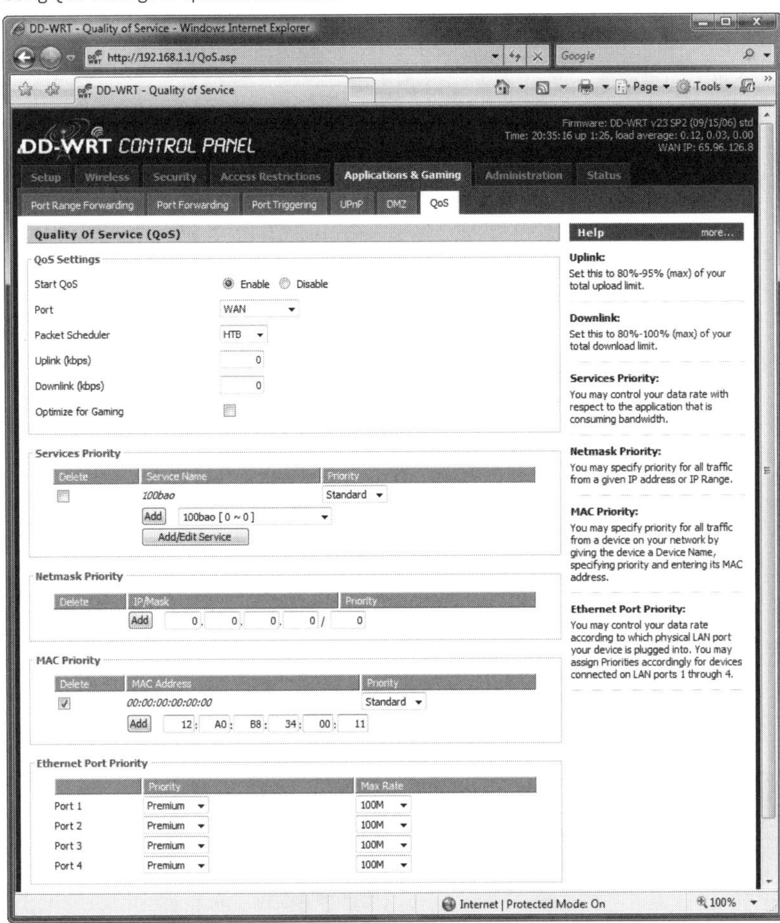

The QoS screen also lets you give certain PCs high priority. For PCs attached to the router via Ethernet, scroll down to Ethernet Port Priority, and make a selection from the Priority drop-down box, to assign different levels to each PC. You can also specify maximum bandwidth rates for each, by selecting them from the Max Rate drop-down list. Rates range from completely disabling access, up to 100 megabits.

You can also assign priorities to wireless PCs. Go to the MAC Priority section, and add the MAC address of any wireless adapter. (To find an adapter's MAC address, go to the command prompt and type ipconfig /all, and press Enter. At the bottom of the entry for your Wi-Fi adapter, look for the number next to Physical Address. That's the MAC address.)

When you're done, click Save Settings.

Restrict Internet Use

If you want to restrict certain PCs from using the Internet during certain hours—for example, if you have children and don't want them online late at night—you can turn off Internet access for any PC on the network for certain hours. You can also block access to certain Web sites or services, either during certain hours, or all the time.

Figure 7-8.
Giving Skype high priority

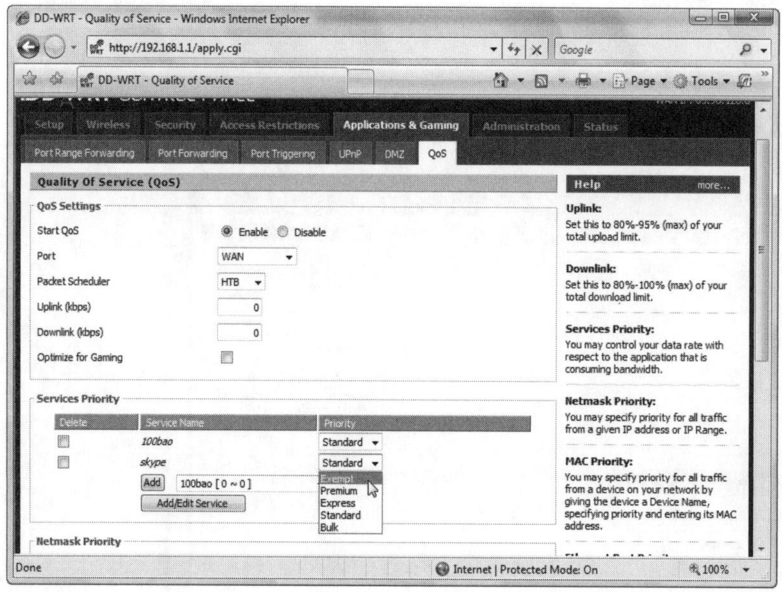

Figure 7-9.
Restricting Internet access

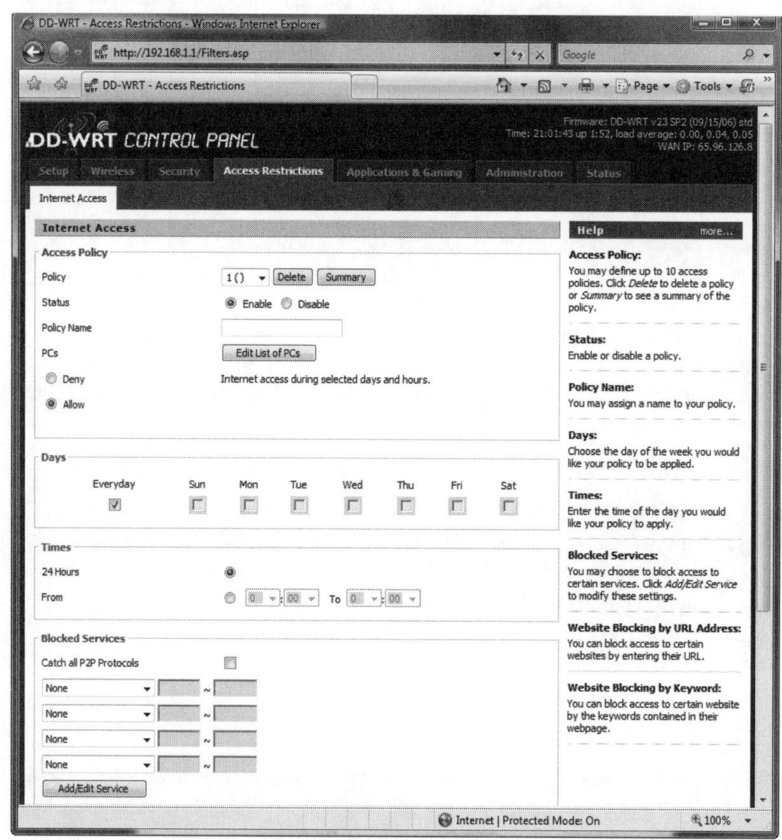

From the main DD-WRT screen, click Access Restrictions, and a screen like Figure 7-9 appears. Click Enable, and from the Policy drop-down menu, select a number. You can create up to 10 separate policies. Enter a name for your profile in the Policy Name box. Then click Edit List of PCs. From the list that appears, select PCs either by MAC address or by IP address or range. Click Deny because you're going to deny access to the Internet or services during certain hours.

Now fill out the rest of the screen. You can restrict access by day of the week, for all day or within a certain time range you can restrict specific services, such as ftp or certain games, you can block specific URLs and so on. It's all pretty self-explanatory. When you're done, click Save Settings.

If you want to block all P2P applications, you don't need to select them individually from the Blocked Services list. Instead, check the box next to Catch all P2P Protocols.

HACK 98: Troubleshoot Wireless Interference Woes, and Extend Your Range

V XP The efficiency and throughput of Wi-Fi networks can vary dramatically. Make sure you get maximum throughput from your wireless network.

Setting up a wireless network sounds so simple: buy a router, do a little basic configuration for it and your wireless PCs, turn everything on, and you're done. Everyone in your house gets full access to the network and high-speed Internet.

Ah, if life were only that simple.

In the real world, using a wireless network at home can be maddening. Put the router downstairs, and your upstairs PCs may barely make the connection; put the router upstairs, and the downstairs PC goes without.

Worse yet, everything may work according to plan, but every once in a while, your PCs may lose their connection for no apparent reason.

Don't put it all down to cosmic rays, sun spots, or the will of the gods. There are a number of reasons why your home wireless network may have problems. And there are many simple ways you can extend your network's range and make sure that all the PCs in your house can connect. Here's what you should do to:

Centrally locate your wireless access point
This way, it's most likely that all your wirelessly equipped PCs will get reasonable throughput. If you put your wireless access point in one corner of the house, nearby PCs might get high throughput, but throughput for others might drop significantly.

Change your Wi-Fi channel
You may have neighbors with Wi-Fi networks, and if so, those networks may interfere with yours. In the United States, Wi-Fi networks should broadcast on any one of three channels (eleven are available, but only three do not overlap: 1, 6, and 11), and if you're using the same channel as a neighbor, your reception can suffer. To find out what channel your neighbor's Wi-Fi network uses, you'll need to use software. If you use the software that came with the adapter—instead of the built-in Windows software—for managing your Wi-Fi adapter, use that software. If not, use the free NetStumbler **[Hack #103]** (netstumbler.com). Run the software, and see if any nearby networks use the same channel as yours (Figure 7-10).

Interference can be caused not only by networks using the same channel, but nearby channels as well. It's best to have a spacing of about five channels. So if you use channel 3, and a nearby network uses channel 2, and you're running into problems, set your network to use channel 7. However, in

Figure 7-10.
Three networks near each other all use the same Wi-Fi channel

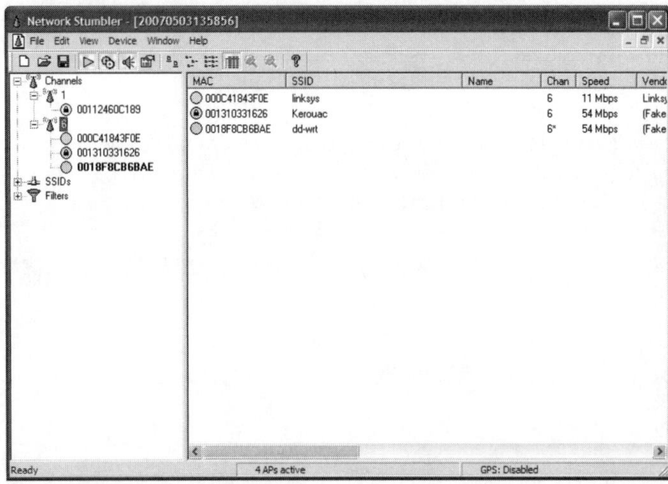

the United States, you can get the largest number of non-overlapping channels by choosing 1, 6, and 11. If you live in a densely populated area, you'll have to coordinate channel assignments with your neighbors.

 Many routers ship with a default channel of 6, so if you're using that channel, you're most likely to run into interference from nearby Wi-Fi networks.

How you change the channel depends on your specific router. For most Linksys routers, though, open a browser to http://192.168.1.1, and log in. By default, there's no username, and the password is admin. Click the Wireless tab (Figure 7-11), and from the Wireless Channel drop-down box, select the channel you want to use. Then click Save Settings.

Check for interference

Cordless telephones, microwave ovens, and other devices use the same frequency as your Wi-Fi network. They may be the cause of intermittent connection problems. Move your access point away from any cordless phones or microwave ovens. If you're using a 2.4-GHz phone system, consider switching to a 5-GHz phone, which won't interfere with anything but the less common 802.11a (so if you are using 802.11a, you should avoid 5-GHz devices).

Change the orientation of your access point's antennas

Moving them from vertical to horizontal, or vice versa, or anywhere in between may have a surprising effect on signal strength to distant PCs. So experiment with antenna orientation until you find one that's best.

Point the antennas of your wireless PCs toward the access point

Although 802.11 technology does not require a direct line of sight, pointing antennas in this way tends to increase signal strength. USB wireless cards generally have small antennas that can be positioned, but frequently wireless PC cards don't, so you might have trouble figuring out the antenna orientation in a wireless PC card. If you have a wireless PC card that doesn't have what appears to be an antenna, the antenna is generally located at the periphery of the card itself, so point that at the access point. If Wi-Fi is built into your notebook, the antenna may be built into the frame of your display.

A newer standard, 802.11g, operates in the same part of the spectrum and has a maximum throughput of 54 Mbps, significantly faster than 802.11b. Much of what you'll buy these days is 802.11g.

The equipment for the 802.11b and 802.11g standards work with each other, although with one "gotcha" you need to watch out for. If you mix and match 802.11g and 802.11b equipment, your

Figure 7-11.
Changing the wireless channel on a Linksys router

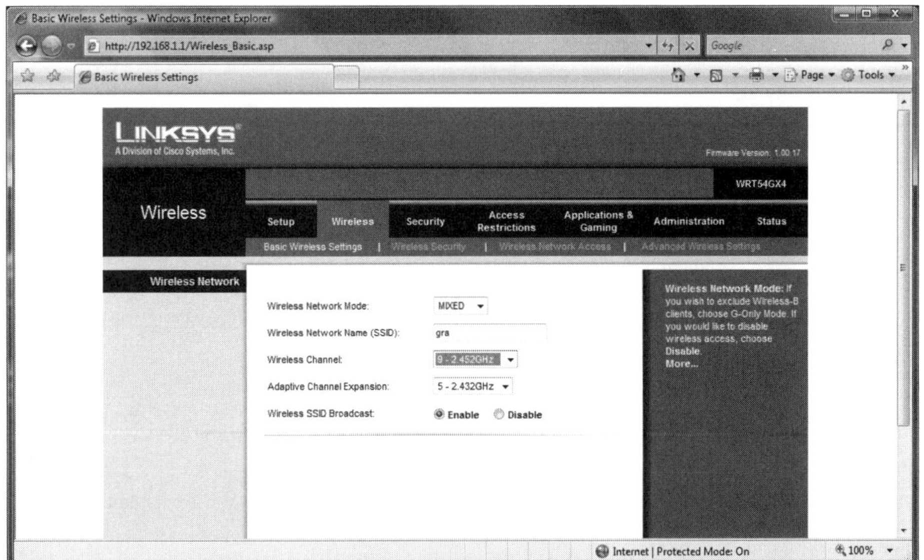

entire network may operate at the lower 802.11b speed, depending on your manufacturer. If you have an 802.11g router and 802.11b adapters, the network will run at the slower speed, of course. But in some instances, if you have an 802.11g router, three 802.11g adapters, and one 802.11b adapter, the entire network may *still* run at the lower speed, even between the 802.11g adapters and the 802.11g router. The upshot: to be safe, make sure every piece of your equipment is at least 802.11g, not 802.11b.

You'll also find 802.11g routers and adapters that promise speeds far greater than 802.11g, commonly at 108 Mbps. This technology goes by different names from different vendors, such as Linksys's SpeedBooster. It works only when you buy all the hardware from the same manufacturer because they use proprietary protocols to reach those speeds. If you mix and match components from different manufacturers, you'll get normal 802.11g speeds, not the faster ones.

There's a newer, higher-speed standard just coming out as well, 802.11n. This promises exceedingly high speeds greater coverage areas. It uses the 2.4-GHz spectrum, like 802.11b and 802.11g, and has a maximum data rate of a whopping 540 Mbps. It promises an indoor range of 50 meters, compared to 25 meters for 802.11g.

As this book went to press, the standard hadn't been formally accepted, but it may have been by the time you read this. Until the standard is formally accepted, manufacturers sell what they call pre-802.11n gear, which adheres to the preaccepted standard. Although 802.11n promises much higher speeds, pre-802.11n gear was topping out near 248 Mbps—but that's the "rated" maximum—real-world performance is closer to 90 Mbps (similarly, 802.11g's 54 Mbps translates to about 20 Mbps in real-world tests). Manufacturers say that the hardware can be upgraded via firmware to the standards when it's finalized. To be absolutely safe, though, you may want to hold off until the standard has been accepted, and hardware is released based on the standard.

Don't place your access point next to an outside wall
If you do that, you'll be broadcasting signals to the outside, not the inside, of the house. That's nice if you want to give your neighbors access to your network, but not great if you want to reach all the PCs in your house.

Avoid placing the antennas of access points or PCs near filing cabinets and other large metal objects
They can cause significant interference and dramatically reduce throughput.

QUICK HACK

WI-FI AND BUYING NEW EQUIPMENT

There are several versions of the 802.11x Wi-Fi standard, so before you buy Wi-Fi gear, you should know what you're paying for because some are much faster than others. The old 802.11 legacy standard was the first one to be ratified, and it was soon followed by 802.11a and 802.11b. The 802.11b standard was the first to gain massive popularity, and equipment that adheres to it is the least expensive. (This is the standard commonly used by public wireless hotspots in coffee shops, airports, hotels, and other locations.) It operates in the 2.4 GHz part of the spectrum, and its maximum throughput is 11 Mbps. Not much new Wi-Fi equipment uses this standard.

Consider using external and booster antennas

Some PC cards will accept external antennas that you can buy or build on your own. They have a small connector to which you attach a pigtail and wire, and then attach that wire to an antenna. (For information about building your own antenna, see "Hacking Wi-Fi Antennas" **[Hack #106]**.) Some access points often accept booster antennas that you can buy as well.

If you have a Linksys wireless network and are looking to improve its signal strength, you can buy a number of different add-ons that promise to extend its range and strengthen its signal. Linksys High Gain Antennas will strengthen your network's signal. Unscrew the antennas from your existing Linksys router, and screw these new ones into place. It also works with 802.11b and 802.11g routers.

Many routers can cooperate to extend the range of your network using a mode called Wireless Distribution System (WDS). This takes a Wi-Fi signal and relays it, expanding your network's range. However, for each relay you use, the wireless throughput is cut roughly in half (because the relay has to resend each message to and from the main router).

You can use two WRT54GL routers in WDS mode to extend the range of your network. But there are less expensive dedicated WDS devices available, such as the WRE54G Wireless-G range expander, for example. Try to avoid mixing WDS equipment from multiple vendors, and make sure the two routers you plan to use in WDS mode are compatible with one another.

Other manufacturers sell similar products, so check your router manufacturer's web site for details.

Update your firmware

Manufacturers regularly update the firmware of their routers to squash bugs and improve performance. So update your router's firmware. How you update firmware varies from router to router, so check for instructions. For a Linksys WRT54GX4 router, first download the firmware from Linksys. Then log in to administrator screen and select Administration→Firmware Upgrade. Follow the instructions on that screen for upgrading the firmware. If you're using custom firmware, follow the instructions in "Turn Your Home Router Into an Enterprise-Level Powerhouse" **[Hack #97]**.

Try and try again

The ultimate way to find the best placement for your access point and wireless PCs is to continuously experiment and see what kind of throughput you get. Each house and office is so different that no single configuration can suit them all.

HACK 99: Impersonate Another Computer on the Network

V XP If you're looking to test your wireless security, a good way is to change your adapter's MAC address, which is a kind of serial number. Here's how to do it.

Every piece of networking equipment has a unique identifying number, called a Media Access Control (MAC) address. This MAC address is used for a variety of different purposes, but primarily as a globally unique identifier. For example, DHCP servers use the MAC address as a way of keeping track of devices before they've been assigned an IP address.

You can use MAC address filtering **[Hack #101]** to help keep nonmalicious users from attaching to your wireless network: draw up a list of MAC addresses of all of the wireless adapters you want to grant access to, and then ban every other MAC address.

MAC address spoofing is commonly used by malicious hackers for a variety of different purposes. So be aware that any security system built using MAC addresses as its foundation will never be a truly secure one.

But how can you really know that's working? The simple way is to use a computer whose address is not in the list of permitted addresses. Once you've done that, you can change that computer's MAC address to one that is permitted and see if you can join the network. That's what you'll learn how to do in this hack.

Understanding MAC Addresses

Before you spoof a MAC address, it's a good idea to get a basic understanding of the addresses. MAC addresses are made up of six groups of two alphanumeric characters, separated by colons, like this: `00:0F:3D:EE:8E:F7`

Those numbers and letters may appear to be random, but in fact they're not. There's some method to the madness. Manufacturers are assigned specific blocks of MAC addresses. For example, Netgear equipment typically has this prefix: `00-0F-3D`

Linksys equipment typically uses this: `00-18-F8`

If you know a MAC address, it's easy to find out the manufacturer of the equipment because there's a public database you can search. Go to the IEEE Standards Association Organizationally Unique Identifier (OUI) database at standards.ieee.org/regauth/oui. Then type in the first three sets of numbers, and press Enter. You'll see the name of the equipment manufacturer. Be aware, though, that the manufacturer you see listed may not match your hardware's name. That's because companies often subcontract out hardware or else buy it from other firms. So, for example, the MAC address of the built-in adapter for my Dell laptop is listed as the Taiwan-based Hon Hai Precision Ind. Co., Ltd., even though the adapter is a Broadcom wireless adapter.

Spoofing Your MAC Address

Before spoofing your MAC address, write down your real MAC address, so that you can reinstate it. To find out your MAC address, go to a command prompt, and type ipconfig /all. The MAC address will be listed as the Physical Address for the adapter.

Now you're ready to spoof the address. Download the free Mac MakeUp (www.gorlani.com/publicprj/macmakeup/macmakeup.asp). Run the program, shown in Figure 7-12, and then choose an adapter from a list of them at the top of the page. If you have a wireless adapter, you will most likely have an Ethernet adapter as well, so make sure that you choose the wireless adapter, rather than the Ethernet adapter.

 Make sure that you run Mac MakeUp as an administrator; if you don't, it won't run. To run it as an administrator, right-click its executable file, and choose "Run as administrator".

There are several ways to create a spoofed address. If you want to spoof the address of a specific manufacturer, choose the name of the manufacturer from the drop-down list, and the new, spoofed MAC address will appear in the New Address box.

You can also click the Generate Random button, and a menu will appear with several choices. From the menu, you can generate a completely random MAC address, or you can generate one randomly from the manufacturer drop-down list (called the OID).

Finally, if you know a MAC address you want to spoof, type it directly into the New address box.

 Don't use the same MAC address on more than one devices on your network. If you do, you could cause conflicts, and devices may not work properly.

You've generated the address, but you haven't yet applied it. To apply it, make sure that the box next to Auto Nic Off/On is checked. Then click the Change button. That will apply the new address.

Now that you have a spoofed MAC address, test your wireless network's security. If you've filtered by MAC address, when you try to connect using a permitted address, you should be able to get in. If you can't get in, double-check to be sure you're using a MAC address from the permitted list. If your router has a log of denied connections, check it out to see if the attempt was listed.

To get back to your real MAC address, type it into the New address box, and click Change.

Hacking the Hack

The Auto Nic Off/On selection disables and then enables your network adapter. The adapter needs to be disabled and then enabled in order for the new MAC address to be applied. If you're the type that likes to do things manually, you can disable and enable the adapter yourself. It's also worth doing this if for some reason your new MAC address doesn't take.

In Windows Vista, select Control Panel→Network and Internet→Network and Sharing Center→Manage Network Connections. Then right-click your adapter, and select Disable, as shown in Figure 7-13. Right-click it again, choose Enable, and you've just spoofed your MAC address.

In XP, select Control Panel→Network and Internet Connections→Network Connections. Then right-click your adapter, and select Disable. Right-click it again and choose Enable.

Figure 7-12.
Use Mac MakeUp to impersonate another computer on the network

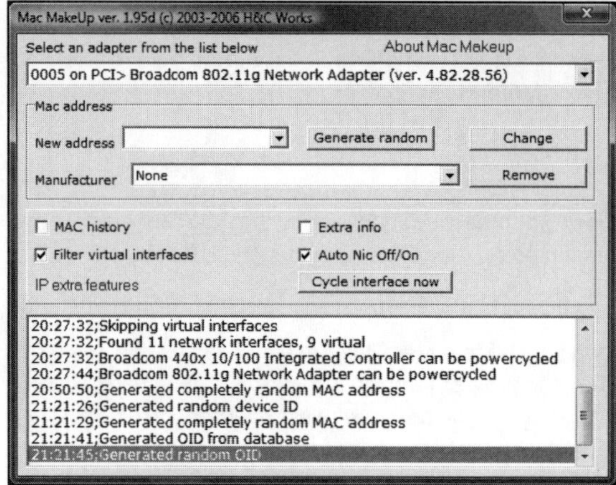

Figure 7-13.
Before your new MAC address takes effect, you need to disable, then enable your network adapter

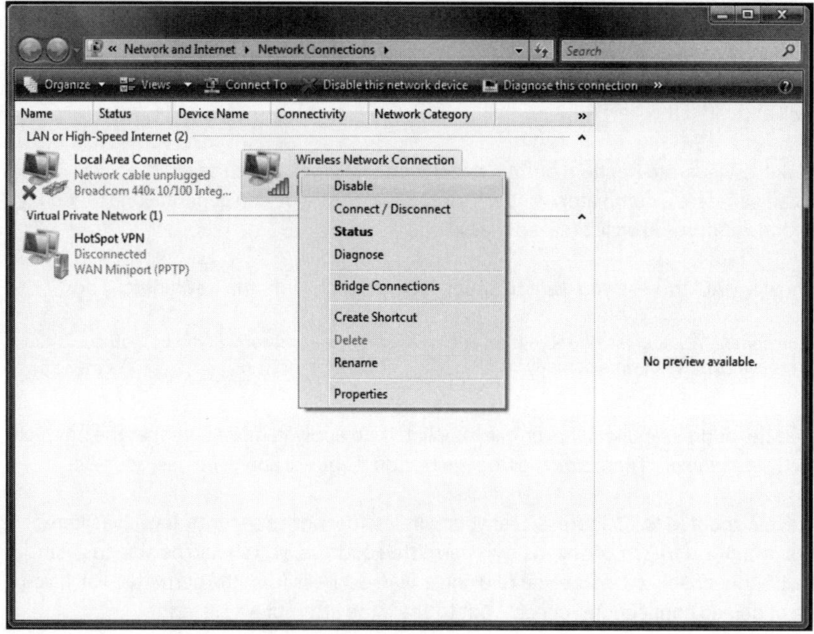

HACK 100: Protect Yourself Against "Free Wi-Fi" Scammers

Next time you see a network calling itself "Free Wi-Fi" beware: it could be a scammer. Here's how to make sure you don't get victimized.

It seems simple enough: You're at an airport, and you see a hotspot calling itself "Free Wi-Fi." You figure you might as well connect. But if you do, you could be victimized by a hotspot scam that's been hitting airports across the country. The hotspot may not be a legitimate one; it could simply be a nearby scammer, using his laptop to lure in the unwitting. Connect, and you could be victimized by a "man in the middle" attack in which a scammer is able to steal the information you send over the Internet, such as usernames and passwords. You could also have your files and identity stolen, end up with a spyware-infested PC, and your PC could be turned into a spam-spewing zombie.

If you're a Windows Vista user, you're especially susceptible to this attack, because of the difficulty in identifying it when using Vista. But XP users can be victimized as well. In this hack, I'll show you how the attack works, and how to keep yourself safe from it.

How the Attack Works

First, let's take a look at how the attack works. In the scam, the "Free Wi-Fi" hotspot isn't in fact a hotspot. Instead, it's an ad hoc, peer-to-peer network, set up by someone with a laptop nearby. Unless you know where to look, you won't know it's an ad hoc connection. And in many cases, you can use the Internet when you connect to the ad hoc network because the attacker has set up his PC to let you browse the Internet via his connection. But because you're using his connection, all your traffic goes through his PC, and so he can see everything you do online, including all the usernames and passwords you enter for many web sites.

Because you've directly connected to the attack PC on a peer-to-peer basis, if you've set up your PC to allow file sharing, the attacker can have complete run of your shared folders, stealing files and data, and planting malware on it.

 But even if you're on a public hotspot, you may be vulnerable to snooping and unwanted visitors. To avoid this, enable your firewall while you are on a public network; be sure to use encrypted connections for POP, SMTP, or IMAP email clients; and if possible, connect to your work VPN or a VPN service provided by a third party (such as JiWire's Hotspot Helper, www.jiwire.com/hotspot-helper.htm).

You can't actually see this any of this happening, so you'd be none the wiser. The hacker steals what he wants to or plants his malware, such as a virus- infected document, then leaves, and you have no way of tracking him down.

 The security company Authentium has found dozens of ad hoc networks in airports in Atlanta's airport, New York City's La Guardia, the West Palm Beach airport, and Chicago's O'Hare. And Internet users have reported finding them at Los Angeles's LAX.

Authentium did an in-depth survey www.computerworld.com/action/article.do?command=viewArticleBasic&articleId=9008399) of the ad hoc networks found at O'Hare, visiting on three different occasions. It found more than 20 ad hoc networks each time, with 80 percent of them advertising free Wi-Fi access. The company also found that many of the networks were displaying fake or misleading MAC addresses, a clear sign that they were bent on mischief.

How to Protect Yourself in Windows XP

Protecting yourself against these kinds of attacks can be quite easy: never connect to an ad hoc network unless someone you know has set one up and specifically asks you to connect. Keep in mind, though, that someone can name an ad hoc network anything they want, so they can even duplicate the name of a legitimate network. For example, if you're at an airport, and the name of the airport's free hotspot is AirNet, someone can set up an ad hoc network with that exact same name. You'd see two networks called AirNet, one the legitimate one, and the other a scam ad hoc network.

 Keep in mind that even a network in infrastructure mode can be a scam: an attacker could bring a modified router running custom firmware or use software to put a computer's Wi-Fi card into infrastructure mode. The only way to be absolutely sure you are connecting to a legitimate network is to use connection software provided by a Wi-Fi operator (such as T-Mobile) who has also implemented 802.1X security on their network.

To protect yourself, you need to differentiate between an ad hoc network and a normal Wi-Fi network. (Microsoft calls a normal Wi-Fi network "infrastructure mode").

In Windows XP, connect to a wireless network, right-click the wireless network icon in the system tray, choose "View Available Wireless Networks", and the "Choose a wireless network" connection screen appears. You'll see a list of all nearby wireless networks. As you can see in Figure 7-14, each network includes a name and a description. Look at the description. If it's an ad hoc network, it will be called a "computer-to-computer" network; normal wireless networks are simply called wireless networks. In the figure, the Free Airport Wi-Fi network is an ad hoc network. You should stay away from it.

There are other steps you can take to make sure you don't accidentally connect to an ad hoc network created by a scamster. For example, you can make sure that XP never connects to an ad hoc network. Here's how:

1. Right-click the wireless icon in the System Tray, and select Open Network Connections.

2. Right-click your wireless connection, and choose Properties.

3. Select the Wireless Networks tab.

4. Click Advanced.

5. On the screen that appears (pictured in Figure 7-15), select Access point (infrastructure) networks only.

6. Click Close, and keep clicking OK until the dialog boxes disappear.

When you're at the Advanced screen, you should also make sure the box next to "Automatically connect to non-preferred networks" is not checked. If that box is checked, your PC will connect to any nearby wireless network, without alerting you, which is a serious security risk.

It's also a good idea when you're on the Wireless Networks tab to look at all the wireless networks listed in the Preferred networks area. These are networks that you've connected to in the past. Highlight any that you are not absolutely sure are secure, then click Remove. That way, your PC won't attempt to connect to them.

There's more you should do as well. You should also configure your remaining preferred networks so that you don't connect to them automatically. Why do that? Let's say your home network uses the default name it shipped with—for example, Linksys for a Linksys network. A scamster can create an ad hoc network called Linksys, and then anyone nearby who has Linksys listed as a preferred network will automatically connect to that ad hoc network.

So, in the Preferred networks area, highlight each network, select Properties, then click the connection tab. Uncheck the box next to "Connect when this network is within range", and keep clicking OK until the dialog boxes close.

Figure 7-14.
Windows XP displays the details of every nearby wireless network, including whether it's an ad hoc network. In this screen, the Free Airport Wi-Fi network is an ad hoc network

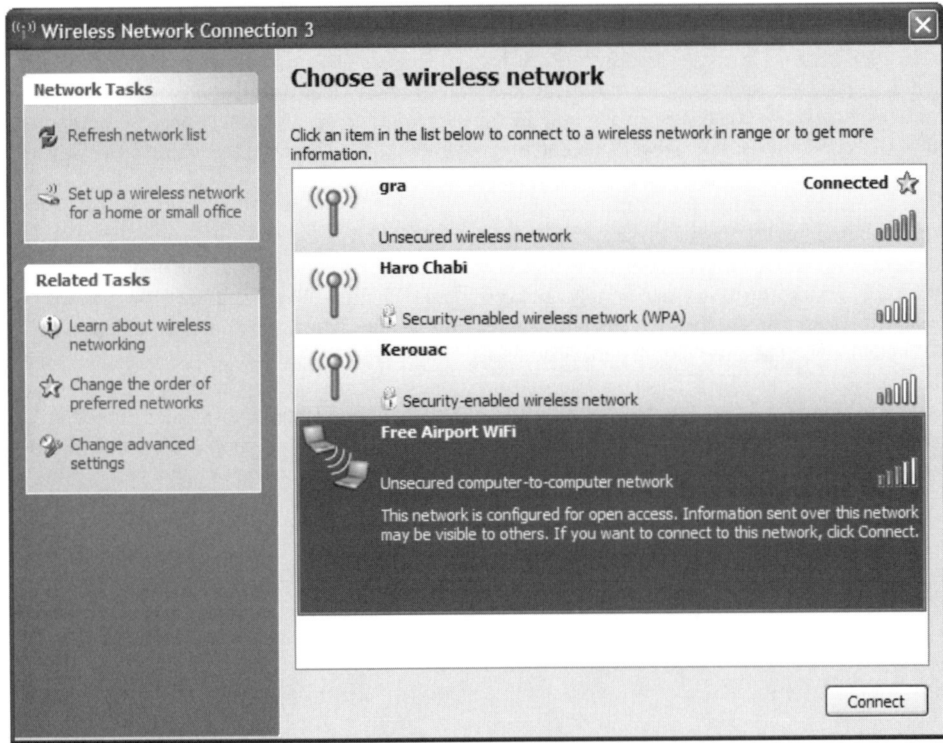

Figure 7-15.
This screen lets you tell your PC never to connect to ad hoc networks

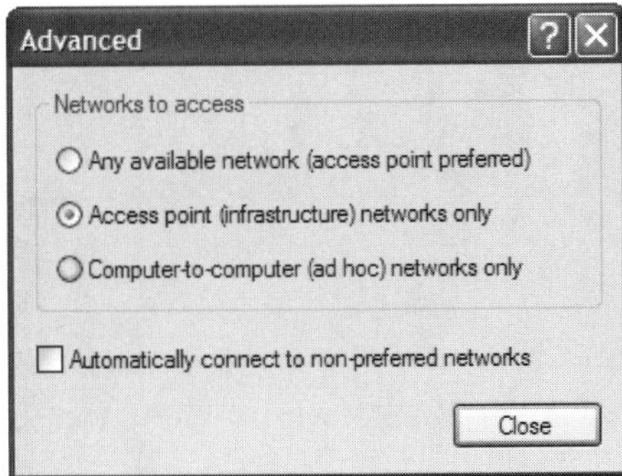

Keeping Safe in Windows Vista

Microsoft spent a considerable amount of effort making Windows Vista more secure than Windows XP, but when it comes to wireless networking, you're more at risk in Windows Vista from a rogue ad hoc network than you were in Windows XP. That's because in Windows Vista, it's not as easy to distinguish an ad hoc network from a normal Wif-Fi network as it in Windows XP. However, once you know the trick, it's easy to do.

In Windows Vista, you connect to a wireless network by first clicking the network icon in the System Tray, then selecting Connect or disconnect. The Connect to a Network screen shows up, with a list of nearby wireless networks. You see the name of each and whether the network is encrypted or not; to get more details about any, hover your mouse over it, as shown in Figure 7-16. But those details don't include whether the network is a true hotspot or instead an ad hoc network.

Before you connect to a new wireless network, the only way to tell the difference between an ad hoc network and one in infrastructure mode is to look at the network icon next to it on the "Connect to a Network" screen. As you can see in Figure 7-16, the icon for a normal Wi-Fi network is one computer, while the icon for an ad hoc network instead is several computers. That's it; there's no other way to distinguish between the two.

Here's another oddity: if you right-click the list of available networks, on the menu that appears, some of them have a Properties menu item, and others don't. Only those networks that you've previously visited and saved to your network list will have the Properties menu item. If you choose Properties, select the Connection tab, and look next to Network Type, you'll see whether it's an ad hoc network or an access point (a normal hotspot).

But if you haven't yet connected to the network (or if you have connected previously, but haven't saved it), it won't have the Properties menu item. So you can't use that method of distinguishing between ad hoc and normal Wi-Fi networks when you're on the road, looking for a hotspot.

 Windows Vista will not automatically connect to an ad hoc network without your knowledge, so there is no need for you to tell it not to automatically connect to ad hoc networks as you do in Windows XP.

Figure 7-16.
The only way to distinguish between ad hoc and normal wireless hotspots is to look at the network icon on this screen. An ad hoc network's icon is made up of several PCs; a normal ad hoc network is made up of one PC.

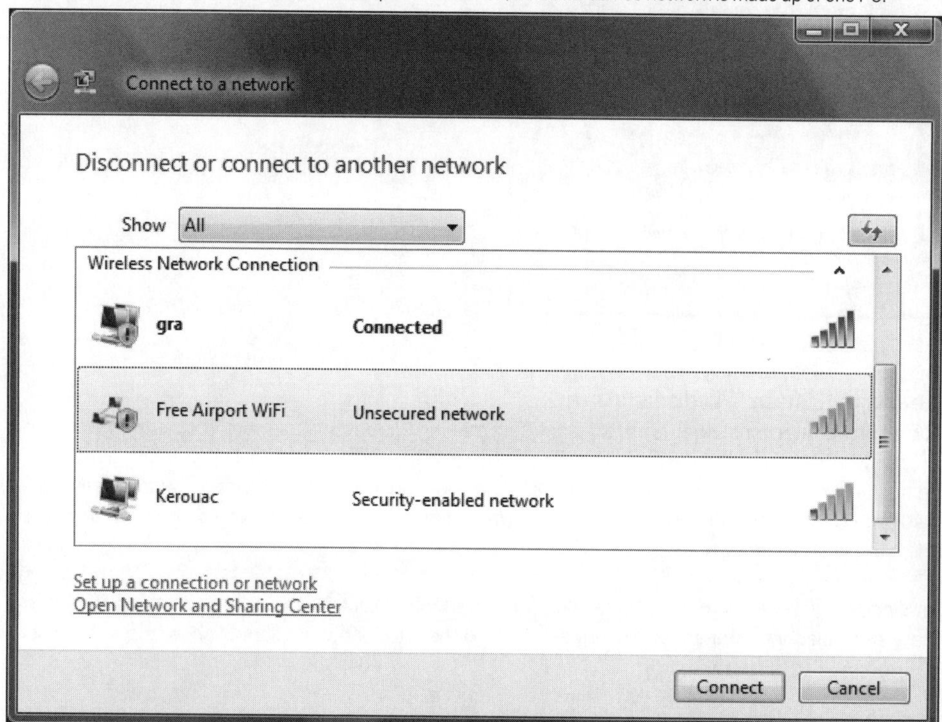

HACK 101: Protect Your Home Wi-Fi Network

V XP The bad guys don't just target corporate networks. If you have a Wi-Fi network at home, intruders are after you as well. Here's how to keep your network and all your PCs safe from malicious intruders as well as prevent novice users from connecting to your network by mistake.

Your home Wi-Fi network is an open invitation to intruders. It's like leaving your front door wide open and putting a sign out front saying, "Come in, and take anything you want."

That's because Wi-Fi broadcasting doesn't stop at your front door, or even the walls of your house or apartment. It leaks out through them. Anyone with a Wi-Fi-connected device passing by can detect the signal and easily connect to your network. And once they've connected, they can do much more than just steal your bandwidth; if you've enabled folder-sharing on any PCs, they can get at your personal information and files, delete files, and wreak a lot more havoc than that.

But there's a lot you can do to keep out intruders and protect your network and PCs. First, and foremost, make sure you use encryption on your network [Hack #102].

That's just the beginning, though. There's a lot more you need to do. No single hack will keep your network protected, so you should use all of what follows.

Even if you're not worried about malicious attackers connecting to your network, consider the damage that a novice user can cause. Suppose you purchase a Linksys router and don't configure anything—just take the plug-and-play route. A month later, your neighbor buys the same model of Linksys router but decides to lock it down with a new admin password, change the SSID from the default, and put a WPA2 password on the router. All of the sudden, you lose a few bars of signal. Can you guess why?

Turns out your neighbor accidentally reconfigured *your* router instead of his. And from that day on, you were connecting to his router, and he was connecting to yours. Even if you want to run a wide open network that anyone can connect to, you should take a few steps (changing the SSID and putting a password on the configuration interface) to keep people from confusing your network with theirs.

Change Your Administrator Password

Before you do anything else, do this: Change the administrator password on your router. Every model of router comes preconfigured with a standard password, which means that it is exceedingly easy for someone to hop onto your network, gain full control over administrative rights, and wreak havoc.

How you do it varies from router to router. In a Linksys router (the SRX400, also called the WRT54GX4), log into the setup screen by opening your browser and going to http://192.168.1.1. When the login screen appears, leave the username blank. In the password section, type `admin`, and then press Enter. Click the Administration link, then click Management. At the top of the page, you'll see the Router Password area. Type a password into the Router Password box, then retype it in the "Re-enter to confirm" box. From now on, when you log in, use that password instead of `admin` when you log into your router.

Stop Broadcasting Your Network's SSID

Your service set identifier (SSID) is your network's name, and if people know what your SSID is, it's easier for them to find your network and connect to it. Your router broadcasts its SSID, and that broadcast tells passersby there's a network there. It also gives out the name, which makes it easier to connect to.

So, if you turn off SSID broadcasting, you'll go a long way toward keeping casual users from seeing your network. But doing that, by itself, won't necessarily solve the problem. Even if you stop broadcasting your network's name, people might still be able to connect to your network. That's because manufacturers generally ship their wireless routers with the same generic SSID; for example, Linksys routers all have the SSID "Linksys" by default. So, even if you stop broadcasting your SSID, intruders can easily guess your router's name and log on.

The answer? First change your SSID's name, and then hide it. That way, passersby won't see it, and they won't be able to guess it either. How you do this varies from manufacturer to manufacturer, and even from model to model from the same manufacturer. But for many models of Linksys routers, here's what to do.

Even with SSID broadcast turned off, a determined attacker using widely available tools can determine your SSID. As with all the security tips in this hack, combining layers of security will give you stronger protection.

To change your SSID name and stop broadcasting it, log into the setup screen by opening your browser and going to http://192.168.1.1. When the login screen appears, leave the username blank. In the password section type `admin`, and then press Enter. If you've changed the password, as outlined earlier in this hack, use your new password instead.

Click the Wireless tab, and look for the Wireless Network Name (SSID) box. Enter the new name of your network. On the same screen, look for the Wireless SSID Broadcast setting, and choose Disable (Figure 7-17). Then, click Save Settings. If you are doing this from a wireless PC, you will immediately lose your connection to the access point and the Internet.

After you change your network name, reconnect each Wi-Fi computer to the network, using the new network name.

Limit the Number of IP Addresses on Your Network

Your wireless router uses DHCP to hand out network addresses to each PC on your network. So, another way to stop intruders from hopping onto your network is to limit the number of available IP addresses to the number of computers you actually have. That way, no one else will be able to get

Figure 7-17.
Changing your SSID name from the default

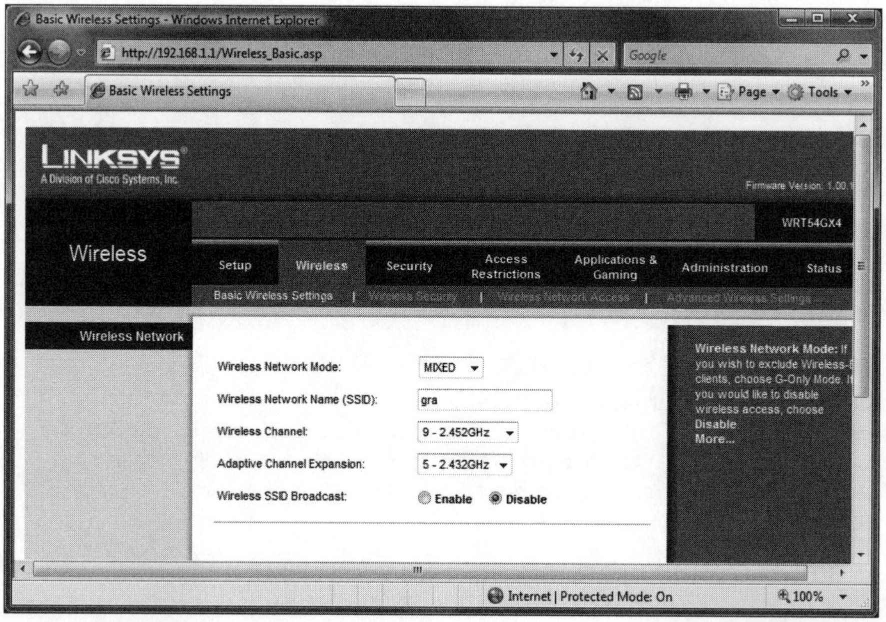

an IP address from your network's DHCP server because your PCs will use up all the available IP addresses.

This will not deter a determined attacker because he can simply use a static IP address. However, it will keep casual users from connecting accidentally.

Your router's built-in DHCP server hands out IP addresses whenever a computer needs to use the network, and the router lets you set the maximum number of IP addresses it hands out. To limit the number on a Linksys router, go to the Setup screen and scroll to the bottom. In the Maximum Number of DHCP Users box, type the number of computers that will use your network, and click Save Setting, as shown in Figure 7-18. If you add another computer to your network, make sure you go back to the screen and increase the number of DHCP users by one.

If you use this technique, you'll also have to change the number of IP addresses your router hands out if you turn off one of your PCs or take it away from the network. For example, if you take a laptop with you on the road, remember to change the number of IP addresses your router hands out, and decrease the number by one.

Check and Filter MAC Addresses

The simplest way to check if you have an intruder is to see a list of every PC on your network. If you see an unfamiliar PC, it means you have an intruder.

To see all the computers currently on your network and their MAC addresses, log into the router's administrative interface, and see if it lets you monitor this. For example, on a a Linksys SRX400 router, also called the WRT54GX4 router, click Status, and then click Local Network. Click the DHCP Client Table button, and you'll see a list of all the PCs on your network, their IP addresses, and their MAC addresses. If you see an unfamiliar computer listed there, you have an intruder. To kick the intruder off the network, check the box next to its listing, and click Delete.

That will only temporarily solve the problem, though. The intruder can simply reconnect to your network and get a new IP address. You can, however, permanently ban all outside specific PCs from ever connecting to your network.

To do so, you'll need to know the MAC address of all the wireless adapters on your PCs. You're going to tell the network only to allow those adapters to connect to the network; you'll ban all other PCs.

Figure 7-18.
Limiting the number of IP addresses your DHCP server hands out

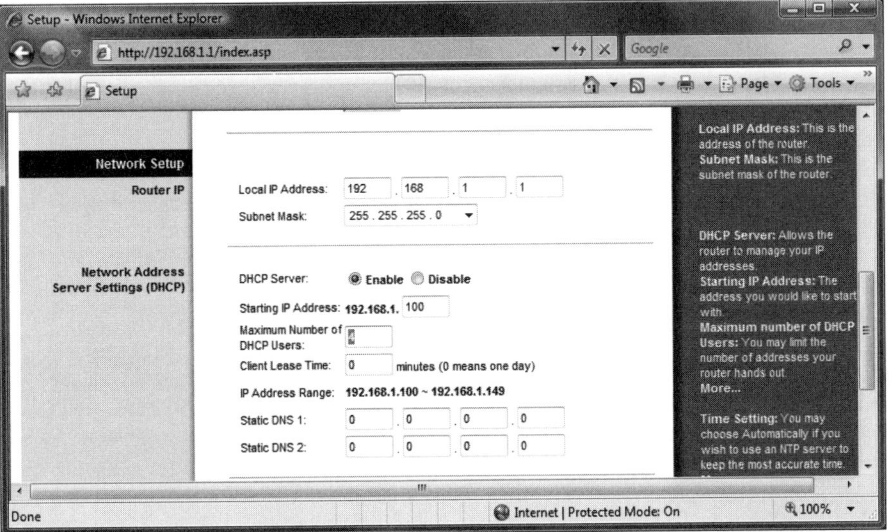

To find the MAC address of each adapter, open a command prompt on each computer, type `ipconfig /all`, and press Enter (if you have Mac OS X or Linux systems, use `ifconfig interface`, where `interface` is the name of your Wi-Fi network interface). The screen will display a good deal of information. Look for the numbers next to `Physical Address`, such as `00-08-A1-00-9F-32`. That's the MAC address. Write all those MAC addresses on a piece of paper.

Now log back into your router, and configure MAC address filtering. For example, on the Linksys SRX400 router, also called the WRT54GX4 outer, click Wireless, and then click Wireless Network Access to get to the Wireless Network Access screen. Select Permit only, and type in the MAC addresses into the text boxes (See Figure 7-19). Click Save settings. Now, only computers you specify will be allowed onto your network.

If you want to allow a new computer with a different MAC address onto your network, you need to add that MAC address.

Check Your Router Logs and Traffic

Your router may keep logs that track all the activity on your network. So, if you regularly check those logs, you can find out whether you've been targeted or whether an intruder has made his way onto your network.

How you check the logs varies from router to router. But on many Linksys routers, you can examine both your incoming and outgoing logs. Log into the router, click Administration, and then click Log. You'll see two buttons: Incoming Log and Outgoing Log.

Click Incoming Log to display a screen that shows the most recent inbound traffic, including the source IP from which the traffic is and the destination port number on a PC on your network. It's tough to decipher this screen, and there's not much immediately useful information here. Much more useful is the Outgoing Log, which shows all outbound traffic. It shows the LAN IP address of each piece of originating traffic, as well as the destination and the port number used. If you see unfamiliar destinations and LAN IP addresses, you have an intruder.

These two screens provide only a current snapshot of your network use, and they don't provide immediately useful information. But there's downloadable software that examines your router logs in much more detail and can give you much useful information, including whether you're under attack, where the attack is coming from, the type of attack you're under, and similar information.

The best of the bunch is shareware, rather than freeware. Link Logger (www.linklogger.com) works with routers from Linksys, Netgear, and ZyXEL. When you run it, it automatically gathers information from your router logs, monitors your network, reports on what exploits and weaknesses are being targeted, and provides a wide range of reports and graphs. If you do find you're being attacked, it will list the attacker's IP address and computer name and identify the ports on his PC where the attack is coming from, as well as the IP address, computer names, and ports on your network being attacked

So, for example, you can create a report that lists for you all the attacks and alerts over a given period of time and includes a breakdown of the number of each type of attack.

Hacking the Hack

Despite all your precautions, there's a chance that someone has broken into your network, or at least uncovered information about it. People who go *wardriving* **[Hack #103]** (basically, driving around with a computer connected to a GPS that can log signal strength, location, and SSID of any wireless network they find) often tell the whole world about unprotected Wi-Fi networks they've found by uploading their logs to servers that generate maps of open wireless networks. So, there's a chance that information about your network is listed on a publicly available web site, for all the world to see.

Figure 7-19.
Filtering MAC addresses

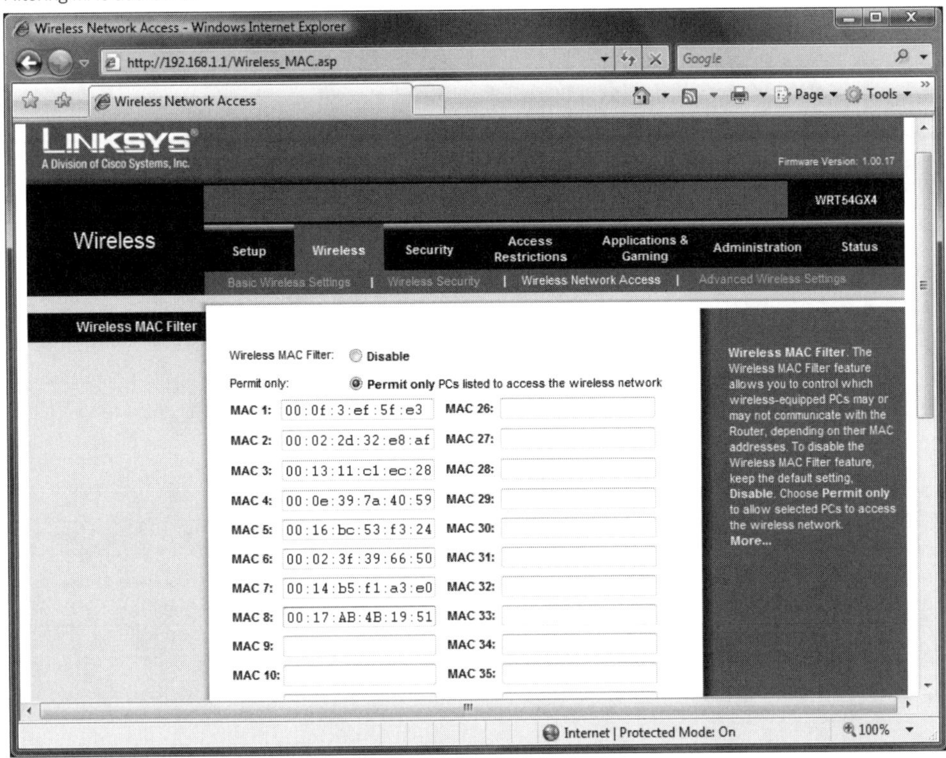

If so, someone can use that information to try and get into your network.

Not all wardriving is malicious. For example, Skyhook wireless has turned wardriving on its head. Instead of using GPS coordinates to find an open wireless network for you, they use information about wireless networks in your vicinity to guess at your location. Of course, they need to do some wardriving to build up this database of networks and coordinates.

First, you need to find the MAC address of your router. It's often listed on one of your router's screens, but if you don't know it, it's easy to find. To find it, first go to the command line, and ping your router's IP address. You'll find it in your router documentation. For a Linksys router, the default IP address is 192.168.1.1. So, for a Linksys router, at the command line, type the following, and press Enter: `ping 192.168.1.1`

Strictly speaking, you don't need to ping the router. But it's a good idea to do it because when you ping it, the router's MAC address information will be put into your PC's Address Resolution Protocol (ARP) cache. Then it's easy to grab the information out of the cache.

After you ping your router, stay at the command prompt, issue the following command, and press Enter: `arp -a`

A screen like the one shown in Figure 7-20 will appear. The MAC address will be listed directly under Physical Address.

Now that you know your router's MAC address, you can see whether information about your router is posted on a public web site. Go to www.wigle.net. Click the Search link on the left side of the screen. You'll have to register at the site, but it's free, so before you search for your MAC address, fill out the registration information.

Figure 7-20.
Finding your router's MAC address

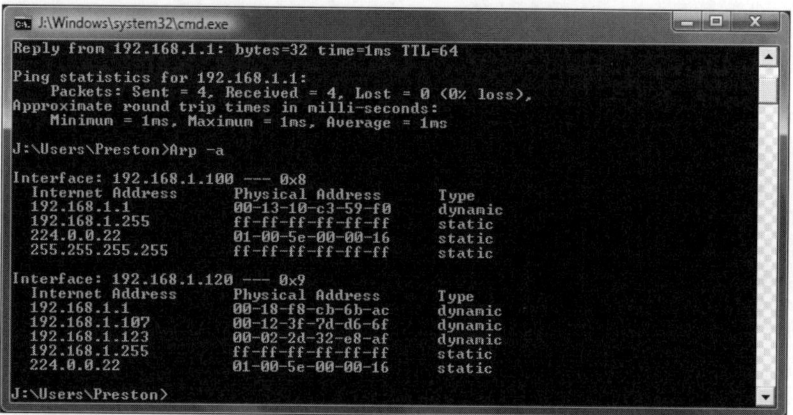

Figure 7-21
Checking the WiGLE web site to see whether a wireless network has been "outed"

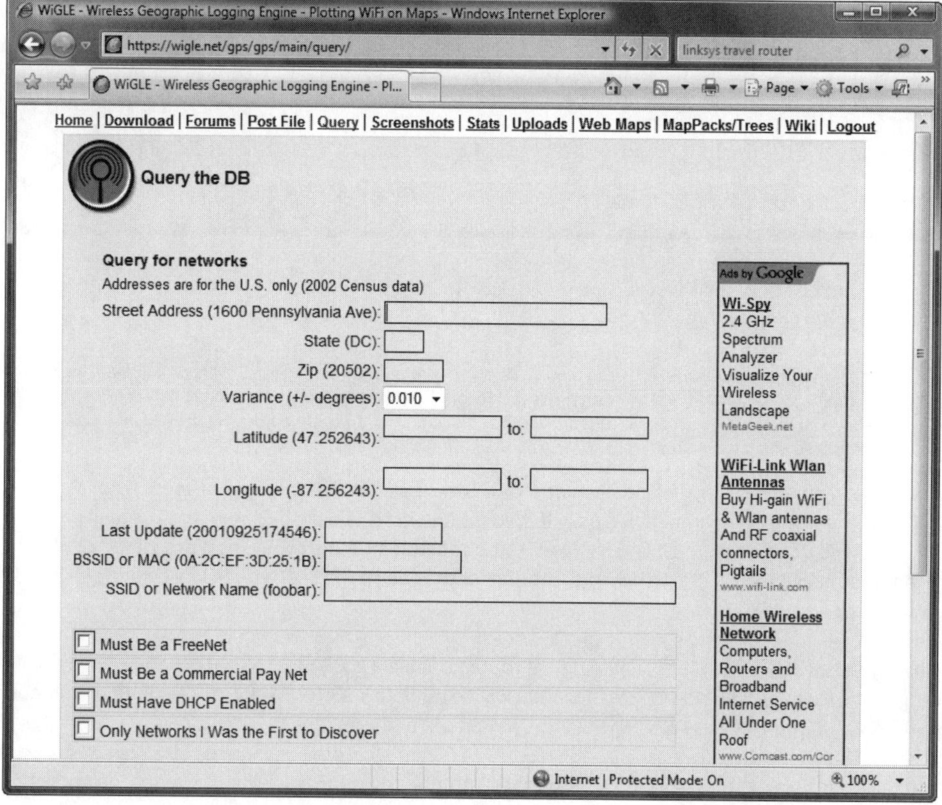

Once you've registered, log in, and click the Searching link. The screen shown in Figure 7-21 appears. In the BSSID or MAC box, type in the MAC address of your router, making sure to put colons between the numbers, instead of the hyphens that ARP shows you. For example, you would type in a MAC address like this:

```
00:0b:db1c:7b:3b
```

Click Query. If a blank screen comes up, information about your network hasn't been posted to the site. But if your network is there, there will be a great deal of information about it, including its SSID, the channel it is broadcasting on, and other identifying information.

If your network is found, and you don't want people to use it, you should take quick action. Use the techniques in this hack and also turn on wireless encryption.

See Also

- "Protect Yourself Against 'Free Wi-Fi' Scammers" **[Hack #100]**
- "Turn On Wi-Fi Encryption" **[Hack #102]**
- "Protect Yourself at Hotspots" **[Hack #105]**

HACK 102: Turn On Wi-Fi Encryption

V XP Using an unencrypted Wi-Fi network can invite trouble. Here's how to put a virtual lock on your Wi-Fi network.

Wi-Fi networks are incredibly convenient—and incredibly easy to snoop on. All that data going out over the air between your PCs and between your PCs and the Internet can easily be snooped on by anyone nearby using simple, off-the-shelf software such as packet sniffers. Virtually every piece of data that goes out across your network can be read.

"Protect Your Home Wi-Fi Network" **[Hack #101]** discusses a variety of precautions that help protect your wireless network. Those hacks will help keep out casual snoopers. But the determined ones will be able to bypass them, so you should use encryption.

You can use two encryption standards to protect your network: Wired Equivalent Privacy (WEP) and Wi-Fi Protected Access (WPA). Don't use WEP: it's not nearly as safe as WPA.

How you turn on encryption varies from manufacturer to manufacturer, and even from model to model from the same manufacturer. It also varies depending on your wireless adapter. This hack shows how to set up encryption on a Linksys router, the SRX400, also called the WRT54GX4, but the instructions will be similar for other routers.

Go to the Setup screen of your router. For a Linksys router, open a browser, type `http://192.168.1.1` (if you've modified the network your router uses, this will be different) in the address bar, and press Enter. A login screen appears. Leave the "User name" field blank; in the Password field, type `admin`, and press Enter. If you've changed the username and password, use those instead.

From the Setup screen, choose Wireless→Wireless Security. In the Security Mode drop-down box, choose WPA/WPA2 Personal. A new set of options will appear on your screen (Figure 7-22).

You can enable either WPA Personal or WPA2 Personal. WPA2 is a more secure method, but your hardware and software may not support it. Check your network adapter manufacturer's web site to see if they support WPA2 Personal. Windows Vista supports WPA2 Personal, but not all versions of Windows XP do. To see if your version of XP supports WPA2 Personal, select Control Panel→Add or Remove Programs. If the Show Updates checkbox is not selected, check it. Scroll to the Windows XP - Software Updates section, and look for Windows XP Hot fix KB893357. If it's not there, your version of Windows XP won't support WPA2 Personal. You can, however, go to the Microsoft updates site, and download KB 893357 to turn on WPA2 functionality.

If you're not sure if your hardware and software supports WPA2 Personal, use WPA Personal.

On the screen shown in Figure 7-22, enable the version of WPA you want to use, and disable the other. In the Encryption Algorithms drop-down list, choose TKIP, which is the approved, certified algorithm for WPA. Some products support Advanced Encryption System (AES), but that hasn't been certified for interoperability among different vendors' hardware.

Figure 7-22.
Setting up WPA encryption on your router

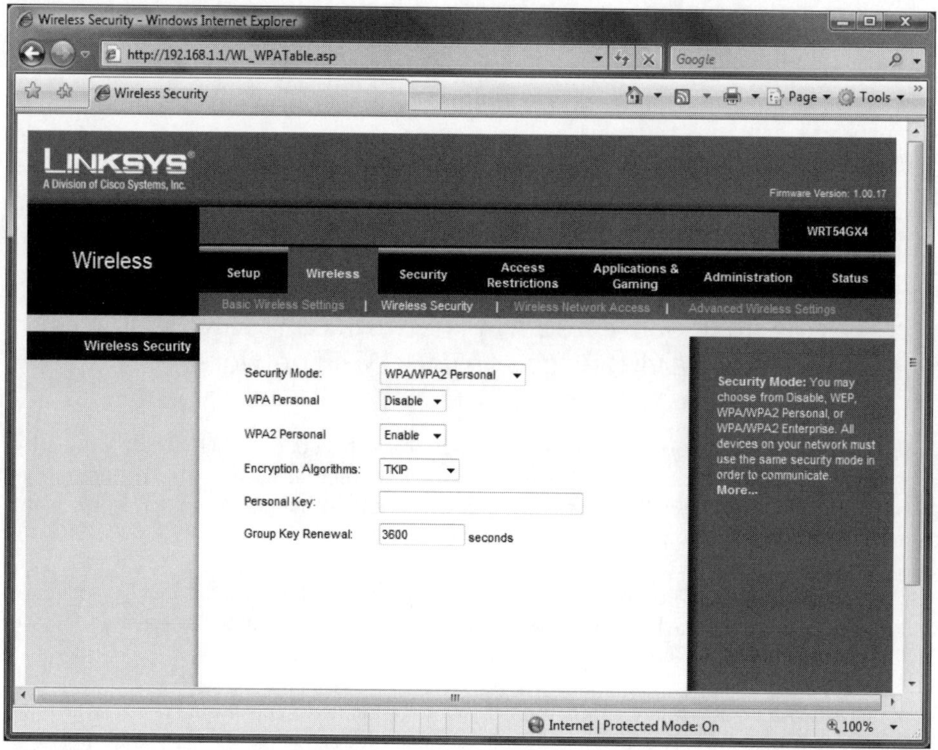

In the Personal Key box, type a key between 8 and 63 characters in length. The longer it is and the more random the characters, the more secure it will be. Write down the key. You'll need to use this on each wireless PC on your network.

Leave the Group Key Renewal row at 3600. Click Save Settings. That applies the key to your network. Now, only PCs that use WPA encryption and the key you just generated will be able to get onto your network.

Now that you've configured your router to use WPA, you have to configure each wireless computer on your network to use WPA and the key you just generated. How you do this varies from Windows XP to Windows Vista. For each Windows XP PC, click the wireless connection icon in the system tray. Then, click Properties, click the Wireless Network tab, highlight your network, click Properties, and then click the Association tab.

In the Network Authentication drop-down box, select WPA-PSK. In the Data Encryption dialog box, choose TKIP. When you do that, the box that reads "The key is provided for me automatically" is checked. Uncheck this box. Enter your WPA key in the "Network key" box, and type it again in the "Confirm network key" box. Click OK and then OK again. Now the Windows XP PC can connect to your network using WPA encryption.

In Windows Vista, select Control Panel→Network and Internet→Network and Sharing Center→View Status. From the screen that appears, click Wireless Properties, and then from the new screen that appears, click Security. A screen like that in Figure 7-23 appears.

From the "Security type" drop-down box, select WPA-Personal, or WPA2-Personal, depending on your encryption method. From the "Encryption type" drop-down box, select TKIP. In the "Network security key" box, type in the security key you used on your router. Click OK. Your Windows Vista PC can now connect using encryption.

Figure 7-23.
Configuring WPA encryption in Windows Vista

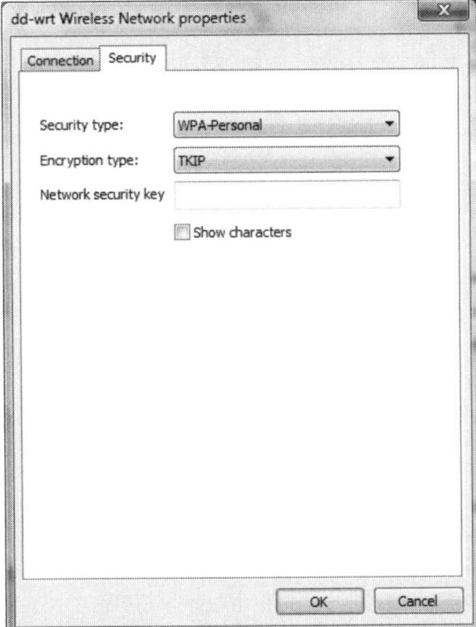

For both WPA and WEP, it's a good idea to change your key regularly: if someone monitors your network and captures network packets for a long enough period of time, they might be able to crack your encryption. If you regularly change your key, it will be much harder for them to crack the encryption because they'll have less time and data to do so. WEP is especially vulnerable in this respect because it is possible for an attacker to discover your key by analyzing the data. WPA is vulnerable to what's called an *offline dictionary attack*, in which the attacker archives some sample traffic from your network and tries one word after another to decrypt the data sample. If you choose a really weird key, especially a word that's not in any dictionary in any language, you'll make it hard for an attacker to learn your WPA key.

See Also

- For more information about WPA, see the Microsoft Knowledge Base Article 815485 (support.microsoft.com/default.aspx?scid=kb;en-us;815485).
- "Protect Your Home Wi-Fi Network" **[Hack #101]**

HACK 103: Go Wardriving for Wi-Fi Access

V XP Wi-Fi networks are everywhere, it seems; you can get free Internet access on wireless community FreeNets armed with your laptop, a car, and software called NetStumbler.

Everyone and their mother has a Wi-Fi network, it seems. Their ubiquity has led to a grassroots community wireless networking movement. The idea is simple: allow people passing by to use your Wi-Fi network to hop onto the Internet, and they in turn let you and others use their Wi-Fi networks for Internet access when you pass near their homes or places of business. These wireless grassroots organizations are often called *FreeNets*. You'll find them in cities including New York, Seattle, Houston, and the San Francisco Bay area, as well as others. For more details about them and how to participate, go to the Free Networks.org web site (www.freenetworks.org). In fact, some cities are creating free wireless zones in downtown business areas to allow anyone with a wireless-enabled computer to get Internet access.

Frequently you'll find dozens of hotspots in one location, particularly in certain urban neighborhoods and suburban office parks that house high-tech companies. Where I live—Porter Square in Cambridge, MA—there are dozens of wireless networks in private homes, apartment buildings, and businesses within a very short walk from my home. There are at least a half dozen on my three-block street alone, in addition to mine. From my back porch, I not only get access to my own wireless network, but can also often pick up signals from four nearby Wi-Fi networks, and sometimes more.

How do you find these wireless networks? As mentioned earlier, the best way is to hop in your car and wardrive through neighborhoods with your laptop, special software, and, if you want to pick up more networks, an antenna hooked up to your Wi-Fi card.

The extremely environmentally conscious prefer to go *warwalking*, though walking around with a laptop is not particularly easy. A better way is with a Wi-Fi-equipped PDA, like the Palm Tungsten C using a product called NetChaser (www.bitsnbolts.com).

Run the software, and it not only locates the network but also provides a variety of information about it that you can use to connect to it, such as its SSID, whether it uses encryption, and the wireless channel it's on. Armed with that information, you should be able to connect to it if it's a FreeNet—for example, if it is set to allow anyone to connect to it, or if it uses a commonly agreed-upon security scheme that everyone in the FreeNet uses for their Wi-Fi networks.

To go wardriving, or if you just want to get the rundown on Wi-Fi networks near your home, download the free NetStumbler program (www.netstumbler.com), which shows you detailed information about any nearby wireless networks. Figure 7-24 shows what happens when I run the software from my home office. I can detect signals from four nearby Wi-Fi networks in addition to my own.

For each Wi-Fi network it uncovers, NetStumbler tells you the network's SSID, name, manufacturer, channel, type, signal strength, signal-to-noise ratio, and whether the network's encryption is enabled, among other details. Armed with that information, you can try to connect to the network. If a network uses encryption, a small lock appears next to it; look closely at the Kerouac network in Figure 7-24 and you might be able to see it.

Once you've found a network, exit NetStumbler. Then, connect to it using Windows as you would normally.

The software built into Windows Vista and Windows XP lets you see nearby networks, just as NetStumbler does. But they don't show you information such as the channel, signal-to-noise ratio, and so on.

Be aware that NetStumbler does not work with all network cards, and may not work with some Windows configurations. For details, see www.stumbler.net/compat.

If you use NetStumbler with Windows XP, it automatically turns off Windows' Wireless Zero Configuration service. This may prevent you from connecting to wireless networks in Windows. When you exit NetStumbler, the Wireless Zero Configuration service will be automatically turned back on, and you'll be able to connect.

NetStumbler will find all wireless networks near you, not just those that are part of FreeNets. So, you might well find the wireless networks of people who don't realize others outside their homes or businesses can tap into their networks. Depending on local, state, and federal law, tapping into those people's networks may be illegal, so do your research before connecting.

Mapping Wireless Networks

NetStumbler lets you save your wardriving information in a file, and if you're using a GPS when you gather data, you can then upload that information to a web site (such as www.wigle.net, shown in Figure 7-25) that uses your information and information provided by many other wardrivers to create maps of Wi-Fi networks across the country. You can zoom in and out on these maps, so

> **QUICK HACK**
>
> **GET WORLDWIDE ACCESS TO FREE WI-FI NETWORKS**
>
> How's this for a deal: Get free access to thousands of Wi-Fi networks around the world? That's what FON Wireless Ltd. (www.fon.com) promises you. You buy an inexpensive router from FON and use it for your network at home. The FON network is set to share your bandwidth with other FON users, so any nearby FON users get to hop onto your network for Internet access. In return, wherever you go, you get to hop onto their networks.
>
> Be aware that using a Fon Wireless Ltd. (FON) router may violate your ISP's terms of service. But ISPs are beginning to get the FON religion. Time Warner, for example, has signed a deal with FON that will let Time Warner customers run FON wireless access points and provide free Wi-Fi access to Time Warner and FON customers.

Figure 7-24.
Detecting nearby wireless networks with NetStumbler

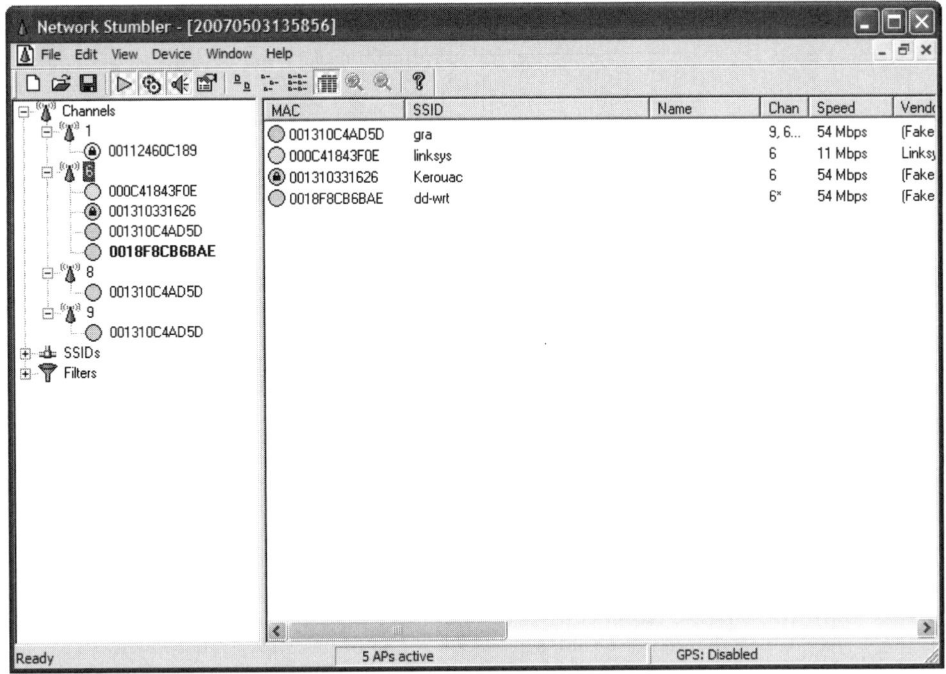

Figure 7-25.
A map of Wi-Fi networks in my neighborhood

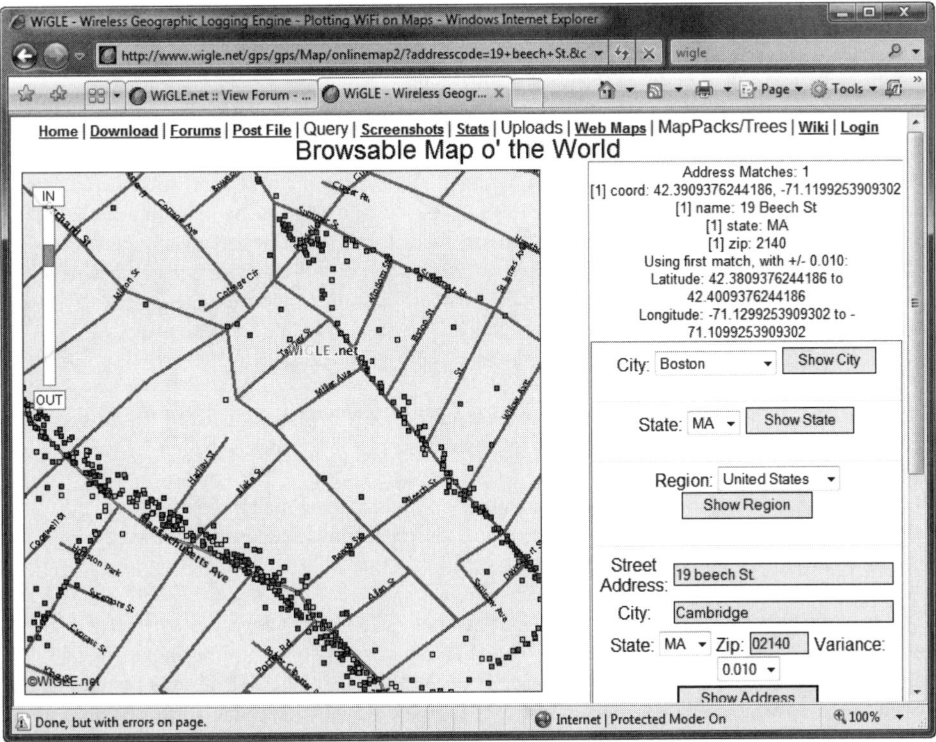

you can get a view of the concentration of Wi-Fi networks in a metropolitan area, or you can see individual Wi-Fi networks on individual streets.

Go to www.wigle.net to view the maps or to upload your NetStumbler information.

See Also

- "Protect Yourself Against 'Free Wi-Fi' Scammers" **[Hack #100]**
- "Protect Yourself at Hotspots" **[Hack #105]**

HACK 104: Solve Hotspot Email Woes

V XP How to send mail at a hotspot, even if your ISP won't let you do it.

If you've ever been unable to send email from your mail client while you're at a hotspot, you're not alone; plenty of other people have had the same problem. In this hack, I'll explain why it happens and how to get around the problem.

First, some background about why you may not be able to send email. The Internet is not the cooperative, friendly place it used to be several years ago, particularly because of the spamming scourge. When spam and scams weren't much of a problem years ago, it was easy to send mail even when you were outside of your normal ISP's network. You're outside your ISP's network when you're at a hotspot rather than at home or an office on a broadband connection, or when you're dialing directly into your ISP.

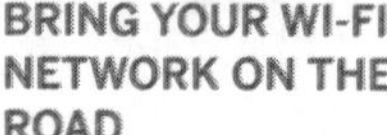

BRING YOUR WI-FI NETWORK ON THE ROAD

Many hotels provide high-speed Internet access via Ethernet, but not as many do so via Wi-Fi. So if you don't want to be tethered to a cable in your hotel room, you can bring along a lightweight travel router that lets you turn your room into your own Wi-Fi network. Apple's AirPort Express (www.apple.com/airportexpress) and the Linksys Travel Router (tinyurl.com/23eaxn) are both good bets, although there are plenty of other travel routers to choose from as well.

ISPs used to allow anyone to use their SMTP servers to send mail. But when spam became a big-time problem, they cracked down on that because it allowed spammers to hide the true source of the origin of their spam. Now, most ISPs won't allow anyone outside their network to use their SMTP servers to send mail. So, when you're at a hotspot outside your ISP's network, you're treated like any outsider, and you won't be able to use the normal SMTP server to send mail.

There are several ways around this problem. If your ISP allows remote access, it probably requires a change to your configuration. So while your ISP's SMTP server works fine on their network default settings (port 25 with no security), you need to use special settings when you are outside their network. For example, Comcast users can follow special instructions for using Secure Sockets Layer (SSL), a user ID, and password to connect to incoming and outgoing email servers (see www.comcast.net/help/faq/index.jsp?faq=EmailOutlook_Express17717). You should contact your ISP and ask them for instructions on using their email servers while you are traveling.

If your ISP doesn't allow remote access, you can try using the SMTP server used by the hotspot. Find out the server address, configure your email software to use it, and you're ready to go.

Of course, that's a whole lot easier said than done. Ask your local barista for the address of the hotspot's SMTP server, and you'll get a blank stare, several seconds of silence, and then the question, "Do you want that grande?"

If you're at the hotspot of a big hotspot provider, such as T-Mobile or Boingo, though, you're in luck, because many of them have SMTP servers. They just don't bother to tell anyone about it. In fact, often, their technical support departments don't even know they have SMTP servers. I made several calls to T-Mobile asking about it and was told each time the servers don't exist. In fact, they do.

Here are the SMTP servers for popular hotspot providers:

T-Mobile
myemail.t-mobile.com

Boingo
mail.boingo.com

Wayport
mail.wayport.net

Surf and Sip
mail.surfandsip.net

If you connect to a hotspot at a hotel, ask whether the hotel has an SMTP server you can use.

Now that you've got the SMTP address, you need to tell your email software how to use it. How you configure SMTP varies according to the email software you use. If you use Outlook 2007, choose Tools→Account Settings, and highlight your email account (Figure 7-26).

Click Change. From the screen that appears, in the "Outgoing mail server (SMTP)" box, type in the name of the SMTP server you want to use (for example, myemail.t-mobile.com), as shown in Figure 7-27. Click Next, and then click Finish. Now you'll be able to send email at a T-Mobile hotspot.

Before you change your SMTP server address, write down your original one. Make sure when you leave the hotspot, you change the address back to the original because if you don't, you won't be able to send mail when you're at your normal ISP.

Figure 7-26.
The main screen for configuring email accounts in Outlook 2007

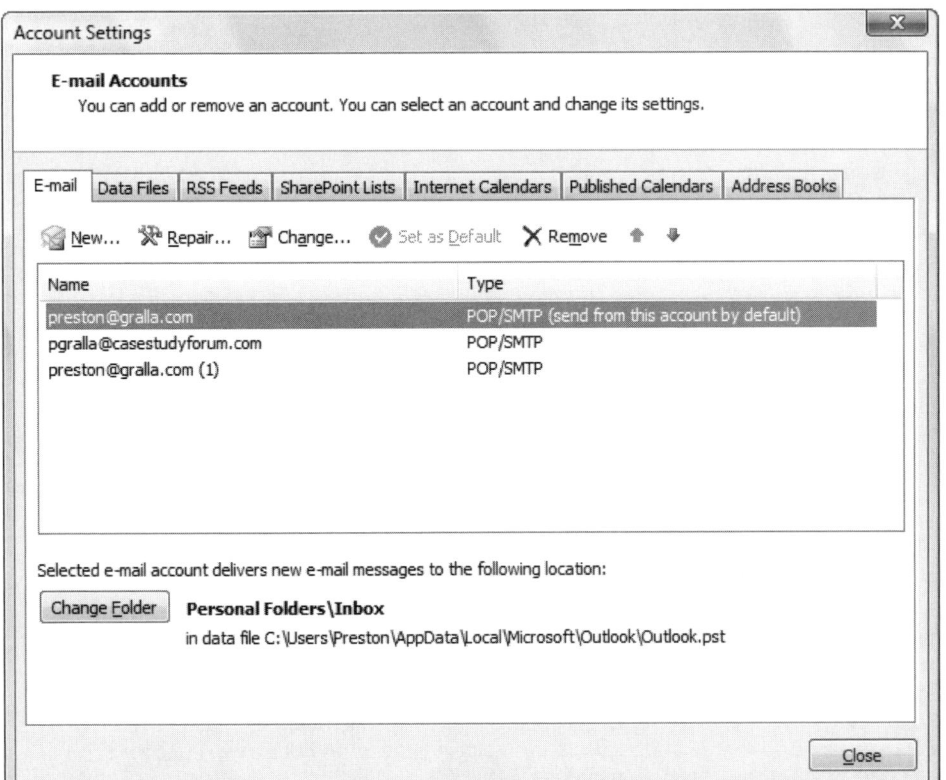

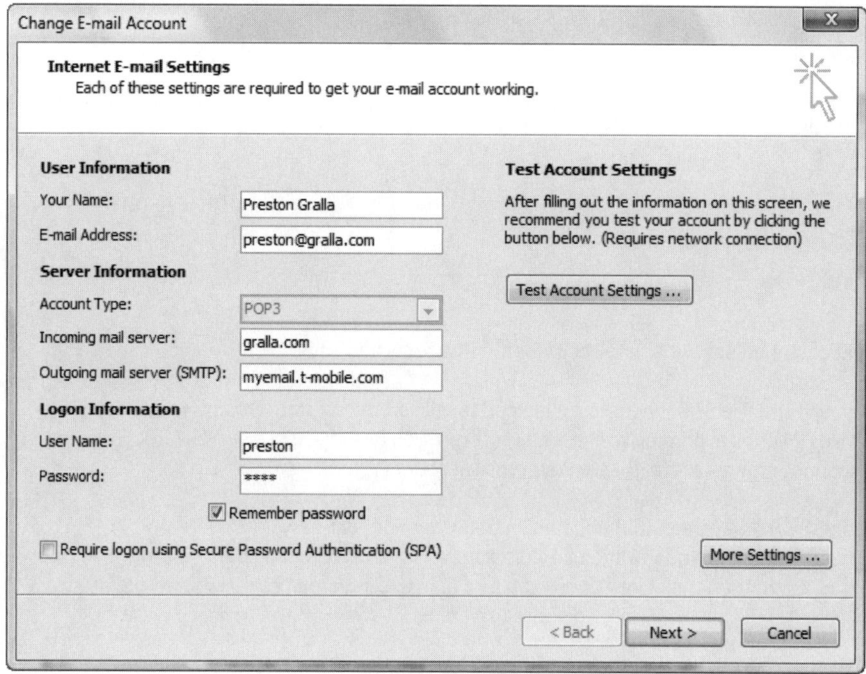

Figure 7-27.
Configuring Outlook 2007 to use T-Mobile's SMTP server

If you use Outlook Express, choose Tools→Accounts, select the Mail tab, click the Properties button, and then select the Servers tab. In the "Outgoing mail server (SMTP)" box, enter the name of the hotspot's SMTP server. Click OK, then OK again, and then Close. You're all set.

In Windows Vista's Windows Mail, choose Tools→Accounts, highlight your mail account, click the Properties button, and then select the Servers tab. In the "Outgoing mail server (SMTP)" box, enter the name of the hotspot's SMTP server. Click OK, then OK again, and then Close. You're all set.

If you've followed these steps, checked that the SMTP address is accurate, and checked that your hotspot won't let you send email, the SMTP server might require authentication. If so, on the screen in Outlook or Outlook Express that requires you to enter the SMTP address, check the "My server requires authentication" box, and click the Settings button. From the screen that appears, select "Log on using", and enter your hotspot account name and password where indicated.

What if your hotspot provider doesn't have an SMTP server? There are still a few solutions for you. One is to pay an SMTP relay service so that you'll be able to send mail from any hotspot, even if the hotspot provider doesn't have an SMTP server. Pay the relay service, and you can use its SMTP server no matter where you are. In general, it's as simple as configuring your email software to use the server, as outlined earlier in this hack. However, you should check with the service, in case it has any special setup instructions.

Here are two reputable relay services:

AuthSMTP (www.authsmtp.com)
Pricing plans start at $24 per year, which lets you send 1,000 messages or 100 MB of mail per month, and go up to $168 per year, which lets you send 10,000 messages or 1 GB of mail per month.

SMTP.com (www.smtp.com)
Has a variety of pricing plans, including a monthly $10 plan, which lets you send 30 emails per day; a $50-a-year plan, which lets you send up to 50 emails per day; and all the way up to a a $280-a-year plan, which lets you send up to 600 emails per day.

There's another solution you can turn to. You can forgo your email software entirely and use your ISP's web-based mail when you're away from home. Just about every ISP should have one. If yours doesn't, you can use Gmail to fetch mail from your ISP, and then forward to you in Gmail [Hack #92].

HACK 105: Protect Yourself at Hotspots

V XP It's a wireless jungle out there. Keep yourself safe when you're away from home.

Wi-Fi hotspots mean more than an always-on, ubiquitous Internet experience. It also means ubiquitous, always-on security risks. Connecting to a hotspot can be an open invitation to danger. Hotspots are public, open networks that practically invite malicious hacking and snooping. They use unencrypted, insecure connections, but most people treat them as if they are secure, private networks.

This can allow anyone nearby to capture your packets and snoop on everything you do when online, including stealing passwords and private information. In addition, it also allows an intruder to break into your PC without your knowledge.

But there's plenty you can do to keep yourself safe, as I'll show you in this hack.

Turn Off File Sharing

Depending on the network you use at work or at home, you may use file sharing to make it easier to share files, folders, and resources. That's great for when you're at a secure network, but when you're at a hotspot, it's an invitation to data theft.

Make sure that you turn off file sharing before you connect to a hotspot. To turn it off in Windows XP, run Windows Explorer, right-click on the drives or folders you share, choose the Sharing and Security tab, and uncheck the box next to "Share this folder on the network." (Figure 7-28).

If you're a Windows Vista user, it's even easier. When you connect to a hotspot, designate it as Public. When you do that, Windows Vista automatically turns off file sharing. You can also turn off file sharing manually. Choose Control Panel→"Set up file sharing", click "File sharing", select "Turn off file sharing", and click Apply. Then click "Password protected sharing," select "Turn off password protected file sharing", and click Apply.

Turn Off Network Discovery

If you're a Vista user, a feature called *network discovery* makes your PC visible on a network, so that other users can see it and try to connect to it. On a private network, this is useful; at a public hotspot, it's a security risk. When you connect to a hotspot and designate the network as public, network discovery is turned off, so again, make sure to designate any hotspot as public. However, you can also make sure that network discovery is turned off for your hotspot connection. When you're connected, choose Control Panel→"View network status and tasks". Then in the Sharing and Discover section, click the "Network discovery" button, choose "Turn off network discovery", and click Apply, as shown in Figure 7-29.

Disable Ad Hoc mode

You don't need a hotspot or wireless router to create or connect to a wireless network. You can also create one using ad hoc mode, in which you directly connect wirelessly to another nearby PC. If your

Figure 7-28.
Protect yourself by turning off file sharing in Windows XP

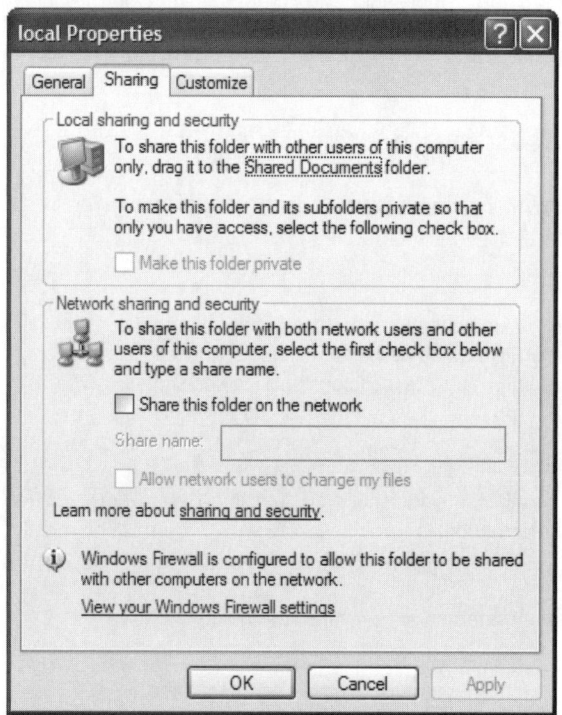

Figure 7-29.
Vista users should turn off "Network discovery" for maximum safety

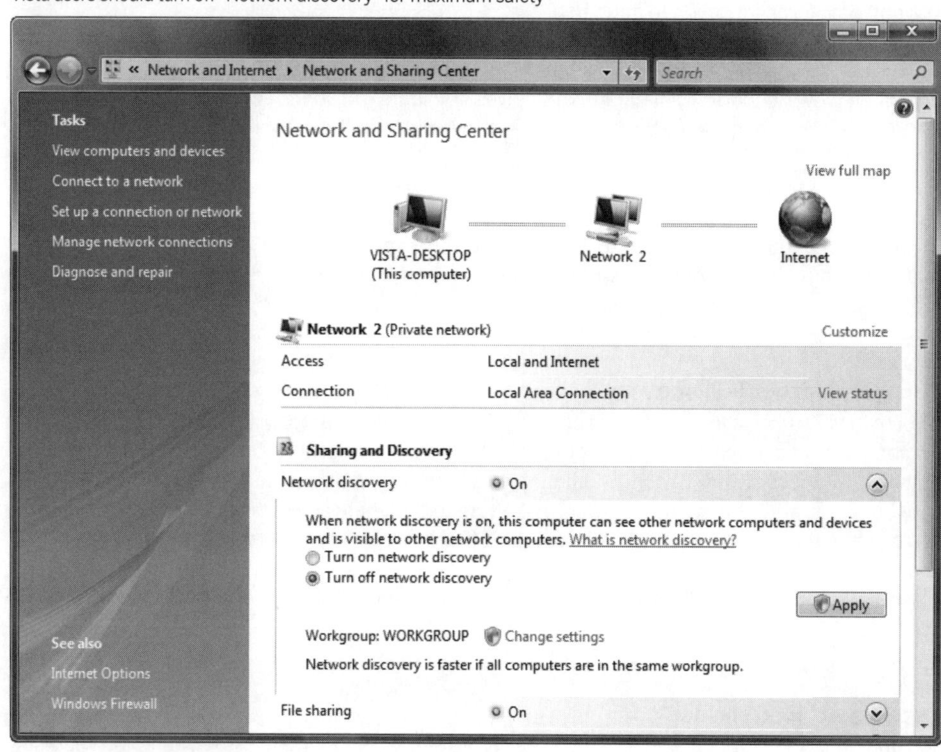

PC is set to run in ad hoc mode, someone nearby could establish an ad-hoc connection to your PC without your knowing about it. They could then possibly wreak havoc on your system, and steal files and personal information.

The fix is simple: turn off ad hoc mode [Hack #100]. Normally it's not enabled, but it's possible that it's been turned on without your knowledge.

Carry an Encrypted USB Flash Drive

USB flash drives are cheap and getting cheaper by the day. For under $50, you can buy a 2-GB flash drive, which is more than enough space to carry all your data. Make sure to get a drive that can use encryption. On your laptop, keep no private data on your hard drive. Use only data on the encrypted USB drive. That way, even if someone somehow gets into your PC, they won't be able to read or alter any of your data because the data is encrypted on the USB drive.

Protect Yourself with a Virtual Private Network

Most hotspots are not secure and don't use encryption. That means anyone with a software sniffer can see all of the packets you send and receive.

But you don't need to rely on the hotspot for encryption. You can use a for-pay virtual private wireless network that encrypts your connection. There are several available, but the one I've been using for years is hotspotVPN (www.hotspotvpn.com). No special VPN software is needed; you can use XP's or Vista's built-in VPN capabilities. The service costs $8.88 per month, or in one-, three-, and seven-day increments for $3.88, $5.88, and $6.88. You can also pay for more secure VPN encryption from the service for between $10.88 and $13.88 per month. (People have also said that the JiWire Hotspot Helper, www.jiwire.com/hotspot-helper.htm, available for $25 a year, is a very good service as well. It's available as a download.)

Once you subscribe to hotspotVPN, you'll get a user name, password, and IP address of a wireless VPN server. At that point, you run a Windows network connection wizard, fill in the user name, password, and IP address information, and you'll be ready to go. In Windows XP, choose Control Panel→Network and Internet Connections→"Create a connection to the network at your workplace". From the screen that appears, choose "Virtual Private Network connection", and follow the wizard.

In Windows Vista, choose Control Panel→"View network status and tasks". Then click "Set up a connection or network", choose "Connect to a workplace", and then "Use my Internet connection (VPN)" as shown in Figure 7-30. Follow the wizard after that.

To use the VPN, first connect to the Wi-Fi network, then run the VPN. To run the VPN in Windows Vista, click the network icon in the system tray, select "Connect or disconnect", then click the HotSpot VPN icon. To run it in Windows XP, double-click the HotSpot VPN desktop icon, and click Connect.

Disable Your Wireless Adapter

There may be times when you're at a hotspot when you actually don't want to connect to the Internet. In that case, you can guarantee absolute safety: disable your wireless adapter so you can't connect.

If you have a wireless PC card, simply remove it. If you have a wireless adapter built into your PC, you can disable it. In XP, right-click the wireless icon, and choose Disable. If you're using the adapter's software to manage your connection, check the documentation to find out how to disable it.

Figure 7-30.
Setting up a wireless VPN using Windows Vista

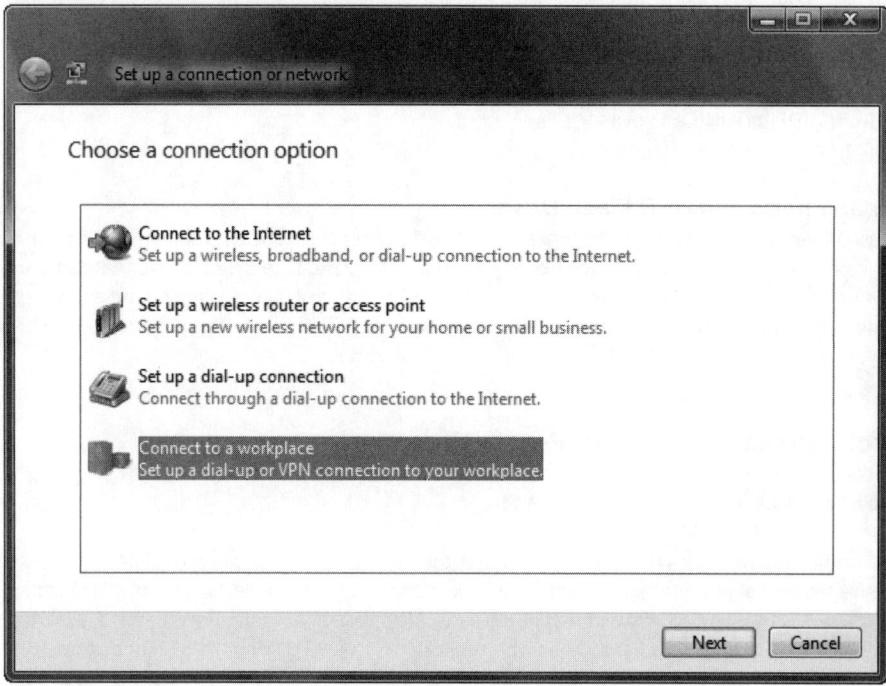

Figure 7-31.
Click Disable to turn off a wireless adapter in Windows Vista

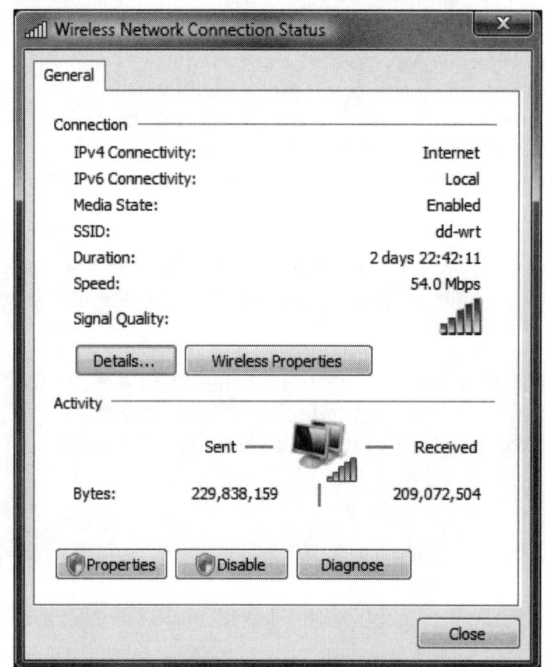

If you're using Windows Vista, choose Control Panel→Network and Internet→Network and Sharing Center. Then in the Connection area, click "View status" and from the screen that appears (see Figure 7-31), click Disable.

Watch Out for Shoulder Surfers

Think all malicious hacking is high-tech programming? Think again. "Shoulder surfers" don't need to know how to write a line of code to steal your password; all they need to do is peer over your shoulder as you type. So make sure no one seems to be paying too close attention when they're directly behind you.

In addition, if nature calls because you've had too many double lattes, don't leave your laptop unattended when you go to the rest room. Laptop theft has become common in some places, most notably San Francisco, which was subject to a laptop crime wave. Consider bringing along a laptop lock, and locking your laptop to a table. Some cafes even include ports to which you can lock your laptop.

Beware Phony Hotspots

Watch out for this latest hotspot scam: someone surreptitiously sets up a hotspot near a cafe, created for the sole purpose of stealing personal information. You're asked to type in sensitive information in order to log in, and the thief makes off with your passwords and financial information. Ask a staffer at the cafe if there is, in fact, a hotspot available, and what it's name is. Only connect to that network. And if you see two hotspots with the same name, don't connect to either: one might be a so-called "evil twin" set up by a snooper to trick you into connecting to the phony hotspot. If you're using a for-pay hotspot, and your hotspot provider makes a connection tool available to you (such as Boingo's connection software), you should use it because it is likely to have a way of verifying that you are connecting to a legitimate hotspot.

Turn On Your Firewall

Windows XP and Windows Vista both have personal firewalls built in, so turn them on. In Windows XP, choose Control Panel→Security Center, then click the Windows Firewall icon at the bottom of the screen. From the page that appears, select On, and click OK.

In Windows Vista, choose Control Panel→Security→ Windows Firewall. The screen that appears will tell you if the firewall is turned on. If it's not, click Change Settings, select On, and click OK.

See Also

- "Protect Yourself Against "Free Wi-Fi" Scammers" **[Hack #100]**

HACK 106: Hacking Wi-Fi Antennas

V XP Not happy with the reception on your Wi-Fi card? You can build your own antenna from materials laying around your house and watch your reception soar.

I've been using a wireless Ethernet card in my laptop for several years. The change from wired networking to wireless was an amazing shift. I was no longer tethered to a thick cable. I could wander around my office or my home and connect to the Web. However, in many situations, I found that the range of the built-in antenna in the PC card was limited, and I desired additional range.

Throughout this hack, I refer to 802.11, which is another term for Wi-Fi. The hacks should work with both 802.11b and 802.11g network cards.

In this hack, I will show you how to build two different range-extending antennas for your wireless LAN card. The first design is made from a used soup or coffee can. It is inexpensive and easy to implement, and will send and receive a signal in one direction that's up to 16 times more powerful than the built-in antenna on your wireless card. The second design uses a discarded Primestar satellite TV dish antenna. It is highly directional and can theoretically send and receive data to another dish up to 10 kilometers away under ideal conditions.

Project Overview

This project uses the Lucent Orinoco 802.11b card, but any brand of 802.11 network card will do. Whichever design you choose to build, you'll need a "pigtail" connector that has the proprietary Lucent connector (for the PCMCIA card) on one end and an N connector on the other. The pigtail can be obtained from a number of online stores for $35 to $40.

You'll also need to know the basics of soldering for this project. The construction of either range-extending antenna for your wireless LAN card can be completed in a few simple steps.

Before attempting either of these hacks, you need to be aware of the FCC regulations on maximum allowed power output from an antenna at the frequencies that the 802.11b cards operate. Read FCC part 15.247 at www.access.gpo.gov/nara/cfr/waisidx_00/47cfr15_00.html.

Hardware Assembly Instructions for Recycled Can 802.11b Antenna

This hack is quick and can be very useful. I put together a can-based antenna in about two hours. I then took it to a local café that offers a for-pay 802.11 service. After powering up my laptop and connecting the antenna, I slowly moved the antenna around, scanning for other networks. Within one minute, I had located another network and "borrowed" access instead of having to use the pay service.

If you are interested in using these antennas at other radio frequencies, the dimensions can be scaled appropriately.

It is quite simple to take an ordinary metal can and transform it into a directional antenna for your 802.11 network card in four simple steps. See Table 7-1 for a complete list of materials you'll need.

Table 7-1. Bill of materials for recycled can

ITEM	QUANTITY	NOTES
Metal can 3 inches to 3.25 inches in diameter and 4 inches long	1	Metal soup or veggie can works well.
N-style RF connector	1	DigiKey Part #ARF1005-ND.
4-40 screws and nuts	4	Hardware store.
12-gauge copper wire	3 inches	Hardware store.
A pigtail connector that has the proprietary Lucent connector on one end and an N connector on the other	1	The pigtail can be obtained from a number of online stores for $35 to $40.
Low-loss coaxial cable	20–50 feet	Time Microwave Part #LMR-400.
Soldering iron		

QUICK HACK 

802.11B/G AND 802.11A RADIO FREQUENCIES

The 802.11b and 802.11g wireless network cards operate at a frequency of approximately 2.4 GHz. This antenna was designed with that frequency in mind. 802.11a operates at 5.8 GHz; if you shrink the can-assembly parts by 50%, it should work at that frequency.

1. SELECT AND PREPARE THE CAN: Locate a metal food can that is between 3 and 3.25 inches in diameter. A longer can is better. Be sure the can is clean and dry, and that the open end is free from any ragged metal edges.

2. MEASURE AND PUNCH HOLES IN THE CAN: Drill a hole approximately 2.5 inches from the closed end of the can for the N connector. You can find this connector from Digi-Key, RadioShack, and ham radio stores. Depending on where you buy it, the exact dimensions may be different from those shown in Figure 7-32, so check the dimensions of your connector. Also drill several smaller holes for the mounting screws. Figure 7-32 shows where the connector will be mounted on the can.

3. BUILD AND INSTALL THE ANTENNA PROBE: Next, take the N connector (see Figure 7-33), and add a short piece of 12-gauge wire so that the wire sticks up 1.21 inches above the edge of the connector. Mount the N connector to the hole you drilled in the previous step. Figure 7-34 shows a cut-away view of the completed antenna. On the left you can see the N connector with added wire "stub." Hold the N connector in place with four 4-40 screws and nuts.

4. ADD A CONNECTION CABLE AND TEST: The radio signal from your 802.11 wireless card must now be connected to the antenna. The Lucent Orinoco PCMCIA card has a tiny (and proprietary) connector at the end of the card. A small plastic cap usually covers this connector. Remove the cap.

You will now need to either locate an adapter connector cable that changes the tiny Lucent connector to a standard N connector, or open up your PCMCIA card and solder a wire to the antenna inside.

If you choose to purchase a connector, do a quick web search for "Orinoco Pigtail" or try this online store, www.hyperlinktech.com. I cannot personally vouch for this store, but they carried the appropriate part at the time this hack was written.

It is possible for you to open up your Orinoco card and solder a thin length of microwave coaxial cable directly to the connector internally. See Building Wireless Community Networks (O'Reilly) for more details.

Try to keep the length of the cable between the antenna and the wireless card as short as practical. At the frequencies at which your 802.11 wireless card operates, the cable will exhibit loss of your signal.

Project Demo

You have now completed construction of the antenna. Connect it to the wireless card, and start up your computer. Aim the open end of the can toward another wireless-enabled computer or an access point (see Figure 7-35). Make note of the signal level as reported by the wireless software on your computer. Remove the antenna, and make another note of the signal strength. The antenna should make a noticeable improvement. Because the signal it emits is polarized, you may need to rotate the can to get the best signal strength.

You should never look into the open end of your antenna when it is operating. Although the signal levels from the built-in antennas in your wireless card have been deemed safe by the FCC, your antenna focuses the signal to levels that could be harmful.

Hardware Assembly Instructions for Primestar Dish 802.11 Antenna

The Primestar antenna hack described here is the brainchild of Rob Frohne, who details some of the steps at www.wwc.edu/~frohro/Airport/Primestar/Primestar.html.

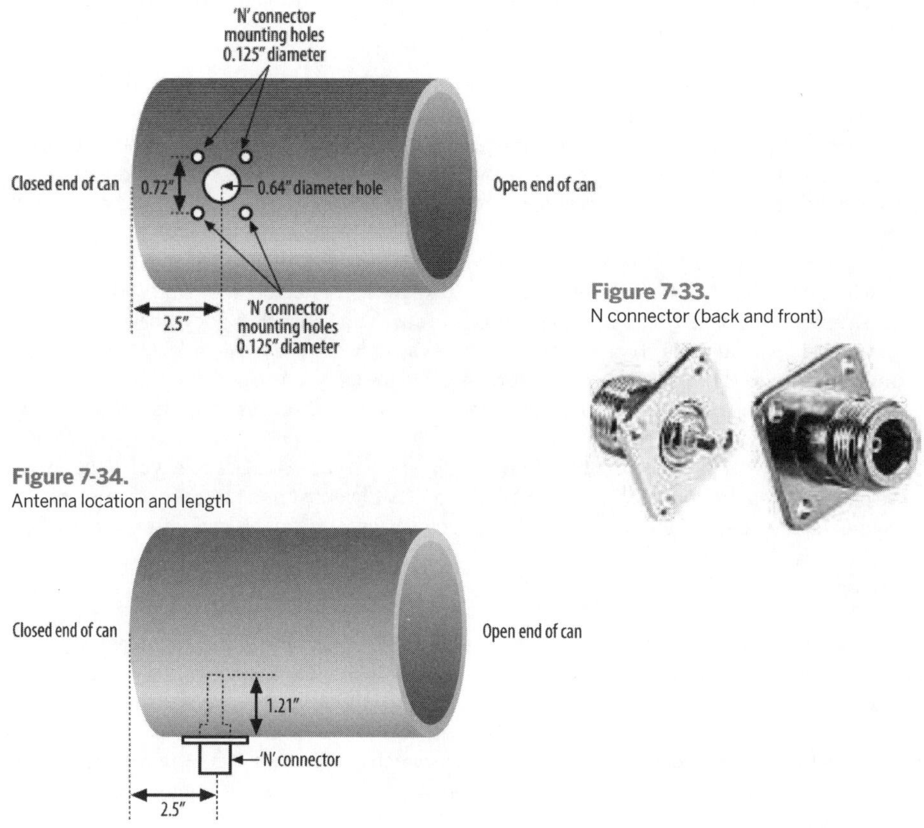

Figure 7-32.
Antenna connector location

Figure 7-33.
N connector (back and front)

Figure 7-34.
Antenna location and length

SIGNAL LOSS IN CABLES

Loss can vary from 1-2db to over 16db per 100 feet. The "db" stands for decibel and is a logarithmic unit of measure. Each 3db of gain represents a linear doubling, and each 3db of loss represents a 50% decrease. By way of example, a 6db loss represents a 75% loss from the original signal (50% x 50% = 25%). A 12db loss represents 93.75% loss.

signal gain (loss) = log (strength of signal 1 / strength of signal 2)

First, a little background. Primestar (a satellite TV company) was purchased by DirecTV (another satellite TV company), which is phasing out all the Primestar equipment. This means many dishes are abandoned and are available for other uses such as that described here. If you can't locate a Primestar dish, you may be able to use a DirecTV or other satellite TV system dish antenna. A little experimenting will be required to get them to work. Primestar antennas can be found at tag/yard/garage sales, local newspaper classifieds, or on the Internet.

It is easy to transform a surplus Primestar dish into a highly directional antenna for the very popular IEEE 802.11 wireless networking. The resulting antenna has about 22 db of gain (this means that the signal is amplified in one direction about 128 times) and is fed with 50-ohm coaxial cable. Usually LMR400 or 9913 low-loss cable is used if the source is more than a few feet from the antenna. (See the Quick Hack on low-loss cable.)

The resulting range of your wireless system using two of these antennas with a line-of-sight path should be close to 10 miles at full bandwidth. I must stress the line-of-sight path, though. Leaves and trees weaken the signal significantly, so you will want to make sure that the path between antennas is clear. Even rain and fog can limit the range.

The long-range link you will create can connect remote homes to the Internet or allow retrieval of audio/video data from remote locations. Imagine being able to set up a web camera on the side of a mountain to monitor wildlife or connect to a hard-to-reach local network with full bandwidth.

In the following easy steps, you will construct and set up a highly directional antenna. See Table 7-2 for a complete list of materials for this project.

Table 7-2. Bill of materials for primestar dish

ITEM	QUANTITY	NOTES
Primestar dish	1	eBay or yard sale
Metal can about 4 inches in diameter and at least 8 inches long	1	Metal soup or veggie can works well
Chassis-mount N connector	1	DigiKey Part #ARF1023-ND
A pigtail connector that has the proprietary Lucent connector on one end and an N connector on the other	1	The pigtail can be obtained from a number of online stores for $35 to $40
Low-loss RF cable	20–50'	Times Microwave Part #LMR400 or 9913
Soldering iron		
12-gauge wire	2"	DigiKey or hardware store

QUICK HACK

LOW-LOSS COAXIAL CABLE

Low-loss cable can be expensive and stiff, making it hard to install and work with. A cable with reasonably low loss for a decent price is the LMR-400 cable from Times Microwave Systems (www.timesmicrowave.com). The company has information on distributors. If you buy this cable, it will not have any connectors on the ends; you will have to add them yourself. This will require you to purchase the male termination connectors and solder them in place. You may also want to purchase a few female-female adapters to make sure that everything connects together. Ham Radio Outlet also carries these parts (www.hamradio.com).

Figure 7-35.
Using the can antenna

Your resulting hacked dish should look something like Figure 7-36. You can see the can antenna at the bottom of the figure.

1. **DECIDE WHERE TO MOUNT THE ANTENNA:** Decide on a place to mount your antenna (which hopefully has a line-of-sight path to the access point or to another 802.11 site) and remove the apparatus at the feed position of the dish (the end of the arm sticking out from the dish). Save the mounting hardware for later. Finding a good location can be time-consuming if you have to crawl up on your roof, but it is important for good performance.

2. **PREPARE A CAN:** Locate and prepare a metal can with dimensions close to those described in Step 1 of the previous section.

3. **SOLDER WIRE TO THE N CONNECTOR:** Solder a 1.15 inch length of stiff wire onto the center conductor of the chassis mount N connector. The 1.15 inches should be measured from the wall of the can to the tip of the wire. You can see what this looks like in Figure 7-37.

4. **MOUNT THE N CONNECTOR TO THE CAN:** Using a punch or whatever other tools you deem necessary, mount the N connector so that it is about 1.2 inches from the closed end of the can, as shown in Figure 7-37. It is also a good idea to put a drip hole at the lowest point of the can to insure that water doesn't build up inside. In fact, you might want to put a plastic lid on the open end of the can. If left exposed to the rain and the elements, the inside of the can will likely rust and lose some sensitivity (and therefore range). If you look inside the can at the N connector with the short wire sticking out, it should look like Figure 7-38.

5. **MOUNT THE CAN TO THE DISH:** If you are certain of the polarization you will need, mount the can so that that polarization is achieved. (You want the antenna you are communicating with to be lined up with yours.) If you don't know the polarization, you can set everything up and experiment to get the maximum signal strength by rotating the can around its axis before mounting the can. Most commercial antennas I've seen use vertical polarization (the orientation of the antenna). Figure 7-39 shows this orientation. You want to mount the can so that the opening is just at the focus of the dish. Even without a perfect alignment and with a long run of cable, you will likely have a decent signal. The easy route is to mount the can as far back as you can, punch two holes through the can, and bolt it in. The best way would be to find the best feed place (which I found to be just a little farther back), and use some PVC tubing or other material that allows you to extend the mount so the feed is in the perfect position. In some installations, every decibel of extra signal will count, and this should be considered.

6. **ALIGN THE ANTENNA:** This antenna is very directional; therefore, you must have it aligned very carefully, or you will lose a lot of signal. It also needs to be mounted securely so that the wind

QUICK HACK 

ALTERNATE DISHES

You may use any satellite dish, but if it is much bigger than the Primestar used in this hack, the gain might be higher than that allowed by the FCC rules for use within the United States.

Figure 7-36.
Mounted dish antenna

Figure 7-37.
Dish antenna connector close-up

Figure 7-38.
Inside the dish antenna

Figure 7-39.
Can mounting

Figure 7-40.
Pointing the dish

doesn't blow it out of alignment. Even a few degrees of movement will make a big difference. This antenna is an offset feed dish, which means that the feed horn (the can) is not positioned in the way of an incoming signal and doesn't shadow the dish. This makes the aiming a bit tricky because it actually looks like it is aimed down when it is aimed at your target antenna. Figure 7-40 shows an antenna aimed just a few degrees above the horizon. Most dishes have an angle scale on the side that can be used to determine the approximate angle. The dish isn't as directional in the vertical direction as it is in the horizontal direction. This is good, because without turning the mounting upside down, you can only set it a few degrees above the horizon. You will lose a little signal by not mounting the antenna upside down, but is it much easier to mount on a roof.

You can mount the antenna on an old roof TV antenna mount or on a roof vent pipe. You will probably need an assistant to help you align the dish toward your target. One person will need to be on the roof (or wherever the dish is mounted), and the other at the computer with the wireless card.

QUICK HACK

POLARIZATION

You've probably heard this term used when looking for sunglasses. You may have even taken two pairs of polarized sunglasses and placed the lenses back to back while rotating one of them. The lenses will turn completely black at one angle and will be clear at an angle 90 degrees later. This is because the light that passes through one of the lenses becomes polarized or oriented in one direction. The other lens, when oriented 90 degrees from the first, blocks the polarized light.

Radio waves behave the same way. If you want two radios to communicate, their antennas must be pointed in the same direction.

Most card utilities include a signal strength meter.

Start by pointing the antenna in from the bottom to the top position. Move it a little bit to the right and repeat this sweep. Now move it a little to the left and repeat. Have the person watching the signal strength meter report its reading frequently. Stop moving the antenna when you have found the best location. Tighten down all screws, and check the signal strength again.

The alignment process can seem tedious and sensitive, but do not give up. Make small alignment adjustments in direction and elevation. You are trying to align two tight radio "spotlights" over great distances without the luxury of being able to see the beam with your eyes.

But the reward is that you should now have a working, highly directional 802.11 antenna!

— *Scott Fullam with photos from Rob Frohne, from the book Hardware Hacking Projects for Geeks*

HACK 107: Using a Bluetooth Headset in Vista

V One of the limitations of Windows XP was its reluctance to use a Bluetooth headset as a sound and recording device—and the problem still exists in Windows Vista. In this hack, I will show how you can use your Bluetooth headset as a sound and recording device in Windows Vista.

If you are the owner of a Bluetooth headset, you will be glad to know that besides using it with your cellular phone, you can also use it with your Windows Vista PC. However, you may have attempted to pair up the headset with your PC only to find out that the built-in Bluetooth stack in Windows Vista does not support the headset.

In this hack I am going to show you how to prepare your PC so that it can work with your Bluetooth headset. I will be using the Billionton USB Bluetooth adapter as well as the Motorola HS820 Bluetooth headset (see Figure 7-41).

Bluetooth Stack in Windows Vista

Windows Vista includes a Bluetooth stack that is automatically launched when you plug in your USB Bluetooth adapter (or if you have a built-in Bluetooth radio on your PC).

The problem with the Bluetooth stack built into Windows Vista is that even though it supports the headset profile required to connect with your Bluetooth headsets, you won't be able to use it in Vista.

To see this for yourself, plug the USB Bluetooth adapter into your computer, and you should see the Bluetooth icon located in the System Tray. Double-click on this icon to bring up the Bluetooth Devices window (see Figure 7-42).

Turn on your Bluetooth headset to set it up for pairing. Click the Add... button to look for the Bluetooth headset so that you can pair it with your computer. When the Bluetooth headset is found, you will be prompted to enter its passkey (PIN).

Most Bluetooth headsets use the default "0000" for passkey. Check the documentation of your device for the correct passkey to use.

WHAT IS A BLUETOOTH STACK?

A Bluetooth stack is a collection of drivers, libraries, and applications installed on your computer that interacts with your Bluetooth devices.

If the pairing is successful, you should see your Bluetooth headset appearing in the Bluetooth Devices window. To view the services offered, you can select the Bluetooth headset icon, and click the Properties button. In the Services tab of the Properties window, notice that you can check the Headset service offered by your Bluetooth headset (see Figure 7-43).

Oddly enough, checking the Headset checkbox does not enable your headset to be used in Windows Vista. Instead, Windows will prompt you to install additional driver software for this new Bluetooth device that you have just paired (see Figure 7-44).

Installing Manufacturer-Supplied Bluetooth Drivers

To overcome the limitations in the Windows Vista Bluetooth stack, you need to install the Bluetooth stack driver that comes with your Bluetooth adapter (or radio). You can download the latest drivers and support software from the adapter vendor's web site. Because each vendor customizes the software slightly, you should not use drivers from a vendor other than the one that manufactured your Bluetooth adapter.

Figure 7-41.
The Billionton USB Bluetooth adapter and the Motorola HS820 Bluetooth headset

Figure 7-42.
The Bluetooth Device window in Windows Vista

Figure 7-43.
Using the Headset service offered by the Bluetooth headset

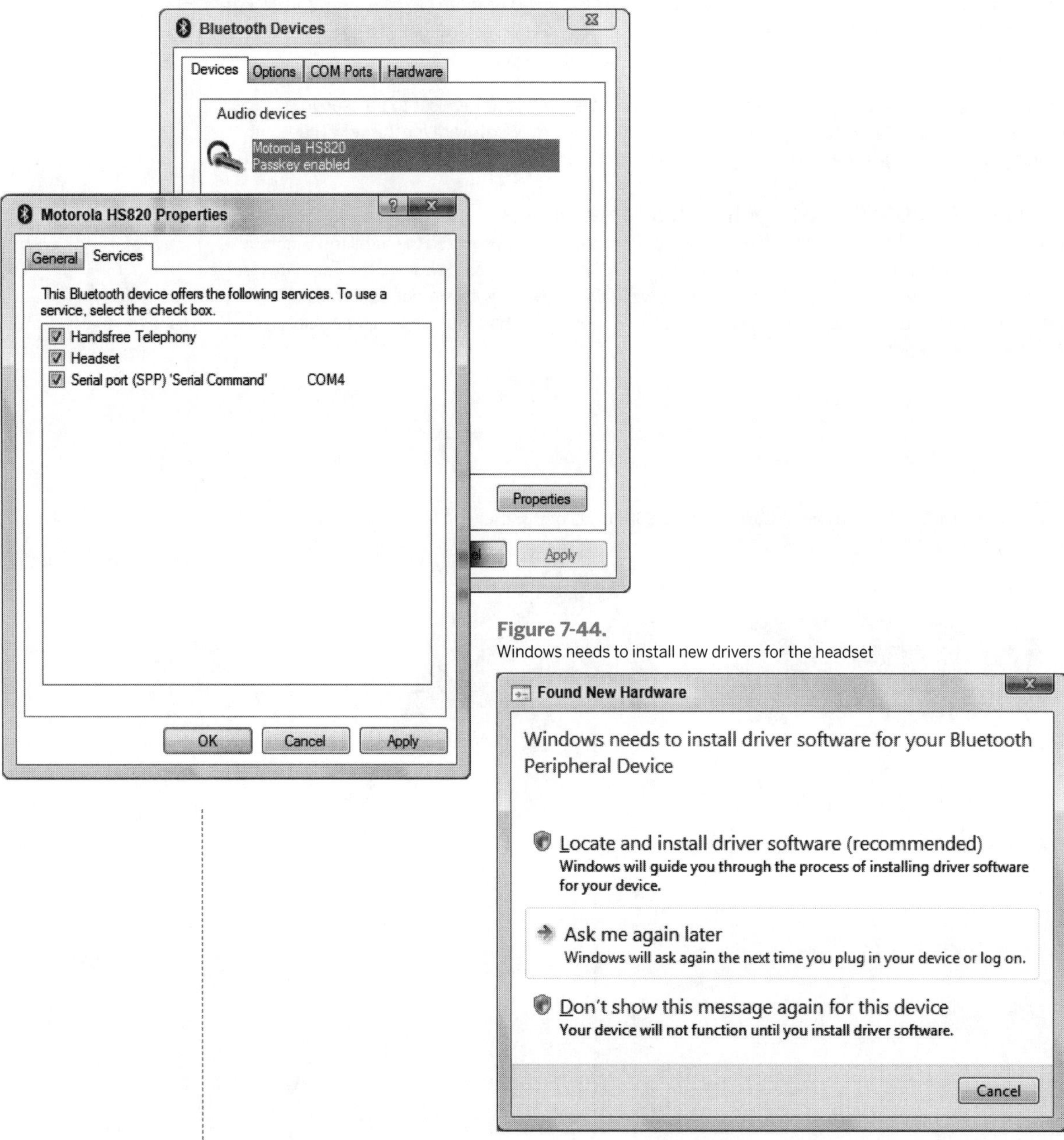

Figure 7-44.
Windows needs to install new drivers for the headset

For my Billionton Bluetooth adapter, I download the "Bluetooth 2.0 - Bluetooth 2.0 driver (Toshiba Stack)" driver found on: www.billionton.com.tw/website/download/driver/Bluetooth_old/1.4.2.11-B/BT2.0.htm.

After the driver is downloaded, extract the files in it, and run *setup.exe*. Once the installation is done, repeat the steps outlined in the last section to pair a new device with your computer.

After pairing, Windows can now automatically search for the additional drivers it needs for your Bluetooth headset (see Figure 7-45).

Figure 7-45.
Installing the additional drivers needed by Windows

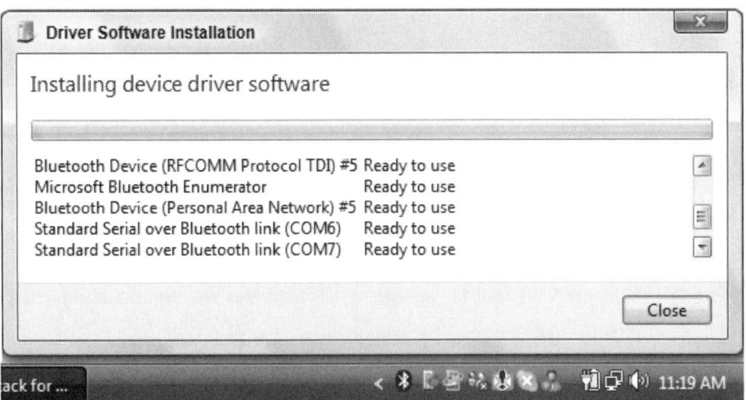

Figure 7-46.
Launching the new connection wizard

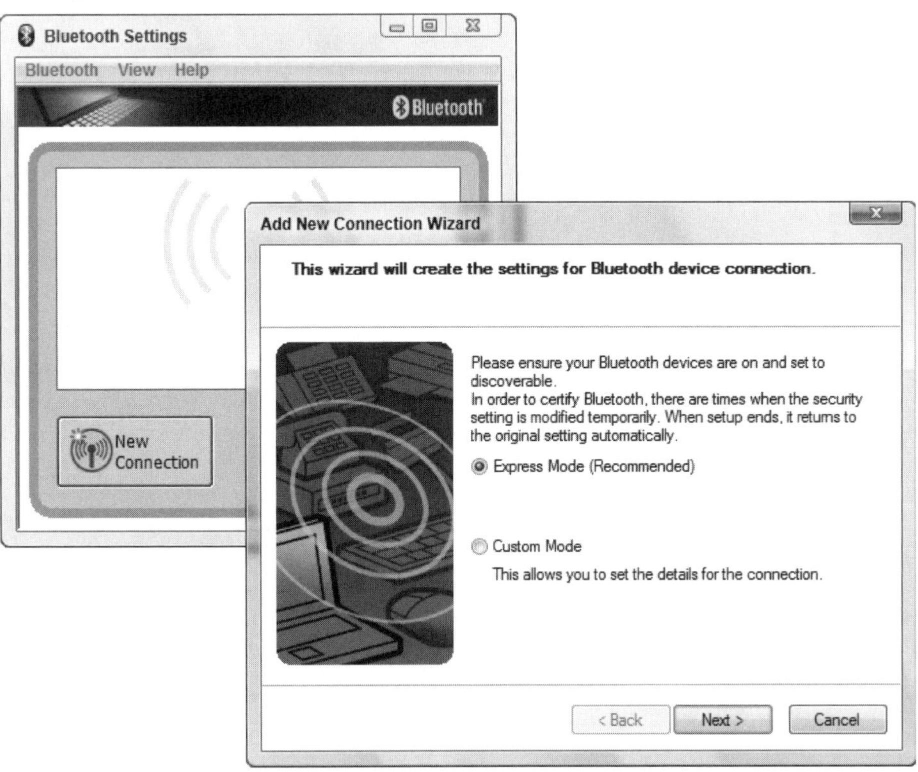

Once the installation is done, you will be asked to restart your computer. The Microsoft Bluetooth stack will now be replaced with the Bluetooth stack provided by the manufacturer (in this case, it is the Bluetooth Stack by Toshiba).

When you double-click on the Bluetooth icon in the System Tray, you can now see a window titled Bluetooth Settings. To pair up with your Bluetooth headset, click the New Connection button (see Figure 7-46). Click Next to launch the connection wizard.

If your headset is turned on and ready for pairing, you should be able to locate the device. Select the headset, and click Next. As usual, you will also be asked to enter the passkey. Finally, click Next to finish the pairing process. You should now be able to see the headset in the Bluetooth Settings window (see Figure 7-47).

To verify that Windows Vista is indeed able to recognize the Bluetooth headset, go to Control Panel, and launch the Sound application. You should see the additional Speakers in the Playback tab. If it is not the default device, right-click on it, and select "Set as Default Device" (see Figure 7-48).

Likewise, you should also be able to see the Bluetooth headset used as a recording device in the Recording tab (see Figure 7-49).

Windows should now redirect all sounds to your Bluetooth headset. To be sure it really works, use a VoIP application such as Skype or Windows Live Messenger, and see if you can make a voice call. Have fun!

See Also

- Getting Your Bluetooth Headset to Work in XP: www.windowsdevcenter.com/pub/a/windows/2005/07/05/bluetooth.html.

— Wei-Meng Lee

Figure 7-47.
Viewing the paired Bluetooth headset

Figure 7-48.
Setting the newly added Bluetooth headset as the default playback device

Figure 7-49.
The Bluetooth headset as a recording device

08 SECURITY

Like it or not, your PC is at risk the moment you turn it on. Even if you don't connect to the Internet, there are dangers; someone walking by could log on and read your files while you're gone, for example. Worse yet, if you have a laptop, it may be stolen, or you may lose it, and your personal data could end up in someone else's hands.

Then, of course, there are the myriad dangers you face when going onto the Internet, where crackers try to take control of your PC and turn it into a spam-spewing zombie.

This chapter includes hacks to protect you against all that and more. You'll be able to hack the Windows firewall for greater protection, use Vista's BitLocker even if you don't seem to have the right hardware, find out how to protect files and folders with encryption, and much more. You'll even learn how to control Windows Vista's outbound firewall.

Windows Vista users will be pleased to know that I spend a lot of time telling you how to hack User Account Control. I will show, in fact, that you don't have to hate UAC; you can hack it to make it more usable. If, however, you truly do despise it, I'll show you how to turn it off.

HACK 108: Hack Windows Vista's User Account Control

V Vista's User Account Control is one of Vista's new security tools—and is without a doubt, Vista's most annoying feature as well. Here's how to bend it to your will.

Quick, answer this: What's the most maddening feature of Windows Vista? If you're like 99% of the world, you'll probably answer User Account Control (UAC). When you try to make any one of a variety of changes to Windows Vista, a UAC prompt appears, and you have to click the Continue button or enter a password before you proceed.

There's some method to this madness. UAC is designed to stop your system and its files from being tampered with. If malware gets loose on your PC, the thinking goes, UAC will help stop it from doing damage because the malware won't be able to click a Continue button or type in a password. You'll get some warning before you try to make a change that will launch a UAC prompt. As you can see in Figure 8-1, a setting protected by UAC has a shield next to it.

The kind of UAC prompt that appears—either one that asks you to continue or one that asks you to type in your password—depends on whether you're logged in as a standard user or an administrator. If you're logged in as an administrator, you'll only have to click Continue. If you're logged in as a standard user, you'll have to type in an administrator's password. If there are multiple administrators set up on the computer, the prompt will include a list of all the administrators. You'll have to type the password underneath the right administrator account.

Figure 8-1.
Settings protected by UAC have shield icons next to them

UAC and Elevating Privileges

Before you hack UAC, you need to understand its guiding principle—that of the *least-privileged user*. Under it, an account is set up that has only the minimum amount of privileges needed in order to run the computer for most tasks. A standard user, in Windows Vista, is this least-privileged user.

But when a change needs to be made that can affect the overall operation or security of the operating system, the user's privilege needs to be elevated. In other words, someone with greater privileges than the least-privileged user must make the change. That's why a standard user will need to type in an administrator password to make a change, and why an administrator will have to confirm she wants to make a change.

Hacking UAC

You're not stuck with Windows Vista's default behavior when it comes to UAC; you can change how UAC works on your PC. To do it, run Local Security Policy by typing *secpol.msc* in the Search box or command prompt and then typing Enter. Now go to `Security Settings/Local Policies/Security Options`. This lets you edit various security policies on your PC, including those related to UAC. To edit a policy, double-click it, and fill in a dialog box—for example, choosing Enable or Disable.

secpol.msc is not available in the home editions of Windows Vista. However, you can use the Registry to make changes to UAC's behavior. Launch the Registry Editor by typing regedit at the Start Search box or a command prompt (see Chapter 13 for details). Go to `HKEY_LOCAL_MACHINE\SOFTWARE\Microsoft\Windows\CurrentVersion\Policies\System\EnableLUA` and give it a value of 0 to turn off UAC. You may need to reboot in order for the change to take effect. The rest of this hack includes registry keys for many of the settings you can change in UAC.

You'll need to edit these policies to hack UAC:

User Account Control: Admin Approval Mode for the Built-In Administrator Account

Registry key: `FilterAdministratorToken`. This determines whether the main Administrator account is subject to UAC. Enabling it means that the account will be treated by UAC like any other administrator; the prompt will appear as normal. If it is not enabled, no prompt will appear for the Administrator account but will appear for standard user accounts.

There is a great deal of confusion about administrator accounts in Windows Vista. There are in fact two different types of administrator accounts—the single, all-powerful, built-in Administrator account, and accounts that are part of the Administrators group. The Administrator account can do anything on the computer, while members of the Administrators group run much as standard users, except they can elevate their privileges by clicking a Continue button in a dialog box when prompted.

User Account Control: Behavior of the elevation prompt for administrators in Admin Approval Mode

Registry key: `ConsentPromptBehaviorAdmin`. This determines what prompt appears for administrators (members of the Administrators Group, not the built-in Administrator account). The default is Prompt for Consent, which means that a UAC prompt will appear, and the administrator needs to click Continue or Cancel. You can also choose Prompt for Credentials, in which case the administrator password will have to be typed in. If you choose No Prompt, a UAC prompt won't appear, and you can make the change.

User Account Control: Behavior of the elevation prompt for standard users

Registry key: `ConsentPromptBehaviorUser`. This determines what prompt appears for standard users. The choices are Prompt for Consent, Prompt for Credentials, or No Prompt. The default is Prompt for Credentials.

User Account Control: Detect application installations and prompt for elevation

Registry key: `EnableInstallerDetection`. By default, this is enabled, and so before software can be installed, UAC will ask for a prompt or a password. Disabling it allows software to be installed without the prompt.

User Account Control: Elevate only executables that are signed and validated

Registry key: `ValidateAdminCodeSignatures`. When enabled, UAC allows programs to be installed without a prompt if those programs have been properly signed and validated by their creators. By default it is disabled, and all programs, whether signed and validated or not, require the prompt.

User Account Control: Run all administrators in Admin Approval Mode

Registry key: `EnableLUA`. This setting requires all administrators (except for the built-in Administrator account) to give consent or supply credentials (depending on the setting of ConsentPromptBehaviorAdmin). By default, it is enabled.

User Account Control: Switch to the secure desktop when prompting for elevation

Registry key: `PromptOnSecureDesktop`. This determines whether Windows Vista will switch to the secure desktop when the prompt appears. You'll notice that when the UAC prompt appears, the screen first goes black, and that when the prompt appears, the rest of the screen is dark. That's the secure desktop. By default, the secure desktop is enabled.

User Account Control: Virtualize file and Registry write failures to per-user locations

Registry key: `EnableVirtualization`. This controls whether changes to the Registry made by standard users should be written to a special, virtual area, rather than directly to the Registry. This protects the Registry. By default, it is enabled.

Turn Off UAC

If UAC prompts drive you around the bend, you can turn them off. Choose Control Panel→User Accounts and Family Safety→User Accounts, and click Turn User Account Control on or off.

Alternately, you can run the MSCONFIG tool by typing MSCONFIG at the command line or search box. When the tool runs, click the Tools tab, and scroll down until you see Disable UAC. Highlight it, and click the Launch button, then reboot. To turn it back on again, follow the same steps, except choose Enable UAC instead.

Hack the Elevated Command Prompt

When you try to run certain commands from the command prompt, you're told that you don't have administrative rights to run them, even if you're currently logged in as an administrator.

What gives?

The problem is that these commands are protected by UAC. So if you want to run them, you'll have to run the command prompt itself as an administrator; what's called running an *elevated command prompt*.

One way to run an elevated command prompt is to type cmd into the Search box on the Start menu, right-click the command prompt icon that appears at the top of the Start menu, then select "Run as administrator." You can also type cmd.exe into the search box, and press Ctrl-Shift-Enter to launch it as an administrator.

Do you really want to have to do that every time you want to run an elevated command prompt? Most likely not. Instead, create a Desktop shortcut for an elevated prompt, or pin an elevated prompt to the Start menu.

To create a shortcut to an elevated prompt on the Desktop:

1. Right-click the Desktop, and select New→Shortcut.
2. In the text box of the Create Shortcut dialog box that appears, type CMD, and then click Next.
3. On the next screen, type a name for the shortcut, for example, Elevated Command Prompt. Then click Finish.
4. Right-click on the shortcut you just created, and select Properties.
5. Click the Shortcut tab, and click Advanced.
6. Check the box entitled "Run as administrator", and click OK, and then OK again.

If you'd like the elevated command prompt to appear on the Start menu, drag it from the Desktop to the Start button, and place it where you would like it to be.

 When a user is asked to type in an administrator password, it's called *credential prompting*; when an administrator is asked to permit an operation, it's called *consent prompting*.

See Also

- "Unlock the Super-Secret Administrator Account" **[Hack #109]**

HACK 109: Unlock the Super-Secret Administrator Account

V XP Hidden in the bowels of Windows is a super-secret Administrator account. Here's how to unlock it, in case you ever need to use it.

Deep inside Windows, there's a secret Administrator account, and it's different from the normal administrator account you most likely have set up on your PC. Oddly enough, this Administrator account is not part of the Administrator group. (Note the differentiation between the secret Administrator account, and the administrator account you've set up. In describing this hack, we'll always use the capital "A" for the secret account, and a lowercase "a" for an administrator account you've set up.)

What's the difference between the secret Administrator account and a normal administrator account? On Vista, the difference is more than the name: the Administrator account is not subject to User Account Control. So the Administrator can make any changes to the system and will see no UAC prompts.

For this reason, you may want to unlock the Administrator account, and use it only for those times when you want to make a series of system changes and don't want to be bothered by UAC. True, you could instead simply disable UAC on your system, but it's a pain to do this, and you may forget to turn it back on.

Turning on the Administrator account is pretty straightforward. On Vista, open an elevated command prompt by typing cmd.exe into the Search box on the Start menu and pressing Ctrl-Shift-Enter. Next, enter this command:

```
Net user administrator /active:yes
```

On XP Professional, fire up TweakUI [Hack #19], go to the Logon section, and choose "Show Administrator on Welcome Screen".

On Windows XP Home, the Administrator account is only available when you boot into safe mode.

From now on, the Administrator account will appear on the Welcome screen. Use it like any other account. Be aware that it won't have a password, so it's a good idea to set a password for it by going to Control Panel→User Accounts and Family Safety (Vista) or Control Panel→User Accounts (XP).

If you want to disable the account and hide it, enter this command at an elevated command prompt:

```
Net user administrator /active:no
```

See Also

- "Bypass the Windows Vista Logon Screen On Multi-Account PCs" [Hack #5]
- "Hack Windows Vista's User Account Control" [Hack #108]

HACK 110: Root Out Rootkits

V XP Rootkits are malicious programs that can do immeasurable damage to your PC and data, and invade your privacy. Normally, you can't detect them. This hack tells you how to find out if one has embedded itself in your system.

The most dreaded of all PC infections are *rootkits*, the superbugs of the malware world. Rootkits embed themselves deep inside your Windows system, and they use a variety of techniques to hide themselves from antispyware software, antivirus software, and system management utilities. In fact, they can appear completely invisible to Windows, hiding their services, processes, and registry keys. Not all rootkits are malignant, but many are. They can open "backdoors" into your system, giving someone else full control over your PC; can turn your PC into a "zombie" or "bot" that can spew spam or spyware; or be used to launch denial of service attacks on web sites. They can also be used to spy on your activities, for example, by stealing your passwords and usernames for logging into web sites such as for financial institutions.

The most infamous rootkit of all time was one that Sony installed on people's PCs without their knowledge when they played a Sony CD on their PC. The rootkit limited what people could do when playing CDs, for example, limiting their ability to rip or burn music. In addition, the rootkit made people's CD drives impossible to use if they tried to uninstall the rootkit. It also could have opened a backdoor into their systems that malicious people could exploit. Sony ultimately stopped including the rootkit on its PCs.

There are four main categories of rootkits:

Persistent rootkits

These are rootkits that stay persistent on a system. Every time the system boots or a user logs in, they activate, which means that they must store their code somewhere permanently, such as in the Registry or in files.

QUICK HACK 

USE WHOAMI TO SEE ACCOUNT INFORMATION

Windows Vista has a cool new command-line tool called Whoami that shows plenty of information about the currently logged on user, including the account name, a list of group memberships, and much more as well. At any command line, type whoami, and you'll be shown the name of the logged-on user. Type whoami /all to see a wide variety of information, including a list of groups to which the account is a member, user privileges, and much more. For a list of all parameters, type whoami /?.

Memory-based rootkits

These are rootkits that do not stay persistent on a system. They have no permanent code, and do not start each time a system reboots or the user logs in. They don't survive a reboot; once the system restarts, they're gone.

User-mode rootkits

These rootkits use a variety of different means to evade detection, including intercepting all calls to Windows APIs that enumerate running processes and remove the rootkit from the list. However, as their name suggests, they run in user mode instead of kernel mode; as such, they can be detected by kernel-mode tools, which includes many antivirus and antimalware tools. User-mode rootkits can be persistent or memory-based.

Kernel-mode rootkits

These are particularly powerful rootkits, because they can directly manipulate the Windows kernel. Kernel-mode rootkits can be persistent or memory-based.

The most dangerous rootkits typically can't be found by antivirus and antispyware software. Your best protection, in fact, is to make sure you're not infected in the first place **[Hack #52]**.

If you notice odd behavior on your PC, and antispyware and antivirus software can't detect a problem, there's a possibility that a rootkit may be the cause. Your best bet is to download and use the free RootkitRevealer (www.microsoft.com/technet/sysinternals/utilities/RootkitRevealer.mspx) from Microsoft.

This isn't the easiest program to understand, and it won't give you a definitive answer to whether you have a rootkit. But if you suspect you have a rootkit, it's the best place to start. Download it, and run it, and its results will be a screen like you see in Figure 8-2. RootkitRevealer scans your system at two different levels—using Windows APIs, and in the contents of the filesystem and the Registry. Because rootkits manipulate portions of the Windows API to hide themselves by altering the output of directory listing and process listing APIs, RootkitRevealer compares its scans, and then reports on anomalies, such as whether a file or Registry setting is hidden from the relevant Windows API. Figure 8-2 shows the results of a scan.

You should close all programs before running RootkitRevealer because any running programs may cause it to report false results.

You'll see plenty of results you don't understand. Don't worry about them. Mainly look for any descriptions that say "Hidden from Windows API", because that's a possible tip-off you've got a rootkit.

RootkitRevealer needs some special care running under Windows Vista. When you run it, a screen will appear, telling you that a program is sending you a message that can't be displayed on your desktop. Click "Show me the message", and your screen will go dark for a moment, and you'll then be sent to a screen running RootkitRevealer. But you won't be able to get to your desktop or any other application. Run the program, see the results, and to return to your desktop, exit the program, and click Return Now. If you don't exit the program before clicking Return Now, you'll constantly get a reminder that a program is sending you a message that can't be displayed.

Keep in mind, though, that not all "Hidden from Windows API" messages mean there's a rootkit present. These messages can be generated for a number of different reasons. For example, if a process such as an antivirus update runs between the time the API scan and the file and Registry scan is done, you may generate those message. So it's a good idea, in fact, to do at least a second system scan. Compare Figure 8-3 to Figure 8-2. They were done on the same system, one after the other. The second scan reports no major anomalies.

QUICK HACK 

WHAT'S THE MOST EFFECTIVE ANTIVIRUS ?

Antivirus makers all claim their programs are the best at detecting and killing viruses. But which is really the best? The site AV Comparatives (www.av-comparatives.org) claims to know. It tests antivirus programs at how well they detect thousands of viruses, compares then all, and gives them ratings from no certification to Standard, Advanced, and Advanced+. You can see the results of the tests, not just the final ratings.

Figure 8-2.
The Hidden from Windows API message appears to indicate there may be a rootkit here...

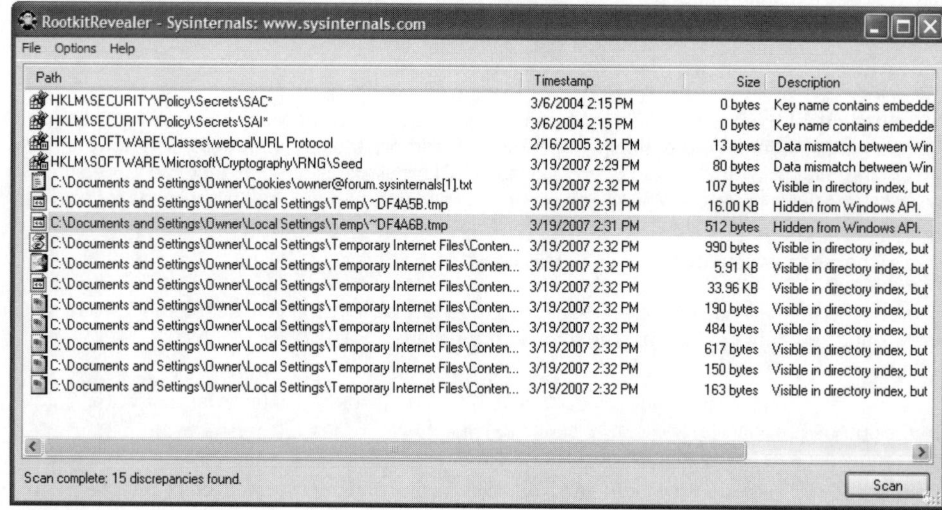

Figure 8-3.
...but a second scan shows that's not the case.

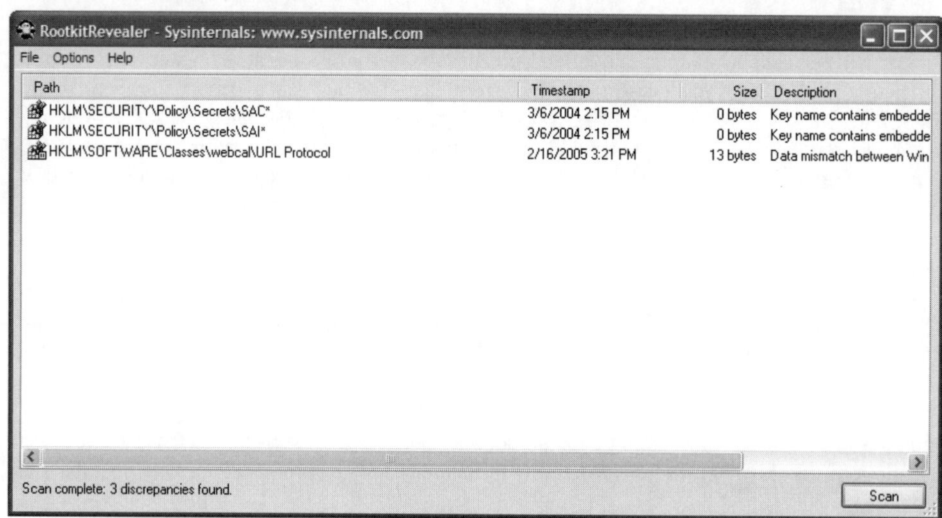

If you still see "Hidden from Windows API" messages, it may mean you have a rootkit. Look at the path of the file or key, and find the filename or the Registry key name. Do a Google search on them; if they're rootkit files, you'll most likely uncover than during your search.

In addition, check the RootkitRevealer page (www.microsoft.com/technet/sysinternals/utilities/RootkitRevealer.mspx) for more instructions on how to interpret your results. And you should also check the Sysinternals RootkitRevealer Forum (forum.sysinternals.com/forum_topics.asp?FID=15) for more information about how to detect rootkits.

As this book went to press, McAfee was in the process of creating the McAfee Rootkit Detective, which promises to detect and kill rootkits. The software was still in beta, and works only with Windows XP SP2, Windows 2000 with SP4, Windows 2000 Server, and Windows 2003 Server SP1. Download it from vil.nai.com/vil/stinger/rkstinger.aspx.

What to do if you think you have a rootkit? You're again going to have to rely on Google, because instructions for removing rootkits vary significantly from one to another; there are no overall guiding directions on how to do it. Keep in mind, though, that there's a possibility that once you've been infected by a rootkit, there may be no way to remove it. Your only solution may be to reformat your hard disk and reinstall Windows. However, there is a chance you can take the rootkit on in a knock-down, drag-out fight **[Hack #111]**.

Hacking the Hack

If you run RootkitRevealer from the command line, you can use several switches with it:

```
rootkitrevealer -a -c -m -r outputfile
```

Here's what each switch does:

-a
Do an automatic scan and exit when the scan is done.

-c
Create output as a *.csv* file. These can be read in spreadsheets and database programs, as well as text editors such as Notepad.

-m
Show NTFS metadata files. These are files the NTFS filesystem uses for disk management. Normally they are not included in a scan, because NTFS normally hides them, and so including them in a scan may result in false "Hidden from Windows API" messages.

-r
Don't scan the Registry.

outputfile
If you are creating a *.csv* file, you need to include a filename. Make sure to include the full path.

For example, if you want to have RootkitRevealer run automatically, do a scan, and create a file of the output named *rootkit.log* in your *C:\Security Files* folder, you'd issue this command at the command line:

```
rootkitrevealer -a -c C:\Security Files\rootkit.log
```

See Also

- "Kill Viruses, Spyware, and Web Bugs—for Free" **[Hack #52]**
- www.rootkit.com contains sample code for rootkits, as well as discussions about how to develop rootkits.

HACK 111: Kill Spyware and Pests With Your Bare Hands

V XP Some spyware and viruses are so nasty that even antispyware and antivirus programs can't kill them. Here's how to go one on one against them and come out the winner.

Most of the time when you're infected with spyware or viruses, your security software will kill the pest dead. Occasionally, however, you need to roll up your sleeves and do the dirty work, especially if the software detects a new pest it can't eradicate. Some pests are so downright nasty, that automated pest-killing using software simply won't work.

If that happens to you, you'll have to go *mano a mano* against the pest and kill it with your own hands.

QUICK HACK 

GET A FREE ROOTKIT KILLER

If you're looking for a simple, one-step way to root out and kill rootkits, try the free AVG Anti-Rootkit (www.grisoft.com/doc/products-avg-anti-rootkit/us/crp/2). Run it, and it searches your system for rootkits. It alerts you if it finds any, and then kills them.

There's no single way to kill pests manually. Each one requires very specific instructions. But this hack will show you the general steps you need to take to kill PC infections your antimalware software can't handle.

First, get the name of the pest from your antispyware or antivirus software. If it can't tell you the name of the pest, all bets are off. You won't be able to eradicate it manually without knowing its exact name. So if your antispyware or antivirus software can't find the name, try a different piece of software until one finds it.

Before you delete any pests manually, try the McAfee Stinger tool. It can often remove stubborn pests left alone by your antivirus software. To download Stinger, see a list of pests Stinger can remove, and get removal instructions, go to vil.nai.com/vil/stinger.

Once you know the name, you're ready to kill the pest. The three best web sites for providing step-by-step manual instructions on pest-killing include McAfee Threat Center (www.mcafee.com/us/threat_center/) which is shown in Figure 8-4, Computer Associates Spyware Information Center

Figure 8-4.
The McAfee Threat Center, a good place to go to get advice on how to kill pests manually

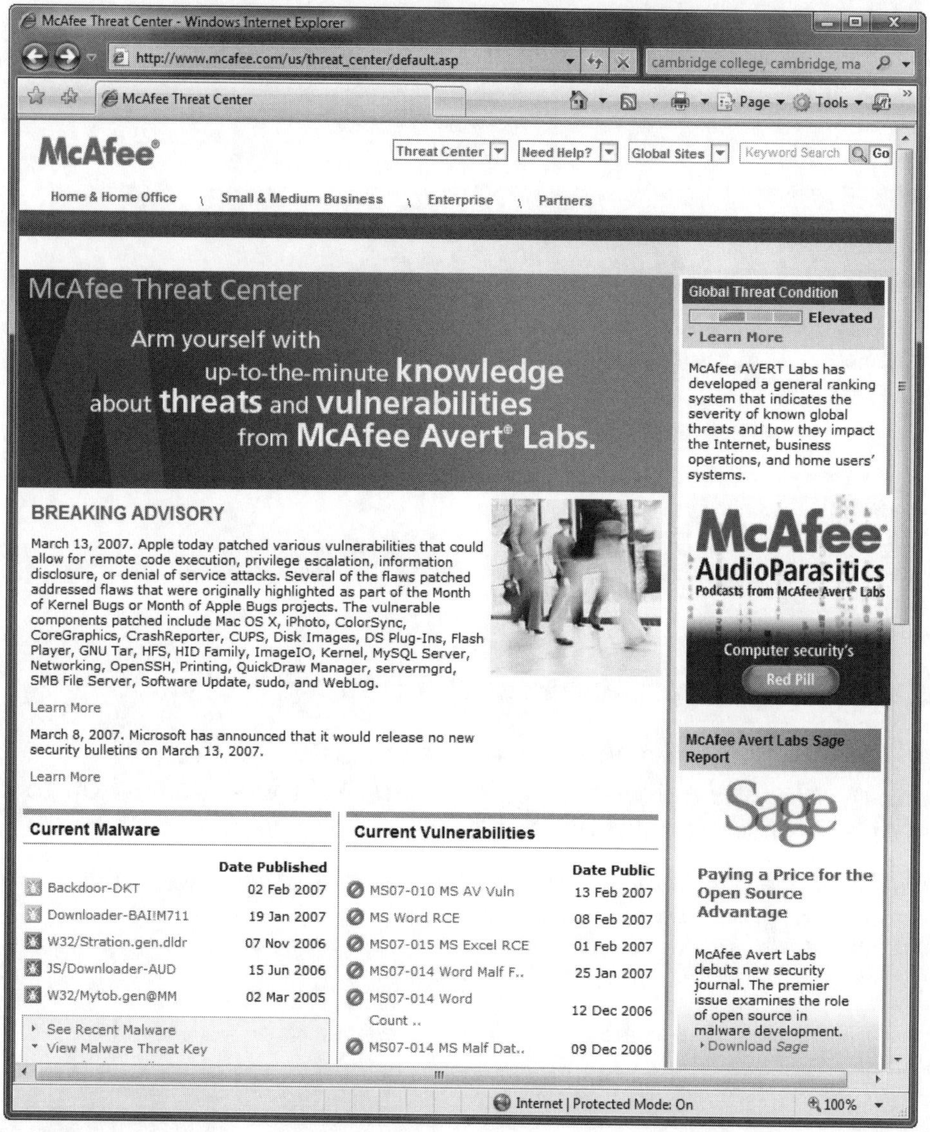

(www3.ca.com/securityadvisor/pest), and Symantec Security Response (www.symantec.com/avcenter).

Let's assume that you've noticed your system behaving oddly, and you suspect that it's been infected with some piece of malware. Your security software, though, hasn't detected it. Download several other pieces of security software **[Hack #52]** until you find one that finds the pest.

Write down the pest name. For example, suppose that you've found the Bagle worm, specifically the *W32/Bagle.aa@MM* variant.

First turn off System Restore, and delete all your restore points. Normally, System Restore is your friend because it can restore your system to a working state if you run into a problem. But if the pest is lurking in one of your restore points, the pest can reinfect your system after you kill the pest.

To turn off System Restore and delete restore points in Windows XP, right-click My Computer, and choose Properties. Click the System Restore tab. Check the Turn off System Restore box, as shown in Figure 8-5.

Click OK. The warning box is shown in Figure 8-6. Click the Yes button to delete all your old Restore Points. It will take a short while for XP to delete all your old Restore Points and turn off System Restore.

To turn off System Restore and delete your old restore points in Windows Vista, select Control Panel→System and Maintenance→Backup and Restore Center→Create a restore point or change

Figure 8-5.
Check the box, and click OK to turn off System Restore

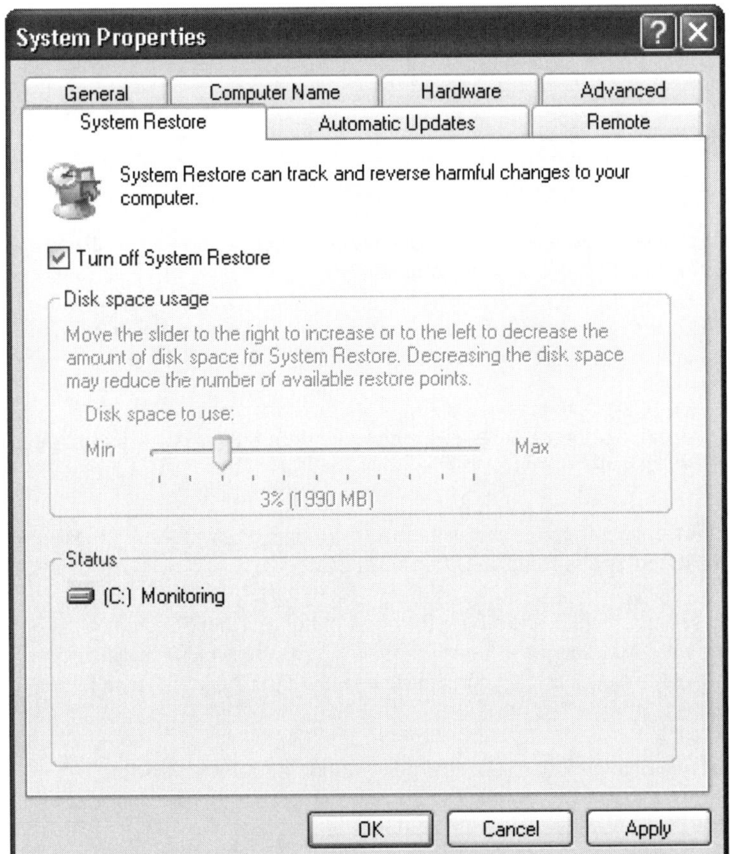

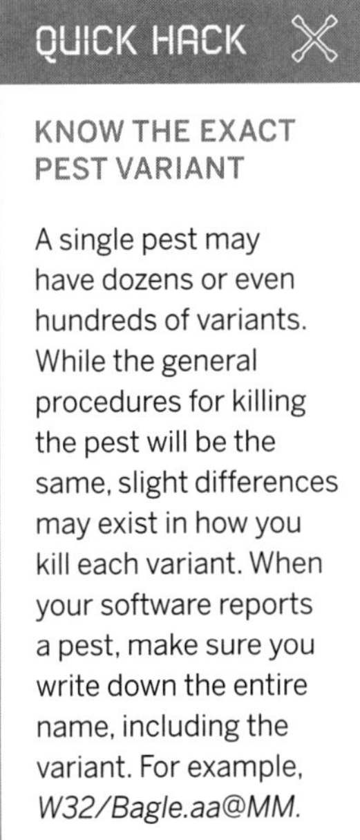
QUICK HACK

KNOW THE EXACT PEST VARIANT

A single pest may have dozens or even hundreds of variants. While the general procedures for killing the pest will be the same, slight differences may exist in how you kill each variant. When your software reports a pest, make sure you write down the entire name, including the variant. For example, *W32/Bagle.aa@MM*.

Figure 8-6.
Click the Yes button to delete all your old Restore Points

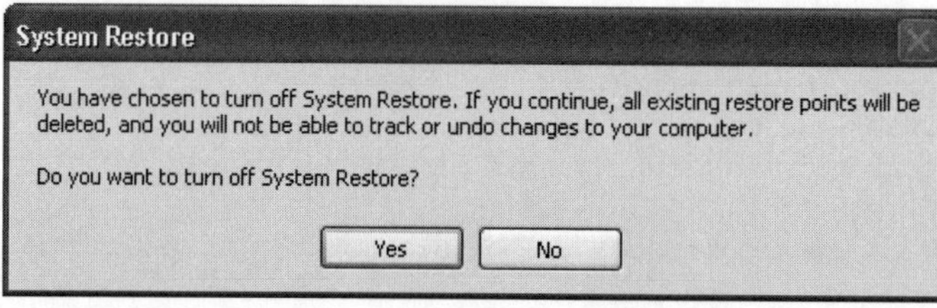

Figure 8-7.
Uncheck the box next to a disk to turn off System Restore for it

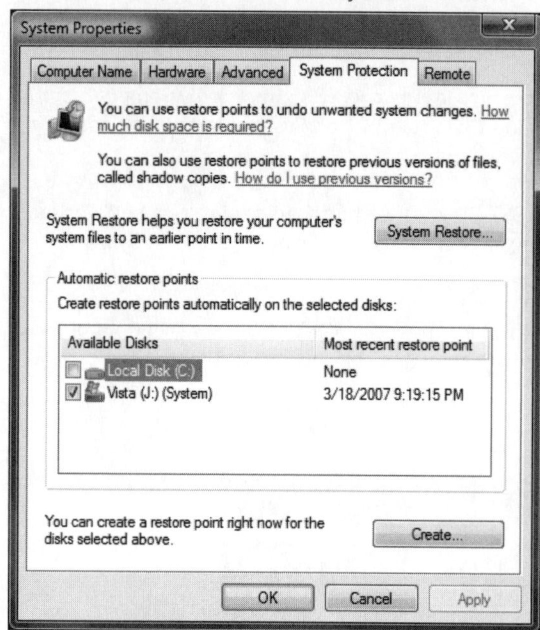

settings. A screen like one shown in Figure 8-7 appears. Uncheck the box next to your disk. If you have more than one disk, uncheck the boxes next to both.

The warning box shown in Figure 8-8 appears. Click the Turn System Restore Off to delete all your old restore points. It will take a short while for Windows Vista to delete all your old restore points and turn off System Restore.

 When you delete restore points, you will lose any shadow copies of files in them. Shadow copies **[Hack #38]** function as backups of files, and earlier versions of files.

Now that System Restore is turned off, update your antimalware's pest definitions. After you kill the pest, do a virus scan to make sure you're completely free of the pest.

Go to www.mcafee.com/us/threat_center, and type in the name of the pest in the Search box. In our case, we type in W32/Bagle.aa@MM, and press Enter. Click the top search result, which should be the most relevant. It will display a page like that shown in Figure 8-9. (If the top search result doesn't display this page, keep clicking until you find one.)

This page provides a great deal of information about the pest, including its characteristics, symptoms, the way in which it infects PCs, and most important, instructions for removing it. Click the Removal link and follow the instructions for removing the pest.

Figure 8-8.
Turning off System Restore in Windows Vista

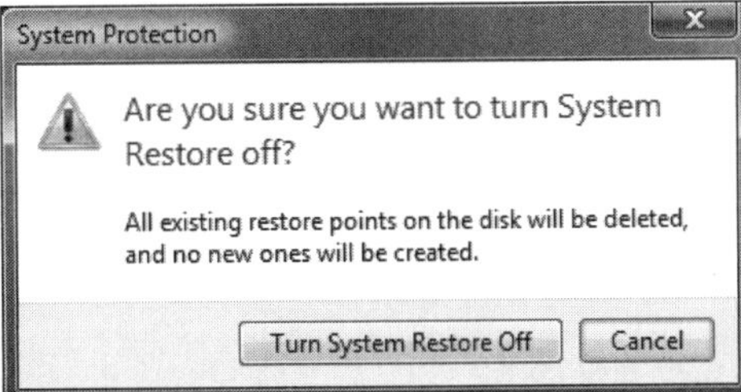

Figure 8-9.
This page provides information about the Bagle pest

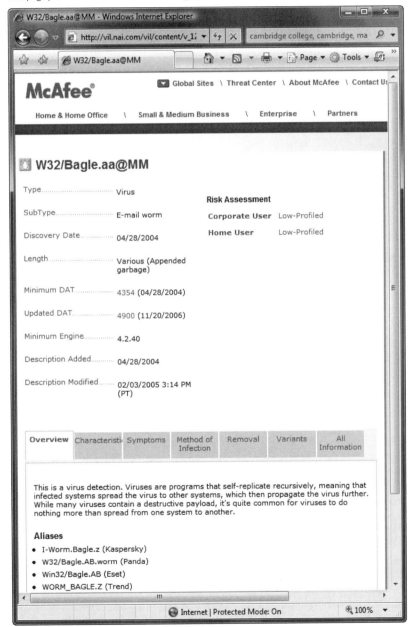

The instructions will vary according to the pest. It will often involve booting into safe mode, deleting specific files, editing the Registry, and then rebooting. (For details about how to edit the Registry, see Chapter 13.) For killing this Bagle variant, boot into safe mode (restart your system, then hit the F8 key, and choose Safe Mode). Next, delete the files *drvddll.exe*, *drvddll.exeopen*, and *drvddll.exeopenopen* from the Windows system directory and delete the `drvddll.exe` value from `HKEY_CURRENT_USER\Software\Microsoft\Windows\CurrentVersion\Run`. After that's done, reboot. (The Stinger tool can also do all this automatically.)

After you kill the pest and reboot, scan your system again to make sure you're free of all traces of the pest. If not, repeat the steps for removing the pest, or use McAfee's Stinger tool (vil.nai.com/vil/stinger) to kill the remaining traces of the pest.

Finally turn System Restore back on. You should now be free of the pest. Remember, if you have to remove a different pest manually, the steps may differ. Again, check one of the sites cited earlier in this section to find out how to manually delete the pest.

HACK 112: Hacking Windows Vista's Outbound Firewall

V Windows Vista's firewall includes outbound filtering: that's the good news. There appears to be no real way to control it: that's the bad news. This hack shows you how you actually can do it, though, and that's the best news of all.

Microsoft touts the Windows Firewall in Windows Vista as a big improvement over the firewall in Windows XP because it offers outbound filtering as well as inbound filtering as a way to improve security. But as shipped, the Windows Firewall offers little outbound protection, and it doesn't appear there's any way to tweak it to use outbound protection to protect against spyware, Trojans, and bots.

Firewalls such as the Windows Firewall work by halting dangerous connections a PC makes over the Internet. The Windows XP firewall offered inbound protection but did not offer outbound protection. Some malware makes unwanted, invisible outbound connections to malicious hackers, which lets them take control of a PC. In some cases, a computer can be turned into a zombie or a bot, spewing out thousands of pieces of spam over outbound connections without the owner's knowledge.

Competing firewalls such as ZoneAlarm, the Norton Personal Firewall, and the McAfee Personal Firewall offer user-configurable outbound protection, also known as *outbound filtering*. When Microsoft reworked its firewall for Windows Vista, it added the ability to perform outbound filtering.

But by default, most outbound filtering in the Windows Vista firewall is turned off. To configure the Window Vista Firewall, choose Control Panel→Security→"Turn Windows Firewall on or off". You'll see the screen shown in Figure 8-10.

There's no way to configure outbound filtering from here. You can only turn inbound filtering on or off, and through the various tabs, configure how inbound filtering works. You wouldn't even know from this screen that the firewall did any outbound filtering.

If you want to try and hack around to configure outbound filtering, you'll have to turn to the Windows Firewall with Advanced Security Group Policy applet of the Microsoft Management Console. Run it by typing wf.msc at the Search box or command prompt and pressing Enter. To see the outbound rules set up for your PC, click the Outbound rules icon on the left side of the screen (see Figure 8-11). Here's the kicker: the rules allow every single outbound action. Not a single configured rule blocks any connection.

Figure 8-10.
Windows Vista Firewall's basic configuration screen

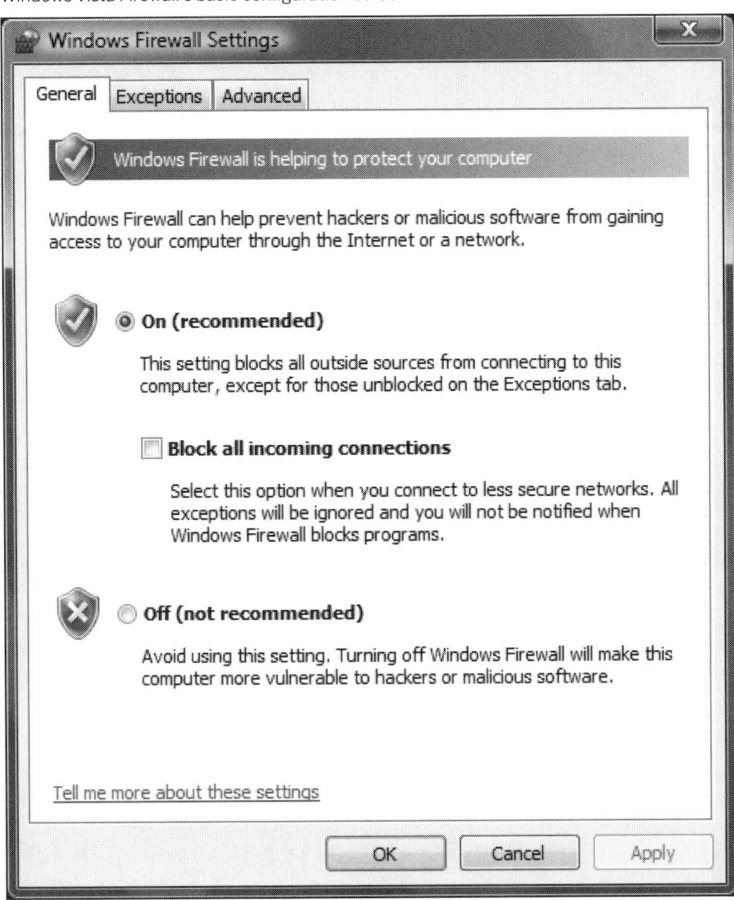

Figure 8-11.
All outbound connections are allowed by default,
as you can see in the Windows Firewall with Advanced Security Group Policy applet

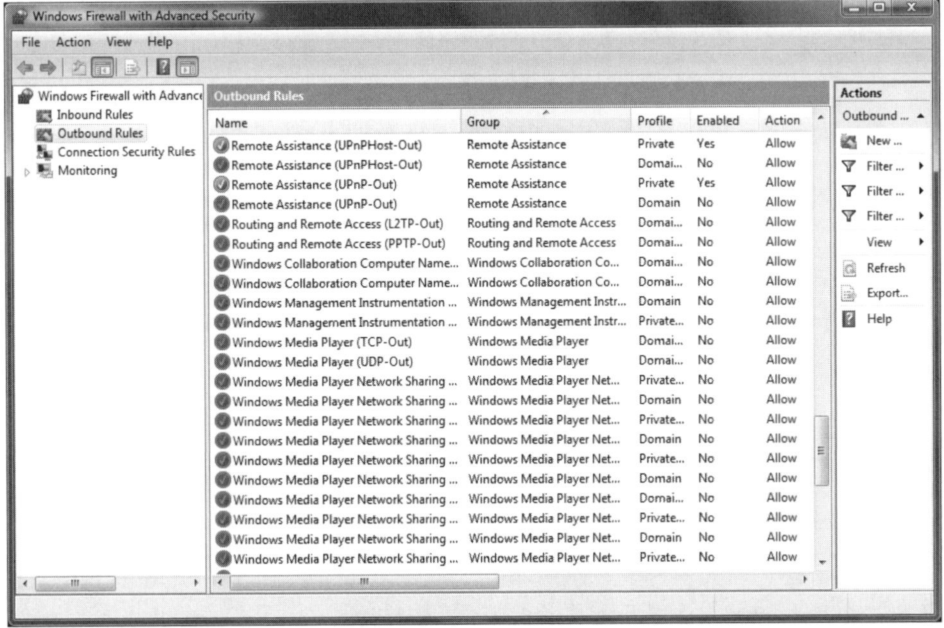

There is no way for you to create an all-purpose rule that will block malware from making outbound connections. You can only create a rule to block a specific piece of malware, and doing that is an extremely difficult task, requiring that you know quite an extraordinary amount of information about that piece of malware, including its location on your PC, the port it uses to make outbound connections, and so on.

To stop all malware from making outbound connections, you'd have to know every one of these details for all the thousands of pieces of malware in existence and create rules for each one individually. But even that wouldn't work because you wouldn't know about malware that has not yet been detected.

In other words, it appears you can't do it.

Competing firewalls often use built-in intelligence to allow certain programs to make outbound connections and then issue alerts when other programs make connections. You're told the program name and executable, and given a recommendation as to whether the program should be allowed. You can then block or allow the program to make a connection on a one-time or permanent basis. For example, ZoneAlarm does this. Get a free version at tinyurl.com/359nrn.

Microsoft says that even though the Windows Vista Firewall doesn't display any outbound filtering rules, it works in concert with a security feature called Windows Service Hardening to block some outbound connections. With Windows Service Hardening, the firewall can understand specific behaviors that various Windows services should have, and if they do something unexpected, such as exploiting a vulnerability, it will block them.

There's also another freebie firewall that lets you configure outbound protection on a program-by-program basis. Get the free VistaFirewallControl at www.sphinx-soft.com/Vista/. Install it, and then every time an application tries to access the Internet, a screen pops up, as shown in Figure 8-12. It tells you the application name, the publisher, and similar information, as well its path and filename. You can enable or disable inbound or outbound connections it tries to make, either permanently, or just this one time.

Figure 8-12.
VistaFirewallControl asking whether to allow an application to access the Internet

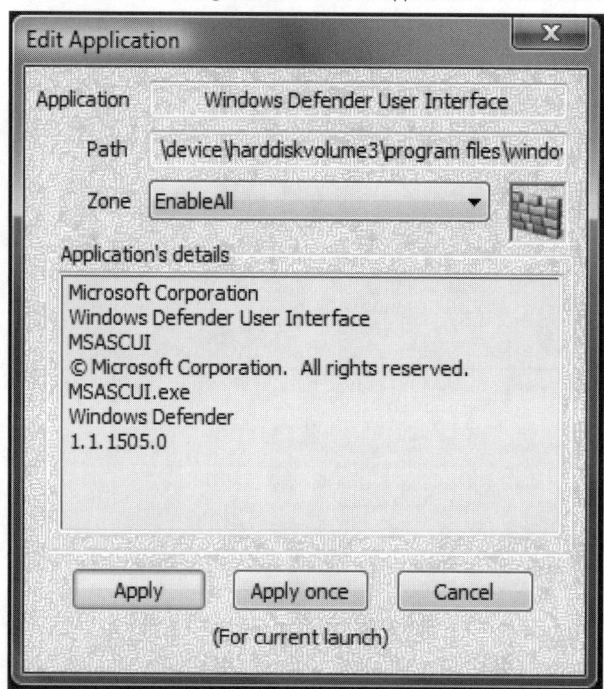

Figure 8-13.
A list of all programs you've configured using the VistaFirewallControl

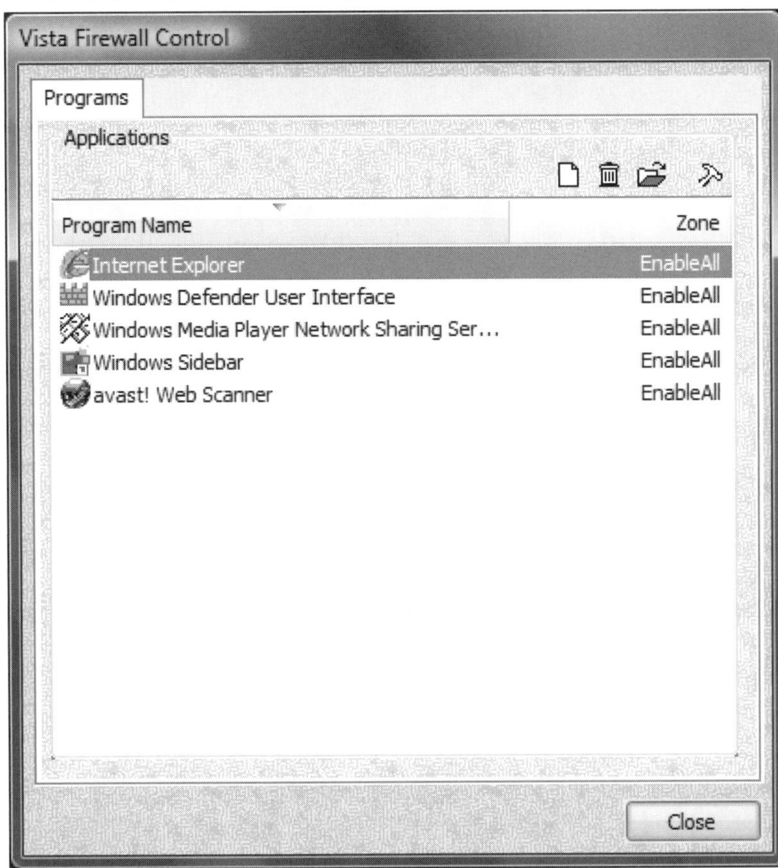

If it's a program you're familiar with, let it through. If you're not familiar with it, go to ProcessLibrary.com (www.processlibrary.com) and search for the filename. It will tell you if it's a valid program or potential malware. Do a Google search as well.

The first several times your run it, you may be inundated with pop ups, but pretty soon you'll have configured all your programs to work with it, and you can use the Internet as you would normally. You can also see all the programs you've configured and make changes to those configurations by double-clicking the VistaFirewallControl icon running in the System Tray. A screen like Figure 8-13 appears. To edit how you've configured the program for the firewall, double-click it.

HACK 113: Punch an Escape Hole Through Your Firewall

V XP Sometimes, firewalls offer too much protection; they block unsolicited incoming traffic that you want to receive, for instance, if you're hosting a web site. Here's how to open a hole in your firewall to let only specific incoming traffic through.

Most firewalls block all unsolicited inbound traffic and connections, which can be a problem if you're running a web site, email or FTP server, or other service that requires you to accept unsolicited inbound packets. But you can punch a hole through your firewall to let only that traffic in, while still keeping potentially dangerous intruders out.

First, decide what kind of unsolicited inbound traffic and connections you want to let through, and then find out which ports they use. For example, if you have a web server, you'll have to allow traffic through that's bound for port 80. Table 5-1 **[Hack #68]** lists common ports; for a complete list, go to www.iana.org/assignments/port-numbers.

How you allow traffic through a firewall varies from firewall to firewall, and it differs between Windows XP and Windows Vista. I'll show you how to do it for both.

Allowing a Program Through the Firewall

In Windows Vista, select Control Panel→Allow a program through Windows Firewall. The Windows Firewall Exceptions dialog box appears, as shown in Figure 8-14. To get to this screen in Windows XP, first choose Control Panel→Security Center. (If a Security Center icon shows in the system tray, you can instead click that icon.) Then, click the Windows Firewall icon at the bottom of the screen. Click the Exceptions tab.

To enable a service and allow its incoming traffic through the firewall, put a check next to the service you want to allow through, and click OK. For this screen, you won't have to know the port numbers for the services whose incoming traffic you want to let through; you just need to know which service you want to allow. Windows will know to block or unblock the proper port.

If the program you want to let through the firewall isn't listed in the Windows Firewall Exceptions dialog box, click Add Program, browse to the program you want added as an exception, and click OK. It will now show up on the list. Make sure the box next to it is checked when it appears on the Windows Firewall Exceptions dialog box.

Figure 8-14.
Enabling specific incoming services and traffic to bypass the Windows Firewall

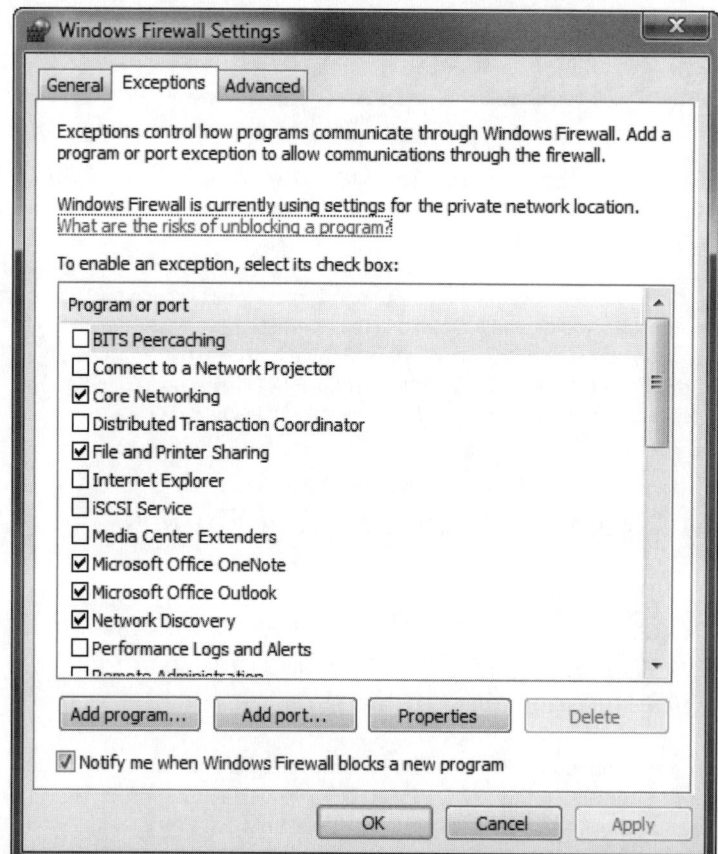

Allowing a Service Through the Firewall

In addition to programs that you allow through the firewall, you might also want to allow services through. For example, if you're running a web server, FTP server, or other server, or you have a VPN that you want to allow others to use, you'll have to tell the firewall to let those requests through.

Windows XP

In Windows XP, this is easy to do, but Microsoft made it much more difficult to do this in Windows Vista, for reasons that aren't at all clear. To do it in Windows XP, go to the Control Panel, choose Security Center, and click the Windows Firewall icon at the bottom of the screen. Click the Advanced tab, highlight the connection for which you want to allow the service through, and click Settings. The Advanced Settings dialog appears as shown in Figure 8-15. Now, select the service you want to allow to pass through, and click OK and then OK again. That service will now be able to bypass the Windows Firewall for the connection you had selected. If you want to allow it for other connections, go to the Advanced tab, and select a different connection, and repeat the steps.

There's a chance the default settings for the services you want to allow won't work properly. If that's the case, you can edit them. Depending on the service, you can change the service's name or IP address, its description, the internal and external port numbers the service uses, and whether it uses the TCP or UDP protocol. For example, if your business uses a VPN with a different port number than the one used by the Windows Firewall, you can change the port number the Windows Firewall uses so that your VPN will work. Some services include hardcoded properties that you can't change, while others will let you edit them. For example, the Remote Desktop service can use only 3389 for external and internal ports and TCP as its protocol, and those can't be edited. But a few of the services, notably the VPN connections, let you edit the ports and protocol.

To edit the properties for one of the services, select it, choose Edit, and you'll see the Service Settings screen, as shown in Figure 8-16.

This process lets you select from a number of services that you want to bypass the Windows Firewall. Table 8-1 describes what each service does. Note that the entry `msmsgs` might or might not show up in your system; Windows Messenger appears if you've used Windows Messenger or Outlook Express (which uses some Messenger components). Unlike all the other services listed, it is enabled by default, so it can already bypass the Windows Firewall.

Table 8-1. Services that can be allowed to bypass the Windows Firewall

SERVICE	WHAT IT DOES
FTP Server	Allows others to connect to an FTP server on your PC.
Incoming Connection VPN (L2TP)	Allows for the use of a Virtual Private Network using the L2TP tunneling technology.
Incoming Connection VPN (PPTP)	Allows for the use of a Virtual Private Network using the PPTP tunneling technology.
Internet Mail Access Protocol Version 3 (IMAP3)	Allows others to connect to an IMAP3 email server on your PC to retrieve email.
Internet Mail Access Protocol Version 4 (IMAP4)	Allows others to connect to an IMAP4 email server on your PC to retrieve email.
Internet Mail Server (SMTP)	Allows others to use an SMTP server on your PC for sending email.
IP Security (IKE)	Allows for the use of the Internet Key Exchange (IKE) security technology.

Table 8-1. Services that can be allowed to bypass the Windows Firewall *(continued)*

SERVICE	WHAT IT DOES
Msmsgs	Allows for the use of Windows Messenger, plus any software that uses its components, such as Outlook Express.
Post-Office Protocol Version 3 (POP3)	Allows others to connect to a POP3 email server on your PC to retrieve email.
Remote Desktop	Allows others to connect to your PC and take control of your desktop using the Remote Desktop feature available in XP Professional only.
Secure Web Server (HTTPS)	Allows others to connect to a web server on your PC that uses the HTTPS security protocol.
Telnet Server	Allows others to use a Telnet server on your PC to use your PC's resources.
Web Server (HTTP)	Allows others to connect to a web server on your PC.

Just because a service isn't listed in Table 8-1 doesn't mean you can't allow its incoming traffic to bypass the Windows Firewall. You can add any service if you know its port information; you'll also have to supply the name or IP address of the PC on your network where you want the traffic routed (unless you're configuring a PC that's acting as a router for another PC, this will usually be the IP address of your PC). For example, to play some instant messenger games, you'll need to allow port 1077 to get through. To add a new service, get to the Advanced Settings dialog box described earlier and shown in Figure 8-15. Then click the Add button, and fill out the dialog box shown in Figure 8-17.

Windows Vista

In Windows Vista, there's no direct way to let services through; you'll have to use a workaround. Tell Windows Firewall to open up the port that the service uses; by doing that, you'll allow through the service that uses that port.

First you have to know the port number of the service you want to let through. Table 5-1 **[Hack #68]** lists common ports used by services; for a complete list, go to www.iana.org/assignments/port-numbers. Note that some services may use multiple ports, so write down all the ports.

Once you have that information, select Control Panel→"Allow a program through Windows Firewall". The Windows Firewall Exceptions dialog box appears, as shown back in Figure 8-14. Click Add Port, and fill out the dialog box shown in Figure 8-18. Click OK. Add any other ports the service requires, and keep clicking OK. Then click OK on the Exceptions tab.

Windows Firewall Killed My File Sharing!

When you use the Windows Firewall and try to browse to another computer on your network to share its files, you might get an error message, and you won't be able to connect to those files. If this happens, open UDP ports 135 through 139, TCP ports 135 through 139, and TCP and UDP port 445 in the Windows Firewall.

Figure 8-15.
Choosing to let a service bypass the Windows Firewall in Windows XP

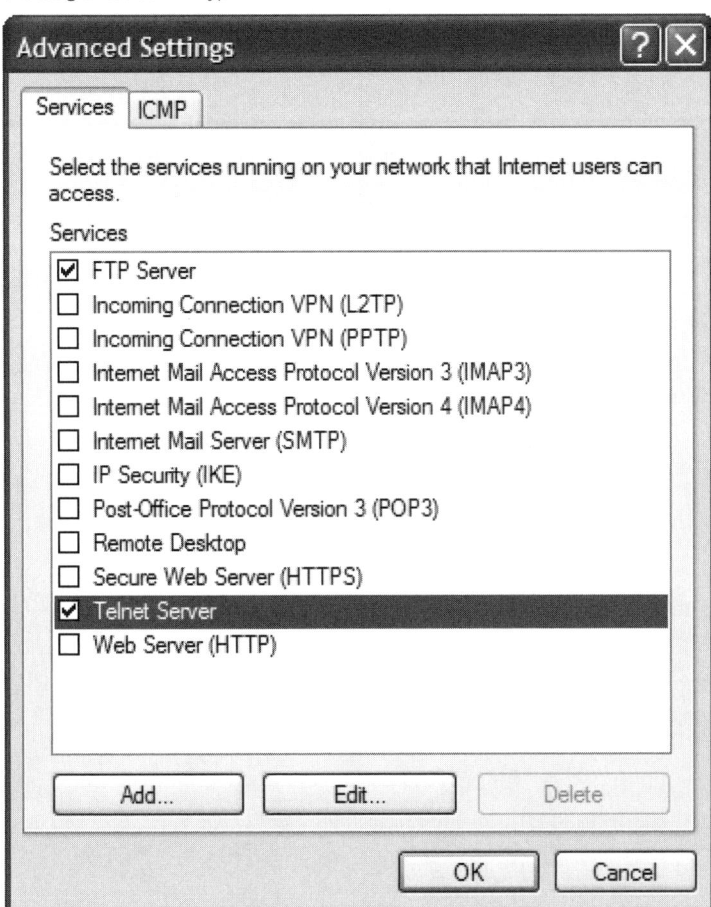

Figure 8-16.
Customizing an inbound service that you want to pass through the Windows Firewall in Windows XP

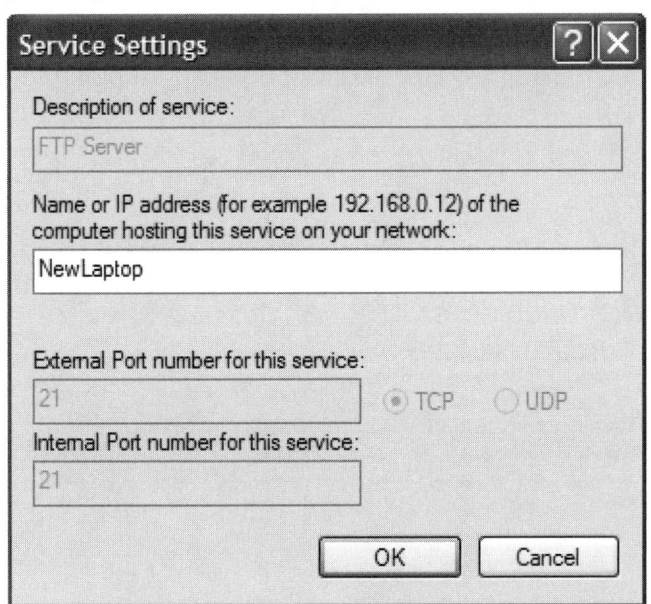

Figure 8-17.
Adding a new service that can bypass the Windows Firewall

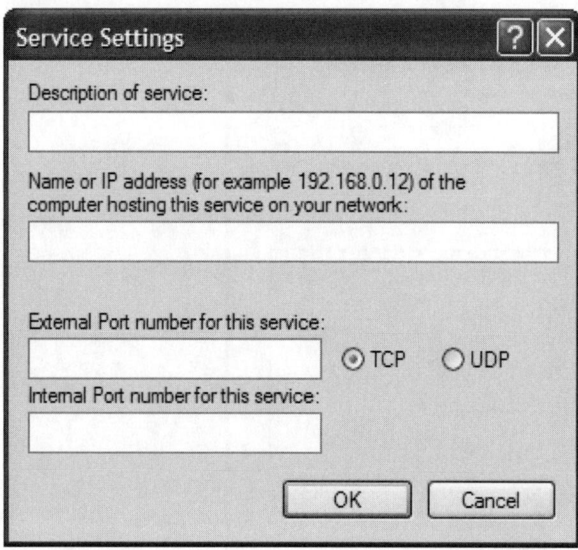

Figure 8-18.
This dialog box lets you add a port to the Windows Firewall exception list

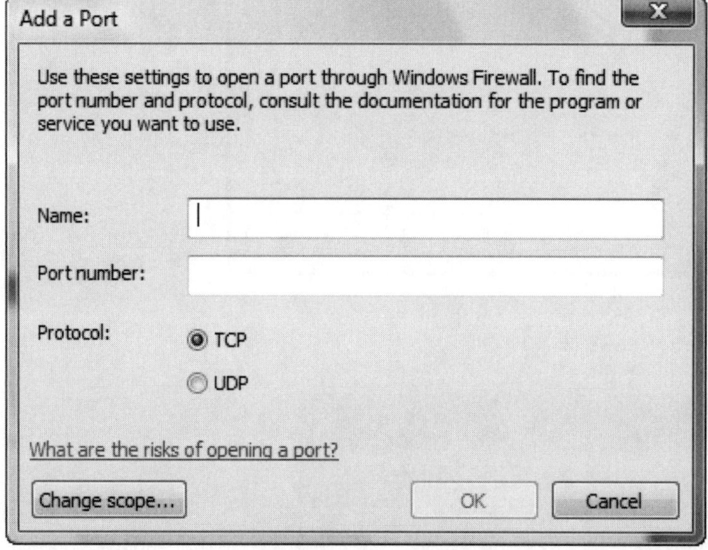

HACK 114: Track Firewall Activity with a Windows Firewall Log

V XP Get the rundown on would-be intruders who have tried to get onto your PC, then wreak revenge.

The Windows Firewall can do more than just protect you from intruders; it can also keep track of all intrusion attempts so that you can know whether your PC has been targeted, and what kinds of attacks the Windows Firewall has turned back. Then you can send that information to your ISP so it can track down the intruders.

How you do this varies from Windows XP to Windows Vista; I'll show you how to do it for each.

First, create a Windows Firewall log. In Windows XP, go to the Control Panel, and open Security Center, choose Windows Firewall→Advanced, and click the Settings button in the Security Logging section. The dialog box shown in Figure 8-19 appears.

Choose whether to log dropped packets, successful connections, or both. A *dropped packet* is a packet that the Windows Firewall has blocked. A successful connection doesn't always mean an intruder has successfully connected to your PC; it refers to both incoming connections as well as any connection *you* have made over the Internet, such as to web sites. If you decide to log successful connections, your log will become large quickly, and you'll need to search through the logs to find just the entries you are looking for. After you've made your choices, choose a location for the log, set its maximum size, and click OK. I don't let my log get larger than 1 MB, but depending on how much you care about disk space and how much you plan to use the log, you might want yours larger or smaller.

The log will be created in a W3C Extended Log format (*.log*) that you can examine with Notepad or another text editor or by using a log analysis program such as the free AWStats (awstats.sourceforge.net).

In Windows Vista, creating a log is a bit more complicated. At a command prompt or the Search box on the Start menu, type wf.msc, and press Enter. The Windows Firewall with Advanced Security screen appears. Click Windows Firewall Properties, and from the dialog box that appears, click the Private Profile tab, and in the Logging section, click Customize. From the screen that appears in Figure 8-20, choose your maximum log size, location, and whether to log only dropped packets, or both logged packets and successful connections. Click OK.

Now Click the Public Profile tab, and follow the same steps you did for the Private Profile tab. You've now turned on the log.

Now that you have a log, what can you do with it? Read it, of course, and send along any information about attackers to your ISP.

Figure 8-19.
Creating a Windows Firewall log in Windows XP

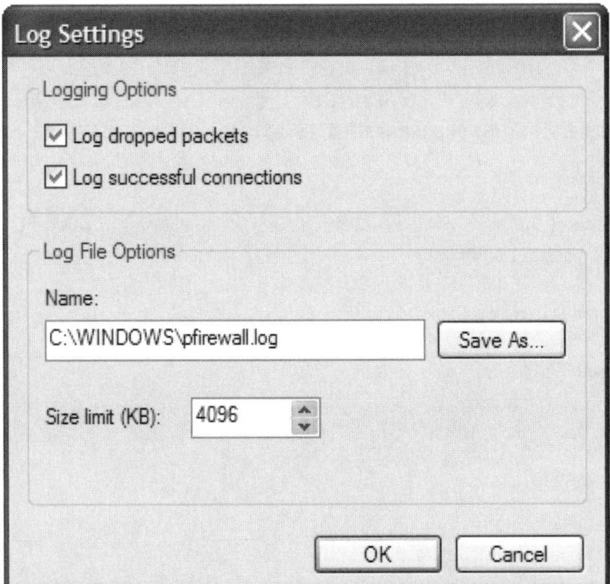

Figure 8-20.
Turning on firewall logging in Windows Vista

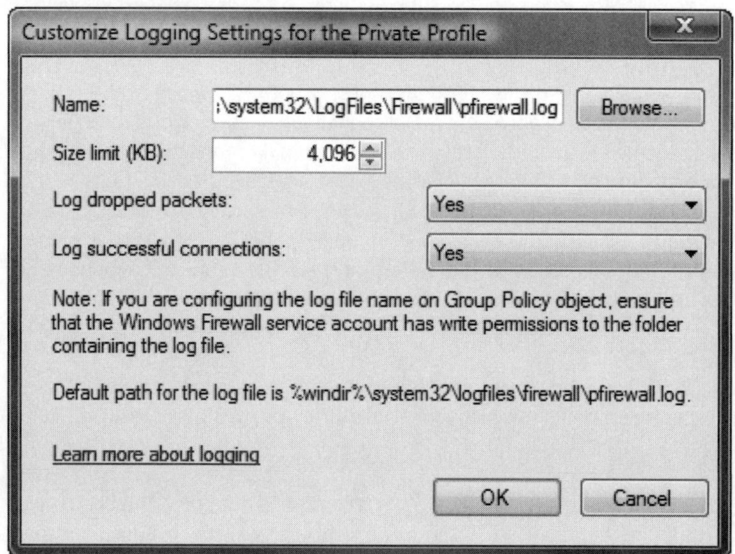

 If like many people, you use a wireless or wired broadband router, then all incoming connections (except those you've enabled as shown in "Give the World Access to a Server or PC Behind your Home Router" **[Hack #68]**) will be stopped at your router. Check your router's documentation to see if it keeps its own log (many routers let you get to the log through the router configuration utility or web-based interface).

In Windows Vista, from the Windows Firewall with Advanced Security screen, scroll down until you see the Monitoring link. Click it, and from the screen that appears, go to the Logging Settings section. Click the link for your log. The log will open in Notepad, as you can see in Figure 8-21. In Windows XP, open Notepad, browse to the log location, and open it (you will need to disable logging temporarily in order to open the logfile in Notepad). You can also use a command-line utility to inspect the log. For example, to find successful incoming connections, open a Command Prompt, change to the *C:\Windows* directory (or wherever the logfile happens to reside), and use FindStr to locate the string "OPEN-INBOUND". In this example, you can see that the PC (192.168.254.9) received a connection on port 139 (Windows file sharing) from another PC (192.168.254.5) on the same network:

```
C:\WINDOWS>findstr OPEN-INBOUND pfirewall.log
2007-07-18 02:22:45 OPEN-INBOUND TCP 192.168.254.5   192.168.254.9 55625 139 - - - - - - - - -
2007-07-18 02:22:45 OPEN-INBOUND TCP 192.168.254.5   192.168.254.9 55626 139 - - - - - - - - -
2007-07-18 02:23:01 OPEN-INBOUND TCP 192.168.254.5   192.168.254.9 55627 139 - - - - - - - - -
2007-07-18 02:23:01 OPEN-INBOUND TCP 192.168.254.5   192.168.254.9 55628 139 - - - - - - - - -
```

Each log entry has a total of up to 16 pieces of information associated with each event, but the most important columns for each entry are the first eight.

 In a text editor, the names of the columns may not align over the data, but they will align in a log analyzer.

Table 8-2 describes the most important columns.

Figure 8-21.
A log generated by the Windows Firewall

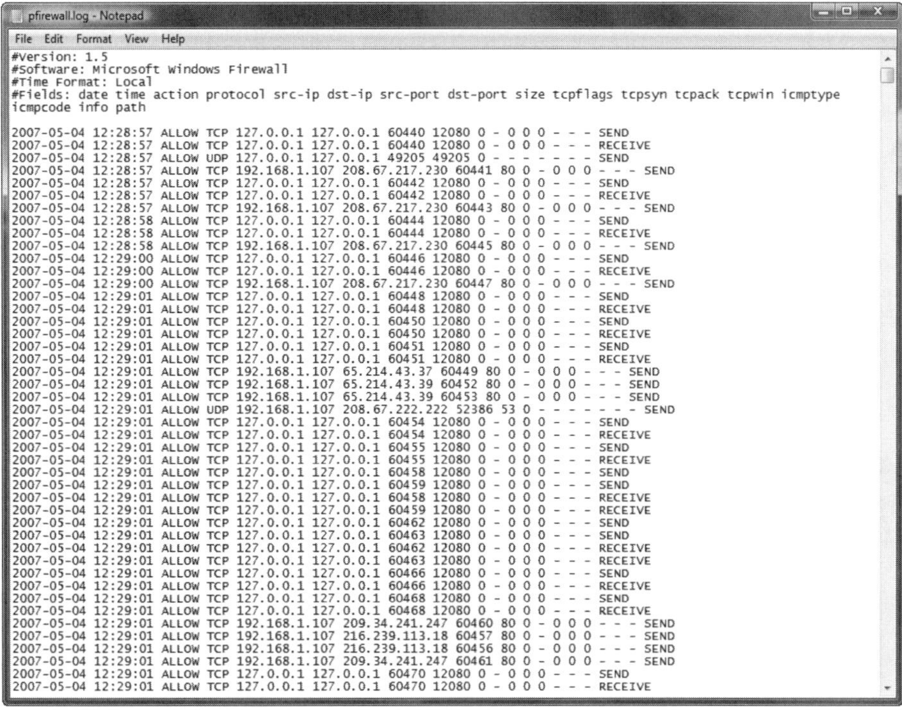

```
#Version: 1.5
#Software: Microsoft Windows Firewall
#Time Format: Local
#Fields: date time action protocol src-ip dst-ip src-port dst-port size tcpflags tcpsyn tcpack tcpwin icmptype
icmpcode info path

2007-05-04 12:28:57 ALLOW TCP 127.0.0.1 127.0.0.1 60440 12080 0 - 0 0 0 - - - SEND
2007-05-04 12:28:57 ALLOW TCP 127.0.0.1 127.0.0.1 60440 12080 0 - 0 0 0 - - - RECEIVE
2007-05-04 12:28:57 ALLOW UDP 127.0.0.1 127.0.0.1 49205 49205 0 - - - - - - - SEND
2007-05-04 12:28:57 ALLOW TCP 192.168.1.107 208.67.217.230 60441 80 0 - 0 0 0 - - - SEND
2007-05-04 12:28:57 ALLOW TCP 127.0.0.1 127.0.0.1 60442 12080 0 - 0 0 0 - - - SEND
2007-05-04 12:28:57 ALLOW TCP 127.0.0.1 127.0.0.1 60442 12080 0 - 0 0 0 - - - RECEIVE
2007-05-04 12:28:57 ALLOW TCP 192.168.1.107 208.67.217.230 60443 80 0 - 0 0 0 - - - SEND
2007-05-04 12:28:58 ALLOW TCP 127.0.0.1 127.0.0.1 60444 12080 0 - 0 0 0 - - - SEND
2007-05-04 12:28:58 ALLOW TCP 127.0.0.1 127.0.0.1 60444 12080 0 - 0 0 0 - - - RECEIVE
2007-05-04 12:28:58 ALLOW TCP 192.168.1.107 208.67.217.230 60445 80 0 - 0 0 0 - - - SEND
2007-05-04 12:29:00 ALLOW TCP 127.0.0.1 127.0.0.1 60446 12080 0 - 0 0 0 - - - SEND
2007-05-04 12:29:00 ALLOW TCP 127.0.0.1 127.0.0.1 60446 12080 0 - 0 0 0 - - - RECEIVE
2007-05-04 12:29:00 ALLOW TCP 192.168.1.107 208.67.217.230 60447 80 0 - 0 0 0 - - - SEND
2007-05-04 12:29:01 ALLOW TCP 127.0.0.1 127.0.0.1 60448 12080 0 - 0 0 0 - - - SEND
2007-05-04 12:29:01 ALLOW TCP 127.0.0.1 127.0.0.1 60448 12080 0 - 0 0 0 - - - RECEIVE
2007-05-04 12:29:01 ALLOW TCP 127.0.0.1 127.0.0.1 60450 12080 0 - 0 0 0 - - - SEND
2007-05-04 12:29:01 ALLOW TCP 127.0.0.1 127.0.0.1 60450 12080 0 - 0 0 0 - - - RECEIVE
2007-05-04 12:29:01 ALLOW TCP 127.0.0.1 127.0.0.1 60451 12080 0 - 0 0 0 - - - SEND
2007-05-04 12:29:01 ALLOW TCP 127.0.0.1 127.0.0.1 60451 12080 0 - 0 0 0 - - - RECEIVE
2007-05-04 12:29:01 ALLOW TCP 192.168.1.107 65.214.43.37 60449 80 0 - 0 0 0 - - - SEND
2007-05-04 12:29:01 ALLOW TCP 192.168.1.107 65.214.43.39 60452 80 0 - 0 0 0 - - - SEND
2007-05-04 12:29:01 ALLOW TCP 192.168.1.107 65.214.43.39 60453 80 0 - 0 0 0 - - - SEND
2007-05-04 12:29:01 ALLOW UDP 192.168.1.107 208.67.222.222 52386 53 0 - - - - - - - SEND
2007-05-04 12:29:01 ALLOW TCP 127.0.0.1 127.0.0.1 60454 12080 0 - 0 0 0 - - - SEND
2007-05-04 12:29:01 ALLOW TCP 127.0.0.1 127.0.0.1 60454 12080 0 - 0 0 0 - - - RECEIVE
2007-05-04 12:29:01 ALLOW TCP 127.0.0.1 127.0.0.1 60455 12080 0 - 0 0 0 - - - SEND
2007-05-04 12:29:01 ALLOW TCP 127.0.0.1 127.0.0.1 60455 12080 0 - 0 0 0 - - - RECEIVE
2007-05-04 12:29:01 ALLOW TCP 127.0.0.1 127.0.0.1 60458 12080 0 - 0 0 0 - - - SEND
2007-05-04 12:29:01 ALLOW TCP 127.0.0.1 127.0.0.1 60459 12080 0 - 0 0 0 - - - SEND
2007-05-04 12:29:01 ALLOW TCP 127.0.0.1 127.0.0.1 60458 12080 0 - 0 0 0 - - - RECEIVE
2007-05-04 12:29:01 ALLOW TCP 127.0.0.1 127.0.0.1 60459 12080 0 - 0 0 0 - - - RECEIVE
2007-05-04 12:29:01 ALLOW TCP 127.0.0.1 127.0.0.1 60462 12080 0 - 0 0 0 - - - SEND
2007-05-04 12:29:01 ALLOW TCP 127.0.0.1 127.0.0.1 60463 12080 0 - 0 0 0 - - - SEND
2007-05-04 12:29:01 ALLOW TCP 127.0.0.1 127.0.0.1 60462 12080 0 - 0 0 0 - - - RECEIVE
2007-05-04 12:29:01 ALLOW TCP 127.0.0.1 127.0.0.1 60463 12080 0 - 0 0 0 - - - RECEIVE
2007-05-04 12:29:01 ALLOW TCP 127.0.0.1 127.0.0.1 60466 12080 0 - 0 0 0 - - - SEND
2007-05-04 12:29:01 ALLOW TCP 127.0.0.1 127.0.0.1 60466 12080 0 - 0 0 0 - - - RECEIVE
2007-05-04 12:29:01 ALLOW TCP 127.0.0.1 127.0.0.1 60468 12080 0 - 0 0 0 - - - SEND
2007-05-04 12:29:01 ALLOW TCP 127.0.0.1 127.0.0.1 60468 12080 0 - 0 0 0 - - - RECEIVE
2007-05-04 12:29:01 ALLOW TCP 192.168.1.107 209.34.241.247 60460 80 0 - 0 0 0 - - - SEND
2007-05-04 12:29:01 ALLOW TCP 192.168.1.107 216.239.113.18 60457 80 0 - 0 0 0 - - - SEND
2007-05-04 12:29:01 ALLOW TCP 192.168.1.107 216.239.113.18 60456 80 0 - 0 0 0 - - - SEND
2007-05-04 12:29:01 ALLOW TCP 192.168.1.107 209.34.241.247 60461 80 0 - 0 0 0 - - - SEND
2007-05-04 12:29:01 ALLOW TCP 127.0.0.1 127.0.0.1 60470 12080 0 - 0 0 0 - - - SEND
2007-05-04 12:29:01 ALLOW TCP 127.0.0.1 127.0.0.1 60470 12080 0 - 0 0 0 - - - RECEIVE
```

Table 8-2. The columns in the Windows Firewall log

NAME	DESCRIPTION
Date	Date of occurrence, in *year-month-date* format
Time	Time of occurrence, in *hour:minute:second* format
Action	The operation that was logged by the firewall, such as `DROP` for dropping a connection, `OPEN` for opening a connection, and `CLOSE` for closing a connection
Protocol	The protocol used, such as `TCP`, `UDP`, or `ICMP`
Source IP (src-ip)	The IP address of the computer that started the connection
Destination IP (dst-ip)	The IP address of the computer to which the connection was attempted
Source Port (src-port)	The port number on the sending computer from which the connection was attempted
Destination Port (dst-port)	The port to which the sending computer was trying to make a connection
size	The packet size
tcpflags	Information about TCP control flags in TCP headers
tcpsyn	The TCP sequence of a packet
tcpack	The TCP acknowledgment number in the packet
tcpwin	The TCP window size of the packet

Table 8-2. The columns in the Windows Firewall log *(continued)*

NAME	DESCRIPTION
icmtype	Information about the ICMP messages
icmcode	Information about the ICMP messages
info	Information about an entry in the log

The source IP address is the source of the connection. You might notice the same source IP address continually cropping up; if so, you might have been targeted by an intruder. It's also possible that the intruder is sending out automated probes to thousands of PCs across the Internet, and your PC is not under direct attack. In either case, you can send the log information to your ISP and ask them to follow up by tracking down the source of the attempts. Either forward the entire log, or cut and paste the relevant sections to a new file.

See Also

- "Punch an Escape Hole Through Your Firewall" **[Hack #113]**
- "Hacking Windows Vista's Outbound Firewall" **[Hack #112]**

HACK 115: Protect Your Privacy by Removing Windows Vista Metadata

V Nearly invisible metadata can reveal plenty of information you might wish remained private. Here's how to zap it in Windows Vista.

A file's metadata contains plenty of information that's particularly helpful when you want to find files. For example, music files typically contain the name of the composer, type of music, and so on. A digital photograph contains when a picture was taken, who took it, the camera model, and other information such as ISO speed. Documents and spreadsheets contain a wide variety of information about their creators, including who created the document, how much time was spent editing it, who reviewed the document and so on. In many cases, programs automatically create their own metadata when a file is created. Users can also create metadata as well, as you'll see in this hack.

This metadata can be quite useful because Windows Vista search uses it. So if you want to find every music track on your PC written by Mozart, for example, type Mozart into a search box, and it will find every track created by Mozart.

But there are times when you don't want your files' metadata to be viewed by others or by people outside your organization. The analyst firm Gartner points out that businesses might embed metadata into files about a customer—for example "good customer" and "bad customer"—and a company certainly wouldn't want others to see that metadata. It's easy to remove this metadata:

1. Open Windows Explorer, and right-click the file.
2. Choose Properties.
3. Select the Details tab. A screen that displays the document's metadata appears, like the one shown in Figure 8-22.
4. Click Remove Properties and Personal Information. The Remove Properties dialog box appears (Figure 8-23).

Figure 8-22.
Document metadata

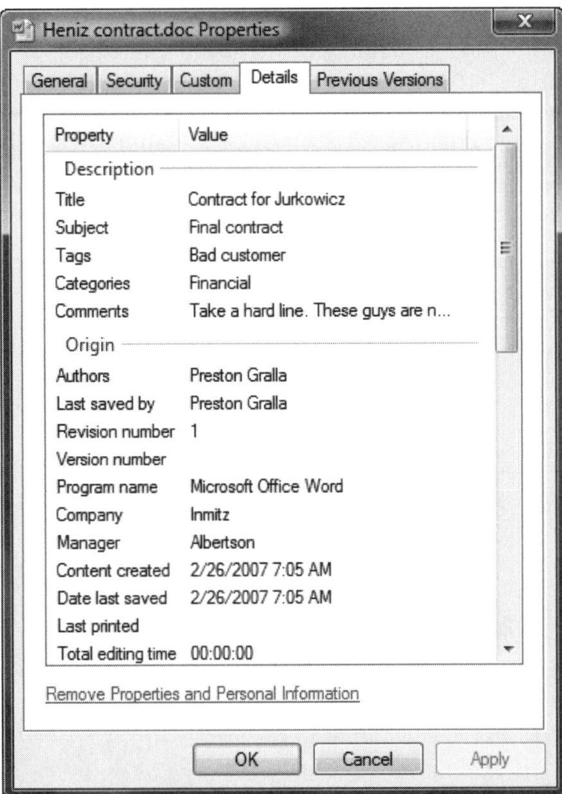

Figure 8-23.
Removing metadata

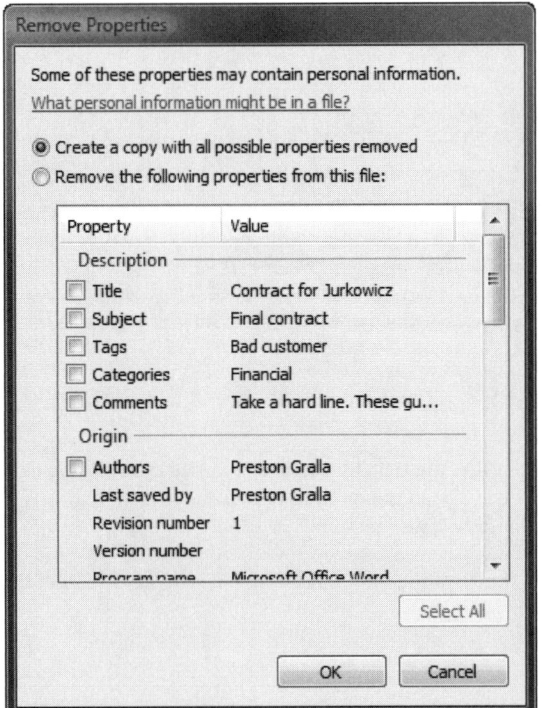

QUICK HACK

WHACK PRIVATE DATA WITH OFFICE 2007'S DOCUMENT INSPECTOR

Office files contain a lot more information than just metadata that you might want to remain private. For example, markup mode reveals every comment that every person has ever made about the file, and this can lead to serious problems if it gets public. In a famous case, hidden comments embedded in a Word document filed in a lawsuit by the tech company SCO against DaimlerChrysler revealed that SCO was also considering extending the suit against IBM.

To view and kill any and all potentially private and embarrassing information in an Office 2007 document, use the Document Inspector. In Word 2007, click the Office buttons, and select Prepare→Inspect Document. You'll be able to find any and all private information, including text formatted as "hidden," metadata, changes made to the document, and so on. You can then delete any information you want.

5. Check the boxes next to all of the metadata you want removed, and click OK. You can create a copy of the document with the metadata removed, and keep the original, or else you can remove the properties from the file.

Hacking the Hack

You can remove metadata from multiple files at once. Select all the files from which you want to remove metadata, then right-click them, and follow the directions in this hack for removing the data. The files, though, will have to have common metadata that can be removed in all of them.

You can also easily create metadata for files or edit existing metadata. Right-click a file, choose Properties, and select the Details tab. Then click any field and type in metadata. Some metadata can't be altered, such as the last time a file was printed.

In Office 2007, it's easy to create, edit, and delete metadata. How you do it varies somewhat from Office application to Office application. To do it in Word 2007, click the Office button, and select Prepare→Properties.

See Also

- "Keep Your Google Search History Private" **[Hack #53]**
- "Surf Anonymously, without a Trace — For Free" **[Hack #49]**

HACK 118: Kill Annoying Software Registration Reminders

V Vista users, are you tired of software bombarding you with registration reminders? There's a surprising and simple way to kill them forever.

Windows Vista users may find themselves bedeviled by a bombardment of registration reminders from programs they've recently installed, such as Adobe Photoshop. Even if you check the box in the reminder saying not to notify you again, the next time you run the program, you get the reminder again.

Have these people taken lessons from telemarketers?

No, believe it or not, the problem is related to the most reviled part of Windows Vista—User Account Control. The problem is that Windows Vista, in order to protect you, performs some nifty UAC tricks related to the Registry. When you check the box saying to stop reminding you about registration, the application attempts to write to the Registry to insert a value telling the program not to pop up registration reminders any more. But UAC restricts how programs can access the Registry, and it writes to a virtualized portion of the Registry. But the application isn't aware of that virtualized location and never actually checks the key.

The result: it's pop-up time.

There's a simple solution. Log in as an administrator, then run the application. When you run the application as an administrator, UAC doesn't do its virtualization trick, and writes straight to the Registry. The value is set properly, and the pop ups will vamoose.

HACK 117: Use Vista's BitLocker with a USB Key

V You don't need special hardware to use Windows Vista's BitLocker encryption to protect your laptop. A USB key can do the trick as well.

Vista's BitLocker drive encryption is available in the Ultimate and Enterprise editions. To use it, you'll need a computer with a supported Trusted Platform Module (TPM), but even if you have one, it may not be enabled properly in your computer (in which case, you'll be waiting on your PC or motherboard vendor to update the BIOS). Figure 8-24 shows what you'll see if you try to turn BitLocker on.

If you followed the media coverage of Vista's capabilities, you may remember some talk about Vista allowing you to use a USB flash drive on systems that don't have a TPM. It's possible, but you need to do a couple of things first.

The first thing you need to do is modify your drive partitions to support BitLocker. At one time, this was a massive hassle: you'd need to repartition and install from scratch. Fortunately, Microsoft has released a Windows Ultimate Extra (available through Windows Update) that will prepare your drive for BitLocker without repartitioning. To install it, go to Windows Update, and install the Windows Ultimate Extra called "BitLocker and EFS enhancements," as shown in Figure 8-25.

Figure 8-24
BitLocker's all-too-common error message

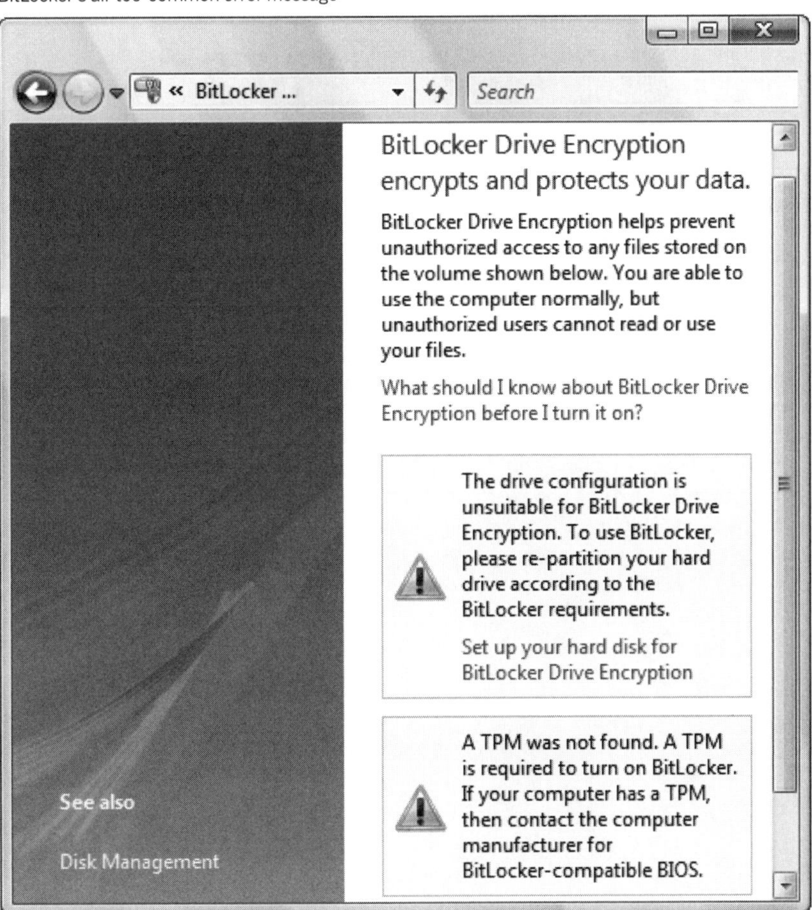

Figure 8-25.
Installing the BitLocker enhancements

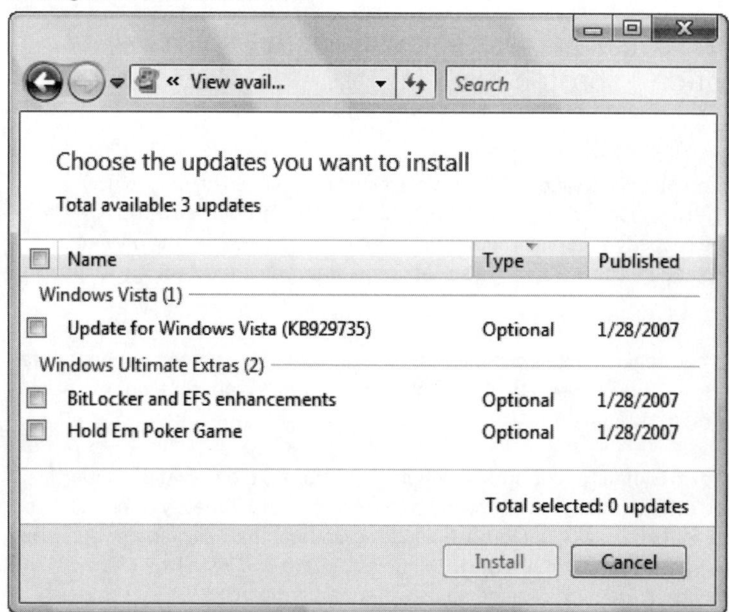

After you've installed the enhancements, open the Start Menu, and choose Programs→Accessories→System Tools→BitLocker→BitLocker Drive Preparation Tool. Follow the instructions (including the warning about backups), and prepare your drive. After it finishes, you'll need to reboot, and you'll find that the BitLocker control panel still isn't ready to cooperate, as shown in Figure 8-26.

To sort it out, you need to run the Group Policy Object Editor (open the Start menu, type gpedit.msc into the search field, and press Enter. You can also launch *gpedit.msc* from the Run dialog or Command Prompt). Once you get into the Group Policy Object Editor, drill down to Local Computer Policy→Computer Configuration→Administrative Templates→Windows Components→BitLocker Drive Encryption. In the right pane, double-click on "Control Panel Setup: Enable advanced startup options". In the dialog that appears (see Figure 8-27), enable this option, then press OK and close the Group Policy Object Editor.

Next, run the command gpupdate /force from the command prompt, search box, or Start menu (you might need to launch the command prompt with Admin privileges, which means you need to find Command Prompt in the Start menu, right-click it, and choose Run as Administrator; or you can type cmd.exe into the Start Search box and press Ctrl-Shift-Enter). After gpupdate runs, close the Control Panel, and open it again to the BitLocker options, and if all went well, you should be able to configure BitLocker, just as if you had a working TPM (see Figure 8-28).

—Brian Jepson

Figure 8-26.
BitLocker, still complaining about that TPM

BitLocker ...
Search
BitLocker Drive Encryption encrypts and protects your data.
BitLocker Drive Encryption helps prevent unauthorized access to any files stored on the volume shown below. You are able to use the computer normally, but unauthorized users cannot read or use your files.
What should I know about BitLocker Drive Encryption before I turn it on?
A TPM was not found. A TPM is required to turn on BitLocker. If your computer has a TPM, then contact the computer manufacturer for BitLocker-compatible BIOS.
Volumes
See also
Disk Management
Vista (C:\)

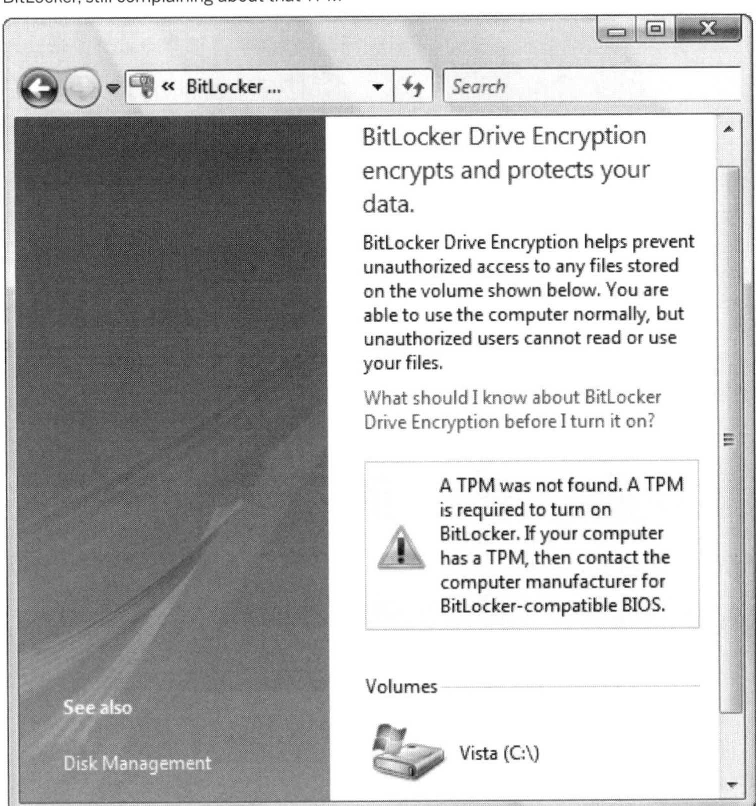

Figure 8-27.
Advanced startup options

Control Panel Setup: Enable advanced startup options Prop...
Setting
Explain
Control Panel Setup: Enable advanced startup options
Not Configured
Enabled
Disabled
Allow BitLocker without a compatible TPM
(requires a startup key on a USB flash drive)
Settings for computers with a TPM:
Configure TPM startup key option:
Allow user to create or skip
Configure TPM startup PIN option:
Allow user to create or skip
IMPORTANT: If you require the startup key,
Supported on: At least Windows Vista
Previous Setting
Next Setting
OK
Cancel
Apply

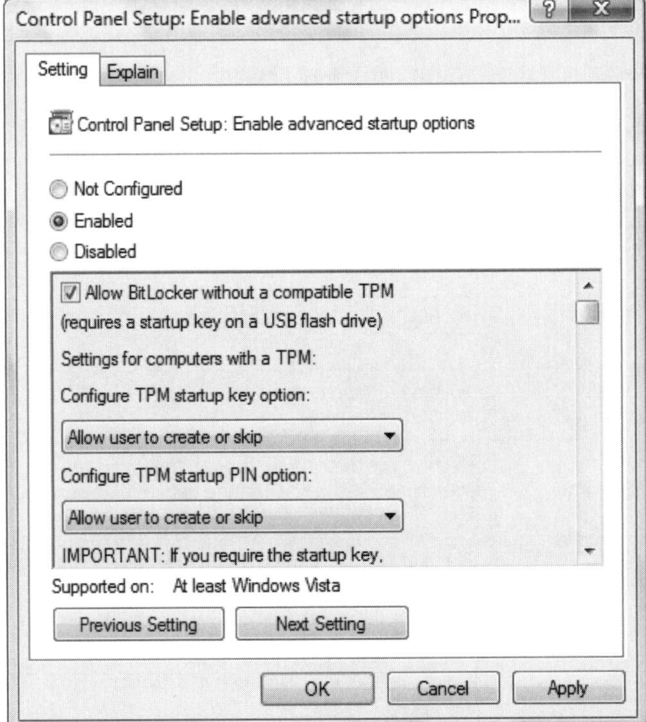

Figure 8-28.
BitLocker is now enabled

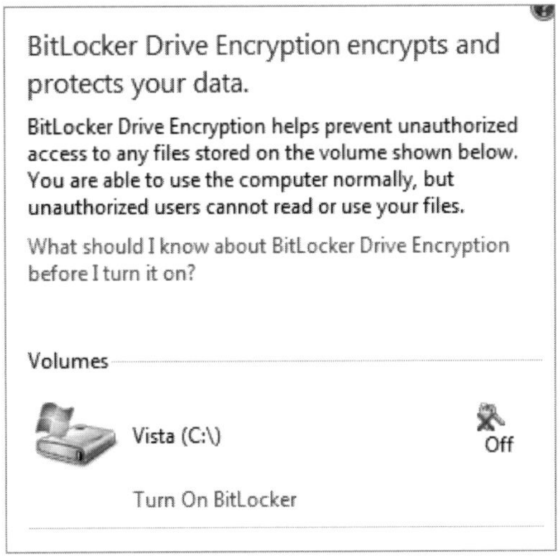

BitLocker Drive Encryption encrypts and protects your data.
BitLocker Drive Encryption helps prevent unauthorized access to any files stored on the volume shown below. You are able to use the computer normally, but unauthorized users cannot read or use your files.
What should I know about BitLocker Drive Encryption before I turn it on?
Volumes
Vista (C:\)
Off
Turn On BitLocker

HACK 118: Hide Folders and Files with the Encrypting File System

V XP Protect all the information on your PC from prying eyes using Windows' built-in encryption scheme.

If you're looking to protect files on a file-by-file basis or a folder-by-folder basis, rather than all at once, you don't need to use BitLocker Drive Encryption. Instead, you can use Windows' Encrypting File System (EFS), which lets you easily encrypt individual files or groups of files.

The Encrypting File System isn't available on the Windows XP Home edition or either version of the Windows Vista Home edition.

EFS lets you encrypt only the files and folders of your choice; you can encrypt a single file or folder or all your files and folders. Encrypted files and folders show up in Windows Explorer in green, so you can tell at a glance which have been encrypted. You can work with encrypted files and folders transparently. In other words, after you encrypt them, you open and close them as you normally would any other file. They're decrypted on the fly as you open them, and then encrypted as you close them. You're the only person who can read or use the files. Encryption is tied to your account name, so even other accounts on the same computer won't be able to read or use them, unless you specifically grant access to certain accounts.

Each time you encrypt a file, EFS generates a random number for that file called the file encryption key (FEK). EFS uses that FEK to encrypt the file's contents with a variant of the Data Encryption Standard (DES) algorithm, called DESX. (DESX features more powerful encryption than DES.) The FEK itself is encrypted as well using RSA public key-based encryption.

EFS have a few minor limitations you should be aware of:

- EFS works only on NTFS volumes. If you have a FAT or FAT32 volume, you'll have to convert it to NTFS **[Hack #42]** if you want to use EFS.
- EFS won't work on compressed files. You'll have to decompress them if you want to encrypt them. Similarly, if you want to compress an encrypted file, you'll have to decrypt it.
- EFS can't encrypt files in the *C:\Windows* folder or any files marked with the `System` attribute.

When you work with encrypted files and folders, they seem to behave like any other files on your hard disk. In fact, though, their behavior is somewhat different, and you might notice files you thought were encrypted suddenly become decrypted for no apparent reason. So, before you turn on encryption, you should understand the common actions you can take with encrypted files and folders, and what the results will be. Table 8-3 lists what you need to know.

Table 8-3. How encrypted files and folders behave

ACTION	RESULT
Move or copy unencrypted files into an encrypted folder.	The files are automatically encrypted.
Move or copy encrypted files from an encrypted folder to an unencrypted folder.	The files remain encrypted.
Move or copy encrypted files from an encrypted folder to a non-NTFS volume.	The files are decrypted, though first you are given a warning and a chance to cancel the move or copy operation.
Back up files using Windows' backup utility.	The backed-up files and folders remain encrypted.
Rename an encrypted file.	The file remains encrypted after it is renamed.
Delete an encrypted file.	The restorable file in the Recycle Bin remains encrypted.

Encrypting Files and Folders

To encrypt a file or folder, right-click the file or folder and choose Properties→General→Advanced. The Advanced Attributes dialog box appears, as shown in Figure 8-29.

If no Advanced button appears on the Properties dialog box, it means you aren't using NTFS, so you can't use encryption.

Check the box next to "Encrypt contents to secure data." Note that you can't check both this box and the "Compress contents to save disk space" box. You can either compress the item or encrypt it, but not both.

Click OK, and then OK again. If you're encrypting a folder, the Confirm Attributes Changes dialog box appears, as shown in Figure 8-30. You have a choice of encrypting the folder only, or encrypting the folder plus all subfolders and all the files in the folder and subfolders. If you encrypt the folder only, none of the files currently in the folder will be encrypted, but any new files you create, move, or copy into the folder will be encrypted.

If you're encrypting a file in an unencrypted folder, the Encryption Warning box will appear, as shown in Figure 8-31. You have the choice of encrypting the file only, or the file and the parent folder. As a general rule, you should encrypt the folder as well as the file because if you encrypt only the file, you might accidentally decrypt it without realizing it. Some applications save copies of your files and delete the original; in those instances, the files become decrypted simply by editing them.

Figure 8-29.
Encrypting files or folders using the Advanced Attributes dialog box

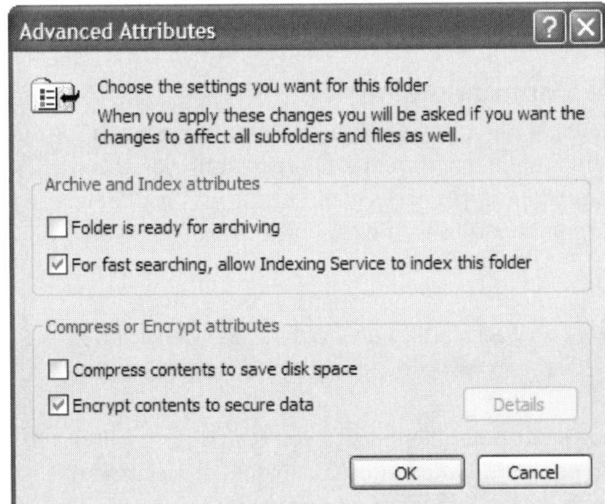

Figure 8-30.
Encrypting the folder only, or all the subfolders and files as well

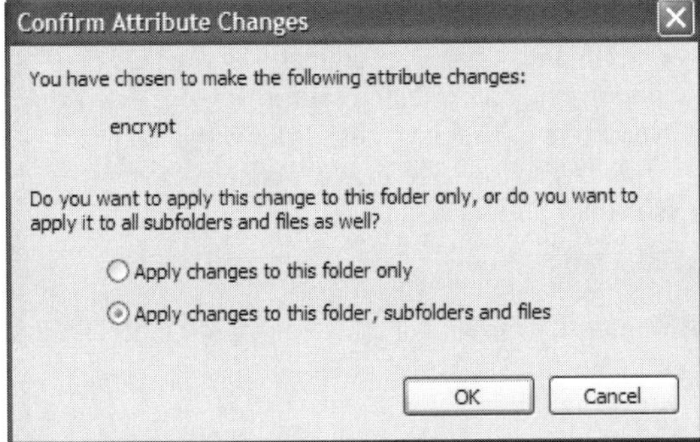

If you encrypt the folder as well, all files added to the folder are encrypted, so the saved file is automatically encrypted. Click OK after you make your choice.

Note that you won't be able to encrypt every file on your system. Files that have the `System` attribute, as well as files located in *C:\Windows* and its subfolders, can't be encrypted.

Decrypting Files and Folders

You decrypt files and folders in the same way you encrypt them. Right-click the file or folder, choose Properties→General→Advanced, clear the check from the box next to "Encrypt contents to secure data," and click OK and then OK again.

QUICK HACK 

TEST YOUR SECURITY WITH SHIELDS UP

Do you really know how secure your PC is from intruders? Probably not. But there's a free online tool that will probe your PC for online security vulnerabilities and report to you on the results.

The Shields UP! site from the Gibson Research Corporation tests your machine, trying to make connections to a handful of the most well-known and vulnerable Internet ports on your PC. The site runs a variety of tests, reports to you on the results, and then explains what the reports mean—where you're vulnerable and how serious those vulnerabilities are. It also has a great deal of useful information about Internet security, as well as free and for-pay security software you can download. Visit the site at www.grc.com. You might have to do some clicking around to find the tests, but keep clicking Shields UP!, and you'll eventually get there.

Letting Others Use Your Encrypted Files

When you encrypt files, you can still share them with others and let them use them as if they were not encrypted—a process that Windows defines as *transparent*. You'll be able to share them this way only with other users on the same computer or with others on your network. You designate who can use the files and who can't. To allow specified people to use your encrypted files, right-click an unencrypted file, and choose Properties→General→Advanced. The Advanced Attributes dialog box appears. Click Details. The Encryption Details dialog box appears, as shown in Figure 8-32. It lists all the users who are allowed to use the file transparently. Click Add.

The Select User dialog box appears. Choose the user you want to be able to use your encrypted files, and click OK. Only users who have Encrypting File System certificates on the computer will show up on this list. The easiest way for someone to create a certificate is to encrypt any file; that automatically creates their certificate.

Encrypting and Decrypting from the Command Line

If you prefer the command line to a graphical interface, you can encrypt and decrypt using the *cipher.exe* command-line tool. To find the current state of encryption of the directory you're in, type cipher without parameters at a command prompt. `cipher` tells you the state of the directory. For individual files, it lists a `U` next to files that are not encrypted and an `E` next to those that are encrypted.

When used with parameters, `cipher` can encrypt and decrypt files and folders, show encryption information, create new encryption keys, and generate a recovery agent key and certificate.

To encrypt or decrypt a folder or file, use the complete path, filename (if you're acting on a file), and any appropriate switches, as outlined in Table 8-4. The `/E` switch encrypts folders or files, and the `/D` switch decrypts them. To perform the task on multiple folders or files, separate them with single spaces. For example, to encrypt the *\Secret* and *\Topsecret* folders, issue this command:

```
cipher /E \Secret \Topsecret
```

Note that you can use wildcards with the `cipher` command. Using the command line instead of the graphical interface is particularly useful for performing bulk or batch operations—for example, simultaneously encrypting or decrypting multiple folders or files, or types of files within folders. Let's say, for example, you want to encrypt every *.doc* file in the *\Secret* and *\Topsecret* folders but not touch any other files in those folders. You issue this command:

```
cipher /E  /A \Secret\*.DOC  \Topsecret\*.DOC
```

Table 8-4 lists the most useful command-line switches for `cipher`. For more help, type cipher /? at the command line.

Figure 8-31.
Encrypting the parent folder as well as the file

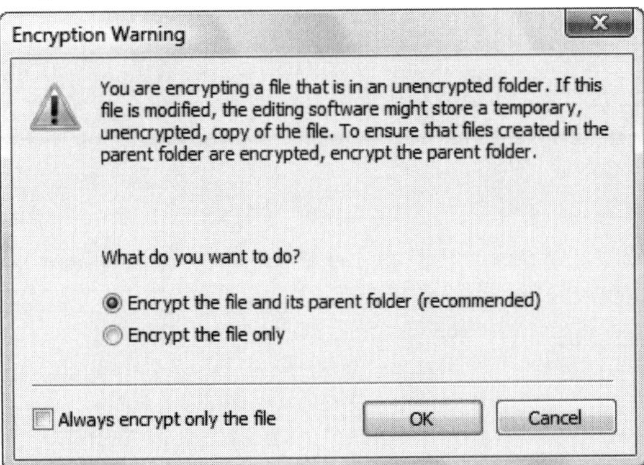

Table 8-4. Command-line switches for cipher

SWITCH	WHAT IT DOES
`/A`	(XP) Acts on individual files within folders.
`/D`	Decrypts the specified file or folder.
`/E`	Encrypts the specified file or folder.
`/F`	(XP) Forces encryption on all specified objects, including those that have already been encrypted.
`/H`	Displays all files in a folder, including those that have hidden or system attributes. (These are not displayed by default).
`/I`	Continues to perform the specified operation, even if errors are encountered. By default, `cipher` halts when errors are encountered.
`/K`	Creates a new file encryption key for the user running `cipher`. If this option is chosen, all the other options will be ignored.
`/R`	Generates an EFS recovery agent key and certificate, then writes them to a *.pfx* file (containing the certificate and a private key) and a *.cer* file (containing only the certificate).
`/S`	Performs the operation on the folder and all its subfolders.
`/U`	Updates the user's file encryption key or recovery agent's key on every encrypted file.
`/U /N`	Lists every encrypted file and does not update the user's file encryption key or recovery agent's key.
`/Q`	Lists only basic information about the file or folder.
`/W`	Wipes data from unused disk space on the drive. (When a file is deleted, its data remains untouched until another file claims the unused space. `/W` deletes all vestiges of this data. It does not harm existing data.)
`/X filename`	Backs up your certificate and keys to *filename*.
`/ADDUSER user`	(Vista) Adds the specified user to the file.
`/REMOVEUSER user`	(Vista) Removes the specified user.
`/REKEY`	(Vista) Updates files to use your current EFS key.

QUICK HACK

USE A PROXY SERVER TO FILTER WEB SITES

If you have a reason for wanting to limit your PC to visiting only certain web sites and banning it from visiting any others—such as for a child's computer, for which you want to have only very limited Internet access—you can easily do it by using a proxy server.

Another way to limit access is to use Vista's built-in parental controls (Control Panel→"Set up parental controls for any user"). There are many third-party parental control programs available for Windows XP as well, such as Safe Eyes and Net Nanny.

Open Internet Explorer, choose Tools→Internet Options→Connections→LAN Settings. (Figure 8-33). Check the box underneath Proxy server. Then, click the Advanced button, and the Proxy Settings dialog screen appears, as shown in Figure 8-34.

For the HTTP entry, type in a word, such as nowhere, or type in an Internet address that doesn't exist. When you do this, you're telling Internet Explorer to use a proxy server that isn't there. This effectively blocks access to the Internet because instead of going to a web site, Internet Explorer will go to a proxy server. But because the proxy server doesn't exist, your browser won't be able to visit any site.

Next, check the box next to "Use the same proxy server for all protocols". This will ensure that you're blocking Internet access for other services, such as FTP, not just for the Web.

Now you've effectively blocked access to the Internet for the PC. At this point you can enable a setting that will let the PC visit only specific web sites. In the Exceptions section, type the locations of the web sites you want to allow to be visited, separated by a semicolon. This Exceptions box tells Internet Explorer to bypass the proxy server for the listed sites, so it will go straight to those sites, bypassing the not-there proxy.

Once you put those settings into effect, whenever your PC tries to access the Web, it will look for a proxy server that doesn't exist, so it won't be able to get onto the Internet. However, it will let you go to the web sites you've put in the Exceptions section.

Figure 8-32.
Deciding which users can share your encrypted files

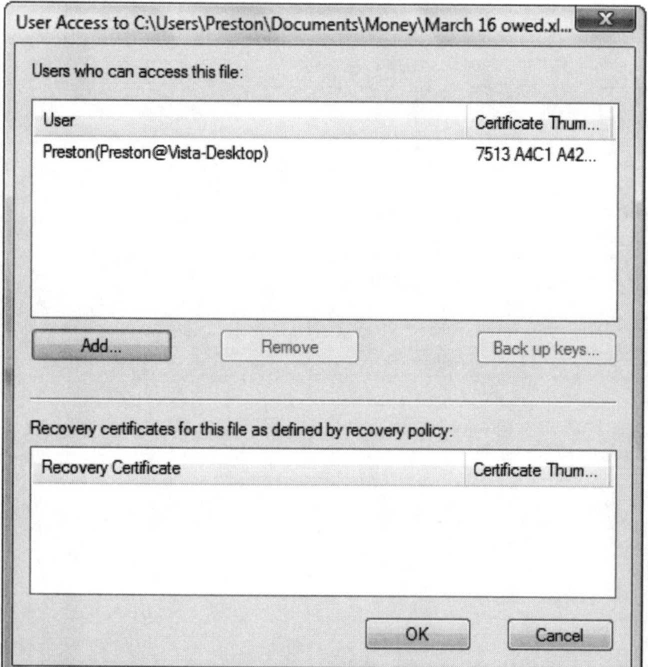

Figure 8-33.
Configuring your proxy settings using the LAN Settings dialog box

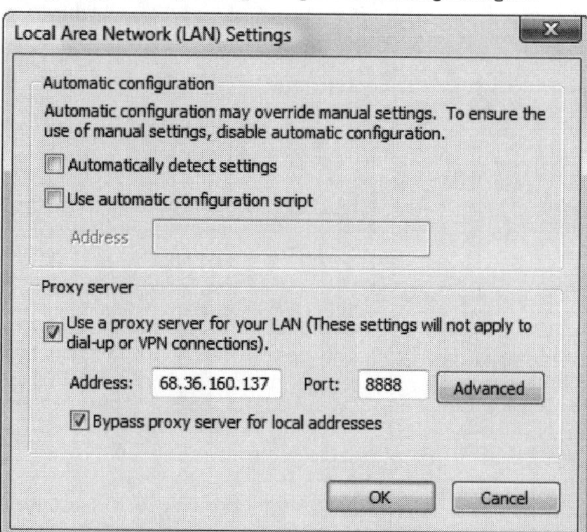

Figure 8-34.
Using the Proxy Settings dialog box to limit the web sites your PC can visit

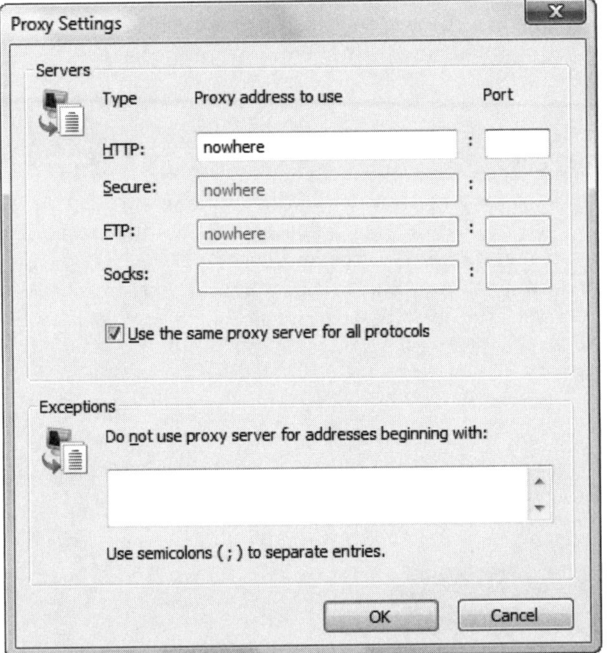

HACK 119: Set Up a Virtual Private Network

V XP If you need to connect to your home machine from work or while traveling, making your home machine a virtual private network (VPN) server is a secure way to accomplish this.

If you've ever taken files home so that you can work on them on your personal computer, you've probably had the experience of arriving to work the next day only to realize you've forgotten to bring the files back with you. If the files were important enough, you probably had to drive all the way back home to get them, or you're had to make a lame excuse to your boss as to why you don't have the TPS report ready yet. Perhaps you're a road warrior who has found yourself stranded in a hotel room on a Monday morning, just hours before a big meeting, without that copy of the presentation you thought you had copied from your home machine. If either of these sounds like a situation you've been in, this is the hack for you.

Both Windows XP and Windows Vista have VPN clients and VPN servers built into them, allowing you, or others you designate to make secure connections into your PC or PC on your home network. While you have an established VPN session with your home machine, you can access files from its hard drive or other machines on the network that have file sharing enabled. All you need is a local Internet connection and a VPN client that supports the Point to Point Tunneling Protocol (PPTP), which the client for all versions of Windows does.

Setting Up a VPN in Windows XP

In Windows XP, preparing your home machine to accept VPN connections is fairly straightforward. Click Start→Control Panel→Network and Internet Connections→Network Connections→"Create a new connection". This will launch the New Connection Wizard. While advancing through this wizard, the options you want to enable are "Set up an advanced connection," "Accept Incoming Connections," and "Allow virtual private connections." The sixth screen of the wizard (Figure 8-35) allows you to specify the users that can use the VPN; make sure you enable at least one account.

QUICK HACK 

GET A FREE, LIGHT, ANTI-VIRUS SOFTWARE

Over the years, antivirus software has become big and bloated, taking up precious system resources and RAM, and bogging down your system. Often, they come as entire suits, including antispyware and firewalls, making them even more bloated. But considering that Windows Vista, for example, already comes with a firewall, and antispyware software, do you really need that bloat?

The answer is no. You can instead get free antivirus software that's lightweight and won't take up RAM or system resources, and that does every bit as good a job as big antivirus bloated software. My favorite is Avast! (www.avast.com). It's free for noncommercial use. I use it on all my PCs at home, and have never gotten a virus. Another good free one is AVG (www.grisoft.com).

If you haven't created a password for your user, now is the time to do so. You are essentially opening up a part of your machine to the Internet, so make sure you choose a good password. After the wizard is complete, nothing further needs to be done; the VPN is ready to accept incoming connections. Later in this hack, I show you how to connect to the VPN using the Windows VPN client.

Setting Up a VPN in Windows Vista

To set up a VPN in Windows Vista, select Control Panel→Network and Internet→Network and Sharing Center→"Manage network connections". The Network Connections folder then appears. Press the Alt key to display the menu, and select File→New Incoming Connection. On the first screen that appears (Figure 8-36), choose who will be allowed to use the VPN. To add someone new, click "Add someone", and follow the prompts. If you haven't set a password for the account you want to connect via the VPN, highlight it, click Account Properties, and set the password.

Figure 8-35.
Make sure to permit at least one account to access the VPN

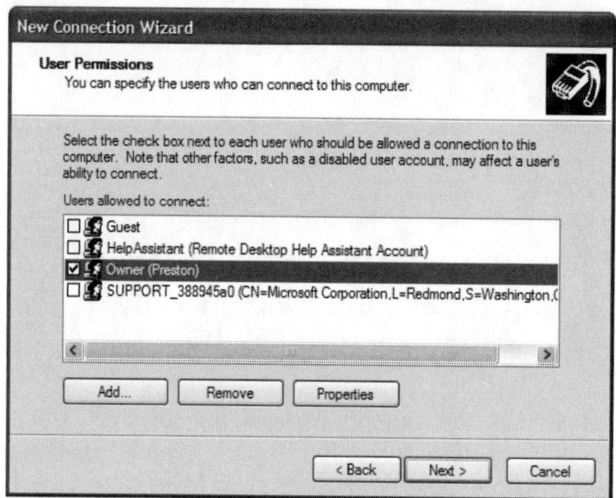

Figure 8-36.
Determining which accounts can access the VPN in Windows Vista

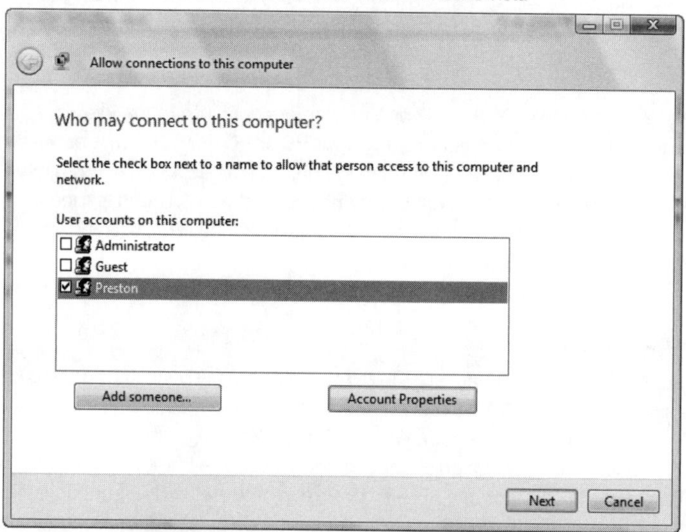

Click Next, and from the screen that appears, check the box next to Through the Internet. Click Next. From the screen that appears (Figure 8-37), select Internet Protocol Version 4, and click Allow Access. Nothing else needs to be done; the VPN is set up.

Connecting to the VPN

Now that you've got the VPN set up, you can connect to it. Assuming that your PC is on a home network with a router, you've got some work to do. There are several issues you'll have to overcome:

- Your router may block VPN connections.
- Your router needs to figure out how to route the incoming VPN connection to the right PC.
- You need to know the IP address of your home network, but because the IP address is DHCP-assigned, it changes from time to time.
- Your firewall may block access to your VPN **[Hack #113]**

Most routers have settings to enable VPN connections, so check your router documentation to see how to turn yours on. VPNs use a variety of protocols for tunneling through the Internet, such as IPSec and the PPTP. Make sure these settings are enabled on your router if you want to use it in concert with a VPN. In a Linksys SRX 400, log into the administration page by opening your web browser, typing 192.168.1.1, leaving the username blank, and typing admin for the password. (Those are the default settings; if you've changed them, use your new settings instead.)

Click the Security tab, and make sure that PPTP Pass through, IPSec Pass through, and L2TP Pass through are all selected (see Figure 8-38). Make sure that the box next to Block WAN Ping is not checked. Click Save Settings.

 You might run into problems running a VPN with a router that doesn't have specific VPN settings, even if the device claims it will work with VPNs. In particular, one default setting, hidden fairly deeply in most router setup screens, can disable VPN access; some routers, such as those made by Linksys, include an option called Block WAN Request or Block WAN Ping. It this option is enabled, it blocks requests into the network from the Internet; for example, it stops ping requests into the network. However, enabling this option also blocks VPN access. VPN access requires that requests get into the network from the Internet, so if you block those requests the VPN won't work. Disable this setting in your router.

Figure 8-37.
Telling the VPN to accept TCP/IP connections

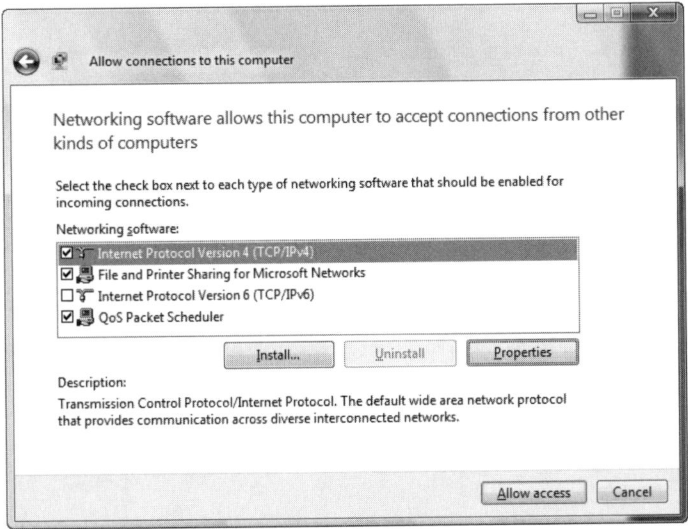

Figure 8-38.
Making sure your home router allows VPN connections

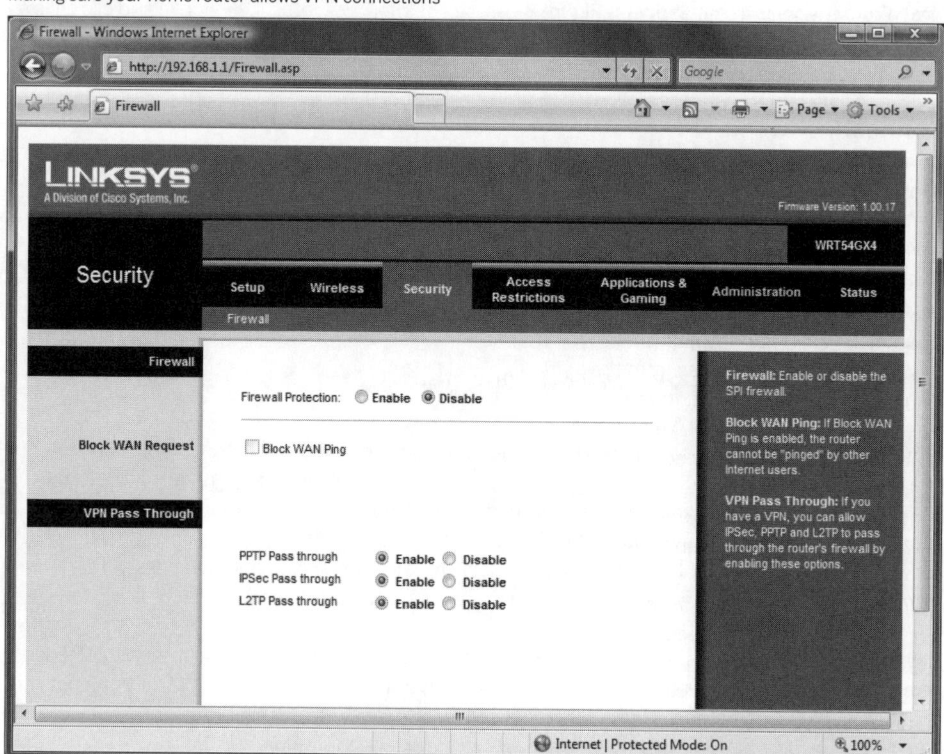

Your router will now allow VPN connections, but you still haven't told your router how to route VPN requests to the proper PC. Normally, you can't connect to the PC because the IP addresses are assigned to it by the router is an internal LAN addresses, unreachable from the Internet.

To get around the problem, use the port forwarding feature of your router. When you do this, whenever a connection is made to a specific port, your router will route the connection to a specific PC **[Hack #68]**—in this instance, the PC with a VPN.

VPNs typically use TCP port 1723 and UDP port 500, so you're going to set up your router to send any requests made via those ports to the PC with a VPN.

Before you start, you need to know the internal IP address of the PC with the VPN. At a command prompt, type ipconfig /all, and press Enter. In the results, look for the IPv4 Address entry, such as 192.168.1.104; that's the internal IP address.

It's also a good idea to disable DHCP on the PC with the VPN and instead give it a static internal IP address. If you continue to use DHCP instead of assigning a static IP address to the PC, the PC's IP address might change and will become unreachable. Check your router's documentation on how to force it to assign static IP addresses to specific devices.

Now you need to tell the router to send all requests via TCP port 1723 and UDP port 500 to 192.168.1.104. For this hack, I use a Linksys router as an example. The instructions are for the SRX-400, but instructions will be similar for all other Linksys router. To start, log into your administrator's screen. Choose Applications & Gaming→Port Range Forwarding (Figure 8-39). Create two entries, one for TCP port 1723 and the other for UDP port 500. For the application, type VPN. Check the Enable box next to each. Then click Save Settings. You'll now forward incoming VPN connections to the right PC.

QUICK HACK 

TURN OFF ANNOYING VISTA SECURITY CENTER NOTIFICATIONS

If you don't use a firewall, antivirus program, or another security feature, Windows Vista will pop up the Security Center shield in the system tray. It will do this even if you do use some of these programs, but for some reason Vista doesn't recognize them. If you want to turn off the annoying reminder, right-click the Security Center icon in the system tray, and select Open Security Center. Then click "Change the Way Security Center Alerts me", and select Don't Notify Me, and Don't Display the Icon. The annoyance will be banished.

You've got one more problem—how to connect to your router, if its IP address might change (many ISPs use dynamically assigned IP addresses)? The answer: you can use a free service that will give you a hostname **[Hack #69]** such as gralla.no-ip.com, and whenever you type in that URL, it will connect you to your router, even if the actual IP address changes. That way, to connect to your VPN, you only need to type in gralla.no-ip.com. Several services do this, including No-IP.com (www.no-ip.com).

Now you're ready to connect to the VPN. You can use the VPN client built right into Windows.

In Windows Vista, select Control Panel→Network and Internet→Network and Sharing Center→"Set up a connection or network". From the screen that appears, select "Connect to a workplace", and click Next. On the next screen, which asks how you will connect to the VPN, choose "Use my Internet connection (VPN)". On the next screen (Figure 8-40), to you'll be asked for the address of the VPN. Type in the URL you use from the dynamic DNS service, such as gralla.no-ip.com. Name the connection. Then click Next. You'll be asked for a username and password. Use the username and password of the account you've enabled on the VPN. Click "Remember this password" if you want to be able to automatically connect in the future. Click Connect, and you'll connect to the VPN.

From now on, to connect to the VPN, click the network icon in the system tray, click Connect to a network, and from the screen that appears, choose the VPN.

In Windows XP, select Control Panel→Network and Internet Connections→"Create a connection to the network at your workplace". Select Virtual Private Connection from the screen that appears, and click Next. Continue filling in the screens in the wizard, including naming the connection and so on. When you get to the screen in which you need to type in the address of the VPN, type in the URL you use from the dynamic DNS service, such as gralla.no-ip.com. At the end, click Finish. You'll create the connection, and also connect to the VPN. You'll have to type in your username and password.

Figure 8-39.
Setting up port forwarding

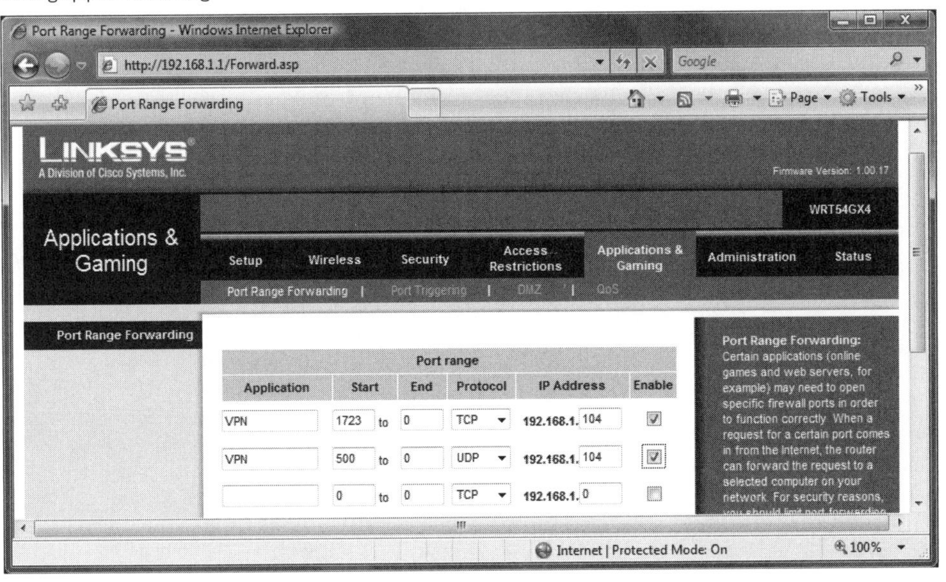

Use the username and password of the account you've enabled on the VPN. A desktop shortcut will also be created so that you can connect to the VPN from now on by just double-clicking it.

— *Wei-Meng Lee and Preston Gralla*

Figure 8-40.
Type in the address of the VPN

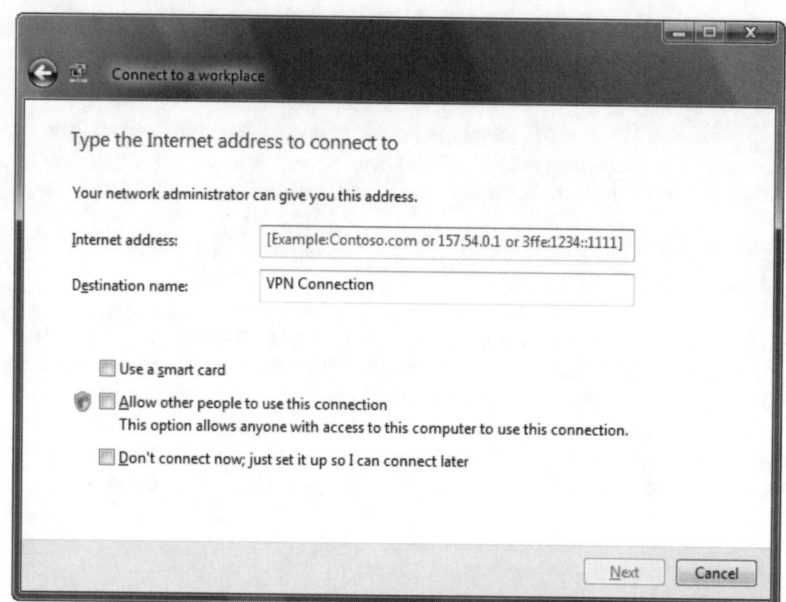

09 APPLICATIONS, HOME SERVER, AND BACKUP

What good is an operating system by itself?

Not much. If you want to actually get anything done, you'll need the applications that run on top of it. So this chapter includes a slew of hacks for applications, including Microsoft Office and beyond. You'll find out how to roll your own PDFs, blog using Word 2007, or automate Excel so that it grabs real-time stock quotes and updates them, and much more.

The chapter also includes hacks for one of Microsoft's newest technologies, Windows Home Server. It lets entire home networks share files and media, backs up all your PCs individually, and even gives you remote access to your PC's files when you're away from home. And you'll also find hacks for backing up your PC—that most important chore that we all hate. You may not love it, but you'll at least be able to do it more effectively.

HACK 120: Fast Hacks for Word 2007

V XP If you've started using Word 2007, you know it's a whole new world compared to Word 2003. Here are some quick hacks to help you bend the new version of Word to your will.

If you're new to Word 2007, you're probably not happy that so many of your shortcuts and customizations from Word 2003 have gone kaput and won't work with the new version of Word. But there are plenty of ways for you to bend Word 2007 to your will. Here are some hacks to get you started.

Turn off the Ribbon

Here's what may be the best tip you'll ever come across for Word 2007—turn off the Ribbon. Doing this will get you back plenty of screen real estate. The Ribbon will still be available when you want it; all you need to do is click on the appropriate menu, and it appears, then discreetly goes away when you are no longer using it. There are several ways to turn off the Ribbon:

- Click the Customize Quick Access Toolbar button (the small, downward pointing arrow to the left of the document name in the title bar), and select Minimize the Ribbon.
- Press Ctrl-F1 (press Ctrl-F1 to make it appear again).
- Double-click the current tab above the Ribbon.

Use Keyboard Shortcuts for the Ribbon

You can also use a clever set of keyboard shortcuts for working with the Ribbon. Press the Alt key and a tiny letter or number icon appears on the menu for each tab—for example, the letter H for the Home tab. (See Figure 9-1.) Now press that letter on your keyboard, and you'll display that tab or

Figure 9-1.
Using the Alt key helps you master the Ribbon

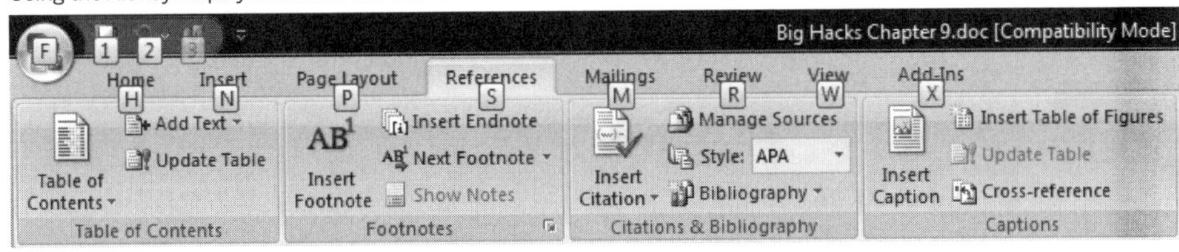

menu item. When the tab appears, there will be letters and numbers for most options on the tab as well, as you can see in Figure 9-1.

If you're a fan of Word 2003's keyboard shortcuts, take heart: the same ones work in 2007. So you can keep using them.

Once you've started to learn these shortcuts, you'll naturally begin using key combinations. So instead of pressing Alt, then H to display the home tab, you can press Alt-H together. The following table shows the Alt key combinations in Word 2007.

Table 9-1. Shortcuts for the Ribbon

KEY COMBINATION	FUNCTION
Alt-F	Office button
Alt-H	Home tab
Alt-N	Insert tab
Alt-P	Page Layout tab
Alt-S	References tab
Alt-M	Mailings tab
Alt-R	Review tab
Alt-W	View tab
Alt-L	Developer tab
Alt-JT	Design tab
Alt-JL	Layout tab

Add Commands to the Quick Access Toolbar

Probably the most helpful customization for Word 2007 is to add buttons to the Quick Access Toolbar. The simplest way to do this is by clicking the Customize Quick Access Toolbar, and selecting a new button to add. But this is quite limited because there's only a small number of buttons you can add in this way.

A better method is to select Office button→Word Options→Customize. The screen shown in Figure 9-2 appears.

Figure 9-2.
Adding buttons to the Quick Access toolbar

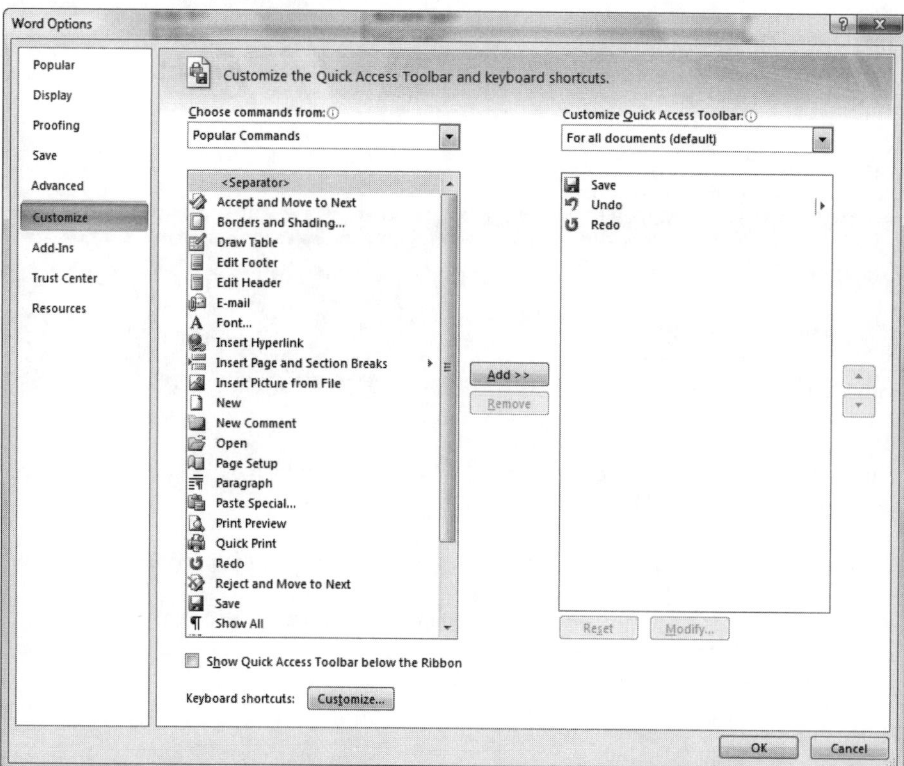

Choose a command from the left side of the screen that you want to add to the Quick Access Toolbar, and click Add. You can change the order of the buttons by highlighting a button on the right side of the screen and using the up and down arrows to move it.

To turn on the Developer tab permanently, select Office button→Word Options→Popular, then check the box next to Show Developer tab in the Ribbon.

The list of commands you see on the left may seem somewhat limited at first. That's because Word is showing you only the most popular commands. There are plenty of other commands you can add. Click the drop-down menu under "Choose commands from" at the top of the screen, and you'll see other lists of commands—All Commands, Home Tab, and so on. Select any, and there will be plenty of commands you can add.

Finally, there's an even easier way to add a command. Right-click any object on the Ribbon, and choose Add to Quick Access Toolbar. You can add not only individual commands in this way, but also entire groups—for example, the Font group.

HACK 121: Blog Using Word 2007

V XP Blogging sites are pretty dismal when it comes to word-processing tools. Here's how to write your blog right inside Word 2007 and then post it automatically.

Is there a person on the planet left who doesn't have a blog? If not, I certainly haven't met them. From the cradle to the grave, we blog, therefore we are.

QUICK HACK

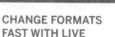

CHANGE FORMATS FAST WITH LIVE PREVIEW

If you often change formatting in your documents and text in Word 2007, you'll welcome the new Live Preview feature. First highlight the text or area of a document you want to change. Then on the ribbon move your cursor over the format you want to apply. The text or portion of the document you highlighted will change so that you can see how it will look with the new formatting. Move the cursor away to revert to the original formatting or move it over a different format to preview different formatting. When you find formatting you want to apply, click it.

But anyone who's blogged knows that the text editing and word processing tools on blog sites are, to put it mildly, dismal. With Word 2007, though, you won't need to go to your blogging site in order to write and post a blog entry because you can do it from right within the program.

First, write your post. You can include text formatting because Word will remember it and use it on your blog. Once you've written your post, here's how to make it live in your blog:

1. Click the Office button, and choose Publish→Blog. A dialog box appears telling you that you need to register with your blogging service if you want to be able to post. Click Register now.
2. From the screen that appears, choose your blog provider from the drop-down list, as shown in Figure 9-3, and click Next.

> If your blog provider isn't listed on the drop-down list, choose Other, and click Next. Fill out the form that appears. You'll need information such as the API your blog provider uses as well as the blog post URL

3. The New Blogger Account screen appears. Enter your username and password for the blog, and check the box next to Remember Password. Click OK. You'll get a warning that Word will send your username and password to your blog service provider, and that it's possible that other people could see it (this is because many blog hosts do not use encryption for the usernames and passwords). Click Yes if you want to proceed.
4. If you have more than one blog on the site, a screen appears asking which blog you want to post to. Select one, and click OK.
5. Your blog post will now appear in a new window. Click Enter Post Title Here, and type in the title of your blog post. You can now type in the rest of your post, as shown in Figure 9-4.
6. At the top left of the screen you'll find the Blog Post group. To publish your blog, click the Publish button. To publish a draft, click the down arrow beneath it, and choose Publish as Draft. Other tools in Blog Post group let you open an existing post for editing, manage your blog accounts (adding, removing, or changing them), assign a category to your post, and view the home page of your bog.
7. When you click Publish you'll receive a warning that Word will send your username and password to your blog service provider. Click Yes to proceed.
8. The post will be published to your blog, and you'll see a notification at the top of your Word document that indicates your post was published. You can either save the Word document with the blog in it or discard it. Even if you discard it, the post is live on your site (see Figure 9-5).

Figure 9-3.
Choosing your blog provider

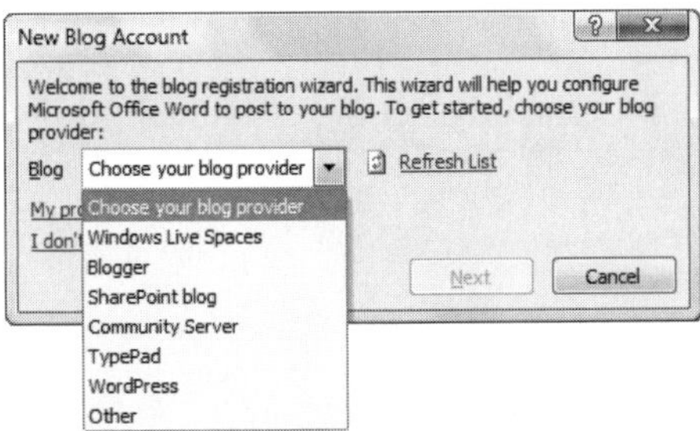

Figure 9-4.
Finish your blog here before posting

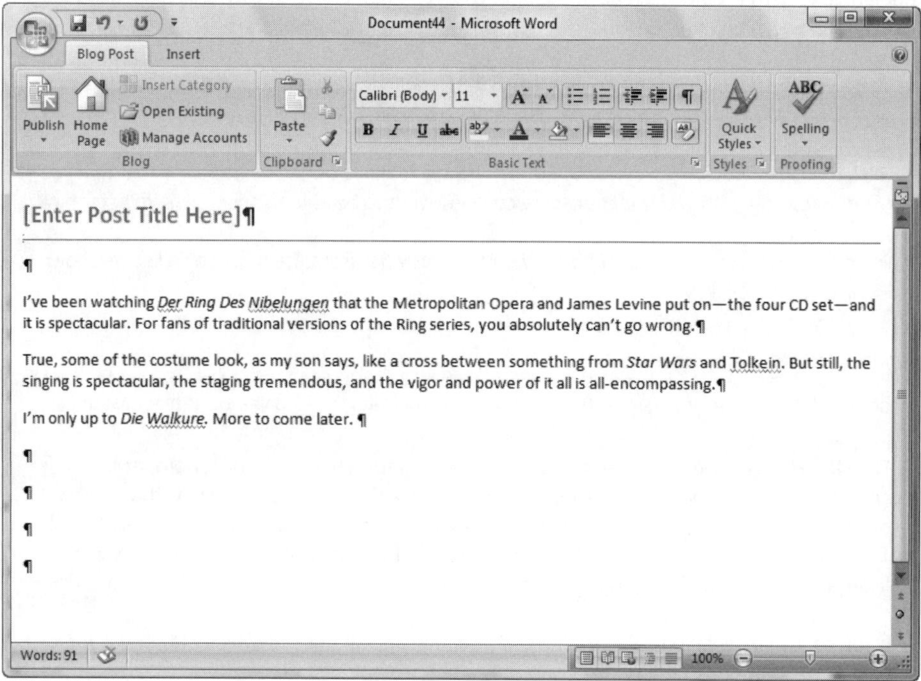

Figure 9-5.
Finally, the post is live

Hacking the Hack

If you include a graphic in your Word document, you may not be able to post it to your site. Your blogging site may require that you use a separate Web site to host graphics for your blog.

If that's the case, how can you get a picture into your blog? When you're asked for your blog user name and password in Word, click Picture Options. Then select My Own Server, enter information about your picture provider, and click OK.

If you forget to do this the first time you set up Word for blogging, you can set it up later. On the Blog Post group, click Manage Accounts, highlight the account for which you want to add pictures, click Change, then click Picture Options and fill in the information.

HACK 122: Create Reusable "Building Blocks" in Word 2007

V XP Here's an easy way to turn text and graphics you often use into building blocks that you can pop into a Word doc in a jiffy.

Do you have boilerplate text or graphics that you constantly reuse? Maybe it's a header or footer, a company logo, or legal or corporate boilerplate. Perhaps you type it in new each time, or you have the text or graphics saved somewhere on your hard disk and have to retrieve it each time you want it, and copy it into Word.

If so, this hack will be one of the simplest time-savers you'll ever come across. You can use Word 2007's "Quick Parts" feature to save any text and graphics, and then pop it into a Word doc with a few clicks. You'll be able to save it with all the formatting intact.

First, in Word 2007 create the text or graphics you want to reuse. Next, select it. If you want to save all the formatting along with it, such as indentation, alignment, line spacing, pagination, and so on, make sure that you select the paragraph mark as well.

By default, paragraph marks aren't displayed in Word. To display them, go to the Home tab, and click the Show/Hide paragraph button (it's at the upper right of the Paragraph group). You can also press Ctrl-Shift-8 to show it, and then press the same key combination to hide it. Note that when you display paragraph marks, you'll display many other items as well, such as tab markers.

Once you select the item you want to save, click the Insert tab, and choose Quick Parts→Save Selection to Quick Part Gallery. The dialog box shown in Figure 9-6 appears.

Fill in a name for your building block, and choose which "gallery" you want to save it in. A gallery is really just a fancy word for the kind of building block it is, for example a header, footer, cover page, and so on. If you save it to the Quick Part gallery, it will show up when you click Quick Parts.

Building block galleries are accessible throughout Word 2007, and you can create building blocks from multiple locations, not just from the Quick Parts. For example, if you are on the Page Layout tab, you can create a watermark and then save it to the Watermark gallery by selecting Watermark→Save Selection to

Figure 9-6.
Saving a building block

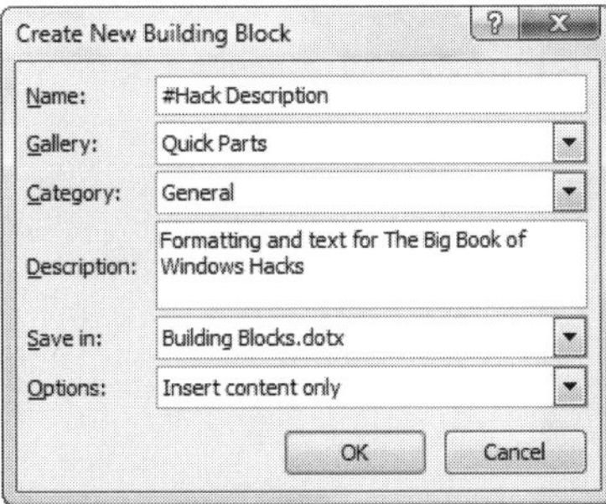

Watermark Gallery. To choose a building block from the Watermark Gallery, click the Watermark button, and select a building block.

After you fill in the gallery where you want to save it, select a category, type in a description, and then save the building block. You'll save the building block to your default Word template. To save it to another template, select it from the drop-down list.

On the bottom of the form, you also have these options available when saving:

Insert content in its own page
This places the building block on a separate page with page breaks before and after the building block.

Insert in own paragraph
This inserts the building block into its own paragraph, even if your cursor is in the middle of the paragraph.

Insert content only
This is the default. It places the building block exactly where you select it on a page.

To insert the building block, go to the Insert tab, click Quick Parts, and choose the building block you want to insert. If it's a specialized building block, such as a watermark, header, or footer, go to the appropriate tab, and make your selection from there—for example, choose Header or Footer from the Insert tab.

USE THEMES IN OFFICE 2007

With Office 2007, you can give all your documents, spreadsheets, presentations and other files a common look and feel, using a new feature called *themes*. A theme includes a layout, colors, logos, paragraph styles, and so on. In most Office 2007 applications, to use a theme, select the Page Layout tab, and click the button under themes to choose a new theme. You can also customize any theme and create new ones. Be aware that themes only work if you're using the new Office XML format; they won't work on old-style Office files.

Figure 9-7 shows how you choose a building block.

Hacking the Hack

To see all your building blocks from every gallery and category, on the Insert tab choose Quick Parts→Building Blocks Organizer. The Building Blocks Organizer, shown in Figure 9-8, appears. From here you can preview all your building blocks, and edit their properties (such as assigning them to a new gallery, renaming them, and so on).

Figure 9-7.
Choosing a building block to insert on a page

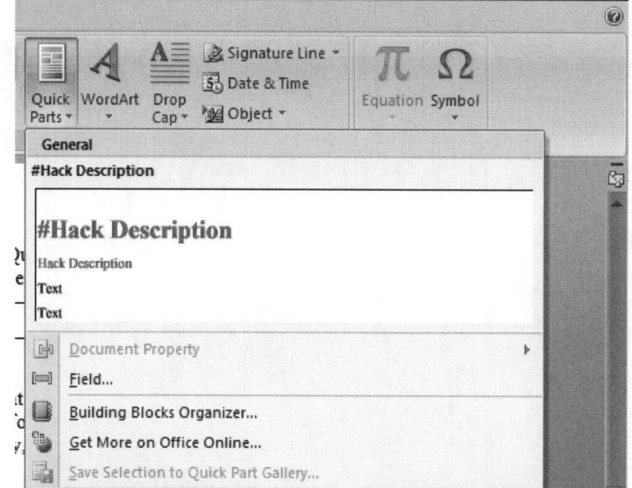

Figure 9-8.
Organize all your building blocks here

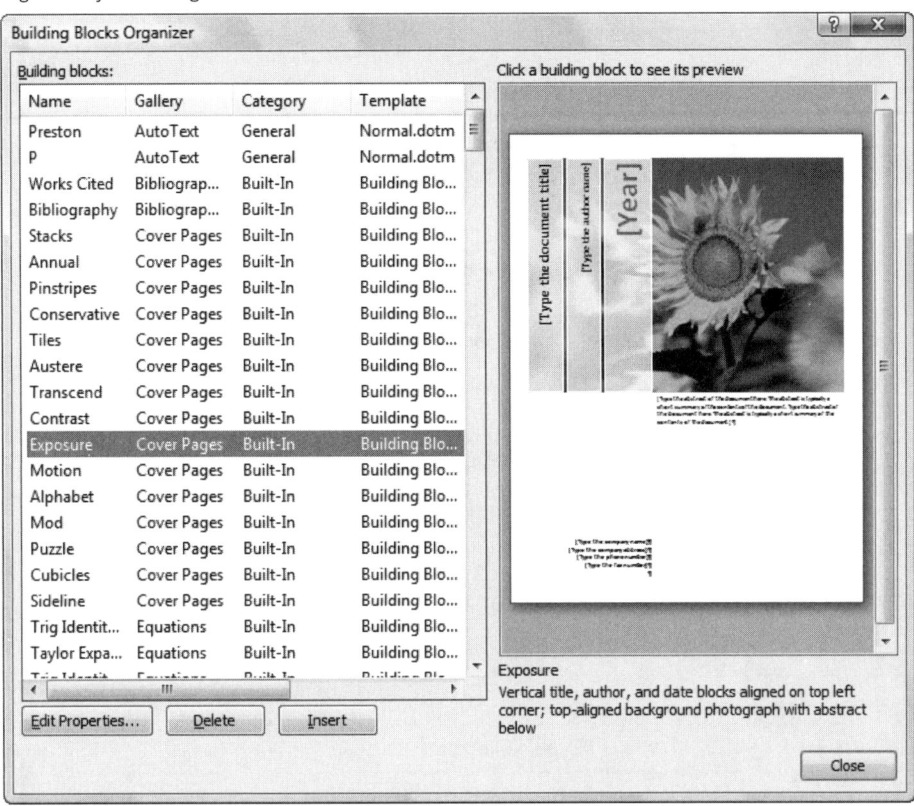

HACK 123: Say Hello to Your New Word 2007 Commands

V XP What happened to your old Word 2003 commands? They're easy to find. Just check out this quick cheat sheet.

Wondering where your favorite Word 2003 commands went in Word 2007? Worry no more. Just use the following quick cheat sheet, which lists the most commonly used Windows 2003 commands and tells you where they are in Word 2007. They're listed here according to the menu on which they're found in Word 2003.

File Menu

WORD 2003 LOCATION	WORD 2007 LOCATION
New	Office Button→New
Open	Office Button→Open
Close	Office Button→Close
Save	Office Button→Save or Quick Access Toolbar→Save
Save As	Office Button→Save As

File Menu *(continued)*

WORD 2003 LOCATION	WORD 2007 LOCATION
Save as Web Page	Office Button→Save As→Other Formats→Web Page
Web Page Preview	Office Button→Word Options→Customize→All Commands→Web Page Preview
Page Setup	Page Layout→Page Setup *or* Office Button→Print→Print Preview→Page Setup
Print Preview	Office Button→Print→Print Preview
Print	Office Button→Print
Recently Used Documents	Office Button→Recent Documents pane on right of menu (disappears if you mouse over a menu with more available options)

Edit Menu

WORD 2003 LOCATION	WORD 2007 LOCATION
Undo	Quick Access Toolbar→Undo
Redo	Quick Access Toolbar→Redo
Cut	Home→Clipboard→Cut
Copy	Home→Clipboard→Copy
Office Clipboard	Home→Clipboard→click arrow in the lower right of the group
Paste	Home→Clipboard→Paste
Paste Special	Home→Clipboard→Paste→Paste Special
Paste as Hyperlink	Home→Clipboard→Paste→Paste as Hyperlink
Clear→Formats	Home→Font→Clear Formatting icon
Clear→Contents	Office Button→Word Options→Customize→All Commands→Contents
Select All	Home→Editing→Select→Select All
Find	Home→Editing→Find
Replace	Home→Editing→Replace
Go To	Home→Editing→Find→Go To

View Menu

WORD 2003 LOCATION	WORD 2007 LOCATION
Normal	View→Document Views→Draft
Web Layout	View→Document Views→Web Layout
Print Layout	View→Document Views→Print Layout

View Menu *(continued)*

WORD 2003 LOCATION	WORD 2007 LOCATION
Reading Layout	View→Document Views→Full Screen Reading
Outline	View→Document Views→Outline
Task Pane	The overall task pane is gone in Word 2007, but some Dialog Box Launchers display task panes.
Toolbars	Word 2007 no longer has toolbars.
Ruler	View→Show/Hide→Ruler *or* Office Button→Print→Print Preview→Preview→Show Ruler
Thumbnails	View→Show/Hide→Thumbnails
Header and Footer	Insert→Header & Footer
Footnotes	References→Footnotes→Show Notes
Markup	Review→Tracking→Show Markup
Full Screen	Office Button→Word Options→Customize→All Commands→ Full Screen Reading
Zoom	Status Bar→Zoom Slider *or* View→Zoom *or* Office Button→Print→Print Preview→Zoom

Insert Menu

WORD 2003 LOCATION	WORD 2007 LOCATION
Break	Insert→Pages→Page Break
Page Numbers	Insert→Header & Footer→Page Number *or* Header & Footer Tools (this appears when your cursor is in a header or footer)→Design→Header & Footer→Page Number
Date and Time	Insert→Text→Date & Time *or* Header & Footer Tools→Design→Insert→Date & Time
AutoText→AutoText	Insert→Text→Quick Parts
AutoText→New	Office Button→Word Options→Customize→All Commands→Create AutoText
AutoText→(List of AutoText Entries)	Insert→Text→Quick Parts

Insert Menu *(continued)*

WORD 2003 LOCATION	WORD 2007 LOCATION
Field	Insert→Text→Quick Parts→Field *or* Header & Footer Tools→Design→Insert→Quick Parts→Field
Symbol	Insert→Symbols
Comment	Review→Comments→New Comment
References	All Reference commands are now located under the References Ribbon tab
Picture→Clip Art	Insert→Illustrations→Clip Art *or* Header & Footer Tools→Design→Insert→Clip Art
Picture→From File	Insert→Illustrations→Picture *or* Chart Tools (this appears when your cursor is on a chart)→Layout→Insert→Picture *or* Header & Footer Tools→Design→Insert→Picture
Picture→From Scanner or Camera	Removed from product
Picture→New Drawing)	Insert→Illustrations→Shapes→New Drawing Canvas
Picture→AutoShapes	Insert→Illustrations→Shapes
Picture→WordArt	Insert→Text→WordArt
Picture→Organization Chart	Insert→Illustrations→SmartArt
Picture→Chart	Insert→Illustrations→Chart
Text Box	Insert→Text→Text Box
File	Insert→Text→Object→Text from File
Object	Insert→Text→Object
Bookmark	Insert→Links→Bookmark
Hyperlink	Insert→Links→Hyperlink

Format Menu

WORD 2003 LOCATION	WORD 2007 LOCATION
Font	Home→Font
Paragraph	Page Layout→Paragraph *or* Home→Paragraph→Dialog Box Launcher (the arrow in the lower right of the Paragraph group)
Bullets and Numbering	Home→Paragraph→Bullets *or* Home→Paragraph→Numbering *or* Office Button→Word Options→Customize→All Commands→ Bullets and Numbering
Borders and Shading	Home→Paragraph→Shading
Columns	Page Layout→Page Setup→Columns
Tabs	Home→Paragraph→Dialog Box Launcher (the arrow in the lower right of the Paragraph group)→Tabs
Change Case	Home→Font→Change Case icon
AutoFormat	Office Button→Word Options→Customize→All Commands→ AutoFormat
Styles and Formatting	Home→Styles
Reveal Formatting	Office Button→Word Options→Customize→All Commands→ Reveal Formatting

Tools Menu

WORD 2003 LOCATION	WORD 2007 LOCATION
Spelling and Grammar	Review→Proofing→Spelling & Grammar
Research	Review→Proofing→Research
Word Count	Review→Proofing→Word Count
AutoSummarize	Office Button→Word Options→Customize→All Commands→AutoSummary Tools
Track Changes	Review→Tracking→Track Changes
Compare and Merge Documents	Review→Compare
Letters and Mailings	Mailings
Macro	View→Macro *or* Developer→Code→Macros
Templates and Add-Ins	Developer→Templates→Document Template
AutoCorrect Options	Office Button→Word Options→Proofing→AutoCorrect Options

Tools Menu *(continued)*

WORD 2003 LOCATION	WORD 2007 LOCATION
Customize	Office Button→Word Options→Customize
Options	Office Button→Word Options

Table Menu

WORD 2003 LOCATION	WORD 2007 LOCATION
Draw Table	Table Tools→Design→Draw Borders→Draw Table *or* Home→Paragraph→Borders→Draw Table *or* Insert→Tables→Table→Draw Table
Insert→Table	Insert→Tables→Table→Insert Table
Insert→Columns, Rows, Cells	Table Tools→Layout→Rows & Columns
Delete→Table, Columns, Rows, Cells	Table Tools→Layout→Rows & Columns→Delete
Select→Table, Column, Row, Cell	Table Tools→Layout→Table→Select
Merge Cells	Table Tools→Layout→Merge→Merge Cells
Split Cells	Table Tools→Layout→Merge→Split Cells
Split Table	Table Tools→Layout→Merge→Split Table
Table AutoFormat	Table Tools→Design→Table Styles
AutoFit	Table Tools→Layout→Cell Size→AutoFit
Heading Rows Repeat	Table Tools→Layout→Data→Repeat Header Rows
Convert→Text to Table	Insert→Tables→Table→Convert Text to Table
Convert→Table to Text	Table Tools→Layout→Data→Convert to Text
Sort	Home→Paragraph→Sort icon *or* Table Tools→Layout→Table→Sort
Formula	Table Tools→Layout→Table→Formula
Hide/Show Gridlines	Table Tools→Layout→Table→Hide/Show Gridlines
Table Properties	Table Tools→Layout→Table→Properties *or* Table Tools→Layout→Cell Size→Properties

QUICK HACK 

MAKE THE MINI TOOLBAR YOUR FRIEND

Having to move back and forth between the Ribbon and the body of your document in order to select formatting or a command is a big time waster and annoying to boot. So Word 2007 includes the clever mini toolbar. Highlight text and point the cursor at it, and a nearly transparent mini toolbar appears above the text, with a set of commands relevant to the text you've chosen. Move your cursor to the nearly transparent mini toolbar, and it becomes solid. Click a command to use it; for example, changing the font, size, and color of text. If the mini toolbar disappears for some reason, right-click the selection or else reselect the text, and it springs back into action.

Window Menu

WORD 2003 LOCATION	WORD 2007 LOCATION
New Window	View→Window→New Window
Arrange All	View→Window→Arrange All
Compare Side by Side with	View→Window→View Side by Side
Split	View→Window→Split
Currently Open Documents	View→Window→Switch Windows

HACK 124: Shrink Supersized Pictures in Office Docs

V XP Office documents with pictures in them can become supersized, and some email servers may reject them as too large. Here's a quick way to shrink them.

Add pictures to a Microsoft Office 2007 document, and all of a sudden your 125 KB file can become 5 MB to 10 MB, and even more. Too many documents of that size can quickly eat up your hard disk space. And if you try sending them via email, you may be in for a surprise: many ISPs reject files over a certain size, so you may not be able to send them.

A new tool built into Office 2007, however, makes it easy to shrink those supersized pictures in a few easy steps. The exact amount of space you'll save depends on the types and number of pictures in a document, and a number of other factors, but you can easily shrink file sizes by a factor of 75%, if you've got files with multiple pictures in them.

This hack shows how to do it in Word, but you do it similarly in all Office applications.

After you've inserted all the pictures in a document, click a picture, then choose the Format tab and click Compress Pictures in the Adjust group. Depending on whether the document is in Word 2007 format (with a *.docx* extension) or a previous Word format (with a *.doc*) extension, the options will be slightly different.

For files with a Word 2007 format, the Compress Pictures dialog box appears. Click Options. You'll see a screen like that shown in Figure 9-9.

In Compression settings, you have three choices of sizes—220 dpi, which is the highest quality for printers and screens; 150 dpi, which is good for web pages and presentations; and 96 dpi, which creates files of the smallest sizes. At least, that's what Microsoft says.

In many instances, you'll find that the 150 dpi choice will be your best bet. The quality difference between 150 dpi and the original pictures is not that great, and in many instances, will be indiscernible. But the space savings can be tremendous.

Keep the default boxes checked in the compression options area, and click OK. Back on the Compress Pictures dialog box, keep the box unchecked next to Apply to selected pictures only if you'd like all the pictures in the document to be compressed. If you check the box, it will compress only the picture or pictures you've selected. (You can select multiple pictures by holding down the Ctrl key as you click each.)

Figure 9-9.
Compressing files in a .docx file

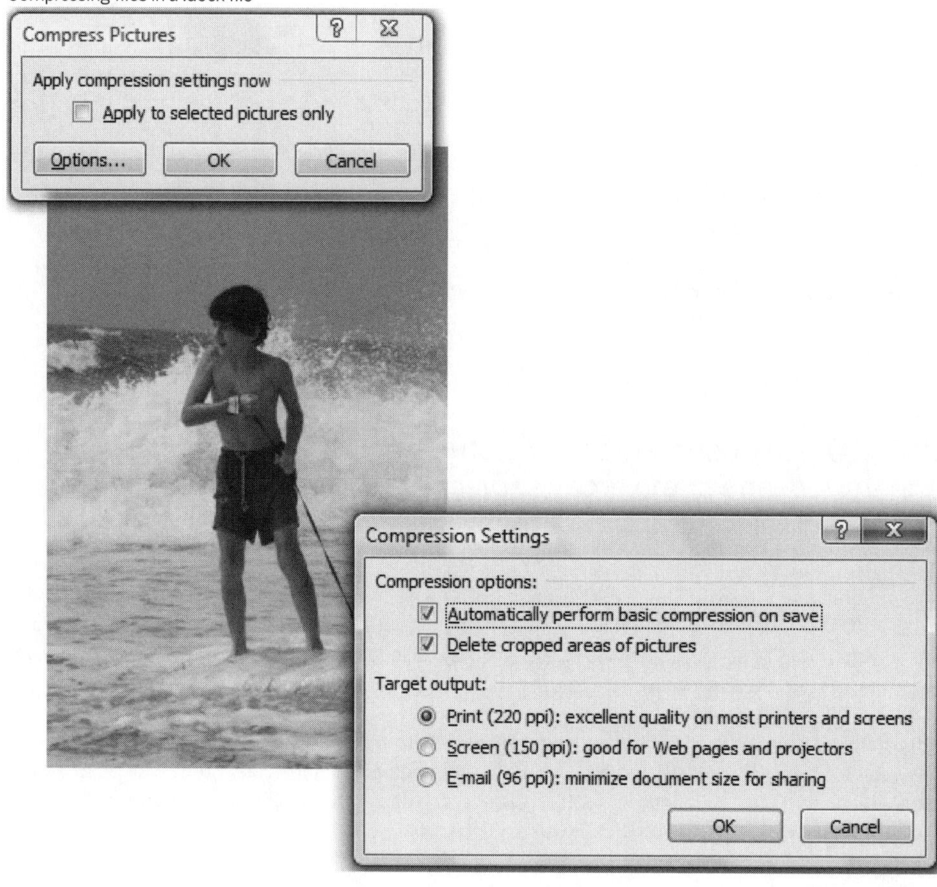

 You have another choice for shrinking the size of a file—saving it as an Acrobat file (*.pdf*) **[Hack #127]**. That, however, won't save you as much space as compressing the pictures and has other drawbacks as well. The person to whom you're sending the file may not have an Acrobat reader, and if he wants to edit it, he will need the file in its original format.

Click OK, and the pictures in the document will compress, shrinking the file size.

If the document is a *.doc* file, you also click a picture, then choose the Format tab and click Compress Pictures in the Adjust group. The screen shown in Figure 9-10 appears.

As you can see, your selection here is more limited. You get only the Print choice, which here, oddly enough, is 200 dpi rather than 220 dpi; and the Web/Screen choice, which is 96 dpi. Your best bet—150 dpi—is nowhere to be seen.

 When you compress the pictures in a document, you won't affect the original pictures on your hard disk. The pictures are compressed only in your document.

How much space can you save by using compression? That varies dramatically, according to how many pictures you have in a document, their file types, and how compressible they are. The results, though, can be surprising. A sample file with multiple large *.tiff* and *.jpg* files was 4.7 MB uncompressed. Here are the surprising results of how compression affects file size:

220 dpi: No change (4.7 MB)

150 dpi: 1.7 MB

96 dpi: 1.1 MB

Here's a useful bit of information about the way Word 2007 handles graphics: a file with the same content and graphics will be slightly larger in *.doc* format than in *.docx* format. For example, a file with plenty of graphics was 4.7 MB in *.docx* format, but 5.4 MB in *.doc* format.

Hacking the Hack

If you need to save a file in the old *.doc* format but still want to be able to take advantage of the 150-dpi compression capabilities for *.docx* files, there's a simple workaround. When you create the file, create it as a *docx* file. Then, when you're done working on the file, shrink the pictures using the *.docx* compression capabilities. Finally, save it as a *.doc* file. You can then delete the *.docx* file if you want.

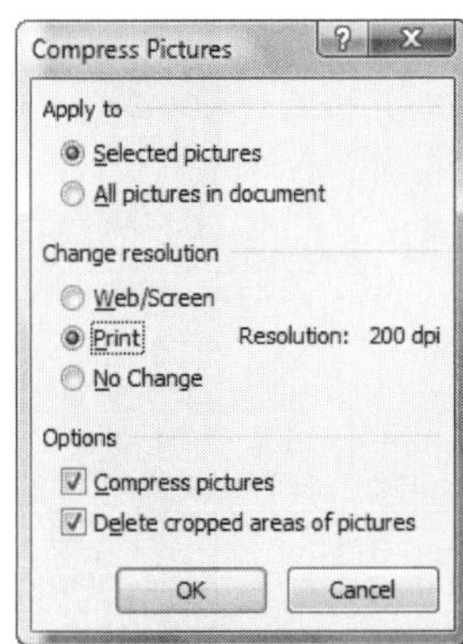

Figure 9-10.
Compressing a file in a .doc file

See Also

- "Instantly Compress Files You Send via Email" **[Hack #84]**

HACK 125: Grab Real-Time Stock Quotes in Excel

V XP Excel 2007 makes it a snap to import any data from the Web, and keep that data fresh and updated. Here's how to import stock quotes that update themselves throughout the day.

Are you a stock watcher, or is there some other kind of data that you like to keep your eyes on and import into Excel? If so, you can use one of Excel 2007's coolest new features—the ability to import any data from the Web, and to automatically update and refresh that data without having to do a thing. So, for example, you could create a spreadsheet tracking your stocks, and it will automatically grab stock quotes live, without you having to lift a finger.

You do it by taking advantage of what are called Web Queries, which are auto-updating links that grab data from the Web as the data changes. The data needs to be in a table on the Web; if it's not in a table, you won't be able to grab it. But most stock quotes online are embedded in table, so it's easy to do. Here's how:

1. Open or create a worksheet, and click the cell where you want the data to appear.

2. Click the Data tab, and in the External Data group, click From Web.

3. The new Web Query dialog box appears. In the Address box, copy the URL of the page that contains the data that you want to import into your worksheet (for example, finance.yahoo.com/q?d=t&s=MSFT), then click Go.

4. The page will be loaded into the dialog box. Every table on the page will have a small yellow arrow next to it. Hold your arrow over any table, and the arrow turns green, and you'll see all the data that you can import if you select that table, as you can see in Figure 9-11.

5. Click the arrows of the table or tables whose data you want to import. The arrows will turn green.

6. If you want the data in your spreadsheet to retain the formatting from the web page, click the Options button, and select Rich Text Formatting Only. Select Full HTML Formatting option if you want all the table properties to be preserved. If you want no formatting, don't click the Options button.

7. Click the Import button. You can select a new location in your worksheet to place the data from the Import Data dialog box that appears, or else keep the currently selected location. Click the OK button.

8. After a few seconds, the data will be imported into your worksheet, as you can see in Figure 9-12.

9. The data is in your worksheet, but it isn't "live" yet: it will not automatically update. To manually update the data, put your cursor inside the data you just imported, and from the Data tab, click Refresh All in the Connections group. (If you have imported multiple tables into your spreadsheet and want to refresh only one table, put your cursor in the table, click the down arrow next to Refresh All, and click Refresh).

10. To have Excel automatically update the data, put your cursor inside the table you want to update, select Properties from the Connections group on the Data tab, and from the form that appears (pictured in Figure 9-13) check the box next to "Refresh every..." Then select how often you want the data updated and click OK. The data will now be updated on the schedule you set.

Hacking the Hack

If you import multiple tables into a single worksheet, there's a simple way to set how often you want to update each table without having to click each one to customize it. On the Data tab, click Connections in the Connections group. The Workbook Connections dialog box appears, and lists every imported table on the page. Highlight any, click Properties, and you'll come to the dialog box pictured in Figure 9-13. From here, you can customize how frequently the table should be updated.

Figure 9-11.
Selecting data to import into your worksheet

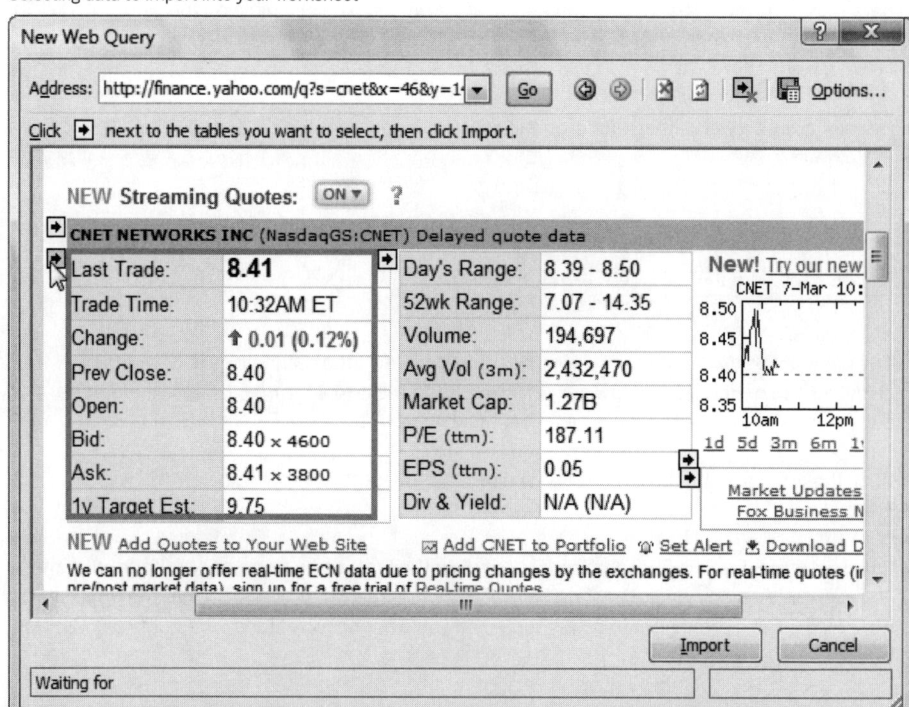

Figure 9-12.
Importing the stock data into the worksheet

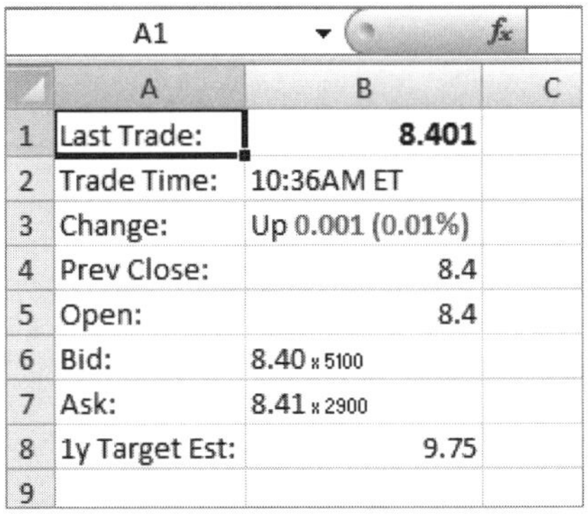

	A	B	C
1	Last Trade:	**8.401**	
2	Trade Time:	10:36AM ET	
3	Change:	Up 0.001 (0.01%)	
4	Prev Close:	8.4	
5	Open:	8.4	
6	Bid:	8.40 x 5100	
7	Ask:	8.41 x 2900	
8	1y Target Est:	9.75	
9			

Figure 9-13.
Telling Excel to automatically refresh your data

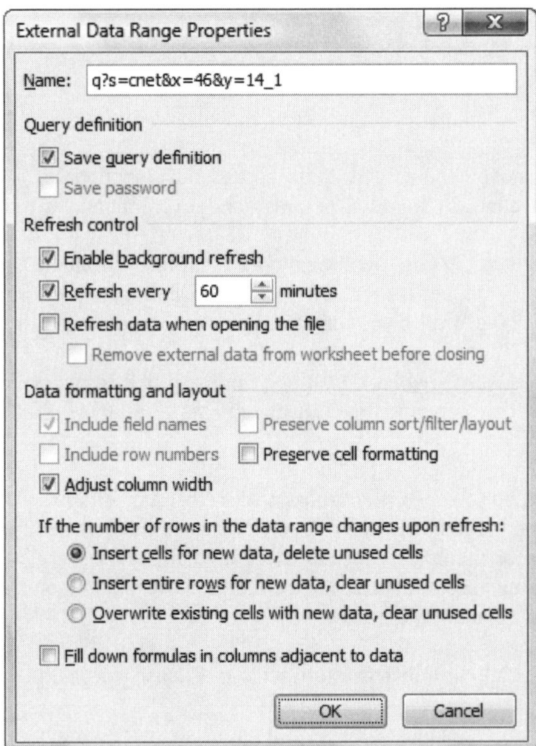

HACK 126: Open and Create Office Docs Without Word or Excel

V XP When it comes to word processing and spreadsheets, it's an all-Microsoft world. But you don't have to pay hundreds of dollars to create and read Microsoft files. You can do it for free, without even having to download or install software.

For better or worse, the Windows world has settled on Word and Excel as the word processing and spreadsheet standards. But as anyone who has recently bought a new computer can tell you, buying an office suite that includes them can push up the cost of your computer by several hundred dollars.

If you want to play well with others, you need to be able to create and read Word and Excel files. That doesn't mean, however, that you need to buy Microsoft Office. In fact, you can use free software that lets you open and create Word and Excel files, and you won't even have to download or install software. You'll also get some features missing in both Word and Excel as well.

Instead, you visit a free, web-based word processor or spreadsheet program. In addition to letting you open and create Word and Excel files, you can open files in other formats. And the sites also let you share your documents with others online, and collaborate on them as well.

The best-known one is Google Docs and Spreadsheets (docs.google.com), pictured in Figure 9-14. It's straightforward to use and works much like any word processor or spreadsheet except, of course, you have to be online to use it.

When you save files, you save them online, rather than on your PC, so that they're available to you wherever you have an Internet connection. However, if you also want them available on your PC, you can choose File→Export, and then save the file to your own PC. If you have a word processor or spreadsheet on your PC, when you export your document, open it in the word processor or spreadsheet, and can then save it locally.

If you're a true spreadsheet jockey, you may not be impressed with the spreadsheet functionality. There are plenty of things it doesn't support, such as macros, pivot tables, or data validation.

If you're anyone else, though—and that means most of us—you'll be more than impressed with it. It includes dozens of built-in spreadsheet functions, and using them is exceptionally easy: click the Formulas link at the top of the page, then click the formula you want to insert, and you're done.

The word processor feature doesn't have all of Word's high-end bells and whistles, but it has a few features that Word isn't very good at. It's great for working with HTML documents, and very good at inserting and handling pictures and links.

Where it shines, as do similar programs, is when you need to collaborate with others. When you want to work with someone else on a document, send them an invitation by clicking the Collaborate tab. (They'll need to sign up for a Google account in order to open the document.) They can then come to the page you're working on, and you can see what each collaborator is doing to the document. Click the Discuss tab, and you can chat live with them.

To publish your document for anyone to see, click the Publish button, and click Publish Now.

There are plenty of other similar web sites that offer similar services, but not all are of the same quality as Google Docs and Spreadsheets. Zoho (www.zoho.com), however, offers similar features. In fact, the Zoho Writer word processor component is superior to Google's in terms of available features.

See Also

- The OpenOffice.org office suite (www.openoffice.org) is a free, open source software suite that includes a word processor, spreadsheet, drawing program, equation editor, and presentation software. It opens and saves Microsoft Office formats as well as many other formats. Versions are available for Windows, Macintosh, Linux, and Solaris.

QUICK HACK

TEACH YOUR MOUSE FLIP 3D

If you have a programmable mouse with a programmable button, you can launch Windows Flip 3D directly from that button, without taking your hand off the mouse. Open the control panel for the mouse, select the button, and then change its button assignment to *C:\Windows\System32\rundll32.exe dwmapi #105*. From now on, when you press the button, you'll launch Windows Flip 3D.

Figure 9-14.
Editing a spreadsheet in Google Docs

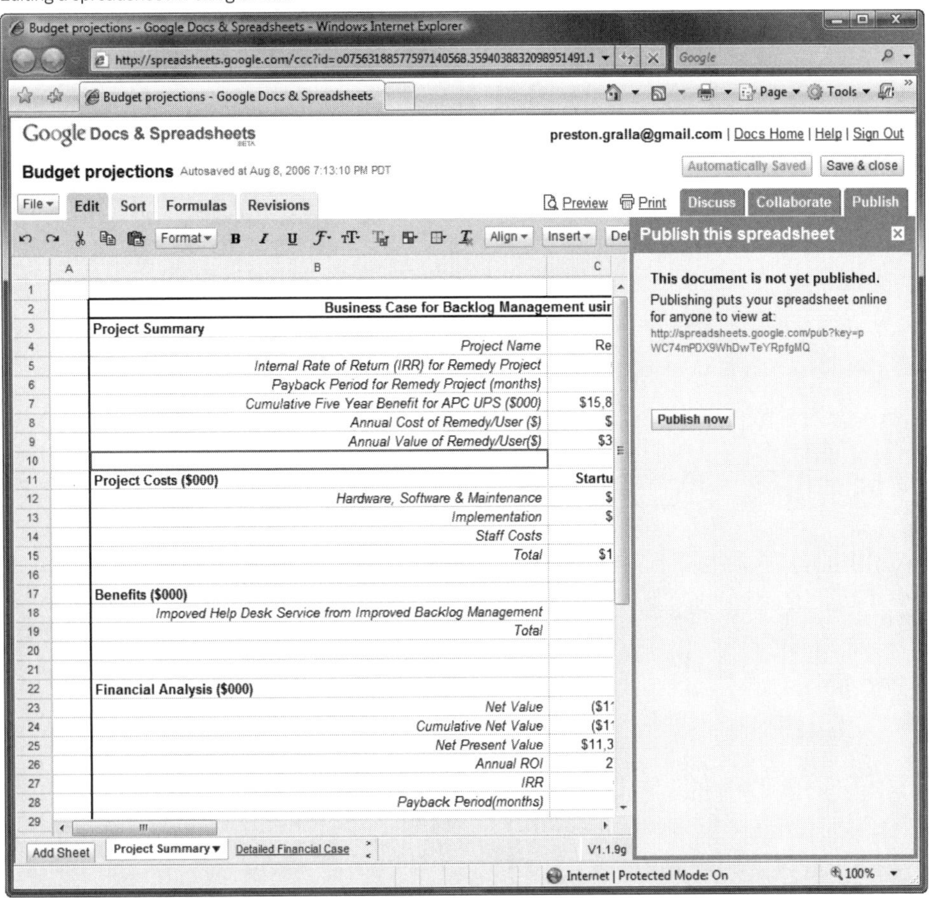

HACK 127: Roll Your Own PDFs

V XP Think if you want to create a file in the Adobe Acrobat .pdf format, you'll have to fork over somewhere in the $300 range to buy Adobe Acrobat standard? Think again. Here's how to do it for free.

The Adobe Acrobat *.pdf* format has become the main worldwide standard for sharing documents that retain all the formatting, layout, and graphics of whatever application you created it with. Adobe makes available a free reader for viewing *.pdf* files. But if you want to create them, you'll have to buy expensive software from Adobe that lists at around $300.

Now, though, you won't have to spend a penny. If you have Microsoft Office 2007, you can create *.pdf* files for free. You'll just have to download free software from Microsoft, and after that, creating a *.pdf* file is as simple as printing a document.

In a Microsoft Office 2007 application, such as Word or Excel, click the Office button and choose Save As→Find Add-ins for other file formats. Click "Install and use the Save as PDF or XPS add-in from Microsoft" and from the page that appears, click "Microsoft Save as PDF or XPS Add-in for 2007 Microsoft Office programs." (If you prefer, you can forgo all this and instead go directly to www.microsoft.com/downloads/details.aspx?familyid=4D951911-3E7E-4AE6-B059-A2E79ED87041 in your web browser.)

Click the Download button, and then download and install the add-in. To create a PDF from any Office 2007 file, click the Office button, then select Save as→PDF or XPS and click Publish. Figure 9-15 shows a file as a Word document; Figure 9-16 shows a PDF of the file, including thumbnail navigation, which is automatically created by the add-in.

Hacking the Hack

When you save a file as a *pdf*, you have several options. If you're going to print the document and distribute it, in the Optimize section choose "Standard." If you're going to publish it online, choose the "Online" option because it will create a smaller file that will download more quickly.

The add-in also lets you create files in Microsoft's new XPS (XML Paper Specification) format, which is similar to Adobe's in that it saves all formatting in a file. Anyone with Windows Vista can view XPS files. Non-Vista users will have to download an XPS viewer at www.microsoft.com/downloads/details.aspx?FamilyId=B8DCFFDD-E3A5-44CC-8021-7649FD37FFEE.

For more control over your *.pdf*, click the Options button. From there, you'll be able to save only a portion of your document as a *.pdf*, publish the markup of a document in addition to the document, and use a variety of other options.

See Also

- If you don't have Microsoft Office 2007, you can still create *.pdf* files for free. Download the free Cute PDF Writer (www.cutepdf.com/Products/CutePDF/writer.asp), and you can create a *.pdf* file from any Windows application.
- The OpenOffice.org office suite (www.openoffice.org) a free, open source software suite, lets you create PDFs.

Figure 9-15.
You can take this Word document...

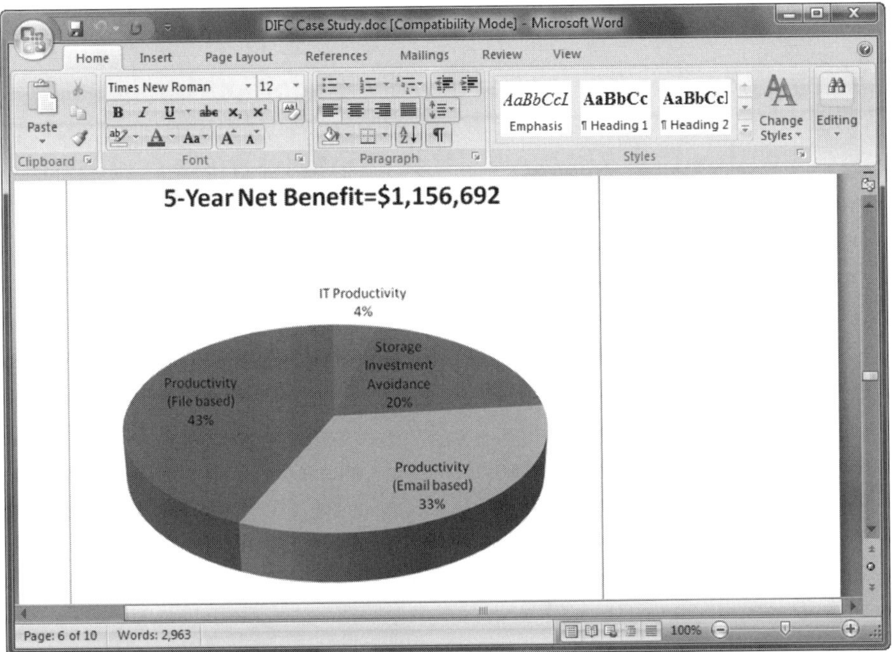

Figure 9-16.
...and turn it into a full-blown PDF, including thumbnail navigation and other features.

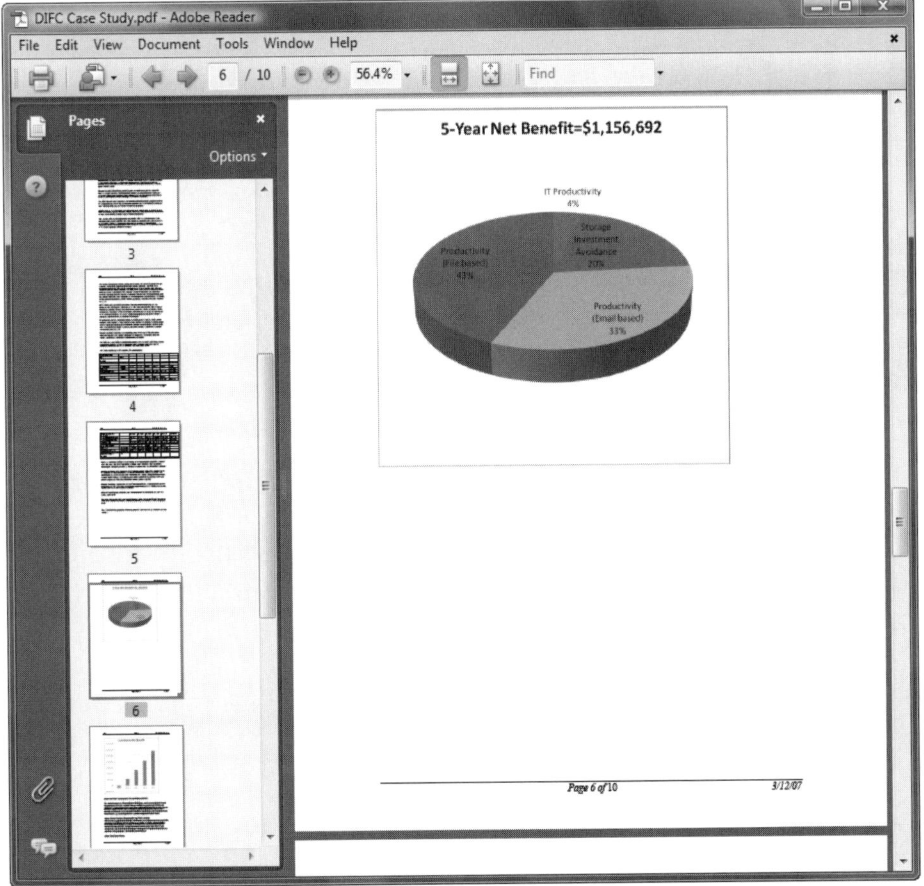

WINDOWS HOME SERVER HACKS

These days, people's homes have as much computing power as entire small businesses. For example, in my house, I've got seven PCs with either Windows XP or Windows Vista on them, several printers, and a scanner or two. A home router, of course, ties everything together and lets all the PCs use the Internet as well.

But having this many PCs presents problems—how, for example, to keep the data on all the PCs backed up? It's simply not practical to think that everyone in the house will do weekly backups.

There are other issues as well, particularly sharing files. We've got several digital cameras, and when someone takes photographs, sharing those photos isn't easy. It's simply too much work, and too confusing to try and set up shared folders on each PC and for everyone to remember the locations of all of them.

To solve problems like these and add some nifty capabilities to PCs at home, Microsoft introduced Windows Home Server. Windows Home Server can automatically back up all the PCs in a home on any schedule you set. In addition, it lets you set up shared folders so that anyone in a home can access and share files that others might want to see. It offers a lot of other extras as well, such as the ability to remotely connect over the Internet to any computer on your network

The following hacks won't teach you the basics of using Windows Home Server—for that, use the manual. Instead, they'll give you advice on using some of its more advanced or hard-to-use features, notably customizing Windows Home Server backups and connecting to Windows Home Server remotely over the Internet.

When you connect Windows Home Server to your network, do it via an Ethernet cable, not wirelessly. If you connect it wirelessly, the enormous amount of data it likes to move around will bog down your wireless network and cause Home Server to disconnect. In that case, you'll only be able to reconnect by rebooting your server.

The hacks assume that you have a working knowledge of Windows Home Server, that you've installed the Windows Home Server Console properly, and that you've set up an account with a strong password, as required by Windows Home Server, for using the Windows Home Server Console.

HACK 128: Customize Windows Home Server Backups

V XP If you use Windows Server's normal backup procedures, you may run out of disk space fast. Use this hack to slim down jumbo-sized backups.

If you've got a home network with three or more computers and back them up to Windows Server, you may find out that their backups take up more disk space than you'd like. That's because by default, when you create a Windows Server backup, it backs up far more files than you may really need.

By default, Windows Home Server won't back up your temporary files, files in your Recycle Bin, your system page file, shadow volume files, and your hibernation file.

You can easily slim down your backups, though. Log into the Windows Home Server Console and click the Computers & Backup button. Select your computer, click Configure Backup, and a wizard launches. Click Next, and you'll come to the Choose Volumes to Back Up screen, shown in Figure 9-17. Uncheck the boxes next to any volumes you don't want to back up. Then click Next, and you'll come to the Choose Folders to Exclude from Backup screen; this lets you pick and choose which folders you *don't* want to back up.

To exclude folders, click the Add button. Click the + sign next to your volumes to see which folders Windows Home Backup will back up (Figure 9-18). Select a folder you don't want backed up, and click Exclude.

By default, Windows Home Server backs up your Windows directory, which takes up between 5 and 6 GB, so you may want to exclude that, as well as any applications. You may want to exclude your Desktop as well.

If you don't back up your Windows folder, you won't be able to use Windows Home Server to restore your entire PC in the event of a crash. You'll be able to restore your data but not Windows itself.

Unfortunately, there's no way to exclude multiple backups in a single operation, so after you click Exclude, you'll be back at the screen shown in Figure 9-17, except that you'll see the folder you just excluded. Click Add to exclude another folder, and repeat the steps for excluding another folder. Keep doing this until you've excluded all the folders you want to exclude. After you do, you'll see a screen like that pictured in Figure 9-19.

Click Next and then Finish. You'll see a screen telling you how many folders you've excluded and the total size that your backup will be. Note that the backup won't start yet; to do that, click the "Backup now" button.

To change the folders you want to back up, simply repeat these steps.

Figure 9-17.
To slim down your backups, only choose volumes you want to back up

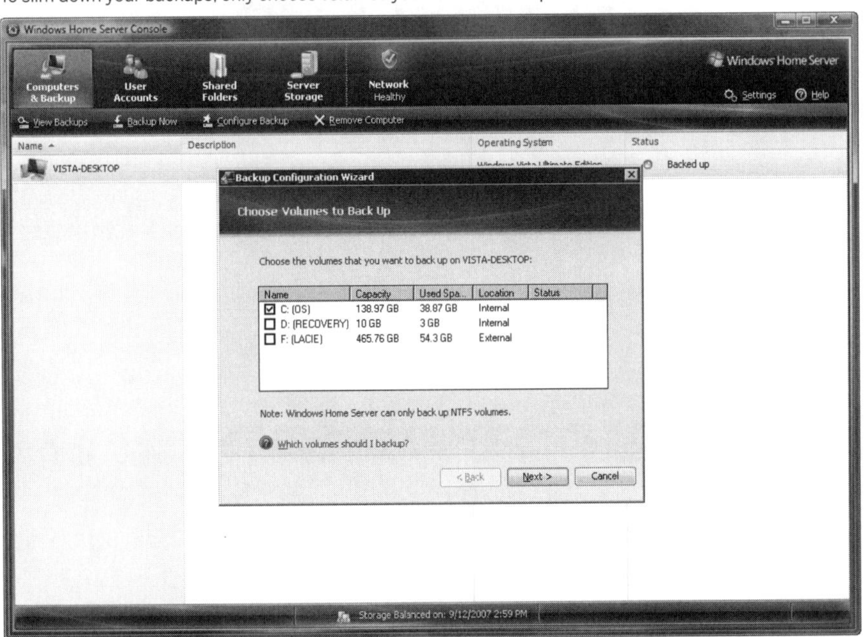

Figure 9-18.
Excluding folders from your backup

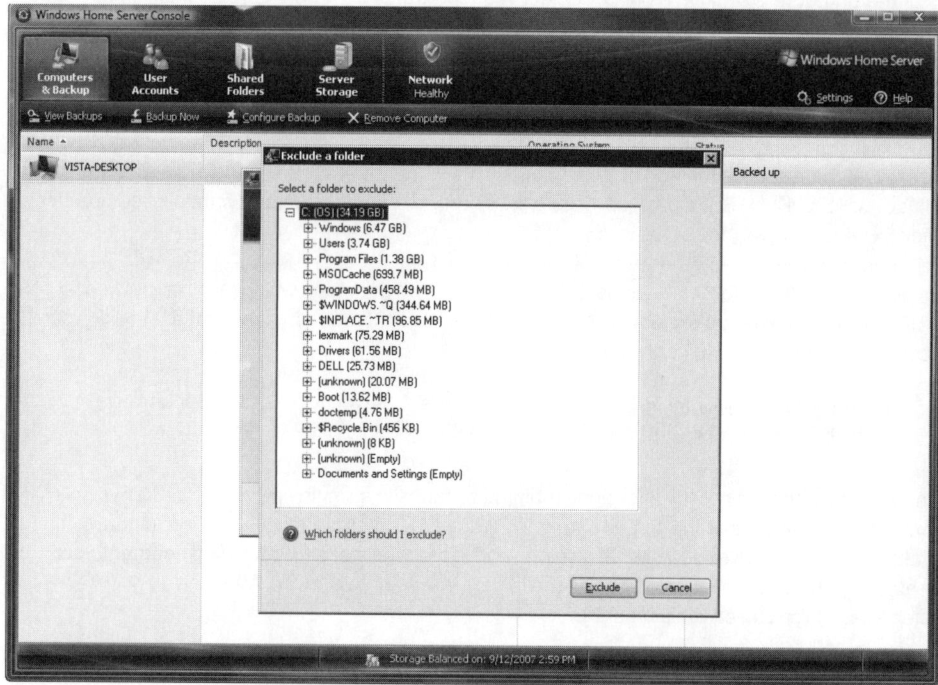

Figure 9-19.
The list of folders excluded from your backup

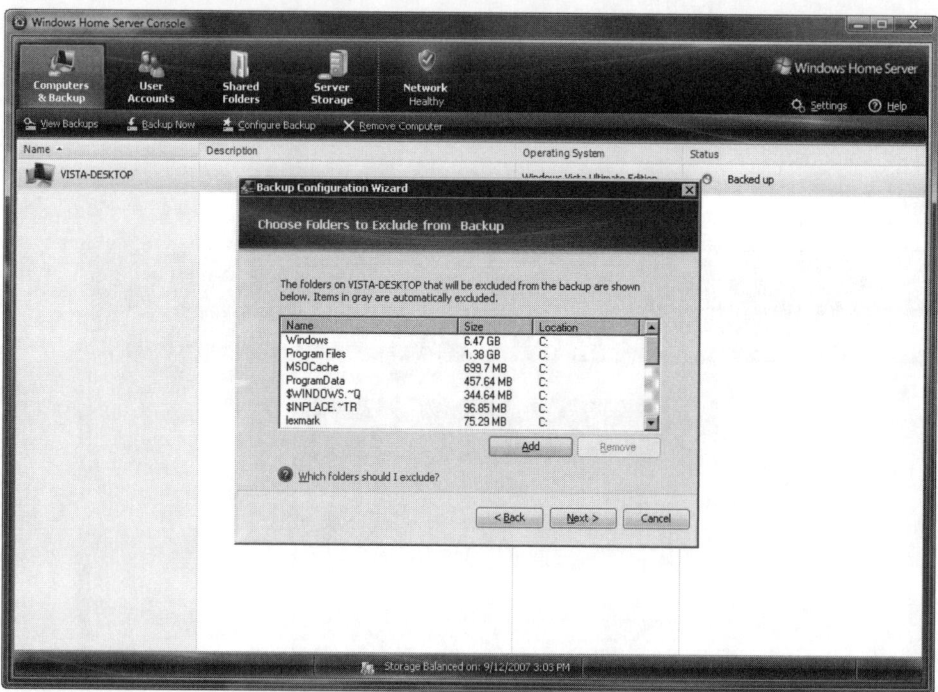

HACK 129: Make a Remote Connection to Windows Home Server Over the Internet

V XP It's not as easy as Microsoft says to get access to your files on Windows Home Server when you're away from home. Here's how to avoid the gotchas and make a connection every time.

For those who travel, one of the more useful features of Windows Home Server is that you can connect to it over the Internet. Make the connection, and you'll have full access to your files.

Or at least, that's the theory. In practice, things are much more difficult than that. Several problems complicate your ability to connect remotely over the Internet to your home server:

- The public IP address of your home server may often change. ISPs hand out dynamic IP addresses, and so your IP address one day may not be the same as your IP address the next day. So even if you copy down the IP address before you leave, that address may change when you get to another location, even only hours later.
- The nature of home routers is that your server doesn't even have a real public IP address, it only has one inside your network. So you need to figure out a way to connect to your server directly.

However, as you'll see, with a little bit of configuring, tweaking, and hacking, you'll be able to make the connection.

Understanding IP Addresses and Windows Home Server

Before you start, you'll need to understand a little about your home router, home server, and their IP addresses. Your router is assigned an IP address by your ISP, for example, 66.32.43.98. Think of that as an external IP address—the IP address that the Internet sees. This IP address is assigned dynamically, and so will change over time; it may be different from one day to another.

Your router uses Network Address Translation that allows multiple computers to access the Internet over a single connection, using the external IP address. With NAT, the single, external IP address is shared among all the computers on the network. But each computer also has its own internal IP address, invisible to the Internet.

With the example IP address just given, each computer looks (to the Internet) as if it has the address of 66.32.43.98, but internally they have different IP addresses, such as 192.168.1.100, 192.168.1.101, and so on. The router has a built-in Dynamic Host Configuration Protocol server that assigns the internal IP address to each PC. These internal IP addresses allow the PCs to communicate with each other and to connect to the Internet.

Setting Up the Connection

With that as background, let's begin. In order to make a remote connection, you need to enable your account to connect remotely. In the Windows Server Home Console, click User Accounts, then right-click the account to which you want to grant remote access, and select Properties. Click the box next to "Enable remote access for this user", then click OK.

Now you need to turn on remote access for Windows Home Server. In the Windows Server Home Console, select Settings→Remote Access. You'll see a screen like the one in Figure 9-20.

If the Web Site Connectivity button is not already turned on, click Turn On. Then, in the Router section, click the Setup button. A screen will appear telling you that Windows Home Server is going to configure port forwarding for your router. Click OK. Depending on your router, it may or may not

QUICK HACK 

LAUNCH PROGRAMS WITH KEYBOARD SHORTCUTS

The fastest way to launch your favorite application in Windows is via keyboard shortcuts. They're easy to build. On the Start menu, right-click the application for which you want to create a shortcut, and select Properties. In the Properties dialog box, put your cursor in the Shortcut Key fields, and press the hotkey sequence you'd like to use for the shortcut, such as Ctrl-Alt-E for Excel. Click OK, and you're done.

Figure 9-20.
Enable remote access to your Windows Home Server from here

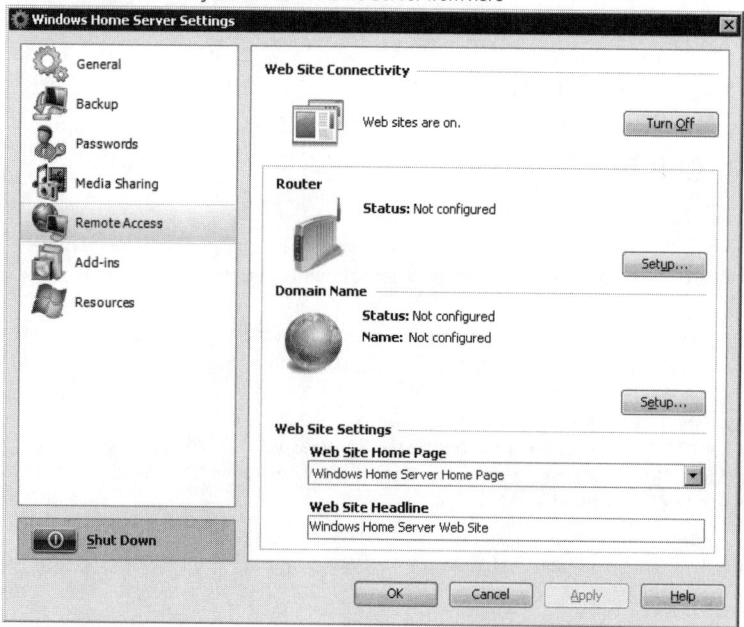

work. If it doesn't, you'll get a warning screen. Don't despair, though, because as you'll see later in this hack, in the "Hacking the Hack" section, you can manually configure port forwarding.

Windows Home Server can only automatically configure your router if it uses UPnP (Universal Plug and Play). If you get an error message saying that your router does not support UPnP, check to see if in fact your router does support it—many routers turn it off for security reasons. Check your router's documentation for details. In the Linksys WRT54GX4, log in to your router, then click Administrator. Scroll down to the UPnP section, select Enable, then click Save Settings. Now go back into the Router section on Windows Home Server and click the Setup button. It should be able to do the automatic configuration now. If it doesn't, you'll need to manually configure port forwarding. See "Hacking the Hack" for details.

Next, click Setup in the Domain Name section. A wizard launches that walks you through the process of creating a domain name that you'll use to connect to your home server over the Internet. You'll need a Windows Live ID in order to complete the wizard, so if you don't have one, you'll get one as part of the process by clicking Get your Windows Live ID.

After you sign into Windows Live and accept a privacy statement, click Next. You'll choose a domain name, as you can see in Figure 9-21. You'll use this domain name to connect to your home server via your browser. The domain will end in homeserver.com, such as `thegrallafamilyhomeserver.homeserver.com`. Click Confirm after you select a name. If it's not already taken, you'll be able to use it. If it is taken, you'll have to choose a new one. Then click Finish, and then Done. Back on the Remote Access screen, you should see green check boxes next to the Router and Domain Name sections. Click OK.

Making the Connection

Now you're ready to make the connection. In your browser, type https://, followed by your domain name, like this: https://thegrallafamilyhomeserver.homeserver.com. If you're using Internet Explorer 7, you may get an error message, saying that there is a problem with the Web site's security certificate. Ignore that message and click "Continue to this website (not recommended)". You'll come to a generic Web logon page, like that shown in Figure 9-22. Click Log On, and type in your user name and password.

Figure 9-21
Choosing a domain name

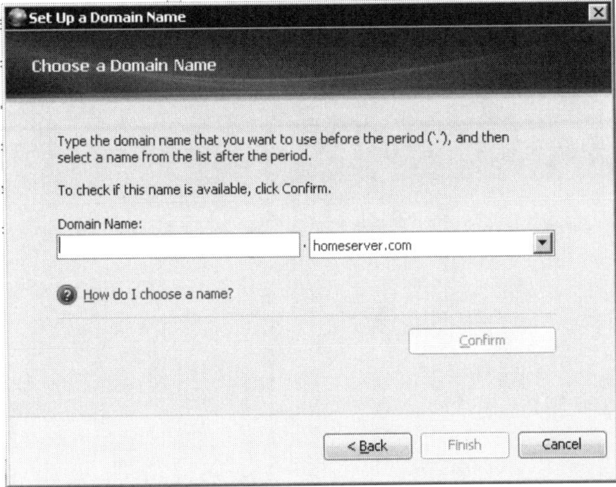

Remember, you can only connect to your home server remotely over the Internet if you log in using an account for which you've set up a strong password, as defined by Windows Home Server. That means the password has to be at least seven characters long, and contain at least three of these character categories: uppercase letters, lowercase letters, numbers, and symbols such as !, @, and #.

After you log in, click the Computers tab in order to connect to your home server via the Windows Home Server Console, and get remote access to any computer connected to your network (Figure 9-23). You'll get a warning in Internet Explorer that the site wants to run the Terminal Services ActiveX Client. Install it by clicking the warning and telling Internet Explorer to run the control.

You're still not quite ready to connect. You first have to add your home server domain to the Trusted Sites zone in Internet Explorer. In Internet Explorer, select Tools→Internet Options→Security, then click Trusted Sites. Click the Sites button, then in the screen that appears, type in the domain of your Windows Home Server, for example, https://grallafamilyhomeserver.homeserver.com. Click Add, Close, and then OK.

Now back on the Computers tab, click Connect to your Home Server. From the screen that appears, type in your password and then OK. A screen will appear asking if you trust the computer to which you are connecting. Click Yes. You'll now connect to your home server via the Web. The screen will look and work exactly as if you were using the Windows Home Server Console via a client, not the Web, as you can see in Figure 9-24.

You've now made the connection, and can use your home server as if you were on the internal network, and gain access to shared folders, and more. In fact, you can take command of any computer on your network **[Hack #130]** as well.

Hacking the Hack

As I've explained earlier in this hack, the Windows Home Server Console may not be able to automatically configure your router for port forwarding. If that's the case, you'll have to configure it yourself. When you configure it yourself, you forward all traffic from specific ports to the internal network IP address of your home server (such as 192.168.1.1). When I refer to ports here, I'm not talking about a physical connection on your PC. Instead, a port is a virtual connection used by network applications.

You're going to configure your home router to route all traffic from the ports that Windows Home Server uses—80, 443, and 4125—to go directly to your own home server. That way, whenever a connection comes in to one of those ports, it will connect to your server. How you do it varies from

Figure 9-22.
Click Log On, then type in your user name and password. Remember that you need to use a strong password if you want to get to your Web site remotely.

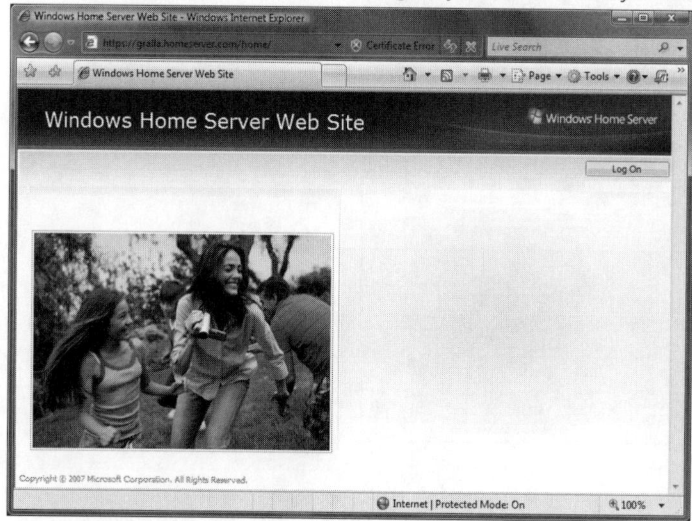

Figure 9-23.
The Computers tab lets you run the Windows Home Server Console remotely, or control computers connected to your network

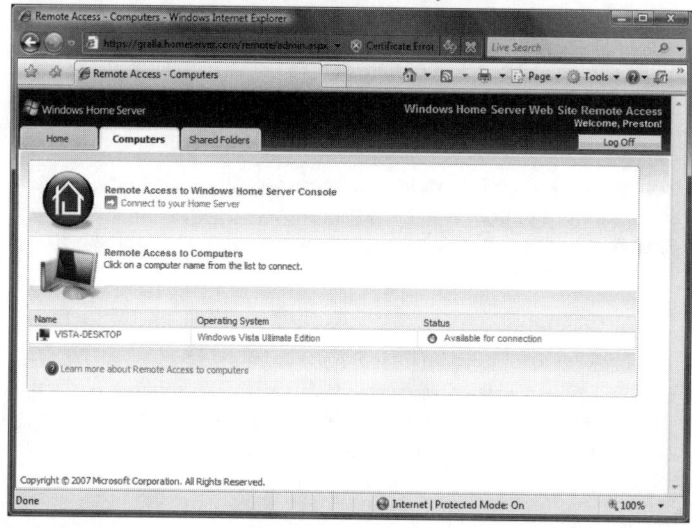

router to router, so check your model's documentation. In this example, I'll show you how to do it for the Linksys router model WRT54GX4.

First, find out the internal IP address of your home server. On any PC on your network, open a command prompt, type net view, and press Enter. After you do, you'll see something like the following:

```
C:\Users\Preston>net view
Server Name            Remark
-------------------------------------------------------------------------------
\\PRESTONSERVER
\\VISTA-DESKTOP
\\VISTA-LAPTOP
The command completed successfully.
```

Figure 9-24.
Congratulations—you've logged into your Windows Home Server

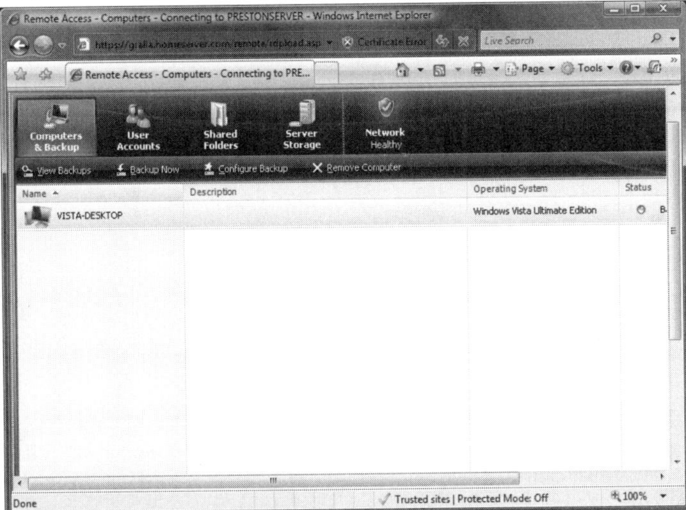

Look for the name of your Windows Home Server, the name you gave it when you first set it up, or that came as part of the default setup. In this instance, it's PRESTONSERVER.

Now at the command line issue the ping command, followed by the name of your home server, like this: ping PRESTONSERVER

The results will look something like this:

```
C:\Users\Preston>ping PRESTONSERVER

Pinging PRESTONSERVER [192.168.1.103] with 32 bytes of data:

Reply from 192.168.1.103: bytes=32 time<1ms TTL=128
Reply from 192.168.1.103: bytes=32 time<1ms TTL=128
Reply from 192.168.1.103: bytes=32 time<1ms TTL=128
Reply from 192.168.1.103: bytes=32 time<1ms TTL=128

Ping statistics for 192.168.1.103:
    Packets: Sent = 4, Received = 4, Lost = 0 (0% loss),
Approximate round trip times in milli-seconds:
    Minimum = 0ms, Maximum = 0ms, Average = 0ms
```

Note the number after Reply from. That's your router's IP address on your network. Write it down; you'll need it in order to configure port forwarding. In this case, it's 192.168.1.103.

If you have Windows Vista on any of the PCs connected to your network, there's an easy way to find out the IP address of your Windows Home Server. First select Control Panel→Network. A list of all devices on your network appears. Right-click your Windows Home Server and select Properties. At the bottom of the screen, in the Troubleshooting Information section, you'll see the server's IP address. Windows XP doesn't have this capability—when you right-click the server from My Network Places, it doesn't display the IP address.

Now you'll need to tell your router to forward all connections from ports 80, 443, and 4125 to the IP address 192.168.1.103. How you do this varies from router to router. In this example, I use a Linksys router, model WRT54GX4 Check your router's documentation for details on how to do it.

QUICK HACK

RUN INCOMPATIBLE PROGRAMS IN WINDOWS VISTA

Got a program that won't run in Windows Vista? Try this trick. Right-click the program's executable file, and select Properties. Click the Compatibility tab, and select Run This Program in Compatibility Mode. From the drop-down list that appears, choose the operating system you used before upgrading to Vista (or choose the operating system on which the program was designed to run). If you need to, select the option to run the program as an administrator. Click OK, and the program may run correctly now.

Log into your administrator's screen by going to http://192.168.1.1 (the address may be different depending on your router model and network configuration) in your browser, and typing in your user name and password. (The default is no user name, and admin as the password, but you should change this so that other people can't modify your router's configuration.) Choose Applications & Gaming→Port Range Forwarding. Fill in the form you see (see Figure 5-4 **[Hack #68]**). For the application, name, use something like Home Server; it doesn't really matter what name you give it. For the first line, in both Start and End, type in 80, and select BOTH from the drop-down list. For IP address, type in the last number of whatever IP address your home server has—in this example, it's 103. Check the Enable box. Do the same for two more lines: one for port 443, and one for port 4125. Click Save Settings. You're done. You can now continue with the rest of the instructions for setting up the remote connection and logging in, as outlined earlier in this hack.

You've now made the connection, and can use your home server as if you were on the internal network, and gain access to shared folders, and more. In fact, as you'll see in the next hack, you can take command of any computer on your network as well.

If the internal IP address of your Windows Home Server changes for any reason, you'll have to go through these steps again, using the new IP address. Why would the IP address change? If you restart your router, for example, the IP address will change. To get around this problem, you might want to assign your Windows Home Server a static IP address. For details on how to assign a static IP address to a computer, see your router's documentation.

See Also

- "Give the World Access to a Server or PC Behind your Home Router" **[Hack #68]**
- "Give Your Home Server a Hostname" **[Hack #69]**
- "Control Another Windows XP PC with Remote Access" **[Hack #73]**
- "Control Another Windows Vista PC with Remote Access" **[Hack #74]**

HACK 130: Take Remote Command of a PC Using Windows Home Server

V XP You've made the connection to your Windows Home Server—now what? You can take total control over any PC connected to it, just as if you were sitting at its keyboard.

Making a remote connection to your home server is useful for gaining access to its shared folders and to the Windows Server Home Console. But there's an even better reason to make the connection: you can control any PC connected to it, just as if you were sitting at the keyboard.

First, you need to enable a remote connection on the PC to which you want to connect. For details, see **[Hack #73]** (XP) or **[Hack #74]** (Vista).

You won't be able to remotely connect to PCs that run the Windows XP Home edition; only Windows XP Professional has the Windows XP Remote Server required for remote connections. The same is true for home editions of Vista; you will need one of the more advanced editions for this.

Now, make a connection to your home server **[Hack #129]**. Then click the Computers tab. You'll come to a screen like the one shown in Figure 9-25, which lists all the computers attached to your server, and shows whether you've enabled remote access to them.

Click the computer to which you want to connect remotely. A screen will appear, like that shown in Figure 9-26, with various options for your connection, including whether you want to connect at full screen size or a different size, whether you want to allow files to be transferred between computers, and so on. Be aware that if you select Full Screen for your size, you'll only be able to run the remote

Figure 9-25.
You can connect to any PC connected to your home server

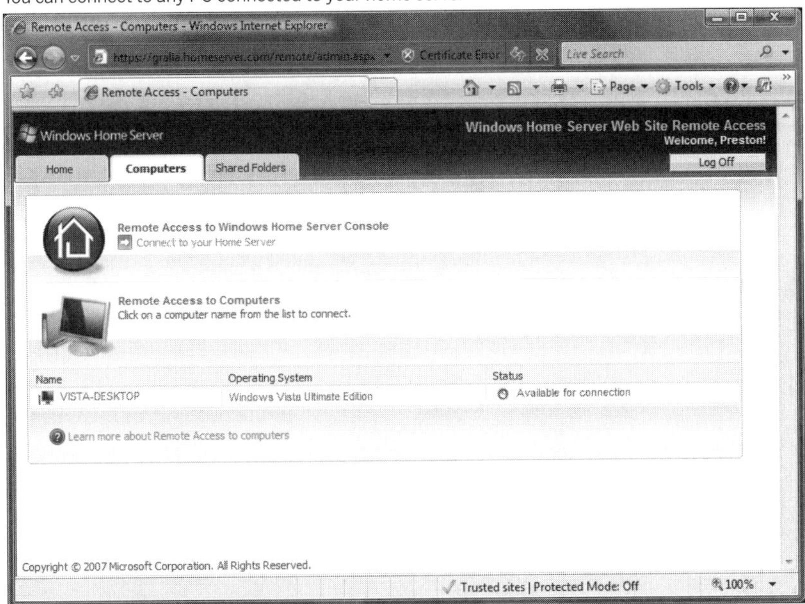

Figure 9-26.
Click OK to make the connection

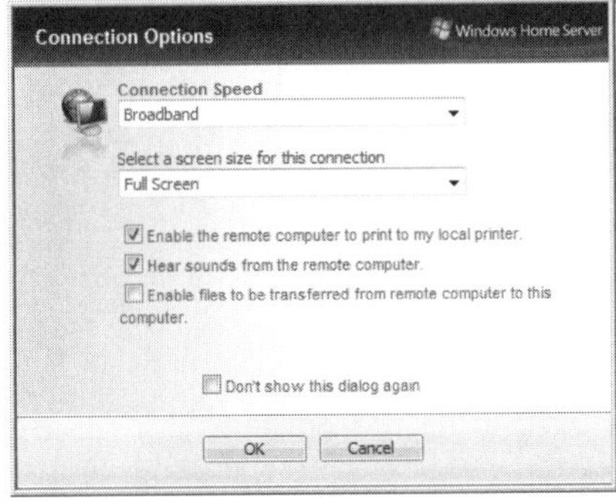

connection full screen or completely minimized—it won't run as a normal window. Also, under connection speed, you may notice there are two selections, Broadband and Modem. It's not a good idea to connect over a modem; the remote connection will be agonizingly slow. Make your choices and click OK.

A warning pops up asking if you trust the PC to which you're about to connect. Click Yes. You'll now make a connection to the PC and can control it using it as if you were sitting at the keyboard (see **[Hack #73]** and **[Hack #74]** for more details, including screenshots)..

See Also

- "Make a Remote Connection to Windows Home Server Over the Internet" **[Hack #129]**
- "Give the World Access to a Server or PC Behind your Home Router" **[Hack #68]**
- "Give Your Home Server a Hostname" **[Hack #69]**

BACKUP HACKS

Backups are the classic example of the thing you don't want to do, but you know that you should. The hacks in this section make it a lot easier—you might even look forward to it!

HACK 131: Hacking Windows Vista Backups

V Windows Vista's built-in backup program leaves much to be desired. Still, there are ways you can wring usefulness out of it.

There's no two ways about it: Windows Vista's backup program is a seriously stupid piece of work. It may be pretty to look at and simple to use, but it lacks some very basic features, as you'll see in this hack. Still, though, it's built into the operating system, it's free, and there are some ways you can improve it. So if you've looked at it once and decided never to use it again, it's time to take a second look.

In Windows Vista, you must initiate all your backup jobs from the Backup and Restore Center. Get there by choosing Control Panel→System and Maintenance→Backup and Restore Center. It's shown in Figure 9-27.

What you'll actually see here, and what you can do here, will vary according to the version of Windows Vista you use. Windows Vista Home Basic includes no backup program at all, so you can't even get here from there. And Windows Vista Home Premium doesn't include Windows Complete

Figure 9-27.
Windows Vista's Backup and Restore Center

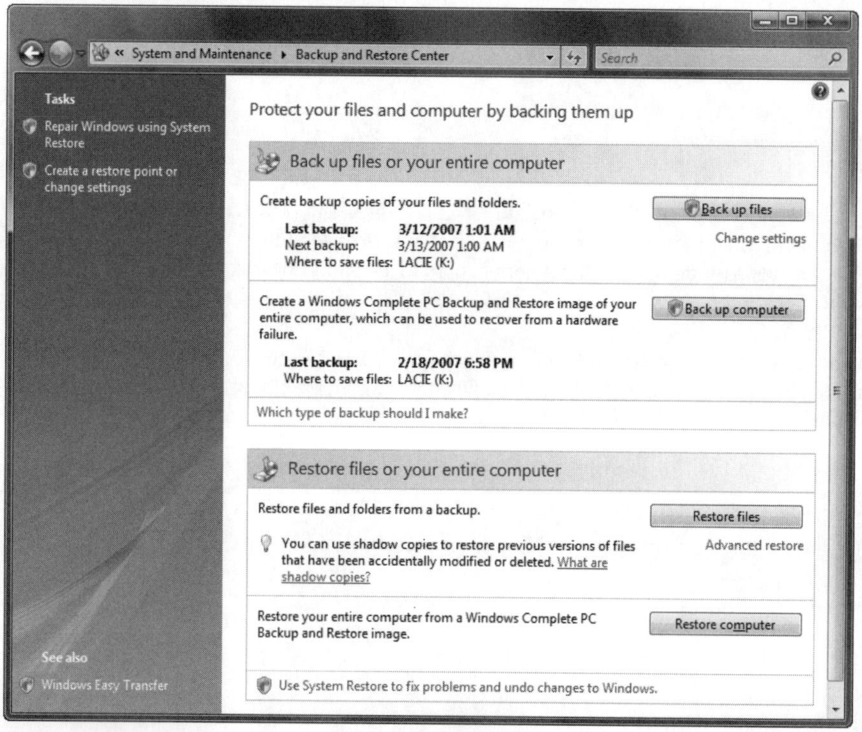

PC Backup, so you won't see that feature if you have Windows Vista Home Premium (or Home Basic, of course).

 If you're a user of a home version of Windows Vista, you can still back up your PC using Microsoft software using Windows XP's Ntbackup **[Hack #132]**.

If you have Windows Complete PC Backup, use it. This is one of Windows Vista's great overlooked features. It creates a snapshot of your PC, including all the system files and applications you've installed. That way, if your system ever goes down the tubes, or your hard disk crashes, you can re-create it with just a few clicks. It's a good idea to create a new snapshot every several months, so that you always have the latest snapshot, ready to rebuild in case disaster hits. Click "Back up computer", and follow the wizard to back it up.

The real problem with backup is the basic program, which you run by clicking "Back up files". Using the program is simple enough; click "Back up files" and a wizard launches, guiding you through the process of creating a backup. So far, so good; what could be easier?

The problem isn't with how easy it is to create a backup; it's how stupidly Windows Vista handles it. Here's the crux of the problem: you can't specify that only certain folders be backed up. You can't specify that only certain *files* be backed up. And you can't specify that only certain file *types* be backed up.

Let's say, for example, that you want to back up 40 or 50 MB of *.doc* files, *.jpg* files, and *.zip* files in some folders but not others. Instead, you have to back up every single datafile, every single graphics file, and every single compressed file on your entire hard disk—and that includes the files that make up Windows, which includes plenty of graphics and compressed files. So you'll have to back up several hundred megabytes of files you will never use and never want to back up, just to back up those 40 to 50 MB of files.

The offending screen is pictured in Figure 9-28, and it's the second screen you'll see after you click "Back up files". (The first asks where you want to back up to.)

Figure 9-28.
Your choices are limited when backing up with Windows Vista's built-in backup program

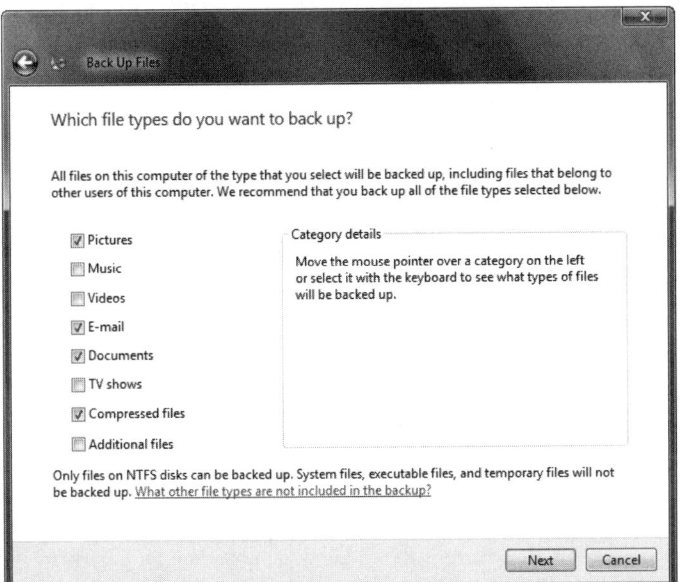

You can only choose to back up broad file types, such as Compressed files or Pictures. Compressed files, though, include not just *.zip* files, which you're likely to want to back up, but also many other compressed file types, such as *.cab* files. The problem is that Windows, as well as many applications, often stores very large *.cab* files on your hard disk, and these files are often only necessary for installing an application or operating system, but are not your data files. They're also often very, very large. So you will end up backing up hundreds of megabytes of unnecessary files just to store some *.zip* files.

Don't try creating a backup or changing backup settings if you're using a laptop running on a battery: it won't work. Windows Vista won't let you do it until you plug in your power cord.

Does this mean you shouldn't use Windows Vista's built-in backup? Not necessarily. There are some ways you can make it more useful:

Get a big, removable USB drive

The big problem with backup is that you will back up hundreds of megabytes of unnecessary files. But if you get a very big removable hard drive, that doesn't matter. Those files will only be backed up once. From then on, only your data files will be backed up. As of this writing, if you look around, you can find a removable USB drive with 500 GB of storage for around $200. As you read this, you may be able to find them for less. At that price, who cares if you waste a few hundred megabytes of space?

Convert the drive to NTFS

You can only back up to an NTFS drive. If your USB drive is not an NTFS drive, you can convert it to NTFS before using it. To do it, type `cmd` at the Search box in the Start menu, then right-click the icon that appears at the top of the search results, and select "Run as administrator". At the command prompt window, type `convert drive: /fs:ntfs`, where `drive` is the letter of the drive you want to convert. Then press Enter. So, for example, if your USB drive is drive E:, type `convert E: /fs:ntfs`.

Bypass the restore screen

To restore files you backed up, you click Restore files, then work your way through a wizard to restore your files. But if you want, you can restore files directly yourself. Your backups are stored using *.zip* compression, and you can browse through the zipped folders to find the file you want. Open Windows Explorer, go to the location where your files were backed up, and look for the backup folder. Look for a folder with the name of your computer, and then in that folder, look for a folder that starts with the name *Backup Set* and may be followed by the date you first created the backup, and then with some random numbers. So the location may be *K:\VISTA-DESKTOP\Backup Set 2007-02-18 181314* for example. Go into that folder, and look for a folder that starts with *Backup Files*, and then has today's date and numbers, for example, *\Backup Files 2007-03-12 010000*. Inside that folder, you'll see a zipped folder, such as *Backup files 1.zip*. Open that folder, and you'll be able to browse through the most recent files that were backed up. Open any you want to restore, and save it to a location of your choice.

Back up late at night

When you first set up your backup, you're asked whether to automatically create backups on a schedule. It's a good idea to do this and to back up at least weekly. If your data is vital, back up every day. Your best bet is to back up at night, or whenever you're not using your PC.

HACK 132: Use Windows XP's Ntbackup in Windows Vista

V Windows Vista's backup features are a step backwards from Windows XP's Ntbackup program. Go back to the future by running Ntbackup on Windows Vista.

Windows Vista's new backup feature in the Backup and Restore Center (Figure 9-29) is very easy to use. It's also very, very dumb [Hack #131]. How dumb? Let me count the ways. You can't back up individual folders and files: you'll have to back up an entire preset group of them. You can't back up

Figure 9-29.
Windows Vista's Backup and Restore Center: Very pretty, and very dumb

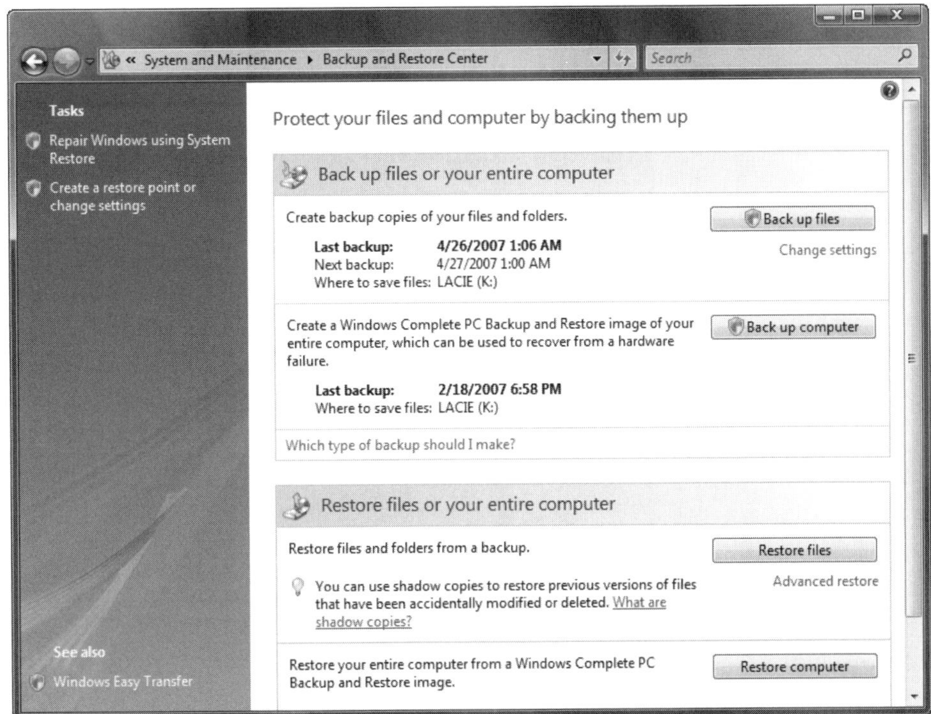

individual file types: again, you have to back up an entire group of them. So, for example, if you want to back up *.doc* and *.jpg* files in your *Budget* folder, you can't do that. Instead, you'll have to back up every single document and every single graphic file on your entire hard disk, including graphics files that are part of Windows itself. That could mean backing up multiple hundreds of megabytes of files, when all you want to back up is a few megabytes.

If you have a copy of Windows XP Professional laying around, there's a simple solution to the problem—install Windows XP's Ntbackup program on Windows Vista and use it there.

First create a new folder on your Windows Vista machine under *C:\Program Files*, for example, *C:\Program Files\Ntbackup*. Go to your Windows XP machine, and from the *C:\Windows\System32* folder, copy these files into *C:\Program Files\Ntbackup* on your Vista machine:

Ntbackup.exe

Ntmsapi.dll

Vssapi.dll

 If you want to get help for Ntbackup when you're using Windows Vista, copy these files from *C:\Windows\Help* on your Windows XP machine to *C:\Program Files\Ntbackup* on your Vista machine: *Ntbackup.chm* and *Ntbackup.hlp*.

Before you use Ntbackup, you'll have to install and turn on Windows Vista's Removable Storage Management feature. Select Control Panel→Programs→"Turn Windows Features on or off". Check the box next to Removable Storage Management (Figure 9-30), and click OK. Windows will take a short while to configure the feature. You'll have to restart for the change to take effect.

You can now double-click *Ntbackup.exe* to run the program. If you'd prefer to make it easier to run the program, you can pin it to the Start Menu, add it to the Quick Launch toolbar, or create a shortcut to it and place that shortcut on your desktop. Right-click *Ntbackup.exe*, and choose one of these options. Figure 9-31 shows it pinned to the Start Menu.

Figure 9-30.
Turning on Removable Storage Management

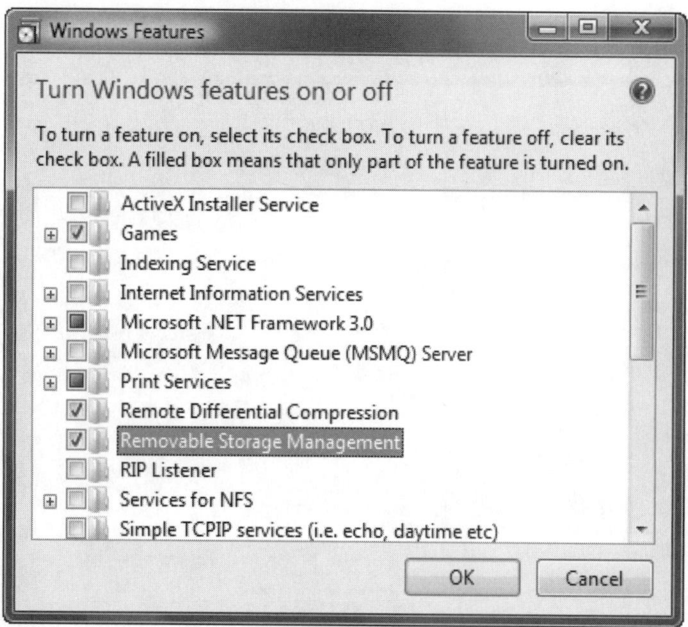

Figure 9-31.
Ntbackup waiting for you on the Start Menu

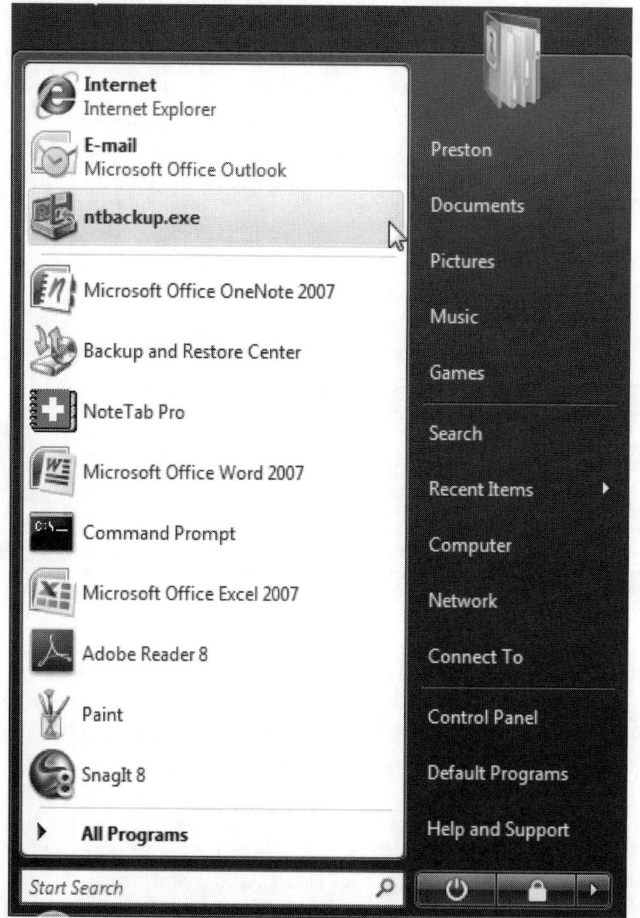

Figure 9-32.
Running Ntbackup in Windows Vista

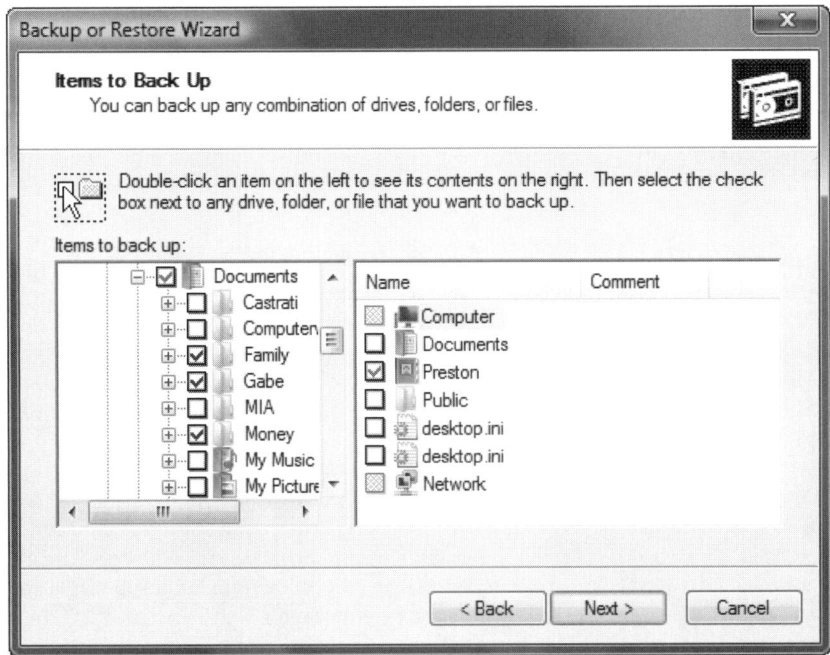

Now you're ready to use Ntbackup. Run it just as you would normally in Windows XP. Figure 9-32 shows it in action.

Hacking the Hack

One good use of Ntbackup is to restore files from a backup you've made on a Windows XP machine—but restore them to your Windows Vista machine. So if you've backed up your Windows XP machine, for example, then realize you need a file from that backup on a Windows Vista machine, you can install Ntbackup, insert your DVD or other media with the backup on it, then restore files from the *.bkf* file.

If the only reason you're installing Ntbackup on your Windows Vista machine is to restore files from a Windows XP backup, there's a simpler solution. You can install Microsoft's free Windows NT Backup-Restore Utility. Get it from tinyurl.com/3chdfk.

HACK 133: Best Backup Plans for Your PC

V XP Backing up isn't hard to do, as long as you've devised a comprehensive plan. Follow this advice, and your data will always be safe.

Maintaining a good set of backups is a critical part of preventative maintenance.

The availability of inexpensive hard drives and motherboards that support RAID 1 mirroring leads many people to depend solely on RAID 1 to protect their data. That's a very bad idea. RAID 1 protects only against the failure of a hard drive, which is partial protection at best. RAID 1 does nothing to protect against:

- Data being corrupted by viruses or hardware problems
- Accidentally deleting, overwriting, or modifying important files
- Catastrophic data loss, such as fire or theft of your equipment

To protect against those and other threats, the only reliable solution is to make backup copies of your data periodically to some form of removable media, such as tapes, optical discs, or removable hard drives.

Backup Hardware

In the past, there weren't any really good hardware choices for backing up home and small office/home office (SOHO) systems. Tape drives were expensive, complex to install and configure, used fragile and expensive media, and were painfully slow. CD writers, although reasonably fast and inexpensive, stored such a small amount of data that many people who used them for backing up were reminded of the Bad Olde Days of swapping floppy disks. External hard drives were expensive and of dubious reliability.

Things have changed. Consumer-grade tape drives are still expensive and slow, although it's easier to install a modern ATAPI tape drive than it was in the days when tape drives used SCSI or proprietary interfaces. CD writers are still reasonably fast and inexpensive, and are a good solution if your data fits on one or two CDs. The most significant change in consumer-grade backup hardware has been the introduction of inexpensive DVD writers and external or removable hard drives. Table 9-2 lists the important characteristics of the types of backup hardware used for home and SOHO backups.

Table 9-2. Important characteristics of backup hardware

METHOD	CAPACITY	TRANSFER RATE	DRIVE COST	MEDIA COST/GB	MEDIA COST/UNIT	RELIABILITY
CD writer	0.65 to 1 GB	Medium	$20 to $50	$0.10 to $0.40	$0.10 to $0.25	Low
Internal DVD writer	4.4 to 8.5 GB	Medium to fast	$40 to $150	$0.05 to $0.50	$0.50 to $4.00	Low
External DVD writer	4.4 to 8.5 GB	Medium to fast	$125 to $250	$0.05 to $0.50	$0.50 to $4.00	Low
External hard drive	80 to 500 GB	Very fast	N/A	$0.50 to $1.00	$100 to $500	Medium
Removable hard drive	80 to 500 GB	Very fast	$75 to $150	$0.40 to $0.80	$75 to $400	Medium
Tape drive	10 to 100 GB	Slow to medium	$200 to $2,000	$0.30 to $5.00	$5 to $150	High
USB hard drive	80 to 500 GB	Medium to fast	$75 to $250	$0.40 to $0.50	N/A	Medium

In addition to cost considerations, you face two issues in choosing backup hardware: capacity and speed. Ideally, the hardware you choose should be capacious enough to store the entire contents of your hard drive—or at least all of your user data—on one disc or tape. Just as important, the backup hardware should be fast enough to complete a full backup and verify in whatever time you have available for backups. It's easy to meet both those requirements if you have an unlimited budget, but most of us have to compromise one or the other to avoid breaking the bank.

For most home and SOHO users, a DVD writer is the best compromise. For $100 or less (possibly much less), you can buy an internal DVD writer and a supply of discs sufficient to implement a comprehensive backup plan. If you have multiple nonnetworked systems or notebooks to back up, you can use an external USB/FireWire DVD writer to back them all up individually.

The capacity of a writable DVD—4.4 GB for single layer and 8.5 GB for dual-layer—suffices for many systems (we'll explain why shortly). Writing and verifying a full disc takes only a few minutes, which makes it practical to back up frequently, even several times during a work day. The only downside to writable DVD is that optical discs have much less robust error correction than tapes, which means there's a small chance that a file won't be recoverable from a backup DVD. That's an easy problem to solve, though. Simply back up more frequently, and keep your older backup discs. If you can't recover the file from the current disc, you'll be able to recover it from the one immediately preceding.

Disc versus tape: We're belt-and-suspenders types when it comes to protecting our data. Before affordable DVD writers became available, we backed up our own systems every day with Travan and DDS tape drives. And we admit that the less robust error correction of optical discs initially gave us pause. But we converted a couple years ago to using DVD+R and DVD+RW for backups, and we haven't looked back. We use top-quality discs (Verbatim premium) and have never had a problem recovering a file. Tape still has its place in corporate data centers, but as far as we're concerned, it's obsolete for home and SOHO users.

If DVD isn't capacious enough, consider using external, removable, or USB hard drives, which store from 80 GB to 500+ GB. In either case, think of the hard drive as the media rather than as a drive. In other words, an external or removable hard drive is really just a funny-looking tape or disc, which you treat just as you would any other removable backup medium. Just as you need several discs or tapes for a good backup rotation, you'll also need several external or removable hard drives. In terms of reliability, hard drives are intermediate between tapes and optical discs. Hard drives have more robust error detection and correction than optical discs but are less robust than tape. Once again, this needn't be of concern if you back up to multiple external/removable hard drives. If you can't recover a file from one, you'll be able to recover it from another.

Advice from Ron Morse about backups: Make sure your latest hardware and software upgrades don't leave your archived data behind. At one time I did most of my backing up to an external CDC SCSI hard drive. At 80 MB, it wouldn't hold the system or application files (I had the original installation media for that). but it was big enough to hold my personal data until things got to the point where it wasn't. The drive got demoted to archive status and fell out of regular service. Didn't think about it too much.

One day I built myself a new machine that didn't have an SCSI adapter because the new machine didn't have any SCSI devices. The old machine got sold to some unsuspecting party. Then one day I needed to access the archive. I *really* needed to access the archive. Duh. Expensive lesson. This applies to software, too. If you have a lot of important data in a proprietary file format, possession of the files themselves is only half the challenge. You need to be able to read them, too. (Insert commercial for open file standards here.)

Organizing Your Data Directory Structure

If you back up to hard drives, you can back up your entire drive every time. If you use a DVD writer, you'll probably do full backups infrequently, with routine backups only of your data files. In that case, it's important to organize your data directories to make it as easy as possible to back up only your data while making sure that you back up all your data. The trick here is to segregate your data into groups that can be backed up with different frequencies.

For example, our data, excluding audio and video files, totals about 30 GB. Obviously, it's impractical to back up that much data to DVDs routinely. Fortunately, it's not necessary to back it all up every time. Much of that data is historical stuff—books we wrote years ago (and that we may update sometime), old email, and so on. That all needs to be backed up, but it's not necessary to back it up every day or even every month. So we segregate our data into subdirectories of three top-level directories:

Data

This top-level directory contains our current working data—email, current book projects, recent digital camera images, and so on. This directory is backed up every day to DVD, and frequently throughout the day to mirror directories on other systems on our network. We never allow this directory to grow larger than will fit on one DVD.

QUICK HACK 

ADD APPLICATION ICONS TO THE QUICK LAUNCH TOOLBAR

The easiest way to run your favorite application may be to put it on the Quick Launch Toolbar just to the right of the Windows Start button. In Windows Vista, open Windows Explorer, right-click the program's executable file, and choose Add to Quick Launch. In Windows XP, you'll have to drag the program to the Quick Launch toolbar manually.

Archive

This top-level directory contains all our old data: files that we may not need from one month to the next, or even from one year to the next. This directory is backed up to multiple redundant sets of DVDs, two of which are stored off-site. Each backup set currently requires six DVDs. Every time we add data to the archive directories, which doesn't happen often, we burn several new sets of backup DVDs. (We keep the old discs, too, but then we're packrats.)

Holding

This top-level directory is intermediate between our working data directories and our archive directories. When the size of our working data directories approaches what will fit on one DVD, usually every two or three months, we sweep older files to the holding directory and burn new copies of the holding directory to DVD. By doing this, we can keep our working data directory at a manageable size, but not have to redo the archive directory backups very often. We also keep the size of this directory to what will fit on one DVD. When it approaches that size, we sweep everything in the holding directory to the archive directory and burn a new set of archive DVDs.

When you plan your data directory structure, it's also important to consider these aspects:

1. The importance of the data
2. How difficult it would be to reconstruct the data
3. How often the data changes

In combination, these three factors determine how often data needs to be backed up, how many generations of backup copies you'll want to retain, and therefore where the data belongs in your directory structure. For example, your financial records and digital photographs are probably critically important to you, difficult or impossible to reconstruct if lost, and change frequently. Those files need to be backed up frequently, and you'll probably want to maintain several generations of backup copies. Those files belong in your working data directories.

Conversely, if you've ripped your CD collection to MP3s, those files are neither important nor difficult to reconstruct because you can simply re-rip the CDs if necessary. Although these files might reasonably be classified as data, chances are you'll categorize them as data that never needs to be backed up and therefore locate them somewhere in your directory structure outside the directories that are routinely backed up.

QUICK HACK 

YOU CAN NEVER BE TOO WELL BACKED UP

Whatever backup means and methods you use, keep the following in mind and you won't go far wrong:

- Back up frequently, particularly data that is important or hard to reconstruct.
- Verify backups to ensure that they are readable and that you can recover the data from them.
- Maintain multiple backup sets, for redundancy and to permit recovering older versions of files.
- Consider using a data-rated firesafe or media safe for on site storage.
- Store a recent backup set off-site, and rotate it regularly.

Although online backup services (including using Google's Gmail for ad hoc backup storage) are reasonable choices for supplemental backups, we suggest that you not use them as your primary form of backup. There are too many things that can go wrong, from your (or their) Internet connection being down to server problems at the hosting company,

continued on next page...

Developing a Backup Rotation Scheme

Whatever backup hardware you use, it's important to develop an appropriate backup rotation scheme. A good rotation scheme requires half a dozen or more discs, tapes, or drives, and allows you to:

- Recover a recent copy of any file easily and quickly
- Recover multiple generations of a file
- Maintain multiple copies of your data for redundancy and historical granularity
- Store at least one copy of your data off-site to protect against catastrophic data loss

The most popular backup rotation scheme, and the one most suitable for backups to DVD+RW discs, is called Grandfather-Father-Son (GFS). To use this backup rotation, label the following discs:

- Five (or six) daily discs, labeled Monday through Friday (or Saturday).
- Five weekly discs, labeled Week 1 through Week 5.
- Twelve monthly discs, labeled January through December.

Back up each working day to the appropriate daily disc. On Sunday, back up to whichever numbered weekly disc corresponds to the number of that Sunday in the month. On the first (or last) of each month, back up to the monthly disc. This method gives you daily granularity for the preceding week, weekly granularity for the preceding month, and monthly granularity for the preceding year. For most home and SOHO users, that scheme is more than sufficient.

You can, of course, modify the standard GFS rotation in whatever way is suitable to your needs. For example, rather than writing your weekly or monthly backups to a DVD+RW disc that will eventually be overwritten, you can write those backups to DVD+R (write-once) discs and archive them. Similarly, there's nothing to prevent you from making a second backup disc every week or every month and archiving it off-site.

If you're backing up to external or removable hard drives, you probably won't want to use the standard GFS rotation, which would require 22 hard drives. Fortunately, you can use fewer drives without significantly compromising the reliability of your backup system. Most removable hard drives have room for at least two or three full backups, if you back up your entire hard drive or a dozen or more data-only backups.

You still don't want to keep all your eggs in one basket, but it's reasonable to limit the number of baskets to as few as two or three. The trick is to make sure that you alternate the use of the drives so that you don't end up with all of your recent backups on one drive and only older backups on another. For example, if you decide to use only two external or removable hard drives for backup, label one of them M-W-F and the other Tu-Th-S, and alternate your daily backups between the two drives. Similarly, label one of the drives 1-3-5 and the other 2-4 for your weekly backups, and one drive J-M-M-J-S-N and the other F-A-J-A-O-D for your monthly backups.

continued from previous page...

to the company going out of business with no notice. When you need your backups, you need them *right now*. Keep your primary backups within easy reach.

Choosing Backup Software

There are four broad categories of software that can be used for backing up. Each has advantages and drawbacks, and which is best for you depends on your needs and preferences.

System utilities

System utilities such as xcopy are free, flexible, easy to use, can be scripted, and create backups that are directly readable without a restore operation. They do not, however, typically provide compression or any easy way to do a binary compare on each file that has been copied, and they can write only to a mounted device that's visible to the operating system as a drive. (In other words, you can't use them to write to an optical disc unless you're running packet-writing software that causes that disc to appear to the operating system as a drive.)

CD/DVD burning applications

CD/DVD burning applications, such as Nero Burning ROM (www.nero.com) are fast, can create directly readable backup copies, and generally offer robust binary verify features, but may not offer compression. Most also have little or no ability to filter by file selection criteria, such as, "back up only files that have changed today." Of course, CD/DVD burning applications have other uses, such as duplicating audio CDs and video DVDs, and chances are that you already have a burning application installed. If so, and if the burning application suits your requirements, you can use it rather than buying another application just for backing up.

Traditional backup applications

Traditional backup applications such as BackUp MyPC (www.stompsoft.com) do only one thing, but they do it very well. They are fast, flexible, have robust compression and verification options, support nearly any type of backup media, and allow you to define standard backup procedures using scripting, detailed file selection criteria, and saved backup sets. If your needs are simple, the bundled Windows XP backup applet **[Hack #132]**, which is a stripped-down version of Veritas Backup Exec (since sold and renamed BackUp MyPC) may suffice. Otherwise, we think the commercial BackUp MyPC is the best option for Windows users.

Disk imaging applications

Disk imaging applications, such as Acronis True Image (www.acronis.com) produce a compressed image of your hard drive, which can be written to a hard drive, optical disc, or tape. Although they are less flexible than a traditional backup application, disk imaging applications have the inestimable advantage of providing disaster recovery features. For example, if your hard drive fails and you have a current disk image, you needn't reinstall Windows and all your applications (including the backup application) and then restore your data. Instead, you simply boot the disaster recovery disc and let 'er rip. Your system will be back to its original state in minutes rather than hours.

We use three of these four software types on our own network. Several times a day, we do what we call "xcopy backups"—even though we now run Linux instead of Windows—to make quick copies of our current working data to other systems on the network. We use a CD/DVD burning application, K3b for Linux in our case, to run our routine backups to DVDs. And, when we're about to tear a system down to repair or upgrade it, we run an image backup with Acronis True Image, just in case the worst happens.

— *Robert Bruce Thompson and Barbara Fritchman Thompson, from* Repairing & Upgrading Your PC

HACK 134: Control How Much Disk Space Windows Vista Uses for System Restore

V Unlike Windows XP, Windows Vista doesn't let you change how much space to devote to System Restore point . . . that is, unless you use this hidden secret.

System Restore points and Shadow Copies can take up a great deal of space on a Windows Vista machine—easily 20 GB or more. That's a lot of space. In Windows XP, you can customize how much disk space to devote to System Restore by selecting Control Panel→Performance and Maintenance→System Restore→System Restore Settings, and then moving a slider to set the amount of space you want to use.

MAKE OFFICE 2007 LOOK LIKE EARLIER OFFICE VERSIONS

Microsoft Office 2007 introduced Ribbon, an entirely new interface for the office suite. If you'd like to make Office 2007 look like earlier versions of Office, try Toolbar Toggle (www.toolbartoggle.com), which lets you use the old Office toolbar, or else switch between the toolbar and the ribbon. It's free to try, and costs $19.95 if you want to continue using it.

Not so in Windows Vista. You appear to be stuck with whatever the operating system wants to devote to it. However, you can use the Volume Shadow Copy Administrative Command-Line Tool to change how much space you want System Restore and Shadow Copies to use.

Run the command prompt with administrative rights by typing cmd in the Search box on the Start menu, then pressing Ctrl-Shift-Enter. To see how much space you're currently using for System Restore and Shadow Copies, and the maximum space allotted to them, type `vssadmin List ShadowStorage` at the command line. It will display information for all your drives, like this:

```
C:\Windows\system32>vssadmin List ShadowStorage
vssadmin 1.1 - Volume Shadow Copy Service administrative command-line tool
(C) Copyright 2001-2005 Microsoft Corp.
Shadow Copy Storage association
   For volume: (C:)\\?\Volume{5ce7de75-bf86-11db-b994-806e6f6e6963}\
   Shadow Copy Storage volume: (C:)\\?\Volume{5ce7de75-bf86-11db-b994-806e6f6e6963}\
   Used Shadow Copy Storage space: 20.983 GB
   Allocated Shadow Copy Storage space: 21.645 GB
   Maximum Shadow Copy Storage space: 21.647 GB
Shadow Copy Storage association
   For volume: (K:)\\?\Volume{3c5c9930-bf71-11db-8775-00123f7dd66f}\
   Shadow Copy Storage volume: (K:)\\?\Volume{3c5c9930-bf71-11db-8775-00123f7dd66f}\
   Used Shadow Copy Storage space: 50.844 MB
   Allocated Shadow Copy Storage space: 2.246 GB
   Maximum Shadow Copy Storage space: 72.157 GB
```

To change the amount of space, used by System Restore and Shadow Copies, use the `vssadmin` command, with these switches and parameters:

```
vssadmin Resize ShadowStorage /on=drive: /For=drive: /Maxsize=size
```

The Maxsize parameter must be at least 300 MB. You can use these suffixes: KB, MB, GB, TB, when telling it how much memory to use.

 When you resize the amount of space you devote to System Restore and Shadow Copies, you may lose some or all of your Shadow Copies, so only do this if you know you don't need older Shadow Copies.

Let's say you want to set the maximum size devoted to System Restore and Shadow Copies to 5 GB, and you're using the C: drive. You'd enter this at the command line and press Enter:

```
vssadmin Resize ShadowStorage /On=C: /For=C: /Maxsize=5GB
```

That's it; you've just resized it.

Hacking the Hack

If you don't mind losing all of your old Restore Points and Shadow copies, you can get space back from System Restore without having to use the command line, by deleting all but the most recent Restore Point, using the Disk Cleanup Manager.

Type clean in the Search box or command prompt, and press Enter. Choose Files from All Users on This Computer from the screen that appears, and click OK. Select the appropriate drive from the screen that appears, and click OK. Windows will spend a little while calculating how much disk space it can regain by doing a cleanup, then displays the Disk Cleanup screen. Click the More Options tab, and a screen like that shown in Figure 9-33 appears.

Click the Clean Up button, and all but the most recent Restore Points will be deleted, saving you a substantial amount of disk space.

Figure 9-33.
Delete all but the most recent restore points from here

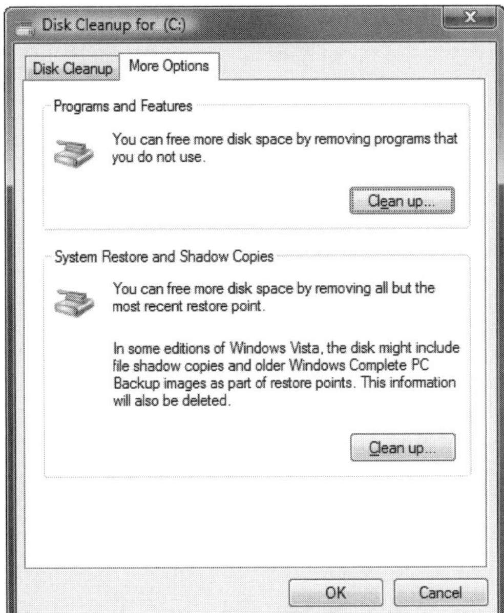

RETRO GAMING HACKS

Your Windows PC can be used for fun, too. And what better fun than a trip down memory lane?

HACK 135: Run 16-Bit DOS and Windows Applications

V XP Yes, you can run 16-bit applications, even in the 64-bit versions of Windows XP and Windows Vista.

Although 16-bit Windows and DOS applications are not common these days, you might feel the need to fire one of them up some day: many excellent retro games are DOS-only, and there are some vintage applications that still haven't quite died: WordPerfect for DOS still commands a following (see www.columbia.edu/~em36/wpdos/ if you don't believe me). There are a few programs, such as VisiCalc and Turbo C, that have been freed by their creators and are worth running just for history's sake.

Unfortunately, the 64-bit versions of Windows XP and Vista do not support 16-bit DOS or Windows applications at all. Even in 32-bit Vista, there are significant limitations: if you're running a WDDM driver, you can't put 16-bit DOS programs into full-screen mode (Microsoft KB article 926657 has detailed information on this).

And you can't rule out the possibility that some day down the road, after you're rich and famous and being sued by the IRS for back taxes, you'll come across a floppy disk with those short stories you wrote in Word 5.5 decades before your career took off—which your fans would pay anything to read today!

The simplest workaround is to use some kind of emulation to run these old applications. Although you could use VMware, Virtual PC, or Parallels to run DOS, that's overkill, and may in fact, run too fast for comfort, especially with older games. Instead, your best bet is DOSBox, which simulates an x86 computer running DOS, and is optimized for retro games. When you run DOSBox, it pops up a window that looks like the command prompt (see Figure 9-34), but is in fact a graphical application that can be run full screen if needed. It can also run graphical programs in a window without going full screen, which is something you couldn't do with the command prompt.

The Command Prompt is not COMMAND.COM: Although the Windows Command Prompt looks a lot like the old DOS shell COMMAND.COM, it's not. The Windows command prompt is a program called CMD.EXE, a full 32-bit application. It recognizes a lot of the same commands that COMMAND.COM does, but it can do much more. Use the HELP command to see a list of cool commands, and HELP `command-name` for more information. Type HELP FOR to see some impressive features.

COMMAND.COM is still there, at least on the 32-bit versions of Vista (you won't find it on the 64-bit version). You can use it if you need compatibility with older DOS programs, but DOSBox is much better, with support for popular audio cards, graphics modes, and better overall compatibility with older programs.

You can obtain DOSBox from dosbox.sourceforge.net. After you've installed it, you should edit the *dosbox.conf* file, which resides in the same directory where you installed DOSBox. Unless you need to change an advanced setting, you can leave everything alone except for the end of the file, where you should insert a command that mounts a directory on your hard drive as your DOSBox C: drive, and then switches to that drive. Create the directory *C:\DOSSTUFF*, and add these commands to the *dosbox.conf* file:

```
mount c C:\DOSSTUFF
C:
```

Figure 9-34.
DOSBox in action

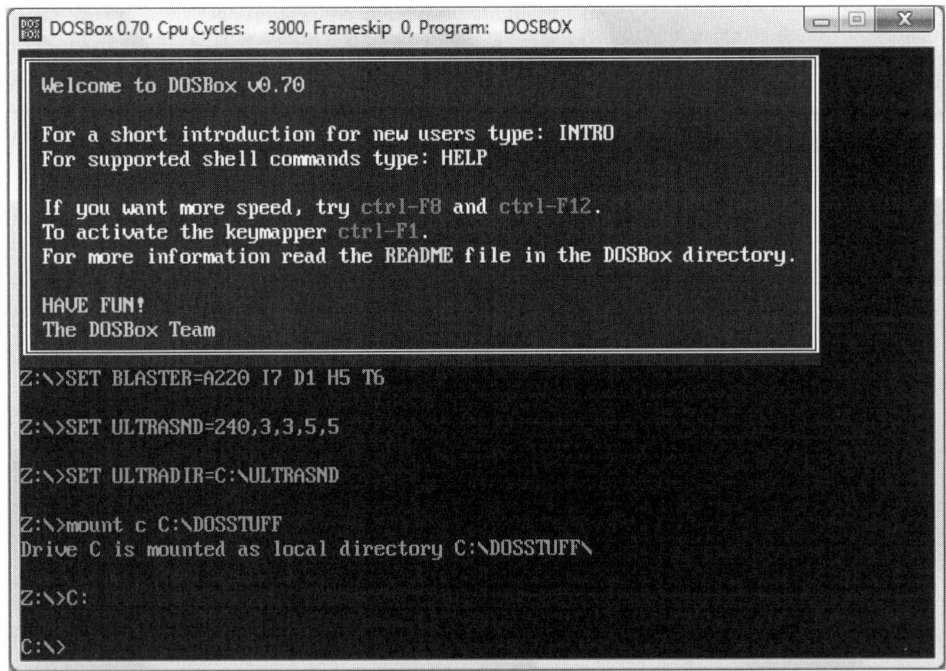

Next, run DOSBox. You'll be sitting at the C: drive, except it won't be the same C: drive as the one on your computer. Instead, it's everything in your *C:\DOSSTUFF* directory. If you have a program you want to run, put it in *C:\DOSSTUFF* or, if you're a neat freak, a subdirectory. If you have a program you need to install, put the install files in a subdirectory, open up DOSBox, and run the installer. For example, to install Borland Turbo C, you need to do the following:

1. Obtain Turbo C from dn.codegear.com/museum/antiquesoftware.

2. Exit DOSBox if it is running (you can type EXIT at the DOSBox prompt to close it).

3. Create a *TMP* subdirectory under *C:\DOSSTUFF*.

4. From Windows (using Explorer or the command prompt), put the installation files into *C:\DOSSTUFF\TMP*.

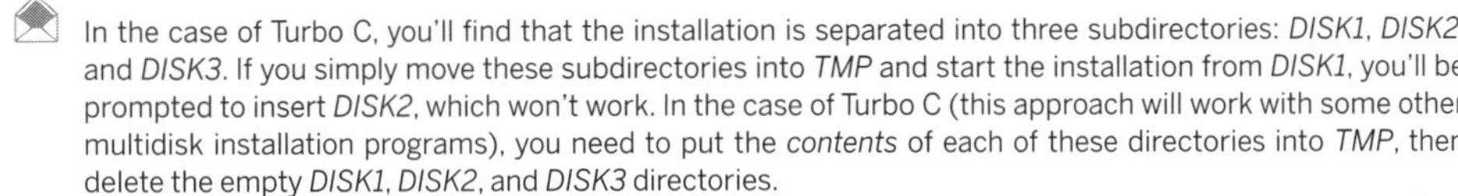
In the case of Turbo C, you'll find that the installation is separated into three subdirectories: *DISK1*, *DISK2*, and *DISK3*. If you simply move these subdirectories into *TMP* and start the installation from *DISK1*, you'll be prompted to insert *DISK2*, which won't work. In the case of Turbo C (this approach will work with some other multidisk installation programs), you need to put the *contents* of each of these directories into *TMP*, then delete the empty *DISK1*, *DISK2*, and *DISK3* directories.

5. Start up DOSBox, change directory to *TMP*, and run the installation program (*INSTALL.EXE* for Turbo C). Specify C as the source drive and *\TMP* as the source path, and install Turbo C to your hard drive.

Now you're ready to run Turbo C. Change directory to *C:\TC*, and run *TC* to launch Turbo C. Figure 9-35 shows a simple program being compiled in Turbo C.

Some Great DOS Games

Here are a few of the DOS games I have in my library. If you feel the urge to play them, look for CD-ROM compilations of these on eBay or in a nearby computer store's $10 bin. Some of these games can be found in GameTap's game subscription service (www.gametap.com), which doesn't require DOSBox at all.

The Ultimate Might and Magic Archives

The Ultimate Wizardry Archives

The Lost Treasures of Infocom

Ultima Collection

Also recommended are Sierra On-Line AGI games such as the King's Quest series, Gold Rush, and Leisure Suit Larry. For lots more DOS games, check out www.abandonia.com, which catalogs and reviews games from the golden age of PC gaming.

You can also enjoy some retro games without DOSBox if you extract the game data and run them under a modern remake of their game engine. For example, there are Inform interpreters such as Windows Frotz (www.d.kinder.btinternet.co.uk/frotz.html) that let you run Infocom games, for Sierra On-Line's AGI games, you need an AGI interpreter such as ScummVM (www.scummvm.org), and there are modern remakes of the game engines for Ultima 7 (exult.sourceforge.net) and Ultima IV (xu4.sourceforge.net). What's more, Ultima IV, considered by many to be the peak of the Ultima series, has been made freely available by its creators (see the xu4 project download pages for more information).

DOS Productivity Applications

It's harder to find word processors, database applications, and spreadsheet from the days of DOS, and people who have copies of these programs often command a high price. However, some publishers have made their programs available for free. Borland has made many of its DOS development tools available for free from dn.codegear.com/museum/antiquesoftware. The authors of VisiCalc, the original spreadsheet, have secured the rights to distribute it for free from www.bricklin.com/visicalc.htm. (If you check out only one vintage DOS application, it should be VisiCalc!) And even Microsoft has gotten into the fun; they've made Word 5.5 for DOS available for free from download.microsoft.com/download/word97win/Wd55_be/97/WIN98/EN-US/Wd55_ben.exe.

Figure 9-35.
Compiling "Hello, DOS" under Turbo C

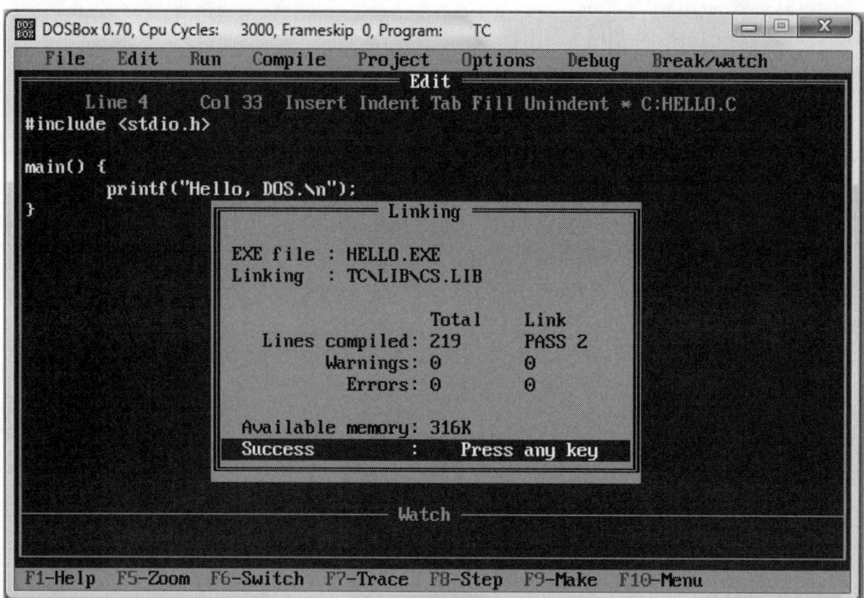

Hacking the Hack

You can also run Windows 3.11 under DOSBox, but you'll have to get your hands on it first. You can probably find it on eBay, a box somewhere in your attic, or at the flea market. If you have an MSDN subscription, you'll find that Microsoft still makes it available in the Operating Systems section of subscriber downloads. The MSDN version is easy to install: it comes as a self-extracting archive, *EN_WIN311.exe*, which you'll need to run under Windows to extract. Shut down DOSBox, delete the contents of *C:\DOSSTUFF\TMP*, and put the Windows 3.11 installation files into *C:\DOSSTUFF\TMP*. Start up DOSBox again, change the directory to *C:\TMP*, and run *SETUP.EXE*. This will give you a basic Windows installation as shown in Figure 9-36. For more information on setting up 16-bit Windows on DOSBox (including enabling higher resolution graphics, sound, and the Win32 subset), visit the DOSBox Guides forums at vogons.zetafleet.com/index.php. If you need a fully-functioning Windows 3.1x system, install it under a full-blown virtual machine **[Hack #32]**.

— Brian Jepson

HACK 136: Emulate the Nintendo Entertainment System on a PC

V XP Find the NES emulator that works best for you.

For some people, Nintendo Entertainment System emulation *is* emulation. It's the only console they've ever emulated; it's the only console they will ever emulate. Sure, they probably know that you can emulate other systems. They might have even messed around with an Atari 2600 emulator once or twice, just to see if it really worked. But that was probably only for a few minutes. NES emulators can suck up hours, days, weeks. (In fact, my "research" for this section took me way longer than I'd planned for.)

Figure 9-36.
Windows 3.11 running under DOSBox

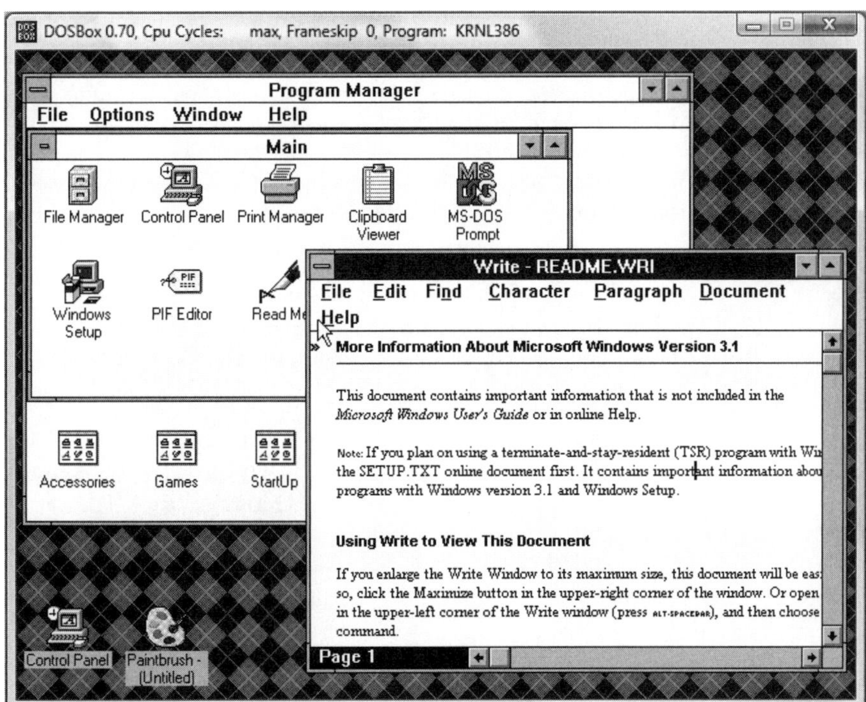

The numbers bear this theory out. While you're lucky to find one working emulator for certain classic game systems, the NES page at the emulation portal Zophar's Domain (www.zophar.net/nes.html) lists more than 75 different programs that run NES games on your home computer!

Thus, the challenge of getting started with NES emulation is not finding the programs: it's figuring out which one you should download. In this hack, I'll take a look at four emulators that are both popular and fully featured. Between these four, you should be able to find something that fits your needs.

The how-to segments of this hack will concentrate on the Windows versions of the emulators. Some of them also have DOS versions. In general, if you check Zophar's Domain you can get a good idea of what DOS emulators are out there.

I suggest that you use the web site PD Roms (www.pdroms.de) to find NES-compatible games that are freely distributed or in the public domain, such as the ones shown in the illustrations accompanying this hack.

RockNES

RockNES (rocknes.kinox.org) has been my emulator of choice for a while. It has that rare combination of being both full-featured and fast— games will run at full speed in a large (800 x 600): window with perfect sound on my three-year-old laptop, something that no other emulator on this list has accomplished. Installation is quick and painless—just download the Zip file, extract the files to a new directory, and then run *rocknesx.exe*. In Figure 9-37, you can see the emulator running the homebrew game Hot Seat Harry.

Even better, its GUI builds a ROM list for you that you can click and scroll through rather than having to click File→Open and then scroll through folders every time you want to load a new game. You can add as many directories as you want to the automatic search feature by clicking Options→Folders, and then the Add button. Then, on the main GUI window, you need only click View→Refresh Game List, and RockNES will search the folders you named for ROMs (which can be in the *.nes* format or zipped), building a handy list.

The reason that RockNES works so efficiently is because it adjusts the frame rate automatically based on your system's performance.

Though it's not likely, you may experience some sound issues: the audio might "pop" or stutter. If that's the case, you'll want to adjust the sound buffer. It's set at a default of 66 milliseconds. If you're having problems, raise this value by clicking Options→Audio Setup, and then moving the sliding bar to the right (towards "Safe"). You can also adjust the Audio Priority by clicking Options→Advanced, just be aware that this can have an adverse effect on your frame rate.

FCE Ultra

FCE Ultra (fceultra.sourceforge.net) is an open source project that has been ported to many other operating systems. It doesn't feature an elaborate GUI; in fact, when you first unzip it and run the *fceu.exe* file, all you'll see is a tiny black window. But it's a window to fun! Just look at FCE Ultra in Figure 9-38.

Since it doesn't feature RockNES' automatic frame-skipping routines, odds are that it will run slowly on your machine if the window size is anything over the standard 320x240. One thing you can do to increase the display size while speeding up emulation (which applies to all the emulators in this hack) is to display in Full Screen mode by hitting Alt-Enter. Note that if you put the emulator into Full Screen mode before you load up a ROM, you won't be able to do anything because you can't access the GUI in Full Screen.

FCE Ultra's claim to fame, besides a generally high level of compatibility and stability, is that it can emulate many different quirky controllers that were released for the Famicom and NES. You can

QUICK HACK 

NSF: NES SOUND FORMAT

If you're following along at home, you've probably noticed that NEStopia also supports a file format called NSF. Short for NES Sound Format, NSF files are basically like NES-format ROM files, but they contain only audio data. Among aficionados of video game music, listening to original sound tracks in NSF format has become quite preferable to MP3 and the like, since it faithfully reproduces the actual sounds of the NES while taking up only a miniscule amount of disk space.

What's more, though the NES homebrewing scene has yet to produce much in the way of full-featured gaming experiences, there is a vibrant community making music in NSF format. The web site 2A03 (www.2a03.org) features over 1,200 different original NSF-format songs as of this writing as well as all the software you'll need to play them. There are standalone players as well as plugins that allow the popular WinAmp digital music player to handle NSF.

continued on next page...

Figure 9-37.
Hot Seat Harry in RockNES

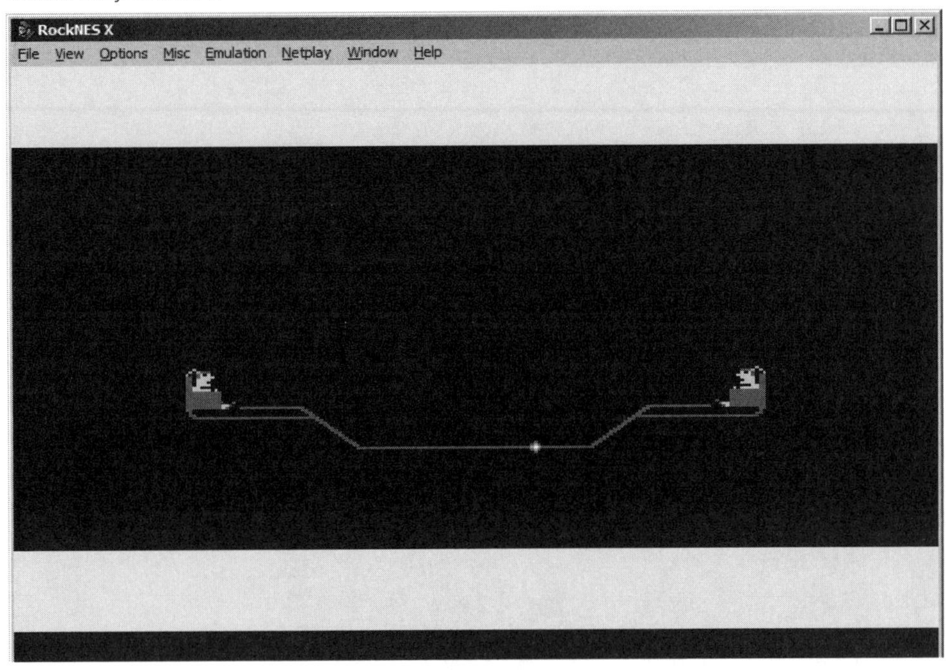

continued from previous page...

Downloading actual game soundtracks in NSF format is legally questionable, although publishers do not seem to be pursuing web sites that offer the files. The legendary NES web site |tsr's NES Archive offers a selection of NSF files for some popular games (www.atarihq.com/tsr/nsf/nsf.html).

switch to these by clicking Config→Input and then selecting Famicom Expansion Port on the bottom drop-down box. FCE Ultra supports:

Zapper (light gun)
Power Pad, sides A and B
Arkanoid Paddle
Hyper Shot (light gun)
Four Score or NES Satellite (4 player adapters)
Family Keyboard
Hyper Shot pads
Mahjongg controller
Oekaki Kids drawing tablet
Quiz King buzzers
Family Trainer, sides A and B
Barcode World (barcode scanner)
Top Rider (handlebar controller for motorbike games)

Sure, using your mouse as a Zapper gun might make Duck Hunt way too easy, but admit it: as a kid, you just put your gun up against the glass of the television screen and fired at point-blank range, too.

NEStopia

The promised land of NES emulation? For some, perhaps. When you boot it up, NEStopia (sourceforge.net/projects/nestopia/) looks very much like FCE Ultra—a small black window (see Figure 9-39). Mess around and you'll see lots of the same options you'll remember from the other NES emulators we've visited in this hack. In the Options→Timing window, you can select the Auto Frame Skip option, which should clear up any speed problems you experience.

You can also turn on and off the NES' different sound channels in the Sound options menu, just in case you want to hear different parts of your favorite tunes separately. And in the Preferences

Figure 9-38.
FCE Ultra running Bomb Sweeper

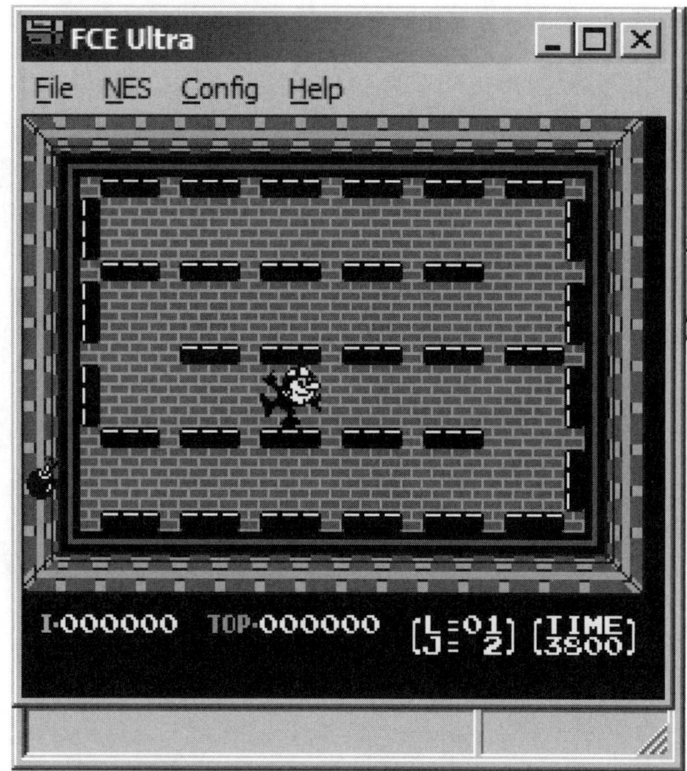

menu you can easily use checkboxes to turn file associations on and off, which means that when you double-click on a supported file in Windows Explorer, it will open automatically in NEStopia. This is not really preferable if you don't want NEStopia to be your one and only emulator, nor if all your ROMs are in zipped format.

Hit Alt+L, and you will bring up the optional Launcher, which is a very useful tool indeed. This provides functionality similar to RockNES, allowing you to search specific directories for ROM files, either in *.nes* format or zipped. Choose Options→Paths, and click Add to name as many directories as you want.

But wait, there's more! Once you've got directories in there, you can check or uncheck them, causing NEStopia to search and skip them, respectively, all without permanently deleting them from the list. There's even a checkbox that will let you eliminate duplicate files from the master list that is generated. As you can see, when combined with some judicious directory organizing on your part, the Launcher can make your emulation experience an easy one.

Nessie

And now for something completely different. The NES emulator Nessie (nessie.emubase.de) takes a very different approach to emulator design. Specifically, the author has taken pains to simplify the entire process, from downloading to running. Nessie is distributed as a single executable file that is not even zipped, so all you need to do is save it anywhere you wish, and then run it. If you want Nessie to support zipped ROMs, you have to save the *unzip.dll* file—also available on the project's web site—to the same directory as Nessie.

Inside, things are even simpler. Click on Options→Preferences; where most emulators would feature screens full of options, Nessie presents you only with the tiny menu shown in Figure 9-40.

Figure 9-39.
NEStopia running the homebrew game Galaxy Patrol

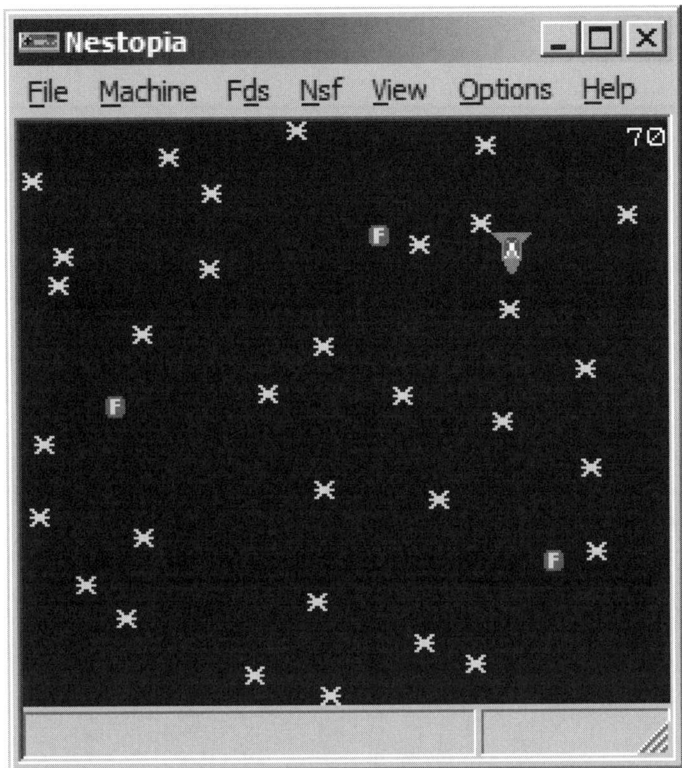

If you leave the settings at default, Nessie will use its built-in database to determine the names of ROMs automatically, power the "system" on as soon as you load a ROM, and hide the menu when you are playing a game.

But this small Preferences screen belies some of the very cool things that Nessie can do. Like most emulators, it can save your game at any point and let you resume it right where you left off. But Nessie doesn't stop there. When you save a game, you can enter one line to describe the save (perhaps a description of where you left off, or even just the date and time). And when you select Load Game, you'll be able to scroll through those descriptions, and each of them will feature a screenshot of the game from where you left off, as shown in Figure 9-41.

The tradeoff here is that, unlike most emulators, you can't instantly save and load games by just tapping a single button; you have to navigate through the menus each time. But you might find that the helpful screenshots and descriptions are more suited to your playing style (especially if you're not saving and loading every time you screw up, cheater).

Oh, and as you might have guessed, there's one more tradeoff with Nessie: you can't manually adjust any of the video or sound options. What this means is that if Nessie doesn't run well on your computer as soon as you boot it up, it's almost definitely never going to run well. But if it does work perfectly, you might really want to stick with it. Either way, with the many different emulators in this hack—and the seventy-odd other NES emulators out there—you're bound to find something that works.

If you're running a very old DOS machine—a 486, for example—you might find that what works is the tastefully named emulator NESticle (bloodlust.zophar.net/NESticle/nes.html). It's been discontinued for over half a decade now, but then again, so has your old 486.

— *Chris Kohler, from* Retro Gaming Hacks

Figure 9-40.
Nessie's basic Preferences menu

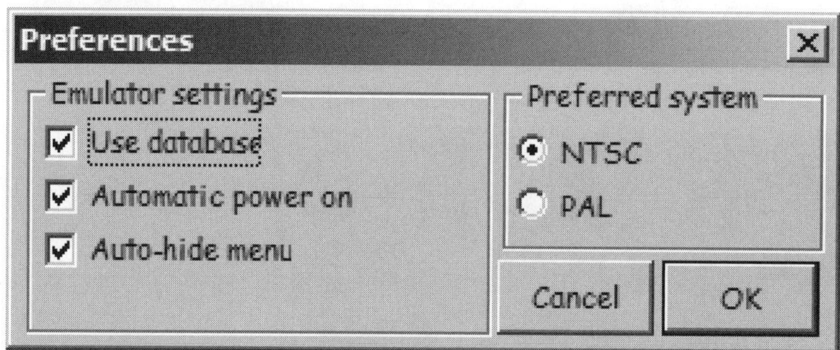

Figure 9-41.
Nessie's Load Game menu

HACK 137: Emulate the Game Boy on Your PC

V XP Make the classic portable not so portable.

Although Nintendo has been producing home video game consoles since the 1970s, soon after the introduction of its portable Game Boy system in 1989, gaming on the go has become the company's main moneymaker. The latest in the line, the Game Boy Advance SP, can play every Game Boy game going all the way back to the original black-and-white cartridges. So there's still quite a bit of nostalgia, even at Nintendo, for the classics.

In fact, the Game Boy (GB) evokes such heartfelt feelings in its fans that there are a tremendous number of homebrew games and tech demos available at public domain ROM sites like www.pdroms.de—over 300 for the original GB and 700 for the Game Boy Advance! If you'd like to play these games quickly and easily, you'll need to use a Game Boy emulator for your personal computer. And with the right equipment and software, you can even play them on a real Game Boy Advance.

Emulating the Game Boy and Game Boy Color

When selecting an emulator, you'll want to make sure that it can emulate all three iterations of the first Game Boy hardware—Game Boy, Super Game Boy, and Game Boy Color. The Super Game Boy was an add-on to the Super Nintendo Entertainment System that let users play GB games on the system, and certain GB games were programmed with Super Game Boy-specific color palettes and extra features such as backgrounds and hidden games.

Although a staggering amount of Game Boy emulators have been developed and are listed on emulation portals such as Zophar's Domain (www.zophar.net), I recommend you stick with an emulator called BGB. It does all of the above, can use the Game Genie cheat add-on, and it runs pretty much any ROM you can throw at it. You can read more about BGB and download the emulator at bgb.bircd.org.

Setting Up BGB

You'll have to unzip the BGB archive into a new directory, but if the ROMs that you download are zipped, you can leave them that way. Run the BGB program, then right-click inside the window to bring up a menu. Click Load ROM, and you'll be able to open the ROMs you have saved (see Figure 9-42).

If you want to explore one of BGB's more advanced features, you might try playing the games online. If you and your friends all have a ROM that allows for multiplayer support, you can play it online. You'll need each others' IP addresses. One player will host the game (select the Link option from the main menu, then select connect), and others will join in (select Link, then listen). At the appropriate prompts you'll put in the IP addresses as requested.

If you want to configure your controller or display settings, you can enter the robust Options menu by right-clicking and selecting Options. Most of the stuff in here is better left untouched unless you know what you're doing, and it's likely you'll never need most of it anyway. You might try messing with the display scheme. The original Game Boy games can display only four colors, but you can pick which colors those are. Select the GB Colors option. Once there, you can use the sliders to tweak the colors some more if you wish. Five preset palettes are available by using the Scheme drop-down box, and you can add your own.

Select the Graphics tab, and you can enable Super Game Boy borders for games that support them, like Donkey Kong and Space Invaders. Also in this tab, you can resize the game play window. Note that if you pick Full Screen Stretched, you'll lose the Super Game Boy backgrounds, but the gameplay area will fill up your monitor, making for a very different experience indeed!

Another useful option is the ability to save your position at any time during gameplay. It's a quick and painless process. Right-click, then look for the seventh option down, State, and click Quick Save. To load, first boot up the ROM, and click Quick Load.

Emulating the Game Boy Advance

Nintendo's Game Boy Advance is one of the most popular game consoles in the history of the industry, so is it any doubt that a thriving emulation and homebrew community exists for the console? Over 700 homebrew Game Boy Advance games and demos are available at the public domain ROMs site www.pdroms.de.

Figure 9-42.
BGB running a homebrew combat game

Although there are many different GBA emulators for Windows, I'll narrow the field down to two excellent choices: BoycottAdvance (boycottadvance.emuunlim.com), which doesn't really require anything other than Windows to get started, and VisualBoyAdvance (vba.ngemu.com). Neither has been updated all that recently, but both seem to fully support any new software. Of the two, Boycott seems to be a bit more stable, is a notch easier to use, and it even comes with a free game. That's not a bad place to start.

Deeper into Boycott

Download and unzip the Boycott archive, and everything should be ready to go. The game Pongfighter v1.2 will be automatically placed into the ROM subfolder. You'll need at least a Pentium III to really run things smoothly, though you should be able to choke decent performance out of a fast Pentium II. Having the latest version of DirectX will help a bit, too.

If you have a joystick hooked up to your system, head into the Options menu, and set that up first. The drop-down menus are a little inconvenient if your joystick's buttons are not labeled, but you should be able to set it up correctly with some trial and error.

It's much easier to get a keyboard set up but not easier to play a game using one. You can configure the keys any which way you want, although you'll probably find that the default settings are acceptable. For certain games, having the auto-fire option turned on can be easier on the thumbs.

Let's play a game of Pongfighter to get things moving. Click File→Load ROM, and you'll arrive at the default ROM folder. There you should see the game's file, still zipped. (The emulator also supports ROMs archived in *.rar* format.) Double-click it to play a GBA version of the classic Pong, augmented with a musical theme from the game Street Fighter II. (Can you guess which character's music it is?)

If games aren't running fast enough for you, there are some options you can toy around with. As is the case with most emulators, skipping frames of animation (done by raising the Frameskip value) can speed things up. You can usually get away with setting it to just 1 or 2, and not lose very much of the detail in the process. You can also resize the window. The smaller the window, the less graphic data there is to process, and the faster the emulation.

A feature unique to Boycott is the ability to adjust accuracy versus speed on a sliding scale. Taking accuracy will make things run smoother, but sacrifice speed. Obviously, speed will try and make things run faster but the game will look "choppier" when it animates. It's a personal choice depending on what you feel is more important. If you're unsure of whether or not the game is running properly (some games look choppy even on the GBA hardware, of course), you can check the frame rate with Show FPS. If it's over or at 60, you're not losing any speed and the game's probably just not very well-programmed. Finally, turning off sound emulation with Sound Enable will lessen the load on the PC, although you might feel that playing a game without the music and sound effects isn't exactly a worthwhile experience.

If you find a game isn't working right, and you're sure it's not your PC, check the History file under Help. There will be a list of games that are known to not work correctly with that version of the emulator. Downloading the last revision as of this writing, Version 0.2.8, should remedy all problems.

— *Matt Paprocki, from* Retro Gaming Hacks

10 GRAPHICS AND MULTIMEDIA

Windows used to take a back seat to the Mac when it came to graphics and multimedia. But with the release of Windows Vista, and with Windows Media Center for both Windows XP and Windows Vista, that's no longer necessarily the case. As you'll see in this chapter, you can do remarkable things when it comes to graphics and multimedia with Windows. You can record TV shows, watch TV in TiVo-like fashion, and as you'll see in one of the hacks in this chapter, you'll even be able to create "mashups" combining several of your favorite TV shows.

The chapter also covers hacking the Zune media player. Whether you want to do something basic like using a Zune as another hard drive, or more complicated, like recording TV shows on your PC, and then automatically transferring them to your Zune, you'll find hacks here.

Also covered are YouTube hacks, graphics hacks, and more.

HACK 138: Set Up Your PC To Record TV Shows

V XP In this hack, I'll show you how you can use set up Windows with a TV tuner card to watch TV shows...and then record them.

In the past, if you wanted to turn your ordinary PC into an all-in-one home entertainment center you had to install the Windows XP Media Center Edition 2005, an enhanced version of Windows XP that let you watch and record TV programs, play DVDs, listen to music, share your digital photos, and more. Best of all, you could continue to do your work on the same computer.

Now, the Windows Media Center is now part of the Windows Vista operating system (Home Premium and Ultimate editions only) and as long as you have the required hardware, you can watch TV, DVDs, as well as record TV shows.

The instructions in this hack for recording TV shows are shown for Windows Vista. But Windows XP Media Center is very similar to Windows Vista, so these instructions will go a long way toward helping you record shows in Windows XP Media Center as well.

Choosing the Hardware Components

The first step towards building your own media center is to select the appropriate hardware based on your budget constraints. Of course, if you have the cash, you can always go for the latest components that money can buy. However, most of us usually have to compromise and decide upon the best value for whatever budget we have. Here is a list of minimum requirements that I suggest:

- CPU: 2Ghz or more
- Memory: 512MB or more
- Hard drive: 80GB or more
- DVD drive: preferably a DVD writer if you want to save TV shows onto DVDs
- Display: 17" LCD Monitor or LCD TV
- Graphics card memory: 128MB or more

For watching TV programs on your computer, you also need a Windows Media Center-compatible TV tuner card. In addition, a remote control that works with Windows Media Center will greatly enhance your usage experience.

TV Tuner cards

One of the important ingredients of a media center is the TV tuner card, which allows you to watch receive TV signals and watch programs on your computer. When it comes to a TV tuner, I turned to Hauppauge (www.hauppauge.com), which is one of the leaders in bringing TV functionality to the PC.

As of this writing, Hauppauge has a series of TV tuners that you can choose from:

- WinTV-PVR-150
- WinTV-PVR-150 MCE
- WinTV-PVR-150 l.p.
- WinTV-PVR-250
- WinTV-PVR-250 MCE
- WinTV-PVR-350
- WinTV-PVR-500 MCE
- WinTV-PVR-USB2

The product names that end with "MCE" are designed specially to work with Windows Media Center Edition. Both the WinTV-PVR-150 MCE (see Figure 10-1) and the WinTV-PVR-250 MCE allow you to watch TV and listen to radio on your PC, while the WinTV-PVR-500 MCE has dual TV tuners that allow you to watch one channel while recording another. The WinTV-PVR-500 MCE uses dual hardware MPEG-2 encoders, so it frees your CPU while you are recording TV programs.

Note that the MCE products previously mentioned do not include a remote control. If you want a remote control, you can buy any of the following MCE kits:

- WinTV-PVR-150 MCE-Kit
- WinTV-PVR-500 MCE-Kit
- WinTV-PVR-USB2 MCE-Kit

If you do not have a spare PCI slot on your computer (or you want to be able to watch TV on your notebook computer), you can opt for the WinTV-HVR-900 (see Figure 10-2), which connects to your computer via USB. The WinTV-HVR-900 (US users should look for the WinTV-HVR-950 for cable TV and over-the-air HD channels) is a digital and analog TV receiver and it comes with an analog aerial/ cable TV receiver plus a Freeview DVB-T digital TV receiver.

Figure 10-1.
The WinTV-PVR-150MCE

Figure 10-2.
The Hauppauge HVR-900 TV tuner

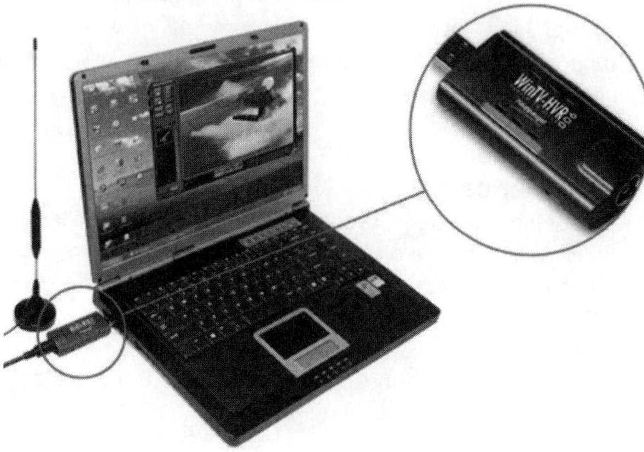

US users can visit www.antennaweb.org to determine which over the air HD signals they can receive and where to best position their antenna for reception.

For Hauppauge's products installation instructions on Windows Vista, you can refer to the online instructions at: www.hauppauge.co.uk/pages/support/support_new_mce.html.

So, which one is suitable for you? It all depends on your budget. For the best performance and features, go for the WinTV-PVR-500 MCE. If you are cash-strapped, the WinTV-PVR-150 MCE is good enough. Finally, if you want to watch TV while traveling, then the WinTV-HVR-900 is probably the best option.

If you plan on putting your media center in the living room, you should equip it with a remote control. Until recently, Microsoft did not directly sell the Windows Media Center remote control to end users; they were only available to system vendors. Fortunately, you can now get one from a hardware retailer (see Figure 10-3). For details, go to www.microsoft.com/hardware/mouseandkeyboard/ProductDetails.aspx?pid=065&active_tab=overview.

Of course, if your TV tuner comes with a remote control (like the Hauppauge's WinTV-HVR-900), then you don't need to buy the additional remote control.

Setting up Windows Vista Media Center Edition

Once you have the appropriate hardware ready, it is now time to configure Windows Vista.

Remember that only the Home Premium and Ultimate editions of Windows Vista have the Windows Media Center.

To launch Windows Media Center, go to Start→Programs→Windows Media Center. Scroll to TV+Movies→set up tv (see Figure 10-4).

Figure 10-3.
The Microsoft Windows Media Center remote control

Figure 10-4.
Setting up the TV signals

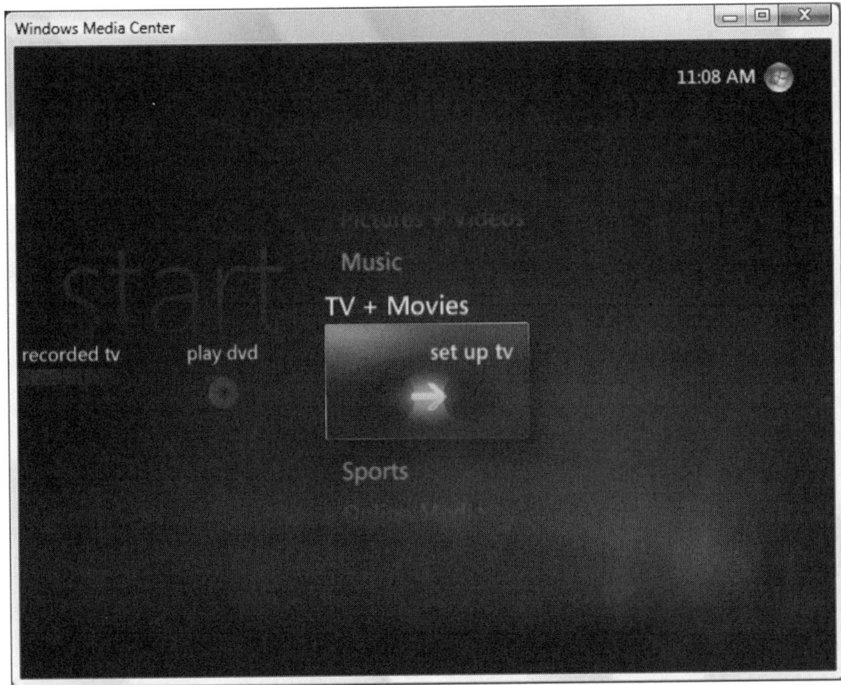

You are now ready to set up your Windows Media Center to receive TV signals.

1. In the Set up Your TV Signal screen, click Next to proceed.
2. In the Confirm Your Region screen, you can either take the default region (United States), or select a different region. Click Next to proceed.
3. Windows will now download the TV setup option based on your selected region.
4. In the Select Your TV Signal screen, select the type of signal you are receiving (see Figure 10-5). I am connecting my HVR-900 TV tuner to a wall antenna, so I will select Antenna. Click Next.

Figure 10-5.
Selecting the type of TV signal you have

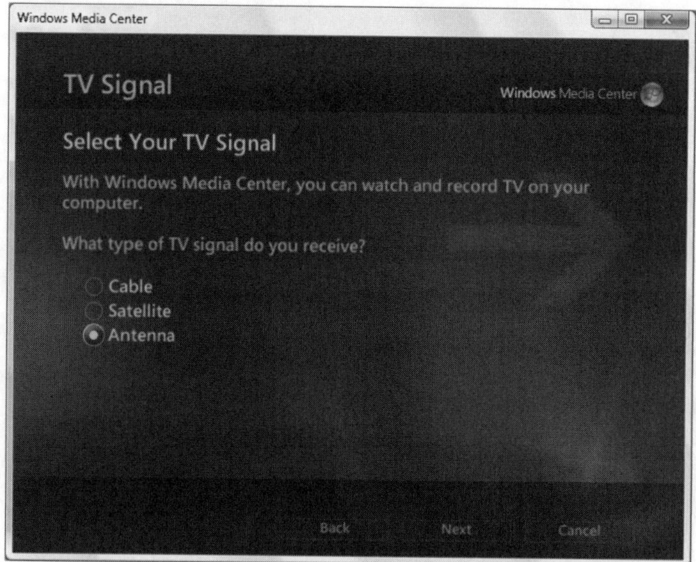

Figure 10-6.
Selecting the TV signal type

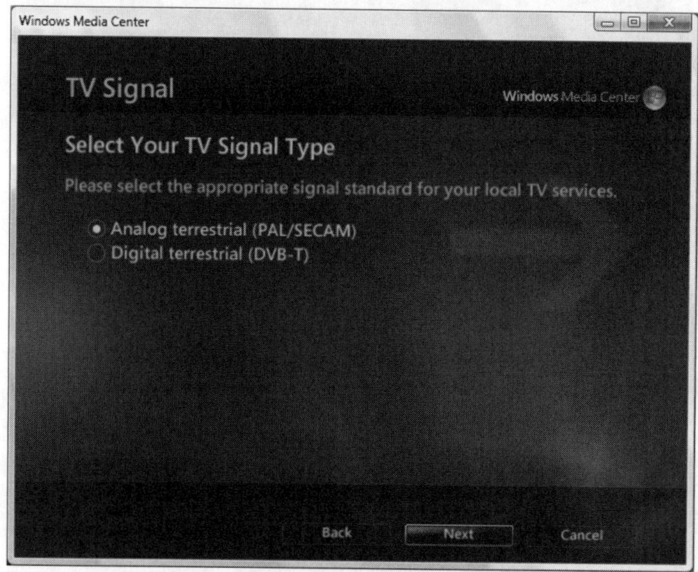

5. In the Select Your TV Signal Type screen, select the signal standard for your local TV services (see Figure 10-6). Click Next to proceed.

You will now set up the TV program guide:

1. In the Set Up Your TV Program Guide screen, click Next to proceed.

2. In the Guide Privacy screen, select whether you want to use the Guide—I selected No so that I could scan for TV signals straight away—and click Next to proceed.

3. You will now scan for TV signals. In the Scan for Services screen, click Next to proceed. You should be able to locate the local TV signals (see Figure 10-7).

Figure 10-7.
Scanning for TV signals

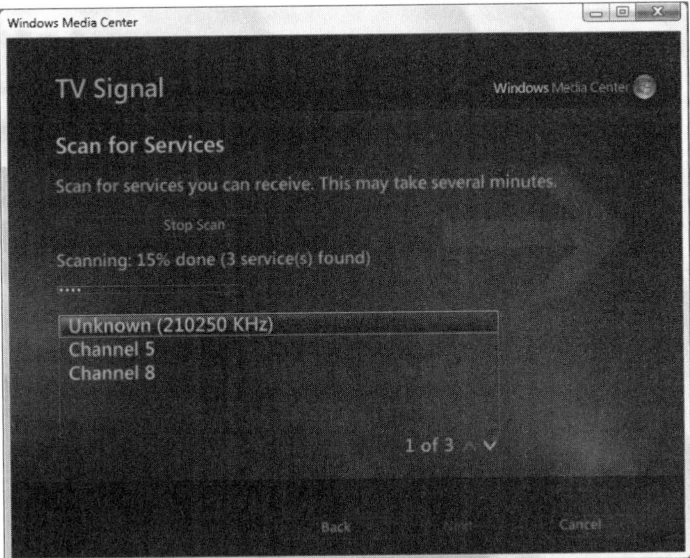

Figure 10-8.
Viewing live TV

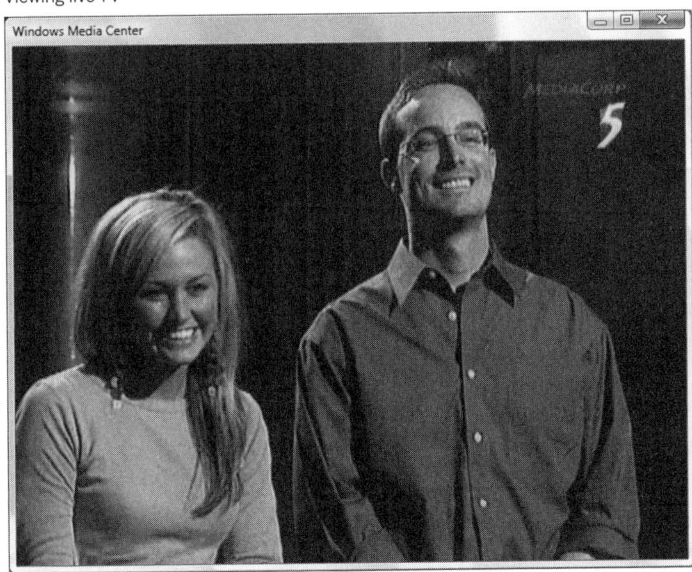

That's it! You can now go back to the main menu of Windows Media Center and select TV+Movies→live tv. Now you can simply select the channel you want to watch (see Figure 10-8).

Recording TV

Now that your computer is set up properly to receive the TV signals, you can use Windows Vista to record TV programs:

1. In the main menu of Windows Media Center, select TV+Movies→recorded tv.
2. To record a TV program, select add recording (see Figure 10-9).

Figure 10-9.
Viewing recorded TV and adding new recordings

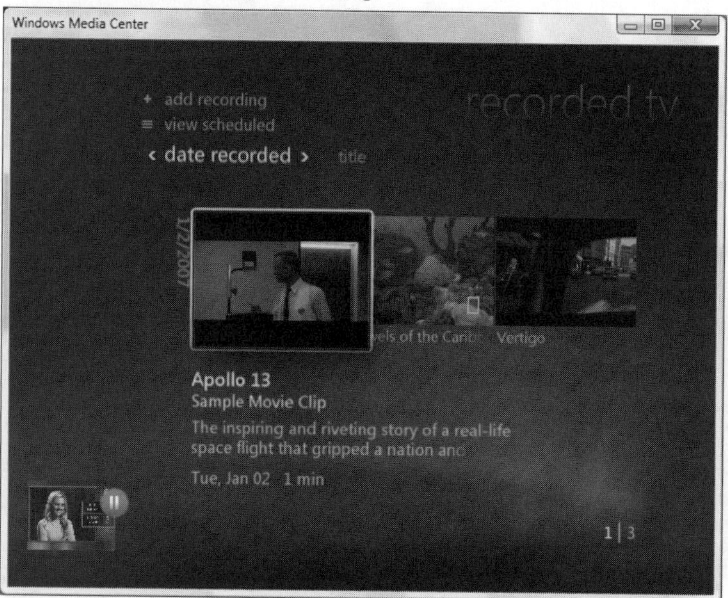

Figure 10-10.
Setting the details of the recording

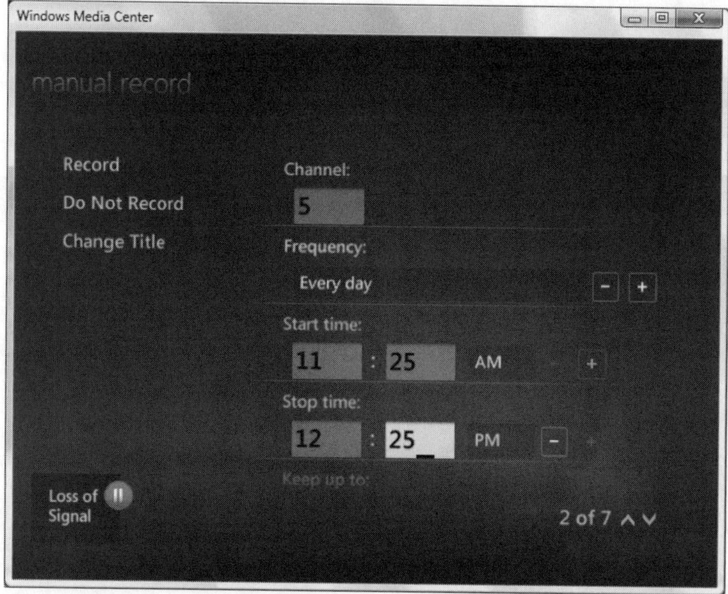

3. There are several options to record TV programs (see Figure 10-10), such as recording only once, or record every day (or alternate day), etc. Once the settings are done, click Record to save the recording.

4. You can now watch your recorded TV programs by going to TV+Movies→recorded tv (see Figure 10-11).

Figure 10-11.
Viewing the recorded TV program

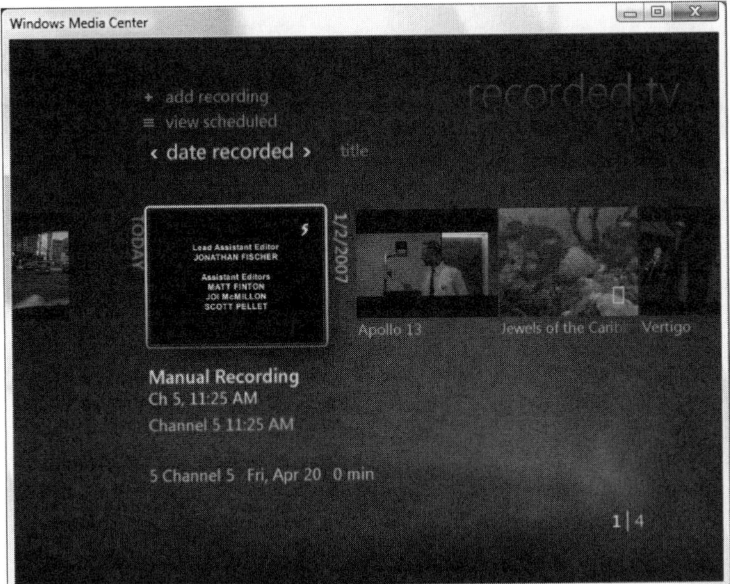

See Also

- For help in managing recorded TV shows in Windows Media Center, go to windowshelp.microsoft.com/Windows/en-US/Help/97flb794-907e-4428-8ae5-69d20aa479c21033.mspx.
- "Make Your Own TV Show Mashup" **[Hack #140]**
- "Burn Recorded TV Shows Directly from Windows Media Center to DVD" **[Hack #141]**
- "Copy Recorded TV Shows To Your Zune" **[Hack #151]**
- "Remove Commercials from Recorded TV Shows" **[Hack #139]**

— Wei-Meng Lee

HACK 139: Remove Commercials from Recorded TV Shows

V XP Want to watch *Lost* re-runs without the commercials? This hack shows you how to record TV shows, edit out the commercials, then save the shows back to disk for commercial-free watching.

Window Media Center does a great job of recording TV shows that you can later watch at your leisure, in much the same way that TiVo works. When you watch those shows, though, you most likely don't want to watch the commercials as well. In this hack, I'll show you how to record TV shows in Windows Media Center, edit out the commercials using Windows Movie Maker, then save the shows back to disk or DVD.

First you need to record TV shows. And before you do that, you need to have a TV tuner installed on your computer **[Hack #138]**.

One you've confirmed everything is working, the easiest way to record a TV show is to use your remote control and select the guide button. This will pull up the electronic TV guide that Windows Media Center uses. You can then select a TV show to get more information and also set up your recording. You can also use the red record button on your Media Center remote to record a TV show

QUICK HACK 

DON'T HAVE A WINDOWS MEDIA CENTER REMOTE?

If you bought a Media Center-powered PC off the shelf, there's a good chance that it came with a Windows Media Center remote control. Some TV tuner cards come with a remote control as well. But if not, Microsoft's Remote Control and Receiver for Media Center PC with Windows will do the trick. Shop around for a good deal. Online computer hardware dealers such as newegg.com and zipzoomfly.com list this as manufacturer part number A90-00007 for under $40.

Figure 10-12.
Getting ready to start recording

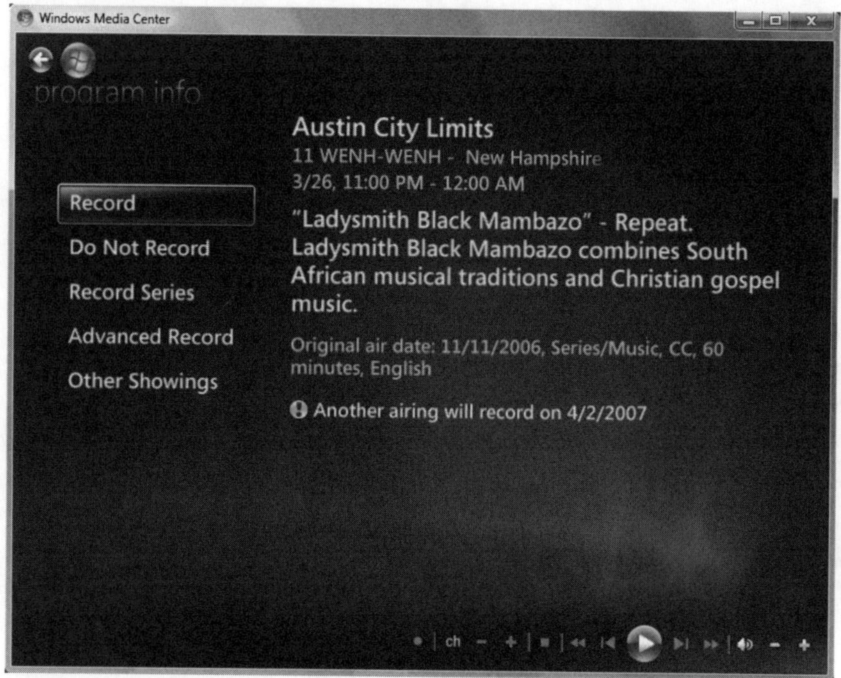

you are currently watching or select one for future recording when you are browsing the electronic TV guide. Figure 10-12 shows Windows Media Center about to record a TV show.

Once you have recorded a TV show, you can go to your recorded TV submenu and see the shows you have recorded. You can also see what is scheduled to be recorded and add a recording by selecting the options at the top of the screen with your Media Center remote control.

Now that you know how to record a TV show we'll move on to editing out the commercials, using Movie Maker, the free digital video editing program that comes with Windows Vista. Movie Maker can import video from your digital camera and edit your home movies. But Movie Maker can also open your recorded TV shows and then you can edit the commercials out.

The version of Windows Movie Maker that comes with Windows XP doesn't have the same full feature set as the one that comes with Windows Vista, and isn't suitable for editing out commercials. VideoReDo Plus (www.videoredo.com) can do the job. Turn to the end of this hack for details.

Start Movie Maker, hit the Import Media button, browse to your recorded TV folder (see Figure 10-13—by default Vista puts it in your *Public* folder under *Recorded TV*; the path is *C:\Users\Public\Recorded TV*) and open up the TV show you want to edit.

You can tell if it is a recorded TV show because Vista will give it a special icon that has the Windows logo surrounded by a Green circle. Also look at the file extension; it should be *.dvr_ms*.

Once you have your TV show open, drag it to the timeline and drop it in the Video section. You will see your TV show in the preview window. To edit out the commercials, drag the green marker in the video timeline to a section of the TV show where the commercial begins. Then select the Split button that is below the video preview window. This splits your TV show into two separate video segments, as you can see in Figure 10-14. Next, drag the green marker to the end of the commercial on the video timeline and select the Split button again. Now you will have three separate video

Figure 10-13.
Recorded TV shows, displayed in Windows Explorer

Figure 10-14.
Editing out the commercials

segments, one of which is the commercial. Right click the commercial segment and delete it by selecting Remove. Do this for each commercial so that they're all gone. Don't worry that you have many separate video segments of the TV show; Movie Maker will put them together as one seamless video file when you publish it.

Now you can save your new commercial-free TV show back to your hard drive as a Windows Media Video file, or else burn it to a DVD. Use the "Publish to" menu on the left hand of the screen and select which option you want. You can even compress your video file so it won't take up so much hard drive space. You'll be prompted to compress the video during the publishing process.

Hacking the Hack

When you open your recorded TV show in Windows Movie Maker, you may get an error saying the show can't be opened. If this happens to you, you can go to the Compatibility tab under Options to disable other video filters installed on your system that may be causing compatibility issues. Get there by choosing Tools→Options→Compatibility, as shown in the nearby figure. I recommend writing down which filters are currently enabled and then disabling all of them while you use Movie Maker (see Figure 10-15). When you are done you can turn back on only the video filters that you wrote down earlier that you were using.

Windows XP users won't be able to use Windows Movie Maker to edit out commercials because the Windows XP version of the program is a pretty anemic thing. There are some free programs available like DVRMSToolbox (babgvant.com/files/folders/dvrmstoolbox/default.aspx) but

Figure 10-15.
If you run into problems opening recorded TV shows, try disabling video filters

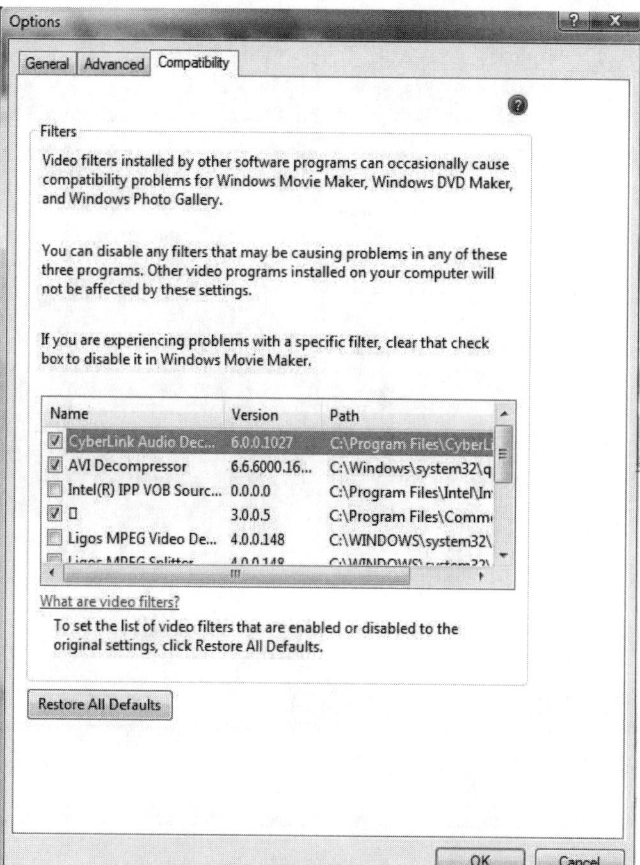

QUICK HACK 

BEST WAY TO SHRINK VIDEO FILES

If you plan to watch videos on in iPod, Sony PSP, Zune or similar media player, you need those videos to be as small as possible. There are a number of different ways you can do this, but the fastest is Instant Video To-Go, available from www.adstech.com for about $80. It looks like a USB flash drive, and shrinks files much faster than software alone can do. The company estimates that using the hardware/software combo, you can speed up the time it takes to compress the video by about 15 times.

By the company's estimates, a 100-minute two-gigabyte video in the MPEG2 format that would take around five hours to shrink down with software alone takes only 20 minutes to be transformed into the high-quality H.264 MPEG4 video used by many portables.

Figure 10-16.
VideoReDo Plus in action

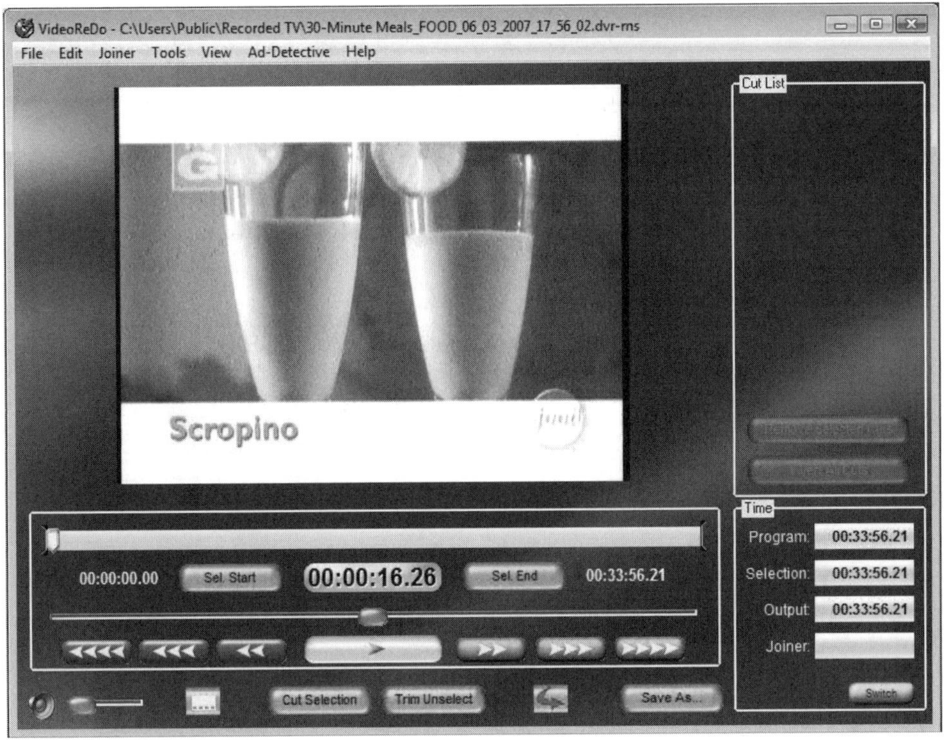

they can be difficult to use. A better bet is VideoReDo Plus (www.videoredo.com), a video editing program that can read and edit the DVR-MS recorded TV format. It's free to try, and $49.99 if you decide to keep it. Figure 10-16 shows it in action.

— Timothy Coyle

HACK 140: Make Your Own TV Show Mashup

V XP Want to mash *I Love Lucy* together with *Lost*? How about *American Idol* with the *Ed Sullivan Show*? With this hack, you can create your own TV show mashup, mashing together any shows you can record.

Now that you know how easy it is to edit the commercials out of your recorded TV shows in Windows Vista **[Hack #139]** the possibilities are endless. One thing I like to do is to make a "mashup" of my favorite scenes from multiple TV shows. A great example is if you like cooking shows, you can take recipes from different shows and put them together into one show—now that's custom television! I'll show you how to do that in this hack.

All you need to do is to import the different recorded TV shows you want to edit into Movie Maker. Then drag each TV show to the timeline and edit out the segments you don't want. Then you can save the TV show to your hard drive in the Windows Media Video format by using the publish option.

First, use Windows Media Center to record the TV shows you want to mash together **[Hack #138]** Then start Windows Movie Maker and use the Import Media button to import two different TV shows that

Figure 10-17.
Time to get cooking: Two TV shows ready to be mashed together

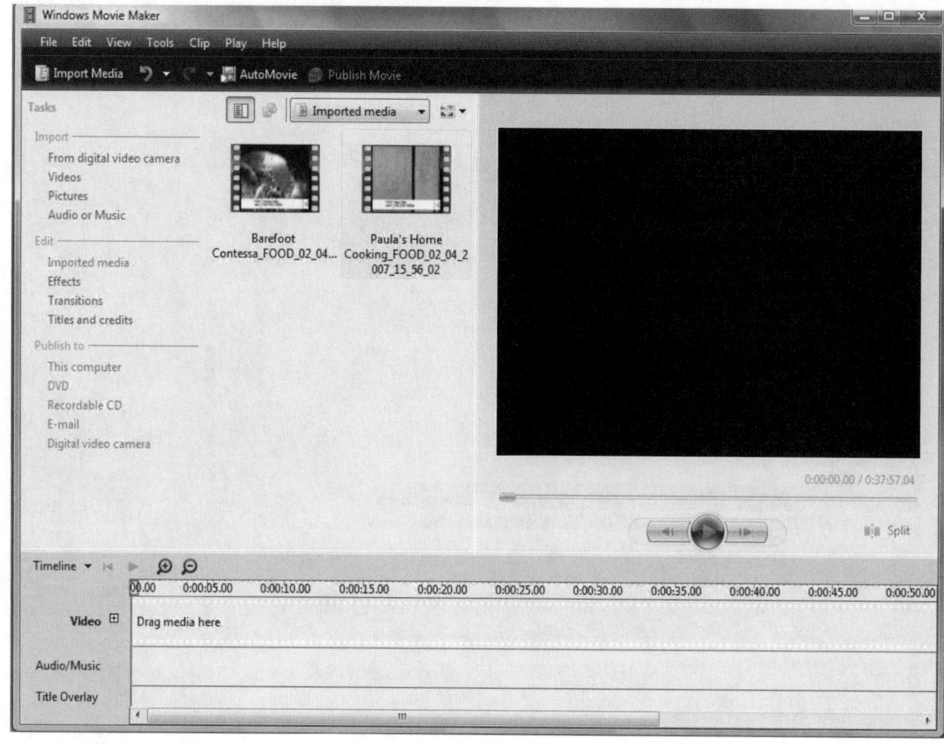

you have recorded. Windows Media Center stores your Recorded TV shows in the *C:\Users\Public\Recorded TV* folder on your main hard drive, so import the shows from there. Figure 10-17 shows Windows Movie Maker with two cooking shows imported, ready to be mashed together.

You mash the two together by dragging each video clip to the Video timeline section. Then you can use the Split button to cut out the commercials and extra scenes you don't want.

For the cooking show example, I'll use the Split button at the beginning and end of every commercial and then delete the commercials. I'll do the same for the other recipe video segments in each show that I'm not interested in. I'll be left with only the parts of the show I want to be in the final mashup. Figure 10-18 shows me in the act of editing out segments from one of the TV shows.

Keep using the Split button to edit your two TV shows until you have only the scenes you want from each show. Once you have done that, select the Timeline drop down arrow and change the view to Storyboard. Now you can add some fancy features to make it a real mashup. Figure 10-19 shows the TV shows put on the storyboard.

In the Storyboard view, you can see two separate video segments that are left from the editing—one recipe segment from each show. Now I want to put them back together.

The first thing to do is add a transition between the two video segments so they look like they belong in the same show. You can do this by selecting "Transitions" under the Edit section on the left hand side. You can use the preview window to the right of the transition menu to see how your transition effect will look.

Figure 10-18.
Editing one of the TV shows

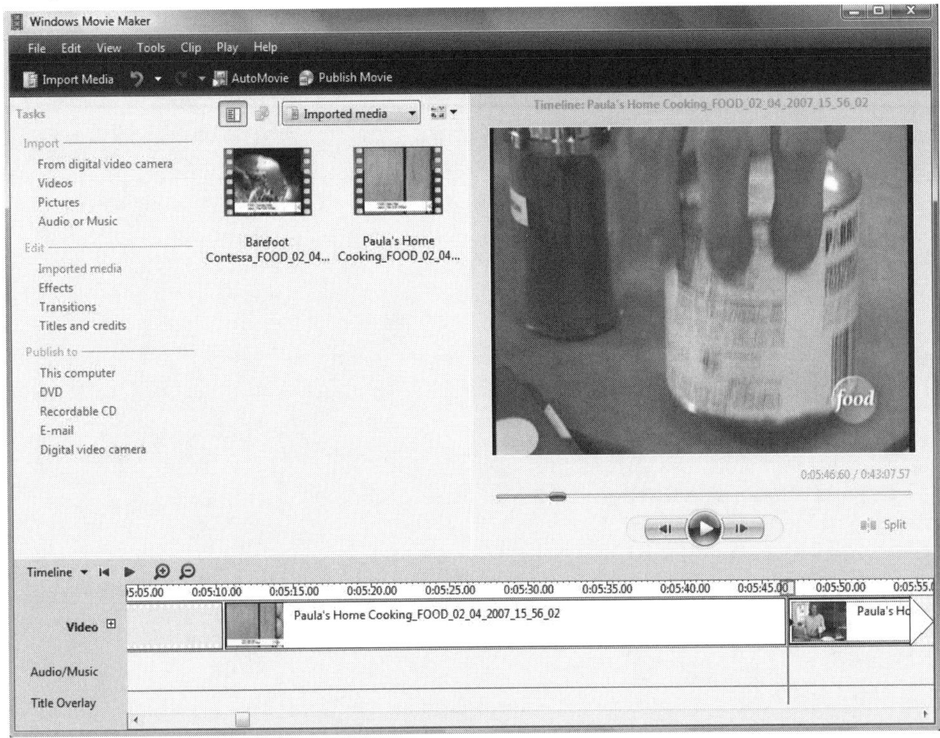

Figure 10-19.
The two TV shows, placed on the storyboard

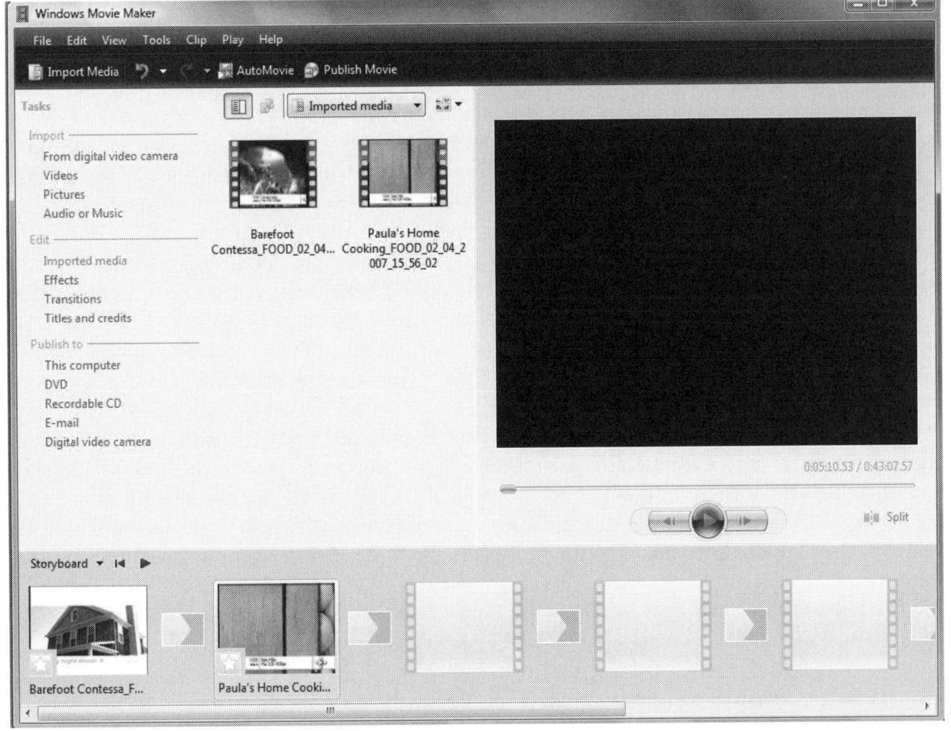

Figure 10-20.
Selecting a transition between the two TV shows

Once you have found one that you like, simply drag it to the transition box between the two video clips. Figure 10-20 shows a transition added between the two clips.

Next, I am going to add a title to the mashup. You can do this by selecting Title and credits under the Edit section on the left hand side. You can add titles anywhere you want in your videos but I are going to add mine at the beginning. Type in the title of your new TV show in the provided space. You can change the color and font of the title under more options. This TV show mashup now has a title and two separate cooking show video segments joined together with a transition, as you can see in Figure 10-21.

Place the title at the beginning of the show, and the mashup is done, as you can see in Figure 10-22.

Obviously, this is a very simple mashup, combining just two segments from two different TV shows. But you can add as many segments as you want, with as many transitions as you want.

Once you've finished your mashup, you can save your TV mashup to your computer or to DVD so your friends can enjoy it as well. This is easy to do using Windows DVD Maker. When you select the Publish to DVD option in Movie Maker it will tell you that it will open Windows DVD Maker so you can create your DVD. When DVD Maker starts it will automatically add your edited TV show mashup and give you the options to add other video or image files, as you can see in Figure 10-23.

You can also see how much time your TV show mashup will take up on a standard DVD. This way, you can make sure that it will all fit on one DVD.

 The title you added in Windows Movie Maker is different than the title you add in Windows DVD Maker. The title you add in Windows Movie Maker will appear when you start actually playing the mashup. The title you add in Windows DVD Maker will appear when you see the DVD menu that appears when you load your DVD.

Figure 10-21.
Creating a title for the mashup

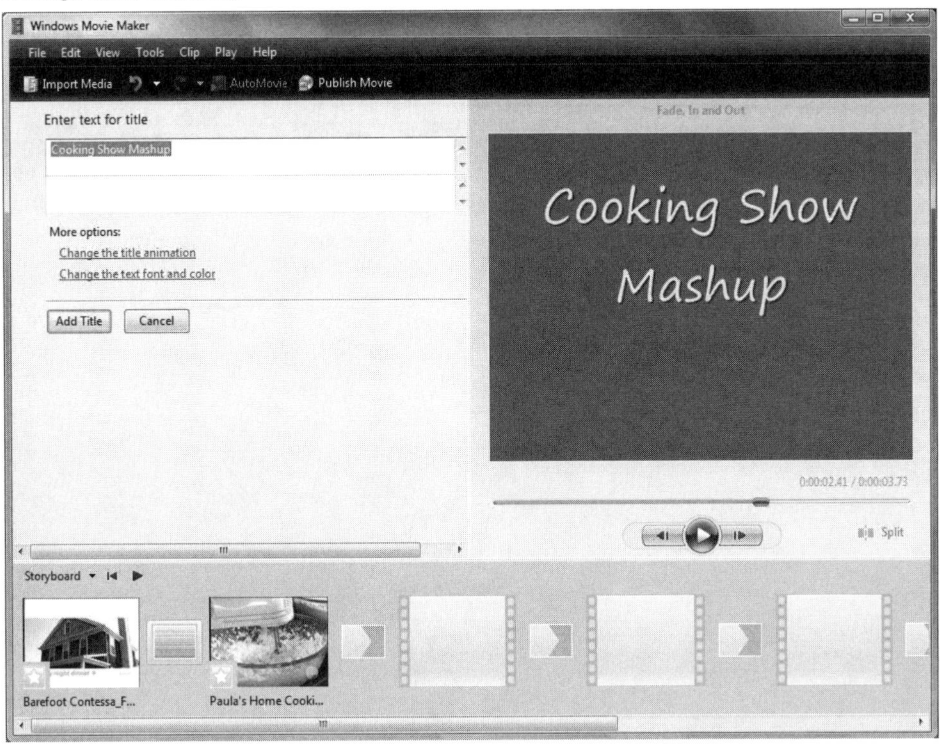

Figure 10-22.
Voila! Mashup du jour!

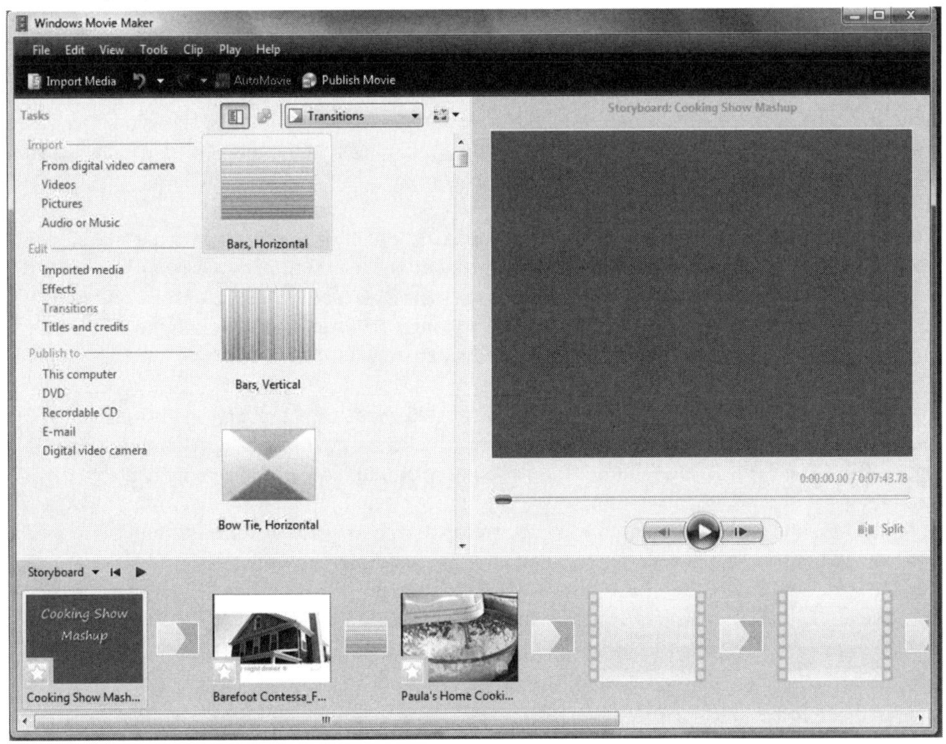

Figure 10-23.
The mashup, imported into Windows DVD Maker

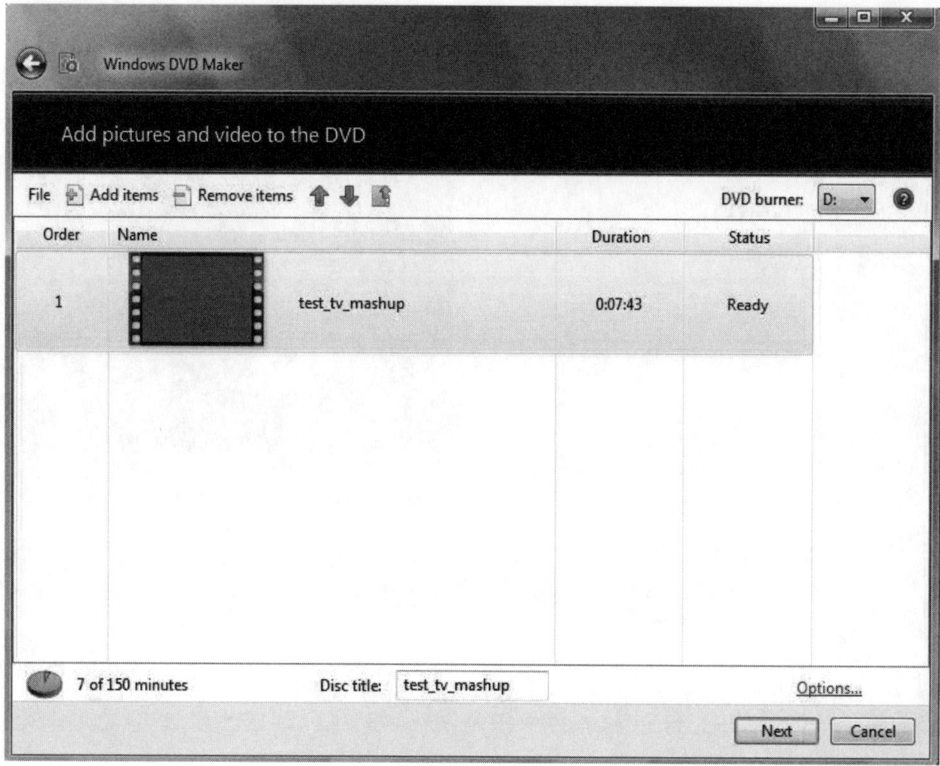

DVD Maker allows you to add custom menus and titles to your DVD. To add them, click Next and DVD Maker will allow you to add and customize them, as you can see in Figure 10-24. On the right hand side of the screen, you can select a DVD menu from the available options. This is the menu that you will see when you put the finished DVD into a DVD player. At the top of the screen, you can change the Menu text by selecting the Menu text button.

When you click the Menu text button, you can choose the font style, the title that shows up on your main menu, and edit the notes section. The notes section is a cool feature that allows you to add note to your DVD that someone can access from the main DVD menu, as you can see in Figure 10-25. Going back to the previous screen you can also change the main menu layout by selecting the Customize menu button. You'll be able to customize it as shown in Figure 10-25.

Here you can change the font style as well as add separate video clips that play in the main menu background. At any time you can use the Preview button to see how your selections look, shown in Figure 10-26. The controls are like the controls you have on your DVD player remote control.

Once you have the menu the way you want you are ready to burn your TV show mashup to DVD. Now you have your own TV show mashup that you can share with your friends!

See Also

- "Set Up Your PC To Record TV Shows" **[Hack #138]**
- "Burn Recorded TV Shows Directly from Windows Media Center to DVD" **[Hack #141]**
- "Copy Recorded TV Shows To Your Zune" **[Hack #151]**
- "Remove Commercials from Recorded TV Shows" **[Hack #139]**

— Timothy Coyle

Figure 10-24.
Adding a custom menu to your DVD

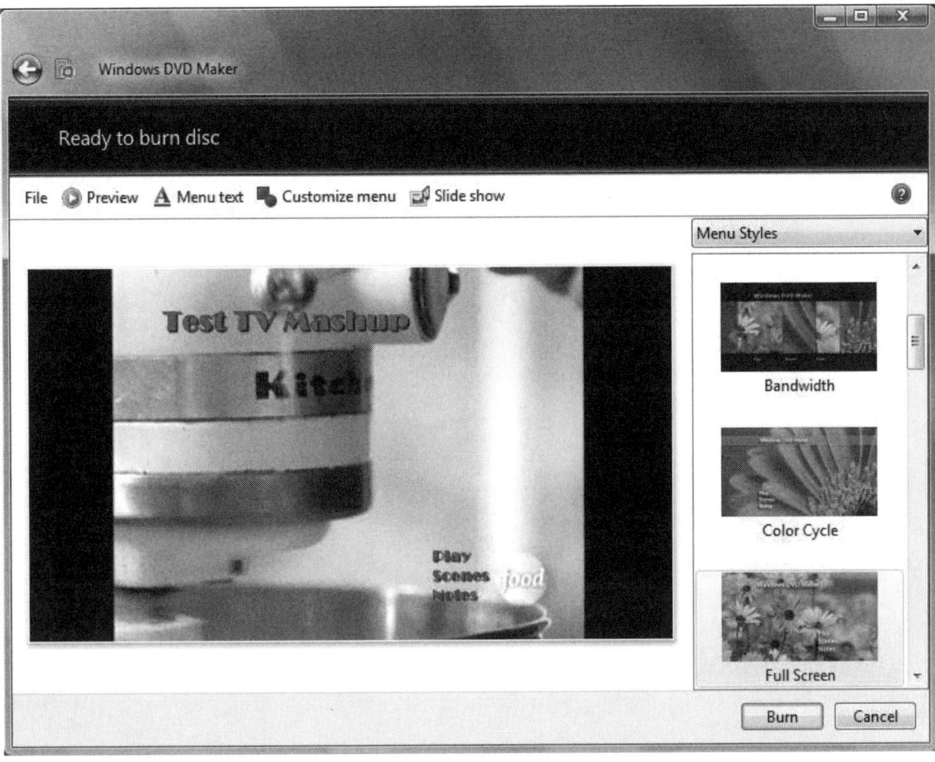

Figure 10-25.
Customizing the menu

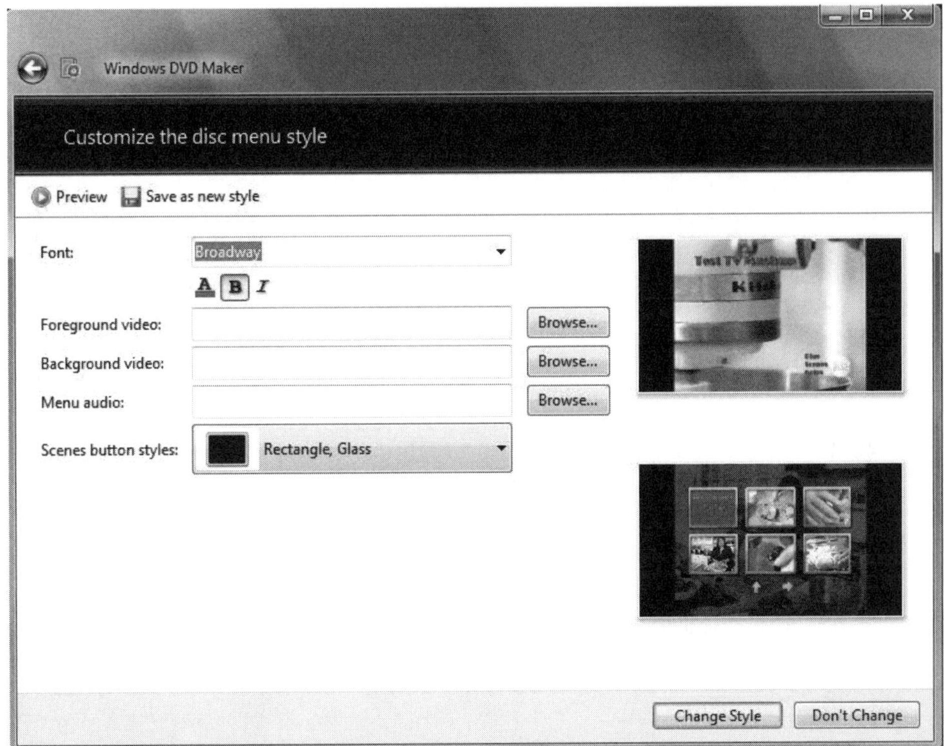

Figure 10-26.
Here's how the mashup will look on DVD

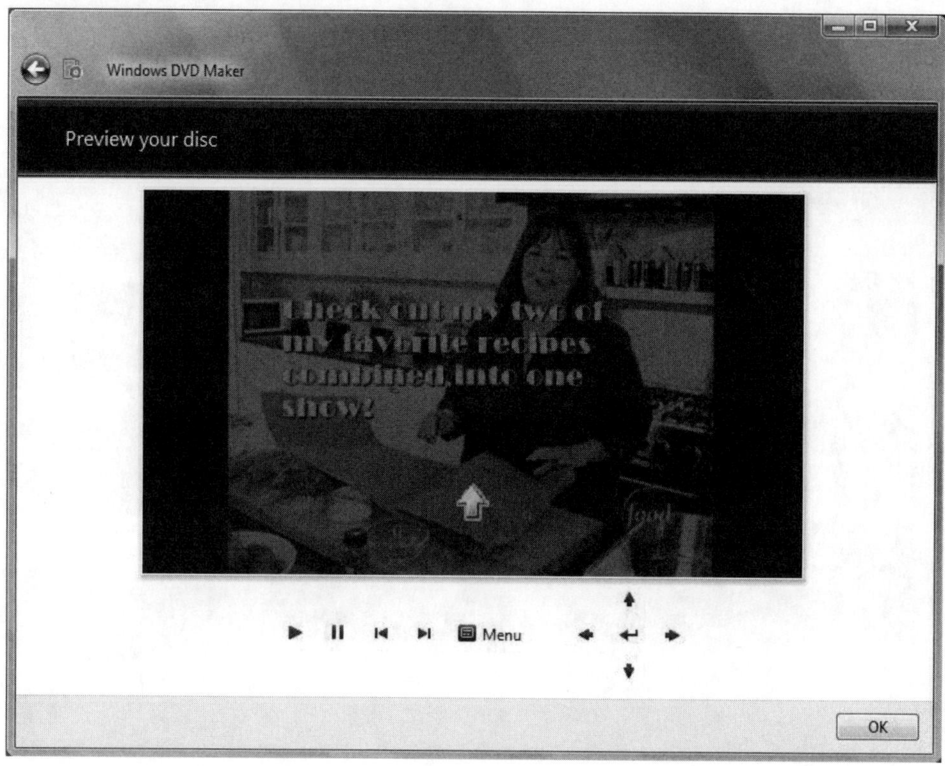

HACK 141: Burn Recorded TV Shows Directly from Windows Media Center to DVD

V XP Want to get a TV show straight from Windows Media Center to a DVD? This hack shows you how.

One of Windows Media Center's best features is its ability to record TV shows and save them on your hard drive so you can watch your favorite programs on your own schedule. The shows are recorded in the *DVR-MS* format that is essentially a *MPEG2* video file with some copyright protection wrapped around it. The size of a recorded TV show is extremely large—figure about 3.2 GB of hard drive space for an hour of recorded TV.

If you record a lot of shows and want to keep them archived, that'll use up your hard disk fast. So your best bet is to burn your recorded TV shows to DVD to archive them or play them on a standalone DVD player. You can burn them to DVD from right within Windows Media Player.

When you record a show to DVD straight from Windows Media Player, you won't be able to edit out commercials **[Hack #139]**.

The easiest way to do this is right inside Media Center using the remote control. When you start Media Center, use your remote control to navigate to the TV and Movies menu and click on the recorded TV submenu. This will show you the TV shows and movies you've recorded. Next, use the remote to navigate to a TV show you want to burn to DVD. When you navigate there, the TV show will be highlighted. (If you are using your mouse to do this, right-click on the highlighted TV show.)

Figure 10-27.
Select Burn from this menu to burn your TV show to a DVD

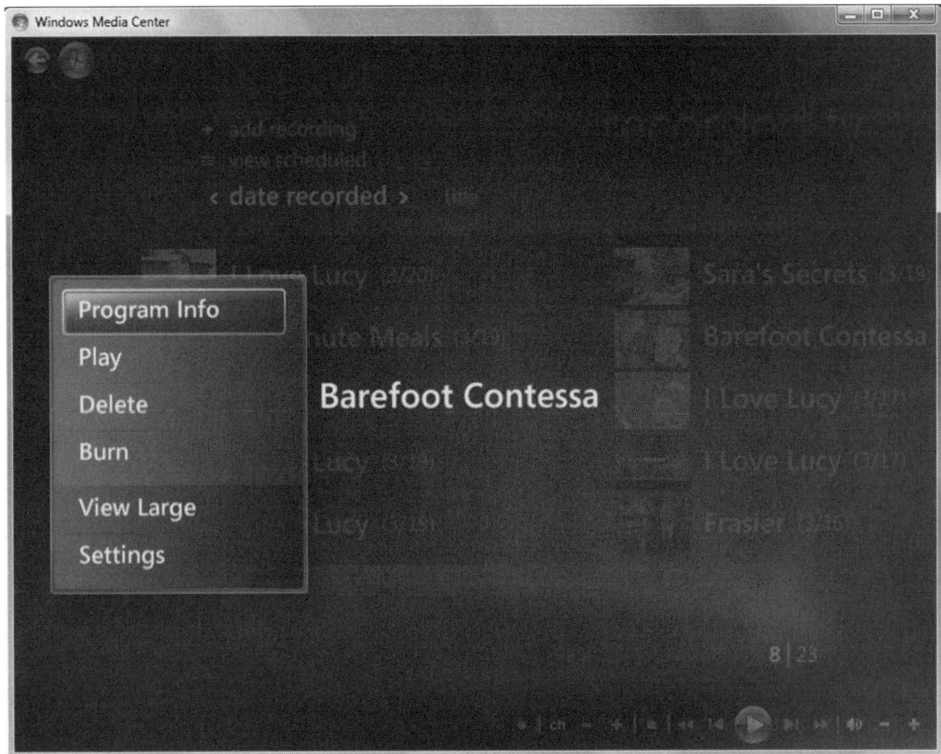

Select the more info button on your remote and a menu will appear with an option to burn your TV show, as you can see in Figure 10-27.

Make sure you have a recordable DVD in your DVD drive. If you don't, Windows will prompt you to put one in. From the next screen that appears (Figure 10-28), you have a choice of burning a Data or Video DVD. You must choose Video DVD if you want to burn a DVD to be played on a standalone DVD player.

Now Media Center will burn your TV show to DVD. Depending on how many TV shows you are burning to one DVD this can take a while since Media Center has to do some transcoding of the video file format.

If you have Media Center Edition 2005 on Windows XP, the screens will be a little different but you can burn TV shows to DVD the same way. On some older versions of Media Center you could not burn TV shows to a DVD because a specific encoder file called *sonic_encoder.msi* was missing. This file can easily be found on the web by doing a simple Google search.

See Also

- You can also use other DVD authoring programs to burn recorded TV shows from Windows Media Center to DVD. Notably, NeroVision 7 Ultra (www.nero.com), which sells for $79.99, supports the DVR-MS format and can burn recorded TV shows to DVD.
- "Set Up Your PC To Record TV Shows" **[Hack #138]**
- "Make Your Own TV Show Mashup" **[Hack #140]**
- "Copy Recorded TV Shows To Your Zune" **[Hack #151]**
- "Remove Commercials from Recorded TV Shows" **[Hack #139]**

— Timothy Coyle

Figure 10-28.
Make sure to select Video DVD to burn it as a DVD you can play on a DVD player

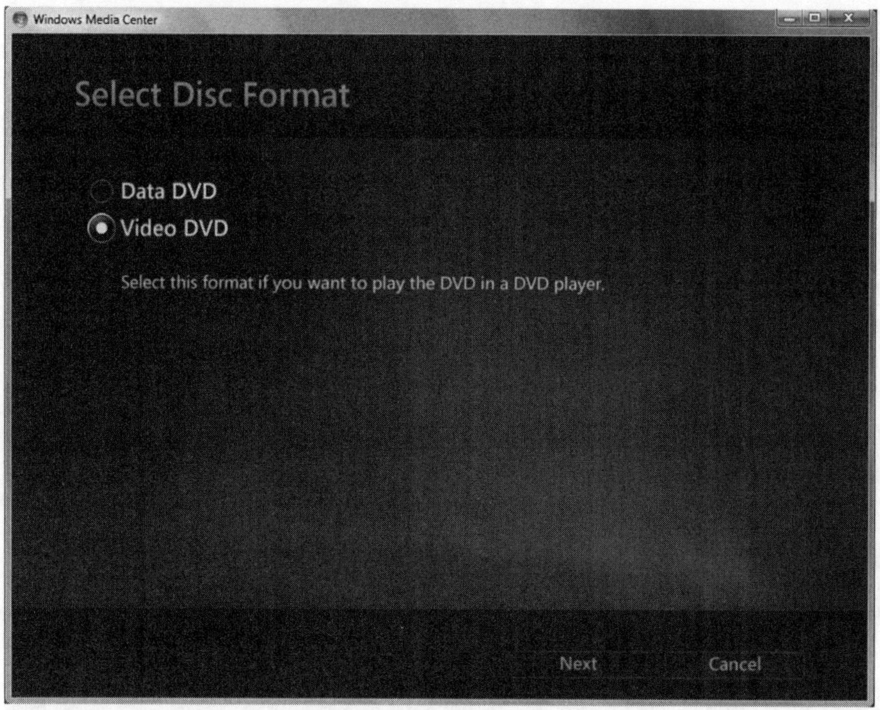

HACK 142: Rip DVDs into Media Center

V XP If you've bought DVDs and want to rip them to your PC like a CD and watch them in Windows Media Center, here's a hack for you.

Windows Media Center gives you the ability to play your DVDs, but wouldn't it be great if you didn't have to put the DVD in the computer? That's one less thing you need to pack when you're going on a trip. In fact, it's not hard to do, and a bonus is that you'll be able to use Windows Media Center's interface to browse all of your DVDs.

There are a lot of different programs that you can use to rip your DVD to your hard drive; all you need is one that will create a video file backup of your DVD in the VOB (DVD-Video Object) file format. My favorite is a freeware program called DVD Shrink (www.dvdshrink.org). It will let you rip DVDs using several different formats for your PC, but I prefer to rip my DVDs in a lossless format with no compression so I have the same quality as the original DVD. Be aware that this will take up a lot of hard drive space (figure about 6 GB per DVD).

Put the DVD you want to rip in the DVD drive in your computer and start DVD Shrink. Select the Open Disc button, select your DVD drive, and DVD Shrink will start to analyze your DVD, as you can see in Figure 10-29. A standard DVD will take about 2 minutes to be analyzed (it will take much longer to rip). You can check the "Enable video preview" box if you want to see a preview of the DVD as the program goes about doing its work.

Once the DVD has been analyzed in DVD Shrink, select the Re-author button to back up the main part of the DVD movie, and skip all the extras such as commentaries. Under the Main Movie section on the right hand side of the screen, double click on the Title 1 icon and the main movie video segment will be added to the DVD Compilation on the left hand side of the screen. This way,

Figure 10-29.
DVD Shrink analyzing a DVD before it starts ripping

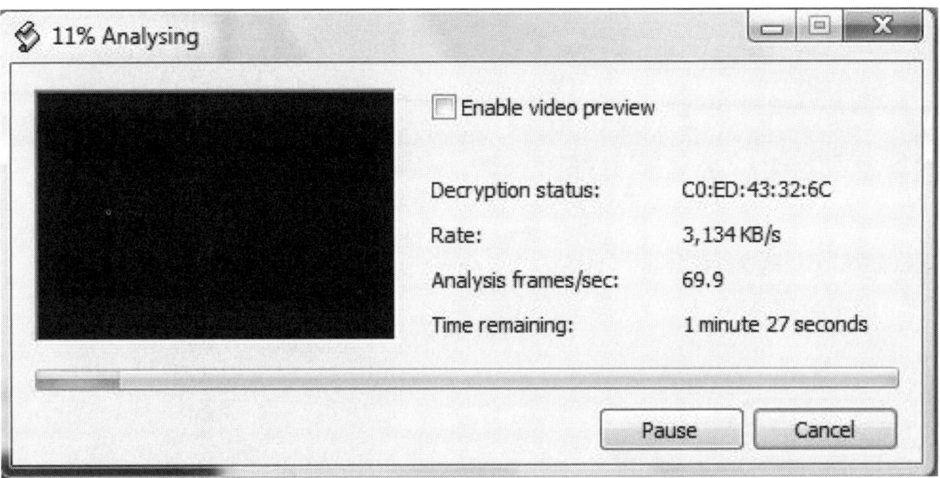

Figure 10-30.
Selecting which parts of the DVD to copy to your hard disk

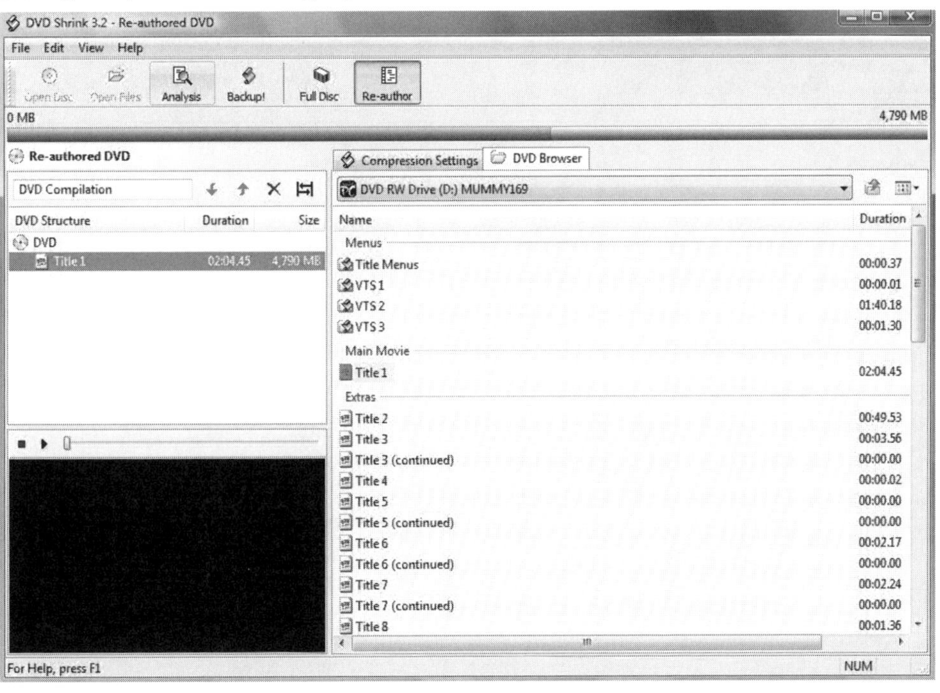

all of the extras that come with standard DVD movies like the menu interface and behind the scene commentaries won't be included. This will save space on your hard drive. Alternatively, you can select the Full Disc option and the entire DVD (menus and all of the extras) will be included. In Figure 10-30, you can see that I just added the main video segment to the DVD Compilation window and it will take up 4.79 GB of hard drive space.

Before you actually rip the DVD to the hard drive, you can reduce the overall size of the ripped DVD video file by clicking the Compression Settings tab, shown in Figure 10-31, and making a compression choice from the drop-down menu on the right side of the screen.

Figure 10-31.
DVD Shrink's Compression Settings tab

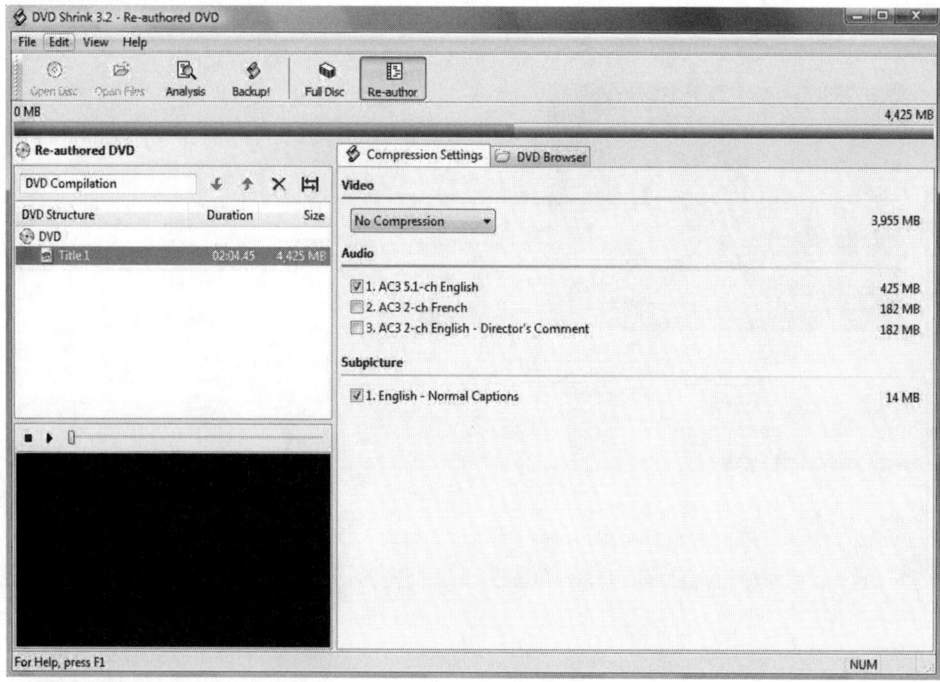

Figure 10-32.
Selecting a backup folder

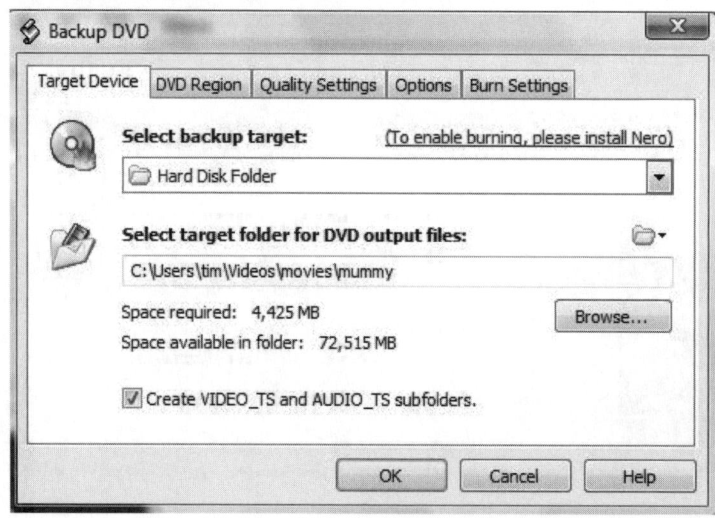

Under the Video section you can choose the level of compression you want. I prefer to have the full video quality of the original DVD so I choose No Compression by default. Remember that if you do choose to compress the DVD video file, although you will save hard drive space, the quality will not be as good as the original DVD. You can also unselect different Audio options to reduce the file size. For example, since I don't speak French I don't need to include the alternative soundtrack in French.

Once you are happy with your settings, select the Backup! button to rip the DVD to your hard drive. Under Select Backup Target choose Hard Disk Folder and then select the folder on your hard drive where you want your DVD to be ripped to, as shown in Figure 10-32. I suggest creating a separate folder for each DVD you back up. Leave all of the other options as default.

Figure 10-33.
DVD Shrink in action, backing up a DVD

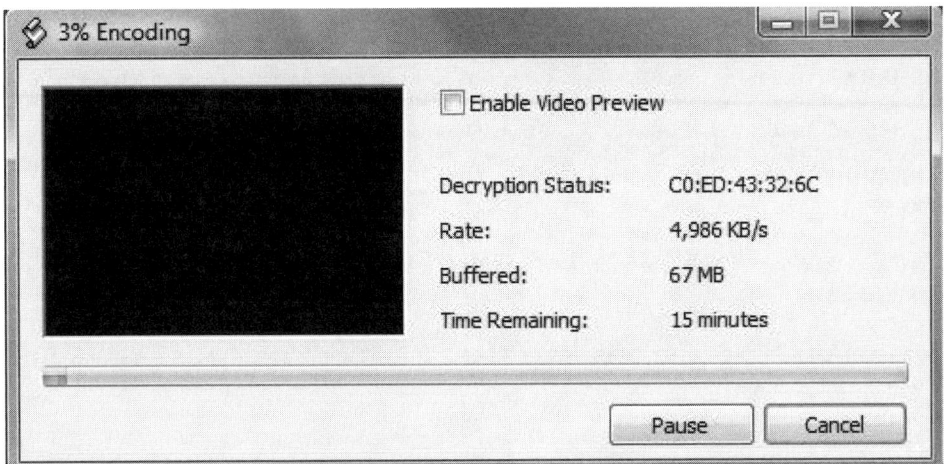

Figure 10-34.
A sample .dvdid file

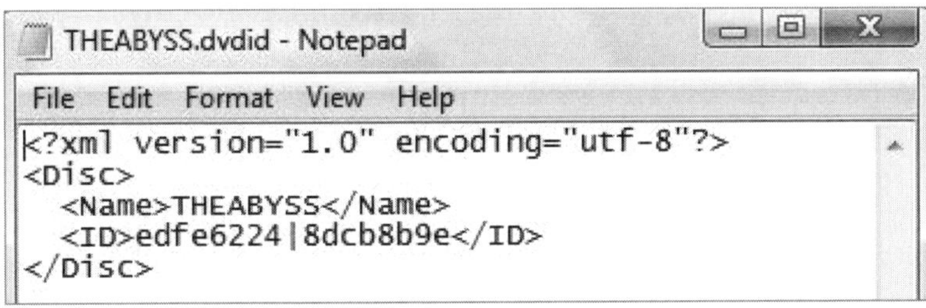

Backing up a standard DVD to your hard drive will usually take about 20 minutes but it could take longer or shorter depending on your compression settings, the file size, and the speed of your computer. Figure 10-33 shows DVD Shrink backing up a DVD to hard disk.

By default DVD Shrink will create two folders; the *VIDEO_TS* folder will contain all of the VOB files and the *AUDIO_TS* folder will be empty. (You need the *AUDIO_TS* folder later on for the DVD library viewer.) The folders will live underneath the folder where you've chosen to back up your DVD.

Once you have your DVD backed up onto your hard drive, you need a DVD XML file in the *.dvdid* format so that Windows Media Center can get the metadata for the DVD in order for you to view the DVD. The file is a plain-text file that you can create in Notepad or another text editor. Its format is like Figure 10-34.

Particularly important is the `<ID> tag` that identifies the DVD title. To get it, you could put each DVD in your computer, start up Windows Media Center, get the ID number that way, and then create the file. But who wants to do that for all of their DVD movies? A better way is to go to www.dvdxml.com and download the DVD XML file you need for free. Make sure you save the file in the same folder that contains your *VIDEO_TS* and *AUDIO_TS* folders that DVD Shrink created so Windows Media Center can find it.

Now you need to configure Windows Media Center to show your DVD library. You'll have to perform a simple Registry hack to do this. Launch the Registry Editor by typing regedit at the Start Search box or a command prompt and pressing Enter (See Chapter 13 for details). Go to `HKEY_CURRENT_USER\Software\Microsoft\Windows\CurrentVersion\Media Center\Settings\DvdSettings\ShowGallery` and change its value to `Gallery`. Exit the Registry, restart Media Center and you should be all set.

QUICK HACK 

RIP DVDS TO YOUR HARD DISK

If you're looking to rip a DVD to your hard disk, here's another way to do it: Get the free Handbrake (handbrake.m0k.org). It'll rip DVD into MPEG-4 format, so that you can watch it on your PC or any MPEG-4-compatible player.

Now when you start Media Center you should see the DVD Library view, as you can see in Figure 10-35.

This Registry hack works with the Windows Media Center in Windows Vista, but not in Windows XP. To enable the My DVD view in the Windows XP version of Windows Media Center, download Tweak MCE PowerToy from Microsoft (www.microsoft.com/windowsxp/downloads/powertoys/mcepowertoys.mspx). There is an option to enable the My DVD view and once you do that you will be all set.

Once you click the DVD Library view, you will see all of your ripped DVDs, as shown in Figure 10-36.

You can click on the DVD you are interested in watching and read the full description as shown in Figure 10-37.

Now your Media Center is a full blown movie database and you don't have to get up to put a DVD in the computer anymore!

Figure 10-35.
You can now see a DVD library in Windows Media Center

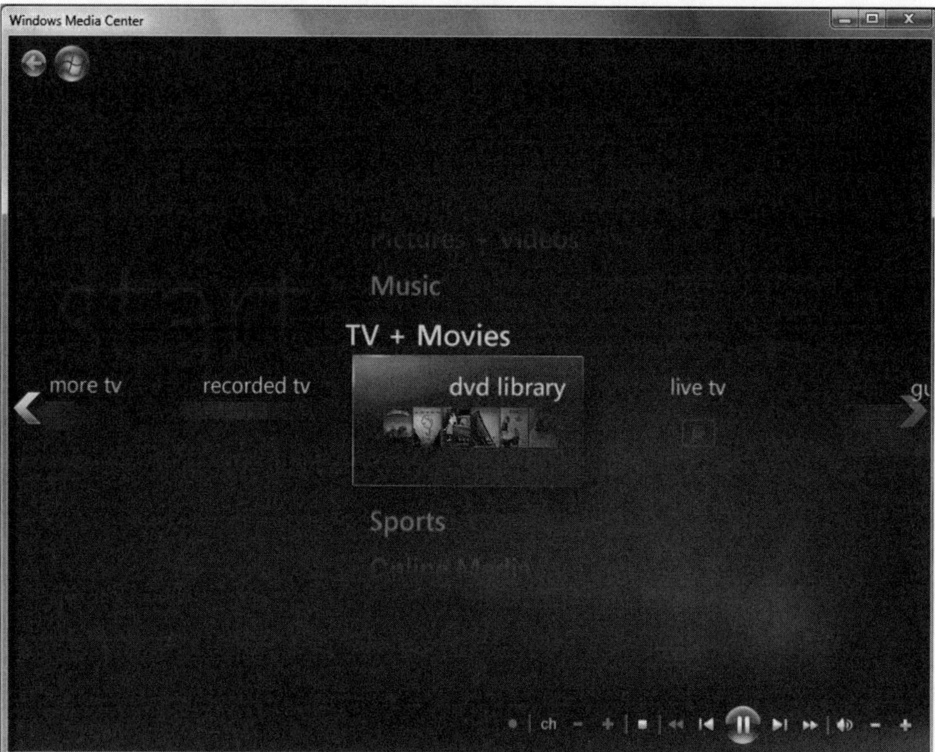

Figure 10-36.
Here's the DVD collection you've ripped to your hard disk

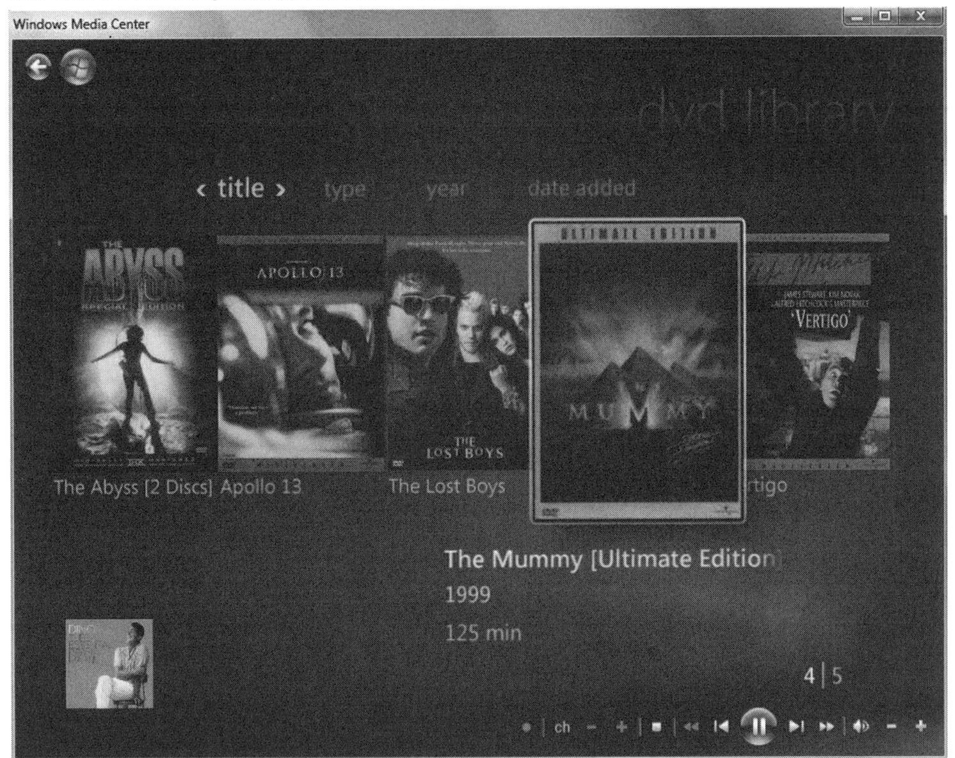

Figure 10-37.
Getting more detail about a DVD before playing it

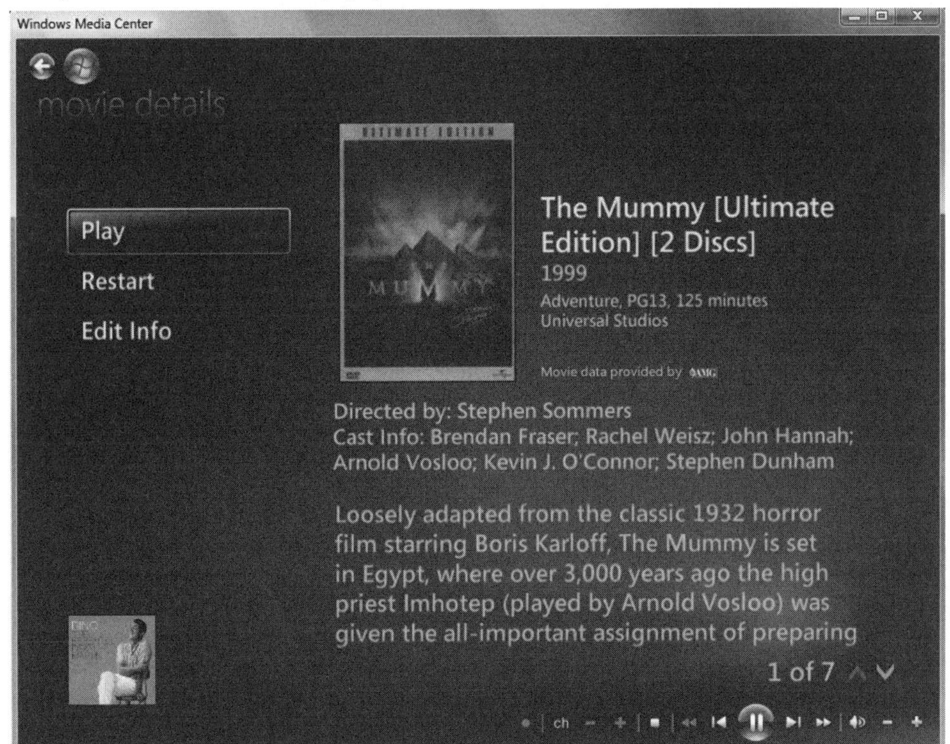

HACK 143: Quick Fix for Video and Animation Woes

V XP Are you having problems playing or working with videos? This quick, easy hack may clear them up for you with a few simple clicks.

Working with or watching video can sometimes be maddening, especially if you have older hardware. Files may become corrupt when you're working with them or converting them, particularly in the MPEG and DVR-MS formats. You may have troubles with your mouse pointer, or display problems with games. Videos may appear jerky. Sometimes, applications won't run at all.

A quick fix often solves the problem—adjust the hardware acceleration in Windows XP or Windows Vista. Hardware acceleration controls how your graphics card handles animations and videos.

In Windows XP, right-click the desktop, and select Properties→Settings→Advanced→Troubleshoot. A screen like the one shown in Figure 10-38 appears.

Move the slider all the way to the left to turn off hardware acceleration, then try running your programs and working with video to see if that solves the problem. If it does, the issue may be that you have an outdated driver. Visit the Web site of your graphics card's manufacturer and download and install the latest drivers; there's a good chance that will solve the problem. You should be able to use the card with full hardware acceleration.

If you still have problems after this, and turn down hardware acceleration one notch from full. Keep doing this until you find a setting at which video runs properly.

In Windows Vista, right-click the desktop, choose Personalize→Display Settings→Advanced Settings→Troubleshoot, and click Change settings to get to the hardware acceleration settings.

Not all graphics cards let you change the hardware acceleration settings. If yours doesn't, you won't be able to move the slider in Windows XP. In Windows Vista, you won't be able to click Change settings, because the button will be grayed out.

HACK 144: Choose the Right Settings for Publishing Your Movie in Windows Movie Maker

V When you save a movie to your PC there are plenty of settings you can choose. But which is the right one? Here's the inside scoop.

Windows Movie Maker in Windows Vista makes it easy to create your own movie, and then publish it in a variety of different ways, such as to a DVD, recordable CD, to a file you send via email to a friend, or as a file on your hard disk. To do it, after you have a movie you want to publish, click Publish Movie, and the screen like the one shown in Figure 10-39 appears.

Click where you want to publish, and Windows Movie Maker automatically selects the right settings for your movie, such as the bit rate, resolution, and so on.

Well, not quite. If you choose to publish the movie to your PC by selecting This Computer, things get a little more complicated. After you choose a location for your file, the screen shown in Figure 10-40 appears.

If you choose the top option, best quality, Windows Movie Maker goes about its merry way and saves your movie, not matter how large the file is. Same with if you choose the "Compress to"

Figure 10-38
Use this slider to turn off hardware acceleration

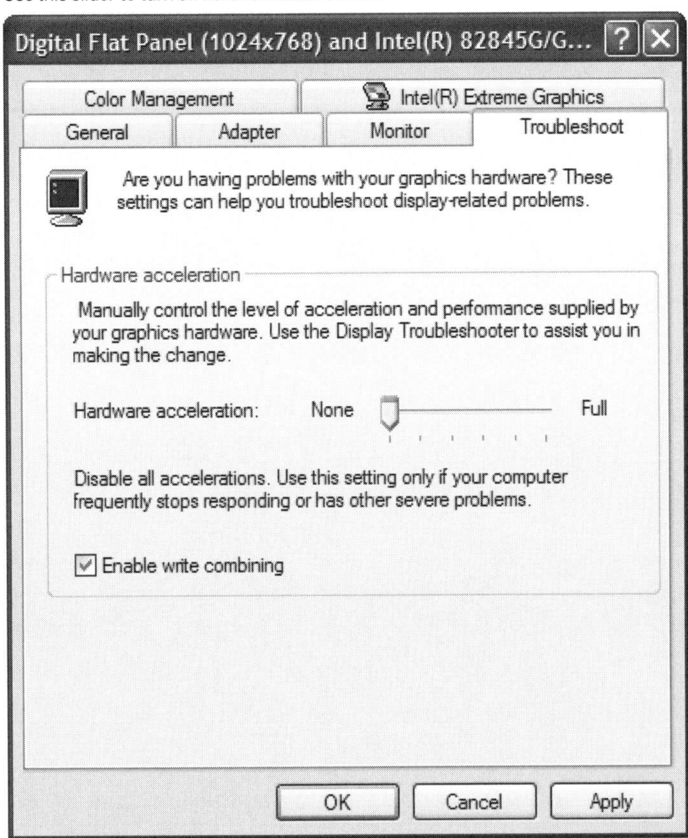

Figure 10-39.
Options for publishing your movie

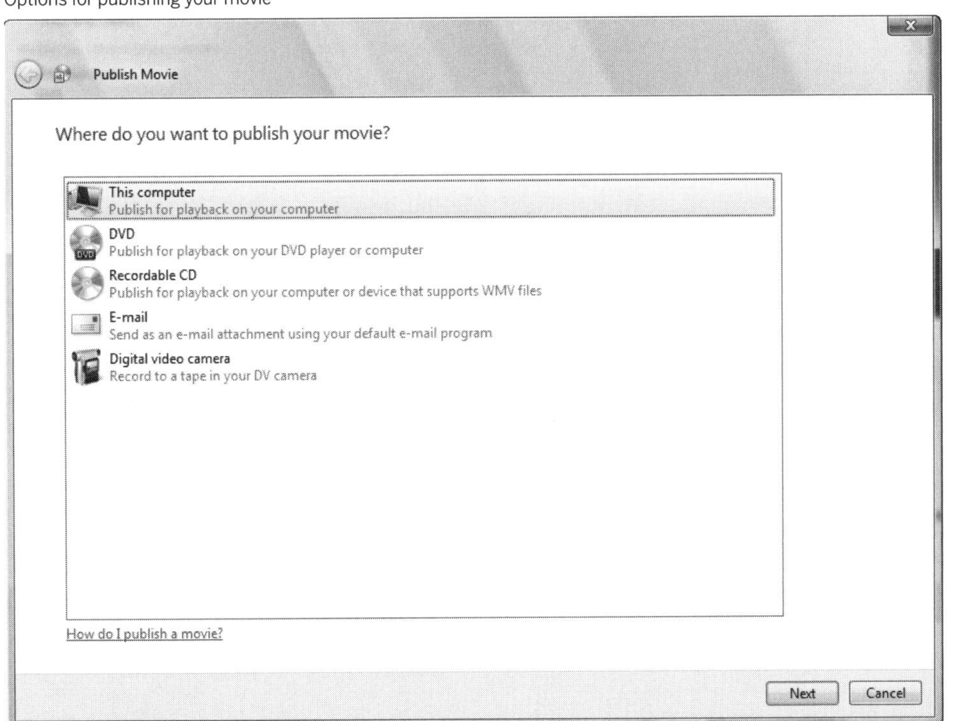

Figure 10-40.
Selecting your options for publishing to your own PC

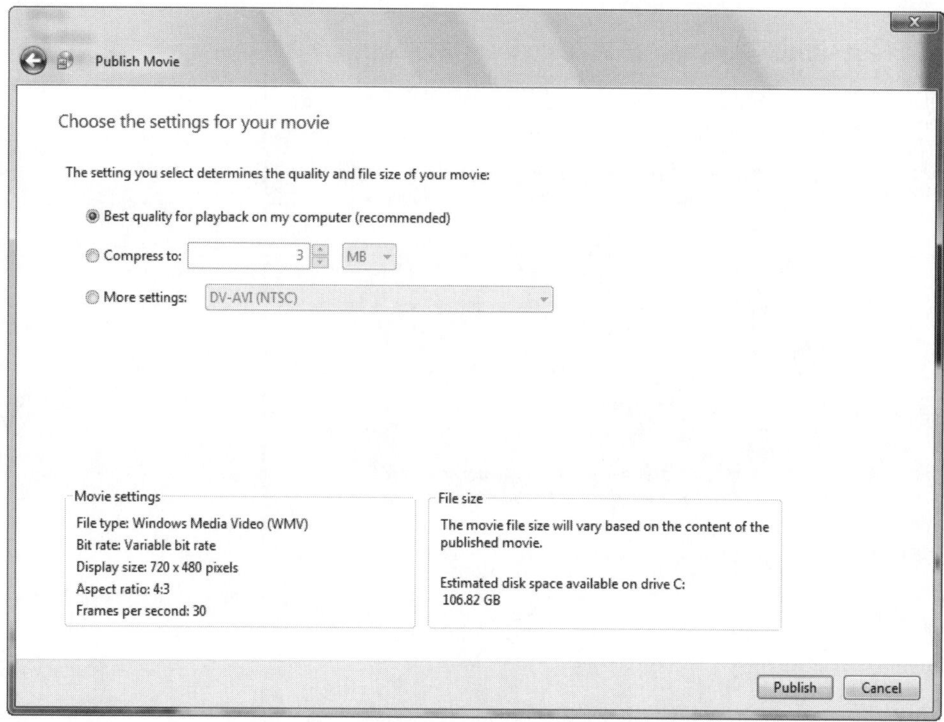

option—select a file size you want, and Windows Movie Maker creates a file of that size, and adjusts the quality accordingly.

But the "More settings" option gives you much more control over how to save your movie. Depending on how you're going to use your movie, you can adjust the quality and other settings of the final file, for the best balance between file size and quality. Table 10-1 shows you your choices, and which options you should choose, according to how you're planning to use your movie.

Table 10-1. Options for saving your movie in Windows Movie Maker

FILE TYPE	RESOLUTION	BIT RATE	RECOMMENDED USE
DV-AVI (NTSC)	720 x 480	25 Mbps	This is the highest-quality output, and generally the largest file size as well. It's a good choice if your movie will be played using an application that does not support Windows Media Video (WMV) files.
Windows Media Portable Device	640 x 480	1 Mbps	If you plan to view the video on a portable device that uses Windows Media Player, this is the one to choose. You won't have to convert this file once you save it; Windows Media Player will automatically convert it to a format that can be played on your supported portable media device.
Windows Media DVD Quality	640 x 480	3 Mbps	This choice is a good balance between file size and video quality. Use this if you've captured video from a digital video (DV) camera, and want a small file size.

Table 10-1. Options for saving your movie in Windows Movie Maker *(continued)*

FILE TYPE	RESOLUTION	BIT RATE	RECOMMENDED USE
Windows Media DVD Widescreen Quality	720 x 480	3 Mbps	This is the same format as the previous choice, except it's good for widescreen (16:9) standard definition output.
Windows Media HD 720p	1280 x 720	5.9 Mbps	You'll only see this setting if you use Windows Vista Home Premium or Windows Vista Ultimate. It creates high-quality high definition (HD) movies in Windows Media Video 9. Use this if you have source content in 720p or your final output display is 720p.
Windows Media HD for Xbox 360	1280 x 720	6.8 Mbps	You'll only see this setting if you use Windows Vista Home Premium or Windows Vista Ultimate. It creates high-quality HD movies at 720p, and is best if you will view your movie on an Xbox 360.
Windows Media HD 1080	1440 x 1080	7.8 Mbps	You'll only see this setting if you use Windows Vista Home Premium or Windows Vista Ultimate. It creates high-quality 1080p HD movies, and is best if you will view the movie on a computer or DVD player that supports WMV HD, or if your source material is 1080p.
Windows Media Low Bandwidth	320 x 240	117 Kbps	If you want a small file size, this is the one to choose—it produces the smallest file size possible, although the movie will not be as good a quality as at higher settings
Windows Media VHS Quality	640 x 480	1 Mbps	If your original content comes from an analog device, such as a VHS tape, and you want a small file size, choose this option. It produces medium-quality standard definition output.

HACK 145: Upload Your Video to YouTube

V XP Time for your closeup? If you want the world to see your video, upload it to YouTube. Here's a quick guide on how to do it.

OK, Fellini-wanna-be, you've used Windows Movie Maker or another program to create a video. Now it's time to share it with the world.

You won't need to find a worldwide distributor, or try to get into the Sundance Festival to do it, though. You can upload your video for free to the YouTube (www.youtube.com) service, for all the world to see.

You can create a video for YouTube in the *.wmv*, *.avi*, *.mov*, and *.mpg* formats. If you want your video to look best on the site, use these specs:

- MPEG4 (Divx, Xvid) format
- 320 by 240 resolution
- MP3 audio
- 30 frames per second

Figure 10-41.
Uploading a video to YouTube

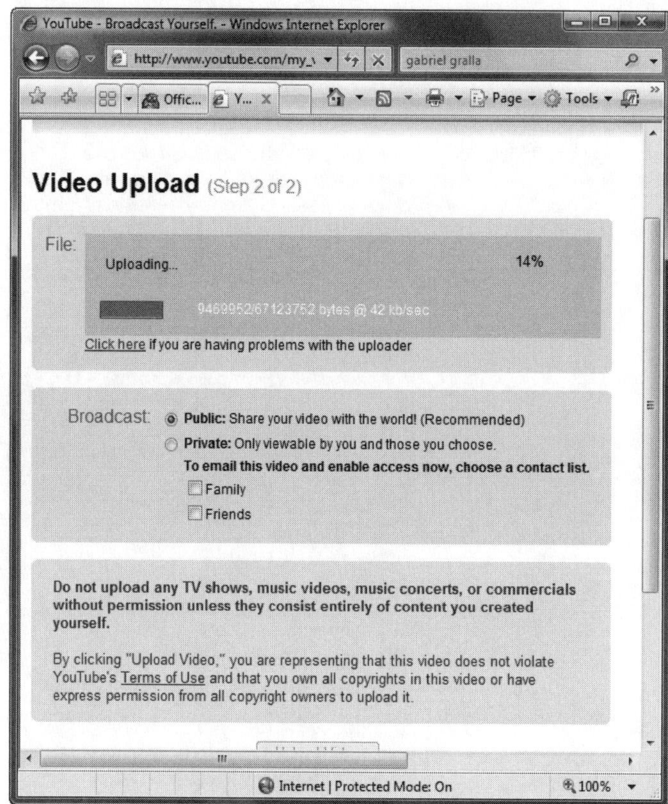

The video file must be under 100 MB, and cannot be longer than 10 minutes.

Before you upload any videos, you have to register with the site and sign in.

There are three ways to upload your video to YouTube: from a video you've created on your PC; via a webcam or digital camcorder attached to your PC; or from a cell phone. Following you'll find instructions on how to upload each way.

From a Recorded Video

After you record your video, head to YouTube, and click the Upload Videos link on the upper right-hand side of the page. From the page that appears, on the left-hand side of the screen, fill in information about your video, including its title, description, category, and so on. At the bottom of the page, click Continue Uploading.

On the next screen that appears, click the Browse button, and select the video. Then choose whether you want the video to be public or private. When you're done, click Upload Video. You'll see a progress bar showing the video being uploaded, as shown in Figure 10-41. Depending on the size of your video and your connection speed, it may take several minutes, or several hours or more to upload it. As a general rule of thumb, figure it will take somewhere between one to five minutes for every 1 MB of file size. But that can vary tremendously depending on your connection speed, and on the amount of traffic on the site.

Once your video uploads, a screen appears that lets you edit information about the video, such as its name, category, and a good deal more information as well. You don't need to edit it; if you're satisfied with the form you filled out, leave it as is.

Once your video is uploaded, it will show up in its category, and be searchable from the site. But keep in mind that it can take a very long time for a video to show up in the search index. In fact, it can take eight hours or more for it to appear in search, and on occasion even takes more than 24 hours.

To see your video, click the My Account link at the top of YouTube, and click My Uploaded Videos. You'll see a screen listing all the videos you've uploaded. You can edit the information associated with the video, and delete the video from here. To play it, click the video as you would any other YouTube video. If you want friends to view it, copy the URL and send it to them. Figure 10-42 shows the YouTube video that was uploaded previously in this hack.

Via Live Recording

If you have a Webcam or digital camcorder attached to your PC, and feel comfortable winging it live in front of a camera, you don't have to record your video ahead of time—you can record a video live and have it uploaded.

Figure 10-42.
Playing your video in YouTube

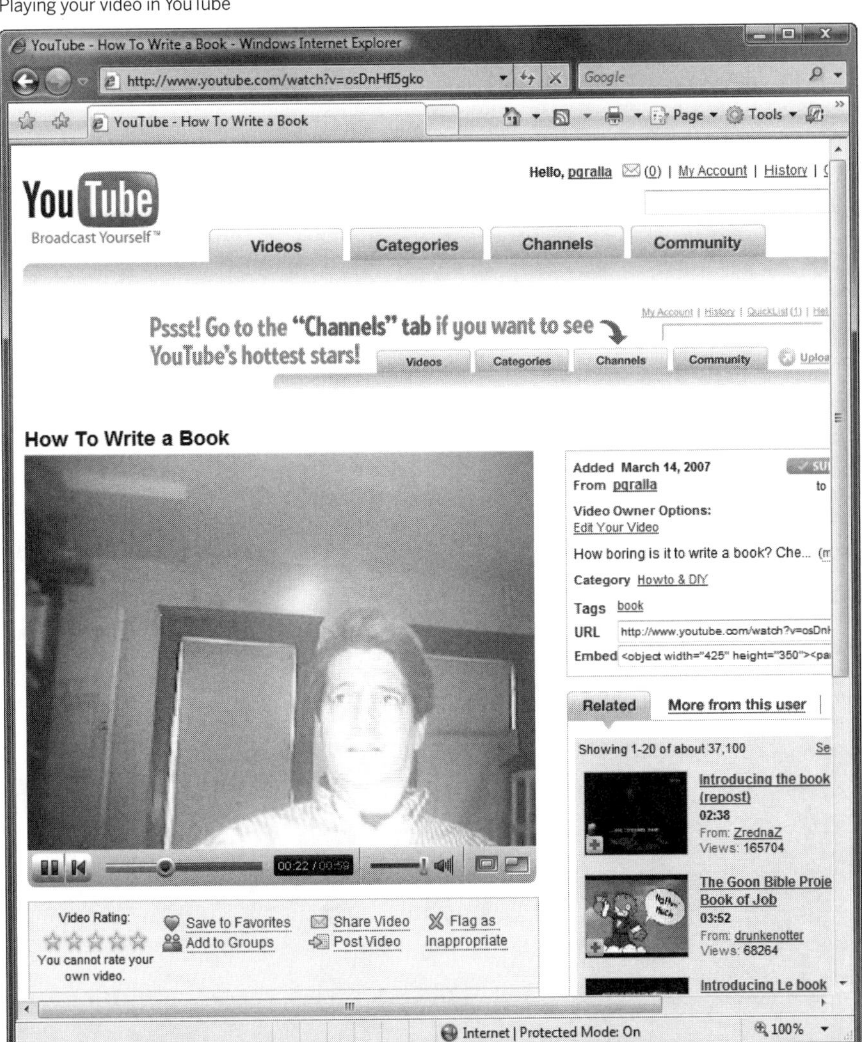

First check to make sure your camera is working properly. Click the Upload Video link—from the page that appears, click the "Try it now" link on the right-hand side of the page just beneath "Record videos directly from your desktop camera!" (After the novelty of this feature wears off, YouTube may put the option in a different location with less fanfare.)

Follow the same directions for filling in information about your video as if you were going to upload it. Before you can begin recording, you'll get a notice on the right-hand side of the screen that a Flash player needs to be installed. Click Allow. Click Auto-Detect Camera and Mic, and click Record. It will start recording. If you click Auto-detect and Mic, you'll see the live video, but it won't start recording yet, as shown in Figure 10-43. This is a good way to test your video before recording it.

From here on it, the instructions are self-explanatory; stop recording when you're done, and follow the forms for uploading your video. You get the same options as if you uploaded a video file.

From Your Cell Phone

To send videos to YouTube from your cell phone, you don't send them directly from the phone using a separate application. Instead, you send it from the phone via the phone's email feature.

First, though, you need to create a profile of your cell phone. To do it, when you click the Upload Video link on the main YouTube page, from the page that appears, click the Set up your preferences link. You'll be prompted to create a "Mobile Profile," which includes the default category for your videos, a default title for your videos, default description for your videos, and so on. You'll also set defaults such as whether you want to receive an email when your upload is complete, or get an SMS message when the upload is complete.

Again, the instructions are self-explanatory from here on in. Record your video on your cell phone, send it via email using your cell phone's email client, and you'll get a chance to be a YouTube star.

Figure 10-43.
Getting ready to record a YouTube video

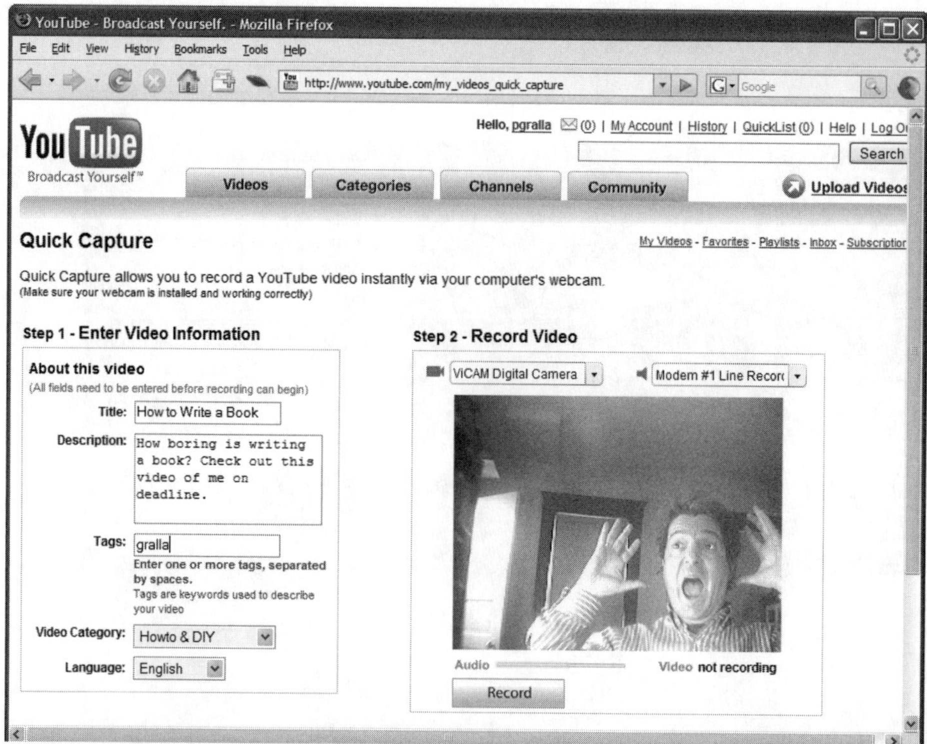

HACK 146: Turn VHS Tapes into DVD Movies

V XP Got aging VHS home movies that you'd like to turn into DVDs? With the right hardware and cables, you can do it.

Back in the pre-digital days, if you made home movies, you shot them on tape, popped the tapes into your VCR, and watched to your heart's content. Plenty of people have lots of these tapes laying around. The tapes, however, don't age well, and degrade over time. So it's a good idea to turn them into DVDs.

But how exactly do you do that? At first, it might seem mind-bogglingly complex to turn old tapes into DVDs. But with the right cables and hardware, you can do it.

The key to getting old tapes into your PC is converting the analog video and audio from the tapes into a digital format. If you have a digital video camcorder, you can use the camcorder to do it, and I cover that in the next part of the hack. If you don't have a digital camcorder, your best bet is to buy a special device that serves as the go-between. You plug your VCR into one end, and then plug the device into a USB 2.0 port. You then use software that comes with the device to capture the video on your PC. Once you have the video captured, use software like Windows Movie Maker or Windows DVD Maker (both supplied with Vista) to edit and then burn a DVD.

There are plenty of inexpensive devices that do the job for about $50, for example Dazzle DVD Recorder (www.dazzle.com), or Video Xpress (www.adstech.com). And you can also bypass your PC altogether, and go straight from tape to a DVD by buying a combo VHS and DVD recorder. There are plenty available; go to your local electronics store, or find them online.

Using Your Digital Video Camcorder to Copy Tapes to DVD

If you have a digital video camcorder, though, you won't need to buy an extra device. You can use it instead to act as your go-between. It takes the analog signal from the tapes, converts them to digital video, then passes them on to your PC. You'll hook up your VCR to your digital video camcorder, then connect the camcorder to your PC and record the video. From there, you can burn it to a DVD.

Before you get started, you'll need to make sure that your DV camcorder supports analog-to-digital conversion, so check the manual. Also check the manual for how to turn on the conversion. In some instances, on the camcorder's playback menu will be a setting such as A/V to DV Out, or something similar.

You'll also need a USB or IEEE 1394 (also known as FireWire or i.Link) cable, depending on the connection your DV camcorder uses, and also a USB or IEEE 1394 port on your PC, again depending on which your camcorder uses. In addition, you'll need a Audio/Video (A/V) cable, which has three RCA connections (one red, one white, and one yellow) on one end, and a mini A/V connector on the other end. If you have an S-Video connection on your VCR or analog video camcorder, you can instead use an S-Video cable and a separate RCA cable that has red and white RCA audio connectors on one end and a stereo mini-jack on the other end. These types of cables may come with your camcorder. If not, you can find them at any electronics store.

Some camcorders that have USB and IEEE 1394 ports cannot transfer video over USB, and instead use USB for transferring still images or for using the camcorder as a webcam. If this is the case, you'll need to use a PC with an IEEE 1394 port.

Figure 10-44.
S-Video connection diagram

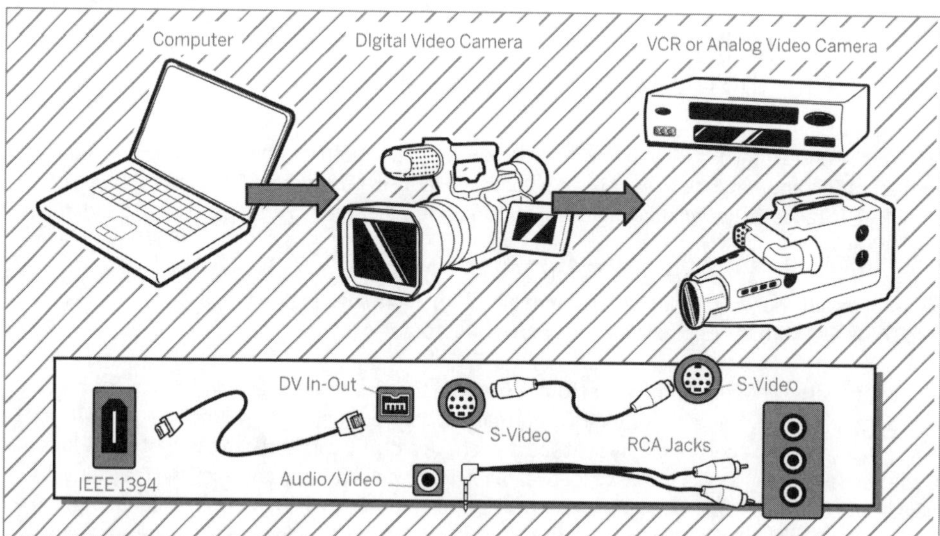

Figure 10-45.
Making the S-Video connection

Making the Connection with S-Video Cables

Now that you have everything you need, it's time to get started. In this section, you'll learn how to make the connection with S-Video cables. If you don't have an S-Video connection, skip to the next section, "Making the Connection with Composite Cables".

First, turn off the DV camcorder, as well as your VCR or analog video camcorder. Now it's time to connect your VCR or analog video camcorder to your DV camcorder. Depending on your setup, you'll connect it either via S-video connection or a composite video connection. If you have an S-video connection, use that, because it's of a higher quality. Figure 10-44 shows all the connections you'll be making if you're using an S-Video connection. Figure 10-45 shows the actual connections.

Plug one end of the S-Video cable into the S-Video jack on the DV camcorder, and the other end of the cable to the S-Video jack on the VCR or analog video camcorder. The S-Video cable carries the video signal from the VCR or analog camcorder to the DV camcorder.

If you have a digital video (DV) camcorder and your home movies reside on DV tape (not VHS), you won't have to go through the lengthy process of transferring it to your PC described in this hack. Connect the camcorder to your PC via a USB or FireWire connection, tell your camcorder to play recorded video, and then in the Autoplay dialog box that appears when your turn on the recorder, select a location and format for the file. You can also import it using Windows Movie Maker. Once you've got the video on your hard disk, burn it to DVD as you would any other video.

Next, plug the red and the white RCA cables into your VCR or analog video camcorder. These cables transfer the audio. Typically, these cables also come with a yellow RCA connector as well, but don't plug that in because that would be used for video if you weren't using S-Video. Also, if you're using a VCR, make sure that the red and white RCA connectors are plugged into the Line Out RCA jacks.

That takes care of connecting your VCR or analog video camcorder to your DV camcorder. Now connect the DV camcorder to your PC via the FireWire or USB ports.

Once the physical connections are made, you'll do the transfer. Jump to "Turn on Analog-To-Digital Conversion" later in this hack to find out how to do it.

Making the Connection with a Composite Cable

First, turn off the DV camcorder, as well as your VCR or analog video camcorder. Figure 10-46 shows all the connections you'll be making if you're using a composite connection. Figure 10-47 shows the physical connections.

Plug the red, white, and yellow RCA connections into their corresponding jacks on your VCR or analog camcorder. The red and white connectors transfer the audio; the yellow transfers the video. If you have a VCR, make sure that the connectors are plugged into the Line Out RCA jacks. Next, plug the mini A/V connector on the other end of the A/V cable is into the Mini A/V jack of the DV camcorder. (The jack is frequently yellow, and may be labeled Audio/Video).

That takes care of connecting your VCR or analog video camcorder to your DV camcorder. Now connect the DV camcorder to your PC via the FireWire or USB ports.

Once the physical connections are made, you'll do the transfer. Head to the next section of this hack to find out how to do it.

Turn on Analog-To-Digital Conversion

Now that you have everything connected, you need to turn on analog-to-digital conversion in your DV camcorder. Eject any tape in the camcorder, then turn the camcorder on, and put it into playback mode. (It may be labeled VCR or VTR). Press the proper buttons or controls to get to the playback settings, then turn on analog-to-digital conversion, then turn off the camcorder.

Your camcorder may not appear to have a specific setting for analog-to-digital conversion. It may instead be called something like A/V to DV Out, A/V to DV, or a similar name. Some camcorders may perform this conversion automatically without needing you to put it in a special mode.

Transfer the Video

Now that everything is connected and your settings are right, you're ready to transfer the video. Insert the tape you want to transfer into your analog video camcorder or VCR. Then turn on the DV camcorder, and put it into playback mode.

On your PC, start Windows Movie Maker in Windows Vista. Select File→Import from Digital Video Camera, or on the left-hand side of the screen, choose From Digital Video Camera under import. Follow the prompts that appear. Start playing the tape on your VCR or analog video camcorder. When it's done, turn it off, and save the file in Windows Movie Maker.

Figure 10-46.
Composite connection diagram

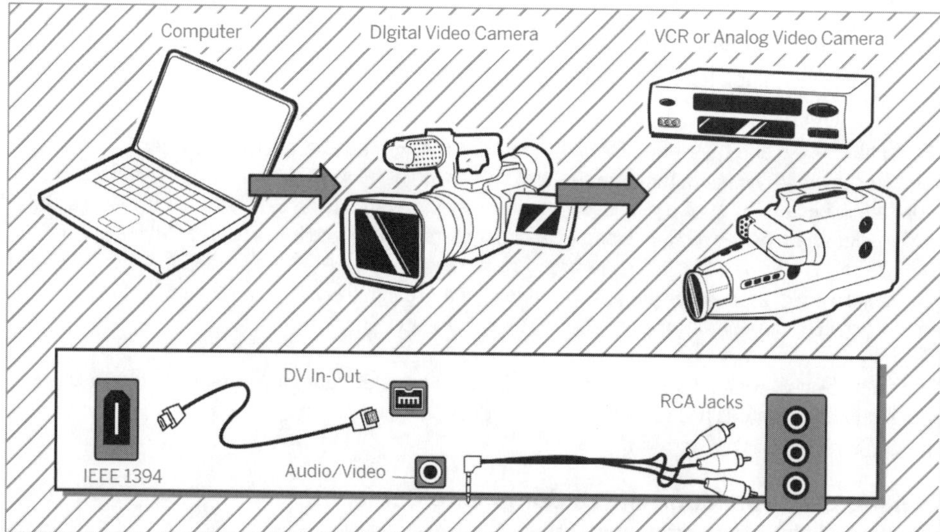

Figure 10-47.
Making the composite connection

You can now edit the video in any way you want, and use Windows Vista DVD Maker to burn it to DVD.

 If you are using Windows XP, import the video by choosing File→Capture Video, or on the left-hand side of the screen choosing Capture from Video Device under Capture Video. Windows XP doesn't include a DVD burning program, so you'll have to use a third-party program for burning a DVD.

See Also

- An excellent choice for turning old videotapes into DVDs is the Sony DVDirect VRD-MC3 DVD, which retails, at press time, for around $250.

HACK 147: Store Any Type of File on Your Zune

V XP You can use the Zune for transferring Zip files and any other kind of files, not just music—and then copying it to your PC. Here's how to do it.

Most people have two reactions to the Zune's built-in Wi-Fi capabilities:

1. Great! What an easy way to transfer music and pictures!

2. What! Is that all it can do with it? What a waste!

This hack shows you how to do more than just transfer music and pictures—it lets you transfer any other kind of file as well. It's a great way to share files with others, because after you send the file to their Zune, they can then copy it to their PC.

If you're going to transfer large files, it's a good idea to first compress them using Windows' built-in Zip compression features, because the file will transfer more quickly that way. So this hack shows you how to transfer a ZIP file, but as I'll show you, you can use it to transfer any other kind of file as well. Here's how to do it:

1. Launch the Registry Editor by typing regedit at the Start Search box or a command prompt (See Chapter 13 for details).

2. Go to `HKEY_LOCAL_MACHINE\System\ControlSet001\Enum\USB`.

3. Right Click on the USB folder and select Find. Search for PortableDeviceNameSpace. You should find a String with the your Zune's ID number in the name.

4. Change `EnableLegacySupport` to 1. Change `PortableDeviceNameSpaceExcludeFromShell` to 0. `ShowInShell` to 1.

5. Exit the Registry. You may need to log off and log on again, or reboot in order for the changes to take effect.

6. Rename the extension of the *.zip* files you want to send to *.jpg*. For example, if you want to send the zip file named *familystuff.zip*, rename it *familystuff.jpg*. (Note: If you're going to send another file type, simply rename that file as well. For example, rename *familystuff.doc* to *familystuff.jpg*.

7. Connect your Zune to your PC, press the Start Sync button, and drag the file or files from your PC into the Zune.

8. Disconnect the Zune, and then use it to send the files to someone as you would normally, using Wi-Fi. Make sure to tell the person the original extension names for the files.

9. The person to whom you've sent the file can now connect the Zune to his PC. After transferring the files to the PC, he can rename them to their original extension, and use them.

— Robert Cox, Zuney.Net Founder

See Also

- "Install a Larger Disk in Your Zune" **[Hack #173]**
- "Watch Any DVD on Your Zune" **[Hack #148]**

HACK 148: Watch Any DVD on Your Zune

V XP Got a DVD that you'd like to watch on your Zune? No problem—just follow these easy steps.

Frustrated because there's no way to watch DVDs from your collection on your Zune? Fret no longer.

DVD, meet Zune. Zune, meet DVD.

All you need to do is convert your DVD into a Zune-friendly format, then transfer it, or part of it, to your Zune, and you'll be ready to go.

There are a number of shareware converters out there, but a very good one is Xilisoft DVD to Zune Converter (www.xilisoft.com/dvd-to-zune-converter.html), which is free to try, but costs $29 if you decide to keep it.

To watch DVDs on your Zune, install the program, run it, insert a DVD into your DVD drive, then follow these steps:

1. Choose File→Add DVD Folder, or click the DVD button. From the window that appears, select the DVD and click OK.

2. If you want to convert the entire DVD, from the screen that appears, highlight the first entry in the list on the left-hand side of the screen. If you want to only convert certain sections (called chapters) on the DVD, click the program's Show Chapters button, and you'll be shown a list of all the chapters.

3. Highlight the chapters you want to convert, or keep the first entry highlighted if you want to convert the entire DVD.

4. From the Profile drop-down box, select a Zune-friendly format (for example, Zune MPEG-4 Video [*.mp4]).

5. After you select your format, the right column will display the audio and video standards, such as video frame rate, audio bit rate, and so on. For the highest quality audio and video, don't make any changes. Doing this will give you high-quality audio and video, but large file sizes. If you want smaller file sizes, choose lower settings, such as a slower frame rate or a lower bit rate.

6. Check the boxes next to any chapters you want to convert.

7. Select the folder to which you want to output the finished files, by clicking the Browse button.

8. Click the Start Ripping button, and the program will convert everything you've selected to a Zune-friendly format.

9. When you're done, copy the files to your Zune as you do any other files. Happy viewing!

See Also

- "Store Any Type of File on Your Zune" **[Hack #147]**
- "Install a Larger Disk in Your Zune" **[Hack #173]**

HACK 149: Delete Music from Your PC without Deleting It from Your Zune

V XP Use this trick to keep music on your Zune, while deleting it from your PC to free up space.

There's good news and bad news about the Zune itself and the Zune software on your PC. First the good news: The music between the two is always automatically kept in sync. Now the bad news: the music between the two is always automatically kept in sync.

The problem is that you want to keep many gigabytes of music on your Zune device, but not necessarily on your PC. That music takes up precious hard disk space. So it would be good to be able to delete music from your PC, but keep the music on your Zune. With automatic syncing, though, that's not possible.

The way around it is to tell the Zune not to sync automatically. That way, when you delete music files from your PC, they won't be automatically deleted from your Zune. When you want to add files to your Zune, you add them manually.

First you need to tell your Zune not to sync automatically whenever you plug it in. Run the Zune software, then right-click the name of your device in the lower left hand portion of the screen and choose Properties→Do Not Sync Automatically (Figure 10-48).

You'll receive a warning that if you make this choice, you'll have to remove files manually from the Zune when you want to delete them. Click Yes.

To add files to your Zune, drag them from your library to the lower-right hand portion of the Zune software screen. Then click Start Sync (Figure 10-49). They will now sync to the Zune.

Figure 10-48.
No, Zune, please don't sync

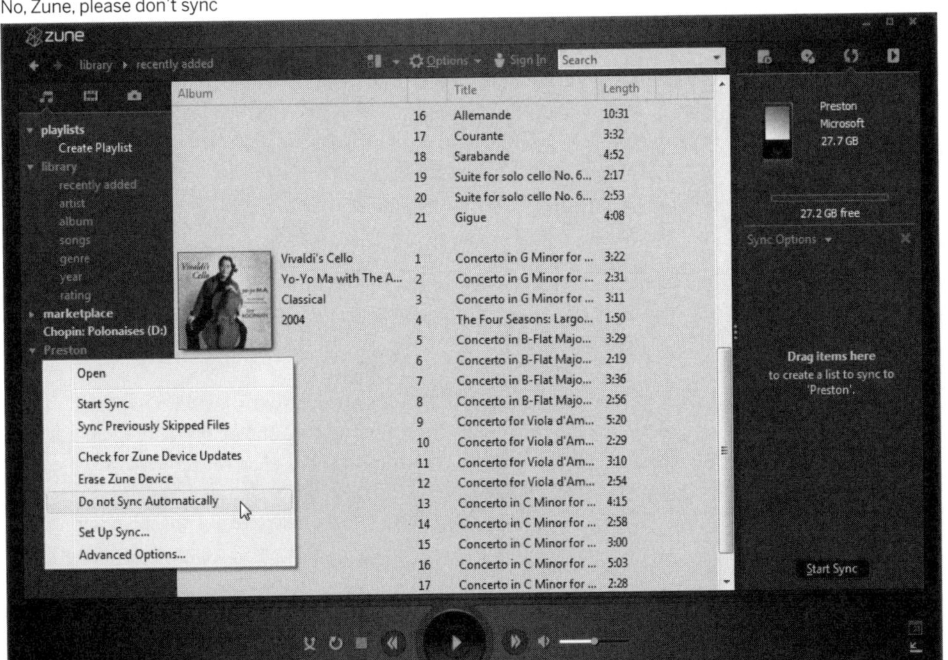

QUICK HACK 

ADD ALBUM ART TO YOUR ZUNE RECORDINGS

If you've added music albums to your Zune by downloading the music, or by ripping the files from a CD you've burned yourself, the album art may not show up in your Zune library or on the Zune itself. There's a simple way to paste in that album art. First go to Amazon, and search for the album, and then view the full description of the album. Right-click on the album art and select Copy. Then in the Zune library on your PC, right-click the album, and select Paste Album Art.

Figure 10-49.
Manually syncing your Zune

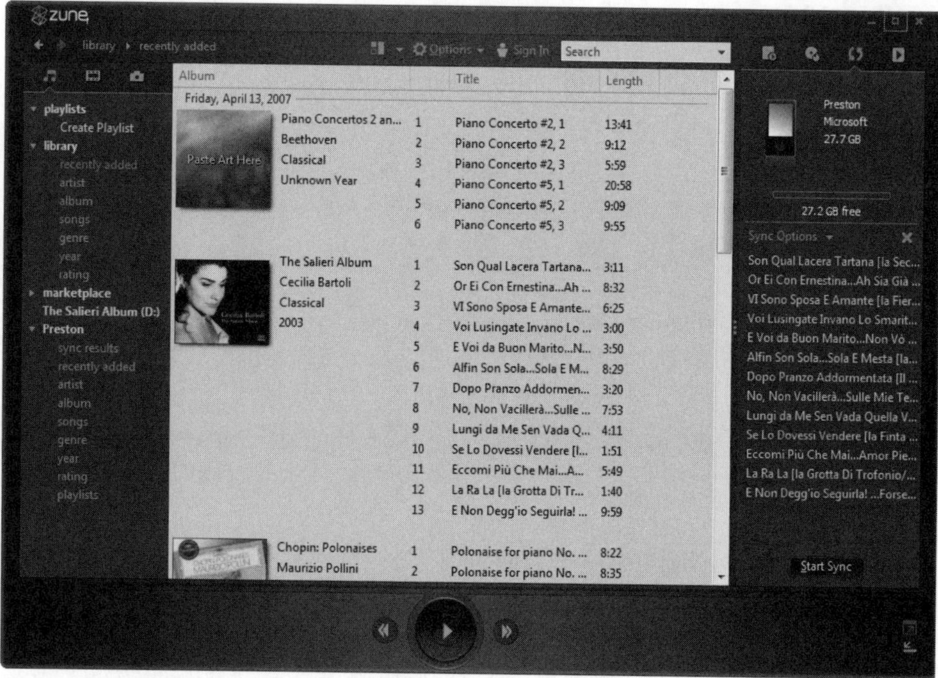

You can now delete any music files from the Zune software or your PC, and they won't be deleted from the Zune itself. If you want to delete files from the Zune, you can delete them manually. Run the Zune software, then under your Zune device name on the left-hand side of the screen, sort your library by artist, album, songs, and so on, and manually delete any files.

HACK 150: Play YouTube Videos on your Zune

V XP Now you can take your favorite YouTube videos with you wherever you go.

There's only one problem with YouTube (www.youtube.com)—its videos reside on its site, and you can't take them with you wherever you go.

Until now, that is. With the Zunemytube (sourceforge.net/projects/zunemytube/) you'll be able to automatically grab any video from YouTube or Google Video (video.google.com), convert it to a Zune-friendly format, and then sync it to your Zune.

The program installs as a plug-in for Internet Explorer; it adds an icon to the Internet Explorer toolbar. However, you may need to do a bit of hacking to make the icon show up after you install the program. Right-click the toolbar and select Customize Command Bar→Add or Remove Commands. On the Customize Toolbar box that appears, click ZuneIt, and click Move Up repeatedly until it's near the top of the toolbar button list. Then click Close. You should now be able to see the ZuneIt icon on the toolbar.

Head over to YouTube and queue up any video you want transferred to your Zune, then click the Zune icon (Figure 10-50).

Figure 10-50.
We'll be sending this YouTube video to a Zune

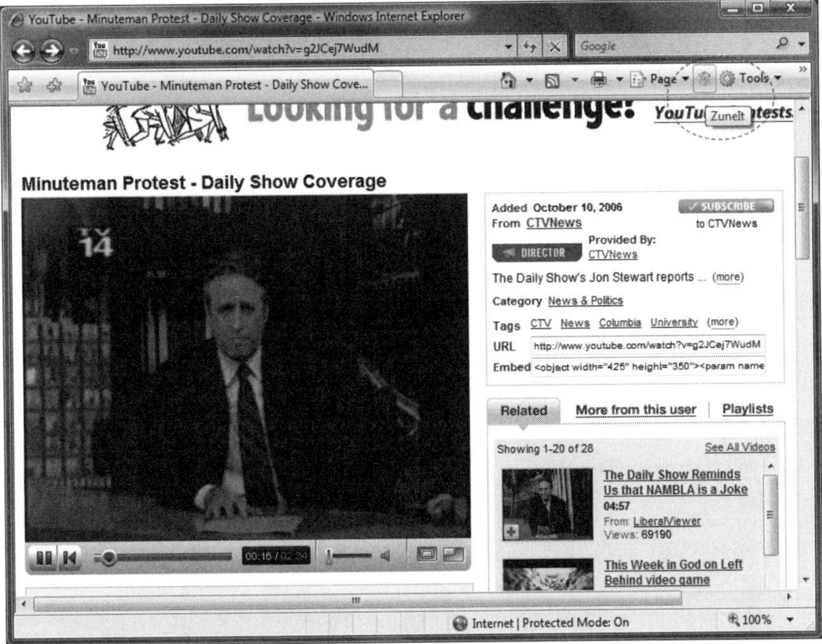

You won't actually see anything happening, but behind the scenes, the video is being converted to *.wmv* format, and being put into a new folder that the program created—a YouTube folder inside your Videos folder (In Windows Vista, the actual path is *C:\Users*`UserName`*\Videos\YouTube*, where `UserName` is your user account name. In Windows XP, it's put into a YouTube folder inside your My Videos folder.) You're now ready to sync it to your Zune. In fact, because it's in *.wmv* format, you can sync it to any media player that supports that format.

See Also

- "Copy Recorded TV Shows to Your Zune" **[Hack #151]**

HACK 151: Copy Recorded TV Shows To Your Zune

V XP Here's how to make Windows Media Center and the Zune the best of friends—automatically send recorded TV shows to your Zune for small-screen watching.

When it comes to videos, to a great extent, the Zune is all dressed up with no place to go. Where can you get all the videos to watch?

If you've got a Media Center PC or Windows Vista, the answer is close at hand, using a free piece of software, ZuneTVWatcher. The program will automatically take all your recorded TV shows, shrink them so they don't take up nearly as much hard disk space, and then put them in the proper folder for automatic syncing with your Zune.

It's quite simple to do. In fact, the hardest part of the entire process may be finding ZuneTVWatcher in order to download it. At times, you can find it on the site ZuneTVWatcher at www.zunetvwatcher.com. At times, though the link there doesn't work properly, or can't be found. So instead, you'll have to go to the forums area of the site (www.zunetvwatcher.com/forums), and register, then go to the main ZuneTVWatcher forum, and download the file from there.

QUICK HACK 

TRANSFER TV AND OTHER VIDEOS TO YOUR IPOD

If you've got an iPod instead of a Zune, you can easily convert TV shows and other videos to an iPod-compatible format and transfer them to your iPod. Download the free iPod video converter (ipodifier.com/download.html) and it will watch any folder for new videos, convert them to an iPod-compatible format, then adds them to iTunes and syncs them with your iPod.

Figure 10-51.
Checking the settings of ZuneTVWatcher

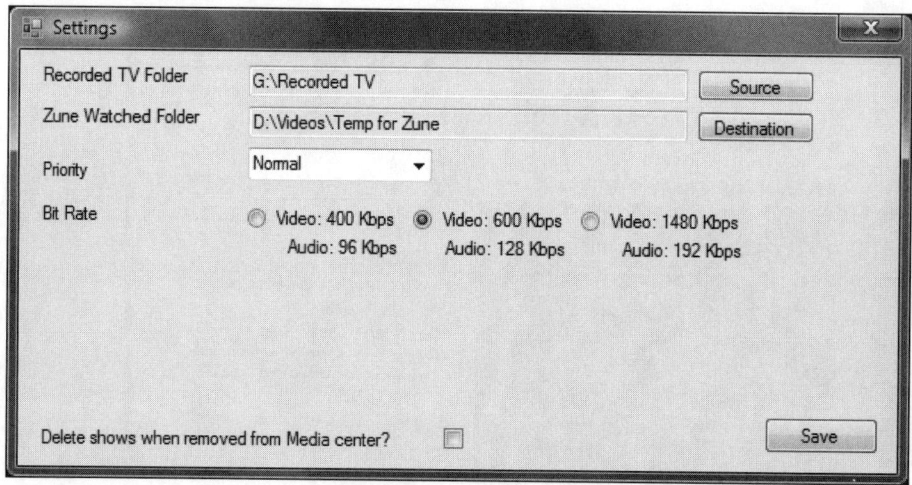

After you download and install it, it's all easy. Run the program to check the settings (Figure 10-51).

Make sure that your recorded TV folder is the right one for your PC, and that your video folder is correct as well. For the bit rate, it's best to keep the default bit rate of 600 kbps, which is the best compromise between quality and size, although you can increase the bit rate for higher quality and larger size, and decrease it for lesser quality and smaller size. Finally, if you want videos to be deleted from your Zune when you delete them from Windows Media Center, check the box at the bottom of the screen. Click Save when you're done.

The program does a very good job of compression. A half-hour TV show that was 30 GB when recorded was shrunk to about 150 MB for transmission to the Zune.

After that, you won't need to do anything special to sync the shows to your Zune. Every time you record a TV show, it will be automatically compressed and placed into a folder for Zune syncing. When you sync your Zune, you'll have TV shows there, ready for watching.

See Also

- "Play YouTube Videos on your Zune" **[Hack #150]**
- "Set Up Your Windows Vista PC To Record TV Shows" **[Hack #138]**
- "Make Your Own TV Show Mashup" **[Hack #140]**

ADD FOLDERS TO WINDOWS VISTA'S PHOTO GALLERY

When you use the Windows Vista Photo Gallery, do you notice that many of your photos and videos seem to be missing? That's because the Photo Gallery only displays photos in your Pictures folder (*C:\Users*`UserName`*\Pictures*) and in your Public Pictures folder (*C:\Users\Public\Pictures*), and videos in your Video folder *C:\Users*`UserName`*\Videos*) and Public Video folder (*C:\Users\Public\Videos*). To have it display pictures and videos from other folders, choose File→Add Folder to Gallery and choose a folder to add.

HACK 152: Organize Your Photos with Metadata

V Windows Vista's Photo Gallery offers a hidden way to easily organize your photos—add metadata to your files. Here's how.

If you've got plenty of photos on your hard disk, browsing through them to find ones you want can be an exceedingly lengthy and frustrating experience. Organizing photos by folder can help only to a certain extent.

The Windows Vista Photo Gallery makes finding photos a snap because of a new technology baked into Windows Vista—the Extensible Metadata Platform (XMP), which was created by Adobe, and is used in high-end, expensive photo-editing programs. With Windows Vista, for the first time it's available directly in the operating system itself.

XMP is unique because it stores keywords—called metadata—as a part of each photograph. There are plenty of image-management programs available that store keywords about photos, but there's a big problem with these programs: The keywords work only in that program itself. So send the photo to someone else, and the keywords are lost. Worse than that, though, is that the operating system won't recognize the keywords, and you can't search through them from Windows. In Windows Vista, because the keyword metadata is part of the files themselves, the metadata travels with the photos. And because the metadata is recognized by the operating system, you can use Windows Search to find photos. For example, add the keyword Hawaii to all the photos of Hawaii, and you can easily search using that keyword in Windows Search.

Photos have several kinds of metadata in them, some of which are automatically placed there by the camera taking them. To see all the metadata in a file, right-click it, choose Properties, then click the Details tab, as shown in Figure 10-52. You'll see all the metadata in the file, which is divided into sections, such as Description, Origin, Image, Camera, and so on. Depending on how you acquired the photo, the metadata in many of these sections might be blank.

If you've take the picture with a digital camera, the file may have information in it such as the manufacturer of the camera, and details about camera settings used when the photo was taken, such as F-stop, ISO speed, exposure time, and focal length.

In this hack, you'll see how to add metadata to your photos to more easily browse through, organize, and search for photos.

Figure 10-52.
Metadata in a photo file

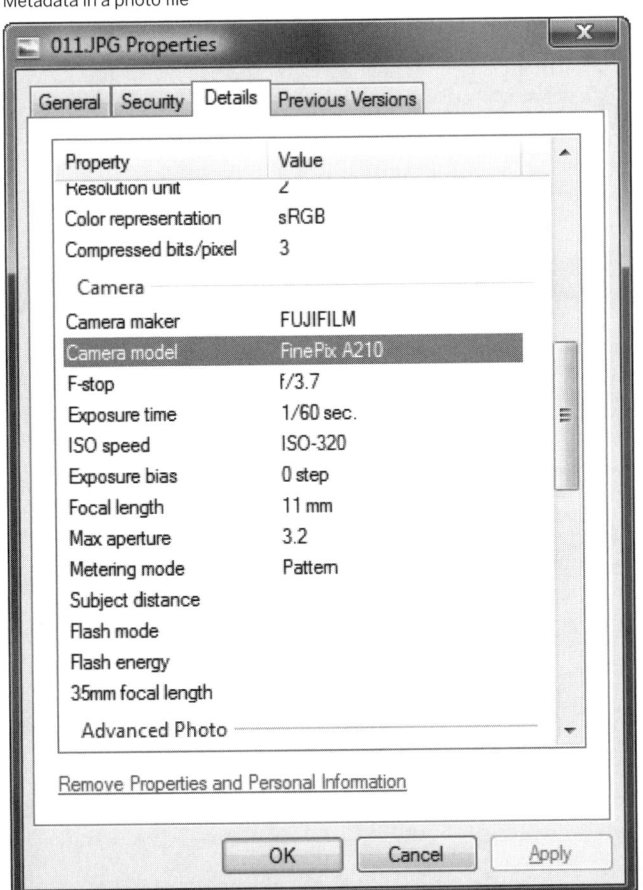

QUICK HACK 

IMPORT PHOTOS FROM VISTA-INCOMPATIBLE CAMERAS

Windows Vista won't recognize some older digital cameras, so it seems as if there's no way to get photos from them into your PC. However, if the camera uses industry-standard memory cards, such as those in the Compact Flash or Secure Digital formats, it's easy to do. Buy an external card reader that plugs into your PC via a USB slot. You then just need to pop the card into the reader, and import them into your PC as you would normally. You'll find plenty of readers in electronics stores and on the Internet. Also check your PC to see if it has any built in slots for memory cards, because increasingly, new PCs have them.

Editing and Adding Tags to Photos

As I've just explained, photos taken by camera have metadata already in them. But that metadata isn't particularly useful for sorting, searching, or browsing through photos. It's unlikely you're going to want to sort your photos by their ISO speed. You're more likely going to want to sort them by, for example, the names of the people in them, or perhaps by date.

To do that, you'll add what Microsoft calls *tags* to your photo—in essence, keywords that describe the photo, and that become part of the photo's metadata. There are several ways to do this. The simplest is to click a file in Windows Photo Gallery, then in the right-hand pane click Add Tags, and type in the tags you want to be associated with the photo. Press Enter after you type in each tag (see Figure 10-53). You can put in as many as you want, and each tag can be made up of multiple words—there is a limit of 255 characters per tag.

If you've already added tags to other photos, you'll see a list of the ten most recent tags you've used when you click Add Tags. Select any, and it will be added as a tag. In addition, as you type, an AutoComplete feature displays a list of tags that match the letters you've typed. Press the down arrow to select a tag, then press Enter to add it to the photo.

You can also assign tags to multiple photos at once doing this. Select multiple files, and add a tag as you would normally. That tag will now be applied to all of the files.

This is the simplest, most straightforward way to add tags, but there are other ways as well:

- In Windows Explorer or Photo Gallery, right-click a file, choose Properties, then select the Details tab. Click in the Tags field, and type in tags. Separate each tag from another by using a semicolon.
- In Windows Explorer, make sure the Details pane is visible at the bottom of the screen by selecting Organize→Layout→Details. Click in the Tags field, and type the tags. Separate each tag from another by using a semicolon.
- In Windows Photo Gallery, in the Navigation pane, click Create a New Tag, then type in the tag. At this point, the tag won't be assigned to any photos. But you can now choose the tag from your list

Figure 10-53.
Adding tags to a photo

of already-created tags when you create a new tag in a photo. And you can also use the method outlined next to add this tag to photos.

- In Windows Photo Gallery, select a file or multiple files, then drag them into the Navigation pane onto the tag you want to apply (see Figure 10-54). You'll see ghosted images of all the photos to which you want to apply the tag. Drop the files onto the tag, and the tag will be applied to all the files.

There's also another quick way to add tags to a group of photos in Windows Photo Gallery. When you select multiple photos, Windows Photo Gallery will display all the tags associated with all the files you've selected. It will put the tags into two groups—"Assigned to all," which means that these tags are in every one of the photos; and "Assigned to some," which means they are present in only some of the photos, as you can see in Figure 10-55. If you want all the photos to have a tag in the "Assigned to some" group, right-click the tag and select Assign to All. If you want to remove the tag from all, when you right-click it, select "Remove tag."

Now that you've got your photos tagged, how will it help you display and find photos? Easy. In the Navigation pane, click a tag, and you'll see all photos that have that tag, as shown in Figure 10-56. In addition, when you use Windows Search, you'll be able to search by that tag as well. And when you search inside Windows Photo Gallery, you'll be able to search by tags as well.

The Search box in Windows Photo Gallery is an especially powerful, often overlooked tool. It will search only through your current selection, so is a great way to find photos fast. For example when you display all photos with a common tag, when you do a search, you'll only search through those photos. Similarly, if you display photos by date, or any other type of metadata, you'll only search through those photos. Keep these things in mind when searching in Windows Photo Gallery:

- If you search for multiple terms, the AND search operator will be used. That means that when you type in two search terms, both terms must be in the metadata of files in order for the files to show up in your search results.
- The search will look through all the metadata of files, including file names, tags, camera name, and so on.

Figure 10-54.
Creating tags by dragging photos to them

Figure 10-55.
Listing all the tags assigned to multiple pictures you've selected

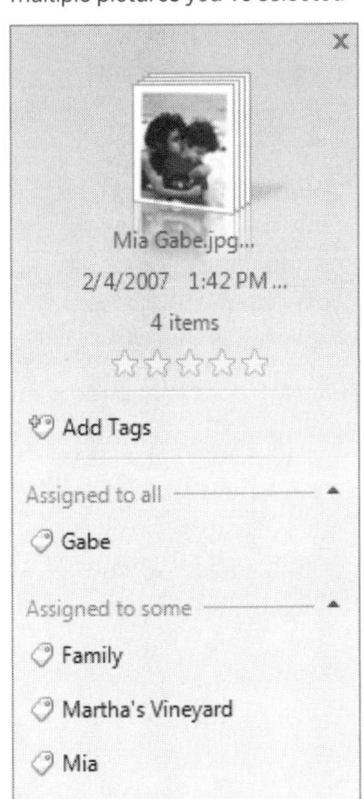

Figure 10-56.
Viewing photos by tag name

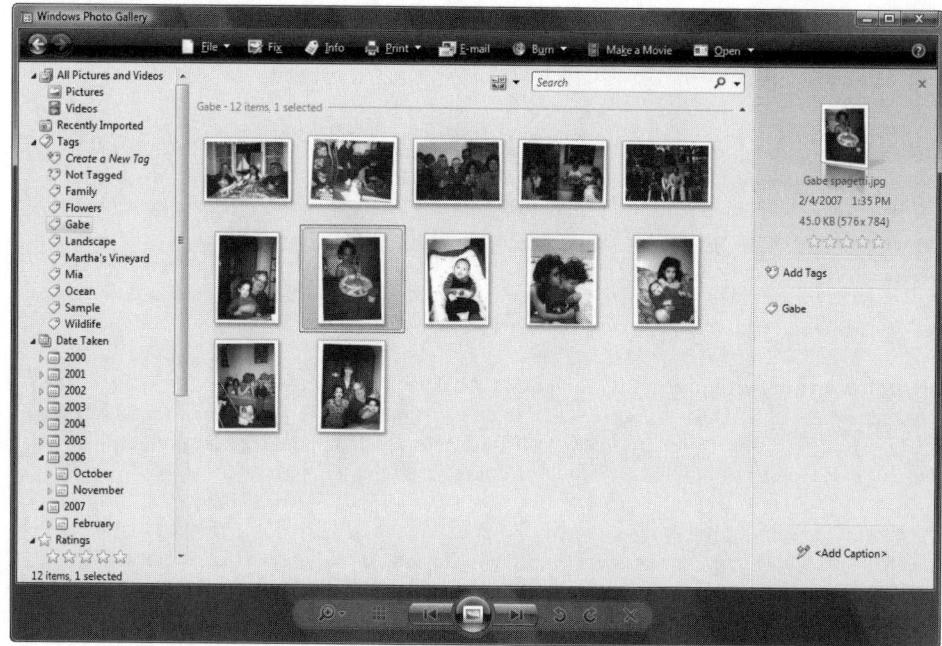

- When you do a search in Windows Photo Gallery, it searches for text strings, not keywords. So, for example, if you search for the term vine you'll see results for files that have the metadata Martha's Vineyard, bovine, and so on.
- If you want to expand your current search for the entire Windows Photo Gallery, not just your current selection, click the down arrow next to the Search box, and select Search All Items in Photo Gallery.

Using Other Metadata

As I explained earlier in this hack, tags aren't the only kind of metadata associated with each file. You can edit the metadata in a file by right-clicking it, choosing Properties, selecting the Details tab, and editing any metadata you see there. Windows Photo Gallery also makes it easy to edit the most useful metadata, including the file name, date, and time the picture was taken as well as a rating on a one-to-five star scale you assign to the file. When you highlight a file, its details appear in the right-hand pane. Click a star rating to assign it a rating, and click the date, time, or name to edit that information.

To sort by rating, date, and so on, simply click the appropriate link in the Navigation pane. This metadata is particularly useful when used in concert with the Thumbnail view button, which is directly to the left of the Search box. Click the button, and choose either Group By or Sort By, and then choose the metadata on which you want to sort or group.

Hacking the Hack

A little-known feature of tags makes them extremely useful when you have hundreds or thousands of pictures on your PC. You can nest tags inside of other tags, and create a hierarchy of tags. For example, you can have a tag for Family, and underneath that, tags for every member of your family. You could then put tags underneath each family member, for example, Age 1 to 5, Age 6 to 10, and so on.

IMPORT PICTURES FASTER

Transferring files from your digital camera to your PC using the Import Pictures Wizard has one drawback—you have to wade through a series of screens and answer a series of questions just to get the photos where you want them to go. There's a faster way. When you connect your camera, choose Open Folder to View Files from the AutoPlay dialog box. Then just use Windows Explorer to copy the files over.

To create this kind of hierarchy, drag one tag onto another one. The tag that you drag will become a subtag of the tag onto which you've dragged it. You can also create new tags in the hierarchy by right-clicking a tag, selecting Create Tag, then typing in the name for the new tag. That new tag will now become of the subtag of the tag on which you've right-clicked. Figure 10-57 shows one example of such a tag hierarchy.

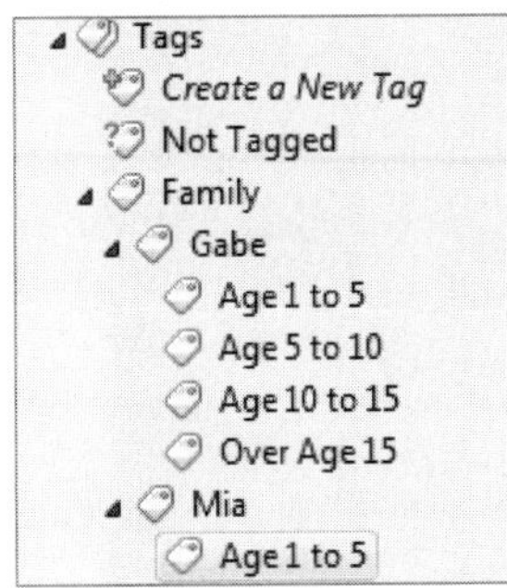

Figure 10-57.
A hierarchy of tags

You'll of course have to then add the appropriate subtags to each photo. It's a bit of work, but when you're done, you have an excellent way of browsing and finding photos.

HACK 153: Use RAW Photos in Windows Photo Gallery

V Some digital cameras use the high-quality RAW file format to take photos. Windows Photo Gallery doesn't seem to handle them—unless you use this hack, that is.

Digital cameras that take high-quality photos can often take them in the RAW format, rather than the more common *.jpg* format. Files taken in the RAW format are of higher quality than those taken in *.jpg*.

Windows Photo Gallery, though, doesn't display RAW files. Transfer RAW files to your PC, and Windows Photo Gallery simply ignores them.

The problem is that RAW isn't really a commonly accepted standard. Each camera manufacturer implements RAW files differently. There is a way, however, to force Windows Photo Gallery to display the photos. You'll need to go to the Web sites of the camera manufacturers and download *codecs*—special software that can decode the photos so you can view them.

After you've transferred the files to your PC, open Windows Photo Gallery and choose File→Update. You'll be directed to Web sites that have the proper codecs for RAW files on your system. (If you have no RAW files on your PC, you won't see the File→Update option.) Go to the Web sites, and follow the directions for downloading and installing the codecs.

Not all manufacturers will have codecs for the RAW files, so you might not be able to view the RAW files from your camera inside Windows Photo Gallery.

When you go into Windows Photo Gallery, you'll see the photos appear. Oddly enough, though, they won't end in a *.raw* extension. Each camera manufacturer has its own specific file type for its highest-quality photos. Generally, they're called RAW files, but the extensions will differ. So, for example, Nikon RAW files have the *.nef* extension, while Canon uses either *.crw* or *.cr2*, depending on the specific camera.

If you edit any RAW files using Windows Photo Gallery, you won't actually change the RAW files themselves. Instead, Windows Photo Gallery leaves the original RAW images intact, and saves a *.jpg* copy of the edited file. The edited *.jpg* file will be of a lower quality than the RAW image.

HACK 154: Play it Loud!

You can pump up the volume and get high-quality surround sound on your PC—but you have to know where to look.

Do your PC speakers sound only ho-hum? The problem may not be that they're not a good enough quality—you may simply now know the right settings to make them sound better.

Many newer PCs have Intel motherboards with High Definition Audio support, which means that they're capable of some pretty cool sound features. But normally, those features aren't turned on. To turn them on, choose Control Panel→Hardware and Sound→Sound. A screen like the one shown in Figure 10-58 appears. If your system supports High Definition Audio, it will say it right on the icon, and there will be a green check mark next to it.

You first need to tell Windows Vista what kind of sound system you have—stereo, quadrophonic, 5.1, 7.1, and so on. Click Configure, and screen like the one shown in Figure 10-59 appears. Select your sound system. To check whether any speaker is working, click it and a sound will come out of it. When you've tested each speaker, click Next to launch a wizard that will confirm your speaker setup.

A 5.1 system is one in which there are five speakers and a subwoofer; a 7.1 system is one in which there are seven speakers and a subwoofer.

You'll come back to the screen shown in nearby. Highlight the speakers again and click Properties, and the Speaker Properties dialog box appears, as shown in Figure 10-60.

There are four tabs; here's how to use each:

General

This lets you turn your audio controller on or off (not the speakers, but the PC sound controller), lists the audio jacks on your PC, and lets you change or configure your sound driver.

Figure 10-58.

You're in luck—this PC supports High Definition Audio

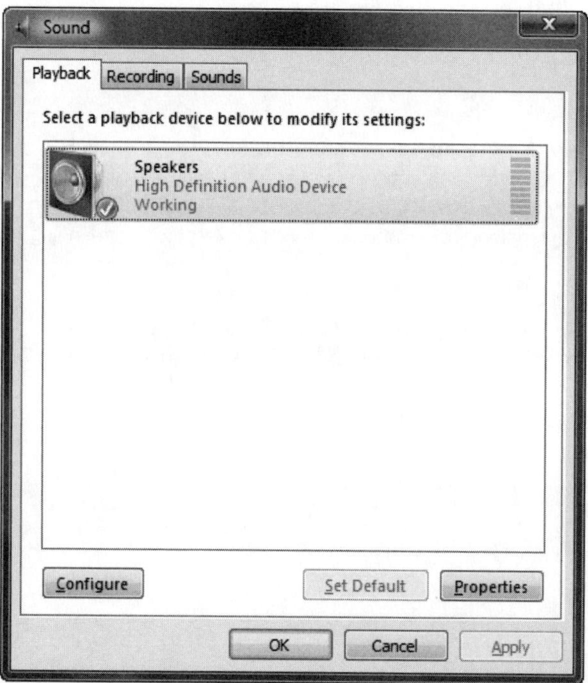

Figure 10-59.
Choosing your speaker system

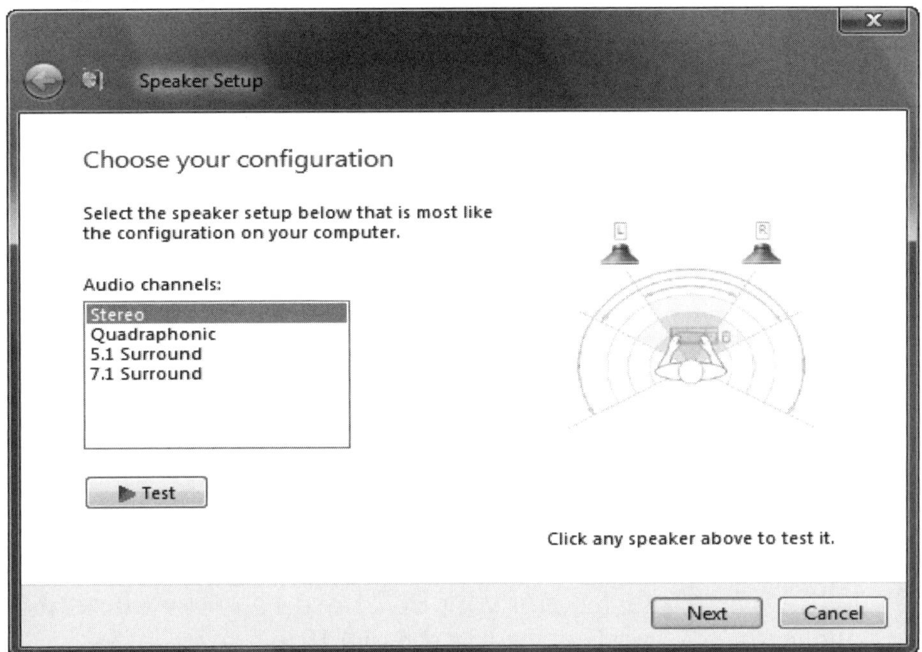

Figure 10-60.
Enabling special features for your speakers

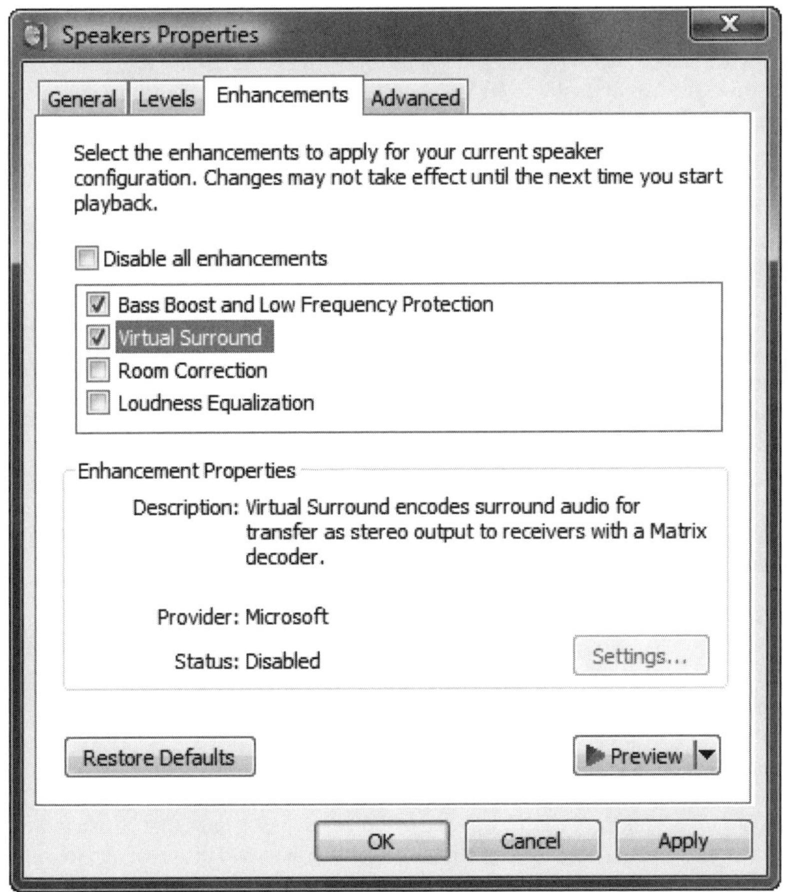

Levels

Change you sound level here; move the slider to the left to make it softer, and to the right to make it louder. You can also change your speaker balance as well. So, for example, if your left speakers are further away from you than your right ones, you might want to shift the balance slightly to your left speakers, so that they both appear equally loud.

Enhancements

Here's where the fun begins for music lover. Here you'll be able to boost your bass, turn on virtual surround sound, and use room correction, which compensates for the characteristics of your speakers and your room and creates the best-sounding sound. You can also turn on loudness equalization, which maintain a relative loudness across different digital audio files or sources. This is particularly important if you're listening to digital audio. Enable each feature you want. Depending on your speakers and your PC's audio capabilities, you may be able to further customize each of these features by clicking Settings. When you're done, click OK.

Depending on your speaker system and your PC's audio capabilities, you may have slightly different enhancements from the ones listed here.

HACK 155: Convert Vinyl and Tapes to MP3s

V XP Got a retro music collection on vinyl and tapes, and wish you had them as digital files for your PC? Here's a groovy, far-out, psychedelic way to help them enter the electronic era.

Contrary to popular opinion, there was music before CDs and MP3s. Plenty of it. And plenty of it was good. And it was all on vinyl LPs and tapes.

What if you've got a collection of vinyl and tapes and want to bring them into the modern era, but don't want to pay for new CDs or digital downloads—or the music may simply no longer be available? Join the club. There are plenty of us out there in the same boat. I've got a big vinyl collection myself, sitting in my basement, with plenty of old blues players like Bukka White, Skip James, and Robert Johnson, not to mention their oddball revivers such as the duo of Backwards Sam Firk and Delta X.

Fear not; it won't take much work to bring that collection into the modern world by turning them into MP3s.

One expensive way to do it is to buy a special turntable or tape deck that connects to your PC via a USB port, then play the music on the turntable, and record it using music recording software such as the free program Audacity (audacity.sourceforge.net). But that won't be cheap. A USB turntable such as the Ion iTTUSB Turntable (www.ion-audio.com/ittusb.php) has a list price of $200, for example.

There's a much cheaper way to do it, it'll only cost you about $10, and it's not any harder, either. All you'll need is inexpensive stereo cable that you can get at a Radio Shack or other electronics store.

First, you need to connect your old turntable or tape player to your PC (don't have one anymore? Head over to eBay or a yard/garage/tag sale). The exact cable you need varies according to the kind of stereo equipment you have. If you have a cassette deck, or a turntable and pre-amplifier that's part of a larger stereo system, you'll most likely need something called a Y-cable. On one end, it has two RCA plugs that hook up to the back of your stereo gear, and on the other end, it has a 3.5-millimeter stereo miniplug that hooks right into your PC's sound card.

If you're going to record from a portable cassette player, you instead need a cable that has stereo miniplugs on both end of it. One miniplug connects to the cassette player, and the other end to your PC's sound card.

If you care about sound quality, consider getting the highest-quality cables you can find. Poor quality plugs can create audio noise, and your MP3s will have that noise in them.

Plug everything in. Before you can start recording, though, you're going to need to know where you can control your PC's audio line-in level—set it too low, and you'll barely be able to hear your MP3s; set it too high and you'll get distortion and noise.

In Windows Vista, right-click the audio icon in the far right of the system tray, and select Recording Devices. Make sure the device is configured properly by highlighting it and clicking Configure and walking through the configuration screen. Click OK. Then double-click the audio icon to bring up the volume control. In Windows XP, double-click the audio icon to bring up the volume control.

You'll need software to record your music. A popular freebie is Audacity (audacity.sourceforge.net), but there are others as well. It will take some work using Audacity, though, because you have to go through both a recording and conversion process. And one more problem with Audacity and other free recording software is that, although they come with a lot of useful filters, cleaning up audio from vinyl and cassette may be something of a manual process. There's a good chance that your file is going to have scratches, pops, clicks, and hiss on it. Vinyl recording software can automatically clean it up for you, and also make recording a one-step process rather than a several-step process.

A good bet is the shareware program Spin It Again (www.acoustica.com/spinitagain/). It's free to try, and $34.95 if you decide to keep it

It's remarkably easy to use. To record from a vinyl LP, for example, connect the cables, click Record A Vinyl LP, or Record a Cassette Tape, and follow the wizard that appears. It will even walk you through setting up the right sound levels. Once you've recorded your tracks, play each of them, and from the Cleaning & Effects Processing drop-down list, select the clean-up you want the program to perform, such as Vinyl Declick & Decrackle, Damaged Records, or Clean Anything, and the program does the rest.

11 SYSTEM PERFORMANCE

Ever since the first version of Windows was introduced, people have complained about system performance. When it comes to PCs, people have three speeds in mind—fast, faster, and fastest, and they only want to go the fastest.

In this chapter, you'll find all kinds of hacks for improving system performance. You'll find out the truth—not the hype—about using USB- and flash memory-based ReadyBoost in Windows Vista, and discover a secret for using it even with USB drives Vista says can't be used. You'll find out how to strip the crud out of your system install, how to make the most of your RAM, how to install a fast RAID hard drive, and plenty more.

HACK 156: Strip the Crud Out of Your Windows Install

V Put your Windows installation on a diet and save your precious disk space for more important things than Windows features you will never use.

Windows has a huge footprint. Vista wants at least 8 GB for an installation, and after you've installed it, you'll find that it takes up almost 7 GB of space just for the operating system, as shown in Figure 11-1.

Wouldn't it be great if you could remove some components? Unfortunately, the "Turn Windows Features On or Off" control panel doesn't actually remove anything from your computer; it just toggles components on and off. Fortunately, there is a way to slim down your Vista installation: Dino Nuhagic's vLite lets you remove components, add drivers, and enable certain tweaks. Once you're done, you can create a new installation DVD and install the slimmed-down version of Vista.

To get started, first download vLite from www.vlite.net and install it. You'll need to install it on a computer that's running Windows and has plenty of free disk space to use as a scratch area for temporary working files. I'd suggest at least 5 GB of free space, but more is always better.

When you run vLite, it notifies you of any needed dependencies and offers to install them. Next, it displays the main vLite screen as shown in Figure 11-2.

Click the Browse button, and choose the location of your Vista install files. This will probably be your Vista installation DVD, so make sure that's in the drive, and choose it. Next, vLite asks you to choose a location to store the installation files. This is where the modified installation files will reside. Once you've done that, vLite copies over the entire DVD, which can take a while.

After vLite has copied everything over, it asks you to choose which Vista version (Business, Home Basic/Premium, Ultimate, etc.) to customize. Choose the one you plan to install. Now you're ready

Figure 11-1.
Free space after a Vista install

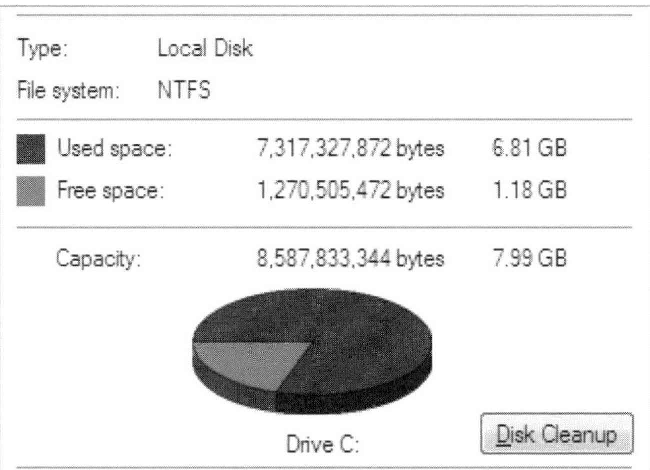

Figure 11-2.
The vLite start screen

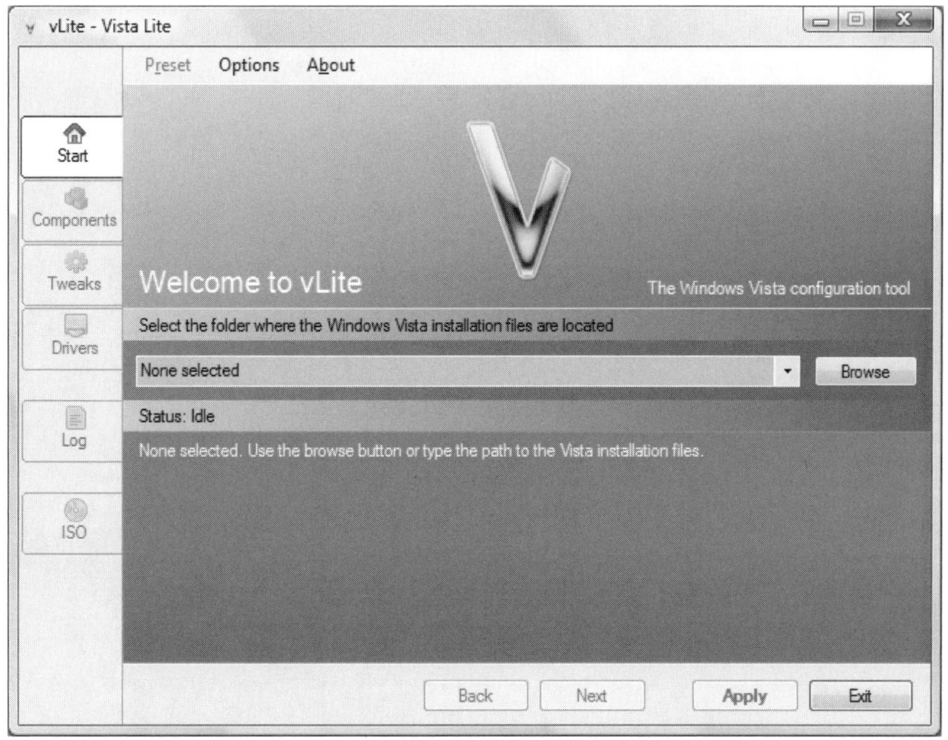

QUICK HACK

"DE-CRAPIFY" YOUR PC

Just about any PC you buy is filled with "craplets"—trial programs that clutter your PC, pop up and ask that you register, and generally sludge up your PC. The solution? Get the free PC Decrapifier (www.pcdecrapifier.com), which searches through your PC and removes as many of the craplets as it can. Among the nearly four dozen craplets it kills are multiple kinds of Norton, McAfee and Trend Micro trial antivirus products, Wild Tangent games, and MusicMatch, among others.

to step through the configuration. Click each of the tabs on the left of the vLite screen to configure your installation media:

Components

Use this tab to choose which components to remove. This can free a lot of disk space, but don't get too greedy, or you might remove something you really need.

Tweaks

You can do some fun stuff here, including forcing Vista to try and enable glass mode even if there's not enough RAM, use a different font for the user interface, disable UAC **[Hack #108]**, get rid of the hibernation file, and more.

Drivers

If you have any drivers you want to add to the installation, here's where to do it.

Once you've made your choices, click Apply; you'll be able to choose whether to "Just apply the changes" (modifies the installation choices without shrinking the size of the installation media; you'll still end up with a smaller installation even if you choose this) or "Apply and rebuild" (removes all but the version of Vista that you selected earlier). You'll also have the opportunity to specify which versions of Vista to remove from the media. After you've made these choices, vLite starts building the final installation set.

Now you can click the ISO tab, as shown in Figure 11-3. From here you can do a few different things. If you just want to create an ISO image of the modified installation files, select Create Image from the drop-down menu. You can then use this with a free virtualization environment (See Chapter 2) such as VMware Server or Virtual PC to test the image out (if not, you can choose Direct Burn from the drop down to burn the image to the DVD drive on your computer, and then you can use the disc to install Vista on a real computer.)

Figure 11-3.
Creating the new Vista image

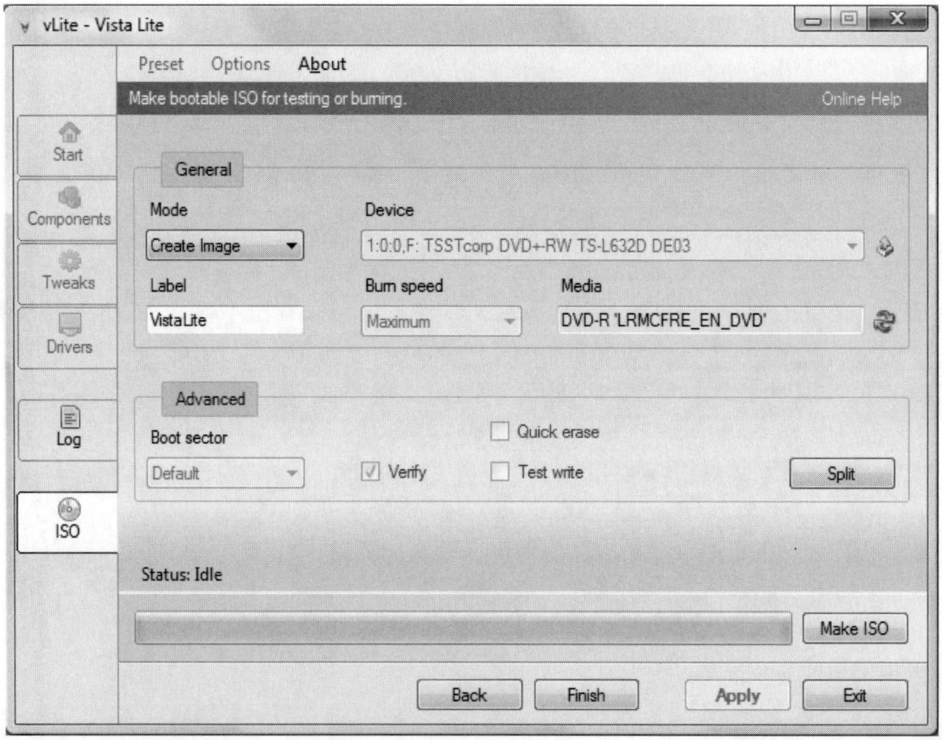

Figure 11-4.
Vista's smaller footprint after customizing with vLite

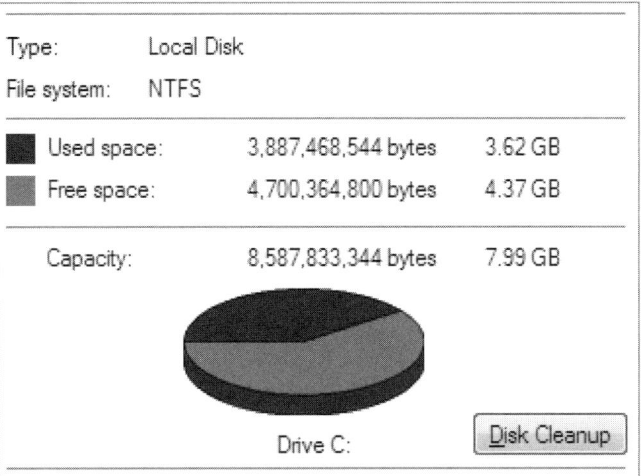

Figure 11-4 shows the free space available on the computer after removing a bunch of stuff. This also includes the 512 MB of disk space saved by disabling the hibernation file, but it's still a big difference!

Windows XP users can also get in on the fun with nLite, which is available at www.nliteos.com and is also one of Dino Nuhagic's creations.

— Brian Jepson

HACK 157: Hack Multicore Performance

V XP What's the use of a dual core PC unless you can hack it?

If you've bought a PC within the last year or so, there's a very good chance that it's got two processors on it, often called a duo-core, or dual core. The idea behind dual core processors is simple: two processors are better than one.

The real benefits of dual core processors won't come until more software is written to take better advantage of it. Windows recognizes dual core processors, though, and lets you control how they run your applications.

If you're interested in hacking your dual core processor, the first thing to do is get a gadget that tracks dual core usage. The CPU Meter gadget that ships with Windows Vista doesn't report on how much of each CPU is being used; instead it averages the two and reports on overall CPU usage. (see Figure 11-5). So if it reports 40 percent CPU use, you have no idea if one processor is using 70 percent and one 10 percent, or one 60 percent and one 20 percent and so on.

 Windows Vista and Windows XP users don't need a sidebar gadget to monitor CPU performance, Task Manager will do the job just fine: start Task Manager (right-click on the Taskbar, and select Task Manager from the menu that appears), and select the Performance tab. A CPU usage history graph appears for each core or CPU you have.

The free Multi Meter gadget, though, will show you how much each processor uses. To get it, first click the + sign at the top of the Sidebar. On the Gadget Gallery screen that appears, click the link at the bottom, "Get more gadgets online". You'll be sent to a page full of gadgets you can download.

QUICK HACK

GET MORE PERFORMANCE GADGETS

The Hobby Lounge (www.betanetwork.net/hobbylounge) makes plenty of other performance-related gadgets, in addition to the Multi Meter. It also makes a gadget that tracks quad core PC performance (the Multi Meter Q gadget), one that reports on hard disk use on multiple hard disks attached to your PC (Multi HDD Meter), and even a gadget that shows you your fan speed, internal PC temperature, voltage use and more (Speedfan Meter). Get them by going to www.betanetwork.net/hobbylounge and clicking Sidebar Gadgets. You'll have to register at the site to download them. Most, if not all, are also available when you go to the Microsoft gadget site [Hack #157].

Figure 11-5.
Windows Vista's CPU gadget reports on overall CPU use, but not on a processor-by-processor basis

Figure 11-6.
Multi Meter tracks dual core performance in real time

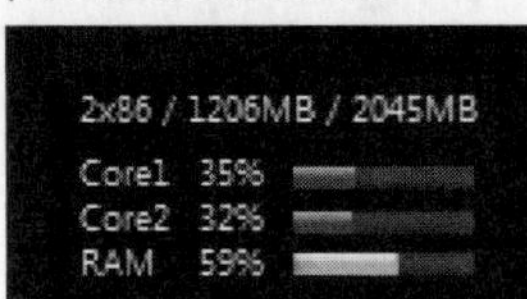

Figure 11-7.
Telling an application to use only one core

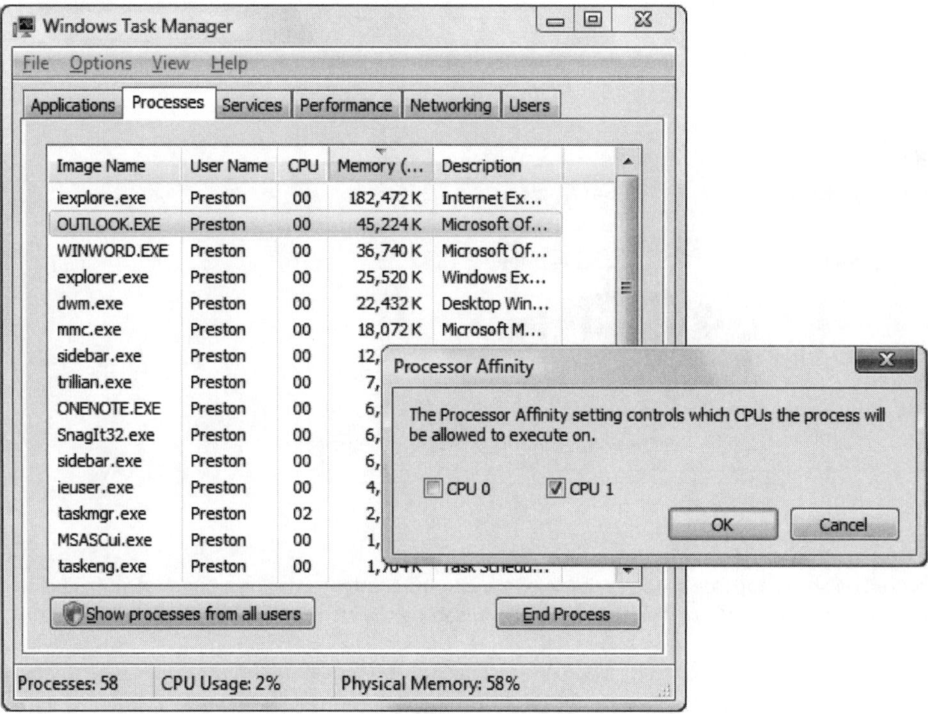

You'll most likely see the Multi Meter gadget listed in the Top Downloads area, because it's been the most popular gadget downloaded for quite some time. However, if it's not there for some reason, browse or search the site for it. You can also find it on www.betanetwork.net/hobbylounge.

Download and install the gadget, and as you use your PC, it will show you how much of each processor is being used, in real time (see Figure 11-6).

If you run a processor-intensive application that takes up a lot of CPU, such as Norton AntiVirus or any other Norton security software, you may be able to improve its performance, and overall performance of your PC, by running that application off of a single core, rather than dividing performance among several cores. To do it, run the Task Manager by typing taskmgr at the Start menu search box or at a command prompt, and pressing Enter. Go to the Processes tab, and right-click the application's filename (in the case of Norton, it's *nprotect.exe*). If you're not sure which file runs the application, look at the Description column. After you right-click, select Set Affinity. From the dialog box that appears (Figure 11-7), deselect one of the cores, and click OK.

When you run the application, watch Multi Meter or Task Manager; you'll notice that the core you assigned that application to is used more heavily. If you find that assigning the application to a single CPU boosts performance, keep the setting; if not, repeat the steps but configure the application to use both cores.

See Also

- "Speed Up System Performance with the Task Manager" **[Hack #168]**

HACK 158: Speed Up Your PC with ReadyBoost

V Windows Vista's ReadyBoost can pump up your PC's power, but it's not as simple to use as you might think. Here's what you need to know to get the most out of it.

One of the simplest and cheapest ways to speed up Windows Vista is to use ReadyBoost, which uses a flash drive (including USB, SD, Compact Flash, and others) to supplement your system's RAM. New to Windows Vista, ReadyBoost prefetches and stores commonly used files on your flash drive.

ReadyBoost speeds up Windows Vista performance in several ways. It increases the size of Windows Vista's normal *prefetch cache* (a memory cache that intelligently stores files that Vista expects you to need soon), so more data can be stored there. Data can be retrieved more quickly from a flash drive than a hard disk, and so commonly used data and programs will run more quickly when you use ReadyBoost. In addition, ReadyBoost frees up RAM that would otherwise be used by prefetch. Depending on your system configuration, you may see a dramatic speed improvement.

These days, there are plenty of flash drives available, in many capacities. Which is the best to get for your system? First, decide on the capacity you want to buy. The smallest size that ReadyBoost can use is 256 MB, and the largest is 4 GB. Microsoft recommends a flash-memory-to-system-RAM ratio between 1:1 and 2.5:1. For example, if you have a PC with 512 MB of RAM, get a flash drive with 512 MB to 1.25 GB of space. A system with 1 GB of RAM should use a drive with a capacity between 1 GB and 2.5 GB. And a 2 GB system would do well with a drive that has a capacity between 2 GB and 4 GB.

Sounds simple enough, doesn't it? It's not. Not all flash drives work with ReadyBoost. A USB flash drive must be at least USB 2.0, and any flash drive you use must be capable of 2.5 MB/sec throughput for 4K random reads and 1.75 MB/sec throughput for 512K random writes uniformly across the entire drive. Unfortunately, those specs are often not published by manufacturer, so it's hard to know before you buy whether the device will work. And even when they are published, the numbers can be very misleading. For example, the manufacturer may publish sequential performance numbers but not publish information about random performance. A device with great sequential performance may fail the random performance test. In addition, on some USB drives, performance isn't consistent across an entire drive. Some USB drives use 128 MB of extremely fast flash memory on one part of the drive, but slower memory for the rest of the drive, and those drives won't work as well. What's more, some flash drive manufacturers use a number such as 60X, which doesn't give a clear indication of the actual speed in megabytes per second.

Luckily, there's a web site that lists USB flash drives that work with ReadyBoost—www.grantgibson.co.uk/misc/readyboost. Keep in mind that it's not an official Microsoft site, and there's no guarantee that the information is absolutely accurate. But I've followed its advice several times, and have yet to go wrong.

One more thing to keep in mind: when it comes to ReadyBoost, faster is better. The faster the flash drive, the bigger the performance boost your PC will get. Check the www.grantgibson.co.uk/misc/readyboost web site because it publishes some speed specs. You can also read the manufacturer's specs, but again, as previously outlined, they may be misleading.

Once you've gotten a flash drive, making it work with ReadyBoost is simple. Connect the flash drive to your PC. Windows Vista will recognize the device, then ask whether to use it to speed up your PC with ReadyBoost, as shown in Figure 11-8. Depending on the drive, you may get a variety of options from which to choose. But if you want to use the drive for ReadyBoost, select "Speed up my system".

If the device meets ReadyBoost specs, a configuration screen appears as shown in Figure 11-9, letting you set the amount of space on the device that you want to devote to ReadyBoost. (The RAM on the device that you don't use for ReadyBoost is available for normal storage.) It's a good

Figure 11-8.
Connecting a new drive

Figure 11-9.
Configuring ReadyBoost

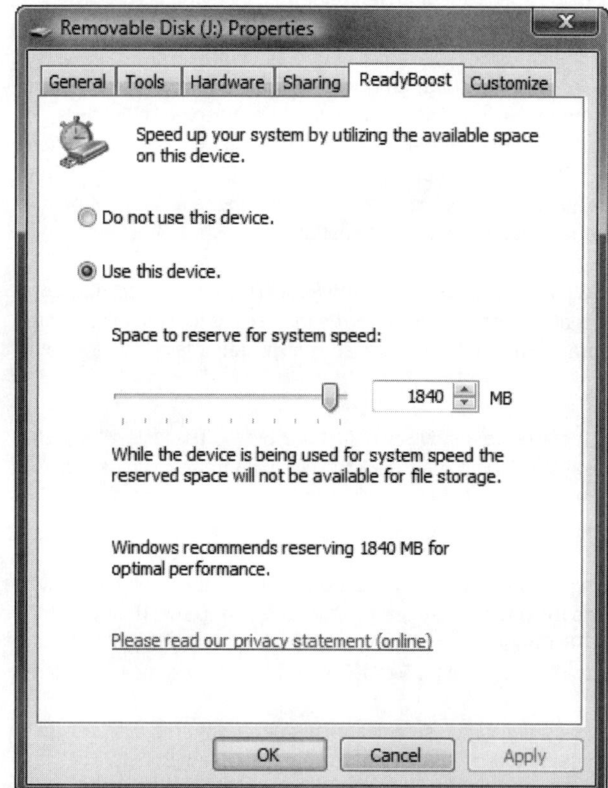

idea to accept at least the minimum, and possibly add more as well. Make sure that you've selected "Use this device". Then move the slider to the right to increase the amount of space or to the left to reduce it. Click OK, and you're done—get ready for your PC to speed up.

If you remove the flash drive and plug it back in again, Windows Vista will automatically recognize that you want to use it for ReadyBoost, so you won't have to reconfigure it. At any point, you can change the amount of RAM for ReadyBoost, or you can use the flash drive entirely for storage instead of for ReadyBoost. Open Windows Explorer, right-click the device, select the ReadyBoost tab, and make your changes.

What If Your Flash Drive Fails the Test?

As I said before, not all flash drives work with ReadyBoost. But Windows Vista doesn't notify you right away whether a drive is compatible. Plug in the drive, then tell Vista to use it for ReadyBoost, as I outlined earlier. If it's not capable of working with ReadyBoost, you'll then see the screen shown in Figure 11-10.

If you're the curious sort, you can see exactly why ReadyBoost failed—which spec it didn't meet. You'll use the Event Viewer to do that. Here's how to do it:

1. Run the Event Viewer by typing *Eventvwr.msc* at the Search box or command prompt and pressing Enter.

2. Select the Applications And Services Logs category in the console tree on the left, then choose Microsoft→Windows→ReadyBoost→Operational. In the center pane, you'll see all events related to ReadyBoost. Scroll through them until you find the one that tells why your USB flash

Figure 11-10.
This drive isn't compatible with ReadyBoost

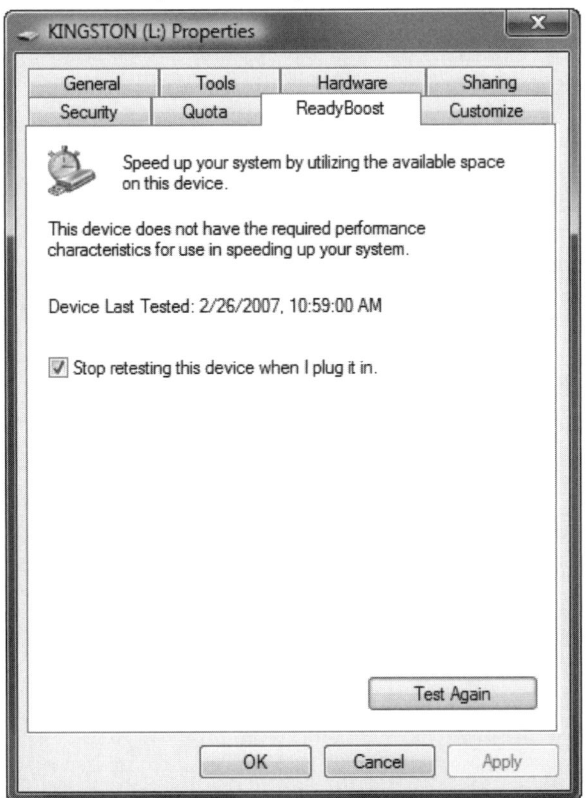

Figure 11-11.
ReadyBoost event listing

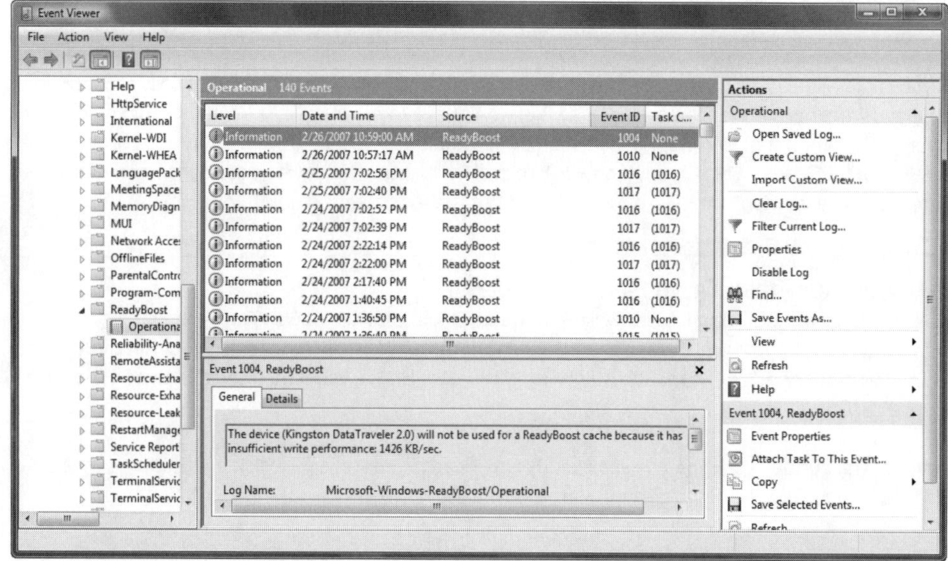

drive wouldn't work with ReadyBoost. In Figure 11-11, you can see that it failed because the drive had an insufficient write performance of 1426 KB/sec.

The Event Viewer reports information in KB/sec rather than of MB/sec. So, for example, 1.9 MB/sec would be reported here as 1900 KB/sec.

Hacking the Hack

If you have more than one flash drive you want to use for ReadyBoost, you can use the Event Viewer to help you choose the faster one to use. First, plug them in one at a time, and use each for ReadyBoost. Then run the Event Viewer, scroll through each event, and you'll come to one event for each drive that details the drive's performance. Compare performances, and then use only the fastest one for ReadyBoost.

You can also use the Event Viewer to get a behind-the-scenes look at the work Windows Vista does to make sure it uses the RAM on your flash drive as effectively as possible. Scroll through all the ReadyBoost events in the Event Viewer, and you'll notice Windows Vista takes a variety of actions for your ReadyBoost drive, such as defragmenting it for maximum performance. This information won't help *you* boost performance, but it's nice to see the hard work that Windows Vista does for you without you noticing it.

See Also

- For a comprehensive Microsoft Q and A about ReadyBoost, head to blogs.msdn.com/tomarcher/archive/2006/06/02/615199.aspx.

HACK 159: Force Windows Vista to Use Any Flash Drive for ReadyBoost

V Don't fret if Windows Vista refuses to use a flash drive for ReadyBoost. Force it to use the drive, whether or not it wants to.

As explained in "Speed Up Your PC with ReadyBoost" **[Hack #158]**, not all flash drives will work with ReadyBoost. Unless your drive meets certain requirements, Windows Vista will flat out refuse to use it.

If you're dead set on using your flash drive with ReadyBoost, though, you can force Windows Vista to use it. Keep in mind that this may or may not speed up your system performance, so it's a good idea to compare before and after performance to see whether it helps.

If Windows Vista tells you that your flash drive won't work in Windows Vista, remove it, and then re-insert the flash drive. If AutoPlay is enabled and a screen pops up asking what you want to do with the device, select "Open folder" to view files.

In Windows Explorer, right-click the drive, and select Properties→ReadyBoost. Uncheck the box next to "Stop Retesting this device when I plug it in", and click OK (Figure 11-12). Then unplug the drive.

Now launch the Registry Editor by typing regedit at the Start Search box or a command prompt (see Chapter 13 for details). Go to `HKEY_LOCAL_MACHINE\SOFTWARE\Microsoft\Windows NT\CurrentVersion\EMDMgmt`. You'll see a list of removable drives that have been connected to your computer. Look for the listing of the one that you just plugged in and then unplugged. You'll see a number of values, as shown in Figure 11-13.

If you're not sure which device matches the one you're interested in, plug the device in, locate it in the Device Manager **[Hack #174]**, view its Properties, and got to the Details tab to examine the Hardware IDs. These should match the items you see listed in the Registry (more or less; for example, a hardware ID that starts with `SD\VID_1C` in Device Manager will start with `_??SD#VID_1C` in the Registry).

Change the `DeviceStatus` value to 2. Then change the value of `ReadSpeedKBs` and `WriteSpeedKBs` to `1000`. Exit the Registry.

Make sure that when you change the values, you use decimal, rather than hexadecimal.

Figure 11-12.
Telling Windows Vista not to retest the flash drive for ReadyBoost compatibility

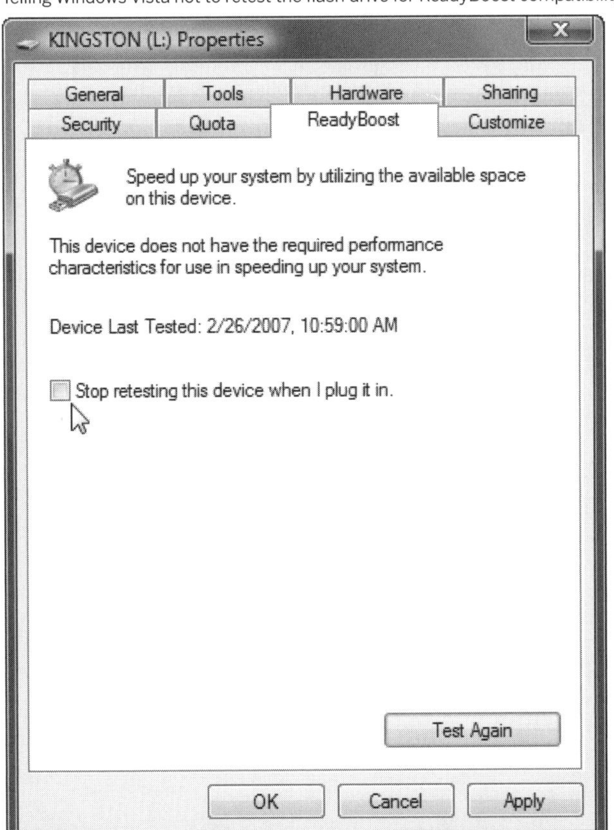

Figure 11-13.
The Registry's listing of removable drives you've connected

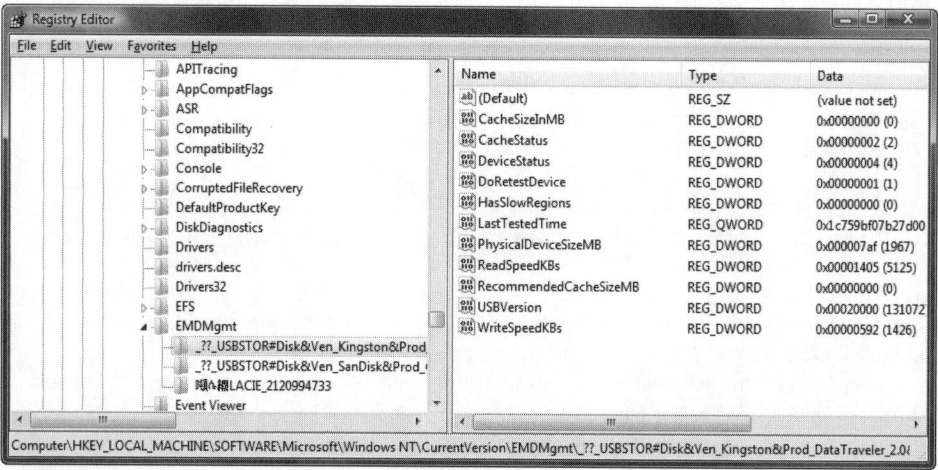

Figure 11-14.
Success! Windows Vista will use the flash drive for ReadyBoost

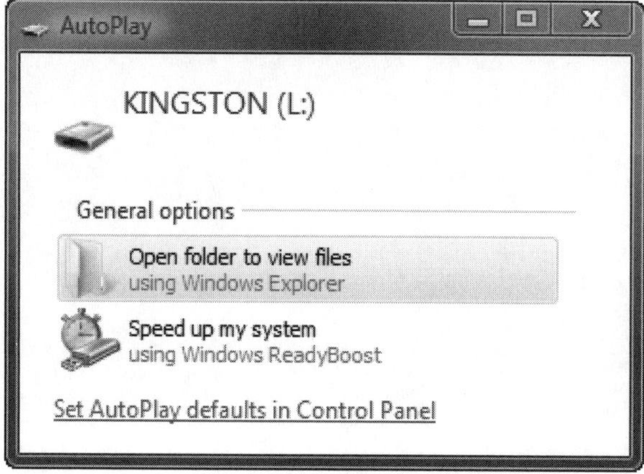

Plug the drive back in to your PC. When you do, you'll see the AutoPlay notification screen that allows you to use the drive for ReadyBoost, as you can see in Figure 11-14.

Click "Speed up my system". A screen like one shown in Figure 11-15 appears. As you can see, Windows Vista defaults to not using the device for ReadyBoost. Select "Use this Device", which tell it to use ReadyBoost. Then move the slide to give as much of the drive's storage to ReadyBoost as you want. Click OK, and you're done.

Again, keep in mind that using a slow flash drive may or may not speed up your system, but considering how easy it is to do, it's worth a shot.

See Also

- "Speed Up Your PC with ReadyBoost" **[Hack #158]**

Figure 11-15.
Select "Use this device", and then select how much memory to devote to ReadyBoost

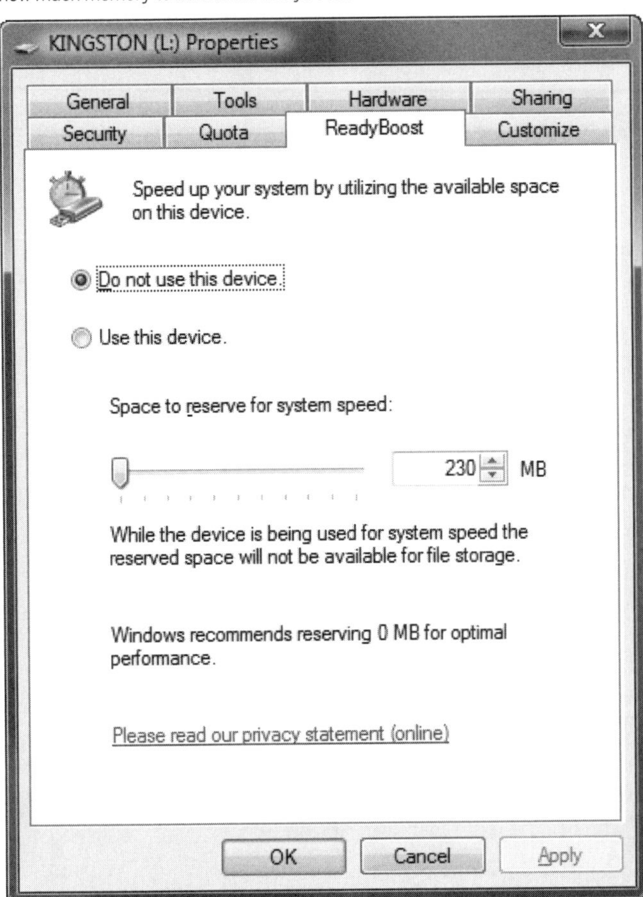

HACK 160: Get the Most Out of Your RAM

V XP The best way to improve system performance is to make better use of your RAM. Here are several hacks to show you how to try this before you buy more.

No matter how much memory you have, you could always use more. Installing more RAM is generally the quickest to better Windows performance. In Windows Vista, using ReadyBoost [Hack #158] is a good way to go as well.

But you can also speed Windows by making better use of the RAM you already have. In this hack, I look at how you can speed up system performance by using your RAM more effectively.

Make Better Use of Your Memory with the Task Manager

If your system doesn't have enough RAM, or if it uses what it has improperly, your system slows down. That's because in those circumstances it moves data and programs to a paging file on your hard disk, and your hard disk is slower than RAM. A certain amount of this is normal, but if you use a paging file too often, or if even your paging file can't handle the memory load, you'll run into system slowdowns and problems.

The Task Manager's Performance tab, shown in Figure 11-16, provides the best way to monitor memory use. To run the Task Manager, press Ctrl-Alt-Del (in Windows Vista, you'll then have to click Start Task Manager from the screen that appears), then click the Performance tab. With it, you can interpret the information and make better use of your memory **[Hack #168]**.

The most important parts of the screen shown in Figure 11-16 are the charts that report on paging file use and the tabular material below it that gives a more detailed view of your current use of memory.

The charts relating to the pagefile are self-explanatory: they show current usage, as well as usage over time. If you see pagefile use is frequently high, it means either your system isn't making the most efficient use of RAM, or you need more RAM. In that case, follow the advice later in this hack for how to better use RAM.

The data below the Pagefile chart can be almost impossible to decipher. Table 11-1 details what the data means, and makes recommendations on how to use that information to improve performance.

Figure 11-16.
The Task Manager's Performance tab

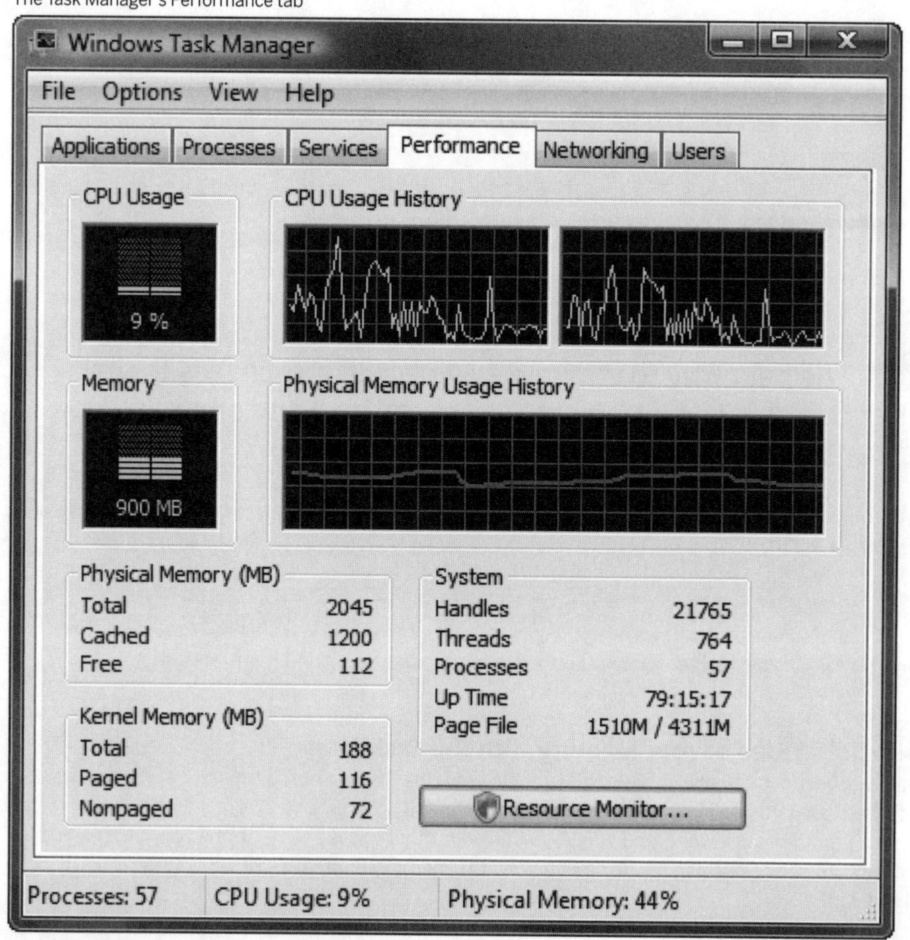

Table 11-1. Understanding Performance tab memory reporting

CATEGORY	SUBCATEGORY	WHAT THE DATA MEANS
Totals	Handles	Lets a program use system resources such as Registry keys, fonts, and bitmaps. Sometimes, poorly written programs don't close down their handles when the program closes, leading to memory loss. As a practical matter, you won't need to monitor this number.
	Threads	A discrete portion of a program executing a single task independently of other parts of a program. Again, as a practical matter, you won't need to monitor this number.
	Processes	Reports on the number of programs and services (processes) currently running on your system. Monitor this to see whether you have too many programs and services running **[Hack #6]** on your PC.
Commit Charge (K)	Total	The total amount of physical memory (RAM) and virtual memory (pagefile) currently in use, in kilobytes. The more programs, files, and data you have open, the greater your commit charge will be. The greater the commit charge, the more demands will be put on your system. To reduce the commit charge, close programs and files, especially large files.
	Limit	Reports on the total amount of physical and virtual memory, measured in kilobytes, that is currently available for your PC. To increase the limit, you can increase the pagefile size **[Hack #169]** or add RAM to your system.
	Peak	Reports on the highest total amount of memory, measured in kilobytes, that has been in use during your current session. Check this value each session to see whether the Peak value is frequently at or near the Limit value. If it is, you need to increase your memory, by either adding RAM or increasing your pagefile size.
Physical Memory (K)	Total	Displays the total amount of RAM in your PC, in kilobytes. This number can be confusing; to find out the amount of RAM in megabytes, divide it by 1,024.
	Available	Reports on the total amount of RAM, in kilobytes, currently available. When available RAM is used up, your system begins to use its pagefile.
	System Cache	Reports on the total amount of RAM, in kilobytes, that is being used for the most recently accessed data and programs. Programs and data can be in the system cache even after they have been closed down; the PC looks to the system cache first when opening a program or file, since it can be opened from the cache faster than from the hard disk.
Kernel Memory (K)	Total	The total amount of memory, in kilobytes, in use by the primary components of the Windows kernel. The kernel comprises the core programs and files that make up the operating system.
	Paged	The total amount of memory in a pagefile, in kilobytes, used by the primary components of Windows.
	Nonpaged	The total amount of RAM, in kilobytes, used by the primary components of Windows.

Here's how to use the information on the tab to improve RAM performance:

- If the Total Commit Charge exceeds the Total Physical Memory, you probably need more RAM. When the Commit Charge is regularly higher than the Physical Memory available, it means you have to regularly use a pagefile, which slows down your system. Buy more RAM; it's inexpensive and will boost system performance.
- Before running a memory-intensive application, use the Processes Tab to identify memory-hogging applications and close them down. The Processes tab of the Task Manager lists every process and program in use and shows the total amount of memory each uses. Click twice on the Mem Usage heading on the tab to reorder the list of programs and processes so that those requiring the most memory show up at the top. Close programs you don't really need before running a memory-intensive application.
- If the Peak Commit Charge is frequently at or near the Limit Commit Charge, you need to increase your memory. When this occurs, it means your PC is frequently out of memory or close to being out of memory. Either add RAM, or increase your pagefile size.

General Advice for Improving RAM Performance

So, you've learned how to use the Task Manager. Here are some additional tips for making better use of your existing RAM:

Remove DLLs from cache memory

If you notice your system running slowly after Windows has been running for some time, or if your RAM seems to be getting low for some reason, the culprit might be left-behind DLLs from programs that are no longer running, but that Windows still keeps in memory. Sometimes Windows keeps DLLs in cache memory even when the program that required them is no longer running, and this cuts down on the memory available to other applications.

You can use a simple Registry hack to have Windows automatically remove from cache memory DLLs that are no longer needed by programs. Run the Registry Editor **[Hack #183]** and go to `HKEY_LOCAL_MACHINE\SOFTWARE\Microsoft\Windows\CurrentVersion\Explorer`. Create a new `DWORD` value named `AlwaysUnloadDll`, and give it a data value of `1`. Exit the Registry, and reboot for the new setting to take effect. Note that this setting might cause problems with some programs. Some Windows programs—especially older and 16-bit programs—can issue error messages with this setting in effect, so if that starts happening, delete the new key, or give it a value of `0`.

Avoid DOS applications

DOS applications may not allow Windows to manage memory properly, and they hold on to the memory they use, not allowing it to be swapped out for use for other programs or processes. If you use any DOS applications, replace them with Windows versions.

Disable Aero

If you're using Aero in Windows Vista, turn it off. Right-click the desktop, and select Personalize. Then choose Window Color and Appearance→"Open classic appearance properties" for more color options. Select a non-Aero theme, and click OK.

Reduce the applications and services running in the background

You might have many programs and services running in the background, without realizing it. Look at your Notification area, and see if there are any programs running that you don't require. Shut them down, and go into their configuration settings to make sure they don't load at startup.

See Also

- "Speed Up System Performance with the Task Manager" **[Hack #168]**
- "Speed Up Your PC with ReadyBoost" **[Hack #158]**
- "Force Windows Vista to Use any USB Flash Drive for ReadyBoost" **[Hack #159]**

SPEED UP YOUR HARD DISK BY DEFRAGGING

Perhaps the simplest way to speed up your PC is to use a disk defragmenter, which will help you open applications and files more quickly. Normally, as you use applications and files, they get spread out in fragments across your hard disk. The next time you use them, they take longer to open because your hard disk has to find each disparate fragment so that they can be assembled when you open the file. A disk defragmenter stores files and applications contiguously (next to one another) so that they can be fetched much more quickly than if they were spread out across your whole disk. The process of defragmenting your hard disk is commonly called defragging.

Both Windows XP and Windows Vista include disk defragmenters. As configured to run, they do a reasonable job. But as you'll see in this next series of hacks, there's plenty you can to juice them up to make them run faster and better, and do a better job of defragging your hard disk.

HACK 161: Improve Defragging in Windows XP

XP Here's how to get the most out of XP's built-in defragmenter that should speed up your hard disk even more.

XP includes a built-in defragmentation program, which you can run by choosing Control Panel→ Performance and Maintenance→"Rearrange items on your hard disk to make programs run faster." But there are ways you can use it more effectively, as you'll see in this hack.

Defragment Boot Files

One of the biggest improvements of XP's defragger over previous Windows versions is that it can perform a *boot defragment*, placing all boot files contiguous to one another so that you boot faster. The boot defragment option is usually enabled by default, but there's a possibility that it could have been disabled, or enabled improperly. You can make sure it's enabled using a Registry hack. Run the Registry Editor [Hack #183], and go to `HKEY_LOCAL_MACHINE\SOFTWARE\Microsoft\Dfrg\BootOptimizeFunction`. Find the `Enable` string. If the `String` value is set to `N`, change it to `Y`. If it is `Y`, leave it as it is because that means boot defragmentation is enabled. Exit the Registry, and reboot. The next time you defragment your disk, the boot files will be defragmented.

You can also defragment the paging file, the hibernation file, and the Registry hives using the freeware program PageDefrag (www.microsoft.com/technet/sysinternals/FileAndDisk/PageDefrag.mspx).

Run the Disk Defragmenter from the Command Line

If you prefer the command line to the graphical interface, you can avoid maneuvering through menus and dialog screens to defragment your hard drive. (Using the command line also gives you greater control over the defragmentation process, as you'll see in this hack.) To defragment a hard drive, type `defrag` C: at a command prompt, where C is the hard drive you want to defragment. When you use the command line, you won't see a visual display of the defragmentation process, and you won't be able to pause it.

`defrag` also works invisibly in the background to make sure your programs load more quickly. It's set up so that every three days, and only during times your computer is otherwise idle, it moves program code to the outside of the disk to make programs load more quickly. You can force it to do that manually, without having to do a full defragment, by using the `-b` switch, like this:

```
defrag C: -b
```

It takes only a few minutes for `defrag` to do this, in contrast with a full defragmentation, which can easily take more than 20 minutes, depending on how fragmented your system is and the speed of your processor and hard drive.

You can use several other command-line switches with the `defrag` command:

`/A`
Analyzes the drive you want to defragment and shows you a brief analysis report, summarizing the hard-disk size and total fragmentation. It only displays the report, however; it does not defragment the drive.

`/V`
Analyzes the drive you want to defragment and shows you a comprehensive analysis report, detailing the size of the hard disk, the percentage of free and used space, total fragmentation, total number of fragments, and other details. It gives the analysis report, defragments the hard disk, and then gives an analysis of the hard disk after defragmentation. It also tells you whether your drive needs to be defragmented. The display will look something like Figure 11-17.

`/F`
Forces the drive to be defragmented, even if there isn't a certain minimum amount of space. Normally, you can defragment the drive only if your hard disk has at least 15 percent of its space free.

What to Do If the Disk Defragmenter Won't Defragment Your Drive

There will be times when the Disk Defragmenter won't defragment your drive or will defragment it only partially. It won't defragment your drive if you don't have at least 15 percent of the drive's space free. To solve the problem, as explained previously, type `defrag C: /F` at the command line, where C is your hard drive.

There are also certain files and areas that the Disk Defragmenter won't defragment: the Recycle Bin; the Windows pagefile; and *Bootsect.dos*, *Safeboot.fs*, *Saveboot.rsv*, *Hiberfil.sys*, and *Memory.dmp*. There's not much you can do about it, though it's a good idea to empty the Recycle Bin before defragmenting. If you have a large amount of RAM, you'll also have a large hibernation file (*Hiberfile.sys*), so it's worth disabling it (see the quick hack titled "Turn Off Hibernation and Get Back Hard Disk Space", later in this chapter) before you defragment and reenable it after. You should also run Disk Cleanup by clicking Start→Run (or Start→Start Search in Vista) and running the cleanmgr command.

Often, the Disk Defragmenter won't defragment every file on the first pass. Your best bet here is to use brute force: run it again until it defragments the files it missed the first time around. Also, keep in mind that the Disk Defragmenter won't defragment any files that are currently in use, so make sure to close all programs; if some files won't defragment, it might be because they're being used by an open program. Sometimes, programs might seem to be shut down but in fact might be running in a kind of phantom mode. For example, Outlook sometimes stays running even after you've shut it down. To make sure your programs are completely shut down before running the Disk Defragmenter, run the Task Manager by pressing Ctrl-Alt-Del or right-clicking the taskbar and choosing Task Manager. Check both the Applications and Processes tabs to see if any programs,

Figure 11-17.
There's no need to defragment this disk

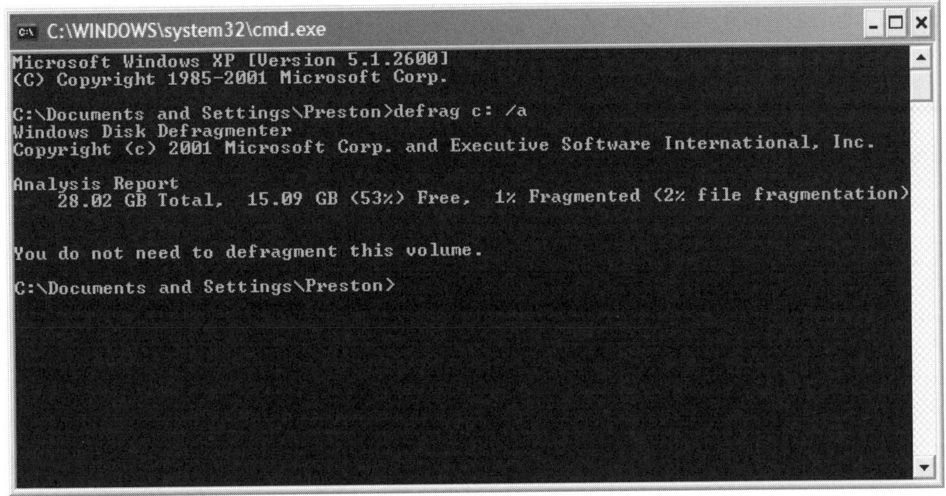
C:\WINDOWS\system32\cmd.exe
Microsoft Windows XP [Version 5.1.2600]
(C) Copyright 1985-2001 Microsoft Corp.
C:\Documents and Settings\Preston>defrag c: /a
Windows Disk Defragmenter
Copyright (c) 2001 Microsoft Corp. and Executive Software International, Inc.
Analysis Report
28.02 GB Total, 15.09 GB (53%) Free, 1% Fragmented (2% file fragmentation)
You do not need to defragment this volume.
C:\Documents and Settings\Preston>

such as Word for Windows (*Winword.exe*) or Outlook (*Outlook.exe*) are still running. These two programs sometimes continue running even after you've shut them down.

The best way to make sure that you aren't running any unnecessary programs is to start your computer in Safe Mode with Command Prompt before you run Defrag from the command line. You won't be able to do anything else while your computer is defragmenting, but at least the process will go a lot faster.

HACK 162: Look, Ma, No Hands! How To Automate Defrag in Windows XP

XP Tired of having to remember to defrag your hard disk on a regular basis? No problem. You can tell XP to defragment your hard disk on your own schedule—for example, when you sleep.

Defragmenting your hard disk is one of those tasks you shouldn't have to remember to do. It should go on all by itself. And there's a simple way to do that in Windows XP—use the Task Scheduler.

Using the Task Scheduler to defrag your hard disk is simple and straightforward. Select Start All Program→Accessories→System Tools→Scheduled Tasks, and the Scheduled Tasks folder will open. Double-click Add Scheduled Tasks, and a wizard appears, that will walk you through the process of creating a new task, in this instance, one that will automatically defragment your hard drive.

When you use the Task Scheduler to defragment your hard drive, you'll tell it to use `defrag` from the command line, not the normal disk defragmenter in Windows XP you get to using the graphical interface.

When the wizard appears, click Next. On the next screen, you'll be asked which program you want the Task Scheduler to run, as you can see in Figure 11-18. Browse to *C:\Windows\System32*, and select *defrag.exe*.

From the next screen in the wizard, type in a name for the task, such as Defragment my Hard Disk, then choose how often you want to defrag, for example daily, weekly, monthly, and so on. Defragmenting weekly will work just fine to keep your PC in tip-top shape, but there's no reason that you can't schedule it to work daily as well if you're the obsessive sort. Then click Next.

Now you'll set the exact time and day that you to schedule your defrag. Depending on the choice you made for how often you want to defrag, this screen may vary slightly. In Figure 11-19, I've chosen to schedule the defragger weekly, so I get choices for time of day and days of the week. There's even a choice for scheduling it on a nonweekly basis, for example once every two weeks, every three weeks, and so on. And you can also schedule it for more than once a week—for example, two or three days a week. Make your choices, and click Next.

Don't schedule your hard disk to be defragmented at the same time that the Windows XP Backup utility, or any other backup program, is backing up your drive. If they're scheduled at the same time, the defragmentation won't complete.

If you have multiple accounts on your PC and have set them up with passwords, another screen appears, asking for your username and password. Enter the username and password of a user with Administrator privileges, click Next, and check the box next to "Open advanced properties for this tasks when I click Finish." You'll need to check this box only if you have more than one hard drive or volume on your PC, and/or if you want to set advanced options for defragging.

If you haven't checked the box next to "Open advanced properties for this tasks when I click Finish," you're done; your disk will be defragged according to the schedule that you've set. If you have more than one hard disk, or if you want to set advanced options, you checked the box, so the screen shown in Figure 11-20 appears.

Here you'll be editing the Run box. It will already have in it the command for running `defrag`, most likely C:\Windows\system32\defrag.exe. To tell it to defrag your *C:* drive, add the *C:*, like this:

```
C:\Windows\system32\defrag.exe c:
```

Figure 11-18.
Starting the Task Scheduler

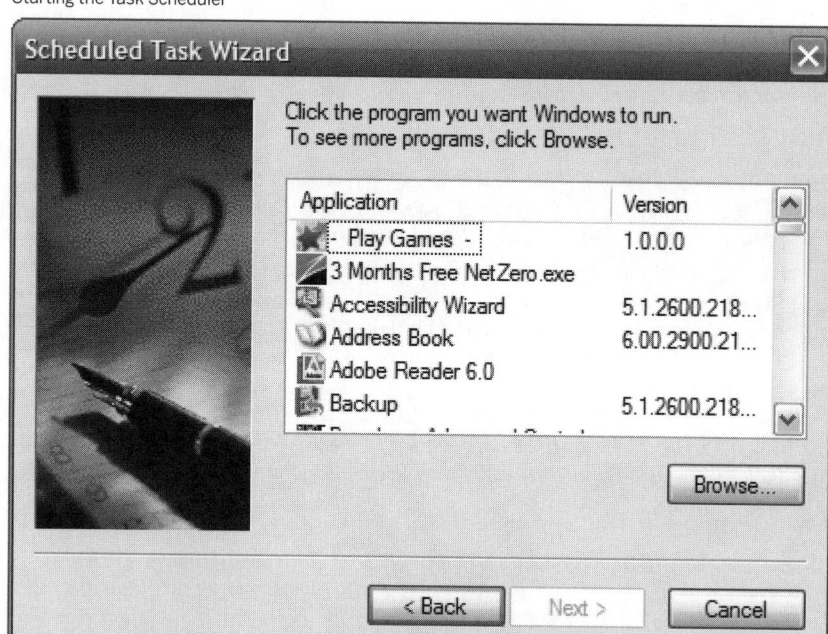

Figure 11-19.
Setting a defragmentation schedule

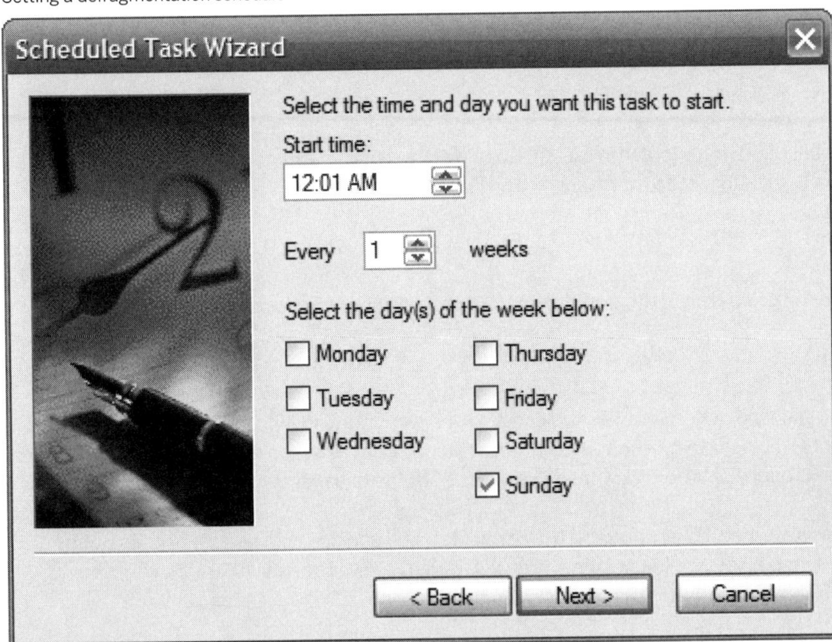

Figure 11-20.
Setting advanced options for your defrag

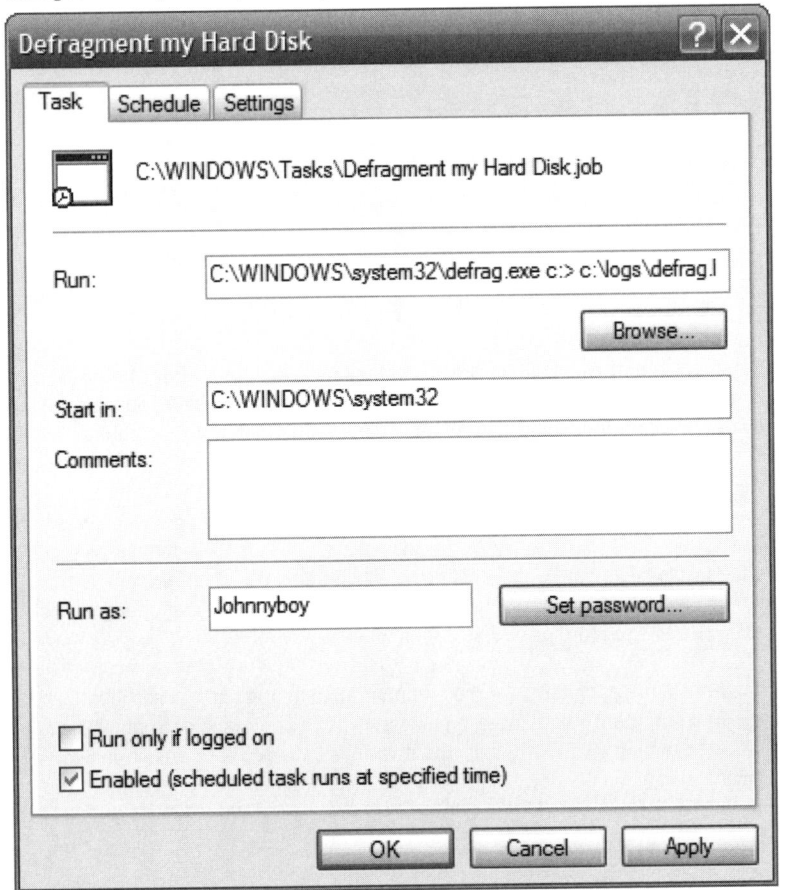

QUICK HACK 

TURN OFF HIBERNATION AND GET BACK HARD DISK SPACE

If you're not a fan of hibernation, you can save yourself some precious disk space by turning it off and recovering the space it normally uses. To turn off hibernation and delete the hibernation file, open the command prompt as an administrator, type this command and press Enter:

```
powercfg -H off
```

You can turn it back on with:

```
powercfg -H on
```

You can also accomplish the same thing on Vista by running Disk Cleanup. Type cleanmgr at the command prompt, and press Enter. From the screens that appear, tell Vista to clean up files from all users of the computer, and select your drive. Then when the Disk Cleanup screen appears, check the box next to Hibernation File Cleaner, and click OK. The files will be deleted.

The files take up about as much space as you have in RAM. So if have 2 GB of RAM, you'll save about 2 GB of disk space.

You can use any of the defrag commands [Hack #161]. So, for example, if you want to force a defrag, even if it isn't advisable because there is less than 15 percent of disk space left on your drive, issue this command:

```
C:\Windows\system32\defrag.exe c: /f
```

You can also tell the defragmenter to create a logfile of its defragmenting activities, which you can later read in a text editor. To do that, type this command:

```
C:\Windows\system32\defrag.exe c: > c:\mylogs\defrag.log
```

And if you want a great deal of detail in that log, tell defrag to run in verbose mode, like this:

```
C:\Windows\system32\defrag.exe c: /v > c:\mylogs\defrag.log
```

Click OK, and you'll be done. However, you can also set even more advanced options, such as running the task if you have a laptop that's running on batteries or stopping the task if it takes more than a certain amount of time. To set them, click the Settings tab, make your changes, and click OK.

Once the task is created, it will appear in the Scheduled Tasks folder. To change any of its options, double-click it, and a screen like the one shown in Figure 11-20 will appear. At any point, if you no longer want to automatically defragment, simply delete the task from the folder.

Hacking the Hack

If you want to automatically defragment more than one drive or volume, create a separate task for each. Make sure that you don't schedule them for the same days and times. So you might want to defrag one on a certain day of the week, another on another day, and so on.

HACK 163: Schedule Defragging in Windows Vista

V Windows Vista's defragger improves on Windows XP's because it runs automatically without intervention. But its schedule might not fit yours.

The Windows Vista defragger is both better and worse than the one in Windows XP. It's better because by default, it runs once a week in the background, keeping your hard disk in top shape. It's worse because it provides no visual feedback; it won't report on disk defragmentation before and after it does its work.

There's a good chance that you never even realized that the Windows Vista defragger was turned on because Windows Vista schedules it to run every Wednesday at 1 a.m.. If you'd like to change that schedule, it's simple to do: select Control Panel→System and Maintenance→"Defragment your hard drive". Click Modify schedule, and a screen like Figure 11-21 appears. Make your changes, click OK and OK again, and it will defrag according to your new schedule.

If you prefer a command-line defragging tool, use the command-line defragger, which is identical to the one in Windows XP. To defragment a hard drive, type `defrag C:` at a command prompt, where C is the hard drive you want to defragment. For details about various switches you can use, including one to force a defragment even when Windows Vista tells you it can't defrag, see the section "Run the Disk Defragmenter from the Command Line" in "Improve Defragging in Windows XP" [Hack #161].

Figure 11-21.
Changing your defrag schedule in Windows Vista

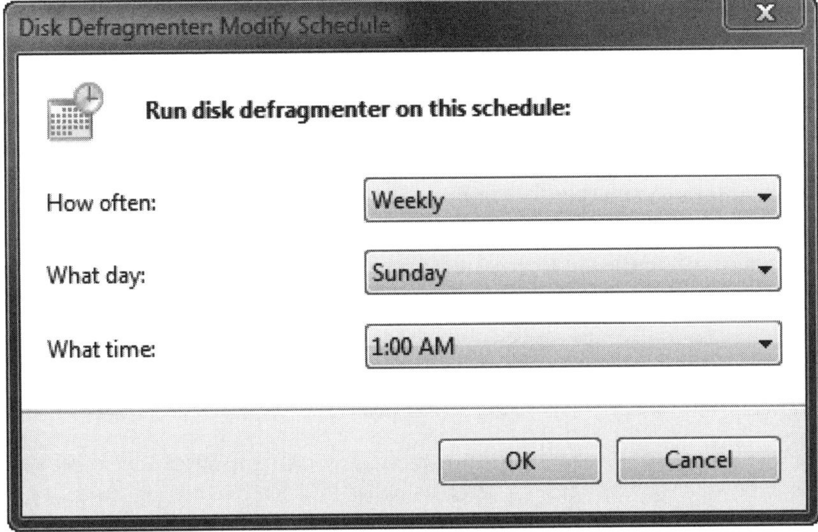

HACK 164: Defragment a Single File

V XP It can as little as a few minutes or as much as several hours to defragment your hard disk. But what if you want to optimize? Do you really want to have to spend as many as several hours waiting for your disk to defrag?

If you just want to optimize a single file, such as a large virtual machine disk image, you can use a tool called Contig, which lets you defrag in a way Windows' defrag utility can't.

Contig (www.microsoft.com/technet/sysinternals/FileAndDisk/Contig.mspx), a free defragger from Microsoft, was made by a company called Sysinternals, which Microsoft bought. It's a command-line defragger, and it works with Windows XP as well as Windows Vista.

Its main benefit is that it lets you defragment individual files and folders instead of your whole disk, but you can also use it to defragment your entire disk. And people have reported that it defragments much faster than Windows Vista's built-in defragger.

To use it on Vista, run the command prompt as an administrator by typing `cmd` at the Search box and pressing Ctrl-Shift-Return. On XP, log in as an administrator, and start a command prompt. Next, go (using the `cd` command) to the folder where you installed Contig. To defrag a single file, use this command:

```
Contig <filename>
```

Make sure that you include the entire path to the file, not only the filename. So, for example, to defrag the file *bigfile.tif* in the folder *C:\Artwork*, you'd issue this command:

```
Contig C:\Artwork\bigfile.tif
```

You can also use wildcards, for example, to defrag all files ending in the *.tif* format in a directory:

```
Contig C:\Artwork\*.tif
```

And if you want to defrag all **.tif* files in *C:\Artwork* and all of its subdirectories, use the -s switch:

```
Contig -s C:\Artwork\*.tif
```

If you want to see how fragmented a file or files have become, but not actually defragment the file or files, use the -a switch:

```
Contig -a C:\Artwork\bigfile.tif
```

To have Contig give you a summary of its actions after it takes them, use the -v switch:

```
Contig -v C:\Artwork\*.tif
```

If you're not a fan of the command line, you can use a simple, graphical frontend for Contig called Power Defragmenter (www.excessive-software.eu.tt). Install it in the same directory as you've installed Contig, and then run it. It lets you defrag up to four files or directories at a time or else your entire hard disk, and includes a so-called "PowerMode Disk Defragmentation," in which it essentially performs a dual defragmentation pass (without taking up twice the amount of time) for maximum defragmentation. Figure 11-22 shows it in action, selecting four folders to defragment.

Figure 11-22.
Defragmenting four folders at a time

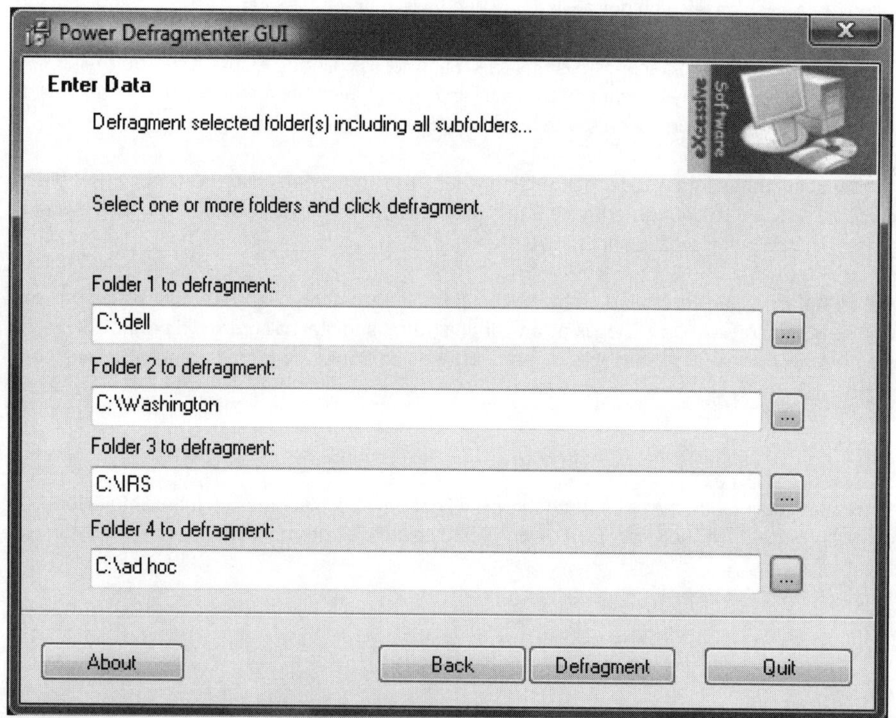

HACK 165: Track Down Vista System Woes

V Here's the best tool you can use for tracking down system performance issues and helping resolve them.

As you use your PC, Windows Vista records an astonishing amount of information. Memory usage, network usage, system startup, application crashes, system slowdowns: all that and far more is captured in mind-boggling detail.

A well-hidden system tool, Event Viewer, lets you get at all that information so that you can see what caused any problems you're having. Based on that, you may be able to fix them.

Launch Event Viewer by typing Event Viewer in the Start Menu's search box, or by typing eventvwr.msc in the Search box or at a command prompt and pressing Enter. The Event Viewer (Figure 11-23) launches; it lets you read a wide variety of Windows Vista system logs and data.

The Event Viewer is an exceedingly complex application with a wide variety of uses, and a full explanation of it is beyond the scope of this book. So what follows are some of the most important ways to use it to track system performance.

In the left pane, click Windows Logs. A variety of subfolders appear, including Applications, Security, Setup, System, and Forwarded Events. The most important of these from a performance point of view are Applications and System, so scroll through them.

When you click either subfolder, you'll see a list of events that happened on your PC—for example, a Restore Point was created, files were backed up, and so on. Mostly, these are purely informational, and frequently, you won't be able to understand much about the event. Events that are normal, and in which no problems were recorded, have a blue icon of the letter *i*.

Problematic events have other icons, and as you scroll through the subfolders, look for these icons. A yellow warning icon, as shown in Figure 11-24, indicates a problem of some sort, although not a severe one.

Figure 11-23.
Windows Vista's Event Viewer

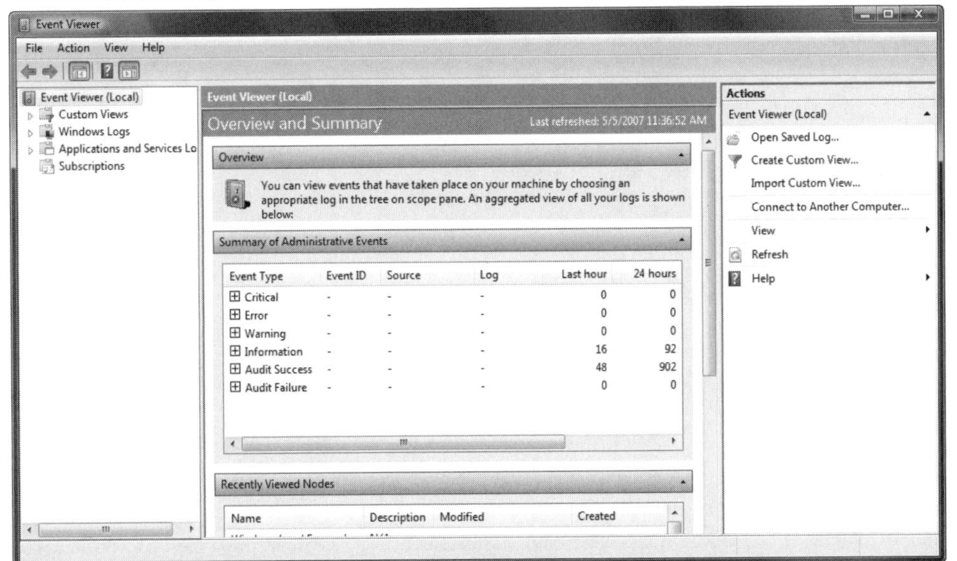

Figure 11-24.
A yellow warning icon indicates a moderate problem

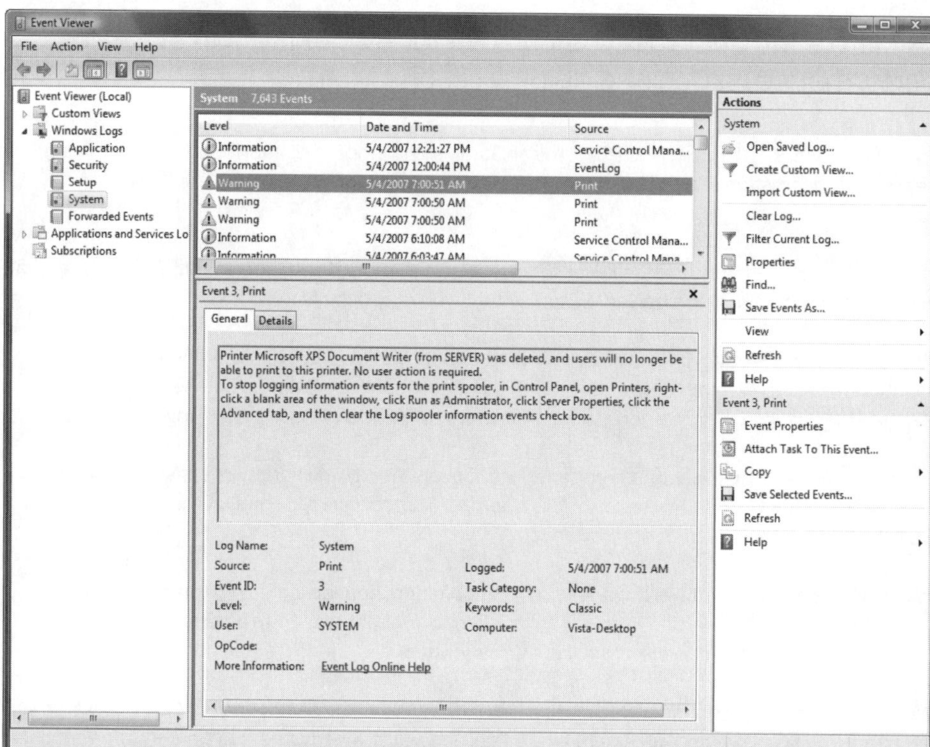

Figure 11-25.
A system health report

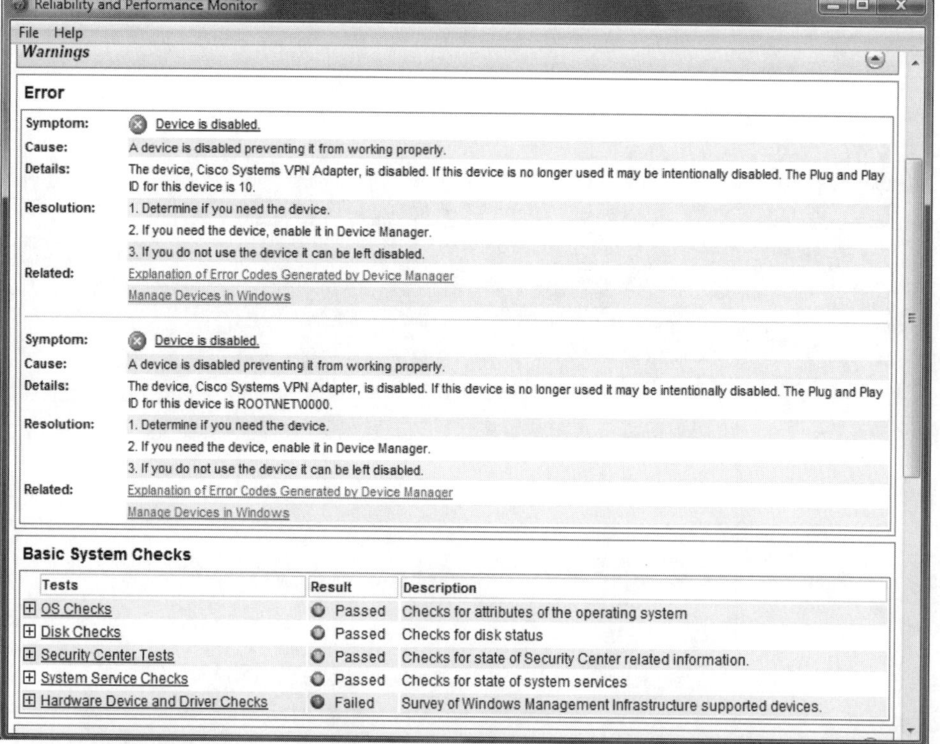

QUICK HACK

HAVE VISTA DO A FAST, FREE, PERFORMANCE CHECK

Windows Vista has a great, little-known tool built into it that performs comprehensive diagnostics on your PC, reports the results in an easy-to-read format, and offers advice on how to fix any problems. Choose Control Panel→System and Maintenance→Performance Information and Tools→Advanced Tools→Generate a System Health Report. After a minute or two, Windows will display a report about the state of your system. If it finds any problems, it flags them with red Xs, offers details about the cause, and offers advice for fixing it. Figure 11-25 shows a typical report.

The Applications and Services Logs top-level folder is where most of the action is if you're interested in system performance. Beneath it you'll find a variety of subfolders, including Antivirus, Internet Explorer, Hardware and so on. The most important subfolder of all is the Microsoft\Windows subfolder, which has far, far more information than the main Windows Log. You'll find dozens of subfolders underneath Microsoft\Windows, and each of these has subfolders, often multiple ones.

Most of the subfolders are self-explanatory. Want to see how ReadyBoost is doing? Head to the ReadyBoost subfolder. There are also subfolders for many other Windows services.

Most useful of all, from a performance standpoint, is the Diagnostics-Performance subfolder. Click to expand it, then click the Operational page (Figure 11-26). This page contains information about system performance, and reports on overall system problems and slowdowns. An event with a red exclamation point means there was a serious error; one with a red X means the error was a critical one.

Scroll through all the errors and warnings. For more detail about any, double-click it, and an Event Properties screen like that shown in Figure 11-27, appears, showing you the details in an easier-to-read format.

As you scroll through the page, look for patterns among the problems. Does a particular application seem to cause issues frequently? If so, consider uninstalling it or upgrading to the latest version, if one is available. Does the problem happen at a certain time of the day? If so, think of what you do on your PC at that time: do you run too many programs at once then?

The Event Viewer won't actually be able to solve problems for you or speed up your system. But by viewing its logs, as outlined in this hack, it can help you see where you have performance issues, and you can take it from there.

Figure 11-26.
This Windows Vista PC clearly has problems

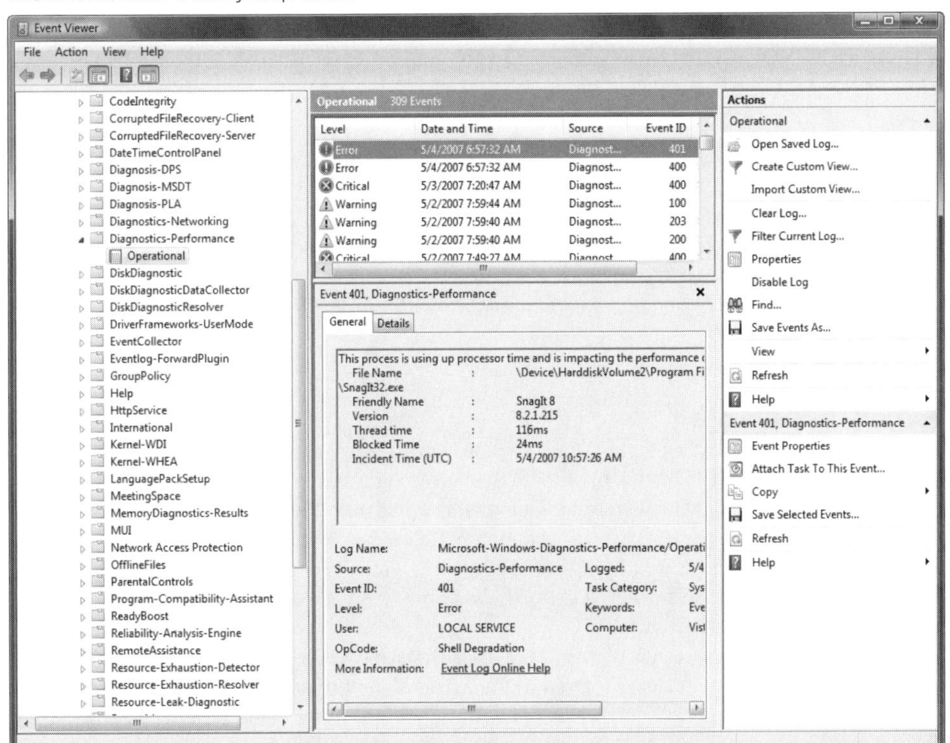

Figure 11-27.
Details about a problematic system event

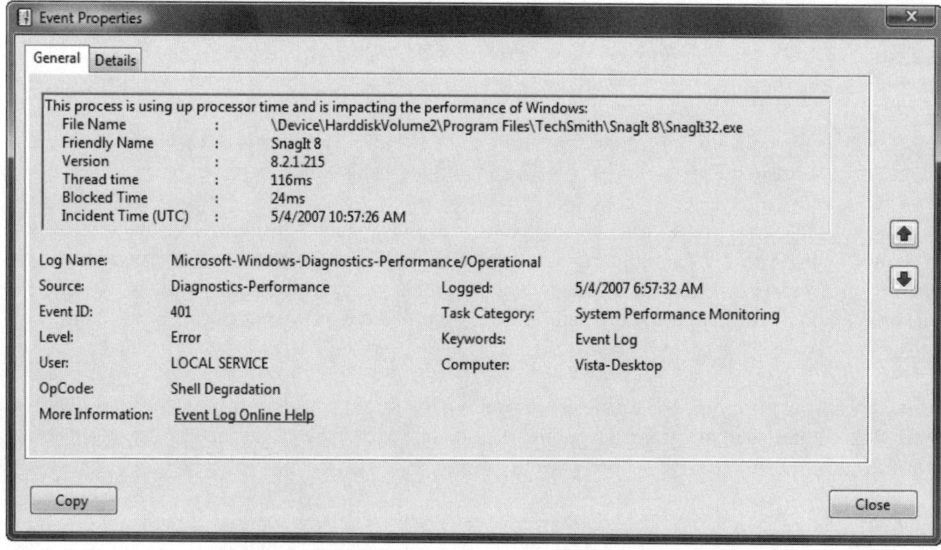

HACK 166: Track System Performance with the XP Performance Console

XP Before you can hack away at things to speed up your computer, you should know how to monitor system performance in the first place. The Performance Console in Windows XP is a great hacker's tool for monitoring and tracking resources of all kinds, and you can use it to find the source of many glitches or slowdowns.

Computers get faster every year, but somehow we sometimes still end up waiting around for them to finish a task.

To figure out what's slowing down your computer and to get to the root of the problem, use the Performance Console (`perfmon`) to track and graph the activities of Windows XP and its components. First, I'll show you how to set up a log, and then I'll give you some ways to put the console logs to good use.

Setting Up Your Logs

Choose Start→Run, and type `perfmon`. You'll see the Microsoft Management Console (MMC) with the Performance title bar. In the left pane, click System Monitor to see a graph of your current system performance, including your processor, memory, and disk (Figure 11-28). You can use the toolbar buttons to configure the graph data and format. This graph is useful for seeing what's going on now, but it's useless for looking at the long-term picture. For this, you'll need to log this information somewhere and see how it changes over time.

To create logfiles of your system's performance, click Performance Logs and Alerts in the left pane of the MMC. You can create counter logs (with the values of performance indicators, measured on a regular basis), trace logs (with the values of performance indicators when something happens, such as a program crash), and alerts (an action for Windows to take when a counter hits a specified value). Logfiles stored in text format contain one line per observation, with values separated by

Figure 11-28.
Windows XP's System Monitor

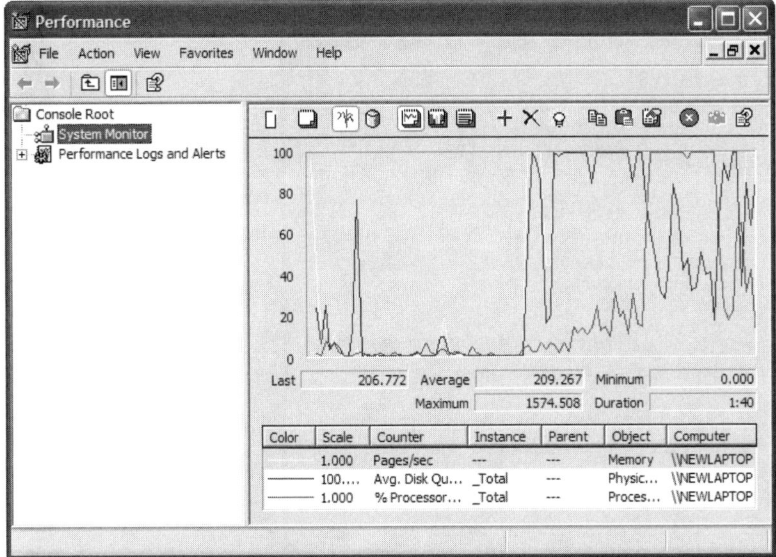

either commas or tabs, and are usually stored in the *C:\Perflogs* folder. You can import these logfiles into a spreadsheet or database for analysis, reporting, and graphing. SQL and binary (nontext) logfile formats are also available. (See article Q296222 in the Microsoft Knowledgebase for how to log data directly to an SQL database.)

Create a counter log by right-clicking Counter Logs in the left pane and choosing New Log Settings from the shortcut menu. Give the new log a name and press OK. Specify the statistics you want to log (see the following section "What to Watch") by clicking Add Counters on the General tab of the Properties sheet for the log (see Figure 11-29). A nice feature of this utility is that you can choose whether to monitor the local computer or another computer on your LAN. Don't add more than a few counters or your logfile will grow quickly and be confusing to analyze. To select a counter, first select the performance object (that is, the part of the computer system you want to monitor, such as memory or disks), and then choose counters from the list.

Set the interval to the frequency at which you'd like to sample the data. Don't choose too frequent an interval, or your logfile will take over your entire hard disk (start with once a minute). On the Logfiles tab, specify the file type, name, and location. If you plan to import this file into a spreadsheet or database program, choose Text File (comma-delimited) for the type. On the Schedule tab, specify when the log start and stops—manually, or automatically on a schedule.

 The Performance console itself can slow down your computer considerably. Run it only when you need it, and don't set the logging interval to be too short. Set logs to stop after a day or two; otherwise, they'll run until your hard disk fills up.

What to Watch

These counters are often worth logging (to select one of them, choose the first word, such as "Memory" from the Performance object drop-down menu, and then pick the counter, such as "Pages/sec" from the list):

\Memory\Pages/sec

Number of pages read from disk or written to disk when Windows runs out of memory. Swapping information to and from the disk can slow down your system significantly. Consider adding more memory.

Figure 11-29
Creating or editing a performance log

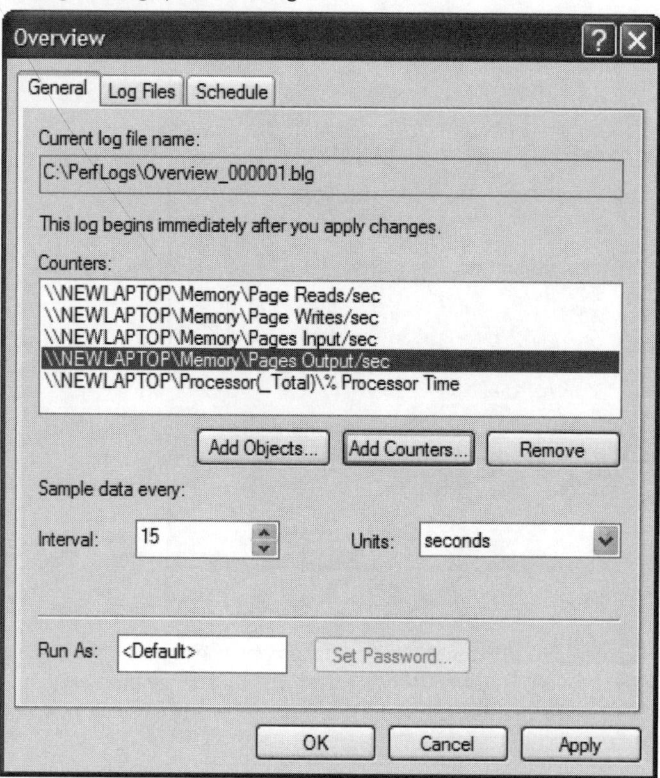

QUICK HACK

REDUCE XP'S VISUAL EFFECTS TO INCREASE PERFORMANCE

Windows XP's visual effects—such as fading and sliding menus, background images for folders, and drop shadows for icon labels—are snazzy-looking. But all those effects can take their toll on system performance.

XP gives you the option of balancing these visual effects against system performance. You can go full-bore and use all the visual effects, you can turn all of them off, you can have your system decide which to use, or you can pick and choose which effects to turn on and off. Right-click My Computer and choose Properties→ Advanced→ Settings (under the Performance section). To turn off all visual effects, choose "Adjust for best performance". To use all visual effects, choose "Adjust for best appearance". To turn individual effects on and off, choose Custom, then check the effects you want to use, and uncheck the ones you don't. Experiment to see how they affect system performance.

\PhysicalDisk\Avg. Disk Queue Length
Number of read and write requests that are waiting for the disk to respond. High numbers indicate that a faster disk drive would speed up performance.

\PhysicalDisk\ percent Disk Time
Percentage of the time the disk was busy. This is another indicator of a slow or overloaded disk.

\Processor\ percent Processor Time
Percentage of the time the processor was busy with all types of processes. This counter can tell you whether delays are caused by an overloaded CPU.

You can click the Explain button to see more information about a counter you've selected in the list.

Viewing Performance Logs

With the System Monitor in the MMC, you can view a log as a graph. Click System Monitor in the left pane of the MMC window, and click the View Log Data icon on its toolbar. Add the logfile, to the list. When you are looking at the graph, click the Properties button on the toolbar to change how the graph looks.

To look at the contents of a *.csv* logfile in Excel or your default spreadsheet program, double-click the filename in Windows Explorer. Excel might complain that the file is still open (since the Performance Console is still appending information to it); click Read-Only or Notify (to open it read-only and be notified when the file is available). This lets you see what's in the file so far. In Excel, you can analyze, graph, and print the counters.

Performance Alerts

You can create an alert to let you know when a counter exceeds a specified value. For example, the Performance Console can let you know when the idle processor time drops lower than 10 percent. Right-click Alerts in the left pane of the MMC window and choose New Alert Settings to create a new alert. Add one or more counters, and specify the limit (upper or lower) beyond which Windows should take action. On the Action tab, specify what Windows does when the alert occurs: specifically, you can have it add a note to an event log or run a program.

— Margaret Levine Young

HACK 167: Track Performance and Reliability with the Vista Reliability Monitor

V Here's the single best place to go in Windows Vista for getting the inside info on system performance and reliability.

Windows Vista has significantly redone Windows XP's Performance Console with the Performance and Reliability Monitor, which for system tweakers offers the best of all possible worlds: a real-time, live snapshot of system performance, as well as a historical view of overall reliability, complete with detailed information about system crashes.

To run it, type perfmon at the Search box of the Start menu or at a command prompt, and press Enter. (For those who prefer to mouse their way there, choose Control Panel→System and Maintenance→Performance Information and Tools→Advanced Tools→Open Reliability and Performance Monitor.)

When it opens, you'll see a screen like that shown in Figure 11-30. The top of the screen offers a snapshot of your system use, including CPU, disk, network, and memory use.

For details, click the options below the graphs. When you click CPU, for example, you'll see something similar to Figure 11-31, which shows all the processes and applications taking up CPU power, along with a description of them, how many threads each use, how much of the CPU they're using, and so on. Keeping an eye on the graphs will help make sure that you don't overstress your system.

The Performance Monitor can do all the same tricks that the Windows XP Performance Console [Hack #166] can. You just get at them in a different way. To add a counter to your page, click Performance Monitor under Monitoring tools in the left pane. Then click the + button at the top of the screen, and from the Add Counter page that appears, browse to the counter you want to use. They're organized by category. Click the category you're interested in, such as Memory, then click the downward-pointing wedge shape to browse through the available counters. Select those you want to add, Click Add, and a list of counters appears. (Figure 11-32). Click OK, and you'll see a screen that monitors those counters. (Figure 11-33).

Using the Reliability Monitor

Click Reliability Monitor to see how reliable your PC has been over time, gives it a reliability rating, and offers details about system crashes. (Figure 11-34).

The Index number at the top of the page is a number Vista calculates gauging your system's overall reliability. The maximum is 10. Every time there's a system failure, application failure, and so on, the index drops, sometimes precipitously, especially if there is more than one failure in a day. For example, on one of my PCs, I had two failures in one day, and the reliability index dropped from 9.21 to 8.26.

Figure 11-30.
Windows Vista's Performance and Reliability Monitor

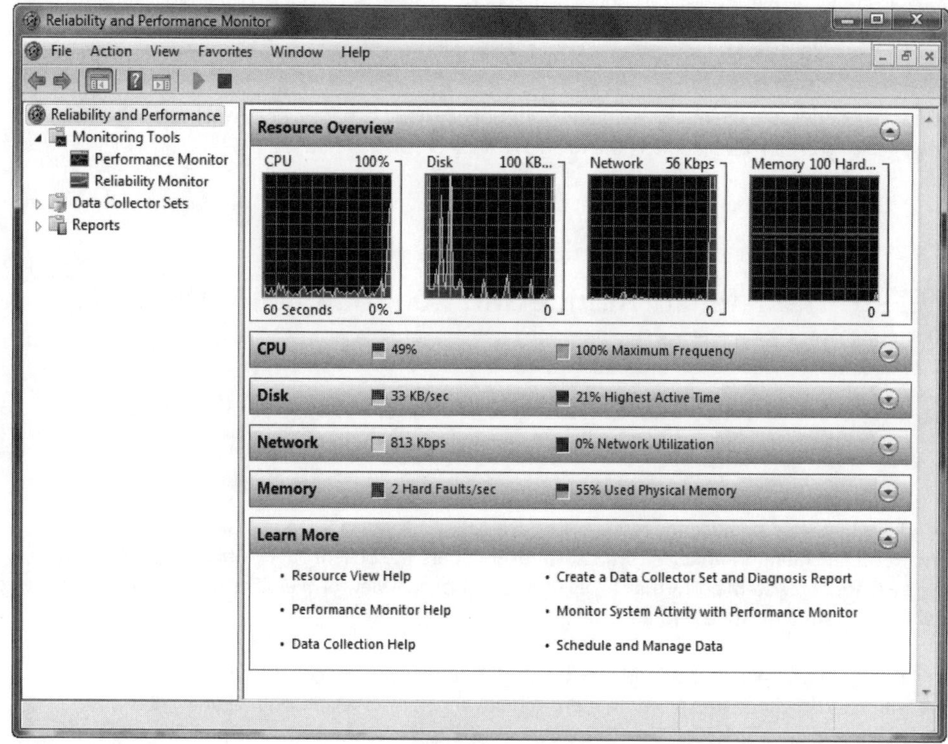

Figure 11-31.
Details of your CPU use

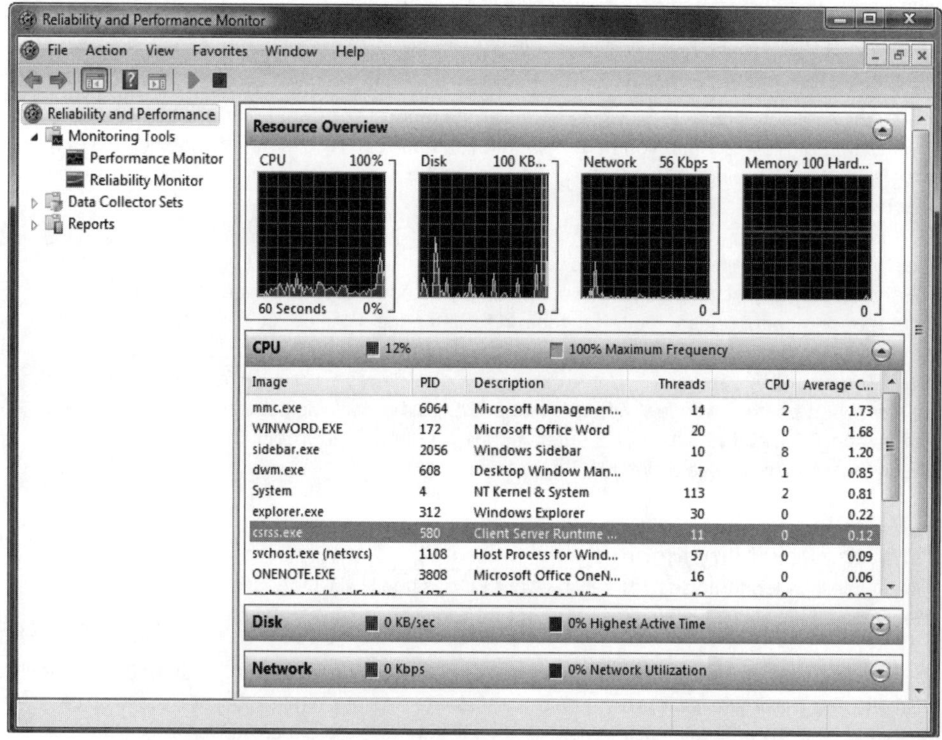

Figure 11-32.
Adding counters to the Performance Monitor

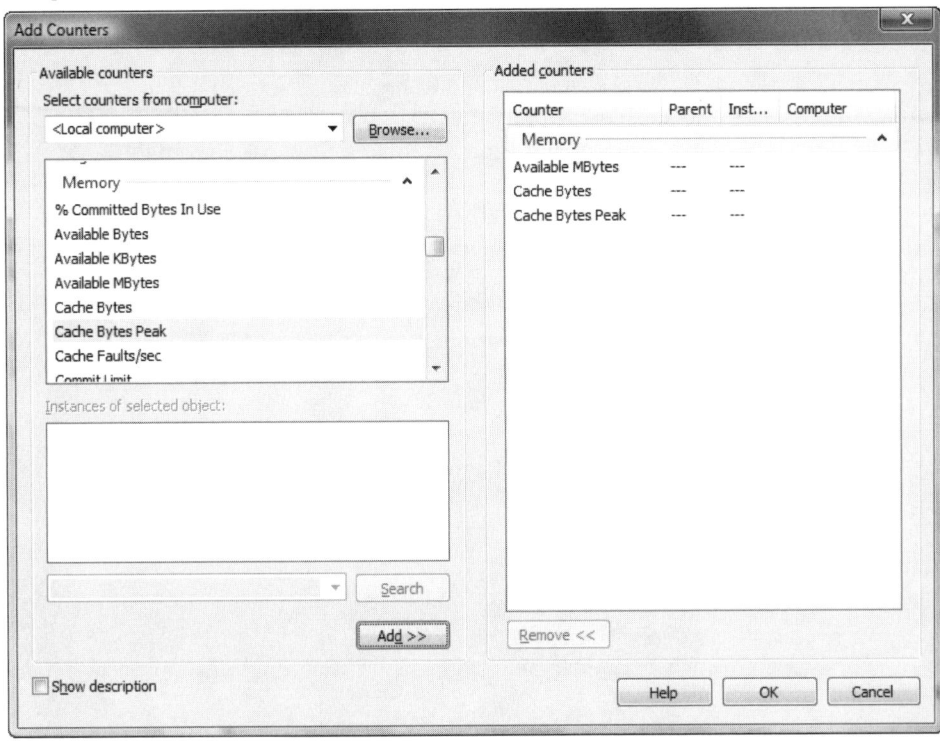

Figure 11-33.
Viewing counters in the Performance Monitor

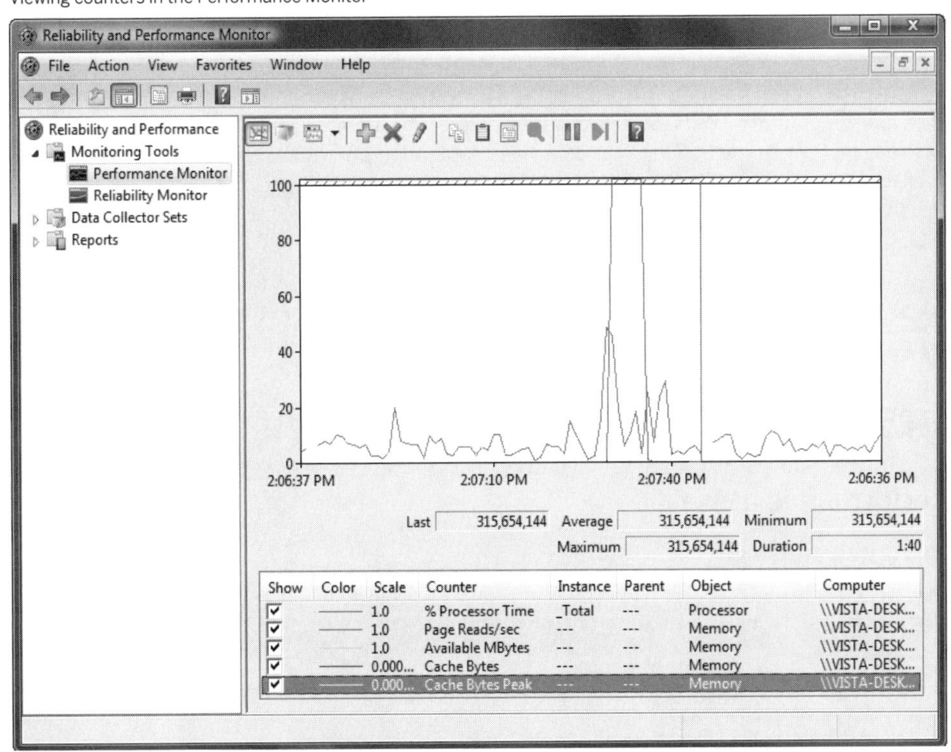

Figure 11-34.
The Windows Vista Reliability Monitor

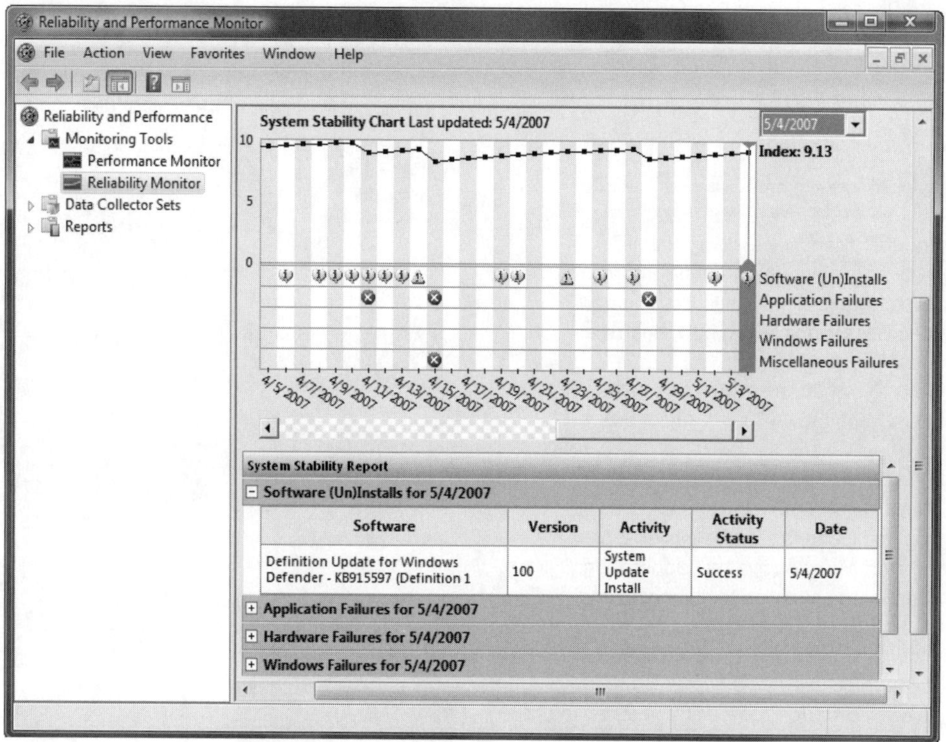

For every day that your system doesn't have a failure, the index rises a little bit, as you can see in Figure 11-34. But exactly how Windows Vista calculates the amount of drops and rises is rather mysterious.

Even more important than the overall reliability index are the details of each system crash. Go to each day that has a crash, and see the cause—an application, an overall system failure, and so on. Look for patterns, such as if an application frequently crashes. If so, uninstall it, or look for an update that fixes the problem.

HACK 168: Speed Up System Performance with the Task Manager

V XP This humble tool does more than show you what applications are running; it can help juice up your PC's performance as well.

Most Windows users know the Task Manager will show them all programs and processes running on their system and that it will let them shut down any they don't want to run any longer. But it can do much more than that; it can also help fine-tune system performance.

The Task Manager can also help you get the most out of your existing RAM **[Hack #160]**.

There are four common ways to run the Task Manager:

- Press Ctrl-Shift-Esc.

- Right-click the taskbar, and choose Task Manager.
- Type taskmgr in the Search box of the Windows Vista Start Menu, and press Enter, or type taskmgr into the command prompt, or Search/Run box in Windows Vista or Windows XP.
- Press Ctrl-Alt-Del (in Windows Vista, you'll then have to choose Task Manager from the screen that appears).

The screens and sequences in this hack are based on Windows Vista, but the Windows XP Task Manager is almost identical to that in Windows Vista, so you can follow the same advice, with only very slight variations.

The Task Manager, shown in Figure 11-35, has six tabs, but you'll use the Applications, Processes, and Performance tabs to help improve system performance. At the bottom of each tab, you'll find a quick summary of the current state of your system, including current CPU use, the number of processes running, and how much memory is dedicated to your system.

Before you can learn how to use these tabs to improve performance, you'll need some background about each tab.

Applications Tab

The Applications tab displays a list of every application currently running on your PC, such as Word, Excel, and any other application. It also reports on the status of each application—primarily, whether the application is running or not responding to input.

When you right-click an application, a menu of choices lets you manage the application in several ways; you can switch to it, move it to the front, minimize it, maximize it, or end it, as shown in Figure 11-36. The Go To Process option takes you to the application's process on the Processes tab. You can get more information about the application this way.

Figure 11-35.
The Task Manager

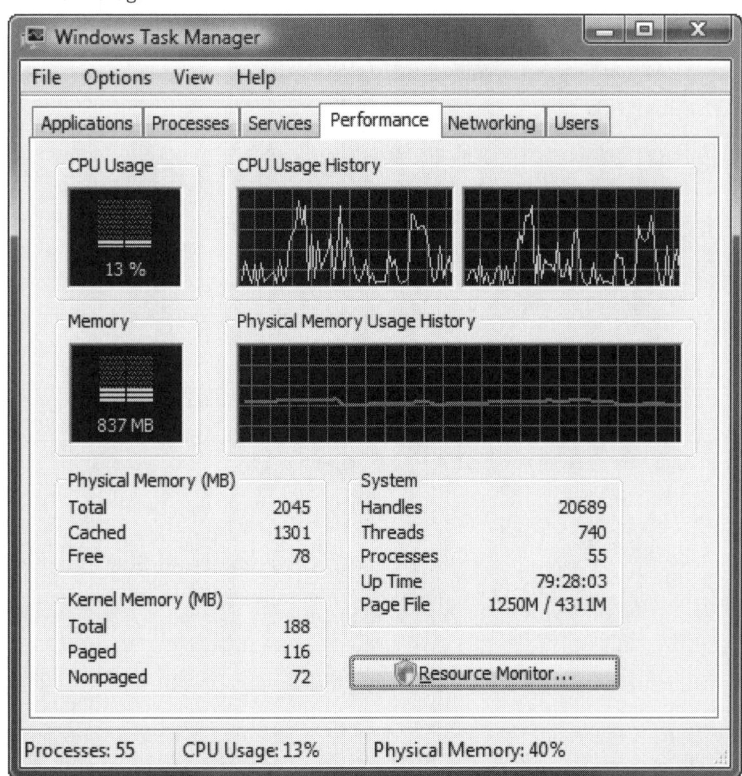

Processes Tab

The Processes tab reports on every process running on your computer, as well as a variety of services run by the operating system. It reports on the percentage of the CPU that each process uses, as well as how much memory each process uses.

When you right-click any process, you get a menu of choices that allow you to manage the process in a variety of ways, including ending that process as well as any related processes, as shown in Figure 11-37. You can see more information about processes by selecting View→Select Columns.

Performance Tab

The Performance tab shows a variety of performance measurements, such as total CPU use, CPU usage history, pagefile usage history, and memory used, as shown in Figure 11-38. You'll use this tab more than any other when tracking system performance and unstopping bottlenecks.

The Performance tab has tabular material and four graphs that detail your computer's current performance. The graphs are straightforward and easy to understand:

CPU Usage	Percentage of your CPU that your PC is currently using
CPU Usage History	Usage over time
Memory (Vista)	How much of your memory you're currently using
Physical Memory Usage History (Vista)	Usage over time
PF Usage (XP)	How much of your pagefile you're currently using
Pagefile Usage History (XP)	Usage over time

Figure 11-36.
The Task Manager's Applications tab

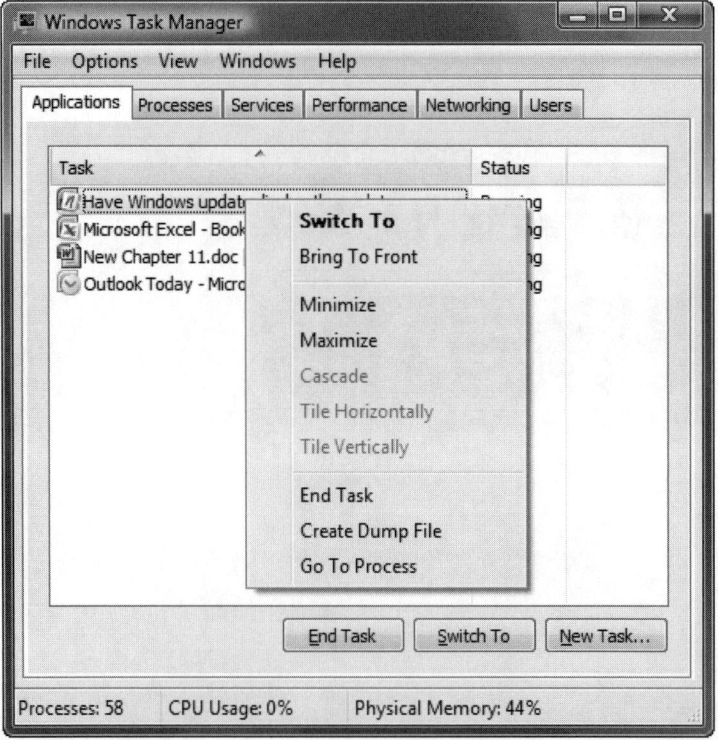

Figure 11-37.
The Task Manager's Processes tab

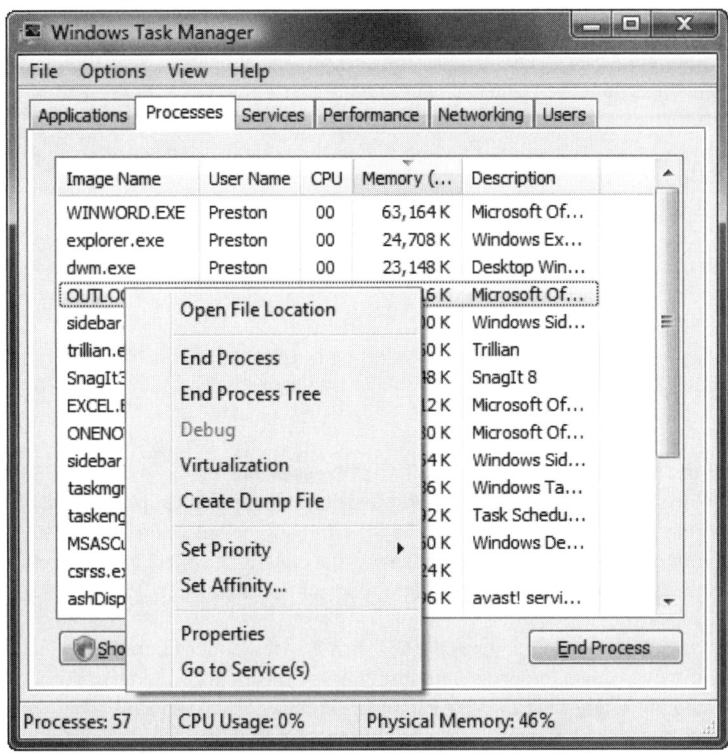

Figure 11-38.
The Task Manager's Performance tab

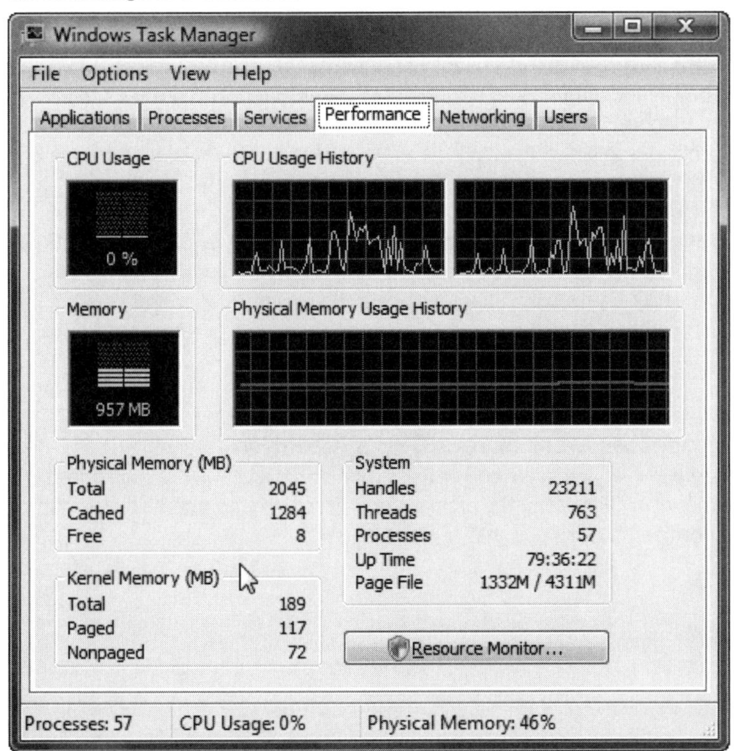

Task Manager updates its data every two seconds, and each vertical line on the graphs represents a two-second interval. To change the update time, from the Task Manager choose View→Update Speed, and select High or Low. When you select High, updates take place twice a second. When you select Low, updates take place once every four seconds. To stop updating altogether, select Paused. To do an immediate update, press F5.

Monitor CPU Use

Today's microprocessors (1 GHz or higher) can handle most tasks easily, but CPU-intensive software or tasks such as computer-aided design (CAD) programs, CD burning, and games can slow down a system significantly. You can use the Task Manager to monitor your CPU use and, based on what you find, take steps to help your system run faster.

You'll monitor your CPU usage using the Processes and Performance tabs of the Task Manager. You'll check two things: total CPU load and how much of the CPU any individual process or program uses.

Finding out how much of the CPU individual programs and processes use

A common cause of CPU slowdown is that one or more programs or processes take up too much of the CPU's attention. You can check the percentage of the CPU that any individual program uses. Once you determine that, close the application; your system will get a quick performance boost. If you need to run that application, close any other applications that take up too much CPU attention.

From the Task Manager's Processes tab, double-click the CPU heading. It will reorder the listing of processes and programs in descending order, listing those that use the most CPU time at the top. Note that, frequently, the top listing will be titled System Idle Process, which reports on the percentage of your CPU that is idle. Look for any programs or processes that use a considerable amount of your CPU. If you find any, close them before starting any other CPU-intensive applications, such as design programs and CD-burning software.

QUICK HACK 

TURN UP YOUR CPU POWER

If you use Windows Vista on a laptop, and it seems sluggish, the problem may be that you're using a power plan that limits CPU power. The Power Saver plan, for example, limits your CPU to a percentage of its power (this depends on the processor models; some low-voltage CPUs can slow down to one-fourth or less of their maximum speed). If you want to turn your laptop up to full throttle, click the power icon in the system tray, and select the High performance plan.

Tracking CPU usage in real time

If your CPU regularly uses a high percentage of its capacity, it means there's a bottleneck. You should upgrade the CPU, buy a new computer, or run fewer programs. But how can you know whether your CPU has a bottleneck? Check your CPU use. Run Task Manager, and make sure Options→Hide When Minimized is selected. Now, whenever you minimize the Task Manager, it will sit in the system tray area of the task bar.

Now, minimize the Task Manager. It will display as a small bar graph in the system tray that lights up green as you use your CPU. To see your current CPU usage, hold your mouse cursor over the Task Manager's icon in the system tray. Try running different combinations of programs, and monitor your CPU use with each combination. If you find your CPU is overburdened on a regular basis, it's time for an upgraded CPU or a new computer.

Give Program and Processes More of Your CPU's Attention

Windows gives a *base priority* to every program and process running on your PC; the base priority determines the relative amount of CPU power the program or process gets, compared to other programs. Here are the priorities Windows assigns:

- Low
- BelowNormal
- Normal
- AboveNormal
- High
- RealTime

Most programs and processes are assigned a Normal priority. But you might want to give a program like a CAD or graphics program more of your CPU's attention. That way, the program will get the CPU power it needs and will therefore run more smoothly and quickly. If there are programs or processes that normally run in the background or rarely need your CPU, you can give them less of your CPU's attention.

If you have a multicore PC, you can tell Windows to assign only one processor to any application **[Hack #157]**.

You can use the Task Manager to change the priorities assigned to any process or program. The priorities of Low, Below Normal, Normal, Above Normal, and High are self-explanatory, but you might not quite understand *Real Time*. Real Time devotes an exceedingly high number of CPU cycles to the given task—so much so that even the Task Manager might not be able to interrupt any program or process assigned that priority. So, you shouldn't assign a Real Time priority to any program or task, unless it will be the sole program or task running on the PC. Of course, if it's the only program or task running, you really don't need to give it a high priority because it already has your CPU's complete attention.

To change the priority of a running program or process from the Processes tab, right-click the program or process whose priority you want to change, highlight Set Priority, and choose the priority for the program, as shown in Figure 11-39.

Be careful when using this feature because it can have unintended consequences and lead to system instability. If you find it causes problems, stop using it.

Keep in mind that when you assign a new priority to a process or program, that new priority sticks only as long as the program or process is running. Once the program or process ends and you restart it, it defaults to the priority assigned to it by Windows.

Figure 11-39.
Devoting more or less CPU power to an individual program or process

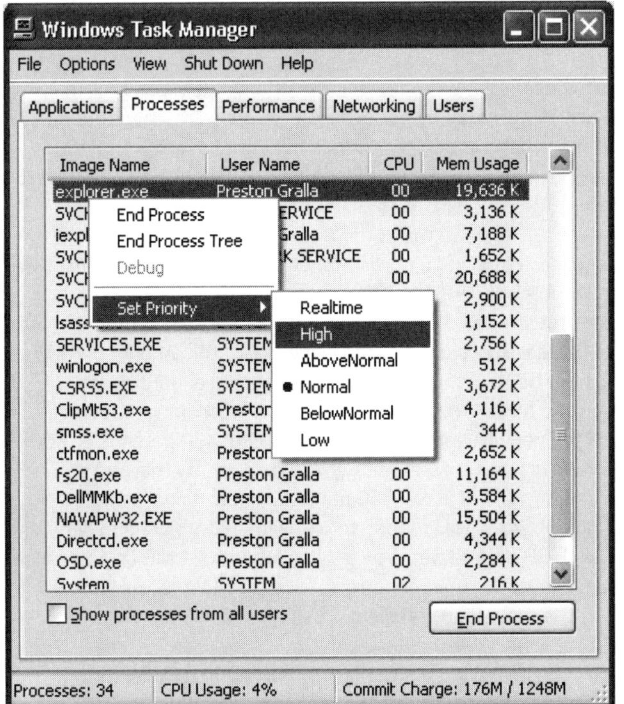

QUICK HACK

FIX WINDOWS VISTA'S 64-BIT DRIVER WOES

Windows Vista 64-bit includes an extremely annoying feature: it will refuse to run any drivers that haven't been digitally signed. Considering how many drivers aren't signed, this can put a crimp in your Vista experience. You can, however, fix the problem. Open an elevated command prompt by typing cmd at the Search box and pressing Ctrl-Shift-Enter. Then at the command prompt, type bcdedit /set loadoptions DDISABLE_INTEGRITY_CHECKS, and press Enter. Reboot, and you should be able to use unsigned drivers.

HACK 169: Manage the Paging File

V XP Windows can get confused about what memory is and how it uses it. Giving Windows some guidance will keep things running smoothly.

Ever encounter an error that indicates Windows is running low on memory? Have you received a chilling notification that "Your system is low on virtual memory. Windows is increasing the size of your virtual memory paging file. During this process, memory requests for some applications may be denied."? These errors are usually *not* about a lack of physical memory, but about how the operating system uses the memory available. Microsoft Windows manages many types of memory—mostly RAM, but within and beyond the obvious system RAM, other resources that store data while the operating system and applications do their thing.

There are three causes for "out of memory" conditions under Windows. The first two involve truly having too little RAM memory to support the operating system and having too little free disk space for the operating system to be able to swap memory contents to the swap file on a hard drive or forcing the pagefile size too small. The third possibility is that some of the RAM is bad—parts of it are unreadable or unwritable—which results in a decrease in the total amount of available RAM.

A solution to truly not having enough memory is of course to add more. When you've given XP and Vista enough memory (1 GB of RAM is usually comfortable), but things are still acting up, it's time to look elsewhere for what's keeping Windows from being happy.

The pagefile is usually controlled by Windows. While users can configure how much disk space to allocate to this file, only Windows decides how and when it is used.

If the hard drive has too little free space available for making or growing the pagefile, Windows can indicate "out of memory". This means it could not swap out enough RAM contents to disk to leave your applications or data and the operating system enough memory to work with. You can easily run out of disk space if your browser cache, Temporary Internet Files, System Restore, or Recycle Bin allocation is way too big; if your applications create a lot of temporary files and do not clean them up; or if you've simply filled your drive with MP3 files and pictures.

If the pagefile size is left for Windows to decide, it may suffer fragmentation and will be broken up across many different regions of the disk drive, reducing performance. Pagefile fragmentation will occur if there is no single area of free space large enough to contain the entire pagefile, or if the pagefile starts out at one size, and files are subsequently stored "around it", then the pagefile has to grow into a separate area of free space.

Performing a disk cleanup and defragmenting your hard drive every week, certainly every month, is an excellent way to improve both filesystem and pagefile performance.

The subject of much debate, there are several rules of thumb that can be applied to configuring the size of the pagefile. In most cases the pagefile size should be at least equal to the amount of RAM installed on the system; that is, if you have 512 MB of RAM, the pagefile should equal at least 512 MB of disk space and preferably two to three times more (1024–1500 MB.) The debate rages at this point whether or not the size of the pagefile should be exactly equal to, 150 percent, or 200 percent, or more of the amount of RAM in the system. Empirically, (determined by trial and error) depending on the amount of RAM installed, most of us use 150 percent as the maximum value, to give Windows a little extra room, but not an excessive amount, to play with. I configure and deploy hundreds of Windows XP PCs that have 2 GB of RAM with a paging file set to 1024 MB and have not heard a single complaint of performance or out-of-memory errors. For a 64 bit Windows Vista PC with 4 GB of RAM, a pagefile size of 2 GB is more than sufficient.

It is important to remember that each version of Windows has a minimum RAM requirement, as shown in Table 11-2. Your system should have enough RAM to accommodate Windows (the minimum requirement) plus your applications and data if you want to reduce pagefile use and manage its size.

Setting the pagefile size tells Windows how much disk space it can play with when it decides it's time to swap a program or data out of RAM and into the pagefile. You want Windows to use the hard drive sparingly, and when it does use it, you want it to use it as efficiently as possible. So how do you determine what "size" to make the pagefile?

All pagefile setting recommendations come with an explicit or implied rule-of-thumb caveat. Most of the recommendations exist for two reasons: a desire or need to limit the amount of disk space the pagefile consumes, and a similar desire to contain or limit the fragmentation of the pagefile and other files on the same drive.

There are as many people who will advise you not to set a specific pagefile size as there are telling you what values to use for setting the pagefile. Nowhere is it documented that manually setting the pagefile size does any harm unless you try to set it too low.

Windows will allow you to configure no pagefile but will "complain" at start-up with a strong message telling you to create a pagefile. As a built-in "self-preservation" feature, even with a zero-byte or no pagefile setting, Windows will create a pagefile anyway.

For XP and Vista, if you have less than 1 GB of RAM set the pagefile to least equal to or up to 150 percent of the amount of RAM: 1500-2000 MB. At less than 512 MB of RAM, Windows is going to swap more than it would with 1 GB of RAM or more simply because you've got less RAM to go around. Going to a 150 percent pagefile size gives Windows room to rattle around, enough space for applications to play in memory, and enough pagefile space to swap it all out if necessary.

If you have 1 GB or more of RAM, you have to start believing that you have more than enough RAM to keep the operating system and most of your applications happy as you've met the minimum RAM requirement for the operating system plus additional RAM for applications. Even a portion of 1 or 2 GB is a lot of disk space to waste and a lot of data to read and write on a disk drive if Windows has to swap out. This considerably slows system performance, but it is better than running out of memory.

It is obviously far better to add more RAM than hit the ceiling of RAM+pagefile size or keep increasing the pagefile size to overcome having too little RAM. For systems with abundant amounts of RAM, certainly with more than 2 GB, setting the pagefile to no less than 50 percent of the amount of RAM typically performs quite well. However, if you frequently use multiple large applications or have multiple large data files open, the pagefile should equal the amount of RAM so Windows has adequate space to swap to. Table 11-2 shows the recommended settings.

Table 11-2. Recommended pagefile sizes based on amount of RAM

TOTAL SYSTEM RAM	RECOMMENDED PAGEFILE SIZE
512 MB	256–512 MB
768 MB	512–768 MB
1024 MB (1 GB)	512– 1024 MB
2048 MB (2 GB)	1024 MB
4096 MB (4 GB)	2048 MB
8192 MB (8 GB) and up	2048–4096 MB

To ensure the best performance of the pagefile and prevent the pagefile from changing size and becoming fragmented, set the minimum and maximum size of the file to the same values. For a recently defragmented PC, setting the pagefile size will create a new unfragmented pagefile. If you set the minimum and maximum sizes to different values, the pagefile can become fragmented and only a disk defragmenter that can defragment the pagefile can put it back together for a short time.

To set the pagefile size in Windows XP, right-click the My Computer icon, and select Properties→ Advanced. In the Performance section, click on the Settings button. The Performance Options dialog appears. Under the Virtual memory section, click the Change button. When the Virtual Memory dialog appears, select the Custom size: radio button. Type in the minimum and maximum amount of disk space you want to allocate for the pagefile size. Click OK to save the information and close the dialogs, and then restart your PC.

In Windows Vista, right-click Computer on the Start menu, and choose Properties. Click Advanced System Settings. In the Performance section, click on the Settings button. The Performance Options dialog appears. Click the Advanced tab, then click Change, and uncheck the box next to "Automatically manage paging file size for all drives" (Figure 11-40). Select the drive for which you want to manage the paging file, and select "Custom size". Type in the minimum and maximum amount of disk space you want to allocate for the pagefile size. Click OK to save the information, close the dialogs, and then restart your PC.

Your paging file and presumably overall disk operation performance can be improved by moving your paging file to a separate disk drive from the one your operating system, applications and data are stored on. Keeping the paging file on a separate drive separates the disk I/O operations for swapping from application and data loading I/O operations. Connecting the paging file drive to a different IDE or SATA drive channel than your main drive should help even more. When you select which drive your paging file uses, go through the steps again, setting no paging file on the original disk drive.

Hacking the Hack

Windows can't defragment the pagefile, because it is open for exclusive use while the system is up and running. Microsoft's PageDefrag (*www.microsoft.com/technet/sysinternals/FileAndDisk/PageDefrag.mspx*) gets around this problem (on NT, 2000, XP, and Windows Server 2003—at the time of this writing, Vista wasn't supported) by defragmenting your pagefile at the next reboot: it uses the same defragmentation mechanism that Windows uses, but it runs before the operating system has opened the pagefile for exclusive use.

— *Jim Aspinwall, from* PC Hacks

Figure 11-40.
Changing the paging file size in Windows Vista

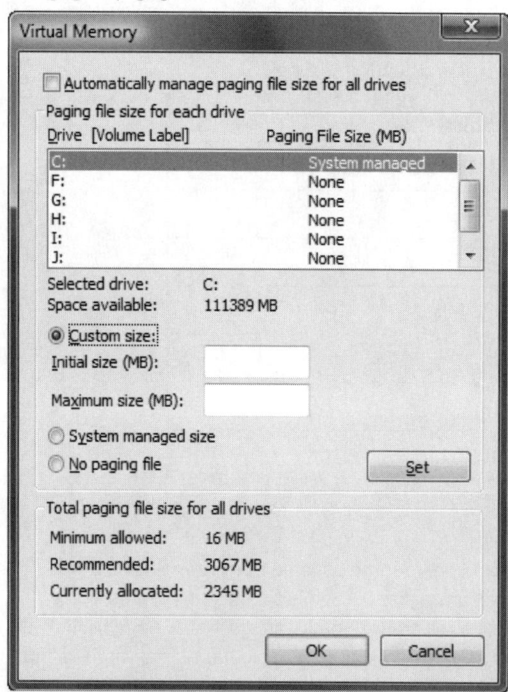

HACK 170: Speed It Up with RAID

V XP If one fast drive is good, then five working together is surely better.

Redundant Array of Inexpensive Disks (RAID) technology has been a significant lifesaver and performance boost for file servers. RAID can be set up in different configurations to provide systems with fault-tolerance or performance enhancements that are crucial to keeping data safe. It can be applied to personal desktop systems to provide significant disk drive performance enhancement.

RAID-0 (zero) is the most basic and highest performing RAID configuration. Portions of data normally stored on one disk drive are spread out across multiple drives, and those drives are accessed in parallel to deliver the data faster. This is because each drive does not have to access all of the data before it can be delivered. RAID-0 is unfortunately and by nature the least reliable in terms of data integrity because a failure in any single drive renders all of the data useless.

In contrast to RAID-0, in a RAID-1 configuration, all the data is stored equally on two drives, in parallel. This slows the storage and reading performance but almost guarantees that the data remains intact even if one of the drives fails.

RAID-5 is somewhat a mix of RAID-0 and RAID-1, striping data across multiple drives but also adding error correction information across the drives, providing the advantages of parallel drives and a high degree of ability to recover data if one drive should fail.

RAID-0+1 is another hybrid implementation of RAID that is very affordable and intended for desktop system. It is a RAID-0 array made up of two or more RAID-1 arrays that will make your drive access faster, while still affording the protection that RAID-1 offers. Upgrading with top-performing disk drives and putting them into a RAID configuration just might knock the dust bunnies out of your keyboard.

The basic steps to install a RAID configuration on your PC are listed below. Be aware that the specific steps will be unique to the RAID controller (system board or add-in card), your system BIOS, and RAID configuration software. After installation, the RAID configuration should appear to your operating system as a single-disk volume.

1. You need a RAID controller or RAID capabilities built into your system board. Promise Technologies is one of the most popular brands of add-in RAID controllers for IDE drives.

2. Have at least two identical disk drives on hand for RAID-0 and 1. Configuration of a simple RAID is a lot easier if the drives are identical: there will be no wasted space, and they should mirror each other and perform equally well. RAID 0+1 will require at least four disks, but it's the best combination of speed and redundancy.

3. If necessary, make a bootable disk/CD with any necessary configuration program for your RAID controller. For BIOS-based RAID setups, familiarize yourself with the RAID setup screens and options in BIOS. It is likely you will have to connect the RAID drives to different IDE connections than the normal non-RAID IDE interfaces.

4. Visit the RAID adapter or motherboard manufacturer's web site, and download the latest drivers for the operating system you intend to install. If you are installing a 64-bit version of Windows, get the 64-bit drivers if they are offered as a separate download. Put these drivers on a floppy disk (for Windows XP or Vista) or CD-ROM, USB drive, or DVD (for Vista).

5. With the system powered down, install and connect the drives to the RAID controller interface connectors.

6. Start the system and either boot with the disk/CD containing the RAID controller configuration program or get into the BIOS setup to access the RAID configuration screens.

7. Select the type of RAID you will be creating—typically 0, 1, or 0+1.

8. Partition the drives with the configuration program or BIOS screens. This process establishes how the RAID controller views and uses the drives.

9. When RAID controller configuration and disk partitioning is complete, start the installation of Windows onto the new RAID system as the primary boot drive. If necessary, have that driver disk or CD-ROM ready in case Windows cannot detect the controller on its own. If XP does not find a usable hard drive, it will ask you for a driver disk; Vista offers the Load Driver button on the "Where do you want to install Windows?" screen; you can use a CD-ROM, DVD, floppy, or USB drive.

10. (RAID 1 and higher only) To test your configuration after installing your operating system, shut down, and disconnect one of the RAID drives, then restart to verify that indeed the RAID system actually mirrors data to one of the drives.

— *Jim Aspinwall, from* PC Hacks

12 HARDWARE

Hardware hacks: just the sounds of it can make grown men and women shiver. Visions of sizzling soldering irons, of system boards, cards, and cables scattered in an unholy mess, of a PC turned into toast.

In fact, though, it's much easier to hack your hardware than you might imagine. As you'll see in this chapter, you'll be able to mod your PC's case, overclock your PC, troubleshoot hardware, and more without having to turn your PC into a wreck. Of course, if you're the type who likes to take things apart, we've got plenty of hacks for you, including a great hack on how to replace a Zune hard drive with a bigger one. And if all you want to do is troubleshoot hardware problems, we've got hacks for you as well.

HACK 171: Mod Your PC's Case

V XP Make an off-the-shelf case suit your decor!

PC case appearance and design have progressed, well, all the way from boring beige to silver, grey, charcoal and black; but none of those may suit your Dutch blue and white, French cottage, radical red, or "environmentally friendly" green motif. While you can shop www.cyberguys.com, www.thermaltake.com, and similar case-modding web sites to find new case colors and designs, you'll make a lot of work for yourself converting from one case to another and may not find the physical size or design you need. With just a touch of mechanical skill, a couple of cans of spray paint, some masking tape and patience, your classic "old" PC can take on a bold new look. Spice up your case with lighting effects and built-in accessories and a customized PC will be a prized contribution to your den.

With this hack you'll see examples of simple do-it-yourself customizations you can complete in a weekend, and probably for under $100. You'll have to shop in advance online for some of the goods if you don't have a well-stocked local PC warehouse like Fry's or Central Computer, and at your local home improvement center for paint and tape. You can then settle into the garage to have some fun tearing your PC down to the bones.

Colorized Case and Display

This part of a custom case hack is probably the most complex and time consuming if you take it down to the smallest details; from screw heads to DVD-drive buttons and drawers, everything gets a touch of color. You will need some basic hand tools for disassembly of the case and a can or two of your choice of spray paint.

First, take one ordinary beige PC and LCD panel (Figure 12-1). Disassemble the case, removing the side, top, and front panels. Then remove the switches and LEDs from the case front panel (Figure 12-2).

Figure 12-1.
Can this case be any more boring than it is?

Figure 12-2.
Removing the switches and LCDs from the front case panel

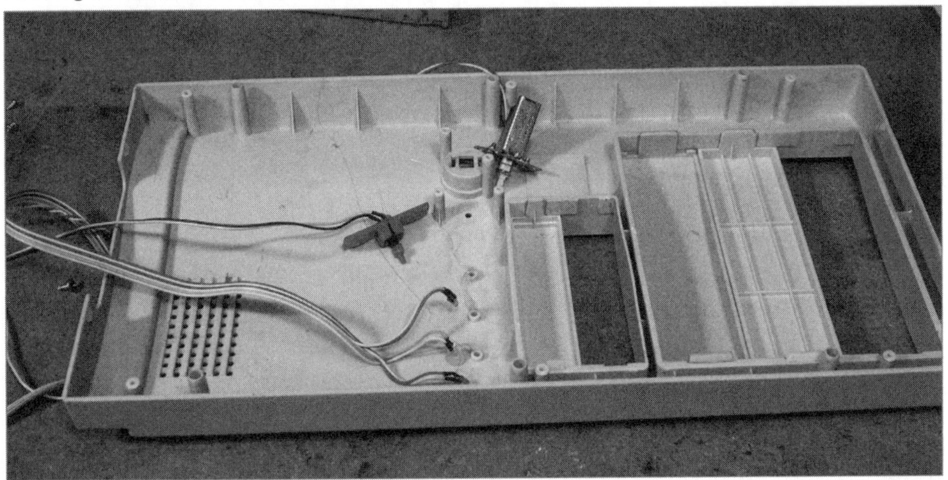

Next, remove the panels and buttons from the CD-ROM and disk drives (Figure 12-3), so that you can paint the panels.

Then, using masking tape and paper, cover the important parts of the LCD monitor, typically the viewing screen and connectors (Figures 12-4 and 12-5). Make sure to cover them carefully; you're covering them so that they don't get any paint on them when you mod your case.

Figure 12-3.
Removing the panels and buttons from the CD-ROM and disk drives, so that they can be painted

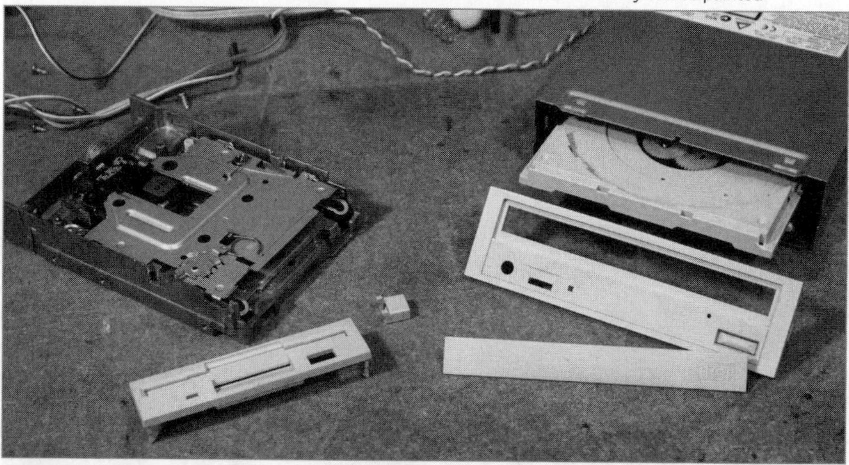

Figure 12-4.
Masking the front of your LCD monitor so that paint won't get on the screen

Figure 12-5.
Masking the back parts of your LCD monitor

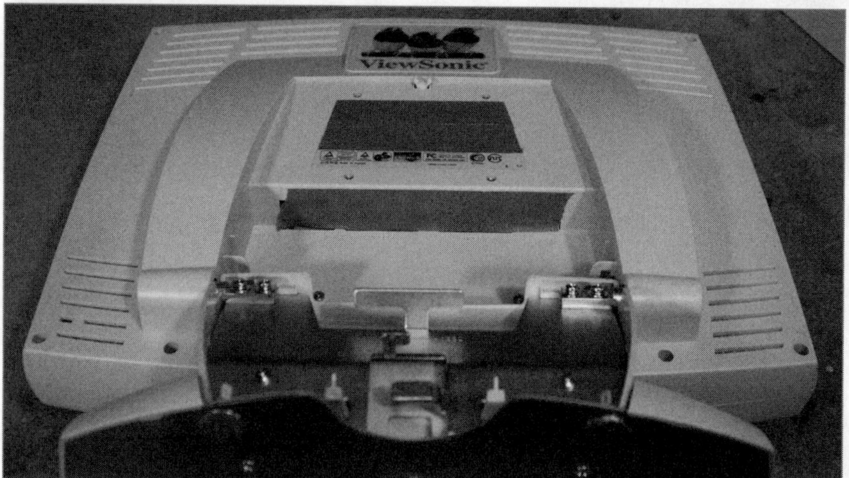

Now wipe down each of the exposed surfaces on your PC and monitor with a multipurpose cleaning product. Then, to ensure the surface is moisture and grease-free, dab a bit of lacquer thinner on a shop rag and wipe over all the surfaces to be painted.

After cleaning and masking the case pieces and LCD, you're ready for the fun: you get to paint with spray paint. Work in a well-ventilated area away from sparks and flame (water heater, furnace, etc.) and with an ambient temperature of 60 degrees F or more so the paint dries and hardens properly. Be sure to use a very large backdrop or drop cloth to ensure that paint does not get onto nearby items.

Most spray paints contain toxic chemicals. Adequate ventilation and respiratory protection is highly recommended. Use plenty of newspaper or other drop-cloth material to avoid damaging your work area.

When spray painting, be patient, and apply four to six light coats of spray, allowing 20–30 minutes or more between coats. By light coats, I mean the first and second coats may not completely cover the surfaces in paint. Alternate paint "stripes" across the surface to fill in the gaps. Being anxious amidst the painting process will result in an uneven, blotchy, runny paint job, so relax and enjoy yourself. Allow the final coat to dry for 30–45 minutes before handling and reassembling the pieces.

The result (Figure 12-6) should be a striking new appearance that will either stand out or blend in amidst your choice of décor.

There's more you can do than just paint your case, though, so read on for more modding.

Ports Front and Center

Most off-the-shelf PC case designs make it difficult to access commonly used I/O ports like USB, headphones/speaker, microphone, and a few PCs give you SD, CF, or Mini-SD memory card ports. In a multimedia world where the PC has become the center of an entertainment universe, including cameras, cell phones, media players, and more, these ports are a must. Your best solution is a little gizmo from www.cyberguys.com, the 20-in-1 5.25 Multi-function Panel. It occupies a single 5.25-inch drive bay and provides multiple data ports, including SATA, media cards, USB, and audio jacks. You also get temperature readings and fan speed control, a perfect up-front geek-out accessory. You may notice in Figure 12-6 the addition of a multiport memory card reader below the disk drive.

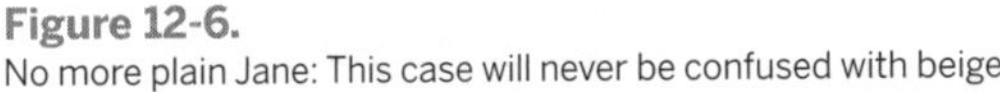

Figure 12-6.
No more plain Jane: This case will never be confused with beige

Light It Off

No, I'm not talking about fuses, blasting caps, rapidly expanding synthetic explosives, or flammable toxic fluids. Instead, I mean light, as in bright and glowing. With the addition of a cold-cathode light tube, you can turn your PC into a high-tech night-light. Get creative, and use a few cold-cathode lighting accessories inside and out; you might want to throw in a Thermaltake USB Dual LED gooseneck lamp on your keyboard, which will keep you lit up in the dark.

I've added a lighted fan to the front of the case for additional cooling (Figure 12-7), and a cold-cathode tube to the side panel (Figure 12-8) as the "night light".

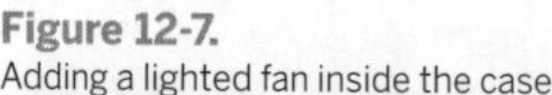

Figure 12-7.
Adding a lighted fan inside the case

Figure 12-8.
Adding a cathode ray tube inside the case—it will be your nightlight

Inside your case you may want to light up and cool down your RAM with something like a Thermaltake Cyclo Memory Cooler with Blue LED Fan. Add a few strands of UV-fluorescent cable wrapping, and your previously middle-aged case will positively glow.

— Jim Aspinwall

HACK 172: Use Your Zune as a USB Hard Drive

V XP Microsoft doesn't want you to use your Zune as a hard drive, and prefers that you only use it via its built-in sync. Here's how to mount your Zune as a hard drive, and do with it whatever you want.

Your Zune has a nice, big hard drive of 30 GB or more, and it's filled with plenty of files. But unfortunately, you can't simply use it like a hard drive; to shuttle files back and forth, you'll have to use Zune's syncing software, which isn't always the easiest way to go about doing things.

However, with a Registry hack, you can treat the Zune like it's just another hard drive, and you can drag and drop files between it and your PC, and do anything else you can do with a hard drive.

To do it, launch the Registry Editor by typing regedit at the Start Search box or a command prompt (see Chapter 13 for details). Then go to `HKEY_LOCAL_MACHINE\System\ControlSet001\Enum\USB`. Right-click on the USB folder, and select Find. Search for `PortableDeviceNameSpace`. Change the `EnableLegacySupport` DWORD value from `0` to `1`, and click OK. Change the `PortableDeviceNameSpaceExcludeFromShell` DWORD from `1` to `0`, and click OK. Change the `ShowInShell` DWORD value from `0` to `1`, and click OK.

Exit the Registry, and attach your Zune to your PC. If it's already connected, unplug it, then reconnect it. In Windows, double-click the Zune icon, and then double-click the storage inside it. You'll see various folders, such as those that store your Albums, Music, Pictures, Playlists, Video, and so on. Even though you can see the Zune's hard drive, you can't yet copy files to and from it. You'll only be able to do that when the Zune lowers its built-in protection. The Zune lowers its protection whenever it performs a synchronization. So, synchronize a large file that takes a long time to transfer, such as a video file. While the file is transferring, you can copy files between your PC and the Zune using Windows Explorer.

HACK 173: Install a Larger Disk in Your Zune

Not happy with the amount of storage in your Zune? Here's how to hack it by taking out the old hard drive, and popping in a newer one with more storage.

No matter how much storage you have for your Zune, it's never enough. If you want more storage, you don't have to buy a whole new Zune, though. Instead, you can install a new disk of your own.

First, of course, you'll need a new hard drive. You can buy them from several places online, including at Rapid Repair (www.rapidrepair.com/shop/microsoft-zune-parts.html), the authors of this hack.

You'll also need some tools for taking the Zune apart. Get a small Phillips head screwdriver, a small flathead or X-Acto razor, and one or more "safe open tools," which are small, plastic devices used to pry open hard-to-open cases. (If you can't find these on your own, you can get a complete kit at www.rapidrepair.com/shop/1051-tool-kit-for-apple-ipod.html).

 When you order a hard drive, you can ask that it be sent to you with the plate already removed, so that you won't have to remove it yourself (Step 7).

Once you've done that, you're ready to start modding. Here's how to install a new hard drive:

1. Start by removing the bottom dock port spacer with your X-Acto razor or flathead, as shown in Figure 12-9. Make sure to insert the razor at one of the long ends and not in the middle of the dock. The dock port spacer should pop off fairly easy.

2. After the dock port spacer is removed, you will have access to both screws. Remove these with the Phillips screwdriver (see Figure 12-10). Now you can crack the shell open.

3. Insert your safe open tool in between the small gap in the case, as shown in Figure 12-11. You will have to insert this fairly hard and work it up and down until the bottom of the shell is open. Make sure not to force the case open near the headphone jack, or you will tear it off the board. Instead, crack it open from the sides down to the bottom.

4. Now that you have the backing off the front panel, you can remove the battery and hard drive casing. (You need to do this in order to get to the hard disk.) Remove the four screws holding the drive case on the board as well as the clip for the battery. Take the battery out as shown in Figure 12-12.

Figure 12-9.
Removing the bottom dock port

Figure 12-10.
Remove these two screws

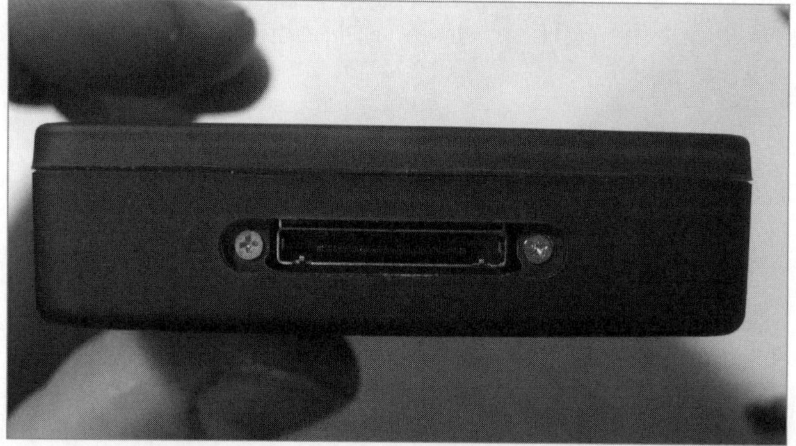

5. Remove both clips for the clickwheel and the battery if you haven't done so. Simply lift up on the brown parts with your fingernail or flathead driver, as shown in Figure 12-13.

Figure 12-11.
Open the case with the safe open tool

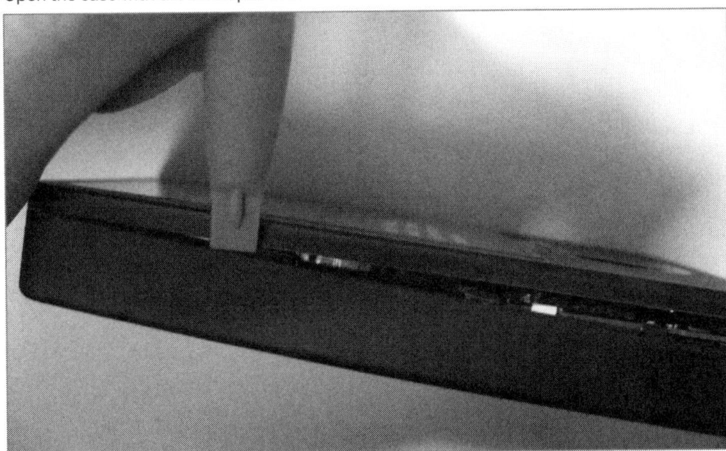

Figure 12-12.
Remove these four screws and the clip for the battery

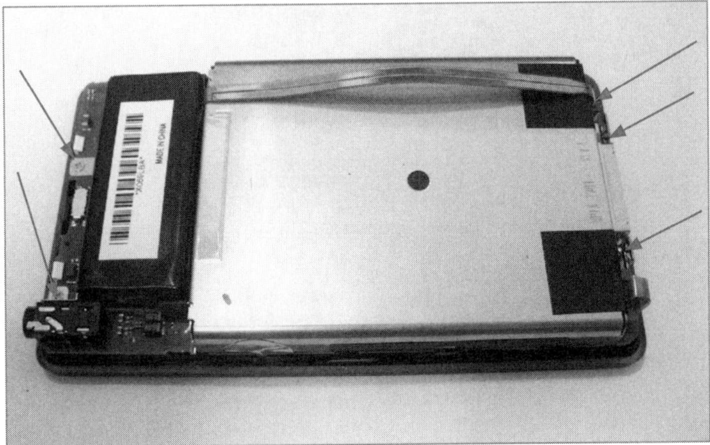

Figure 12-13.
Remove these clips with your fingernail or flathead driver

6. Now you've exposed the hard drive, and you're ready to remove it. Lift the drive with its casing above the top part of the Zune (by the headphone jack). Remove the drive cable clip (lift the black part up with your nail or flathead), and then take the sticky tape off the label side of the drive. After the tape is lifted up, you can remove the hard drive as shown in Figure 12-14.

7. Take the new hard drive, and remove the metal plate label as shown in Figure 12-15. Use your fingernail to pop the label side off of the drive. There are two sticker spots holding this on so it will not come off easily.

After the label plate is removed (see Figure 12-16), you are ready to connect the new drive inside the Zune. This is the tricky part. Depending on the size of your original hard drive and the hard drive you are installing, the new drive may be physically larger than your old drive. For example, a new 40 GB hard drive is the same size as the original 30 GB hard drive in most Zunes, but a 60 GB or 80 GB hard drive is slightly larger:

- If your new hard drive is the same size as the old hard drive, simply put the new drive into the old hard drive cage.

Figure 12-14.
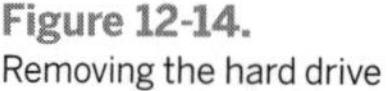
Removing the hard drive

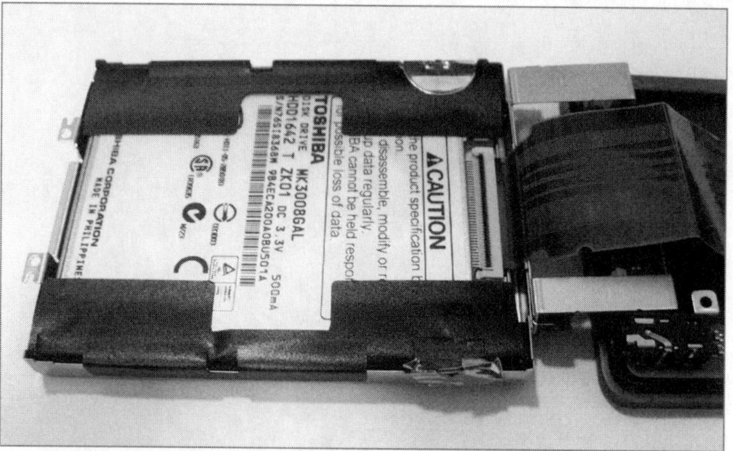

Figure 12-15.
Removing the metal plate from the hard drive

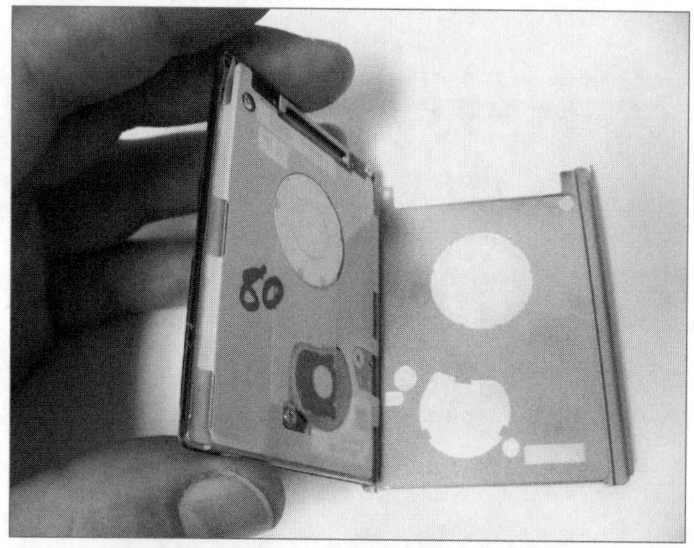

- If your new hard drive is slightly larger than your old hard drive, you won't be able to use the old hard drive cage. Instead, cut your old drive pads to fit two of them on the new drive as shown in Figure 12-17. These pads will seat the drive in the case for you, and perform the function of the cage. Make sure to not make the pads too large, or the drive will not fit properly. You should also reuse the old battery enclosure so the battery is seated properly.

Now you're ready to reconnect everything, by tracing steps 1 through 7 backwards.

— *RapidRepair.com*

See Also

- "Store Any Type of File on Your Zune" [Hack #147]
- "Watch Any DVD on Your Zune" [Hack #148]

Figure 12-16.
A hard drive with the plate removed

Figure 12-17.
Use these pads to seat the hard drive in the Zune

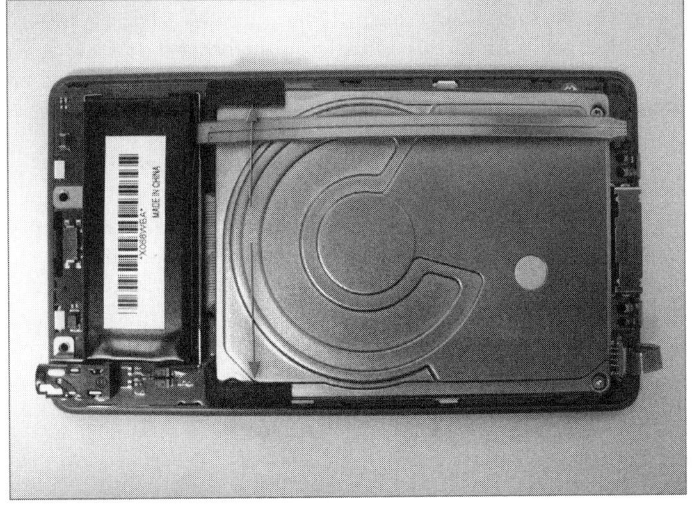

QUICK HACK

FAST WAYS TO RESOLVE HARDWARE WOES IN WINDOWS VISTA AND XP

Both Windows Vista and Windows XP includes wizard-like tools for resolving hardware problems. Sometimes they work, and sometimes they don't, but they're a good place to start. In Windows XP, use the Hardware Troubleshooters. Choose Start→Help and Support→ Hardware→"Fixing a hardware problem," and under "Fix a problem", click Hardware Troubleshooter. It's a wizard-style interface, so follow the prompts.

In Windows Vista, choose Control Panel→System and Maintenance→Problem Reports and Solutions. Look for any "Solutions to install", and click them to resolve your hardware problem. You can also click "See problems to check" to look for any other problems. Highlight any, and click "Check for solutions", and follow the directions. For another automated troubleshooter, in Windows Vista, Choose Start→Help and Support→Troubleshooting, and look for a link that describes your problem. Follow the directions and links.

HACK 174: Troubleshoot Hardware with Device Manager

V XP The Device Manager is a great hardware troubleshooting tool, but you'll need this hack to make sense of the error messages it relays to you. Here's how to decode the cryptic messages and how to use the messages to solve hardware woes.

If you install and uninstall enough hardware on your system, error messages and system conflicts are a way of life. Luckily, Windows Vista and Windows XP include a built-in way to resolve system conflicts by hand: using the Device Manager, Windows' best all-around hardware-troubleshooting tool. Run it by typing devmgmt.msc at a command prompt or in the Run box (in Windows XP), or the Search box (in Windows Vista). You'll see a list of all the devices installed on your system, as shown in Figure 12-18.

To find information about any device, right-click it and choose Properties. The multi-tabbed Properties dialog box appears (Figure 12-19). You'll be able to get comprehensive information about the device from here. You can also troubleshoot by clicking the Troubleshoot button in the General tab in Windows XP. (The Troubleshoot button doesn't appear in Windows Vista.)

When you open the Device Manager to the view shown in Figure 12-18, an icon will be displayed next to any device involved in a system conflict. A yellow exclamation point means the device has a problem or conflict of some sort. A red "X" means the device is disabled. A blue "i" (which stands for information) means the device's resource configuration has been altered via the Device Manager.

The blue "i" icon shows up only when you choose one of two views: "Resource by type" or "Resource by connection." To switch to those views, use the View menu.

Only the yellow and red icons mean there's a problem of some sort. To find out more details about the problem, double-click the device that has an icon next to it, and an error message and error code will appear in the "Device status" section of the General tab shown. Those error messages are supposed to help you solve the hardware problem. Unfortunately, though, they're cryptic at best, and, as a general rule, you won't be any closer to resolving the problem after you read them.

However, armed with the right knowledge, you can resolve the problems based on the error message you see. The advice in Table 12-1 (adapted from Microsoft Knowledgebase Article 125174) tells you how to use the Device Manager to solve the problem.

Figure 12-18.
The Device Manager displaying all the devices installed on your system

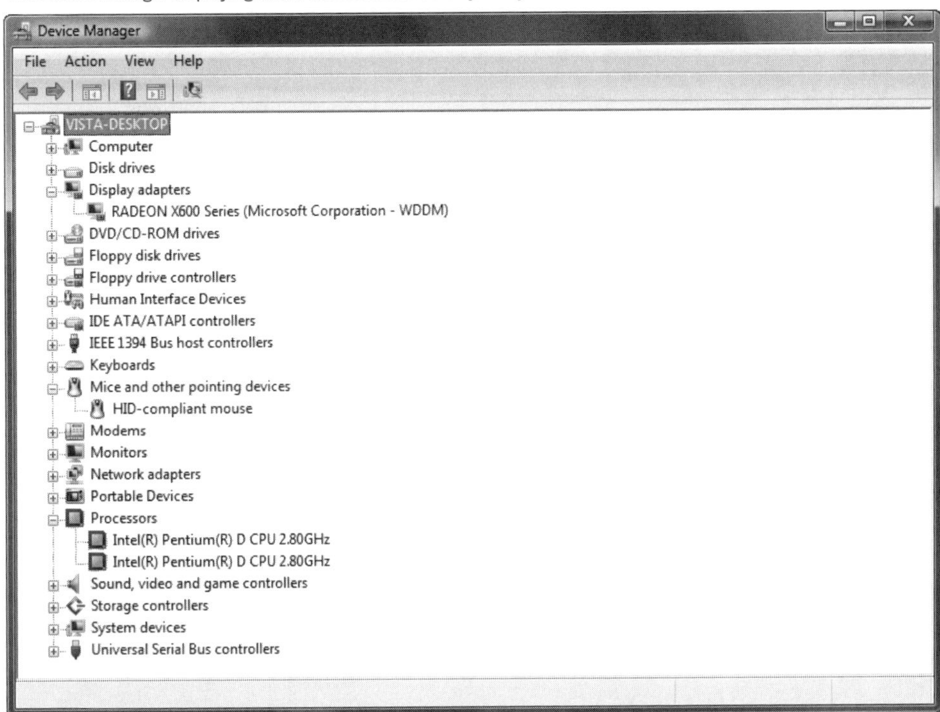

Figure 12-19.
The Device Manager's General tab

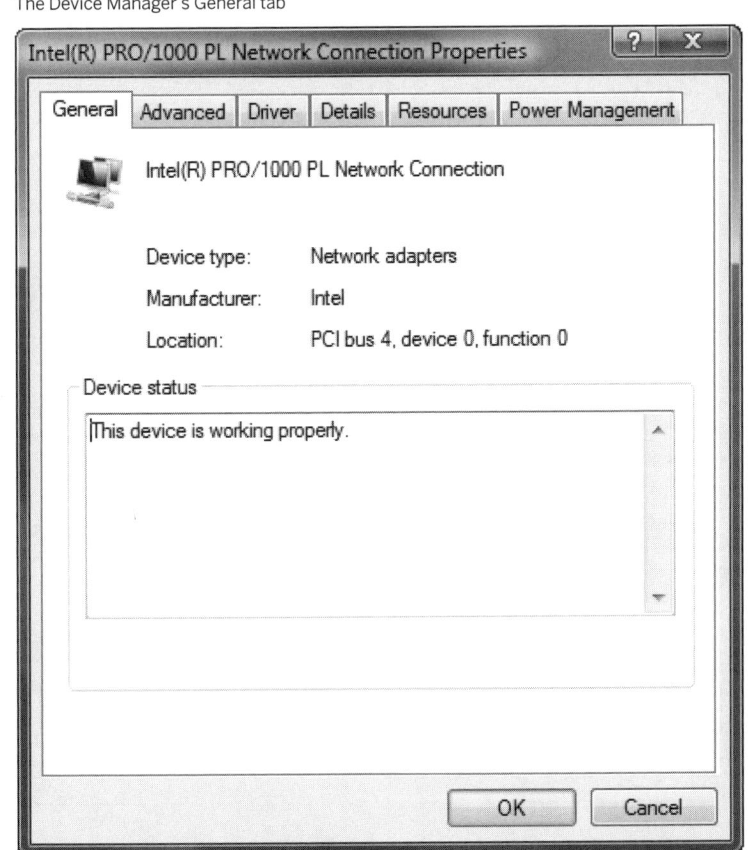

There are several solutions you might need to employ, and some of the common ones are abbreviated:

ABBREVIATION	DETAILS
D	Get and install updated drivers from the hardware manufacturer.
I	Uninstall and then reinstall the driver.
M	Check memory and system resources by right-clicking My Computer, choosing Properties and then the Advanced tab, and then clicking Settings under Performance to see whether that is the problem. (In Vista, click Start, right-click on Computer, select Properties and choose Advanced System Settings→Performance). You might have to install more RAM to solve the problem.
R	You can try removing the device in the Device Manager and running the Add New Hardware Wizard from the Control Panel (under Vista, select Action→"Add legacy hardware" from Device Manager).
T	Click Troubleshoot on the General tab of the device to run the Troubleshooting Wizard. On Windows Vista, Choose Start→Help and Support→Troubleshooting, and look for a link that describes your problem. Follow the directions and links.
U	Update the drivers by choosing Update Driver from the Driver tab, and follow the instructions in the Hardware Update Wizard.

Table 12-1. Device Manager error codes, messages, and potential solutions

CODE	ERROR MESSAGE	RECOMMENDED SOLUTION
1	This device is not configured correctly.	U R
2	The <type> device loader(s) for this device could not load the device driver.	U R
3	The driver for this device might be corrupt or your system may be running low on memory or other resources.	U R M T
4	This device is not working properly because one of its drivers may be bad, or your Registry may be bad.	U R D
5	The device's driver requested a resource that Windows does not know how to handle.	U R
6	Another device is using the resources this device needs.	T
7	The device's drivers need to be reinstalled.	Click Reinstall Driver.
8	This has many associated error messages.	U R
9	This has several associated error messages.	R D Update your system BIOS.
10	This device either is not present, is not working properly, or does not have all the drivers installed. This code may also have a manufacturer-specific error message associated with it, depending on the device.	Make sure the device is physically connected to the computer properly. U

Table 12-1. Device Manager error codes, messages, and potential solutions *(continued)*

CODE	ERROR MESSAGE	RECOMMENDED SOLUTION
11	Windows stopped responding while attempting to start this device and therefore will never attempt to start this device again.	D
12	This device cannot find enough free <type> resources that it can use. Note that <type> is a resource type, such as IRQ, DMA, Memory, or I/O.	T
13	This device either is not present, is not working properly, or does not have all the drivers installed.	Click Detect Hardware. R
14	This device cannot work properly until you restart your computer.	Restart your computer.
15	This device is causing a resource conflict.	T
16	Windows cannot identify all the resources this device uses.	Click the Resources tab, and manually enter the settings as detailed in the manufacturer's documentation.
17	The driver information file <name> is telling this child device to use a resource that the parent device does not have or recognize. <name> is the *.inf* file for the device.	U R
18	Reinstall the drivers for this device.	Click Reinstall Driver.
19	Your Registry may be bad.	Click Check Registry.
20	Windows could not load one of the drivers for this device.	U
21	Windows is removing this device.	Wait several seconds, and then refresh the Device Manager view. If the device appears, restart your computer.
22	This device is disabled.	Click Enable Device.
22	This device is not started.	Click Start Device.
23	Several error messages may appear with Code 23.	Click Properties or Update Driver, depending on which button appears.
24	This device is not present, is not working properly, or does not have all its drivers installed.	Click Detect Hardware or Update Drivers, depending on which button appears.
25	Windows is in the process of setting up this device.	Restart your computer.
26	Windows is in the process of setting up this device.	Restart your computer.
27	Windows can't specify the resources for this device.	R D
28	The drivers for this device are not installed.	Click Reinstall Driver. R D

Table 12-1. Device Manager error codes, messages, and potential solutions *(continued)*

CODE	ERROR MESSAGE	RECOMMENDED SOLUTION
29	This device is disabled because the firmware for the device did not give it the required resources.	Check the device's documentation on how to enable its BIOS. If that doesn't work, enable the device in your computer's CMOS settings.
30	This device is using an Interrupt Request (IRQ) resource that is in use by another device and cannot be shared. You must change the conflicting setting or remove the real-mode driver causing the conflict.	Check the Device Manager to see if another device is using the same IRQ and disable it. If you can't find another device using the IRQ, look for drivers loaded in a *Config.sys* or *Autoexec.bat* file, and disable them.
31	This device is not working properly because Windows cannot load the drivers required for this device.	Click Properties. If that doesn't work, remove the device in the Device Manager, and run the Add New Hardware Wizard from the Control Panel. If the device still does not work, get updated drivers or other assistance from the manufacturer.
32	Windows cannot install the drivers for this device because it cannot access the drive or network location that has the setup files on it.	Restart the computer.
33	Windows cannot determine which resources are required for this device.	T Contact the hardware manufacturer, and configure or replace the device.
34	Windows cannot determine the settings for this device. Consult the documentation that came with this device and use the Resources tab to set the configuration.	T Change the hardware settings by following the manufacturer's instructions and then use the Resources tab to configure the device.
35	Your computer's system firmware does not include enough information to configure and use this device properly. To use this device, contact your computer manufacturer to obtain a firmware or BIOS update.	T Update your system BIOS.
36	This device is requesting a PCI interrupt but is configured for an ISA interrupt (or vice versa). Please use the computer's system setup program to reconfigure the interrupt for this device.	Check your computer's docs for instructions on reconfiguring the IRQ settings in the BIOS. T
37	Windows cannot initialize the device driver for this hardware.	I T
38	Windows cannot load the device driver for this hardware because a previous instance of the device driver is still in memory.	Restart the computer. T
39	Windows cannot load the device driver for this hardware. The driver may be corrupt or missing.	TI
40	Windows cannot access this hardware because its service key information in the registry is missing or recorded incorrectly.	TI

Table 12-1. Device Manager error codes, messages, and potential solutions *(continued)*

CODE	ERROR MESSAGE	RECOMMENDED SOLUTION
41	Windows successfully loaded the device driver for this hardware but cannot find the hardware device.	I T If the device is non-Plug and Play, you might need to run the Add Hardware Wizard. To do that, open the Control Panel and choose Performance and Maintenance→ System→Hardware→Add Hardware Wizard.
42	Windows cannot load the device driver for this hardware because there is a duplicate device already running in the system.	Restart the computer. T
43	Windows has stopped this device because it has reported problems.	Check the hardware documentation. T
44	An application or service has shut down this hardware device.	Restart the computer. T
45	Currently, this hardware device is not connected to the computer.	Reconnect the device to the computer.
46	Windows cannot gain access to this hardware device because the operating system is in the process of shutting down.	No fix should be necessary; the device should work properly when you start your computer.
47	Windows cannot use this hardware device because it has been prepared for "safe removal" but it has not been removed from the computer.	Unplug the device from your computer, and then plug it in again.
48	The software for this device has been blocked from starting because it is known to have problems with Windows. Contact the hardware vendor for a new driver.	D
49	Windows cannot start new hardware devices because the system hive is too large (exceeds the Registry Size Limit).	Uninstall any devices you are no longer using **[Hack #3]**.

See Also

- "Uncover Hidden Hardware with the Device Manager" **[Hack #175]**

HACK 175: Uncover Hidden Hardware with the Device Manager

V XP Hardware ghosts and other hidden devices can cause system conflicts, and the Device Manager won't report on them. This hack forces the Device Manager to uncover all your hidden hardware so that you can resolve any conflicts.

One of the strangest hardware problems you'll encounter in Windows involves hardware devices that are invisible to you but that cause system conflicts. You won't see them in the Device Manager, which stops you from using that troubleshooting tool to resolve the conflicts.

The Device Manager hides several types of these devices. Non-Plug and Play printers and other devices don't show up. Most newer devices are Plug and Play, so you'll most likely encounter this problem only if you have old hardware attached to your PC. (Plug and Play devices are automatically

QUICK HACK 

FIND VISTA DRIVERS FOR YOUR HARDWARE

Because Windows Vista is a newer operating system than Windows XP, not all manufacturers had drivers for their hardware ready when Windows Vista shipped. That means that you may not be able to use that hardware until you get a Windows Vista driver for it. In theory, Windows Update is supposed to deliver any updated drivers to you. In practice, that often doesn't happen. You'll have to spend time visiting the sites of your hardware manufacturers, and then spend a good deal of time trying to find where in the world they've hidden driver information. There's a quicker way, though. Go to the RadarSync VistaDrivers page (www.radarsync.com/vista). You'll find links to drivers from many different manufacturers.

recognized and installed in Windows XP and Windows Vista.) In this instance, the device is physically present on your PC, but the Device Manager doesn't show you it's there.

Then there are the so-called *nonpresent* or *ghosted* devices—devices you've removed from your system without doing an uninstall or whose uninstallation did not work properly. These devices aren't physically present in your system, but Windows treats them as if they were and devotes system resources to them. For example, if you physically remove an old network card without doing an uninstall, it might cause conflicts because Windows treats it as if it were still in your system.

The Device Manager also might not give you details about USB devices that you frequently attach and remove—for example, MP3 players that you attach to your PC only when you want to add or delete MP3 files from them. Even when these devices aren't present in your system, Windows devotes resources to them. If you replace one USB device with another of the same model, it's best to go through the uninstall process rather than just swap them.

And then there are devices you might have moved from one PCI slot to another. Windows might believe they are actually present in two slots, so it devotes resources for both slots to them.

Displaying these hidden devices can help with troubleshooting. For example, a hidden device could possibly conflict with a nonhidden device. And sometimes you might want to uninstall hidden devices—for example, when you've moved a non-Plug and Play network card from one slot to another and want to uninstall it from one slot.

But to do this kind of troubleshooting, you'll need to force the Device Manager to display information about the devices; otherwise, you won't know how to solve the problem.

Forcing the Device Manager to display non-Plug and Play printers and other devices is a simple matter. Run the Device Manager by typing devmgmt.msc at a command prompt, pressing Enter, and then choosing View→Show Hidden devices.

Displaying ghosted or nonpresent devices takes a little more work. You'll set an environment variable that forces the Device Manager to display them.

At the command prompt, type set devmgr_show_nonpresent_devices=1, and press Enter. You won't get a prompt in response; the command prompt will stay blank. At the same instance of the command prompt, type start devmgmt.msc, and press Enter. The Device Manager will launch in a separate window.

Keep in mind that you have to run the Device Manager from the same instance of the command prompt in which you typed set devmgr_show_nonpresent_devices=1. If you run the Device Manager outside the command prompt, it won't display ghosted devices.

So, now you've set the variable properly, but the Device Manager won't display ghosted devices yet. First you have to tell it to display them. Choose View→Show Hidden Devices, and the ghosted devices will appear, as shown in Figure 12-20. You should see quite a few devices now, including a lengthy list of non-Plug and Play drivers. Typically, devices that are not currently present on your PC will be shown as gray, rather than the black that connotes present devices. You might also see some devices listed more than once.

Now, use the Device Manager to troubleshoot any of those ghosted devices **[Hack #174]**. If you find any ghosted devices you no longer use on your PC, uninstall them from the Device Manager by right-clicking the device and choosing Uninstall.

Figure 12-20.
Displaying ghosted devices in the Device Manager

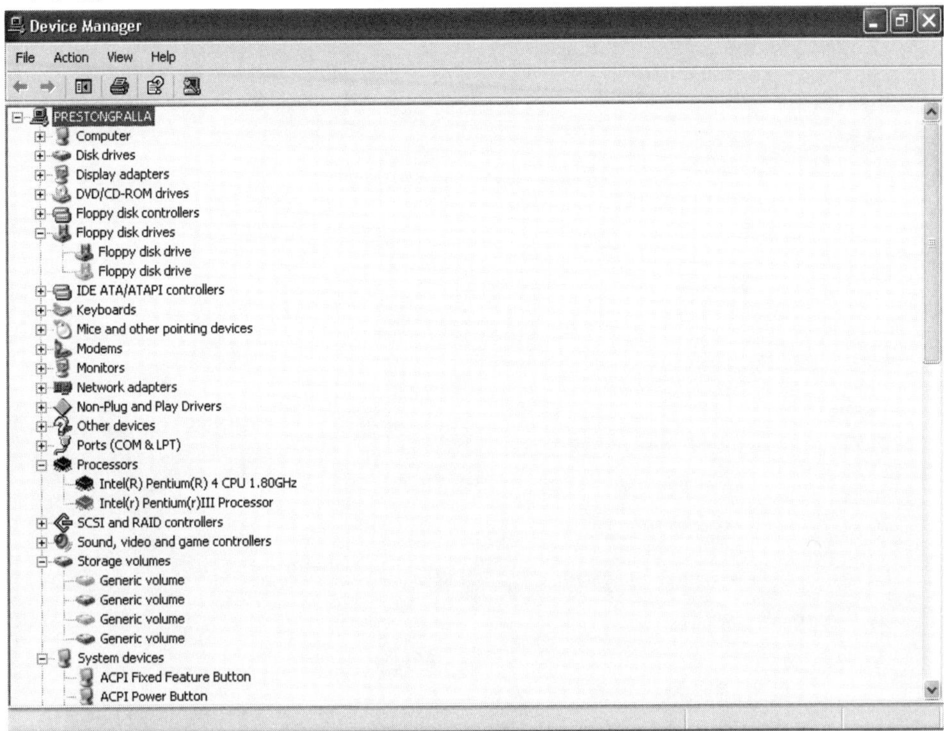

Hacking the Hack

You can permanently turn on the ability to see hidden and ghosted devices if you'd like.

To do that, you need to get to the Environment Variable dialog box. In Windows XP, right-click My Computer, and choose Properties→Advanced→Environment Variables. In Windows Vista, right-click Computer on the Start menu, choose Properties→Advanced System Settings, and click the Environment Variables button.

The Environment Variable dialog box opens. This dialog box lets you set system variables for the entire system or for individual users. Environment variables control a variety of Windows features, such as the location of your *Windows* directory and *TEMP* directories and the filename and location of the command processor that will launch when you run the command prompt.

The Environment Variables dialog box contains two sections: User variables and System variables. To apply the variable to a single user, use the "User variables" dialog box; to apply the variable to all users, use the "System variables" dialog box. In this case, you'll want to create the variable systemwide, so click New in the "System variables" section. The New System Variable dialog box appears. For "Variable name," type devmgr_show_nonpresent_devices. Once you've created the name, you need to give it a value. To turn the setting on, type 1 in the "Variable value" box. You can see the box filled out properly in Figure 12-21. Click OK, and then OK again. Run the Device Manager by typing devmgmt.msc at a command prompt or in the Run box and pressing Enter. Now, enable the Device Manager to show ghosted devices in the same way you did previously in this hack.

Figure 12-21.
Setting the Device Manager to always show ghosted devices

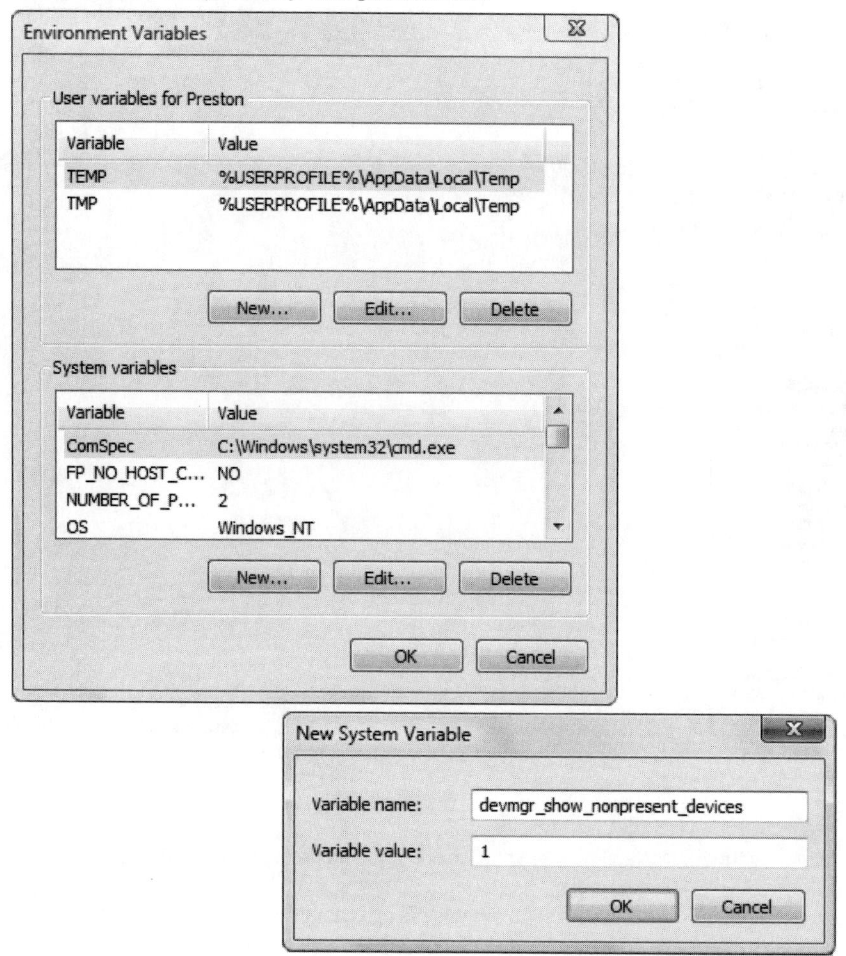

HACK 178: Get a Comprehensive List of All Your Drivers

Not sure what drivers you've got on your system and when they were installed? Use this command-line tool under Windows Vista and Windows XP Professional.

V XP The Device Manager [Hack #174] will list drivers for you, one by one, as you navigate your way through it. But that's an awful lot of work if you're looking to get a list of all the drivers in your system. Why get a list of all your drivers? You might want to print them out, so in the event of a system crash, you'll know all the drivers you need to reinstall. Or if you have multiple systems at home or are a system administrator, you might want to make sure that all the drivers on all your PCs are up-to-date. If you see, for example, that one system has a newer driver than another for the same piece of hardware, you'll know that the older one needs updating.

The command-line tool DriverQuery lists all your drivers, along with information about each, including file size and more.

To see a list of all drivers, type driverquery at a command prompt, and press Enter. You'll see a long list of drivers, along with basic information about each. Here's an excerpt of what you might see:

```
Module Name Display Name           Driver Type   Link Date
======================================================================
ACPI        Microsoft ACPI Driver  Kernel        11/2/2006 4:35:03 AM
adp94xx     adp94xx                Kernel        9/5/2006 3:55:58 PM
adpahci     adpahci                Kernel        9/5/2006 3:51:11 PM
adpu160m    adpu160m               Kernel        10/25/2005 1:00:45 AM
adpu320     adpu320                Kernel        3/13/2006 9:47:51 PM
AFD         Ancilliary Function Dr Kernel        11/2/2006 4:58:41 AM
agp440      Intel AGP Bus Filter   Kernel        11/2/2006 4:35:06 AM
aic78xx     aic78xx                Kernel        4/11/2006 8:20:11 PM
aliide      aliide                 Kernel        11/2/2006 4:51:35 AM
amdagp      AMD AGP Bus Filter Dri Kernel        11/2/2006 4:35:06 AM
amdide      amdide                 Kernel        11/2/2006 4:51:35 AM
AmdK7       AMD K7 Processor Drive Kernel        11/2/2006 4:30:18 AM
AmdK8       AMD K8 Processor Drive Kernel        11/2/2006 4:30:18 AM
arc         arc                    Kernel        8/21/2006 7:08:39 PM
arcsas      arcsas                 Kernel        8/14/2006 6:02:44 PM
aswMonFlt   aswMonFlt              File System   1/5/2007 12:48:25 PM
aswRdr      aswRdr                 Kernel        1/15/2007 12:26:05 PM
```

Some basic information is missing, though, notably the filename and size of the driver. To see that additional information and more, add the /v switch:

```
driverquery /v
```

You'll get the extra information, but it will be hard to read on the screen. So to display the output in a list format type this:

```
driverquery /v /fo list
```

You'll see output like this:

```
Module Name:       vga
Display Name:      vga
Description:       vga
Driver Type:       Kernel
Start Mode:        Manual
State:             Stopped
Status:            OK
Accept Stop:       FALSE
Accept Pause:      FALSE
Paged Pool(bytes): 20,480
Code(bytes):       4,096
BSS(bytes):        0
Link Date:         11/2/2006 4:53:56 AM
Path:              J:\Windows\system32\DRIVERS\vgapnp.sys
Init(bytes):       4,096
```

You can even save the results to a text file with the redirection operator (>):

```
driverquery /v /fo list > drivers.txt
```

For extra security, print it out, and keep it in a safe place.

Hacking the Hack

DriverQuery has other switches as well. Here's how to use them:

`/fo format`

Specify the format of the display: /fo table (the default) for a formatted table, /fo list for a plain-text list, or /fo csv for a comma-separated report, suitable for importing into a spreadsheet or database.

`/nh`

If using the `/fo table` or `/fo csv` format (above), the `/nh` option turns off the column headers.

`/v`

Display additional details about driver other than signed drivers.

`/si`

Display additional details about signed drivers.

`/s system`

Connect to a remote system, where *system* is the name of the computer.

`/u user`

Specify a user account (include an optional domain before the username) under which the command should execute.

`/p password`

The password for the user account specified with `/u`; prompts for the password if omitted.

See Also

- For more information about how to use DriverQuery, see www.microsoft.com/resources/documentation/windows/xp/all/proddocs/en-us/driverquery.mspx?mfr=true.

> **QUICK HACK**
>
> **ROLL YOUR OWN POWER PLAN**
>
> Don't like the settings Windows Vista has created for any of your power plans? It's easy to customize them. From the Power Options screen (Figure 12-22), click "Change plan settings" for any power plan you want to customize. From the Edit Plan Settings screen, make basic changes to when to turn off the display and put the computer to sleep. For more advanced settings, click "Change advanced power settings", make your changes and save them. If you're not happy with your changes, you can restore the plan settings back to the default. From the Edit Plan Settings screen, click "Restore default settings for this plan".

HACK 177: Turn Off Hybrid Sleep Mode in Windows Vista

V Vista's Hybrid Sleep for laptops mode may be more trouble than it's worth. Here's how to turn it off.

Windows' various sleep and hibernation modes are mind-bogglingly confusing. Do you know the difference between hibernation and sleep? Does anyone?

You would have thought that Microsoft would have simplified things with Windows Vista, but it hasn't. There's no need to go into the nitty-gritty details here, particularly because it would bore you all beyond belief. But the key point is this: in Windows Vista, Microsoft introduced a hybrid sleep mode that as I'll explain, has some benefits and some drawbacks. You may want to disable the hybrid sleep mode on a laptop, and in this hack, I'll show you how to do it.

First you need some background about sleep, hybrid sleep, and hibernation. Here are the three modes and how they're different:

Hibernation

In this mode, your work and the state of your PC, including open applications, and so on, is saved to RAM and to your hard disk. Windows Vista turns off the display, the hard disk, and the computer. When you restart, Windows will restore your desktop and work exactly as you left it. It can take 15 to 20 seconds or more to wake your PC from hibernation mode. Hibernation mode uses no power.

Sleep

In this mode, your work and the state of your PC are saved to RAM, but not to your hard disk. Your PC shuts down your monitor, your hard disk, and all other devices, but your RAM doesn't shut off.

Sleep mode uses a little power, enough to power RAM. If for some reason power is shut off to RAM, you'll lose all your work. In sleep mode, the PC can wake up instantaneously.

Hybrid sleep

This mode is an attempt to use the best of hibernation and the best of sleep. In it, your work and the state of your PC is saved to RAM as well as to your hard disk. Your PC shuts down your monitor, your hard disk and all other devices, but your RAM doesn't shut off. Sleep mode uses a little power, enough to power RAM. Unlike sleep mode, if for some reason power is shut off, though, you won't lose your work, because it was saved to disk. It takes longer to wake your PC from sleep mode than it does from sleep.

Why would you shut off hybrid sleep? One reason is that a number of people have reported problems with using hybrid sleep: their laptop simply never wakes up from hybrid sleep. In order to get their laptop restarted, they have to unplug the power cord, take out the battery to cut off power completely, then put the battery back in and plug in the power cord. Their work is lost.

Also, it takes about as long to recover from hybrid sleep as from hibernation. And you'll most likely never need it on a laptop. A laptop, after all, has batteries in addition to a power cord, so if the power cord is unplugged, your batteries take over. Also, many laptops go into hibernation mode when the power drops below a certain level. So you may never need hybrid sleep.

To turn off hybrid sleep, first click the power icon in the system tray, and select More Power Options (if the icon is not visible, open Control Panel→Hardware and Sound→Power Options). Figure 12-22 appears. For the power plan for which you want to turn off hybrid sleep, click "Change plan settings".

From the screen that appears, click "Change advanced power settings". On the Power Options Advanced Settings screen that appears, scroll to Sleep, and expand the options. Click the + sign next to hybrid sleep, and set both "On battery" and "Plugged in" to Off (Figure 12-23). Click OK, then "Save changes". From now on, your laptop will use normal sleep mode, rather than hybrid sleep.

Figure 12-22.

Choose the power plan for which you want to turn off hybrid sleep

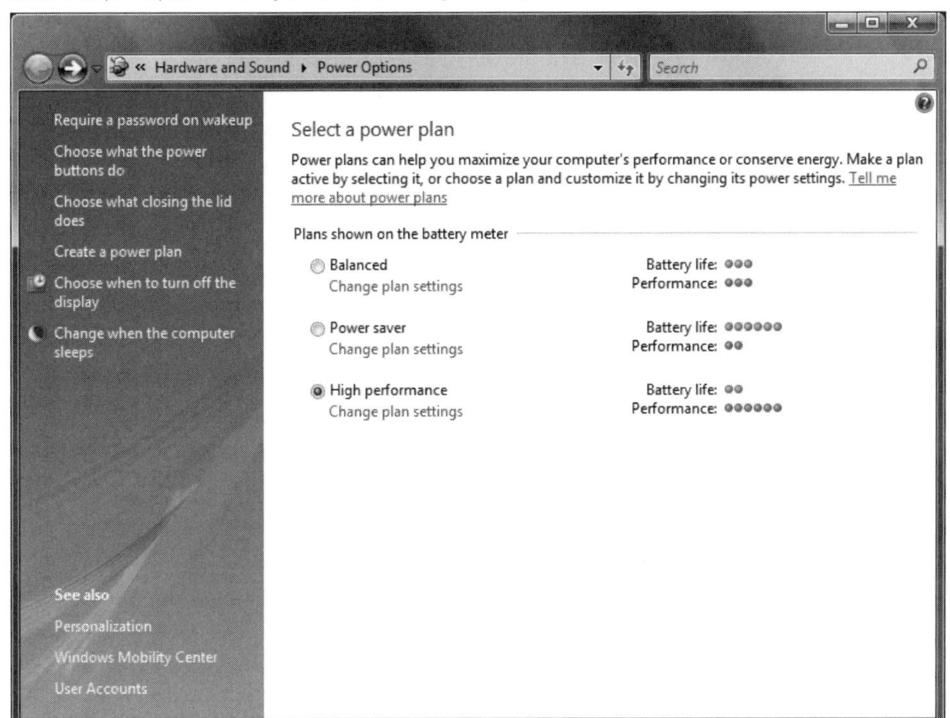

Figure 12-23.
Turning off hybrid sleep

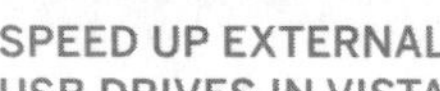

SPEED UP EXTERNAL USB DRIVES IN VISTA

Here's a way to juice up an external USB drive's performance in Vista. Open Device Manager by typing device manager into the Search box on the Start menu and pressing Enter. Browse to the external USB drive that you want to speed up, right-click it, select Properties, then click the Policies tab. Select Optimize for performance, and click OK. You'll have to reboot. Note that you should do this only for drives that you don't usually detach from your PC, because if you unplug the drive from your PC while it's caching, you could lose data.

HACK 178: A Quick Way to Overclock Your PC

V XP If you're looking for a speed boost, here's the simplest way to overclock your PC

Overclocking a PC is an exceedingly complicated business, and on many systems, is simply not possible. But if you're lucky, you may be able to bypass all that—your BIOS, or a utility from the motherboard or chipset maker, may let you overclock your PC without all the hassle.

Overclocking your PC can cause serious damage to your system unless you know what you're doing—and even then, you could do damage. If you're going to overclock, you should replace your heat sink/fan unit with one that will cool your PC as much as possible, because overclocking heats up your CPU **[Hack #179]**.

Each BIOS handles overclocking somewhat differently, and not all let you overclock. To see if yours does, restart your PC, and press the key that boots you into your BIOS. This may be different from system to system, but often is the F2, Del, or Esc key. When you start your PC, and the initial screen appears, press the F2 (or whatever the appropriate key is for your PC), and you'll get to the BIOS screen.

Often, but not always, overclocking options will be found under an Advanced menu, so from the main BIOS menu, go to the Advanced menu. Look for configuration settings such as CPU External Frequency, CPU Frequency Multiplier, and CPU Vcore. How you overclock your PC will vary according to your motherboard manufacturer. A typical example, though, would be for the external frequency to list a number, for example, 166. This would be the default external frequency for your processor, in this instance 166 MHz. The menu may give you a maximum number you can use, such as 200. This number works in concert with the frequency multiplier to determine your CPU speed. For example, a 166 MHz external frequency and a multiplier of 13 would give you a CPU speed of 2158 MHz. If you were to set your external frequency to 200 MHz and your multiplier to 14, you'd kick your CPU up to 2800 MHz.

At those settings, it's very unlikely that your CPU will work; chances are good that you'll get a blank screen, and you'd need to power down, reboot, and in most cases your computer will be smart enough to boot at some incredibly low speed so that you can get into the BIOS and fix the damage that you've done!

Some chipset manufacturers provide Windows-based utilities that let you interactively adjust these settings while Windows is running. NVIDIA's nTune (www.nvidia.com/object/sysutility.html) is one such utility. This is a great way to experiment with the possibilities but also an excellent way to crash Windows and maybe even lose data.

So how do you make it work? Trial and error is a rough way to go, but fortunately, Google will help you out immensely. Simply search for your CPU, motherboard, and the term "overclock," and if your CPU/motherboard combination is indeed overclockable, you will get dozens if not hundreds of web pages with stories about what worked, and what crashed and burned. Here's the search term I used to learn about one of my old PCs that I was hoping to breathe new life into (note that I used double quotes to keep some of the terms together):

```
"a7n8x-e deluxe" "xp 3000+" overclock
```

Be aware that if you overclock too much, you can do damage not just by heating up your processor too much. Other peripherals such as graphics cards may not be able to handle the higher speeds.

See Also

- *PC Hacks* (O'Reilly) is a great place to turn for help with overclocking.
- The web site Overclockers.com (www.overclockers.com) is a superb site for getting help with overclocking. It's pretty techie; you won't find much beginners' help.

HACK 179: Keep It Cool

V XP Better to overcool than undercool. A CPU survives best with adequate cooling to keep it stable.

Hackability of the CPU and system board is not the only consideration for a CPU speed tweak. As the CPU goes faster, the internal temperature rises, stressing the incredibly small wires and component structures inside. With excessive heat comes random lockups of the system and possibly catastrophic failures, with some spectacular but short-lived fireworks as the CPU melts down. To counteract excessive heat, you need significant cooling capability attached to the CPU chip, so you will see a lot of heat-sink and cooling fan gimmicks and gadgets for sale with CPUs. Check the documentation that comes with the CPU chips, and you will find recommendations and warnings about ensuring proper CPU-to-heat-sink contact and adequate ventilation. Figure 12-24 shows an example of a specially milled heavy-duty supercooling heat sink from an HP server with an integrated fan. HP engineers lay claim to inventing this style of cooling device, and it either works very well or just looks cool as heck! This design has been cloned by many aftermarket vendors.

Never run your CPU without a heat sink/fan unit! That said, there are some CPUs that can run *fanless*, such as the ULV (ultra-low voltage) Celerons and the CPUs used in some small form factor PCS.

Anyone who has run a modern CPU, overclocked or not—will tell you that the chip must be fitted with a decent heat sink and fan before any power is turned on, or the CPU will either burn up or refuse to start. Figure 12-25 shows a CPU chips that has suffered catastrophic thermal failure when operated without a heat sink. Try as you might, you cannot put the "magic smoke" back in the chip and have it work again.

Figure 12-24.
This bolt-down heavy-duty heat sink from an HP server keeps the CPU quite cool

Figure 12-25.
A fried CPU

Avoid inhaling the smoke or fumes from a "flamed-out" chip. When the internal elements of a CPU or other semiconductor melt or burn, they give off very foul-smelling and possibly toxic fumes. If a CPU does burn up, ventilate the area well to clear the air and be wary of nausea, dizziness, or other ill effects of toxic contamination.

The stock heat sink that comes with your CPU is adequate for operating the CPU at its rated speed, but overclocking and voltage adjustments can raise CPU temperature dramatically. In most cases of moderate (10–20 percent) clock or voltage (5–10 percent) increase, a slightly bigger heat sink and better ventilation will suffice to keep the chip temperature within safe operating range. In the rare cases when you can kick the CPU speed up by 25–200 percent or more, you need to provide some serious heat removal.

Current CPU types provide internal temperature sensors that can be read by the system BIOS and by some utility programs such as SiSoft Sandra. Reading the temperature of your system running normally will give you a baseline operating temperature to compare with as you overclock. You must avoid reaching or exceeding the thermal limits of your CPU.

The "normal" CPU temperature can vary greatly. The best way to determine what is normal for your CPU is to consult whatever documentation you can find from the manufacturer, but also to observe: when your computer is new and working optimally without a lot of programs running, take note of the temperature. Do the same just after (or while) you've done something CPU-intensive, such as playing the latest 3D shoot-em-up.

The secret to heat removal is to have a large mass of material with low thermal resistance to conduct heat away from the chip into the surrounding cooler air. Alternatively, you can attach a device with a circulating coolant that draws the excess heat away quickly and dumps away from the system components, like the radiator in your car or a home air conditioner does.

Aluminum is the ideal metal for most heat sinks. It has low thermal resistance, so it can accept and dissipate thermal energy very efficiently. It is inexpensive and easily manufactured into a variety of shapes that provide fast thermal dissipation and contact with almost any surface that needs cooling. Copper, also used in some heat sinks, is more expensive but is the material of choice for water-cooled devices. Copper/aluminum hybrids are not uncommon and are usually cheaper than copper-only heat sinks.

In addition to using a highly thermal-conductive material, that material must be as tightly attached to the CPU as possible. It is not adequate to merely place the material next to the CPU: the bond must be as close to being a part of the CPU as possible. The bond is usually made with a very thin layer of thermally conductive grease specifically designed for heat sink bonding.

The layer must be very thin because the compound or adhesive is intended to improve the metal-to-metal contact by filling in minute imperfections in both surfaces to provide optimal contact and thermal transfer. If the layer can be made thin enough, it will cover only the imperfections and leave metal-to-metal contact at the high spots common to both surfaces.

An often neglected attribute of using a thin layer of thermal compound is that it eliminates air bubbles between the surfaces that may trap a small amount of moisture. Moisture trapped between a hot device and its heat sink does not constitute water cooling; instead it could be a small water bomb waiting to go off. See Step 11 in the instructions that follow.

If the temperature of the moisture bubble exceeds 100 degrees Celsius or 212 degrees Fahrenheit (the boiling point of water)—and it can with a souped-up CPU—the water will expand to 2,700 times its volume as steam and demand to go someplace. That will likely be in the direction of destroying the CPU chip or at least weakening the overall thermal bond, causing the CPU to overheat and self-destruct.

If you've removed a heat sink from a CPU (best done with either a slight twisting motion to separate heat sink and CPU or very light prying between the two), beware that some are glued on with high-temperature epoxy and cannot be removed without destroying the CPU. You've probably experienced this thermal grease or heat sink compound—a tenacious white material that looks and feels like toothpaste but stains like red wine in the middle of a new white carpet. Thermal compound is typically a mixture of aluminum oxide for thermal conduction and a silicon paste to hold the aluminum oxide together (see Figure 12-26).

Two new compound mixtures have emerged: one containing aluminum oxide in a fine ceramic form, the other silver and silver oxide. According to product documentation at www.articsilver.com, the typical aluminum oxide-based white paste provides the lowest thermal conductivity and the least CPU temperature drop (2–7 degrees), the ceramic compound is next in the order of effectiveness (2–10 degree drop), and the silver-based compound the most efficient, providing a 3–12 degree drop in CPU temperature. The effectiveness is also represented in the cost of the compound—between $4 and $9 per tube. Unless you see your CPU temperature rising towards its maximum limits, the typical aluminum oxide, and certainly the ceramic paste, are more than adequate for the task.

For a time, Intel prebonded heat sinks to some versions of their Pentium I CPUs using thermal epoxy, making it impossible to separate the two if you wanted to add a larger heat sink.

Figure 12-26.
Thermal compound fills the gaps between heat sink and CPU

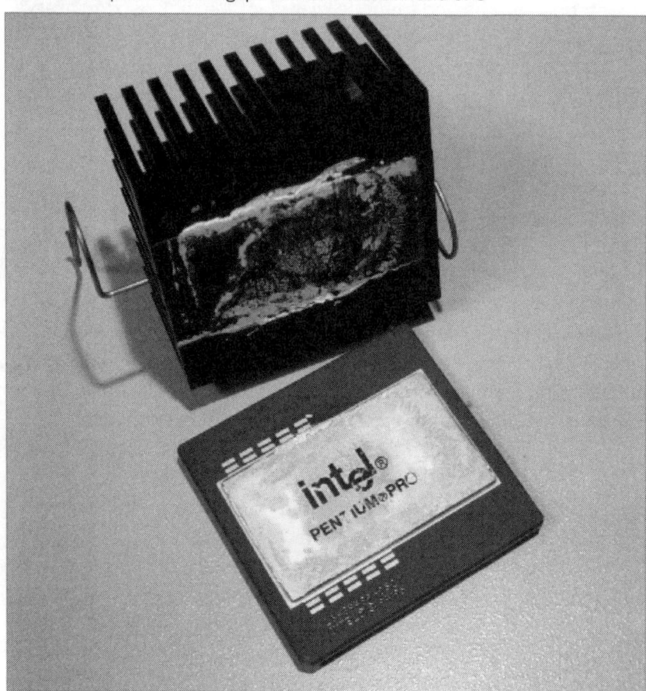

To speed production processes and make applying thermal bonding cleaner, many vendors have chosen to use thermal pads, as shown in Figure 12-27. Thermal pads are fine in lower-temperature applications, but, while they certainly fills gaps between surfaces, they do not give way to allow direct surface contact between high spots. If you separate a CPU and heat sink that were bonded with a thermal pad, it is acceptable to replace the pad with thermal paste instead, unless the warranty on your CPU requires the use of the supplied thermal pad and heat sink.

No matter which compound you choose, the technique for properly applying thermal compound to obtain optimal thermal bonding between a cooling device and a CPU involves a few very simple items and steps.

Here's what you will need (see Figure 12-28):

- Thermal compound
- A clean, dry cloth, something as lint-free as possible
- Isopropyl (rubbing) alcohol
- A vinyl glove or piece of plastic wrap
- A straightedge, such as a single-edged razor blade or used plastic card
- An antistatic pad or chip storage bag to pad the CPU pins and reduce the chance of static damage

Figure 12-27.
Two forms of thermal pads used on CPU heat sinks

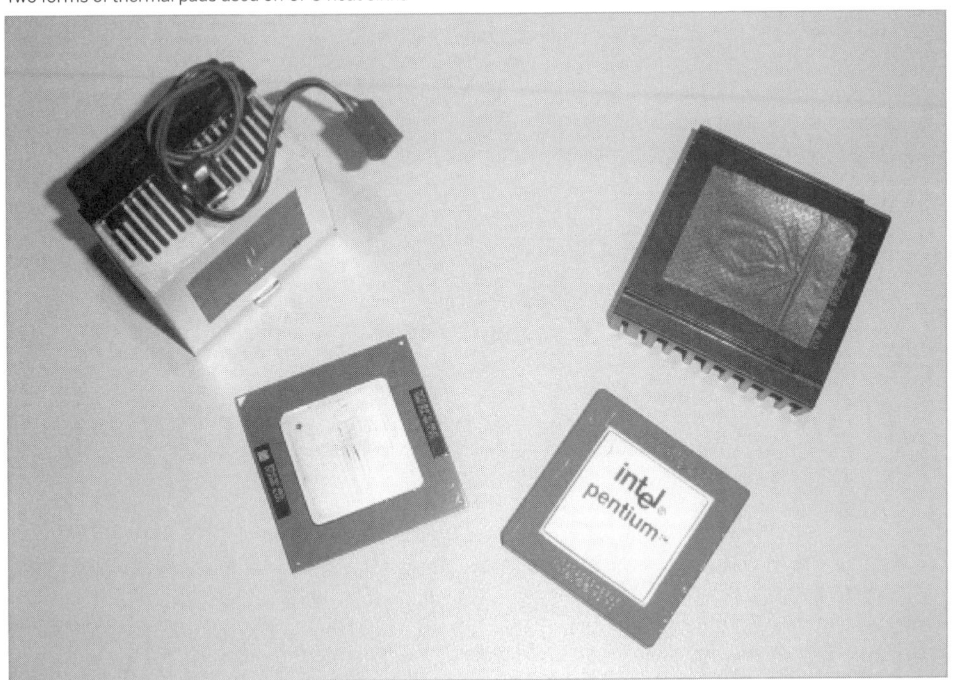

Figure 12-28.
Basic items needed to bond CPU and heat sink

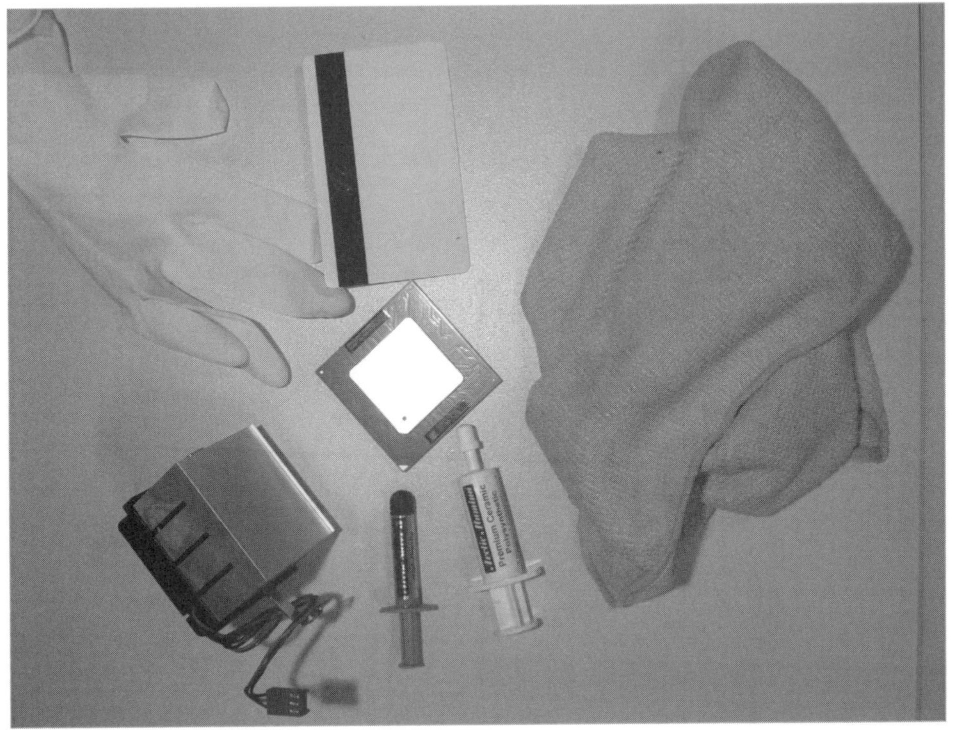

Use these items to install your heat sink as follows:

1. Remove the CPU from its socket, and set it pins-down on the antistatic material.
2. Maintain cleanliness! Apply a few drops of isopropyl alcohol to the clean cloth, and wipe the contact surface area of your heat sink and the top cap of the CPU core. Alcohol will remove most oils and help evaporate moisture from the surfaces.
3. Apply a small bead/drop of thermal compound to the area of the heat sink that will contact the CPU, as shown in Figure 12-29.
4. Protecting your fingers with the vinyl glove or plastic wrap, smear the compound around and into the surface of the heat sink, as shown in Figure 12-30. This will help fill imperfections in the metal surface.
5. Using a clean, dry portion of the cloth, wipe the excess thermal compound off the surface of the heat sink, as shown in Figure 12-31. If the compound is especially thick and hard to wipe off, scrape the excess off with the straightedge and then wipe clean. Do not use alcohol to clean the surface.
6. Apply a small bead of thermal compound to a corner of the CPU's metal die/cap, as you did in Step 1.
7. Using the straightedge, distribute the compound evenly across the surface of the top of the CPU as shown in Figure 12-32.
8. Remove as much excess as possible but leave a thin layer of compound, as shown in Figure 12-33.
9. Install the CPU in its socket on your system board. Be careful not to disturb the thermal compound.
10. Align and place the heat sink as squarely and accurately in its final placement above the CPU as possible.
11. Apply a slight downward pressure evenly on the heat sink, then twist the heat sink to the left and right of its final placement position and back to its final centered position, as in Figure 12-34. This action will press out excess compound and fill in any gaps, reducing any bubbles in the surface-to-surface distance between the heat sink and CPU.

Follow the directions carefully for heat sink fastening. The mechanics and fastening system for your heat sink, CPU, and system-board socket may be different from the one shown.

— Jim Aspinwall, from PC Hacks

QUICK HACK 

DO YOU NEED HIGH-PERFORMANCE RAM?

Companies like Corsair and Mushkin sell "high-performance" memory to the enthusiast market. We're sometimes asked if it's worth paying more for such memory rather than using standard Kingston or Crucial modules. The short answer is that it's usually not.

Even nominally identical memory chips vary from one to the next. Some are faster than others, and performance memory packagers take advantage of that fact. They order large numbers of memory chips and use a process called *binning* to hand-select the fastest chips from that batch. After they've cherry-picked the fastest 5 percent or 10 percent, they resell the remaining chips to other memory packagers. They assemble those hand-picked chips into high-performance modules and verify that they function at higher speeds and tighter memory timings than standard memory.

Many gamers happily pay premiums for such memory, on the assumption that faster memory

continued on next page...

Figure 12-29.
Apply thermal compound sparingly

Figure 12-30.
Rubbing thermal compound into the heat sink surface

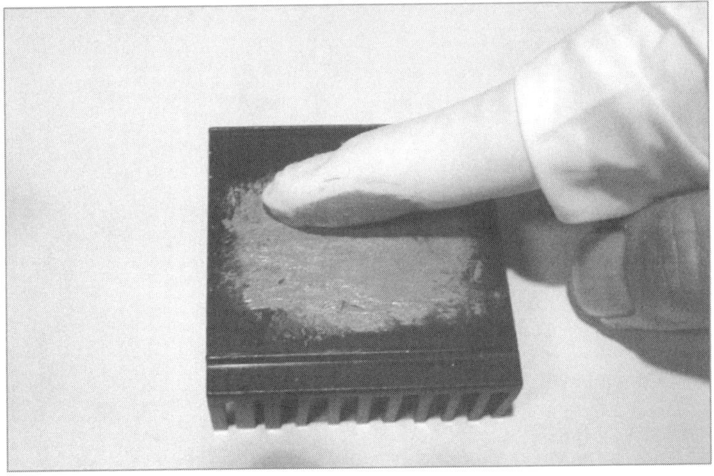

Figure 12-31.
Wiping excess compound from heat-sink surface

continued from previous page...

improves overall performance. Alas, that's not necessarily true. If your memory is fast enough to keep up with the processor, or nearly so, substituting faster memory has very little effect on overall system performance.

Benchmarks may show a difference, but only when they test memory subsystem performance in isolation. But memory performance is only one aspect of overall system performance, and using faster memory helps only if memory speed is the bottleneck. For most gaming systems, it is not.

The one exception is overclocked systems. If you boost the bus speed to run your CPU at higher than nominal speed, which we do not recommend, you're also pushing other system components, including memory, to speeds they were not designed to support. In such cases, it's a good idea to use hand-picked performance memory rather than depend on the tolerances built into standard memory modules.

— *Robert Bruce Thompson, Barbara Fritchman Thompson, from* Building the Perfect PC

Figure 12-32.
Spreading thermal compound on the CPU

Figure 12-33.
CPU with thermal compound ready for installation

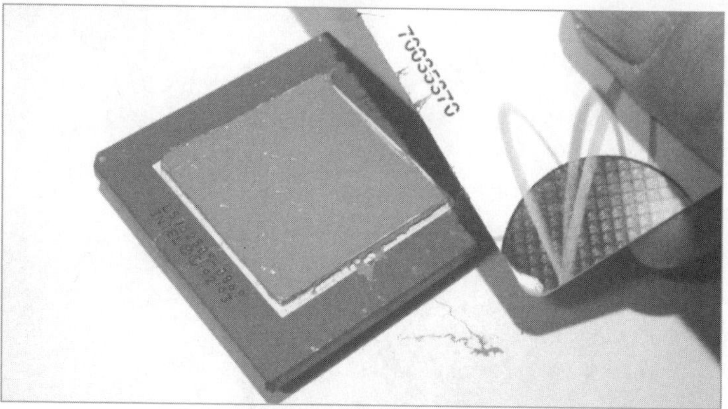

Figure 12-34.
Slight pressure and twisting bonds the heat sink to the CPU

HACK 180: Overclock Any Video Card

V XP The PowerStrip tool has got your overclocking needs covered for almost any card from legacy to present day.

PowerStrip, shown in Figure 12-35, detects and allows overclock settings for dozens of different video adapters.

A trial version of PowerStrip is available for download from www.entechtaiwan.net/util/ps.shtm. The program runs resident and provides access to its settings when you right-click on its icon in the system tray. Myriad general video monitor and performance settings are available. PowerStrip 3.7 can soup up legacy video cards and chips, such as those from ATI, 3dfx, Cirrus Logic, Number Nine, nVidia, Rendition, S3, and Tseng Labs.

Using Powerstrip to overclock a 128 MB nVidia FX 5200 dual-DVI card in a 1.8 GHz Intel Pentium 4 system produced an expected proportional 10 percent frame-rate and 3DMark performance increase for a 10 percent increase in video engine and video memory clock speeds.

— *Jim Aspinwall, from* PC Hacks

HACK 181: Install a Video Card

V XP Getting better video on your PC isn't as tough as you may think. Here's how to do it.

Installing a video card is generally straightforward, but there are a couple gotchas to watch out for:

- If you are installing an AGP card on a motherboard with a non-Intel chipset, you may need to install a GART driver before you physically install the video card or its drivers. Skipping this step

Figure 12-35.
Dozens of video options can be set with PowerStrip

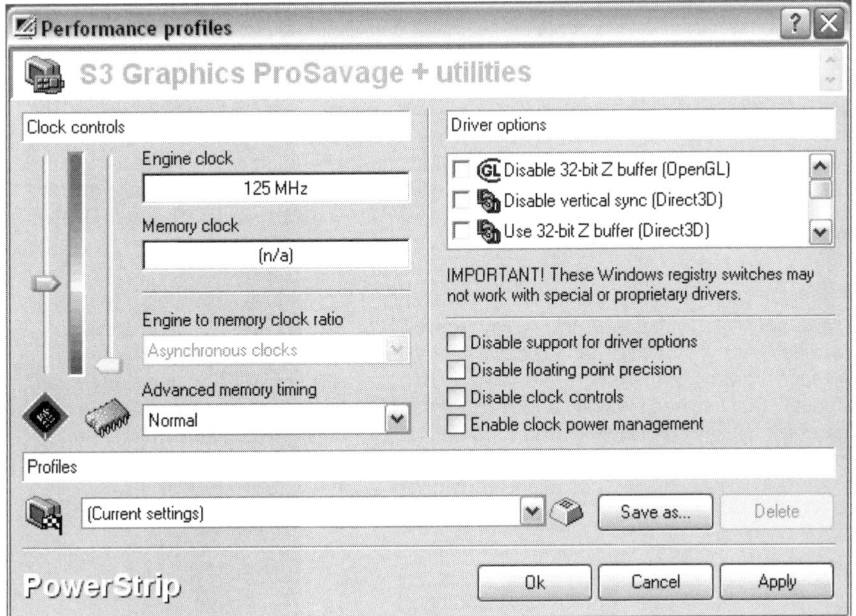

QUICK HACK

GET MORE FROM YOUR USB FLASH DRIVE

If you copy applications to a USB flash drive, and normally run those applications when you plug the drive into a PC or copy files from the drive to a PC, download the free MyPendrive (www.mypendrive.org). This nifty freebie makes your USB flash drive do all kinds of tricks, such as starting up your portable apps as soon as you plug in your USB drive and backing up your folders when you connect your drive.

can cause Windows to black-screen at boot. Follow the instructions supplied with the new video card to install the GART driver.

- The presence of old video drivers may cause problems with the installation of the new card. You may need to use Safe Mode (press F8 while the system boots, and choose Safe Mode from the menu) to uninstall the old video drivers before installing the new video card or, if the current video adapter is dead, as the first step after installing the new video card.

SAFE MODE VERSUS VGA MODE

Pressing F8 during boot displays the Windows Advanced Options Menu, which offers several choices. The first option, Safe Mode, starts the system with everything disabled except the essentials—no networking or sound, only a vanilla 640×480 VGA video driver, and so on. We use Safe Mode during troubleshooting to minimize the number of variables that may be causing the problem. If for some reason you prefer to start the system in what we call "Safe Video Mode"—with all drivers loading normally except that the vanilla 640×480 video driver is used—choose Enable VGA Mode instead of Safe Mode.

If you buy a retail-boxed video card, it will include a comprehensive manual. If you buy an OEM video card that arrives without a manual, your first step should be to download the PDF manual from the maker's web site. (You may also need to download drivers if no driver disc is provided.) The exact sequence of installation steps, including loading drivers, varies from card to card, so follow the instructions provided in the manual.

Here are the top mistakes to avoid when installing a new video card:

Failing to read the manual

Most people don't bother to Read the Fine Manual (RTFM), which is a mistake. If you don't read the manual, you're likely to do something wrong; most commonly, people install drivers too early, too late, or the wrong way. That's best case. Worst case, you may destroy your expensive new video card instantly when you turn on the power. So, RTFM.

Failing to seat the video card

Video cards, both AGP and PCIe, may require significant pressure to seat fully. You may think the card is seated. You may even have heard it snap into place. That doesn't mean it's fully seated. Always verify visually that the card is seated fully in the connector and that the retention mechanism has latched the card in place. A partially seated video card may not work at all. Worse still, it may kinda, sorta work, leaving you with a difficult troubleshooting problem.

Failing to connect supplemental power

Many recent video cards, particularly high-performance models, require more power than the video slot can provide. These cards have a supplemental power connector designed to accept either a special PCIe power connector or a standard Molex hard drive power connector. Failing to connect supplemental power can have several results, none of them good. At best, the video card simply won't work, but nothing will be damaged. At worst, the card may attempt to draw too much power from the video connector, damaging the card and/or the motherboard. (If your card requires a PCIe power connector, and your power supply doesn't provide one, there are adapter cables available with standard Molex hard drive power connectors on one end and PCIe power connectors on the other.) If you do need to connect a Molex hard drive power connector, do not use the ones labeled Fan Only. They do not provide enough power.

Failing to connect power to the fan

Fast video cards generate a lot of heat. Instead of depending on a passive heat sink for cooling, many recent video cards use a small fan to cool the video processor. Failing to connect power to this fan will cause the video processor to overheat, perhaps catastrophically. Running a fast video adapter without its fan for even a few seconds can literally burn the video processor to a crisp. (We try to avoid using such cards because fans fail unpredictably, and a failed fan can have the same result. If you do purchase such a card, be sure to clean it regularly. Not only does the fan motor have to work harder to spin dusty blades, but its cooling capacity is greatly diminished.)

To physically install a video card, proceed as follows (deferring to conflicting instructions in the manual):

1. Disconnect the display and other external cables, and move the system to a well-lit work area. Remove the case access panel(s) to gain access to the case interior. Now, as always when you have the case open, is a good time to clean the system.

2. If you are replacing an existing video card, remove the screw that secures the video card to the chassis, release the retention mechanism, if any, and pull the video card. If you are upgrading integrated video, align the video card with the motherboard video slot to determine which slot cover you need to remove (it's not always obvious).

3. Remove the correct slot cover. You may also need to loosen the screw for the adjacent slot cover temporarily in order to free the slot cover you want to remove. Carefully slide the rear bracket of the video card into place, making sure that the external connectors on the bracket clear the edges of the slot. Carefully align the connector on the video card with the AGP or PCIe slot, and use both thumbs to press the video card down until it snaps into the slot, as shown in Figure 12-36.

4. Verify visually that the card contacts have fully penetrated the video slot, and that the base of the video card is parallel to the slot and in full contact with it. Verify that the retention mechanism, visible here as two brown tabs to the lower right of the heat sink, mates to the corresponding notch on the video card, snapping into place as the card is seated. If you need to remove the adapter later, remember to press those tabs to unlock the retaining bracket before you attempt to pull the card.

5. After you are certain that the video adapter is fully seated, secure it by inserting a screw through the bracket into the chassis, as shown in Figure 12-37.

6. Replace the access panel(s), move the system back to its original location, reconnect all the external cables, and turn on the power. Follow the instructions that came with the video card to install and configure the video drivers and any other software supplied with the adapter, such as a DVD-Video player or TV capture program. If you intend to view DVDs on your PC, the DVD-Video player is essential because Windows cannot play DVDs without it (and in fact, the player software includes a decoder that even Windows Media Player relies on to play DVDs). You should be sure to visit the decoder software vendor's web site for updates because they may not be automatically provided through Windows update or the video card manufacturer's periodic driver updates.

DANGER, WILL ROBINSON!

If the video card has a supplemental power connector and/or a fan power connector, make certain to connect power to them before proceeding. It's always embarrassing to burn a new video card to a crisp, and it isn't covered by warranty.

— *Robert Bruce Thompson and Barbara Fritchman Thompson, from* Building the Perfect PC

Figure 12-36.
Insert the video card and press down firmly to seat it

Figure 12-37.
Secure the video card with a screw

HACK 182: Top Hardware Troubleshooting Hacks

V XP Got problems with your home-made, retail-bought, or mail-order PC? We've got help—multiple ways to sniff out the source of your problem and fix it.

What makes good PCs go bad? More causes than you can count, everything from cable problems to bad drives, bad power supplies, loose card connections, and much more. Tracking down the source of a hardware problem can be immensely frustrating.

But help is on the way. This hack covers some of the most common troubleshooting woes you'll come across and tells you what to do. Whether you're a dedicated hardware hacker, or want help with a system you've bought ready-made, these troubleshooting hacks can help.

Problem: When you apply power, nothing happens.

- Verify that the power cable is connected to the PC and to the wall receptacle, and that the wall receptacle has power. Don't assume. We have seen receptacles in which one half worked and the other didn't. Use a lamp or other appliance to verify that the receptacle to which you connect the PC actually has power. If the power supply has its own power switch, make sure that the switch is turned to the "On" or "1" position. If your local mains voltage is 110/115/120V, verify that the power supply voltage selector switch, if present, is not set for 220/230/240V. (If you need to move this switch, disconnect power before doing so.)

- If you are using an outlet strip or UPS, make sure that its switch (if it has one) is on and that the circuit breaker or fuse hasn't blown.

- If you installed an AGP/PCIe video adapter, pop the lid, and verify that the adapter is fully seated in its slot. Even if you were sure that it seated fully initially—and even if you thought it snapped into place—the adapter still may not be properly seated. Remove the adapter, and reinstall it, making sure it seats completely. If the motherboard has an AGP/PCIe retention mechanism, make sure the notch on the adapter card fully engages the mechanism. Ironically, one of the most common reasons for a loose adapter card is that the screw used to secure it to the chassis may torque the card, pulling it partially out of its slot. This problem is rare with high-quality cases and adapter cards, but quite common with cheap components.

- Verify that the main ATX power cable and the ATX12V power cable are securely connected to the motherboard and that all pins are making contact. If necessary, remove the cables, and reconnect them. Make sure the latch on each cable plug snaps into place on the motherboard jack.

- Verify that the front-panel power switch cable is connected properly to the front-panel connector block. Check the silkscreen label on the motherboard and the motherboard manual to verify that you are connecting the cable to the right set of pins. Very rarely, you may encounter a defective power switch. You can eliminate this possibility by temporarily connecting the front-panel reset switch cable to the power switch pins on the front-panel connector block. (Both are merely momentary on switches, so they can be used interchangeably.) Alternatively, you can carefully use a small flat-blade screwdriver to short the power switch pins on the front-panel connector block momentarily. If the system starts with either of these methods, the problem is the power switch.

- Start eliminating less likely possibilities, the most common of which is a well-concealed short circuit. Begin by disconnecting the power and data cables from the hard, optical, and floppy drives, one at a time. After you disconnect each one, try starting the system. If the system starts, the drive you just disconnected is the problem. The drive itself may be defective, but it's far more likely that the cable is defective or was improperly connected. Replace the data cable, and connect the drive to a different power supply cable.

If you have a spare power supply—or can borrow one temporarily from another system—you might as well try it as long as you have the cables disconnected. A new power supply being DOA is fairly rare, at least among good brands, but if you have the original disconnected, it's not much trouble to try a different one.

- If you have expansion cards installed, remove them one by one, except for the AGP adapter. If the motherboard has embedded video, temporarily connect your display to it, and remove the AGP card as well. Attempt to start the system after you remove each card. If the system starts, the card you just removed is causing the problem. Try a different card, or install that card in a different slot.

- Remove and reseat the memory modules, examining them to make sure they are not damaged, and then try to start the system. If you have two memory modules installed, install only one of them initially. Try it in both (or all) memory slots. If the module doesn't work in any slot, it may be defective. Try the other module, again in every available memory slot. By using this approach, you can determine if one of the memory modules or one of the slots is defective.

- Remove the CPU cooler and the CPU. Check the CPU to make sure there are no bent pins. If there are, you may be able to straighten them using a credit card or a similar thin, stiff object, but in all likelihood you will have to replace the CPU. Check the CPU socket to make sure there are no blocked holes or foreign objects present.

Before you reinstall the CPU, always remove the old thermal compound and apply new compound **[Hack #179]**. You can generally wipe off the old compound with a paper towel, or perhaps by rubbing it gently with your thumb. (Keep the processor in its socket while you remove the compound.) If the compound is difficult to remove, try heating it gently with a hair dryer. Never operate the system without the CPU cooler installed.

- Remove the motherboard, and verify that no extraneous screws or other conductive objects are shorting the motherboard to the chassis. Although shaking the case usually causes such objects to rattle, a screw or other small object may become wedged so tightly between the motherboard and chassis that it will not reveal itself during a shake test.

- If the problem persists, the most likely cause is a defective motherboard.

Problem: The system seems to start normally, but the display remains black.

- Verify that the display has power, and the video cable is connected. If the display has a noncaptive power cable, make sure the power cord is connected both to the display and to the wall receptacle. If you have a spare power cord, use it to connect the display.

- Verify that the brightness and contrast controls of the display are set to midrange or higher.

- Disconnect the video cable, and examine it closely to make sure that no pins are bent or shorted. Note that the video cable on some monitors is missing some pins and may have a short jumper wire connecting other pins, which is normal. Also check the video port on the PC to make sure that all the holes are clear and that no foreign objects are present.

- If you are using a standalone AGP/PCIe adapter in a motherboard that has embedded video, make sure the video cable is connected to the proper video port. Try the other video port just to make sure. Most motherboards with embedded video automatically disable it when they sense that an AGP/PCIe card is installed, but that is not universally true. You may have to connect the display to the embedded video, enter BIOS Setup, and reconfigure the motherboard to use the AGP/PCIe card.

- Try using a different display if you have one available. Alternatively, try using the problem display on a known-good system.

- If you are using an AGP/PCIe card, make certain it is fully seated. Many combinations of adapter card and motherboard make it very difficult to seat the card properly. You may think the card is seated, and may even feel it snap into place. That does not necessarily mean it really is fully seated. Look carefully at the bottom edge of the card and the AGP/PCIe slot, and make sure the card is fully in the slot and parallel to it. Verify that installing the screw that secures the adapter card to the chassis did not torque the card, forcing one end up and out of the slot.

- If the system has PCI expansion cards installed, remove them one by one. (Be sure to disconnect power from the system before you remove or install a card.) Each time you remove a card, restart the system. If the system displays video after you remove a card, that card is either defective or is conflicting with the graphics adapter. Try installing the PCI card in a different slot. If it still causes the video problem, the card is probably defective. Replace it.

Problem: When you connect power (or turn on the main power switch), the power supply starts briefly and then shuts off.

All of the following steps assume that the power supply is adequate for the system configuration. This symptom may also occur if you are using a grossly underpowered power supply. Worse still, doing that may damage the power supply itself, the motherboard, and other components.

- This may be normal behavior. When you connect power to the power supply, it senses the power and begins its startup routine. Within a fraction of a second, the power supply notices that the motherboard hasn't ordered it to start, so it shuts itself down immediately. Press the main power switch on the case, and the system should start normally.

- If pressing the main power switch doesn't start the system, you have probably forgotten to connect one of the cables from the power supply or front panel to the motherboard. Verify that the power switch cable is connected to the front-panel connector block, and that the 20-pin main ATX power cable and the 4-pin ATX12V power cable are connected to the motherboard. Connect any cables that are not connected, and press the main power switch, and the system should start normally.

- If the preceding steps don't solve the problem, the most likely cause is a defective power supply. If you have a spare power supply or can borrow one from another system, install it temporarily in the new system. Alternatively, connect the problem power supply to another system to verify that it is bad.

- If none of the preceding steps solves the problem, the most likely cause is a defective motherboard. Replace it.

Problem: When you apply power, the floppy drive LED lights solidly and the system fails to start.

- The FDD (floppy disk drive) cable may be misaligned. Verify that the FDD cable is properly installed on the FDD and on the motherboard FDD interface. You may have installed the FDD cable backward or installed it offset by one row or column of pins.

- If the FDD cable is properly installed, it may be defective. Disconnect it temporarily, and start the system. If the system starts normally, replace the FDD cable.

- If the FDD cable is known-good and installed properly, the FDD itself or the motherboard FDD interface may be defective. Replace the FDD. If that doesn't solve the problem, and you insist on having an FDD, either replace the motherboard or disable the motherboard FDD interface, and install a PCI adapter that provides an FDD interface.

Problem: The optical drive appears to play audio CDs, but no sound comes from the speakers.

- Make sure the volume/mixer is set appropriately, i.e., the volume is up, and CD Audio isn't muted. There may be multiple volume controls in a system. Check them all.
- Try a different audio CD. Some recent audio CDs are copy-protected in such a way that they refuse to play on a computer optical drive.
- If you have tried several audio CDs without success, this may still be normal behavior, depending on the player application you are using. Optical drives can deliver audio data via the analog audio-out jack on the rear of the drive or as a digital bit stream on the bus. If the player application pulls the digital bit stream from the bus, sound is delivered to your speakers normally. If the player application uses analog audio, you must connect a cable from the analog audio-out jack on the back of the drive to an audio-in connector on the motherboard or sound card.

Few optical drives or motherboards include an analog audio cable, so you will probably have to buy a cable. In the past, audio cables were often proprietary, but modern drives and motherboards all use a standard ATAPI audio cable.

- If you install an audio cable and still have no sound from the speakers, try connecting headphones or amplified speakers directly to the headphone jack on the front of the optical drive (if present). If you still can't hear the audio, the drive may be defective. If you can hear audio via the front headphone jack but not through the computer speakers, it's likely the audio cable you installed is defective or installed improperly.

QUICK HACK

SEE ALL OF YOUR USB DEVICES

Given how many USB ports PCs come with these days, it can be tough to keep track of what, exactly, you have connected to them. You might have a mouse, keyboard, printer, external hard drive, USB flash drive . . . the list goes on. If you'd like to get a quick list of all USB devices connected to your PC—or that have ever been connected to your PC—along with details about them, get the free USBDeview (www.nirsoft.net/utils/usb_devices_view.html). As you can see in Figure 12-38, it lists the USB device's name, the port to which it's connected, whether it's currently connected, whether it's safe to unplug it, and so on.

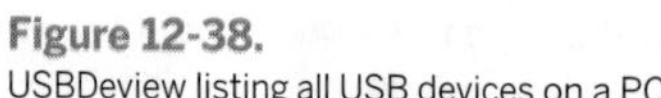

Figure 12-38.
USBDeview listing all USB devices on a PC

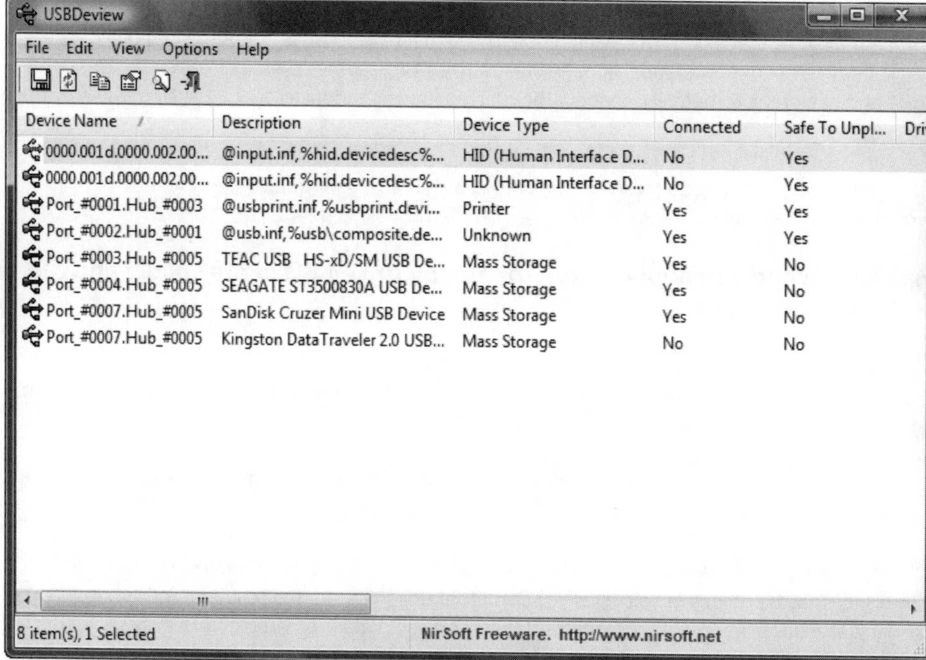

Problem: SATA drives are not recognized.

- How SATA drives are detected (or not detected) depends on the particular combination of chipset, BIOS revision level, SATA interface, and the operating system you use. Failing to recognize SATA devices may be normal behavior.

- If you use a standalone PCI SATA adapter card, the system will typically not recognize the connected SATA drive(s) during startup. This is normal behavior. You will have to provide an SATA device driver when you install the operating system.

- If your motherboard uses a recent chipset, e.g., an Intel 945 or later, and has embedded SATA interfaces, it should detect SATA devices during startup and display them on the BIOS boot screen. If the drive is not recognized, update the BIOS to the latest version if you have not already done so. Restart the system, and watch the BIOS boot screen to see if the system recognizes the SATA drive. Run BIOS Setup, and select the menu item that allows you to configure ATA devices. If your SATA drive is not listed, you can still use it, but you'll have to provide a driver on disk, CD, or USB drive during OS installation [Hack #170].

- Recognition of SATA drives during operating system installation varies with the OS version and the chipset. The original release of Windows 2000 does not detect SATA drives with any chipset. To install Windows 2000 on an SATA drive, watch during the early part of Setup for the prompt to press F6 if you need to install third-party storage drivers. Press F6 when prompted, and insert the SATA driver floppy. Windows XP may or may not recognize SATA drives, depending on the chipset the motherboard uses. With recent chipsets, e.g., the Intel 865 series and later, Windows XP recognizes and uses SATA drives natively. With earlier chipsets, e.g., the Intel D845 and earlier, Windows XP does not recognize the SATA drive natively, so you will have to press F6 when prompted and provide the SATA driver on floppy. Most recent Linux distributions (those based on the 2.4 kernel or later) recognize SATA drives natively.

- If the SATA drive is still not recognized, pop the lid, and verify that the SATA data and power cables are connected properly. Try removing and reseating the cables and, if necessary, connecting the SATA drive to a different motherboard interface connector. If the drive still isn't accessible, try replacing the SATA data cable. If none of this works, the SATA drive is probably defective.

Problem: The monitor displays BIOS boot text, but the system doesn't boot and displays no error message.

- This may be normal behavior. Restart the system, and enter BIOS Setup (usually by pressing Delete or F1 during startup). Choose the menu option to use default CMOS settings, save the changes, exit, and restart the system.

- If the system doesn't accept keyboard input, and you are using a USB keyboard and mouse, temporarily swap in a PS/2 keyboard and mouse. If you are using a PS/2 keyboard and mouse, make sure you haven't connected the keyboard to the mouse port and vice versa.

- If the system still fails to boot, run BIOS Setup again and verify all settings, particularly CPU speed, FSB speed, and memory timings.

- If the system hangs with a DMI pool error message, restart the system, and run BIOS Setup again. Search the menus for an option to reset the configuration data. Enable that option, save the changes, and restart the system.

- If you are using an Intel motherboard, power down the system, and reset the configuration jumper from the 1-2 (Normal) position to the 2-3 (Configure) position. Restart the system, and BIOS Setup will appear automatically. Choose the option to use default CMOS settings, save the changes, and power down the system. Move the configuration jumper back to the 1-2 position and restart the system. (Actually, we do this routinely any time we build a system around an Intel motherboard. It may not be absolutely required, but we've found that it minimizes problems.)

- If you are still unable to access BIOS Setup, power down the system, disconnect all the drive data cables, and restart the system. If the system displays a Hard Drive Failure or No Boot Device error message, the problem is a defective cable (more likely) or a defective drive. Replace the drive data cable, and try again. If the system does not display such an error message, the problem is probably caused by a defective motherboard.

Problem: The monitor displays a Hard Drive Failure or similar error.

- This is almost always a hardware problem. Verify that the hard drive data cable is connected properly to the drive and the interface and that the drive power cable is connected.
- Use a different drive data cable, and connect the drive to a different power cable.
- Connect the drive data cable to a different interface.
- If none of these steps corrects the problem, the most likely cause is a defective drive.

Problem: The monitor displays a No Boot Device, Missing Operating System, or similar error message.

- This is normal behavior if you have not yet installed an operating system. Error messages like this generally mean that the drive is physically installed and accessible, but the PC cannot boot because it cannot locate the operating system. Install the operating system.
- If the drive is inaccessible, verify that all data and power cables are connected properly. If it is a parallel ATA drive, verify that the master/slave jumpers are set correctly and that the drive is connected to the primary interface.

Problem: The system refuses to boot from the optical drive.

- All modern motherboards and optical drives support the El Torito specification, which allows the system to boot from an optical disc. If your new system refuses to boot from a CD, first verify that the CD is bootable. Most, but not all, operating system distribution CDs are bootable. Some OS CDs are not bootable, but have a utility program to generate boot floppies. Check the documentation to verify that the CD is bootable, or try booting the CD in another system.
- Run CMOS Setup, and locate the section where you can define boot sequence. The default sequence is often (1) floppy drive, (2) hard drive, and (3) optical drive. Sometimes, by the time the system has decided it can't boot from the FDD or hard drive, it "gives up" before attempting to boot from the optical drive. Reset the boot sequence to (1) optical drive and (2) hard drive. We generally leave the system with that boot sequence. Most systems configured this way prompt you to "Press any key to boot from CD" or something similar. If you don't press a key, the system then attempts to boot from the hard drive, so make sure to pay attention during the boot sequence, and press a key when prompted.
- Some high-speed optical drives take several seconds to load a CD, spin up, and signal the system that they are ready. In the meantime, the BIOS may have given up on the optical drive and gone on to try other boot devices. If you think this has happened, try pressing the reset button to reboot the system while the optical drive is already spinning and up to speed. If you get a persistent prompt to "press any key to boot from CD," try leaving that prompt up while the optical drive comes up to speed. If that doesn't work, run CMOS Setup, and reconfigure the boot sequence to put the FDD first and the optical drive second. (Make sure there's no disk in the FDD.) You can also try putting other boot device options (e.g., a Zip drive, network drive, or boot PROM) ahead of the optical drive in the boot sequence, even if you don't have these devices connected. The goal is to

provide sufficient delay for the optical drive to spin up before the motherboard attempts to boot from it.

- If none of these steps solves the problem, verify that all data cable and power cable connections are correct, that master/slave jumpers are set correctly, and so on. If the system still fails to boot, replace the optical drive data cable.

- If the system still fails to boot, disconnect all drives except the primary hard drive and the optical drive. If they are parallel ATA devices, connect the hard drive as the master device on the primary channel and the optical drive as the master device on the secondary channel, and restart the system.

- If that fails to solve the problem, connect both the hard drive and the optical drive to the primary ATA interface, with the hard drive as master and the optical drive as slave.

- If the system still fails to boot, the optical drive is probably defective. Try using a different drive.

Problem: When you first apply power, you hear a continuous high-pitched screech or warble.

- The most likely cause is either that one of the system fans has a defective bearing or that a wire is contacting the spinning fan. Examine all the system fans—CPU fan, power supply fan, and any supplemental fans—to make sure they haven't been fouled by a wire. Sometimes it's difficult to determine which fan is making the noise. In that case, use a cardboard tube or rolled-up piece of paper as a stethoscope to localize the noise. If the fan is fouled, clear the problem. If the fan is not fouled but still noisy, replace the fan.

- Rarely, a new hard drive may have a manufacturing defect or may have been damaged in shipping. If so, the problem is usually obvious from the amount and location of the noise and possibly because the hard drive is vibrating. If necessary, use your cardboard-tube stethoscope to localize the noise. If the hard drive is the source, the only alternative is to replace it.

— *Robert Bruce Thompson and Barbara Fritchman Thompson, from* Building the Perfect PC

13 THE REGISTRY AND GROUP POLICY EDITOR

When it comes to hacking Windows, you need to know how to use the Registry. It contains the underlying organization of the entire operating system, and its often-incomprehensible settings hold the key to countless hacks. In simpler days, you could hack Windows without bothering with the Registry; a solid knowledge of such things as .ini files would suffice. But no longer. If you want to get hacking, the Registry holds the key—literally, since it's organized by way of keys.

Even if you've edited the Registry before, you'll find a lot in this chapter to help. It not only teaches the mechanics of using the Registry, but also explains its underlying organization. You'll find ways to keep your Registry safe, learn how to back it up, and find downloadable tools to make the most of the Registry. As a bonus, this chapter includes a grab bag of other great hacks.

This chapter also covers Group Policy Editor. Don't be confused by its name; it's not just a tool for system administrators looking to handle file permissions and the like. In fact, it's an exceedingly powerful tool for hacking many parts of Windows.

Differences Between the Registry in Windows Vista and Windows XP

Whether you use Windows Vista or Windows XP, the Registry works the same, so the following hacks will work, no matter which operating system you use. But there are some differences in the Registry between the two versions of Windows, and it's a good idea to know them before you start hacking away.

Because the two versions of Windows have different interfaces and features, there naturally will be some Registry settings that work on one version of Windows and not the other. In addition, Microsoft has made some changes having to do with safety and security, and with ensuring that the operating system doesn't accidentally become damaged. In Windows Vista, only accounts with administrator privileges can make changes to the Registry. This affects not just editing the Registry directly, but when the user takes an action that will change the Registry, such as installing software.

But what if a standard user wants to edit the Registry, or make a change that affects the Registry? Windows Vista uses several ways to handle that:

- When a standard user tries to run the Registry Editor, User Account Control (UAC) asks for an administrator password. If the user provides one, the Registry Editor can be used, and changes made. Otherwise, the Registry Editor will not start.
- When a standard user installs software, UAC will ask for an administrator password. If the user provides them, the software makes the appropriate changes to the %SystemRoot% and %ProgramFiles% folders as well as to the Registry.

- If a legacy application fails to work correctly with UAC, Windows Vista will use a new feature called *file and registry virtualization*. This creates virtual %SystemRoot% and %ProgramFiles% folders, and a virtual HKEY_LOCAL_MACHINE Registry entry. These virtual folders and entry are stored with the user's files. The Registry itself—as well as the %SystemRoot%, and %ProgramFiles% folders—are not altered in any way, so that system files and the Registry are protected.

HACK 183: Don't Fear the Registry

V XP The Registry is the single best tool available for hacking Windows. Here's an introduction to how it's organized and how to use it.

If you haven't spent much time in the Registry, you can easily be cowed by it. At first glance, it's a maze of apparently incomprehensible settings. In fact, though, there's a method to the madness. The Registry is a hierarchical database of information that defines exactly how your system works, including virtually every part of Windows and its applications. Editing the Registry database is often the best way to hack Windows. In fact, it is the only way to make certain changes to the operating system.

Even if you've never used the Registry directly before, you've changed it without realizing it. Whenever you change a setting using the Control Panel, for example, a Registry change is made behind the scenes that puts that new setting into effect. The menus and dialog boxes you see in Windows are often little more than a visual front end to the Registry.

If you want to optimize Windows and master every part of it, you'll have to use the Registry. Windows contains so many different settings and customizations that it simply wasn't possible for Microsoft to build a graphical interface for every conceivable option. And many times it's easier, and you get more options when you edit the Registry instead of using the graphical Windows interface. You can use Windows without ever editing the Registry—many users do—but advanced users understand its power tool status.

The way to edit the Registry is by using the Registry Editor, also called RegEdit, which is shown in Figure 13-1.

Before you edit the Registry, though, first you should get a basic understanding of its structure.

Sometimes, power users like to jump in without reading the manual. The Registry is not the best place to experiment and learn as you go until you understand at least a little of what's going on. You could render your system useless and unrecoverable with just a few changes. So, we recommend making a backup [Hack #186] and reading at least most of this chapter first. You'll be glad later if you do this now.

Figure 13-1.
Controlling Registry settings by using the Registry Editor

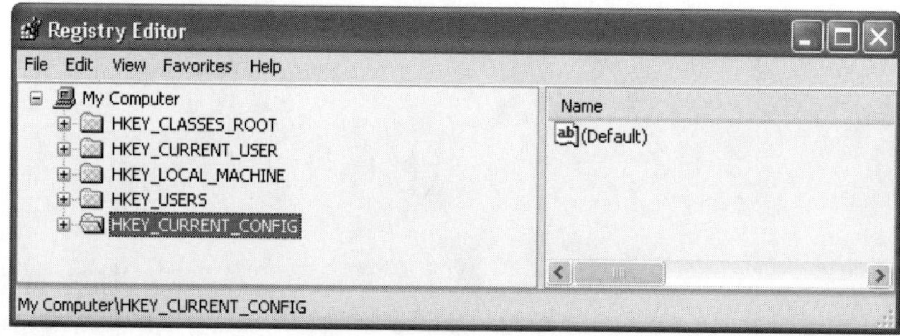

The Five Logical Registry Hives

The Registry has many thousands of settings; in fact, it often has tens of thousands of them. They are organized into five main Registry sections, called *Registry hives*. Think of each hive as a root directory. Each hive has a different purpose. When you start to delve into the Registry, you might notice that many of the settings seem to be exact duplicates of one another; in other words, the settings in one hive mirror the settings in another hive. In fact, frequently one set of settings is merely an alias (called a *symbolic link*) of another, so when you change those settings in one hive, the changes are made in both hives.

 The hives themselves are stored in the *C:\Windows\system32\config* and *C:\Documents and Settings* `username` (*C:\Users*`username` on Vista) directories.

Following are the five hives and what each does:

`HKEY_CLASSES_ROOT`

This hive contains information about file types, filename extensions, and similar information. It instructs Windows on how to handle every different file type and controls basic user interface options, such as double-clicking and context menus. This hive also includes class definitions (hence the word `CLASSES` in its name) of unique objects, such as file types or OLE objects. Frequently, classes associated with file types contain the `Shell` subkey, which defines actions, such as opening and printing, that can be taken with that file type.

`HKEY_CURRENT_USER`

This hive contains configuration information about the system setup of the user that is currently logged in to Windows. It controls the current user's desktop, as well as Windows' specific appearance and behavior for the current user. This hive also manages network connections and connections to devices such as printers, personal preferences such as screen colors, and security rights. Also included in this hive are Security Identifiers (SIDs), which uniquely identify users of the PC and which have information about each user's rights, settings, and preferences.

`HKEY_LOCAL_MACHINE`

This hive contains information about the computer itself, as well as the operating system. It includes specific details about all hardware, including keyboard, printer ports, storage—the entire hardware setup. In addition, it has information about security, installed software, system startup, drivers, services, and the machine's specific configuration.

`HKEY_USERS`

This hive contains information about every user profile on the system.

`HKEY_CURRENT_CONFIG`

This hive contains information about the current hardware configuration of the system, in the same way `HKEY_CURRENT_USER` contains information about the current user of the system.

Using Keys and Values

Each hive is at the top of the hierarchy, and underneath each hive are keys, which can in turn contain subkeys, and those subkeys can contain subkeys, and so on, organized in folderlike fashion, much like a hard drive.

Keys and subkeys contain a value, which controls a particular setting. For example, this key:

```
HKEY_CURRENT_USER\Control Panel\Mouse\DoubleClickSpeed
```

determines the amount of time between mouse clicks that must elapse before Windows won't consider it to be a double-click. To set the amount of time, you change the key's value. In this case, the default value is `500`, measured in milliseconds, and you can edit the Registry to change it to whatever value you want, as shown in Figure 13-2. You can also make the changes using the Mouse Properties dialog box (Start→Control Panel→Printers and Other Hardware→Mouse). When you make changes to that dialog box, the changes are in turn made in the Registry, which ultimately controls the setting. In essence, the dialog box is merely a convenient front end to the Registry.

A key can contain one or more values. Here are the six primary datatypes of values in the Registry:

`REG_SZ` *(string value)*
This datatype is easy to understand and edit because it is made up of plain text and numbers. It is one of the most common datatypes in the Registry. The value for `DoubleClickSpeed`, mentioned earlier in this hack, is of this type.

`REG_MULTI_SZ` *(string array value)*
This datatype contains several strings of plain text and numbers. The Registry Editor will let you edit these values, but it won't let you create them.

`REG_EXPAND_SZ` *(expanded string value)*
This datatype contains variables that Windows uses to point to the location of files. For example, to point to the location of the Luna theme file, the expanded string value in the Registry is `%SystemRoot%\resources\Themes\Luna.theme`.

Figure 13-2.
Editing a Registry key's value

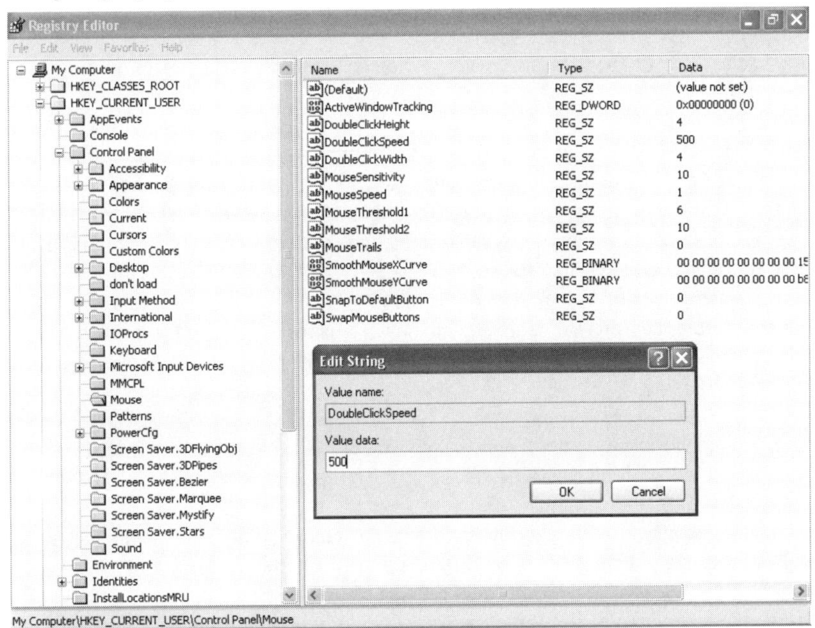

REG_BINARY *(binary value)*

This datatype is made up of binary data: *0*s and *1*s. Figure 13-3 shows a typical example of a binary value. As a general rule, you won't edit binary values; instead you'll edit string values because they're made up of text and numbers, as shown in Figure 13-4.

REG_DWORD *(DWORD values)*

This datatype is represented as a number. Sometimes a `0` turns on the key or a `1` turns off the key, though it can use other numbers as well. While you see and edit the value as a number, such as `456`, the Registry itself views the number as a hexadecimal number, `1C8`. Figure 13-5 shows a `DWORD` value being edited.

REG_QWORD *(QWORD values)*

This is like REG_DWORD, except that it can hold larger values. A DWORD holds 32 bits (D stands for double, and Q stands for quad), and a QWORD holds 64 bits.

Launching the Registry Editor

There's an upside and a downside to using the Registry Editor. The upside is that it's relatively simple to use. The downside is that it doesn't offer much functionality beyond basic Registry editing.

In some instances, when you make changes using the Registry, the changes take effect as soon as you exit the Registry. In other instances, they'll take effect only after you log out and then log back in. And, in yet other instances, they'll take effect only after you restart Windows.

To run the Registry Editor, select Start→Run (on XP) or Start→Start Search (Vista), type regedit, and press Enter (you can also type regedit at the Command Prompt). If this is the first time you've run the Registry Editor, it will open, highlighting the `HKEY_CURRENT_USER` hive as shown in Figure 13-6. If you've previously used the Registry Editor, it will highlight the last key you edited or the last place you were in the Registry.

You can browse through the Registry with the Registry Editor in the same way you browse through a hard disk using Windows Explorer. Clicking a + sign opens a key to reveal the next level down the hierarchy. Clicking a – sign closes the key.

The Registry can be several levels deep in keys and subkeys, so navigating it using a mouse can take a substantial amount of time. (Every time you open it, it jumps to the last-used key.) You can use shortcut keys, though, to more easily navigate through the Registry. The right-arrow key opens a Registry key to reveal subkeys; the left-arrow key closes a key and moves one level up in the key hierarchy. To jump to the next subkey that begins with a specific letter, press that letter on the keyboard.

You use the Registry Editor to edit existing keys and values, create new keys and values, or delete existing keys and values. Again, sometimes the changes take effect as soon as you make the change and exit the Registry Editor; other times, you'll have to reboot for them to take effect. Keep in mind that there is no Save button. When you modify a value, it changes right then and there. There is also no Undo button, so make your changes carefully.

If you want to edit a particular key, an even faster way to navigate is to use the Find command from the Edit menu. (You can also use the Find command by pressing Ctrl-F.) To find successive keys with the same value, press the F3 key.

To edit the data associated with a value, double-click the value in the right pane of the Registry Editor; a box appears that lets you edit the value, as shown in Figure 13-7.

When you're editing the Registry, it's often hard to tell what key you're editing because the Registry Editor doesn't highlight that key. Instead, it shows only an open folder icon next to it, but it's easy to miss that icon. Check the status bar at the bottom of the Registry Editor; it should display the key you're editing. If it doesn't, choose View→Status Bar from the Registry Editor menu.

Figure 13-3.
Binary values

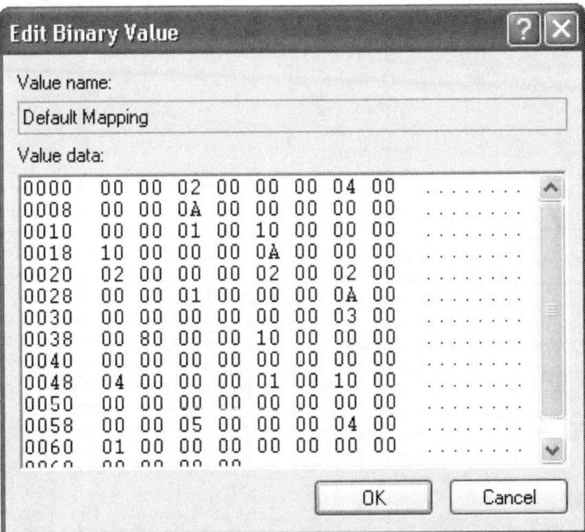

Figure 13-4.
Editing string values

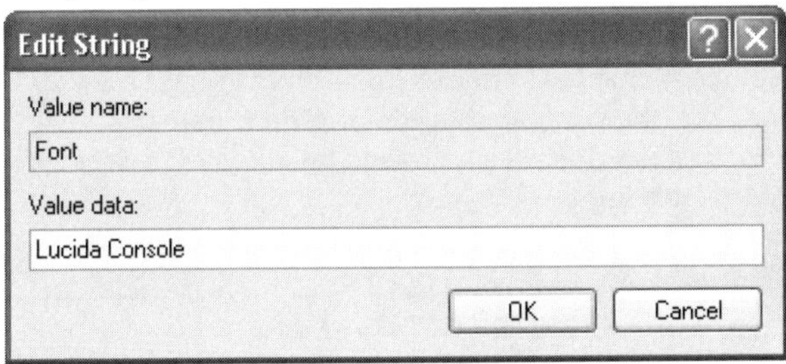

Figure 13-5.
Editing DWORD values

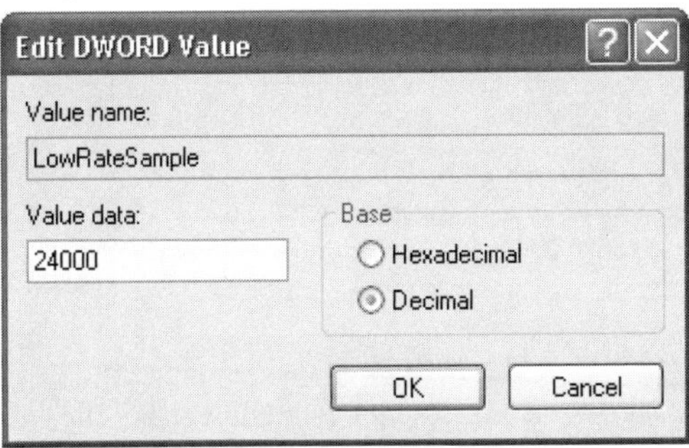

Figure 13-6.
Using the Registry Editor for the first time

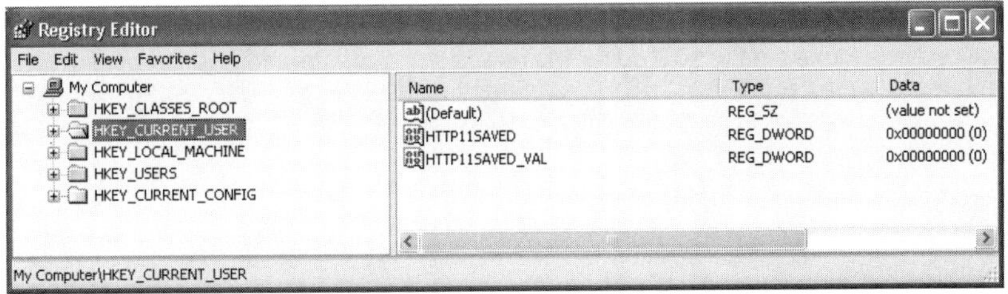

Figure 13-7.
Editing a value

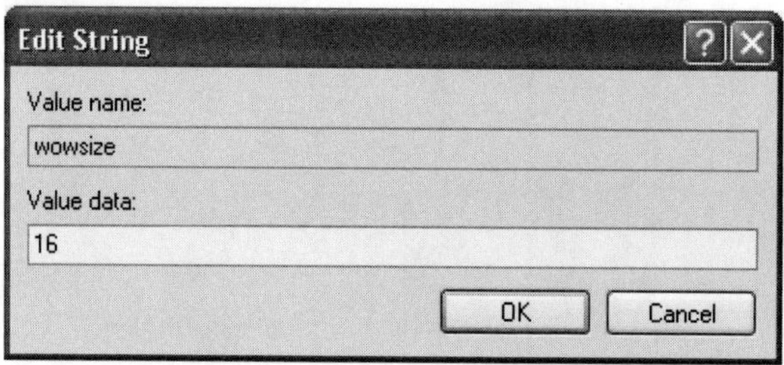

To rename a key or value, select it, and choose Edit→Rename from the menu. You can also right-click the key and choose Edit→Rename.

Adding and Deleting Keys and Values

Editing the Registry often requires that you add and delete keys and values. To add a new key, select the new key's parent key in the left pane. Then, choose Edit→New→Key from the menu. Type in the new key's name. You can also right-click the new key's parent key and choose Edit→New→Key. To delete a key, select it, and press the Delete key.

Very often, you need to add values to a key for its changes to take effect. To add a value to a key, select the key's parent key in the left pane. From the menu, choose Edit→New, and from the submenu, select the type of value you want to create. I've already covered the six types of values you can create; as a reminder, they're detailed in Table 9-1.

Table 13-1. Values you'll encounter in the Registry

VALUE NAME	REGISTRY DATATYPE
String value	`REG_SZ`
Binary value	`REG_BINARY`
32-bit value	`REG_DWORD`
64-bit value	`REG_QWORD`
String array value	`REG_MULTI_SZ`
Expandable string value	`REG_EXPAND_SZ`

To create a new value, type in the name of the new value, and press Enter. Press Enter again. The Edit String dialog box appears, as shown in Figure 13-7. Enter your data, and press Enter.

See Also

- For an excellent collection of Registry hacks, go to the Registry Guide for Windows at www.winguides.com/registry. Make sure to sign up for the newsletter that offers Registry advice and hacks.

HACK 184: Hack Away at the Registry

V XP Here are eight great hacks that use the Registry to do their magic.

You'll find dozens of Registry hacks sprinkled throughout this book, but to give you a sense of the breadth of the kinds of hacks you can accomplish using the Registry, I've included a wide-ranging sample of Registry hacks here as well.

Automatically Close Programs at Shutdown

XP When you shut down Windows, if you have any programs running you'll get a message box warning you that a program is still running. Then you have to close the program and tell Windows again to shut down. It's a fairly pointless warning—better yet would be if Windows automatically killed the programs without issuing the warning. That way, you wouldn't get error messages and wouldn't have to close each individual application before shutting down your computer. Beware, though; if you forcibly close an application that has unsaved changes (such as a word processor), you'll lose all your work.

To have Windows automatically close programs at shutdown, run the Registry Editor, and go to `HKEY_CURRENT_USER\Control Panel\Desktop`. Edit the `AutoEndTasks` key so that is has a value of `1`. If the key doesn't exist, create it as a `DWORD` value and give it the value of `1`. To disable it, either delete the key, or set the value to `0`.

Disable Shutdown

V XP There might be times when you want to make sure XP can't be inadvertently shut down. You can use a Registry hack to disable the normal shutdown. Run the Registry Editor, and go to `HKEY_CURRENT_USER\Software\Microsoft\Windows\CurrentVersion\Policies\Explorer`. (In Vista, you may need to create the Explorer key.) Create a new `DWORD` value named `NoClose` with a data value of `1`. Exit the Registry, and reboot for the change to take effect. You won't be able to shut down Windows in the normal manner from now on; you'll have to run Task Manager by pressing Ctrl-Alt-Del or right-clicking the toolbar, choosing Task Manager, and then using the Task Manager's Shut Down menu to close Windows. If you want to reenable normal shutdowns, delete the `NoClose` value. Under Vista, this setting may not take effect until you shut down and start Windows back up.

Change the Names of the Registered User and Company

V XP When you install Windows or when it comes factory-fresh on a PC, a username and company name are entered as the owner of the system. And that's the way it stays, like it or not. But a Registry hack will let you change both. Run the Registry Editor, go to `HKEY_LOCAL_MACHINE\SOFTWARE\Microsoft\Windows NT\CurrentVersion`, and look for the values `RegisteredOwner` and `RegisteredOrganization`. Edit their value data to whatever username and company name you want.

Change the Amount of Time Before Programs Time Out

V XP When an application hangs and no longer responds, and you click the End Task command button in Task Manager, Windows displays a dialog that prompts you to kill the application or wait a while longer. By default, the dialog appears after the application hasn't responded for five seconds.

This can cause problems. For example, if a program is doing heavy-duty calculations in the background, it won't respond until the calculation is done, so the operating system will report that the application is hung, even though it isn't. You can use a Registry hack to increase or decrease the amount of time it takes before Windows reports that the program has hung.

Run the Registry Editor, and go to HKEY_CURRENT_USER\Control Panel\Desktop. Select the HungAppTimeout entry, and put in a new value (in milliseconds) If the entry does not exist, create it as a DWORD value. The default is 5000. Exit the Registry. You might need to reboot for the new setting to take effect. Try increasing the number in increments of 1,000 until you find a number that works.

Disable the Disk Cleanup Warning

V XP If your hard disk has what Windows decides is too little space left on it, the operating system will pop up a warning and recommend that you run Disk Cleanup. But you might be like me and not want a virtual nanny nagging you to clean up your mess. You can turn off the warning with a Registry hack. Run the Registry Editor, and go to HKEY_CURRENT_USER\Software\Microsoft\Windows\CurrentVersion\Policies\Explorer. (In Vista, you may need to create the Explorer key.) Create a DWORD value called NoLowDiskSpaceChecks and give it a value of 1. Exit the Registry, and reboot. You can also do this on XP by using Tweak UI **[Hack #19]**.

Change the Default Location for Installing Programs

V XP Windows uses the *C:\Program Files* directory as the default base directory into which new programs are installed. However, you can change the default installation drive and/or directory by using a Registry hack. Run the Registry Editor, and go to HKEY_LOCAL_MACHINE\SOFTWARE\Microsoft\Windows\CurrentVersion. Look for the value named ProgramFilesDir. By default, the value will be C:\Program Files. Edit the value to any valid drive or folder; Windows will use that new location as the default installation directory for new programs.

Allow Laptops to Enter Power-Saving State

XP Some laptops' processors might not be able to enter their power-saving state, even when they're idle, because USB polling fools the processor into thinking the laptop is active. Your system polls your USB ports once every millisecond to see whether a device is present. So, even if a device isn't present, it continues polling. The problem is that some laptop processors won't go into their power-saving state because the constant polling makes them think the laptop is active.

With a Registry hack, you can increase the polling interval from the default of one millisecond, letting the processor enter its power-saving state. Run the Registry Editor, and go to HKEY_LOCAL_MACHINE\System\CurrentControlSet\Control\Class\{36FC9E60-C465-11CF-8056-444553540000}\0000. Create the new DWORD value IdleEnable, and set the data value to a number between 2 and 5. This will set the polling interval in milliseconds. If there are additional subkeys for HKEY_LOCAL_MACHINE\System\CurrentControlSet\Control\Class\{36FC9E60-C465-11CF-8056-444553540000} (such as 0001, 0002, etc.), repeat the procedure, and create the IdleEnable DWORD in each of them. Exit the Registry. You might need to reboot for the new setting to go into effect. You also might need to try several different values until you find one that works.

Change the Size of Your Mouse and Keyboard Buffer

V XP If you get an error message telling you that you have an overflow in your mouse buffer or keyboard buffer, it means the buffer isn't large enough, and you need to increase its size. To increase your mouse buffer, run the Registry Editor, go to HKEY_LOCAL_MACHINE\SYSTEM\CurrentControlSet\Services\Mouclass\Parameters, and find the MouseDataQueueSize subkey. The default setting is 100 (64 hex). Increase the decimal number to increase the size of the buffer; then exit the Registry and reboot. You might need to try several different settings until you find the right one.

To increase the keyboard buffer, look for the KeyboardDataQueueSize subkey in HKEY_LOCAL_MACHINE\SYSTEM\CurrentControlSet\Services\Kbdclass\Parameters. The default setting is 100 (64 hex). Increase the number to increase the size of the buffer; then exit the Registry and reboot. Again, you might need to try several different settings until you find the right one.

HACK 185: Safely Edit the Registry Using .reg Files

V XP Forgo the dangers and inconvenience of editing the Registry directly. Instead, use plain-text .reg files.

When you're editing the Registry, it's easy to make small errors that cause major repercussions. You might inadvertently edit the wrong key, put in a wrong value, or—given how confusing the Registry is—make changes without realizing it. The Registry is unforgiving when this happens. It doesn't keep a backup, so you're stuck with the new setting unless you've made backups yourself [Hack #186].

When you edit the Registry directly, you're also apt to make errors if you're making multiple changes because you have no chance to look at all the changes you're making at once.

There's a way to solve both problems: use *.reg* files to edit the Registry. These are plain ASCII text files you can create or read with Notepad or any text editor, and merge into the Registry to make changes. You can create a *.reg* file from scratch, or you can export it from a portion of the Registry, edit it with Notepad or another text editor, and then merge it back into the Registry. You'll find that *.reg* files are particularly useful if you're going to make changes to the Registry of several computers or if you are leery about editing the Registry directly.

You should also consider creating *.reg* files to copy the parts of the Registry you're about to edit using the Registry Editor [Hack #183]. Then, if you make a mistake with the Registry Editor, you can revert to the previous version of the Registry by merging the *.reg* file into the Registry. They're also useful if you need to do search-and-replace operations on parts of the Registry because the Registry Editor doesn't include search-and-replace functionality. You can do the search-and-replace operation in your text editor and then merge the edited file back into the Registry.

To create a *.reg* file from an existing portion of the Registry, run the Registry Editor, highlight the key or portion of the Registry you want to export, and choose File→Export. Choose a name and location for the file. You can export an individual key, a branch of the Registry, a hive, or the entire Registry. Here is an example of a *.reg* file exported from the `HKEY_CURRENT_USER\Control Panel\Accessibility` branch:

```
Windows Registry Editor Version 5.00

[HKEY_CURRENT_USER\Control Panel\Accessibility]
"MessageDuration"=dword:00000005
"MinimumHitRadius"=dword:00000000

[HKEY_CURRENT_USER\Control Panel\Accessibility\AudioDescription]
"Locale"=""
"On"="0"

[HKEY_CURRENT_USER\Control Panel\Accessibility\Blind Access]
"On"="0"

[HKEY_CURRENT_USER\Control Panel\Accessibility\HighContrast]
"Flags"="126"
"High Contrast Scheme"=""
"Previous High Contrast Scheme MUI Value"=""

[HKEY_CURRENT_USER\Control Panel\Accessibility\Keyboard Preference]
"On"="0"

[HKEY_CURRENT_USER\Control Panel\Accessibility\Keyboard Response]
"AutoRepeatDelay"="1000"
```

```
"AutoRepeatRate"="500"
"BounceTime"="0"
"DelayBeforeAcceptance"="1000"
"Flags"="126"
"Last BounceKey Setting"=dword:00000000
"Last Valid Delay"=dword:00000000
"Last Valid Repeat"=dword:00000000
"Last Valid Wait"=dword:000003e8

[HKEY_CURRENT_USER\Control Panel\Accessibility\MouseKeys]
"Flags"="62"
"MaximumSpeed"="80"
"TimeToMaximumSpeed"="3000"

[HKEY_CURRENT_USER\Control Panel\Accessibility\On]
"On"=dword:00000000
"Locale"=dword:00000000

[HKEY_CURRENT_USER\Control Panel\Accessibility\ShowSounds]
"On"="0"

[HKEY_CURRENT_USER\Control Panel\Accessibility\SoundSentry]
"Flags"="2"
"FSTextEffect"="0"
"WindowsEffect"="1"
"TextEffect"="0"

[HKEY_CURRENT_USER\Control Panel\Accessibility\StickyKeys]
"Flags"="510"

[HKEY_CURRENT_USER\Control Panel\Accessibility\TimeOut]
"Flags"="2"
"TimeToWait"="300000"

[HKEY_CURRENT_USER\Control Panel\Accessibility\ToggleKeys]
"Flags"="62"
```

Edit a *.reg* file as you would any other text file. As you can see, the first line of the *.reg* file starts with `Windows Registry Editor Version 5.00`. Don't change this; Windows uses it to confirm that the file does in fact contain Registry information. Previous versions of Windows have a different first line; for Windows 95/98/Me and Windows NT 4.0, the first line reads either `REGEDIT4` or `Registry Editor 4`.

The names of Registry subkeys are surrounded by brackets, and they include the full pathname to the subkey, such as `[HKEY_CURRENT_USER\Control Panel\Accessibility\Keyboard Response]`. Following each subkey are the subkey values and data. Values and data are both surrounded by quotation marks. Here is the full section of a subkey, along with its associated values and data:

```
[HKEY_LOCAL_MACHINE\SYSTEM\CurrentControlSet\Services\mouclass]
"DisplayName"="Mouse Class Driver"
"Group"="Pointer Class"
"ImagePath"=hex(2):73,00,79,00,73,00,74,00,65,00,6d,00,33,00,32,00,5c,00,44,00,\
  52,00,49,00,56,00,45,00,52,00,53,00,5c,00,6d,00,6f,00,75,00,63,00,6c,00,61,\
  00,73,00,73,00,2e,00,73,00,79,00,73,00,00,00
"ErrorControl"=dword:00000001
"Start"=dword:00000001
"Type"=dword:00000001
"Tag"=dword:00000002
```

```
[HKEY_LOCAL_MACHINE\SYSTEM\CurrentControlSet\Services\mouclass\Enum]
"0"="Root\\RDP_MOU\\0000"
"Count"=dword:00000002
"NextInstance"=dword:00000002
"1"="ACPI\\PNP0F13\\4&25ee97c0&0"
```

As you can see, quotes surround data for `String` values. `DWORD` values, however, are preceded by `dword:` and don't have quotes surrounding them. Similarly, binary values are preceded by `hex:` and don't have quotes surrounding them.

Edit the value and data, and save the file. When you've made your changes, import the file back into the Registry by choosing File→Import in the Registry Editor and opening the file. An even easier way to import it is to double-click the file. Windows will ask whether you want to import it; when you answer yes, Windows will import it and make the changes to the Registry. This is somewhat counterintuitive and can be confusing; at first you might think double-clicking a *.reg* file will open it for editing. But it won't; it will merge it into the Registry. To edit a *.reg* file, open Notepad or another text editor, and then open the *.reg* file. Alternatively, you can right-click the *.reg* file and choose Edit.

 Because double-clicking a file merges it back into the Registry, it's easy to mistakenly make Registry changes when you really just want to edit a *.reg* file. I explain how you can protect yourself against this kind of mistake later in this hack.

Delete Registry Keys and Values Using .reg Files

You can use a *.reg* file not just to create new keys or values or to modify existing ones, but also to delete keys and values. To delete a key with a *.reg* file, put a minus sign in front of the key name, inside the bracket, like this:

```
[-HKEY_CURRENT_USER\Control Panel\Accessibility\Keyboard Response]
```

When you import the *.reg* file, that key will be deleted. Keep in mind that you won't be able to delete a key this way unless all its subkeys have been deleted first, so you'll have to delete them first.

To delete a key's value using a *.reg* file, put a minus sign after the equals sign in the *.reg* file:

```
"BounceTime"=-
```

When you import this into the Registry, the value will be deleted but the key will still stay intact.

Protect the Registry by Changing the Default Action for .reg Files

As mentioned earlier in this hack, when you double-click a *.reg* file, the file doesn't open for editing; instead, it gets merged directly into the Registry. This can cause serious problems since most of us are used to double-clicking to open files in Windows. But the file will end up merging into the Registry and making Registry changes you didn't want to make.

To solve the problem, change the default action so that a *.reg* file is opened for editing in Notepad rather than merged when you double-click it. In XP, go to Windows Explorer, choose Tools→Folder Options→File Types to open the File Types dialog box. Highlight the REG entry, and click Advanced. Highlight the Edit action, and click Set Default. The Edit action should turn bold. Click OK. In Vista, click Start→Default Programs, then select "Associate a file type or protocol with a program", locate *.reg* in the list, and double-click it. Click Browse to locate *C:\Windows\system32\notepad.exe*, and select it as the default for *.reg* files.

Change the Default Editor for .reg Files

Notepad is the default editor for editing *.reg* files, but if you have another text editor you'd rather use you can force that to be the default instead. First, follow the directions from the previous section to open the File Types dialog box, and highlight the REG entry's Edit action. Then, click the Edit button, and type in the full path and filename of the text editor you want to use to edit *.reg* files, followed by %1—for example:

```
C:\Program Files\TextPad 4\TextPad.exe %1
```

Then click OK twice. In Vista, follow the same instructions given for *notepad.exe*, but select your preferred text editor instead.

 Never use a word processor such as Word to edit *.reg* files (unless you *make sure* to save it as a plain-text file from within the word processor!). Word processors add extra codes that the Registry can't understand. Always use a text editor such as Notepad or WordPad.

HACK 186: Better Registry Backups

V XP Avert disaster by backing up the Registry so that you'll always be able to revert to a clean copy.

The Registry is unforgiving; once you make a change to it, the change is permanent. There is no Undo. To get the Registry back to the way you want it, you'll have to remember and revert the often arcane and complicated changes you make—if you can. And, unlike most Windows applications, the Registry Editor doesn't ask you whether you want to save your changes. Changes happen instantly. To paraphrase F. Scott Fitzgerald, there are no second acts when you edit the Registry.

Because of this, you should take precautions to keep your Registry safe and ensure that you can restore it to its previous safe settings whenever you want to. The best way to do that is to back up your Registry before you edit it. You should make copies of your Registry not only to protect against accidentally doing damage while you're editing it, but also to ensure that you can restore your system in the event of a system crash.

Here are the best ways to back up your Registry:

System Restore
One of the simplest ways to back up and restore the Registry is by using System Restore. System Restore creates a snapshot of your entire system, including the Registry, and lets you revert your system to that snapshot. To use System Restore, before editing the Registry choose Start→Control Panel→Performance and Maintenance→System Restore (on Vista, choose Control Panel→System and Maintenance→System→System Protection→Create) and then follow the wizard to create a restore point. If you want to restore the Registry to its preedited state after you edit it, use the same wizard to do so (on Vista, click System Restore instead of clicking Create).

Backup utility
You can also use the Windows Backup utility to back up and restore the Registry.

 By default, the Backup program is installed in XP Professional but not XP Home Edition. If you have the Home Edition, you must install Backup manually. For more on backup strategies, see Chapter 9.

Run the Backup utility by choosing Start→All Programs→Accessories→System Tools→Backup (on Vista, choose Control Panel→System and Maintenance→Back up your computer).

On XP, if you use the Backup Wizard, choose "Only back up the System State data" on the What to Back Up screen. Then, follow the Wizard's directions. It will back up the Registry and other system files, including files used to boot XP. If you don't use the Backup Wizard, click the Backup tab in the Backup utility, check the box next to System State, and then click Start Backup. When you want to restore your system, run the Backup utility. Click Restore and Manage Media→Start Restore.

Registry Editor

You can also use the Registry Editor to back up the Registry. This is probably the easiest way to back up the Registry, but it won't back up two Registry keys: the `SAM` and `Security` keys that control password policies, user rights, and related information. Unless you have a complex system with many users, though, these keys are not absolutely vital.

Run the Registry Editor by typing **`Regedit`** in the Run box or a command prompt and pressing Enter. Highlight My Computer. If you highlight an individual Registry hive instead, only that hive will be backed up. Next, choose File→Export. The Export Registry File dialog box appears, as shown in Figure 13-8. Give the file a name, choose a location, and save it. For safety's sake, also make backups to another machine and to a CD.

To restore the Registry, run the Registry Editor, choose File→Import, and then import the file.

HACK 187: Track and Restore Registry Changes

V XP Protect your Registry and track changes to it made by programs with this downloadable goodie.

An excellent way to keep your Registry safe is to use RegSpy, which watches the changes programs make to the Registry, tracks and reports on those changes, and then lets you restore your Registry or use your knowledge about the changes the program makes to fine-tune the way the program runs. One of the program's more useful features is the way it lets you undo changes on a program-by-program basis by building a `RollBack` script for that program. When you roll back the Registry, you'll roll back changes made only by that one program, not by any others. This is far superior to Windows' System Restore because System Restore makes changes en masse; there's no way to use it to save some changes and delete others.

My favorite RegSpy feature is SnapShots, which creates files in JavaScript or Visual Basic format, and lets you review and repeat all the Registry changes that took place, step by step. That way, you can get a better understanding of the changes programs make during the installation process, and you can better undo or customize any changes made. It's also a great way to learn more about the Registry; watching the changes made by several different programs gives you insight into the Registry's inner workings.

Figure 13-8.
Using the Export Registry File screen to back up the Registry

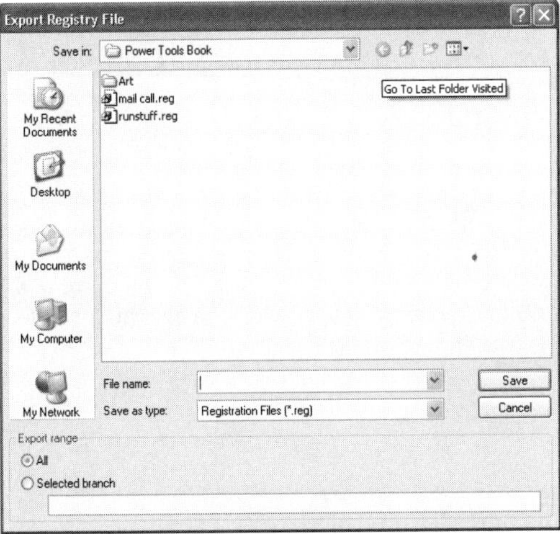

RegSpy is shareware and free to try, but it costs $19.95 if you continue to use it. It's available from www.utils32.com/regspy.htm. At the time of this writing, it did not list support for Vista, so you may need to check out some of the similar utilities listed next.

See Also

- Registry First Aid (shareware from www.rosecitysoftware.com) cleans up the Registry by deleting old and unneeded Registry entries that clog up your system. Registry First Aid supports Vista.
- Registry Commander (www.aezay.dk/aezay/regcmd) is a free utility that gives you many features that the Registry Editor leaves out, such as a history list that lets you jump to recently edited keys, the ability to copy and paste entire keys and bookmark keys, and advanced search tools.
- Resplendent Registrar (www.resplendence.com) is shareware that includes even more tools that the Registry Editor leaves out, such as search-and-replace, a Registry defragmenter to reclaim wasted disk space, an activity monitor that tracks all Registry activity, and a tool that lets you compare the contents of two Registry keys. Resplendent Registrar supports Vista, as well.

HACK 188: Hack Away at Windows with the Group Policy Editor

V XP This tool offers simple but powerful ways to hack Windows.

The Group Policy Editor, shown in Figure 13-9, was primarily designed for system administrators on networks, but is also a powerful tool for single machines as well, not only for creating policies for every user of the single computer but also for offering access to settings and controls not otherwise accessible. Like the Registry, it works in both Windows Vista and Windows XP. It is not available in the Home editions of XP or Vista. To start the Group Policy Editor, click Start→Run (Start→Start Search in Vista), type gpedit.msc, and press Enter.

The Group Policy Editor's options can be found in a handful of folders in (sometimes) plain English, such as "Hide Add New Programs Page" and "Turn off Windows Sidebar". (And there are obscure ones as well, such as "User Group Policy loopback processing mode".)

Be very careful when using the Group Policy Editor. It makes it possible to restrict or reconfigure almost every security setting on your computer, so it's very easy to break something. And there's no undo feature.

There are two major folders in the Group Policy Editor: Computer Configuration and User Configuration. Computer Configuration lets you set policies computer-wide (or network-wide), while User Configuration lets you set them for individual users. To some extent, the folders mirror one another, with the same subfolders and settings in each. However, there are some settings available only in Computer Configuration, and others available only in User Configuration.

To change a setting, double-click it, and select Enabled or Disabled, as you can see in Figure 13-10. There are plenty of things you can do with the Group Policy Editor; here are a few of the more entertaining and useful ones:

Pretty-Up Internet Explorer

Several settings in this subfolder let you do things you most likely never thought possible: change the Internet Explorer title bar, change the Internet Explorer logo, and change the background of the Internet Explorer toolbar. Go to *User Configuration\Windows Settings\Internet Explorer Maintenance\Browser User Interface,* and double-click the Browser Title entry to change the IE title bar; the Custom Logo and Animated Bitmaps entry to change the IE logo and logo animation; and the Browser Toolbar Customization to change the background of the IE toolbar. Note that when you change the logo and toolbar background, you'll have to create or find suitable graphics.

Choose Places for your Places Bar

Go to *User Configuration\Administrative Templates\Windows Components\Windows Explorer\ Common Open File Dialog*, and double-click the Items Displayed in Places Bar option. Click Enabled, and then type the full pathnames of up to five folders on your hard disk. Click OK, and these folders will appear in the gray "Places" bar on the left side of most File→Open and File→Save dialog boxes.

There aren't any Browse buttons in this dialog, but you can specify folder paths without typing by opening Windows Explorer, navigating to the folders you want, highlighting the text in the Address bar, copying it, and pasting the text into the Group Policy Editor's dialog box. Alternatively, you can use the Places Bar in Microsoft Office file dialogs to customize your Places Bar. Doing that, of course, will affect only Office applications.

Turn off CD/DVD Autoplay

Go to *Computer Configuration\Administrative Templates\Windows Components\AutoPlay Policies*, and double-click the Turn off Autoplay option on the right. If you enable this option, Windows will no longer play CDs and DVDs automatically when you insert them.

Disable User Tracking

Go to *User Configuration\Administrative Templates\Start Menu and Taskbar*, double-click the "Turn off user tracking" entry to the right, and click Enabled. This will stop Windows from recording every program you run, every document you open, and every folder path you view, thus hobbling such features as "personalized" menus and the Recent Documents menu.

Figure 13-9.
The Group Policy Editor gives you complete administrator's access to Windows' deepest settings

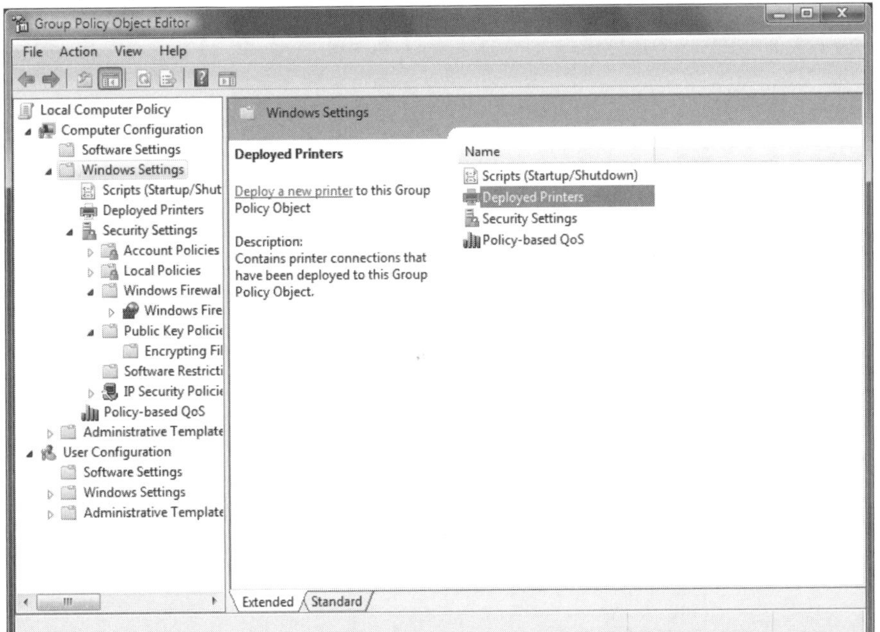

Figure 13-10.
Change settings from this screen

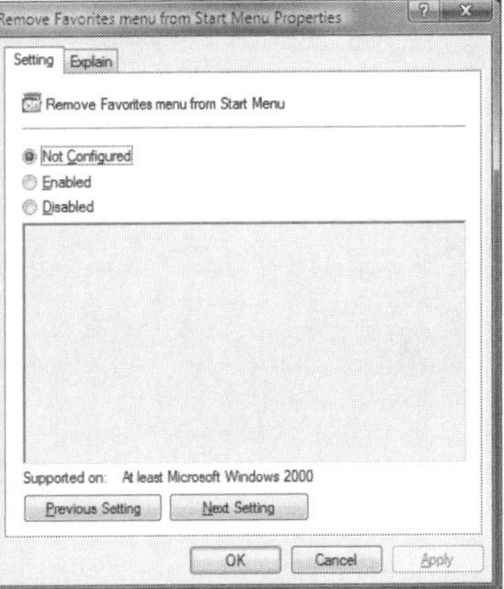

CREDITS

About the Author

Preston Gralla is the author of nearly 40 books, including O'Reilly's *Windows Vista in a Nutshell*, *Windows XP Hacks*, 2nd Edition, and *Windows Vista Pocket Reference*. He is a contributing editor for *Computerworld*, and has written about technology for many national magazines and newspapers, including *The Los Angeles Times*, *USA Today*, the *Dallas Morning News* (where he was a technology columnist), *PC World*, *PC Magazine*, and many others.

Gralla's books have been translated into 20 languages, and sold multiple hundreds of thousands of copies worldwide. His commentaries about technology have been featured on National Public Radio's *All Things Considered*, and he has won the award for the Best Feature in a Computer Publication from the Computer Press Association. Under his editorship, *PC/Computing* was a finalist for General Excellence from the National Magazine Awards.

He has written about technology since the dawn of the PC age, and was the founding editor of *PC Week*; a founder, then editor, then editorial director of *PC/Computing*; and executive editor for ZDNet and CNet. A well-known technology expert, Gralla has made numerous TV and radio appearances, including on the *CBS Early Show*, *CNN*, *MSNBC*, *ABC's World News Now*, and many others. He lives in Cambridge, MA with his wife and two children.

Contributors

Jim Aspinwall is the author of *PC Hacks*, from O'Reilly, and manages the global configuration and deployment of over 4000 PCs and SMS worldwide. He's authored multiple books and PC support articles and columns for CNet and McGraw-Hill. In his spare time he works on a number of amateur radio data and voice projects for disaster communications services. You may contact him at: *hacks@raisin.com.*

Paul Bausch Paul Bausch is a co-creator of the weblog software Blogger, maintains a directory of Oregon-based weblogs at ORblogs.com, and has contributed several books to O'Reilly's Hacks series. Bausch currently works behind the scenes at the community weblog Metafilter.com, and has his own infrequently updated blog at onfocus.com.

Justin Blanton (justinblanton.com) has a B.S. in computer engineering and is currently attending law school in Silicon Valley, where he is focusing on intellectual property law, and will likely practice both patent prosecution and litigation. Much of his "free time" is spent writing about various things on his web site, including Mac OS X, mobile phones and other gadgets, general tips and tricks for the Movable Type CMS, and life in general.

Tara Calishain is the creator of the site, ResearchBuzz. She is an expert on Internet search engines and how they can be used effectively in business situations.

Eric Cloninger was one of the original contributors to the Palm OS, working on tools for software developers. After 15 years in the Real World, Cloninger decided that living in a small town in Oklahoma wasn't so bad after all. When he's not writing software, he enjoys spending time with his family, tinkering with his John Deere tractor, and watching tornadoes roll across the plains. While he doesn't miss the traffic in the Big City, he does occasionally yearn for a Spicy Tuna Roll.

Robert Cox is the founder of the former web site www.zuney.net, which was a source of news, how-to articles, and forum posts about the Zune.

Tim Coyle enjoys writing on his blog The F-Stop Blues (www.fstop-blues.com) about digital media including Windows Media Center, digital photography, and other new and interesting technology. He also has an interest in hardware hacking and robotics and plans on building some cool robots this year. His dream is to operate a low power community radio station and bring understandable technology to the masses. He resides in Portland, ME with his wonderful wife Nicky.

Rael Dornfest is founder and CEO of Portland, Oregon-based Values of n. Dornfest leads the Values of n charge with passion, unearthly creativity, and a repertoire of puns and jokes—some of which are actually good. Prior to founding Values of n, he was O'Reilly's chief technical officer, program chair for the O'Reilly Emerging Technology Conference (which he continues to chair), series editor of the bestselling Hacks book series, and instigator of O'Reilly's Rough Cuts early access program. He built Meerkat, the first web-based feed aggregator, was champion and co-author of the RSS 1.0 specification, and has written and contributed to six O'Reilly books. His programmatic pride and joy is the nimble, open source blogging application Blosxom, the principles of which you'll find in the Values of n philosophy and embodied in Stikkit: Little yellow notes that think.

Kevin Farnham is owner of a small consulting and publishing company, Lyra Technical Systems, Inc. He works on software engineering projects involving mathematical modeling, simulation, and scientific data acquisition, analysis, and presentation. Farnham is also community manager of the ThreadingBuildingBlocks.org open source project. He is an active blogger, writes technology articles, and is co-author of the book *MySpace Safety: 51 Tips for Teens and Parents*.

Jim Foley, a.k.a. The Elder Geek (www.theeldergeek.com), owns and operates a small consulting and web design firm in Cambridge, N.Y., that specializes in the integration of Windows XP technology into home and business environments. He is also the creator and owner of The Elder Geek on Windows XP, a web site that strives to provide relevant information related to Windows XP, including a notification service and Windows XP forum to keep readers informed of the latest XP tips, troubleshooting, and update developments.

Scott Fullam has been hacking hardware since he was 10 years old with his first RadioShack 100-in-1 electronic kit. He built an "intruder" alarm to keep his sister out of his room. Fullam attended MIT earning bachelors and masters degrees in electrical engineering and computer science. While an undergraduate he built a "shower detection" system so that he could see if the community shower was in use. After graduating from MIT, he designed children's toys and built close to 50 prototypes in 2 years. He then went to work at Apple Computer in the Advanced Technology Group designing digital still cameras. In 1995, Fullam co-founded PocketScience, which develops revolutionary mobile e-mail communications products and services. As the chief technology officer, Fullam personally developed all of the algorithms for the company's products. He now works as an independent consultant helping consumer electronics companies design high quality products. Never satisfied with how the consumer electronics products he owns work, he often takes them apart and enhances their capabilities.

Brian Jepson is an editor for Maker Media, the division of O'Reilly Media, Inc. that publishes MAKE Magazine and the Hacks series of books. He's also a volunteer system administrator and all-around geek for AS220, a non-profit arts center in Providence, Rhode Island. AS220 gives Rhode Island artists uncensored and unjuried forums for their work. These forums include galleries, performance space, and publications. Jepson sees to it that technology, especially free software, supports that mission.

Chris Kohler is a video game journalist and editor who has written for several publications in the past decade, including *Wired*, *Animerica* magazine, and *Nintendo Official Magazine UK*. After graduating from Tufts University with a degree in Japanese, Kohler attended Kyoto Seika University on a Fulbright Fellowship, and completed major research for a book tentatively titled *Super Mario Nation: The Cinematic Japanese Video Game*. At Tufts, he taught a for-credit undergraduate course titled "A History of Video Games" and continues to study Japanese at an advanced level.

Wei-Meng Lee (weimenglee@learn2develop.net) is a technologist and founder of Developer Learning Solutions (www.learn2develop.net), a technology company specializing in hands-on training of the latest Microsoft technologies. Lee speaks regularly at international conferences and has authored and coauthored numerous books on .NET, XML, and wireless technologies, including *ASP.NET 2.0: A Developer's Notebook* and the *.NET Compact Framework Pocket Guide* (both from O'Reilly).

Margaret Levine Young has coauthored many books, including *The Internet for Dummies*, *Windows XP: The Complete Reference*, *UNIX for Dummies*, *Internet: The Complete Reference*, and *Poor Richard's Building Online Community*. She has a bachelor's degree in computer science from Yale and lives in Vermont.

Mark Lyon (marklyon.org) is the creator of the Google Gmail Loader. A former programmer for the U.S. Army Corps of Engineers, he gave up his aspirations of programming greatness after an unsuccessful interview at Google. He is now a law student at Mississippi College in Jackson and plans to practice intellectual property and technology law. In his spare time, he writes novel but mediocre software in whatever language strikes his fancy.

John Moscarillo worked with Microsoft's Sidebar team to deliver the default gadgets that are currently installed with Vista. He currently works with 3Tier, an environmental forecasting company, delivering their next generation of web applications. He hacks at sidebar gadgets when he's not spending time with his wife and two children in Seattle.

Matt Paprocki has played video games since he was five, but he began writing about them back in 1999 with his own fanzine titled "Gaming Source". Once the cost became too much of a burden, he found the web site Digital Press (www.digitpress.com) and has been writing reviews for them ever since. His current total is over 500, covering a variety of consoles. He also editorializes on the games industry at his blog www.breakingwindows.com. His articles have been published in *G-Fan* magazine as well as the *Toledo City Paper*.

Kyle Rankin is a system administrator for Quinstreet, Inc., the current president of the North Bay Linux Users Group, and the author of Knoppix Hacks, Knoppix Pocket Reference, Linux Multimedia Hacks, and Ubuntu Hacks. Kyle has been using Linux in one form or another since early 1998. In his free time he does pretty much the same thing he does at work—works with Linux.

RapidRepair.com is dedicated to the service, repair, and modification of all iPod & Zune models.

Marco Shaw has been working with computers for about ten years, from working in a call center environment, to being a system administrator. These days, he likes playing with Windows PowerShell. You can check out his Windows PowerShell blog at marcoshaw.blogspot.com. He can be contacted at *marco.shaw@gmail.com*.

Andrew Sheppard is the author of *Skype Hacks* from O'Reilly. After earning a first-class honor's degree in astrophysics, he made the mistake of going on to earn higher degrees: a master's in astronomical technology at Edinburgh University (UK) and a master's in business administration at the London Business School (UK). This period of time and that which followed was punctuated with work as a scientific researcher at Oxford University, as a software developer, and later, as a "Rocket Scientist" at Bankers Trust Company in the financial square mile of the city of London, as well as in New York and Tokyo.

A lot of heartache and financial anguish could have been avoided throughout had he become what is clearly the optimal career choice for anyone anywhere: a master plumber. Nowhere on the planet is there a poor or unemployed master plumber! Too late to correct past follies, Sheppard now makes his living writing software, books, and magazine articles.

Robert Bruce Thompson is coauthor of *Building the Perfect PC* and *PC Hardware in a Nutshell*. Thompson built his first computer in 1976 from discrete chips. It had 256 bytes of memory, used toggle switches and LEDs for I/O, ran at less than 1MHz, and had no operating system. Since then, he has bought, built, upgraded, and repaired hundreds of PCs for himself, employers, customers, friends, and clients. Thompson reads mysteries and nonfiction for relaxation, but only on cloudy nights. He spends most clear, moonless nights outdoors with his 10-inch Dobsonian reflector telescope, hunting down faint fuzzies, and is currently designing a larger truss-tube Dobsonian (computerized, of course) that he plans to build.

Barbara Fritchman Thompson is coauthor of *Building the Perfect PC* and *PC Hardware in a Nutshell*. She worked for 20 years as a librarian before starting her own home-based consulting practice, Research Solutions, and is also a researcher for the law firm Womble, Carlyle, Sandridge & Rice, PLLC. During her leisure hours, Thompson reads, works out, plays golf, and, like Robert, is an avid amateur astronomer.

Theodore Wallingford is an executive technologist and the cofounder of Best Technology Strategy Inc., a company that helps entrepreneurs and established companies alike in the adoption, integration, and successful use of communication systems and business processes. A global thought leader on the subject of VoIP and Internet Protocol communications, Wallingford has emerged as an expert in the fields of network convergence and unified business communication. He has written two technology books for O'Reilly Media, and has appeared on NPR Science Friday. He also periodically writes for *Macworld* Magazine and maintains the Signal to Noise blog. He resides in Cleveland, OH.

INDEX

16-bit, 460–463
20-in-1 5.25 Multi-function panel, 571
32-bit, 460
64-bit, 21, 460, 561
802.11a/b/g, 362

A

abandonia.com, 462
Access logs, router, 246–249
Acronis True Image, 458
activation, Vista, 25–27
ad hoc mode, 357–359
Ad-Aware, 194
add-ins, Internet Explorer, 201–204
Administration Console, RSSBus, 239–240
administrator
  accounts, Vista, 375
  Administrator account, super-secret, 377–378
  command prompt, Windows Explorer, 138–140
  Internet Explorer settings, 209
  login, 76
  Mac MakeUp, 337
  password, 343
  Registry access, 610–611
Aero
  Java-based apps, 228–229
  overview, 62–65
  RAM performance, 538
AIM. *See* instant messaging
album art, Zune, 511–512
alerts, performance, XP, 553
alternative verb forms, search, 172
Amnesty Generator, 96
analog-to-digital conversion, 507
animation
  interface, slow motion, 64
  troubleshooting, 498
  Vista network icon, 68
anonymous
  email, 186
  surfing, 182–187
Anonymouse AnonEmail, 186
antennas, wireless, 334–335, 361–368
antivirus software, 193–194, 409
applets
  cascading menu, 81
  recategorizing, 80–81
  running hidden, 79
  unused, 78–80
applications. *See* programs
archives
  backing up, 455–456
  Outlook storage space, 291–294
arrows, shortcut, 67, 98
art. *See* graphics
Atom InterSoft proxy server list, 186
attachments
  file size, 303
  opening blocked, 300–303
  Outlook storage space, 291–294
  zipping, 290–291
Audacity, 522–523
audio
  Bluetooth headset, 368–372
  MP3s, vinyl and tapes, 522–523
  NES Sound Format, 464–465
  optical drive, troubleshooting, 606
  PC speakers, 520–522
  system beeps, 74
  VoIP (*See* VoIP)
  Zune, syncing, 511–512
Aurora, 19
AuthSMTP, 356
auto logons, 28
auto-tuning, 260
automated disk defragmentation
  Vista, 544–545
  XP, 541–544
AV Comparatives, 379
Avast!, 194, 409
AVG, 409
AVG Anti-Rootkit, 381
AWStats, 395

B

BackUp MyPC, 457
backups
  archives, 455–456
  data directory structure, 455–456
  disk defragmentation, scheduling, 542
  hardware, 454–455
  Ntbackup, 449, 450–453
  NTFS drive, 450
  planning, 453–457
  Registry, 622–623
  rotation, 456–457
  software, 457–458
  USB drive, 450
  Vista, 448–452
  Windows Home Server, 438–440
bandwidth
  measuring, 266
  optimizing, 330–331
  router congestion, 180–182
  speed, 330
  vampires, 330
batch files, 140
BCD store, 42
BCDEDIT, 42–44
beeps, system, 74
BGB, 469–470
BIOS
  boot text, 607–608
  OEM, 36–38
  speeding up startup, 23, 34–35
  unhackable, 36–38
  upgrading, 38–39
BitLocker, 401–403
blacklists, email, 296–297
Blaze Audio Voice Cloak, 281–282
blinking cursor, Vista, 64
blogging, 418–421
Bluetooth
  headset, Vista, 368–372
  stack, 368
boilerplate text, 300, 421–423
Boingo, 355
bookmark icons, Firefox, 216
Boolean operators, search, 171
boot defragment, 539–541
boot screen
  Vista, 18–21
  XP, 21–22
boot.ini file, 45–50
booting
  Knoppix, 124–132
  Linux from disc, 124–132
  multiboot systems (*See* multiboot systems)
  multiple versions, 36
  speeding up, 22–25, 29–33, 34–35
  Ubuntu Linux, 58–60
BootSkin, 21–22

borders, Aero interface, 62–64
Borland Turbo C, 461
Boycott Advance, 470–471
Breezy Badger, 55
bridge, network, 261–263
browsers
    Firefox (*See* Firefox)
    Internet Explorer
        (*See* Internet Explorer)
    multiple, testing web sites, 227
Browsershots.org, 227
BrowserSpy, 182
browsing
    anonymous, 182–187
    speed, 187–190
buffers, mouse and keyboard, 618
Bugnosis, 197
bugs, web, 193–197
building blocks, Word, 421–423
burning DVDs
    copying video tapes, 508
    Media Center, 490–492
    TV mashup, 486–490
bypass logon screen, 27–28

C

cables
    signal loss, 364, 365
    video tapes, copying to DVDs, 505–507
cache
    DNS, 191–192
    Firefox, 219–220
calendars, Vista, 231–235
camcorder
    uploading video, YouTube, 503–504
    video tapes, copying to DVDs, 505–508
cameras, Vista-incompatible, 515
Caps Lock key, 70
capture, screen, 104
cards, TV tuner, 473–474
cascading menu, applets, 81
case-modding, 568–573
cassettes, converting to MP3s, 522–523
cathode ray tube light, case-modding, 572–573
CD writer, 454–455, 457
cell phone, uploading YouTube videos, 504
change tracking, Registry, 623–624
channel, Wi-Fi, 333–334
checkboxes, selecting with, 68
Chipmunks, Alvin and the, 281–282
ClearType, 66–68
clients
    remote access, Vista, 268–270
    remote access, XP, 264–267
    VPN, 409–414
cloaking, voice, 281–282
CNet Bandwidth Meter Test, 330
    cold-cathode light, case-modding, 572–573
command line
    decrypting from, 406–407
    disk defragmentation, 539–540
    encrypting from, 406–407
    shortcuts, Windows Explorer, 146–150
command prompt
    Administrator, 138–140
    elevated, 376–377
    Windows Explorer context menu, 135–136
command startlet, 165–167
COMMAND.COM, 460
commands
Word, 2007 versions of 2003, 423–429
    Word, Quick Access Toolbar, 417–418
commercials, removing, 479–483
common controls, 103–104
Community Server, RSS feeds, 242–244
company name, changing, 69
composite video connection, 507–508
compressing files
    DVDs, 493–494
    NTFS, 155–158
    Office, 429–431
    video, 482
    ZIP, 155, 157–158, 290–291
Computer Associates Spyware Information Center, 382–383
confirmation box, file deletion, 68–69
congestion, router, 180–182
connection. *See also* networks
    HyperTerminal, 229–231
    remote access, Windows Home Server, 441–446
    settings, Internet Explorer, 208–209
    VPN, 409–414
    Windows Home Server, 438
contact information, xvii
CONTAINS operator, 170
context menu, Windows Explorer, 134–137
Contig, 545–546
Control Panel
    applets, cascading menu, 81
    applets, recategorizing, 80–81
    applets, running hidden, 79
    applets, unused, 78–80
    customized, 81–82
controls, common, 103–104
conventions, xvi
cookies, Google, 198–200
Cool Desk, 103
cooling
    heat sink, 591–598
    Thermaltake Cyclo Memory Cooler Fan, 573
Copy To Folder, 134–135
copying
    files, 151
    path, 165
    video tapes to DVDs, 505–508
CPU Gadget, 86
CPU Meter gadget, 527–528
CSV file, Gmail contacts, 313–314
cursor, Vista, blinking, 64
Cute PDF Writer, 436

D

data directory structure, backups, 455–456
Data Encryption Standard (DES), 404
date and time expressions, search, 171
Dazzle DVD Recorder, 505
DD-WRT firmware, 324–333
DDNS, 252–254
dead spots, wireless, 329
Decrapifier, 525
decryption, 406–407
default location, installing programs, 618
defragmentation
    boot, 22–23, 539–541
    single files, 545–546
    Vista, 544–545
    XP, 539–541
    XP, automating, 541–544

deleting
commercials, 479–483
files, confirmation box, 68–69
keys, Registry, 616, 621
music files, PC, 511–512
restoring shadow copies, 145–146
values, Registry, 616
viruses manually, 381–386
DES, 404
DeskSpace, 70–72, 103
DESX, 404
development tools, DOS, 462
Device Manager
hidden hardware, 583–585
troubleshooting, 578–583
devices. *See* hardware
DHCP IP address, 271
diagnostics. *See also* performance; troubleshooting
Performance Console, XP, 550–553
Reliability Monitor, Vista, 553–556
system performance, Vista, 547–550
directories
listing, Windows Explorer, 140–142
moving, 150–152
structure, backups, 455–456
disable shutdown, 617
dish antenna, 363–368
Disk Defragmenter, 539–541, 544–545
disk drives
cleanup warning, 618
defragmentation, Vista, 544–545
defragmentation, XP, 539–541
defragmentation, XP, automating, 541–544
failure, 608
floppy (*See* floppies)
imaging, 458
letters, hiding, 177
RAID, 565–566
space, hibernation, 544
space, NTFS compression, 155–158
space, Vista, Disk Cleanup, 544
space, Vista, smaller installation, 524–527
USB, backing up, 450, 454–455
USB, speed, 590
Disk Management Console, 153
display, troubleshooting, 604–605
disposable email address, 295
DNS
OpenDNS, 187–190
speed, settings, 190–193
Docs and Spreadsheets, 431–433
Document Inspector, 399
documents. *See also* files
Google, 431–433
PDFs, 435–437
domain-connected PCs, auto logons, 28
DOS
games, 460–463
productivity applications, 462–463
RAM performance, 538
DOSBox, 460–463
downloading
MD5sum, 125
multiple files, 229
spyware, 196
DriverQuery, 586–588
drivers
64-bit, Vista, 561
GART, 599–600
hardware, Vista, 583
listing, 586–588
video, 599–601
drives
detection, 34–35
floppy, troubleshooting, 605
floppy, USB, 118
hard drives (*See* disk drives)
optical, troubleshooting, 606, 608–609
SATA, troubleshooting, 607
USB flash, BitLocker, 401–403
USB flash, encrypted, hotspot security, 359
USB flash, gadgets, 94–96
USB flash, MyPendrive, 599
USB flash, ReadyBoost, 529–535
Zune, file storage, 509, 573
Zune, replacing, 573–577
dropped packets, 395
DSL Reports, 330
dual core processor, 527–528
dual-boot
alternatives, 105
XP/Linux, 54–61
DVD Maker
TV mashup, 486–490
video tapes, copying to DVDs, 508
DVD Shrink, 492–497
DVDs
compression, 493–494
Media Center, burning, 490–492
Media Center, ripping, 492–497
tapes, copying from, 505–508
TV mashup, 486–490
writer, 454–455, 457
Zune, watching, 510
DVRMSToolbox, 482
Dynamic DNS (DDNS), 252–254
DynDNS, 254

E

EasyBCD, 52
ECN, 180–182
Edelman, Ben, 197
Edit menu commands, Word, 424
editing
photo tags, 516–519
Registry Editor, 614–616
Registry, safely, 619–622
removing commercials, 479–483
EFI, 42
EFS, 404–407
elevated command prompt, 376–377
email
anonymous, 186
compressing files, 290–291
disposable address, 295
Exchange Messaging, 304
file size, 303
forwarding Skype voicemails, 288–289
Gmail as POP3, 310–312
Gmail universal inbox, 308–309
Gmail, importing contacts, 313–318
Gmail, importing mail, 319–323
Gmail, privacy, 198
Gmail, virtual hard drive, 312–313
international spam, 297–299
newsletters, 296–297, 299

email (continued)
opening blocked attachments, 300–303
publishing calendar to Web, 304–307
spam prevention, 293–295
storage space, 291–294
wireless, 354–357
emulators
DOSBox, 460–463
Game Boy, 468–471
NES, 463–468
PearPC, 111–112
Virtual PC, 116–117
VMware Server, 105
Encrypting File System (EFS), 404–407
encryption
BitLocker, 401–403
Encrypting File System (EFS), 404–407
home Wi-Fi, 349–351
USB flash drive, 359
EQUALS operator, 170
error messages, Device Manager, 578–583
ESupport.com, 36
Eusing Free Registry Cleaner, 23–24
Event Viewer, Vista, 547–550
Excel stock quotes, 431–433
exception list, firewall, 394
Exchange Messaging, 304
Explicit Congestion Notification (ECN), 180–182
Explorer
Internet (*See* Internet Explorer)
Windows (*See* Windows Explorer)
expressions, search, 170–172
extended tests, disabling, 34
Extensible Firmware Interface (EFI), 42
Extensible Metadata Platform (XMP), 514–519
extensions
file, blocked, 301–302
Firefox, 210–213, 217–219
external hard drive, 454–455

F

failure, hard drive, 608
fan, Thermaltake Cyclo Memory Cooler, 573
fanless CPUs, 591
FAT32, 158
FCE Ultra, 464–465
FDD, troubleshooting, 605
Feed Headlines, YouTube videos, 92–94
feeds, RSS, 238–244
FEK, 404
file encryption key (FEK), 404
File menu commands, Word, 423–424
files
backing up (*See* backups)
compressing, NTFS, 155–158
compressing, Office, 429–431
compressing, video, 482
compressing, ZIP, 155, 157–158, 290–291
copying, 151
CSV, Gmail contacts, 313–314
defragmentation, 545–546
deleting, confirmation box, 68–69
Document Inspector, 399
downloading multiple, 229
email, compressing, 290–291
Encrypting File System (EFS), 404–407
extensions, blocked, 301–302
file encryption key (FEK), 404
folders, Windows Explorer context menu, 134–135
Gmail, virtual hard drive storage, 312–313
listings, Windows Explorer, 140–142
metadata, 398–400
offline, 172–179
opening blocked attachments, 300–303
Outlook storage space, 291–294
properties, search, 161–162
RAW, 519
sharing, 172–179, 357–358
sharing, firewalls, 392–394
sharing, speed, 246–249
size, email, 303
synchronizing, 172–179
Zune, 509, 573
filtering
outbound, 386–389
search noise, 172
Firefox
bookmark icons, 216
cache, 219–220
extensions, 210–213, 217–219
gmail, 198
interface, 214
memory leaks, 216–220
search, 220–223
tab, active, 216
testing web sites, 227
toolbar graphic, 214–215
Torbutton, 184
firewalls
file sharing, 392–394
hotspot security, 361
inbound, bypassing, 389–394
log, 394–398
ports, exception list, 394
Skype, 283–285
Vista, outbound, 386–389
ZoneAlarm, 195
flamed-out chip, fumes, 592
flash drive
gadgets, 94–96
ReadyBoost, 529–532, 532–535
Flip 3D, Vista, 70, 163, 434
floppies
booting Knoppix, 126–127
booting Linux, 126–127
drive, troubleshooting, 605
USB drive, 118
FolderBox, 151
folders
backing up (*See* backups)
Encrypting File System (EFS), 404–407
gadgets, 85
listings, Windows Explorer, 140–142
moving, 150–152
offline files, 172–179
Open dialog box, 73–74
Startup, 29–30

synchronizing, 172–179
Windows Explorer context menu, 134–135
FON Wireless Ltd., 352
fonts, ClearType, 66–68
formatting
Format menu commands, Word, 427
Live Preview, 418
themes, Office, 422
forums, RSS feeds, 242–242
forwarding Skype voicemails, 288–289
Free Wi-Fi scam, 339–342
FreeDOS, 117
Freemeter, 266, 310
FreeNets, 351–354
Frotz, 462
fumes, flamed-out chip, 592
FxVisor, 98

G

gadgets
built-in, 85–86
CPU, 86
Feed Headlines, YouTube, 92–94
flash drive, 94–96
folders, 85
gadget.xml, 86
overview, 84–85
performance, 527
restoring, 87–88
settings, 87
Slide Show, videos, 88–91
uninstalling, 87–88
user-installed, 85–86
Web, 96–99
galleries, building blocks, 421–423
Game Boy emulator, 468–471
games
16-bit, 460–463
DOS, 460–463
Game Boy emulator, 468–471
NES emulator, 463–468
GameTap, 462
gaming, optimizing network, 330
GART driver, 599–600
Gentoo Linux 2.4 Live, 55
gExodus, 321
ghosts, hardware, 583–585
Gmail
importing contacts, 313–318
importing email, 319–323
POP3, 310–312
privacy, 198
universal inbox, 308–309
virtual hard drive, 312–313
GmailerXP, 321
GNOME, 127
Gold Rush, 462
Google
calendars, 231–235
Docs and Spreadsheets, 431–433
Firefox search, 220–223
Gmail (*See* Gmail)
Mail Loader, 319
privacy, 198–201
video, Zune, 512–513
GParted, 53, 153
graphics
blogging, 420–421
boilerplate, Word, 421–423
compressing, 429–431
user account, 74–75
Vista boot screen, 18–21
XP boot screen, 21–22
Zune, album art, 511–512
Group Policy Editor
Internet Explorer, 207–209
options, 624–625
Start menu, 82–83
unused applets, 79–80
GRUB, installing, 58–59
GUIDs, command line shortcuts, 149–150

H

Handbrake, 495
hard-disks. *See* disk drives
hardware
acceleration, video playback, 498
backup, 454–455
case-modding, 568–573
Device Manager, hidden hardware, 583–585
Device Manager, troubleshooting, 578–583
drivers, listing, 586–588
drivers, Vista, 583
ghosts, 583–585
Hardware Troubleshooter, 578
heat sink, 591–598
overclocking, 590–591, 592, 597
overclocking, video cards, 599
PC, TV recording, 472–473
Problem Reports and Solutions, 578
troubleshooting, 603–609
USB drives, speed, 590
video card, installing, 599–602
Zune drive, replacing, 573–577
Hardware Troubleshooter, 578
Hauppauge, 473
HBB1 Broadband Booster, 287
headset, Bluetooth, 368–372
heat sink, 591–598
hibernation, 544
hidden hardware, 583–585
hiding
drive letters, 172–179
icons, notification center, 73
unused applets, 78–80
High Definition Audio, 520–522
high-performance RAM, 596–597
history
search, Google, 200
sync, 178
hive keys, Registry, 613–614
hives, Registry, 612
Home Server. *See* Windows Home Server
hostname, home server, 252–254
HOSTS file, 191
hotspots. *See* wireless
hotspotVPN, 359
HTML, plain text, converting, 182
HTMLAsText, 182
hybrid sleep mode, laptops, 588–589
HyperTerminal, 229–231

I

icons
bookmark, Firefox, 216
Device Manager messages, 578
favicons, 223
Quick Launch Toolbar, 455
resizing, 71, 137
shortcut arrows, 67, 98
system tray, hiding, 72–73
text, 68

Icons *(continued)*
- Vista desktop, versions, 69
- Vista network, animating, 68

ICQ. *See* instant messaging
IIS, 262
images. *See* graphics
imaging, disk, 458
ImgBurn, 118
importing
- contacts, Gmail, 313–318
- mail, Gmail, 319–323
- photos, speed, 518
- photos, Vista-incompatible cameras, 515

IMs
- spyware, 196
- timeouts, 249

inbound firewalls, bypassing, 389–394
incompatible
- cameras, Vista, 515
- programs, Vista, 445

index, search, 159–160
Indexing Service, XP, 167–172
Insert menu commands, Word, 425–426
installing
- FreeDOS, 119–120
- GRUB, 58–59
- programs, default location, 618
- RSSBus, 238
- Ubuntu Linux, 58
- Ubuntu Linux within Windows, 108–111
- video card, 599–602
- Vista, smaller, 524–527
- Windows 3.11, 120–124

instant messaging
- spyware, 196
- timeouts, 249

Instant Video To-Go, 482
interface
- 3D virtual desktop, 70–72
- common controls, 103–104
- Control Panel, 78–82
- Feed Headlines, YouTube, 92–94
- Firefox, 214
- flash drive, gadgets, 94–96
- Internet Explorer, 207–208
- Linux, booting from disc, 124–132
- Registry, 72–75
- running Linux within Windows, 105–111
- running Mac OS X within Windows, 111–116
- running Windows 3.11 within Windows, 116–124
- Slide Show, videos, 88–91
- speeding up, 76–77
- Start Menu, 82–83
- Tweak UI, 75–77
- user account graphic, 74–75
- virtual desktops, 100–103
- Vista, 66–70
- Vista Aero, 62–65
- Vista, gadgets, 84–88
- Web gadgets, 96–99
- XP taskbar, 84

interference, wireless, 333–336
international spam, 297–299
Internet. *See also* networks
- calendars, Outlook, 235–237
- calendars, Vista, 231–235
- downloading multiple files, 229
- favicons, 223
- filtering, proxy server, 408–409
- Firefox (*See* Firefox)
- Internet Explorer 7 problems, 201
- Internet Information Services (IIS), 262
- Java-based apps, Vista, 228–229
- privacy, 182–187, 198–201
- publishing Outlook calendar, 304–307
- remote access, Windows Home Server, 441–446
- RSS feeds, 238–244
- speed, DNS settings, 190–193
- speed, Explicit Congestion Notification (ECN), 180–182
- speed, OpenDNS, 187–190
- spyware, 193–197
- use, restricting, 331–333
- viruses, 193–197
- web bugs, 193–197
- wireless (*See* wireless)

Internet Explorer
- add-ins, 201–203
- connection settings, 208–209
- default programs, 209
- downloading multiple files, 229
- Group Policy Editor, 207–209
- interface, 207–208
- printing, 204–206
- privacy, 182–187, 198–201
- search, 224–228
- security, 209
- speed, Explicit Congestion Notification (ECN), 180–182
- speed, OpenDNS, 187–190
- tab order, 204
- testing web sites, 227
- Tools menu, 203–204
- URL settings, 209
- version problems, 201–203
- YouTube videos, Zune, 512–513
- zoom, 144

Internet Information Services (IIS), 262
Ion iTTUSB Turntable, 522
IP addresses
- home server hostname, 252–254
- limiting on home network, 344–345
- router, 249–251
- troubleshooting, 271
- Windows Home Server, 441–446

ipconfig, 277–278
iPod, video converter, 513
IrfanView, 18, 223
ISO Recorder, 55

J

Java-based apps, Vista, 228–229
JiWire's Hotspot Helper, 339, 359

K

K Desktop Environment (KDE), 127–131
KDE, 127–131
kernel-mode rootkits, 379
keyboard buffer, 618
keyboard shortcuts
- Flip, 163
- launching applications, 441
- Ribbon, Word, 416–417
- switching desktops, 102

keys
  hive, Registry, 613–614
  product, 21
  Registry, 621
King's Quest, 462
Knoppix, 124–132
Knoppix Hacks, 132

L

languages, search noise filters, 172
Lantronix connection, 229–230
laptops
  hybrid sleep mode, 588–589
  power-saving, 588–589, 618
least-privileged user, 375
LED light, case-modding, 572–573
Leisure Suit Larry, 462
license information, Vista, 26–27
light, case-modding, 572–573
Link Layer Topology Discovery (LLTD), 261
Link Logger, 346
Linux. *See also* Knoppix; Ubuntu
Linux
  booting from disc, 124–132
  multiboot systems (*See* multiboot systems)
  Windows, running within, 105–111
Live Preview, 418
live recording, uploading, YouTube, 503–504
LLTD, 261
LMR-400 cable, 365
location, default, installed programs, 618
login, Administrator, 76
logon screen, bypassing, 27–28
logs
  firewall, 394–398
  Performance Console, XP, 550–553
  router, 246–249, 346
LPs, converting to MP3s, 522–523

M

MAC address, 336–338, 345–346
Mac MakeUp, 336–338
Mac OS X, Vista, running within, 111–116
mail. *See* email; voicemail
malware. *See* security
maps
  network, 258–261
  wireless network, 352–354
mashup, TV, 483–490
McAfee
  Rootkit Detective, 380
  Stinger, 382
  Threat Center, 382
MD5sum, 125
Media Access Control (MAC) address, 336–338, 345–346
Media Center
  DVDs, burning, 490–492
  remote control, 474, 479
  ripping DVDs, 492–497
  TV commercials, removing, 479–483
  TV mashup, 483–490
  TV, recording, 472–479
  Zune, TV, 513–514
memory. *See also* RAM, performance
  based rootkits, 379
  leaks, Firefox, 216–220
metadata
  Photo Gallery, 514–519
  security, 398–400
Microsoft Virtual PC, 106
mini toolbar, Word, 428
modding, case, 568–573
mouse
  buffer, 618
  programming, Flip 3D, 434
Move To Folder, 134–135
Movie Maker
  commercials, removing, 480–483
  saving movies, settings options, 498–501
  TV mashup, 483–490
  video tapes, copying to DVDs, 505–508
movies
  ripping DVDs, 492–497
  saving, settings options, 498–501
  YouTube, 501–504
MP3s
  recording calls, 282–283
  vinyl and tapes, 522–523
Multi Meter gadget, 527–528
multiboot systems
  BCDEDIT, 42–44
  boot.ini file, 45–50
  Linux, XP, 54–61
  overview, 40–42
  Vista, partitions, 53–54
  XP, boot.ini file, 45–50
  XP, Linux, 54–61
  XP, VistaBootPRO, 50–53
multiple
  accounts, PCs, bypassing logon screen, 27–28
  email accounts, 308–309
  networks, connecting, 261–263
  operating systems (*See* multiboot systems)
  PCs, controlling, 265
  Windows versions, 36
music
  MP3s, vinyl and tapes, 522–523
  optical drive, troubleshooting, 606
  PC speakers, 520–522
  Zune, syncing, 511–512
MyPendrive, 599

N

NAT, 249–251, 441
Nero Burning ROM, 457
NeroVision 7 Ultra, 491
NES
  emulator, 463–468
  Sound Format, 464–465
Nessie, 466–468
NESticle, 467
NEStopia, 465–467
Net Nanny, 408
NetChaser, 352
NetLimiter, 286
netsh, 275–276
netstat, 276–277
NetStumbler, 333, 352
Network Address Translation (NAT), 249–251, 441
networks
  backups, Windows Home Server, 438–440
  connecting multiple, 261–263
  connection shortcuts, 254–256
  discovery, 357–358

networks *(continued)*
home server blocking, 249–251
icon, animating, 68
map, 258–261
performance, router, 329
rebooting settings, 271
remote access, Vista, 268–270
remote access, XP, 264–267
renewing IP address, 271
speed, file sharing, 246–249
SSID, 343–344
Sync Center, 172–179
troubleshooting, IP address, 271
troubleshooting, ipconfig, 277–278
troubleshooting, netsh, 275–276
troubleshooting, netstat, 276–277
troubleshooting, pathping, 274–275
troubleshooting, ping, 271–273
troubleshooting, tracert, 274
VPN, 409–414
XP/Vista communication, 256–261
newsgroups, RSS feeds, 238–244
newsletters, preventing blocking, 296–297, 299
nightlight, 572–573
Nintendo
NES Sound Format, 464–465
NES emulator, 463–468
Game Boy, 468–471
NNTP newsgroup, RSS feed, 240–242
No-IP.com, 252
noise filter, Indexing Service, 172
noise, screeching, 609
nonpresent devices, 583–585
Norton antivirus, 194
notification area, 72–73, 412
NSF, 464–465
Ntbackup, 449, 450–453
NTFS
compression, 155–158
drive, backing up, 450
nTune, 591
NVIDIA nTune, 591

O

OEM BIOS, 36–38
Office. *See also* Excel; Word
Document Inspector, 399
documents, 433–435
folders, dialog boxes, 73
Google Docs and Spreadsheets, 431–433
graphics, compressing, 429–431
Online, publishing calendar, 304–307
PDFs, 435–437
spreadsheets, 431–433
themes, 422
versions, 458
offline
dictionary attack, 351
files, 172–179
Open dialog box, folders, 73–74
Open With, 136
OpenDNS, 187–190
OpenOffice.org, 432, 436
operating systems
error messages, troubleshooting, 608
Linux, booting from disc, 124–132
Linux, running within Windows, 105–111
multiboot
(*See* multiboot systems)
running Mac OS X within Windows, 111–116
running Windows 3.11 within Windows, 116–124
Vista (*See* Vista)
XP (*See* XP)
operators, search, 170–172
optical drive, troubleshooting, 606, 608–609
order, search results, 172
Orinoco Pigtail, 362–363
outbound firewalls, 386–389
Outlook
calendars, 235–237
Exchange Messaging, 304
Gmail, POP3, 310–312
opening blocked attachments, 300–303
publishing calendar to Web, 304–307
storage space, 291–294
overclocking, 590–591, 592, 597, 599
overseas spam, 297–299

P

packets
dropped, logging, 395
prioritizing, VoIP, 279–281
router congestion, 180–182
PageDefrag, 564
paging files, RAM performance, 535–538, 562–564
painting, case, 568–571
Pamela, 288–289
parental controls, 408
Partition Magic, 53, 153
partitions
managing, 152–154
moving folders, 150–152
moving, Vista, 53–54
multiboot, XP/Linux, 55–58
shared, Ubuntu Linux, 60–61
Vista installation, 155
password, administrator, 343
pasting, path, 165
path, copy and paste, 165
pathping, 274–275
PC Decrapifier, 525
PC Hacks, 591
PCs
backing up, planning, 453–457
(*See also* backups)
deleting music files, 511–512
multiaccount, bypassing logon screen, 27–28
multiple, controlling, 265
networks (*See* networks)
remote access, router blocking, 249–251
remote access, Vista, 268–270
remote access, Windows Home Server, 446–447
remote access, XP, 264–267
saving movies, settings options, 498–501
speakers, 520–522
TV shows, recording, 472–479
PD Roms, 464

PDFs, 435–437
PearPC, 111–112
performance
  Aero interface, 65
  bandwidth, speed, 330
  compression, 155
  CPU use, 527–528
  defragmentation, single files, 545–546
  disk defragmentation, Vista, 544–545
  disk defragmentation, XP, 539–541
  disk defragmentation, XP, automating, 541–544
  DNS settings, 190–193
  dual core processor, 527–528
  Firefox memory leaks, 216–220
  gadgets, 527
  hibernation, 544
  importing photos, 518
  interface, 76–77
  Internet, router congestion, 180–182
  network, wireless, 329
  overclocking, 590–591
  paging files, 535–538, 562–564
  Performance Console, XP, 550–553
  QoS, Skype, 285–287
  RAID, 565–566
  RAM, 535–538
  RAM, high-performance, 596–597
  ReadyBoost, 529–532, 532–535
  Reliability Monitor, Vista, 553–556
  shutdown time, 22–25
  startup time, 22–25, 29–33, 34–35
  surfing, web, 187–190
  system health report, Vista, 548
  system, Vista, 547–550
  Task Manager, 556–561
  USB drives, speed, 590
  Vista, smaller installation, 524–527
  visual effects, XP, 552
Performance Console, XP, 550–553
permissions, xvi
persistent rootkits, 378
phishing, 187–190
phone calls. *See* VoIP
Photo Gallery, Vista
  metadata, 514–519
  RAW photos, 519
PhraseExpress, 300
pictures. *See* graphics
ping, 271–273
plain text
  converting HTML, 182
  editing Registry, 619–622
plan, backup, 453–457
polarization, 367
pop-up ads, 196
POP3, Gmail as, 310–312
ports
  adding, 571
  firewall exception list, 394
  TCP, common, 251
  USB serial port, HyperTerminal, 229
  USB, case modding, 571
power
  plan, Vista, 588
  saving, laptops, 588–589, 618
  troubleshooting, 603–605
Power Defragmenter, 546
Power Saver, 560
PowerGadgets, 242
PowerStrip, 599
prefetch cache, 529
Primestar dish 802.11 antenna, 363–368
printing, Internet Explorer, 204–206
privacy
  anonymous surfing, 182–187
  Google, 198–201
Privacy.net Analyzer, 182–183
privileges, UAC, 374–377
Privoxy, 184
Problem Reports and Solutions, 578
ProcessLibrary, 389
processor, dual core, 527–528
product keys, 21
programmable mouse, Flip 3D, 434
programs
  backup, 457–458
  default, Internet Explorer, 209
  DOS, 462
  firewalls, allowing through, 390
  incompatible, Vista, 445
  installing, default location, 618
  launching, shortcuts, 441
  Quick Launch Toolbar, 455
  RAM performance, 538
  retro games, 460–463
  shutdown, close at, 617
  startup, halting, 29–33
  Task Manager, 557
  timing out, 617–618
properties, search, 161–162, 168–170
proxy servers
  anonymous, 186–187
  filtering Web sites, 408–409
Public Proxy Servers, 186
PuTTY, 229–230

Q

QoS
  DD-WRT, 330–331
  Skype, 285–287
Quality of Service (QoS)
  DD-WRT, 330–331
  Skype, 285–287
query language, search, XP, 167–172
Quick Access Toolbar, Word, 417–418
Quick Launch Toolbar, 455
QuickSilver, 186

R

RadarSync VistaDrivers, 583
RAID, 565–566
RAM, performance
  high-performance, 596–597
  paging files, 535–538, 562–564
  Task Manager, 556–561
Rankin, Kyle, 132
Rapid Repair, 573
RAW photos, 519
ReadyBoost, 529–532, 532–535
recording
  Bluetooth headset, 368–372
  calls, 282–283
  MP3s from vinyl, tapes, 522–523
  TV with PCs, 472–479
  TV, removing commercials, 479–483
records, converting to MP3s, 522–523
recycled can 802.11b antenna, 362–364

Redundant Array of Inexpensive Disks (RAID), 565–566
regions, BIOS, 35
registration
  activation, Vista, 25–27
  name, changing, 69
  reminders, Vista, 400
  user name, 617
Registry
  adding keys and values, 616
  applets, unused, 78–80
  backups, 622–623
  change tracking, 623–624
  default location, installing programs, 618
  deleting keys and values, 616, 621
  disable shutdown, 617
  disk cleanup warning, 618
  editing safely, 619–622
  Editor, 614–616
  folders, moving, 151–152
  hive keys, 613–614
  hives, 612
  keyboard buffer, 618
  laptops, power-saving, 618
  mouse buffer, 618
  Open dialog box folders, 73–74
  overview, 610–616
  programs, close at shutdown, 617
  programs, timing out, 617–618
  registered user name, 617
  restoring, 623–624
  speeding up startup, 23–24
  startup, halting programs, 31
  system beeps, 74
  system tray icons, 72–73
  Vista, 610–611
  XP, 610–611
Registry Commander, 624
Registry First Aid, 624
Registry Guide for Windows, 616
Registry Registrar, 624
RegSpy, 623
relational operators, search, 170–171
Reliability Monitor, Vista, 553–556
reminders, registration, 400
remote access
  router blocking, 249–251
  VPN, 409–414
  Windows Home Server, 441–446
  Windows Home Server, PC, 446–447
  XP, 264–267
remote control, media center, 473, 479
Remote Desktop Connection
  Vista, 268–270
  XP, 264–267
removable hard drive, 454–455
restoring
  backups, Vista, 450
  backups, Windows Home Server, 438–440
  files, shadow copies, 143–146
  gadgets, 87–88
  Registry, 623–624
results, search order, 172
retro games, 460–463
Ribbon, Word, 416–417
ripping DVDs, 492–497, 510
RockNES, 464
Rootkit Revealer, 379
rootkits, 378–381
rotation, backups, 456–457
router. *See also* wireless
  administrator password, 343
  congestion, 180–182
  encryption, 349–351
  FON Wireless Ltd., 352
  home server blocking, 249–251
  Internet use, restricting, 331–333
  IP addresses, 249–251
  limiting IP addresses, 344–345
  logs, 246–249, 346
  MAC address filtering, 345–346
  network performance, 329
  OpenDNS configuration, 188–189
  optimizing bandwidth, 330–331
  prioritizing packets, VoIP, 279–281
  remote access, PC, 249–251
  remote access, Vista, 268–270
  remote access, Windows Home Server, 441–446
  remote access, XP, 264–267
  security, 330
  signal, 329
  speed, file-sharing, 246–249
  SSID, 343–344
  travel, 354
  upgrading firmware, 324–333
  VPN, 409–414
RSS feeds, 238–244
RSSBus, 238–244
Running Mac OS X on Windows, 116

S

S-Video cable, 505–507
Safe Eyes, 408
Safe Mode, 600
SATA drives, troubleshooting, 607
saving
  movies, settings options, 498–501
  PDFs, 435–437
  searches, 160–161
scheduling disk defragmentation
  Vista, 544–545
  XP, 541–544
screeching noise, 609
screen capture, 104
screensavers, 99–100
ScummVM, 462
search
  Firefox, 220–223
  Google, privacy, 198–201
  Internet Explorer, 224–228
  noise filter, 172
  photo metadata, 517–518
  results, order, 172
  startlets, 166–167
  Vista, 158–164
  Vista, speed, 164–165
  Vista, Start++, 165–167
  XP, 167–172
secret Administrator account, 377–378
security
  Administrator account, super-secret, 377–378
  antivirus comparisons, 379
  Avast!, 409
  AVG, 409
  BitLocker, 401–403
  Document Inspector, 399
  Encrypting File System (EFS), 404–407
  firewall, bypassing inbound, 389–394
  firewall, log, 394–398
  firewall, Vista, outbound, 386–389

free Wi-Fi scam, 339–342
Internet Explorer, 209
Internet, anonymous surfing, 182–187
Internet, OpenDNS, 187–190
Internet, spyware, 193–197
Internet, viruses, 193–197
metadata, Vista, 398–400
opening blocked attachments, 300–303
rootkits, 378–381
router blocking, 249–251
Shields UP!, 406
Skype, firewalls, 283–285
spoofing MAC address, 336–338
User Account Control (UAC), Vista, 374–377
variants, pests, 383
virtual private network (VPN), 409–414
viruses, manual removal, 381–386
VPN, 359–360
Wi-Fi (*See* wireless)
wireless (*See* wireless)
Security Center notifications, 412
Send To, 135
SendThisFile, 303
serial ports, Hyperterminal, 229–231
servers
anonymous proxy, 186–187
DNS, OpenDNS, 187–190
home, hostname, 252–254
home, router blocking, 249–251
remote access, Vista, 268–270
remote access, XP, 264–267
RSSBus, 238–244
VPN, 409–414
Windows Home Server (*See* Windows Home Server)
Service Hardening, 388
service set identifier (SSID), 343–344
services
firewalls, allowing through, 390
RAM performance, 538
startup, halting, 29, 31–33
Shadow Copies, 458–459
sharing
files, 172–179, 357–358
files, firewalls, 392–394
Shields UP!, 406
shortcuts
command line, Windows Explorer, 146–150
Flip, 163
icon arrows, 67, 98
launching applications, 441
network connections, 254–256
Ribbon, Word, 416–417
Startup folder, 29
switching desktops, 102
shoulder surfers, 361
shrink volume, 153
shutdown
disable, 617
programs, closing, 617
speeding up, 24–25
Sidebar, gadgets, 84–88
Sierra On-Line AGI games, 462
signal
cable, loss, 364, 365
wireless, 329
Sisoft Sandra, 592
Skype
Bluetooth headset, 372
firewalls, 283–285
forwarding voicemails, 288–289
prioritizing, 330–332
service quality, 285–287
super nodes, 285
wardriving, 347
sleep
button, 100
mode, hybrid, 588–589
Slide Show, videos, 88–91
SMTP.com, 356
SnapShots, 623
software
backup, 457–458
product keys, 21
retro games, 460–463
startup, halting, 29–33
Sony DVDirect VRD-MC3 DVD, 508
sound. *See also* music
Bluetooth headset, 368–372
NES Sound Format, 464–465
screeching noise, 609
system beeps, 74
VoIP (*See* VoIP)
spam
disposable email address, 295
international, 297–299
newsletters, 296–297, 299
preventing, 293–295
SpamCheck, 299
Speakeasy Speed Test, 330
speakers, PC, 520–522
speed
Aero interface, 65
bandwidth, 330
defragmentation, single files, 545–546
disk defragmentation, Vista, 544–545
disk defragmentation, XP, 539–541
disk defragmentation, XP, automating, 541–544
DNS settings, 190–193
Firefox memory leaks, 216–220
importing photos, 518
interface, 76–77
Internet, router congestion, 180–182, 246–249
network, wireless, 329
overclocking, 590–591
paging files, 535–538, 562–564
Performance Console, XP, 550–553
QoS, Skype, 285–287
RAID, 565–566
RAM, 535–538
RAM, high-performance, 596–597
ReadyBoost, 529–532, 532–535
shutdown time, 22–25
startup time, 22–25, 29–33, 34–35
surfing, 187–190
system health report, Vista, 548
system, Vista, 547–550
Task Manager, 556–561
USB drives, 590
Vista search, 164–165
visual effects, XP, 552
Speedfan meter, 527
Spin It Again, 523
splash screen, Windows Mail, 318
spoofing MAC address, 336–338

spreadsheets
- Google, 431–433
- stock quotes, Excel, 431–433

spyware. *See* security
Start menu, 82–83
Start++, 165–167
startlet
- command, 165–167
- search, 166–167

startup
- multiboot systems
  - (*See* multiboot systems)
- programs, halting, 29–33
- services, halting, 29, 31–33
- speeding up,
  - 22–25, 29–33, 34–35
- troubleshooting, 603–609
- Vista boot screen, 18–21
- XP boot screen, 21–22

Stinger, 382
stock quotes, Excel, 431–433
storage
- email, space, 291–294
- files, Zune, 509, 573
- Gmail, virtual hard drive, 312–313

super nodes, Skype, 285
Surf and Sip, 355
surfing, web
- anonymous, 182–187
- shoulder, 361
- speed, 187–190

switches, boot.ini file, 45–50
Symantec Security Response, 383
Sync Center, 172–179
synchronizing
- files, 172–179
- Zune, 511–512

Synctoy, 173
Synergy, 265
syntax, search, 161–162
system
- beeps, 74
- performance (*See* performance)
- tray icons, hiding, 72–73
- utilities, backup, 457

System Configuration Utility, 30–32
System Rescue, 55
System Restore, 458–459

T

T-Mobile, 355
tab
- active, Firefox, 216
- order, Internet Explorer, 204

Table menu commands, Word, 428
tags, photo, 516–519
tape drive, 454–455
tapes, converting to MP3s, 522–523
Task Manager, 556–561
taskbar
- XP, 84
- XP, thumbnails, 96

TCP ports, common, 251
telephony. *See* VoIP
testing
- security, 406
- web site, multiple browsers, 227

text
- boilerplate, 300, 421–423
- converting HTML, 182
- editing Registry, 619–622
- icons, 68

The Cloak, 185
themes, Office, 422
Thermaltake Cyclo Memory Cooler Fan, 573
thumbnails, XP taskbar, 96
time expressions, search, 171
timing out
- instant messaging, 249
- programs, 617–618

titles, TV mashup, 486–488
Toolbar Toggle, 458
toolbar, mini, Word, 428
Tools menu add-ins, 203–204
Tools menu commands, Word, 427–428
Tor, 184
Total Recorder, 282–283
tracert, 274
tracking changes, Registry, 623–624
travel router, 354
troubleshooting
- animation, 498
- Device Manager,
  - 578–583, 583–585
- disk defragmentation, XP,
  - 540–541
- display, 604–605
- drive failure, 608
- Firefox memory leaks, 216–220
- floppy drive, 605
- Hardware Troubleshooter, 578
- Internet Explorer, 201–203
- networks, IP address, 271
- networks, ipconfig, 277–278
- networks, netsh, 275–276
- networks, netstat, 276–277
- networks, pathping, 274–275
- networks, ping, 271–273
- networks, tracert, 274
- operating system error messages,
  - 608
- optical drive, 608–609
- optical drive, audio CDs, 606
- Performance Console, XP,
  - 550–553
- performance, Vista, 547–550
- power, 603–605
- printing, Internet Explorer, 206
- Problem Reports and Solutions,
  - 578
- router firmware upgrade, 326–327
- SATA drives, 607
- screeching noise, 609
- system health report, Vista, 548
- video, 498
- Vista boot screen, 20–21
- wireless interference, 333–336
- wireless security, 343–349

tuner cards, TV, 473–474
Turbo C, 461
TV
- commercials, removing, 479–483
- DVDs, burning, 490–492
- DVDs, mashup, 486–490
- iPod video converter, 513
- mashup, 483–490
- PCs, recording with, 472–479
- Zune, 513–514

Tweak UI, 75–77
TweakVI, 81

U

UAC
- overview, 374–377
- registration reminders, 400

Ubuntu Linux
- installing, 58
- shared partition, 60–61
- Windows, running within, 105–111

Ultima, 462
UltraExplorer, 164
UltraISO, 112
unhackable BIOS, 36–38
uninstalling gadgets, 87–88
unsigned drivers, Vista, 561
upgrading
- BIOS, 38–39
- router firmware, 324–333

uploading videos, YouTube, 501–504
URLs, settings, Internet Explorer, 209
USB
- Bluetooth adapter, headset, 368–369
- devices, listing, 606
- FireWire DVD writer, 454
- flash drive (*See* USB flash drive)
- floppy drive, 118
- hard drive, backing up, 450, 454–455
- hard drive, speed, 590
- ports, case modding, 571
- serial port, HyperTerminal, 229
- turntable, 522
- TV tuner, 473
- Zune, file storage, 573
- USB flash drive BitLocker, 401–403
- encrypted, hotspot security, 359
- gadgets, 94–96
- MyPendrive, 599
- ReadyBoost, 529–535

USBDeview, 606
User Account Control (UAC), 374–377, 400
user account, graphic, 74–75
user-mode rootkits, 379

V

Vader, Darth, 281–282
vampires, bandwidth, 330
variants, pests, 383
VCR, video tapes, copying to DVDs, 505–508
verb forms, search, 172
Veritas Backup Exec, 457
Vern, 103
VGA Mode, 600
video
- card, installing, 599–602
- card, overclocking, 599
- compressing files, 482
- converter, iPod, 513
- Feed Headlines, YouTube, 92–94
- saving, settings options, 498–501
- Slide Show, 88–91
- tapes to DVDs, 505–508
- troubleshooting, 498
- TV mashup, 483–490
- TV shows, recording, 472–479
- TV shows, removing commercials, 479–483
- YouTube, 501–504
- Zune, DVDs, 510
- Zune, TV, 513–514
- Zune, YouTube, 512–513

Video Express, 505
VideoReDoPlus, 480, 483
View menu commands, Word, 424–425
vinyl, converting to MP3s, 522–523
Virtual Desktop Manager, 100
virtual desktops
- 3D, 70–72
- overview, 100–103

Virtual PC, 116–117
virtual private networks (VPN)
- hotspotVPN, 359–360
- security, 409–414

viruses. *See* security
VisiCalc, 462
Vista
- 64-bit drivers, 561
- activation, 25–27
- administrator accounts, 375
- Aero interface, 62–65
- Aero, RAM performance, 538
- animate network icon, 68
- auto-tuning, 260
- backup, 448–450, 450–453
- BCDEDIT, 42–44
- BitLocker, 401–403
- blinking cursor, 64
- Bluetooth headset, 368–372
- boot screen, 18–21
- bypass logon screen, 27–28
- calendars, 231–235
- checkboxes, 68
- ClearType, 66–68
- desktop icons, versions, 69
- disk defragmentation, 544–545
- Event Viewer, 547–550
- Explicit Congestion Notification (ECN), 180–182
- Feed Headlines, YouTube, 92–94
- file deletion confirmation box, 68–69
- file listings, Windows Explorer, 141–142
- firewalls, outbound, 386–389
- flash drive, gadgets, 94–96
- folders, moving, 150–152
- FxVisor, 67
- gadgets (*See* gadgets)
- hardware drivers, 583
- High Definition Audio, 520–522
- hybrid sleep mode, 588–589
- HyperTerminal, 229–231
- icon shortcut arrows, 67, 98
- icon text, 68
- icons, resizing, 71
- incompatible cameras, 515
- incompatible programs, 445
- installation, managing partitions, 155
- installation, smaller, 524–527
- Internet Information Services (IIS), 262
- Java-bases apps, 228–229
- license information, 26–27
- Mac OS X, running within, 111–116
- metadata, 398–400
- multiboot systems (*See* multiboot systems)
- network connection shortcuts, 254–256
- network map, 258–261

Vista *(continued)*
network XP communication, 256–261
Ntbackup, 449, 450–453
offline files, 172–179
opening blocked attachments, 303
partitions, moving, 53–54
path, copy and paste, 165
Photo Gallery, 514
power plan, 588
Power Saver, 560
Problem Reports and Solutions, 578
ReadyBoost, 529–532, 532–535
registration, activation, 25–27
registration, reminders, 400
Registry, 610–611
Reliability Monitor, 553–556
remote access, 268–270
screen capture, 104
screensavers, 99–100
search, 158–164
search speed, 164–165
search, Start++, 165–167
Security Center notifications, 412
shadow copies, 143–146
Shortcut Overlay Remover, 67
Slide Show, videos, 88–91
splash screen, Windows Mail, 318
Sync Center, 172–179
system health report, 548
system performance, 547–550
System Restore, space, 458–459
TV, recording with PCs, 472–479
UAC, 374–377
UAC, registration reminders, 400
USB drives, speed, 590
virtual desktops, 70–72, 101
Web, gadgets, 96–99
Whoami, 378
Wi-Fi scam, 341–342
Windows 3.11, running within, 116–124
Windows Flip 3D, 70
VistaBootPRO, 50–53
VistaFirewallControl, 388
Visual Tooltip, 96
VisualBoyAdvance, 470
vLite, 524–527
VMware Server, 105
voice cloaking, 281–282
Voice Over IP. *See* VoIP
voicemail, 288–289
VoIP
Bluetooth headset, 372
packet prioritization, 279–281
recording calls, 282–283
Skype, firewalls, 283–285
Skype, forwarding voicemails, 288–289
Skype, QoS, 285–287
voice cloaking, 281–282
VPNs
hotspot, 359–360
security, 409–414

W

wardriving, 346–349, 351–354
WAV files
recording calls, 282–283
Skype, forwarding voicemails, 288–289
Wayport, 355
Web
calendars, Outlook, 235–237
calendars, Vista, 231–235
downloading multiple files, 229
favicons, 223
filtering, proxy server, 408–409
Firefox (*See* Firefox)
gadgets, 96–99
Internet Explorer 7 problems, 201
Java-based apps, Vista, 228–229
multiple browsers, testing site, 227
privacy, 182–187, 198–201
publishing Outlook calendar, 304–307
RSS feeds, 238–244
speed, DNS settings, 190–193
speed, OpenDNS, 187–190
speed, router congestion, 180–182
spyware, 193–197
viruses, 193–197
web bugs, 193–197
Web Queries, Excel, stock quotes, 431–433
Webcam, uploading videos, YouTube, 503–504
WEP, 349–351
whitelists, newsletters, 296–297
Whoami, 378
Wi-Fi. *See* wireless
widgets, 96–99. *See also* gadgets
wildcard operators, search, 172
WinAmp, NSF, 464
Window Clippings, 104
Window menu commands, Word, 429
Windows 3.11
DOSBox, 463
Vista, running within, 116–124
Windows Explorer
Administrator command prompt, 138–140
checkboxes, 68
command line shortcuts, 146–150
command prompt, 135–136
context menu, 134–137
file listings, 140–142
files, copying, 151
folder listings, 140–142
icons, resizing, 71
NTFS compression, 155–158
partitions, managing, 152–154
path, copy and paste, 165
search speed, Vista, 164–165
search, Vista, 158–164
search, Vista, Start++, 165–167
search, XP, 167–172
shadow copies, 143–146
UltraExplorer, 164
zoom, 144
Windows Flip 3D, 70
Windows Home Server
backups, 438–440
connecting wirelessly, 438
IP addresses, 441–446
remote access, Internet, 441–446
remote access, PC, 446–447
Windows Service Hardening, 388
WinZip, 155, 158
Wired Equivalent Privacy (WEP), 349–351
wireless
adapter, disabling, 359–361
antennas, 334–335, 361–368
Bluetooth headset, 368–372

email, 354–357
encryption, 349–351
home, security, 343–349, 349–351
interference, 333–336
Internet use, restricting, 331–333
limiting IP addresses, 344–345
MAC address, filtering, 345–346
MAC address, spoofing, 336–338
network performance, 329
optimizing bandwidth, 330–331
router, upgrading firmware, 324–333
security, 330, 357–361
signal, 329
SSID, 343–344
wardriving, 346–349, 351–354
Wi-Fi channels, 333–334
Wi-Fi Protected Access (WPA), 349–351
Wi-Fi scam, 339–342
Windows Home Server, 438
Zune, 509

Word
5.5, 462
blogging, 418–421
boilerplate text, 421–423
commands, 2007 versions of 2003, 423–429
commands, Quick Access Toolbar, 417–418
Document Inspector, 399
graphics, compressing, 429–431
keyboard shortcuts, 416–417
Live Preview, 418
metadata, 398–400
mini toolbar, 428
Ribbon, 416–417

workgroup name, XP, 256–261

WPA, 349–351

X

xcopy, 457

Xilisoft DVD to Zune Converter, 510

XP
applets, unused, 78–80
boot screen, 21–22
common controls, 103–104
disk defragmentation, 539–541
disk defragmentation, automating, 541–544
dual-boot Linux, 54–61
file listings, Windows Explorer, 140–142
folders, moving, 151–152
Hardware Troubleshooter, 578
multiboot systems (*See* multiboot systems)
network Vista communication, 256–261
Ntbackup, 449, 450–453
Performance Console, 550–553
Registry, 610–611
remote access, 264–267
search, 167–172
taskbar, 84
taskbar thumbnails, 96
Tweak UI, 75–77
virtual desktops, 70–72, 100–103
visual effects, 552
Wi-Fi scam, 339–341
workgroup name, 256–261

XPS, saving, 435–436

Y

YouTube
Feed Headlines, 92–94
uploading videos, 501–504
Zune, watching, 512–513

YPOPs!, 321

Z

ZIP files, 155, 157–158, 290–291, 509

Zoho, 432

ZoneAlarm, 195, 388

zoom, 144

Zophar's Domain, 464, 469

Zune
album art, 511–512
drive, replacing, 573–577
drive, storing files, 509, 573
DVDs, watching, 510
syncing, 511–512
TV, 513–514
YouTube, watching, 512–513

Zunemytube, 512

ZuneTVWatcher, 513–514